W0081010

BAKERY TECHNOLOGY AND ENGINEERING

Third Edition

Other books by the same author—

Chemistry and Technology of Cereals as Food and Feed
First and Second Editions

Bakery Technology and Engineering
First and Second Editions

Equipment for Bakers

Cereal Technology

Cereal Science

Food Texture

Water in Foods

Bakery Technology

Ingredients for Bakers

Cookie and Cracker Technology
First and Second Editions

Formulas and Processes for Bakers

Technology of the Materials of Baking

Snack Food Technology
First and Second Editions; Japanese Edition

* * * * * *

This book was written, designed, and manufactured to give you maximum value and long use. It is printed on good quality, heavy base-weight paper of superior opacity and whiteness, so that it will last longer and be easy to read. The type face is New Century Schoolbook, an open style which is esthetically pleasing and can be scanned quickly and accurately.

The book has been bound by a process called "Smyth sewn in signatures," a method selected to give you a sturdy book with convenient handling properties. The binding has been made of stronger-than-usual papers and boards to support the weight of 850 pages without sagging. The cover is a plastic impregnated cloth which is resistant to wear and damage; its blue and gold stamping helps to make the book an attractive addition to your library.

BAKERY TECHNOLOGY AND ENGINEERING

Third Edition

by

SAMUEL A. MATZ, PH. D.

President, Pan-Tech International, Inc. Formerly, Vice President for Research, Development, and Compliance, Ovaltine Products, Inc. At one time, Vice President for Research and Development, Robert A. Johnston Co.; Technical Director of the Refrigerated Dough Program, Borden Foods Co.; Chief of the Cereal and General Products Branch, Quartermaster Food and Container Institute for the Armed Forces; Chief Chemist, Harvest Queen Mill and Elevator Co.; Instructor, Department of Flour and Feed Milling Industries, Kansas State University; Chemist, Iglehart Mills Division of General Foods.

CBS Publishers & Distributors Pvt. Ltd.

New Delhi • Bengaluru • Chennai • Kochi • Kolkata • Mumbai
Hyderabad • Nagpur • Patna • Pune • Vijayawada

CBS Pubs ISBN: 81-239-0481-9
Chapman ISBN: 0-442-30855-8

First Indian Edition: 1996
Reprint: 2003, 2008

Copyright © 1991, The Open University

This edition has been published in India by arrangement with
Hodder & Stoughton, UK

All rights reserved. No part of this book may be reproduced or transmitted in
any form or by any means, electronic or mechanical, including photocopying,
recording, or any information storage and retrieval system without permission,
in writing, from the publisher.

This reprinted edition is authorised for sale in India only

Published by:
Satish Kumar Jain for CBS Publishers & Distributors Pvt. Ltd.,
4819/XI Prahlad Street, 24 Ansari Road, Daryaganj, New Delhi - 110002
delhi@cbspd.com, cbspubs@airtelmail.in • www.cbspd.com
Ph.: 23289259, 23266861, 23266867 • Fax: 011-23243014

Corporate Office: 204 FIE, Industrial Area, Patparganj, Delhi - 110 092
Ph: 49344934 • Fax: 011-49344935
E-mail: publishing@cbspd.com • publicity@cbspd.com

Branches:
• *Bengaluru:* 2975, 17th Cross, K.R. Road, Bansankari 2nd Stage,
  Bengaluru - 70 • Ph: +91-80-26771678/79 • Fax: +91-80-26771680
  E-mail: cbsbng@gmail.com, bangalore@cbspd.com
• *Chennai:* No. 7, Subbaraya Street, Shenoy Nagar, Chennai - 600030.
  Ph: +91-44-26681266, 26680620 • Fax: +91-44-42032115
  E-mail: chennai@cbspd.com
• *Kochi:* Ashana House, 39/1904, A.M. Thomas Road, Valanjambalam,
  Ernakulum, Kochi • Ph: +91-484-4059061-65
  Fax: +91-484-4059065 • E-mail: cochin@cbspd.com
• *Kolkata:* 6-B, Ground Floor, Rameshwar Shaw Road, Kolkata - 700014
  Ph: +91-33-22891126/7/8 • E-mail: kolkata@cbspd.com
• *Mumbai:* 83-C, Dr. E. Moses Road, Worli, Mumbai - 400018
  Ph: +91-9833017933, 022-24902340/41 • E-mail: mumbai@cbspd.com

Representatives:

• Hyderabad: 0-9885175004   • Nagpur: 0-9021734563
• Patna: 0-9334159340   • Pune: 0-9623451994
• Vijayawada: 0-9000660880

Printed at:
Neekunj Print Process, Delhi

PREFACE

The first edition of "Bakery Technology and Engineering," which I edited, appeared in 1960. I was also responsible for the second edition, which was published in 1972. The lengthening time between editions makes it rather unlikely that I will be around to work on a fourth version. I was determined to get it right this time.

The format of the present book is generally the same as that of the first and second editions. A series of chapters on bakery ingredients is followed by twelve chapters about formulas and processes, and after that, by several chapters on equipment and engineering. Finally, a chapter on staling and spoiling reactions and means of preventing or delaying them, a chapter on computer applications in the bakery, and a chapter on sanitation and safety complete the book. In the first and second editions the final section consisted of lengthy discussions of the administration and practice of product development and quality assurance. These topics are certainly of great interest and importance, but I felt that the size of the third edition would be too unwieldy if they were included. As it is, the length of the text exceeds 800 pages as compared to about 650 pages in the first edition and about 550 pages in the second edition. The other alternative would have been to make this a two-volume set and I had objections to that course.

"Bakery Technology and Engineering" is not directed just to cereal chemists and bakery engineers, although its most obvious appeal is to those groups. Food technologists connected with industries that supply ingredients, equipment, and packaging materials to bakeries should find the book helpful in directing new product development and product improvement studies. Marketing and sales personnel should find the subject matter to be of value in orienting themselves with respect to factors affecting product quality and the economics of production. Administrators who are not technically trained will find in this single volume a unified treatment of the technology and engineering aspects of their business that can make more meaningful the reports of their research, development, and quality control personnel.

This book covers much the same ground as the set of four books, "Ingredients for Bakers," "Formulas and Processes for Bakers," "Equipment for Bakers," and "Bakery Technology," which were issued during the years 1987 through 1990, but the information in the older books has been updated and condensed. Also, some of the previous topics have been omitted from the present volume, while others have been added.

Samuel A. Matz
Edinburg, Texas
October 15, 1991

A FEW WORDS ABOUT FORMULAS AND PROCEDURES

I have used two ways of presenting formulas. In some cases, formulas and procedures are incorporated into the running text, using a more or less conventional format. In other cases, tables summarizing several formulas are used to condense information into as small a space as possible.

Ingredient quantities given in the tables are all stated as percentages on an "as is" basis. The total batter, dough, or other mixture is considered to be 100%; that is, the total ingredients, as weighed out, are taken as the basis. Converting these percentages to grams, kilograms, pounds, ounces, or any other unit of weight is greatly simplified by this method of presentation. The technologist simply chooses a desired batch size stated in the units most convenient for a particular operation, divides by 100, and then multiplies each figure in the formula by the factor so obtained. It is assumed that all readers of this book will understand that water must be considered variable when flour constitutes a substantial portion of the mixture. This does not affect the stated proportions of other ingredients.

The formulas include basic ingredients but not necessarily all flavoring ingredients. Extracts and other flavoring substances vary in strength. It would be a practical impossibility to specify quantities of flavors that would be applicable to the ingredients present in the storeroom of every bakery. Furthermore, different markets may require different strengths or different types of flavor. These factors cannot be predicted and so have been left to the discretion of the individual operator. Also, bakers may wish to exercise their creativity by using flavoring blends of their own devising.

The procedures have been given in outline form—there was no intention of giving complete cookbook directions for preparing finished products. Details are limited to critical steps or to techniques that differ in some way from those used for other products of the same type. The decision to use this approach was partly due to limitations of space, but there was a more basic consideration. The more details set out in a process description, the greater the number of shops or laboratories that will find the process unsuitable for their equipment and layout. By relying on their own experience and skills, readers will be able to flesh out the bare bones of the skeletonized procedures given in the text.

Formulas and processes have been taken from three sources. Many of them are based on products I developed or helped develop in the course of my 40+ years of directing and performing studies on food preparation and formulation. A fairly large number of formulas have been modified from examples found in publications of suppliers or government agencies—in these cases, I have either tested the formula myself or used other methods of verification. A rather small percentage of formulas (mostly those for exotic or old-time products), which have been included mainly to stimulate the reader's imagination, are untested but have been selected from publications thought to be reliable.

Contents

chapter one

INGREDIENTS MADE FROM WHEAT

INTRODUCTION

Wheat flour is the ingredient that, more than any other, influences the processing response of most doughs and batters and determines the finished quality of most bakery products. Among the reasons for the strong influence of flour are: (1) Unique proteins in wheat give most bakery products a characteristic highly expanded structure; and (2) Wheat flour is generally present in a larger proportion than any other ingredient. It follows that bakers must be certain the flours they are using have predictable and uniform properties appropriate to the products being made.

Many bakers do not have adequate facilities for testing their flour and also have limited sources of supply. They must often procure flour in bags from local distributors who sell a few types obtained from mills having many other customers. Each type will be identified by a different brand name. This situation forces the baker to depend heavily upon the reliability of the miller. For satisfactory results, the flour must be uniform from bag to bag and from shipment to shipment. Uniformity is nearly always preferable to a so-called "improvement" that makes the ingredient less compatible with the baker's processing system.

Virtually all millers, large and small, will attempt to maintain uniformity in flour sold under a specific brand name or produced to meet a published set of specifications. Millers are, however, subject to certain constraints in producing uniform products. Chief among these limitations is an unavoidable variability in their raw material, wheat. Grain, even wheat of a given variety grown in a specific area, will show differences in composition from year to year, and this variability in raw material cannot always be compensated for by adjustments in milling conditions.

The baker must, therefore, have a dependable supplier, preferably one that will furnish technical assistance when problems arise. The miller must be selected with care and the buyer must insist on receiving rapid and complete input on expected changes in flour quality. Often defects in the flour will not become apparent until items made with it come out of the oven—or even later. These situations can be disastrous, since substandard products can alienate customers or even be totally unsalable at any price to any type of customer. By the time the defect is identified and corrective action taken, the losses may be sufficient to put the baker out of business or, at least, set back growth for many months. Price is important and must be considered, of course, but no bargain can compensate for the harm that results from delivery of inconsistent or defective ingredients.

In this chapter, characteristics of wheat important to the baker will be described, followed by a review of flour tests and specifications as related tc baked product quality.

WHEAT

It is generally agreed that wheat was one of the first cereal grains to be cultivated. According to their traditions, the Chinese were growing wheat as long ago as 2700 BC. It has been cultivated around the Eastern Mediterranean and in Mesopotamia for at least 5,000-6,000 years. There is abundant evidence that the ancient civilizations of Babylon, Egypt, Crete, Greece, and Rome were dependent upon wheat as a principal food. Its use in Abyssinia and India antedate written records.

The type of wheat for which we have the oldest records of cultivation is emmer. It is true that durum wheat was found in Egypt in some tombs dated to about 4000 BC, but emmer has been found in far greater abundance and at more sites. Emmer is not, however, cultivated anywhere in Egypt at the present time, durum having totally displaced it.

Some primitive wheats are still grown to a limited extent in southern Europe. These are einkorn, emmer, and spelt. They can be called primitive because they share certain characteristics with the wild grasses of the genus *Tritcum* to which they belong. Like these grasses, the primitive wheats have a fragile, articulated head, which breaks into segments on threshing, and the mature grain does not separate readily from its enveloping structures. In other cultivated species, *T. aestivum*, for example, the axis of the head is stout and not articulated, so that it resists breakage, while the ripe kernel separates easily and cleanly from its husk. These characteristics adapt the plant to efficient harvesting and threshing procedures.

There are several different types of wheat grown in the U.S., and commercial production of the different types is usually fairly well separated by regions. The principal wheat types by areas are hard spring wheat in the northern Midwest states, hard winter wheat in the Southwest, hard and soft wheat in the Pacific Northwest, soft wheat in the area east of the Mississippi River, and durum wheat in North Dakota and South Dakota. Of course, there is some overlapping and shifting of these types: for example, in some of the northernmost states, hard red winter wheat may be planted, but if winter kill is excessive, it may be replaced by durum in the same field the following spring.

Commercial Wheat Varieties

Bread wheat, the grain formerly classified as *T. vulgare* but now known as *T. aestivum*, consists of several varieties that have quite different applications. Hard wheats yield flours that are particularly useful for bread, bread rolls, pizza shells, and other products requiring a very elastic, extensible dough. Hard red spring wheat is normally higher in protein and has a stronger gluten than hard red winter wheat. It normally sells at a premium and is used for the very strong flours needed for multigrain breads, bagels, and premium bread and rolls. Hard red winter wheat provides the raw material for most of the bread and bread roll flours sold in the U.S., as well as for nearly all of the family or all-purpose flours. Soft wheats are milled into flours used for a wide range of products—cakes, biscuits, cookies, pancakes, quickbreads, etc., which do not require a highly extensible and tough gluten. Club wheat, of which only a small amount is grown in the U.S., has many of the same characteristics as other soft wheat varieties. Durum wheat, to be discussed in more detail in the following chapter, is not a bread wheat and is seldom, if ever, used in the U.S. as an ingredient in bakery products.

It is important for agronomists, grain buyers, millers, and other persons involved in buying, selling, and processing wheat to be able to determine the variety of a sample of the grain with a high degree of confidence. Although identification of class—hard red, soft red, white, etc.— is routinely done to nearly everyone's satisfaction by inspectors in the grain trade, it is difficult or even impossible to identify every variety of wheat within a class if reliance is placed only on visual and tactile clues. Field appearance and many plant characteristics usually need to be studied before identification can be clearly established..

It is important to be able to recognize by visual inspection certain varieties that have doubtful baking quality. Identification is usually based on kernel characteristics such as: color, texture, shape, and appearance of the germ, back, crease, and brush. Other clues are wrinkling, depressions, fine lines, or sharply outlined germ. In some cases, kernel characteristics are sufficiently different to be recognizable by non-specialists who have had some instruction in wheat kernel identification. Various instrumental methods have been developed for determining hardness and other factors of importance.

Table 1.1. RANGES OF MAJOR COMPONENTS IN U.S. WHEAT[1]

Determination	Range of Analytical Results, %	
	Low	High
Protein (N X 5.7)	7.0	18.0
Mineral matter (ash)	1.5	2.0
Lipids (fat)	1.5	2.0
Starch	60.0	68.0
Cellulose (crude fiber)	2.0	2.5
Moisture	8.0	18.0

[1] Data assembled from several sources.

Varieties within the classes of hard red spring, hard red winter, or hard white wheat can exhibit wide differences from the norm of gluten quality for the class. To be of top quality, a variety of hard wheat should yield flours that have high dough absorption and good tolerance to variations in mixing and fermentation conditions, and that are capable of producing bread of good volume, grain, and texture. Some wheat varieties possess these neccessary attributes to a high degree while others do not. The selection of satisfactory wheat for a specific purpose depends upon a determination of the gluten characteristics essential to that purpose.

Composition of Wheat

Wheat composition can vary considerably from one area to another as well as from year to year within any given area. A fairly typical range in composition of wheat samples collected within the U.S. in one crop year is indicated in Table 1.1. The samples represented many different varieties of all commercial grades. The reader will understand that samples will be found exhibiting values falling outside these ranges, but such lots would be rather rare so far as material found in commercial channels is concerned.

In addition to publications on the proximate composition of wheat, which indicate only broad classes of chemical constituents, a vast amount of analytical data has been assembled on the amino acid content of wheat proteins, the elements constituting the ash or mineral matter, enzyme activity, vitamin content, and the properties of wheat starch and other carbohydrate materials. Investigators caught up in the current enthusiasm for knowledge about fiber components have expended considerable effort in identifying and characterizing the indigestible materials in wheat kernels. A short basic review of the current state of knowledge of wheat constituents is given in the following discussion.

Table 1.2. WHEAT ENDOSPERM PROTEINS CLASSIFIED BY OSBORNE'S METHOD[1]

Protein Class	Solvent	Percentage of total nitrogen
Globulin+albumin	NaCl in water	12-18
Gliadins	70% ethanol	20-43
Glutenins	Acetic acid	6-12
Glutenins	HgCl	19-28
Glutenins	2-mercaptoethanol	10-27

[1] Based on Blanco et al. (1988)

Proteins.—As a cereal plant develops and eventually forms seeds, two basic metabolic processes are predominant—photosynthesis and formation of proteins from smaller nitrogen-containing compounds. Photosynthesis leads to the formation of carbohydrates from carbon dioxide, water, and energy. Protein is developed from simpler nitrogen-containing substances extracted from the environment. The uniqueness of wheat among cereal grains depends mostly upon the characteristics of its protein content.

The storage proteins in wheat kernels include gluten, which is the complex mixture of nitrogenous compounds that gives wheat flour doughs their cohesive and elastic properties. Gluten can be separated from wheat flour by making a stiff dough from a mixture of flour and water, then washing (manually or mechanically) this dough in an excess of water (as in a stream of water) until the starch granules and all soluble materials have been removed. Gluten appears to be a mixture of two major fractions called glutenin and gliadin. The gliadin fraction is soluble in neutral 70% aqueous ethanol. It consists mainly of monomeric proteins that associate by non-covalent hydrogen bonding and by hydrophobic interactions, but also contains polymeric molecules that are related structurally to some glutenin subunits. Glutenins are essentially insoluble in 70% ethanol, and appear to consist of proteins or subunits that are aggregated into high molecular weight polymers by covalent disulfide bonds. See Shewry *et al.* (1987) for more details. The solvent methods for separating gluten into fractions conforming to Osborne's well-known classification are shown in Table 1.2. The albumins and globulins include enzymes. Structural details are shown in Figure 1.1, slightly modified from Bietz (1979).

The protein of the wheat kernel is not a well balanced nutrient for the human diet. It has a PER considerably below that of egg, milk, or soybean protein, although it is superior to corn protein. The limiting amino acid is lysine, as is the case with the proteins found in most other cereals.

Table 1.3 lists essential amino acids in various mill products. Generally speaking, the more refined the product, the less lysine is present. Germ contains the most. Various attempts have been made to develop strains of wheat that have better than average protein quality, as by increasing the content of lysine. Some success has been achieved, but high lysine strains often have defects, such as poor yield, reduced bread-making quality, etc.

Table 1.3. ESSENTIAL AMINO ACIDS IN WHEAT FRACTIONS[1]

Amino Acid	Milled Fractions						
	Whole grain	Patent flour	Clear flour	Bran	Germ	Shorts	Red dog
Isoleucine	3.8	3.9	4.0	3.5	3.5	3.5	3.8
Leucine	6.7	6.7	6.7	6.0	6.2	6.0	6.4
Lysine	2.7	1.9	2.0	4.0	5.4	4.4	3.9
Methionine	1.7	1.8	1.8	1.6	2.0	1.7	1.9
Cysteine	2.2	2.3	2.1	2.0	1.7	1.6	2.1
Phenylalanine	4.6	4.9	5.0	3.9	3.8	3.8	4.3
Tyrosine	3.1	2.9	3.2	2.8	2.8	2.7	2.9
Threonine	2.9	2.7	2.7	3.3	3.7	3.3	3.2
Tryptophan	1.2	1.0	1.0	1.6	1.1	1.4	1.3
Valine	4.7	4.3	4.5	5.0	5.1	5.0	5.0

[1] Expressed as gm per 16 gm N; based on Pomeranz (1988).

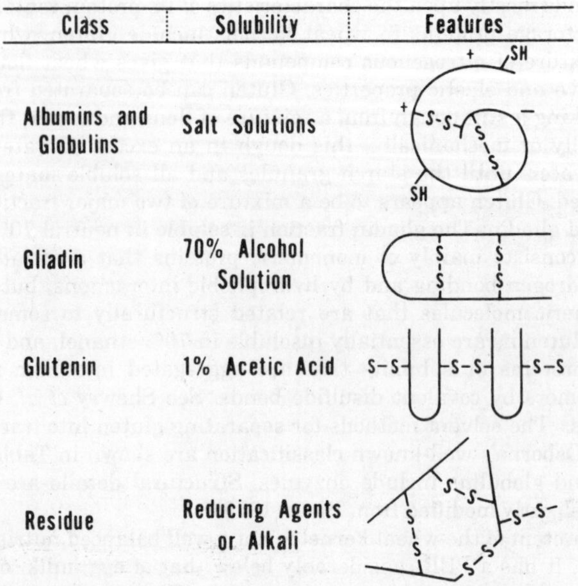

Class	Solubility	Features
Albumins and Globulins	Salt Solutions	
Gliadin	70% Alcohol Solution	
Glutenin	1% Acetic Acid	
Residue	Reducing Agents or Alkali	

Figure 1.1. Solubility and structural features of wheat proteins.

Carbohydrates.—Carbohydrates are formed from carbon dioxide and water by the process of photosynthesis. They serve as some of the supporting structures in the plant and seed, act as energy sources for many of the plant's reactions, and are deposited in the seed to furnish energy for the early development stages of a new plant.

Mono- and di-saccharides can be found in the dormant wheat kernel, but they are present in very small amounts. As percentages of dry matter, the following values may be considered fairly representative: fructose 0.06, glucose 0.08, galactose 0.02, sucrose 0.54, difructose 0.26, and maltose 0.05. Sugars of higher molecular weight are found in very small amounts. For example, about 0.19% raffinose has been reported as being present. Table 1.4 gives the results of a compilation by Cerning and Guilbot (1974) of numerous analyses performed by several laboratories investigating the carbohydrate content of wheat.

Starch is the carbohydrate present in the greatest amount in the mature wheat kernel. It is a polymer of D-glucose, most of the hexose units being joined together by α-(1-4) bonds. There are varying proportions of amylose and amylopectin, molecules of the former being essentially straight chains of glucose residues with only a few branch points, while molecules of the latter contain numerous side chains attached by 4% to 5% α-(1-6)-D-glucosidic linkages and have a molecular weight greater than about 10^8.

Table 1.4. SUGARS AND POLYSACCHARIDES IN WHEAT KERNELS

Component	Content	Component	Content
Total alcohol soluble sugars	2.15-3.96	Glucose	0.03-0.09
Glucofructosans	0.94-1.14	Fructose	0.06-0.08
Raffinose	0.19-0.68	Galactose	0.02
Glucodifructose	0.26-0.41	Starch	62.9-75.0
Maltose	0.01-0.18	Crude fiber	1.70-3.02
Sucrose	0.54-1.55	Pentosans	5.57-9.00

Starch is deposited in plant cells as microscopic particles of varying size and conformation. Many genes are involved in determining the shape, crystalline pattern, and chemical properties of starch granules. In wheat starch, the granules have a bimodal size distribution, with about 3% to 4% (50% to 75% by weight) being lenticular and 15 to 40 microns in size while the remainder are small granules, approximately spherical and ranging in size from about 1 to 10 microns. In spite of the apparent bimodal distribution, there is actually a continuous gradation in size of granules from smallest to largest, especially evident during development of the kernel, as would be expected since the sudden appearance of large granules without any intermediate growth stages would indeed be a curious phenomenon. In the ripe kernel, the intermediate size granules are not numerous, constituting in many cases only a fractional percentage of the total weight of starch.

Polysaccharides other than starch are found in cell walls of the parenchymatous and lignified tissues of the wheat plant. In the cell wall parenchymatous tissues, these compounds are present mainly as arabinoxylans and soluble β-D-glucans. Small amounts of cellulose and glucomannans may be present, but pectins and pectic substances are absent. Wheat endosperm is comparatively rich in arabinoxylan and very low in β-D-glucans, unlike the condition existing in barley and oats. Cell walls of the lignified bran layers of the kernels contain appreciable amounts of cellulose. Arabinoxylans are present, but they are acidic rather than neutral, as in the endosperm. Lignin and protein can be found in the isolated polysaccharide fraction (Lineback and Rasper 1988). The starch-protein matrix and the size of the starch granules in the wheat kernel are important considerations in flour milling and in bakery processes.

Lipids

Among the lipids reported to have been found in wheat kernels are free fatty acids, simple glycerides, galactosylglycerides, phosphoglycerides, sterol lipids, sphingolipids, diol lipids, tocopherols, carotenoids, wax esters, and hydrocarbons. In amount, the principal lipids are acyl lipids containing the fatty acids palmitic, stearic, oleic, linoleic, and α-linolenic. Reports have indicated minor amounts of many other fatty acids. Triglycerides predominate, with minor amounts of diglyceride and monoglyceride. Table 1.5 (based on data from Lockhart and Nesheim 1978) summarizes the typical distribution of fatty acids in wheat lipids, with the polyunsaturated fatty acids being included in the unsaturated fatty acid figures.

Table 1.5. FATTY ACID COMPOSITION OF WHEAT AND PRODUCTS[1]

Material Analyzed	Total lipid	Saturated fatty acids	Unsat'd fatty acids	Poly- unsaturated fatty acids
HRS wheat	2.7	0.37	1.56	1.30
HRW wheat	2.5	0.35	1.47	1.18
SRW wheat	2.4	0.35	1.40	1.14
White wheat	2.0	0.30	1.14	0.95
HRSW flour	1.5	0.23	0.84	0.72
HRWW flour	1.5	0.20	0.74	0.67
SRWW flour	1.4	0.22	0.76	0.68
All-purpose flour	1.4	0.23	0.72	0.61
Bran	4.6	0.74	3.09	2.36
Germ	10.9	1.88	8.18	6.60
Durum wheat	3.3	0.54	1.88	1.47
Durum semolina	1.8	0.33	0.90	0.72

[1] Values as grams of lipid per 100 g material, 14% MB

Minerals and vitamins.—Minerals form a small part of the wheat kernel, and an even smaller proportion of the endosperm—less than 1%. Major constituents of the mineral fraction are the phosphates and sulfates of potassium, magnesium, and calcium. Some of the phosphate is present in the form of phytic acid. There are significant quantities of iron, manganese, zinc, and copper as well as trace amounts of many other elements. One report shows the following ranges for wheat (in mg per kg): iron 18-31, zinc 21-63, copper 1.8-6.2, manganese 24-37, and selenium 0.04-0.71. Hard wheat generally contains more of these elements than soft wheat. Potassium is present at about 0.37% in whole soft wheat (air dry basis), magnesium at 0.15%, phosphorus at 0.42%, and calcium at 335 ppm (O'Dell *et al.* 1972). The sodium content of wheat is quite low. The results of one extensive set of analyses is reproduced in Table 1.6.

Bioavailability of the wheat minerals must be considered in any nutritional evaluation of the grain. Phytate, most of which is found in the aleurone layer, forms insoluble complexes with some minerals, and these complexes are poorly absorbed from the digestive tract. Zinc may be rendered totally unavailable as a result of this chelation, and the availability of other essential minerals may be adversely affected. Calcium is said to increase the binding effect of phytin on zinc.

There are substantial variations in published figures for the vitamin content of wheat, but the grain is known to be a significant source of thiamin, niacin, and B_6. The vitamin content of 406 wheat cultivars from five market classes was reported by Davis *et al.* (1981). Mean values, in mg per kg, were thiamin 4.6, riboflavin 1.3, niacin 55, and pyridoxine 4.6. Ranges were 3.3 to 6.5, 1.0 to 1.7, 38 to 93, and 1.6 to 7.9, respectively.

Table 1.6. MINERAL AND PHYTATE CONTENT OF WHEAT KERNELS[1]

Element or compound and unit	Content in kernel or part				
	Whole kernel	Germ	Endosperm	Aleurone	Hull
Total P,%	0.42	1.66	0.11	1.39	0.08
Phytate P, %	0.32	1.10	0.001	1.16	0
Zn, ppm	40.4	222.	14.1	119.	88.7
Fe, ppm	54.6	.235.	21.5	186.	110.
Mn, ppm	56.4	402.	8.80	130.	182.
Cu, ppm	4.25	18.	2.80	12.	22.6
Ca, ppm	335.	1760.	173.	730.	2570.
Mg, %	0.15	0.54	0.02	0.58	0.13
K, %	0.37	0.91	0.12	1.10	0.24

[1] O'Dell et al. (1972). The kernel was composed of 3.5% germ, 70.5% endosperm, 23% aleurone, and 3% hull. All analyses reported on an air dry weight.

Fiber.—In all discussions of dietary fiber, quantitative presentations are clouded by the almost continual changes in definition and concept of this category of substances which have occurred over the past decade, as well as by the lack of standardization in test conditions which existed until quite recently. It is very clear, however, that wheat endosperm contains only minor amounts of substances which could be called fiber even by the most liberal definition, and this condition carries through to white flour. "Wheat flour" (containing some of the outer layers) and whole wheat flour (containing all the fractions in the same proportion as in the kernel) are somewhat better, but not superior, sources of dietary fiber. White flour, whole wheat flour, and wheat bran contain, on the average, 2.78%, 12.57%, and 42.65% dietary fiber (dry matter basis) according to Cummings and Englyst (1987).

Pigments.—Ripe wheat grain varies from light buff or yellow to red-brown, according to the concentration of red pigments in the seed coat. The color will vary little in true breeding cultivars, allowing wheat varieties to be reliably classified as red or white. Red pigmentation is controlled by three genetic loci, with the result that depth of color can differ between varieties classified as red. The amber color of some durum wheats results from endosperm pigments seen through the translucent exterior layers. Nearly all bread wheat grown in the U.S. is red, but Australia produces white bread wheat exclusively. Canadian wheat is all, or nearly all, of the red type. In some emmer wheats, a purplish kernel color has been observed. Soft, chalky endosperm increases the paleness of white wheats and decreases the color of red wheats, while hard, vitreous endosperm has the opposite effect.

The endosperm of wheat has a pale yellow color that is slightly darker in hard wheat, as compared to soft wheat, and durum endosperm has even more color. The outer layers of wheat have a slight red to dark brown color, depending on the cultivar. These pigments are not considered desirable in white bread, but the yellow color is much less objectionable than the grayish effect given by bran particles. The yellow color is highly desirable in pasta, and therefore is a quality factor in durum semolina. Bran specks are at least as objectionable in pasta as in bread, and probably more so.

The yellow pigments are primarily carotenoids, hydroxylated xanthophylls (lutein), mono- and di-esters of lutein, and flavones (primarily tricin). Very small amounts of other xanthine compounds and chlorophyll decomposition products have also been reported. The bleaching agents added by millers to some types of flour oxidize carotene; nutritionally this is not important since there is not enough provitamin A in flour for it to be a significant source for humans. Xanthophylls are easily oxidized to colorless compounds. Both carotenes and xanthophylls are insoluble in water but readily dissolve in many organic solvents. Tricin is the major flavone in wheat. The flavone pigments range in color from yellow to brown.

A preparation of the enzyme(s) called lipoxygenase is commercially available for use as a bleaching agent in bread doughs. In a rather complex series of reactions, carotene is oxidized by this enzyme preparation, so that a lighter-colored bread crumb is obtained.

Enzymes.—There are certainly hundreds, perhaps thousands, of different enzymes in wheat. Virtually all of the reactions that make up the metabolic activities of the plant are expedited and guided by these organic catalysts. In the intact, dry, ungerminated grain, the total enzyme activity appears to be very slight, but this picture changes dramatically when germination begins. Then, activity becomes pronounced as new enzymes are generated and preformed but hindered enzymes are released. The enzymes that have received the most attention from investigators are the amylases, or starch-digesting enzymes, primarily because the effects of these enzymes are so important in baking and, particularly, in malting and brewing.

Among the carbohydrases in cereals are α-amylases, β-amylases, debranching enzymes, cellulases, β-glucanases, and many glucosidases. Alpha-amylase appears to be the most important carbohydrase. Wheat also contains a large number of proteolytic enzymes, such as endoproteolytic enzymes (cleaving peptide bonds some distance from the ends of protein molecules) and exoproteolytic enzymes (attacking either the carboxyl or amino termination of a protein molecule). The acid carboxypeptidases, which are exoproteolytic enzymes reacting at the carboxyl termination, are relatively abundant. Ester hydrolases include enzymes such as lipases, esterases, and phosphatases; the first two are differentiated by their ability to break ester linkages from water-insoluble esters and soluble carboxylic acid esters, respectively. Phosphatases act primarily on esters of orthophosphoric acid.

Phytase catalyzes the hydrolysis of phytic acid to inositol and free orthophosphate. Lipoxygenase, which catalyzes the peroxidation of certain polyunsaturated fatty acids by molecular oxygen, is found in wheat. Polyphenol oxidases (catechol oxidase, tyrosinase, etc.) oxidize phenols to quinones and are evidently more concentrated in the bran than in the endosperm; some of their reaction products are colored. Peroxidases and catalase are classed as hydroperoxidases that catalyze the oxidation of certain aromatic amines and phenols by hydrogen peroxide; they are also more active in bran than in the endosperm. All of these, and other enzymes, are discussed in much detail in the recent review by Kruger and Reed (1988).

Utilization of Wheat

Most wheat grown in the U.S. is milled into flour. The amount of the unmilled grain used as animal feed depends on its price relative to other feed grains such as corn and sorghum, but is usually fairly small. A comparatively constant amount is used as seed, and some is used in breakfast cereals, distilled spirits, etc.

When wheat is milled, those portions of the kernel not used for flour go into some combination of bran, shorts, red dog, germ meal, and mixed feed. The nutritional attributes of such products have been studied extensively, but a difficulty with comparisons is that these materials vary widely in composition from one lot to another. The raw materials themselves vary: wheat, for example, can vary in protein content from 7% to 18%. Obviously, the by-products obtained from milling wheats of different composition will themselves vary. And, the efficiency of the milling operation and the way the operator combines the millstreams affects the quality of the millfeed. Products that can be produced by roller mills of conventional design and operation are shown in Figure 1.2.

A fairly large amount of gluten, both "vital" and denatured, is produced. Quite a lot is made in Australia. The U.S. gluten industry seems to be increasing. Vital gluten is being increasingly used for supplementing weak flours and for giving adequate structure to health breads loaded with non-wheat grains and other ingredients that give no gas-retaining properties to the dough. A considerable amount of the undenatured gluten is also being used in hamburger bun and hot dog roll formulas to give the desired low density and a texture that stands up to the abuse given these products. Small amounts of gluten are processed into liquid dietary supplements and flavoring hydrolysates.

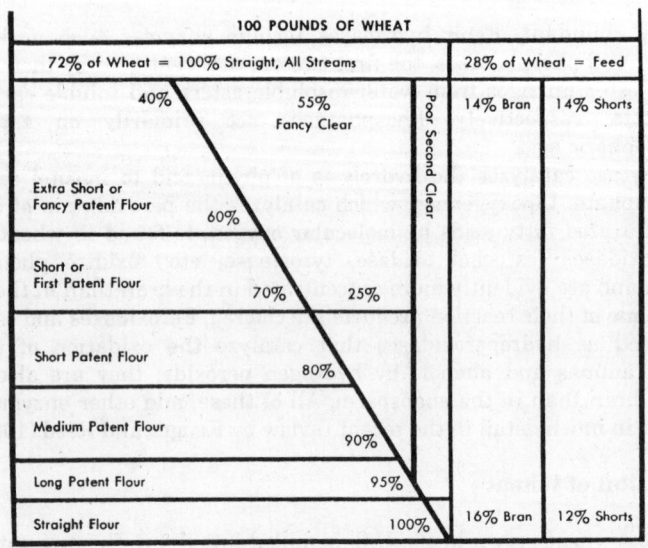

Figure 1.2. Products produced by conventional milling of wheat.

Applications specific to soft wheat.—According to Finney (1989), soft wheats are a preferred source of flour for four product categories and at least 25 product types. He names the product categories of chemically-leavened and yeast leavened baked products, non-baked confectionery, and industrial uses. Most authorities would probably not agree that soft wheat is preferred for yeast-leavened bakery products. He lists the following yeast-leavened products as often being made with soft wheat flour: saltines, pretzels, French-type bread, Chinese steamed bread, and many flat breads. Non-baked products include soups, batters, breadings, gravies, and various noodle types. Of course, it is well known that many chemically-leavened products, such as cakes, cookies, doughnuts, biscuits, and pancakes are most often made with soft wheat flour, and so are many non-leavened products such as cream wafers, pie crusts, and ice cream cones.

When milled, the endosperm of soft wheat breaks yields smaller flour particles than does hard wheat endosperm. The bran usually separates readily from the endosperm, and the latter is easily disintegrated to flour particle size by the reduction rolls. This means the mill requires less energy to grind a given amount of flour, and often the number of steps (roll stands) is reduced.

Applications specific to hard wheats.—The market price of hard wheat is usually slightly higher than the price of soft wheat, so hard wheat products are generally restricted to those uses for which they are particularly well suited. For all practical purposes, this means applications requiring an elastic, extensible dough with good gas-retaining properties. Breads, bread rolls, many kinds of Danish pastry and certain other sweet dough products, yeast-leavened doughnuts, crackers, pretzels, and pizzas are typically made with hard wheat flour. There are many other products that could be listed. It is certainly true that some of these products are being made with soft wheat flours, or with mixtures of soft wheat flours with hard wheat flours or gluten, but products of superior quality are almost always made with flours relatively high in protein and containing gluten which is "strong."

It is not only the quality of the finished product that is dependent on the strength of the flour ingredient; processing efficiency is also affected. Weak flours tend to give soft, sticky doughs. which hang up in the equipment or are torn apart by some of the machinery. Strong flours give doughs that can absorb relatively high levels of water but still give pieces that are not unduly sticky after light applications of dusting flour. They also tend to recover quickly and more or less completely after the abuse given them by the divider, rounder, and molder. They resist gas loss during these processing steps.

Strong flours also give doughs with a high degree of extensibility, so that the repeated laminating and reduction steps encountered in soda cracker processing and in the formation of Danish or puff pastry doughs do not cause the thin layers to break down. Pizza doughs, especially for thin crust pizzas, also need to be highly extensible and to resist the formation of holes; they must be able to expand while supporting a topping layer of considerable weight and rather low viscosity.

These characteristics are not obtainable with the ordinary type of soft wheat flour, no matter how low the absorption or how high the level of flour in the formula. The difference in performance between soft wheat and hard wheat lies not only in the percentage of protein but in its intrinsic quality. This tells us that a simple measurement of the protein content of a wheat or flour is not sufficient to allow an informed judgement to be made of the material's adequacy as an ingredient for bread and the like—it is necessary to test for the quality/strength of the protein as well.

Determining the Quality of Wheat

What Should be Tested?—It is certainly obvious that, in order to be meaningful to the processor or consumer of wheat, the intended use of the grain must determine the characteristics that should be measured in order to evaluate its quality. Wheat that is to be milled into flour for sale to bakeries must have many properties of no interest to operators of feed plants. Good quality durum wheat is expected to have characteristics which, if found in a lot of hard wheat winter wheat, would make the latter unacceptable to a miller of bread flour. Furthermore, manufacturers of baked products may have flour specifications that require the use of very specific types and qualities of hard or soft wheat. Hundreds of tests have been developed by millers, bakers, agronomists, quality control people, and academic scientists for the purpose of providing a basis for selecting the best wheats for specific applications. Most of these procedures have been abandoned because they are too difficult to perform, not specific enough, inaccurate, insufficiently sensitive, of no practical value, or are unpopular for some other reason. In this section, several of the most important tests that are being used today or have been used in the past will be described and related to the characteristics they are supposed to measure. Tests for durum wheat will be discussed in the next chapter.

There are some very general standards used to describe virtually all lots of wheat sold in the U.S., so they can be thought of as perhaps the most important of all quality specifications for wheat. These are the U.S. Official Standards, and they are briefly described below.

Official United States Standards for wheat.–Official Standards define eight classes of wheat: Durum, Hard Red Spring (HRS), Hard Red Winter (HRW), Soft Red Winter (SRW), Hard White (HW), Soft White (SW), Unclassed, and Mixed wheat. Durum wheat is divided into three subclasses based on the percentage of dark, hard, and vitreous kernels of amber color: Hard Amber Durum. Amber Durum, and Durum wheat. Hard Red Spring wheat is divided into three subclasses: Dark Northern Spring, Northern Spring, and Red Spring wheat, based on its content of dark, hard, and vitreous kernels. The classes of Hard Red Winter wheat and Soft Red Winter wheat are not divided into subclasses. White wheat was formerly a class divided into four subclasses, Hard White, Soft White, White Club, and Western White wheat, but in 1990 this class was divided into two new classes, Hard White and Soft White (Sanders 1990).

Any lot of wheat not classifiable under other criteria provided in the wheat standards is "Unclassed Wheat," for which no subclasses are provided, although the class includes red durum wheat and any wheat not red or white in color. "Mixed Wheat" is a mix that consists of less than 90% of one class and more than 10% of one other class, or a combination of classes that meet the definition of wheat. The Standards give other criteria important to wheat producers and buyers but of less interest to flour purchasers.

Tests for "hardness".–It has been suggested by Sanders (1990) that wheat hardness may form the basis of future Standards. Wheat hardness, protein content, and protein quality have been reported to be the major characteristics that differentiate wheat classes. Protein content ranges, however, overlap class boundaries. Protein quality tests are time-consuming and the results are often ambiguous. On the other hand, instruments based on the measurement of near-infrared reflectance (NIRR) can rapidly determine the "hardness" of samples of ground wheat or even of a slice from a single grain.

Kernel hardness affects such factors as the energy required for milling and the mill settings during flour production, and it is also related to the percentage of damaged starch granules found in the flour. It profoundly affects the processing response of cookie and cracker doughs and the texture of the finished products (Faridi *et al.* 1987).

Quality Assurance Testing of Soft Wheat

Some of the quality factors for soft wheat are very similar to those for hard wheat, but, since the products for which the two kinds of flour will be used often require quite different characteristics in their ingredients, the tests applied to the flour and the wheat from which the flour is milled must take these differences into consideration. The major soft wheat quality predictors were reviewed by Finney (1989). He considered five milling and seven end-use properties to be the most important factors characterizing milling and end-use quality of eastern U.S. soft winter wheats and flours. The milling quality predictors are: (1) milling flour yield; (2) break flour yield; (3) endosperm separation index or ESI; (4) friability; and (5) sievability and flowability. The end-use quality predictors are: (1) protein content; (2) protein quality; (3); alkaline water retention capacity; (4) sugar-snap cookie test bake; (5) layer cake test bake; (6) pasting viscosity; and (7) α-amylase activity. Because of the general applicability of these quality tests, each of them will be discussed briefly here. Of course, an individual mill producing specialty flours for limited uses may not need to apply all, or even most, of these tests.

Quality Assurance Testing of Hard Wheat

Milling quality predictors.—Milling quality is a broad term used to summarize the many factors affecting the wheat's response to milling processes. Among these factors are the response of the wheat to conditioning, the millability or reduction response of grain, and the flour yield.

The following physical tests are commonly applied to hard wheat: (1) federal grade, including test weight; (2) kernel hardness; (3) gluten washing; (4) internal infestation evaluation; (5) density; (6) thousand-kernel weight; (7) pearling index; and (8) granulation and particle size. Methods for performing physical tests are included in the handbook of the Official Grain Standards of the U.S. and in Cereal Laboratory Methods (Anon. 1991).

The moisture determination is useful as a basis for setting up the storage and conditioning requirements for wheat and should be conducted on all incoming shipments. The ash determination need not, in all cases, be considered a part of the specifications applied to wheat intended for milling, but it can often be useful. If wheat is purchased from an area where the mineral content in the kernel is unusually high, then it is advisable to have a record of the wheat ash. The ash content is also a valuable check on the uniformity of flour deliveries from a single mill. A mill attempting to meet a given specification, using wheat from a single crop year, should be able to keep the ash content within a very narrow range.

To obtain the most complete evaluation of wheat quality, it is necessary to mill the wheat and subject the flour so obtained to tests not only of protein quality but also of baking strength. The Brabender farinograph is an instrument frequently used to measure absorption and the physical dough properties of wheat and flour. This instrument measures plasticity and mobility of dough when a simple dough is subjected to mixing at a constant temperature. Although the farinograph is useful as a basis for estimating absorption and dough development properties of both soft and hard wheat flour, it gives more meaningful results for hard wheat.

Samples of wheat intended to be milled into flour are often subjected to indirect measurements for amylase activity. Gas production determinations, falling number tests, or amylograph procedures can be employed for this purpose. Most hard wheat flours require adjustment of their amylase activity in order to function optimally in baking. Wheats unusually high or low in amylase activity may not be suitable for use in these mill blends.

In North America it is common practice for quality assurance managers in the milling industry to require a standardized evaluation of the baking quality of wheats used to make up their mill mix. Standardized tests have been developed to help appraise the quality of wheat for bread and some other products. The experimental bread baking test has reached a high level of acceptance as a measure of wheat quality. Many users and suppliers of hard wheat flour have, however, introduced variations into the official procedure which they believe make the test more informative for their particular applications.

GENERAL TESTS FOR CEREAL FLOURS

There have been many reviews of tests that have been suggested and/or used for evaluating wheat and flour quality, particularly quality of flour for bread baking. Papers and booklets on this specific subject include those by Miller and Johnson (1954), Shellenberger and Ward (1967), and Finney and Yamazaki (1967), while books written or edited by Matz (1959, 1969, 1987, 1989), Pomeranz (1988), and Inglett (1974) contain lengthy discussions of this topic as well as many references to original publications. Space limitations prohibit a complete discussion of all the important aspects of this topic. In the following paragraphs, the reader will be directed to the basic references on the subject, and brief reviews and comments applying to the most commonly used tests will be added.

It is widely recognized that the standardized bread baking test is a practical and effective method for measuring the overall quality of flours, though it is labor intensive.

An authoritative source of test procedures relied upon by nearly all quality control technologists is the Official Methods of the Association of Official Analytical Chemists (Anon. 1990).

Chemical and Physical Tests

The tests that quality control analysts have for many decades applied to nearly all flours, whatever the intended purpose of the flour, are moisture, protein, and ash. To these were added tests designed to measure the suitability of the flour for its intended purpose.

Air ovens are often employed to determine the moisture in flour samples. The most common conditions are 266°F for one hour with constant air movement. A number of semiautomatic ovens have been developed using a variety of heat sources. The Carter-Simons moisture tester and the Brabender moisture tester are two of this type.

There is only one chemical method of importance for measuring the protein content of cereal products, the time-tested Kjeldahl procedure. In this technique, the sample is digested by the application of heat and strong sulfuric acid, usually in the presence of a catalyst. The nitrogen in protein and other compounds is converted to ammonia, which forms a salt with the sulfuric acid. After the digest has cooled, ammonia is released from it by adding a strong base. The freed ammonia is distilled into a standard acid solution and the remaining acid determined by a back titration with a standard alkali. End points are determined colorimetrically or electrometrically. Although the Kjeldahl procedure measures the total combined nitrogen content in the flour, not just the protein, this seems to be a minor point so far as flour quality is concerned.

Modifications of the Kjeldahl method have reduced the hazards and ecological deficiencies of the procedure. The original method involved dealing with relatively large amounts of strong acids and with very hot digests that gave off acrid and corrosive fumes, and it was very time-consuming. Ecology-wise it was not very green. Many methods intended to replace the Kjeldahl procedure have been suggested over the years, and some have achieved moderate popularity. New methods and equipment enable the test to be conducted with much smaller samples and much less reagent; they are faster and cheaper, and they involve less danger to the analyst. It would serve no purpose to go into further details of the Kjeldahl test since a complete description is given in readily available references.

Near-infrared reflectance instruments seemingly do a good job in estimating protein content and are much quicker, cleaner, and ecologically desirable than the Kjeldahl analysis.

Although the importance of ash content measurements has been downgraded in recent years, the ash test has a long history of providing a way to estimate flour grade or extraction, subject to the input of other information on the type of wheat being milled, etc. Since the ash content of bran is about twenty times that of endosperm, the ash test can be a reliable indicator of the efficiency with which the bran and germ were separated from the endosperm. There is considerable variation in the amount of mineral matter in wheat, depending on the class of wheat and the area it was grown; therefore the ash test is often applied to wheat as well as to flour, but its significance is somewhat less certain in the case of wheat. In the author's opinion, the real value of the ash test is that it gives another clue to the uniformity of the flour, compared with previous deliveries, and provides a check on the miller's control of his process. The test is simple and inexpensive and not very labor intensive, so it should be routinely applied to incoming flour shipments unless there is some valid reason not to do so.

Starch damage is a subject of concern to wheat processors and to the baker. The extent of starch damage alters flour characteristics and can affect final product quality. The amylase activity of wheat and flour can be measured or estimated by the Falling Number test, the Blish-Sandstedt method, and the amylograph evaluation. Descriptions of these tests can be found in test compilations previously cited.

Tests of gluten quality.—The meaning of "quantity of protein" in a wheat or flour is readily understood since the protein determination is a standardized procedure that can be duplicated in almost any cereal laboratory. The meaning of gluten "quality" is not as uniformly defined, because the definition is affected by characteristics inherent in the wheat kernel and by the purposes for which the flour is to be used. However, there are three rather clearly delimited categories of gluten quality: strong (hard wheat) gluten, weak (soft wheat) gluten, and durum-type gluten. The last is not considered satisfactory for bread dough, but it is ideal for pasta.

Many attempts have been made to appraise flour quality on the basis of the amino acid composition of gluten. Determining the amino acid composition of a sample of protein is no longer a tedious and labor intensive procedure (though it still requires expensive equipment), so it might not be impractical as a quality control test, but various investigators have failed to find essential differences in the amino acid profiles of good and bad flours. It appears much more work is needed before evaluations based on the amino acid distribution will tell the baker what he needs to know about the baking quality of flour. The value of the test to wheat breeders and cereal scientists is more obvious.

A large number of tests based on the imbibitional properties of wheat proteins have been developed and, in some cases, used fairly extensively to estimate the bakery potential of wheat and flour. In this category are measurements of viscosity, sedimentation, and swelling properties of gluten. The Zeleny sedimentation test consists of suspending flour particles in a graduated cylinder containing dilute lactic acid. The rate of sedimentation is a measure of the hydration capacity of the flour proteins and, thus, supposedly is an index of quality. Sedimentation test values obtained from 360 cargoes of wheat in world commerce showed a correlation of 0.726 with the overall quality scores of the wheat. This was a significantly higher correlation than that between protein contents and quality scores.

Although there is wide agreement that many properties of a dough are reflections of the gluten characteristics, most cereal chemists prefer to study the properties of doughs rather than to separate gluten and then attempt to appraise its quality. Regardless of the methods used, differences in gluten properties can be clearly shown to be related to the variety of wheat from which the flour was milled, extraction rate, and proteolytic activity.

Dough testing instruments.—Elaborate mechanical and electro-mechanical devices have been developed for evaluating the baking properties of flour. Some of these have achieved considerable commercial success. They are of definite value in policing the uniformity of flour deliveries from a given miller. The Farinograph and the Extensograph are widely used, particularly for determining the quality of hard wheat flours. Although data obtained from these instruments reflect mainly the quality and quantity of protein, these factors are not the only characteristics affecting results. The Mixograph is an earlier, simpler, instrument which has been used in many labs for about the same purposes as the Farinograph and Extensograph. Mixograms obtained under conditions of uniform absorption and adjusted to a constant ash basis are supposed to permit an experienced operator to estimate a flour's hydration properties.

The Alveograph or Chopin extensimeter is an apparatus that measures a dough's extensibility and resistance to expansion. A thin sheet of dough is clamped between two metal plates, the upper plate having a circular hole through which the dough can expand while the lower plate is provided with an air valve leading to a small air chamber. Pressure in the chamber is increased at a constant rate by supplying air from the top of a burette into which water is flowing. Pressure is recorded by indicators or sensors connected to the chamber and charted against time. Temperature is maintained at 77°F. The manometer record normally shows a rapid initial rise in pressure as the dough sheet resists expansion, then a decline as the thinning sheet loses strength and stretches, forming a bigger "balloon." Ultimately, the bubble will burst and the graph will show a sudden complete loss of the excess pressure. The volume of the bubble is often a good indication of the baking strength of the flour.

Extensographs measure the resistance to stretching of a cylinder of flour-water dough. Dough samples may be measured at various intervals after mixing to show changes in extensibility with time. The processing response of doughs in the bakery and the quality of final products are related to these measurements. Force required to stretch the dough is automatically plotted against the distance it stretches, so that a curve is drawn.

The Farinograph has a steel bowl in which two mixing arms turn. The resistance of the dough to movement of the agitator arms is recorded on a chart as a function of time. Resistance increases as the dough develops and then decreases as the dough breaks down, as it always does under prolonged, excessive mixing. Factors measured on the curve include absorption (percentage of water added to reach a predetermined height in the curve), initial development (time required for maximum development), stability (resistance of the dough to breakdown with continued mixing),

mixing time, mechanical tolerance index, etc.

The Amylograph is employed to measure the viscosity changes of starch suspensions which are being heated at a controlled rate. The data so obtained are related to the performance of soft wheat flours in certain applications where starch gelatinization characteristics are important.

BIBLIOGRAPHY

ANON. 1990. Official Methods of Analysis of the AOAC, Fifteenth Edition. Assoc. Official Analytical Chemists, Arlington, VA

ANON. 1991. Approved Methods of Analysis, Compiled Version. Eighth Ed. Am. Assoc. Cereal Chemists, St. Paul, MN

BASS, E. J. 1988. Wheat flour milling. In Wheat. Vol 2. Third Edition. Y. Pomeranz, Ed. Am. Assoc. Cereal Chemists, St. Paul, MN

BIETZ, J. A. 1979. Recent advances in the isolation and characterization of cereal proteins. Cereal Foods World 27, 199-204

BLANCO, A., DE PACE, C., PORCEDDU, E., and MUGNOZZA, G. T. S. 1988. Genetics and breeding of durum wheat in Europe. In Durum Wheat: Chemistry and Technology. G. Fabriani and C. Lintas, Editors. American Association of Cereal Chemists, St. Paul, MN

BOLLING, H. 1987. Milling quality of wheat. In Cereals in a European Context. I. D. Morton, Ed. Ellis Horwood Ltd., Chichester, England

BUSHUK, W. 1986. Wheat: Chemistry and uses. Cereal Foods World 31, 218-220, 222, 225-226

CERNING, J., and GUILBOT, A. 1973. Carbohydrate composition of wheat. In Wheat: Production and Utilization. G. Inglett, Ed. AVI Publ. Co., Westport, CT

CUMMINGS, J. H., and ENGLYST, H. N. 1987. The development of methods for the measurement of "dietary fibre" in food. In Cereals in a European Context. I. D. Morton, Editor. Ellis Horwood, Chichester, England

DAVIS, K. R., CAIN, R.F., PETERS, L. J., LETOURNEAU, D., and MCGINNIS, J. 1981. Evaluation of the nutrient composition of wheat. II. Proximate analysis, thiamine, riboflavin, niacin, and pyridoxine. Cereal Chem. 58, 116-120

DAVIS, K. R., PETERS, L. J., and LE TOURNEAU, D. 1984. Variability of the vitamin content in wheat. Cereal Foods World 29, 364-367

EVERS, A. D., and BECHTEL, D. B. 1988. Microscopic structure of the wheat grain. In Wheat: Chemistry and Technology, Vol. I. Third Edition. Y. Pomeranz, Ed. Am. Assoc. Cereal Chemists, St. Paul, MN

FARIDI, H. A., FINLEY, J. W., and LEVEILLE, G. A. 1987. Wheat hardness: A user's view. Cereal Foods World 32, 327-329

FINNEY, K. F., and YAMAZAKI, W. T. 1967. Quality of hard, soft, and durum wheats. In Wheat and Wheat Improvement. American Society of Agronomy, Madison, WI

FINNEY, P. L. 1989. Soft wheat: View from the eastern U.S. Cereal Foods World 34, 662, 664, 666-667

FORD, M., and KINGSWOOD, K. 1987. Milling in the European economic community. In Soft Wheat: Production, Breeding, Milling, and Uses. W. T. Yamazaki and C. T. Greenwood, Editors. Am. Assoc. Cereal Chemists, St. Paul, MN

GAINES, C. S. 1990. Influence of chemical and physical modificaton of soft wheat protein on sugar-snap cookie dough consistency, cookie size, and hardness. Cereal Chem. 67, 73-77

GEDDES, W. F. 1951. Cereal grains. In The Chemistry and Technology of Food and Food Products. M. B. Jacobs, Editor. Interscience Publ., NYC

GREENWELL, P., and SCHOFIELD, J. D. 1986. A starch granule protein associated with endosperm softness in wheat. Cereal Chem. 63, 379-380

HOSENEY, R. C. 1987. Wheat hardness. Cereal Foods World 32, 320-322

INGLETT, G. E. (Editor) 1974. Wheat: Production and Utilization. AVI Publishing Co., Westport, CT

JACKEL, S. S. 1987. More wheat with superior baking quality is needed. Cereal Foods World *32*, 323-325

KRUGER, J. E., and REED, G. 1988. Enzymes and color. *In* Wheat: Chemistry and Technology, Vol. I. Third Ed. Y. Pomeranz, Ed. Am. Assoc. Cereal Chemists, St. Paul, MN

LINEBACK, D. R., and RASPER, V. F. 1988. Wheat carbohydrates. *In* Wheat: Chemistry and Technology, Vol. I. Third Edition. Y. Pomeranz, Ed. Am. Assoc. Cereal Chemists, St. Paul, MN

LOCKHART, H. B., and NESHEIM, R. O. 1978. Nutritional quality of cereal grains. *In* Cereals '78. Y. Pomeranz, Ed. Am. Assoc. Cereal Chemists, St. Paul, MN

MATZ, S. A. (Editor) 1959. The Chemistry and Technology of Cereals as Food and Feed. AVI Publishing Co., Westport, CT

MATZ, S. A. 1969. Cereal Science. AVI Publishing Co., Westport, CT

MATZ, S. A. 1987. Ingredients for Bakers. Pan-Tech International, Inc., McAllen, TX

MATZ, S. A. 1989. Technology of the Materials of Baking. Elsevier Science Publishers, Barking, England

MILLER, B. S., and JOHNSON, J. A. 1954. A review of methods for determining the quality of wheat and flour for breadmaking. Kans. Agr. Expt. Sta. Tech. Bull. *76*

MORRISON, W. R. 1988. Lipids. *In* Wheat: Chemistry and Technology, Vol. I. Third Edition. Y. Pomeranz, Ed. Am. Assoc. Cereal Chemists, St. Paul, MN

NIERNBERGER, F. F. 1978. Near-infrared reflectance instrument analysis of grain constituents: A cost study. USDA ESCS Rept. *ESCS-20*

O'DELL, B. L., DE BOLAND, A. R., and KOIRTYOHANN, S. R. 1972. Distribution of phytate and nutritionally important elements among the morphological components of cereal grains. J. Agr. Food Chem. *20*, 718-721

PERTEN, H. 1990A. Method for determining the quality of gluten in wheat. U. S. Pat. 4,953,401

PERTEN, H. 1990B. Rapid measurement of wet gluten quality by the gluten index. Cereal Foods World *35*, 401-402

POMERANZ, Y. (Editor) 1988. Wheat: Chemistry and Technology, Third Edition. American Association of Cereal Chemists, St. Paul, MN

SANDERS, K. F. 1990. Wheat hardness may form basis of future U.S. grain standards. The Wheat Grower (Apr. 1990) 12-14

SHELLENBERGER, J. A. 1980. Advances in milling technology. Adv. in Cereal Science and Technology *3*, 227-274

SHELLENBERGER, J. A., and WARD, A. B. 1967. Experimental milling. *In* Wheat and Wheat Improvement. American Society of Agronomy, Madison, WI

SHEWRY, P. R., FIELD, J. M., AND TATHAM, A. S. 1987. The structures of cereal seed storage proteins. *In* Cereals in a European Context. I. D. Morton, Editor. Ellis Horwood, Chichester, England

chapter two

INGREDIENTS FROM OTHER GRAINS

INTRODUCTION

Although wheat flour is the indispensable ingredient in leavened bakery products as we know them, flours and meals from many other grains (not necessarily cereal grains) are frequently used as ingredients for the purposes of enhancing flavor or color, reducing ingredient cost, meeting requirements of certain ethnic markets, and improving nutritional aspects. They may also be used solely for marketing purposes to distinguish one commercial item from a multitude of similar products. No doubt there are additional reasons for adding non-wheat flours and meals to bakery foods.

The purpose of this chapter is to give basic information on all the grains that might reasonably be expected to perform some useful function in bakery products, so that the reader can decide whether further investigation is justified when formulation studies are contemplated. Brief discussions of rye, triticale, barley, oats, corn, rice, millet, and durum, and of the baking properties of ingredients made from them will be found in the following paragraphs. These grains, and others, are discussed in much more detail in "The Chemistry and Technology of Cereals as Food and Feed," Third Edition (Matz 1991).

The U.S. Grain Standards, often quoted in this chapter, can be found in the Code of Federal Regulations (CFR), current edition, title 7, part 810 and can also be obtained from the USDA or the U.S. Printer's Office, Washington, DC. Standards of Identity for Cereal Flours and Related Products are found in 21 CFR 137. These sources have not been repeated in the Bibliography.

DURUM

Durum is a grain that has been in existence for much longer than bread wheat, but it is now mostly used as a raw material for pasta. It is not a preferred ingredient for leavened bakery products, because durum flour will not make the extensible, elastic, cohesive doughs necessary for proper functioning of those formulas. Small amounts are used in flat breads—mostly in the Middle Eastern countries—but that usage is largely based on economic and traditional considerations rather than on quality factors.

Production of durum wheat is rather widespread. In Europe, at least seven countries produce commercially significant quantities of this grain. In North America, durum wheat is an important crop in the north central states of the U.S. and in Canada. Argentina has the largest durum production in Central and South America, followed by Mexico, Chile, Bolivia, and

Peru, all with less than 100,000 acres planted to this crop in normal years.

Special Quality Considerations

Nearly all published research studies involving quality of durum are concerned with the function of semolina in pasta. Review of these applications is outside the scope of this book.

Starchy kernels, which are opaque and, when cut across, show endosperms that are completely white and starchy, are considered a defect in durum. Milling performance of durum, but not of hard wheat, is adversely influenced by the presence of starchy kernels in the mill blend because they tend to break down readily into fine flour, reducing the yield of the coarser semolina. The simplest way to detect starchy or piebald (partly starchy) kernels is by visual examination, although it has been shown that starchy kernels contain less protein than vitreous kernels (Dexter *et al.* 1989).

For durum that is to be used to make flour for bread, a use that is described below, the gluten qualities must be taken into account. According to Boggini and Pogna (1989), breadmaking quality is associated with the viscoelastic properties of gluten, protein content, and protein composition. Among the Farinograph indices, development time and mixing stability were positively correlated with bread volume.

Utilization

In Europe and America, the principal use of durum wheat is for the production of semolina to be used as a raw material in pasta, but durum can also be made into flour for bread and this was its major application for thousands of years. It is not nearly as satisfactory as hard or soft wheat for breadmaking, however, because doughs made from it are not as extensible, and the bread cannot be made as light and tender as the sophisticated consumers of today demand. In the Middle East and North Africa, local breadmaking still accounts for about half the consumption of durum. The doughs will often consist of imported hard wheat flour mixed with a fairly large percentage of locally produced durum flour.

Quaglia (1988) described the production of Altamura bread in Italy. Varying proportions of durum and hard wheat flour are used in these doughs. Durum flour has a positive value in that it contributes a yellow color in the finished product. Leavening is by sourdough starters. A sponge is prepared by mixing soft wheat flour and hard wheat flour with water and allowing the dough to ferment until the following day. One part of sponge is then mixed with 0.7 parts of durum flour and 1.4 parts of water, and the new sponge is allowed to stand for two hours. To reduce acidity, another dough-up follows in which one part of the previous blend is mixed with 0.5 parts water and 0.9 parts durum flour. After four hours of fermentation, three parts of the final sponge are doughed up with 10 parts of flour, 0.3 part salt, 0.09 parts compressed yeast, and eight parts of lukewarm water.

Mixing is for about 30 min in a reciprocating dual-arm machine. The dough is wrapped in a cotton cloth and allowed to rest for 2 hr after which it is divided into 1.2 kg or 2.4 kg pieces. The rounded pieces are fermented for about 60 min on wooden trays. Traditional shapes are formed by folding the dough at the center, refolding it on itself, then pressing it with the back of the hand. Loaves are baked for 2 hr at 200°C without steam.

RYE

Rye can be considered a minor cereal crop in the Americas, but it is important in Europe and in parts of Asia where it finds substantial use as a bread grain. Its ability to produce acceptable crops under conditions of soil, temperature, and precipitation that make wheat cultivation impractical, is the principal reason for its dominance in these regions. Of course, tradition plays an important role, as it always does, and farmers continue to grow rye long after they have access to varieties of wheat capable of producing acceptable crops in their areas.

It is clear from centuries of experience that people given a free choice between rye bread and wheat bread will eventually switch to the latter product. The persistence of rye as an ingredient for bread is based not on any superiority of the taste, texture, or appearance characteristics the grain contributes to the finished product but to: (1) adherence of millers, bakers, and consumers to traditional products; (2) a possible price advantage in some very limited market situations; (3) a desire by affluent consumers for "something different"; and (4) a perception, not necessarily correct, that rye has some sort of health-giving features not found in wheat.

Chemical and Physical Characteristics

The rye kernel, like other cereal grains, is a caryopsis, a small, dry, indehiscent, one-seeded fruit varying to as much as 6 to 8 mm in length and 2 to 3 mm in width. Ripe grain is free-threshing and of various colors, but commonly grayish yellow. The seed consists of an embryo attached through a scutellum to the endosperm and aleurone tissues. The endosperm and aleurone are enclosed by the remnants of the nucellar epidermis and the testa or seed coat. The pericarp or fruit coat surrounds the whole seed and adheres closely to it. A crease or furrow extends the full length of the grain on the ventral side. The outline of the embryo can be seen at the base of the dorsal side. Mature kernels often have a shrivelled appearance. Developing kernels are served by four vascular traces emanating from a basal vascular bundle. Three of the traces extend through the pericarp while the fourth passes up the crease of the kernel on the ventral side. Some chemical components of rye and its milling products are shown in Table 2.1.

Protein content of the rye kernel ranges from 6.5% to 14.5%; samples near the latter figure apparently originated from fields given very high levels of nitrogen fertilizer. In general, rye is lower in protein content than is wheat. Some uncertainty is introduced into the discussion by disagreements over the factor to be used in converting Kjeldahl nitrogen of rye grain to protein. Factors from 5.64 to 6.25 have been used by various writers. The World Health Organization recommends 5.83, while Simmonds and Campbell (1976) used 5.7.

Table 2.1. CHEMICAL COMPOSITION OF RYE GRAIN AND PRODUCTS[1]

Sample	Protein	Fat	Crude fiber	Minerals	N-free extract
	%	%	%	%	%
Rye grain	12.6	1.7	2.4	1.8	70.9
Rye flour	11.2	1.3	0.6	0.9	74.6
Rye middlings	16.6	3.4	5.2	3.8	61.2

[1] Based on data of Morrison (1956).

Ash determinations typically yield a figure of 2.1% for rye, comparable in amount to the ash of wheat. Composition of rye ash is similar to that of other cereals. The mineral content is particularly high in the aleurone layer because of the presence of phytin granules, which are made up mostly of potassium and magnesium salts of myoinositol hexaphosphate.

There is about 1.5% to 2.0% crude fat in rye, not far different from the amount found in wheat and barley, but considerably lower than the fat content of oats. Rye lipids differ from those of most other cereals by having a slightly greater proportion of the unsaturated linolenic acid. Because such fatty acids are very susceptible to oxidation, rancidity development tends to be the factor limiting the storage life of rye flour, assuming the product is protected against insect infestation and is not of sufficiently high moisture content to encourage mold growth.

The nitrogen-free extract consists primarily of starch. Rye starch granules have a mean particle diameter greater than those of other cereals, and the size distribution covers a wider range. The granules fall into two classes depending on shape, one type being lenticular and the other being smaller and approximately spherical. Like other cereal starches, rye granules show birefringence in transmitted polarized light and, as usual, this birefringence disappears when the starch gelatinizes. The birefringence endpoint temperature and gelatinization temperature range of rye starch granules are similar to those of wheat starch. Rye flour suspensions give very low peak amylograph viscosities as compared to wheat, but this is due to high alpha-amylase activity in the former. Although there is some dispute about the amylopectin:amylose ratio in rye starch, most authorities seem to think that, in most cultivars, it is about the same as in wheat starch.

In rye the nonstarchy polysaccharides are more important than protein in determining the quality of bread (Kuhn and Grosch 1989). This is the principal reason that rye bread has larger pores and seems moister than wheat bread. These substances, predominantly pentosans, are present at levels of about 8% in rye, compared to about 3% in wheat. Crude fiber content is similar to wheat kernels, perhaps slightly less, depending on the cultivar and the method used for determining fiber.

Rye has a significant content of a few micronutrients such as thiamin, nicotinic acid, riboflavin, pyridoxine, pantothenic, and tocopherol. These substances are present mainly in the embryo, scutellum, and aleurone. Typical figures on content in the whole kernel, in mg per 100 g dry basis, are thiamin 0.44, riboflavin, 0.18, niacin 1.5, pantothenic acid 0.77, and pyridoxine 0.33. Rye is essentially devoid of vitamin C and vitamin A.

Typical mineral content of rye grain in mg per kg includes calcium 60, iron 10, magnesium 120, phosphorus 340, potassium 460, sodium 1, copper 0.78, manganese 6.7, and zinc 3.0 (Lockhart and Nesheim 1978).

There are, of course, many enzymes in fresh rye kernels (i.e., those not damaged by heat or long storage). Many of these enzymes are substantially inactive in mature dry grain. Some of the enzymes that have received a great deal of researchers' attention are α-amylase, proteases, esterases, and beta glucosidases.

In summary, the analytical report for a typical sample of rye kernels might be expected to show 13.4% protein, 1.8% ether extract, 2.6% crude fiber, 2.1% ash, and 80.1% nitrogen free extract, all on a moisture-free basis.

There appear to be anti-nutritional factors in the grain. When rye is fed as a high percentage of the diet to domestic animals, such as chickens, deleterious physiological effects are often observed. Studies have shown that these effects are the result, at least in part, of the presence of relatively high amounts of such toxic substances as 5-alkyl resorcinols. Phytic acid and its salts also occur, and act as anti-nutritional factors by chelating calcium, iron, magnesium, and zinc. Anti-trypsin factors have been reported by a number of authors. Further details about toxic substances in rye can be found in the article by Hulse and Laing (1974).

TRITICALE

Triticale is a hybrid of wheat and rye that has been known for over 100 years. It is planted on about four million acres worldwide, most of it in France, Russia, and Poland. A much smaller acreage is planted in the U.S. The plants currently cultivated as triticale apparently breed true, and seed can be used through numerous generations, unlike usual hybrids.

General Characteristics

Triticale plants are generally similar to wheat plants, except the former have larger spikes and kernels and show greater vigor of growth. Both winter and spring types are known. The plant appears to be more resistant than rye to ergot infection but less resistant than wheat. Triticale grain has few, if any, advantages over wheat for food manufacturing purposes. It doesn't yield bread that tastes better, looks better, or has better texture than bread made from wheat flour. Its dough processing properties are inferior to those of doughs made from hard wheat. It may give some of the flavor and color of rye to bread doughs, but it seems easier and more reliable to get the same results using a blend of rye meal and wheat flour. Its nutritional quality may be somewhat better than that of wheat, but even this is debatable. Promoters of this grain emphasize that triticale contains higher amounts of lysine than wheat does. Under favorable conditions, triticale is able to match or surpass wheat's vitamin, mineral, and protein levels, but its quality is still inconsistent. Protein levels average over 11% but can vary by as much as 50% in a single year.

This grain can be used to make flour for baked goods that normally require soft wheat flours such as cakes, cookies, and pancakes. Low gluten content is a problem for applications such as loaf bread.

Quality, Composition, and Nutritional Factors

The basic quality specifications for triticale introduced into commerce are the U.S. Standards for Triticale. In this publication, triticale is defined as the "Grain that, before the removal of dockage, consists of 50% or more of triticale (X Triticosecale Wittmack) and not more than 10% of other grains for which standards have been established, and that, after the removal of dockage, contains 50% or more of whole triticale." There are four numerical grades and a U.S. Sample grade for triticale not meeting the numerical grades. The numerical grades are distinguished from one another by their test weights, percent of damaged kernels, content of foreign material, limits on shrunken and broken kernels, and "defects." Minimum bushel weights for the four numerical grades run from 41.0 to 48.0 lb. There is no division of triticale into classes or sub-classes.

Total protein content of triticale is known to be quite variable among cultivars. In one report, triticale grain is said to have 13.1% protein (dwb), or 12.1% true digestible protein, compared to wheat's 12.6% and 11.3% and rye's 9.1% and 7.0%, respectively (Eggum 1977). From another source, we learn that triticale has (mg per kg) 20 calcium, 4 iron, 385 potassium, 0.52 copper, 4.26 manganese, and 2.00 zinc (Lockhart and Nesheim 1978).

Four whole triticale flours showed total lipids varying from 3.19% to 4.61% (dry basis), free lipids being in the range of 1.70% to 2.17%, and bound lipids ranging from 1.47% to 2.56% (Chung and Tsen 1974). These authors concluded: "Neither triticale lipid composition nor quantity was intermediate between analogous properties of its wheat and rye parents."

In a review of publications on triticale starch, D'Appolonia (1974) stated ". . .there does not appear to be any physical, chemical, or structural properties in triticale starch that is so different that it cannot be accounted for by the starch of one of the parents." Percent amylose in the starch of one cultivar was 23.7%. Birefringence end point temperature was 61.5°C. Mean granule diameters of six varieties varied from 17.8 to 25.6 microns. Analyses showed 0.04% N, 0.39% ash, 0.78% fat, and 0.042% P in the starch.

Triticale kernels contain inhibitors for both chymotrypsin and trypsin. The trypsin inhibitor was probably inherited from its rye parent, since wheat has little of this anti-nutritional factor. The anti-chymotrypsin activities of triticale, wheat, and rye are comparable (Madl and Tsen 1974).

Utilization

The characteristics and genetics of triticale suggest that the grain could be milled by a combination of the processes used for milling wheat and rye. Farrell *et al.* (1974) milled many small lots and came to the following conclusions: (1) Cleaning and tempering could use the same equipment as is used for wheat; (2) A rather white flour of 0.55% ash obtained at about 60% yield seems feasible using corrugated and smooth rolls with selected sifting arrangements; (3) In the break process, the cleanup is somewhat difficult because the bran is tender like soft wheat bran, so bran dusters will be required after the break rolls; (4) sifting seems less difficult than with rye mills or soft wheat mills; (5) the spread in protein between the grain and the straight grade flour is from 1.5 to 2.0% compared with 0.8% to 1.2% for milled hard wheat bread flours; and (6) air classification is possible.

The baking quality of triticale flour is inferior to that of wheat flour. The poor performance is largely due to the lower percentages of gluten in triticale flour. Tsen (1974) reviewed uses of triticale flour in baked foods. Acceptable sugar cookies can be made from the flour, but soft red winter wheat flour gives superior results. Other cookies, such as oatmeal, coconut, and chocolate chip, can be made from triticale flour. When used in layer cakes, chlorination improved performance of the flour but the finished products were still not equal to those made from soft wheat flour. Cake doughnuts were mostly satisfactory, but had lower volume. Pancakes were mostly satisfactory though they had a different flavor than conventionally formulated products. Muffins were generally good, but darker.

RICE

Rice, one of the oldest and most important food crops, is the staple food of over half the world's population. Harvested area of rice land has fluctuated between about 350 and 360 million acres during the last few years. Annual world production of rough rice probably approached 475 million metric tons last year. Only about 2% or 3% of this enters world commerce because most rice is consumed in the country where it is produced. Most rice is eaten as the whole grain. Rice flour will not make an extensible dough, so its use in leavened baked products is very limited. It has been used in cookies and crackers, where its mild flavor, white color, and neutral textural qualities are of some value. Its presumed low or nonexistent "gluten" content has prompted investigations of its possible use to replace other cereal flours in bakery products for celiac disease victims.

Structure and Composition

As harvested, rough rice consists of the outer covering tissues comprising the hull, or husk, and the inner kernel, i.e., the caryopsis. The caryopsis is enveloped by the caryopsis coat consisting of the pericarp, seed coat, and nucellar layers. Just inside it is the seed coat, a layer of cells having a thick cuticle and representing what remains of the inner integument. Proceeding inwardly, the next layer, only about 2.5 microns thick, consists of the remains of the nucellus. Inside this layer is the aleurone, which completely encloses the endosperm and the embryo.

The composition of typical samples of rice and rice products is shown in Table 2.2. The changes that occur as the grain is milled reflect the uneven distribution of its components relative to the distance from the surface of the kernel. As layers are successively removed, the proportion of protein, fats, and vitamins in the remaining kernel decreases, while the proportion of carbohydrates increases.

Table 2.2. REPRESENTATIVE COMPOSITION OF RICE PRODUCTS[1]

Component and unit	Brown rice	Milled rice	Rice polish	Rice bran
Carbohydrates, %	87.2	91.5	66.8	46.6
Protein, %	8.3	7.6	13.2	14.6
Ash, %	1.7	0.5	7.1	10.6
Fat, %	2.0	0.3	10.7	13.4
Crude fiber, %	1.1	0.4	3.3	12.7
N-free extract	82.4	88.8	62.5	45.0

[1] Compiled from a number of sources, see especially Matz and Beachell (1969). Data reported on moisture-free basis.

Proteins.—The nutritional quality of rice protein is high relative to that of most other cereal proteins. This is due to rice's relatively high content of lysine, which is the first limiting amino acid. Most of the so-called storage proteins in rice kernels are found in discrete protein-rich bodies (aleurins) in the endosperm, similar to the situation in many other seeds. This protein is largely insoluble in water. Most of it—80% or more in milled rice—is the type called glutelin, soluble only in dilute acids or alkalies. The second most abundant type of protein is the salt-soluble globulin. Both of these are composed of a number of molecular species that are generally isoelectric around pH 7. The amount of protein and the amino acid composition of the protein of rice will vary with growing conditions and variety.

Starch.—Milled rice contains from about 84% to over 90% starch (dry basis). Starch is present in the form of angular granules measuring about 2 to 7 microns in their largest dimension. Many of these particles are roughly pentagonal in outline. In size and shape, they are somewhat like the granules of oat starch, but differ in that few if any rounded particles occur. The hilum is centric and indistinct, and birefringence is weak.

Waxy (glutinous) rice has been grown in Asia for many centuries. In some countries, most of the crop consists of these varieties. The principal differences between waxy and normal rice depend upon the starch. Typically, waxy rice will contain 2% or less of amylose.

Lipids.—There is not much lipid material in milled rice, perhaps 0.3% to 0.4% by acid hydrolysis could be considered average. Rice bran contains a much higher percentage of lipids, perhaps 21%. Nearly all the studies of rice lipids have concentrated on rice bran oil, and there is a substantial trade in the fatty materials extracted from rice bran and refined.

Fatty acids in the glycerides of rice bran oil contain mostly even numbers of carbon atoms from 14 to 20 as well as odd-numbered fatty acids of chain length 11, 13, and 15. These odd-numbered chains are present in the small amounts of 0.2%, 0.6%, and 0.9%, respectively, in one sample. Gas-liquid chromatography indicates that bran lipids have significantly higher mean contents of linoleic and linolenic acids, but lower contents of myristic, palmitic, palmitoleic, and stearic acids, than the lipids of milled rice.

Vitamins and minerals.—Only thiamin and niacin are important vitamins in rice. The following data are in mg per 100 g, first figure for raw, second for parboiled rice. Thiamin was present at levels of 0.13 and 0.15, niacin at levels of 1.54 and 3.2, pyridoxine at a level of 0.14 for raw, and riboflavin at 0.04 and 0.044. According to Kennedy (1980), "When compared on an energy basis with the RDA for adult women and when rice is a large part of the diet (2,000 Kcal), brown rice would give more than sufficient niacin, thiamin, and phosphorus. . .Protein needs would be nearly enough—91%. . .but calcium and riboflavin needs would be low, both about 23% [zinc about 60%]. Milled rice, however, would be deficient in all nutrients with only protein, niacin, and phosphorus supplying more than 50% of the RDA."

Milled rice is not an important source of minerals. The content of ash in a large series of samples ranged from 0.26% to 1.95%, dry basis, with a mean of about 0.65%. There is a considerably higher concentration of minerals in the bran, but the availability of at least some of these is adversely affected by the high concentration of phytin in the bran.

Potassium and phosphorus are the most abundant mineral elements in rice (e.g, 88 mg and 140 mg per 100 g DWB, respectively). Calcium, iron, sodium, silicon, magnesium, sulfur, and minor amounts of other elements have also been found in the ash. Appreciable amounts of silicon are found in the mature rice plant, and slight amounts in milled rice. Sodium, magnesium, and calcium were found at mean concentrations of 8.1, 28, and 25 mg, respectively, in whole kernels of six varieties of milled rice.

Of the trace minerals, iron is present in brown rice and white rice at 1.8 and 0.9 mg per 100 g, dry weight basis, respectively, and zinc is present at 1.6 and 1.4 mg per 100 g, as is basis, respectively.

Other constituents.—Sugars, hemicellulose, nucleic acids, pigments, phytin, and numerous other substances have been found in small amounts in rice. Phytin, the principle phosphorus compound in rice, is said to constitute more than 8% of the bran in some samples. There is a small, but important, amount of sugars, brown rice containing about 0.8% to 1.4% total sugars. Reducing sugars are typically near 0.1%. Parboiled rice can be expected to contain around 0.7% to 1.1% total sugars, and about 0.16% reducing sugars. Milled rice will typically contain much lower amounts of total sugars, about 0.4%, and perhaps 0.06% reducing sugars.

The amount of fiber varies greatly, depending on the method of analysis, the variety of rice and its growth conditions, the processing that has been applied to the rice, and other factors. Among reported values for fiber in brown, milled, and parboiled rices are 0.9%, 0.3%, and 0.2%, respectively.

Quality Factors

The U.S. Standards control commercial definitions of rice and thus serve as the foundation for any purchasing specifications for rice and rice products. There are actually three sets of standards: U.S. Standards for Rough Rice, U.S. Standards for Brown Rice for Processing, and U.S. Standards for Milled Rice. Rough rice is defined as "Rice (*Oryza sativa* L.) which consists of 50 percent or more of paddy kernels of rice." Brown rice for processing is defined as "Rice . . . which consists of more than than 50.0 percent of kernels of brown rice, and which is intended for processing to milled rice." Milled rice is defined as "Whole or broken kernels of rice . . . from which the hulls and at least the outer bran layers have been removed and which contain not more than 10.0 percent of seeds, paddy kernels, or foreign material, either singly or combined."

It is rather obvious that the U.S. Standards are too general to serve the needs of the average commercial processor, although they may be suitable for packagers of raw rice. Furthermore, they do not deal with rice flour, which would be the ingredient of most interest to developers of bakery products. Of course, there are some general quality factors, such as freedom from insect infestation and absence of toxic chemicals that will apply to virtually all food uses. Color and flavor would be of interest to users of flour, as would particle size. Characteristics of the starch would also be important.

Classification as long grain, medium grain, or short grain is based on the length:width ratio of unbroken kernels, with limits as defined in the Rice Inspection Handbook. Long grain rice is characterized by a comparatively high amylose content and a fairly high gelatinizing temperature.

Use of Rice in the Baking Industry

The use of whole or broken rice kernels in baked products is certainly of minor importance. Rice flour made by impact milling of the broken grains does have some applications. There is no theoretical reason why roller milling cannot be applied to rice, but this would not be an efficient use of the complex roller milling system. The simpler method of pearling, then impact milling works very well for rice.

Rice flour is far from ideal as the structural component of leavened bread rolls or loaves; it does not contain the gluten proteins that give wheat flour its unique ability to form highly expanded, tender, white, and flavorful yeast-leavened or chemically-leavened baked products. Nonetheless, much research has been done into ways of preparing bread substitutes from rice flour. Part of this interest has been the result of the demand from persons who are allergic to wheat flour. Some of the experiments reported in the literature of this field have been summarized by Bean and Nishita (1985). Many gums have been tested as gluten replacements; only certain hydroxy-propyl methylcelluloses gave promising results in bread formulas. Only flour from short- and medium-grain rice had the necessary physicochemical properties to give soft-textured bread crumb.

Flat breads of the unleavened "chapati" type can be made from rice instead of the traditional wheat flour, but, of course, the texture and flavor of the two products are entirely different. Red rice has been used in some places in Pakistan for making rice bread, because the product remains softer for a longer period of time than when ordinary rice is used. There are many varieties of oriental snack crackers containing rice.

MILLET

Most authorities agree that pearl millet was first domesticated somewhere in Africa, then spread throughout that continent, and finally moved into Southeast Asia in prehistoric times. The point of origin may have been Western Ethiopia or somewhere along the southern margins of the Saharan highlands and the time of origin perhaps 5,000 years ago. There is evidence this grain reached northern India about 3,000 years ago.

Although millets are among the world's most important food plants, their cultivation is restricted mostly to the Eastern Hemisphere, and, in particular to regions where population density is high and the climate is arid. During the Medieval era, millet was one of the principal grains produced in Europe. Millet declined in popularity because foods prepared from it have a relatively strong flavor that is not generally appreciated by persons having access to blander grains such as wheat. Furthermore, the flour or meal cannot be made into leavened bread because it lacks an exten-sible protein, so it must be consumed as a gruel, made into flatbreads, or used as an ingredient in mixed dishes.

Varieties and Distribution

The name "millet" has been applied at different times and in different places to a considerable number of cereals, some of which are only distantly related, but the grains most generally recognized as millets belong to two tribes of the grass family, the Chlorideae and the Paniceae. The tribe Chlorideae includes *Eleusine coracana*, finger millet, as the only species of economic importance. It is grown in India, and there is called "ragi."

Pearl millet, *Pennisetum americanum* (L.) K. Schum, syn. *P. typhoides*, is the species having the largest seeds and is probably the most widely grown of all these grains. *Panicum milaceum*, called hog millet or proso, is not raised for grain to any extent in the U.S. except in the northern plains where the growing season is too short for grain sorghum production. Foxtail millet, *Setaria italica* (L.), is grown in Russia and China, and is a staple food crop for many people in India (Naren and Virupaksha 1990). Its seed head is a long, compacted cylindrical spike, similar to that of pearl millet. Other varieties, such as German millet and Siberian millet, are grown in China and Russia for human use, but in the U.S. only for forage.

Sorghum vulgare has been erroneously called pearl millet, and in some parts of the world all varieties of sorghum and millet are known by the latter name, but sorghums belong to one genus (*Sorghum*) in one tribe (Andropogoneae) of the grass family.

Structure of the Seed

The generally tear-shaped kernels of pearl millet are about a third the size of sorghum kernels and weigh an average of 9 mg. Size of the seed does vary substantially because of variety, cultural conditions, etc. Shellenberger (1980) lists average length (mm), width (mm), and weight (mg) for millet kernels as 1.5, 1.5, and 8.5, compared to sorghum 4, 3.5, and 23, and wheat 7, 3.5, and 35. Colors range from yellow to black in different cultivars, but most varieties yield slate-gray seeds. Hand dissection of kernels gave the following proportions: 75.1% endosperm, 17.4% germ, and 7.5% pericarp plus endosperm. There was a large variation in thickness and weight of the pericarp in different pearl millet lines (Abdelrahman and Hoseney 1984).

Food Uses

In the U.S., food use of millet constitutes a very small fraction of the cereal's total disappearance and an insignificant amount of all grain used for food. It is known that millet is offered in many health food stores, but the total value of these sales cannot be determined. It is believed that some millet is sold in stores having substantial patronage by recent immigrants from the areas in Africa and Asia where the grain constitutes a major part of the diet. The small amount of millet that enters the food distribution chain, i.e., its status as a specialty food, inevitably causes it to sell at a higher price per pound than any of the common food grains.

In some parts of Africa and India, where millet has for centuries been an important cereal crop, the grain has multiple applications. It may be boiled and pounded into a porridge or mush, or it can be ground into a flour, formed into thin disks with water, then cooked on a hot surface to make one form of the Indian flatbread called chapatis. Whole grain millet is also used as an ingredient in soups; the ground grains are made into puddings and deep-fried doughs, and may be mixed with pulses, vegetables, milk, cheese, or dates. The grains are also prepared by popping, roasting, sprouting, malting, and fermenting. In short, millet is being used in almost every kind of food for which other grains have been used. Millet is usually supplemented with pulses, which contain a greater percentage of protein, though pulses are also relatively low in the sulfur-containing amino acids.

CORN

Corn *(Zea mays* L.) originated in the Western hemisphere. It was the only cereal systematically cultivated by the American Indians, although some other grains were harvested from the wild state. Columbus found corn being cultivated on Haiti, where it was called "mahiz." From this Arawak Indian word was derived the name maize that is used in Europe to distinguish this cereal from other grains that were called "corn". Locations that have been suggested as possible centers of origin of corn are Central America (including southern Mexico) and the highlands of Peru.

There are more than 250 races of corn in about 14 groups, according to one study. The classification into races was based on: (1) recognizable characteristics of the plant tassel and ear; (2) physiological, and genetic differences; (3) cytological differences; and (4) geographic origin of the variety. Racial groups were based on further examination of the ear and kernel characteristics (Poehlman 1979). Most of these races are grown in very small amounts in restricted areas of Central and South America.

By far the greatest production of corn is field corn of the dent and flint types, with the former greatly predominating in this country. When the unqualified term "corn" is used, dent corn is generally meant. Sweet corn and popcorn are also of considerable economic importance in the U.S., but are seldom used in bakery products—sweet corn kernels are sometimes added to corn muffins or fritters to give texture contrast.

Structure and Composition

Distribution of some of the components within the dent corn kernel is given in Table 2.3. There is a characteristically high level of oil in the embryo and of starch in the endosperm. There are also relatively high concentrations of sugar and ash in the embryo.

Carbohydrates. Starch is the predominant component of corn kernels. Other carbohydrates are present in relatively small amounts. In waxy corn, close to 100% of the starch will be in the branched molecule form, i.e., amylopectin. In ordinary varieties, the proportion of amylose averages about 27% and seems to vary within a rather narrow range. In a series of nonwaxy varieties comprising 190 samples from the U.S. and 167 varieties from abroad, the amylose content of the starch was found to vary from 20% to 36%. Varieties containing from 55% to 80% of the total starch as linear fractions have been developed.

Starch from dent corn includes rounded granules from the floury endosperm and polyhedral granules from the horny endosperm. The latter show pronounced pressure facets, which are attributed to tension developed during field drying. Diameter of the granules lies between 2 and 30 microns. The hilum is centrally located, the lamellae indistinct or invisible, and the polarization crosses are of moderate intensity. High-amylose varieties tend to have grossly irregular granules, which show little or no birefringence and are usually smaller than normal. Waxy constarch granules are similar but, usually, somewhat larger than those of ordinary cornstarch.

Table 2.3. DISTRIBUTION OF COMPONENTS OF YELLOW DENT CORN KERNELS AMONG THE FRACTIONS[1]

	Endo-sperm	Embryo	Peri-carp	Tip cap
	%	%	%	%
Proportion of the part to the whole kernel	82.0	11.6	5.5	0.8
Protein	73.1	23.9	2.2	0.8
Oil	15.0	83.2	1.2	0.6
Sugar	28.2	70.0	1.1	0.7
Starch	98.0	1.3	0.6	0.1
Ash	18.2	78.5	2.5	0.8

[1] Based on data of Earle et al. (1946). Percentages may not total 100% because of rounding.

Cell walls of the pericarp contain quite a bit of fibrous material. Cellulose and pentoglycan, in about equal amounts, are the principal dietary fibers. Isolated pentoglycan forms viscous pastes in water and may have some commercial use. It contains residues of D-xylose, L-arabinose, DL-galactose, D-glucose, and glucuronic acid in highly branched molecules.

About 0.1% to 0.3.% raffinose, 0.9% to 1.9% sucrose, 0.2% to 0.5% glucose, 0.1% to 0.4% fructose, and smaller amounts of myo-inositol and glycerol are present in sound corn kernels. Maltose and probably other saccharides appear during germination while raffinose disappears.

Nitrogenous Compounds.—Most of the nitrogen of the corn kernel is present in the form of protein. The proteins can be separated into various fractions based on their solubility in different reagents. The significance of such fractionations can be debated, but the predominant protein of corn, zein, is a prolamine; that is, it is soluble in dilute alcohol. Most of the proteins, including zein, are located in the endosperm. The hull contains little protein. Germ usually accounts for between 15% and 25% of the total protein of corn and may contribute 25% to 40% of the total kernel lysine.

Relatively small amounts of nonprotein nitrogen are found in corn. Christianson *et al.* (1965) found that over 50% of the nonprotein nitrogen in whole corn is in the form of amino acids, which are distributed almost equally between the endosperm and the germ fractions. Their percentage concentration in the germ is, however, several times that in the endosperm. Quaternary-N and heterocyclic-N compounds have been found in the germ.

Lipids and Related Compounds.—Analyses of a series of 125 inbreds showed oil content of the whole kernel varies between 1.2 % and 5.7% (Quackenbush *et al.* 1963). Varieties developed particularly for high oil content are known to yield as much as 14% of this constituent. Fatty acids that have been reported by various investigators are 56% linoleic, 30% oleic, and 0.7% linolenic, while stearic, palmitic, arachidic, and others were present in relatively insignificant amounts.

The study by Quackenbush and associates reported iodine values from 111 to 151, and tocopherols from 0.03% to 0.33%. Appreciable amounts (around 1%) of phosphatides are present. Lecithin content is about 0.5%.

The oil from the total kernel takes on many of the characteristics of the germ lipids, of course, since the embryo is the preponderant source of fatty material. Although few studies have been published on the subject, it appears that the endosperm oil is similar in most respects to germ oil.

Corn oil is one of the seed oils known to have a hypocholesterolemic effect in man and animals. The property of reducing cholesterol in the blood may be partly due to the large amounts of plant sterols, such as β-sitosterol.

Table 2.4.　MINERAL AND PHYTATE CONTENT OF CORN KERNELS[1]

Element or compound and unit	Content in kernel or part			
	Entire kernel	Germ	Endosperm	Hull
Total P, %	0.30	2.04	0.05	0.13
Phytate P, %	0.25	1.80	0.01	0.02
Zn, ppm	18.8	106.	6.66	20.3
Fe, ppm	20.9	145.	10.7	31.8
Mn, ppm	5.20	34.6	2.25	15.8
Cu, ppm	1.50	7.28	0.87	7.2
Ca, ppm	44.0	109.	29.5	582.
Mg, %	0.11	0.84	0.02	0.08
K, %	0.35	1.69	0.07	0.25

[1] O'Dell et al. 1972. Kernels contained 12% germ, 82% endosperm, 6% hull. Data reported on an air dry basis.

Vitamins and Minerals.—Distribution of minerals in the fractions of corn kernels is shown in Table 2.4. Since it is known that phytate affects the absorption of some of these minerals, and thus controls their biovailability to a considerable extent, phytate content is also shown in this table. Most of the phosphorus is present as the phytate, and nearly all of the phytate is in the germ.

Corn is not a particularly good source of vitamins. Although yellow corn is a good source of vitamin A and is important in animal feeding for this reason (among others), white corn has little or none of this fat-soluble vitamin. Of course, most of the vitamin A is found in the oil, and therefore the germ is the principal repository for this nutrient. According to data of Watson (1987), dent corn kernels contain the following (units per kg): Vitamin A, 2.5 mg; vitamin E, 30 IU; thiamin 3.8 mg; riboflavin, 1.4 mg; pantothenic acid, 6.6 mg; biotin, 0.08 mg; folic acid, 0.3 mg; choline, 567 mg; niacin, 28 mg; and pyridoxine, 5.5 mg.

Other Constituents.—A topic of considerable interest to many cereal scientists is the subject of pigments in corn. The system of carotenoid pigments in yellow corn grain is quite complex, and separation of the original compounds has proved to be difficult. When fractions are eluted from a magnesia column, spectrophotometry provides values for three provitamins as well as eight carotenoids with little or no vitamin activity. In addition to *cis* isomers of the major polyenes, a number of minor components have been observed. This method showed wide differences existed in carotenoid and tocopherol distribution in 125 inbred lines of corn. Provitamin A ranged from a trace to 7.3 ppm. Lutein, the predominant xanthophyll, ranged from 2 to 33 ppm. The total tocopherol content fell between 0.03% and 0.33%.

Xanthophylls of typical double-cross hybrid yellow dent corns varied from 10 to 30 ppm and carotenes from 1 to 4 ppm. Some exotic strains from South America contained about 60 ppm, the highest found up to that time. Analyses of several samples indicated that xanthophylls and carotenes may be independently inherited. Outward appearance of the seed was not correlated with xanthophyll content.

Quality Factors

In discussing the factors affecting quality of corn, it is necessary to keep in mind that the analytical values to be given the most weight will vary depending upon the intended use of the grain. For example, many of the quality factors important in sweet corn will obviously be quite different from those looked for in field corn, and both field and sweet corn will have different requirements from popcorn. On the other hand, some specifications will remain the same, for example, freedom from significant mold damage and from rodent contamination would be required for all food items and most industrial raw materials. Some of the specifications for dent corn will be discussed in the following paragraphs.

Field corn is a standard item of commerce for which closely defined classes and grades have been established by the federal government. The commercial quality of corn as grain cannot be discussed intelligently without consideration of these basic specifications. For the purposes of the Official Grain Standards of the United States, "corn" is any grain that consists of 50% or more of the whole kernels in the dent or flint variety of *Zea mays* L. and not more than 10.0% of other grains for which standards have been established under the U.S. Grain Standards Act. The balance may be made up of other varieties of maize.

A very serious quality problem that affects corn is aflatoxin contamination. This can be so severe that the grain is unsuitable for any use connected with food or feed. Aflatoxin is a metabolite elaborated by the fungus *Aspergillus flavus* as it grows on corn in the field. There are several types, and some of them are among the most potent carcinogens known and can, in addition, cause acute symptoms of poisoning. High temperatures accompanied by drought conditions during maturation of the corn kernel favor the growth of the mold and production of the poison. Aflatoxin contamination of corn has proved to be a very difficult regulatory problem.

Dry millers of corn are insistent on having supplies as free as possible of certain contaminants. Among these unwanted inclusions are insects, the excreta of rodents and birds, toxic weed seeds, kernels invaded by mold growth, and soybeans. The latter are undesirable because they follow the process all the way through and appear in prime grits causing interference with processing into food or beverage products. Corn should not show excessive levels of physical damage such as split and broken pieces because they pick up moisture at a faster rate than whole kernels in the tempering process and give an inconsistent response to subsequent treatment. There should not be a large proportion of small kernels. Tough bran that is difficult to break from the endosperm is objectionable. Color is important for most uses of the meal or grits, but special precautions must be taken if the corn is destined for alkali-treatment (as for tortilla chips) because the high pH the corn encounters during processing affects the pigments.

Traditional Food Products from Corn

In some "underdeveloped" areas of the world, corn constitutes a substantial part of the diet of most of the population. At one time, this was the situation throughout much of the southern U.S., and health of the people suffered because of the poor nutrient profile of corn. Economic improvement and education on dietary factors gradually reduced and finally eliminated the problem. In South and Central America, corn is still the staple food. Physiological disorders attributable to nutritional deficiencies can be observed in these populations. As a result, considerable effort has been devoted to the study of means for improving the nutritional adequacy of corn. It has been well documented that the limiting factor in the growth promoting ability of corn protein is its relatively low content of lysine residues, while niacin is the limiting vitamin.

In Central and South America, corn is generally consumed in the form of tortillas, i.e., flat thin disks of baked masa. Preparation of masa involves heating and soaking whole kernels of corn in lime water, washing the cooked kernels to remove most of the lime, and grinding the softened endosperm to a paste or dough.

Substantial percentages of nutrients are lost during the preparation of masa. For white corn, the combined physical and chemical losses average 60% of the thiamin, 52% of the riboflavin, 32% of the niacin, 44% of the ether-extractables, and 10% of the nitrogenous substances. Comparative figures for yellow corn are 65%, 32%, 31%, 33%, and 10%, respectively. Yellow corn also loses 21% of the carotene originally present. The hot lime water treatment does, however, increase the rate of release of most of the essential amino acids, so that masa is, in this respect at least, somewhat more nutritious than the corn from which it has been made.

OATS

When agriculture began, a form of wild oats apparently existed as a weed in widely separated regions of the world. Oat (*Avena* spp.) kernels, it is not clear whether cultivated or not, were found in the Franchthi Cave in Greece at a level dated to 10,500 BC. Primitive agriculturists, however, concentrated their efforts on the cultivation of the forerunners of modern wheat and barley. Oats continued to appear in the fields and was harvested along with more desirable grains. It made its way as an adventitious interloper in seed stocks of barley and emmer carried to other parts of the world from the cradle of civilization around the eastern end of the Mediterranean.

Oats now rank sixth in world cereal production behind wheat, corn, rice, barley, and sorghum. World production of oats has been trending downward because other crops give higher yields, particularly as improved varieties of rice and wheat are introduced. The grain is not nearly as important in commerce as wheat and corn. It is generally consumed in the locality, and frequently on the same farm, where it is produced. The chief use in most countries is as animal feed, with human consumption in second place, and industrial usage a distant third.

There is a large and increasing use of oats for food in the U.S. Most of this is consumed as breakfast cereals, very little as bakery products.

Classification

Most species of oats known today were described as early as 1750 by Linneus, the great Swedish taxonomist. Stanton (1955), in his comprehensive studies on the identification and classification of oats, described twelve species or subspecies of *Avena*. Among these are *A. abyssinica, A. byzantina, A. fatua, A. nuda, A sativa,* and *A. byzantina.* Space limitations prevent the discussion of all but the commercially important species. There are annual and perennial oats, but all cultivated varieties are annuals.

Common oats (*Avena sativa*) are grown in the cooler and moister regions of the temperate zones. This species constitutes most of the oats produced today. The red oat is grown in regions considered to be too warm for satisfactory growth of the common oat. If it were not for these heat-tolerant red oats, production of the grain would be much less important in the southern U.S., South America, Australia, and the Mediterranean countries of Europe.

Structure and Composition

The gross physical structure of the oat groat is similar to that of the kernels of wheat and barley. It is, however, covered with numerous trichomes or hairlike protuberances. The groat can be seen to be divided into three major parts—bran, endosperm, and germ.

Compared to other cereals, oat groats are characterized by lower carbohydrate content, and higher protein and fat content. By using selective stains followed by microscopic observation of sections, lignin has been identified in the epidermis, aleurone cell walls, endosperm cell walls, and germ cell walls. The epidermis yielded the most positive test. Cellulose was found in the hyaline layers, aleurone cell walls, endosperm cell walls, and germ cell walls. Protein would be expected to be widely distributed, but positive reactions for it were found in the aleurone cells, germ cells, and endosperm cell walls. Starch was confined to the endosperm, where it occurred in well-defined aggregates. The germ and the aleurone cells were the main lipid depots. There were traces of pectin in the horny endosperm and epidermis.

Table 2.5. COMPOSITION OF OATS, GROATS, AND MEAL[1]

Component and units	Dry milling oats	Finished groats	Oat meal
Moisture, %	7.5	7.5	8.1
Crude protein, % (N X 6.25)	13.0	17.0	16.8
Crude fat, %	5.5	7.7	6.7
Crude fiber, %	11.8	1.6	3.9
Ash, %	3.7	2.0	2.2
Nitrogen free extract, %	66.0	71.6	70.5
Iron, ppm	51.0	47.0	51.0
Calcium, ppm	700.0	570.0	580.0
Phosphorus, %	0.37	0.50	0.445
Manganese, ppm	34.0	34.0	48.0
Thiamine, mg/100 g	0.65	0.77	0.78
Riboflavin, mg/100 g	0.14	0.14	0.17
Niacin, mg/100 q	1.15	0.97	1.25
Pantothenic acid, mg/100 g	0.86	1.36	1.19
Folic acid, mg/100 g	0.034	0.06	0.06
Choline chloride, mg/100 g	107.0	120.0	120.0
Pyridoxine, mg/100 g	0.20	0.12	--

[1] Adapted from "Facts on Oats," Quaker Oats Co. Components reported on dry weight basis.

The percentages of ash, fiber, and nitrogen-free extract seem to vary only slightly among samples of oat grain taken from many different places throughout the world. The different streams of oats separated before milling are also similar in composition for most samples, but there is a considerable variation in the composition of samples if they are widely different in hull percentage. The data in Table 2.5 illustrate the effect of processing on the composition of oat products.

Carbohydrates.— Whole oats, including hulls, will yield about 65% nitrogen-free extract, on a dry basis. Starch and other carbohydrate polymers make up about 90% of this material. Reducing sugars in the extract are quite low, usually less than 0.1%, while total sugars are often near 1.4%. Whole oats contain about 14% pentosans, mainly araban and xylan.

The highest concentration of pentosans is in the hulls, though groats will have around 4%. Their content of pentosans make oat hulls an important raw material for the manufacture of furfural, a chemical intermediate and solvent. Beta glucan, discussed later, is present in significant amounts.

The fiber of oats is found mainly in the hulls and consists principally of cellulose, hemicellulose, and lignin. Dry oat hulls contain about 16.7% lignin (not a carbohydrate) and 29.4% α-cellulose.

Between 33% and 43% starch (DWB) can be extracted from whole oats, but the actual starch content is somewhat higher. The granules are very irregular in shape, often assuming a polyhedral configuration, but ovoid and hemispherical particles are also seen in quantity. An occasional spindle-shaped or pointed-oval granule will be seen; these are characteristic of oats. Average size varies according to the location within the kernel, the largest and most densely packed granules being found in the cheek near the crease, while the horny endosperm contains smaller particles. Most granules will fall within the size range of 3 to 10 microns in their largest dimension, giving oats the smallest starch particles of all the cereal grains except rice. The hilum is faint or invisible, and lamellae are seldom seen.

The individual granules develop in bundles or clusters about 60 microns in diameter. These compound clusters, which fill most of the central space in the endosperm cells, are usually broken up during processing of the kernel, yielding the irregularly shaped granules seen in most starch preparations. Birefringence of the granules is relatively weak, with the polarization cross being centrally located in most cases. The amylose content is about 23% or 24%. No references to waxy oat varieties have been located.

Nitrogenous Substances.— Various references indicate that from 85% to 94% of oat nitrogen is present in amide or amino groups. The usual data presented as protein in oats are the Kjeldahl-determined nitrogen contents multiplied by the factor 6.25. There is some dispute about the applicability of this factor, but when it is used, the protein of a typical example of milling oats will average about 13.1%, hulls about 4.5%, and finished groats about 16.9% (dry weight basis).

Oats generally contain a higher percentage of protein than other cereals, and this constituent has a higher biological value than the protein of any other common cereal. This situation is due, of course, to higher amounts of essential amino acids such as lysine, which are limiting in wheat, corn, etc. The protein of oats differs from the protein of other cereal grains in that its major (about 55%) protein is a globulin type rather than a glutelin (about 21% to 27%). These figures are subject to considerable uncertainty, varying substantially depending on the extraction method and subsequent technique, but probably not varying much with different cultivars.

Lipids.—Oat groats have the highest lipid concentration of all the cereal grains. The ether or petroleum extractables of oats can vary from about 4% to 10%, and are distributed among the parts of the grain as follows (percentages on dry basis): whole grain 5.4%, groats, 7.6%, hulls 0.62%, germ (hand-dissected) 11.2%, germ-free groats 5.8%, germ plus bran coats 7.4% to 9.0%, and endosperm 6.2% to 6.7%.

The amount of lipid that is extracted depends on the solvent. When the amount extracted by diethyl ether is taken as 100%, the equivalent figures for material extracted by other common solvents are: petroleum ether 97, carbon tetrachloride 104, chloroform 110, benzene 113, acetone 113, and ethanol 128. Values for ethanol and acetone extractables are in the same range as the figures obtained by acid hydrolysis methods. Oats is an excellent source of linoleic acid, an essential fatty acid for the human diet. Solidification points vary in the range of 41° to 68°F.

Gums.— Stimulated by the interest in "dietary fiber," a great deal of research activity has gone into investigations of oat gums, which appear to be largely β-glucan. As described by Wood (1986), "The mixed-linkage β-glucan of oat and barley endosperm belongs to a family of unbranched polysaccharides composed of (1-4)- and (1-3)- linked β-D-glucopyranosyl units in varying proportions." Whole oats will contain about 4% to 5% of these substances. Water extracts of oats will normally contain both starch and β-glucan, with the former in excess, so that separation of the glucan generally leads to a preparation considerably contaminated with starch. Analysis for glucan is aided by the use of enzymes that preferentially attack β-glucans.

Oat gums dissolve in hot water, but more readily in dilute alkalies, to give highly viscous solutions that slowly lose viscosity on standing.

Vitamins and Minerals.—Mineral components of the groat are concentrated in the outer bran fraction. It would appear that oats can be considered a fairly good source of manganese, magnesium, iron, calcium, zinc, and copper. The phosphorus content also appears fairly high, but the bioavailability of this element has been called into question by some nutritionists because of the relatively inert form (phytic acid) in which it exists in oats. Four strains of oats grown in Finland showed ranges of means of 3.89 to 5.42 of iron, 0.99 to 2.23 of copper, and 1.87 to 2.52 of manganese—all in mg per 100 g dry weight (data of Koivistoinen quoted by Sandstrom 1986). There is a paucity of published information on the amounts of trace nutrients such as chromium, nickel, cobalt, vanadium, silicon, and tin.

Oats and oat-based products contribute a small but significant amount of vitamins to the human diet (Lockhart and Hurt 1986). They are good sources of thiamin and pantothenic acid.

Quality Factors in Oats

Nearly all U.S. trade in cereal grains relies on the Official Grain Standards to establish the basic quality requirements for the merchandise, and this applies to oats. Domestic oats transactions can be conducted on unofficial grades, if the participants so agree, but all exports must have official grades and must be weighed at the port of export. Equipment and procedures used must be standardized and checked regularly for accuracy, and inspectors are tested for proficiency. The Federal Grain Inspection Service (FGIS) administers and supervises the official U.S. inspection system.

Per capita consumption of oats has averaged slightly above 3 lb per year, compared to wheat's 115 to 120 lb. Products that account for the disappearance of oats within the food catgegory include oatmeal, oat flour, natural cereals, meat product extenders, cookies and breads, granolas, and baby food, but the main consumption is as breakfast foods and snacks. The chief food use of oats is as a breakfast cereal. Hot cereals are made from oat groats, which may be "pan-toasted," and which are either flaked or "steel-cut" to reduce the size and decrease the cooking time.

Oat groats as collected from the field do not have much flavor, and the flavor they do possess is not particularly appealing. Desirable flavor notes are developed by the heating steps applied during processing. Hayda-nek and McGorrin (1986) say, "Oat flavor has been shown to be a complex, precursor-dependent, heat-induced collection of volatile flavor components."

Recent research seems to show that oats have the ability to lower cholesterol content in the blood serum of humans. Because high cholesterol levels have been shown (in some studies) to be correlated with the presence, or development, of atherosclerosis, and the latter to be correlated with ischemic heart disease and other circulatory disorders, many people have become convinced that it would be a wise move to eat more oats. It is this situation, plus the perceived benefits based on the high fiber content of oats, that has led to the recent increase in food usage of this grain.

Anderson and Chen (1986) reviewed the literature on the cholesterol-lowering properties of oat products. They found studies showing that the intake of certain plant fibers lowers serum cholesterol concentrations in humans. Several water-soluble fibers such as pectin, guar, and Bengal gram give a hypocholesterolemic effect, whereas most water-insoluble fibers such as cellulose do not lower serum cholesterol levels. Based on this work, they conducted experiments which showed that a diet supplemented with oat bran significantly reduced the blood cholesterol levels of hypercholesterolemic patients. The decrease in serum total cholesterol concentrations observed with oat bran diets occurred primarily in the LDL cholesterol concentrations, whereas HDL either increased or remained stable. It is generally accepted that LDL (low-density lipoproteins) carry most of the serum cholesterol and are the most atherogenic. These authors also found that oat products had beneficial effects on glucose metabolism and fecal bulk.

It is quite evident that controversy will surround the oat vs. cholesterol question for years to come.

BARLEY

It is widely agreed that barley was an important food grain in many parts of the world during prehistoric times. It was probably used mostly as a porridge and as a base for fermented beverages. Although it does not form an extensible dough, it was used to make baked cakes or flatbreads.

Description of Plant and Seed

Barley is one of the cereal members of the grass family. Winter and spring types exist. The plant consists of roots, leaves, stems, and flower parts. The grain is produced in spikes, or heads, at the tops of the stems. Mature barley plants vary in height from 12 to 48 inches (typically 38 inches), the height depending upon type or variety and growing conditions.

Most cultivated barleys have been classified into the two groups, *Hordeum vulgare* L., the six-rowed barleys, and *H. distichum* L., the two-rowed types. In the six-rowed barleys, three kernels develop at each rachis node. The median kernel is slightly larger than the lateral kernels on each side and is symmetrical in shape. The two lateral kernels are twisted, and the twist is more pronounced at the attachment end of the kernel.

In the common two-rowed group, the lateral florets are sterile and greatly reduced. Only one row of kernels develops on each side of the spike. The kernels are all symmetrical and more uniform in size than the six-row barleys, but the kernels that develop at the base and at the tip of the spike are often somewhat smaller than those in the center.

Utilization of Barley

There are two categories of uses for barley grown in the U.S. — food and feed. Utilization of barley for non-nutritive industrial purposes is very small, as compared to the numerous applications available for, say, corn starch or wheat gluten. The major food/beverage use is as an ingredient for alcoholic beverages, mostly in the form of malt. As might be expected, specifications for barley intended for food applications are much more restrictive than those for the grain intended to be used in animal rations. In the U.S., more barley is used for feeding animals than for any other purpose.

The major non-feed use of barley is in the production of malt and by far the largest part of this malt is used for brewing beer. Some malt is used by distillers and a substantial amount is used in ground form as a diastatic enzyme source in yeast-leavened baked products. Other uses are known.

Barley has been used in snacks, breakfast cereals, baby foods, cookies, breads, and grain yoghurts (Sparrow *et al.* 1989). The sprouts have been used as a health food. It is used for production of pot and pearl barley, and small quantities of barley flour are used for baby foods. Barley meal and cracked barley are two of several grain components found in multi-grain breads. The grain is high in fiber and so could be considered as an enriching ingredient whenever that miracle "nutrient" is required.

Although food uses of malt are numerous, the quantities consumed are relatively small. Diastatic and non-diastatic malt syrups are used in bread and other yeast-leavened products, non-diastatic syrups are sometimes used as a coloring agent in rye breads and the like although caramel color has taken over most of this market, one or more pancake/waffle dry mixes rely on malt as a flavor, some "health" crackers contain malt.

Structure and Composition of Barley Kernels

A typical hulled barley kernel from the outside inward is composed of lemma and palea enclosing and cemented to the caryopsis. The rachilla lies within the crease of the kernel near the base and on the ventral or palea side. It is covered with hairs, which may be long or short. The lemma is five-nerved and somewhat angled at the nerves. Lateral and marginal nerves may have few to numerous small teeth or they may be smooth. The lemma may have a depression consisting of a transverse crease at its base just above the point of attachment. The caryopsis is composed of pericarp, integuments, starchy endosperm, and germ. The outer layer of the endosperm is made up of the aleurone cells. In blue barleys, the anthocyanin pigment is blue in the alkaline aleurone cells, while the same pigment in the pericarp or hull appears as red. The aleurone of many varieties is colorless.

The germ is partly embedded in the endosperm at the base of the kernel on the lemma or dorsal side and is held at an oblique angle to the axis of the kernel. The germ is composed of the embryonic axis, which develops into a seedling at germination, and the adjacent scutellum. The latter structure secretes hormones that stimulate enzyme release and synthesis. The enzymes hydrolyze constituents of the endosperm to produce nutrients for the growing seedling.

Typical proximate analyses of barley types are given in Table 2.6. In common with other cereal grains, barley is low in the essential amino acids lysine and methionine, but barley contains more lysine than regular corn and may even be equivalent to high lysine corn if the Opaque-2 gene doubles the lysine content. High lysine feed barleys inevitably have substantially lower yields, however, and are seldom, if ever, grown commercially. Protein can be increased to a limited extent by using extra nitrogen fertilizer. Very early maturing varieties tend to have high protein contents.

Table 2.6. PROXIMATE COMPOSITION OF THREE TYPES OF BARLEY[1]

	Kernel weight	Hull	Pro- tein	Fat	Starch	Fiber	Ash	N-free extract
	mg	%	%	%	%	%	%	%
Midwestern six row	36	12	12	2.0	58	5.7	2.7	66.6
California six row	45	14	11	2.0	58	6.6	3.0	65.4
Western two row	40	10	10	2.0	60	5.2	2.5	72.3

[1] Based on data from Kneen and Dickson (1967).

In general, barley contains somewhat larger amounts of vitamins, as compared to corn, except for pyridoxine and carotene.

As a basic material for beer, barley's content of human nutrients is more or less irrelevant, and it must be evaluated for those constituents which contribute to reliable production of well flavored beer.

Sugars and polysaccharides.—Starch makes up almost two-thirds of the total dry weight of barley, thus being not only the predominant poly-saccharide in the grain, but larger by far than any other component. Barley starch has A- and B-granules similar to those making up wheat starch. The smallest granules (<2.7 microns) constitute about 74% of the total, the largest (>13.6 microns) about 9.4%, and those of intermediate size about 16.6% (MacGregor 1979). The larger starch granules of barley have a higher amylopectin percentage and a lower gelatinization temperature than the smaller granules. In addition to the starches of normal amylose and lipid contents, there are waxy mutants with 1% to 2% amylose and low levels of lipids, and high-amylose mutants with over 40% amylose and elevated levels of lysophospholipids (Morrison 1987).

The main polysaccharides, besides starch, are β-D-glucans, pento-sans, and cellulose. The glucans and pentosans, or at least part of them, form the "gum" fraction. Barley, like oats, has a relatively high β-glucan content. The β-D-glucans and part of the pentosans are constituents of the cell walls in the endosperm and aleurone. The thickness of the cell walls, and presumably the content of β-glucans and arabinoxylans, is under genetic control and is also affected by environmental factors. The small amount of cellulose that is present in the grain (about 4% to 5%) is located mainly in the cell walls of the aleurone-testa tissues. Small amounts of fructosans can be detected. There are very small amounts of reducing sugars in the ungerminated grain, probably less than 0.1% in most samples. Sucrose will generally be present at about the 1% level.

Nitrogenous compounds.—The two major groups of storage proteins in barley are the glutelins and the prolamines, present at levels of about 4% each, with somewhat more glutelin than prolamine (hordein). The albumins plus globulins will about equal the amount of glutelin. Total protein can be expected to fall in the range of 10% to 12%, dry basis.

Hordein seems to serve as the major component of the endosperm matrix, which surrounds the starch granules. Some hordein is also present in the protein bodies of the aleurone cells. The albumins and globulins include the enzymes; they are found mainly in the embryo and aleurone.

The content of peptides and free amino acids in ungerminated barley is low, normally less than 0.2% of the grain. Nucleic acids and their hydrolytic products represent about 0.2% of the dry weight of the grain, with 30% of the nucleic acids being DNA and 70% RNA.

Lipids.—The total amount of lipids in barley range from about 2.5% to 3.2%. It is generally accepted that environmental growing conditions have a significant effect on lipid levels. Most of these substances are found in the embryo, scutellum, and aleurone. About 78.2% of the total is neutral lipid, 7.3% glycolipid, and 14.5% phospholipid (Price and Parsons 1975). Low levels of waxes, free sterols, alkyl resorcinols, carotenoids, xanthophylls, and tocopherols have been reported. The principal fatty acids of the lipid fraction are linoleic, palmitic, and oleic. Over 4% of total lipid occurs as linolenic acid, about four times the level in corn oil. Less than about 1% of stearic, palmitoleic, and myristic are typically present. A complete review of barley lipids can be found in the article by Morrison (1978).

Vitamins and minerals.—According to Foster and Prentice (1987), vitamin levels in barley have not been determined reliably. Apparently, there are wide variations in reported values which might be real or be a result of imprecise analytical procedures.

There is virtually no vitamin A and no vitamin D in barley, though precursors for these vitamins may be present. Vitamins C, B_{12}, and K are also absent. Vitamin E is present in the oil as a mixture of tocopherols, which is found at levels of about 6 to 45 mg per gram of oil. Other vitamins have been reported at the following levels (values are per gram): choline (as the chloride) 0.9 to 2.2 mg; thiamin 1 to 16 micrograms; riboflavin 0.8 to 3.7 micrograms; nicotinic acid 47 to 147 micrograms; pantothenic (as calcium salt) 3.7 to 4.4 micrograms; combined pyridoxin, pyridoxal, and pyridoxamine 2.7 to 11.5 micrograms; biotin 0.05 to 0.1 micrograms; and inositol 1.4 to 3.2 micrograms. Embryo, scutellum, and aleurone contain more vitamins than the other tissues (Briggs 1978).

In the whole kernel of barley, the minerals present in greatest amount are phosphorus, potassium, and magnesium, reported at levels of 2.97, 4.39, and 1.29 grams per kg, respectively. Calcium and sodium are found in much lower levels, 0.257 and 0.138 grams per kg, respectively. Still lower, but significant quantities of iron, zinc, magnesium, and aluminum are present, 28, 23, 11, and 10 micrograms per kg, respectively. Traces of copper and molybdenum can be found. See the article of Liu *et al.* (1974). Barley, especially the hull-less waxy cultivars, contains tocotrienol, a fat-soluble isomer of vitamin E which is said to repress cholesterol synthesis.

Quality Factors

Quality factors of interest will be determined primarily by the application for which barley is intended —food, malting, feed, or seed. The grain must meet the requirements of the USDA Official Grain Standards if it is to qualify as malting barley. "Barley" is defined as grain that, before the removal of dockage, consists of 50% or more of whole kernels of cultivated barley (*Hordeum vulgare* L.) and not more than 25% of other grains for which standards have been established under the U.S. Grain Standards Act. The term "Barley" does not include hull-less barley or black barley. There are three classes for Barley: Six-rowed barley, Two-rowed barley, and Barley. Six-rowed barley is divided into three subclasses: Six-rowed Malting barley, Six-rowed Blue Malting barley, and Six-rowed barley. Two-rowed barley is divided into two subclasses: Two-rowed Malting barley and Two-rowed barley. Instructions for applying the Standards are published by, and actual inspections are performed by, the Federal Grain Inspection Service (FGIS).

BIBLIOGRAPHY

ABDELRAHMAN, A. A., and HOSENEY, R. C. 1984. Basis for hardness in pearl millet, grain sorghum, and corn. Cereal Chem. *61*, 232-235

ANDERSON, J. W., and CHEN, W. L. 1986. Cholesterol-lowering properties of oat products. *In* Oats: Chemistry and Technology. F. H. Webster, Ed. Am. Assoc. Cereal Chemists, St. Paul, MN

ANON. 1968. Barley: Origin, Botany, Culture, Winterhardiness, Genetics, Utilization, Pests. USDA Agr. Hdbk. *338*

ANON. 1989. Triticale: Has its time finally come? Agricultural Outlook *157*, 12-13.

ANON. 1990. Official Methods of Analysis of the AOAC, Fifteenth Edition. Assoc. Official Analytical Chemists, Arlington, VA

ANON. 1991. Approved Methods of Analysis, Compiled Version. Eighth Ed. Am. Assoc. Cereal Chemists, St. Paul, MN

BAUM, B. R. 1977. Oats: Wild and Cultivated. Printing and Publishing Supplies and Services of Canada, Ottawa

BEAN, M. M., and NISHITA, K. D. 1985. Rice flours for baking. *In* Rice: Chemistry and Technology. B. O. Juliano, Ed. Am. Assoc. Cereal Chemists, St. Paul, MN

BHATTY, R. S. 1986. Physiochemical and functional (breadmaking) properties of hull-less barley fractions. Cereal Chem. *63*, 31-35

BIZZARRI, O., AND MORELLI, A. 1988. Milling of durum wheat. *In* Durum Chemistry and Technology. G. Fabriani and C. Lintas, Editors. American Association of Cereal

BOGGINI, G., and POGNA, N. E. 1989. The breadmaking quality and storage protein composition of Italian durum wheat. J. Cereal Sci. *9*, 131-139

BRIGGS, D. E. 1978. Barley. John Wiley & Sons, NYC

BUSHUK, W. 1976. History, world distribution, production, and marketing. *In* Rye: Production, Chemistry, and Technology. Amer.Assoc.Cereal Chemists, St.Paul, MN

CASEY, P. and LORENZ, K. 1977. Millet functional and nutritional properties. Bakers Digest *51*, No. 1, 45-51

CHEN, W. L., and ANDERSON, J. W. 1981. Soluble and insoluble plant fibers in selected cereals and vegetables. Am. J. Clinical Nutr. *34*, 1077-1082

CHRISTIANSON, D. D., WALL, J. S., and CAVINS, J. F. 1965. Location of nonprotein nitrogenous substances in corn grain. J. Agr. Food Chem. *13*, 272-276

CHUNG, O. K., and TSEN, C. C. 1974. Triticale lipids. Nutr. *28*, 349-400. *In* Triticale: First Man-made Cereal. C. C. Tsen, Editor. Am. Assoc. Cereal Chemists, St. Paul, MN

D'APPOLONIA, B. L. 1974. A review of the starch of triticale. *In* Triticale: First Man-made Cereal. C. C. Tsen, Editor. Am. Assoc. Cereal Chemists, St. Paul, MN

DEXTER, J. E., MARCHYLO, B. A., MACGREGOR, A. W., and TKACHUK, R. 1989. The structure and protein composition of vitreous, piebald, and starchy durum wheat kernels. J. Cereal Sci. *9*, 19-33

DICKSON, A. D. 1959. Barley. *In* The Chemistry and Technology of Cereals as Food and Feed, S. A. Matz, Ed. AVI Publishing Co., Westport, CT

DREWS, E., and SEIBEL, W. 1976. Bread baking and other uses. *In* Rye: Production, Chemistry, and Technology, W. Bushuk, Ed. Amer.Assoc.Cereal Chemists, St.Paul, MN

EARLE, F. R., CURTIS, J. J., and HUBBARD, J. E. 1946. Composition of the component parts of the corn kernel. Cereal Chem. *23*, 504-511

FORSBERG, R. A. (Editor) 1985. Triticale. Crop Science Society of America, Madison, WI

FOSTER, E., and PRENTICE, N. 1987. Barley. *In* Nutritional Quality of Cereal Grains: Genetic and Agronomic Improvement. Agronomy Society of America, Madison, WI

FULCHER, R. G. 1986. Morphological and chemical organization of the oat kernel. *In* Oats: Chemistry and Technology. F. Webster, Ed. Am. Assoc. Cereal Chem., St. Paul, MN

HAYDANEK, M. G., JR., and MCGORRIN, R. J. 1986. Oat flavor chemistry. *In* Oats: Chemistry and Technology. F. H. Webster, Ed. Am. Assoc. Cereal Chemists, St. Paul, MN

HOSENEY, R. C., ANDREWS, D. J., and CLARK, H. 1987. Sorghum and pearl millet. *In* Nutritional Quality of Cereal Grains. R. A. Olson and K. J. Frey, Ed. American Society of Agronomy, Madison, WI

HULSE, J. H., and LAING, E. M. 1974. Nutritive Value of Triticale Protein. International Development Research Centre, Ottawa, Canada.

HULSE, J. H., LAING, E. M., and PEARSON, O. D. 1980. Sorghum and the Millets: Their Composition and Nutritive Value. Academic Press, NYC

INGLETT, G. E. (Editor) 1982. Maize: Recent Progress in Chemistry and Technology. Academic Press, New York

JULIANO, B. O. 1980. Properties of the rice caryopsis. *In* Rice: Production and Utilization. B. S. Luh, Ed. AVI Publishing Co., Westport, CT

JULIANO, B. O., and BECHTEL, D. B. 1985. The rice grain and its gross composition. *In* Rice: Production and Utilization. B. S. Luh, Ed. AVI Publishing Co., Westport, CT

KENNEDY, B. M. 1980. Nutritional quality of rice endosperm. *In* Rice: Production and Utilization. B. S. Luh, Ed. AVI Publishing Co., Westport, CT

KRAMER, N. W., and MATZ, S. A. 1969. Sorghum. *In* Cereal Science. S. A. Matz, Ed. AVI Publishing Co., Westport, CT

KUHN, M.C., and GROSCH, W. 1989. Baking functionality of reconstituted rye flours having nonstarchy polysaccharide and starch contents. Cereal Chem. *66*, 149-154.

LI, C., and LUH, B. S. 1980. Rice snack foods. *In* Rice: Production and Utilization. B. S. Luh, Ed. AVI Publishing Co., Westport, CT

LIU, D. J., ROBBINS, G. S., and POMERANZ, Y. 1974. Composition and utilization of milled barley products. IV. Mineral components. Cereal Chem. *51*, 309-316

LOCKHART, H. B., and HURT, H. D. 1986. Nutrition of oats. *In* Oats: Chemistry and Technology. F. H. Webster, Ed. Am. Assoc. Cereal Chemists, St. Paul, MN

LORENZ, K., and WELSH, J. R. 1974. Food product utilization of Colorado-grown triticales. *In* Triticale: First Man-made Cereal. C. C. Tsen, Editor. Am. Assoc. Cereal Chemists, St. Paul, MN

MADL, R. L., and TSEN, C. C. 1974. Trypsin and chymotrypsin inhibitors of triticale. *In* Triticale: First Man-made Cereal. C. Tsen, Ed. Am. Assoc. Cereal Chemists, St. Paul, MN

MATZ, S. A. 1969. Cereal Science. AVI Publishing Co., Westport, CT

MATZ, S. A. 1991. The Chemistry and Technology of Cereals as Food and Feed, Third

Edition. Pan-Tech International, McAllen, TX

MCGINNIS, J., REDDY, S. J., and PETERSON, C. J., JR. 1985. Nutritional value of triticale. *In* Triticale. R. A. Forsberg, Ed.

MILLER, D. F. 1958. Composition of Cereal Grains and Forages. Nat. Acad. Sci. Nat. Res. Council Rept. 585

NAREN, A. P., and VIRUPAKSHA, T. K. 1990. Alpha- and beta-setarins: Methionine-rich proteins of Italian millet. Cereal Chem. 67, 32-34.

PETERSON, D. M., SENTURIA, J., YOUNGS, V. L., and SCHRADER, L. E. 1975. Elemental composition of oat groats. J. Agr. Food Chemistry 23, 9-13

POEHLMAN, J. M. 1979. Breeding Field Crops, Second Ed. AVI Publ. Co., Westport, CT

PRICE, P. B., and PARSONS, J.G. 1975. Lipids of seven cereal grains. J. Am. Oil Chem. Soc. 52, 490-493

QUACKENBUSH, F. W., FIRCH, J. G., BRUNSON, A. M., and HOUSE, L. R. 1963. Carotenoid, oil, and tocopherol content of corn inbreds. Cereal Chem. 40, 250-259

QUAGLIA, G. B. 1988. Other durum products. *In* Durum Chemistry and Technology. G. Fabriani and C. Lintas, Editors. American Association of Cereal Chemists, St. Paul, MN

ROZSA, T. A. 1976. Rye milling. *In* Rye: Production, Chemistry, and Technology, W. Bushuk, Ed. Amer. Assoc. Cereal Chemists, St. Paul, MN

SANDSTRÖM, B. 1986. Cereals as a source of minerals in human nutrition. *In* Cereals in a European Context. I. D. Morton, Ed. Ellis Horwood Ltd., Chichester, England

SHANDS, H.L. 1969. Rye. *In* Cereal Science, S.A.Matz, Ed. AVI Publ. Co., Westport, CT

SIMMONDS, D. H. 1974. The structure of the developing and mature triticale kernel. *In* Triticale: First Man-made Cereal. C. C. Tsen, Ed. Am. Assoc. Cereal Chem., St. Paul, MN

SLIMAK, K. M. 1990. Process for products from amaranth. U.S. Pat. 4,911,943

SMITH, A. K., and CIRCLE, S. J. 1972. Processing soy flours, protein concentrates, and protein isolates. *In* Soybeans: Chemistry and Technology. A. K. Smith and S. J. Circle, Eds. AVI Publishing Co., Westport, CT

SPARROW, D. H. B., LANCE, R. C. M., and HENRY, R. J. (EDITORS) 1989. Alternative End Uses of Barley. RACI, Parkville, Australia.

STANTON, T. R. 1953. Production, harvesting, processing, utlilization, and economic importance of oats. Economic Botany 7, 43-64.

STANTON, T. R. 1955. Oat identification and classification. USDA Tech. Bull. 1100

TANNER, F. W., JR., PFEIFFER, S. E., and CURTIS, J. J. 1947. B-complex vitamins in grain sorghums. Cereal Chem. 24, 268-274

TSEN, C. C. 1974. Bakery products from triticale flour. *In* Triticale: First Man-made Cereal. C. C. Tsen, Ed. Am. Assoc. Cereal Chem., St. Paul, MN

WALL, J. S., and BLESSIN, C. W. 1970. Composition of sorghum plant and grain. *In* Sorghum Production and Utilization. J. Wall and W. Ross, Ed. AVI Publ. Co., Westport, CT

WATSON, S. A. 1987. 1987. Structure and composition. *In* Corn: Chemistry and Technology. S. A. Watson and P. E. Ramstad, Editors. American Association of Cereal Chemists, St. Paul, MN

WEBER, E. J. 1987. Lipids of the kernel. *In* Corn. Chemistry and Technology. S. A. Watson and P. E. Ramstad, Ed. American Association of Cereal Chemists, St. Paul, MN

WEBSTER, F. H. 1986. Oat utilization: past, present, and future. *In* Oats: Chemistry and Technology. F. H. Webster, Ed. Am. Assoc. Cereal Chemists, St. Paul, MN

WESTERN, D. E., and GRAHAM, W. R., JR. 1961. Marketing, processing, uses. *In* Oats and Oat Improvement. F. A. Coffman, Ed. Am. Soc. Agronomy, Madison, WI

WOLFE, M. J., BUZAN, C., MAC MASTERS, M., and RIST. C. E. 1982. Structure of the mature corn kernel. Gross anatomy and structural relationships. Cereal Chem. 29, 321-333

YOUNGS, V. L., and FORSBERG, R. A. 1987. Oat. *In* Nutritional Quality of Cereal Grains. R. A. Olson and K. J. Frey, Ed. Am. Soc. Agronomy, Madison WI

chapter three

LEAVENERS AND YEAST FOODS

INTRODUCTION

The "raising" or expansion of dough and batter products during some phase of their preparation can result from the operation of several agencies. The generation of carbon dioxide from reactions going on within the dough or batter is the principal leavening force in the majority of bakery products, including most bread and rolls, cakes, muffins, pizza, doughnuts, cookies, pancakes, etc. The two methods of generating this gas that are of the most practical significance to bakers involve chemical leavening systems and yeast fermentation.

It is believed that in excess of 90% of all chemical leavening systems in bakery foods involve the reaction of sodium bicarbonate with acid-reacting ingredients. Yeast fermentation, in which carbon dioxide is generated by the action of *Saccharomyces cerevisiae* on carbohydrates, is responsible for the typical form and flavor of nearly all bread and rolls. These two processes can be used jointly or in sequence. For example, combined yeast fermentation and chemical leavening is always used in soda cracker production and sometimes in other products such as English muffins (Juers 1982).

Other systems are used in a minority of cases. Bacterial fermentations have been used for preparing specialty breads, often in combination with yeast. Ammonium bicarbonate is a "self-contained" leavening agent helpful in the manufacture of certain types of cookies, frequently as part of a formula that includes sodium bicarbonate.

In this chapter, the basic mechanisms operating in systems dependent on yeast or chemical leaveners will be discussed, while other effects of leavening materials and their reaction products will be covered in subsequent chapters dealing with formulas and procedures. The roles of water vapor and incorporated air on the expansion of specific bakery products will also be dealt with in those chapters.

Yeast foods are discussed in this chapter because their functions and uses are more closely associated with yeast than with any of the other materials discussed in the series of ingredient chapters.

YEAST

Large quantities of bakers' yeast are used in the production of bread, rolls, sweet doughs, pretzels, pizzas, crackers, doughnuts, bagels, Danish pastry, and the like. The chief advantages of yeast leavening, as compared to chemical leavening, are that it contributes characteristic tastes and aromas and that the evolution of carbon dioxide can be made to continue over a much longer period of time. The main disadvantage is that it is somewhat more difficult to control. Also, in some food, fermentation flavors can be undesirable—certain cookies, for example. The yeast leavening process is generally more costly than chemical aeration, not only because yeast can be more expensive than chemical leaveners, but because the yeast cells consume other materials (sugars) as a result of their activity.

Gas is generated during fermentation as part of the metabolic activity of yeast. Many microorganisms can ferment sugars with the production of carbon dioxide, but the organism that seems to function best in doughs is *Saccharomyces cerevisiae*, or bakers' yeast. Special strains of this species particularly suitable for leavening have been developed over many years by commercial producers.

Every live yeast cell can perform many different chemical reactions, but those of most importance to the baker are in the group called fermentation. The most obvious manifestation of these changes is the production of carbon dioxide and ethyl alcohol, but these substances are merely the end result of an extremely complex series of reactions that are largely controlled by enzymes. Sugars such as glucose and fructose are the substrates transformed by fermentation. A simplified equation that describes the substrate and principal end products of the fermentation reactions is $C_6H_{12}O_6 = 2\ C_2H_5OH + 2\ CO_2$.

The equation is one way of indicating that a molecule of a hexose sugar is converted by yeast to two molecules of ethyl alcohol and two molecules of carbon dioxide. Of course, in practice, the yield is not quantitative, because other compounds (some quite complex) are formed from the sugars.

Carbon dioxide is responsible for leavening the dough, while ethyl alcohol helps to make up the complex aroma of baked products. A large part of both these compounds is lost during the baking and cooling stages.

The sugars that are consumed in fermentation are the simple sugars glucose and fructose, which result from the action of enzymes on the larger molecules of sucrose, maltose, starch, or other more complex carbohydrates. Enzymes for hydrolyzing sucrose and maltose are present in the yeast, but these organisms cannot break down starch to its individual glucose residues. Amylases from diastatic malt or fungal enzymes can be added to hydrolyze starch. There is also a small amount of amylase activity naturally present in most flours. Sucrose is broken down extremely rapidly by enzymes always on, or in, the cell wall of yeast, but the maltose digesting enzyme requires a certain activation period before it becomes effective.

Side reactions accompanying alcoholic fermentation provide relatively small amounts of flavoring substances. Not all of these have been identified, but they are known to include acids (such as acetic acid), aldehydes, and esters. Compounds that are not in themselves desirable as flavors may react during baking to give some of the essential components of baked bread flavor. The question of what comprises the flavor of yeast-leavened products such as bread and rolls is a complex problem that is gradually being resolved through the use of instrumental methods of analysis. It is also a matter of common observation that the most desirable components of bread flavor are fugitive, either evaporating or changing into compounds that are odorless or have unpleasant odors shortly after baking.

A single cell of bakers' yeast will average from 4 to 6 microns in width and from 5 to 7 microns in length. They grow as single cells, or sometimes pairs, and reproduce asexually by forming buds or daughter cells that ultimately separate and continue their life cycle. Commercial yeast is prepared by adding a pure inoculum of a specially selected strain of *Saccharomyces cerevisiae* to a vat or fermenter of perhaps 40,000 gallon capacity containing molasses (or some other fermentable substrate) and other nutrients. The cells are allowed to grow and reproduce under controlled conditions of temperature, agitation, and aeration (Reed 1982). The process is described as a "highly aerobic, fed-batch fermentation" (Sanderson 1985). Substrates are fed into the fermenter at a rate that varies over the course of the process. When maximum cell count attainable with the substrate has been achieved, the cells are concentrated by centrifugation, then washed, filtered, combined with additives, and further processed as necessary. Efforts have been made to develop a continuous yeast-growing procedure; it is not known whether any of these processes are in commercial use at the present time.

Bacteria that produce lactic acid are always present in commercial yeast. Their numbers vary from a low of perhaps 10,000 per gram to several million per gram. Although the number of cells may seem large, the amount of active material they represent is relatively small, because a yeast cell weighs about 50 times more than one of these cocci, and there are about 20 billion to 24 billion yeast cells per gram of the compressed product.

Yeast received by the baker can be as the moist but solid form called compressed yeast, as a fluid "cream," or as dried pellets or granules. Manufacturers offer modifications of size, shape, and composition in each type. There are claimed advantages for each variable: better storage stability, improved functionality, or the economic one of lower price. In all cases, the product consists mostly of yeast cells. Minor amounts of additives will be present—either substances added because they were needed to improve processing response during yeast manufacture, materials left over from the culture medium in which the yeast was grown, or compounds added to improve the storage stability, dispersability, or activity of the yeast cells.

Compressed Yeast

In making compressed yeast, the washed yeast suspension is filtered and extruded to form a firm cake containing about 69% to 70% water. On a dry weight basis, extruded material will contain 50% to 60% protein, 4% to 5% fat, 2.8% to 3.0% phosphorus, and 6% to 8% ash. Fractional percentages of additives such as emulsifiers may be present. Compressed yeast is delivered as rectangular cakes of 1 lb weight wrapped in waxed paper and packed 24 or 48 to a box, or as small chunks (crumbles) packed 50 lb to a bag.

Compressed yeast stored at refrigerator temperatures of 42°F will lose about 10% of its activity in four weeks. At higher storage temperatures, the yeast rapidly loses its leavening power and develops unpleasant odors, and the cakes turn brown at the edges. Of course, compressed yeast should never be stored at room temperature. Many baking problems can be traced to the use of compressed yeast that has deteriorated in storage. Compressed yeast with a higher content of carbohydrate and a lower protein content is said to be considerably more resistant to storage deterioration.

Yeast in a totally dormant state can be frozen without much damage. But, if the yeast is actively fermenting at the time of freezing, some of the cells may be killed. Apparently, this toxic reaction is due to freezing concentration of the ethanol that is present. This is the reason for recommending that the fermentation time given to doughs that are to be frozen be kept at the absolute minimum. Special strains of S. cerevisiae have been developed for use in frozen doughs that are intended to be thawed and given some proof time before baking, i.e., in which the yeast must retain good fermentative power (Nakatomi et al. 1985).

Active Dry Yeast

Regular active dry yeast.—There are several types of active dry yeast (ADY). Most, if not all, of these products are manufactured from strains selected to be resistant to dehydration damage. Yeast "cream" is the raw material. Free water is removed by vacuum filters or filter presses. If a vacuum filter is used, the yeast cream is first treated with an aqueous solution of a salt such as sodium chloride to extract some internal water from the cells through osmotic action. Pomper et al. (1989) disclose that use of salts of calcium or magnesium at this stage, instead of common salt, gives an intermediate that loses less of its activity during the drying stage.

The most common type of ADY has been dehydrated at low temperatures until it reaches a moisture content of about 7.5% to 8.5%. Otherwise, its composition is very similar to that of compressed yeast. It can be produced as short thin strands, small pellets, small granules, or powder, and it is normally packed in polyethylene-lined fiber drums or in flexible pouches containing 2 lb of the yeast. About 1% of its activity will be lost per month of room temperature storage if the yeast has been packed in nitrogen or carbon dioxide, while up to 8% per month may be lost if it has not been packed in one of these inert gases.

Regular ADY must be rehydrated with water having a temperature of 105° to 110°F if maximum fermentative activity is to be obtained. It should never been rehydrated with either chilled water or hot water. Rehydration of the individual cells is very rapid, but it may take a few minutes for water to penetrate to the center of the granules. After rehydration is complete, the yeast may be chilled, or even heated to slightly above the rehydration range, without causing significant damage to its fermentation ability.

When substituting ADY for compressed yeast in a formula which has been designed for the latter, multiply the compressed yeast weight by 0.6 to

0.75, and add enough water to make up the difference.

All active dry yeasts must be clearly distinguished from inactive dry yeast, which is manufactured as a nutritional additive or as a raw material for preparing flavors and other greatly modified products. It has no fermentative ability at all, and is probably never used in bakery products. Some inactive dried yeasts are made from species other than *S. cerevisiae*.

Instant ADY.—This product differs from regular dried yeast in that the instant version does not require a separate rehydration step. That is, the instant product can be added directly from its container to the dough mixer. The difference results both from the yeast's genetic constitution and the method used for processing it. According to Oszlanyi (1980), faster drying leads to a reduced loss of activity. Consequently, a method was developed to rapidly dry small (0.4 mm diameter) threads of yeast with 320°F air in a fluid bed dehydrator. Although this temperature may seem to be excessive, the yeast itself never rises above 105°F during its relatively brief (20 minute) exposure to the drying gas, and damage to cell membranes and enzymes is minimized (Lehmann 1981). Sorbitan monostearate is used as a wetting agent to accelerate rehydration. This form of yeast is more potent than regular ADY, on an equal "as is" weight basis. It is nearly as effective as compressed yeast in gas production, on a dry weight basis.

A method of preparing instant active dry yeast was described by Percel (1988). Fresh compressed yeast (special strain of *S. cerevisiae*) containing about 1% to 3% of methyl cellulose and about the same amount of a wetting agent is divided into a mass of particles having a particle size of 0.2 mm to 2.0 mm. The particles are dried by passing through them a drying gas (e.g., air) at a temperature of not more than 160°C. In not more than 120 minutes, a dry matter content of 85% or more is achieved without raising the temperature of the particles above 50°C.

Because instant ADY is dried to a moisture content lower than 5%, it will absorb water from air at normal ranges of relative humidity. This partial rehydration can lead to rapid deterioration with loss of gassing power. Oxygen uptake is also detrimental to the shelf life of ADY. Consequently, the package is designed to have low gas transmission rates. It usually is a pouch of four ply construction including layers of aluminum foil and polyester. Pouch and contents are vacuumized before heat sealing.

Three methods have been recommended for adding instant ADY to doughs. Method No. 1 requires combining all ingredients except yeast, mixing for about one minute, then adding yeast and continuing to mix as usual. The second method involves adding yeast to the mixer with other dry ingredients; these components are agitated to blend them, water is then added, and finally mixing is continued until desired results are obtained. Method No. 3 specifies prior rehydration of the yeast with approximately five times its weight of 95°F water; after ten minutes the yeast suspension is added to the other ingredients and mixing continued for the usual length of time.

When a compressed yeast formula is modified for using with instant

ADY, the water content should be increased by one to two parts for each part of instant ADY to compensate for the difference in moisture content of the two yeasts. If this is not done, reactivation of the yeast may be impaired.

Table 3.1. COMPARISON OF YEAST ACTIVITY[1]

Description of yeast	Moisture content	Protein content	Gas production
	%	%	%
Compressed	70	50	390
Belt dried	7	41	150
Drum dried	7	42	172
Spray dried	7	42	127
Fluidized bed dried	5	47	341

[1] Based on Oszlanyi (1980) and Jackel (1983). Data are representative but are not industry averages. Moisture content, "as is" basis. Protein, dry weight basis. Gas production in ml CO_2 in 165 min per 300 mg yeast in a simple dough mix.

It is claimed that instant ADY is less sensitive than regular ADY to temperature extremes at the time it is mixed. It rehydrates readily—even though the cells are packed together in the tiny rod-shaped particles, there are pores present through which water can penetrate. Rehydration is facilitated by the surfactant usually added by the manufacturer.

Jackel (1983) says that a major disadvantage in the use of instant ADY is a proof-time lag, which causes a delay of 5 to 15 minutes at this stage of processing, as compared to compressed yeast usage.

All forms of ADY can be expected to be more expensive than compressed yeast, whether compared on a solids or a gassing power basis. Lower freight costs and simpler handling and storage may offset the premium.

Yeast for Frozen Doughs

Doughs that are frozen and then thawed and proofed frequently exhibit unacceptably low leavening action because some of the yeast cells have been damaged. A type of yeast developed especially to prevent this type of deterioration contains 25% moisture, so it could be considered a partially dehydrated yeast. According to Oszlanyi (1989), a special *S. cerevisiae* variety is dried under mild conditions until only the "unbound" water has been removed. Frozen storage is required, but ice crystals don't form in the cells. The yeast is vacuum packed.

In the initial dough preparation stages, this yeast is slightly less active than compressed yeast. A separate reconstitution phase is not desirable; the yeast should be added in its frozen form. This does increase the lag phase, but a slow start is an advantage in preparing doughs for frozen distribution, since any substantial amount of fermentation during mixing and make-up is detrimental to yeast survival when the dough is frozen. If reduced-moisture yeast is substituted for compressed yeast, equal solids contents should be used, and extra water should be added to provide the same moisture:solids proportion found in compressed yeast.

Harmful Effects of Deteriorated Yeast

A number of methods have been suggested for improving the storage stability of yeasts. Patents have been granted for coating yeast cells with fats and oils. Percel (1988) points out what he regards as deficiencies in these approaches, and discloses a process for preserving active dry yeast by applying polyethylene glycol having a molecular weight in the range of 3,350 to 4,600 to the surface of the yeast. The coating is applied in a fluid bed dryer by spraying the molten glycol on to the surface of the particles.

Glutathione, a reducing agent, is one of the substances released from dried yeast when the yeast is rehydrated. The physical properties of doughs may be adversely affected by this substance—they may become softer, stickier, and less retentive of gas. Glutathione is present in all yeast, including compressed yeast, but semi-permeable membranes in the cell prevent it from leaking out if the cells are fully hydrated. The membrane's control of permeation is lost (or greatly reduced) when it is dehydrated, however, and soluble substances inside the cell can be dissolved and eluted before permeability is completely re-established after the cell contacts liquid water. Published data indicate that the amount of glutathione released from instant ADY is considerably less than that extracted from regular ADY, when the rehydration conditions are similar.

It might be thought that addition of oxidizing agents would counteract the reducing action of glutathione, but there does not seem to be any practical way of balancing these reactions.

Compressed yeast cells that have been killed, as by high temperature storage, will also release glutathione when they are mixed with water. The effects on dough properties are similar to those described above. Of course, the loss of organized metabolic activity in heat damaged cells will eliminate any significant gas formation by these cells.

Dead yeast cells autolyze, i.e., they break down completely, producing compounds having unpleasant flavors that carry through to the baked loaf.

Quality Control of Yeast

The principal evaluations applied to yeast by bakery quality assurance departments fall into the two categories of gassing power determinations and baking tests.

The quality control of yeast can be measurably improved by using receiving records patterned on that described by Hirt (1984), including entries for brand, date, time, yeast temperature, yeast pH, yeast code number, condition of delivery vehicle, and condition of container. At the very least, the manufacturer's control or batch numbers (as shown on the container) should be recorded in case questions arise as to the yeast's performance. More elaborate quality assurance systems would probably necessitate comparing the gassing rate of a new shipment with that of a standard.

All gassing power evaluations are based on observations of the amount of carbon dioxide produced over a given time by a standard dough or, less commonly, by yeast in a nutrient solution. The amount of evolved gas is determined either by measuring the volume at atmospheric pressure or by measuring the pressure increase at constant volume. In all cases, the temperature is held constant at some prescribed level. Devices used for these tests range from simple inexpensive pressure cups to rather costly precision instruments fitted with an automated recording apparatus. The rate at which gas is evolved is often as important, or even more so, than the total amount of gas generated.

Directions for making bake tests of yeast performance can be found in the Approved Methods of Analysis of the American Association of Cereal Chemists (Anon. 1991). The procedures are based on the preparation of a standard formula dough under standard conditions, using the test yeast as the variable and a control yeast as the comparison. The results, though helpful in comparing two nearly identical samples of yeast, cannot realistically be expected to determine the relative responses of the samples to all variations of times, temperatures, sugar concentrations, and salt concentrations that may be encountered in shop practice.

YEAST FOODS

Discussed in this section will be those proprietary mixtures that are added to yeast-leavened doughs for the purpose of improving fermentation, either by increasing the overall rate of gas production or by making it more uniform throughout the bench time. Sometimes it is said these materials permit achieving the same fermentation results even though a smaller amount of yeast is added to the dough, thus permitting a reduction in usage of this relatively expensive ingredient.

The use of ammonium salts, phosphates, and sulfates in yeast foods is based on the hypothesis that they improve the fermentation capacity of yeast in doughs, principally by encouraging growth and reproduction of the cells. Investigators have shown that some of the substances commonly considered to be necessary for yeast growth also have an accelerating effect on gas production in synthetic media. Potassium, magnesium, ammonium, sulfate, and phosphate are the principal inorganic ions found to be required. Vitamin B_1 can also markedly influence the rate of fermentation. Most, if not all, of the accelerating substances are normally present in doughs in sufficient amounts to support fermentation at optimal rates. If the gassing power of a dough seems to be inadequate, it may be due to an insufficient amount of yeast or fermentable carbohydrate, or an excessive salt concentration. None of these problems would be significantly affected by adding yeast foods.

Table 3.2 includes examples of yeast food formulations. Some of the ingredients have been selected to act as buffers, while others (bromates, iodates, peroxide) are oxidizers added specifically to strengthen the dough.

Table 3.2. COMPOSITION OF DOUGH IMPROVERS AND YEAST FOODS (in percent, as is basis)

Type No. 1	
Calcium sulfate	24.93
Ammonium chloride	9.38
Potassium bromate	0.27
Sodium chloride	24.93
Starch and moisture	40.49
Type No. 2	
Potassium bromate	0.12
Potassium iodate	0.10
Ammonium sulfate	7.01
Sodium chloride	19.35
Monocalcium phosphate	50.06
Starch and moisture	23.36
Type No. 3	
Calcium peroxide	0.65
Diammonium phosphate	9.00
Dicalcium phosphate	90.00
Starch	0.35

OTHER BIOLOGICAL LEAVENING SYSTEMS

Bread doughs were originally leavened with "sours" or portions of old doughs that were kept over from preceding batches and used to inoculate a fresh batch with the mixture of wild yeasts and bacteria that had accumulated and stabilized during many such transfers. Some specialty breads are still made with sours in order to achieve a more intense flavor and the unusual texture and appearance characteristic of such fermentations.

The word "barm" may be found in older books and articles from the U.K. and Australia to describe a leavener used in doughs. Its meaning appears to be rather inexact, but it seems to refer, in most of its occurrences, to a yeast preparation that is rather more enriched or more active than a common sourdough but not as pure as a commercial bakers' yeast preparation. A crude yeast mixture procured from a brewery, or even from a vintner, for the purpose of making bread might be called a barm. One of the definitions of barm given in the Oxford dictionary is: "The froth that forms on the top of fermenting malt liquors, which is used to leaven bread. . ." A dried form of what the inventor calls a "barm" is described in the patent granted to Spiller (1990). It consists mainly of a whole grain base containing *S. dairensis* and *L. brevis*, as well as other materials.

Role of Microorganism in Sours

The sour used in a non-conventional fermentation may be composed of several different yeasts and bacteria that act in concert or in sequence in complicated ways. Identification of the predominant species, and duplicating that mixture with pure strains of the same organisms will seldom provide results equivalent to the targeted system. Furthermore, transfer of samples of the sour from one plant to another may cause loss of one or more of the essential organisms and lead to failure of the leaven to perform satisfactorily. Additionally, the sour may be inoculated or modified by microorganisms in the original plant as, e.g., contaminants on equipment, and these conditions may not be easily reproducible in the second plant.

Some specialty doughs are leavened primarily by bacterial fermentations. Usually there is some yeast fermentation as well—not necessarily as a result of adding *S. cerevisiae*. The reactions occurring during the gas evolution phases, the changes in dough constituents resulting from metabolic by-products of bacterial activity, and many other aspects of these fermentations are poorly understood, mainly because there has not been as much research done on them as there has been on traditional yeast-leavened doughs. According to Sanderson (1985) and Spooner (1990), the yeast species other than *S. cerevisiae* which have been reported as being used in bakery products are: *Candida krusei*—starter for sour doughs in Germany; *C. lusitaniae*—for more rapid development of fermentation flavor, sometimes combined with bakers' yeast; *C. milleri*—San Francisco sourdough bread and pannetoni; *Klyvermyces fragilis*—bread and buns; *Pichia saitoi*—starter for sour doughs in Germany; *S. delbrueckii*—for more rapid development of fermentation flavor, sometimes combined with bakers' yeast; *S. exiguus*—San Francisco sourdough bread and pannetoni; *S. rosei*—frozen dough products; *S. rouxii*—very sweet dough products; *Torulopsis celluculosa*—torsh starter for Iranian Sangek bread; *T. candida*—torsh starter for Iranian Sangek bread; and *T. holmii*—German sour doughs.

In addition to the yeasts, San Francisco sourdough will typically contain large numbers of the bacteria *Lactobacillus sanfrancisco*. This same organism is found in panettone (sometimes spelled pannetoni), where it is accompanied by *L. brevis* and *L. plantarum*.

From time to time, various types of sourdough breads acquire a regional popularity, which leads bakers in other parts of the country to attempt to duplicate them. It is important to recognize that the typical flavors of these breads are heavily dependent on the organisms present in the culture or sour and the conditions of fermentation being used by the originator(s). Dough composition, i.e., the formula, also has an influence on the flavor and texture, of course, but it is futile to attempt to reproduce a specific sour dough flavor by manipulating other ingredients, in the absence of the culture used in the original bread.

Examples of Sourdough Breads

San Francisco sourdough.—This product, sometimes called Pacific Slope sourdough French bread, generated tremendous interest in the trade, probably more interest than the consuming public showed. Typical examples have a rather pungent aroma, a definitely acidic taste, a thick crust, and a dense chewy crumb. Many elaborate fermentation and proofing schemes and many formulations were proposed to solve the "secret" of San Francisco sourdough bread. None were, or could be, completely successful unless the doughs were inoculated with sours containing the mixed culture of microorganisms developed in the originating shops. The predominant yeast in this culture (*Saccharomyces exiguus*), is a different species from standard bakers' yeast. A major difference is that it does not ferment maltose, so this sugar can provide more nutrient for the bacteria that are present. A luxuriant growth of a specific bacteria generates many of the substances that contribute unique flavor notes to this bread. Commercial cultures in frozen form are now available for bakers (Johnson 1978).

Rye Breads.—There are many different kinds of rye breads. They differ from one another in the type of rye meal used, in acidity of the crumb, and in the flavoring adjuncts such as spices that are included in the formula. A typical formula for American-style rye bread will include about 30 to 40 parts white or light rye flour and 60 to 70 parts of high-protein spring wheat clear flour in addition to salt, malt extract or sugar, yeast food, shortening, caramel color, and yeast. It can be made by either the straight dough or the sponge method. Processing is similar to the procedure used for wheat bread, with care being taken to avoid overmixing and overdevelopment. Sour or Jewish rye breads will be made with a sourdough or a commercial culture or a flavoring composition that includes citric or lactic acid. Each of these options will respond in different ways to changes in processing conditions, and each will yield a product having features that may appeal to a specific market.

At one end of the organoleptic spectrum are such items as Westphalian pumpernickel, which undergoes virtually no leavening action and contains 100% whole rye in the form of slightly broken kernels. It is baked for hours in a slow oven with steam applied (often throughout the baking) to prevent drying. Westphalian pumpernickel is a very dense, dark, and chewy loaf with a flavor strongly reminiscent of wet hay. The flavors are affected by enzymic and other reactions occurring during the long, slow bake. The true Westphalian pumpernickel is rarely made in the U.S.; the breads sold as pumpernickel or even Westphalian pumpernickel in this country being merely darker versions of the regular rye formulas, usually strongly colored with caramel. Westphalian pumpernickel rarely, if ever, contains caraway.

Some kinds of rye breads are made with sours. For the sake of convenience and uniformity, most rye bread nowadays is made without a sourdough, substituting for it one of the special flavors distributed by bakery supply houses. These compositions often rely on caraway to create a distinctive and familiar flavor in the finished products, and many also include organic acids and other natural and artificial flavors. Most quality rye breads are prepared with commercially available dehydrated sours that contain viable microorganisms of the type found in natural sour doughs.

Salt-rising Bread.—This product is a specialty bread that owes its unusual texture and distinctive pungent aroma to a combined yeast and bacterial fermentation. It was formerly prepared by a natural sour dough method that used a high concentration of salt at one point in the process to guide the survival and growth of the types of organisms needed to give the typical flavor. Practically all of the commercial salt-rising bread now being made in this country contains a dry "yeast" preparation or culture. As is the case with many strong-flavored products, it exhibits a dichotomous distribution of acceptance, many people finding it very desirable while others dislike it extremely. The odor is said to be suggestive of cheese—since cheeses can be found with a wide variety of flavors, most of which are due to bacterial action, this description is neither unexpected nor particularly helpful.

The interior, or crumb, of salt-rising bread is close-grained and firm so that its specific volume will be three-fourths, or less, that of ordinary bread. The loaves have a tendency to crack on the sides, so it is customary to mold the loaf in two parts or to pan as a double loaf so that the split comes in the middle. It must be emphasized that true salt-rising bread cannot be made with ordinary bakers' yeast, either compressed or dry. There is a hot water reconstitution step for the special culture which would completely inactivate any preparation of *S. cerevisiae*.

Potato Bread.—Potato bread can also be made using a primary ferment. Although a sour dough based on the action of wild yeasts on a boiled potato mash was the former source of the typical flavor of potato bread, it is now much more common to use a mixture of bakers' yeast, potato flour, and water to develop the initial sour. Most examples of wholesale potato bread aren't made with a sour dough, but simply use some potato flour in a yeast-leavened white bread formula.

CHEMICAL LEAVENING SYSTEMS

Chemical leavening systems include a source of gas, almost always sodium bicarbonate (baking soda), and one or more acid-reacting substances. If these essential components are combined in a "baking powder," other materials will usually be included to dilute the powder to a standard strength, or for other purposes. The acid-reacting substances are included to neutralize the alkalinity of the soda and to generate the maximum amount of carbon dioxide. When a baked product is formulated for low-sodium diets, sodium bicarbonate is sometimes replaced with potassium bicarbonate.

Acid-reacting components may include ingredients that perform other functions in the final mix, such as molasses, fruit juice, or buttermilk. The baker can also neutralize the soda with an appropriate amount of a proprietary "acid cream" powder that contains one or more phosphates plus some diluents and, perhaps, some other functional or non-functional ingredients. Substances other than phosphates, which have been used as acid-reacting components of chemical-leavening systems, include cream of tartar (potassium acid tartrate) and alum (sodium aluminum sulfate).

Ammonium bicarbonate is a self-contained leavening system which decomposes into water, carbon dioxide, and ammonia when heated. It is used in some crackers and cookies.

Sodium Bicarbonate

Sodium bicarbonate's widespread use as a leavener is based on its low cost, lack of toxicity, ease of handling, relatively tasteless end products, and the high purity of commercial supplies. An additional advantage is that its solutions tend to be less alkaline than, for example, the carbonates so that localized regions of high alkalinity are less apt to be formed around granules as they dissolve in doughs. When high pH regions are formed, undesirable colored and flavored spots may occur when the mixture is baked.

Sodium bicarbonate has some disadvantages. Among them is its rather rapid rate of solution at room temperature, a feature that reduces the amount of control that can be exercised over its leavening action. It also tends to deteriorate upon storage unless it can be kept very dry.

Table 3.3. TYPICAL ANALYSIS OF U.S.P. SODIUM BICARBONATE

Substance or component	Percent of total
Carbonates	99.8300
Sodium carbonate	0.7060
Sodium chloride	0.0071
Sodium sulfate	0.0012
Sodium sulfite	0.0005
Silica	0.0010
Iron oxide	0.0007
Aluminum oxide	0.0023
Calcium carbonate	0.0168
Magnesium carbonate	0.0015
Other substances	0.0637

The United States Pharmacopeia (U.S.P.) and Food Chemicals Codex include specifications for sodium bicarbonate. Typical examples of U.S.P. sodium bicarbonate offered for ingredient use will yield 52.32% of the total weight as carbon dioxide and contain 36.88% total alkali. A representative analysis is shown in Table 3.3.

Specifications for purchasing baking soda should include a purity requirement and particle size limitations. The latter will be influenced by the use to which the soda will be put. U.S.P. powdered grade dissolves rapidly and completely to assure total availability for reaction with the acidic ingredients. It is used for scratch-mixed biscuits, cookies, instant or quick breads, and most cakes. A version of the powdered grade that has been treated with calcium phosphate has the advantages of being free-flowing and is particularly useful in self-rising flours and packaged mixes. U.S.P. Fine Granular is recommended for those products where minimal leavening during mixing and holding is desired; these include cake products, which require long baking time and refrigerated or frozen doughs, which require minimal leavening during dough preparation and storage. It is also useful in baking powders where premature reaction during storage can be a problem.

U.S.P. granular contains larger size particles than the grades previously mentioned, and is useful in refrigerated doughs and some doughnut mixes. In most other products, the relatively large particles of this soda may be detrimental. If sodium bicarbonate granules remain undissolved in the dough or batter, they may decompose to the carbonate salt during baking. This results in excess residual alkalinity, which causes a soapy off-taste and an undesirable dark crumb color. Dark spots on the crusts and yellow spots in the crumb develop if particles remain undissolved at the time the dough enters the oven.

When sodium bicarbonate is dissolved in water, there results a mixture of sodium ions, carbonate ions, bicarbonate ions, undissociated carbonic acid, and dissolved carbon dioxide. Proportions of the last four components are determined by the temperature of the system, the concentration of hydrogen ions, and the partial pressure of carbon dioxide over the solution. If other substances are added to the solution, the situation becomes much more complex, so that calculating theoretical gas yields of dough systems gives values that differ by unpredictable amounts from the observed values. Predictions of the direction of changes resulting from variations in composition can usually be made, however.

Considerable amounts of carbon dioxide can exist in aqueous solutions above pH 8. Below the point of neutrality, very little of the compound will exist in dissolved form, and below pH 6 the amount present in this state can be considered negligible for all practical purposes. In more complex systems, particularly those involving colloidal components, much carbon dioxide (in one or more of its states) can exist in bound form. Evidently the ions are held by loose bonds to the electrophilic sites on proteins and other substances. These bonds are weak and readily broken at higher temperatures, or by competition for the carbon dioxide-containing sites by increased concentrations of hydrogen ions.

Evolution of carbon dioxide from pure solutions of sodium bicarbonate is slow, especially near room temperature. When soda is added to dough, gas evolves at an appreciable rate, at least initially, because doughs usually have a pH between 5 and 6 and hydrogen ions force the equilibrium toward the gaseous form of carbon dioxide, not favoring the bicarbonate or carbonate ion forms. In the absence of added acids, dough pH quickly becomes alkaline and gas production decreases. To obtain the maximum yield of gas, and to control its rate of evolution, acids (or acid-reacting substances) are added to the dough along with the sodium bicarbonate. Soda crackers are a special case in which the neutralizing acid is formed as a result of the activity of yeast and other microorganisms. Only a few bakery products utilize both yeast and soda in their leavening systems, however.

Leavening Acids

The function of a leavening acid is to promote a controlled and nearly complete evolution of gas from a dough in which carbon dioxide exists in its dissolved or bound form. Obviously, the acid must be nontoxic and must yield edible and nearly tasteless end products. It should exist in a solid form at normal storage temperatures; it should be economical and easy to handle; and it should not have any deleterious effects on other dough constituents (e.g., it should not weaken the gluten). Several acids have been developed which meet most of these requirements and are capable of releasing gas from doughs at desirable rates. Some of these are listed in Table 3.4.

The substances commonly described as leavening acids are not acids in the usual chemical sense of that word. The initial pH of water solutions or suspensions of these chemicals is often in the range of 4 to 5, and this is only slightly below the pH of some unleavened doughs. The phosphates and cream of tartar commonly used as leavening acids are actually metal salts of partially neutralized acids, while sodium aluminum sulfate (and some others) react with water to form acids.

The chemical formulas of these compounds do not adequately define their function in doughs. Small amounts of additives included during manufacture can have important modifying actions. For example, companies specializing in leavening acids usually offer several different types of sodium acid pyrophosphate. Although the chemical formula of the main constituent is the same and analysis reveals variations only in trace elements, the slowest reacting member of the series will cause an inital rate of gas evolution considerably slower than the rate caused by the fastest acting type. One method of modifying the reaction rate of a leavening acid is to add potash and alumina to the crystallization mixture of calcium acid phosphate; impurities from these additives concentrate on the surface of the crystals as they are forming; upon further heating, the impurities are converted to the corresponding glassy metaphosphates, which restrict access of water molecules to the inner crystal.

Monocalcium phosphate (MCP) monohydrate was the first of the phosphate leavening acids, and it has been used commercially for about a century. When used as the only leavening acid in a system, it reacts very rapidly with bicarbonate to release 60% or more of the available carbon dioxide from batters during a two-minute mixing period at 80°F. It becomes virtually dormant during the bench period, possibly due to the formation during the initial mixing of an intermediate form of dicalcium phosphate containing only one hydrogen ion. The heat of baking renews the reaction and causes release of the remaining carbon dioxide. The reaction characteristics of MCP monohydrate limit application of the compound to doughs and batters in which early fast release followed by a dormant period are appropriate. Some examples of such products are pancake mixes, cookie mixes, and pizza doughs. In combination with slower acting phosphates, monocalcium phosphate monohydrate can be used to expedite initial gas release without impairment of bench and oven reactions. It is valuable in forming gas cells and increasing their number during mixing of batters and doughs.

Table 3.4. CHARACTERISTICS OF SOME COMMON LEAVENING ACIDS

Chemical Name	Abbreviated or common name	Reaction rate*	Neutralizing value
Monocalcium phosphate monohydrate	MCP.H$_2$O	V. fast	80
Monocalcium phosphate anhydrous	MCP	Slow	83
Dicalcium phosphate dihydrate	DCP	None	33
Sodium acid pyrophosphate	SAPP	Variable	72
Sodium aluminum sulfate	SAS	Slow	100
Sodium aluminum phosphate hydrate	SALP	Slow	100
Sodium aluminum phosphate anhydrous	SALP	Medium	110
Potassium acid tartrate	**	***	50
Glucono-delta-lactone	GDL	Slow	55

* At room temperature. **Cream of tartar. ***Medium fast.

Anhydrous monocalcium phosphates are normally very fast acting, but the granules can be coated with a slowly soluble layer of potassium and aluminum phosphate to delay leavening action. The outer layer's resistance to penetration by water causes a slow but rather steady release of acidity, so that only about 20% of the available carbon dioxide will be released during mixing of the dough or batter, while 40% to 50% additional will be generated during a 10- to 15-minute bench period. Anhydrous MCP is used in combination with MCP monohydrate in pancake mixes to improve texture and tenderness, and in cake mixes, self-rising flour, and baking powder.

Dicalcium phosphate is never used alone as a leavening acid, but it can be used in a combination system to provide some acid release very late in the baking cycle. It does not function during the bench period but only when the temperature of the batter reaches 135° to 140°F, usually after 20 to 30 minutes baking time. Its chief function is to adjust the pH level.

Sodium acid pyrophosphate (SAPP) is a versatile leavening acid. By controlling certain variables during processing of the substance, a whole range of baking acids can be produced. Some of these variables are, addition of dissolution-retarding chemicals, heat treatment, and particle size. The fastest grade that is readily available has a dough reaction rate of 40, the slowest a rate of 22. All grades of SAPP are double-acting. Fast grades of this acid are often used for machine made doughnuts. Medium-slow grades are regarded as general purpose leavening acids. The slowest acting grade is particularly useful in refrigerated doughs. It reacts slowly enough to permit the dough to be sheeted, cut into individual rolls, packaged in the can, and sealed before the dough has "proofed" too much to fit its container.

Sodium aluminum phosphate has a high neutralizing value and so is economical to use. Its reaction rate is relatively slow, but several grades differing in rate of gas release are available. For example, one grade will release about 22% of its gas during mixing and 8% during 10 to 15 minutes on the bench, with the remaining carbon dioxide being generated after the batter reaches about 120°F. Advantages of these acids are their apparent improving effects on the structure of bread and some other bakery products (perhaps due to the aluminum ions) and the bland flavor of the end products of their reaction. Sodium aluminum phosphates have good buffering action leading to pH levels near 7 in many systems. They are best used in combination with other leavening acids in cakes and quick breads.

Glucono-delta-lactone, an organic compound, reacts slowly but continuously with soda. It is relatively expensive and has found application primarily in a few specialty uses.

All ingredients with an acid reaction will participate in neutralizing sodium bicarbonate, as previously mentioned. These include not only such obviously acidic materials as fruit juices, buttermilk, and the like, but molasses, honey, corn syrup, and many other ingredients not commonly considered to be acidic.

Two important properties that are related to the suitability of a compound for use as a leavening acid are neutralizing value and dough rate of reaction. Neutralizing value, sometimes called neutralizing strength, represents the number of parts of sodium bicarbonate which can be neutralized by 100 parts of the leavening acid. This "NV" number is a measure of available acidity. It is used by formulators to determine the proportions of leavening acid and bicarbonate needed to produce an approximately neutral pH in the baked product. Neutralizing values are helpful as starting points in formulating leavening systems, but it is important to recognize that the amounts of acids required to give neutrality (or any other targeted pH) in a baked product may be significantly different from the amounts calculated on the basis of neutralizing value.

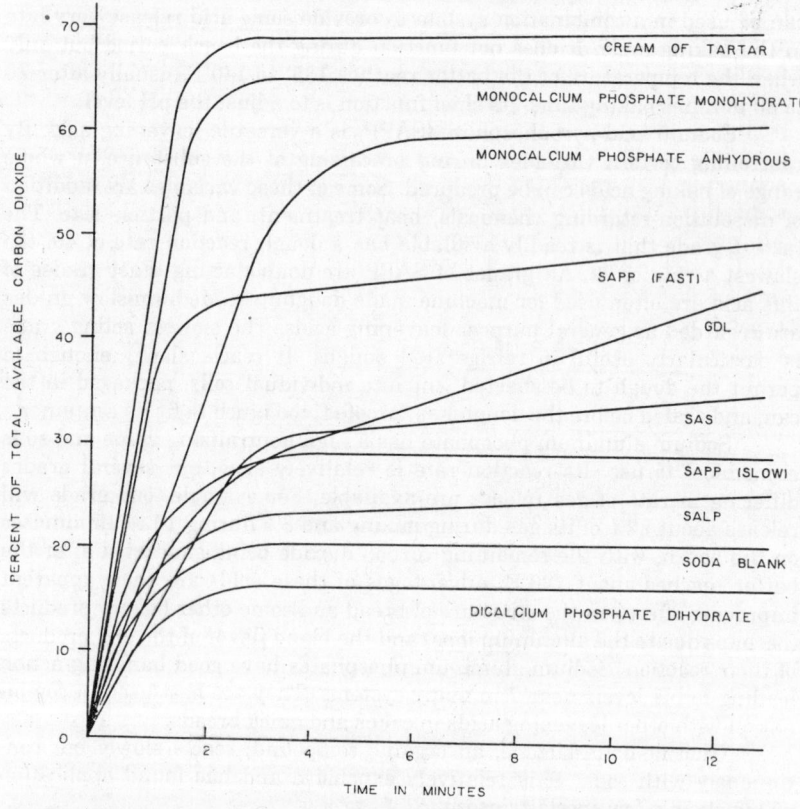

Figure 3.1. Typical reaction rates of several leavening acids
Adapted from LaBaw (1986)

"Dough rate of reaction" (DRR) is a measure of the speed of reactivity of the leavening acid in a dough or batter; it is not the same as neutralizing value (NV). DRR is determined by measuring the amount of carbon dioxide released from a dough over a period of time. These measurements are recorded after a short mixing time of 2 to 3 minutes and after a standing period of 5 to 8 minutes (called "bench action"). The rate number is the percentage of carbon dioxide released compared with the total amount available from the soda that has been added. Figure 3.1 illustrates typical rates of reaction curves for several leavening acids tested in biscuit doughs.

Baking Powder

By FDA definitions, baking powder must contain sodium bicarbonate in sufficient quantity to release a minimum of 12% carbon dioxide when tested under standard conditions. The compounded baking powders which are offered to consumers and bakers are generally classified as "Fast-Acting," "Slow-Acting," and "Double-Acting." Fast-acting powders release most of their gas at room temperature. Slow-acting powders also release a portion of the available carbon dioxide during mixing, but generate most of it by reactions occurring at elevated temperatures, i.e., in the oven. Double-acting powders are really a version of the slow-acting type which exhibit somewhat more gas producing potential during mixing and on the bench. All, or virtually all, retail baking powders are of the double-acting type. Most of the bulk powders offered to retail and wholesale bakers are also of the double-acting type. Figure 3.2 shows the reaction rates of these three types of baking powder, as tested in a simple batter.

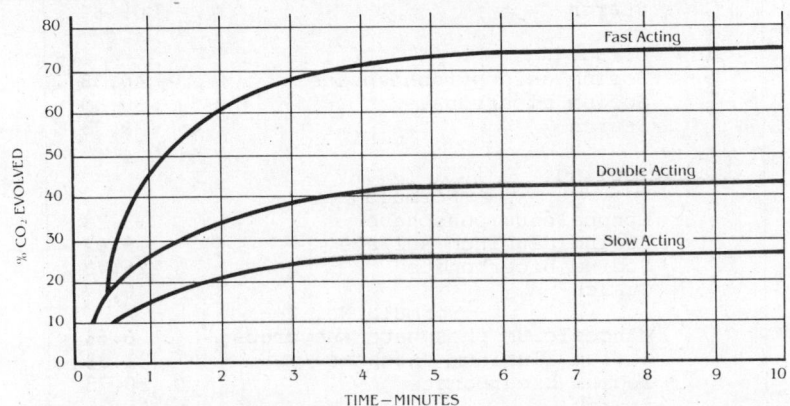

Figure 3.2. Typical reaction rates of three types of baking powder
Courtesy: Church and Dwight

Table 3.5 contains typical formulas for all three types of baking powders. There are many other possible combinations, but, in general, the formulas tend to be fairly simple. Two formulas for fast acting powders are shown. They give off nearly all their available carbon dioxide during mixing and while the batter is being held and portioned. The slow acting powder formula given in the table leads to a product that will release about one-third of its gas at room temperature and the remainder in the oven. The two formulas for double-acting powders contain an acidic ingredient that causes release of considerable gas at room temperature and another acidic ingredient that functions primarily at elevated temperature.

Baking powders are manufactured by simple dry-mixing operations. These powders must be kept dry and clean in the bake shop if uniform results are to be obtained. Dipping out a quantity of powder with a damp or dirty scoop (which is done all too often) is absolutely contraindicated.

Table 3.5. REPRESENTATIVE FORMULAS FOR BAKING POWDER
(in percent)

Fast Acting:	
--Formula No. 1--	
Tartaric acid	5.97
Cream of tartar	44.90
Sodium bicarbonate	26.73
Starch	22.40
--Formula No. 2--	
Monocalcium phosphate	33.43
Sodium bicarbonate	26.73
Starch	39.84
Slow Acting:	
Sodium acid pyrophosphate	40.38
Sodium bicarbonate	30.59
Starch	29.03
Double Acting:	
--Formula No. 1--	
Monocalcium phosphate	13.28
Sodium aluminum sulfate	19.92
Sodium bicarbonate	26.73
Starch	40.07
--Formula No. 2--	
Monocalcium phosphate anhydrous	6.68
Sodium aluminum phosphate	21.38
Sodium bicarbonate	26.73
Starch	45.21

Ammonium Bicarbonate

Ammonium carbonate and ammonium bicarbonate are used as leavening agents in applications where a very low final moisture content is reached in the baked products. Because of this requirement they are usable only in products that are expected to be crisp such as certain cookies, crackers, and crisp pretzels. One advantage of using this carbon dioxide source is that it is self-contained; no leavening acid is required.

When they are heated, ammonium bicarbonate and ammonium carbonate decompose completely into ammonia, carbon dioxide, and water. The ammonia generated in this reaction will bake out, provided the final moisture content is low enough and the product is thin and porous enough to allow the gas to escape. Otherwise, some ammonia may be retained in the food that reaches the consumer, with disastrous effects on acceptability.

At room temperature, ammonium bicarbonate dissolved in water begins to convert slowly into its products. When the temperature exceeds about 104°F, as in the early stages of baking, ammonium bicarbonate dissociates rapidly. The release and initial expansion of carbon dioxide gas throughout the dough increases its volume. As the baking temperature rises, ammonia gas and water vapor add slightly to the leavening effect.

Ammonium bicarbonate is generally used as a supplementary leavener in formulas that also contain some sodium bicarbonate. It is known to increase spread in cookies, a phenomenon partly due to its early release of gas (before the cookie has "set up") and partly due to its effect on dough pH.

Commercial ammonium carbonate is made by the sublimation of a mixture of ammonium sulfate and calcium carbonate. It has been described as a mixture of ammonium bicarbonate and ammonium carbamate, but the Chemical Abstracts name for the pure substance is ammonium hydrogen carbonate. At room temperature, it is a hard white (or translucent) mass which, when ground, becomes a white powder. Temperatures above 140°F will cause the rapid decomposition of dry ammonium bicarbonate. Addition of alkalies will liberate ammonia, while acids cause rapid evolution of carbon dioxide. A small amount (1%) of magnesium carbonate is usually added to the powder as a flow agent.

Other specifications of interest include composition of 21% minimum ammonium, 55% carbon dioxide, and 0.5% (maximum) water. Bulk density is 50 lbs per sq ft; pH of a 1% solution is 7.8; and solubility in 20°C water is 21.6% (w/w). The nominal formula is NH_4HCO_3.

The term "vol" has been used in the UK to describe a chemical preparation of this type, i.e., a commercial mixture of ammonium carbonate, ammonium bicarbonate, and ammonium carbamate.

These ingredients have a pronounced ammoniacal odor, even at room temperature, which leads to the possibility of contaminating other ingredients and finished products and causes unpleasantness in handling.

BIBLIOGRAPHY

ANON. 1981. Food Chemicals Codex, Third Edition.

ANON. 1986. Sodium bicarbonate specifications. Church & Dwight Co., New York

ANON. 1988. Extra effort pays off as company responds to customer's special needs. Bakery *23*, No. 1, 142

ANON. 1990. Official Methods of Analysis of the AOAC, Fifteenth Edition. Assoc. Official Analytical Chemists, Arlington, VA

ANON. 1991. Approved Methods of Analysis, Compiled Version. Eighth Ed. Am. Assoc. Cereal Chemists, St. Paul, MN

BRUINSMA, B. L., and FINNEY, K. F. 1981. Functional (bread-making) properties of a new dry yeast. Cereal Chem. *58*, 477-480

CICCIU, A. P. 1982. Distribution of yeast. Proc. Am. Soc. Bakery Engrs. *1982*, 92-97

CONN, J. F. 1981. Chemical leavening systems in flour products. Cereal Foods World *26*, 119-123

DZIEZAK, 1990A. Acidulants: Ingredients that do more than meet the acid test. Food Technol. *44*, No. 1, 76-83

DZIEZAK, J. D. 1990B. Phosphates improve many foods. Food Technol. *44*, No. 4, 80-82, 85-86, 90, 92

FIELDS, M. L., HOSENEY, R. C., and VARRIANO-MARSTON, E. 1982. Microbiology of cracker sponge fermentation. Cereal Chem. *59*, 23-26

HIRTS, N. F. 1984. Trouble-shooting in the bakery. Proc. Am. Soc. Bakery Engrs. *1984*, 112-118

JACKEL, S. S. 1981. Ingredient research for bakery applications. Cereal Foods World *26*, 400-401

JACKEL, S. S. 1983. Leavening is basic to baking—what's new. Bakers Digest *57*, No 5. 38-39, 41-42

JOHNSON, F. E. 1978. Sourdough products. Proc. Am. Soc. Bakery Engrs. *1978*, 43-46

JUERS, A. A. 1982. English muffins. Proc. Am. Soc. Bakery Engrs. *1982*, 46-51

KICHLINE, T. P., and CONN, T. F. 1970. Some fundamental aspects of leavening agents. Bakers Digest *44*, No. 4, 36-40

LABAW, G. D. 1977. Chemical leavening agents defined. Proc. Am. Soc. Bakery Engrs. *1977*, 77-81

LEE, J. L. 1976. Reconstitution of dry yeast in dough preparation. U.S. Pat. 3,959,495

LEHMANN, T. A. 1981. Instant dry yeast. Proc. Am. Soc. Bakery Engrs. *1981*, 155-159

NAKATOMI, Y., SAITO, H., NAGASHIMA, A., and UMEDA, F. 1985. Saccharomyces species FD612 and the utilization thereof in bread production. U.S. Pat. 4,547,374

OSZLANYI, A. G. 1980. Instant yeast. Bakers Digest *54*, No. 4, 16, 18-19

OSZLANYI, A. G. 1989. Stable yeast for frozen dough. Proc. Am. Soc. Bakery Engrs. *1989*, 133-140

PELLETIER, R. F. R. 1990. Method of combining baking additives and baker's yeast prior to use in preparing baked goods. U.S. Pat. 4,935,249

PEPPLER, H. J. 1981. Fermentation technology: Past and present. Cereal Foods World *26*, 609-611

PERCEL, P. J. 1988. Encapsulated yeast. U.S. Pat. 4,719,114

PIZZINATTO, A., and HOSENEY, R. C. 1980A. A laboratory method for saltine crackers. Cereal Chem. *57*, 249-252

PIZZINATTO, A., and HOSENEY, R. C. 1980B. Rheological changes in cracker sponges during fermentation. Cereal Chem *57*, 185-188

POMPER, S., and DAVIS, J. R. 1989. Active dried yeast. U.S. Pat. 4,797,365

REED, G. 1982. Manufacture of yeast. Proc. Am. Soc. Bakery Engrs. *1982*, 84-90

REIMAN, H. M. 1981. Chemical leavening. Proc. Am. Soc. Bakery Engrs. *1981*, 83-87

SANDERSON, G. W. 1985. Yeast products for the baking industry. Cereal Foods World *30*, 770-775

SAUSSELE, H., JR. 1980. Trends and the future of yeast. Proc. Am. Soc. Bakery Engrs. *1980*, 97-101

SEIGHMAN, J. T. 1987. Process for encapsulating liquid acids. U.S. Pat. 4,713,251

SPILLER, M. A. 1990. Preparation of dried forms of leavening barms containing an admixture of certain lactobacillus and saccharomyces species. U.S. Pat. 4,950,489

SPOONER, T. F. 1990. Yeast in a biotech age. Baking & Snack Systems *12*, No. 10, 20-24

TURNER, J. E., SR. 1980. Liquid pre-ferments. Proc. Am. Bakery Engrs. *1980*, 176-181

VAN HORN, D. R. 1989. Cream yeast. Proc. Am. Soc. Bakery Engrs. *1989*, 144-152

ZELCH, R. H. 1988. The role of yeast in fermentation. Proc. Am. Soc. Bakery Engrs. *1988*, 122-128

chapter four

SHORTENINGS, EMULSIFIERS, AND ANTIOXIDANTS

INTRODUCTION

The ingredients described in this chapter are either based on fats and oils or are compounds added to modify the functionality or storage stability of fats and oils. The major sources of vegetable oils are annual field crops of soybeans, peanuts, cottonseed, rapeseed, and sunflower seed and the tree-borne crops of palm, palm kernel, coconut, and olive. Important animal fats include butter, lard, and tallow. Relatively small amounts of fats and oils are derived from marine sources (whales, menhaden, etc.), but these materials are seldom, if ever, used as components of bakery products in the U.S.

"Shortenings" is a word used to describe fats, oils, and various processed versions of fats and oils that are used as ingredients in doughs and batters. Strictly speaking, these same materials, if used in whipped toppings, buttercream icings, fatty coatings, and the like, or as frying fats and pan release agents, would not be described as "shortenings," but this is a difference that need not concern us here. Shortenings may contain substances other than fats and oils, for example, flavors, colors, and emulsifiers.

Fats and oils, and their derivatives, are important ingredients in the baking industry. They modify the physical and chemical properties of doughs and batters so that these intermediate products can be processed more efficiently. They lubricate the internal structure of intermediates to allow greater expansion during proofing and baking, and they make the texture of finished products more tender. Shortenings modify the visual and tactile texture of the crust in desirable ways. In some cases, natural fats contribute highly desirable flavor notes to bakery products.

Fats and oils are indispensable ingredients in many adjuncts: toppings, fillings, icings, frostings, coatings, etc. The unique texture of real chocolate products is a direct consequence of the special kind of fat contained in cocoa beans. Whipped cream and its imitations are also dependent on fat structures. In addition to their direct use as ingredients, fats and oils are important as heat transfer media in the frying of doughnuts and similar products; as release agents applied to the baking surface of pans, they facilitate production operations and reduce the amount of damaged products.

THE CHEMISTRY OF FATS AND OILS

Fats and food oils are triglycerides of fatty acids, that is, three fatty acid molecules are chemically combined with one glycerol molecule to yield one molecule of lipid. True fats and oils do not contain any atomic species besides carbon, hydrogen, and oxygen, and they do not have any chemical bonds except carbon to carbon, carbon to hydrogen, carbon to oxygen, and oxygen to hydrogen. They are neutral in reaction and essentially non-polar.

All three fatty acids on a triglyceride can be chemically identical, or they can be mixed. In a natural fat, a rather wide assortment of fatty acids can be expected, but the fat from each source (e.g., butter) shows a characteristic fatty acid profile when the fat is hydrolyzed and the fatty acids are identified and quantified. Fatty acids are unbranched chains of methyl groups bearing a carboxyl group at one end. Naturally occurring fatty acids almost always have an even number of carbon atoms between 4 and 26. If these long carbon chains are completely saturated, they are relatively resistant to chemical attack. In some cases, however, a carbon atom lacks the full complement of hydrogen atoms and is double-bonded with the adjacent carbon. At that point, the chain is more reactive and can acquire oxygen with relative ease, giving undesirable deterioration products which are often detectable as rancid odors.

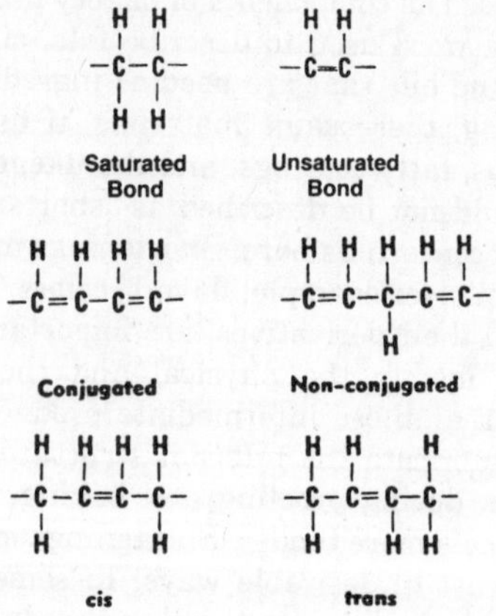

Figure 4.1. Some structural features of fatty acids

At the point of unsaturation, the adjacent carbon atoms will each be provided with only one hydrogen atom. Because of the relative rigidity of the double bond, these hydrogen atoms will retain a position either both on the same side of the molecule or on opposite sides. The first condition leads to a "cis" molecule, the latter to a "trans." This is not an insignificant difference, since some variation in physical properties and perhaps in nutritional properties is found in fats containing cis as compared to trans bonds.

If the fatty acid contains two or more double bonds, the unsaturation can appear on both sides of a pair of carbon atoms joined by a single bond, in which case the molecule is said to have conjugated double bonds. If the double bonds are be more widely separated, a non-conjugated condition exists. Conjugation normally results in a more reactive molecule and causes other differences. Figure 4.1 illustrates a few of the structural features found in fatty acids.

Melting points increase with chain length, and saturated fatty acids with twelve or more carbon atoms are solid at room temperature. Mono-unsaturated fatty acids have much lower melting points than their fully saturated counterparts, and polyunsaturated fatty acids (i.e., those containing two or three double bonds per molecule) carry this phenomenon even further. Fatty acids with more than three double bonds are apparently not found in foods, except for some fish oils that contain 4, 5, and 6 double bonds. Polyunsaturated fats have been claimed to be of great value as dietary components, being anticholesterolemic, etc.

Table 4.1 contains names and some chemical information, as well as the melting points, of some common fatty acids.

Table 4.1. CHARACTERISTICS OF SOME FATTY ACIDS

Common Name	Systematic name	Carbon atoms	No. of double bonds	Melt. point °C
SATURATED FATTY ACIDS				
Butyric	Butanoic	4	0	-8
Caproic	Hexanoic	6	0	-3
Caprylic	Octanoic	8	0	17
Capric	Decanoic	10	0	32
Lauric	Dodecanoic	12	0	44
Myristic	Tetradecanoic	14	0	54
Palmitic	Hexadecanoic	16	0	63
Stearic	Octadecanoic	18	0	70
Arachidic	Eicosanoic	20	0	75
Behenic	Docosanoic	22	0	80
UNSATURATED FATTY ACIDS--CIS CONFIGURATION				
Caproleic	9-Decenoic	10	1	NA
Lauroleic	9-Dodecenoic	12	1	NA
Myristoleic	9-Tetradecenoic	14	1	18
Palmitoleic	9-Hexadecenoic	16	1	NA
Oleic	9-Octadecenoic	18	1	16
Linoleic	9,12-Octadecadienoic	18	2	-6
Linolenic	9,12,15-Octadecatrienoic	18	3	-13
Gadoleic	9-Eicosenoic	20	1	NA
Arachidonic	5,8,11,14-Eicosatetraenoic	20	4	-50
Erucic	13-Docosenoic	22	1	33
UNSATURATED FATTY ACIDS--TRANS CONFIGURATION				
Elaidic	9-Octadecenoic	18	1	44
Vaccenic	11-Octadecenoic	18	1	44

Butterfat is a typical source for butyric, caproic, myristic, caproleic, lauroleic, myristoleic, elaidic, and vaccenic; coconut oil for caprylic, capric, lauric, and myristic; peanut oil for arachidic and behenic; beef fat for palmitoleic; lard for arachidonic; and soybean oil for linolenic. Of course, these fats and oils also contain other fatty acids. Most fats and oils contain the fatty acids palmitic, stearic, oleic, and linoleic.

SHORTENINGS FROM NATURAL SOURCES

Animal Fats and Oils

In this section, the composition and characteristics of butter, lard, and rendered beef fat will be discussed because they are the only commercially significant shortenings (in the U.S.) derived from animals.

Butter.—Butter contains over 80% butterfat, about 16% water, 0.5% lactose, and 0.1% to 3.0% ash (mostly from added salt). The physical structure of butter consists of a continuous phase of butterfat enclosing globules of liquid fatty material and droplets of aqueous solution. The aqueous phase of butter contains milk proteins, native minerals plus any added salt, lactose, and skim milk and washwater components. The aqueous phase is the principal repository of flavor in butter, and it contains numerous microorganisms that strongly affect the product's flavor. Crystals or agglomerates of solid fatty substances may also be present in particles large enough to be detected microscopically.

Butterfat is a mixture of many different glycerides, the relative proportions of which will not be the same in every sample of the fat, but will be found to be affected by the breed of cattle, by the season of the year, and, particularly, by the type of feed that has been provided to the animal.

Since butter is quite expensive relative to most other fats, its use is restricted to those products in which its flavor makes a significant contribution to consumer acceptability or in which its presence permits advertising claims that have marketing value. Butter is classified in the following grades depending on its flavor, color, etc.: U.S. Grade AA or U.S. 93 Score, U.S. Grade A or U.S. 92 Score, U.S. Grade B or U.S. 90 Score, and U.S. Grade C or U.S. 89 Score. The price difference between these grades is not particularly large, because of the commercial demand for the lower scores with their stronger flavors. Low-score butter is often preferred by bakers to AA score because of its stronger flavor.

The low melting point of butterfat can lead to the appearance of greasiness in products containing moderate to high levels of this ingredient. Although this greasiness may cause annoyance when the product is handled, and tends to smear packaging material and be related to early development of rancidity, there are indications that it has organoleptic attractions for some customers.

Lard.—Lard is the material prepared from pig fat by various rendering operations. It has a distinctive natural flavor that is thought to be desirable in some foods. In its unmodified forms, it has a tendency for early development of rancidity.

Lard is classified on the basis of the rendering method as either prime steam, dry rendered, open kettle rendered, or continuous process lard. Lard sold commercially to bakers and other food processers is generally the type called refined pure lard, and it can be made by any of the preceding methods. The characteristics of lard are governed by the composition of the hog fat from which it is made, by the method of rendering, and by the refining and modification methods applied to the extracted fat.

Variations in hardness of the lard depend upon the body location of the fat that has been rendered. For example, internal fats such as leaf fats, are always higher in melting point than fat taken from locations nearer the surface of the animal. The refiner controls and standardizes his product by selecting and blending different fats. Special grades are produced by segregating certain fats and by using special rendering methods.

Pure leaf lard, which has the highest melting point of the unmodified lards, is made only from fat taken from the body cavity. If a still firmer fat is required, hydrogenated lard flakes can be added to the natural fats. By varying the amount of hydrogenated material, a wide range of melting points can be obtained.

Beef fats.—Beef tallow is made from edible fatty tissues of cattle. As with lard, its physical properties vary depending on the feeding history and genetic constitution of the cattle from which the fat is taken. It is normally a hard plastic fat having a melting point of about 110° to 120°F. Because of its hardness, it may be subjected to further processing rather than used in its native form.

Beef fats rendered by special methods can be separated by fractional crystallization into oleo oil (the low melting fractions) and oleostearin (the high melting fractions). Its short plastic range (from about 70° to 80°F) and relatively low melting range make oleo oil a fair substitute for coconut oil in some applications. Minimally refined beef fats retain a slight meaty flavor that has been found valuable in, for example, french frying potatoes.

Vegetable Shortenings

Soybean oil and cottonseed oil are the principal raw materials for hydrogenated vegetable oil shortenings made in the U.S. Where bland flavors (or label claims of all-vegetable origin) are important, hydrogenated fats prepared from soybean or cottonseed oil are the shortenings of choice. Coconut oil is widely used as a spray fat and as an ingredient fat in fillings and coatings. Palm oil and palm kernel oil have received much attention as their supply increased and quantity improved in recent years. Peanut oil, corn oil, sesame seed oil, and sunflower oil are used primarily for specialty applications because they are generally more costly than other vegetable oils. Olive oil is seldom used as a bakery ingredient in this country.

Rapeseed oil has faced some problems related to health questions and nomenclature, but an improved version called canola oil appears to have received a modest amount of consumer usage, probably mostly among the health food coterie. The major problem with the conventional variety of rapeseed is that a large percentage of the fatty acid content of the oil is erucic acid, which can cause substantial health problems if ingested in more than minor amounts. The FDA limits the erucic acid component of rapeseed intended for human consumption to 2% of the fatty acid content, whereas the figure for rapeseed for industrial use is 45% or more (Anon. 1989). Canola oil is currently marketed as a salad oil and perhaps for other purposes. Its principal appeal to the health-conscious consumer is that 94% of its fatty acid content is unsaturated.

All vegetable oils offered to food manufacturers have been refined and deodorized. They are also bleached, in most cases. Cottonseed and partially hydrogenated soybean oil may, in addition, be treated to remove the higher melting fractions to give a "winterized" or "salad" oil. Although for many purposes, soybean oil and cottonseed oil may be used interchangeably, the latter has the reputation of being more resistant to oxidation and flavor reversion. Table 4.2 contains some flavor descriptors that have been applied to vegetable oil by one investigator in this field, both before and after storage in the light and in the dark (Warner 1988).

Table 4.2. FLAVOR DESCRIPTORS APPLIED TO VEGETABLE OILS

Processing & storage	Vegetable oil			
	Soybean	Canola	Sunflower	Cottonseed
Refined, bleached, diluted*	grassy/hay grass/green beany	cabbage sulfur grassy/ green	pine/cedar weedy acrid	weedy sulfur woody
Deodorized, zero time	nutty buttery	nutty butter	nutty buttery	nutty buttery
Storage in the dark	buttery rancid painty grassy	cabbage rancid painty fishy	woody rancid burnt nutty	waxy rancid
Storage in the light	light- struck grassy sour buttery	buttery grassy metallic	stale sour	light- struck

*Diluted 5:95 in deodorized oil.

If they are intended for use as ingredients in bakery products, soy and cottonseed oils that have received the basic refining treatment are usually further improved by blending, hydrogenating, adding emulsifiers and antioxidants, and other processing steps.

Peanuts yield a high-quality cooking and frying oil that is seldom used in the baking industry because of its relatively high price. It has some special advantages for deep fat frying because of its high smoke point. It is among the lightest (lowest in density) of the common unsaturated vegetable oils. Since it contains natural antioxidants, it has a fairly good resistance to the development of rancidity. The flavor is distinctive, but pleasant and mild.

Coconut oil is one of the so-called lauric acid fats. These fats, although relatively highly saturated, have melting points not far above room temperature because their glycerides contain high percentages of fatty acids having short chain lengths. The most popular coconut oil varieties are the 76° and 92° types, the numbers referring to their nominal melting point. The 92° oil is a partially hydrogenated variety. A "fully hardened" or 110° oil can also be obtained, and doubtless products of other degrees of hydrogenation would be made available if the demand was sufficient.

Coconut oil seems to be more susceptible than most fats to hydrolytic rancidity. If hydrolysis of its glycerides occurs (usually the result of enzymic activity), the short chain fatty acids that are liberated give rise to an unpleasant soapy flavor in the product. Some unblanched nuts contain active lipases that can catalyze these deteriorative reactions and so should not be fried in coconut oil. If lipolysis has not occurred, coconut oil has an above average resistance to oxidative rancidity.

Palm and palm kernel oils are obtained from the fruit of the oil palm. The fleshy covering of the fruit is processed to obtain palm oil, while palm kernel oil is extracted from the seed that lies at the center. The quantity of palm oils entering international commerce has increased markedly during the past decade, and the quality and uniformity of the product has improved substantially. Recently, considerable adverse publicity has been generated by publicists who have implied these oils (and coconut oil) are, somehow, less healthful than, for example, hydrogenated soy oil. There is no compelling evidence on this point, and it is difficult to understand how palm oil of a given degree of unsaturation would be less healthful than a soy oil or cottonseed oil of similar degree.

Cocoa butter is obtained from cocoa beans. Slightly more than 50% of the dry matter of cocoa nibs is fat that can be removed by filter pressing or solvent extraction. It does have a mild chocolate aroma unless it has been bleached and deodorized. This is a very high priced fat that is used in large quantities as an ingredient in chocolate candy. Its unique SFI profile causes it to be firm and "dry" at room temperature while allowing it to quickly soften at body temperature, and makes it peculiarly valuable in applications where the consumer must handle the fat coated product.. Cocoa butter contains natural antioxidants and seldom turns rancid.

QUALITY ASSURANCE OF FAT AND OIL PRODUCTS

Tests

As with most ingredients, the best test for fats and oils is a performance test under actual conditions of use and consumption. Since tests of this sort are often impractical and too time consuming for routine use, other procedures have been developed to evaluate those shortening characteristics likely to affect the quality of the finished product. Some of the most useful of the present day analyses are described briefly in the following paragraphs. A description of all common tests applied to fats and oils can be found in the latest edition of "Official and Tentative Methods" of the American Oil Chemists Association (Anon. 1980).

Melting point.—Fats, being mixtures of compounds, do not have the sharp melting points of pure compounds. Any natural fat will contain some liquid and some solid material over a wide range of temperatures. Of course, at some temperature any mixture of triglycerides will consist entirely of solid material, and at some higher temperature it will be totally liquefied. Because the proportion of liquid components will increase as the temperature is raised, a gradual softening and, finally, liquefaction will be observed as the material is heated. Conversely, on cooling the fluid, clouding is first noticed, followed by development of a soft plastic mass that gradually hardens and finally becomes quite firm. "Plastic range" is a term used to describe the range of temperature in which the fat appears to be solid but can still be readily deformed. Because of these considerations, determination of the melting point is rather inexact in most cases. There are several methods that have been used to establish this datum; they differ primarily in their definition of the end point.

The capillary melting point is the temperature at which a sample of the fat contained in a small glass tube becomes completely clear. The open-tube slip point, also called the softening point, is the temperature at which a solidified plug of fat in an open tube immersed in water will soften sufficiently to rise under the buoyant effect of the water.

In the Wiley melting point test, a molded tablet of the fat is allowed to float at the interface of an aqueous ethanol bath. The temperature of the bath is gradually raised and the end point is taken to be the temperature at which the tablet assumes a spherical form.

Ordinarily, each of these "melting point" tests will provide a different temperature for the same fat. In most cases, the closed-tube melting point will be the highest of the three, while the open-tube test will give the lowest temperature. The congealing point, determined by cooling liquid fat until it becomes cloudy, then transferring the sample to a 68°F air bath and observing the highest temperature reached as the fat congeals, will in most cases be different from any of the melting points.

Stability tests.—The extent to which a fat or oil will resist rancidity development is one of its most important characteristics. Fresh products can be tested for content of free fatty acids or peroxides to get a rough idea of the extent to which deterioration has already occurred. Tests based on the principle of bringing samples to a stage of detectable rancidity by controlled heating are perhaps more meaningful from a practical point of view.

The active oxygen method, or AOM test, is widely used for determining a fat's stability to oxidative deterioration. In this procedure, air is bubbled through fat held at 208°F. The end point is the time at which a peroxide value of 100 mEq per kg is reached. Other peroxide value end points may be specified for certain fats to give better correlations with sensory perceptions of rancidity. A modification of the AOM test based on a temperature of 230°F is widely used because deterioration occurs more than twice as fast at the higher temperature, so that results are available much sooner than they would be when the lower temperature is used.

The Schaal test consists of holding a sample of the fat, or a product containing it, in an oven maintained at 145°F. Other temperatures can also be used. The sample is examined daily, or even more frequently, and the time required to reach a condition of detectable rancidity is recorded. Crumbled or ground bread, rolls, crackers, etc., that have been made with the fat in question, can be tested in this manner and the results can frequently be correlated with problems associated with distribution times and shelf-life. The interrelation of product and packaging can also be estimated by placing strips of packaging material in contact with crumbs of the food.

Peroxide value can be determined by reacting a sample of the fat with potassium iodide, and titrating the excess iodide with potassium thiosulfate. It is expressed as milliequivalents (mEq) of oxygen per kilogram of fat. Peroxide value is an indication of the extent to which the fat has already reacted with oxygen and thus indicates approximately how much storage life remains. The deodorization process applied to fats and oils reduces their peroxide value to zero. Consequently the storage conditions and history of the fat must be taken into account when determining and using peroxide values to estimate the remaining shelf-life of a fat (Clark 1987).

The free fatty acid content of a fat is essentially a measure of the amount of hydrolysis that has occurred. Since hydrolysis and oxidation are the reactions leading to organoleptically detectable rancidity, the peroxide value and the free fatty acid content considered together give a reasonably good picture of a fat's current status and future prospects. Free fatty acid is determined by titration with a standard solution of alkali.

Solid fat index.—The proportion of solid fat to liquid fat in a shortening held at a given temperature is related to the performance of the shortening at that temperature. This proportion cannot be deduced from the melting point (however it is determined) of the fat or from the consistency of the shortening at the given temperature. It can be accurately determined by a technique called dilatometry, however. This test is based upon measurement of the change in volume of samples of constant mass held at a series of temperatures. The density of a liquid triglyceride will differ from that of its solid form. Therefore, as the temperature of a fat is progressively raised, additional molecular species will liquefy and lead to changes in volume of the total sample. The situation is complicated somewhat by the mutual solubility of the various glycerides, which also varies with temperature.

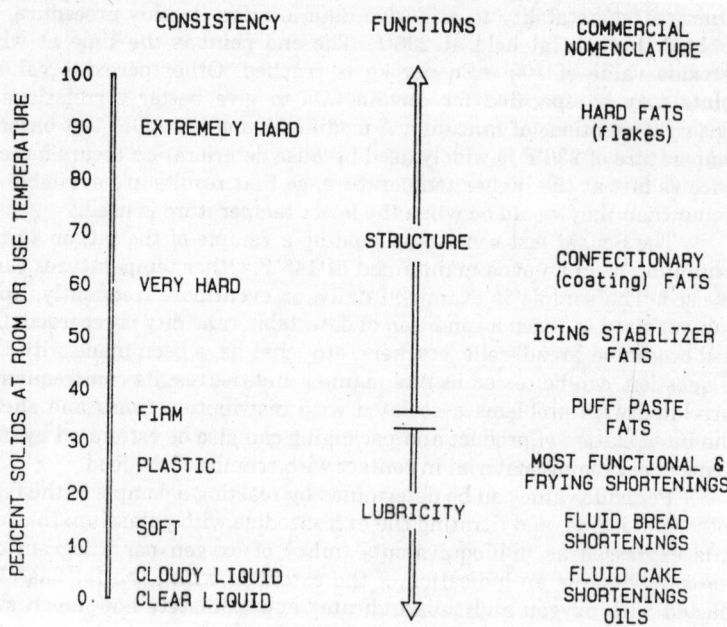

Figure 4.2. Percent solids vs. consistency and functions

Figure 4.2 shows the relationship of percent solids at room temperature (or at temperature of use) to the consistency and function of the fat.

An apparatus of the type described by Pontius (1965) is used in conjunction with a series of water baths to determine the solid fat index (SFI), also called the solids factor index. The sample of melted fat is placed in a chamber attached to a calibrated and graduated capillary tube, then solidified. The instrument containing the solidified fat is allowed to stand ("temper") at a standard temperature and is then heated gradually until the sample melts. The increase in volume is read by observing the movement of an indicator fluid in the capillary tube. Examples of the percentages of solids found in different shortenings by this method were published by Stingley *et al.* (1961). These figures can be converted into a chart or graph. Data from fats with a wide plastic range will exhibit a flatter curve with small differences in the SFI at each temperature. Fats having a shorter plastic range will give a steep curve that is generally high at the low temperatures and low at the higher temperatures.

Other tests.—Saponification value tests involve measuring the quantity of alkali required to saponify a given amount of fat; the results indicate the average molecular weight of the fatty acids. The refractive index, determined by an optical instrument, correlates with the degree of unsaturation and is used to follow the progress of catalytic hydrogenation. The amounts of moisture and insoluble unsaponifiable matter are important parameters that tell how much non-fatty impurities are present in a fat. Bleaching tests measure residual color and are used primarily on cottonseed, soybean, and sunflower seed oils. Cloud point tests determine the highest temperature at which a haze can be observed in an oil sample and is an indication of the level of winterization. Dilatometry tracks the change in volume with change in temperature and detects phase transformations.

Iodine value is a measure of the number of double bonds present in the fatty acids of a glyceride. It indicates the degree of unsaturation of the fat or oil and is a rough indication of its storage stability. If the material is unhydrogenated, the iodine value can help identify the type or origin of the oil. Hydrogenation decreases the iodine value of a fat, as does oxidation of the double bonds.

Most consumers want shortenings, except butter and lard, to have bland flavors. As Thomas (1968) points out, all shortenings do have a characteristic flavor, though it may be very faint in fresh, highly purified samples. Taste panels consisting of a few experienced members can be used to verify the absence of off-flavors in samples of shortenings received for use as ingredients. Evans (1955) described procedures for setting up, conducting, and evaluating panel tests. Experience has shown that good agreement and reproducibility can be obtained in these tests, according to Evans.

Smoke point, flash point, and fire point are valuable tests for frying fats. The involve gradual heating of the fat in standard equipment under rigidly specified conditions and noting the temperature at which the material emits smoke or catches fire. Table 4.3 contains data on FFA, smoke points, flash points, and fire points of some vegetable oils (Morgan 1942).

Table 4.3. CHARACTERISTICS OF SOME VEGETABLE OILS

Oil	Description	Free fatty acids	Smoke point	Flash point	Fire point
Cottonseed	Crude, hydraulic	1.1	310	565	650
Cottonseed	RBO*	0.18	365	605	675
Corn	RB*	0.06	400	618	678
Soybean	RD*	0.01	453	623	685
Olive	Edible grade	2.1	280	550	670

* R = alkali refined; B = bleached; D = deodorized

If it is desired to determine the content of individual fatty acids with a great deal of precision, the procedure of choice involves gas-liquid chromatography. The fatty acid profile can give warning of adulteration of batches with unwanted types of fats and oils.

Specifications

A specification is a document that can be used by a purchaser to notify a supplier of the limits within which the qualities of an ingredient must fall. Often, the user accepts a manufacturer's specification sheet that sets forth the characteristics of one of the standard products made by the supplier. Although this procedure works out satisfactorily in many cases, the food processor should always be aware that the specification has been written to protect the supplier's interest. If the buyer has some special requirements, it is very likely that the specification will not protect him or her if the fat or oil turns out to be defective in that particular characteristic.

Before establishing a specification, the purchasing agent should circulate specification sheets obtained from shortening suppliers among the technical and production people of his company and make such changes as they deem necessary. It is desirable to insert in the specification a general requirement that the ingredient must function satisfactorily when used in the equipment, formulas, and processes for which it is intended. Although suppliers often object to clauses of this type, it seems perfectly reasonable provided that the sales agents or the supplier's technical people are aware of any special conditions existing in the processor's plant.

According to Vernon (1981), specifications for fats and oils should be based on the following ten rules: (1) Specify only those items required to provide proper functionality of the product; (2) Use only standard testing procedures; (3) Specify test procedures; (4) Make ranges broad enough to include inherent variations in the test procedures and production variations in the manufacturing plant; (5) Don't specify limits that are incompatible with each other or that duplicate one another; (6) Specify only those items that can be controlled; (7) Consider time delays in outlining analytical requirements; (8) Specify delivery temperature only if necessary; (9) Specify only the critical points in the SFI curve (usually three temperatures will provide enough information); and (10) Confer with suppliers to be sure that requirements are realistic and compatible. Vernon claims that peroxide values should not be specified because they are subject to rapid and unpredictable changes caused by light, temperature, time, and other factors; suppliers lose control of peroxide values when the products are transported by rail car because of time delays and different temperatures encountered.

EMULSIFIERS

Emulsifiers are natural or synthetic substances that promote the formation and improve the stability of emulsions, e.g., dispersion of fat droplets in aqueous solutions or of water droplets in a continuous lipid phase. In some cases, they can be used to improve wetting properties—change the surface tension—of water or aqueous solutions. Surface active agents are widely employed in the baking industry for these purposes.

The unifying characteristic of emulsifier molecules is the presence of a hydrophilic group (attracted to water) and a lipophilic group (attracted to fatty substances). Not all such molecules have practical value as surface-active agents, however. It is not necessary that the hydrophilic and lipophilic groups have equal effectiveness; as a matter of fact, it is usual to find that one or the other plays a dominant role in the action of the emulsifier. The variability in performance of different emulsifiers is the result of the relative potency of the two kinds of regions, their spatial relationship, the size of the entire molecule, and certain other factors. There are some very potent emulsifiers that cannot be used in foodstuffs because of legal restrictions. There are a few that are acceptable in most standardized foods, however, and several more are permitted in nonstandardized foods.

Without a screening system, the time required for selecting an emulsifier of optimum function for a given application might prove to be prohibitive. A prescreening system or emulsifier rating scale that has been rather widely used is the HLB (hydrophile-lipophile balance) scheme (Anon. 1963). In brief, this method provides rules for assigning an HLB number to the combination of ingredients that are to be emulsified, and then directs the selection of an emulsifier or blend of emulsifiers having the same number. The HLB numbers of all common emulsifiers can be found in the literature. Unfortunately, it is not as easy to secure the HLB numbers of ingredients.

Some (but not all) emulsifiers form complexes with starch, and particularly with amylose. Apparently, the HLB numbers are of little or no value in predicting the starch-complexing ability of surfactants. It appears that starch must be gelatinized before the full effect of this complexing action is observed. The exact nature of the reaction is a subject of continuing debate, but the most recent opinions seem to favor the view that a kind of clathrate is formed, with the long amylose molecule wrapped around an extended molecule of, for example, monoglyceride.

The starch-complexing ability of emulsifier-like substances appears to be related to an initial crumb-softening effect and/or a slowing of the starch retrogradation that is widely believed to be the cause of texture staling and firming of baked products such as bread. In addition to their fat-dispersing and starch complexing properties, some emulsifiers also appear to strengthen the gluten and assist aeration. Other functions have been claimed for some of them, as summarized in Table 4.4.

Lecithin

Lecithin, a mixture of phospholipids, is widely distributed in nature but is commercially prepared almost exclusively from soybean oil at the present time. It exists preformed in crude soybean oil, and the commercial method of preparing the emulsifier involves precipitation of the phospholipids from the oil and subsequent purification. It may be further processed by bleaching the purified mixture. It may be mixed with adsorbents to improve dispensing and mixing at point of use, or standardized by blending with small amounts of oil. Most of the lecithin products offered to bakers do have a flavor that may be found objectionable in some applications.

Table 4.4. EFFECTS OF DOUGH CONDITIONERS ON BREAD[1]

Dough conditioner	Loaf volume	Delay of firming	Bread quality
Polysorbate 60	v. good	v. slight	good
Calcium stearoyl-2-lactylate	v. good	good +	v. good
Lactylic stearate	good +	good +	v. good
Sodium stearyl fumarate	fair	v. good	good
Sodium stearoyl-2-lactylate	v. good	v. good	v. good
Succinylated monoglyceride	v. good	good +	v. good
Ethoxylated mono- & di-glycerides	v. good	v. slight	fair

[1] Stutts et al. 1973.

Commercial grades of lecithin are classified according to their total phosphatide content, color, and fluidity. The concentration of total phosphatides in commercial lecithin products ranges between 54% and 72%. Specifications usually report the concentration of active ingredient as "percentage acetone insolubles." Color will be stated as unbleached, single bleached, or double bleached. Bleaching processes tend to reduce the effectiveness of lecithin as a surface-active material. The consistency is described as "plastic" or "fluid." Lecithin can be dispersed in water to form hydrates, and similar responses occur when it is mixed with propylene glycol, glycerine, etc.

Flavor is an important factor to be considered in testing lecithin because off-flavors in the lecithin itself, or in the carriers mixed with it, can often be detected in the finished baked product. Rancidity can occur in the oleaginous vehicle.

Monoglycerides and Diglycerides

These emulsifiers consist of either one or two fatty acids chemically combined with a glycerol molecule. The uncombined OH groups on the glycerol moiety act as the hydrophilic portion of the molecule. It has been shown that monoglycerides are far more effective than diglycerides in reducing surface tension, but the nature of the manufacturing process is such that some diglycerides (and for that matter, some triglycerides and some free glycerol) are inevitably included in the reaction mixture except, perhaps, in the purest of molecularly distilled emulsifiers.

The common basic raw materials for monoglyceride manufacture are lard and vegetable oils such as cottonseed oil (usually hydrogenated). This results in a mixture of fatty acid moieties combined in random fashion with glycerol. Special mixtures and more or less purified fatty acids can be used to give monoglycerides of specific composition.

Commercial blends of mono- and diglycerides contain 35% to 55% monoester, with the balance being predominantly diglycerides. The physical forms of the products may vary from semiliquid or plastic to flaked or beaded solids. High-vacuum distillation techniques can be used to prepare pure (i.e., 96% to 98%) monoglycerides, but at a considerable cost. A commonly used crumb softener is a hydrate (water emulsion) containing about 22% to 25% of distilled monoglycerides. The physical status of the monoglycerides in these preparations causes it to disperse more readily in doughs, and it is therefore a more effective emulsifier than the pure monoglyceride when equal quantities of the active ingredient are compared. There are now available powdered water-dispersible distilled monoglycerides containing sufficient unsaturated fatty acids to permit rapid hydration of the emulsifier in doughs or brews.

Krog (1979) described two stages of monoglyceride activity in dough. In the first stage, if the monoglycerides are present in the form of fine crystals, hydrates, or extremely fine powders, they will absorb on the surface of starch granules during mixing. In the second stage, as the temperature of the dough reaches about 120° to 125°F during baking, the monoglycerides will form a semisolution with part of the water. When the temperature rises to a point where starch begins to gelatinize, the monoglycerides will come into contact with hydrated amylose outside as well as inside the swollen granules. A water-insoluble helical complex will form between the amylose moleule and the monoglyceride. The amylose fraction is virtually immobilized and forms a gel phase between the starch granules. This results in a softer crumb structure in the freshly baked bread, and staling is delayed because the amylose molecules cannot easily aggregate to form quasicrystalline regions. When monoglycerides are used in cake shortening, the functional value of the shortening is less dependent on the amount and crystalline form of the triglyceride than it would be otherwise (Knightly 1981).

Modified monoglycerides are made by reacting food acids with monoglycerides. The most common types are lactated (lactic acid), acetylated (acetic anhydride), and succinylated (succinic anhydride). Ethoxylated mononglycerides are prepared by reacting ethylene oxide with monoglycerides. The resulting product has a stronger affinity than normal monoglycerides for water.

Other Food Emulsifiers

Polyglycerol esters are formed by polymerizing three or more glycerine units and reacting the resulting molecule with stearic acid, oleic acid, or fat. The key characterizing factors are chain length of the glycerol polymer, iodine value, and number of fatty acid esters per molecule.

Propylene glycol monostearate (PGMS) is produced by reacting propylene glycol with stearic acid. Propylene glycol monoester (PGME) is made by reacting propylene glycol with glycerine and fats. PGMS contains only propylene glycol esters, while PGME contains mixed esters of propylene glycol and glycerine. Factors related to functionality include iodine value and monoester type and quantity (normally, 35% to 90%).

Sorbitan monostearate is made by dehydrating sorbitol and reacting it with stearic acid. To make polysorbate 60, sorbitan monostearate is reacted with ethylene oxide—this increases its water affinity and modifies its functionality.

Sodium stearoyl lactylate has become a widely accepted emulsifier for bakery foods. It has the advantages of ready dispersibility and high potency in many applications. To manufacture it commercially, stearic acid is reacted with lactic acid and the product converted to the sodium salt. Calcium stearoyl-2-lactylate is similar but is less dispersible in water.

There are many other chemical species that have a certain amount of surfactant or emulsifier potential, but most of these are unsuitable for food use or, at least, have not been approved for that application.

ANTIOXIDANTS

All bakery foods contain some fat, even if it is only the percent or so of lipid that is naturally present in flour. All of these fats, including the flour fat, are subject to oxidative and hydrolytic rancidity, with resultant objectionable odor and flavor.

Antioxidants are materials that can retard the development of oxidative rancidity during storage of foods containing fat. Natural antioxidants are found in many foods, including "nonpurified" fats such as unbleached cocoa butter, and certain chemical compounds can be added to fats to retard their deterioration.

From a chemical standpoint, rancidity is of two types: (1) hydrolytic rancidity, which can lead to the occurrence of soapy flavors, and (2) oxidative rancidity, which causes the pungent or acrid odor characteristic of badly deteriorated fat. When hydrolytic rancidity has occurred, oxidative deterioration is facilitated. Oxidative rancidity is unquestionably the most important of these two mechanisms so far as its effects on food acceptability are concerned. The susceptibility of a fat to oxidation depends to a considerable extent on the number of unsaturated bonds in the fatty acid moieties. Polyunsaturated fats are very prone to the development of oxidative rancidity, whereas fully saturated fats and oils are more resistant. The amount of surface area exposed to oxygen is also a factor; if fat is absorbed into a material such as paper, with consequent increase in the surface exposed to air, oxidative rancidity may develop in a few days.

In the development of hydrolytic rancidity, moisture and enzymes cause splitting of the triglyceride molecule into glycerol and free fatty acids.

The rate of lipolysis of the fat is strongly influenced by temperature. Optimum temperature for this reaction is near 100°F. Hydrolytic rancidity can be controlled by inactivation of the responsible enzymes by sterilization, low moisture content, and low storage temperatures.

The predominant fatty acids in cereal grains are palmitic, stearic, oleic, linoleic, and linolenic, with the unsaturated acids oleic and linoleic accounting for perhaps two-thirds of the fatty acids in the oil. The reactions leading to oxidative rancidity attack the unsaturated portion of the fatty acid, the double bond. The steps in the process are not fully understood, but probably there is autoxidation by a free radical mechanism catalyzed by heat, light, and trace quantities of metal ions, especially copper and iron. When the fatty ester free radical captures a hydrogen atom, the action of the free radical is terminated and autoxidation is inhibited. The chain reaction can be broken by adding phenolic-type antioxidants, which readily give up a hydrogen atom to the free radical.

The review, "Rancidity in Foods," edited by Allen and Hamilton (1989) contains many useful observations on this subject.

Synthetic Antioxidants

A great amount of research has been directed toward finding substances that will retard the development of oxidative rancidity in foods and at the same time be acceptable to federal regulators as food additives. At the present time, only a limited number of synthetic chemicals are available, and a few "natural" antioxidants. Some of these will be discussed below.

Tertiarybutyl-4-hydroxyanisole, or butylated hydroxyanisole (BHA), is a synthetic antioxidant that has been used effectively for many years to protect the flavor of fat-containing foods. It is practically odorless, flavorless, and colorless when used in the quantities permitted by regulations. It is a solid at room temperature, and it is usually offered in the form of white tablets or flakes. It is particularly valuable for its high degree of persistence even at temperatures used for baking or frying foods.

Butylated hydroxytoluene (BHT) is also an old-timer, relatively speaking. It is available as a pure white crystal. It is partially soluble in benzene, methanol, mineral oil, linseed oil, and lard. It is considered to be slightly more effective than BHA in retarding rancidity of vegetable oils, but acts synergistically with BHA when blends of these two materials are used in some applications.

Tertiary-butyl-hydroquinone (TBHQ) is another antioxidant that has been approved by the FDA for use in foods. The concentration must be such that the combined total of BHA, BHT, TBHQ, and propyl gallate does not exceed 0.02% of the weight of the fat and oil in the finished product (including any essential oil present). The regulations concerning antioxidants in animal fats, as promulgated by the USDA, are slightly different. According to data released by the manufacturer, TBHQ seems to be somewhat more effective than BHA in slowing the development of rancidity in dry cereals, and can reasonably be expected to act similarly in many other products.

Propyl gallate (PG), is the common name for n-propyl 3,4,5 trihydroxybenzoate. Formulations containing PG are not recommended if there will be substantial contact of the treated material with iron equipment, since a colored compound results when PG reacts with ferric iron. This reaction can be reduced if citric acid is present. Citric and phosphoric acid are included in many antioxidant mixtures because they chelate some metal ions and reduce the rancidity-promoting effect of iron, copper, etc.

Although the synthetic antioxidants described above can be obtained separately, many suppliers offer proprietary mixtures of two or more kinds that are said to be more effective than any single compound. All of these substances are insoluble in room temperature water for all practical purposes, the common commercial diluent for BHA, BHT, and TBHQ being vegetable oil. PG is almost insoluble in vegetable oil at room temperature. They are all very soluble in ethyl alcohol. Table 4.5 gives more details on commercial versions of these antioxidants.

Table 4.5. CHARACTERISTICS OF SYNTHETIC ANTIOXIDANTS[1]

Common name	Food additive regulation	Melting range, °C	Odor	Solubility, %
BHA	21 CFR 182.3169	48–63	Slight	50
BHT	21 CFR 182.3173	70	Slight	30
TBHQ	21 CFR 172.185	126–129	Very slight	10
PG	21 CFR 184.1660	146–150	Very slight	1

[1] Eastman Kodak Co. Publ. ZG-109H, and other commercial publications. Solubility: In soybean oil at 25°C.

Antioxidants behave differently in different foods, so that it is advisable to conduct a storage test before selecting the antioxidant for a new product. For example, in AOM stability tests of five antioxidants at 0.02% in lard, PG, BHA, and BHT were about equally effective and all increased the stability of the control about 7 to 8 times, while tocopherol was about 50% to 60% as effective and TBHQ about twice as effective as the other three antioxidants. On the other hand, when used on pecans, TBHQ was only about half as effective as BHA. In most products, however, TBHQ seems to be more protective than the other antioxidants.

Natural Antioxidants

Many substances naturally occurring in foods and food ingredients act as fat antioxidants to some extent. They are usually of limited practical value for one or more of the following reasons: (1) They are of low potency; (2) They are accompanied by flavors, odors, or colors that are undesirable in most foods; (3) They would be inordinately expensive to produce in commercial quantities; and (4) Their legal status as ingredients is questionable. An example that can be suggested as having some of these drawbacks is the extract of black tea leaves patented as a food lipid antioxidant by Mai *et al.* (1990). Tea extract evidently owes its antioxidant properties to gallic acid.

A widely promoted "natural" antioxidant is mixed tocopherols, a material derived from vegetable oil distillates. "Mixed" indicates that alpha-, beta-, gamma-, and delta-tocopherols may be present. It is said these additives, or some of them, as an additional advantage increase the vitamin E content of the finished product. It is said by the manufacturer that the ingredient may be described on the label as "natural mixed tocopherols, a natural source of vitamin E, used to protect freshness"

A commercial preparation of mixed tocopherols containing 70% of these compounds is described as a reddish brown, slightly viscous liquid having a refractive index of 1.559 at 20°C and a specific gravity of 0.92 at 25°C. It has a mild, slight vegetable oil flavor and is easily soluble in vegetable oils, essential oils, and ethanol but insoluble in water. Recommended addition levels are 0.015% to 0.045% of tocopherols, based on fat as 100%. Levels greater than 0.1% may actually increase the oxidation rate.

A spice extract called Rosemary AR has been shown to have antioxidant properties, at least for some foods. It suffers from the disadvantage of having a very intensive characteristic herb flavor that is not compatible with most products. It is also quite expensive.

FAT SUBSTITUTES AND REPLACEMENTS

Since it is quite obvious that fats and oils, with their nine calories per gram, create major problems in the designing of diets for persons desiring to reduce weight, these foods and ingredients are among the most favored candidates for elimination or change by nutritionists seeking to encourage "healthful" eating habits among the American public. An impediment to the effectiveness of these efforts is that foods containing less than the expected or customary amount of fat often have very low acceptability. This situation has provided the impetus for much research into means for replacing fat and oil ingredients with low caloric or no-calorie substitutes. There are two major approaches: (1) The fat is replaced by hydrocolloids or similar materials that increase solution viscosity so as to simulate the mouthfeel and/or viscosity of oil—this approach has been successful in preparing reduced-calorie salad dressings, and perhaps could be used in formulating reduced-calorie icings, toppings, etc.; or (2) The fat is replaced by a chemical having some of the same physical characteristics, but having no caloric value.

Another approach, somewhat similar to the first but having important differences, is that used in making the product called Simplesse, which is essentially tiny drops of aqueous solution encapsulated in microscopic vesicles of egg white or milk protein. This material has a viscous, lubricating type of texture and appears to function very well in certain limited applications, as a ingredient in no-fat ice cream, as a cream replacer, etc. It probably would be of little or no use in a cooked dough or batter, but might be useful in adjuncts such as buttercream-type icings, whipped toppings, salad dressings, etc. It is apparently of no value as a frying medium.

Some of the viscosity-modifying materials that have been suggested as the first type of fat mimetic are polydextrose, maltodextrins, tapioca dextrins, potato starch, microcrystalline cellulose, and gums such as alginates, xanthans, carrageenan, and locust bean. An ingredient trade-named N-flate has been proposed as an aid in producing shortening-free cakes. The product, essentially a blend of emulsifiers, modified food starches, and guar gum on a nonfat milk base, aids in the incorporation of a large number of air cells during batter preparation, so that (it is said) a cake with fine uniform cell structure and good volume can be made with no shortening.

The second type, sometimes called engineered fats (though they really aren't fats), include sucrose polyesters, polyglycerol esters, triglyceride esters of alpha-substitute carboxylic acids, and alkyl glycoside polyesters. Probably the most work has been done with sucrose polyesters. Olestra is the trade name for sucrose combined with six, seven, or eight long chain fatty acids. This substance is claimed to not be absorbed in the human intestine, and so it is devoid of calories when used as a component of the diet. Sucrose polyesters are differentiated from other fat substitutes by their reasonable stability at high temperatures, such as those encountered in baking or frying. Other possibilities have been listed by Nelson (1990).

The technological challenges posed by fat replacement formulas are but a small part of the picture. All of these products face present or potential problems with legal clearance and labeling, although Simplesse is now being used in a number of commercial products after having surmounted these obstacles at great expense and after several years legal work.

BIBLIOGRAPHY

ALLEN, J. C., and HAMILTON, R. J. (Editors). 1989. Rancidity in Foods, Second Edition. Elsevier Science Publ. Co., New York, NY

ANON. 1963. The Atlas HLB System. Third Edition. Atlas Chemical Industries, Wilmington, DE

ANON. 1973. Tenox TBHQ antioxidant for fats, oils and fat containing foods. Eastman Chem. Prod. Publ. ZG-210

ANON. 1980. Official and Tentative Methods, Third Ed. Am. Oil Chemists Soc., Chicago

ANON. 1982. Food Fats and Oils. Inst. of Shortening and Edible Oils, Washington, DC

ANON. 1986. Food Chemicals Codex. Second Supplement to the Third Edition. National Academy Press, Washington, DC

ANON. 1989. Fatty acid content is critical. Agricultural Outlook AO-159, 11.

D'ALONZO, R. P., KOZAREK, W. J., and WADE, R. L. 1982. Glyceride composition of processed fats and oils as determined by glass capillary gas chromatography. J. Am. Oil Chemists Soc. *59*, 302-303

EVANS, C. D. 1955. Flavor evaluation of fats and oils. J. Am. Oil Chemists Soc. *32*, 596-604

FRIEDERICH, J. P., LIST, G. R., and HEAKIN, A. J. 1982. Petroleum-free extraction of oil from soybeans with supercritical carbon dioxide. J. Am. Oil Chemists Soc. *59*, 288-292

GREENWELL, B. A. 1981. Chilling and crystallization of shortenings and margarines. J. Am. Oil Chemists Soc. *58*, 206-208

KINCS, F. 1990. Choosing shortenings and oils. Proc. Am. Soc. Bakery Engrs. *1990*, 73-77

KNIGHTLY, W. H. 1981. Shortening systems: Fats, oils and surface-active agents—present and future. Cereal Chem. *58*, 171-174

KROG, N. J. 1979. Dynamic and unique monoglycerides. Cereal Foods World *24*, No. 1, 10-11

KROG, N. M. 1981. Theoretical aspects of surfactants in relation to their use in breadmaking. Cereal Chem. *58*, 158-164

MAI, J., CHAMBERS, L. J., and MC DONALD, R. E. 1990. Process for inhibiting lipid oxidation in food. U.S. Pat. 4,891,231

MORGAN, D. A. 1942. Smoke, fire, and flash points of cottonseed, peanut, and other vegetable oils. Oil and Soap *19*, 193-199

MORRISON, W. R. 1976. Lipids in flour, dough, bread. Bakers Digest *50*, No.4, 29-35, 47

MOYER, J. 1965. Selection, maintenance and protection of frying fats. Proc. Am. Soc. Bakery Engrs. *1965*, 273-278

NEWBOLD, M. W. 1976. Crumb softeners and dough conditioners. Bakers Digest *50*, No. 4, 37-40

NELSON, K. J. 1990. Fat substitutes in baking. Proc. Am. Soc. Bakery Engrs. *1990*, 79-84

PONTIUS, W. I. 1965. The Meaning of Solids Factor Index. Armour & Co., Chicago, IL

RACCACH, M. 1984. The antimicrobial activity of phenolic antioxidants in foods: A review. J. Food Safety *6*, 141-170

RUSCH, D. T. 1981. Emulsifiers: Uses in cereal and baked foods. Cereal Foods World *26*, 111-114

SCOTT, E. A. 1984. Product release agents. Proc. Am. Soc. Bakery Engrs. *1984*, 157-165

STINGLEY, D. V., and WHEELER, F. G. 1956. The meaning of commonly quoted analytical values of shortening as related to shortening performance. Cereal Sci. Today *1*, 39-42

STUTTS, R. L., DEL VECCHIO, A. J., and TENNEY, R. J. 1973. The role of emulsifiers and dough conditioners in foods. Food Product Development *1973*, No. 10, 35-42

SUGGS, J. 1982. Powdered cake emulsifiers. Proc. Am. Soc. Bakery Engrs. *1982*, 110-116

THOMAS, B. L. 1968. Specifications: What do they really mean? Snack Food *57*, No. 12, 30-32

TUBB, G. O. 1966. The use of liquid shortening in bread. Proc. Am. Soc. Bakery Engrs. *1966*, 102-106

VERNON, H. R. 1981. Writing fats and oil specifications. Cereal Foods World *26*, 441 443

WARNER, K. 1988. Sensory evaluation of flavor quality of oils. *In* Flavor Chemistry of Fats and Oils. D. B. Min and T. B. Smouse, Editors. Am. Oil Chemists Soc., Champaign, IL

WEISS, T. J. 1982. Food Oils and Their Uses, Second Ed. AVI Publ. Co., Westport, CT

WERNER, L. E. 1981. Shortening systems. Proc. Am. Soc. Bakery Engrs. *1981*, 61-70

WOERFEL, J. B. 1960. Shortenings. *In* Bakery Technology and Engineering. S. A. Matz, Ed. AVI Publ. Co., Westport, CT

chapter five

SWEETENERS AND MALT SYRUP

INTRODUCTION

Very few bakery products are made without some added sweetener. Even plain bread and rolls generally contain small amounts of sugar or syrups, which function not only as flavorants but also as sources of food for the yeast early in the fermentation process and, sometimes, throughout all stages of fermentation. Many cakes and cookies will contain at least as much sugar as flour, and many adjuncts such as icings and frostings will owe most of their texture and structure to the sweetener that makes up a large part of their composition.

The types of sweeteners most commonly used are sucrose (cane or beet sugar) and various hydrolysates of corn starch (corn syrup, dextrose, etc.). Depending on the amount added, these ingredients can affect not only the taste but also the texture and appearance of the baked product.

Malt syrup, a product derived from extracts of germinated grain, is discussed in this chapter. Although it functions in present day bakery practice mainly as a sweetener, flavoring material, and colorant, some forms supply enzymes that convert part of the wheat starch (from the flour) into fermentation substrates for yeast. Its enzyme contribution was the original reason for using malt in doughs, but enzymes derived from cultures of fungi or bacteria have partially supplanted the barley product for this purpose.

In addition to the common types of nutritive sweeteners added to foods, there are several other substances that are basically sweeteners, but that are only used for special purposes such as added flavor, health or natural food connotations, or reduced calorie possibilities. Several of these ingredients are discussed toward the end of the chapter.

SWEETENERS FROM SUGAR CANE AND SUGAR BEETS

Granulated Sugar

Commercial sucrose—cane sugar and beet sugar—is one of the purest ingredients available to the food manufacturer. The composition of the fractional percentage of nonsucrose material in beet sugar differs slightly from that in refined cane sugar, but for all practical purposes the two refined sugars can be used interchangeably if the sieve analyses are similar.

The manufacturing of either cane or beet sugar can be separated into sequences of operations, the sequences sometimes being performed in different plants. The first set of operations leads to the production of raw sugar, the second set converts raw sugar into the refined product found on the shelves of retail grocery stores and in the warehouses of bakeries. Manufacture of raw sugar from beets is significantly different from cane sugar processing, especially in the early steps.

Beet sugar factories slice beets, extract them with water, concentrate the solution, and crystallize the sucrose. Various cleaning operations, mostly of a filtering type, are included between these steps. Sucrose crystals are separated from the impurities that accompany them by washing, recrystallizing, etc. Molasses obtained from beet sugar manufacture is used mainly in cattle feed, often as a mixture with spent beet pulp.

Cane sugar starts with the crushing and pressing of sugar cane. The conventional extraction process involves grinding the canes with an impact disk mill in order to open the cells, and then passing this preparation through cane mills consisting of fluted rollers that exert a high pressure of 50 to 100 bars (Gautier 1989). The juice that is obtained in the pressing operation is concentrated and purified, then sucrose is crystallized from the concentrate under controlled conditions. The dark, moist, sticky sugar (about 95% sucrose) is sent by the raw sugar factory to a refinery, where it is further purified by dissolving, precipitating impurities, recrystallizing, and washing, to yield the granular white sugar of commerce. At various stages in these processes, molasses is removed by centrifuging or (seldom) draining mixtures of crystals and syrup.

The average particle size and the particle size range of granular sucrose can be accurately controlled by adjusting processing conditions. For the finer varieties such as confectioners' sugar, the crystals are ground, as in a hammer mill. Usually a small amount (about 3%) of cornstarch is added to prevent caking. Sugar particle size has an important effect on the behavior of certain kinds of bakery mixtures. Of course, if the sugar is going to be dissolved, as it is in making syrups and many doughs and batters, its particle size has little or no influence on the finished product. In icings where the sugar does not completely dissolve, in fat-based fillings where the original particle size is maintained until the product is consumed, in chocolate coatings, and in many cookie formulas where the dough moisture is insufficient to completely dissolve the sugar before the piece encounters oven temperature, particle size specifications must be carefully considered.

Molasses

Molasses is an inexact term that has different meanings to the raw sugar manufacturer, the sugar refiner, and the baker. The various grades and types of molasses that are offered to the food manufacturer can be loosely defined as concentrated cane juice with (1) some of the sucrose removed; (2) some of the sucrose inverted; (3) various processing aids added; and (4) various reaction products accumulated. All types of molasses tend to be dark brown in color, acidic in reaction, and bitter in flavor.

Whole cane juice molasses is, ostensibly, all the juice as pressed from the cane, concentrated by boiling. Since sucrose will dissolve to give a concentration of only about 67% in water and at this concentration is not sufficiently stable microbiologically to allow safe storage and distribution, manufacturers of molasses invert part of the sucrose to give a total solids concentration of about 78% to 80% in the finished product. At this Brix level, molasses will resist fermentation by most microorganisms and can be distributed through normal channels without spoiling. This type of syrup is relatively light in color. Though mild in flavor, it is sweeter than a saturated solution of sucrose. Some of these syrups will have been treated with sulfur dioxide. Since whole cane juice molasses is expensive compared to other types of this sweetener, and the supply is limited, it is sold mostly through retail stores as a table syrup and as an ingredient for home baking.

Other grades of molasses are collected in the sugar manufacturing process as liquids removed from the mass of crystallized sucrose that forms at various stages in the procedure. First strike molasses is the syrup removed from the first crystallization. It can be sold as syrup or subjected to a further crystallization of sucrose after various treatments have been applied. Molasses removed from the second crystallization step is called second strike molasses. Third strike molasses is removed from the third crystallization vessel, etc. The molasses becomes progressively darker, more bitter, and lower in sucrose content as the number of "strikes" proceeds. Furthermore, nonfermentable carbohydrates, minerals, and other unwanted materials accumulate in the syrup, and some can have unwanted physiological effects. Blackstrap molasses is the end point in this sequence and it is generally considered unfit for human consumption.

First strike, second strike, blackstrap, etc., are terms used by raw sugar manufacturers and sugar refiners, but these two groups of processors tend to have different definitions for the terms, and they are of little significance to purchasers of bakery ingredients who buy syrups from manufacturers of blended molasses products. The latter products are formulated to have the color, flavor, stability, and fermentability needed by bakers, and can often be modified to meet a unique specification. Year to year variation in quality, resulting from differences in the growing conditions encountered by the cane, is also minimized by using blends.

In addition to blending syrups from various sources, the manufacturer of ingredient molasses will invert part of the sucrose content to get a finished product with true solids of 78% to 79% (spindle Brix reading of about 79.5). In the best quality molasses, about 72% to 74% total sugars will be present, divided about equally between sucrose and invert sugar. A syrup of this composition, when hot-filled into containers, will be sufficiently resistant to microbiological spoilage to maintain its quality during prolonged storage. Analysis will show the presence of about 2% to 2.5% ash and some organic non-sugars (mostly browning products and Krebs cycle acids). Molasses of stronger flavor and darker color will usually contain more non-fermentable carbohydrates, more ash, and less sugar.

Final composition of molasses can vary depending on the cane variety, climate, soil conditions, and the method and extent of processing. There can be considerable variation in the composition of the same type of molasses made at different mill locations or in different years at the same mill.

It has been reported that molasses has a significant antioxidant effect on prime steam lard (Morano 1984). See Table 5.1. The "extract" was not clearly characterized in this publication.

Table 5.1. ANTIOXIDANT EFFECT OF MOLASSES EXTRACT[1]

| | | Days sample held at 60°C | | | |
| | | 0 | 2 | 4 | 10 |
Additives	Amount	peroxide values			
Nothing	None	0.7	4.0	8.0	50.0
BHA	200 ppm	0.7	2.2	5.0	12.6
Molasses extract	200 ppm	0.7	1.8	3.7	23.3

Brown Sugar

So-called "soft" or "brown" sugars can be regarded as sugar crystals coated with molasses. Their total sugar content ranges from 90% to 95%, and their moisture content from about 2% to 4%. They are composed of small crystals covered with a film of highly refined, dark-colored, cane-flavored syrup. On a solids basis, these sugars are always slightly more expensive than ordinary granulated sugar. They contribute characteristic colors and flavors that are considered desirable in several kinds of bakery foods, e.g., graham crackers and ginger snaps. At one time, sugar refiners produced 15 grades of brown sugars, ranging from No. 1, with a slight creamy tint, to the very dark brown No. 15. Because of limited demand for the finer gradations of color, most refiners now produce only four grades, No. 6, No. 8, No. 10, and No. 13. The retail varieties are Light Brown (No. 8), Medium Brown (No. 10), and Dark Brown (No. 13).

Moisture contents range from about 2% in the lightest colored type to about 4% in the darkest type. The total sugar content varies from about 95% in No. 6 to 91% in No. 13. From 1% to 5% of the sugar is present as invert.

Brown sugars remain "soft" and easy to measure and dispense as long as their moisture content remains constant. If the sugar is exposed for weeks to atmospheres of low relative humidity, much of the water will evaporate and the sugar crystals will become cemented together. It is this familiar change that creates numerous difficulties in the commercial use of brown sugar. A bag of brown sugar that has become cemented into a solid block is very difficult to handle in the plant. To circumvent this problem, suppliers offer brown sugar syrup, brown sugar flavors (to be used with granulated sugar), and granulated brown sugar. Another expedient is to use a good grade of cane molasses in combination with granulated sucrose as a substitute for an equal quantity of brown sugar.

Because of the differences in the way beet sugar is refined, molasses prepared from beets is not condidered suitable for human consumption and, therefore, brown sugars can not be made from beet sugar by withdrawing partially purified sugar crystals during the refining process. The solubles found in beet extract are different, and less acceptable, than those in sugar cane juice. Some of the processing aids used in the initial stages are also different from those added in cane sugar refining. As a result of these differences, molasses obtained during beet sugar processing is not a food ingredient. Large quantities are, however, used as fermentation substrates and in animal feeds. Brown sugar can be made from beet sugar by coating the beet sugar crystals with a type of molasses made from cane.

Sucrose and Invert Sugar Syrups

In many applications, the obvious advantages of handling sugar in a dissolved form has led to the extensive distribution and use in bakery products of sucrose and invert sugar syrups. Liquid sugars can be roughly classified into sucrose types, invert (or mixed) types, and refinery syrups or liquid brown sugars. Sucrose is available at 66.5% to 68% solids content. This is the limit of solubility of sucrose at ordinary temperatures. Two or three grades, varying mostly in color, are usually available.

If part of the sugar is inverted (hydrolyzed to glucose and fructose), the resulting syrup will retain higher concentrations of solids in solution. Common commercial types are syrups of 73% or 76% solids with 30% or 60% invert. "Totally" inverted syrups contain 72% to 73% solids with perhaps 5% being sucrose. All of these syrups are reasonably resistant to microbiological spoilage, but the invert syrups are probably somewhat superior in this regard because of their lower water activity. There has been some controversy about the relative sweetness of sucrose and invert sugar in foods, but, when solutions of the same concentration are compared directly, it is generally agreed that invert sugar is sweeter.

Liquid sugars are usually cheaper, on a solids basis, than bagged sucrose. In comparison with dry sugar shipped in bulk, the situation is not as clear-cut, and the economic advantage may vary with the date of delivery and location of the purchaser. There are formulas, particularly of cookies, in which the granular form of sucrose has a specific function and it cannot be satisfactorily replaced by dissolved sugar.

Refiners' syrups are obtained by special processing of material obtained at intermediate stages in the manufacture of cane sugar. They have a relatively strong flavor and a dark color that can be advantageous in certain food uses and undesirable in others. They are usually priced lower than pure granulated sugar, so substitution is desirable when it is feasible. Refiners' syrups contain a total of 50% to 75% sucrose and invert solids combined, and other substances making up a total of 70% to 80% solids.

All of these syrups (sugar, invert, and refiners') have viscosities low enough so they can be transferred, stored, and dispensed at normal room temperatures. They are less viscous than low DE or high solids corn syrups. Heat tracing of pipes is not needed under the usual conditions of use.

In the U.S. and some other countries, the price of sucrose is kept artificially high (compared to the world market for raw sugar) by government support programs. This has led to market opportunities for corn sweeteners that can be sold at unregulated prices. These corn sweeteners, which have supplanted cane and beet sugar in many of the latter's traditional bakery food applications, will be discussed in the next section.

CORN STARCH DERIVATIVES

Starch, from whatever source, is composed of anhydroglucose units. The long and often branched molecules can be split by acids or enzymes to yield the simple hexose sugar D-glucose. Although starch from many sources can be treated in this manner, the sweeteners of greatest commercial importance in the U.S. are made from corn starch. The starch portion of the corn endosperm (the raw material for these sweeteners) is separated from other fractions of the kernel by wet milling processes. Because of space limitations, it is not possible to give details of these manufacturing processes here; readers interested in learning about wet-milling should consult "The Chemistry and Technology of Cereals as Food and Feed" (Matz 1991).

Corn Syrup Processing

Starch conversion processes.—The most common methods used in the commercial production of corn syrups are the acid process, the acid-enzyme process, and the multiple enzyme process.

In the acid conversion process, a starch slurry is acidified to about pH 2 and then pumped to a converter vessel where it is heated and stirred until all the starch has been hydrolyzed to the desired extent. The conversion process is terminated by reducing the pressure and neutralizing the reacted mixture with alkali. Small amounts of sodium chloride are produced by the neutralization. The mixture is clarified to remove suspended solids and then concentrated by evaporation to an intermediate density.

The intermediate syrup is further clarified, decolorized, and concentrated in evaporators to the final density. The syrup may then be treated with ion-exchange resins to remove some of its impurities.

The acid-enzyme process is similar to the acid process except that the starch slurry is partially converted by acid until a predetermined dextrose equivalent is reached, after which it is treated with appropriate enzymes to complete the conversion. For example, in the production of 42 DE high maltose syrup, the acid conversion is halted at a point where the D-glucose concentration is negligible. Then the maltose-producing enzyme (beta-amylase) is added and conversion continued under appropriate conditions. Finally, the enzyme is deactivated and the purification, clarification, and concentration procedures are performed in much the same ways as described in the preceding paragraphs.

The distribution of saccharides in corn syrup (i.e., the relative proportions of mono-, di-, and tri-saccharides, as well as larger molecules) is related to the dextrose equivalent and will also vary according to the conditions of hydrolysis.

Isomerization processes.

—To manufacture high fructose corn syrups, D-glucose solutions or high DE substrates produced by acid-enzyme or dual enzyme methods are refined by carbon and ion-exchange systems and further treated enzymatically with purified isomerase—an enzyme that converts glucose to fructose. Isomerase reactors employ an immobilized enzyme system that is capable of continuously isomerizing a stream of glucose solution. Isomerization is usually carried to a point where the substrate contains 42% fructose. Following this step, the product is again purified by passing it through carbon and ion exchange systems before it is finally evaporated to a viscous syrup containing about 71% dry substance.

If the manufacturer desires to produce a syrup having a fructose concentration above 42%, the feedstock described in the preceding paragraph is passed through separation columns that retain fructose while allowing D-glucose to pass. This is possible because of the greater affinity of fructose for divalent calcium and other cations that are present in the column's packing. The fructose retained in the column can be flushed out with de-ionized water, while the D-glucose is taken back to the isomerization reactor. Both batch and continuous systems for the separation process are used, with the continuous systems being based on a simulated moving bed process.

Fructose fractions are generally recovered at an 80% to 90% concentration. This fraction and the 42% fructose feedstock are mixed to produce the common industrial product having 55% fructose content. Blended syrups are refined with both carbon and ion exchange systems before they are evaporated to a dry substance level of 77%.

The high level fructose feedstock may be refined and evaporated for users who demand a very high fructose product. For example, there is available a high fructose corn syrup with a solids content of 71%, of which 43% is fructose, 52% is D-glucose, and 5% other sugars. Its color is water white and the pH is 4.0. Another version contains 77% solids, of which 55% is fructose, 42% is D-glucose, and 3% is other sugars. These ingredients command premium prices as compared to corn syrups with lesser amounts of fructose, but, presumably, they will be priced below inverted sucrose syrups.

Crystalline fructose is also available and may have some appeal for certain specialty applications although its price is estimated to be about 1.5 to 2 times that of sucrose. A process for making this material has been described by Schollmeier (1985). Crystalline maltose derived from plant starch has also become available in commercial quantities.

Characterizing Corn Sweeteners

Although corn syrups may be, chemically, rather complex mixtures, they can be characterized for most ingredient purposes by fairly simple tests. In addition to evaluations of color and flavor, which ought to be applied to all food ingredients as a matter of course, and any microbiological tests deemed necessary, conventional corn syrups can be described by the three parameters of dextrose equivalent, solids content, and viscosity.

Dextrose equivalent.—Corn syrups are usually classified into four types on the basis of their dextrose equivalent (DE or D.E.). "Dextrose equivalent" is based on an analysis for reducing sugars, the results being expressed as glucose calculated as a percentage of the total dry substance. That is, it is the percent of glucose that would give the same analytical effect as is actually given by the total of all the different reducing sugars present in the syrup. It is considered to be a rough indication of the sweetness, fermentability, and viscosity of the syrup, although these comparisons must be tempered with caution when they are used to predict performance in bakery products. The syrup called by the trade "Type I" falls in the more than 20 but less than 38 DE range, Type II will test 38 to less than 58 DE, Type III has 58 to less than 73 DE, and Type IV has 73 DE or higher. High fructose corn syrups are not classified according to their dextrose equivalent, but are identified by their fructose content (e.g., 42%, 55%, 90%).

The performance of corn syrups in foods, including bakery products, can often be related to their conversion level. Specialty syrups, such as high maltose syrup, require more complicated specifications. A more-or-less complete profile of the carbohydrate composition as obtained by chromatographic analysis is often very useful.

Solids content.—In addition to the carbohydrate composition, corn syrups are also classified, or described, according to their solids content. Most commercial corn syrups are sold on a Baumé (Bé) basis, an estimate of the density based on a measurement of the specific gravity of the syrup by a type of hydrometer. When the degrees Baumé and the dextrose equivalent of a syrup are known, its dry matter can be determined by reference to published tables. For example, a 43° high conversion syrup has about 2% more solids per unit volume than does 43° regular conversion corn syrup.

The Baumé designation has been largely superseded by determinations of the refractive index. The latter is a simpler and faster procedure and just as accurate. High fructose corn syrups are sold on a dry substance specification without reference to Baumé tests. Most corn syrups are available in the range of 41 to 45 Bé corresponding to a dry substance content of about 77% to 85%.

Viscosity.—From a practical standpoint, it is important to recognize that syrup viscosity varies inversely with the DE and directly, but not linearly, with the solids concentration. A low DE, high Bé syrup can be very viscous and therefore very difficult to transfer and to disperse unless it is heated and mixed with water. If, for some reason, one of these syrups is allowed to cool in a pump or transfer line, a tedious and difficult clean-up situation is created. In most cases, a 43° or 44° Bé syrup offers insufficient economic advantages to compensate for the more difficult handling problems, as compared to 42° Bé syrups. High fructose syrups are always less viscous than regular corn syrups of the same concentration, and are usually offered at concentrations of about 71% to 77% dry substance; the higher the proportion of fructose to glucose, the higher the concentration. These concentrations are quite adaptable to normal storing and transfer systems.

Freezing point—Freezing point depression is related to the molecular weight of the sweetener and, of course, to its concentration in a water solution. Figure 5.1 (Anon. 1988A) illustrates this effect for four sweeteners. These considerations are of minor concern in handling corn syrups and sucrose syrups but may affect the behavior of frozen dou ghs and baked products and, especially, adjuncts.

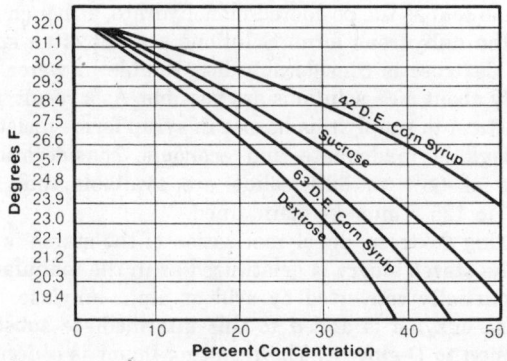

Figure 5.1. Freezing point relations of sweetener solutions

Dried Corn Sweeteners

To produce dried corn syrups, completely refined corn syrups are dehydrated in spray dryers or vacuum drum dryers. This process forms granular, semi-crystalline, or powdery amorphous products depending on the conditions and equipment. Dried corn syrups are comparable in chemical composition to their liquid counterparts. The dry substances are mildly sweet in taste and moderately hygroscopic. Because of their hygroscopicity, corn syrup solids are packed in multiwall moisture-resistant bags.

Dextrose, or alpha-D-glucose, is a readily available sweetener derived from corn starch. It is nearly always cheaper, pound for pound, than sucrose, although it is not nearly as effective a sweetener. Dextrose has been used in cookie fillings to reduce sweetness. It also produces a cooling sensation in the mouth when ingested in the dried form, since it has a negative heat of solution. The cooling effect (heat of solution, latent heat of crystallization) of dextrose hydrate and four other sugar preparations is shown in Table 5.2. Data from Anon. (1986A), which see for original sources.

Table 5.2. HEAT OF SOLUTION OF CARBOHYDRATES[1]

Material	Latent heat of crystallization
Lactose, anhydrous	+7.33
Sucrose	-3.85
Dextrose, anhydrous	-14.5
Lactose, hydrate	-10.3
Dextrose, hydrate	-25.2

[1] Calories per gram at 25°C

Most dextrose is sold as the powdered monohydrate, although there is also a demand for the anhydrous form. Solutions are not often specified. Below about 130°F, dextrose is considerably less soluble in water than is sucrose. At 75°F, only about 50% solutions are possible. As a result, it is not often considered practical to supply this hexose in syrup form—resistance to bacteriological spoilage is inadequate and economic considerations are unfavorable. Syrups of 68% to 69% solids are available, but holding temperatures of 120° to 125°F must be maintained.

In manufacturing dextrose, depolymerization of the starch is carried as far as possible. The starch slurry is gelatinized as in the manufacture of corn syrup and is partially converted by acid or alpha-amylase. Then a purified glucoamylase enzyme is added to this intermediate substrate to complete the conversion to D-glucose. The resulting liquor is concentrated, cooled, and pumped to crystallizers where the temperature is gradually reduced. Crystallization is controlled by the amount of seed crystals added. Dextrose monohydrate crystallizes and is separated from the mother liquor by centrifugation. The moist crystals are washed in centrifuges and dried in continuous dryers to about 8.5% moisture.

Anhydrous dextrose is usually produced by dissolving dextrose hydrate and evaporating the solution to a very high solids content. Anhydrous alpha-D-glucose is then crystallized on added (or induced) seed crystals at elevated temperatures. The anydrous dextrose is separated by centrifugation, washed, and dried.

Preparation of dried fructose has been approached by fractional crystallization techniques. One commercially-used aqueous crystallization process involves a two-stage batch procedure in which both stages operate as constant supersaturation systems, being cooled from 60°C to 30°C over a

50 hr cycle. Crystals are separated from the residual syrup by centrifugation and gently dried at about 40°C in vacuum ovens. A patented continuous process (Gautier 1989) requires the rapid and thorough mixing with seed crystals of a 95% solids syrup at a temperature of 55° to 70°C.

Solubilities of sucrose, lactose, dextrose, and fructose are shown in Table 5.3 (data from Pancoast and Junk 1980). Figure 5.2 shows the solubility of dextrose (and sucrose) over a wide range (Source: Corn Products).

Table 5.3. EFFECT OF TEMPERATURE ON WATER SOLUBILITY

| Temperature, °C | Grams of sugar dissolved in 110 g water | | | |
	Sucrose	Glucose	Fructose	Lactose
0	181	349	--	11.9
10	188	412	--	--
20	199	478	789	18.3
30	214	546	815	24.6
40	233	618	843	31.5
50	258	709	869	44.1
60	288	748	--	60.1
70	325	782	--	75.8
80	370	813	--	98.4
90	426	--	--	140.4
100	--	--	--	157.6

Maltodextrins

Maltodextrins are not really "sweeteners," but they are produced in a manner very similar to that used for making corn syrup, so they will be discussed briefly at this point. When making maltodextrins, the starch conversion process is stopped at an early stage to keep the DE below about 20. At this DE level, very little sweet taste is detectable. Both acid and enzyme processes are used. Refining of the syrup is conducted much the same as with corn syrup. Maltodextrins are usually spray dried to provide white free-flowing powders that are only slightly hygroscopic. They are used mainly as viscosity inducers in liquids or as bulking agents in foods where sweetness would be objectionable. Chemically, maltodextrins are relatively large molecular weight polymers of glucose.

MALT PRODUCTS

Malt is prepared from a cereal grain, usually barley, by moistening it with water, allowing it to sprout under controlled conditions, drying it with warm circulating air, and removing the sprout. Witt (1970) has given a detailed account of malt manufacture. The natural processes accompanying sprouting create or release in active form relatively large quantities of enzymes and change the original components of the grain in many other ways. Manufacturers of alcoholic beverages, especially brewers, use much more malt than any other industry, but considerable quantities are also used by millers and bakers.

Malt products available to bakers may conveniently be classified as malt flour, malt syrup, dried malt syrup, and blends. Each of these categories may be further subdivided into diastatic and nondiastatic products. Malt flour is the ground modified grain, malt syrups are concentrated water extracts of the grain, and dried malt syrups are derived from their liquid precursors by removing most of the moisture at elevated temperatures. Blends are mixtures of malt syrup with corn syrup and they are being sold in both liquid and dried forms.

Malt is fairly high in vitamins and essential amino acids, and so is a nutritionally valuable additive. Malt syrup contains 60% to 65% carbohydrates, 5.5% to 6% protein, 1.5% ash, 20% to 25% water, and other substances. The minerals and low molecular weight nitrogenous compounds present in malt may have some value as yeast nutrients.

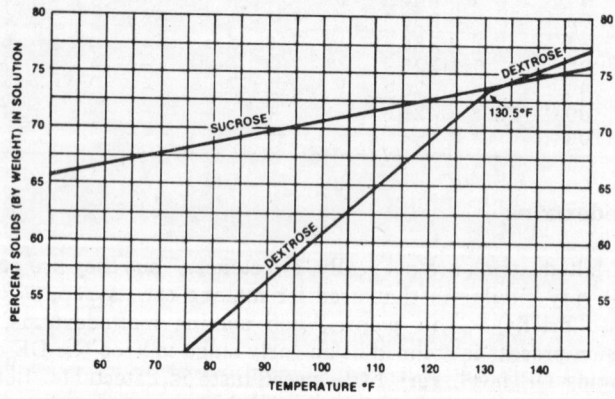

Figure 5.2. Effect of temperature on solubility of dextrose and sucrose

Malt as a Source of Fermentable Sugars

Both diastatic and nondiastatic malts contain considerable quantities of sugars including glucose and maltose. Glucose is a monosaccharide that is used very rapidly by fermenting yeast. Maltose is a disaccharide that is fermented by bakers' yeast late in the breadmaking process when glucose and fructose have been used up. If a dough does not contain maltose, the other fermentable sugars may be exhausted before the end of pan proof, a critical time when sustained gassing power is necessary in order to produce loaves having good volume. If maltose is present in the dough, either added as an ingredient or produced subsequent to mixing as a result of the action of amylolytic enzymes, the monosaccharides glucose and fructose (or sucrose, which is rapidly split into these hexoses by an enzyme bound to the cell wall of yeast) are used first; then a lag period ensues during which little gas is produced, and finally the maltose is attacked leading to a final, fairly rapid stage of gas production. This means there is an inherent mechanism for securing adequate gassing during pan proofing if the doughs contain adequate maltose and the fermentation conditions are appropriate.

There are two ways of getting maltose into doughs. One method is to add this sugar to the dough in the form of malt or as a high maltose corn syrup, and the other is to rely on the production of maltose from the flour starch by diastatic enzymes. In recent years, the enzymic action of diastatic malt syrup has been largely replaced by standardized enzymes isolated from bacterial or fungal cultures. The latter will be discussed in another chapter.

Diastatic Malt

Diastatic malt products differ from their nondiastatic counterparts in possessing considerable enzymic activity. The malted grain from which these products are derived is a veritable storehouse of enzymes, most of which have never been adequately investigated. The two types that are of greatest interest to bakers are proteolytic enzymes and amylolytic enzymes. The latter group, comprising the "diastase" of older writers, contains at least two different enzymes, commonly designated alpha-enzyme (sometimes called the dextrinizing enzyme) and beta-amylase (also known as the saccharifying enzyme). Alpha-amylase splits the starch molecule at random points, forming smaller molecules of widely varying size. Two important effects of this action are the reduction of the viscosity of susceptible starch suspensions and the production of relatively small amounts of fermentable sugars. End products of the reaction are chiefly dextrins (compounds containing several glucose residues) that cannot be used as substrates by bakers' yeast. There is some doubt that the amounts of alpha-amylase normally encountered in sound wheat flour have any significant effect on its baking properties in the absence of native or added beta-amylase.

The action of beta-amylase on starch results in the production of maltose by the progressive release of terminal sugar residues from the starch molecule. Beta-amylase cannot attack the starch molecule inside the points at which it is branched, and so a residue of limit dextrin of high molecular weight remains after beta-amylase has completed its action. These limit dextrins cannot be fermented, but they are customarily produced in smaller amounts than the dextrins resulting from the action of alpha-amylase.

When the two types of amylase act in conjunction, a much greater conversion of starch into fermentable sugars results than when either of them acts alone. Alpha-amylase can sever bonds between the branch points that halt hydrolysis by beta-amylase. The new end groups exposed by this action are then subject to attack by beta-amylase. As a result, the amount of limit dextrin is decreased and the effective concentration of molecules capable of being hydrolyzed by beta-amylase is increased so that both the rate and final yield of glucose are considerably increased in starch suspensions containing mixtures of the two enzymes. For example, the rapid and relatively complete conversion of starch to fermentable sugars, typical of the action of malt, is a consequence of the combined action of alpha- and beta- amylase. Conversely, the slow rate of sugar development in unsupplemented flour suspensions or doughs results from a deficiency of these enzymes and particularly of beta-amylase.

The action of beta-amylase on undamaged and ungelatinized starch granules is very slow. Alpha-amylase does attack granules with no visible damage at an appreciable rate. Both enzymes attack gelatinized starch very rapidly, but this reaction cannot be of much importance in the breadmaking process because the starch in dough does not become gelatinized until virtually all of the enzyme activity has been destroyed by heat. Starch granules that have been mechanically damaged during milling are also broken down by both alpha- and beta-amylase. Perhaps 3% or 4% of the starch granules in a typical hard wheat flour sample are visibly damaged. This mechanical damage is due to shearing forces and pressures encountered during milling of the grain. Consequently, the proportion of damaged granules is a function of the milling conditions, and may vary not only from mill to mill, but also between flours of different extraction rates. However, flours of similar extraction rates made from the same types of wheat and ground at the same mill should contain a rather constant proportion of damaged granules.

The capacity of malt to convert starch to reducing substances (e.g., maltose) can be expressed as the Lintner value, °L, or as maltose equivalent. When tested by the standard procedure, degrees Lintner equal about one-fourth of the maltose value. In each system, the rating of nondiastatic malt is theoretically zero, although in practice malts of 10°L or less are classified as non-diastatic malts. A good barley malt flour might rate as high as 124°L. Commercial diastatic malt syrups usually have ratings of 20°, 40°, or 60°L, and are described as low, medium, and high diastatic products, respectively.

Diastatic malt syrups are frequently recommended for use in bread formulas at the rate of 1 lb to 1.25 lb of syrup per hundredweight of flour. Larger amounts may darken the crumb, cause excessive fermentation, and make the dough too sticky to process efficiently.

Nondiastatic Malt

The amylolytic activity of malt products can be reduced by heat treatment. If this process is carried far enough to deactivate nearly all of the amylases, the product is called "nondiastatic," even though traces of hydrolyzing activity can still be detected. Such malts are used principally to supply flavor and color to baked products. They also have some effect on texture and supply fermentable carbohydrates and other yeast nutrients.

Nondiastatic malt syrups tend to be darker in color and stronger in flavor than their enzymatically active counterparts. These differences result from the more extreme heat treatment that has been applied to the nondiastatic malt during processing, especially during the condensing step. It is necessary to minimize heat treatment if substantial enzymic activity is to be retained, while the nondiastatic products can be evaporated at high temperatures since amylase activity is not desired. Both color and flavor are intensified by heat-mediated reactions thought to be chiefly of the Maillard type. Although the flavor of a highly heat-treated syrup tends to be strong, it is also inclined to be more bitter and less aromatic than that of a lighter-colored syrup. Malt syrups will also change color during storage, becoming darker but losing some of the reddish hue that adds richness to the brown color. Some vitamin and protein content is lost due to the heat treatment.

Nondiastatic malt products are high in sugars and dextrins of low molecular weight that have been to some extent reacted with other components under the influence of the high temperature processing they have encountered. Consequently, they can contribute considerable sweetness to products in which they are used. In addition, there is a peculiar and characteristic flavor to malt products that many people find very attractive. The use of malt in malted milk and in the confection called "malted milk balls" is a clear indication that there is a true liking for malt flavor in a large segment of the population.

The color changes accompanying caramelization and other nonenzymatic browning reactions resulting from the high temperature processing applied in the manufacture of nondiastatic malt make the product valuable as a coloring agent. Dark rye breads often contain large amounts of nondiastatic malt syrup, although caramel color replaces malt in many present-day formulas. Special dietary breads may also be colored with dark malt syrups. On the other hand, addition of malt ingredients as enzyme sources, and especially high roasted malts, in white breads is definitely limited by the darkening that is observed even when the usage level is moderate.

Blended Syrups

Mixtures of malted barley syrup with various types of corn syrup are very common today. Also, barley malt may be combined with other carbohydrate sources (mostly corn derivatives) to produce worts (i.e., the initial grain extract, usually relatively dilute) that is further processed to yield a malt blended syrup. These combination syrups are then condensed to make syrups that can be more highly colored than simple blends of malt syrup with corn syrup. Many of the non-diastatic "malt" syrups being offered to bakers are probably blends. The potency of the syrup in flavoring and, perhaps, in coloring the finished baked product will depend to a large extent on the proportion of malt syrup the blend contains. Dried malt preparations (other than ground malted barley or wheat) almost always contain substantial percentages of corn derivatives, partly because of economic considerations and partly because it is more difficult to dry a pure barley malt syrup.

Methods for Drying Hygroscopic Syrups

Syrups such as honey, molasses, and HFCS contain large percentages of hygroscopic compounds. They are viscous and sticky, may crystallize, and when overheated develop off-flavors and dark colors. As a result, they pose significant problems in storing, metering, transporting, and dispensing. These problems could be considerably alleviated by converting the syrups into dry powders, and much research effort has been directed toward developing products of this type.

One process requires mixing the syrup with an ungelatinized starch to form a slurry, then heating, gelatinizing, and dehydrating. Other methods use non-fat dry milk as a drying aid. Molasses has been n ixed with wheat flour to form a slurry that is then dehydrated as a thin film on a heated surface. Soy protein flour is another additive said to allow preparation of a dried powder. The means of dehydration is variously drum drying, spray drying, fluid bed drying, or extrusion drying.

An approach that does not use a carrier substance specifies adjustment of the pH of molasses with an alkaline agent before it is dried. In a patented process, ungelatinized starch or soy protein is mixed with a syrup to form a slurry that is dried; the thin film is separated into flakes that are later mixed with water to form a mixture that can be extruded.

A solid dry molasses product containing no starch or protein additives has been described in a fairly recent patent. After a conventional drying step, the thin layer of molasses is cooled immediately. The cooled molasses is pre-crushed to coarse particles, and then reduced to a powder by impact without crushing or significant friction.

A patent by Bateson *et al.* (1990) discloses what is said to be an improved method for making dried honey and molasses without the use of starch or other additives. For example, the syrup is applied as a thin film (0.1 to 1 mm) to a surface heated to above 75°C but below about 150°C. Drum dryers or thin film evaporators are suggested types of equipment. Water is driven off and removed from the dryer until the material has reached a desired moisture content. Pressures above the drying surface are maintained at, preferably, 0.5 mm to 20 mm. The plastic material is removed from the drying surface, as by doctor knives, and rapidly cooled (as by the surface of a cooled rotating cylinder) in a space having a substantially moisture-free atmosphere. Honey of about 2% moisture and molasses of about 2.6% moisture content can be prepared by this method. Finished products can be ground to a powder, it is said. The Bateson *et al.* patent also describes a process using an extrusion dryer to prepare solid honey or molasses compositions containing the additives hydroxylated lecithin, soya flour, corn syrup, and starch in various combinations.

A somewhat different approach (Anon. 1987) has been applied to drying HFCS, which has characteristics similar to honey. This product was made by using pulse-combustion drying, a technology that combines acoustics with spray dehydration. The temperatures used are typically around 90°F, much cooler than conventional spray-drying. Earlier problems with hygroscopicity in dried HFCS were said to be alleviated by a proprietary encapsulation process.

Commercially available dried honey and dried molasses generally contain substantial amounts of additives. They are easier and more sanitary to handle, but probably do not have quite as much flavor as their liquid counterparts, simply because the dehydration process drives off some of the aromatics. Malt syrup, sorghum syrup, and maple syrup are also available in dry powdered forms.

OTHER SWEETENERS

Many substances are perceived as being sweet in taste. A list of some pure compounds and commercial preparations that have been tested for sweetness by taste panels is given in Table 5.4. The reader is cautioned that the values given in the table are only approximations, since the data were assembled from several different sources, and the way a taste panelist rates the intensity of sweetness of a sample is dependent on many factors, including concentration, temperature, viscosity of the medium, other substances consumed with the sweetener, etc. In the following paragraphs, only materials that have some potential as food sweeteners will be discussed.

Table 5.4. RELATIVE SWEETNESS OF VARIOUS SUBSTANCES[1]

Alitame	2,000.	Xylitol	1.00
Sucralose	600	Honey	1.00
Saccharin	300.	Glucose	0.74
Acesulfame K	200.	Sorbitol	0.54
Aspartame	150.	Mannitol	0.40
Glycyrrhizin	100.	Xylose	0.40
Cyclamate	30.	Maltose	0.32
Erythritol	2.+	Rhamnose	0.32
Fructose	1.73	Galactose	0.32
Invert sugar	1.30	Malt syrup	0.30
90% HFCS	1.06	Raffinose	0.23
Sucrose	1.00	Lactose	0.16

[1]Sweetness compared to sucrose as 1.00

Honey

The composition of honey depends upon the source and other factors, but a typical analysis would be: water 17.1%, 38.5% fructose, 31% glucose, other carbohydrates 12.8%, protein 0.3%, ash 0.2%, and no fat (Anon. 1989B). There is a small amount of sucrose present. It is said that over 80 organic compounds have been identified, including carboxylic acids, aldehydes, alcohols, and phenols.

It can be said that honey contributes about the same sweetness as an equal amount of invert syrup, but any other generalizations about its flavor (or color) are likely to be misleading. This is due to the fact that the floral sources from which the bees collect nectar affect the color and flavor of the product. From 20 to 30 floral types account for nearly all of the honey sold in the U.S. (Johnson *et al.* 1959). Most bulk honeys come from mixed sources. Distributors can supply commercial quantities of honey from single floral sources, but these premium ingredients will seldom be required by bakers.

It has been stated frequently that the flavor of honey is desirable in bakery foods, but this ingredient is often used (as in graham crackers) where it makes no appreciable contribution to the overall flavor (except sweetness) of the final product. Honey has achieved great popularity as a "natural" and "organic" sweetener in recent years, although it is difficult to understand why it is more natural than sucrose, which undergoes no chemical change during its extraction from sugar cane, while honey undergoes very substantial modification by the bees and by human intervention.

There is a considerable history of adulteration of honey with invert sugar and corn syrup, but this practice seems to have been pretty well suppressed by government action in recent years. Truthfully labeled commercial mixtures of honey mixed with sucrose, glucose, invert syrup, etc., are available to those who find this form of the flavoring material convenient.

It is important both ethically and legally that bakery product manufacturers observe federal and local regulations and common sense (assuming that . is compatible with regulations) in nomenclature and ingredient labeling of honey-containing products. FDA has set a minimum level of 8% (FWB) honey content for bread that is labeled "honey bread."

Some suggested conversion ratios are: To replace granulated sugar, use the same weight of liquid honey, and reduce the water in the formula by 0.18 lb for each pound of honey used. When replacing high fructose corn syrup (42/52 type) having a 71% total solids content, replace one pound of corn syrup with 0.71 pounds of honey and add 0.1 pound of water.

As a basis for purchasing pure liquid honey meeting U.S. Grade A standards, to be used in high-quality bakery items, the following specifications have been recommended by the National Honey Board Food Technology Program (Anon. 1989B):

Color—most applications call for an extra-light, amber, or light amber honey. A common specification is 70 mm maximum on the Pfund scale. Amber and dark amber honeys are suitable for use in dark breads, fruit cakes, brownies, etc.

Moisture—the maximum moisture content is 18.6% for both Grade A and Grade B. A range of 17.0% to 18.6% is often specified. The moisture content of honey influences its viscosity and should be monitored for accurate pumping and metering.

Refractive index—this test provides a rapid, accurate, and simple measurement of the water content of honey. A range of 1.400 to 1.494 at 20°C is often specified.

Flavor and odor—honey to be used in bakery products should possess a typical honey flavor and aroma with no objectionable taste and odor notes.

Density—one gallon of honey weighs approximately 12 lbs at 80°F, and a minimum of 11.75 is a reasonable requirement.

Packaging—honey is shipped in various containers, such as metal drums, tote bins, pails, and tankers. When shipped in bulk tankers, the temperature of the honey should not exceed 130°F and the tankers should be equipped with in-line strainers.

Honey can be pumped, stored, and metered with the same kind of equipment used for corn syrup. The viscosity of honey decreases as its temperature increases, and holding honey at 90° to 130°F facilitates transfer by fluid handling systems. Temperatures over 130°F should be avoided, since they can affect the flavor and odor of the product. The glucose:fructose ratio of honey influences the tendency of honey to crystallize and granulate. Heating redissolves the glucose crystals and reverses granulation.

The color of honey can be affected by several factors, including the kind of flowers from which the bees collect nectar. Among the floral sources, sweet clover, alfalfa, white clover, tupelo, tulip-poplar, and buckwheat honeys, in that order, will result in very light to dark gold loaves.

Maple Syrup

This material, the partially dried sap of a certain kind of maple tree, has a mild and pleasant flavor. It is a very expensive source of sweetening. Characteristics, including color and flavor, may vary considerably depending on conditions existing during processing and collection and the weather conditions affecting the trees from which the sap was collected. Most of the flavor appears to be developed during collection and processing, rather than being inherent in the sap. Some flavor may be due to bacterial action.

Maple syrup contains no more than 34% water. The solids are 88% or more of sucrose, up to 12% hexose sugars, small amounts of raffinose and oligosaccharides, organic acids, ash, and protein. The acids may include various combinations of malic, citric, succinic, fumaric, and glycolic, as well as traces of others. The minerals include potassium, calcium, silicon oxide, manganese, sodium, and magnesium. The principal flavoring components have not all been identified, but a syringaldehyde appears to be important.

There are United States Standards for "Maple sirup" (7 CFR 52.5963, et seq.) that define the basic product (minimum of 66 Brix) and three grades: U.S. Grade A, U.S. Grade B for Reprocessing, and Substandard. Furthermore, Grade A is divided into three color classifications: U.S. Grade A Light Amber, U.S. Grade A Medium Amber, U.S. Grade A Dark Amber. The colors are established by comparison with colored glass standards maintained by the USDA. Some other factors that are important in grading include cloudiness, cleanliness, scorching, fermentation, "buddy flavor," and other off flavors.

Most consumers like the flavor of maple syrup, but its high cost and the ready availability of good artificial flavors, limit the use of the pure ingredient in bakery products.

Maple sugar and dried maple syrup, both usually containing a few percent of water, can be obtained but have few or no bakery applications.

Sugar Alcohols

The chemical reduction of conventional corn syrups under certain condtions can give mixtures of sugar alcohols, the so-called hydrogenated starch hydrolysates. These materials have a sweet taste and, generally, reduced fermentability, increased resistance to non-enzymic browning reactions, decreased tendency to crystallization, and increased hygroscopicity, as compared to the original corn syrup.

By hydrogenating a more or less pure sugar of the proper type, specific sugar alcohols such as sorbitol, xylitol, mannitol, and maltitol can be produced. All except maltitol are less sweet than sucrose. They are also less susceptible to fermentation by microorganisms commonly found in the mouth and so have been touted as non-cariogenic sweeteners. Some sugar alcohols have value as humectants. They are utilized at varying levels by the human digestive system, maltitol (for example) being of low caloric value, though its sweetness is about 175% that of sucrose (Hirao *et al.* 1990).

The moisture binding of a few compounds is shown in Table 5.5 (data of Sloan and Labuza 1975).

Lactose

Lactose is developed from the fractionation of milk or its byproducts such as whey. It is nearly always more expensive than sucrose and is much less sweet (about 0.16 compared to śucrose as 1.00). For applications where a bland bulking agent is needed, as in cases where a baker wants to reduce the sweetness of a filling and starch or corn syrup solids are unsatisfactory for some reason, lactose may be helpful. This sugar is offered in crude, edible, and pharmaceuticl grades, in several particle sizes, and in at least two crystal forms. A bland grade of dehydrated whey may be substitutable for lactose in some applications. Purified whey that has been enzymatically hydrolyzed to galactose and glucose has been suggested as a corn syrup replacement and may be useful for this purpose.

Fruit Syrups

Bland fruit syrups can be used as sweeteners. They have been used in bakery and confectionery items where label claims of "no added sugars" have been made, though this claim is clearly misleading. One supplier offers a blend of grape, apple, pineapple, and peach concentrates with "substantially reduced flavor, color, and acid and standardized to ensure continuity of quality." It is intended to replace processed sugars, honey, and other liquid sweeteners, and offers "combined benefits of natural sweetness and humectancy." The Brix is 70°, the pH 3.7 to 4.2, and the color "Extra White on honey scale." It is to be expected that sweeteners of this type will be more expensive than corn syrup or sucrose, but they may permit label claims that have some marketing advantages.

Table 5.5. MOISTURE BOUND AT TWO WATER ACTIVITIES

Substance	Grams water bound per 100 g solids	
	Intermediate water activity (0.6)	High water activity (0.95)
Glycerol	41	625
Propyelene glycol	40	650
Sorbitol	30	485
Fructose	18	380
Dextrose	11	207
Sucrose	3	188

Non-nutritive Sweeteners

Saccharin.—This substance, 2,3-dihydro-3-oxobenzisosulfonazole, is about 300 to 500 times sweeter than sucrose when the two substances are compared in dilute aqueous solutions. An exact match to sucrose cannot be obtained because saccharin has flavor notes that are not present in sugar, and vice versa. Many people find that saccharin has bitter, astringent, or metallic tastes, especially at high concentrations. These off-flavors tend to be particularly objectionable in delicately flavored fruit products, but may be partially concealed in foods that contain sucrose or corn sweeteners in addition to saccharin, and they are also less obvious in cola beverages, hot cocoa and other chocolate products, coffee, etc. Saccharin is very stable under conditions normally encountered in the preparation and storage of foods and beverages, retaining its identity in very acid environments and during extended heat treatment.

The negative flavor notes of saccharin should regarded in their proper perspective. Tons of the sweetener are used each month in products that are consumed with every indication of satisfaction by tens of millions of consumers. All things considered (including economics), this is probably the best of all artificial sweeteners on the market for general purpose use.

Aspartame.—This compound does have some caloric content, but the energy value it adds to finished products is negligible in most applications. Aspartame is the methyl ester of 1-aspartyl-1-phenyalanine and it is prepared by chemical synthesis, as is saccharin. The substance is said to taste about 180 times as sweet as sucrose, but its sweetening power depends on the conditions under which the two materials are compared. In many systems, the potency of aspartame is probably less than the preceding figure would indicate.

Although aspartame is only about a half to a third as sweet as saccharin, and is much more expensive, aspartame does not contribute the bitter and metallic notes frequently observed when foods and beverages containing saccharin are ingested. When the patent on the aspartame manufacturing process expires toward the end of 1992, it is expected that the price of this sweetener will fall considerably. The reader should remember, however, that several patents applying to the use of aspartame in specific products were granted subsequent to the basic manufacturing patent and will remain effective until their own expiration dates.

Aspartame tends to slowly hydrolyze and become ineffective as a sweetener under certain rigorous conditions. The reaction is accelerated by high temperatures and high pH.

Glycyrrhizin.—This substance has been described as a non-caloric extract of liquorice root. Ammoniated glycyrrhizin is the most common form of the sweetener. It is said to be 100 times sweeter than sugar, but its strong liquorice flavor appears to be inseparable from the sweetening effect, so its use in bakery products is attended with difficulty. It has been applied mostly in tobacco and pharmaceutical manufacture, but a few confectionery products have also been made with it. It has foam-enhancing properties that can be useful in beverage formulation.

Acesulfame K.—In 1988, FDA approval was given for the use of the potassium salt of 6-methyl-1,2,3-oxathiazine-4(3H)-one-2,2-dioxide, known as acesulfame K, in several food products. It is believed to be on the market in the form of tabletop sweeteners, chewing gum, instant coffee and tea, and dry bases for beverages, gelatins, puddings, pudding desserts, and dairy product analogs. There is an intent to use it in confections, baked goods, and soft drinks. It has been used in many other products in Europe, where it has been an accepted food ingredient for several years.

Acesulfame K is a white crystalline material with very good stability in the solid state. It does not have a defined melting point, but begins to decompose when brought above 225°C. The compound also has good stability in most liquid environments. Solublity in water is high. By one method of measurement, it appears that acesulfame K is about 200 times as sweet as sugar. The manufacturer states that the best performance of this compound is observed when it replaces the taste impact contributed by an 8% to 10% solution of sucrose. It displays sweetness synergy when it is used in combination with other high-intensity sweeteners such as aspartame (Hood and Schoor 1990).

Other non-caloric sweeteners.—There are several non-caloric (or low calorie) sweeteners that seem to have some potential for dietetic foods but have not received FDA clearance. Some of these have been under investigation for decades. Examples are neohesperidin, sucralose, L-sugars, neosugar, stevioside, monelin, miraculin, and thaumatin (see Nabors and Gelardi 1986, Newsome 1986, and Anon. 1987 for further details). Stevioside, thaumatin, monelin, and miraculin can be extracted from certain plants. They often have curious flavor side-effects such as delayed action or lingering off-flavors. Stevioside, which is a glycoside extracted from the leaves and twigs of a herb found in South America, is actually being used there and in Japan. It is about 300 times as sweet as sucrose and has not been approved for use in the U.S. (Stamp 1990).

Thaumatin, tradenamed Talin, is a mixture of sweet-tasting proteins extracted from the African katemfe fruit, and is about 1,500 times as sweet as sucrose. It has been classified as GRAS for use as a flavor enhancer in chewing gum.

Neohesperidin is made by processing a substance found in rinds of grapefruit and some other citrus fruits. L-sugars are stereoiosomers of common natural D-sugars such as D-glucose—although these compounds stimulate human taste buds, the body cannot metabolize them and so they contribute sweetness without calories. Sucralose, a chlorinated derivate of sugar, is said to be about 600 times sweeter than sucrose. Neosugar is a derivative of sucrose produced by a fungal enzyme and it, too, is non-metabolizable.

Alitame is a dipeptide-based amide about 2,000 times sweeter than sugar. It is not approved for food use, as of the date of this writing. Like aspartame, it does have some caloric value, about 1.4 calories per gram (Freeman 1989).

Sucralose (4,1',6'-trichloro-4,1,6'-trideoxy-galactosucrose), a chlorine-containing compound approximately 600 times sweeter than sucrose, is under FDA review for use in 15 food categories, including baked goods. It appears to have good stability, maintaining its integrity throughout baking (Barndt and Jackson 1990, also see Hood and Campbell 1991). This as yet unapproved sweetener is said to have synergistic sweetening effects with other artificial sweeteners, especially cyclamate (Beyts 1990).

Sweeteners derived from beta-substituted beta-amino acids are as much as 20,000 times sweeter than sucrose. Trisubstituted guanidines are said to be up to 170,000 times as sweet as sucrose (Anon. 1990).

BIBLIOGRAPHY

ANON. 1986A. Food Applications and Formulations; Technical Data. CPC International, Inc., Englewood Cliffs, NJ

ANON. 1986B. Nutritive Sweeteners from Corn, Fourth Edition. Corn Refiners Assoc., New York, NY

ANON. 1987. New technology produces dry HFCS. Food Engineering *59*, No. 5, 79

ANON. 1988A. High fructose corn syrup comes of age. Dairy Field *171*, No. 3, 22, 45

ANON. 1988B. FDA clears Hoechst's non-caloric sweetener for use in dry foods. Food Technol. *42*, No. 10, 108

ANON. 1989A. Lite sweeteners maneuver for heavyweight title. Prepared Foods *158*, No. 11, 91-92

ANON. 1989B. Specifying and handling honey. Honey Hotline *2*, 1

ANON. 1990. Synthetic sweeteners developed by design. Chem. Eng. News *68*, No. 18, 8

BARNDT, R. L., and JACKSON, G. 1990. Stability of sucralose in baked goods. Food Technology *44*, No. 1, 62-66

BATESON, G. F., MORRIS, C. A., and HEUER, G. C. 1990. Methods for drying honey and molasses. U.S. Pat. 4,919,956

BEYTS, P. K. 1990. Sweetener for beverages. U.S. 4,915,969

DZIEZAK, J. D. 1989. Ingredients for sweet success. Food Technology *43*, No. 10, 94-116

FREEMAN, T. M. 1989. Sweetening cakes and cake mixes with alitame. Cereal Foods World *34*, 1013-1015

GAUTIER, A. 1989. Process and outfit for the extraction of sugar from sugar cane. U.S. Pat. 4,804,418

GOMERAC, W. L. Bees, Beekeeping, Honey, and Pollination. AVI Publ. Co., Westport, CT

GOODACRE, B. C., and SMITHSON, A. 1989. Sugar process. U.S. Pat. 4,861,382

HICKENBOTTOM, W. J. 1983. Malts in bakery foods. Am. Inst. of Baking, Res. Dept. Tech Bull. *5*, No. 3

HIRAO, M., HIJIYA, H, and MIYAKA, T. 1990. Food containing anhydrous crystals of maltitol and the whole crystalline hydrogenated starch hydrolysate. U.S. Pat. 4,917,916

HOOD, L. L., and CAMPBELL, L. A. 1990. Developing reduced calorie bakery products with sucralose. Cereal Foods World *35*, 1171-1172, 1177-1181

HOOD, L. L., and SCHOOR, M. 1990. Evolution, properties, and applications of an approved high intensity sweetener. Cereal Foods World *35*, 1184-1186

HORN, H. E. 1981. Corn sweeteners. Functional properties. Cereal Foods World *26*, 219-223

JOHNSON, J. A., MILLER, D., and WHITE, J. A., JR. 1959. Honey in your baking. Kans. State Univ. Extension Circ. *281*

KULP, K., LORENZ, K., and STONE, M. 1991. Functionality of carbohydrate ingredients in bakery products. Food Technology *45*, No. 3, 136-142

MATZ, S. A. 1991. The Chemistry and Technology of Cereals as Food and Feed, Second Edition. Pan-Tech International, McAllen, TX

MORANO, J. 1984. Functional properties of molasses. Bulletin *A-15*. Specialty Products Div., Ingredient Technology Co., Woodbridge, NJ

NABORS, L. O., and GELARDI, R. C. (Editors). 1986. Alternative Sweeteners. Marcel Dekker, Inc., New York, NY

NEWSOME, R. L. (Editor). Sweeteners: Nutritive and non-nutritive. Food Technol. *40*, No. 8, 196-206

PANCOAST, H. M., and JUNK, W. R. 1980. Handbook of Sugars, Second Edition. AVI Publ. Co., Westport, CT

PANGBORN, R. M. 1963. Relative taste intensities of selected sugars and organic acids. J. Food Sci. *28*, 726-730

SCHOLLMEIER, C. E. 1985. Semi-crystalline fructose. U.S. Patent 4,517,021

SLOAN, A. E., and LABUZA, T. P. 1975. Humectant water sorption isotherms. Food Product Dev. *9*, 68

STAMP, J. A. 1990. Sorting out the alternative sweeteners. Cereal Foods World *35*, 395-400

STONE, H., and OLIVER, S. M. 1969. Measurements of the relative sweetness of selected sweeteners and sweetener mixtures. J. Food Sci. *34*, 215-222

WHITE, J. S., and PARKE, D. W. 1989. Fructose adds variety to breakfast. Cereal Foods World *34*, 392-398

WITT, P. R., JR. 1970. Malting. *In* Cereal Technology. S. A. Matz, Editor. AVI Publishing Co., Westport, CT

chapter six

WATER AND SALT

INTRODUCTION

Discussions of the ingredients water and salt are combined in this chapter. These two materials, though having many separate and distinct actions, also have related effects on dough properties. The concentration of dissolved salt, or relation of salt content to free water content, has important effects on fermentation rate, on gluten strength, and, of course, on taste.

WATER

Water is, in many respects, a unique compound. It has properties not exhibited by any other substance and it imparts unusual and often unpredictable properties to those materials dissolved in it. Water has been called "the universal solvent." This is, of course, an exaggeration, but water does dissolve so many other compounds that obtaining a totally pure sample seems to be a practical impossibility. One authority (Anon. 1989) states that, due to the aggressive nature of water, ultrapure water stored in glassware experiences an increase of three to four times in the concentrations of heavy metals and, if stored in plastic, increases its content of total organic carbons by about five times within a few days. The water supplied to our homes has dissolved, entrained, suspended, and otherwise become contaminated with many particles, ions, gases, microorganisms, etc.

It is not surprising, then, that the chemical, physical, and microbiological characteristics of ingredient water can have significant effects on the quality of bakery goods. Chemical reactions and physical interactions in which water participates on the ionic or molecular scale influence every gross characteristic of foodstuffs. The amounts and types of dissolved minerals and organic substances that are present in the water can affect the color, flavor, and texture of the finished product as well as the response to machining of doughs, batters, fillings, marshmallows, icings, etc. The average temperature of the water and the range around the average can be important factors in the performance of any given formula. The differences in bacterial and yeast flora and other suspended contaminants are of obvious interest to any food producer.

The quality of ingredient water is established by the initial status of the water, the treatments applied to it inside and outside of the plant, and the conditions of storage and transport subsequent to treatment. Most bakeries use either municipal supplies or water from deep wells. In either case, the water will very likely be potable. However, water that is perfectly acceptable for drinking and suitable for most food processing applications may have to be further treated before it will be adequate for certain specialized food and beverage uses. Most people know that manufacturers of carbonated beverages must pay special attention to the quality of their water supply and, that they apply in-plant purification procedures.

Even though doughs are less sensitive to minor differences in water quality than are some other foods and beverages, this does not mean they totally lack response to fluctuations in this ingredient. Marshmallow, jellies, and similar adjuncts may be more sensitive than doughs.

The initial requirement for any water put into a food product is that it must comply with legal specifications for drinking water. Federal standards have been established for drinking water, and often there are applicable state and municipal standards as well. In the following sections, some of the regulations will be reviewed, but the reader is cautioned that changes are constantly being put into effect. When questions arise as to the suitability of a water source or a water processing method, it is advisable to contact the responsible authorities for copies of current standards.

Regulations Affecting Potable Water

Water Quality Act.—The Water Quality Act passed by Congress in 1967 required each state to establish quality criteria for all interstate waters and to develop a plan for the implementation and enforcement of these criteria. In general, the standards promulgated by the states must be such as to enhance the quality of natural waters for their use and value for public water supplies, propagation of fish and wildlife, recreational purposes, agricultural, industrial, and other legitimate uses. Numerical values should be stated for these quality characteristics where available and applicable. Biological or assay parameters may be used where appropriate.

Safe Drinking Water Act.—The Environmental Protection Agency (EPA) has the responsibility under the Safe Drinking Water Act (SDWA) for establishing standards for drinking water contaminants that may lead to adverse health effects. The 1986 amendments to the SDWA require the EPA to regulate 83 contaminants within a three-year period according to a specified schedule, and 25 more contaminants every three years starting in 1990. All current drinking water regulations issued as of July 1st in any year will be found in the Code of Federal Regulations (CFR), Volume 40. Some important Parts to search are Part 131 (Water Quality Standards), Part 133 (Secondary Treatment Regulations), Part 141 (National Primary Drinking Water Standards), and Part 143 (National Secondary Drinking Water Standards). Regulations promulgated between CFR editions will be found in the Federal Register.

The Federal Drinking Water Standards for Maximum Contaminant Levels (MCL) which became effective January 9, 1989 are listed in Table 6.1 (Source: Hobbs 1990 and Cotruvo et al. 1989). Some proposed standards are also included. Federal standards for coliforms, heterotrophic plate count, and total coliforms are not shown in the table. Also not shown are proposed standards for color, corrosivity, foaming agents, total dissolved solids, turbidity, and odor. In the Federal Register for January 25, 1991 were published "final" drinking water standards for 38 contaminants including 17 pesticides, 10 volatile organic chemicals, polychlorinated biphenyls, eight inorganic chemicals, and two chemicals used to treat drinking water.

Table 6.1. MAXIMUM CONTAMINANT LEVELS AND PROPOSED STANDARDS FOR DRINKING WATER

Contaminant	Maximum level, mg/L	Contaminant	Maximum level, *
Arsenic	.050	Benzene	5
Barium	1.	Carbon tetrachloride	5
Cadmium	.010	p-a,4-dichlorobenzene	75
Chloride**	150.	1,2-dichloroethane	5
Chromium	.05	1,1-dichloroethane	7
Copper**	1.	2,4-D	100
Fluoride	4.	Endrin	0.2
Iron**	0.3	Gamma lindane	4
Lead	.05	Methoxychlor	100
Manganese**	.05	pH limits	6.5-8.5
Mercury	.002	Toxaphene	5
Nitrate (as N)	10.	1,1 1-Trichloroethane	200
Selenium	.01	Trichloroethene	5
Silver	.05	Trihalomethanes	100
Sulfate	250.	2,4,5-TP (Silvex)	10
Zinc**	5.	Vinyl chloride	2

*In micrograms per liter, unless otherwise specified.
** Proposed

Public Health Service drinking water standards.—Standards for drinking water used on common carriers (e.g., trains, planes, buses) engaged in interstate commerce were prepared by the U.S. Public Health Service in 1946 and issued in revised form in 1962 by the U.S. Department of Health, Education, and Welfare (Anon. 1962). These federal standards were used as guidelines by many states and municipalities in setting up specifications for potable water. The American Water Works Association regards these standards as being minimum requirements for the protection and well-being of individuals and communities, and it advocated the establishment of the standards as criteria of quality for all public water supplies in the U.S. Water that does not conform to the standards should not be used as an ingredient in foods regardless of the legal status of the standards in the locality of the manufacturer.

The standards specify that the water supply shall be obtained from the most desirable source that is feasible, and efforts should be made to prevent or control pollution at the source. If the source is not protected by natural means, the supply must be adequately protected by treatment.

Responsiblity for conditions existing in a water supply system is held by: (1) the water supplier, from the sources of supply to the connection of the customer's service piping; and (2) the owner of the property served and the municipal, county, or other authority having jurisdiction from the point of connection in the customer's service piping to the free-flowing outlet of the ultimate consumer. As can be seen from the preceding discussion, the food manufacturer would be responsible for the condition and quality of the water in his service piping before and after any treatment in his plant.

Water Treatment

Basic operations.—Nearly all water obtained from surface sources (rivers, lakes, impounding reservoirs, etc.) must be treated to remove suspended material, dissolved color and flavor vectors, and microbiological contaminants. Water from shallow wells contains dissolved minerals and gases, and perhaps impurities from infiltrating surface water. Deep wells will generally deliver water that contains dissolved minerals and gases but that is almost always free of surface water contamination provided adequate care is used in pumping and piping it to the plant outlets.

Iron is probably the water constituent most often responsible for adverse effects on taste, color, and texture of processed foods. In this respect, it is followed closely by manganese and hydrogen sulfide. All of these impurities are routinely and easily removed by oxidation, using such treatments as superchlorination or addition of oxidizing minerals, followed by good filtration (Beaumann 1983). The details of these treatments are too complex to be set forth in this book, and the reader who is interested in such information as it applies to food is referred to "Water in Foods" (Matz 1965), Chemistry of Water Treatment (Faust and Aly 1983), and similar texts. In general, sedimentation with or without added coagulants, filtration, and chlorination are treatments needed for most water supplies.

A thorough course of treatment for making potable a raw water of low quality could involve: (1) sedimentation in a large impounding reservoir; (2) coagulation (i.e., the formation of a voluminous flocculent precipitate by adding salts of iron or aluminum under the proper conditions); (3) allowing nearly all of the precipitate to settle out in a reservoir or tank; (4) filtering the decantate from the preceding step through specially prepared beds of sand or gravel to remove residual precipitates and other impurities; (5) filtering through activated charcoal to absorb most or all of the dissolved substances affecting color, odor, and taste; and (6) chlorination. In recent years, synthetic organic polymers and polymeric inorganic compounds have found use as coagulants or in combination with iron and aluminum compounds in pre-treatment (Amirtharajah 1990)

It is often desirable to treat municipal or well water in the plant to eliminate off-flavors or other undesirable characteristics. Some firms offer modular systems that can be used to furnish ingredient water of the needed purity. Operations available in such plants include: (1) Prefiltration using filter media; (2) Adsorption of organic compounds by activated charcoal or by special weak-base organic scavenger resins; (3) Reverse osmosis pretreatment to reduce the salt content of saline water or reduce the amount of other dissolved materials; (4) Cation or anion exchange for removal of specific ions; and (5) Ultrafiltration for final removal of particulates. Packaged water treatement plants range in capacity from quite small throughput to hundreds of thousands of gallons per day. Their compact stand-alone design allows multiple modular installations of even higher capacity (Lisk 1991B).

In some cases, processors will have to consider the effects of water on their processing equipment. Corrosion, lime scale, and grit are some of the factors affecting boilers, pumps, pipes, valves, and meters.

Disinfection.—In industrial water treatment practice, disinfection (the killing of disease-causing organisms) can be considered to be virtually synonymous with chlorination. Various other disinfection methods such as heating, irradiation with ultraviolet rays, application of ultrasonic energy, and the addition of ozone, chlorine dioxide, lime, bromine, iodine, or colloidal silver have been advocated from time to time, and some of these methods are doubtless being used today, but no other technique has proved to be more effective than, or as inexpensive as, chlorination for general water treatment purposes.

Although other sources of chlorine, such as hypochlorite of lime, have been used for disinfection, chlorine gas is particularly suitable for water disinfection because it is inexpensive, easy to apply, and has harmless end products. It is very effective in destroying bacteria, but a few other kinds of microorganisms are more resistant—at least, at the usual dosages. Among the resistant organisms is *Entamoeba histolytica*, the causative agent of amoebic dysentery. Many viruses are markedly more resistant to chlorine than are such bacteria as *Escherichia coli*. Among the more resistant viruses are the Coxsackie A2 virus, some at least of the polioviruses, and probably the causative agent of infectious hepatitis.

Chlorination may be accomplished by injection of the substance from cylinders containing 100 lb, 150 lb, or 2,000 lb of the liquid element, or by means of hypochlorinators that feed small quantities of sodium or calcium hypochlorite into the system. Use of the latter equipment is generally restricted to the smaller plants. Automatic control of chlorine application has been made possible by amperometric techniques for measuring residual chlorine. Such tests are based on the ability of chlorine and iodine to generate a current proportional to their concentration in an amperometric cell.

The point of application must be selected to allow thorough mixing of the chlorine with the water before it reaches the first user outlet. The chlorination apparatus and spare cylinders should be located in a separate gas-tight room that can be ventilated to an unoccupied area if leakage occurs. Doors to the room should have glass inspection panels. A gas mask furnished with a chlorine-absorbing cannister should be stored near the entrance to the room.

It is often desirable to add an excess of chlorine so there will be a carryover that will exert a continuing disinfectant action at subsequent points in the distribution system. This "residual" chlorine is obtained by applying a dosage in excess of that needed for destruction of the micro-organisms found to be present in the water at the point of application. It is of two types: (1) Free residual chlorine, and (2) Combined residual chlorine.

Chlorine has other functions beside disinfection. Its oxidant action is useful in removing iron and manganese and for converting some of the organic materials responsible for taste, odor, and color into imperceptible compounds. The use of chlorine for removing taste and odor vectors demands careful control. Not only does chlorine itself have an objectionable taste and odor, but the products of its reactions with organic compounds may have worse organoleptic properties than the original substances. If progressive increments of chlorine are added to water containing organic contaminants, it is commonly observed that the off-flavors will first increase to a higher level and then decrease to a relatively low level.

Ozone has been suggested, and used, as a replacement for chlorine in disinfecting water. Irradiation by ultraviolet light of certain wavelengths is also being used in certain specialized disinfecting operations.

Ozone has a germicidal effectiveness exceeding that of chlorine. It is very effective in reducing taste, odor, and color problems present in many fresh water sources, and it is an effective disinfectant against cysts and viruses. It decomposes into molecular oxygen and avoids the development of trihalomethanes, which have been a concern of the EPA (Lorenz 1990).

Ozone must be generated on site since it is an unstable gas. The raw material is either air or pure oxygen. Multiple dryers and air filters are used to supply uncontaminated gas to the medium- or low-frequency generator that manufactures the ozone and feeds it to the contactor. A wide variety of water-ozone contactor systems are used; the predominant one in the U.S. is an over/under baffled basin. It is essential to destroy the gas that is not consumed in the contactor, that is, the excess ozone, and this is usually accomplished in a thermal/catalytic destruct system. Ozonation is sometimes used both before and after flocculation, and it can be used in combination with chlorination (Tate 1991).

In an ultraviolet system, water is pumped through a cylindrical stainless steel chamber where it is irradiated by 20 to 30 low-pressure low-intensity arc tubes supplying UV light within a narrow set of wavelengths (Warne 1986 and Mans 1987). In a more recent version, one high output arc tube is mounted axially within a quartz sleeve to treat up to 200 cubic meters of water per hour. Although UV light can quite satisfactorily disinfect water, it cannot provide the residual or delayed effect of chlorine. On the other hand, UV light does not add odorous or chemically reactive material to the water.

Other processes.—Air stripping, or packed tower aeration, is a technology for reducing volatile organic compounds to acceptably small levels. These compounds are difficult to remove in other ways, although granular activated carbon systems are sometimes effective.

Desalinization is a relatively expensive method for obtaining potable water from brackish or saline sources, but there are situations where it seems to be the only practical solution. In a few areas where energy supplies are abundant and fresh water very scarce, as in some Middle Eastern countries, large scale desalinization plants have been installed. We will probably see more applications of this technology in the U.S., as natural water supplies become increasingly depleted. Methods for reducing the salt content of water include reverse osmosis, electrodialysis, and vapor compression units for both commercial and military applications, and smaller reverse osmosis plants for coastal communities. Freeze desalinization is a relatively simple, low energy process that involves limited corrosion and fouling and requires no pre-treatment. Distillation is, of course, a familiar and widespread process, and in some plants of newer design involving very efficient energy recycling, is not as prohibitive in cost as may first appear (Lorenz 1990).

Effects of Water Impurities on Bakery Products

Hard water.—The "hardness" of water is traditionally an indication of its ability to form insoluble precipitates with soaps. The term is used in water technology to mean a specific index of the calcium and magnesium (and, sometimes, iron and aluminum) content calculated as carbonates. Water hardness can be expressed either as grains per gallon or parts per million of calcium carbonate equivalent. One grain per gallon is equal to 17.1 ppm. Hardness has been measured by observing the so-called sudsing power of the water when it is mixed with a soap solution that has been standardized against a calcium salt solution of known strength. The U.S. Geological Survey classifies water as follows: Soft, 0 to 60 ppm; Moderately hard, 60 to 120 ppm; Hard, 120 to 180 ppm; and Very hard, over 180 ppm. In the U.S., water hardness of supplies have been found to vary from about 1 to 350 grains per gallon, but most will fall in the range of 3 to 50.

Although variations of hardness within the normal range found in potable water supplies have no hygienic significance, they do affect taste, response of foods during preparation, and suitability of water for industrial purposes such as steam generation. The ions responsible for hardness can affect the color, flavor, and texture of foods, and it may be necessary to remove them in order to improve the quality of finished products.

Water that is either too soft or too hard causes difficulties in dough handling and quality problems in finished products. Use of softened water as an ingredient can lead to soft, sticky doughs, primarily as the result of the reduction in calcium ions. Hard water can increase mixing times, and have a retarding effect on fermentation. Alkaline water is considered undesirable because it can neutralize the acidity developed during fermentation, this being an important factor affecting dough quality. The general effect of divalent ions on polymers bearing carboxyl groups is to create more or less transient bonds between molecules with a resultant toughening or strengthening of gels and increased viscosity of solutions. Hardening is quite apparent when traces of calcium ions are added to many kinds of fruits and vegetables. This is due to interaction of the calcium ions with pectic substances. Less pronounced results are observed with gluten, gelatin, etc. Stronger concentrations of sodium or potassium (or certain other monovalent ions) can cause a reversal of the calcium effect, in some instances, provided the pH remains constant.

The two main types of water-softening processes are those in which offending substances are precipitated by adding appropriate reactants and those in which calcium and magnesium are replaced by hydrogen or sodium ions in some sort of ion exchange process. The former type includes the cold-lime or lime-soda processes used by many municipal water plants. These methods are not as common in industrial plants, where some modification of the zeolite or resin ion-exchange processes is more likely to be found.

Water Treatment Methods Used by Bakeries

Most bakeries can obtain water from a municipal plant that has already applied the necessary primary treatments. It may be desirable, however, for the bakery to further purify the water by removing suspended particles, pigments, ions present in excessive quantities, undesirable flavors and their precursors, and organic materials. Filtration (including carbon filtration) reverse osmosis, and resin decolorizing are some of the methods used. Processes for correcting excessive hardness have been discussed in a preceding section. Distillation is the oldest technology for producing pure water, but it is so expensive from an energy standpoint that it cannot be considered except for producing laboratory solvent and other situations where cost is a secondary consideration.

Removal of iron and manganese.—In water from deep wells that have the bicarbonate type of alkalinity, iron will be present as colorless and soluble ferrous bicarbonate. Iron in this form may be removed by oxidizing it to insoluble feric hydroxide and then settling and filtering the water. Ion exchange processes can also be used. Manganese zeolite filters can be used to extract iron present at concentrations of 1 ppm or less. The sodium cation exchanger or zeolite water-softening processes will remove iron as well as hardness minerals. Ion exchange resins in which the iron displaces hydrogen ions are used by some industries. Manganese can be removed by analogous methods, but a higher pH is required if the oxidation-precipitation technique is used. Oxidation can be effected by aeration or through such chemical oxidants as chlorine.

If the water is acidic, iron, and manganese may be present as the divalent sulfates $FeSO_4$ and $MnSO_4$. These can be removed by successively applying aeration, neutralization, settling, and filtration. Ferric hydroxide constitutes the major part of the iron content of "red waters." Since this compound is insoluble, it may be removed by coagulation, settling, and filtration. Often, the particle size is such that coagulation is not required. Aeration may precede the other steps in order to bring additional forms of iron into a more insoluble state. Iron and manganese chelated by compounds of relatively high molecular weight are frequently found in intensely colored waters. These chelates can also be removed by aeration, coagulation, settling, and filtration.

Carbon filters and deionization.—Beds of activated carbon can be used to remove chlorine and certain objectionable tastes and odors that are virtually impossible to take out by any other practical method. Carbon beds are not filters, in the strictest sense, because their principal action depends not on passing the fluid through a sieve-like barrier that restricts the passage of particles exceeding a specific size, but rather on the adsorption of charged particles on surfaces of the carbon grains. It is true that carbon beds trap and remove some suspended matter, but other types of filters are cheaper and more effective for this function.

Deionization systems consist of beds of resins or minerals through which water is passed. They can be used to remove ionic species that may be harmful to the dough. The three types of deionization systems encountered in food plants are the weak base, strong base, and mixed bed systems. Weak base systems provide maximum capacity but do not remove either carbon dioxide or silica. Silica causes few if any problems. Since carbon dioxide is not removed, pH of the water will remain below 7.0 after it passes through the bed. Strong base systems remove carbon dioxide and silica, and generally produce water having a relatively high pH, often around 9. Mixed bed systems are combinations of cation resins and strong base resins. They remove carbon dioxide and silica.

Because deionized water is very pure, it has less surface tension and acts wetter than untreated water. Flour takes up more deionized water, often as much as 3% to 5% more than untreated water, according to some reports; also, the deionized water is taken up faster by the dry ingredients. These effects can be either advantageous or disadvantageous, depending on circumstances. The more consistent quality resulting from the elimination of ionic fluctuations would normally be considered an advantage. Of course, once the water contacts other ingredients, it dissolves organic and inorganic substances from them and is no longer "pure."

Reverse osmosis.—This method relies on the use of pressure to force water through a semi-permeable membrane. Reverse osmosis will ordinarily remove about 90% to 95% of the total impurities from raw water. Particulate matter, colloidal suspensions, organic substances, and microorganisms can be extracted. Generally, gases are not taken out effectively. Ions are removed at varying rates, depending on the chemical structure of the membrane, its thickness, and the pressure applied. A typical cellulose acetate membrane operating at 200 psi will remove 96% to 98% of the calcium and magnesium, 85% to 90% of the sodium and potassium, 95% to 98% of the manganese, 89% to 99% of the aluminum, 60% to 80% of the silica, 92% to 94% of the copper and cadmium, 93% to 95% of the nickel, 85% to 90% of the chromium, and over 90% of the zinc ions.

The removed materials form a concentrated solution of impurities that must be disposed of in some manner, and this is usually done by directing the effluent to the sewer. Since these materials are not toxic (having originated from drinking water), this should cause no problem.

Adjusting pH.—Most municipal treatment systems do not have means for adjusting the pH of water emerging from the plant. Substantial pH variations can be observed in some supplies. For example, Collins (1978) described a cycle from 5.8 to 7.2 occurring about every two hours in water received from one source. He pointed out this meant there were about 25 times more hydrogen ions present at the lower pH. The author has found even wider fluctuations in some municipal supplies.

Fluctuations on the alkaline side could be corected, if necessary, by additions to the system of small amounts of food acids (water supplies significantly on the acid side are uncommon). Only small amounts of acid should be necessary because water is not a good buffering agent in the neutral range. Generally speaking, however, it is better to adjust formulas and processes to the water that is available rather than try to add acids directly to the supply pipe. Other ingredients have buffering capacities usually far exceeding that needed to correct a pH imbalance in added water.

Analyses of Water

Standardized techniques are available for determining nearly all of the water quality factors thought to be important to food manufacturers. Some of the procedures have attained official, or at least quasi-official, status through inclusion in "Standard Methods for the Examination of Water and Waste Water" (Anon. 1975). Nearly all of the tests referred to in "Drinking Water Standards" (Anon. 1962) are included in that book.

Some of the analyses that have been standardized are acidity, alkalinity, aluminum, arsenic, boron, calcium, carbon dioxide, chloride, chlorine (residual chlorine), chlorine demand, chromium, color, specific conductance, copper, cyanide, fluoride, grease, hardness, iodide, iron, lead, lignin, magnesium, manganese, albuminoid nitrogen, ammonia nitrogen, nitrate nitrogen, nitrite nitrogen, oxygen, oxygen consumed, pH, phenol, phosphate, potassium, residue, selenium, silica, sodium, sulfate, sulfite, tannin, taste and odor, temperature, turbidity, and zinc. There are alternative or tentative methods for some of these factors. Since the standard methods are readily available, there is no point in reproducing them here.

In modern laboratory practice, the determination of inorganic ions in environmental water samples is performed mostly by automated wet chemistry analyzers. Equipment based on the technology of flow injection analysis have the largest number of methods approved by the U.S. Environmental Protection Agency. Ion analysis can also be performed by ion chromatography; however, the only method currently approved for EPA compliance monitoring is for nitrate in drinking water, so that this equipment is broadly applicable only to preliminary or screening tests in which formal approval is not required (Ranger 1989).

Three more or less traditional bacteriological tests are applied to water: (1) counts of colonies grown on gelatin plates incubated at 68°F; (2) counts on agar plates incubated at 90°F for 24 hours; and (3) the coliform count. The third criterion has been largely superseded as a standard by the "Most Probable Number (MPN)" of *Escherichia coli*, which has been defined as "the bacterial density, which, if it had actually been present in the sample under observation, would more frequently than any other have given the observed analytical results."

Plate counts made after incubation at 68° or 99°F are not particularly important as indicators of water safety, but they are useful as routine quality control tests in the various water treatment procedures and as means for determining the sanitary conditions of basins, filters, etc. The coliform test is the ultimate measure of bacteriological safety of water supplies.

It is sometimes necessary to make an estimate of the planktonic organisms (e.g., algae, diatoms) in a reservoir or other water source. This is usually done by direct microscopic count on a sample concentrated by filtration or other means.

Biological oxygen demand (BOD) is an important indicator of the degree of pollution of a water source and the potential for spontaneous recovery of this supply. BOD is the total amount of oxygen taken up by the microorganisms that are present and that act on the available nonliving organic matter. The BOD has been defined by the American Public Health Association as "the oxygen in parts per million required during stabilization of the organic matter by aerobic bacterial action." It has also been stated that "complete stabilization requires more than 100 days at 68°F but such long periods of incubation are impractical in any but research investigations, consequently a much shorter period of incubation is used." The bacterial consumption of oxygen may be partially offset by photosynthetic processes of microscopic plants that produce oxygen and consume carbon dioxide.

Turbidity, color, and odor are routinely determined when a complete water analysis is performed. Turbidity is a measure of the extent to which light passing through the fluid is reduced in intensity by suspended materials such as clay, organic debris, and certain industrial wastes. It was originally determined with a Jackson candle turbidimeter, but now is measured by devices that continuously evaluate and record the attenuation of a beam of light. Until about 1962, the goal for filtered water was 10 turbidity units (TU), but in that year the U.S. Public Health Service lowered the goal to 5 TU. Then in 1977, the EPA reduced the allowable turbidity to 1 TU, and in 1989 the primary standard was dropped to 0.5 nephelometric TU with a goal of 0.1 TU. For most bakery products, a rather high level of turbidity can be tolerated, unlike many clear beverages, jellies, etc. This is not to say that the substances causing turbidity are free of other effects that may be very deleterious to the quality of a bakery product.

Color of water is defined as the difference in hue caused only by those substances actually in solution. It can be the result of mineral or vegetable pigments of natural origin or it can be caused by soluble organic or inorganic materials from sewage or industrial effluents. To obtain a quantitative estimation of "color," the analyst visually compares a sample of water to standard platinum-cobalt solutions or to colored glass tubes or discs under standard lighting conditions—methods that are being replaced by electronic colorimetric equipment.

All users of municipal water for ingredient purposes should maintain good contacts with their supplier. Although it is often true that water treatment plants in small communities (and in some larger ones) have surprisingly little quality control information that they can give out, the user should take what is available and use it as a basis for his own decisions as to analyses that must be applied after the water reaches his factory. It is unwise, however, to accept the data uncritically, since the civil servant collecting the samples or performing the analyses may lack scientific training. Additionally, the water changes as it goes through the piping from municipal plant to the bakery, and it is the quality as the manufacturer receives it that is important.

SALT

Salt in the Human Diet

Hundreds of chemical compounds are classified as salts, and many of the water-soluble ones exhibit what we recognize as a salty taste, but only sodium chloride seems to give this flavor in a form not modified by sour, bitter, or sweet tastes. Neither the sodium ion nor the chloride ion alone causes the typical salty flavor. Substances other than sodium chloride may provide a similar flavor, but they generally have off-notes that are described by consumers as disagreeable or atypical. For examples, sodium sulfate has a less pronounced salty flavor and potassium chloride has a bitter, cooling aftertaste. Some salts are more or less toxic and so are not suitable for food use regardless of their flavor.

The mechanism of salty taste is very specific. All other taste-inducing substances in foods, such as sucrose or acetic acid, bind to a receptor on one of the hundred or so taste cells present in every taste bud. This receptor, to which a number of different chemical compounds possessing a specific reactive region can bind, then generates impulses that are conducted to the brain and recognized as "sweet," "sour," or "bitter." The lack of specificity of these receptors enables the design of sweet-tasting substances that have little or no chemical similarity to sugars. Sodium, on the other hand, enters taste cells by passing through specialized pores (called the sodium ion channels) in the cell membrane. Entry of sodium cells causes depolarization of the cells and triggers the release of neurotransmitters that excite the nerves carrying impulses recognized by the brain as "salty." Only sodium and lithium can pass through these pores, and, it is said, only these two ions taste salty (Anon. 1990, attributed to G. K. Beauchamp).

In addition to having a pronounced and generally agreeable taste of its own, sodium chloride modifies other flavors. In test situations, it has been found to enhance the sweetness of sugars and decrease the sourness of acids (Fabian and Blum 1943). In some liquid products, the addition of small amounts of salt, even below its threshold concentration, will increase the perceived sweetness of sucrose.

Although food-grade salt is unusually pure compared with many other food ingredients, it always contains other ions that may affect its taste. For example, calcium and magnesium ions cause a stronger, more bitter flavor. These foreign ions tend to concentrate near the surface of sodium chloride crystals and therefore have an even more potent effect than they would have if they were evenly distributed throughout the particle. This is, of course, only observed where particles are consumed, as in the topping salt on crackers, pretzels, salt rolls, etc.

The appetite for salt flavor is widespread in the animal kingdom; this liking is not restricted to humans. Infants appear to be attracted by moderately salty flavors in foods. This is clearly not a learned response, as some writers would have us believe. Beauchamp (1987) reviewed the evidence for an innate, genetically determined preference for salt. Evidence shows there are two distinct shifts in the appetite for salt that occur during early human development. At about four months of age, the infant reaction shifts from indifference to relative preference. Then, at about the third year, there is a change from acceptance to rejection of salt in water while salt is still preferred in other ingestibles. These reactions seem to bear no relationship to the history of exposure of the infant to salt.

Sodium is an essential nutrient. Symptoms related to sodium deficiency in the diet are rare because of the widespread presence of sodium in foods. Some people (a minor percentage of the population) are said to have their tendency to high blood pressure exacerbated by sodium consumption above certain levels, but there is no persuasive evidence that chronic hypertension is initiated by intake of sodium at any reasonable level.

Although there has been a great deal of agitation by various so-called consumer groups which demand that the level of salt in prepared foods be reduced, manufacturers have experienced limited consumer demand for foods promoted as no-salt or low-salt varieties. At present, most reduced-salt foods are being distributed as "health foods" or special dietary foods. Among food manufacturers, there does appear to be an increasing interest in applying sodium labeling or in calling attention to low sodium content if their products already fall in that category.

Containers and Storage

Ingredient salt is usually delivered in 50- or 80-lb multiwall paper bags having a 1.5 mil polyethylene liner. These packages give good protection against moisture absorption and caking as long as the liner remains intact. If the salt contains antioxidants or nutrients, a special liner of glassine/wax laminate may be included to prevent evaporative loss of the additives. Bulk delivery in trucks or rail cars can be arranged if the rate of usage justifies the installation of a bulk handling and storage facility. Bulk handling tends to reduce the average particle size because of the abrasion that occurs during transfer. Some specialty types of salt are considerably more susceptible to this type of damage than is regular vacuum salt.

Bags of salt should be stored on pallets in a dry warehouse away from condensate drip and damp floors and walls. Unlike most other food ingredients, pure salt does not undergo chemical deterioration in storage. Absorption of foreign odors is rarely a problem. Undesirable physical changes, such as caking, can occur, however. Caking is a response to fluctuations in relative humidity around a critical point. In the temperature range of 32° to 240°F, saturated brine has a vapor pressure approximately 75% that of water.

Above about 75% RH, salt becomes deliquescent. Moisture from the atmosphere condenses on the surface of the crystals and forms a layer of saturated brine. These layers will coalesce where the crystals touch and, when the water evaporates as the ambient relative humidity falls below 75%, they will form a re-crystallized bridge or weld of solid salt between the crystals. Obviously, the salt should either be protected from fluctuations in atmospheric humidity by packaging it in containers having very low moisture vapor transfer rates or it should be stored in rooms where the relative humidity can be controlled below 75%.

Fine grades of salt that contain added tricalcium phosphate are somewhat more resistant to caking than unmodified salt. Dendritic salt is resistant to caking because of its moisture absorption characteristics. Any kind of salt will cake if it is exposed to severe condensation, however.

According to Kaumann (1960), the terms "free-flowing" and "non-caking" are not synonymous. Free-flowing salts are probably non-caking, but non-caking salts are not necessarily free flowing. Regardless of how dry the salt seems, or how great the drying temperature to which it has been heated, a film of saturated brine will be present on the salt surfaces. The degree and seriousness of caking will vary according to several factors, the principal ones being: (1) variation in moisture content; (2) impurities; (3) particle size; (4) particle shape; (5) crystal abnormality or injury; (6) characteristics of the storage container; (7) storage humidity and temperature; (8) pressure of overlying product; (9) transit duration; (10) storage duration; and (11) freezing.

Types of Salt

The types of salt offered to bakers differ mainly in the size and shape of their particles. The available types can be described as vacuum granulated, grainer or Alberger flake, ground/pulverized, solar, dendritic, compacted flake, rock, and pelletized. Size and shape of the salt particle are related to its function in processing and to consumer acceptance. Table 6.2 contains information on particle size and related physical characteristics of several types of salt; it is based on data supplied by Morton Thiokol Co.

Table 6.2. PHYSICAL CHARACTERISTICS OF SALT TYPES

Grade or name of salt	Mean screen size	Mean particle thickness	Surface area	Particles per gram
	microns	microns	sq cm/g	thousand
Rock pretzel	1050	600	50	0.7
Top flake coarse	900	330	85	1.8
Top flake topping	600	300	95	4.3
Dendritic	220	220	290	100.
Purex fine prepared	200	200	140	60.
Flour	100	100	460	460.
Pulverized (EF 200)	40	40	1150	7,200.

Granulated salt.—Granulated or common salt is made from brine that has been evaporated in a vacuum pan. The resultant cube-shaped crystal is relatively hard and has a medium solubility rate. Alberger process flake salt is made from brine that has been treated to remove much of the calcium and magnesium. The Alberger method of crystallization gives small flake-like crystals that dissolve more rapidly than granulated salt.

Dendritic salt.—Dendritic salt is made by a unique process that also involves vacuum pan evaporation. A distinctive crystal formation is achieved by chemically pre-treating the brine with yellow prussiate of soda (sodium ferricyanide decahydrate). A maximum of 13 ppm of this additive is permitted in the finished product. Unlike the cubical structure of vacuum pan (granulated) salt or the rather flat crystal aggregates of flake-type salt, dendritic crystals are branched or somewhat star-like in shape and contain numerous microscopic cavities. This salt has a relatively low bulk density, high specific surface area, good resistance to caking, and a rapid rate of solution. Because it is porous, dendritic salt is a fairly good absorbent for some non-aqueous liquids, taking up comparatively large amounts of oil, for example, before becoming wet or pasty. It also demonstrates excellent blending properties when mixed with powders. Some manufacturers offer dendritic or flake salt mixed with antioxidants as a convenient means of retarding rancidity development in snacks and the like.

As an example of typical specifications for dendritic salt, the following description of Star Flake brand of the Morton Salt Company may be of interest. Star Flake dendritic salt complies with the Food Chemicals Codex tolerances for sodium chloride. Guaranteed tolerances on a moisture-free basis are 99.9% sodium chloride, 0.01% maximum calcium and magnesium expressed as calcium, 1.0 ppm maximum copper, and 2.0 ppm maximum available iron. The moisture level should not exceed 0.1%. The level of residual yellow prussiate of soda does not exceed the federal tolerance of 13 ppm. The USDA Standard for No. 1 salt specifies a limit for coarse, water-insoluble sediment of 0.5 mg per 250 g sample, which is equivalent to 2.0 ppm. A typical chemical analysis of dendritic salt on the moisture-free basis is 99.94% sodium chloride, 0.05% sodium sulfate, and 0.01% calcium salts. The pour bulk density is required to fall in the range of 53 lb to 58 lb per cu ft. Particle size specifications are 5% maximum retained on a U.S. Standard 40-mesh screen, and 20% maximum passing through a 100-mesh screen.

One of the main advantages of dendritic salt is that it is nearly dustless when applied either by a mechanical salting roller or by forced air. It flows freely and uniformly through mechanical salters, providing a more even distribution on the product. This type of salt adheres well when used as a topping, especially if the surface is tacky or oily at the time of application. The sharp-pointed edges of the crystals tend to penetrate the surface fat and become firmly attached. There is also greater oil absorption by dendritic salt, which contributes to the adhesion. If the product to be salted is relatively dry at the time of application, a finer screen size of "flour" salt is needed to secure adequate adhesion.

Flour salt and pulverized salt.—Certain applications call for very fine mesh sizes of salt. This form of the ingredient is used mainly in premixes and the like where separation might be a problem. In low moisture doughs, as in some cookie formulas, rapid and complete solubility is made possible by the use of very fine salt.

Flour salt can consist of the finest grindings of flake, granulated, or ground-granulated production. These grades are extremely dusty and difficult to dispense by conventional roll-type salters. Flake flour salt is usually the least dusty but is not universally available.

Flour salts have a particle size range of 70 to 200 mesh and must be treated with an anticaking agent—usually 1.0% to 1.5% tricalcium phosphate or calcium polysilicate—to ensure free flow.

For applications where the salt is to be incorporated into an oil or oil and cheese topping, pulverized (through 200 mesh) salt is often employed. Pulverized salt must contain 1.7% to 2.0% tricalcium phosphate to prevent caking. It is extremely dusty and cannot be fed through ordinary dispensers as a dry topping because of its flow characteristics.

Pretzel salt.—There are various kinds of pretzel salt. One company offers selected screenings of crushed rock salt obtained from a dome deposit on the Gulf Coast of Louisiana. It is a peculiar characteristic of this material that it breaks up into uniformly flat, rectangular particles when it is crushed. These granules adhere particularly well to pretzels. They have a mild saline flavor with a note of "huskiness" that is provided by the traces of mineral impurities they contain. The average bulk density is 72 lb per cubic foot. Pretzel salt is offered in coarse and fine varieties.

Salt with Additives

Various additives have been applied to salt. Most salt manufacturers can supply salt containing anti-caking or free-flow agents, and some offer preparations containing antioxidants as functional additives. Vitamins and mineral nutrients are other additives that are commercially available in mixtures with salt (Anon. 1972).

Fortification with nutrients.– If nutritional supplements are to be added to doughs or batters, the powders or tablets supplied by repackagers are convenient and effective means of applying them. For certain types of snacks requiring topping salt, another way of adding the nutrients is through the medium of enriched topping salt. At least two salt companies have offered vitamin-fortified snack toppings based on either a 40-mesh salt or a flour salt. The nutrients are agglomerated onto the salt to avoid segregation and dusting during application.

The standard formula is designed to furnish 100% of the RDA of five vitamins per pound of potato chips when it is added at the rate of at least 1.5% of the finished product. The added nutrients in this product are vitamin A, thiamin, riboflavin, niacin, and ascorbic acid. Custom formulations were also supplied if large quantities were ordered.

Iodized salt contains approximately 0.01% of added potassium iodide. The purpose of this additive is to reduce the incidence of goiter in susceptible populations. Because potassium iodide tends to decompose, forming free iodine that can have adverse effects on the color and flavor of foods, stabilizers such as dextrose are usually added along with it. Ingredient salt sold to food manufacturers is not normally iodized, though it can be obtained in this form at a very small additional cost.

Free-flow agents and antioxidants.–At least two manufacturers can supply dendritic salt with added free-flow agents or antioxidants. The free-flow agents are usually water-insoluble materials in fine powdered form. Tricalcium phosphate, sodium silicoaluminate, and calcium silicate are three common anticaking substances. They function by preferentially adsorbing water vapor while maintaining the solid particle form that acts as a separator between the salt crystals. Yellow prussiate of soda acts in a different manner. Due to the method of crystallization, this substance (when added in dissolved form to the brine) separates as fine particles on the surface of the salt crystals. In humid atmospheres, the solid yellow prussiate of soda preferentially absorbs water and dissolves. When the relative humidity drops below about 75%, the substance dehydrates to form bridges between the salt crystals. Up to this point, its behavior is very similar to that of sodium chloride. The bridges of yellow prussiate of soda are, however, much more fragile than sodium chloride welds and are easily broken by normal handling procedures. Figure 6.1 illustrates this effect (Source: Morton Thiokol).

1.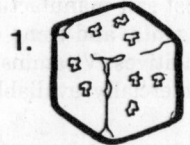
TRACES OF FINE PARTICLES OF YPS ON SURFACE OF SALT CRYSTALS

2.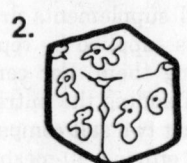
ABOVE 75% rH, ABSORBED MOISTURE DISSOLVES SOME SALT AND YPS TO FORM BRINE ON CRYSTAL SURFACE

3.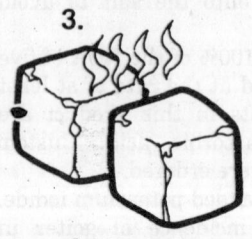
BELOW 75% rH, BRINE EVAPORATES AND PRESENCE OF YPS RESULTS IN WEAK NEEDLE-SHAPE SALT WELD BETWEEN CRYSTALS

4.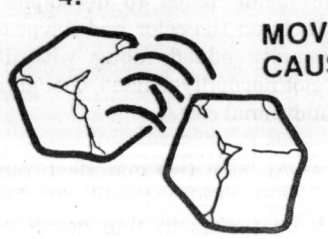
MOVEMENT OF SALT MASS CAUSES WELD TO BREAK.

Figure 6.1. Anticaking function of yellow prussiate o soda

Antioxidant-treated salt is designed primarily for use on oil-fried products such as corn chips. The formulation of R. G. dendritic salt of Morton Salt Co. is: dendritic salt 99.092%, BHA 0.130%, propyl gallate 0.048%, citric acid 0.130%, calcium polysilicate 0.500%, and propylene glycol

0.100%. When this salt is added at the 2.0% level to products containing 40% oil, it will contribute approximately 65 ppm BHA, 65 ppm citric acid, and 25 ppm propyl gallate to the oil. Federal tolerances, based on the fat content of the food are 100 ppm for any one antioxidant, 200 ppm for total antioxidants, and 100 ppm for citric acid.

Salt Substitutes in Bakery Products

The concentration of salt in dough affects a number of processing responses, but the main reason bakers use this ingredient is its enhancement of the flavor of the finished product. Replacements for sodium chloride have been offered as a basis for formulating products that might appeal to persons with health problems (particularly those afflicted with high blood pressure), but none of them completely reproduces the flavor effects of salt.

Potassium chloride is probably the most widely used salt substitute. This material does have a somewhat salt-like flavor, but it also contributes some off-flavors, variously described as metallic, bitter, chemical, etc. Strietelmeier (quoted by Best 1989) believes the bitterness of potassium chloride becomes a consumer negative only when it is used in certain products such as soups and yogurts. Furthermore, he says some spices, particularly Italian-type spice mixtures, will mask the off-flavors of potassium chloride. A 50:50 mixture of salt and potassium chloride has frequently been used with fair results in reduced-sodium products.

A mixture containing approximately equal portions of salt and potassium chloride with traces of fumaric acid, potassium glutamate, and monocalcium phosphate was used at about the 2% level in bread doughs (Adams 1983). This blend gave a well flavored, but rather bland, bread containing only 100 mg of sodium per serving of two ounces. Some processing characteristics of the dough were affected. Additional yeast and oxidants were required with a preferment process, and about 30 minutes additional fermentation time was required when using sponge-dough processes. Other ingredients that have been used to divert the attention of consumers from the lack of salt flavor include spices, MSG, meat extracts, protein hydrolysates, autolyzed yeast, soy sauces, and nucleic acid derivatives.

Gillette (1985) correctly pointed out that flavor studies conducted with aqueous solutions of sodium chloride or its substitutes give results that are of limited value to food technologists. When her panels tested soups, rice, potato chips, and scrambled eggs with various levels of salt and salt substitutes, they reported that the addition of sodium chloride did more than just add a "salt" flavor. This ingredient increased the perception of "fullness" and "thickness," giving the impression of a less watery product. It enhanced the perception of sweetness. In some cases, a metallic or chemical off-flavor was decreased or masked by salt. Overall, the most significant effect of sodium chloride was its improvement of the flavor balance. These results were obtained even when "saltiness," *per se*, was not noticeable.

In the Gillette work, potassium chloride enhanced sweetness but did not improve mouthfeel or flavor balance significantly. It did, however, impart bitter, metallic, and chemical notes to foods. Glutamate also lacked the overall improving effect of sodium chloride. The net effect of all this experimentation is to confirm something most of us already suspected, that is, bakery products taste better if they contain some salt. Persons who must avoid sodium can learn to like salt-free bakery products, but like most other educational programs, the learning is accompanied by considerable discomfort.

In addition to being a nearly universal flavoring agent in bakery foods, salt has important effects on the physical properties of dough and on fermentation. Indirectly, it can have effects on color of crust and crumb and on other characteristics.

Salt is commonly added to bakery formulas at levels from 1% to 2.5% of the flour weight, with most of the additions probably being nearer the low rather than the high side of the range. In addition to having salt in the dough, some specialty products such as saltine crackers, salt sticks, and pretzels contain an even larger amount as sprinklings of fairly large salt particles on their surfaces (see Table 6.3, based on information received from D. M. Strietelmeier). Placing the granules on the surface has two beneficial effects, an immediate flavor impact is obtained when the product is placed in the mouth and the salt does not affect dough properties.

Since salt must be dissolved in order to be detected by the taste buds, the particle size of topping salt and its dissolving rate are important quality parameters. Generally, dissolving rate is a direct function of exposed surface area, which is related, in a general but inexact way, to the particle size. Given the same crystal form, surface area increases geometrically with decreasing particle size. In practice, this rule seems to apply fairly well to different sizes of the coarse topping salt used with crackers and pretzels, but not as well to finer toppings employed on chips, nuts, and popcorn. No doubt, the firmness with which the particles adhere to the underlying product also has an effect on the speed and intensity of the flavor impact.

Sodium chloride affects both the fermentation rate of yeast and the rheology of the dough. Salt inhibits or "controls" fermentation. This effect is not due solely to the increased osmotic pressure that results from the addition of salt to the dough formula, but is partly a specific manifestation of the action of sodium and chloride ions on the semipermeable membranes of yeast cells. Salt affects many metabolic activities of yeast but the effect on fermentation that is of most importance to the baker is the reduced rate of gas production and the consequent lengthening of proof time. Data in the literature indicate that, for some doughs at least, the reduction in rate of gas production is approximately linearly related to salt concentration. If proof time can be extended to compensate for the lower rate, loaf volumes need not be smaller. Inadequate salt will allow yeast to ferment excessively, leading to gassy, sour doughs that are difficult to process ("wild") and give loaves with open grain, poor texture, and other defects.

As a result of its effect on dough, salt generally improves the crumb color and grain in bread.

Table 6.3. COMMON LEVELS OF TOPPING SALT[1]

Product	Topping salt, %
Crackers-	
-soda	3.0
-saltines	3.0
-snack	1.5-2.0
Corn chips	1.5
Tortilla chips	1.0-1.2
Cheese collets	2.0
Nuts-	
-oil roasted	1.5
-dry roasted	1.0
Potato chips	2.0-2.5
Pretzels	4.0-5.0
Popcorn	1.0-1.5

[1] Amounts refer to salt retained on the product.

Sodium chloride has a modifying effect on the physical properties of gluten. This is usually described by bakers as a binding or tightening of the dough. Increases in salt lengthen the mixing time—the more salt, the longer the dough must be mixed in order to achieve proper development. Furthermore, the energy required for adequate mixing is greater. Experiments conducted more than 40 years ago led researchers to attribute the effect of salt on gluten to an inhibition of proteolytic enzymes. If this does occur, it is a relatively minor part of the effect, however. More likely, the sodium ions compete with hydrogen ions for loci on the gluten molecule, reducing the hydrogen bonding that tends to tie molecules together (though with weak bonds). Fortmann (1967) saw the phenomenon as a coagulation or hardening of the gluten with a release of water; the gluten molecules are bent and interlocked so that work in the form of additional mixing is required to unwind and unravel the gluten strands into more nearly linear alignments.

To offset the effect of salt on mixing time, some workers have recommended a delayed addition of this ingredient. In these schemes, the essentially salt-free dough is developed nearly to its optimum, then the formula amount of salt is added and mixing completed. Overall mixing time and the total energy requirement are reduced appreciably by this method. Another approach that has been attempted is to coat the salt particles with a water-resistant coating that is expected to delay the dissolving of the ingredient. The author's experience with coated readily-soluble ingredients has convinced him that, as a practical matter, this approach is extremely unlikely to be worthwhile, because (1) it is virtually impossible to completely enrobe irregular particles with a continuous layer without using large amounts of coating material, and (2) it is unrealistic to expect to retain the protective layer during the abrasive action of dough mixing.

Analytical methods

Solubility rate.—The dissolving rate of salt, which is often an important property for the bakery technologist, can be estimated by means of standardized procedures. This test requires the use of a simple apparatus that provides conditions of maximum exposure to solvent. In a typical test, 17.3 g of salt will be dropped through a 100 ml column of water 9.5 inches in height, and the volume of undissolved salt that collects in the graduated bottom part of the tube can be recorded. Another procedure, the float method, limits the exposure to solvent by suspending or floating the salt on the surface of the water. A weighed amount of salt is placed on the screen, and the time required for complete solution is recorded. Table 6.4 describes the relationship of solubility indexes and solubility rates of salt types; it is based on data supplied by Morton Thiokol Co.

A new universal test was developed by International Salt Research to compare solubility rates. In this tests, 1,000 grams of the salt to be tested is placed in a large glass beaker fitted with a stationary column that contains a salt hydrometer. Three liters of water adjusted to a temperature of 60°F are quickly added to the beaker. Agitation is provided by a laboratory mixer adjusted to a speed of 240 rpm and fitted with a four-blade stirrer. Time required for reaching 90° on the hydrometer is measured with a stopwatch.

Table 6.4. SOLUBILITY INDEXES AND RATES

Name or type	Particle size microns	Percent dissolving "instantly"	Time to dissolve 20 g, seconds
Dendritic	150-420	98	380
Fine flake	150-420	95	240
Fine granulated	150-420	87	140
Medium flake	300-850	83	295
Coarse flake	420-1200	78	350
Coarse granulated	200-600	74	180

Analyses for "salt".—For many years, salt was determined by a silver nitrate titration using potassium chromate to indicate the end point. Of course, it is really the chloride ion that is measured by this technique and chloride can enter the product in forms other than common salt, but the results give a sufficiently accurate indication of the concentration of salt to be useful for most purposes. Analytical methods for sodium ions were much more time-consuming and somewhat less accurate, so they were seldom conducted unless there was a special reason for wanting to establish the concentration of this constituent.

At least one company made a fiber strip impregnated with silver dichromate that can be immersed in a hot sample solution to determine salt concentration. The strip is brown in color to begin with, but turns white along its length to a distance that is related to the chloride ion concentration. The amount of water required to saturate the strip is a relatively constant amount, and the chloride dissolved in this amount of water reacts with the silver dichromate from the bottom to a point on the strip that represents complete reaction of the chloride. Reaction above this point does not occur because no more chloride ions are available. A reading is made by comparing chart figures with the length of the reacted portion when a moisture-sensitive indicator at the top of the strip changes color, indicating the water has traveled the entire length of the strip by capillary action; this more or less establishes a set amount of solution. Simplicity is the principal advantage of this method.

Sodium and potassium can be measured specifically and accurately by atomic absorption spectroscopy. The equipment required for making these determinations is often considered to be too expensive or complex for routine quality control tests, so considerable development effort has been expended in designing instruments that will rapidly and inexpensively determine either sodium or chloride concentrations with sufficient accuracy to satisfy the needs of production control personnel.

At least two firms are distributing automated devices based on the old silver nitrate titration method for determining chlorides. The procedure has been upgraded and mechanized by employing automatic titrators that use the principle of coulometric silver ion generation to titrate chloride ions. A generator-set of high purity silver electrodes is energized by a stabilized direct current to develop the silver ions, while a smaller set of electrodes is used to detect the end point. During titration, a small current flows between the detector electrodes. When titration of the chloride is complete, there is a sudden increase in the concentration of free silver ions in the solution. These free silver ions cause a surge of current between the detector electrode, activating the titration endpoint circuit. Since silver ions are generated at a constant rate, the elapsed time is related to the total amount of silver ions and thus to the amount of chloride in the sample.

Another instrument uses mercuric nitrate as the titrating substance and diphenylcarbazone as the indicator. Disposable plastic cartridges filled with mercuric nitrate are connected with a titrator that controls a plunger and a digital counter. Titrations are performed automatically and the end point sensed electronically. Mercuric nitrate concentrations are adjusted so the numbers shown on the digital counter at the endpoint can be multiplied by a constant factor to yield the percent sodium chloride in the sample.

Several inexpensive and fairly accurate devices have been developed for measuring sodium ion or chloride ion concentration by electronic means. Specificity, accuracy, and simplicity of these instruments vary depending on the design, but most of them are good enough for routine quality control testing (Anon. 1985). The selective ion electrode was one of the first approaches to be widely accepted. Both chloride and sodium electrodes are available. In both, an impermeable membrane separates the test solution from an internal solution of fixed concentration. Because of its composition and physical attributes, the membrane has an affinity for the ion, thus making it ion specific. Generally, other ions with the same positive or negative charge will be attracted to a much lesser degree. Supposedly, a charge separation occurs at the surface of the electrode, creating a difference in potential that can be measured and which is proportional to the effective concentration of the ion. The ion-selective electrode method has been refined to the point where an automated sampling and measuring device can be used to determine sodium and potassium with 5% and chloride with 7% accuracy and 1% to 2% precision using only a simple slurry of the food in deionized water (Balulescu 1985).

Table 6.5. HOW TO SELECT THE RIGHT SALT

Characteristic of interest	Factors to specify
Clean saline taste	Purity and impurities
Flavor profile	Impurities and solubility rate
Visual cleanliness	Extraneous and foreign matter
Microbiological	Expected to be very low
Adherence	Particle shape; size distribution
Appearance	Particle shape, color, size distribution
Controlled solubility	Solubility rate
Control flowability	Particle size distribution, moisture, chemical impurities, caking, free-flow additives
Shelf life	Caking resistance
Controlled pH	Anti-caking & free-flow additives
Blendability	Particle shape; size distribution
Non-segregating	Particle shape; size distribution
Bulk density	Bulk density range (loose)
Controlled Ca & Mg	Calcium and magnesium content
Suspendibility in oil	Particle shape, size distribution anti-cake & free-flow additive
Non-dusting	Particle size distribution, anti-caking and free flow additives
Liquid absorption capacity	Particle size & shape distribution
Low pro-oxidant potential	Copper-iron (free) content
Sediment	Water insolubles, anti-caking and free-flowing additives
High surface area	Particle shape & size distribution

A small portable device that measures the conductance of solutions is available for testing for sodium ions. Although the relationship between conductivity and percent salt is not linear, the circuitry is designed to correct for the deviation and provides a linear readout for percent salt over the whole range of the instrument. The conductivity probe is small enough to be placed in a test tube and it contains a temperature-sensing device that applies a correction signal to the conductance measurement. Range can be switched between zero to 1.999% salt and zero to 19.99% salt at the operator's discretion. Readout is on a liquid crystal display. The Diamond Crystal DSA-1000 "DiCromat" Salt Analyzer is similar in principle to the preceding device, but has some novel features (Anon. 1986).

Other tests.—Some of the determinations not given detailed consideration here are blendability, specific surface area, crystal count, bulk density, and adherence. Most of these involve strictly empirical tests.

Specifications

To provide the best value for price, specifications for ingredient salt should be written to describe clearly the functions that the material is expected to perform in your product. It is probably counterproductive to use a generalized specification. The Morton Salt Company, in one of its bulletins, has provided guidelines for criteria to be used in selecting the right salt. Table 6.5 contains this information in slightly modified form.

BIBLIOGRAPHY

ADAMS, M. E. 1983. Salt. Proc. Am. Soc. Bakery Engineers *1983*, 152-155

AMIRTHARAJAH, A. 1990. Coagulation: Rejuvenation for a classical process. Water Eng. Mgmt. *137*, No. 12, 25-27

ANON. 1962. Drinking water standards. U.S. Public Health Serv. Publ. *956*

ANON. 1972. Vitamin fortified toppings for fried snacks. Morton Salt Co. Tech. Serv. Bull 72-5 A

ANON. 1975. Standard Methods for the Examination of Water and Wastewater, 15th Edition. American Public Health Association, Washington, DC

ANON. 1979A. Methods for the chemical analysis of water and wastes. Environ. Prot. Agency Bull. *EPA 600/4-79-020*

ANON. 1979B. National secondary drinking water regulations. Fed. Reg. *44* (140)42195-42202

ANON. 1980. Interim primary drinking water regulations. Fed. Reg. *45* (168) 57332-57357

ANON. 1985. Rapid techniques for analyzing sodium. Prepared Foods *154*, No. 4, 163-164, 166

ANON. 1986. How to avoid the "salty-not salty" syndrome. Dairy Field *196*, No. 5, 42, 66

ANON. 1989. The Water Book. Barnstead-Thermolyne Corp., Dubuque, IA

ANON. 1990. Trick of the tongue. Scientific American *262*, No. 5, 80-81

BALULESCU, L. 1985. An automated ion-selective electrode method for salt determination in foods. Food Technol. *39*, No. 7, 38-40

BEAUCHAMP, G. K. 1987. The human preference for excess salt. Am. Scientist *78*, No. 1, 27-33

BEAUMANN, W. H. 1983. Personal communication. Everpure, Inc., Westmont, IL

BEST, D. 1989. Compensating for sodium: the low-salt solution. Prepared Foods *158*, No. 2, 97-98

BRIGHTON, T. B., and DICE, C. M. 1931. Increasing the purity of common salt. Ind. Eng. Chem. *23*, 336-339

BROOKE, M. M. 1939. Survey of basic work on the effects of various minerals on fermentation. Proc. Am. Soc. Bakery Engineers *1939*, 84-86

BROWN, E. R. 1939. The effect of minerals on baking, using sponge and straight doughs. Proc. Am. Soc. Bakery Engineers *1939*, 88-91

COLLINS, J. J. 1978. Water as an ingredient. Proc. Am. Soc. Bakery Engineers *1978*, 36-41

COTRUVO, J. A., PERLER, A. H., BATHIJA, B. L. 1989. Drinking water analysis regulatory report. Environmental Lab *1*, No. 3, 22, 25-27, 46

DUBOIS, D. K., BLOCKCOLSKY, D., and DREESE, P. 1984. Effect of salt level on processing and flavor of white pan bread. Am. Inst. Baking Res. Dept. Tech. Bull. *6*, No. 8

DUNN, J. A. 1941. Salt and water. Proc. Am. Soc. Bakery Engineers *1941*, 70-71

FABIAN, F. W., and BLUM, H. B. 1943. Relative taste potency of some basic food constituents and their competitive and compensatory action. Food. Res. *8*, 179-183

FAUST, S. D., and ALY, O. M. 1983. Chemistry of Water Treatment. Butterworth Publishers, Woburn, MA

FORTMANN, K. 1967. Theory of mixing. Proc. Am. Soc. Bakery Engineers *1967*, 64-70

GILLETE, M. 1985. Flavor effects of sodium chloride. Food Technol. *39*, No. 6, 47-52

HAAS, L. W. 1927. Water in baking. Proc. Am. Soc. Bakery Engineers *1927*, 80-81

HESTER, A. S., and DIAMOND, H. W. 1955. Salt manufacture. Ind. Eng. Chem. *47*, 627-683

HIRT, N. F. 1984. Troubleshooting in the bakery. Proc. Am. Soc. Bakery Engineers *1984*, 112-118

HOBBS, W. E. 1990. Don't forget to check your water. Prepared Foods *159*, No. 5, 149-150

INGOLS, R. S., WYCKOFF, H. A., KETHLEY, T. W., HOGDEN, H. W., FINCHER, E. L., HILDEBRAND, J. C., and MANDEL, J. E. 1953. Bactericidal studies of chlorine. Ind. Eng. Chem. *45*, 996-1000

JACKEL, S. 1982. Cereal chemists research salt and instant active dry yeast. Bakery Prod. Marketing *17*, No. 3, 126, 128

KAUFMANN, D. W. 1960. Sodium Chloride—The Production and Propeties of Salt and Brine. Van Nostrand Reinhold, New York, NY

KIRK, D. J. 1951. Effects of hardness and acidity of water and fermentation. Bakers Digest *25*, No. 6, 28-30, 34

LEUNG, H. K. 1981. Structure and properties of water. Cereal Foods World *26*, 350-352

LISK, I. 1989. Water treatment systems and equipment. Water & Wastes Digest *29*, No. 3, 10

LISK, I. 1991A. Disinfection gets complicated. Water & Wastes Digest *31*, No. 3, 10

LISK, I. 1991B. Package treatment plants for water/wastewater. Water & Wastes Digest *31*, No. 2, 8

LORENZ, W. T. 1990. Innovation in the water and wastewater markets. Water & Wastes Digest *30*, No. 5, 14

MANS, J. 1987. Disinfect water with ultraviolet light. Prepared Foods *156*, No. 3, 72-74

MATZ, S. A. 1965. Water in Foods. AVI Publishing Co., Westport, CT

MC FAUL, R. 1981. Quality water for the baking industry. Proc. Am. Soc. Bakery Engineers *1981*, 70-74

NIMAN, C. 1981. Salt in bakery products. Cereal Foods World *26*, 117-118

PICKERING, C. S. 1936. The interpretation of a water analysis and the effect of water on dough fermentation. Am. Soc. Bakery Engineers Bull. *104*

RANGER, C. B. 1989. New tools for testing water samples. Environmental Lab *1*, No. 3, 36-39

RICE, R. G. 1990. Ozone Drinking Water Treatment Handbook. Lewis Publishers, Boca Raton, FL

SIMPSON, R. A. 1954. Tailored salts provided many plus values. Food Eng. *26*, No. 7, 78-79

SKOVHOLT, O. 1948. Water in baking. Bakers Digest *22*, No. 4, 65-66, 81

SNOEYINK, V. L., and JENKINS, D. 1980. Water Chemistry. John Wiley & Sons, New York, NY

STRIETELMEIER, D. M. 1974. A new incentive for controlling salt content. Snack Food *63*, No. 10, 36-38

STRIETELMEIER, D. M. 1986. Personal communication. Morton Salt Co., Chicago, IL

STUCKI, S. (Editor) 1988. Process Technologies for Water Treatment. Plenum Press, New York, NY

SWANSON, A. T. 1966. The effect of water on the fermentation process. Proc. Am. Soc. Bakery Engineers *1966*, 48-57

TATE, C. H. 1991. Latest study finds utilities satisfied with ozone. Water Eng. Mgmt. *138*, No. 2, 24-25

THAYER, A. M. 1990. Water treatment chemicals: Tigher rules drive demand. Chem. Eng. News *68*, No. 13, 17-18, 20-21, 24, 28, 30, 32-34

WARNE, S. 1986. Water treatment—the secret of UV. Food Manufacture *61*, No. 9, 59, 63

WEAVER, F. B. 1983. Water—the forgotten ingredient. Proc. Am. Soc. Bakery Engineers *1983*, 136-141

chapter seven

INGREDIENTS FROM MILK AND EGGS

INTRODUCTION

Eggs and milk are enriching ingredients that have been used in pastries for centuries. They were not so common in bread-type products, although certain specialty breads and rolls used for celebrations or on holidays are well known. In recent years, the improving effects of milk, especially, and eggs, to a lesser extent, have been made of in bread and bread rolls. Still more recently, concerns about the adverse health effects of the fats and cholesterol in these two kinds of ingredients have tended to reduce their use.

INGREDIENTS DERIVED FROM MILK

Federal Requirements for Specific Standardized Milk and Cream (Anon. 1991) describe "milk" as being the lacteal secretion, practically free from colostrum, obtained by the complete milking of one or more healthy cows. Milk that is in final form for beverage use shall have been pasteurized or ultrapasteurized and shall contain not less than 8.25% milk solids not fat and not less than 3.25% milkfat. Milk may have been adjusted by separating part of the milkfat therefrom, or by adding thereto cream, concentrated milk, dry whole milk, skim milk, concentrated skim milk, or nonfat dry milk. Milk may be homogenized. There are also provisions allowing the addition of vitamin A, vitamin D, carriers for these vitamins, and certain flavoring ingredients if label declarations of these additives are made.

In addition to fresh fluid products, milk and its fractions can be concentrated, dried, and mixed with other substances to improve their utility for baking purposes or to achieve economic advantages. Bakers seldom use fresh whole milk. As ingredients, they are more likely to use lowfat dry milk, nonfat dry milk, sweetened condensed milk, sweetened condensed sweet milk, concentrated milk, evaporated milk, evaporated skim milk, dry whole milk, and dry cream, for all of which there are Federal Standards given in the same regulations cited above. Other, more modified, derivatives of milk are used by bakers—cheese and whey being examples.

There are Federal Standards of Identity for many types of cheese, but there are also on the market many cheese varieties and mixtures of dried cheese with other ingredients that are not standardized. Whey (in dried form) is a common bakery ingredient, either by itself or combined with other materials that are supposed to complement its functions. Consult 7 CFR 58 (Anon. 1991) for Standards for Grades of Whey and other dairy products.

Composition of Milk

Milk is a biologically derived commodity and varies in its properties according to the breed of cow, geographical location of the herd, climatic conditions, composition of feedstuffs, and other factors. The principal constituents of milk are butterfat, milk protein, lactose, minerals, and water. Most states establish a minimum either for total solids or for milk solids not fat. Dairy products other than milk may also be subject to regulation of fat and solids content, depending on the state. If the food is introduced into interstate commerce, it must meet federal standards as well.

The principal proteins of milk are casein, lactalbumin, and lactoglobulin. These should be regarded as classes of proteins rather than as single molecular species. Casein is the structure-forming, water-binding protein. When coagulated by acids or enzymes, it forms the basis for virtually all cheeses. When casein is removed from skim milk, it leaves behind the whey proteins.

Lactose is the only carbohydrate present in milk in any appreciable quantity. There are usually traces of glucose, galactose, and sucrose. Lactose is a reducing disaccharide containing glucose and galactose moieties. It is considerably less soluble than either glucose or sucrose, and it is also less sweet than these sugars, being rated by some investigators as being only about 16% as sweet as sucrose.

Milk fat is a mixture of triglycerides, with less than 1% of diglycerides present as intermediates in the milk fat synthesis process. The triglyceride portion is relatively complex, containing over 60 different fatty acids. The presence of appreciable amounts of fatty acids with ten carbon atoms or less, together with the presence of hydroxy and keto fatty acids, adds to the complexity of the milk fat system and gives it properties that are distinctly different from other fats. In addition to triglycerides, the lipid portion of milk contains small quantities of lecithin, cephalin, and probably other phospholipids, as well as cholesterol, fat-soluble vitamins, etc.

Table 7.1. AVERAGE VALUES FOR MILK MINERAL CONSTITUENTS[1]

Constituent	Content	Number of samples
Calcium	1.23	824
Magnesium	0.12	759
Phosphorus	0.95	829
Sodium	0.58	491
Potassium	1.41	472
Chlorine	1.19	1579
Sulfur	0.30	80
Citric acid	1.60	307

[1] Adapted from a compilation by Corbin and Whittier (1965). Concentrations in grams per liter of whole milk.

Milk ash contains seven major components. Many more minerals are present in trace amounts (Table 7.1). The primary salts of milk are the chlorides, phosphates, and citrates of calcium, magnesium, sodium, and potassium. From functional and nutritional viewpoints, calcium and phosphorus are the most important minerals of milk and exist mostly as calcium salts or complexes with phosphorus. The distribution of phosphorus in milk is 18% esterified to the various caseins, 7% as organic esters such as sugar phosphates, 1.5% in phospholipids, 38.5% as colloidal calcium phosphate, and 35% in the form of soluble phosphate salts (Harper and Hall 1976).

The mineral constituents of milk play important roles in the coagulation of proteins during heat processing. Calcium and magnesium facilitate the precipitation of proteins while phosphates and citrates tend to protect them or keep them in suspension during sterilization procedures or other heat treatments. It is common practice to stabilize milk that is going to be canned or otherwise heat-shocked by adding, for example, disodium phosphate or citric acid.

Milk contains trace amounts of numerous organic substances, many of which have unknown significance. They are probably either (1) intermediates in the biosynthesis of major milk components, (2) products of degradation by enzymes normally accompanying milk or elaborated by bacteria that have contaminated the milk, or (3) components carried through from the feed consumed by the cows. The materials derived from feed or enzymatic reactions are frequently associated with undesirable flavors and include mercaptans, sulfides, and a wide variety of carbonyl compounds.

On either a wet weight basis or a caloric content basis, milk is not a particularly good source of vitamins (see Table 7.2). The water-soluble vitamins present in more than trace amounts are thiamin, riboflavin, niacin, pyridoxine, pantothenate, biotin, folic acid, choline, ascorbic acid, inositol, and vitamin B_{12} (Posati and Orr 1976).

Types of Milk Ingredients

Fluid milk products.—The fluid milk products of commerce include whole milk, skim milk, buttermilk, cream, and whey. They are characterized by containing relatively large percentages of water and so they are bulk and more expensive to store and ship than are the dried equivalents. In addition, they are quite perishable and must be kept under refrigeration and used within a short time of collection. Because of these disadvantages, they become relatively high-cost ingredients even though their base price may seem low. Some bakers have been able to utilize nearby sources of fluid milk and cream, where local supplies are plentiful and reliable, and delivery can be made in a timely manner. Composition and organoleptic quality of fresh liquid milk products can be expected to vary more than for concentrated and dry ingredients made from milk.

Table 7.2. VITAMINS IN FRESH MILK[1]

Vitamin	Concentration
Vitamin A	0.34
Carotenoids	0.38
Vitamin D	23.6
Vitamin E	0.6
Vitamin K	1000.
Ascorbic acid	16.0
Biotin, total	0.035
Choline	130.0
Choline, free	40.0
Folic acid	0.0023
Inositol, total	130.0
Inositol, free	60.0
Nicotinic acid	0.85
Pantothenic acid	3.5
Pyridoxine	0.48
Riboflavin, total	1.57
Thiamin, total	0.42
Thiamin, free	0.23
Vitamin B-12	0.0056

[1] From a compilation of Corbin and Whittier (1965).
Concentrations expressed in mg per liter, except
vitamin D is in USP units per liter and vitamin K
is in Dam-Glavinal units per liter.

Concentrated milk products.—This class of ingredients includes whole milk, skim milk, buttermilk, and whey from which a major portion of the water has been removed, but which still contain enough moisture to give some fluidity to the finished product. These ingredients are referred to as "condensed" if partial dehydration is the only change involved, "sweetened condensed" if sucrose has been added and water removed, and "evaporated" if water has been removed and the product canned and sterilized.

In concentrated milk products, the increased total solids content plus the added sugar (in the sweetened versions) result in finished products that have useful storage lives varying from weeks to months. Being concentrated, they also occupy considerably less storage space, weigh less per unit of active ingredient, and can be economically transported.

Concentrated milk products do undergo deteriorative changes in storage, however. The protein can gel, lactose can crystallize, browning reactions can occur, and microbiological spoilage is possible. For these reasons, refrigeration of the material, rather close scheduling of deliveries, and careful inventory control are required if quality problems are to be minimized. Concentrated milk products are viscous fluids that are adaptable to bulk handling and liquid metering operations.

Cheese and cream are concentrated in the sense that butterfat and/or nonfat solids have been increased per unit of finished product weight. In commercial terminology, however, they are not usually included in this category.

Dried milk products.—Dried milk products are based on the raw materials described under "Fluids," but they have had nearly all of their moisture removed and are in powdered or granular form. The commercial usage of these materials far exceeds the industrial consumption of fluid milk and milk concentrates, at least so far as bakery ingredients are concerned. They occupy a minimum of storage space per unit of active ingredient and have good storage stability at ordinary temperatures. These advantages lead to dependability and uniformity of supply, less critical inventory control, uniformity of quality at time of use, and relatively stable costs.

Dried skim milk, or milk solids not fat (NFMS), is certainly the predominant item of commerce in this category. The three principal stages of converting skim milk into NFMS are: (1) preheating of the fluid milk; (2) condensing the liquid; and (3) drying. Other treatments such as agglomerating can precede or following the basic process. Variations of conditions existing in any of these treatments can change the characteristics of the finished material. Adjustment of time and temperature in the preheating step is the most common technique for modifying the qualities of the dried milk in a desired direction. The primary effect of these changes in processing conditions is a modification of the status of the protein molecules.

When produced under optimum conditions, milk will incur very little additional heat damage during the drying process. Milk powder prepared under these conditions is almost completely soluble/dispersible and has a mild flavor and light color.

Dry whole milk contains not less than 26% milk fat and not more than 4% moisture. Both spray- and roller-dried types are available. As with most other dried milk products, food-grade dried whole milk is available in Standard Grade and the higher quality Extra Grade. Dry whole milk is subject to rancidity development and stocks should be stored, controlled, and rotated with great care. In many bakery applications, especially where the ingredient is to be mixed into a dough, dry whole milk can generally be replaced by appropriate combinations of butter and NFMS.

As a first approximation, whey can be regarded as skim milk from which the casein has been removed. Commercially, whey is the liquid residue remaining from the cheesemaking process. Although whey was originally a roller-dried product, virtually all whey drying is now done in spray equipment. There are acid wheys that are derived from cottage and cream cheese operations, regular or sweet wheys that are by-products of cheddar and Swiss cheese manufacture, and modified wheys containing additives such as casein and soy proteins. In addition to the usual milk constituents, wheys may contain processing additives remaining from the cheese-making operation—e.g., coloring materials.

Sweet whey has a maximum titratable acidity of not more than 0.16%, and an ash alkalinity of not more than 225 ml of 0.1N per 100 grams. The acidity of whey and whey products may be adjusted by the addition of safe and suitable pH-adjusting ingredients (Clark 1986).

Dried whey contains about 12% protein, and this protein has high nutritional quality. The remainder of the product is mostly lactose which can improve crust color and add slightly to the sweetness of products containing it. There is also a considerable amount of mineral matter in whey, and it can be detected as a salty or metallic flavor if the concentration is high enough in the finished food. Whey proteins have very adverse effects on bread doughs and other developed doughs, causing stickiness and loss of strength. These effects can be overcome, or at least substantially reduced, by adequate heat treatment of the whey before it is dried.

The chief reason for using dried whey instead of NFMS is the economic advantage although, in a few situations, improvements in organoleptic properties can result from using whey. It does not possess as much water-binding or toughening action as MSNF but it is more effective, gram for gram, in promoting browning reactions. Its rather low solubility and the reduced sweetness as compared to sucrose can be helpful in a few cases. The flavor contributions of whey and skim milk are different; this can be either advantageous or undesirable. The high mineral content of whey can contribute an excess of salt-like or mineral flavor to products containing substantial amounts of the ingredient, but it is not effective as a salt substitute.

Modified wheys usually are dried materials made from whey in which the protein content has been increased by reverse osmosis, gel filtration, coprecipitation, or other means. Lactose and/or mineral content is reduced by the treatment, and there are changes in the proportions of other constituents. Singer et al. (1988) give a good, brief summary of the methods by which whey concentrates can be formed. These ingredients can be useful in improving protein content and other nutritional properties of bakery foods. Their functional properties may also be important in certain applications.

According to USDA specifications, dry buttermilk product (made by the spray process or the atmospheric roller process) is the product resulting from drying the liquid derived from churning milkfat from whey, or milkfat from whey commingled with sweet cream, or a commingling of the liquid product derived from such following churning. The product shall have been pasteurized either before or during the process of manufacture at a temperature of 161°F for 15 seconds or an equivalent in bacterial destruction. Dry buttermilk product contains less than 30% protein—the label on the container must specify its minimum protein content. Butterfat content shall not be less than 4.5%. It is the butterfat content that makes this ingredient particularly desirable to manufacturers who wish to make claims based on the total butterfat content of a product.

There are two kinds of dried buttermilk; regular and high acid. High acid buttermilk has a distinctive flavor that may or may not be desirable, depending on the product in which it is used. The lactic acid it contains (about 5%) will react with sodium bicarbonate in a chemically leavened system, causing loss of leavening power unless the quantity of soda is adjusted to compensate for the loss. Dried buttermilk is generally cheaper than nonfat milk solids although the difference in price fluctuates according to supply and other market conditions.

Other dried products that are used to a limited extent in the baking industry are malted milk powder, chocolate crumb, dried cream, and dried sour cream. Dried yogurt also seems to be available.

Dried cream designates dried milk products containing 40% to 70% milk fat. Most of the commercial products fall into the range of 50% to 60% fat. It can be spray dried either by conventional methods or by foam drying techniques. The latter process is said to give products with less heat damage, a "drier" (i.e., less greasy) body and texture, and superior flowability. Dried creams provide a simple means for introducing butterfat into doughs and batters and may be useful in icings and frostings.

Foam spray drying is recommended for sour cream to avoid the discoloration that often occurs when this material is dehydrated by other methods. It can be used in doughs, batters, and frostings although, as a rule, the "fresh" undried material is preferred if a good source can be found, since desirable volatiles are lost in the drying process. Yogurt, which has some similarities to buttermilk and sour cream, can also be dried and used as a flavor.

Milk Protein Concentrate

Protein concentrates can be prepared from milk or its fractions by various chemical and physical methods. These ingredients are occasionally used in bakery foods because of their improving action on certain qualities or to enhance the nutritional value of the food.

Acid casein is made by adjusting fluid skim milk to a pH of about 4.6 by adding mineral acid or by lactic fermentation. The casein curd that forms is separated, washed, and dried. Acid caseins contain relatively low amounts of calcium and phosphate ions that are solubilized during the pH adjustment and carried over in the whey.

Rennet, a preparation of the proteolytic enzyme chymosin, can also cause casein precipitation. This is the same reaction used in most cheese manufacture. The protein curd is isolated, washed, and dried somewhat like the acid casein, but it has a pH of about 7.1 and a calcium-phosphate complex is retained in it. To solubilize this form of dried casein, the calcium must be sequestered by adding, for example, trisodium phosphate.

Caseinates are made by dissolving casein, using alkalies or sequestering agents as needed, and drying the resulting solution. Sodium caseinates are probably the most common form of this ingredient, and they can be dispersed in water to form translucent solutions with high viscosity and excellent water-binding properties. Calcium caseinates form opaque solutions with low viscosity but good whitening power. They are widely used in coffee whiteners.

Whey protein concentrates, previously mentioned, are separated from lactose, soluble ions, and some other unwanted constituents of whey by ultrafiltration or use of other methods (Chaveron and Neumann 1989). Protein levels of the dried materials vary, with commercial products mostly falling in the 35% to 80% range. Generally, whey protein concentrates are soluble over a wide pH range and gel when heated.

Lactalbumin is a preparation of whey proteins that have been coagulated by heat. In a typical process, liquid whey is heated to about 194°F and the protein particles centrifuged out, washed, and dried. Lactalbumin is insoluble under most conditions encountered in food preparation.

Whey proteins can be co-precipitated with casein under certain conditions. Heat, calcium addition, and pH adjustment may be needed. The precipitate is separated, washed, and dried in the usual sequence. These preparations are not used much in bakery products (Swartz and Wong 1985).

Dairy Blends and Milk Replacers

There have appeared on the market many spray-dried blends of milk constituents that are intended to be substituted in bakery formulas for nonfat dry milk. These blends are made up of various combinations of caseinates, whey, modified whey, soy protein, and corn syrup solids, as well as additives intended to improve drying properties or functional characteristics. Whey often predominates in the list of ingredients, because of the cheapness of this raw material. Simple blends of the separately dried ingredients are also being offered.

Nearly all of these substitutes are powders; few, if any, are liquids. They can be blended as powders or dehydrated from liquid mixtures. Stahel (1982) categorized this type of ingredient as either dairy blends or milk substitutes. Dairy blends are combinations of dairy ingredients used to provide functionality equivalent to nonfat dry milk. Frequently used components are skim milk, sweet cream buttermilk, whey, caseinates, defatted soy flour, soy protein concentrate, and whey protein concentrates. The lowest poriced all-dairy milk replacer would be sweet dairy whey, but this substitute would be very different in many of its functions from nonfat dry milk. Dairy substitutes are products designed to provide functionality similar to dairy ingredients while containing either little or none of these materials. For example, a half-and-half mixture of soy flour and whey would yield a blend containing about 31% protein.

Because of the diversity in composition of "blends," it is impossible to generalize on their usefulness. Flavor can be a problem, because caseinates (especially) can contribute stale or other off-flavors that greatly reduce the acceptability of the baked product.

Cheese

Cheese is used in the bakery as an essential ingredient in cheese cake and cheese Danish. It is an almost essential part of the topping for pizza. It is a popular flavor for snack crackers. In some areas, cheddar-flavored bread and rolls attract a limited but devoted clientele. Possibly, cheese could be used more widely than it now is as a flavor for different kinds of bakery foods.

A listing of cheese varieties with their physical and organoleptic characteristics was published by Sanders (1953), and thorough descriptions of the production methods and quality factors have been given by Kosi-kowski (1966) for many kinds of cheeses. Although it would not be appropriate to give a lengthy survey of these subjects in the present volume, some general information should be valuable to the bakery technologist in the event that the basic ingredients must be used in formulas.

Experts say there are perhaps 18 different kinds of cheese, although hundreds of different names have been applied. These basic types are brick, Camembert, Cheddar, cottage, cream, Edam, Gouda, hand, Limburger, Neufchatel, Parmesan, Provolone, Roman, Roquefort, sapsago, Swiss, Trappist, and whey cheese. Cheese can be classified by other systems, as the one based on texture: (1) very hard (grating) cheese ripened by bacteria, such as Parmesan; (2) hard cheese ripened by bacteria, but without eyes, such as Cheddar; (3) hard cheese ripened by bacteria, with eyes, such as Swiss; (4) semisoft ripened principally by bacteria, such as brick; (5) semisoft ripened by bacterial surface microorganisms, such as Limburger; (6) semisoft ripened principally by blue mold in the interior, such as Roquefort; (7) soft ripened, such as Camembert; and (8) Unripened, such as Neufchatel.

Two factors to be considered when selecting the cheese component of a bakery formula are the degree of ripeness and the quality of flavor. Objective tests for these factors are of questionable validity. It would seem to be desirable for the quality assurance person to compare samples from new shipments to samples from previous shipments that have been maintained in a frozen and sealed condition.

Powdered cheese.—Instead of using natural cheese, which is perishable and varies widely from lot to lot in color and flavor, it is customary for bakers to use powdered cheese flavors. These may consist entirely of dehydrated and ground natural cheese, but more often they contain a minor amount of cheese supplemented with dried buttermilk, acid or sweet whey powder, artificial flavors and colors, etc. Cheese powders are generally made by spray drying an emulsion of cheese and other ingredients. Spray drying of cheese can be performed by regular, foam, vacuum, and silo processes (Hedrick 1981). Often, a combination of medium and aged cheddar cheeses are used. The liquid slurrying medium is often water, but sweet or acid whey, buttermilk, and sweet or acid skim milk have been employed for this purpose.

Table 7.3. COMPOSITION OF MILK AND MILK DERIVATIVES

Product	Water	Fat	Protein	Carbo-hydrate	Ash
Fluid whole milk	87.4	3.5	3.5	4.9	0.7
Fluid skim milk	90.5	0.1	3.6	5.1	0.7
Cream, 30% butterfat	63.4	30.0	2.5	3.6	0.5
Butter, salted	15.5	81.0	0.6	0.4	2.5
Buttermilk	90.5	0.1	3.5	5.1	0.8
Cheddar cheese	37.0	32.2	25.0	2.1	3.7
Cheese whey	93.2	0.3	0.9	5.1	0.5
MSNF	3.5	1.0	35.6	52.0	7.9
Dried buttermilk	3.5	5.0	34.7	49.0	7.8
Dried whey	6.2	1.2	12.5	72.4	7.7
Condensed whole milk	70.0	8.5	7.8	11.9	1.8
Condensed skim milk	70.0	0.2	11.1	15.2	2.5
Evaporated milk	73.7	7.9	7.0	9.9	1.5
Sweetened condensed whole milk*	27.9	8.6	7.7	54.2	1.6
Malted milk	2.6	8.3	14.7	70.8	3.6

* 42% added sucrose.

Table 7.3 contains information on the composition of a number of milk products, obtained from various sources. Data are based on the "as is" weight as 100%.

Quality Tests for Milk and Milk Products

Each type of dairy ingredient has its own specification. There are certain quality tests that are common to all (or most) of these, however. These tests involve analyses of components, which are useful for all food manufacturers, and tests of functionality, which are of particular interest to bakers. In the following discussion, some of the most important of these tests will be discussed briefly. For complete details on applying the test, the original references must be consulted.

Butterfat.—Commercially, the butterfat content of most liquid dairy products is determined either by the Babcock test or the so-called Mojonnier determination. The Babcock test has been around for several decades, but procedural details and equipment have been modernized from time to time. It is very sensitive to small variations in operator technique, and it gives results that are not exactly the same as those obtained from the Mojonnier test (Bradley 1986). The test includes a volumetric measurement of the fat present in a previously weighed or measured portion of the fluid after the digestion of milk proteins by sulfuric acid.

Mojonnier determinations involve the ether extraction of butterfat from a measured sample, separating the ether solution and evaporating the solvent, and weighing the dry fat.

Since milkfat (butterfat) is usually the most valuable milk constituent pricing of any dairy product is strongly influenced by its fat content.

Moisture.—Vacuum oven techniques, in which samples are dried to constant weight, are the most widely accepted methods for determining moisture content, but there are more rapid methods that may often be used where convenience and speed are important and official accuracy is not required. These include lactometry, toluol distillation, and infrared drying.

The lactometer is a form of hydrometer or density bob calibrated to read in terms of the specific gravity of fluid milk products. Under constant temperature conditions, fluid milk products of known fat content will vary in specific gravity depending on their solids-not-fat and (by difference) their water content. Lactometer measurements are commonly used for quality control in the production of fluid and concentrated milk products.

The toluol method for moisture determination is based on evaporation of water from a known weight of dried milk product. The vapor is condensed and measured volumetrically. Toluol is used as a heat transfer medium and extractant because it forms with water an azeotrope having a boiling point of about 185°F. This is the commercial test commonly used for moisture determinations of dried milk. Moisture contents above about 4% will cause rapid flavor deterioration, and possibly browning and lumping, in dried milk products. Low moisture content is a paramount factor in allowing maximum stability in these products.

There are several forms of equipment that rely on infrared heating of powdered dairy products to drive off the moisture. The balance pan and sample holder are often combined in these devices. They have the advantage of convenience, but great care must be taken to avoid heat degradation of the sample, which would lead to high readings.

Acidity.— Virtually all fresh milks are slightly acidic. The acidity is measured by determining the quantity of a standard alkali solution required to neutralize the acidity in a given quantity of product. The value so obtained is expressed as a percentage of titratable acidity calculated as lactic acid. Acidities above those known to be normal for any specific milk product are indicative of bacterial decomposition, while those below normal indicate that some neutralization chemical has been applied at a prior stage in the product's history.

Bacteriological quality.—The bacteriological quality of milk products can be estimated by several techniques. Three procedures that have considerable popularity are reduction tests, microscopic clump counts, and standard plate counts. Reduction tests for bacterial activity can be applied to raw fluid milks. Results are reported as hours "reduction time" required for methylene blue or resazurin dyes to be reduced to a colorless state or intermediate hues. The microscopic clump count involves the staining and counting of numbers of bacteria in an aliquot of milk. Counts are usually expressed as clumps per milliliter (for fluids) or per gram (for powders). Standard plate counts are the most widely used industry technique for estimating the living bacteria in raw or pasteurized fluid, concentrated, or dried milk products. Specifically, this test estimates the number of organisms that will grow in standard plate count media at 92°F.

There are several other tests for bacterial quality that focus on specific organisms. The coliform test, thermophilic spore count, and blood agar count are examples. Specifications relating to such characteristics are often worked out between the supplier and the purchaser.

Flavor and odor of all sweet milk products should be bland, slightly sweet, and free from acid, feed, and other foreign flavors. Flavor and odor of dried dairy products is usually determined after reconstitution. With certain highly heated milk powders, cooked flavors of varying degrees are expected and may even be considered desirable. Whey, fluid or dried, will have relatively strong odors and flavors, and it is up to the purchaser to specify those notes that are unacceptable. Describing these flavor notes is difficult, and quantification nearly impossible. Comparison to standard samples, which have been stored in the freezer since receipt, is a practical alternative.

The scorched particle test, formerly referred to as a sediment test, involves the reconstitution of a specific quantity of milk powder, which is then filtered through a cotton pad of 1.25 inch diameter to determine the number of discolored milk particles or any other extraneous material. Modern drying techniques should produce powders containing a minimum of scorched particles.

The solubility index test is performed by reconstituting known quantities of powders under carefully controlled conditions and, after centrifuging to accelerate the separation of insoluble material, measuring the quantity of precipitate in the bottom of the centrifuge tube. Solubility index is a measure of the relative quantity of destabilized milk protein (particularly casein) in dried milk powders. A high solubility index can be caused by excessive heat in drying, developed acidity in a raw milk supply, or physiologically unstable milk. Roller process powders are characterized by high solubility indices while spray process powders characteristically have low solubility numbers.

Dried milk powders used as dough ingredients must have certain qualities beyond the characteristics required for Extra Grade Powder. Whey protein denaturation and its associated chemistry, water absorption, and, of course, overall baking performance are among the special qualities that will be required of powders procured for bakery use.

The Harland-Ashworth whey protein test is applied to both spray- and roller-dried NFMS which will contain on the average 9.12 mg of serum protein per gram of solids. The principle of the test is the comparison of turbidity of samples heated under standardized conditions, but the procedure is too lengthy and complex to reproduce here. Since denaturation of this whey protein fraction is associated with good baking quality, a high degree of denaturation and a low level of undenatured serum protein is desirable for NFMS intended for use in developed doughs. Opinions vary among technologists as to the exact values required in the baking industry. From experience, it is apparent that undenatured whey protein values of 1.0 mg per gram or lower are generally very adequate, and values of less than 2.0 mg per gram are satisfactory for most bread baking purposes.

Farinograph mixing tests are used to estimate the "absorption" of dairy products. Doughs mixed with and without the addition of the dairy product are tested in the farinograph, and the amount of extra water required to bring the consistency of the milk dough to a standard height on the chart is converted to absorption. Low-heat NFMS will exhibit absorptions well below 40%, while high-heat powders will vary from about 40% to as high as 60%. Values of 45% to 50% are common for high-heat powders. Values of 50% to 55% represent spray process powders of relatively high absorption.

Next to actual tests in the plant, laboratory-scale baking tests come closest to providing definitive evaluations of a dairy product's suitability for a given purpose. These tests have been standardized and the detailed procedures can be obtained from the American Dairy Products Institute.

INGREDIENTS FROM EGGS

Many bakery products contain no eggs, and the total amount of eggs used by bakeries must constitute a small percentage of the total weight of their ingredient procurements. Even so, eggs can have substantial effects on the flavor, color, and texture of bakery products. In some air-leavened items, such as angel food cakes or meringues, egg whites constitute a large part of the batter and form an indispensable part of the structure of the finished food, while whole eggs or egg yolks are important determinants of the physical and organoleptic properties of sponge cakes and chiffon cakes. In other types of baked products where eggs are only a small percentage of the total ingredients, they can still have significant effects on the structure, since the proteins and emulsifiers they contain greatly enhance the air-entrapment properties of batters and doughs. In the following discussion, "egg white" is regarded as being synonymous with "albumen," as is the common practice.

Eggs can make important contributions to the nutritional value of bakery products. Both egg yolks and egg whites contain nitrogenous compounds having very high protein efficiency ratios, allowing them to enhance the nutritional value of dessert type bakery products which would, in their absence, have limited nutritional justification. Some vitamins and minerals are also present in significant amounts. There is, however, a certain degree of popular prejudice against eggs because the yolks contain a fairly high level of cholesterol, which is thought by some medical people to have adverse effects on health, especially if ingested in excess of published guidelines and over long periods of time. On the other hand, studies by Margaret Flynn at the University of Missouri have indicated that blood cholesterol was not increased noticeably or was even lowered, in 85% of persons consuming three eggs per day (Bergquist 1987).

Functional Properties

The three physical properties of egg products that are of most importance to bakery formulators are foaming power, emulsification, and coagulation. These properties are uniquely combined in eggs, and many bakery products would be impossible to make in their present form if eggs were not available.

Whippability.—Foaming power is the ability of the ingredient to incorporate air in small bubbles and to maintain the bubbles or foam structure long enough so that the batter can be firmed up by the heat and dehydration of baking. Egg white proteins have the capacity to form a very stable foam. When egg whites are whipped, large areas of new surface area are formed and the protein molecules will unfold and spread as a monomolecular layer over the new surfaces. Proteins that change in this way have some properties similar to heat denatured proteins. In egg white foams, a relatively strong three-dimensional network of denatured proteins is formed, giving a structure with considerable stability. Dried egg whites that are employed for their foaming ability, as in angel cake batters, often are improved by the addition of a whipping aid such as sodium lauryl sulfate.

Food foams based on egg white have a tendency to separate, that is, the liquid phase tends to collect in droplets, pools, or layers. This phenomenon, which is especially observable in such things as soft meringues, is usually accompanied by shrinking, and perhaps cracking, of the foam portion. There are two interrelated mechanisms that cause the separation: the gel portion (coagulated egg protein) shrinks due to aggregation and dehydration of the protein molecules, and the liquid phase moves downward through the foam network in response to the force of gravity.

The shrinkage of baked egg white foams has obvious commercial disadvantages and there have been numerous attempts to prevent it, or at least to slow its development. Suggested methods usually involve the addition of some other hydrocolloid to the meringue formula. Modified starches can be helpful and, if used in moderation, do not have very noticeable effects on the mouthfeel of the baked product. Other gums, as well as pH modifiers, have been recommended for the same purpose.

The foaming of whole eggs and yolks is similar to the foaming of egg white, but additional factors enter the picture. There is a large amount of lipid present in yolks (and, of course, in whole eggs since they contain yolks), and these lipids must be in a highly emulsified state in order for the product to develop a stable foam. Processors who dry whole eggs or yolks have found that carbohydrates must be added to the liquid material if whipping power is to be maintained through the drying process. In any case, the potential specific volume attainable in batters using egg yolks or whole eggs as foaming agents is much less than that achievable using egg white foams.

Coagulation.—Egg products have good binding and thickening properties in batters and doughs because their proteins bind water and, perhaps, establish interlacing networks of hydrogen-bonded molecules. They form more or less permanent foam-like structures in baked products because their proteins coagulate during heating—a phenomenon familiar to anyone who has ever fried an egg.

The ability of eggs to coagulate into a firm gel-like mass upon the application of mild heat is one of their most important properties. The different proteins in eggs denature and coagulate over a fairly wide range of temperatures, from about 135° to 180°F, and this is the reason egg white can furnish the framework for the very tender and highly aerated structure of an angel food cake. When the cake is baked, some of the proteins will begin to coagulate at the lower end of the temperature range, setting up the foam batter structure. This structure is elastic since all the proteins do not coagulate until the angel cake structure has expanded and set in its final form as the upper end of the critical temperature range is approached.

Emulsification.—The emulsifying properties of eggs reside principally in the yolk fraction although egg white does have some emulsifying ability. The current view is that lecithin, cholesterol, lipoproteins, and proteins are the emulsifying substances in egg yolk (Stadelman and Cotterill 1986). Proteins and lipoproteins are the most important emulsifying materials in whole eggs, and the emulsifying capability of whole eggs is not altered by changes in the fatty acid composition of the egg yolk. Workers in the field have concluded that the most efficient emulsifiers are mixtures and complexes, such as occur in egg yolk. Egg yolk is a very efficient emulsifier as shown by its long-time use in preparing mayonnaise, a stable oil-in-water emulsion having 65% to 75% oil content. Emulsions stabilized by egg yolk tend to be viscous and stable. They are not as stiff as a well-made meringue.

Composition

It would be overly optimistic to attempt to define a "typical" egg. For eggs entering commercial channels, there is a wide variability in total weight, proportion of white to yolk, and chemical composition. Conditions having an influence on some or all of these factors include storage time and condition, the hen's age, breed, and strain, environmental conditions including temperature, length of day, and many other such factors, and composition of the diet. The latter factor has a surprisingly large effect on, for example, the concentration of pigments, fatty acids, vitamins, and trace minerals.

Proportions of white and yolk.—It is apparent even from casual observation that the white and the yolk are not homogenous components but are, themselves, compound structures. This complexity causes difficulties in separating yolks from whites and in securing a uniform processed liquid egg. Liquid whole eggs and the frozen and dried products derived from them can vary in composition depending on the characteristics of the shell eggs used in the breaking operation, but average figures are given in Table 7.4. Some of the variation is the result of different proportions of white and yolk in eggs and may be affected by the genetics of the chicken and its nutritional history. Small eggs from pullets tend to have a lower proportion of yolk, while the small eggs laid by old hens have a greater proportion of yolk to white, as compared to larger eggs.

Table 7.4. COMPOSITION OF LIQUID AND DRIED EGG PRODUCTS

Component or test	"As is" composition in percent					
	Liquid egg white	Liquid egg yolk	Liquid whole egg	Dried egg white	Dried egg yolk	Dried whole egg
Solids	11.7	43.5	24.7	--	--	--
pH	9.0	6.6	7.6	7.0	6.6	8.5
Protein	10.1	14.5	11.5	80.5	31.8	46.0
Lipids	--	26.5	10.5	0.06	57.5	42.0
Free glucose	0.4	0.2	0.3	0.1	0.44	1.16
Ash	0.6	1.7	1.0	4.8	3.7	3.9
Moisture	--	--	--	7.5	4.5	4.5

Although contamination of yolk with a small amount of egg white has few practical disadvantages in bakery product formulation, accidental contamination of white with yolk during the breaking operation results in decreased whipping response when the ingredient is used in meringues, angel food cakes, and marshmallows. It is also possible that some yolk lipid migrates into the albumen during storage of intact eggs. There are other changes during storage that affect the proteins and, consequently, affect the foaming ability of the egg white. In spray-dried egg white, the intense shearing forces to which the fibrils of protein are subjected during the atomizing process may also affect whipping quality.

Microstructure of white and yolk.— Yolk has been described as a system of a variety of different kinds of particles suspended in a protein solution. When yolk is separated by high-speed centrifugation, the granules sediment, leaving a clear fluid supernatant called plasma. The plasma constitutes about 78% of the yolk and contains about 49% water, 40% lipid, 1.1% ash, and about 9% other materials (mostly proteins). The granules contain about 44% water, 19% lipids, 34% protein, and 3% ash. Granules are said to be composed of 70% alpha- and beta-lipovitellins, 16% phosvitin (a phosphoprotein), and 12% low-density lipoprotein.

Albumen has been described as a protein system of ovomucin fibers in an aqueous solution of numerous kinds of globular proteins. The relative proportions of these two categories of substances determine whether the albumen will be of the thick or thin type. Normally, the white as it exists in the intact egg can be seen to consist of an outer thin white, then proceeding inwardly, thick white, thin white, and chalaziferous layers (thick inner white). The relative proportions of these layers can vary greatly, depending upon numerous factors.

Lipids.—The lipids of egg, all of which are located in the yolk, are composed of glycerides and phospholipids in a ratio of approximately 2:1. About 30% of the fatty acids in the glycerides are saturated. The phospholipids, which are mainly responsible for the emulsifying properties of yolk, are made up of about 60% lecithin, 25% cephalin, and 15% "others." There is also a significant amount of cholesterol in egg yolk.

Because of the intense interest in egg lipids by nutritionists and the general population, a summary of the distribution of lipids and their components is given in Table 7.5. These data have been excerpted from "Eggs in Brief" (Anon. 1985). The data are based on a 60.9 g shell egg weight, with 55.1 g total liquid whole egg of which 38.4 g is white and 16.7 g is yolk. Egg white is not included in this table because it contains essentially no lipids.

Pigments.—Fat-soluble carotenoids in the lipid portion of lipoproteins are responsible for the yellow-orange color of yolk. These carotenoids are mostly xanthophylls, with minor amounts of carotenes. The intensity of yellow color in some egg-containing products—cakes, noodles, bread, etc.—is regarded by many consumers as a token of "richness" or nutritional quality. Yolk color is not, however, a reliable measure of the nutrient content of an egg. Eggs with pale yellow yolks can have as high a content of vitamins, proteins, and minerals as eggs with intensely colored yolks. Most food manufacturers prefer to buy egg yolks and whole eggs with uniform color so that their finished products do not vary in appearance. On the other hand, egg noodle producers desire egg yolks and whole eggs with the highest possible color to improve the appearance of their product.

The color of whole eggs and egg yolks depends to a very great extent on the plant pigments that are in the feed consumed by the chickens. Feed ingredients such as ground yellow corn, corn gluten meal, and alfalfa meal contain significant amounts of lutein, zeaxanthin, and cryptoxanthin, which are absorbed in the hen's digestive tract and then translocated to the ovary for deposition in the yolk as it is forming. The genetic capability of absorbing xanthophylls and depositing them in the yolk varies among individual hens. Also, other feed components (particularly fats and antioxidants) and the hen's condition affect the efficiency of pigment translocation. Therefore, color of the egg products may vary with the season, source, method of processing, and other factors. If the premium for dark yellow yolks is sufficiently high to justify the added cost, the egg producer may add feed supplements that contain large amounts of xanthophylls. Among these supplements are marigold petal meal and dried algae meal.

Table 7.5. LIPID DISTRIBUTION IN WHOLE EGG AND YOLK[1]

Component	Liquid whole egg	Liquid yolk
Fatty acids, g--		
--Saturated:		
Total	2.01	1.95
8:0	.027	.027
10:0	.082	.080
12:0	.027	.026
14:0	.022	.022
16:0	1.37	1.31
18:0	.462	.459
20:0	.022	.022
--Monounsaturated:		
Total	2.53	2.50
14:1	.005	.005
16:1	.214	.211
18.1	2.31	2.28
--Polyunsaturated:		
Total	.73	.72
18:2	.660	.650
18:3	.011	.014
20:4	.055	.051
Cholesterol, mg	264.	258.
Lecithin, g	1.27	1.22
Cephalin, g	.253	.241

[1] Weights related to one large egg. See text for details.

Carbohydrates.—About 0.4% to 0.5% glucose is present in egg albumen, and this represents virtually the entire amount of uncombined carbohydrate in eggs. There is about 0.5% of mannose and glucose chemically combined with glycoprotein. Yolks may contain as much as 1% of carbohydrate, but this is mostly in combined form, with only 0.2% as free glucose.

The small amount of glucose in dried egg white can lead to darkening and the development of off-flavors during storage as a result of the nonenzymatic browning (Maillard) reactions that occur between this reducing sugar and the amino groups of the proteins. In the manufacture of dried albumen or dried whole egg, glucose is removed either by fermentation (using pure strains of yeast or bacteria) or by enzymatic oxidation using a commercial preparation of enzymes. Albumen treated by these techniques is called "stabilized."

There is some glucose in liquid yolk (about half that in liquid white), but it is less of a storage problem in the dried yolk, as compared to dried white, perhaps because staling or spoilage usually occurs as a result of reactions other than non-enzymatic browning, and the odors, tastes, and colors resulting from these other reactions cover up changes involving glucose. Furthermore, because of the different percentages of solids in the liquid materials, dried yolk contains only about 0.4% glucose versus about 3.2% in dried unstabilized white. Stabilized yolks can be prepared by procedures similar to those used for stabilizing whites.

Vitamins and minerals.—Although egg white is low in vitamin content, except for riboflavin, yolk is a good source of many of these nutrients, particularly vitamins A, D, E, folic acid, biotin, and choline.

The mineral content of albumen is quite variable, being influenced by the hen's diet and age, as well as environmental factors such as temperature, season, lighting, etc. The main influence, however, is the composition of the feed. Among the elements found are sulfur, potassium, sodium, phosphorus, calcium, magnesium, and iron. There is about 1.1% "ash" in yolk. The major elements present are phosphorus, calcium, and potassium. These are present in free and combined forms, the phosphorus being present mainly as phospholipids. There seems to be no clear-cut relationship of mineral content with egg quality.

Pseudo-quality factors.—Color of the shell, whether brown or white, is not related to composition of the egg contents. "Organic" eggs and eggs from field-raised chickens do not differ in any significant way from ordinary commercial eggs. Fertile eggs are essentially the same as non-fertile eggs in all known chemical factors.

Standards of Identity and Quality

There is no federal definition or Standard of Identity for shell eggs, but 7 CFR 56, containing part of the Agricultural Marketing Act controls their interstate distribution. *U.S. Standard Grades and Weight Classes for Shell Eggs* and *Regulations Governing the Grading and Inspection of Egg Products* are quality guides in the absence of Standards of Identity.

Requirements for standardized egg products other than shell eggs are found in 21 CFR 160, current edition. The categories include: (1) dried eggs; (2) frozen eggs; (3) liquid eggs; (4) egg whites; (5) dried egg whites; (6) frozen egg whites; (7) egg yolks; (8) dried egg yolks; and (9) frozen egg yolks. "Liquid eggs" is regarded as a synomym for mixed eggs, liquid whole eggs, and mixed whole eggs. Frozen eggs can also be called frozen whole eggs or frozen mixed eggs. Dried eggs is the same as dried whole eggs. Egg whites is synonymous with liquid egg whites and liquid egg albumen; dried egg whites with egg white solids, dried egg albumen, and egg albumen solids. Egg yolks, liquid egg yolks, yolks, and liquid yolks are equivalent names, as are dried egg yolks and dried yolks. Frozen egg yolks is the same as frozen yolks. Details of these regulations will not be reproduced here. Many libraries have copies of the entire set of Code of Federal Regulations. Separate titles (in the case of food standards, Title 21) can be purchased from the Superintendent of Documents, Washington, DC and government book stores.

The standards allow certain additives to be mixed with standardized products provided the added substance is clearly described on the label. It is common practice to add whipping improvers to egg whites and to add caking preventatives to dried eggs, for example. Furthermore, manufacturers can (and do) offer nonstandardized egg products provided they do not identify them by the names set forth in 27 CFR 160.

Commercial Products

Bakeries can buy their ingredient eggs as eggs in the shell, in refrigerated liquid form, frozen, or dried.

Shell eggs.—Fresh eggs in the shell are normally sold on the basis of "cases" of 30 dozen eggs. The different size designations, as related to total weight of the eggs in a case of 360 eggs are: Jumbo, 56 lb; Extra Large, 50.5 lb; Large, 45 lb; Medium, 39.5 lb; Small, 34 lb; and Peewee, 28 lb. The approximate equivalent weights in ounces per dozen are 30, 27, 24, 21, 18, and 15, respectively. Price relationships of the different sizes are interesting; they change according to the season, geographical areas, temporary demand cycles, and for more obscure reasons. If the total net yield of whole egg per dollar is the important parameter, it will be necessary for the purchaser to compare the prices for the different sizes at the time of each procurement. Shell eggs may be graded for interior and exterior qualities by federal and state agencies, and by other services.

If eggs have been graded by the USDA, there will be an inspection shield on the container with an indication of the grade—AA, A, or B.

Purchasing and processing of shell eggs is a job for specialists, and bakeries should not attempt these operations unless very compelling circumstances exist. Egg breaking, separating, and pasteurizing are done by highly specialized and automated egg processing plants. To briefly summarize the unit operations, the eggs are first washed, then individually inspected by candling before being broken and separated by machine. Up to 24,000 eggs per hour can be processed by each egg breaking and separating machine. The liquid egg products must be pasteurized, the conditions for whole egg being a minimum of 140°F for at least 3.5 minutes.

Egg products.—In commercial practice, the term "egg products" refers to convenient forms of eggs processed for industrial, manufacturing, foodservice, and home use. In other words, shell eggs are not included in this classification. The industry classifies products as refrigerated liquid, frozen, dried, and specialty products.

Refrigerated liquid egg products are distributed by bulk tank-truck in quantities of 6,000 or 2,500 gallons, in 2,000-lb stainless steel containers equipped with a dedicated self-contained refrigeration units, in smaller returnable sanitary containers, in 30-lb cans, and in cartons containing 4, 5, 8, or 10 lb. Egg whites, egg yolks, and whole eggs as well as proprietary mixtures are distributed in this form. The terminology is somewhat inexact, particularly in the case of commercial egg yolk, which contains about 15% egg white. This contamination cannot be prevented in normal breaking operations because some white clings to the yolk during separation. High quality egg white has less than 0.03% yolk contamination. Whole egg is a mixture of yolk and white in the natural proportions (i.e., about one-third yolk and two-thirds white). Sometimes, specialty products are made by "fortifying" whole eggs with (usually) additional yolk.

A common container for frozen eggs to be used by bakers is a metal can with a friction-fit lid holding 30 lb of egg product. Containers other than the 30-lb tin, including unit containers designed to hold the exact amount of egg required for one batch of a specific formula are also being offered. These include 4-, 5-, 8-, and 10-lb pouches or waxed or plastic cartons. Among the varieties widely available are egg whites, whole eggs, whole eggs with yolks added, egg yolks, whole eggs with corn syrup added, whole eggs with yolks and corn syrup added, sugared egg yolks, salted egg yolks, and salted whole eggs. The carbohydrates and salt additives are intended to give smoothness to thawed whole eggs and fluidity to the thawed yolks, that otherwise tend to have a very thick gelatinous consistency.

Dried eggs for ingredient use are ordinarily packed in 25- or 50-lb boxes and 150-, 175-, and 200-lb drums. Among the varieties of dried egg products that can be obtained by food processors are spray-dried egg white solids, flake albumen, instant egg white solids, whole egg solids, stabilized (glucose-free) whole egg solids, whole egg solids with free-flow agent added, and blends of whole egg with additives such as extra yolk, sugar, corn syrup, or mixtures of these ingredients. In addition, dried egg products can be custom formulated for a specific use.

Most egg white solids will have been desugared; whole eggs and yolks are desugared if specified in the procurement document. Egg whites, egg yolks, whole eggs, and whole eggs "fortified" with yolks are available in dried or frozen form. There are also many combination products consisting of one or more of the egg fractions combined with additives such as salt, corn syrup, sugar, or defatted soy flour.

Specialty and imitation egg products.—Some companies offer so-called "egg replacers" to the bakery trade. These ingredients are usually cheaper and often have better storage properties than natural eggs. They may contain small percentages of eggs, but often consist primarily of fats and oils, emulsifiers, gums, flavors, and colors. If the emulsifying and texturizing properties of eggs are the only functions needed, egg replacers are probably worth testing, but they are of doubtful value in duplicating the thermal setting and structure-building properties of eggs (Ash 1979).

Conversion factors.—The question is frequently asked, "How do I convert a recipe (or formula) from shell eggs to dried eggs?" Other conversion factors are also of interest. These calculations assume greater difficulty when the technologist tries to convert a cookbook recipe to a form usable in the plant. The factors in Table 7.6 can be used, but it should be noted that the unit figures are approximate (i.e., valid to one significant figure only) and that refrigerated products are considered equivalent in composition to frozen products. These factors are only approximations. The amount of liquid egg removed from the shell in home preparation and in commercial processing can be expected to be different, but valid data on the home method as related to the egg requirements in cookbooks does not seem to be available. In fact, most cookbooks do not even specify egg size. Of course, both home and commercial results will differ from the yield obtained in laboratory tests where careful and complete removal of egg contents can be made.

It is possible to reconstitute dried egg products to their original moisture content before adding them to a mix, but it is more convenient (and for most purposes just as satisfactory) to use standard ratios. The recommended ratio to yield the equivalent of 4 lb of liquid whole eggs is 3 lb of water to 1 lb of whole egg solids. One part of dried yolk plus 1.25 parts of water is the approximate equivalent of 2.25 parts of fresh or frozen yolk. Addition of 7 lb of water to 1 lb of spray dried albumen yields 8 lb of liquid white.

Table 7.6. COMMERCIAL PRODUCT EQUIVALENT OF SHELL EGGS[1]

Product	Frozen product, pounds	Dried product, ounces	Grams of fresh* product	Number of shell eggs
Whole eggs	1	4.2	477	9
Yolks	1	7.3	462	22
Whites	1	1.9	448	14
Whole eggs	0.12	0.48	53	1
Yolk	0.05	0.36	21	1
White	0.07	0.13	32	1

[1] Adapted from Cotterill (1981). Conversions based on 61 gm shell egg (25.8 oz per doz) yielding 53 gm whole, 21 gm yolk, and 32 gm albumen per egg.
* Or refrigerated product.

Storage

A number of chemical and physical changes related to functional quality occur during the refrigerated storage of shell eggs. The albumen portion increases in pH from between 7.6 and 8.5 in a new laid egg to a maximum of about 9.7. The rate of increase is temperature-dependent and is caused by effusion of carbon dioxide through the pores of the shell. It has been established that the pH of albumen is controlled by an equilibrium between dissolved carbon dioxide, bicarbonate ion, carbonate ion, and carbon dioxide bound to protein. The pH of albumen exerts a substantial effect on the rheological properties of the gels formed as a result of cooking operations. Fresh egg yolks separated by normal commercial procedures will have a pH of about 6.4 to 6.6. This gradually increases during storage.

Both frozen and dried eggs deteriorate with time at a rate dependent upon the storage conditions. Initial quality, before freezing or drying, is very influential in determining the rate of storage deterioration, especially as far as the flavor of the product is concerned. Generally, frozen eggs retain their original properties better. Powdered eggs are unquestionably more convenient to use and store. Thawing an dispensing of frozen eggs can lead to sanitation problems. On the other hand, reconstitution and sequence of addition are critical factors in the use of dried eggs.

All dried egg products must be kept from contamination by moisture. For dried egg whites, room temperature storage is acceptable and probably even preferable to refrigeration. Dried egg white is stable for long periods of time if glucose has been removed, as is the case with virtually all these commercial products. Whipping ability actually improves with storage. As long as it is protected from moisture, dried albumen can be expected to retain good quality for several months, even when stored at room temperature. Normal rotation should, however, avoid the necessity for keeping this ingredient for such long periods of time.

Dried unstabilized whole eggs and yolk solids may be stored for several months if kept under refrigeration, while dried whole eggs and yolk with glucose removed before spray drying may be stored for several months without refrigeration. The "Tex" type products, in which corn syrup or sugar have been added to the liquid before drying, can be stored for relatively long periods of time at room temperature without signs of deterioration.

Freezer storage of dehydrated materials is not essential, but it does provide additional shelf life and maintains flavor quality better than cool storage. When large containers are received, it is usually considered good practice to repackage dried egg products in smaller sealable containers, because moving the containers in and out of the refrigerator to remove batch-sized portions can lead to an undesirable amount of condensation on the powder surface. Re-packaging is not necessary if the contents of a complete container are used up in a short time.

It should be emphasized again, that it is not good practice to keep any ingredient in storage for several months, even dehydrated or frozen products. Normal rotation and good procurement policies should maintain a constant turnover as two facets of good operating procedures.

Liquid whole eggs, whites, and yolks should be held at a temperature below 40°F. Shelf life and storage conditions should be based on recommendations of the supplier. Generally, these products will be pasteurized and delivered in sealed tanks. All fresh and thawed frozen products should be used within one or two days.

Bacteriology of Egg Products

Egg products are very susceptible to contamination by microorganisms, including some pathogenic species. These organisms can originate from the egg itself (especially from the egg exterior), from egg handlers, from equipment, from containers, from dispensing utensils, and from the air. If the liquid materials are held at room temperature, proliferation of bacteria or molds can occur very rapidly. Considerable progress has been made over the years in improving the microbiological quality of commercial egg products. Part of the impetus for this improvement has been the establishment of government regulations that require all egg products to be pasteurized or treated so they are rendered Salmonella-negative. It is also necessary that all egg products be inspected by the USDA.

In spite of the generally good quality of commercial egg products, it is important to establish and enforce bacteriological standards for egg ingredients used in the bakery. Reasonable standards include maximums of 10,000 viable bacteria per gram in all frozen and dried products except for frozen whites where a limit of 50,000 per gram is more realistic. Yeasts, molds, and coliforms should be restricted to less than ten per gram.

There has been much concern about contamination of egg products by *Salmonella*. This is an organism that can cause food poisoning, rarely fatal. As early as June 1, 1966, all egg products were ordered to be free of viable salmonellae when tested by a specific procedure. Although this regulation was highly commendable from a public health standpoint, its implementation caused certain difficulties to users of frozen and dried egg products. Whole egg and egg yolk can be pasteurized in high temperature-short time equipment with little loss of functionality, but treatment of albumen in a similar manner leads to deleterious changes in whipping quality. It was discovered that use of additives and modification in the conditions of heat treatment greatly reduced the loss of foam-forming ability. It is generally conceded, however, that treating egg whites to make them *Salmonella*-free causes some reduction in their response to whipping procedures.

There are three general methods for pasteurizing egg products. One method is particularly applicable to whole eggs. It is based on the application of carefully controlled heat for a given time (minimum of 60°C for at least 3.5 minutes). A slight reduction in viscosity of treated product is frequently observed. The hydrogen peroxide-catalase method is more suitable for egg whites. A quantity of hydrogen peroxide solution is added to the egg white, the mixture is heated to within the range 52° to 54°C for 3.5 minutes, then cooled. When the mixture is cool, catalase is added to remove any residual hydrogen peroxide. A slight reduction in viscosity and some white clumps result. The third method is also suitable for egg whites. Aluminum sulfate and lactic acid are added, the eggs are heated to 60°C for at least 3.5 minutes and then cooled. There is a reduction in viscosity, some white clumps appear, and turbidity develops in the liquid phase.

The rapidity with which egg white can be whipped to the desired volume, the maximum specific volume of the foam, and the stability of the foam can be improved by certain additives. It has long been known that lowering the pH improves the functional properties of egg albumen. The type of acid used to accomplish this effect is a factor in the degree of improvement; that is, the anionic portion of the additive as well as the hydrogen ion concentration determines the effectiveness of the acid. Citric acid and lactic acid seem to be the preferred additives. When dry mixes are being formulated, phosphoric acid salts or tartaric acid salts are often used.

Surface-active agents also influence whipping properties. Triethyl citrate and various anioni surface-active agents (e.g., some common detergents) are effective. Apparently, these additives act to partially overcome the effects of the traces of yolk as well as to increase the speed of surface denaturation, thus permitting the more rapid formation of a stiff foam.

Quality Control Tests

Even if the user does not intend to perform many quality control tests, it is advisable to present the egg supplier with specifications that can correctly assign responsibility if a quality problem arises.

Tests for protein, fat, total solids, and inorganic matter are common tests applied to egg products. Obviously odor, taste, and color of the product should closely approximate those of typical fresh eggs. For the baker who does not have facilities to make elaborate tests of the functional properties of each shipment of egg products he receives, a sensitive performance test based on the most critical recipe in his formula book might be devised. The next best solution is to buy from a reliable supplier and trust in his quality control. Egg products packed in continuously inspected plants can be identified by the USDA emblem on each package. This mark can be considered an indication of excellent sanitary quality and the absence of inferior materials. It is not, of course, any protection against storage deterioration. Eggs are standard commodities and any material that is being offered substantially below published market prices is undoubtedly inferior in some manner.

The quality control of dried egg products has been influenced by regulations requiring pasteurization of egg products by the FDA, mandatory USDA inspection, and the establishment of E-3-A standards for equipment.

Details of chemical, microbiological, and functional tests for all egg products can be found in *Egg Science and Technology* (Stadelman and Cotterill 1986). Chemical methods of analysis include determinations of: (1) Total solids or moisture; (2) Color; (3) Salt; (4) Sugar; (5) Percentage of yolk in egg whites; (6) Total fat; (7) Protein; (8) Ash; (9) Pesticide residues; and (10) pH. Microbiological methods of analysis commonly performed include: (1) Total count; (2) Coliforms; (3) Salmonellae; (4) Yeasts and molds; (5) *Escherichia coli*; and (6) Coagulase-positive organisms. Functional performance tests for general purposes include: (1) Whip tests; (2) Test baking in angel food cake or sponge cake formulas; (3) Performance in salad dressings; and (4) Solubility of dried products.

BIBLIOGRAPHY

ANON. 1969. Egg Pasteurization Manual. USDA Agr. Res. Serv. *74-48.*

ANON. 1977. Land O Lakes Ingredient Blends. Land O' Lakes, Minneapolis, MN

ANON. 1984. Standard Methods for the Examination of Dairy Products, Fifteenth Edition. American Public Health Association, New York, NY

ANON. 1985. Eggs in Brief. American Egg Board, Park Ridge, IL

ANON. 1986. Milk and cream. 21 CFR 131. Cheeses and related cheese products.

ANON. 1987. Dehydrated Food Products. Henningsen Foods, Omaha, NE

ANON. 1990. Guide to Real Wisconsin Cheese. Wisconsin Milk Marketing Board, Madison, WI

ANON. 1991. Grading and inspection, general specifications for approved plants and standards for grades of dairy products. 7 CFR 58

ARBIGE, M. V., FREUND, P. R., SILVER, S. C., and ZELKO, J. T. 1986. Novel lipase for cheddar cheese development. Food Technol. *40*, No. 6, 91-96, 98

ASH, D. 1979. Small cake items. Proc. Am. Soc. Bakery Engineers *1979*, 83-91

ATHERTON, H. W., and NEWLANDER, J. A. 1967. Chemistry and Testing of Dairy Products, Fourth Edition. AVI Publishing Co., Westport, CT

ATKIN, L. 1966. Egg products and how to use them. Proc. Am. Soc. Bakery Engineers *1966*, 248-256

BÄCHLER, R., FOSSEUX, P-Y., and JOST, R. 1988. Preparation of gelled food products. U.S. Pat. 4,720,390

BALDWIN, R. E. 1986. Functional properties of eggs in foods. *In* Egg Science and Technology, Third Edition. AVI Publishing Co., Westport, CT

BANWART, G. J., and AYRES, J. C. 1956. The effect of high temperature storage on the content of *Salmonella* and on the functional properties of dried egg white. J. Food Technology *10*, 68-73

BERGQUIST, D. H. 1979. Sanitary processing of egg products. J. Food Protection *42*, 591-595

BERGQUIST, D. H. 1987. Personal communication. Omaha, NE

BRADLEY, R. L., JR. 1986. Intricacies of the Babcock test for milkfat. Dairy Field *169*, No. 6, 28-29, 43

CHEVRON, M., and NEUMANN, F. 1989. Process for treating dairy by-products. U.S. Pat. 4,803,089

CLARK, W. S., JR. 1986. Personal communication. American Dairy Products Institute, Chicago, IL

CORBIN, E. A., and WHITTIER, E. O. 1965. The composition of milk. *In* Fundamentals of Dairy Chemistry. B. H. Webb and A. H. Johnson, Editors. AVI Publishing Co., Westport, CT

COTTERILL, O. J. 1981. A Scientist Speaks About Egg Products. American Egg Board, Rosemont, IL

DIXON, R. P., DE MAN, J. M., and WOOD, F. W. 1969. Production of volatile acids during cheddar cheese ripening. Canadian Inst. Food Technol. J. *2*, 127-135

DZIEZAK, J. D. 1986. Enzyme modification of dairy products. Food Technol. *40*, No. 4, 114, 116, 118-120

FORSYTHE, R. H. 1963. Chemical and physical properties of egg products. Cereal Science Today *8*, 309-310

FUJIMARA, G., SOTOMA, K., KUNIYOKO, H., HATA, M., and INOUE, H. 1986. High speed egg breaking method. U.S. Pat. 4,605,562

HALL, C. W., and HEDRICK, T. I. 1971. Drying of Milk and Milk Products, Second Edition. AVI Publishing Co., Westport, CT

HARPER, W. J., and HALL, C. W. 1976. Dairy Technology and Engineering. AVI Publishing Co., Westport CT

HEDRICK, T. I. 1981. Spray-drying of cheese. Proc. Second Biennial Marschall International Cheese Conference, Madison, WI. Sept. 15-18, 1981

HENDERSON, J. L. 1971. The Fluid Milk Industry, Third Edition. AVI Publishing Co., Westport, CT

HONER, C. 1989. Egg processor lays claim to latest technology. Prepared Foods *158*, No. 7, 122-123

HUGUNIN, A. G., and EWING, N. L. 1977. Dairy Based Ingredients for Food Products. Dairy Research Inc., Rosemont, IL

KOSIKOWSKI, F. 1966. Cheese and Fermented Milk Foods. Edwards Brothers, Ann Arbor, MI

POSATI, L. P., and ORR, M. L. (Editors) 1976. Composition of Foods—Dairy and Egg Products. Agric. Handbook *8-1*. Agr. Research Service, USDA

SANDERS, G. P. 1953. Cheese varieties and descriptions. U.S. Dept. Agric. Handbook *54*

SINGER, N. S., YAMAMOTO, S., and LATELLA, J. 1988. Protein product base. U. S. Pat. 4,734,287

SINGLETON, A. D., HANEY, H. N., and HABIGHURST, A. B. 1965. Adapting dried whey products to present-day bakery operations. Cereal Science Today *10*, 53-55, 62

STADELMAN, W. J., and COTTERILL, O. J. 1986. Egg Science and Technology, Third Edition. AVI Publishing Co., Westport, CT

STAHEL, N. G. 1982. Milk replacers. Proc. Am. Soc. Bakery Engineers *1982*, 68-73

SWARTZ, M., and WONG, C. 1985. Milk proteins: Nutritional and functional uses. Cereal Foods World *30*, 173-175

TALBOTT, L. L., and MCCORD, C. 1981. The use of enzyme modified cheeses for flavoring processed cheese products. Proc. Second Biennial Marschall International Cheese Conference, Madison, WI. Sept. 15-18, 1981

WEBB, B. H., JOHNSON, A. H., and ALFORD, J. A. 1974. Fundamentals of Dairy Chemistry, Second Edition. AVI Publishing Co., Westport, CT

ZICK, W. F. 1969. Lipid and protein-derived flavors for snack foods applications. Cereal Science Today *14*, 205-206

chapter eight

FRUITS, VEGETABLES, AND NUTS

INTRODUCTION

There are a great many fruit and nut ingredients used in bakery foods, and quite a few vegetable products. Although most of the individual items in these categories are consumed in quantities that seem almost insignificant as compared to, say, flour or sugar, they are all important characterizing ingredients, that is they are factors controlling the appearance, flavor, or texture of a product. They are also, frequently, the most expensive ingredients with which the baker deals, with the possible exception of some of the artificial or natural flavor preparations. Too often, they are the ingredients about which the bakery technologist knows the least. Their importance, then, justifies an extensive discussion, which is the purpose of this chapter.

NUTS

Most nuts have a relatively low content of moisture when in the condition in which they are usually distributed, thus they tend to have fairly good shelf lives. Rancidity is a frequent problem, however. All common varieties, with the sole exception of the chestnut, contain high levels of fat; this allows them to be ground into pastes or "butters." When in large pieces they are usually crunchy in texture and rather mild in flavor. Roasting or frying often intensifies and improves their flavor. If available in whole or half kernels, they can be used to give a decorative touch to the surfaces of foods. These characteristics combine to make nuts desirable ingredients for bakery products.

Almonds, Almond Butter, and Almond Paste

There are two species of almond, the bitter and the sweet or edible. Of the latter, there are two types, the hard shell and the soft shell. The almonds of commerce are mainly the soft-shelled type.

In world trade, the major producers of almonds are Spain, Italy, Portugal, Morocco, Iran, and the U.S. Some almonds are imported into the U.S., but the greater part of the almonds consumed here are domestically grown and processed. California is the only important almond-growing state. Seven varieties that dominate the U.S. market are Nonpareil, IXL, Ne Plus, Peerless, Drake, Mission, and Jordanolo.

The USDA has established Standards for Grades of Shelled Almonds, including the grades U.S. Fancy, U.S. Extra No. 1, U.S. No. 1, U.S. Select

Sheller Run, U.S. Standard Sheller Run, U.S. No. 1 Whole and Broken, and U.S. No. 1 for almonds of similar varietal characteristics, as well as Mixed Varieties and Unclassified. There are also standards for grades of almond in the shell, but these are not of much significance for the bakery trade.

Standard Sheller Run, the lowest quality class, consists of kernels just as they come from the cracking machines, of mixed sizes, free of dust and shell but containing some broken pieces. These nuts are satisfactory for making almond paste, chopped or sliced nuts, and the like. Select Sheller Run contains few broken pieces and is offered in different sizes.

Fancy consists of almonds closely sized and without defects, as regular in shape, size, and color as is practicable. They are free of double-nuts, shell, and broken pieces. For garnishing or decorating, where appearance of the piece is of primary importance, this is the grade that should be specified. The size, which should also be specified, is defined as the number of almonds in each avoirdupois ounce.

In the U.S., many almonds are marketed through growers' federations, such as the California Almond Growers' Exchange, which enforce quality standards and market the nuts cooperatively. A substantial amount of almonds is also bought and sold by independent companies.

For many applications, it is desirable that the kernels be blanched, i.e., the brown skin removed. A typical blanching treatment consists of placing the almonds in contact with 180°F water for 3 min and then skinning them manually or by special machines. If the nuts are to be stored for more than a few hours, the absorbed moisture must be removed. California almonds can be purchased already blanched and with the moisture content brought back to safe levels. Nuts should always be stored in air-tight containers to prevent moisture pick up and minimize insect infestation.

Almonds are relatively resistant to rancidity development as compared to pecans or peanuts, but they will deteriorate with time, and the decrease in acceptability is accelerated by blanching or roasting. It is desirable to place the nuts in the freezer if they are to be held for several months. If roasted nuts are to be stored for several days or weeks, it is helpful to apply antioxidants such as TBHQ, BHA, and BHT in spray form or add them to the roasting oil.

Almonds are normally fried or dry roasted before use. In some applications, blanching may be disadvantageous because the light-colored smooth nut does not show up well on many cakes and confections. Almonds can be sliced, diced, halved, and chopped to give the baker a wide choice in piece size and shape.

Almond butter is an item of commerce. It consists of finely ground roasted almonds. The composition is reported to be 15% protein, 21.2% carbohydrates (9.1% fiber), and 59.1% fats.

Almond paste is an adjunct that for a very long time has been used to fill, flavor, decorate, and otherwise enhance bakery products. It is the basis for marzipan and other ancient confections. Long ago, bakers used to make their own almond paste using one part powdered sugar and one part blanched and dried almonds pounded together in a mortar, with some egg white mixed in later to make a paste (Ranhofer 1893). It is said that there are two manufacturing processes that may be distinguished, the so-called French process (a combined cooking and crushing procedure) and an evaporation-crushing method. Nowadays, bakery supply houses grind the nuts and sugar together on roll refiners, and the proportion is likely to be two parts sugar to one part almonds, with some cheaper binding material replacing the egg white. Mange and Allard (1989) disclosed a continuous method requiring the use of a screw conveyor type of cooking extruder.

Marzipan is a variant of almond paste that is used in confections and bakery adjuncts including cake decorations. An old description of commercial preparation of marzipan was published by Bennion and Stewart (1930). Almonds are first blanched in the usual way, then steeped in cold water to prevent oil separation during grinding. After steeping, they are chopped and put through the grinding machine three or four times, with the rollers being set closer together each time. After a smooth paste is formed, a nearly equal quantity of icing or pulverized sugar is added, and the mixture transferred to a steam jacketed kettle where it is boiled until it reaches the desired consistency. The paste must be continuously stirred to prevent it from sticking to the pan and scorching. When the mass shows no tendency to stick to the pan, it is ready to be transferred to air-tight containers for storage. Properly made marzipan should be as smooth and plastic as potters' clay. Colors, flavors, and extra sugar may be added to the marzipan as desired; this is sometimes done in the factory, but more often by the baker. To make cake icings, up to equal quantities of confectioners' sugar may be added to the marzipan.

Coconut

Coconut is available in the form of the dried meat of the ripe coconut in various sizes and shapes of particles (usually called "desiccated" coconut), as sweetened preparations, and as toasted sweetened preparations.

If the purchaser wants unsweetened coconut, the only available variables are particle size and particle shape. This material will consist of about 65% fat, 2% to 3% moisture, 3.9% fiber, 5.9% sugars, 8.3% protein, 8.9% pentosans, and 2.4% minerals. The fat is inclosed in cell walls, so that desiccated preparations do not appear to be oily unless they have been ground very fine. Desiccated coconut is available in 100-lb and 25-lb units commonly packed in four-ply natural Kraft bags fitted with polyethylene liners. The coconut is cut into small chunks or shreds. There are a dozen or more forms available. For example, extra fine has a particle size similar to that of granulated sugar, rice cut is 1/8 to 1/4 inch in length with an overall appearance similar to rice, medium shred passes through a 10-mesh screen and is approximately 1/16 to 1/4 inch in length, etc. These materials are widely used in and on sweet rolls, pies, cookies, doughnuts, and confections.

Sweetened coconut is made by cooking the chopped coconut with sugars and glycerol or propylene glycol to give the soft white moist material found in retail packages of this ingredient. The usual composition is 14% moisture, 33% total sugars, 0.5% salt, 2% propylene glycol, and coconut solids. Various shapes and sizes are available, depending on the supplier. Industrial users can obtain this type of coconut in 2-lb plastic bags or in 25-lb or 50-lb polyethylene-lined cartons.

Sweetened toasted coconut is roasted in ovens to give a medium brown color and a toasted flavor. It is used almost exclusively as a topping, and principally on cookies, doughnuts, confections, and meringue-topped pies. Creamed coconut, which is a kind of stiff white paste with free oil present, is made by fine-grinding, aerating, chilling, and whipping desiccated coconut to a smooth consistency. Primary applications are fillings, icings, and confections.

Filberts and Hazelnuts

The terms filbert and hazelnut are apparently used interchangeably for all plants in the genus *Corylus* (Woodroof 1979B). Principal commercial production of these nuts is in Italy, Spain, and Turkey. The U.S. does produce some filberts, but this nut has never been very popular with U.S. consumers. The situation is quite different in Europe, where the nut is ubiquitous as an ingredient in bakery products and candies. When U.S. bakers put filberts in their products, which they seldom do, the nut fills many of the same functions as almonds or walnuts. The nut can also be ground to give a paste analogous to peanut butter. Approximate composition of the kernels is 3% to 4% moisture, 15% to 17% protein, 63% to 66% ether extract, 5% to 6% sucrose, 3% to 4% starch, 2% crude fiber, 2% to 3% ash, and traces of reducing sugars.

Kernel Paste

Kernel paste is an analog of almond paste in which almonds have been largely or entirely replaced by pulverized apricot pits. It is used as a cheap replacement for almond paste in pastry fillings, etc., but it has a distinctive and rather attractive flavor of its own.

Peanuts and Peanut Butter

Peanuts are used to decorate bakery foods and to add texture and flavor contrast. Although whole or half nuts perform these functions admirably, it is more common to use chopped peanuts as it is easier to distribute them and the economics are generally better. In every case roasted nuts are used, and they are nearly always blanched because, otherwise, the skins tend to come loose and form unsightly debris on the product.

According to Woodroof (1983), the classification of types and varieties of peanuts is loose and many intermediate forms are found. The relatively small, somewhat spherical Spanish type is grown in the Southwestern and Southeastern U.S. The Virginia peanut is considerably larger and the kernel is longer or football-shaped. The runner variety is approximately intermediate between these two in shape and size, but it is not as uniform as the Virginia and Spanish peanuts. There are also Tennessee red or white types and Valencias, but they are currently of relatively minor economic importance. There are USDA grades and classes for the major varieties.

The number of kernels per pound of Spanish peanuts will vary from about 1,100 to 2,000, of runners from 900 to 1,100, and of Virginias from 512 to 864. Peanuts when freshly dug have a moisture content of 25% to 60%. Upon air drying in the shell, this drops to 5% to 10%. Roasted peanuts will have a moisture content of about 1%, roughly the same as peanut butter.

For most commercial applications, the roaster buys cured shelled peanuts packed in burlap bags. This stock retains good organoleptic properties for six months at room temperature, or even more if kept free of infestation and protected from foreign odors the nuts might absorb. At 47°F storage, the life is nearer nine months. When shelled, the storage life is reduced by about one-third; if blanched and split, another third of the potential stability is lost. In most supplier warehouses, shelled peanuts are stored in refrigerated rooms, substantially increasing their shelf life. Chopping and roasting can further reduce stability.

Spoilage results from development of oxidative rancidity, absorption of foreign odors, and color changes. The purchaser should keep in mind that storage life begins at harvest, and it is essential to insist that nuts from the latest crop year be supplied. If possible, purchases should be deferred in the last three months of the crop year until new crop peanuts become available.

Depending on their intended application, whole peanuts, split peanuts, or granules will be procured by the food manufacturer. Some bakers may want to roast peanuts in their plant to obtain fresher taste in the pastry, but the average bakery will not command enough volume to justify on-premises roasting, blanching, and chopping, so purchases of whole kernels, splits, or granules of the appropriate size will be made directly from a roaster. It is very important to have a reliable supplier who will roast and cut the nuts to order and not ship from a stock of material that might have been processed weeks or months before shipping. Nuts that are rancid will ruin any bakery product, and the greatest precautions are necessary to prevent usage of such defective material. If no other quality control test can be made, the roasted nuts should be tasted immediately before they are applied to the finished product.

Table 8.1 lists some of the components of normal peanut kernels. These data are from Freeman *et al.* (1954).

Peanuts can be either fried or dry roasted. Both processes yield acceptable products. It appears the latter process is more common at this time. Blanched nuts are preferred for frying because of equipment fouling by loose skins when unblanched nuts are so treated.

Table 8.1. TYPICAL COMPOSITION OF PEANUT KERNELS

Constituent	Range	Average
Moisture	3.9–13.2	5.0
Protein	21.0–36.4	28.5
Lipids	35.8–54.2	47.5
Crude fiber	1.2–4.3	2.8
Nitrogen-free extract	6.0–24.9	13.3
Ash	1.8–3.1	2.9
Reducing sugars	0.1–0.3	0.2
Disaccharides	1.9–5.2	4.5
Starch	1.0–5.3	4.0
Pentosans	2.2–2.7	2.5

Peanut butter can be made from either blanched or unblanched roasted peanuts, according to Federal Standards, but it is more common to use blanched nuts, i.e., with skins removed and, often, with the germs ("hearts") removed. Fat content must be 55% or less. Up to 10% of seasoning and stabilizing ingredients may be included. Artificial sweeteners, artificial flavors, chemical preservatives, vitamins, and colorants are not acceptable additives. The usual ingredients other than peanuts and partially hydrogenated vegetable oil are salt, sugar or corn sweeteners, and mono- and diglycerides.

Packers of bulk peanut butter will make products to meet their customer's requirements. The texture can be smooth—with all of the peanuts ground to a size small enough to eliminate all grittiness, or chunky, in which granular pieces of peanuts have been added to a smooth butter. The Federal Specification for peanut butter (Anon. 1978A) requires that the peanuts be either runner, Virginia, or Spanish variety.

The manufacture of peanut butter consists of shelling, dry roasting, cooling, blanching, and inspecting the peanuts, followed by grinding. Salt is then put in, along with peanut chunks, if desired. Hydrogenated peanut oil or other vegetable oil is added to prevent separation during storage. The final mixture is cooled to about 85° to 110°F before it is filled into containers. All of these steps are done continuously in modern large factories. Various devices have been used for grinding, including comminuters, attrition mills, homogenizers, disintegrators, hammer mills, and colloidal mills.

Color and flavor of the finished product are very much influenced by the degree of roast applied to the peanuts. Generally speaking, nuts should be roasted to a point just short of the development of burnt or bitter flavor if they are intended to be packaged as bulk peanut butter for the bakery trade. This results in developing a maximum amount of flavor and color per pound of ingredient. Once the desired roast has been obtained, it is very important to cool the peanuts quickly to avoid further heat-induced reactions. Ideally, peanuts should be separated by size before roasting since the size (or, at least the thickness) affects the response to heat, i.e., thinner nuts will roast to a darker color than thicker peanuts of the same initial moisture content, given the same time and temperature of heat treatment. In commercial practice, size segregation is probably never done.

For industrial use, peanut butter can be packed in steel drums, in fiber drums with plastic linings, and in plastic bags placed in cardboard boxes. It is important to avoid entrapping air bubbles during filling. Peanut butter has a rather long shelf life if it is stored in unopened containers. If the oil leaks out and saturates, for example, the fiber box, rapid development of oxidative rancidity can be expected. Light accelerates rancidity development, but salt has no effect. Because of the very low moisture content (i.e., low water activity), microbiological spoilage will not occur unless the surface has been wetted, which could only result from very poor storage conditions. The flavor of bulk packed peanut butter gradually decreases, but glass packed product with nitrogen in the headspace will stay palatable for a long time.

Peanut butter, or peanut butter mixed with other materials, can be used as an adjunct in Danish pastry, as an ingredient in icings, in cookie doughs or fillings, etc. It is not used much in bread products.

Pecans

Pecans are highly regarded as flavoring ingredients and decorative toppings for pies, cakes, cookies, and sweet rolls. Although their flavor is pleasant, it is mild and can easily be overpowered by spices and other flavors. Because they are expensive, pecans are found mostly in premium goods, except when token amounts are used in chopped form to justify the claim of pecan flavor. Pecan pieces are often mixed with chunks of walnuts or almonds to make toppings for doughnuts, cupcakes, and Danish pastry and for ingredients in cheap versions of pecan pies—particularly the small individual pies.

The pecan is a native American tree. It will not survive severe winters and so is restricted to the milder climatic areas of the U.S. Nuts are harvested from both wild and cultivated trees. There is more variability in the pecan crop than in most other nut crops. In recent years, brokers have been storing the nuts under refrigerated or freezing temperatures, so that they can be kept in good condition for longer periods of time and the year-to-year fluctuations in supply are reduced.

After harvesting, pecans are put in dry storage to undergo curing. During this holding period of about three weeks at room temperature, the moisture of the entire nut decreases to about 8.5% to 9.0%, and that of the meat to about 4.5%. Free fatty acid content and the peroxide value of the lipids increase, and the tannins of the seed coat oxidize with a resultant color change from pale to medium brown. The overall effects of these changes result in the development of a characteristic pecan flavor, appearance, aroma, and texture. The nuts will gradually develop staleness—both a loss of desirable flavor and the appearance of non-rancid flavors such as bitterness—and, finally, rancidity will develop at a rate dependent on the temperature. Conditions of 40°F and 70% to 80% relative humidity are necessary if the fresh flavor is to be retained more than three months. At 0°F the in-shell kernels will retain good quality for more than five years.

Heating pecan meats to an internal temperature of 176°F in dry air or oil doubles the shelf-life by inactivating oxidative enzymes. Higher temperatures produce a partially cooked flavor, while roasting at 365°F for about 15 minutes by means of hot air or infrared radiation destroys natural antioxidants, accelerating rancidity development but increasing the flavor and aroma many times. This is a favorable condition for nuts that are to be consumed soon after roasting but has undesirable implications for products entering a long distribution system. Antioxidants such as BHA or BHT can be added to increase shelf life. Development of the so-called amber color is a kind of storage deterioration probably related to high temperature and high moisture content.

If pecan meats are dried below about 3.5% to 4.0% moisture content, they become brittle and suffer excessive breakage during handling.

There are USDA standards for shelled pecans that establish four grades: No. 1 Halves, Commercial Halves, No. 1 Pieces, and Commercial Pieces. There is also a catch-all "Unclassified" category that is not regarded as a grade. The size of halves are specified according to the number of halves per pound; pieces are classified in accordance with a sieve test.

Poppyseeds

It is recognized by the author that most readers will consider poppyseed to be inappropriately classified as a nut. It is true that such a classification cannot be justified on a botanical basis. Many writers in this field have included poppyseeds in their discussion of spices, which makes even less sense. Poppyseeds are included in bakery products for their effects on appearance and texture. Their contribution to flavor is not particularly significant, which would seem to rule out their positioning as spices and quasi-spices.

Poppyseeds are tiny (less than 1 mm diameter) seeds of a plant of the poppy family. They are used in bakery products both as the whole seed and crushed or ground with other ingredients to form pastes. The seeds are slightly crunchy and they have a somewhat nutty aroma and taste.

Edible poppyseeds will typically contain 6.8% moisture, 18.0% protein, 44.7% fat, 23.7% total carbohydrate (6.3% fiber), 6.8% ash, and 5.3 calories per gram. Blue poppyseed, a type made famous by the Dutch, is considered the highest quality. There is a Federal Specification for poppy seed that describes it as the clean, dried, seed of *Papaver somniferum* L., having an agreeable nutty taste free from evidence of rancidity.

Poppyseeds have been used as a source of edible oil, though there is no known commercial production at this time.

Walnuts

The American black walnut (*Juglans nigra*) is prized for its distinctive flavor but creates problems because of its tendency to stale rapidly. The price of this nutmeat is high and it must be used in granules or chunks since it is practically impossible to obtain complete half kernels from the nut cracking operation. Black walnuts are used mainly in cakes and cake icings, but commercial consumption of the natural product is probably very small. Some artificial black walnut flavor is used in commercial cookies.

It is more common to use Persian/English walnuts (*J. regia*), which are cheaper and can easily be obtained as recognizable pieces. The flavor of the English walnut is milder and of a different quality than that of the black walnut. It is also develops rancidity more slowly, under similar conditions.

The English walnut is widely cultivated today, with centers of production in middle and southern Europe as well as in California and some other parts of the southern U.S. Some of the popular varieties in this country are Payne, Eureka, Hartley, and Franquettes.

When harvested, the kernel moisture content may be as high as 35%. This is reduced by mechanical drying, and the in-shell nuts are stored at about 4.0% kernel moisture until they are shelled. The protein content is about 25.2%, fat at least 48%, ash about 3.3%, carbohydrates about 19.9%, and crude fiber about 2.5% Shelled walnuts quickly darken and develop rancidity when exposed to moisture, heat, light, and air. There is an approximately linear increase in stability with decreasing temperature of storage. Antioxidants can be applied to the kernels to retard rancidity development.

Flavor deterioration in walnuts appears to be related to reactions occurring in the skin. This nut is seldom blanched, but a process based on dry heating the nutmeats, then blowing off the skins with pressurized air was developed for blanching, and the skinless nuts were found to have much improved stability (Anon. 1989B).

U.S. Standards for Grades of shelled walnuts were first issued in 1959. The Grades consist of U.S. No. 1 and Commercial. There is also an "Unclassified" category for portions of walnut kernels that do not fall into the two Grades. Suppliers describe quality categories of Light, Special Light, Light Amber, and Standard Amber in order of their decreasing desirability. Some of the piece sizes offered are halves, halves and pieces, sliced, diced, syruper pieces, small syruper pieces, and meal.

Shelled walnut pieces are packed in cans, cartons, and or bags. Cans typically contain 3 lb or 4 lb of nuts. Cartons contain 25 lb or 30 lbs.

Less Important Nuts

Table 8.2 gives the nutritional profile of some of the less common nuts bakers may wish to consider as ingredients. The factor used for converting total nitrogen to protein is 5.30. No vitamin B_{12} was found in these nuts.

Table 8.2. COMPOSITION OF SOME NUTS AND SEEDS[1]

Component	Unit	Brazil nuts (1)	Cashew nuts (2)	Chest- nuts (3)	Pecans (1)	Sesame seeds (4)
Water	g	3.34	1.70	40.48	4.82	4.69
Food energy	kcal	656.	574.	245.	667.	573.
Protein	g	14.34	15.31	3.17	7.75	17.73
Total lipid	g	66.22	46.35	2.20	67.64	49.67
Carbohydrate	g	12.80	32.69	52.96	18.24	23.45
Fiber	g	2.29	0.70	1.90	1.60	4.60
Ash	g	3.30	3.95	1.20	1.56	4.45
Calcium	mg	176.	45.	29.	36.	975.
Iron	mg	3.40	6.00	0.91	2.13	14.55
Magnesium	mg	225.	260.	33.	128.	351.
Phosphorous	mg	600.	490.	107.	291.	629.
Potassium	mg	600.	565.	592.	392.	468.
Sodium	mg	2.	16.	2.	1.	11.
Zinc	mg	4.59	5.60	0.57	5.47	7.75
Copper	mg	1.77	2.22	0.51	1.18	4.08
Manganese	mg	0.77	NA	1.18	4.51	2.46
Ascorbic acid	mg	0.7	0	26.	2.0	0
Thiamin	mg	1.00	0.20	0.24	0.85	0.79
Riboflavin	mg	0.12	0.20	0.18	0.13	0.25
Niacin	mg	1.62	1.40	1.34	0.89	4.52
Pantothenate	mg	0.24	1.22	0.55	1.71	0.05
Vitamin B-6	mg	0.25	0.26	0.50	0.19	0.79
Folacin	mcg	4.0	69.2	70.0	39.2	96.7
Vitamin A	IU	NA	0	24.	128.	9

[1] McCarthy and Matthews (1984). Protein is N x 6.25.
Notes: (1) Dried, unblanched; (2) Dry roasted; (3) European, roasted; and (4) Whole, dried.

Brazil Nuts.—The principal consumption of Brazil nuts is as a component of mixed nuts and as an ingredient in confections. A relatively small amount is used in bakery products. The large nut is sliced or chopped to give piece sizes appropriate to bakery foods.

Cashews.—Cashew nuts are produced in India, Brazil, and East Africa. Virtually all cashews consumed in the U.S. are imported from India, but these may include some East African nuts processed in India. Brazil is assuming increasing importance as an exporter of cashews. There is no commercial production of cashew nuts in the U.S., and there are no federal standards. The India Cashew Export Promotion Council has established grading and marketing rules that apply to nuts shipped out of that country. These rules define grades for whole cashews, scorched wholes, dessert wholes, white pieces, scorched pieces, and dessert pieces. Whole cashew kernels are identified according to size by the identification symbols W210, W240, W280, W320, W400, and W500. In each instance, the number part of the symbol designates the maximum number of kernels per pound.

Cashews are imported in square metal tins that are hermetically sealed. Generally, a vacuum of a few inches is drawn before the tins are soldered shut. These tins, of about 4-gallon capacity, contain 28 lb of Baby Bits or 25 lb of other sizes. The nuts, which are processed by a heat treatment but are not roasted before shipment, are comparatively stable when stored in the unopened tin at room temperature, and a year of useful shelf life can be expected when they are refrigerated.

Distributors in the U.S. import cashews and oil-roast them for bakers, confectioners, and other users. The roasted nuts may be packed 25 lb to a corrugated box with polyliners.

Chestnuts.—Chestnuts are rarely used in manufactured food products in the U.S. but are very commonly employed as ingredients in other countries. They are unlike the rest of the nuts described in this chapter in that they contain relatively little oil, less than 5% in fresh chestnuts, and a large amount of carbohydrates—about 40% to 45%. Chestnuts as harvested contain about 50% moisture. They may be held for more than one year at 40°F if they are reduced to 10% moisture within four days.

The forms in which chestnuts have usually served as ingredients in baked foods are as a puree of cooked nuts or as marrons glacé. The puree can be used as a component of fillings, pastry creams, and the like, while the latter product mostly fills a decorative role. Further details can be found in Woodroof (1979B).

Macadamias.—This nut is native to Australia, but new plantations of significant size have been established in Hawaii and other parts of the world. It appears to have excellent acceptability from the standpoints of flavor and texture. A relatively high cost has prevented its widespread application to commercial bakery products, but it does have a prestige image that may be a considerable advantage in marketing upscale goods.

The nuts in their husks fall from the trees when mature and are gathered by hand. The husks are removed by mechanical devices leaving the nuts in a very hard and thick shell. Freshly husked nuts contain up to 20% moisture, which must be reduced to about 3.5% immediately if good quality is to be maintained. Drying can be done in forced air dryers at ambient temperatures or at temperatures below 110°F for a few days and then at 135° to 140°F.

Removing the nutmeats from the hard shells is difficult and can lead to a considerable number of damaged kernels. Cracking machines force open the shells, and automatic separators shake out the loose kernels. The kernels are graded according to density by immersing them in solutions of known specific gravity and separating those that float and those that sink.

Grade 1 kernels will float in tap water at room temperature. Grade 2 kernels have a specific gravity higher than 1.0 but no higher than 1.25. Grade 3 nuts are those that have a still higher density.

Macadamia nuts are cooked either by immersion in oil or by dry roasting. The color, texture, and flavor of Grade 1 dry roasted and oil roasted nuts are about equal, because of their high content of oil, but Grade 2 nuts dry out and become dull when dry roasted.

Shelf life of the roasted kernels increases with decreasing moisture content and decreasing storage temperatures. At moisture contents of 1.4%, only very small changes occur in flavor and chemical composition during 18 months storage at room temperature. Flavor deterioration closely parallels darkening of the kernels. Deterioration in texture first appears as a loss of crispness and the development of a slight mealiness. Stability can be improved by adding antioxidants to the roasted nuts or by storing in a vacuum or under inert gases.

Pistachios.—Pistachios are nuts that are seldom used in bakery products but deserve greater consideration because they do have unique flavor, appearance, and texture. Their high cost is certainly a discouraging feature, but the increased production from California plantations has already led to substantial declines in the cost of this nut. The domestic product is also far superior to the Iranian exports in uniformity and cleanliness. Shelled and roasted (optionally salted) pistachios are available as Whole, Whole & Broken, Large Pieces, and Small Pieces. Sizes are, for example, 21/25, 24/26, and 26/28—the designations indicating the approximate number of kernels per ounce. The nuts in shell nuts are available in the natural off-white shell or in shells colored red with edible dyes. Packing of ingredient pistachios is often 25 lb in cardboard cases with polyethylene liners.

Nut Substitutes and Defatted Nuts

Because the usual varieties of nuts are expensive relative to other food ingredients, and are generally non-uniform and lack storage stability, there is a constant search for manufactured replacements that will not have these disadvantages. One approach is the artificial nut piece, such as provided by the invention of Maloney *et al.* (1970).

Bitsyn is a trademarked and patented simulation in form, texture, and taste of various kinds of nutmeats (e.g., pecans). Organoleptically, it has good quality, but it is fairly expensive and could create labeling problems in certain situations. Tamanuts and other versions of glandless cottonseeds have reasonably good texture and fairly bland flavor, but they are small in size and rather unattractive in color. In addition, the supply situation is unclear.

Great strides have been made in processing soybeans so that they resemble nuts in appearance, texture, and flavor. There are commercial imitations of roasted salted nuts made from soybeans, and they appear to have a certain amount of consumer acceptance. Their use in bakery products is not great. Soybeans have the great advantage, for a raw material, of always being in plentiful supply at prices that are low compared with the prices of nuts. What would advance this research more than any other step would be the genetic improvement of soybeans so that their typical "beany" or "green" flavors were not apparent.

One of the major problems with nuts as food ingredients is that their high fat content makes them unsuitable for persons who wish to reduce their caloric intake. There have been many schemes suggested for reducing the fat content of nuts while maintaining their texture and flavor. Most of these methods involve pressing nuts until the desired quantity of oil is removed, then steaming or cooking the pieces until they resume approximately their original shape. The net effect is a substitution of water for oil. The hydrated nuts can be dry roasted to give a simulation of regular nuts. In general, it appears that the finished product resembles natural nuts only superficially. Gannis and Wilkins (1990) review some of the prior art and disclose a process that does not require rehydration before roasting.

FRUITS

Dried Fruits

Some fruits are used by bakers almost entirely in the partially dried forms, because the fresh forms are so perishable and expensive that they could only be used seasonally and in high priced goods. Many common traditional products, such as fig bars and date bread, are based on the dried fruit. Table 8.3 gives the nutritional composition of four items.

Dates and date paste.—Whole dates (*Phoenix dactylifera*), with or without the seed, are used in confections more often than in baked goods. The predominant flavor in dates is sweetness—not surprising since they are 75% to 80% sugar, In dry varieties such as Deglet Noor the sugar is mostly sucrose, while the moist varieties contain much invert sugar. The natural tannins of dates and the enzymatic and Maillard browning that take place during storage impart a brown color and a somewhat caramelized flavor (Boyle 1974).

Date paste has been suggested as a possible sugar source in bread doughs (Yousif *et al.* 1991), but this would seem to be economically logical only in a few areas where there is an excess of dates and a lack of sugar. Date paste is sometimes found in specialty cakes or cookies as a characterizing ingredient, similar in this respect to fig paste.

Figs and fig paste.—The amount of whole or cut figs used in bakery products must be very small, although one occasionally sees recipes for tarts, pies, or pastries in which fresh or canned figs are called for. Fig paste made from ground dried figs is an important ingredient, however.

Table 8.3. COMPOSITION OF SOME DRIED FRUITS[1]

Component	Unit	Apples, sulfured	Apricots sulfured	Zante currants	Prunes
Water	g	31.76	31.09	19.21	32.39
Food energy	kcal	243.	238.	283.	239.
Protein	g	0.93	3.65	4.08	2.61
Total lipid	g	0.32	0.46	0.27	0.52
Carbohydrate	g	65.98	61.75	74.08	62.73
Fiber	g	2.87	2.95	1.57	2.04
Ash	g	1.10	3.05	2.36	1.76
Calcium	mg	14.	45.	86.	51.
Iron	mg	1.40	4.70	3.26	2.48
Magnesium	mg	16.	47.	41.	45.
Phosphorous	mg	38.	117.	125.	79.
Potassium	mg	450.	1378.	892.	745.
Sodium	mg	87.	10.	8.	4.
Zinc	mg	0.20	0.74	0.66	0.53
Copper	mg	0.191	0.429	0.468	0.430
Manganese	mg	0.090	0.275	0.469	0.220
Ascorbic acid	mg	3.9	2.4	4.7	3.3
Thiamin	mg	0	0.008	0.160	0.081
Riboflavin	mg	0.159	0.151	0.142	0.162
Niacin	mg	0.927	2.998	1.615	1.961
Pantothenate	mg	0.125	0.753	0.045	0.460
Vitamin B-6	mg	0	0.156	0.296	0.264
Folacin	mcg	NA	10.3	10.2	3.7
Vitamin B-12	mcg	0	0	0	0
Vitamin A	IU	0	7240.	73.	1987.

[1] Gebhardt et al. (1982). Protein is N x 6.25.

The chief domestic varieties of figs are Calimyrna, White Adriatic, Kadota, and Black Mission. Calimyrnas are large, onion-shaped, tender, green-skinned figs with an excellent flavor; they have been highly recommended as an ingredient for fig jam to be used in bakery products. Calimyrna is the domestic version of the Smyrna, probably the best fig for jam use.

The White Adriatic has a bright green skin that turns light amber as it dries. These fruits do not make good jam unless they are supplemented with other ingredients because they lack natural sugars and flavors and contain a slight excess of crude fiber. When they are blended with other varieties of figs containing a high percentage of sugar and with more pronounced flavor, a very satisfactory jam can be produced.

The Kadota fig does not contain noticeable seeds. Its flesh has a light color and a pleasing taste. The thickness of its skin causes these figs to be very hard to dry, so that their susceptibility to spoilage is great and they must be ground into paste near where they are grown. Due to its lack of seeds and the toughness of its skin, the Kadota is not recommended as the sole fig ingredient for jam. It can be used as part of a blend, depending on the user's preference for jam characteristics.

Black Mission figs have excellent flavor and texture, but when dried they turn very dark, in many cases becoming almost black. Dark fig jam is associated in consumers' minds with poor flavor, low-grade raw materials, and poor manufacturing practices. If used in the proper blend with other varieties, Black Mission figs can enhance the flavor and texture of jams.

Ripe figs on the tree will analyze approximately as follows: 78.0% moisture; 1.4% protein; 0.4% fat; 2.4% ash; 1.7% fiber; 16.0% sugars; and 0.1% acids. After drying, the typical fig will have the following analysis: 24.0% moisture; 4.0% protein; 1.2% fat; 2.4% ash; 5.8% fiber; 62.0% sugars; and 0.6% acids.

A large amount of fig paste is used as an ingredient for the jam centers in fig bar cookies. Fig paste is usually ground to the customer's order from whole figs. It is frequently packed in 80-lb cases with polyethylene liners. Moisture content of the paste will be about 23%.

In order to produce an ideal jam, it is necessary to combine a fig of high color and flavor with one of good texture and seed quality because these characteristics are seldom if ever combined in a single variety of fig. For the ideal jam, use of an imported Smyrna fig for color and flavor and a White Adriatic for texture has been suggested.

Figs for jam should preferably not be treated with sulfur dioxide. Fig paste will darken with time. Storage at 45°F or lower will retard this undesirable change. Figs should be stored in a conditioned room with a relative humidity between 50% and 60%. High humidity may cause loss of sugars due to condensation of water on the fig and formation and subsequent draining of syrup. It may also lead to mold growth. Low humidity will tend to dry out and harden the figs, making them difficult to work with.

Before grinding figs into jam, the blocks should be broken up and inspected for foreign matter. The broken pieces are usually washed by being conveyed through a water spray. Soaking is to be avoided. Figs are often ground immediately after washing.

Raisins, raisin paste, and currants.— The raisins of commerce are dried grapes of the Thompson seedless or Muscat varieties. Natural Thompson raisins (the dark kind) are dried untreated grapes, while golden Thompson raisins have been subjected to a sulfur dioxide treatment that bleaches out the natural pigments and prevents darkening during drying. Fagrell (1990) described test methods that can be applied to raisins to determine their quality for specific uses. Table 8.4 includes the compositional profile of Thompson seedless raisin (adapted from Ziemke 1982).

Raisins in normal packaged condition, i.e., exhibiting a moderately flexible structure, will have a moisture content of about 15% to 17% and will be in equilibrium with a relative humidity of about 50% at room temperature. Adding 6 lb of hot water to 100 lb of raisins and allowing the mixture to stand for three to four hours is sufficient to soften the fruit enough to make it suitable for use in soft cookies (Bergholz 1957). In high-moisture bakery products such as bread and rolls, raisins are often soaked before they are mixed into the dough. Such a treatment is often desirable if it brings the fruit to a moisture content in equilibrium with the water activity of the dough. Excessive water in the raisins will, however, lead to the effusion of acid, sugar, and pigments into the dough, with consequent deleterious effects. If the fruit has been softened too much by soaking, it will also be more susceptible to breakage during mixing.

Raisin paste has the same composition as Thompson seedless raisins and meets the USDA raisin standards. It is soft and spreadable as purchased. If the paste dries out and becomes hard, it can be softened by adding corn syrup or simple syrup (not water). This product can be used in fillings and toppings for Danish and yeast-raised sweet doughs as well as in cookies and crackers.

Muscat raisins are seldom used in bakery products. The grape is large and has several seeds that are usually removed for manufacturing purposes. The raisin is normally soft, moist, sticky, fairly dark in color, and has a unique flavor. It will contain 14% to 19% moisture. There are several size categories covering the range of 500 to 1,200 raisins per pound.

Currants of the kind offered for use as an ingredient in bakery products are not closely related to the true or bush currant. The latter fruit is not dried but rather made into jams, jellies, and preserves. The Zante currant is a very small, dark, round grape that yields, when dried, a small raisin of excellent quality for baked goods. Their small size makes currants easy to distribute uniformly throughout an individual portion of a baked product, giving greater consumer satisfaction. The California product is generally referred to as the Zante currant, but there are imported dried fruits of similar type under different names.

Zante currants will contain 17% to 19% moisture and about 70% reducing sugars. There will be about 4,000 currants per pound. Some suppliers will oil coat or sugar coat the currants to reduce sticking.

Puffed raisins of 2% moisture content have been manufactured for use in thin batters where settling to the bottom is a problem (Webb 1989).

Other dried fruits.—Many of the cheaper fruits are available as dehydrated powders, with moisture content in the 2% to 5% range. These are useful as natural flavoring ingredients. Apple, citrus, and banana powders are three varieties used in considerable quantity by bakers.

Candied or glacé fruit

Candied or glacé fruits and peels are certainly reduced-moisture products, but they are generally considered to be in a different category than the dried materials described in the preceding chapters. They are mostly used as decorative adjuncts since they cost much more than the canned or frozen raw ingredients and often contribute little of the fruit's typical flavor (although flavors added to them in the manufacturing procedure can be quite important to their acceptability). In all candying processes, some of the original color and flavor of the fruit are lost. The texture also changes. The color and flavor of maraschino cherries, for example, are entirely due to added dyes and essences. In materials like candied ginger, however, some of the color and much of the flavor is retained.

Table 8.4. COMPOSITION OF NATURAL THOMPSON RAISINS

Component	Amount per 100 g raisins	Component	Amount per 100 g raisins
	grams		mg
Total solids	83.00	Sodium	15.60
Moisture	17.00	Potassium	673.00
Protein (Nx6.25)	3.41	Calcium	54.20
Ash	1.61	Magnesium	35.30
Fat	0.31	Phosphorus	102.00
Fiber	0.96	Iron	2.10
Carbohydrate	77.04	Copper	0.38
Sugar (as invert)	70.20	Zinc	0.20
Acid (as tartaric)	2.12	Vitamin C	0.88
		Niacin	0.56
		Riboflavin	0.022
		Thiamin	0.153
		Vitamin A, in IU	15.80

For some of these products, the raw material may be fresh peels or fruits, but in perhaps the majority of the cases, the fruit is first treated with sulfur dioxide or sodium bisulfite and calcium in solution ("brined") in order to preserve, decolorize, and firm the pieces. Before they are candied, the fruit must be washed and soaked to remove the sulfite.

In simplest terms, the candying process consists of replacing the juices of the fruit with a concentrated sugar solution. For glacé fruit, this replacement is carried to the point where the aqueous phase is totally saturated with sugar, and the fruit pieces are then dried so that a coating of sugar forms on the outer surface. Pigments and flavorings can be added to the syrups or applied by soaking the fruit pieces in special solutions before the sugaring process starts.

Preservation of these items is due to the initial sulfite treatment, heat from the syrups that are added, and the low water activity in the finished product. Chemical preservatives (benzoates, sorbates) are sometimes employed.

Canned fruits

Many kinds of fruit ingredients are obtained in cans for preparation of pie fillings, Danish toppings, and the like. The usual container is a No. 1 (603x700) can with a nominal capacity of 3.1 liter or a total capacity of 109.45 avoirdupois ounces of water at 68°F. Ready-to-use pie and pastry fillings such as apple, blueberry, and cherry are also available in these containers. Although frozen fruit has to some extent replaced canned water packs as the basic ingredient for preparation of bakery fillings, especially for premium goods, such ingredients as pumpkin and mince meat are not available in frozen form and, if they were, the difference in finished product quality would not be sufficient to justify replacement of the canned item with a frozen preparation.

There are FDA standards of identity for canned applesauce, apricots, ten kinds of berries, cherries, figs, fruit cocktail, seedless grapes, grapefruit, peaches, pears, pineapple, plums, and prunes. The Code of Federal Regulations, Title 21, Part 145 can be consulted for details of these requirements. There are USDA Quality Grade Standards for canned apples, apple juice, apple sauce, apricots, RTP cherries, sweet cherries, fruit cocktail, fruits for salad, grapefruit, grapefruit juice, grapefruit-orange juice, orange juice, cling peaches, pears, and tangerine juice. The appropriate CFR section can be consulted, or there are convenient summaries available. (Anon. 1991).

The FDA Standards of Identity and USDA Quality Grades are helpful in composing specifications for canned fruit products, but of course they are not always sufficiently complete to permit a clear description of the exact type of material desired by some manufacturers. Often, this will require negotiations between the supplier and purchaser. It is important to know the age of the product, or more particularly, the storage history. Canned fruits do deteriorate with time, although brokers have a tendency to disregard this point.

Frozen fruits

Where quality products are particularly desired, frozen fruits can be used as the basis for pie fillings, etc. The usual industrial container encountered by bakers is the 30-lb metal can with a friction-fit lid. Sometimes sugar or sweetener syrup has been added, up to half the finished product, to help preserve flavor, color, and texture. Individually quick frozen pieces are nearly always superior in flavor and texture to bulk frozen products.

There are many critical factors in selecting a frozen ingredient for bakery use. Variety of the fruit, size and shape of the pieces (e.g., whole, diced, sliced), ripeness, post-harvest handling, rapidity of freezing, and storage history are some of the factors that have to be considered. There are USDA Grades for frozen apples, apricots, berries, blueberries, peaches, pineapple, plums, red tart pitted cherries, raspberries, rhubarb, strawberries, and some other fruits of interest to the baker. These regulations should be consulted before writing company specifications.

Apple slices, whole blueberries, whole RTP cherries, whole or sliced strawberries, blackberries, and boysenberries are some of the frozen products available from distributors, brokers, and bakery suppliers.

Fruit jams, jellies, and preserves

Most fruit butters, jellies, preserves, and related products are covered by FDA regulations that closely control their composition. Bakers do not customarily procure these standardized materials. They will likely use as ingredients not only the basic fruit raw material, but also natural or imitation flavors, coloring materials, and gel-forming substances such as starch. The finished fillings can also be obtained from bakery supply houses.

Although economy is one of the reasons for making or procuring nonstandardized adjuncts, almost as important are the needs for stronger flavored and colored finished products when the filling is used in small amounts (as in Danish pastries and cookies, but not in pies) and for uniformity. Preparation of these "fabricated" fillings will be discussed in the chapter on formulas and processes for making adjuncts, found later in this volume. Basic guidelines for procuring fruit for jams and jellies were published by the International Jelly and Preserve Association (Anon. 1978B).

VEGETABLES

Many kinds of vegetables have been used in bakery products. Everyone is familiar with carrot cake, potato bread, tomato sauces for pizza, and onion rolls, but have you heard of sauerkraut fritters, ketchup cake, or baked bean muffins? All of the latter, and many more highly imaginative recipes featuring vegetables can be found in cookbooks. The commercial demand for these innovative products seems, somehow, to be less than vigorous, but there is always the possibility that one or more of them will catch the fancy of present-day consumers who worship the deified veggie.

Limitations of space prevent the detailed discussion of all the vegetables that have been used in bakery products, but brief descriptions of a few of the most important varieties and the forms in which they will be offered to the baker will be included.

Potatoes

It is believed that most variety breads containing potatoes as an ingredient are made with potato powder (dried cooked potatoes). Many years ago, potato bread, even that made in bakeries, included as one of the ingredients a mash of peeled and cooked potatoes, often allowed to ferment for a time before it was added to the dough. Potatoes are also used in the fillings for knishes, some types of pasta, and other ethnic specialties. Doubtless most of these fillings are prepared from fresh or frozen potatoes.

The two general types of dehydrated potatoes are the dried pieces, such as dices, probably having a very limited market, and the dried mashed potatoes, which meet a big retail and wholesale demand. The latter product comes in two basic forms, granules and flakes.

The process for making granules consists of conditioning a potato mash so that it can be divided into single cells without excessive disruption of the cell walls. If cell breakage occurs, the starch that is released impedes the processing and causes the reconstituted potato to be pasty and sticky. The basic granule process is sometimes called the "add back" method. A brief description of this process follows.

The peeled raw potatoes are heated in atmospheric steam cookers for 30 to 40 minutes. To the cooked potatoes are added dried granules from a preceding batch to give an average of 35% to 40% moisture for the total. Sulfite is usually added during cooking. The mash is transferred to a cooler, where gentle agitation and air currents are used to cool it to 60° to 80°F. The mechanical action separates the cells until the bulk of the material is unicellular. Conditioning of the cooled mix for about one hour allows the starch to retrograde. Drying is typically done in two or more stages. First, a pneumatic or airlift dryer brings the granules to about 12% moisture. Then, a fluidized bed dryer brings the mass to 6% to 7% moisture. Between the stages, the granules are sieved and the larger particles, with some of the finer particles, are used in the add-back step.

Granules are packaged in No. 10 cans or 5-gallon cans, or in plastic-foil pouches. In all cases, nitrogen or carbon dioxide is used to replace air.

Onions

Because onions are used almost entirely for their flavor, the exceptions being when some textural contribution is desired, the pre-dominant quality factors are determined organoleptically or by some chemical tests related to sensory effects. It should be obvious that sanitation and microbiological requirements must also appear in the specification.

Onions have frequently been used in and on breads and bread rolls to give added appeal to otherwise rather bland foods. The dehydrated form is often used because preparation of the fresh bulbs is hardly a suitable activity for the bakery. Also, greater uniformity results from the use of standardized dehydrated material. It it believed that canned onions are not a factor in bakery formulas, but frozen onions offer a practical alternative to the dehydrated form and in some cases are more convenient.

Processing for dehydration begins by grading the onions for size. The onions may have been stored for several weeks to a few months before processing, although fresh onions are also processed during the harvesting season. Length and temperature of storage of the bulbs do have effects on the color and flavor of the dried product. The bulbs are flame-peeled and then washed to remove the organic debris and other undesirable material. High-velocity air streams and then high-pressure water jets are used to wash away the charred skins and dirt. After inspection and removal of damaged material, the tops and roots are trimmed off. The cleaned and trimmed bulbs are sliced or chipped by automatic equipment. There is no blanching step in onion dehydration, since enzyme activity is needed to develop the typical flavor. The characteristic odor of onions and other members of their genus arises from enzymatic reactions initiated by cutting or otherwise damaging the tissue.

Dehydration occurs in hot-air tunnels. The older type of dehydrator uses stacks of wooden trays to convey the onion pieces through the tunnel. In newer dehydrators, the onion slices or dices are placed on stainless steel belts. In either case, hot air is blown in alternate directions in successive compartments of the dryer, entering first at the exit end. The total drying period of about three hours is divided into three temperature stages, 165°F. 145°F, and 130°-140°F. The onions do not reach the necessary dryness in the tunnel, so they are put into finishing bins where warm air currents complete the drying and facilitate equilibration of the remaining water. The resulting pieces may be milled to give products of varying particle size.

Dehydrated onions are very hygroscopic. Moisture absorption leads to physical and chemical instability and causes the powdered forms to cake severely. If kept cool and dry, dehydrated onions can be stored for several years (Jones and Mann 1963). Some of the readily available dehydrated onion products are sliced, chopped, diced, minced, ground, granulated, and powdered. In flavor replacement value, approximately one pound of sliced, chopped, or minced onions has the flavor of eight pounds of prepared raw onions. One pound of ground, powdered, or granulated onions has the equivalent flavor of ten pounds of raw, finely ground onions (Anon. 1989A).

Shallots, chives, leeks, and garlic are other members of the onion genus available in dehydrated form. The baker will seldom have a need for shallots or leeks, but chives may have some application where their appearance provides consumer appeal. Garlic is common in many flavor combinations used in snack products, and, of course, in pizza toppings, but very likely the baker will for these applications procure the ready-mixed spices that include powdered garlic.

Tomatoes

The pizza manufacturer will buy canned tomato products. There are Federal Standards of Identity for tomato pulp or puree, tomato paste, and concentrated tomato juice that cover the composition of most commercially available tomato concentrates. These are in the class of foods prepared by concentrating one or any combination of two or more of: (1) The liquid obtained from mature tomatoes of the reddish varieties (*Lycopersicum esculentum* P. Mill); (2) The liquid obtained from the residue obtained from preparing such tomatoes for canning; or (3) The liquid obtained from the residue from partial extraction of juice from such tomatoes. Optional ingredients, which must be declared on the label, include salt, lemon juice, sodium bicarbonate, water, spices, and flavoring. "Tomato puree" and "tomato pulp" contains 8.0% or more, but less than 24.0% of tomato soluble solids. "Tomato paste" contains not less than 24.0% tomato soluble solids.

U.S. Standards for Grades of Canned Tomato Paste include provisions for the following levels of concentration, as measured by the content of natural tomato soluble solids: "Extra heavy concentration," 39.3% or more solids; "Heavy concentration," 32% or more but less than 39.3% solids; "Medium concentration," 28% or more but less than 32%; and "Light concentration," at least 24% but less than 28% solids.

U.S. Standards for Grades of Canned Tomato Puree (Tomato Pulp) also contain provisions for designations of concentration, as follows: "Extra heavy concentration," 15.0% or more, but less than 24% solids; "Heavy concentration," 11.3% or more, but less than 15% solids; "Medium concentration," 10.2% or more, but less than 11.3% solids; and "Light concentration," 8% or more, but less than 10.2% solids.

Table 8.5. COMPOSITION OF SOME COMMERCIAL TOMATO PRODUCTS[1]

Component	Unit	Amount per 100 g, edible portion			
		Red ripe canned, whole	Paste, canned	Puree, canned	Powder
Water	g	93.67	74.06	87.26	3.06
Food energy	kcal	20.	84.	41.	302.
Protein	g	0.93	3.78	1.67	12.91
Total lipid	g	0.24	0.89	0.12	0.44
Carbohydrate	g	4.29	18.82	10.12	74.68
Fiber	g	0.46	0.95	0.82	6.65
Ash	g	0.87	2.45	0.94	8.91
Calcium	mg	26.	35.	15.	166.
Iron	mg	0.61	2.99	0.93	4.56
Magnesium	mg	12.	51.	24.	178.
Phosphorous	mg	19.	79.	40.	295.
Potassium	mg	221.	932.	420.	1927.
Sodium	mg	163.	65.	20.	134.
Zinc	mg	0.16	0.80	0.22	1.71
Copper	mg	0.11	0.592	0.163	1.241
Manganese	mg	NA	NA	NA	1.951
Ascorbic acid	mg	15.1	42.3	35.3	116.7
Thiamin	mg	0.045	0.155	0.071	0.913
Riboflavin	mg	0.031	0.190	0.054	0.761
Niacin	mg	0.735	3.223	1.715	9.133
Pantothenate	mg	0.167	0.753	0.440	3.760
Vitamin B-6	mg	0.090	0.380	0.152	0.457
Folacin	mcg	NA	NA	NA	119.9
Vitamin A	IU	604.	2468.	1361.	17247.

[1]Haytowitz and Matthews (1984). Protein is N x 6.25.

There are U.S. Standards for Grades of Tomato Sauce that specify color, consistency, and flavor levels for "U.S. Grade A" (also called "U.S. Fancy), "U.S. Grade C" (also called "U.S. Standard"), and "Substandard." There is no Grade B. Grading principles are similar to those for catsup except that flowability is greater than for equivalent grades of catsup.

Table 8.5 summarizes the content of some of the nutrients and other components in actual commercial samples of canned and dried tomato products. When insoluble dietary fiber was determined by the neutral detergent fiber method, a value of 0.7 g was obtained for canned whole tomatoes.

Carrots

Carrot cake has become a popular dessert item in the U.S., largely because of its supposed health benefits. Formulators have done a commendable job in flavoring the product so that the carrot flavor is hardly detectable. Even the texture one would expect to encounter from the shredded vegetable is rarely in evidence in the usual examples.

Carrots are available as fresh/refrigerated, canned, frozen, and dehydrated. It is assumed that very little, probably none, of the canned and dehydrated versions are used in making carrot cake.

There are U.S. Standards for Grades of Frozen Carrots, which are described as the clean and sound product prepared from the fresh root of the carrot plant (*Daucus carota*) by washing, sorting, peeling, trimming, and blanching, then frozen in accordance with good commercial practice. Styles include "Whole," "Halves," "Quarters," "Slices," "Diced," "Double-diced," "Strips," "Chips," and "Cut." The last term defines cut units that do not conform to any of the other styles. Grades are "U.S. Grade A" (or "U.S. Fancy"), "U.S. Grade B" (or "U.S. Extra Standard"), and "U.S. Substandard."

Very likely Grade B in the form of chips would be satisfactory for carrot cake, or alternatively, "Cut" in forms specially designed for this use. Color may or not be a quality factor, but flavor should be relatively bland.

BIBLIOGRAPHY

ANON. 1978A. Peanut butter. Federal Specification 2-P-196E. June 6, 1978

ANON. 1978B. Raw Materials Guidelines. International Jelly and Preserve Association, Atlanta, GA

ANON. 1989A. The case for dehydrated onions. Pizza Today 7, No. 10, 73-74

ANON. 1989B. Walnuts: flavor's only skin deep. Prepared Foods *158*, 95

ANON. 1991. The Almanac of the Canning, Freezing, Preserving Industries, Edition 76. Edward E. Judge & Sons, Westminster, MD

BENNION, E. B., and STEWART, J. 1930. Cake Manufacture. Leonard Hill, Ltd., London

BERGHOLZ, B., JR. 1957. Elements of raisin bread production. Proc. Am. Soc. Bakery Engineers *1957*, 77-82

BOYLE, F. P. 1974. Dates. In Encyclopedia of Food Technology. A. H. Johnson and M. S. Peterson, Editors. AVI Publishing Co., Westport, CT

FAGRELL, E. A. 1990. Some quality comparisons of raisins from around the world. Cereal Foods World *35*, 1016-1018

FREEMAN, A. F., MORRIS, N. J., and WILLICH, R. K. 1954. Peanut butter. U.S. Dept. Agr. *A1C-370*

GANNIS, P., and WILKINS, H. 1990. Products and process for preparing low-fat roasted nuts. U.S. Pat. 4,938,987

GEBHARDT, S. E., CUTRUFELLI, R., and MATTHEWS, R. H. (Editors) 1982. Composition of Foods: Fruits and Fruit Juices. USDA Human Nutrition Information Service Ag. Hdbk. *8-9*

HAYTOWITZ, D. B., and MATTHEWS, R. H. (Editors) 1984. Composition of Foods: Vegetables and Vegetable Products. USDA Human Nutrition Information Service Ag. Hdbk. *8-11*

MALONEY, J. F., SANDER, E. H., and WILHELM, A. 1970. Edible food product and process. U.S. Pat. 3,505,076

MANGE, C., and ALLARD, G.-A. 1989. Process for preparing almond paste. U.S. Pat. 4,839,193

MCCARTHY, M. A., and MATTHEWS, R. H. (Editors) 1984. Composition of Foods: Nut and Seed Products. USDA Human Nutrition Information Service Ag. Hdbk. *8-12*

MURPHY, R. J. 1981. Variety breads, Part II. Proc. Am. Soc. Bakery Engineers *1981* 46-53

PATTEE, H. E. 1985. Evaluation of Quality of Fruits and Vegetables. AVI Publishing Co., Westport, CT

PATTEE, H. E., PEARSON, J. L., YOUNG, C. T., and GIESBRECHT, F. G. 1982. Changes in roasted peanut flavor and other quality factors with seed size and storage time. J. Food Sci. *47*, 455-460

RANHOFER, R. 1893. The Epicurean (from the reproduction issued in 1971 by Dover Publications, New York, NY)

WEBB, W. A. 1989. Process for dehydrating and puffing food particles. U.S. Pat. 4,844,931

WOODROOF, J. G. 1979A. Coconuts: Production, Processing, Products, Second Edition. AVI Publishing Co., Westport, CT

WOODROOF, J. G. 1979B. Tree Nuts: Production, Processing, Products, Second Edition. AVI Publishing Co., Westport, CT

WOODROOF, J. G. 1983. Peanuts: Production, Processing, Products, Third Edition. AVI Publishing Co., Westport, CT

WOODROOF, J. G., and LUH, B. S. 1986. Commercial Fruit Processing, Second Edition. AVI Publishing Co., Westport, CT

YOUSIF, A. K., MORTON, I. D., and MUSTAFA, A. I. 1991. Functinality of date paste in breadmaking. Cereal Chem. *68*, 43-47

ZIEMKE, W. H. 1982. Raisins—character profile of their use and application. Am. Soc. Bakery Engineers Bulletin *215*

chapter nine

SPICES, FLAVORS, AND COLORS

INTRODUCTION

It hardly needs to be said that the flavor and color of a bakery product must meet the expectations of the final consumer if the manufacturer is to achieve lasting success in the marketplace. Some of the color and flavor will be due, of course, to the major ingredients such as flour, sugar, shortening, and (if they are present) milk and eggs. In the case of fermented doughs, the tasty and pleasantly aromatic products of yeast action will enhance the acceptability of the finished products. More is needed, however, to pique the taste of the modern consumer. Fortunately, bakers have access to a wide selection of spices, flavors, and colors.

COLORING ADDITIVES

Both artificial and natural coloring agents are used in the bakery industry to enhance the visual appeal of products. In cases where Standards of Identity for a product have been promulgated, the options available for improving color with additives are very limited, but in products for which such Standards have not been established, a fairly wide choice of coloring ingredients is available.

All food colors must be selected from substances approved by government agencies, principally the FDA. Food ingredients such as cocoa, green peppers, grape juice, or tomatoes which contribute their own natural color when mixed with other foods are not regarded as "color additives," but food substances deliberately added for the purpose of coloration (as when beet juice is used in pink lemonade) are "color additives."

There are two categories of acceptable color additives: certified colors and uncertified colors. Uncertified colors are all permitted color additives not falling into the "Certified" category. Certified colors include chemically synthesized dyes and their lakes. Lakes are made by adsorbing or chemically combining water-soluble dyes with certain specified insoluble materials. Table 9.1 lists all of currently permitted uncertified additives while Table 9.2 lists the certified pigments. Citrus Red No. 2 and Orange B are certified colors, but are not approved for use in bakery products.

Any manufacturer who plans to use these materials as food ingredients should verify their status by consulting the appropriate government bulletins. The federal regulations affecting the status of food color additives can be found in the Code of Federal Regulations (mostly in 21 CFR 74 and 21 CFR 82). Most color suppliers will have this information on file and should be willing to furnish it upon request.

Table 9.1. CERTIFIED COLOR ADDITIVES FOR FOODS

Type of Listing	
Permanent	Provisional
FD&C Red No. 3	FD&C Yellow No. 6 Lake
FD&C Blue No. 2	FD&C Red No. 3 Lake
FD&C Yellow No. 5	FD&C Blue No. 1 Lake
FD&C Green No. 3	FD&C Blue No. 2 Lake
FD&C Blue No. 1	FD&C Green No. 3 Lake
FD&C Red No. 40	FD&C Yellow No 5 Lake
FD&C Red No. 40 Lake	
FD&C Yellow No. 6	

The chemical compounds making up the category of certified color additives have been subjected to a very thorough program of toxicity tests. According to Borzellaca *et al.* (1982), there were no consistent, statistically significant and biologically relevant compound-related effects when these colors were fed to mice and rats at varying levels up to 5% of their diets.

The uncertified color additives listed in Table 9.2 include pigments extracted from fruits, vegetables, and other common edibles, inorganic substances that are not expected to be absorbed by the body (e.g., titanium dioxide), and some synthesized materials that are more or less similar to certain natural products. Among the last group, carotenoids are particularly useful as bakery product colorants because they simulate the color of butter and eggs. Algae meal, corn endosperm oil, ferrous gluconate, grape skin extract (enocianina), synthetic iron oxide, tagetes meal and extract, and ultramarine blue have been approved for some food uses but not for bakery foods and so are not included in Table 9.2.

Only those food dyes of significance to bakers will be discussed in detail in the following section. Worthwhile discussions of other food colorants can be found in the article edited by Newsome (1986) and the review by Zuckerman and Senackerib (1979).

Uncertified Color Additives

Carotenoids.—The class of chemicals called carotenoids is comprised of a large group of compounds, some of which have potent biological activity (Gordon and Bauernfeind 1982). About 400 of these substances have been identified, but only beta-apo-8'-carotenal, beta-carotene, and canthaxanthin are marketed for food applications in the U.S. Beta-carotene produces a bright yellow color and has been recommended as a replacement for FD&C Yellow No. 5. Apocarotenal gives an orange-yellow color similar to that obtained from FD&C Yellow No. 6. Both beta-carotene and apocarotenal have provitamin A activity, with the former compound equivalent to 1,667 IU of vitamin A per milligram, and the latter equivalent to 1,200 IU per mg.

These substances are insoluble in water and slightly soluble in fats and oils. They are somewhat unstable in air because oxidative reactions occur, and light increases the rate of oxidation. In their marketed forms, beta-carotene and apocarotenal are either suspended or dissolved in an oil or are emulsified into a water-soluble matrix that can be converted into beadlets or spray-dried powders (Emodi *et al.* 1980).

Table 9.2. UNCERTIFIED COLOR ADDITIVES FOR FOODS

Colorant	Upper limits of use
Annatto extract	--
Beta-apo-8'-carotenal	15 mg per lb or per pt
Beta-carotene	--
Beet powder	--
Canthaxanthin	30 mg per lb or per pt
Caramel	--
Carrot oil	--
Cochineal extract (carmine)	--
Cottonseed flour (toasted, etc.)	--
Fruit juice	--
Grape color extract	--
Paprika and its oleoresin	--
Riboflavin	--
Saffron	--
Titanium dioxide	Maximum of 1%
Turmeric and its oleoresin	--
Vegetable juice	--

Beta-carotene is used in such bakery products as sweet doughs, cakes, and rich yeast breads. A suspension of 30% beta-carotene in vegetable oil has been recommended for production systems where it is convenient and practical to color the fat phase. This is also the most economical version of the colorant. If a water dispersible form is needed, the usual choice is a beadlet which includes surfactants and other dispersing agents in addition to about 2.4% of the beta-carotene. A stock solution is prepared shortly before addition to the doughs by adding 1 lb of the beadlets to four pounds of water. From 1.5 to 4 fluid ounces of the stock solution is used for each 100 lb of batter, depending on the final color desired.

Some loss of color can occur during mixing and baking, because of chemical alterations in the compound. Extended exposure to direct sunlight will also fade bakery goods colored with beta-carotene.

Caramel colors.—Caramel colors are important ingredients for the food industry because they can give rich brown shades that are difficult to achieve using dyestuffs, and they are relatively inexpensive.

Caramel colors have no relationship to caramel candy. They are usually manufactured by heating high-DE corn syrups in the presence of reactants (or catalysts) such as certain alkalies. These ingredients are supplied to bakers as a dark, almost black syrup having a density of about 11 lb per gallon and a solids content near 65%. These syrups are fairly low in viscosity compared to corn syrups of similar solids. Their flavor is mild, slightly bitter, and not particularly appealing. They are never used for flavoring purposes.

Although the hues or the spectral distribution of color from the different kinds and brands of caramel are similar, this ingredient imparts varying shades to the finished product, depending on the amount used and the background colors. The color of the finished product may range from a light tannish yellow to a very dark brown. Caramel color is not as potent as most synthetic colors; a larger quantity has to be used to give the same color intensity. Color may lighten and hues change after prolonged exposure to light. Francis and Clydesdale (1972) described measuring the intensity of caramel colors by Lovibond Tintometers and and absorptimetric methods.

Table 9.3. SPECIFICATIONS OF SOME CARAMEL COLORS[1]

Description	Baume* or moisture content	Color intensity	Shelf life	pH
Double strength acid proof Caramel color	*30.5–31.5	239–247	Min. 2 yr	2.5–3.0
No. 111 Caramel color	*34.7–35.6	145–150	Min. 2 yr	3.0–3.6
No. 252 Powdered caramel	*29.3–31.7	180–200	Min. 6 mo	4.0–5.0
color No. 600 Powdered caramel	Max. 4.0%	240–280	Unlimited	4.5–5.5
color No. 602 Powdered caramel	Max. 4.0%	455–515	Unlimited	4.5–5.5
color No. 643	Max. 4.0%	270–310	Unlimited	7.5–8.5

[1] Data from literature of D. D. Williamson & Co.

The colloidal particles that make up the bulk of a mass of fluid caramel color are held in suspension by small electrical charges. Caramel can be made with these charges either negative or positive. Charge has an effect on the tendency of colloidal particles to coalesce and precipitate. It is necessary that caramel used in soft drinks such as colas be of the negatively charged type so that it is not precipitated in the acid environment; these caramels are called "acid proof." Bakers need not specify this type of ingredient.

Rather large quantities of caramel color are used in rye breads and whole wheat breads. The consumer expects these products to be dark in color and equates a light color with poor quality, while most bakers know that breads made with large percentages of whole wheat flour or dark rye flour would be unacceptable to most consumers because of poor texture or harsh flavor. The solution is to use light rye flour and smaller amounts of

whole wheat flour while achieving the desired dark color by adding caramel.
Common containers for caramel color are 5-gal steel pails, 30-gal steel
or fiber drums, and 56-gal steel drums. Bulk deliveries in rail tankers and
tank trucks are available. Color changes occur in stored caramel color, but
even so, high quality caramel colors can be stored a year or longer at room
temperature. Under certain adverse conditions, caramel can polymerize into
an amorphous gel, and this change cannot be reversed.

Dry, powdered versions of caramel color are sold by some manufacturers, but they are considerably more expensive than the syrups.

Table 9.3 gives some of the specifications for 3 powdered and 3 liquid
caramel colors. Color intensity is determined by a Food Chemicals Codex
method involving measurement of absorbence at 610 nm; pH of liquids is on
an "as is" basis, for dry materials a 1% solution is measured.

Carmine.—This material is a relatively expensive natural colorant
sometimes used in food adjuncts such as icings. Carminic acid is extracted
by acidic aqueous solvent from the dried bodies of certain insects gathered
in Mexico, Central America, South America, and the Canary Islands. The
pigment is precipitated (laked) on to a substratum of aluminum hydrate
using aluminum and calcium ions as precipitants. The resultant lake is
called carmine (Stern and Leon 1984). The die is pH sensitive, becoming
yellow at pH 4.8 and below, and violet at pH 6.2.

Fruit and vegetable extracts.—The colored juices from certain
plants have been used as colorants for millenia. Some of the old favorites
are no longer in good repute, however, because they were found to contain
toxic materials. Annatto extract, beet powder, carrot oil, fruit juice (any
edible kind), grape color extract, grape skin extract (also called enocianina),
and vegetable juices are currently in the list of uncertified colors for foods.
Some of these have good potential for bakery foods. Although the hues they
contribute are perhaps not often called for in doughs and batters, they
might be helpful in coloring pie fillings, icings, and other adjuncts.

Riboflavin.—This vitamin is a permitted food colorant, but its cost
and flavor would seem to rule it out for nearly all food applications.

Spices.—Certain spices can be effective natural colorants. Many
spices have this effect (which is sometimes undesirable), but only turmeric
and paprika have mild enough flavors and strong enough colors to be of
practical value as food pigments. These spices are described in the flavor
section of this chapter. Turmeric oleoresin and paprika oleoresin are more
potent forms of these natural coloring materials. Saffron is also used as a
food color, but its extremely high cost makes it prohibitive for all but a very
few specialty items.

Titanium dioxide.—This manufactured mineral substance is useful where an insoluble non-nutritive white color is needed. One percent is the maximum that can be added. The cost of the material is reasonable and it has practically infinite stability. Icings would be the most likely application for this ingredient.

Table 9.4. COMPARISON OF LAKES AND DYES[1]

Characteristic	Dyes	Lakes
Solubility	Soluble in water, glycerol, etc.	Insoluble in most solvents
Method of coloring	By being dissolved	By dispersion
Pure dye content	Primary colors: 90% to 93%	Mostly 10% to 40%
Rate of use	0.01% to 0.03%	0.1% to 0.3%
Particle size	12 mesh to 200 mesh	Aver. <0.5 micron
Stability--		
--to light	Good	Better
--to heat	Good	Better
Coloring strength	Directly related to dye content	Not proportional to dye content
Shade or hue	Constant	Varies with dye content

[1] Adapted from Anon. (1986)

Certified Color Additives

The two kinds of colors in the certified list are lakes and dyes. Dyes are almost chemically pure pigments, with perhaps 10% of non-coloring matter, which is difficult or impossible to remove or is included to promote solubility, etc. Lakes are dyes that have been deposited on microscopic particles of some insoluble material. The FDA regulations describe lakes as being made by ". . .extending on a substratum of alumina a salt prepared from one of the certified water-soluble straight colors hereinbefore listed in this subpart by combining such color with the basic radical aluminum or calcium." Dyes and lakes differ in several important characteristics, as shown in Table 9.4. Dyes are generally more suitable for doughs, batters, pastry cremes, pie fillings, etc. Lakes might be better for icings, fat-based fillings, etc. Solicit advice from your supplier for specialized applications.

NATURAL AND ARTIFICIAL FLAVORS

Vanilla

Vanilla is one of the most common flavorings added to bakery foods. It is not only a very desirable flavor by itself, but is also an essential note in chocolate goods and many other compound flavors. Vanilla comes from the fruit of an orchid cultivated in tropical and semi-tropical countries. These pods, much like long (4 to 12 inch) string beans in appearance, are without desirable odor and flavor until they are cured in special ways to develop the characteristic aroma and taste of vanilla.

The following method is said to be followed in Mexican curing of vanilla beans (Riley and Kleyn 1989): (1) The pods are stored in sheds until the pods are shriveled; (2) When the pods have shriveled, they are transferred to large wooden sweating boxes; (3) The boxes are surrounded with mats that help to maintain the sweating temperature until the desired enzymatic reactions are completed; (4) The process is repeated daily until the pods acquire a dark brown color; (5) The frequency of the "sunning/sweating" is reduced to lower the moisture content; and (6) The pods are placed in aging boxes in the warehouse for two to three months.

A recently introduced method of curing requires treating the beans with hot water for enzyme activation and mobilization of substrate by cell wall disruption, reacting for three to four days under controlled humidity and temperature to allow the beans to develop desirable aroma and color, then drying in forced hot air ovens.

Vanillin is the major flavoring component, but at least 170 other volatile compounds are present in cured vanilla beans. Many of these, such as p-hydroxybenzaldehyde, p-hydroxybenzyl methyl ether, acetic acid, and diastereoisomeric vitispiranes, are important factors in the characteristic vanilla flavor and aroma.

Although the ground pod is sometimes added directly to foods as an ingredient, it is far more common to use alcoholic extracts which incorporate nearly all of the desirable flavor notes present in the plant material. Pods are sliced into pieces about one-half inch in length, then immersed in dilute ethanol until extraction is deemed to be complete. Some manufacturers use a cold extraction, said to preserve more of the delicate top notes, while others use warm or hot alcohol. The alcohol is usually circulated constantly through the mass of chopped beans. The extract is clarified by centrifugation and filtration and then aged in glass or stainless steel containers until the reactions that lead to an optimal aroma have taken place.

The vanilla beans of commerce are described by type or region of origin, such as Mexican, Bourbon, Tahitian, etc. It is of little value for the baker to prescribe the bean blend for purchased extracts, however, since there is no reliable practical way to police the deliveries. Mexican and Bourbon vanilla have superior characteristics and are difficult to distinguish from one another.

Pure vanilla extract and some vanilla-vanillin blends have been defined by FDA Standards (21 CFR 169). Vanilla extract is defined in part as follows: ". . .the solution in aqueous ethyl alcohol of the sapid and odorous principles extractable from vanilla beans. In vanilla extract the content of ethyl alcohol is not less than 35 percent by volume and the content of vanilla constituent [as described elsewhere] is not less than one unit per gallon. The vanilla constituent may be extracted directly from vanilla beans or it may be added in the form of concentrated vanilla extract or concentrated vanilla flavoring or vanilla flavoring concentrated to the semisolid form called vanilla oleoresin. Vanilla extract may contain one or more of the following ingredients: (1) Glycerin, (2) Propylene glycol, (3) Sugar (including invert sugar), (4) Dextrose, (5) Corn sirup (including dried corn sirup)."

"Vanilla beans" are elsewhere defined (21 CFR 169.3) as "the properly cured and dried fruit pods of *Vanilla planifolia* Andrews and of *Vanilla tahitensis* Moore." The term "unit weight " means, 13.35 ounces in the case of vanilla beans containing not more than 25% moisture, and, in the case of vanilla beans containing more than 25% moisture, it means the weight of such beans equivalent in moisture-free vanilla-bean solids to 13.35 ounces of vanilla beans containing 25% moisture. The term "unit of vanilla constituent" means the total sapid and odorous principles extractable from one unit weight of vanilla beans by an aqueous alcohol solution in which the content of ethyl alcohol by volume amounts to not less than 35%. Moisture content is to be determined by a referenced method in the AOAC compilation, which is a toluene distillation method. Standards are given for "vanilla extract," "concentrated vanilla extract," "vanilla flavoring" (similar to regular vanilla extract except that it contains less alcohol), "concentrated vanilla flavoring," "vanilla powder" (ground vanilla beans or oleoresin coated on to a powder such as starch), "vanilla-vanillin extract," "vanilla-vanillin flavoring," and "vanilla-vanillin powder."

Because nearly all manufacturers make vanilla extracts by similar processes and which contain concentrations of flavorants established by the Standards, flavor qualities of different extracts will depend mostly on the type of vanilla beans used. Mexican beans are said to yield the finest, strongest flavor. Beans from Indian Ocean growers (Bourbon) are described as generally richer in top aromatics and lacking in the deeper notes. West Indian products are intermediate in character between the Bourbon and the Mexican. Tahitian vanilla is different in aromatic character from all others, having a sweetness that comes from the heliotropine-like compounds developed during the cure. According to Ranadive (1990), Mexican beans have been substantially unavailable since about 1975. True though that may be, liter bottles of ostensibly pure vanilla extract are sold by the thousands to U.S. tourists in Mexico. Ranadive further states that Malagasy is the major supplier of vanilla beans, followed by Indonesia, both supplying *Vanilla planifolia* products.

Oleoresin of vanilla is prepared by evaporating under vacuum the filtered extract of comminuted vanilla beans. It consists mostly of the resinous substances of the vanilla beans with very little of the balsamic flavor of the original extract. Oleoresin can be diluted with solvents to give the 10-fold extracts sometimes offered to bakers. No more than 4-fold concentration is possible using extraction methods only. Powdered vanilla or vanilla sugar is made by mixing ground beans with sugar or by coating sugar granules with an extract.

It is unfortunate that vanilla extracts sold to food manufacturers have the reputation of being the most frequently adulterated of all food ingredients. Of course, mixtures of artificial flavors and pure vanilla are perfectly legal if properly labeled. This does not constitute adulteration, which results when the flavor (as extract or as part of a consumer product) is stated to be, or implied to be, pure vanilla. The baker who wishes to use only pure vanilla, and to label his products accordingly, will find it advisable to buy only from reliable suppliers and to be prepared to pay more than the lowest price quoted on multiple bids. Careful evaluation of incoming shipments is very important as a means of keeping the supplier honest. A retention sample (held in a sealed bottle kept under refrigeration) should always be compared to the contents of each container received. Many cases have occurred where the shipped material did not match the approved sample, even though they bore the same stock number or the same batch number.

Chemical analyses alone cannot determine the quality of the extract or its purity, although gas chromatographers have made great advances in detecting adulteration. Traditional tests for quality include determinations of the lead number, the ash content, and the vanillin content. Each of these tests can be circumvented by fairly simple ruses if the supplier is dishonest. More definitive is the stable isotope ratio analysis (SIRA), which can detect synthetic vanillin additions unless the synthetic molecule is itself labelled (see Riley and Kleyn 1989 for details). High pressure liquid chromatography to determine the presence or absence of some of the trace compounds from vanilla beans is also helpful.

It has been shown by panel tests that consumers prefer bakery products made with pure vanilla extracts as opposed to artificial flavors when the two products are compared side-by-side. The difference in acceptability ratings is usually slight, on the average, and tends to disappear when there is not a comparison sample readily available.

Although it does not appear that artificial flavors can fully reproduce the fine aroma and delicate taste contributed by good quality vanilla extracts, most consumers find vanillin or mixtures of vanillin and ethyl vanillin to be perfectly acceptable substitutes for the natural product.

In very delicately flavored pastry creams and fillings, the differences between vanilla and vanillin are fairly obvious to many tasters, but it is considerably harder to distinguish between chocolate products (for example) that are flavored with the two materials. Many very successful food products, such as the most popular chocolate bars, rely entirely on artificial vanilla flavor, i.e., vanillin. Because the synthetic materials are so much cheaper, on an equivalent strength basis, than vanilla extracts, most bakers are willing to forgo the nuances of flavor, which are usually not appreciated by their customers, in favor of a more competitive ingredient cost.

The aromatic components of both artificial and natural vanilla flavorings tend to be lost in the baking process. Many of the minor constituents of vanilla distill off quicker than vanillin, so the change in flavor during baking is more apparent in products containing pure vanilla. The loss is greatest at elevated oven temperatures and in products baked almost to dryness, such as cookies. Ethyl vanillin is considerably more expensive than vanillin, but it does have a stronger flavor. The flavor character of the two compounds is quite different, however, so a meaningful comparison of effective ingredient cost of the two substances is difficult. Frequently, the best results are obtained by using mixtures of the two compounds.

The Code of Federal Regulations citation given above contains Standards of Identity for vanilla-vanillin extract, vanilla-vanillin flavoring, and vanilla-vanillin powder, in addition to others.

Cacao Products

Federal regulations are frequently found to be useful guides for establishing commercial requirements for ingredients. There are Federal Standards of Identity for Cacao Products, covering cacao nibs, chocolate liquor, breakfast cocoa, cocoa, low-fat cocoa, cocoa with dioctyl sodium sulfosuccinate, sweet chocolate, milk chocolate, buttermilk chocolate, skim milk chocolate, mixed dairy product chocolate, sweet cocoa and vegetable fat coating, sweet chocolate and vegetable fat coating, and milk chocolate and vegetable fat coating. Some of these products are virtually unknown to present day chocolate processors, others are used in large quantities by the baking industry.

The raw material for chocolate and cocoa is the seed of an evergreen tree of the genus *Theobroma*. Many of these seeds are borne in a pod somewhat resembling a large acorn squash. After removing the seeds from their pod and fermenting them to facilitate removal of the surrounding pulp and to develop important flavor precursors, they are dried or cured. Next follows a roasting step that further develops the flavor and loosens the outer covering of the seeds.

Roasting affects many characteristics of the finished chocolate, including flavor and color. Flavor reaches a peak and then declines and acquires off-notes with continued roasting. Color continues to deepen until the finished chocolate (and the cocoa made from it) becomes black, reflecting an essentially charred state. Many of the very dark cocoas are made by intensifying the dutching process applied to the pressed cocoa because high heat treatment of chocolate liquor damages the cocoabutter.

After the hulls (and sometimes the germs) are removed by crushing and air aspiration, the remainder of the seed (now in small chunks called nibs) is ready for processing into chocolate. Roasting can be applied to nibs, meal, ground meal, or the milled paste (Wissgott 1988). The most common, or at least the traditional, roasting pattern is to apply mild heat treatment to the whole beans for the principal purpose of making the hulls brittle and easy to break off, then to separate the nibs from the mixture and complete their roasting.

The nibs are subjected to grinding and milling procedures that reduce the non-fatty substances ("cocoa solids") to colloidal size and develop the texture which is characteristic of chocolate liquor—also known as bitter chocolate and bakers' chocolate. At this point in the process, the chocolate is in the form of a very viscous liquid or paste; if allowed to cool it would solidify into a hard brittle mass. When subjected to the sequence of temperature changes called "tempering," and then placed into molds and cooled, the bars or other shapes supplied to the bakery trade by chocolate manufacturers are obtained.

Tempering is critical to all chocolate usage (not to cocoa use), so a brief discussion will be included here. The principle of the operation is to set the crystals of cocoa butter in a form or state that will resist the movement of lower melting fractions to the surface of the chocolate piece. It must be noted that no form of tempering will prevent the formation of bloom if the temperature of the piece rises above about 105°-110°F for more than a few minutes. To begin the tempering operation, the chocolate must be brought to about 115° to 120°F, at which point the cocoabutter melts rather quickly and all of it becomes liquid. The chocolate must now be cooled under agitation and relatively slowly to the 84°-86°F range; no part of the chocolate must be allowed to fall significantly below this range. Under these conditions of agitation and slow cooling, cocoabutter assumes the form called "beta crystals," and after the entire mass has been at this temperature for at least ten minutes, it can be deposited in molds. As the chocolate chills, it becomes substantially more viscous and it is necessary to vibrate the molds and use other strategems to assure complete filling of all the cavity. The three different kinds of eating chocolate, semi-sweet, sweet, and milk, behave somewhat differently and more detailed references should be consulted for details.

Recent developments (Wiedmann 1989) have demonstrated the possibility of using cooker-extruders to crush, roast, and alkalize the nibs, which are then comminuted in a separate mill, and finally, transferred to another extruder where heat treatment is continued and the paste mixed with other ingredients such as sugar.

Addition of milk solids and/or sugar together with other flavoring materials such as vanilla, and sometimes emulsifiers, to chocolate liquor produces the "eating" chocolate varieties milk chocolate, sweet chocolate, and bittersweet chocolate. These products contain a minimum of 10%, 15%, and 35% chocolate liquor, respectively. Although these materials are seldom used directly as flavors in baked products, they do appear frequently in adjuncts (icings, coatings, etc.) and are often used as small or large pieces in chocolate chip cookies and the like.

Table 9.5 includes data on a few composition factors of some familiar cocoa varieties.

At some point in its manufacture, the chocolate may be conched to improve mouthfeel, flavor, etc. Conching involves lengthy vigorous agitation of heated chocolate, sometimes in a partial vacuum. The changes undergone by the product during this treatment are still matters of debate among the experts. Conching is of greatest value for chocolate that is to be consumed in bar or piece form, and probably has less utility for baking chocolate.

Cocoa is prepared by separating most of the fat from the liquor in a filter press. The hot cocoabutter emerges as a clear, yellowish liquid having a pleasant aroma. The hard filter cake is "kibbled" or broken into relatively small pieces for further processing. The chunks are then ground in various kinds of mills, usually in the presence of refrigerated air currents, until a very fine powder is obtained, or they may be further treated with alkali and heat to give dutched cocoa, assuming the liquor was not alkalized. By adjusting treatment conditions, including the gas present during treatment, various colors can be obtained, including the highly desired dark red-brown. Very dark colors can be obtained, but the flavor of the cocoa suffers.

Table 9.5. COMPOSITION AND pH OF SOME CACAO PRODUCTS[1]

Component	Roasted Nibs	Breakfast cocoa	Dutch breakfast	Sweet chocolate	Milk chocolate	Chocolate syrup
Moisture	3.0	3.9	5.0	1.4	1.1	31.0
Ash	2.8	5.0	8.0	1.4	1.7	1.9
Protein	10.5	8.0	7.7	4.0	6.0	3.5
Fat	55.0	23.8	21.5	33.0	33.5	1.1
Fiber	2.6	4.6	4.3	1.4	0.5	0.6
Alkaloids	1.45	1.9	2.0	0.4	0.4	NA
Carbohydrates	25.2	44.3	40.2	61.3	55.2	56.0
pH	4.9	5.6	6.1-8.8	5.6	5.6	NA

[1] Composition in percent as is. "Carbohydrate" does not include fiber.

The flavor quality of chocolate owes a great deal to the type and origin of the cacao beans from which it is made. Beans are generally named for the port from which they have traditionally been shipped and the crop season—thus, "mid-crop Accra." There are exceptions to this system of nomenclature. The roaster will often blend "basic" beans of strong but perhaps harsh flavor and "flavor" beans that give an aromatic, smooth, blended quality to the flavor of the finished chocolate. There are also some beans that have very little flavor, and they are used largely for economic reasons. Basic beans include those called Accra, Bahia, Lagos, Sanchez, Ivory Coast, Fernando Po, and Cameroon. Flavor beans include Arriba, Trinidad, Caracas, Puerto Cabello, Maracaibo, and Rio Caribe. Varying degrees of heat treatment are used to develop or modify the flavor potential of beans. Because of the difficulty of monitoring the varietal content of a chocolate or cocoa, the baker will usually decide not to specify the blend, relying instead on a requirement that future shipments match the characteristics of retention samples retained from an approved batch.

Alkalizing is a process that can be applied to chocolate nibs, chocolate liquor, or cocoa press cake. The pH of "natural" cocoa is slightly acid, typically about 5.2, as a result of the fermentation the beans have experienced. Treatment of cocoa nibs with alkali (such as potassium carbonate) at some stage during the roasting process profoundly changes their character-istics and gives the "dutched" or alkalized chocolates and cocoas of com-merce with pHs in the range of about 6.8 to 7.5. Some of these changes are: (1) the color of the cocoa becomes darker and this darkening carries over to suspensions of the cocoa provided the pH is not changed by the suspending medium; (2) the flavor changes and becomes less harsh; (3) some of the cocoa butter is saponified; (4) the starch is partly gelatinized; (5) cellulosic materials swell; (6) some of the seed's tissues are disintegrated; and (7) the natural cocoa acids are neutralized so that the slightly acidic pH of a natural cocoa changes to a neutral or slightly alkaline pH. The net changes of importance to the baking industry are the changes in color and flavor that make it possible to use less of the cocoa to get the same organoleptic impact, and an increase in the solution stability of the ingredient. Experts will usually say that only the dispersibility is improved while the solubility remains unchanged when cocoa is dutched. It does appear, however, that some increase in soluble or colloidal materials often results. Some alkalizing treatments change the hue of the cocoa from a dark brown to a reddish-brown, which is preferred in many applications.

The Federal Standard of Identity for Cocoa (21 CFR 163) stipulates that breakfast cocoa must contain at least 22% cacao fat, "cocoa" or medium-fat cocoa must contain at least 10% but less than 22% cacao fat, and low fat cocoa must contain less than 10% cacao fat. Medium-fat cocoa will be chosen by nearly all bakers as the ingredient for all of their formulas in which a chocolate flavor is desired, and cocoa containing 10% to 12% fat will be spe-cified. Breakfast cocoa costs considerably more than medium-fat cocoa but provides few, if any, benefits in flavor and color. On the other hand, low-fat cocoa is not usually significantly cheaper than medium-fat cocoa, and often has flavor or color difficulties arising from the fat extraction process.

Many writers have published tables of correction factors to apply to the shortening percentage when cocoas of varying fat contents are added to, e.g., a plain or vanilla batter. Actually, cocoa butter is not a particularly good shortening agent and probably does not function in this capacity to any great extent in most formulas. At any rate, the use of a universal correction factor for all types of batters and doughs is certain to lead to difficulties. When a product containing cocoa is to be formulated, it should be developed by the usual thorough experimental process and not by calculations based on published correction factors for shortening equivalents.

Tests applied to cocoa products to determine their quality include: (1) fat content; (2) particle size; (3) color—both intrinsic and potential; (4) pH; (5) moisture content; (6) flavor; and (7) microbiological contamination. Color and flavor are best evaluated in the food in which the ingredient will be used, since both of these characteristics can change markedly depending on proccessing conditions and associated ingredients. Color, especially, is much affected by the pH of the finished product. The appearance of the dry cocoa powder can be considered only a rough guide to its coloring power, partly because the status of the fat has an effect on appearance.

Because of its method of manufacture, it is difficult to hold the fat content of the cocoa closer than plus or minus 1% of the specification level. For this reason, it is customary to specify at least a 2% range, such as 10% to 12% fat. There are significant differences between fat content determined by the Soxhlet extraction procedure and by the acid hydrolysis method, so it is necessary to state in the specification the analytical procedure by which the fat will be determined.

The pH of a water slurry of natural (non-alkalized) cocoas will vary depending on many factors in the history of the material, and some of these factors are not controllable by the roaster operator. Alkalized cocoa can usually be held within a range of plus or minus 0.2 pH units by controlling the processing conditions.

Particle size is not quite as critical for bakery use as for some other applications (chocolate milk, etc.). It is more important to get finely ground cocoas for use in icings and fillings than for doughs and batters. A cocoa of very fine particle size might be described as 0.5% maximum on a 325-mesh screen. A reasonably satisfactory fineness for cocoa to be used in batters would be 0.5% maximum on a 200-mesh screen. Low-fat cocoas with granulations allowing 99.5% to pass through a 400-mesh screen are being offered.

Of course, the main reason for adding cocoa is to enhance the flavor and color of the finished bakery product, except for those unusual marketing situations where cacao ingredients are added solely to justify some label claim or legal requirement. There is no sure way of making flavor evaluations except by preparing product samples containing the ingredient in question. Organoleptic evaluations are essential. When there is an existing product for which consumer satisfaction has been established, comparison of the test sample with a control sample is the ultimate test.

When used as enrobing materials, chocolate, milk chocolate, semi-sweet chocolate, and the like must first be tempered. This process involves a sequence of temperature adjustments having as their purpose the establishment of a certain type of fat crystal habit. Properly tempered chocolate enrobing materials are more resistant to the development of fat bloom, which is a disfiguring dull greyish-white "frost" on the surface of the coated piece. Basic information on tempering has been given earlier in this section; further details may be found in the literature.

Artificial Flavors

Artificial flavors are essentially imitation flavors. Artificial does not necessarily mean synthetic. A flavor is artifical if it does not arise directly from the substance that constitutes the food so designated. Combinations of natural substances that give a butter flavor to margarine are still "artificial flavors" if they are not themselves butter. Fenugreek seed (or its extracts), when used to give a maple flavor to sugar syrup, is an imitation flavor. The examples are almost endless. It is certainly true, however, that many imitation flavors contain a substantial proportion of synthesized chemicals.

Mixing pure chemical compounds to obtain imitation flavors is an art and a science much surrounded by secrecy. Two books giving some insight into modern practices in this field are Merory's "Food Flavorings" (1968) and "Flavor Chemistry and Technology" by Heath and Reiniccius (1986). The identification of chemical substances found in natural food materials is a preliminary to simulating the natural flavor with mixtures of synthetic compounds, and it requires the most sophisticated methods of instrumental analysis, including the use of gas chromatography, high-pressure liquid chromatography, mass spectrometry, and infrared spectrophotometry.

Most natural flavors result from a combination of several or many compounds, but others can be imitated fairly well with one or two pure chemicals. As examples, 2-isobutylthiazole is suggestive of tomatoes, methyl- and ethyl-cinnamates are readily recognized as strawberry flavor, methyl anthranilate is used in large amounts as a grape flavoring, and benzaldehyde is an important note of cherry aroma (Whitaker and Evans 1987).

Flavor suppliers vary greatly in their competence and reliability. Some of them merely repackage (often, after dilution) materials obtained from other firms, or, at best, put together simple mixtures such as artificial vanilla or butter flavor. Other firms have extensive research laboratories, either in the U.S. or abroad, and manufacture many of the necessary chemical intermediates themselves. Some large firms sell most of their products to the cosmetic and soap industries, their food and beverage business being a minor factor, but they may still be willing to provide much useful technical service if they can foresee a reasonable sales volume developing.

It is important for the buyer to realize that most artificial flavors contain reactive and unstable substances capable of changing drastically during a relatively short period of storage. These changes can result in a loss of flavor, or even more damaging, the development of unpleasant flavors. Buying small quantities and storing flavor stocks at refrigerator temperatures are suggested. The cooler temperatures may, however, result in precipitation of some of the flavor's components while freezing may break emulsions or cause separation of the components in some other way. Consult the supplier for recommendations.

Flavor ingredients can also react with other dough or batter ingredients during the relatively high temperatures reached during baking, or they can evaporate or be steam-distilled from the product during cooking. It is very difficult to predict the extent or direction of these changes without conducting tests (van Osnabrugge 1989).

Federal approval of the materials used in a flavor can be withdrawn at any time, with unpleasant consequences to the baker if a substantial amount of products containing the banned flavor is in retail channels. Suppliers will not be inclined to accept returns of their flavor if it has been made obsolete by changes in federal regulations, and this is particularly true when the flavor has been custom blended. There may be no use whatever for the obsolete material, with resultant charge-offs of inconvenient size. This is another reason for buying flavoring materials in small lots.

Probably the greatest number of chemical compounds, extractives, etc., used as ingredients in flavor mixtures fall into the category of "Generally Recognized as Safe" (GRAS). Describing this category, the FDA says (21 CFR 182.1) "It is impracticable to list all substances that are generally recognized as safe for their intended use. However, by way of illustration, the Commissioner regards such common food ingredients as salt, pepper, vinegar, baking powder, and monosodium glutamate as safe for their intended use." The 1990 publication of substances specifically lists 28 "Multiple Purpose GRAS Food Substances" (e.g., citric acid, caramel, sodium caseinate), 6 "Anticaking Agents" (e.g., calcium silicate), 20 "Chemical Preservatives" (e.g., sorbic acid, sodium bisulfite, tocopherols), 56 "Dietary Supplements" (e.g., linoleic acid, copper gluconate, iron reduced), 20 "Sequestrants" (e.g., sodium acid phosphate, isopropyl citrate), one "Stabilizer" (chondrus extract), and 19 "Nutrients" (e.g., calcium pyrophosphate, zinc chloride). Also, about 83 "Spices and other natural seasonings and flavorings" (e.g., alfalfa, coriander, star anise), about 159 "Essential oils, oleoresins (solvent-free), and natural extractives" (e.g., asafetida, cacao, kola nut, tea), 5 "Natural extractives (solvent-free) used in conjunction with spices, seasonings, and flavorings" (apricot kernel, peach kernel, peanut stearine, persic oil, and quince seed), 5 "Certain other spices, seasonings, essential oils, oleoresins, and natural extracts" (ambergris, castoreum, civet, cognac oil, and musk), and 21 "Synthetic flavoring substances and adjuvants" (e.g., anethole, ethyl acetate, methyl anthranilate).

Flavors should be packaged in such a way that withdrawal of aliquots is not likely to contaminate the residue. Obviously, packaging in batch-size amounts is an ideal solution, though often costly.

When a flavor has been approved by quality assurance, it is good practice to package several aliquots of the approved batch in bottles, seal the bottles, and store them at refrigerator temperatures. These samples will be withdrawn, as needed, for comparison with future deliveries.

SPICES AND HERBS

General Considerations

Spices have been defined as dried products of plant origin that are used primarily for seasoning food. Rhizones, bark, leaves, fruit, seeds, and other parts of plants can be spices. The flavor and pungency of many spices are due to their content of volatile oils, such as oil of cinnamon, oil of cloves, etc. Other substances, such as the alkaloids piperine in black pepper and capsaicine in cayenne pepper can contribute to the overall flavoring impact of spices. Some writers prefer not to consider onions, garlic, celery, and the like as spices, regarding them as simply flavorful foods. A few spices are also useful coloring agents, among these are paprika, turmeric, and saffron.

For federal definitions of spices, consult 21 CFR 101, which states, "The term 'spice' means any aromatic vegetable substance in which the whole, broken, or ground form, except for those substances which have been traditionally regarded as foods, whose significant function in food is seasoning rather than nutritional; that is true to name; and from which no portion of any volatile oil or other flavoring principle has been removed." Also, in 21 CFR 182 are listed many spices, herbs, essential oils, oleoresins, and natural extractives (including distillates) falling into the category of "Substances Generally Recognized as Safe."

Fresh, high-quality spices offer innumerable opportunities for introducing variety into bakery products. Most spices can be obtained in their whole form (i.e., as the entire root, seed, etc.), in various particle sizes, and as extractives in liquid, paste or encapsulated forms. The particular form best suited for a specific application is a matter for the formulator to decide.

Oleoresins are substances removed from a spice by an organic solvent. They consist of essential oils, organically soluble resins, some nonvolatile fatty acids, and other substances. By combining oleoresins with surfactants, diluents, and other additives, they can be made to disperse rapidly when added to aqueous systems, thus giving the so-called soluble spices.

Most spices are imported. Often there are several different sources for a spice. This gives more than the usual number of opportunities for quality variations and even for adulteration. It is essential to have a reliable supplier and to enforce sensible specifications. Every shipment of spices should be sampled and tested; even every container, if possible. Retention samples from previous approved batches, which have been stored at 0°F or lower, should be compared organoleptically with new shipments.

Spices can be a significant source of bacteriological contamination because of their source and the methods by which they are processed. Chemical fumigants, heat (Sorensen 1988), and ionizing radiation have been used to sterilize these materials. Also, converting the flavors into oils or oleoresins has the effect of destroying any microorganisms that are present.

Spices Used in Bakery Products

There are many spices that are seldom, if ever, used as bakery ingredients. An attempt will be made to discuss, however briefly, all of those that do have some significant utilization for this purpose.

Allspice.—Allspice is the dried, nearly ripe, pea-sized fruit of an evergreen tree (*Pimenta officinalis*). The whole spice comes in the form of a reddish-brown seed with a fairly smooth surface. Most allspice is produced in Jamaica, but alternative sources include Guatemala, Honduras, and Mexico. Jamaican allspice is considered by many to be the best because it has a more rounded flavor, higher oil content, and cleaner appearance. In the spice trade this material is often called "pimento," confusingly similar to "pimiento"—a type of bell pepper.

The predominant flavor of allspice is that of cloves and is due to the presence of eugenol. Jamaican allspice has more clove flavor with woody and cinnamon notes while the Honduran and Guatemalan spices are said to have more of a "bay-rum" aroma. The volatile oil content of the dried material will run from about 2.5% to 3.5% and the moisture content will be 9% to 12%.

Allspice has been used in some cakes, especially dark fruit cake types, and in mince meat. A few cookie formulas also contain some. Usually, it is not the predominant flavor in a product.

Anise seed.—This is the fruit of a small annual plant of the parsley family. It is a small, oval, grayish brown seed with a licorice-like odor and flavor. Although it is seldom used in U.S. bakeries, the recipes for certain Italian specialties and some Christmas cookies specify this ingredient.

Basil.—A herb or spice (*Ocimum basilicum*) native to India, but now widely grown throughout the world. It consists of the leaves of an annual plant allied to the mint family. Major commercial suppliers of basil are the U.S., France, and Egypt. Its essential oil content ranges from 0.15% to 1.1%, and consists largely of d-linalool and methyl chavicol. The flavor is described as pungently aromatic, sweet, and spicy. There are several varieties of basil, such as sweet basil, dark opal basil, and piccolo verde fino.

Basil is often used in pizza sauces, and is sometimes found in stuffing mixes, but otherwise is not a common ingredient in bakery products.

Caraway.—This spice is the dried fruit of a biennial of the parsley family native to Europe (*Carum carvi*). It is exported mainly by Holland though Egypt is also an important supplier. The Dutch spice is more aromatic and bitter than the Egyptian, the latter having the milder flavor.

Caraway has a pleasantly sweet but slightly biting flavor and a spicy, aromatic odor. It contains from 1.5% to 2.0% of volatile oil, carvone being the principal compound. Quality factors other than taste or odor include the amount of stem and chaff present, and the color, which should be light to dark brown.

The greatest bakery use of caraway is in rye bread. Many people wouldn't recognize a loaf as being rye bread if it was not flavored with caraway. The spice is also used in some cakes and cookies. It is also used as a flavoring in liqueurs, as are several of the other spices in this list.

Cardamom.—Cardamom is the dried unopened fruit of a perennial from the ginger family (*Elettaria cardamomum*). From 8 to 16 reddish brown seeds are contained in a fibrous spherical capsule that is greenish brown in its natural state but is often bleached white. The tiny brown aromatic seeds inside this capsule are slightly pungent in taste. Cardamom can be purchased as whole pods, as the decorticated seeds, or as a ground preparation. The powder is the most convenient form to use in the bakery, although adulteration may be a problem.

Quality factors to look for include an appearance free from blemishes, a pod color of bold green (or white, if bleached), a seed color of brownish-black, and an aromatic and sweet flavor and odor. Cardamom flavor has been described as citrus-like, floral, and soapy with green/woody notes. It has a menthol undertone and has some similarities to ginger. The menthol notes seem to predominate in some preparations. The spice contains 2% to 3% volatile oil, of which the principal flavoring component is 1,8-cineole. Chemical composition of cardamom oil has been the subject of numerous studies. More than 70 compounds have been identified; most of them are monoterpenoids (Maurer and Hauser 1988).

Indian Malabar cardamon is supposed to be the best. The Indian Mysore variety has a slightly harsher flavor. Most of the cardamom imported into the U.S. comes from Guatemala, which ships a type considered to be of good quality. Sri Lankan spice is less desirable, according to some experts. The spice is reputed to be an essential ingredient in Indian curries.

Cardamom has been used for flavoring Danish pastries, fillings for eclairs and cream puffs, and fruit pies. It is regarded as being compatible with sugar, blueberry, grape, apple, and pumpkin flavors.

Celery Seed.—This spice is the dried fruit of a herb that is related to, but not identical with, the vegetable (stalk) celery plant. The tiny brown seeds have a celery-like flavor and odor. They contain 1.5% to 2.0% volatile oil in which beta-silinene is the major aromatic component.

The flavor of celery seed has been compared to that of fennel and anise, but it is less mellow than these spices, and it has hay-like and grassy notes. India, China, and France are major exporters of celery seed. The French spice is slightly darker, while the Indian is the most bitter tasting.

Celery seed is not much used in bakery foods, except in croutons and stuffing mixes, and sometimes in pizza sauces and snack crackers.

Cinnamon.—Cinnamon, the most important baking spice, is the dried inner bark of an evergreen tree. Three types of cinnamon are recognized by federal and industry standards: (1) Batavia cassia, the dried bark of a cultivated tree, *Cinnamomum burmanni*; (2) Saigon cassia, the dried bark of cultivated varieties of *Cinnamomum foureirii*—after being processed and packaged for the retail trade, this spice is labeled "cinnamon"; and (3) Korintji cassia, similar to Batavia but containing less volatile oil. The "true" (or Ceylon) cinnamon, which comes from *Cinnamomum zeylanicum* trees, is produced in Sri Lanka, and is not used much in the U.S. (McCormick 1987). It is quite different in color, texture, and flavor strength from cassia and is popular in Mexico and Europe.

The flavor and aroma of cinnamon/cassia have been described as sweet and pungent, with woody, musty, and earthy notes. It causes a mouth-warming sensation. There will be 1.5% to 2.0% of a volatile oil, the flavor intensity of which is largely a function of the cinnamic aldehyde content.

A few examples of the many bakery products in which cinnamon plays an major improving role are pumpkin pie, apple pie, spice cake, many kinds of cookies, etc. It is mixed with fillings for Danish pastry. It is a flavor that is almost universally liked and that is compatible with many other flavors such as apple, peach, pear, blueberry, chocolate, coffee, and butter.

Cloves.—This material is composed of the dried unopened buds of an evergreen tree native to the Molucca Islands. Today, Zanzibar and Madagascar are the major sources for U.S. importers. The spice from Madagascar is supposed to be better than cloves from other sources.

The flavor of cloves is strong, pungent, bitter, astringent, and sweet. The spice leaves a numbing sensation in the mouth, due principally to the content of eugenol, the volatile oil most responsible for clove's odor.

Quality factors include an appearance free from evidences of mold, a bright uniform reddish-brown color, and a pungent and aromatic flavor. There should be about 15% to 20% of volatile oil.

Small amounts of cloves can be used in fruit fillings for bakery products. The flavor is particularly compatible with pumpkin, cherry, and mince. One whole clove is customarily placed in each Kaurabiedes (Greek Easter Cookies).

Coriander.—Coriander is the dried ripe fruit of the herb *Coriandrum sativum*. The round but ridged seeds are tannish brown in color and have a sweetly aromatic flavor which is slightly reminiscent of lemon. They contain a small amount, about 0.3%, of volatile oil.

Most of the world's supply of coriander is produced in Mexico, Romania, Egypt, China, and India. Only a very small amount of coriander is used in bakery products, but some pastry recipes call for the spice.

Dill Seed.—Dill seeds are the dried fruits of a herb. The oval shaped seeds have a pungent, aromatic flavor. They contain about 1.5% to 2.0% of volatile oils, of which d-carvone is the most important constituent.

The flavor of dill is characterized by pungent, woody, and menthol notes. It is warming to the taste. Dill is used only in some specialty breads and rolls, but it could probably be more widely applied in savory snacks because the flavor is appreciated by a large segment of the population. For example, it might be used in pretzels or to differentiate a cheese cracker. Total consumption in the form of bakery products is probably very small.

Fennel.—Fennel is the dried ripe fruit of the perennial *Foeniculum vulgare*. The seeds are oval in shape, yellowish-brown in color, and have a slight anise taste. It has a slight menthol undertone with musty and green flavor notes. It contains about one percent of volatile oils, with anethole being the principal constituent, as it is in anise.

Most fennel comes from China, Egypt, Turkey, and India, with the latter country supplying the best quality. Fennel is used in some pizza sauces but seldom in other bakery products. It might be considered as a flavor in spice cookies and the like.

Fenugreek.—This spice is the dried ripe seed of a herb grown primarily in India and Morocco. The Indian material is considered to be more uniform in color and to have a better appearance than that from Morocco. It contains little or no volatile oil. The flavor of this spice is characterized as being maple-like, and its most important use is as an ingredient in artificial maple flavors. As such, it finds considerable application in icings for pastries, cakes, and doughnuts.

Garlic.—The garlic plant is a small, hardy perennial closely allied botanically to the common onion. The bulb, which develops underground, is made up of several "cloves" or segments inclosed in a tough white skin. Varieties with white, pink, and yellow cloves are grown, and each has a somewhat different flavor. Garlic develops its typical pungent odor when the cloves are bruised or cut, being nearly odorless when intact. Damage to the cells causes them to release enzymes that react on precursors to form allyl disulfide, the compound responsible for most of the characteristic aroma.

Dehydrated garlic has about five times the strength of fresh garlic, while commercial oil of garlic has about 200 times the strength of the dried form although it is usually diluted with vegetable oil to give more practical concentrations. Oleoresin of garlic is available in water dispersible and oil dispersible forms and it is usually regarded as being about 12 times as strong as dehydrated garlic. For food manufacturers, dehydrated garlic is the most useful form. It is available in diced, sliced, minced, granulated, and powdered forms.

Garlic bread (sliced bread toasted with garlic butter) is a food familiar to almost everyone. The seasoning is also used in other savory breads, some snack crackers, and pizza toppings.

Ginger.—The dried rhizome of a tuberous perennial plant of the tropics (*Zingiber officinale*) forms the spice called ginger. It is native to southern Asia but most of today's supply comes from India and China. Jamaica exports fine quality ginger and so does Australia. This spice is hot to the taste and has been characterized as having lemony, soapy, and musty or earthy notes. The root contains about 1.5% of volatile oils, such as the sesqiterpene called zingiberene, and other flavoring compounds including cineole, citral, borneol, zingerone (a ketone related to vanillin and capsaicin).

Gingersnaps and gingerbread are two obvious applications of ginger. It is found in other cookies, sometimes in cakes, and in a few pie fillings such as pumpkin. The spice is claimed to be a natural preservative, antioxidant, bactericide, and meat tenderizer.

Mace.—Nutmeg and mace both are taken from the peach-like fruit of the evergreen tree *Myristica fragrans*. Mace is the fleshy arillode or skin surrounding the seed that becomes nutmeg. Mace comes from Indonesia and Grenada. The spice coming from the East Indies has always been considered superior because of its bright orange color, rich balanced flavor, and high volatile oil content. Mace grown in the West Indies is yellowish in color and has a milder flavor. It contains about 10% to 12% volatile oils. The flavor has been described as strongly aromatic, spicy, and warming to the taste with citrus and terpeny notes

This spice is widely used in bakery products, but it is replaced by the similarly flavored nutmeg wherever possible, because of the price differential. Mace, however, is mellower and better rounded in flavor than nutmeg.

Mint.—This fragrant spice comes from a perennial plant that grows in temperate climates. The genus *Mentha* contains many species that yield valuable flavoring materials. Among these are *M. spicata* (spearmint), *M. cardiaca* (Scotch type spearmint), *M. rotundifolia* (applemint), *M. pulegium* (pennyroyal), and *M. piperita* (peppermint). Some of these are grown as sources of menthol or for perfume. Of these, spearmint and peppermint are undoubtedly the most important in food flavoring. Although it is not widely applied to bakery products, a considerable amount of mint is used as a supplemental flavor in chocolate icings and in cookie fillings.

The common form of mint flavoring used in bakery foods is the essential oil obtained by steam distilling the flowering plant tops. Chemically synthesized versions are also available and are quite satisfactory for many applications. The U.S. is the principal supplier. The flavors and the chemical compositions of spearmint and peppermint oils are significantly different. A major component of peppermint oil is menthol, which is present at levels of 50% or more, while carvone is the major component of spearmint oil—also present in excess of 50%.

Nutmeg.—This spice is the seed that comes from the same plant as mace. The oval seed is dark brown in color and has a ridged surface. It can be as long as 1.25 inches. Producing regions are, of course, the same as for mace. Nutmeg yields from 5% to 7.5% of volatile oil and about 25% of nonvolatile ether extract. The spice is used in doughnuts, particularly cake doughnuts, coffeecakes, apple pies, and many other kinds of sweet goods.

Paprika.—The powder that is called paprika is the pulverized ground pods of *Capsicum annum*, a sweet red pepper. It is prized for its brilliant red color, but it is used both as a coloring agent and a flavor. Most paprika is mild and slightly sweet in flavor with a pleasant fragrant aroma. The "hot" taste found in many peppers is almost absent. Quality factors include the intensity of color—determined by standardized extraction procedures—and the strength and profile of the flavor.

The largest quantities of paprika are produced in Spain, Central Europe, and the U.S. Although both Spanish and domestic paprika are mild and sweet in flavor, domestic peppers are generally fresh, green, and vegetable-like, while the Spanish peppers have a more piquant and fermented flavor. Paprika is used in bakery foods primarily in adjuncts such as pizza sauces, but also as a coloring in some cheese snack crackers and the like.

Pepper.—There are two kinds of pepper coming from two very different kinds of plants. Black pepper is the dried seed of the climbing vine *Piper nigrum*, a native of India but now produced in large quantities in both India and Brazil. These seeds contain the powerful compound piperine, which gives the sensation of "heat" or pain in the mouth. White pepper is merely the decorticated black pepper seed. Red pepper comes from the fruits of many different varieties of the genus *Capsicum*. These fruits contain varying amounts of the chemical capsaicin, which is even hotter than piperine. There are varieties of Capsicum having fruits with little or no "heat" and yellow or green in color, bell peppers being examples.

Although black pepper is not a common seasoning for bakery products, it is found in a few old recipes for cookies (pfeffernusse, etc.) and some savory items. Bell peppers are used in a number of savory muffins and quickbreads, primarily to add color and texture interest. Cornbread with diced red and green pepper bits is an example. Pizza sauces may use either kind of pepper, but mostly capsicums.

The burning mouthfeel that arises when a pepper-containing food is ingested is not really a thermal sensation. It is a chemical sensation and appears to become known through receptors closely allied to the pain-sensing nerve-endings.

The "heat" of pepper is an important quality factor, and it is usually expressed as "Scoville Units." This factor is determined by diluting a sample until the hotness becomes undetectable to a small panel of judges. There have been attempts to replace this procedure with an alternative method based on ratings of perceived hotness. Also, capsaicin can be determined by chromatographic analysis.

Saffron.—Saffron is a very expensive spice consisting of the dried stigmas and styles of a type of crocus flower (*Crocus sativus*). One acre of these plants will yield about five pounds of dried saffron. Three varieties are produced, a light colored (yellow-orange) saffron that is also light in flavor, an orange colored saffron that is stronger in flavor, and a darker colored (reddish-orange) saffron that is strongest in flavor. An important characteristic of this ingredient is its ability to color the products in which it is used. In many cases, the color may be more noticeable than the flavor, which has been described as being a spicy, sweet, floral aroma with an earthy, bitter, fatty, herbaceous taste.

Saffron buns have been made for centuries, but are seldom seen nowadays. The spice can also be used in cakes and other products having a mild background flavor and light color, but the flavor of saffron is easily overwhelmed and other spices and essences must be used with care when formulating such combinations.

Sesame seed—It is a questionable decision to include this ingredient in the category of spices, because the flavor of sesame seeds is very mild. Their principal functions are to provide appearance and texture differentiation on bread rolls. They are the seeds of a small annual plant native to Asia, but now widely grown, especially in the U.S., Nicaragua, Salvador, and Guatemala. The seeds are small, oval-shaped, and shiny. They are known to some ethnic groups as "benne" or "bene."

Hulled seeds are pearly white in color. They are commonly applied to rolls, breads, and buns and give a somewhat nutty flavor and aroma when browned. When scorched, as they so often are, the flavor contribution of sesame seeds is rather negative. The ground seed forms the basis of the Middle Eastern confection halvah.

Turmeric.—This spice is the dried root of the plant *Curcuma longa.* Although it has a flavor resembling a combination of ginger and pepper, turmeric is used mostly for its potent coloring effect. Large quantities are used for this purpose in condiments such as mustard and curry powder. Most of the U.S. supply comes from India—this material being called Alleppey turmeric. The spice can be used in savory crackers, cheese flavored breads and bread sticks, and similar products where a yellow or orange-yellow color is desired.

BIBLIOGRAPHY

ANON. 1986. All About Lake Pigments. Warner-Jenkinson Co., St. Louis, MO

ANON. 1990. Balancing chocolate's advantages. Bakery *25,* No. 1, 37-38, 40, 42, 44-45

BADER, P. 1981. Natural flavoring materials. Cereal Foods World *28,* 281-283

BARSNESS, T. O. 1984. Flavors. Proc. Am. Soc. Bakery Engineers *1984,* 60-66

BEST, D. 1989. Spices, flavors, and oleoresins. Prepared Foods *158,* No. 5, 147-150

BORZELLACA, J. F., HALLIGAN, J., and REESE, C. 1982. Food, drug, and cosmetic colors. Toxicological considerations. Paper delivered at Sept. 12-17, 1982 Meeting, Am. Chem. Soc. Kansas City, MO

BRUHN, W. 1982. Industrial quality control of flavors. Dragoco Rept. *1/1982.* Dragoco, Inc. Totowa, NJ

DZIEZAK, J. D. 1989. Spices. Food Technol. *43,* No. 1, 102, 104, 106-108, 110-114, 116

FARRELL, K. T. 1985. Spices, Condiments, and Seasonings. AVI Publishing Co., Westport, CT

FRANCIS, F. J. 1981. Natural food colorants. Cereal Foods World *26,* 565-567

FRANCIS, F., and CLYDESDALE, F. 1972. Color measurement of foods. Caramel coloring. Food Product Dev. *6,* No. 3, 86-88

GORDON, H., and BAUERFEIND, J. 1982. Carotenoids as food colorants. Critical Reviews in Food Science and Nutrition *18,* No. 1, 59-97

HASSEL, J. 1989. Spice alternatives for microwave applications. Cereal Foods World *34,* 340-341

HEATH, H. B., and REINICCIUS, G. A. 1986. Flavor Chemistry and Technology. AVI Publishing Co., Westport, CT

RILEY, K. A., and KLEYN, D. H. 1989. Fundamental principles of vanilla/vanilla extract processing and methods of detecting adulteration in vanilla extracts. Food Technol. *43,* No. 10, 64, 66, 68, 70, 73, 75, 77

LAWLESS, H. 1989. Pepper potency and the forgotten flavor sense. Food Technol. *43,* 52,

57-58
MAURER, B., and HAUSER, A. 1988. New natural products from essential oils. Chemistry and Industry *18*, 587-591
MCCORMICK, R. 1987. Pungent cinnamon notes offer aromatic potential for microwaveable products. Prepared Foods *156*, No. 8, 145-146
MCCORMICK, R. 1990. Technology widens "natural" color spectrum. Prepared Foods *159*, No. 3, 131-132
MERORY, J. 1968. Food Flavorings. AVI Publishing Co., Westport, CT
METZNER, A. A. 1978. Coloring short shelf life bakery products with beta carotine. Cereal Foods World *23*, 120-126, 128
MURAI, K., and WILKINS, D. 1990. Natural red color derived from cabbage. Food Technol. *44*, No. 6, 131
NEWSOME, R. L. 1986. Food Colors. Food Technol. *40*, No. 7, 49-56
NIELSEN, C., JR. 1985. The Story of Vanilla. Nielsen Massey Vanillas, Lake Forest, IL
RANADIVE, A. 1990. Vanilla—additions and corrections. Food Technol. *44*, No. 4, 34
SJÖSTROM, L. B. 1970. Functionality of flavorings. Am. Assoc. Cereal Chem., Central States Sect., 11th Annual Symp., 1970, Kansas City, MO
SORENSEN, S. 1988. Process for sterilizing spices. U.S. Pat. 4,790,995
VAN OSNABRUGGE, W. 1989. How to flavor baked goods effectively. Food Technol. *43*, No. 1, 74, 76, 78, 80, 82, 94
WHITTAKER, R. J., and EVANS, D. A. 1987. Plant biotechnology and the production of flavor compounds. Food Technol. *41*, No. 9, 86-88, 90, 92, 94, 96, 98, 100-101
WIEDMANN, W. 1989. Methods for preparing chocolate mixtures. U.S. Pat. 4,861,615
WISSGOTT, U. 1988. Process of alkalization of cocoa in aqueous phase. U.S. Pat. 4,784,866
ZUCKERMAN, S., and SENACKERIB, J. 1979. Colorants for foods, drugs, and cosmetics. Kirk-Othmer Encyclopedia of Chemical Technology, Third Ed. *6*, 561-596

chapter ten

OTHER INGREDIENTS

INTRODUCTION

This chapter will cover several kinds of bakery ingredients that do not fit into the subject matter of the preceding chapters. Such a process of selection inevitably makes the present chapter a "mixed bag" of ingredient types. In addition, space limitations dictate that some of the most exotic ingredients won't be discussed at all and some others will receive only brief attention. These deficiencies should not affect most bakery technologists, since they will seldom, if ever, have occasion to use the omitted materials.

Most of the ingredients covered in this chapter can be described as "specialty food additives," which, in total, constitute a $5.5 billion market in the U.S. (Thayer 1991). These materials can be broken down into the following categories: no- or low-calorie sweeteners, $1 billion (with aspartame accounting for three-fourths of this); gums and thickeners, $884 million; flavors and flavor enhancers, $800 million; emulsifiers, $460 million; acidulants, $246 million; colors, $220 million; vitamins and other nutrients, $157 million; enzymes, $143 million; preservatives, $83 million; antioxidants, $24 million; and "others," $500 million.

INHIBITORS OF MICROBIOLOGICAL SPOILAGE

The only form of microbiological spoilage with which the average baker has to contend is mold growth. A couple of generations ago, rope spoilage of bakery products caused by *Bacillus mesentericus* or similar organisms was a serious problem, but today's improved sanitary practices combined with better packaging and sales control have virtually eliminated this form of spoilage. Many bakers in the U.S. have never seen an authentic case of rope. Mold spoilage still remains a problem, however. The principal spoilage organisms are reported to be *Aspergillus nigricans*, *Rhizopus spp.*, and *Penicillium spp.* (McMillan 1983). No feasible amount of sanitation can prevent contamination of bakery products with the ubiquitous mold spores, and an abundant display of mycelia and sporangia can appear on a loaf within three days if the conditions of humidity and temperature are right.

Over the years, a considerable number of compounds have been proposed as fungicides or fungistats for use on, or in, food substances. Most of these materials are no longer heard of because they were shown to be toxic to man or harmless to molds—frequently both. In the following paragraphs, some of the materials currently being used, or having the potential of use, as preservatives will be described.

Organic Acids

Most organic acids having carbon chain lengths of 1 to 14 exert some fungistatic action, but various objections, including inadequate supply and unpleasant odors, have limited commercial use of all except the 2 and 3 carbon chain compounds. It is the acid moiety of these substances that exerts the fungistatic effect, the choice of sodium, potassium, or calcium salts being based on convenience and cost. Effectiveness is, in most cases, related to the pH of the medium.

Use of acetic acid as a spoilage retardant has considerable appeal. In the form of vinegar, it has been used as a food component for thousands of years; it is economical and its flavor and aroma are relatively mild and acceptable. Vinegar has long been regarded as a rope preventative and it is apparently effective for that purpose. Although there is some question about its ability to retard mold growth significantly, vinegar (or acetic acid) is being used in some "no preservative" breads, as is raisin concentrate, in the hope that storage life will be enhanced by it.

Among the types of vinegar commercially available are cider vinegar, wine vinegar, malt vinegar, sugar vinegar, distilled vinegar, corn sugar vinegar, and rice vinegar. Each has a somewhat different composition. Content of acetic acid, price, flavor, and color vary. The amount of acetic acid in vinegar is indicated by the "grain strength." In the U.S., grain strength is equal to 10 times the acid content expressed as acetic acid. Vinegar is generally shipped in concentrated form in 30 or 55 gallon drums, or in tanker trucks. Bulk vinegar has usually been filtered but not pasteurized. When exposed to air, a cloudy growth ("mother") forms in the liquid. This bacterial formation is not harmful and can be removed by filtering, but it does reduce acidity by oxidizing the acetic acid. Distilled (white) vinegar is very stable. Retail strength (50 grain) vinegar has about 64 calories per lb.

Sodium diacetate has been recommended for use in white breads at levels of 3.5 oz to 5 oz per 100 lb flour and in dark breads at 5 oz to 6 oz per 100 lb flour. It reduces the incidence of rope and growth of mold by reducing the dough pH. The "diacetate ion" is said to have a specific inhibitory effect on spoilage organisms. Calcium acetate-propionate at the 0.25% level is claimed to inhibit mold growth. Sodium and calcium salts of propionic acid have been used with good results for many years. Recommended application levels depend upon the product and on the temperatures of distribution and storage, but a dosage of 0.2% (FWB) is sufficient under normal conditions, while up to 6 oz per 100 lb flour may be needed in hot and humid climates. Off-flavors may be noticed at higher dosage levels.

Sorbic acid, or potassium sorbate, is effective as a preservative in many applications of interest to bakery technologists. Sorbate appears to be most effective when it is placed on the surface of products. It is routinely applied to the surfaces of sliced cheese sold by the major manufacturers of that product. Such applications may require sophisticated spraying devices. Sorbates have a distinctive taste and odor, especially when they are heated.

Specially fermented wheat flour or dairy-derived ingredients have been promoted as mold inhibitors for bread. The claim is that the organic acids developed in these fermentations act in the same way as sodium propionate or acetic acid. There do not seem to be any published reports of continuous commercial usage of these materials. Their chief advantage over propionates would be the "natural" origin of the substances developed in the flour or whey that forms the bulk of the additive.

Alcohol

There have been some patents and other publications that claim ethanol, when added to doughs packaged for consumer baking (e.g., refrigerated pizza crusts), greatly extends the shelf life of the product. Partially or completely baked items such as pizza crust or focaccio have also been marketed in this way—probably many others, as well. The product must be packaged in such a way that the ethanol is not lost through evaporation, of course. Hermetically sealed pouches of aluminum foil laminated to plastic films can be satisfactory. Usually, other chemical substances such as propionic acid are also added to aid in preserving the dough. These methods have been extended to cover breads and cakes (Ando 1985). The preservation effects apply to microbiological spoilage; texture and flavor staling are not delayed by these additives.

Polyhydric alcohols (e.g., glycerol) have some value as preservatives when they are added to unbaked doughs and baked products in fairly large amounts, say 5% or more of the liquid ingredients (Durst 1985). Of course, use of polyhydric alcohols to preserve moist foods, such as dog foods, has been practiced commercially for several years. In this role, the alcohols function primarily by reducing the water activity to a safe level. Durst claims, however, his invention also leads to a decrease in the rate of starch retrogradation, a principal factor in texture staling.

Mechanism of Inhibition

There are different mechanisms by which inhibitors can retard microbiological spoilage. Parabens (para-hydroxbenzoic acid esterified with methyl, ethyl, propyl, or butyl alcohol) inhibit enzyme activity and are not dependent on the pH of the medium. Acetic, propionic, benzoic, and sorbic acids inhibit transport of growth substrates through cell membranes and their effectiveness is definitely related to pH of the medium. In addition, sorbic acid inhibits an enzyme system used by the cell.

TEXTURE MODIFIERS

Substances that form gels with water under certain conditions have been used as additives in doughs and batters to enhance their machinability or the sensory properties of finished baked products, but they have their greatest utility in the bakery as components of adjuncts such as icings and pie fillings. There are many options available for a technologist seeking an ingredient that will make a flavored solution into a viscous liquid or a solid gel, but identifying a substance which will fill all the requirements of a particular situation can require tedious and time-consuming experimentation. Brief discussions of some common hydrocolloids are given in the following sections to assist formulators in the initial stages of this selection process.

Starches

Starch, which is found as granules in many seeds, tubers, roots, and other plant parts, has long been recognized as a valuable food ingredient. Of course, it is also the major component of all common flours and meals (wheat, corn, rye, etc.). In fact, these meals and flours are often used instead of the purified starch, as in thickening soups and gravies. It is usually preferred, however, to use a purified starch to avoid unwanted side effects resulting from the presence of other materials, such as proteins, fats, etc. Corn starch is a pure, cheap, versatile thickener for foods.

Corn starch is widely used as a constituent of doughs, batters, and adjuncts, primarily as a texture-modifier (thickener, gelling agent, etc.). It has the great advantages of being uniform from lot to lot, readily available, and wholesome. It is also very bland in flavor and yields nearly colorless gels. Natural (unmodified) starch is frequently the ingredient of choice, but there are chemically and physically modified forms that can be used in foods and that have some functional advantages over the natural starch in special situations. Federal regulations controlling "Food Starch—Modified" can be found in 21 CFR 172.892.

Starches from many other sources, both cereal and non-cereal, are readily available and may have properties that make them more suitable than standard corn starch for certain applications (see Table 10.1).

Table 10.1 CHARACTERISTICS OF UNMODIFIED STARCHES [1]

Source of starch	Amylose content, %	Clarity	Gel structure	Texture
Potato	20	Clear	Doesn't gel	Salve
Dent corn	27	Cloudy	Firm gel	Gel
Waxy corn	0	Clear	Doesn't gel	Paste
Cassava (tapioca)	22	Clear	Soft gel	Gel
High-amylose corn	55	Opaque	Rigid gel	Gel

[1] Adapted from Luallen (1985)

Food starches are separated from the basic raw materials by methods similar to those used in wet milling of corn (see the Sweeteners chapter for a description of this process) or by other methods. Physical modification methods can involve merely gelatinizing and drying the native starch, or can be more elaborate. Chemical methods include dextrinizing by dry heating in the presence of an acid and reacting with chemicals that add functional groups to the carbohydrate molecule. An excellent though brief review of these methods can be found in the booklet "Corn Starch" (Anon. 1986).

The principal value of starch to the food manufacturer is that, when heated in the presence of sufficient water, it gelatinizes to form viscous solutions or rigid gels. When it is allowed to cool, the gelatinized starch becomes more viscous. This change is known in the industry as "setback." The common cereal flours have high setback, while the waxy cereal starches exhibit little setback. As room temperature is reached, starch pastes may set to a more or less rigid gel, their firmness depending on the kind and concentration of starch and the pH of the system. Corn starch pasted in 5% concentration sets to a stiff gel, as seen in homemade starch pudding. Wheat starch forms a much softer gel at this concentration, while rice and oat starch form soft masses that appear more like cold pastes than gels. The waxy starches form soft thick masses; this characteristic, together with the clarity and slow retrogradation of waxy corn and sorghum starch pastes, make these ingredients useful in fruit pie fillings and similar products. Many kinds of confections are based on these gels.

In doughs, starch can be used to offset the excessive toughness caused by a strong flour. When added to batters for cakes, starch increases the tenderness and softness of the finished product. In cookies, it can help to form a tender structure, can sometimes reduce stickiness and oiliness, and can bind water to give soft varieties.

Starch is helpful in forming the soft gels needed in pie fillings, doughnut fillings, pastry creams, etc. It can add strength to meringues and reduce their sweetness. In commercial dry mixes for meringues, starch is used to replace some of the structure-forming function of egg white.

Gels formed from unmodified starch tend to retrograde. This is made apparent by gradual shrinking of the gel and extrusion of a syrupy liquid. Usually, an undesirable opaqueness also develops. These are significant disadvantages, especially if the product is expected to have a storage life of more than a couple of days.

When preparing bakery product constituents based on a starch gel, it is important to recognize the effect preparation conditions have on the viscosity or gel strength of the finished product. The data in Table 10.2 illustrate the effects of some of these conditions. In addition, the following guidelines may be helpful.

1. Hot starch pastes lose viscosity if maintained near boiling temperatures. They should be cooled immediately after cooking to the temperature at which they are to be used.

2. Starch pastes lose viscosity in direct proportion to the intensity of mechanical disturbance.

3. Starch pastes increase in viscosity as they are cooled. Continuous

stirring while cooling the paste makes it smoother in texture and reduces the gelling tendency. If maximum gel strength is to be obtained, stirring should be avoided during cooling.

    4. Undercooked starch pastes yield gels that release water (i.e., "weep") upon standing. This syneresis can be avoided by choosing the correct starch ingredient, cooking it thoroughly, and cooling it properly.

    5. Dilute starch pastes, particularly those of unmodified and acid-modified starches, may develop cloudiness as a result of starch retrogradation. Oxidized, certain derivatized, and most dextrinized starches have reduced tendencies to retrograde, and waxy starches do not retrograde to any significant extent.

    6. Microorganisms can grow rapidly in starch gels. If the gel is to be stored at or near room temperature for more than 24 hours, preservatives should be added. Fillings with a distinctly acid pH and high sugar content are more resistant to bacterial growth.

Table 10.2. EFFECTS OF SOME FACTORS ON PASTE VISCOSITY [1]

Starch concentration	Temperature	Holding time	Stirring rate	Visible granule breakage	Apparent viscosity
%	°F	min.	rpm		centipoise
3	194	30	120	None	15
5	194	30	120	None	1,080
5	194	30	1,800	Appreciable	317
5	212	30	160	Appreciable	754
5	212	30	1,800	Complete	90
10	194	30	120	None	11,800
10	194	30	1,000	Slight	7,290
20	212	30	1,000	Complete	18,500
20	212	60	1,000	Complete	9,480

[1] Unmodified cornstarch.

    Starch consists principally of two different types of molecules: amylose and amylopectin. Many of the commercial starch preparations used as food ingredients contain about 20% to 30% amylose, the remainder being amylopectin. Some properties of amylopectin are similar to those of tapioca starch, which yields pastes that are almost clear when cool, do not congeal, and are slow to retrograde. Amylopectin preparations are used for thickening many kinds of foods. Most comercial waxy starches have been modified by cross-linking or derivatization to enhance their performance.

    Acid-modified starches exhibit reduced viscosities when warm but have a strong tendency to gel when cooled. They are used in large amounts by the confectionery industry for making gum candies. Starches oxidized with sodium hypochlorite yield pastes that are relatively clear and show a reduced tendency to thicken when cooled. The major uses for oxidized starches are in the textile industry, but they are said to be suitable for food applications where high solids and low viscosity are desired.

Dextrins are produced by heating or roasting starches with or without an acid or alkaline catalyst. Many variations in the finished product are possible, but most dextrinized starches produced today are employed as adhesives where bland taste and lack of toxicity are prime requirements, as on envelope flaps, postage stamps, etc.

Some starch acetates are used in foods. Waxy corn starch can be crosslinked by treating with phosphorus oxychloride and then acetylated with acetic anhydride to produce an effective thickener. When succinic anhydride is used instead of acetic anhydride, the starch derivative that results can be used as a thickening agent for foods. Starch can be esterified with monosodium orthophosphate or sodium tripolyphosphate to yield derivatives that are more stable than those produced from the parent starch.

Table 10.3. RANGES OF PROPERTIES IN COMMERCIAL GELATIN

Property and unit	Type of Gelatin	
	A	B
Gel strength in Bloom gm	75 to 300	75 to 275
Viscosity in centipoises	2.0 to 7.5	2.0 to 7.5
Ash, in percent	0.3 to 2.0	.05 to 2.0
pH	3.8 to 6.0	5.0 to 7.4
Isotonic point	9.0 to 9.2	4.8 to 5.0

Gelatin

Gelatin is a substance that gives fluid solutions while hot, and rigid short gels when chilled. The gelatin desserts known and favored by millions of children are typical examples of this behavior. Gelatin can also be used to give a gloss to icings and similar adjuncts. It is usually one of the functional ingredients in marshmallow. Gelatin is not often specified as an ingredient in doughs and batters, but can be used to improve crust gloss under certain conditions.

Gelatin is a generic term used to identify a group of proteinaceous substances prepared by the partial hydrolysis of collagen, the latter being a material found in several animal tissues. Bones and pork skins are the two main raw materials used in gelatin manufacture. Type A gelatins, the so-called acid-reacting gelatins, are produced from pork skins and have pHs in the range of 4.7 to 5.0 and isoelectric points from pH 8.3 to 8.7. Type B, or alkaline-reacting gelatin, is prepared from bones and other animal by-products. Its pH range falls in the range from 5 to 7, and its isoelectric point is from pH 4.7 to 5.0. Isoelectric point differences are chiefly responsible for the differences in behavior of the two materials (Kramer 1967). In the U.S., type A made from pork skins is the more common product. See Table 10.3 for some additional information on gelatin specifications.

The viscosity and other properties of a gelatin vary with the pH. The viscosity is lowest at the isoelectric point. As the pH moves away from this point, viscosity will increase to a maximum that will be several times the minimum. The bloom strength of a gelatin refers to a measurement of the rigidity of a gel of standard composition as made by an instrument called the Bloom gelometer. This simple form of penetrometer measures the weight required to push a circular plunger of 12.7 mm diameter to a depth of 4 mm into the gel, under standard conditions. The gel sample is prepared by dissolving 7.5 gm of the gelatin in 105 gm of distilled water at 140°F. The solution is gelled by holding it at 50°F for 18 hr before making the penetrometer measurement.

Gelatins are offered in the range of 50 to 300 bloom. Selection of the proper bloom-strength of gelatin intended to be used as an ingredient in a particular product will depend to some extent on transient economic factors. Although it is not strictly true that larger amounts of a weaker gelatin can be substituted for high bloom-strength gelatin in a formula, there is an inverse relationshiop of bloom strength and quantity that is reasonably valid in the intermediate ranges of addition. Therefore, the selection of a bloom strength that will give the lowest total cost for the amount required in a given formula, must take into consideration the current market price of the available ingredients.

The flavor (which should be bland) and the color (which should be as light as possible) of gelatin are important, but can be expected to vary only slightly in gelatins of similar bloom strength obtained from different suppliers. Gelatin, although a kind of protein, is not suitable as a protein supplement for foods because of its very low protein efficiency ratio (PER).

Gums

Gums for food use have been described as edible polymeric materials that are soluble in water and cause a viscous or gelled consistency in foods. Important functional properties include proven lack of toxicity, water binding, fat rejection, encapsulating, and structure forming. There are many substances meeting these requirements, including flour, but only a few of them can be mentioned in this article (see Table 10.4).

Microcrystalline cellulose, carboxymethylcellulose, methylethylcellulose, and hydroxypropylcellulose are classes of synthetic gums that include many types useful in foods. Viscosity, thermal gelation temperature, and gel texture can be varied over wide ranges.

Table 10.4. CHARACTERISTICS OF SOME WATER SOLUBLE GUMS[1]

Type of gum	pH range	Characteristics of water dispersions	Uses in the bakery
Gum arabic	4.5-5.5	Cold water soluble, low viscosity, emulsifier	Icings
Tragacanth	5.1-5.9	Creamy texture, emulsifier, acid stable	Adjunct emulsifier
Locust bean	5.5	Adds viscosity, reacts with milk, smooth text.	Jellies, pie filling
Gum guar	5.5-6.1	High visc. Reacts with milk. Dissolves cold.	Thickens; suspends; holds water
Agar agar	7.0	Strong & rigid gels. Stable to heat & pH changes.	Pie filling; icings; meringues
Furcelleran	5.5-9.0	Strong, flexible, clear gels	Flans; fruit fillings
Gum karaya	4.3-5.5	Hydrates rapidly in cold water	Seldom used
Gum ghatti	4.5	Good emulsifier and film former	Seldom used
Carrageenan	7.0	Reacts with casein & other proteins	Cream filling; custard
Alginates	7.5	Thickens; suspends; forms gels	Pie filling; icings

[1] Based in part on data supplied by TIC Gums.

Plant exudate gums include gum arabic, gum ghatti, gum karaya, and gum tragacanth, some of which have from ancient times been used as food ingredients, primarily in confectionery. In recent years, these natural products have been cleaned up, standardized, and modified to meet modern requirements. In bakery science, they would primarily be candidates for applications where thickening is needed or soft gel structures have to be formed. Specifically, gum arabic has been used in icings and glazes, gum karaya has been used in emulsion stabilization, and gum tragacanth has been suggested as a texture-modifying ingredient for pie fillings.

Plant seed gums include guar gum, locust bean gum, and psyllium seed gum. The latter product is used mostly as a component of bulk laxatives and has not found its way into general purpose foods, though patents exist describing its use as an ingredient in, for example, cookies (Pflammer *et al* 1990). Locust bean gum has been used to a limited extent for texture modification in fruit gel fillings and the like. Guar gum has been used in considerable amounts in the food industry as a water binding ingredient and for stabilizing emulsions.

There are several important gums derived from seaweeds, including agar, alginates, carrageenans, and furcelleran. Many of these are very effective water binders and gel formers. Agar is typical, forming gels that are stiff at low concentrations, clear, and reversible. These gels form the structural basis of some icings, piping jellies, and pie fillings. Alginates have been used in icings.

Carrageenan is widely used as a thickener for chocolate milk and to stabilize ice cream. In dough products, carrageenans can form stable complexes between cereal and milk proteins, though they are seldom used for this purpose. They have been suggested for use in cheesecake mix and lemon pie filling, and perhaps used for these purposes. Carrageenan can be separated by chemical and physical manipulations into three or four fractions, each of which has distinctive charcteristics and applications.

Vital Wheat Gluten

Gluten is derived from wheat flour or, in recently developed processes, from ground whole wheat, by kneading a dough or batter under conditions such that the protein components known as gluten form a curd or cohesive mass from which the soluble materials and starch can be washed. The gluten so obtained is dried and ground, or sometimes dispersed in an ammonia solution and spray dried. There are two main types, devitalized gluten and vital gluten. The latter material retains its capability of forming a cohesive elastic mass when mixed with water.

The protein fraction obtained from the wet milling process applied to corn is also called gluten, but it has properties entirely different from those of wheat gluten and is used mostly as animal feed. Corn gluten and devitalized wheat gluten will not be discussed further in this chapter.

Commercial gluten is a tan, free-flowing powder with a bland flavor. It is used primarily in bread and roll doughs to supplement the flour gluten when the latter is not present in sufficient amounts (or is not strong enough) to perform its intended purpose. Typically, it will find use in multigrain breads or in rolls high in fruit content, where the cell structure must support a rather heavy load of inert material. When low protein flour, or weak flour, must be used because of a supply problem, supplementation with gluten may be needed to get adequate handling properties and satisfactory finished product quality even when ordinary white bread is being made. Vital wheat gluten has been called "the baker's universal crutch" (Murphy 1981, Shields 1982, Lanham 1978).

DOUGH MODIFIERS

It has been found that certain chemicals generally described as oxidizers or reducing agents can greatly modify the physical properties of doughs, even when they are added in very small amounts. It is usually found that oxidizers make doughs "stronger" and reducing agents make doughs "weaker." These materials are in common use and can be added either at the flour mill or by the baker (see Table 10.5).

Oxidizers

Oxidizing agents are added to doughs to make them tougher, drier, and easier to machine. Underoxidized doughs tend to be weak, soft, sticky, and easy to stretch; they often do not retain gas very well. Finished loaves made from them show reduced volume, weak crusts, uneven grain and texture, poor break and shred, and poor symmetry. Overoxidized doughs tend to be tight, firm, dry, bucky, and difficult to mold. Bread made from such doughs may have less volume than expected, rough break and shred, and uneven grain with large holes. It is widely accepted that oxidizing agents perform their function by changing sulfhydryl groups on gluten protein molecules into disulfide groups that connect adjacent chains.

The oxidizing compounds available to the baker are potassium iodate, potassium bromate, calcium peroxide, azodicarbonamide, and ascorbic acid. The maximum addition level for the first four is 75 ppm, for azodicarbonamide it is 45 ppm, and there is no maximum for ascorbic acid. There are indications that bromate may lose its FDA approval in the near future (Kamman 1991, Spooner 1990). Calcium peroxide by itself is not very satisfactory, but combined with other ingredients it is a good dough conditioner (Tieckelmann and Steele 1991). Oxygen from the air, as well as oxygen dissolved in the aqueous phase of the dough, can cause the same changes as other oxidants. Some of these changes do in fact occur during mixing, but they are slower and may never become as pronounced as those caused by the more powerful oxidants.

Reducing Agents

Reducing agents act in an opposite manner to oxidants. They change some of the disulfide bonds between protein molecules into sulfhydryl groups. This makes the gluten network weaker, and the dough tends to become less resistant to extension, wetter in appearance, softer, and stickier. The dough requires less mixing, i.e., it becomes overmixed with less energy input. It expands well up to a point, but may collapse partially during later stages of proofing or during baking.

Sulfite, L-cysteine, and reduced glutathione have been used as reducing agents in dough. L-cysteine is said to significantly reduce mixing time when used at concentrations up to 90 ppm (FWB). Inactive dry yeast has been used as a source of reduced glutathione, and it is effective in weakening the dough structure but the flavor and color added by the yeast could create acceptability problems. There are statements in the literature that sorbic acid, at levels between 25 to 50 ppm, acts as a reducing agent in dough (Powell 1977). Sulfite has been used in cracker doughs to soften and weaken them, thus reducing the tearing that sometimes occurs when the dough is stretched excessively during sheeting and laminating. Regulatory problems may affect the use of sulfite.

Table 10.5. OXIDIZERS AND REDUCING AGENTS[1]

Common Name	Action or function	Used in	Reaction rate
Potassium Bromate	Oxidizes, improves	Bread flour & doughs	Slow
Potassium Iodate	Reduces mix time, oxidizes, improves	Bread dough	Fast
Azodicarbonamide	Oxidizes, matures, improves	Bread flour & doughs	Fast
Chlorine dioxide	Bleaches, matures, oxidizes	Bread flour	Fast
Chlorine	Bleaches, matures, oxidizes	Cake flour	Fast
Benzoyl peroxide	Bleaches, oxidizes	Bread & cake flour	1-3 days
L-ascorbic acid	Reduces mix time, reduces/oxidizes	Bread flour & doughs	Medium
L-cysteine	Reduces mix time, reduces, relaxes	Miscellaneous doughs	Fast

[1] Based on material from P. M. Ranum and Pennwalt Corp., greatly modified.

Minerals and Buffers

The effect of the cations of water on dough quality has been explained in some detail in the earlier chapter on water. If ingredient water is very low in such ions as calcium, gluten may be adversely affected with resultant poor dough quality. Use of the salts that are included in most commercial dough improvers can be helpful in such cases. After an optimum level of concentration is reached, further addition of these ions has little positive effect and may even be deleterious.

If the ingredient water is alkaline, the buffering action of some of the salts which are found in dough improvers may bring the pH down slightly. It is difficult to see how this effect can be very pronounced, considering the small amounts of these substances that are customarily added to doughs and the large amounts of buffering materials ordinarily present in the other ingredients.

Enzymes

Enzymes are protein molecules that catalyze, or accelerate, reactions without undergoing a net change themselves. No doubt there are many enzymes functioning in doughs and batters since wheat flour contains many of them. Only a few have any significance for the baker, however. It has been found that certain types of enzymes give the baker better control over dough processing or result in a superior finished product. Suppliers offer these enzymes in standardized strengths as liquid, powder, or tabletted ingredients. Most commercial enzyme preparations are obtained by culturing selected strains of bacteria or fungi and recovering the enzyme from the medium. Plant extracts (papain, ficin, etc.) have also been used.

Lipoxygenases.—Enzymes that selectively oxidize certain lipids can have both beneficial and deteriorative effects on bakery products. As bleaching agents they can increase the whiteness of doughs and baked products; as oxidizers they can increase the mixing stability of doughs. They also promote oxidative deterioration. Soybean preparations containing active lipoxygenases are added to doughs specifically for their bleaching action. They are also used occasionally for their gluten oxidizing action, which differs from the chemical oxidizers in that it can be more prolonged and selective.

Proteases.—Enzymes known as proteases catalyze the hydrolysis of peptide bonds and thus cause splitting of protein molecules. The oldest intentional use of proteases that we know of was the addition of rennin from animal tissue to milk so as to cause casein to precipitate. From this precipitate, cheese was made. The principal application of proteases in bakery products is to reduce the strength of gluten in extensible doughs—to make the dough softer, smoother, more extensible, and easier to mix. If there is too much proteolytic action, the doughs will become sticky, tear easily, fail to retain gas, and hang up in the molding equipment.

Because proteases added to the dough continue to act on the gluten and other proteins until they are denatured by heat, the time factor is critical. Variations in processing time lead to variations in dough quality. Once a peptide bond has been severed by the enzyme, there is no way of reversing the action in dough. This is somewhat different from the softening action of reducing agents, which can sometimes be reversed by the addition of oxidizers. Obviously, proteases must be used with great caution.

Proteases offered by suppliers as bakery product ingredients are obtained from fungal or bacterial cultures. Trypsin and chymotrypsin from animal intestines and papain and ficin from fruit extracts have been used or suggested for use in bakery products.

Amylases.—Starch-splitting enzymes are very important agents in the processing of fermented dough products. By hydrolyzing starch molecules to fermentable sugars, they continuously generate a substrate (mostly maltose) that can be used by yeast throughout a long proofing period. The traditional source of amylases has been barley malt flour or diastatic malt syrup, the formerly normally added to wheat flour at the mill and the latter product added by the baker to his dough mix.

In recent years, fungal and bacterial amylases have been manufactured and offered to bakers and millers as replacements for malt enzymes. They have been used by millers to maintain the amylase activity of their flour at a uniform level, so that bakers need not make any adjustments in their formulas. They are used by bakers to even out differences in flours and to solve specific production problems. Sometimes they are used by bakers to adapt a flour to a formula for which it was not intended. Although there are many similarities in the actions of malt and fungal amylases, there are also differences that can affect the quality of dough and bread. One of these is the difference in their inactivation temperatures. Fungal alpha amylase of the type usually supplied for bakery use has a slightly lower inactivation temperature than the malt enzyme.

According to Ranum (1979), only slight variations in the other factors affecting diastatic activity occur when fungal amylases are used, so that the level of enzyme supplementation can be adjusted to control glucose production in doughs. All other factors are either constant or non-limiting. These other factors include starch damage, the small amount of sugars naturally present in flour, and the beta amylase originating from the wheat. Actually, this simplification would seem to apply only where the flour is a constant. Also, see Ranum and De Stefanis (1990).

Various enzyme preparations, mostly based on amylases, have been suggested as additives for reducing texture staling (Boyle and Hebeda 1990, Hebeda et al. 1990. and others). All commercial alpha amylase preparations contain varying amounts of other enzymes, including traces of proteases.

NUTRITIONAL SUPPLEMENTS

The discussions under this heading will relate to the ingredients available for nutritional supplementation of bakery products. Details concerning the physiological basis of supplementation, legal considerations, and other factors affecting nutrient addition will be found in references listed in the Bibliography.

Protein Supplements

Supplementation of bakery products with significant amounts of protein is difficult because most of the available additives alter one or more of the organoleptic aspects of the finished item. Protein supplementation is also expensive; unlike vitamins which, though costly on a per pound basis are added in micro-amounts, several grams of protein must be added to each portion to achieve an increase sufficient to be claimed on the label.

Protein supplementation takes two forms: (1) Adding purified amino acids or complementary proteins to increase the PER (an indication of the nutritional quality) of the proteins already present in the food, and (2) increasing the total amount of protein present by adding some purified nitrogenous material such as casein, isolated soy protein, or egg white. For labeling purposes, the latter method is the more desirable one.

Soy protein preparations are used far more than any other protein supplement. Next in importance are the milk protein preparations whey and casein. Egg proteins are generally too expensive for this purpose unless they also contribute other essential properties to the dough or batter.

Whey protein concentrates have an excellent PER, they interfere only slightly with most of the handling properties of the dough (if the whey has been properly processed), and they are relatively inexpensive. Unfortunately, many of these preparations have unpleasant flavors that carry through to the finished product. Careful screening of suppliers and rigid policing of deliveries is absolutely essential when buying these materials.

Defatted soy flour and grits are the most economical sources of soy protein available, and the nutritional value of these products is somewhat superior to that of the concentrated (refined) protein products made from soybeans. That is to say, the protein of the flour and grits has a slightly higher PER. Unfortunately, the organoleptic properties of most bakery foods decline in direct proportion to the amount of these enrichments added to the dough. Soy protein concentrates have had some, but not all, of the offending components removed, but they are considerably more costly than defatted soy flour. They have been used in milk replacers, mostly in combination with whey solids. They do affect the flavor adversely, if used in significant amounts, and can affect the color and have some effect on physical dough properties and on volume and texture of the finished product. Protein isolates contain the highest percentage of protein of the various soy enrichments and they are the most expensive. They usually have less influence on color, flavor, and texture. Nutritionally, soy protein is complementary to wheat protein (that is, it contains substantial amounts of the amino acids that are limiting in wheat), so its use is justifiable from that standpoint.

Certain amino acids are available as almost pure synthetic compounds. Lysine and methionine can be purchased in this form and may be useful for supplementation. Because they tend to be destroyed by heat, it would be advisable to add them to an icing or filling if the baked product includes such an adjunct. These purified amino acids have some significant drawbacks for supplementation purposes. Among these are high cost and undesirable flavor. The increased cost might be acceptable in certain specialty items, if the consumer can be convinced of the added value, but the flavor defects may be more difficult to overcome.

The use of protein hydrolysates, consisting mostly of individual amino acids or peptides of low molecular weight, has been suggested as a means of increasing the PER of bakery products, but their use is attended with some difficulties. Some of the amino acids are inevitably destroyed, regardless of how mild the proteolysis conditions are, so the hydrolysate is never as nutritionally effective as the original protein. And, in the manufacture of these materials, chemical recombinations or rearrangements may occur that could lead to compounds having a deleterious effect on health, even though the original protein was completely wholesome. Flavor and color factors are often undesirable. These may result from colors and flavors present in the raw material, or from Maillard reactions involving the added amino acids and reducing sugars present in other ingredients.

Casein for protein supplementation is obtained from milk by acid precipitation of this material, which also constitutes the major part of cheese. It is used for protein supplementation to an extent varying with the economics. It can cause some flavor problems because of the tendency of manufacturers to use as a raw material milk that has undergone some deterioration. The PER of casein is very good. It is difficult to disperse casein; sodium caseinate is considerably better but far from ideal.

Other protein-containing materials that have been used for, or suggested as, nutritional supplements for baked products include preparations from oil seed press cakes, analogous to defatted soy meal. Cottonseed meal, sunflower seed meal, and sesame seed meal are some of the materials that have been investigated or used in small amounts.

Vitamins

Vitamin supplementation is somewhat simpler than mineral or protein supplementation because of the smaller quantities of vitamins required. The cost is reasonable, just a fraction of a cent per portion if supplementation is restricted to the five vitamins in the list of seven commonly analyzed nutrients. Cost becomes much more important if Vitamin E and biotin are included at high percentages of the U.S. RDA.

Vitamins can definitely affect flavor. Thiamin is the primary offender, but other vitamins can contribute noticeable off-flavors when used in relatively large amounts. Color is generally not a problem, except with riboflavin, which is highly colored. The yellow hue of riboflavin may, however, be compatible with many baked products or be concealed by other colors (as in rye bread or chocolate cake). Processing and storage deterioration of these labile substances must be compensated for by addition of an excess so that the consumer receives the full claimed quantity.

There are several sources for most of the individual vitamins, but only a few large firms maintain stocks of all of them. Full-service companies will supply premixes of any specified combination and guarantee potency. These premixes can be obtained preweighed in batch-size containers or formed into tablets like those often used for bread dough enrichment.

A substantial percentage of some of the vitamins may be destroyed because of conditions existing in baking. Vitamin C is particularly labile, and vitamin B_1 is fairly sensitive, while niacin is relatively stable. To prevent undue loss during processing, the vitamin supplement can be sprayed on some baked products after they have cooled (nonstandard products only). Concentrated aqueous suspensions should be used to avoid the adverse effects on texture, appearance, and stability, which would result from contact of the product with excess water. Consideration should be given to spraying the bottom to avoid appearance defects. An oil suspension might also be used. Dusting with a dry mixture of the vitamins may leave a detectable residue and presents difficulties in securing uniform distribution. If the product has a filling or icing, consider adding the enrichment there.

Vitamins can be obtained in encapsulated form; this reduces the odor and flavor problem (as long as they remain dry), and to some extent lengthens their storage life. Encapsulation is of little value if the vitamins are put through a wet-processing step, especially if heat is applied. The fat-soluble vitamins are often supplied in oil solutions or in minute pellets composed of fatty substances, in which case it is advisable to specify an antioxidant content since the corn oil vehicle can become rancid in time.

If a product is supplemented with vitamins, or with any nutritional factor, the manufacturer must establish a quality control program that will make certain every portion contains the amount of nutrient stated on the label. The necessary QA analyses can add substantially to the overall cost of enrichment.

Minerals

The large amounts of calcium and phosphorus needed to supply meaningful percentages of the U.S. RDA to the consumer of a product can lead to seemingly insuperable problems in formulating certain types of highly enriched baked products. These nutrients are usually added as some form of calcium phosphate (e.g., monocalcium phosphate) for economic, organoleptic, and functional reasons. None of the available calcium phosphates contain nutritionally equivalent weights of the two nutrients, so that it is not possible to add just the minimum amount of each. This further complicates the enrichment problem. Even 10% of the U.S. RDA of phosphorus and calcium would require the addition of about 0.5 gm of tricalcium phosphate per portion of food. Textural and visual defects can result from the inclusion of such amounts to portion quantities of most cookies or crackers, and perhaps of bread and rolls. In some cases, the enrichment may also affect the consistency and baking response of the dough or batter.

Iron, which is one of the "commonly analyzed nutrients," along with calcium and five vitamins, must be declared as a percentage of the U.S. RDA on the nutrition information panel. It also is one of the nutrients that must be added to enriched bread. Iron salts can cause problems related to adverse organoleptic properties. Soluble iron salts, such as ferrous sulfate, can react with cocoa to produce blue, gray, or black hues which are quite objectionable in many foods. Reduced iron may be observed as small black specks, and because of its high density separates from the lighter ingredients and moves toward the bottom of the container when in a dry mix. Some iron additives may greatly accelerate the development of rancidity in cookies or other fat-containing foods. Sodium iron pyrophosphate is less damaging in this respect and has a number of other advantages over other iron enrichments, being bland in flavor, white in color, and relatively insoluble. Its main disadvantages are a rather high cost and an apparently low level of bioavailability.

Different iron compounds differ in availability of iron for nutrition of animals, including humans. The bioavailability of iron compounds is affected by other materials in the diet, e.g., calcium, phytates, and ascorbic acid (Morck and Cook 1981). It is also affected by the condition of the consumer's metabolism. Iron from animal sources is more readily available than iron from plant sources, evidently due to the heme structures in the former. Of the iron sources that have been suggested for enrichment, ferrous sulfate, ferric ammonium citrate, ferrous fumarate, and ferrous gluconate seem to have high availability. Some forms of elemental iron also have rather high availability, while sodium iron pyrophosphate and ferric orthophosphate appear to have low bioavailability, at least under some circumstances.

Loss of mineral supplements due to deterioration during processing and storage generally does not occur, with the possible exception of iodine. Reactions of soluble additives with other dough or batter constituents or segregation because of density differences may be observed, however. If the baked product contains icings or fillings, consideration should be given to adding the mineral supplement to the adjuncts. Additions to coatings such as chocolate may not be feasible because of changes in the appearance, viscosity, and mouthfeel (smoothness).

Mineral supplements can be obtained from several manufacturers. They can be ordered in bulk containers, or arrangements can be made to receive them in preweighed packets containing sufficient nutrients for addition to one batch of product. Tablets containing vitamin and mineral enrichment in the proportions required for enriched bread are also available. And, of course, enriched flour is available from nearly every wheat miller.

Fiber Sources

The use of high fiber materials as dietary supplements justifies their inclusion in this section even though they are not "nutrients" in the strict sense of that word—quite the contrary.

Publications by some medical researchers and nutritionists seem to indicate that increased incidences of gastrointestinal and cardiovascular diseases (and perhaps cancer) are correlated with decreased dietary fiber intakes. It has been shown that transit time of food residues in the colon, stool weight/concentration, and the binding of bile salts are directly affected by the amount of dietary fiber consumed. These factors singly or in combination are thought to result in more generalized physiological benefits. The rationale presented by proponents of the beneficial nature of dietary fiber is rather convoluted (not to say circular) in many cases, but there is some experimental evidence that increased consumption of whole cereal grains (which are relatively high in fiber) can decrease cholesterol levels in rats. Statistical and demographic date have been assembled to support some of the other claimed benefits (Anon. 1985). The popular press latched on to the preliminary reports of possible fiber benefits and, as usual, inflated their significance far out of proportion. This whetted the appetite of consumers for foods of high fiber content and gave an opportunity for the marketing of foods specially formulated to fill the demand.

There is no doubt that the tremendous publicity given to the supposed beneficial effects of high fiber diets has strongly influenced a large segment of the population. Consequently, the fiber content of a bakery food can be a selling point which has to be taken into account when the formula is designed. First of all, the question to be asked is, "What is fiber?" There is more than one answer (see, for example, Schneeman 1986). A definition handed down by a committee is, "Endogenous components of plant material in the diet which are resistant to digestion by enzymes produced by man. They are predominantly nonstarch polysaccharides and lignin and may include, in addition, associated substances" (Anon. 1985). Another definition is, ". . .the portion of plants which is not broken down by chemical action in the digestive system" (Harland and Hecht 1985). The components of fiber that can be chemically characterized include the insoluble fibers (cellulose, hemicellulose, lignin, insoluble pectins, insoluble gums, and pentosans) and the soluble fibers (soluble gums, soluble pectins, and polysaccharides not digested by amylases), according to Aaron and Stauffer (1986).

Crude fiber can be determined by first digesting the product in dilute acid, then in dilute alkali, and measuring what remains. The figures obtained for most common foods by this method are quite low. Another method is arithmetical, and simply involves substracting from 100% the sum of the figures obtained in the proximate analyses. Neither method is suitable for measuring dietary fiber. The Neutral Detergent Fiber Procedure is regarded as an improvement but not as the final answer. It relies on extractions with neutral and acidic detergents for isolating fractions. A third approach, intended to provide a single value for the soluble and insoluble fiber content of a food, involves the enzymatic removal of protein and starch from fat-extracted samples. The residue is corrected for ash and residual protein, and the fiber is determined gravimetrically. The so-called Southgate method analyzes separately for each of the fiber components (soluble and insoluble), and is the most informative of all methods but is very time consuming and labor intensive. It would seem to allow cumulative errors, as well.

Dietary fiber estimation by enzymatic analysis yielded the following values for some ingredients of interest to technologists who may be considering fiber supplementation of bakery foods: Corn bran 89.02%; wheat bran 42.25%; whole wheat flour 23.31%; oats 12.47%; raisins 4.43%; rice 3.67%; and white flour 3.07%. Other supplements that might be considered are purified cellulose, which should be close to 100% fiber on a dry weight basis, pectin, lignin, and various gums such as guar. The author's experience suggests that any of these supplements, when included in formulas in more than trace amounts, can impair the flavor, texture, and appearance of the finished product. Highly flavored, dense cookies are one of the best mediums for delivering fiber in a form acceptable to consumers. Corn bran is perhaps the best choice for a fiber supplement, especially if cost is a significant consideration, but it, too, poses substantial problems in flavor and texture.

BIBLIOGRAPHY

AARON, J. S., and STAUFFER, C. E. 1986. Dietary fiber: Accessing its ingredient function and marketing role. Baking Industry *153*, No. 4, 46-48

ANDO, H. 1985. Method for preserving food using a preservative gas atmosphere. U.S. Pat. 4,550,026

ANON. 1965. The corn refining industry. Corn *21*, No. 1, 2-4

ANON. 1985. Report of Expert Advisory Committee on Dietary Fibre. Health Protection Branch, Health and Welfare Dept., Canada. Information Letter *700*

ANON. 1986. Corn Starch, Seventh Edition. Corn Refiners Assoc., Inc., Washington, DC

BELSHAW, F. R. 1980. Effects of modified starches on modern cake formulas. Cereal Foods World *25*, 648-649

BEST, D. 1990. Dietary fiber: down, but far from out! Prepared Foods *159*, No. 5, 82-84

BOYLE, P. J., and HEBEDA, R. E. 1990. Antistaling enzyme for baked goods. Food Technol. *44*, No. 6, 129

DUBOIS, D. K., and COTTLE, F. E. 1969. Vital wheat gluten applications in bakery foods. Am. Soc. Bakery Engineers Bulletin *188*,

DURST, J. R. 1985. Storage stable, ready-to-eat baked goods. U.S. Pat. 4,511,585

HAHN, R. R. 1969. Tailoring starches for the baking industry. Bakers Digest *43*, No. 4, 48-53, 64

HARLAND, B., and HECHT, A. 1985. Grandma called it roughage. U.S. Dept. Health and Human Services Publ. No. (FDA) *78-2087*

HEBEDA, R. E., BOWLES, L. K., TEAGUE, W. M. 1990. Developments in enzymes for retarding staling of baked goods. Cereal Foods World *35*, 453-457

HICKEY, C. S. 1980. Proper use of preservatives. Proc. Am. Soc. Bakery Engineers *1980* , 62-68

HURT, H. D., and CROCCO, S. C. 1986. Dietary fiber: marketing implications. Food Technol. *40*, No. 2, 124-126

KAMMAN, P. 1980. Oxidizing and reducing agents. Proc. Am. Soc. Bakery Engineers *1980*, 138-144

KAMMAN, P. 1991. Baking bread and rolls without potassium bromate. Bakery *26*, No. 3, 178-179

KRAMER, F. 1967. Gelatin—how it's made. Food Eng. *38*, No. 11, 74-77

LANHAM, F. B., JR. 1978. Vital wheat gluten—reasons and usage. Proc. Am. Soc. Bakery Engineers *1978*, 54-57

LIGHT, J. M. 1990. Modified food starches: why, what, where, and how. Cereal Foods World *35*, 1081-1092

LUALLEN, T. E. 1985. Starch as a functional ingredient. Food Technol. *39*, No. 1, 59-63

MC MILLAN, T. 1983. Retaining product freshness in bread. Proc. Am. Soc. Bakery Engineers *1983*, 141-148

MONGEAU, R., and BRASSARD, R. 1990. Determination of insoluble, soluble, and total dietary fiber: Collaborative study of a rapid gravimetric method. Cereal Foods World *35*, 319-324

MORCK, T. A., and COOK, J. D. 1981. Factors affecting the bioavailability of dietary iron. Cereal Foods World *26*, 667-671

MURPHY, R. J. 1981. Variety breads. Proc. Am. Soc. Bakery Engineers *1981*, 46-53

NEIDLEMAN, S. L. 1991. Enzymes in the food industry: A backward glance. Food Technol. *45*, No. 1, 88

PFLAMMER, P. E., SMITH, E. D., III, and HUDSON, W. G., JR. 1990. Cookies containing psyllium. U.S. Pat. 4,950,140

POWELL, A. G. 1977. Agents to reduce mixing time. Proc. Am. Soc. Bakery Engineers *1977*, 99-103

RANUM, P. M. 1979. Advantages of fungal amylase-treated bakery flour. Proc. Am. Soc. Bakery Engineers *1979*, 50-55

RANUM, P. M. 1987. Personal communication. Buffalo, NY

RANUM, P., and DE STEFANIS, V. A. 1990. Use of fungal alpha-amylase in milling and baking. Cereal Foods World *35*, 931-933

RUSCH, D. T. 1981. Emulsifiers: Uses in cereal and bakery foods. *26*, 111-115

SCHNEEMAN, B. O. 1986. Dietary fiber: physical and chemical properties, methods of analysis, and physiological effects. Food Technol. *40*, No. 2, 104-110

SHIELDS, D. W. 1982. Total cost of flour in bread and buns. Proc. Am. Soc. Bakery Engineers *1982*, 73-77

SPOONER, T. F. 1990. The fate of potassium bromate. Baking & Snack Systems *12*, No. 7, 12-16

THAYER, A. M. 1991. Use of specialty food additives to continue to grow. Chem. Eng. News *69*, 9-12

TIECKELMANN, R. E., and STEELE, R. E. 1991. Higher-assay grade of calcium peroxide improves properties of dough. Food Technol. *45*, No. 1, 106, 108, 112

TOMA, R. B., and CURTIS, D. J. 1986. Dietary fiber: effect on mineral availability. Food Technol. *40*, No. 2, 111-116

WORTHY, W. 1990. Evidence mounts for dietary soluble fiber benefits. Chem. Eng. News *68*, No. 22, 23-24

chapter eleven

UNLEAVENED BAKERY PRODUCTS

INTRODUCTION

The products discussed in this chapter typically do not contain any added yeast or chemical leavening materials and they are not made in such a way that an appreciable amount of air is entrapped in expansible vesicles. As a result, they do not "rise" significantly during baking or other processing steps. Indeed, many of them actually shrink in the oven. They are not solid masses of baked dough or batter, however, for there is nearly always a multitude of small holes throughout the finished product. These cavities result from incomplete coalescence of the mixed ingredients and from the drying of particles.

To some extent, products in this category overlap both in formulation and processing the air-leavened and steam-leavened products to be discussed in subsequent chapters. A decision on the category to which a product belongs has been based on whether or not it contains added leavening materials as well as on the presence or absence of processing steps deliberately intended to establish a structure enhancing the entrapment of leavening gas and significantly affecting the eating texture of the finished product. The presence of large surface blisters, as in some tortillas or matzos, does not mean the product is "leavened" in the sense in which the word is used in this book.

In developing most unleavened bakery products, two major goals are to avoid the entrapment of gases and the development of gluten—almost the opposite of what the formulator of leavened products is looking for.

PIE CRUSTS

General Considerations

This is probably the most important commercial type of unleavened bakery product. Leavening agents are not always absent from pie crust formulas; some recipes do call for small amounts of baking powder or sodium bicarbonate, but conventional and typical recipes omit such ingredients and they are not needed to obtain pie crusts having desirable eating qualities.

Formulas and basic procedures for pie crusts and a few allied products are included in this section. Descriptions of equipment for making pie crusts in commercial operations will be covered in the next section of this book. Fillings, glazes, streusels, meringues, coatings, washes, etc., to be used on and in pies will be discussed in the chapters devoted to formulations and procedures for adjuncts.

Types of Pie Crusts

There are several methods of merchandising pies and pie crusts, and they can determine which type of pie crust is the most desirable. Among these methods are:

(1) Raw pie crusts sold either as rolled out circles of dough or as trimmed dough fitted into foil pans. The dough-sans-pans is sold either as a frozen, refrigerated, or shelf-stable product and represents the smaller part of the market. Dough in foil pans is more convenient in some ways, but it causes inconveniences when two-crust pies are being made, because some hassle is involved in manually forming the top crust. The total amount of pie dough sold as unfilled raw crusts is thought to be relatively small.

(2) Baked pie crusts. There is a low but consistent volume of sales of graham cracker and cookie crusts pressed into foil pans and offered for use in preparing cream pies, certain kinds of cheesecakes, etc. They are available in small sizes for "tarts" and in large sizes for 8- or 9-inch pies. These crusts are not actually "baked," since the crusts themselves are merely pressure-formed from ground-up crackers or cookies which have been mixed with shortening and some other ingredients. There may be some regular unfilled baked crusts sold regionally in small amounts, but there are no brands marketed regularly on a national basis because these products are too fragile to withstand the transportation and warehousing abuse they would encounter in normal distribution channels.

(3) Unbaked pies. More crusts are sold as constituents of frozen unbaked pies than in any other form, except for crusts in bakery pies sold "fresh." The fillings in frozen pies are usually traditional pie fruits such as apple and cherry. Most frozen pies are probably sold through retail channels but there is a considerable foodservice market as well. There is also a comparatively small market for frozen unbaked "cobblers," which are deep dish, usually rectangular, fruit pies often with a top crust that is not attached to the bottom crust.

(4) Fresh baked pies. These pies are sold within a few days of baking by retail and wholesale bakeries, in bake-off sections of supermarkets, and in other outlets for purchase by consumers and foodservice customers. To reach the table in good condition, they should be sold within two or three days of baking, but many unquestionably exceed this shelf life before they are consumed.

(5) Frozen baked pies. An increasing volume of sales is developing for "thaw and eat" pies, especially cream topped pies. Some manufacturers are offering individually packaged, portion-sized slices for thawing and eating by people who do not wish to buy a whole pie. There is a considerable and increasing foodservice market for both whole and baked pies and prebaked slices in frozen form.

(6) Portion-size fried pies. There is a very large sale of individual fried pies through quick food chains such as McDonald's, and these items are also sold as snack items through various outlets such as convenience

stores. The latter market invariably requires fully cooked products.

In addition to serving as the basis for the familiar fruit, cream, or meringue dessert pies, crusts of the same general type are used for baked meat and fish pies, quiches, tarts, apple dumplings, one type of turnover, and deep dish covered pies. Many of these applications require only minor modifications in crust formula.

Baked Pies

Ingredients and formulation principles.—Pie doughs are made with a high level of shortening. They contain a relatively small amount of water to begin with and are kept in the oven until their moisture content is quite low compared with many other baked foods. The ratio of ingredients together with the method of preparation prevent the formation of a strong gluten network throughout the dough mass and result in baked products that are fragile and more or less friable or flaky.

The porous or spongy structure that typifies nearly all leavened bakery products is not wanted in pie crusts because they must support and retain, without leakage, fillings of moderate viscosity and high moisture content. It is also necessary that the pies can be cut in serving-size pieces without fragmenting and that soaking of filling into the crust be minimized. Flavor of the crust should be bland to avoid interference with the filling flavor, unless the crust is especially designed to complement a specific flavor, as when a chocolate cookie crust is used with a vanilla- or mint-flavored filling or a graham cracker crust is used to contain banana filling.

Some experts have divided pie crusts into three classes based on their flakiness, a term that may be loosely defined as the tendency of the crust to separate into strata or layers when it is broken. Flaky or long-flake crusts when broken tend to show fractures along different lines at different levels and to separate in layers parallel to the surface. Mealy crusts can be broken in a fairly straight line and exhibit a fracture surface more like that of a cookie. Short-flake or flaky-mealy crusts have characteristics intermediate between the two extremes.

Flaky crusts are esteemed by connoisseurs and by trade experts, but they show the abuse of handling more quickly than the mealy type, and they pose difficulties in serving. They are also more difficult to process properly than is the mealy type. Mealy crusts can be cut readily, usually support fillings adequately, and are not particularly sensitive to processing conditions. Most manufacturers catering to the general public make pies with mealy-type crusts. Home recipes are generally designed to produce flaky or semi-flaky crusts, but most packed mixes yield the mealy variety. Refrigerated or frozen, pre-shaped crusts for home pie baking usually yield semi-flaky crusts.

The basic formula for pie crusts requires flour and water for structure formation, shortening to provide the desired textural qualities, and salt to enhance the flavor. Sugar, dextrose, or nonfat dry milk may be added to ensure adequate coloration and improve the flavor. The amount of water used, the kind of shortening, and the method of mixing are the chief determinants of crust characteristics. Table 11.1 contains formulas for pie crusts of the conventional type.

Table 11.1. FORMULAS FOR CRUSTS OF FRUIT PIES[1]

Ingredient	Type of crust			
	Simple	Top crusts	Low fat	Rich
Pastry flour	49.2	49.4	50.9	46.2
Shortening	29.5	34.5	24.4	38.1
Salt	1.6	1.2	1.8	1.4
Water, cold	19.7	12.5	15.3	13.3
Corn sugar (dextrose)	--	1.8	--	1.0
Nonfat dry milk	--	0.6	--	--
Maltodextrin (10 grade)	--	--	6.1	--
Granulated sugar	--	--	1.5	--

[1] Proportions are stated in percent, as is basis.

The formulas in Table 11.1 will yield crusts suitable for fruit pies. Differences in formulas for top and bottom crusts will be discussed in later paragraphs. To process these formulas on the bench, mix the dry ingredients by cutting or rubbing in the shortening until most of the lumps are about the size of peas. Add water by sprinkling, and mix only until it has been absorbed. Remove dough from the mixer in one mass, if possible, flatten it slightly, and cut pieces of desired weight (about 6.5 oz to 7 oz for the usual crust). Shape each piece into a circular mass and roll it out to about 3/16th inch thick and place it in the pan. Deposit the fruit filling. Apply top crust, crimp, seal, and bake. Crust ingredients such as glucose, sucrose, and nonfat dry milk should be dissolved in the ingredient water. Maltodextrin should be mixed with the flour before shortening is added.

The weakest flour that is commercially available is suitable for pie crusts, though some gluten binding is necessary to provide the rheological properties required for proper processing. Any factor tending to strengthen gluten structure is to be avoided. In practice, this means that the flour used in pie crusts should be unbleached, with a protein content of 7.0% to 8.5%, ash content of 0.38% to 0.48%, and a MacMichael viscosimeter reading of 30° to 40°. Struckmann (1956) recommends even narrower limits of 7.0% to 7.25% for protein and 32° to 36° for viscosity. The flour should be milled from a soft white winter wheat and should be slightly granular. Soft red winter wheats yield somewhat stronger flours that may or may not be satisfactory for the purpose, depending on how critical the finished product requirements are. If a stronger flour must be used because of inventory or supplier problems, it may be possible to dilute it with corn starch, but the results are seldom satisfactory. Bleached flours generally make poor crusts.

In spite of the preceding comments about the need for very weak flours, starch, durum flour, etc., are not satisfactory as the sole cereal ingredient.

A coarse, rather than fine, granulation is desired in pie flour. High diastatic activity is considered undesirable in the crust of frozen, fruit-filled pie (Loving and Brenneis 1981), and it certainly is not necessary in any type of crust. Color can vary within fairly wide ranges, and a few small specks are probably of little concern to the consumer.

It is generally believed that ingredient water should have a pH near the neutral point for best results in processing and baking. Very hard water will make a firmer dough and may improve machinability of a mealy type dough. Very soft water will lead to a softer, more flexible dough that shrinks relatively little. Adding vinegar has been suggested as a means of bringing alkaline water to neutrality. Baking soda is used for the opposite effect.

Shortening for pie crust doughs is used at levels of about 70% to 75% (FWB) in household recipes, about 50% to 60% in commercial pie crusts, and as low as 35% in fried pie doughs. The type of shortening has an effect on the amount that must be used. Ingredient fats and oils can be assigned shortening values which reflect their efficiency in promoting tenderness and flakiness in pie crusts. Table 11.2 shows the shortening values obtained for several common bakery fats and oils in one study.

Table 11.2. SHORTENING VALUES OF SOME BAKERY INGREDIENTS

Fat or Oil Ingredient	Shortening value
Totally hydrodgenated shortening	100
Partly hydrogenated shortening, usual type	110
Partially hydrogenated lard	110
Open-kettle lard, plasticized	125
Special grainy type lard	130–135
Vegetable oil	150

The higher the value shown in the table, the more effective the fat or oil is in promoting "shortness" (not necessarily flakiness) in the crust. These shortenings were evaluated by preparing crusts from a standard recipe, varying only the type and quantity of fat. Other bakery technologists may regard vegetable oils as having a lower shortening value than lard, which is frequently called for in household recipes. Some retail pie crust mixes contain hydrogenated lard from which part of the lard oil has been removed. Lard is also much used commercially and the tough, "fibrous" variety (leaf lard) is preferred over the soft, grainy type. The former gives a short and tender pie crust without the undesirable greasy quality sometimes seen in crusts made from other shortenings.

The use of highly hydrogenated shortenings with elevated melting points may make it easier to prepare flaky crusts but they can cause a waxy eating texture that is undesirable.

Emulsifiers should not be used in pie doughs. They tend to disperse shortenings and thus reduce flakiness, which is the opposite effect to that which is usually desired. Antioxidants can be added, though their effects on shelf-life are doubtful, since most crusts are consumed before rancidity can levelop.

Salt is used at levels from 1.5% to 4% of the flour weight. If salt is mixed with the dry ingredients before water is added, it may not dissolve completely because of the short mixing time and the relatively small amount of liquid available. This may not be a serious problem if fine grain salt is used, because incomplete dispersion may not then be detectable by the average consumer. As a precautionary measure, the salt should be dissolved in the ingredient water.

It is quite a common practice to add sugar, corn syrup, or dextrose in proportions of about 3% to 8% (FWB). Amounts in this range lead to adequate browning of the crust without contributing a sweet taste. Sometimes the sugars are dispersed in the absorption water along with the salt and milk solids, if the latter are used. The need for a sweet taste in the crust is a matter for debate. On general principles, it would seem a slightly sweet flavor can hardly be objectionable since the crusts are eaten with fillings that are usually high in sugar content. Reducing sugars are more effective than sucrose in promoting browning, so corn syrup or corn sugar are the ingredients of choice if the problem is a crust that is too light in color.

At one time, it was fairly common to add a little egg white to the dough to give a drier and crisper crust. This additive is probably not used in any commercial crusts at this time, economic reasons such as cheaper alternatives having been the cause of its decline.

Whey powder or milk solids can be included for much the same purposes as sugar; their lactose content contributes to the development of an appetizing brownish crust color during baking. They also contain proteins that can participate in the browning reaction. Spray-dried milk is considered to be preferable to roller-dried material. Wheat or corn proteins may be added to improve machinability of the dough and add to the crispness of the finished products.

Propionates or sorbates are sometimes included in the formula to retard mold formation. They are often added to crusts used in baked pies distributed in unfrozen form, since mold can develop rapidly when the water activity of the crust rises as a result of its contact with the moist filling. There is less logic to adding these preservatives to frozen pies, although this is sometimes done.

Many of the early publications on the influence of dough ingredients on crust quality were reviewed by Miller and Trimbo (1970). These researchers also made quantitative measurements—and some subjective judgements—of various dough and crust characteristics. They found that the tensile strength of their test doughs decreased as the water or shortening content of the mixture increased. A somewhat similar response of consistency (shear press values) to variations in these ingredients was observed. The stretchability of pie dough was a linear function of water content, but passed through a maximum as the shortening content or mixing time of the dough was increased. Stickiness increased linearly with increasing water level, shortening level, and mixing time.

An increase in the flour's protein content resulted in a linearly related increase in tensile strength and shear values, a non-linear increase in stretchability, and a linear decrease in the stickiness of the dough. Stickiness decreased while tensile strength and shear press values increased with increasing hardness of the shortening. There appeared to be no relationship between the stretchability of the dough and hardness of the shortening. Increasing the mixing time or raising the shortening or water levels in the formula caused the pie doughs to become softer and easier to roll out, but dough stickiness was also increased by these changes. Doughs made with high-protein flour had high water absorbing characteristics and tended to be both bucky and difficult to roll out. Diluting a high protein flour with starch produced a dough with greatly improved rollability.

Continuing with the results of Miller and Trimbo as related to pie crusts, it was found that crust became more tender with increasing shortening content and decreasing water level. With increased mixing, the crusts became mealy, but more tender. Tenderness was found to be inversely related to the protein content of the flour, and the effect of protein was accentuated when the water content of the dough was increased. Pie crust made with soft shortenings were more tender than crusts made with hard shortenings. Shrinkage during baking increased with increased flour protein content, but was little affected by varying the shortening or water content of the dough. When the doughs shrank, a noticeable increase in thickness of the upper crust occurred.

Softer shortenings appeared to produce crusts with shorter flakes, whereas excessively hard shortenings tended to produce crusts that were tough and quite tight in structure. There were no observable differences in flakiness when the shortening level was varied between 40% and 80% (FWB). Crust made from dough containing starch but no protein was tender but very mealy, while crust made from dough containing a high protein flour was very flaky. Flakiness was not a requisite for tenderness, i.e., these two properties did not appear to be directly related. These authors confirmed that a certain (small) amount of gluten development is needed to give adequate processing qualities to doughs.

In general, flaky crusts are obtained by mixing all of the shortening with all of the flour for a period just sufficient to reduce the shortening to small lumps. The recommended size for fat chunks varies somewhat according to the authority consulted. One writer says the mix should resemble "very coarsely ground corn meal mixed with kernels of uncooked rice." It also is related to the type of shortening employed, the temperature of the dough, the intensity of subsequent processing steps, and the thickness of the finished crust.

In preparing doughs for mealy crusts, however, the shortening may be completely dispersed in the dough. Consequently, the processing conditions are much less critical for these crusts. It is usually convenient to mix flour and shortening blends until the fat is completely absorbed and the flour particles are coated with it. Refrigeration of ingredients and doughs is of no particular value in these cases.

Semi-flaky crusts represent a compromise between the two extremes of flaky and mealy crusts. They are often made by bakers who consider the flaky method too sensitive or difficult for the conditions in their plants, but who do want to give their customers something better than mealy crust pies. One method for obtaining the semi-flaky crust is just to continue the mix a little longer than is required for flaky crust dough. Two other methods that have been developed for this intermediate type of crust are the flour-paste method and the slurry method (Knuepfer 1960).

In the flour-paste method, half the flour is mixed with all the shortening to form a paste. Then the remainder of the flour is added, and the batch mixed to a lumpy consistency. Finally, water is added and mixing continued until it is all absorbed.

The slurry method requires that 15% to 20% of the total flour be withheld from the first stage. The remainder of the flour is blended well with all the shortening, as in making a mealy crust. The flour that has been held back is dispersed in the ingredient water so as to make a slurry. The flour and water mix is added to the first stage and blended only enough to make the dough uniform. High fat levels (65% to 70%, FWB) are necessary in order to obtain maximum mixing tolerance. When lower fat levels (e.g., 50%) are used, conditions during the second stage are critical, with a slight overmixing resulting in shrinkage and toughness.

An extreme example of flakiness is seen in the so-called "extra flaky" crust that is sometimes used in one-crust chicken or meat pies and for deep dish fruit pies, where a very distinct crispness and flakiness is required. This type of pie crust is made by cutting the shortening into the flour to give lumps of fat about the size of a walnut. The consistency of shortening must be such that it will not smear into the flour too easily and both flour and shortening have to be chilled to 55° to 60°F. About 70% to 80% of shortening (FWB) will be required for best results. After the mix, the dough is given one three-fold and rolled out. The similarity with blitz process puff pastry (see the next chapter) is obvious. Advantages of this crust are a high degree of tenderness, an excellent flaky appearance, and very good color. Disadvantages are that it has poor resistance to soaking by the filling, it is difficult to make, and it has a high raw materials cost due to the large amount of shortening required.

It is desirable to have all of the pie crust ingredients refrigerated, or, at least, the flour and water should be chilled to 35° to 40°F before mixing. Most processing instructions call for only the water to be chilled. In some cases, it is recommended that the flour be brought to refrigerator temperatures before used. In addition, the dough itself may be chilled for several hours after mixing and before it is sheeted and cut so as to keep the shortening particles discrete. This cool rest period allows the water to distribute itself more thoroughly in the dough mass and hardens the shortening so that it is less likely to liquefy during subsequent handling and shaping operations. These chilling steps are particularly important in the manufacture of dough for long-flake crusts. Chilling is not necessary for mealy-type doughs, which should come out of the mixer at about 65°F and be held in a covered container at this temperature for about 3 to 4 hours to allow the water to become more uniformly distributed.

Large amounts of scrap dough may be generated in the cutting of pie crust circles, and the problem of efficiently utilizing this scrap is of great concern to pie manufacturers. Most authorities recommend that scrap dough be blended into fresh dough in quantities not exceeding 50% of the total. Use of scrap dough in this manner is essential in most operations but it does adversely affect texture, particularly if the manufacturer is trying to produce a flaky crust. Some bakers restrict the use of scrap blends to bottom crusts, where the effect on texture is thought to be less evident to the consumer. This plan often results in bottom crusts being nearly 100% scrap. Other operators believe that it is more desirable to take advantage of the greater dilution of scrap that is possible when it is blended into both the bottom and top crusts. If the crusts are pressed from lumps of dough (eliminating the cutting of circles from a basically rectangular sheet), the amount of scrap generated is drastically decreased, but other texture problems are introduced.

To summarize the processing of pie crusts, two steps common to nearly all pie dough mixing processes are: (1) Blending the shortening and the flour until the fat has reached a desired degree of subdivision, and (2) Adding the water and the water-soluble ingredients to the fat and shortening mixture and agitating until the water has been absorbed. Flaky crusts require a short first stage that leaves the shortening in the form of discrete lumps while mealy crusts are thoroughly mixed during the first stage so that the flour particles are completely coated by fat. Intermediate types of crust may be prepared either by reducing the shortening to very small lumps, e.g., about the size of peas, or by a two-stage addition of fat, during the first step of which the fat is uniformly dispersed while in the second stage mixing is carried only to the point where the fat has been broken down to fairly small uniform particles. Mixing the dough after the water has been completely absorbed is not good practice, since it tends to develop the gluten, making the dough bucky and leading to crust shrinkage.

Practical formulas and procedures.– The preceding discussion will serve as the background for the following review of some work that has been reported on specific formulas and methods for good quality pie crusts. It must be pointed out that each of the individual discussions represents the viewpoint of one authority, and authorities may differ in the details of their formulas or procedures.

Spannuth (1962) suggested a formula consisting of 100 parts flour, 65 parts shortening, 27 parts water, 5 parts dextrose, and 2 parts salt. The flour is to be unbleached, 8% protein, pastry type, and tempered to 50° to 60°F. Shortening is to be a non-grainy, plastic lard with antioxidants; it is to have good feathering and be conditioned at 50° to 60°F. Ingredient shortening should be firm but not hard at the time of use. Shortening that has been chilled until it is brittle will not distribute properly throughout the dough. The water can be typical drinking water refrigerated to 50°F or lower, if required.

The flour and shortening are dry mixed to a stage where the blend is crumbly but beginning to gather, so that there is a rubbing action causing relatively rapid fat dispersion as compared to the initial period. "Marbles or globs" of fat will still be visible, particularly if a sample of the mass is compressed and then cut with a spatula. The dry mix stage can be varied considerably to adjust for differences in consistency of the shortening, the latter being affected by the composition of the fat, type of fat, type of crystal structure in the fat, actual temperature of the fat, and its previous storage history. Regardless of the length of the mixing time, which may vary with a given formula depending upon the ingredient characteristics and the conditions, the goal is to stop at a point where the blend is capable of yielding a flaky crust. When arm-type pie mixing equipment, of which the Artofex is one example, is being used, four minutes is usually sufficient time.

To make a semi-flaky crust, the mixing is extended until a fine crumbly mixture with small pea-sized lumps is obtained. Often, a change in color of the mix will be noted at this point; it will become slightly darker or yellower. Sometimes it will be found necessary to reduce the water by 2% to 4% to maintain good machinability. Such doughs will usually bake more uniformly and color faster than a very flaky dough.

Additional mixing will lead to a mealy crust. A dough of this type will be a fine meal, almost a paste, with little or no fat particles visible. The water content will probably have to be reduced to give the dough adequate handling properties. It will color well during baking and show very little shrinkage. The eating texture resembles that of a cookie (Dietrich 1962).

Salt and dextrose are dissolved in the water, which is added in a single portion to the dry mix. Use of a stock solution of salt and dextrose is acceptable and saves time, but this should be mixed fresh every day. The solution is distributed over the mix to minimize any tendency to develop wet spots. Mixing is then continued until the dough begins to form a lump and clean the bowl. At this stage the dough should feel fairly dry, with not much stickiness. If the dough is cut, specks of fat will be visible. Further working of the dough will result in increased stickiness and toughness. Doughs should come out of the mixer at 60°F or cooler; 65°F is definitely too warm. It is desirable to rest the doughs for four hours at 50° to 60°F.

The doughs should be rolled to a thickness of about one-eighth inch and cut. Trimmings can be used for bottoms, adding to them as much fresh dough as possible. Often, the amount of scrap is such that the bottoms are made entirely of recycled dough. This does affect the finished consistency, of course. Circles cut or otherwise shaped for the bottoms are fitted into pans so that minimum space is left between the dough·and the pan at all points. Then, the filling is deposited and leveled out. If a two crust pie is being made, the rim of the bottom dough is thoroughly wetted, the top is fitted on this rim, and the edges are pressed together and crimped. Tops should be made entirely from fresh dough. The top is punctured to vent the vapors that develop during baking. Washing the top crust with milk is optional.

It is instructive to examine a slightly different approach to making the most preferred type of pie crust. Elling (1952) gave a formula and procedure for making a 211 lb batch of long-flake dough suitable for use during warm weather months. He indicates the same formula can be adapted for producing short-flake or mealy crusts if the processing techniques are changed appropriately.

Long-flake Crust

(1) Mix smooth but do not cream:
    45 lb steam rendered lard
    15 lb partially hydrogenated vegetable shortening
(2) Add the following ingredients to the above and mix until the fat is in pieces the size of walnuts:
    100 lb soft pastry flour at 35° to 40°F
    6 lb nonfat milk solids
(3) Add the following to the above and mix just enough to blend well:
    38 lb ice water
    4 lb salt
    3 lb corn sugar

Struckmann (1956) described the production of doughs yielding a short-flake pie crust suitable for fruit pies and a mealy crust especially suitable for small individual pies and custard shells. Slightly modified versions of these are given below.

Short-flake Crust

(1) Place in an arm-type mixer the following ingredients and blend them together until the shortening and flour are well combined:
    100 lb flour
    25 lb margarine or soft shortening
(2) Continue to mix the flour and margarine until it attains the appearance of a coarse streusel with no raw flour spots in evidence, and then add:
    45 lb lard
(3) After mixing has reduced the lard to chunks about the size of eggs, add:
    4 lb spray dried skim milk powder
    3 lb salt
    2 lb corn sugar dissolved in
    28 lb ice cold water

(4) Continue mixing until all of the ingredients are thoroughly dispersed. Stop mixing when the pie dough is dry with no wet spots evident, and the shortening is in tiny lumps well distributed throughout the entire batch.

Mealy Crust

(1) Place in the mixer and blend thoroughly:

    100 lb pie flour

    45 lb lard

    20 lb margarine or soft shortening

(2) When the above is well mixed and no raw flour spots are visible, add:

    3 lb spray dried skim milk powder,

    4 lb corn sugar, and

    3 lb salt, dissolved in

    24 lb ice water

(3) Continue to mix until the water has been completely taken up.

Doughs are usually scaled at about 6.25 oz to 6.5 oz for the top crusts of 9-inch fruit pies containing 26 oz to 28 oz of filling. The top crusts would be scaled at 5.25 oz to 6.25 oz. Crusts for the bottoms of 9-inch custard pies can be scaled at about 7 oz.

Variations.—Prebaked pie shells for cream pies and the like are made by carefully fitting and shaping a standard pie dough (mealy formulas work best) into a pan, thoroughly docking the bottom with some utensil such as a fork that makes small holes all the way through, and baking at 450°F for about 10 min. Of course, there are production lines that do this continuously and automatically. Some automatic pie shell formers press the shell from a lump of dough, i.e., the dough is not sheeted out and circles cut from the sheet. Two serious problems encountered in making prebaked pie shells are shrinkage and the formation of "blisters" on the bottom. Both of these defects are very troublesome since they are likely to cause breakage of the crust when it is filled or cut. Docking helps to prevent blisters but it is not a sure cure; other methods are to bake the crusts between two pie pans (perforated pans should be used) or to add many small round pieces, such as beans, clean pebbles, or marbles, to the crust before it goes into the oven.

It is also possible to bake pie shells by draping the dough over an inverted pie tin and sending the assembly through the oven. Docking is essential in this case. Although blistering is not particularly inhibited by this strategy, a somewhat more uniform bake is obtained. The extent of the bake, or, in effect the coloration, is a matter of personal judgement and can vary from market to market. The coloration should certainly be as uniform as possible and entirely free from blotches or spots, although a pattern of spots from docking holes does not seem to be objectionable. Blotches, or fairly large irregular areas of different color will probably be the result of insufficient incorporation of trimmings.

The formulas for tart shells tend to be different from those recommended for large pies. Flakiness is less of a consideration and it is common to add more sweeteners to the dough. Often, other enriching ingredients such as butter or even eggs are included, and sometimes flavors such as vanilla. Table 11.3 gives representative formulas for tart shells. The Czarina crust is traditionally flavored with a slight amount of brandy, which may be added to the dough or sprinkled on the baked crust. Butter flavor has been recommended for some of these, especially the cream cheese, while lemon flavor (or grated rind plus a slight amount of juice) is preferred for some lighter fillings. For savory pies, such as meat pies, using a higher level of salt and deleting the sugar or dextrose are the changes commonly made.

Table 11.3. FORMULAS FOR TARTS[1]

Ingredient	Short	Rich short	Sweet crisp	Czar-ina	Cream cheese
Pastry flour	53.5	50.5	49.0	41.5	41.3
Shortening	7.1	18.5	--	--	31.0
Salt	0.9	0.3	--	0.3	0.5
Water, cold, variable	3.0	12.2	5.9	--	--
Liquid whole eggs	14.2	--	--	--	--
Fresh whole milk	--	--	--	10.0	--
Butter (or *Lard)	7.1	18.5*	31.8	36.6	--
Granulated sugar	14.2	--	5.1	4.3	3.1
Liquid egg yolks	--	--	8.2	7.3	--
Cream cheese	--	--	--	--	24.1

[1] Proportions are stated in percent, as is basis.

A generic preparation method for the formulas in Table 11.3 consists of cutting cool shortening into the flour with a pastry blender until the mixture assumes the appearance of coarse meal; the remainder of the shortening is added and blending continued until the fat pieces are the size of peas; water (or milk or eggs) is added gradually while mixing very slowly; the dough is removed from the mixer and pressed together until no cracks or open spaces are visible; pieces of desired size are cut from the mass and pressed or rolled to fit tart pans. Sugar and salt are blended with the liquid ingredient before it is added. Cream cheese is added after the shortening.

Pâte brisée and pâte sucrée.—These two crusts, mainstays of Italian and classic French cuisine, are very similar in composition to pie crusts. In fact, if you are able to make ordinary pie crusts you can make pâte brisée and pâte sucrée. The former is a simple non-sweet crust made of pastry flour, butter, and salt, often with spices such as parsley, thyme, and pepper added. There seems to be no reason why a pie crust formula made up using margarine or butter cannot be called pâte brisée. The spiced crusts are often used with a tomato filling to give tomato pie, in Italian "crostata di pomodori." Pâte sucrée can be made from 50% to 55% pastry flour, 10% to 14% powdered sugar, 25% unsalted butter, 10% to 12% liquid whole egg, and, if necessary to get a cohesive crust, a percent or so of ice water. Cut the chilled butter into the flour and sugar until a mixture resembling bread crumbs in size is obtained. Blend in the egg only until the dough sticks together; it may be necessary to add a very little ice water at this point. Press into a lump and then into a thick disc, then roll out very carefully, keeping the dough cool at all times. Bake in a special tin or large tart tin. Fill the baked crust with custard, fruit, etc.

Fillings and washes.—The amount of filling deposited in a standard pie is highly variable, depending on demands of the market, economic exigencies, and competitors' practices. The type of filling and the amount of crust also have an effect on the amount of filling needed to reach optimum eating quality. Highly flavored fillings, such as cherries, rhubarb, and mince can be used in smaller amounts than less flavorful fruits such as apple and blueberry. Density of the filling (weight per unit volume) should also be taken into account. The optimum amount of filling is also related to pan specifications, being affected (for example) by the depth of the pan, the width of the rim, and the slant of the sides, as well as by the diameter. For premium quality fruit pies, one set of recommendations is to place 1.5 lb to 2 lb of filling in a 7-inch pie, 2 lb to 2.5 lb in an 8-inch pie, and 2.5 lb to 3 lb in a 9-inch pie. Some general guidelines for standard pies are: 10 oz filling in 6- inch pies, 19 oz in 8-inch pies, and 30 oz for 9-inch pies. No doubt, many economy grade pies contain even less filling.

Baking conditions and time are very dependent on weight and thickness of the pie, temperature of the pie as it goes into the oven, type of filling and its temperature, amount of filling, amount of moisture in the crust, thickness of the crust, type of pan, oven characteristics, and many other variables that cannot be considered in detail here. The baker will frequently base his decision on doneness by the color of the crust, but a few general guidelines for baking times and temperatures and other conditions will be given here, with the caution that they cannot be used without conducting tests using the exact equipment and product in question. Pies should be baked on a solid metal surface, not on racks or screens. Typical pies should be baked in a standard oven at 375°F for 55 to 60 minutes, 400°F for about 50 minutes, at 425°F for 40 to 45 minutes, or for 28 to 32 minutes at 450°F. In a convection oven, about 35 minutes at 350°F might be satisfactory.

There is a considerable difference of opinion regarding the merits of "washes" for the top crusts of pies. The theory is that washes add visual attraction to the top crust, which otherwise has little esthetic appeal. Washes of egg or milk, or combinations of these, result in glossy and relatively dark crusts. Some bakers regard this appearance as highly desirable while others consider it to be somewhat artificial and of no marketing benefit. There seems to be no published consumer research study on this point.

Struckmann (1956) suggested the application of a spray of skim milk to the top crusts of pies just before they enter the oven. This gives a golden brown crust color and a drier and crisper texture. Some bakers spray the top crust with melted shortening, or even butter, in attempts to enhance both the appearance and texture.

Pressed Crumb Crusts

Cookie crusts have been mentioned previously in this article. Graham cracker crusts for cheesecakes and banana pies, chocolate cookie crusts for vanilla cream pies, etc., and vanilla wafer crusts for banana cream pies are the most frequent combinations. Gingersnap crusts have been suggested for pumpkin chiffon pies. These crusts are made by grinding graham crackers, chocolate wafers, vanilla wafers, etc., in a food processor or some other kind of mill, mixing in enough melted shortening to get good adherence of the particles, and pressing the mixture into a pie tin or tart cup. Some sugar is usually added to the mixture, and occasionally other ingredients are included to improve flavor, strength, color, or resistance to soaking.

Table 11.4. FORMULAS FOR PRESSED-CRUMB CRUSTS[1]

Ingredient	Type of crust				
	Cheese cake	Choco- late	Ginger snap	Van- illa	Coco- nut
Graham cracker crumbs	63.2	--	--	--	--
Nonfat dry milk	7.9	--	--	--	--
Sugar, fine	7.9	--	11.6	2.0	25.7
Margarine or butter	21.0	32.0	30.4	34.1	22.3
Choc. wafer crumbs	--	68.0	--	--	--
Gingersnap crumbs	--	--	58.0	--	--
Vanilla wafer crumbs	--	--	--	63.9	--
Sweet grated coconut	--	--	--	--	52.0

[1] Percent, as is basis

Chilling the crust until the shortening fully congeals is necessary before the product is packed and shipped, but the crust never develops any substantial amount of mechanical strength, and it must be kept in the tin in which it has been made until the pie is served. The particles should be granules of medium size, perhaps an eighth of an inch in their greatest dimension, at the time they are put into the mixer, where some attrition does occur. Powder does not perform well as an ingredient, and, for the best quality crusts, dust should be sieved out before the crumbs are mixed with shortening. Mass produced cookie pie shells and tart shells for retail and foodservice sale are produced automatically, but in essentially the same manner as described above, except that the plunger that forms the inside of the crust spins as well as presses the fat and crumb mixture. Tests have shown it is apparently impossible (or at least very difficult) to get a satisfactory shell by baking cookie dough in a pie tin. Several formulas and procedures for pressed-crumb crusts are given in Table 11.4.

Savory Pies

Up to this point, the discussion has been concerned solely with dessert pies—those made with sweet fillings. Individual savory, or meat-containing, pies have a very old tradition (e.g., the Cornish "pasty") and can be made as either fried or baked items. Regulatory problems are somewhat more complicated than for dessert pies because the USDA gets involved in plant inspections when meat-containing products are manufactured. Nonetheless, egg-filled ("omelet") and meat-filled turnovers are being made and distributed in respectable amounts. Quiches, similar in their basic structure to custard pies, are also popular. In general, crusts for these pies can be made by following the same principles as used for dessert-type fried pies even though the fillings are obviously different both in composition and consistency. Certain brands of frozen pizza "rolls" and Chinese-style egg rolls are made on lines differing only slightly from those used for fried fruit pies.

Meat pies are a prominent item of commerce in the United Kingdom, and an excellent review by Taylor (1963) covers this industry. Probably more steak and kidney pie is sold than any other variety, but there are may other types, some with a strictly local popularity. The critical features of meat pie preparation will be discussed in the following paragraphs.

Although a weak flour will give the best eating pastry, it also leads to a dough that may be too short and difficult to handle and the pies are often so fragile that they break on handling. The high gluten content of a strong flour can lead to shrinkage during baking and at other points in the process, and to extreme brittleness in the finished product. It is best to use a medium strong flour that will give the crust strength to withstand depanning and transportation while at the same time contributing shortness and crispness to the eating quality.

Lean doughs for these pies will contain about 31% fat (FWB) while better quality pastes will be made with about 50% fat. Both lard and shortening are being used. The fat should be selected so as to set up quickly and firmly and show no exudation of grease in the hot paste step, yet it must be soft enough to rub into the flour easily.

The quantity of water required will depend on the strength of the flour and the process used. The amount of fat will also be related to the water requirements since both of these ingredients cooperate in controlling gluten formation in the paste. Water percentage also influences paste handling and the shrinkage and eating quality of the baked pie.

Taylor described five methods of making short paste for meat pies: (1) The cold water method; (2) The boiling water method; (3) The half-boiled method; (4) The full boiled method; and (5) The hot fat method. In the cold water method, the fat is rubbed into the flour until it is finely distributed, water (containing the salt) is added to the fat-flour blend, and a smooth paste is formed. This dough is rested for 0.5 to 1 hour and then processed into crusts. Such crusts have good texture after reheating.

The boiling water method is mainly for pies that will be eaten cold since the pastry stays crisp longer than crusts made by the cold water process. The dough also holds its shape better. These crusts are often used for steak pies because gravy does not soak into the pastry as quickly. In this method, the water is brought to boiling, added hot to the fat-flour mixture, and the composition blended to give a smooth paste. The paste is rested until cold and set, then processed further. The water must be near the boiling point when added, because the purpose of this procedure is to gelatinize the starch.

In the half-boiled method, only half the fat is dispersed in the flour. The salt is dissolved in the ingredient water, and the remaining fat added to the solution, which is then heated to boiling added hot to the flour-fat blend, and the compound blended until it is smooth. This method gives a paste that sets up more firmly than paste made by the boiling water method, and results in a pie that will stay crisp for much longer after baking. Little or no resting period is needed.

In the full boiled method, the salt is dissolved in the water and the fat added to the solution. This combination is boiled and added to the flour in the mixer bowl, where it is mixed to a smooth paste. The dough is allowed to cool, and then made up into crusts.

The hot fat method involves placing half of the flour in the mixer bowl, heating the fat until it is completely melted, adding it to the flour, and mixing the combination for 5 to 10 min. The remaining flour is added and mixed, bringing the paste to a crumbly condition. The salt is dissolved in cold water and added to the flour-fat mixture and the whole blended to a smooth paste. This method has little advantage over the more conventional pie paste methods unless the baker is using a very soft fat that will not set up in hot paste methods.

Many of the pies made with the above-described crusts will be eaten cold, often in slices but sometimes as portion-sized pies. In parts of the U.K., pies intended to be eaten hot have a puff pastry as the top crust, giving a more attractive and crisper crust. Three recipes for meat pie paste, as produced in the U.K, are shown in Table 11.5

The dough, or paste, is taken to the divider for scaling of pieces suitable for an individual pie. The dough chunks are formed in the pie tins and allowed to stand until cold and set, then filled with the meat and gravy. In the meantime, some of the dough has been sheeted out for the top crusts, pierced with holes to serve as steam vents, then placed on the moistened edges of the bottom dough. Finally, the tops are pressed to seal the edges and trimmed.

Table 11.5. FORMULAS FOR MEAT PIE CRUSTS, UK STYLE[1]

| Ingredient | Type of crust | | |
	Low quality	Medium quality	High quality
Flour	14	14	14
Shortening	5	6.25	7
Salt	3.5	3.5	3.5
Water	5	3.75	3.4

[1] In parts by weight.

Although formulas and procedures for most pie fillings have been reserved for a later chapter, a typical English meat pie filling (steak and kidney) will be described here for the convenience of the reader.

Cook 6 lb stewing beef and 1 lb kidney in 7.5 lb water (with added seasonings) until tender. Strain off the stock to use in the gravy and cut the meat into small cubes. Mix 9 oz of flour into the cooled stock, add 2 oz meat extract (or hydrolyzed vegetable protein, etc.), 3 oz onion powder, and caramel color as required. Cool and add to the meat. It is customary to coat the crust with an egg wash or other glaze before it is baked.

A typical individual pie will include a 2.5 oz pastry base, a 1.25 oz lid, and 3.5 oz of filling. A family size pie will typically contain 7 oz base, 6.5 oz lid, and 12.5 oz filling.

Fried Pies

Fried pies constitute an interesting variant type that has achieved constantly increasing popularity during the last twenty years or so. They are by no means a new product, being based on such predecessor foods as empanadas, pasties, etc. The present-day fried pie is a single-serving pastry most often weighing about 4 oz to 6 oz. It is a typical convenience food, to be held in the hand while it is being eaten rather than put on a plate and eaten with a fork. The method of consumption as well as the method of distribution dictate many of its physical characteristics. For example, the crust must be sturdy enough to allow the pie to be transported and sold without breaking, even though individual pies are packaged only in flexible pouches (some fried pies sold through fast food outlets are packaged in semi-rigid fiberboard containers after they are cooked). The crust must be tender enough, however, to allow the consumer to bite through the pie without squeezing out all the filling. The filling should be short and somewhat firm, rather than slightly stringy and fluid as usually found in a large baked pie. These necessities force compromises with flavor and texture that often lead to items falling considerably short of being culinary masterpieces.

Although the all-important crust characteristic is structural strength, since the crusts of fried pies are not supported by pans during their transportation from the factory to the point of consumption, there are other problems that must also be considered. According to Burris (1979), several processing details are important: (1) The dough should not be overmixed since this would produce a dough that would shrink during frying, producing a ball-shaped object rather than a pie which lies flat, and the crust would be too tough; (2) The dough should be kept cool—65°F or less; (3) The dough should be kept on the stiff side to provide a better handling product and to retard gluten development; (4) Trimmings from the crust-forming operation should be mixed with the dry ingredients before water is added; and (5) The dough should have a rest period or floor time of about 15 minutes to permit more uniform distribution of the limited water content.

In most cases, the fat content of a fried pie dough will be much lower than that of a dough intended for a baked pie crust. Sugar content will normally be considerably higher than for a fried pie dough. Baking powder has been used in many fried dough formulas, although this ingredient would seem to decrease the mechanical strength of the cooked dough.

A basic formula for fried pie dough was said by Keathley (1956) to be: 100 lb pastry flour, 35 lb vegetable shortening, 35 lb water, 3 lb salt, and 4 lb corn sugar. Lard is not recommended for use in the dough or as the frying fat. Mixing procedures and equipment are similar to those used for baked pies except that fried pie doughs may be mixed a little longer and to a smoother consistency than those used for baked pies. Flakiness is not generally aimed for in these crusts, but to get a flakier crust some producers use a short mixing cycle that leaves minute lumps of shortening throughout the dough.

Dietrich (1962) gave these production details for fried pie crusts:
(1) Blend together thoroughly,
  100 lb pie flour
  25 lb hydrogenated shortening
  100 lb dough scraps from previous production
(2) Blend together the following, then add the liquid to the above,
  30 lb water (variable)
  2 lb salt
(3) Add and mix until a smooth dough results,
  1 lb corn sugar (optional)
  3 lb wheat or corn protein
  3 oz mold inhibitor

The dough can be made up immediately if desired, but holding does not cause it to deteriorate. After mechanical or hand scaling into pieces of desired size, the dough is sheeted through rollers or by other means. About 1.5 oz of dough to 2 oz of filling is the recommended proportion for fried pies. The filled pies are fried submerged at a temperature of about 380°F for three minutes and then thoroughly cooled by forced air before wrapping.

A bubbly or blistered crust can be formed by adding a wash after an initial frying step, then frying the product again. This type of processing, which is applied to fried pies distributed in large amounts by drive-in restaurant chains, is thought to improve both the appearance and the texture of the finished crusts. Large blisters are regarded as quality defects, however.

If ice is to be used in the dough to keep its temperature low, pockets of high moisture can be formed where chips of ice remain at the end of the mixing period. The dough is poorly consolidated at this point. As a result, steam can form during frying and separate the dough into layers, forming a large bubble. Even in the absence of pockets of moisture, steam can be trapped between layers of dough if the gluten is mistakenly overdeveloped during mixing or processing.

Two more pie dough formulas, which may be useful for comparison, are given in Table 11.6. The flour specified by Taylor is Michigan white winter wheat straight flour.

Table 11.6. FORMULAS FOR CRUSTS FOR FRIED PIES[1]

	Formulas	
Ingredient	No. 1	No. 2
Flour	100.00	100.00
Shortening	29.25	25.00
Salt	2.75	3.00
Corn sugar	4.00	3.75
Soy flour	2.50	2.75
Sodium bicarbonate	0.31	0.31
Preservative	0.19	0.19
Water	24.25	28.25

[1] Taylor (1971)

Each of these formulas defines a dough for a separate type of equipment. Formula No. 1 is primarily designed for the molded pie machine, which demands more elasticity from the dough. The moisture level is fairly low to provide the tenderness that is possible with this process. The second formula is designed for the guillotine cut, two layer crimping, and cutting equipment. This machine demands a tougher dough to resist tearing. The flour is described as having the following characteristics: protein content 8.65%, moisture content 13.2%, ash content 0.43%, MacMichael viscosity 31°, pH 5.26, and bleached. Baking soda is said to be included in this formula to improve the "flakiness" of the crust, but it is doubtful it has this effect. It is also claimed to promote moisture release during frying, which it might do.

In processing the above formulas, the shortening, salt, corn sugar, soy flour, soda, and preservative are creamed for six minutes at low speed in a horizontal dual-armed dough mixer, a twin-arm shearing action machine, or a vertical mixer provided with a dough hook. The flour is added to the creamed mixture and mixing continued for 1 to 2 min. Then, all the water is

added at one time and blending continued at low speed for six minutes.
Fried pie dough has been successfully mixed in vertical mixers using dough hooks, or in double-arm kneading mixers. At least one manufacturer uses horizontal dough mixers with spiral agitators (Zones and Robe 1976). The dough must sheet well in a continuous ribbon while requiring a minimum of dusting flour. The sheeted dough should be free of pinholes. Reducing agents have been used by some producers to achieve the desired physical state. Doughs are transferred manually or automatically to sheeter rollers that compress the dough to the required thickness. The dough strips feed over a series of clam shell pie formers, extending slightly beyond the edges on both sides of the "shell." Filling is metered and deposited on one side, then the molds close, folding the dough around the filling. Fluted edges on the clam shells crimp the dough, seal the filling within the pie, and sever the dough strip. The individual pies are then transferred by conveyor to a fryer that has a device for holding the pie beneath the surface of hot fat until cooking is complete. If they are to be glazed, the topping can be applied while the pies are still hot (Havighorst 1976).

The preceding method is the usual one for crescent-shaped pies. For rectangular pies, a somewhat different method may be used. A wide strip of dough is placed so as to cover the bottom of a large mold with, e.g., 50 cavities. Plungers press the dough into these cavities, then fillings are deposited. A second sheet of dough is used to form the top crusts. The crusts are sometimes docked to allow steam to escape during frying (Pacyniak 1986).

A brief description of the method used for producing McDonald's fried pies, probably the volume leader in this field, has been published by Sjerven (1991). Equipment in a line having a capacity of 5,000 pies per hour includes a Kemper spiral mixer, a Chester-Jensen cooking/cooling unit for fruit filling, a Murzan pump, a Rykaart pie make-up line, a Koppens batter mixing and enrobing unit, Bundy Industries' pans and racks, a Rondo reversible sheeter, and Bader candling units for fruit inspection. To prepare the filling, apples are inspected, peeled, cored, sliced, and frozen until required. Sliced apples are mixed with other ingredients then steam cooked. After cooling, the filling is pumped to the pie line. The dough is mixed and divided into 15-lb blocks that are sheeted to the final thickness and rolled on to pastry reels for later transfer to the make-up line. From the reels, the dough enters the molding device where the filling is applied, a second sheet of dough is dropped on top of the filling, the continuous combined web of filling and dough sheets is crimped into individual pie sizes, and then cut into separate units by a guillotine blade. The pies are placed on pans, which are conveyed to the freezer. The frozen pies are transferred to restaurants, where they are fried shortly before serving.

A fried pie to be sold as a 4-oz item would normally weigh nearly five ounces in the raw state, with the dough making up 3 oz to 3.5 oz of this. During frying, the crust picks up one-third to one-half ounce of frying fat.

There are numerous variations in formulas and processing methods for fried pies that have been introduced by manufacturers to expedite processing or to get special characteristics they believe to be important. In one operation, fried pies are dipped into a kettle of constantly boiling water immediately after frying. This sets the crust and floats off excess cooking fat. Such pies are said to keep well during summer months and have a slightly glossy surface. In another variant process, the crusts were made up with high protein spring wheat flour. Then, before frying, the pies on the screen were dipped quickly into boiling water and immediately submerged in the frying kettle. Pies prepared by this method had crusts that were less greasy than those prepared without the preliminary water bath. In other variations, pies were steamed without subsequent drying or steamed followed by drying in attempts to use fat absorption, but with results in the opposite direction to that desired (Finley and Simpson 1976). Addition of soy flour apparently reduces fat absorption during frying, a result similar to that found by other experimenters working with doughnuts.

Brody (1969) reported than the internal temperature of a fried pie filling rose at approximately the same rate whether the temperature of the frying fat was 360° or 400°F, but the crust darkened faster at higher temperatures. The trick is to get proper crust color and complete setting of the crust before the filling starts to boil out and burst the crust. Typically, these products are fried at 380° to 390°F for about four minutes. It is obvious that the weight and conformation of the piece, and the proportion of filling to crust, will influence the time required for proper frying.

Fried pies can be filled with fruit pieces surrounded by starch thickened juice, or with puddings or imitation custards (e.g., lemon or chocolate flavored). Probably about half of all these pies are of the apple variety. The fruit component of the filling can be a puree or pieces made by chopping or dicing fruits, the latter being preferred by the consumer. The pies are usually glazed on one surface, or they may be partially covered with icing. Some premium items have been enrobed with chocolate-flavored coatings. The expected shelf-life is apparently about a week or ten days at room temperature. No doubt many are sold that are two weeks old or more. The pies can be frozen, although they lose the convenience feature when this method of distribution is chosen. There seems to be only a limited food service demand for frozen individual fried pies although a large volume is sold fresh in fast food restaurants. Some of the present fillings would doubtless break down when frozen, though this problem could be solved by reformulation along known lines.

It is unfortunate that more innovative thought has not gone into designing portion-sized fried savory pies. Frozen, unbaked versions would seem to have good potential in fast food outlets and perhaps for institutions. Cracker-like crusts with chili- or stew-type fillings, toast-flavored crusts containing welsh rarebit compositions, even pasta-based fillings, are some of the directions an imaginative product development technologist might take.

Causes of Faults in Pie Crusts

For trouble shooting crust problems in baked pies, the following suggestions have been made by authorities in this field:

(1) Excessive shrinkage of the crust. May be caused by (a) not enough shortening, (b) too much water, (c) dough that has been worked too much, or (d) flour that is too strong.

(2) Crust not flaky. May be caused by (a) dough that has been mixed at too high a temperature, (b) shortening that is too soft, or (c) overmixing.

(3) Bottom crust absorbs too much liquid from the filling. May be caused by (a) insufficient baking, (b) crust formula that is too rich, or (c) an oven that is not hot enough.

(4) Tough crusts. May be caused by (a) flour that is too strong, (b) overmixing the doughs, or (c) using too much water.

(5) Soggy crusts. May be caused by (a) not enough bottom heat in the oven, (b) an oven that is too hot, or (c) using a filling that is too hot.

To eliminate crust shrinkage, (1) use high-quality, medium-protein, high-ash pie flour, (2) increase shortening content to the highest percentage consistent with material cost targets and handling requirements, (3) adjust formula to assure the lowest practicable moisture in the dough, and (4) rest the dough for at least 4 hr under refrigeration before sheeting and cutting.

To eliminate raw spots in crusts, (1) check to make sure the oven baking surface is level and evenly heated, (2) make sure the oven is free from flash heat, (3) adjust mixing procedure to insure uniformity of the dough mass, and (4) use clean trim dough in the remix for tops.

To eliminate soggy bottom crusts, (1) check formula balance, (2) control oven temperature carefully, (3) keep fillings at 70°F, (4) do not use only remixed trim doughs for bottoms, and (5) consider substituting for your present thickener a gelling agent that has a higher viscosity when it is in hot solutions.

STRUDEL, PHYLLO, AND EGG ROLLS

Strudels are made by wrapping fillings in many layers of very thin dough. The dough usually is made up of flour, egg, water, salt, and oil. There is no leavening and the method of preparation discourages incorporation of bubbles. Home methods of preparation, which involve hand stretching of the dough while brushing it with oil, are time consuming and tedious. Commercial methods have been developed to prepare strudel dough leaves that are distributed in frozen form. Details of the commercial method have apparently not been published.

Fillo (phyllo) dough is the basis for several kinds of Greek pastry, including baklava, and some savory dishes. It is made in somewhat the same way as strudel dough, i.e., by stretching an extremely flexible dough until it becomes very thin and then stacking layers of the film. The film is usually brushed with oil before rolling or stacking to form a many-layered structure that is then baked. The fillings for strudels and fillos desserts (nut pieces, fruit chunks or pastes, spice powders, etc.) may be sprinkled between layers or inclosed in a wrapping of several layers. At least one firm is distributing fillo dough in frozen form for home baking purpose and apparently for foodservice use as well.

Although neither strudel dough or fillo ever contains leavening agents, the many-layered structures making up the finished dessert product tend to expand as a result of the wrinkling and distortion of individual strata that occur during baking. This leaves voids between layers, even though the individual strata do not expand at all and, in fact, contract.

Egg rolls are the dough wrapped, fried, cylindrical items offered by virtually every Chinese restaurant as appetizers or main courses. The fillings can be combinations of everything that didn't sell as well as expected the day before, or traditional mixtures of shrimp, bean sprouts, etc. The dough is usually a thinly sheeted mixture of flour, water, salt, and perhaps egg white or whole egg. The dough is often bought ready-sheeted from a specialty distributor rather than made in the restaurant. According to Hee (1990), the dough mass is extruded into ribbon-like form, aged, then passed through calendering rolls to produce a continuous sheet of pastry material, commonly of 24-inch width. Because of the manner of forming, the grain of the sheet (its axis of maximum strength) extends longitudinally of the sheet. This strip is then cut into squares (7 inches each way), stacked with a powdering of cornstarch between, and allowed to age. Hee's patent describes an elliptically shaped dough sheet that obviates some of the problems encountered in folding the square sheet around a cylindrical filling.

UNLEAVENED COOKIES

Most cookies are leavened with sodium bicarbonate plus an acid-reacting substance, with ammonium bicarbonate, or with a combination of these two gas generating systems. A very few examples are yeast-leavened, others undergo a significant volume increase as a result of expansion of entrapped water vapor during baking, and some are unleavened in the sense that the dough blank does not undergo permanent expansion during baking or at any other time during its preparation, although there may be a small amount of temporary expansion in the oven due to water vapor pressure. It is this last group which will be discussed here.

The fact that a cookie is unleavened doesn't mean it must be a solid mass of flour, fat, and sugar. Many cookies of this type have a coarse chewy texture due to the inclusion of substantial amounts of oat flakes, puffed rice, corn flakes, or other large pieces which are stuck together with sugar syrup or some other adhesive, leaving empty spaces that contain but do not entrap gases. Some cookies of the shortbread type are unleavened and have such ineffective gas entraining structures that they expand very little, if at all, during baking. They are solid appearing, and dense, but do not have a tough structure because of the large amount of shortening and sugar and the small amount of flour they contain. Their similarity to pie crust will, no doubt, occur to the reader. Of course, there are cookies called "shortbread" that contain both leavening materials and a slight amount of gluten structure, and these do expand somewhat during baking and show a primitive type of cellular mechanism in the finished product. It is instructive to compare an old formula for shortbread cookies, more or less of the original type, and a modern rotary molded cookie.

There is a semi-traditional ratio of four parts (by weight) of flour, two parts butter, and one part sugar used in making the paste or dough that is rolled out or pressed out and then baked to make shortbread. Some sources claim the oldest formulas called for 5-lb flour, 2-lb butter, 2-lb sugar, and one dozen eggs. For shortbread/shortcake cookies by the first mentioned formula, cream four pounds of butter or margarine with eight pounds low protein content unbleached cake flour. Add 2-lb powdered sugar and mix to make a soft paste. Roll out on a lightly floured surface to about one-third inch in thickness. Cut into desired shapes—flute edges as for pie crust to reduce cracking. Bake on an ungreased sheet at about 325°F for 20 minutes or until the cookies are very lightly browned. Cool. The product tends to be fragile because of the insignificant development of gluten during mixing.

There are probably hundreds, maybe even thousands, of different variations on this theme. They include formula, process, and shape differences. Sometimes the paste is baked in fairly large thick disks that have been scored in pie wedge shapes. Addition of about 0.5% salt improves the flavor. Flavoring with spices can give innumerable varieties, but is, in fact, seldom done. Adding one-half part liquid whole eggs, lightly whipped, to the traditional recipe will give some expansion during baking, if that is desired. This variation is sometimes called "sweet paste." A few examples of shortbread formulas will be found in Table 11.7. For commercial processing, most of these cookies could be run on rotary molding machines.

Table 11.7. UNLEAVENED COOKIES--SHORTBREAD TYPE[1]

Ingredient	Regular	Coconut	Butter milk	Chocolate	Oat
Flour, pastry/cake	56.4	41.4	54.2	47.0	46.0
Shortening	23.5	15.7	23.5	28.7	26.0
Sugar, powdered	16.8	20.0	7.0	12.3	8.0
Water, variable	6.8	4.8	10.0	10.0	9.0
Salt	--	0.3	0.3	--	0.5
Whole milk powder	0.8	0.9	--	--	--
Liquid whole eggs	5.0	--	--	--	--
Molasses, medium	--	5.6	--	--	2.5
Macaroon coconut	--	11.3	--	--	--
Buttermilk powder	--	--	5.0	--	--
Dark dutched cocoa	--	--	--	2.0	--
Instant oats	--	--	--	--	8.0

[1] Percent, as is basis

Shortbread cookies retain the die design very well when made as rotary molded cookies, but the dough tends to crack as it moves across transfer points, especially if the dough blank is thick. Some water is often added to the mixture for this reason and also because the use of hydrogenated vegetable shortening eliminates the water that would otherwise come into the dough as part of the butter or margarine.

A simple formula for shortbread cookies is: Mix together until thoroughly blended 400 lb weak pastry flour, 120 lb powdered sugar, 150 lb shortening, 5 lb flour salt, and 25 lb to 35 lb water. If the mixture is allowed to set for up to 30 minutes, it will machine better. The dough is molded into pieces of the desired shape and weight in the usual manner and baked in a hot oven until the high points and edges of the pieces just begin to show color. For larger pieces, cooler baking temperatures will be required. Not much moisture bakeout is expected on this item, since the original water content is around 80 lb to 85 lb, and the finished moisture (when cooled) should be around 28 lb. If desired, a minimum amount of leavening can be obtained by adding about 4 lb of a mixture containing 50% sodium bicarbonate, 25% acid cream, and 25% ammonium bicarbonate.

The following formula will give a shortcake cookie with a mild chocolate flavor, but for a rich chocolate appearance, additional coloring materials will be needed. Quantities are pounds or parts: Flour, very soft, 500; shortening 125; powdered sugar 100; high fructose corn syrup 50; fine salt 5; lecithin 2.5; dutched cocoa 35; vanillin 2.5; and water 90. Mixing is a one stage process, and the other steps are essentially as described in the preceding paragraph.

Macaroons of the original type are also unleavened cookies (or confections), although the name has been applied over the years to almost every kind of coconut cookie, including some rather highly leavened types containing substantial amounts of flour. The original macaroon seems to have been an almond confection. Formulas and procedures for some other kinds of unleavened cookies are shown in Table 11.8.

Outline procedures for the cookies in Table 11.8 are as follows (numbers in parentheses refer to formula numbers in table, not to steps):

(1) Mix egg whites and sugar together at medium or fast speed. Add almond paste and rice flour and mix until stiff. Use deposit machine or hand bag on to paper or floured surface. Bake at about 450°F.

(2) Mix flour, sugar, butter, dried milk, salt, spice, and pecans until they are uniformly distributed. Then add water, eggs, and molasses and mix at slow speed for about three minutes. Run on a wire-cut machine. Bake about seven minutes at 450°F.

(3) Cream butter and sugar. Beat eggs slightly. Mix all ingredients only until blended. Chill in the refrigerator. Sheet out very thin. Cut into shapes. Bake at 350°F for 12 to 15 minutes.

(4) Mix flour, sugar, and ground pecans. Blend in soft butter at low speed until the mixture is uniform. Roll out to 1/8 inch thickness on a floured surface. Bake on an ungreased pan or belt at 375°F for 8 to 10 minutes.

Table 11.8. FORMULAS FOR VARIOUS UNLEAVENED COOKIES[1]

Ingredient	(1) Almond macaroon	(2) Molasses crisp	(3) Sand tart	(4) Pecan crisp
Butter	--	21.8	32.4	30.5
Almond paste	25.4	--	8.2	--
Light molasses (*HFCS)	--	13.4	--	--
Sugar, gran. (*powdered)	51.9*	11.8	18.9	19.8
Liquid egg whites (*whole)	16.9	1.8*	5.9*	--
Cake flour (*rice flour)	5.8*	36.4	34.6	32.8
Corn syrup, regular	--	3.5	--	--
Water	--	3.6	--	--
Dried skim milk	--	1.8	--	--
Salt	--	0.4	--	--
Pecans, finely chopped	--	5.5	--	16.9

[1] Percent, as is basis. Formulas do not include flavors such as vanilla extract, which should be added "to taste."

TORTILLAS

There are two major kinds of tortillas, the older type developed by American Indians and made from masa, and the wheat flour tortilla, which is a more recent development. The corn tortilla is almost always unleavened, while some flour tortillas include a small amount of baking powder. The market for tortillas in the U.S. increased dramatically within the last 10 or 15 years until reaching a present value of about a billion dollars (Davis 1991). Consumption in the U.S. is still small compared to the intake in Mexico where the per capita consumption of this item of diet amounts to about 260 lb per year. Of course, the price of this food is extraordinarily low in Mexico because of government subsidies, and many people there eat a lot of tortillas because they are about the only kind of food they can afford.

There are many Central and South American countries where the tortilla is not a prominent item of diet. In some South American countries, the regular tortilla is replaced by a toasted unleavened flatcake produced from degerminated maize dough and called "arepas," and there are additional variations to be found in other localities.

Tortillas are used not only as a staple food (as rice, bread, pasta, and potatoes are used in other areas of the world) but also as a base for tacos, enchiladas, burritos, envueltos, flautas, and other items of Mexican cuisine. In these applications, tortillas may be baked, fried, used as a soup ingredient, etc. In a commercially significant development, they also form the basis of some of the fried snack chips sold in very large amounts in the U.S.

The masa tortilla is always made from alkali-treated corn dough. The method for tortilla preparation varies between geographical areas and ethnic groups. The description that follows is a generalization of most of the home processes. Preparation starts with the addition of one part of whole dry corn kernels to two parts of a solution containing about 1% (corn weight basis) hydrated lime. This mixture is heated to about 200°F for 50 to 90 minutes and then allowed to stand for about 12 to 14 hours. The liquid is decanted, and the remainder, consisting of gelatinized corn kernels called nixtamal, is washed two or three times with water. The germs are usually not removed by the washing procedure, and parts of the skins also remain. The nixtamal is ground to a smooth dough, called masa. About 35 g to 50 g of masa are hand patted into a disc about 15 cm to 20 cm in diameter and 2 mm to 3 mm thick. This cake is cooked or toasted on a heated flat surface for 1 to 2 min. When it swells, the cake is turned over and cooked on the other side for about 30 seconds (this description is essentially that of Parades-Lopez and Saharopulos-Parades 1983).

The texture of masa is affected by the the type of corn kernel and its history of drying, storing, and cleaning. Extrusion cooking can be used (Bedolla and Rooney 1982).

Havighorst (1971) and Clark (1981) described mechanized plants used to prepare this type of tortilla. The cooking cycle begins by charging a kettle with 2,000 lb white corn and a measured amount of water. The kettle contains an upper perforated ring from which water is sprayed over the corn. A steam injection ring in the bottom part of the kettle maintains the contents within the desired temperature range and agitates the corn.

The corn is first hydrated with water maintained at about 120°F. Then the temperature is raised to 165°F to gelatinize the corn, after which the heat is shut off. During the cooking cycle, hot water is sprayed over the corn and continuously recirculated by a pump connected to the discharge valve. When the temperature drops below 140°F, recirculation is discontinued and the corn allowed to steep undisturbed for about 12 hours. The steep water contains 12 oz hydrated lime for each 100 lb corn.

After the steeping period is completed, fresh water is used to flush the corn to a draining conveyor. From the discharge, the kernels fall into a screw-type elevating conveyor in which the corn is again washed to remove free starch before it is milled.

The mill consists of a stationary lower stone disc and a rotating upper stone, both of 16-inch diameter and 4-inch thickness. This burr mill of generally conventional design is powered by a 30 hp motor and grinds about 3,000 pounds of corn per hour.

The ground alkalized corn dough, or masa, is conveyed to the hopper of a tortilla cutting head by a screw-type extruder. A thick sheet of masa is extruded between sizing rolls, and the resulting ribbon is cut into discs of appropriate size.

Gas-fired ovens held at 600°F bake the tortilla discs in 30 to 32 seconds. Tortillas discharged at 175°F are cooled to 85° to 90°F in a multi-tiered conveyor through which ambient temperature is circulated.

Fried corn chips were originally made from regular tortillas. Indeed, many restaurants still make them from stale table-style tortillas. Such corn chips tend to be oily, blistered, and hard in texture. They are often used as the base for nachos, with some kind of topping. Modern commercial plants specializing in snack chips have improved the product by using coarse masa prepared by decreasing cooking and steeping times and temperatures and by using a wider separation of the grinding stones (Gomez *et al.* 1987).

Taco shells are rigid, trough-shaped items made from masa disks (i.e., tortillas). They are normally deep-fat fried before they are filled with cooked ground meat, shredded lettuce, refried beans, etc. It is customary to either set the shape before frying or to fry the soft uncooked tortilla in some sort of a mold. The tortilla may be pre-baked and folded while hot or baked while draped over mold, then allowed to cool and become more or less firm before being fried (Ghiasi and Skarra 1990). Devices that form and cook taco shells were invented by Schy (1976) and Caridis *et al.* (1985). The former continuously forms tortillas into the familiar trough-shape of tacos and cooks them in a hot oil tank. The latter forms tortillas into cooked taco shells using a conveyor with many forming elements that shift from a nested to an open condition as the conveyor passes between the feed and discharge points. The formed taco is cooked to a rigid (or semi-rigid) condition as it passes through the cooking oil under the restraint of the nested molds.

Flour tortillas are, quite simply, the wheat flour analog of masa tortillas. The composition appears to be, in most cases, low-grade wheat flour, salt, perhaps a small amount of shortening, and enough water to prepare. Of course, the wheat flour is not alkalized like masa. Some of these products contain a small quantity of baking powder. A very soft dough is made and formed into flat sheets which are toasted on a baking surface until part of the starch has been gelatinized and the moisture has been reduced to acceptable levels. Completion of cooking is usually judged by observing the changes in texture of the dough piece. Flour tortillas are very bland in flavor, even blander than corn tortillas. Gringos generally prefer flour tortillas and there even seems to be a trend to greater use of them by persons having a Mexican background.

Schmidt (1985) gave a detailed description of the manufacture of a "hand-stretched flour tortilla" that is important as being representative of a modernized process actually being used to manufacture thousands of pounds of this product every day. The formula is: wheat flour (high gluten, bleached) 100 lb; water (tempered) 46 lb; shortening (lard or vegetable oil) 8 lb; salt 1.5 lb; baking powder 6 oz; dough conditioner 8 oz; mold inhibitor 12 oz; oil for dough balls 2 lb; and dusting flour 6 lb. It will be noted that about 0.2% baking powder has been specified so as to give a slight lift as the product is baked and to form the blisters that are thought to be desirable, but it is believed it is possible to make a satisfactory product without leavener. High gluten flour is required for this product. The water should be at about 100°F for best results. Lard is generally used as the shortening because most customers prefer the flavor it adds.

A two-speed dough mixer is recommended by Schmidt, and it can be either the conventional horizontal mixer or the vertical type. The dough is very stiff, so the batch size should be reduced below that considered accep-table for bread doughs. The dough is divided into 25 gram sizes for tortillas of 6-inch diameter, 60 grams for the 10- and 12-inch diameter tortillas, etc. Almost any kind of dough divider can be used. Rounding follows dividing almost immediately. A rest period is then given so the dough can recover from the punishment it undergoes in the preceding stages. The dough ball is pressed into a circle 0.006 to 0.01 inch in thickness by passing it through two or more sets of sheeting rolls. In this particular process, the sheeted circle is irregular and must be finished by handstretching the tortilla as it rests on (or travels across) a heated platen. Shaped tortillas then spend 20 seconds on mesh bands or baking plates passsing through an oven heated to 500°F. There is little radiation or convection heating, most of the energy transfer occurring by conduction. The tortillas will be near 212°F when they emerge from the oven and will show some puffing. They must be cooled to prevent them from adhering to one another when they are stacked and to prevent condensation of moisture inside the container.

Details of another modern tortilla plant can be found in a recent article by Gorton (1980). It was also reported by Gorton (1984) that the addition of 0.1% or less of vegetable gums to tortilla doughs decreases the incidence of cracking that often occurs when the product is folded, especially if the tortilla is rather dry or stale.

Tortillas have about the same shelf life as bread. Except for tortillas that are to be converted into frozen burritos, etc., the usual package is ten or a dozen tortillas in a tied plastic bag or sealed pouch.

MATZOS

Although matzos or matzoth, the Jewish specialty which is tradi-tionally consumed during Passover, is an unleavened bread in the sense that no fermentation is permitted, it does undergo a moderate amount of volume increase during cooking, as a result of the expansion of entrapped air bubbles and evolution of water vapor within the dough piece. If it were not for this leavening effect, the product would be much less palatable.

The formula for matzos is essentially flour, salt, and water, although some varieties flavored with onion and garlic have been offered commer-cially. The product is baked in very thin sheets at moderately high tempera-tures until a moisture level of 2% to 5% is reached. Docking is essential to prevent permanent separation of the top and bottom surfaces during baking. It is desirable to have a substantial contribution of radiant (top) heat in the oven to brown the tops of the wafers so as to produce some flavor in this otherwise quite insipid product. Shelf-life is good (about the same as soda crackers) if the matzos are protected from moisture absorption.

BIBLIOGRAPHY

BEDOLLA, S., and ROONEY, L. W. 1982. Cooking maize for masa production. Cereal Foods World 27, 219-221

BRODY, H. 1969. Fried pie production tips. Food Engineering 41, No. 5, 111, 113-114, 117

BURRIS, J. B. 1979. Fried pies. Proc. Am. Soc. Bakery Engineers 1979, 111-118

CARIDIS, A. A., BENSON, C. K., and KLEIN, L. F. 1985. Taco shell forming and cooking method. U.S. Pat. 4,510,165

CARMAN, W. E. 1960. Streamlined production of pies. Proc. Am. Soc. Bakery Engineers 1960, 305-309

CLARK, D. B. 1981. Corn tortilla and tortilla chip processing. Cereal Foods World 26, 499

DAVIS, K. 1991. Tortillas have become a billion-buck biz. The Monitor (McAllen TX), Jan. 6, p. 21A

DIETRICH, F. B. 1962. Basic pie crust production. Proc. Am. Soc. Bakery Engineers 1962, 287-291

ELLING, J. W. 1952. Types of crust. Proc. Am. Soc. Bakery Engineers 1952, 275-280

FINLEY, J. W., and SIMPSON, I. H. 1976. Fried pie crust with less fat, more protein. Food Product Dev. 10, No. 4, 92, 94

GHIASI, K., and SKARRA, L. L. 1990. Taco shell and method of manufacture. U.S. Pat. 4,950,490

GOMEZ, M. H. ROONEY, L. W., WANISKA, R. D., and PFLUGFELDER, R. L. 1987. Dry corn masa flours for tortilla and snack food products. Cereal Foods World 32, 372-373, 375-376

GORTON, L. 1984. Tortilla improvements. Bakers Digest 58, No. 6, 26

GORTON, L. 1990. Fresher tortillas faster. Baking & Snack Systems 12, No. 8, 6-7. 9-11, 13

HAVIGHORST, C. H. 1971. Mechanizes age-old process. Food Engineering 43, No. 6, 60-61

HAVIGHORST, C. H. 1976. Perky produces pies by the millions. Food Engineering 48, No. 6, 62-63

HEE, D. L. 1990. Egg roll leaf. U.S. Pat. 4,938,981

KEATHLEY, M. F. 1956. New ideas in mechanized quality pie production. Proc. Am. Soc. Bakery Engineers 1956, 293-300

KNUEPFER, W. H. 1960. Pie crust and fillings. Proc. Am. Soc. Bakery Engineers 1960, 292-302

LANNUIER, G. L. 1970. The future of quality control in pie production. Proc. Am. Soc. Bakery Engineers 1970, 123-128

LOVING, H. J., and BRENNEIS, L. J. 1981. Soft wheat uses in the U.S. In Soft Wheat Production, Breeding, Milling, and Uses. W. Yamazaki and C. Greenwood, Editors. Am. Assoc. Cereal Chemists, St. Paul, MN

MILLER, B. S., and TRIMBO, H. B. 1970. Factors affecting the quality of pie dough and pie crust. Bakers Digest 44, No. 1, 46-49, 52-55

PARADES-LOPEZ, O., and SAHAROPULOS-PARADES, M. E. 1983. Maize—a review of tortilla production technology. Bakers Digest, Sept. 13, 1983, 16-18, 20, 22, 25

PACYNIAK, B. 1986. Pudding pies may firm up soft snack cake/pie market. Prepared Foods 155, No. 9, 200-202

SCHMIDT, C. O. 1985. Tortilla production. Proc. Am. Soc. Bakery Engineers 1985, 112-4-124

SCHULTZ, G. A. 1986. Method for toasting a bakery product. U.S. Pat. 4,569,851

SCHY, F. R. 1976. Taco shell cooking apparatus. U.S. Pat. 4,3,946,655

SJERVEN, J. S. 1991. Supplying Moscow McDonald's. Baking & Snack Systems 13, No. 1, 6-8, 10-12

SKLOSS, L. C. 1985. Tortilla making apparatus. U.S. Pat, 4,504,209

SPANNUTH, H. T. 1962. Techniques for freezing pies. Proc. Am. Soc. Bakery Engineers 1962, 279-286

STRUCKMANN, E. 1956. The importance of good tasty pie crust. Proc. Am. Soc. Bakery Engineers *1956*, 300-304

TAYLOR, J. C. 1971. Fried fruit pies, production methods. Proc. Am. Soc. Bakery Engineers *1971*, 182-190

TAYLOR, W. F. 1963. Meat pie production. Food Trade Review *33*, No. 12, 65-76

ZONES, J., and ROBE, K. 1976. One million pies a week. Food Processing *37*, No. 6, 60-61

chapter twelve

PRODUCTS LEAVENED PRIMARILY WITH WATER VAPOR

INTRODUCTION

The expansion of water vapor at elevated temperatures (not necessarily at the boiling point) plays an important role in the leavening of many baked products, including all those containing yeast or baking powder, but there are some doughs that depend almost entirely upon the increase of water vapor pressure during their passage through the oven to develop the volume expansion that is such an important factor in establishing their characteristic appearance and texture. The products that benefit most from water vapor-leavening are those that can be baked at high oven temperatures so the interiors of the products get hot enough for the leavening effect to take place before the structure of the piece becomes rigid. To be included in this chapter, a product has to contain little or no chemical leaveners or yeast and not be whipped into a foam during some stage of its preparation.

It may seem to the critical reader that products described here are not clearly differentiated in leavening effects from the air-leavened baked goods described in the following chapter. It is certainly true that a small to moderate amount of entrapped and dissolved atmospheric gases does exist in the doughs of vapor-leavened products, and these gases do expand during baking to add to the volume of the finished piece; conversely, a certain amount of water vapor expansion can be expected in air-leavened products. As the discussion continues, the justification for separating the products into these two groups should become clearer, however.

A chart of the increase of vapor pressure as water is brought from 32° to 212°F shows an acceleration in the rate of expansion beginning at about 140°F. This allows for a considerable effect of water vapor on volume increases in dough and batter products before the gluten and starch components are substantially altered by heat.

It should be pointed out that ethanol, when present, can contribute to the vapor pressure of the gas phase inside the vesicles of the dough or batter. Ethanol and its azeotrope with water boil at substantially lower temperatures than does pure water. The participation of ethanol in oven spring has been discussed in a few published studies. But ethanol can only be an important factor in oven spring if yeast-leavened products are under consideration, or in those rare cases when a substantial amount of ethanol is added to a batch as part of a flavoring material (e.g., when alcoholic beverages such as rum are added to batters). Therefore, it does not contribute significantly to expansion of the products described in this chapter.

Some of the products to be discussed are sugar wafers, crispbreads, puff pastry, and popovers.

PUFF PASTRY

The principle underlying the preparation of puff pastry is the interleaving of thin layers of fat with thin layers of dough so that, upon baking, a partial separation of dough strata occurs. The individual dough layers contain no leavening and undergo very little expansion during baking. Water vapor is generated in the dough but quickly passes from the dough into the intervening spaces formed by shortening layers. These spaces are not completely open to the atmosphere because of the many dough adhesions that have formed during the repeated sheeting operations. As a result, steam is trapped in the pockets formed by partial fusion of the dough layers. These vesicles or bubbles tend to be comparatively large and irregular; their greatest dimension is nearly always in the horizontal direction. The expanding water vapor can cause a very substantial puffing of the piece.

Products made with puff pastry include turnovers and millefeuille pastries such as napoleons, vol-au-vents, and patty shells. Simulated strudel can also be made with puff pastry, although the genuine article is made from a single, very thin sheet of dough that is painted with oil or melted butter before it is wound around the filling in many layers.

Table 12.1 contains five puff pastry formulas selected from the literature.

Table 12.1. REPRESENTATIVE FORMULAS FOR PUFF PASTRY[1]

Ingredient	I	II	III	IV	V
Bread flour	39.3	37.1	36.5	36.9	38.4
Margarine or butter	6.6	6.2	7.2	9.2	3.8
Eggs, liquid whole	4.1	3.1	0	1.8	0
Cream of tartar	0.3	0.8	0	0	0
Salt	0	0.2	0.1	0.3	0.5
Water, variable	23.6	21.7	27.2	24.1	22.9
Roll-in shortening	26.1	30.9	29.0	27.7	34.4

[1] Percentages on as is basis. Formulas do not include food colors or flavors, which may be added, though not generally recommended.

Theoretical Considerations Affecting Layering

It is well recognized that one of the factors affecting the quality of puff pastry is the number of layers that have been formed in the raw dough piece. It is also generally understood that dough which is stretched too far, or dough layers that are too thin, will break down and ruin the structure that is necessary for a good quality puff pastry, since a uniform and maximum expansion depends upon maintaining the separation and integrity of the dough and fat layers. Therefore, it is common to specify the number of layers that are to be achieved in the folding and sheeting proceses.

What is not so widely re alized is that it is useless to define the number of layers that are to be achieved unless the thickness of the total puff pastry dough sheet is specified. That is, the thickness of the dough and fat layers in a sheet having a given number of laminations will depend upon the total thickness of the dough. Thus, a dough sheet which is one inch thick and contains 100 total layers will be composed of layers averaging 0.01 inch in thickness, while a dough sheet 0.1 inch thick and having 100 layers will contain layers averaging only 0.001 inch in thickness. It is, in fact, the thickness of the dough layers in the finished product—not the total number of layers or even the thickness of the fat layers—which is primarily responsible for the texture and expansion of this kind of pastry. The total number of layers and the thickness of the fat layers may, however, influence other characteristics of the product. The purpose of the preceding comments is to emphasize the interrelationship of total piece thickness and the point at which breakdown of the fat and/or dough laminations will occur. It is pointless to discuss the number of layers in a piece of puff pastry unless the piece thickness is also specified.

Maintaining the continuity of each stratum throughout the entire series of processing operations is a highly desirable goal. Its achievement depends upon the dimensions and rheology of the two separate phases (dough and fat) at the temperature of processing. It would be ideal if the fat and gluten could be stretched indefinitely while retaining the form of continuous unbroken layers, but both the roll-in shortening and the dough have elastic limits beyond that they will break down and continuous layers will not exist. They will then merge into a more or less homogeneous mass. The thickness at which the dough will break down is usually different from the thickness at which the fatty layers will be disrupted. In addition, the fat layers will ordinarily differ in thickness from the dough layers at each step in the folding and sheeting operations. Therefore, it is logical to assume that one of the systems will be limiting in any dough piece and will break down while the other component still has some potential for extension. The more closely the breakdown points of the two phases approach each other, the less roll-in shortening will have to be used for any given set of conditions.

The amount of force and the way it is applied in thinning out the doughs are important factors in maintaining intact layers. The ideal type of force is a gradually increasing pressure applied simultaneously all over the surface of a flat piece of dough by some method that would allow the free flow of the top and bottom layers. There is no production device which allows this type of uniformly-applied pressure to be applied, and, in practice, the dough sheets are reduced in thickness by roller systems that often cause excessive localized distortion and premature breakdown of the layers.

Multiplication of layers is best accomplished by cutting pieces of identical shape from the rolled out dough and stacking them. This may not be practical in commercial manufacturing procedures. When layers are multiplied by folding the dough upon itself, which is the universally accepted technique, added stress occurs at the extended surface of the fold (i.e., at the curled edges) and it is here that tearing is most likely to occur. Although folding is supposed to prevent oozing out of the fat when pressure is applied, this phenomenon is not usually observed after the first set of folds, and not even then if the initial fat layer is thin enough and the fat is firm enough.

Squeezing out of fat is minimized and dough integrity is assisted by reducing the thicknesses of the dough and fat layers in the initial folded sandwich. Let us assume it has been determined that a final structure of 100 total layers per inch of thickness is necessary in order to get the structure, volume, texture, and appearance desired in the baked products. If three folds of dough and two layers of fat, each one inch thick, are used in the initial structure, and a three-fold operation is used after each sheeting step, the initial three folds plus two additional three folds will be necessary. This will yield a theoretical 109 layers of fat and dough when we consider that contacting layers of dough (surfaces brought into contact during the folding operation) will merge during the sheeting-out process. This structure will have to be sheeted to a thickness of 1.09 inch to achieve the goal originally specified, that is, 100 layers per inch of thickness. Assuming that the initial layers of fat and dough are the same thickness (this assumption is made to improve simplicity and clarity of the calculation), this means the original one-inch thickness of each layer will have to be reduced one hundred times by the three sheeting steps. Obviously, great stress will be placed on the dough by stretching of this degree. Next, we will examine the situation that exists when we start out with thinner layers of dough and fat.

If the initial structure is comprised of dough and fat layers 0.1 inch thick, then it is obvious that these layers must be reduced ten times in order to achieve the desired 0.01 inch layers in the final product. It is important, however, to understand that these thin layers must be of uniform thickness—if the specification is 0.1 inch thick, then the fat and dough layers musst be 0.1 inch thick everywhere in the original sandwich preparation. This cannot be accomplished by slicing off irregular chunks of shortening and throwing them haphazardly on a crudely rolled dough piece, but it can be approximated by carefully pre-sheeting the dough and the fat layers using standard methods. Pre-sheeted puff pastry fat of the desired thickness might be obtainable from suppliers if the quantity ordered is large enough. It is rather obvious that it is easier to maintain layer integrity through a 10-fold reduction than it is through a 100-fold thinning.

It is also clear that sheeting pressure applied to thick layers of fat and dough is going to cause greater extension of one than the other component unless their rheology is identical, which is practically impossible to achieve. Thus, there will be relatively greater distortion of one of the components than will happen when much thinner layers are used. If butter is used, for example, it is likely that starting out with thick layers will result in some extrusion of the fat from edges of the sandwich, unless the butter is chilled to the extent it becomes hard (which may cause other problems), while thin shortening layers are much more likely to be retained within the laminated structure.

There are other phenomena that occur during the folding and sheeting of puff pastry doughs. Layering and reduction (thinning) processes improve the grain and texture by reducing the size of large gas bubbles and by forming many nuclei for steam evolution by subdividing pockets of entrapped air. These actions are separate from the layering effect and will occur even in the absence of any laminating medium such as shortening, although the latter may facilitate steam entrapment when it is present as a discontinuous phase. The practice of braking cracker or biscuit doughs to improve texture is based on these considerations, althoug dough development is another factor in such processes. Some treatises on puff pastry speak of the heat insulating effect of the fat layers. It is not clear how this is supposed to work. The insulating effect of a layer about a thousandth of an inch thick cannot be very great.

In the theoretical discussion found in the preceding paragraphs, a finished product containing layers averaging about 0.01 inch thick was postulated. This figure was chosen only to illustrate a point. In nearly all cases, the layers in a good quality puff pastry product will be considerably thinner. In the case of a dough laminating process during which the dough undergoes six folding steps, each fold forming a three-layered piece, the product will contain 486 layers of fat and 487 layers of dough. If the final dough sheet is reduced to 0.5 inches (thicker than most products will require), the layers will have an average thickness of about 0.0005 inch. Now, in order to ensure the proper thickness of each layer and an adequate expression of each layer in the final dough piece, certain processing conditions must be maintained. These conditions are as follows: (1) The gluten must be developed to the point where it will properly stretch during reduction by the sheeting rolls, but consideration must be given to the fact that a form of dough development occurs as a result of the sheeting, so mixer development must be stopped at an early stage; and (2) The roll-in shortening, though plastic and a semisolid, must be gradually stretched along with the dough in order not to destroy the symmetry of its ultimate shape.

If these conditions are not met, the following will occur: (1) The gluten will exceed its elastic limit and the molecular network will break down, causing breaks in the dough layers. In the finished product, this will lead to coarse layering, dull surfaces, irregular expansion, greasiness, and other defects; and (2) The roll-in fat will separate, leaving empty areas within the shortening layers where dough layers will touch each other. Also, a fast reduction under intense pressure will tend to push unevenly spread roll-in shortening through the thin gluten films that are above and below it, especially if the fat is relatively hard.

Gradual reduction through repeated sheetings is preferable to a one-step reduction. Results of an operation where the thickness of the dough piece is reduced in a single pass through a set of rollers (as in a dough brake) instead of by a gradual reduction, will be as follows: (1) The gluten matrix will break down because of the too rapid application of intense shearing forces; (2) There will be physical destruction of the gluten strata by fat pieces that are forced through the gluten layers as a result of intense localized pressure; and (3) The fat will not be distributed evenly because it does not have time to flow under the influence of the pressure.

And, the final product will suffer in the following ways: (1) Layering will be destroyed because of disruptions in the fat and dough laminations. This will result in reduced flakiness, poor volume, and coarse and uneven texture. Volume is lost because the layers, that normally entrap the water vapor that causes the major part of expansion in the oven, are merged together and are not capable of performing this function; (2) The crust may be dull and uneven—dull because the fat is all taken up by the dough and no free fat is left to impart a shine to the crust when the piece is baked, and uneven because the strata, which are normally aligned horizontally, are either destroyed completely or are misaligned so that the ends are directed haphazardly; (3) Holes that wend through the internal structure of the product will result from ruptured vesicle walls. This will cause lack of symmetry or collapse of the product during baking, with loss of the desired shape; and (4) Crusts will be tough due to coalescence of gluten layers.

The ultimate failure of the dough laminating process occurs when the shortening is completely incorporated into the dough, forming a single substantially homogeneoous mass. When this happens, the dough piece will bake out much like a high shortening dough, with no layering, malformed products, and a greasy or waxy mouthfeel. Thus, it appears the production of a high quality dough piece having many laminations and carrying a relatively high ratio of roll-in shortening must be based on a slow reduction of piece thickness between the folding steps.

Practical Methods of Puff Pastry Production

Butter was the original shortening of choice for puff pastries, but shortening manufacturers have developed ingredients that improve considerably on the performance characteristics of the soft dairy product. When butter is used, frequent resting of the dough at refrigerator temperatures is absolutely essential if the fat is to be prevented from being absorbed into the dough layers. These cool rest periods allow the butter layers to firm up again. Puff pastry margarines have higher melting points so that the laminating steps can be conducted at somewhat higher temperatures and with fewer (or no) rest periods. The special shortenings developed for layering puff pastries are generally composed of meat fats, vegetable oils, water, and salt. Lecithin and monoglycerides may be included, although their surfactant effect in this type of shortening may not, in fact, be desirable. Sometimes the water is replaced by skim milk or cultured milk for added flavor.

Shortenings used in the dough itself should preferably be softer than the roll-in fat, since softer shortenings tend to make the dough more extensible. Regular margarine is suitable, but some fairly soft hydrogenated vegetable oil will do about as well. The amount of this ingredient should be kept to the minimum necessary to obtain satisfactory dough handling properties. The total product will have plenty of fat for eating purposes from the roll-in, and the dough shortening will tend to add to the greasiness of the finished pastry. The best choice is to avoid adding shortening to the dough unless it is necessary to obtain proper dough handling characteristics.

Bread flour is customarily used for puff pastries. The speckiness and off colors of high extraction flours show up plainly in puff pastry, so a patent flour should be used. Bleaching is optional. A strong flour is recommended because it is necessary to have a tough but very extensible dough for this process. If the dough is bucky, however, considerable difficulties will be encountered in sheeting it, especially in the early stages. Cream of tartar, or some other acid salt, can be used to improve the handling properties. Possibly, L-cysteine could also be used. Sodium metabisulfite works well, but may not be an acceptable ingredient at this time.

The dough portion of the pastry has a simple composition: flour, water, salt, and (usually) shortening. Colors or flavors are sometimes added. As indicated previously, a small amount of acid or acid salt may be added to improve the extensibility of the dough. Leaveners are never used, and all insoluble granules must be avoided. The amount of roll-in fat is variable, depending on the process and the care taken to preserve the layers, but 35% of fat based on the dough weight seems to be an absolute minimum for an acceptable product if it is made by the usual factory or shop methods. Good pastry can probably be made with as little as 30% roll-in shortening if it is optimal in all its characteristics and exceptional care is taken in the laminating process. A larger percentage of roll-in fat is required for top quality puff pastry and for commercial processes that severely punish the dough.

A kind of puff pastry can be made by the so-called Scotch (McGill 1975) or blitz method which involves a brief blending of shortening cubes into a previously mixed dough. This final blending step is stopped while most of the cubes are still pretty well intact, and the dough rolled out, then folded and rolled an additional two or three times. The hypothesis is, the cubes will sheet out into layers that will form the desired laminated structure. Such products are never as good as those made with uniform layers of shortening folded into sheeted dough and then rolled out, because the pieces of shortening used in the blitz method are partially absorbed by the dough no matter how gentle the mixing step is. As a result, layering in blitz products is erratic and coarse. Furthermore, the finished products are nearly always greasy because excess fat must be used in this method to compensate for the inefficient layering technique. Blitz methods are not recommended if the baker intends to make a high quality product.

In the hand folding and rolling of puff pastry, many techniques have been advocated. Some of the names given to these methods are the French, the English, the Classic, the Bourgeoise, the Viennese, the Italian, etc. These differ primarily in the way the dough is initially folded around the sheet(s) or lumps of shortening. Methods have also been suggested that specify mixing of the fat, or a part of it, with flour, but it is not believed that such mixtures are required for the preparation of top quality puff pastry. Instead, the author advocates the following method: Step 1—shape the shortening into a sheet of convenient uniform thickness (but fairly thin) and cut the sides straight so that a square or rectangle is formed that does not contain voids or empty spaces; Step 2—Calculate the correct amount of dough needed for the weight of shortening contained in the square sheet, then roll this amount of dough into two square or rectangular sheets just slightly larger than the shortening; Step 3—Place the shortening on one of the dough sheets and cover it with the other dough sheet (optionally, prepare a five-layer sandwich of three layers of dough and two layers of fat); Step 4—Without attempting to seal the edges, roll the sandwich out to about one-third its former thickness, this proportion to be adjusted according to conditions; Step 5 and subsequent steps—Fold the rolled-out dough to give three thickness and continue the rolling and folding (with rest periods and cooling as necessary) until the desired number of layers is obtained, or, preferably, cut the rolled-out sheet into three pieces of the same size and shape and stack them before sheeting.

The method described above avoids some of the excess extension of dough that occurs when the original folding style used in other methods brings the dough sheet around the edges of the shortening. This excess extension often shows up later in the rolling and folding process as cracks and tears at the edge of the dough piece. If the consistencies of the dough and shortening are compatible, there is no more reason to expect squeezing out of the fat at the cut edges in this procedure than there is in, e.g., the English method where exposed shortening is also present. The suggested method also gives a somewhat more uniform distribution of shortening.

Most technologists who are reading this book will be using mechanical processing methods for rolling in the shortening, so the preceding discussion is of more value in establishing the principles of laminating roll-in doughs than it is in helping to design manufacturing methods. It will be helpful in setting up laboratory and pilot plant procedures.

Traditional Puff Pastry Method

(1) Mix a dough consisting of 10 lb bread flour, 1 oz salt, 2 lb shortening, and 7 lb water (variable) at 40°F.

(2) Let the dough stand for 15 minutes, then sheet it and fold it over 8-lb of puff pastry shortening.

(3) Sheet this out to about a third of its original thickness, then give it a three fold. There should be three, four, or five of these sheeting and folding sequences depending on the other factors involved. Rest one-half hour between folds.

(4) In the final sheeting, bring to thickness needed for final dough piece. Cut out and shape pieces. Place them on an ungreased baking surface.

(5) Bake at 400°F for a time governed by piece thickness and other factors.

Automated Puff Pastry Production

The latest development in puff pastry production is based on a piece of equipment that does all of the fat application and sheeting in a continuous operation (Shoup 1978, Haarsgaard 1980). Dough and shortening are separately fed into two hoppers. They are formed by an extruder into a double-layered continuous tube of which the peripheral layer consists of dough and the inner layer is shortening. Following extrusion, the tube is flattened to give a thick continuous sheet. The sheet is then greatly reduced in thickness by a dough stretcher, after which the sheet is folded upon itself by a swinging, paddle-type mechanism. The folded dough, consisting of many layers, is stretched again into a thin sheet.

The dough stretcher, so-called, is an assembly of many small rollers which are drawn across the dough with their axes at right angles to the direction of travel. According to the manufacturer, this machine is capable of reducing the dough to one-tenth its original thickness (e.g., one-sixteenth inch) without tearing. The advantage of this system is said to be that the stretcher handles the dough more gently, since it thins the dough by pulling it horizontally rather than squeezing it vertically. Thinning is assisted by passing the dough to conveyor belts, each of which runs faster than the one preceding it. The manufacturer states that doughs formed in this way will expand ten times or more while retaining a very symmetrical conformation.

Forming and Baking Puff Pastry

In the last sheeting operation before the pieces are cut to their final shape, it is essential to keep the dough sheet of uniform thickness throughout. If this is not done, the pieces will expand in an erratic and asymmetric manner when baked.

Patty shells are made by rolling out the finished dough sheet to about one-eighth inch thickness, cutting into circles, cutting the centers out of half of the circles (making doughnut shapes), washing the top of the whole disks with water and placing the doughnut shapes on top of them. Greased paper or parchment is placed on top of the patty shells to prevent them from tipping and they are baked at about 400°F. In baking puff pastry items, it is highly desirable to have steady uniform heat from beginning to end of the bake period. Large sizes of patty shells are sometimes called vol-au-vents and, after baking, can be filled with creamed chicken and the like to serve as main courses.

For cheese sticks, roll the dough very thin. Sprinkle with a high flavored grated cheese that has been mixed with a small amount of paprika (for color) and fine salt. Fold one half over the other (trapping the cheese inside) and again sprinkle with cheese. Cut into narrow strips about 3.5-in long. Place on a pan and allow to rest for an hour. Bake in a moderate oven. For variety in shape, the strips may be twisted one time before baking.

Turnovers are common forms of puff pastry. To make them, roll out the finished puff pastry dough to about one-eighth inch thick. Cut in squares about 4- to 6-inches on each side. Place about 2 oz to 3 oz of filling in the center of the square. Highly spiced fillings such as mincemeat would be used in smaller amounts than less potent fillings such as blueberry. Brush around the rim of the dough piece with a wash, which can be water, sugar syrup, egg, starch gel, or milk, but not fat. Enclose the filling by folding the dough over the filling to make a triangle. Seal the edges by pressing them together. One or two cuts can be made over the filling to allow steam to escape, but this can be omitted depending on the appearance desired. Place on an ungreased, undusted surface protected from boiled out fillings with paper or foil. Bake at 450°F for 20 to 25 minutes.

Sugar crisps or sugar puffs are simple but rather popular products. Sheet out the finished puff pastry dough to about one-quarter inch thick. Cut in circles of about two inches in diameter. Dock with a few holes. Press the pieces on both sides in fine granulated sugar, place on pans, and bake. Sprinkle with cinnamon after removal from the oven.

Trouble Shooting Puff Pastry

If the pastry does not expand enough, the oven may be too cold, the pastry may have been put through too many sheeting and folding operations, the flour may be too weak, or the fat may be too soft or not plastic enough.

If the finished product is too tough and doughy, the oven may be too cold, the dough sheet may have been too thick, or there may not have been enough sheeting and folding operations.

If the pastry is hard and flinty, the oven may have been too cold, the flour may be too strong, or the dough may have been too stiff.

If the pastry shrinks in the oven, the dough may not have been sufficiently rested between processing steps.

If the pastry is excessively greasy or fat runs out of it during baking, too much total fat (dough shortening plus roll-in) may have been used, or the fat may have remained in chunks in the finished dough sheet (common in blitz method doughs). Roll-in fat that is too soft, such as butter, may also contribute to these problems.

If the pastries rise too high during baking, the oven may have been too hot, the number of foldings may have been too few, or the flour may be too strong.

If there is no puff or layering, the roll-in has probably been completely mixed into the dough phase as a result of excessive rolling and folding, inadequate cooling of dough between steps, inadequate resting between steps, or excessive reduction in thickness at some point.

Waxy taste or texture in the finished (cooled) product is related to the type of roll-in shortening used. It is probably too hard (SFI too high). An excessive amount of shortening often contributes to this fault.

CRISPBREAD

The kind of products described in this section are wafer-like in form and crisp or hard in texture. They are sometimes called flatbreads. Ry-Krisp (a trademark) is a typical example, although it may not be made by any of the procedures to be described here. These products were originally made by traditional methods involving the rolling and sheeting of doughs, but a much more efficient procedure based on the use of extrusion cooking equipment has been gaining favor. The extruded products generally contain no leavening compounds, their expansion depending upon the evolution of steam within the interior of a hot dough as it emerges from a pressurized cooking and mixing chamber. The structure of these products has a lot in common with the structures of extrusion-expanded snack products such as corn curls (Fulger *et al.* 1986).

The basic ingredients of the extruded crispbreads are soft white wheat flour, salt, whole milk powder, corn starch, and sugar. Optional ingredients include rye flour, whole wheat flour, and shortening. Flavors, colors, and other additives are possibilities the formulator may consider.

The following description is based on a Baker Perkins plant. Dry ingredients are mixed in a ribbon blender that discharges into a service bin from which the mixture is fed into the extruder hopper by a variable speed conveyor. The extruder section is preceded by a smaller twin screw feeder section that is adjustable in speed. It ensures the delivery to the main extruder section of a solid pack of material at a predetermined rate. About 5% to 10% of water is normally added to give the desired plasticity and expansive properties to the dough, and it is injected directly into the extruder barrel via a high pressure pump. The contents of the extruder are mixed and cooked by the screw assemblies. The principal source of heat is the shearing work performed by the augers, although the extruder barrel can be fitted with jackets heated by steam or electricity.

Conformation of the augers, their spatial relationship to one another, their speeds, and the load of material in the barrel are among the factors controlling dwell time and heat generation. Temperatures as high as 355°F can be reached in cooking extruders. Cooked dough is extruded through a die plate with four to six slits. Because of the high temperature of the dough, it expands almost instantaneously as it emerges from the die, the drop in pressure allowing most of the water content to flash into steam.

The hot plastic strips emerging from the die orifices are picked up by a conveyor that subsequently passes beneath one or more gauging rolls used to control thickness of the product. Further down the line, a cut is made across the strips by a four-disc rotary cutter. The cuts do not go entirely through the dough, so that the strips can be conveyed in continuous form through the toasting oven. Before entering the oven, the moisture content of the dough will be about 8% to 10%.

The oven of the Baker Perkins plant uses porous bricks as burners. A gas and air mixture passes through the bricks to burn on their surfaces at temperatures as high as 2,000°F. The intense radiant heat generated in this manner dries and toasts the crispbread strips in 5 to 10 seconds. As the strips emerge from the oven, they are nearly dry (5% moisture or less) but still plastic because of their temperature. They then pass through cooling sections where air streams cool and set them. After a few seconds of this cooling, the product becomes hard enough to be broken under rolls of the type called "cracker breakers"—very similar to the arrangement used to separate sheets of soda crackers. The individual wafers of crispbread are stacked and packed by conventional devices.

Anderson *et al.* (1981) obtained a product with the texture, structure, and taste of Swedish crispbread by cooking in a twin-screw extruder a mixture of 30% wheat bran, 60% starch, and 10% gluten. During extrusion, the total sugar content was reduced by 70% to 80%, the breakdown being accentuated by decreasing screw speed or addition of more water, while omission of gluten had the opposite effect. The loss of sugar is due to thermally mediated chemical reactions involving nitrogenous compounds, presumably of the Maillard type.

Rusks, "bread crumbs," and croutons can also be made by extruding unleavened doughs from high pressure extruders and forming the extrudate into appropriate sizes and shapes. Corn flake preforms can be made in the same manner, although this is not the traditional method for manufacturing breakfast cereals. Corn meal, with no additives, can be made into many different shapes of low density by high pressure extrusion to form popular snack foods. Other cereal flours—wheat, rice, sorghum, and rye, for example—can also be extrusion expanded.

ECLAIR SHELLS, CREAM PUFFS, AND POPOVERS

Popovers are a type of hot bread while eclair and cream puff shells are components of dessert foods. These products typically have an extremely coarse and irregular grain, the interior being formed of a few large cells. Water vapor contributes the greater part of the leavening action, although entrapped air also has some effect. Neither chemical leaveners nor yeast is used in these products.

Popover batters are made from a simple formula and procedure. In an average formula, about 85 to 130 parts by weight of liquid whole eggs and 200 parts of liquid whole milk will be used for each 100 parts of flour. Small amounts of shortening, salt, and flavorings constitute the remainder of the batter. Bread flour is generally used, and it should be sifted.

Popover batter should be deposited in muffin tins or in specially designed pans. The cavities are filled about one-third full of batter. Before the batter is added, the pans are greased and placed in the oven to heat. These utensils should be heavy-walled to provide a good initial source of heat and should be transferred to the oven immediately after they are filled, as it is essential for the batter to undergo a rapid temperature increase if it is to expand properly.

Baking conditions are very critical in the successful production of popovers. The filled pans should be placed in a hot oven (about 450° to 475°F) so that water vapor pressure will increase rapidly in the batter and expand the piece before the crust is set by radiant heat. After the expansion has reached its maximum, temperature of the oven should be reduced to about 350°F to dry the popover and firm up the interior without burning the crust. When the pastries are removed from the oven, the shells should be punctured immediately to allow water vapor to escape and drying to continue. If properly baked, the crust will be crisp in texture and medium dark brown in color, while the interior will be nearly dry but not tough or crumbly. A common defect is overbaked crusts resulting from an excess of radiant heat, the crusts become too dark in color, either too brittle or too powdery in texture, and rather bitter in flavor.

Grated cheese, rye meal, whole wheat flour, or other characterizing materials can be added to the batter without ruining the popovers if the batter is kept at a very fluid consistency and the total fat content is low.

The preparation method for cream puffs and eclair shells is unusual in that the batter is cooked before it is deposited and baked. This so-called pate a chou has a fairly simple composition of about 150 to 200 parts of liquid whole eggs, 100 parts flour, 100 parts shortening, and about 200 parts of water. Part of the whole eggs can be replaced by egg white, but some egg yolk is needed because the eggs must not only contribute to the structure of the finished shell, but must also emulsify the fat so that it does not leak out of the batter during baking. The quality of the eggs has an important influence on both flavor and appearance of the cream puff.

The shortening (often butter) and the water are brought to a boil, then the heat is reduced, and the flour and salt are added in one portion. The mixture is stirred until a ball of dough is formed. The source of heat is then removed and the ball of flour paste is allowed to cool slightly so that it will not cause coagulation of the egg proteins, the eggs being added at this time with vigorous stirring. At the completion of mixing, the paste should be stiff enough to remain in a peak when a spoon is drawn out of it. It may be necessary to adjust the egg content to attain this consistency. The batter must be homogeneous, lumps being a distinct liability. The paste should be chilled before it is formed into units.

Mounds of the paste are extruded on to a lightly greased baking sheet from a pastry bag, or by any equivalent method. A hot oven temperature (450°F) is generally recommended although some authorities indicate 375°F is adequate. In any case, satisfactory performance depends upon a fast transfer of heat into the paste. The pastries are baked until they are golden brown and beads of moisture are no longer seen on the surface. Then the heat is turned off and the shells are punctured to allow an escape route for trapped water vapor. It is important that both the interior and the exterior parts of the case be firm enough to retain their shape at this time. The punctured puff shells are allowed to dry out in the oven for a few minutes before they are removed for cooling.

Size and shape are important factors in getting good expansion and an interior that is slightly moist but not wet and soggy. If the batter deposit is too large, heat penetration under any achievable oven conditions may be too slow to get adequate expansion before the crust sets up. Then, the interior may be soggy and stringy due to insufficient baking of the batter at the center of the mass. On the other hand, pieces that are too small may not entrap the vapor well enough to get good expansion.

Eclair shells are made in exactly the same way as cream puffs except that the paste is extruded in strip form. It cannot be said that eclair shells or cream puff cases have flavors that are particularly appealing. Added flavors, such as vanilla, will in large part be dissipated due to the baking conditions, so taste appeal must be added in the form of fillings and coatings. Cases can be filled with pastry cream, whipped cream, or other fillings, as desired. Cases and shells may either be slit open for the filling operation, or the cream may be injected through holes in the ends. Often, the filled case is iced or enrobed.

Eclair shells, cream puffs, and popovers are not commonly made for commercial distribution, although at least one brand of frozen eclairs has enjoyed a modest success. These products have a short shelf life when stored at room temperature, because they tend to absorb moisture and shrink or collapse and become tough. They could serve as the basis of new and unique desserts and appetizers if properly packaged and distributed. Enrobing with chocolate could be considered as a means of retarding moisture absorption.

Cream puff dough (pâte a chou) can be fried as well as baked; puffed fritters (beignets soufflés) are the most common example. Cream puff dough made as described above is formed into small balls (about the size of a walnut) and dropped into 370°F frying fat. The balls will expand and turn over without further manipulation. After they are removed from the fat, they are drained, then rolled in powdered sugar. Beignets can be served with sauces such as sabayon or apricot sauce. Commercial application of these fried doughs is somewhat questionable, although they could provide an additional variety for doughnut shops. They are much better in flavor and texture when eaten very fresh.

Cream puffs and eclair shells would seem to be good candidates for microwave cooking. Generation of heat in the interior would create good expansion without prematurely coagulating the outer layers. Some radiant heat might have to be applied separately to set up and color the crust. An interesting experiment would be to place the eclair batter deposits (on a non-metallic tray) in a microwave oven until they have reached their limit of expansion and steam evolution has markedly declined, then transfer them to an oven with a high amount of radiant heat (broiler?) until they are adequately browned.

Table 12.2 contains representative formulas for eclairs, popovers, and two types of cream puffs.

Table 12.2. FORMULAS FOR POPOVER-TYPE PRODUCTS[1]

Ingredient	Eclairs	Cream puffs I	Cream puffs II	Popovers
Bread flour	20.5	17.4	22.5	24.4
Butter	0	17.4	0	3.4
Shortening	11.2	0	15.0	0
Whole eggs, liquid	24.2	30.4	30.0	21.0
Whole milk, liquid	4.6	0	1.9	50.6
Salt	0.5	0.2	0.6	0.6
Water, variable	31.6	34.6	30.0	0
Egg whites, liquid	7.4	0	0	0

[1] As is basis.

COOKIES AND CRACKERS

Some cookies and crackers depend primarily on water vapor generation in the dough for their leavening action. A few of these are made by processes analagous to the puff pastry laminating technique, while others depend on different principles. Several examples will be discussed in the following paragraphs.

Beaten Biscuits

Beaten biscuits are a southern specialty that achieved their greatest popularity in Maryland. These crackers have a crisp texture somewhat resembling that of soda crackers or ship biscuits and the crust is pale in color—almost white, in many cases. The method of preparation has some resemblances to the preparation of puff pastry, although roll-in shortening is not used. The dough does not contain any yeast or chemical leavening. A structure is formed by repeated folding and thinning out of the dough piece. This sheeting is usually done by pounding the dough for the better part of an hour with a rolling pin or similar implement, although sets of rollers driven by a hand-turned crank have been marketed.

The formula for beaten biscuits is simple, consisting of flour, salt, lard (a small amount), and water. A little sugar is sometimes added. The flour should be strong and only enough water is added to make a very stiff dough. The dough should be developed before the beating and folding process begins. The dough piece is folded and sheeted out, or beaten out, perhaps 20 or 30 times. If sheeting rollers are available, the dough will break down and tear long before this many steps are reached, unless rest periods are provided for it. An old-time formula having some unusual features is: flour 100 parts, sugar 3 parts, salt 2 parts, shortening 20 parts, and fresh whole milk 35 parts.

The dry ingredients are blended together, then creamed with the shortening. Finally, the milk is mixed in and a stiff dough developed. This is beaten continuously by hand, with occasional folding, for about 30 minutes. As the process continues, bubbles or blisters will be seen just below the surface of the dough.

Small circular pieces, about 1 to 1.5 inches in diameter and not more than 0.5 inch thick are cut from the dough sheet, and indentation is made in the center and the top is docked with several holes. These discs are then placed about a half inch apart on an ungreased baking sheet and put in a 325° to 350°F oven until they are substantially dried out, i.e., until they reach about 5% moisture content. Some expansion does occur, but the finished product is still dense. Baking at higher temperatures should promote greater expansion. The biscuits are generally consumed cold, and should be stored in a closed container to delay moisture absorption.

Attempts have been made to commercialize this product, which is inexpensive and easy to prepare using a dough brake or similar equipment, but there is little consumer demand for the product except as a novelty.

Puff Biscuits

Puff "biscuits" or crackers are more common in European markets than they are in the U.S. Formulas and procedures are reminiscent of puff pastry preparation, but the crackers or cookies are much less expanded and generally are made with less fat. They are also smaller in piece size, and thinner, which, of course, accounts for some of the reduction in expansion. A representative formula as given by Whiteley (1971) is: strong flour 100, malt extract 2.6, salt 2.5, and water as required (e.g., 40%). He suggests 18% layering fat for lean biscuits and 36% for rich biscuits. Whey or other dough mellowing agents may be used to facilitate the sheeting and folding steps. Sodium metabisulfite has also been added for this purpose.

According to Manley (1983), puff biscuits may be consumed as unsweetened carriers for butter, cheese, jam, etc., or as shells for sweet or savory cream sandwiches. If used as sweet biscuits, it is customary to garnish their surfaces with sugar before baking so that a glossy, lightly browned surface is produced. Since puff biscuits are always eaten at room temperature, unlike some puff pastry items like patty shells, which are eaten warm, the fat used as a roll-in must not give a waxy sensation in the mouth. Lower melting point fats are therefore used for puff biscuits and the doughs are always processed while chilled.

Puff doughs can also be made into fancy shaped cookies. One of these varieties is palmier biscuits, made by slicing across the laminations of a puff dough sheet that has been folded inward from the edges in two steps. The baked biscuit looks something like two broad leaves spreading from a common base, hence the name. Manley described the various fat interleaving methods that can be used for making these products, and they greatly resemble the processes used for making puff pastry, except one process where "flakes" of hard fat are spread across the dough sheet, either by hand or by braking. About 72 layers are considered to be near the optimum for puff biscuits.

Puff biscuits are baked using an oven temperature profile that is very hot at the entrance end. If the early bottom heat is too high relative to the top heat, the biscuits will tend to curl into a saucer shape with the edges high. Increasing top heat will encourage the centers to rise more, giving either flat cookies with even thickness or a doming effect with the centers high. Control is facilitated if light wire mesh bands are used. Final moisture contents around 2.5% are considered satisfactory.

Extruder-Cooked Cookies

The processing of flatbreads in auger-type extruder-cookers has been discussed. There is no theoretical reason why sweet goods, particularly cookies, cannot be processed with the same type of equipment. The patent of Keller and Reed (1990) discloses the use of, e.g., a twin-screw extruder to process a mixture of 15% to 35% plasticized crystallizable sugar, 15% to 35% shortening, and 40% to 60% flour. The moisture content is about 15%. Little or no post-extrusion drying is required. Many shapes can be formed, including cylinders with cavities for filling with creams, etc.

SUGAR WAFERS

The base cake for sugar wafer cookies is entirely different from any other biscuit, but it has many similarities in texture and structure to certain puffed snack foods, although it is not made like them. Structurally, it is a foamed, dehydrated starch gel with an associated gluten network that contributes some additional support. Most of the leavening action results from the evolution of steam during the baking process. The batter is closely confined between hot molds so that the steam cannot readily escape, and the inflating effect of the water vapor under these conditions is much greater than it would be if the thin sheet of batter were exposed to the atmosphere. The hot metal also rapidly creates a thin, but more or less impervious, surface layer that inhibits the loss of water vapor and has important textural effects.

The basic principles used in making the flat, cream-filled sugar wafers are also employed in manufacturing ice cream cones (cake cones) and novelty cream-filled shapes such as circles, hemispheres, half-cylinders, peanut shells, etc. All of the fillings used in these shells must be fat based, since any appreciable amount of moisture completely ruins the texture of the base cake, causing it to first become tough and flexible, and then to collapse. Apparently, some types of caramel have such low water activities that they can be successfully combined with sugar wafers and this principle has been used to make some popular confections.

Batters for these products are fluid mixtures of flour and water to which small amounts of of other ingredients are added. A recommended formula would be 100 parts flour, 140 parts water, 0.5 part sodium bicarbonate, 0.5 part salt, 0.1 part lecithin, and 1 part coconut oil. The other ingredients sometimes used include flavors, colors, ammonium bicarbonate, nonfat dry milk, dried whole milk, corn starch, egg yolk, and lecithin. A yellow color is commonly added to the vanilla or plain base cake. Flavors tend to be lost through steam distillation during baking, so most of the finished product's flavor is expected to come from the cream filling. "Chocolate" or dark-colored wafers sometimes do not contain any cacao products; instead they are colored with caramel color or food dyes. For a chocolate taste, about 10% of cocoa has been used—this would necessitate an increase of about 15% in the water.

Old-time formulas for sugar wafer base cakes often contained enriching ingredients such as milk or eggs, and sometimes even sugar, but batters made with these components tend to cause excessive build-up of carbon on the oven plates, especially at their corners. Carbon deposits cause sticking of the wafer sheet with resultant difficulty in extracting the sheet from the plate. Shortening (usually 76° coconut oil) can be added to facilitate release of the wafer. Lecithin has also been used for this purpose.

Table 12.3 gives averages, ranges, and recommended amounts of ingredients for sugar wafer batters, collated from numerous sources.

Table 12.3. AVERAGES AND RANGES FOR SUGAR WAFER BATTERS

Ingredient	Average	Range High	Range Low	Recommended
Flour	100.	100.	100.	100.
Water	135.	150.	125.	140.
Sodium bicarbonate	.38	.75	.1	.5
Ammonium bicarbonate	.22	.5	0	0
Nonfat dry milk	1.8	5.	0	0
Dried whole milk	0.5	3.	0	0
Corn starch	1.7	5.	0	0
Dried egg yolk	0.96	2.5	1.25	0
Salt	0.32	0.75	0	0.5
Lecithin	0.13	0.4	0	0.1
Coconut oil	0.8	2.	0	1.

Flour should be short extraction soft wheat flour. Flour from white wheat is sometimes used. Both bleached and unbleached flour work satisfactorily. Any speckiness in the flour shows up clearly in white wafers. The amount and quality of gluten seem to have some effect on expansion so that a very weak flour may give a wafer that is too dense or close in texture. On the other hand, strong gluten can cause the wafer to be hard and flinty in texture. Thus, the protein content or strength of the flour should be chosen to achieve a compromise between excessive hardness and excessive fragility. The precise requirements for flour strength will depend upon the kinds and amounts of other ingredients, the type of end product desired, and the characteristics of the equipment being used. Corn starch has been suggested to improve the texture, that is, to make the wafer more tender.

Water is variable, the amount being chosen to give a batter viscosity that will enable the fluid to spread rapidly over the plate and between the plates while still retaining a substantially uniform internal structure without large voids or other defects. These very fluid batters have a tendency to show gluten separation in strands during mixing, a serious defect.

Some other ingredients that have been suggested for sugar wafer shells are heat-treated, defatted cottonseed flour and degerminated white corn flour. Such materials add viscosity to the batter without increasing the possiblity of gluten separation during mixing.

Although sugar wafer shells have been regarded here as among those products that normally contain no added leavening agent, some formulas do, in fact, contain ammonium bicarbonate or sodium bicarbonate. It is generally acknowledged that these sources of carbon dioxide contribute only slightly to expansion of the batter. Soda is used in such limited amounts that leavening acids are rarely needed because the flour has enough buffering action to cause release of the carbon dioxide. However, cream of tartar may be added to leavened or unleavened formulas in an amount sufficient to bring the pH slightly below 7.0 so as to improve the color of white shells.

Mixing of sugar wafer batters is relatively simple. Almost any equipment that can produce a smooth, lump-free batter is suitable for the purpose. The dry ingredients are first blended, then the water is added gradually while mixing. If shortening is used, it is blended in while the mixture is still of a doughy consistency. Some authorities recommend using melted shortening. Eggs and milk solids can be added to the mixer at the start, with about half the water, and allowed to become rehydrated before the remainder of the dry ingredients are added; finally, the rest of the water is gradually brought in.

Batters are preferably mixed at high speed although there are many cases where low speed horizontal mixers have been used successfully. Under certain conditions, as when the batter is overmixed, gluten may develop into strands and separate. Settling-out of starch and other particles is also a problem and some agitation is needed while the batter is being held for depositing. Keeping the batch size small is highly recommended, while holding for longer than about 30 minutes is definitely not recommended.

Small scale equipment which allows the production of, for example, waffle cones at an ice cream store is available. Most of the batter mixes provided by suppliers for use with these devices appear to be unleavened. That is true of the mix disclosed in the patent of Ito (1990), and intended to be used with his invented machine in retail outlets.

BIBLIOGRAPHY

ANDERSSON, Y., HEDLUND, B., JONSSON, L., and SVENSSON, S. 1981. Extrusion cooking of a high-fiber cereal product with crispbread character. Cereal Chem. *58*, 370-374

ANON. 1982. Extruded crispbread fast mover in Europe. Snack Food *71*, 28, 30

CHARM, S. E. 1971. Fundamentals of Food Engineering, Second Ed. AVI Publishing Co., Westport, CT

DOW, W. T. 1958. Puff pastry--production fundamentals. Am.Soc. Bakery Engineers Bull. *159*

FULGER, C. V., LAZARUS, C. R., LOU, W. C., STOCKER, C. T., and TU, C. 1986. Process for preparing a cooked extruded flour-based product. U.S. Pat. 4,568,550

GLABAU, C. A. 1959. Puff pastry. Bakers Weekly, Apr. 13, Apr. 20, Apr. 27, May 4, May 11, May 18, May 25, June 1, June 8, and June 15.

HAARSGAARD, E. E. 1980. Automatic production of puff pastry. Bakers Digest *54*, No. 1, 16-18, 42

ITO, S. 1990. Method of producing edible vessel. U.S. Pat. 4,927,656

KELLER, L. C., and REED, R. B. 1990. Continuous production of cookie-like product. U.S. Pat. 4,948,612

MANLEY, D. J., JR. 1983. Technology of Biscuits, Crackers, and Cookies. Ellis Horwood, Ltd., Chichester, England

MC GILL, E. A. 1975. Puff pastry production. Bakers Digest *49*, No. 1, 28-29, 33-34, 36-38

SCHMIED, K. H. 1959. Fat distribution in puff pastry prepared by different methods. Brot Gebäck. *13*, 225-233 (in German)

SHOUP, G. 1978. Automated puff pastry production. Proc. Am. Soc. Bakery Engineers *1978*, 139-144

WHITELEY, P. R. 1971. Biscuit Manufacture. Elsevier Publishing Co., London

WOOLLEN, A. 1985. Higher productivity in crispbread. Cereal Foods World *30*, No. 5, 333-334

chapter thirteen

AIR-LEAVENED PRODUCTS

INTRODUCTION

All doughs and batters contain gases derived from the atmosphere, even if they have been mixed in vessels under reduced pressure. These gases are enfolded by the material as it is tossed around, cut, folded, and deformed in other ways during mixing. Nitrogen, oxygen, and carbon dioxide also dissolve in the aqueous phase and are adsorbed on the insoluble solids. These gases will be at least partially released when the mixture is heated. The uptake of gas can be increased by mixing the dough or batter in pressurized chambers.

Among other procedures that facilitate the incorporation of gas are: (1) Sifting the flour or air-conveying it under pressure; (2) Creaming the shortening with a particulate ingredient such as flour or sugar; (3) Adding whipped liquid egg products, especially egg whites; (4) Repeated folding and sheeting of dough, with or without interleaving of shortening; and (5) Vigorous mixing of doughs or fairly stiff batters, particularly under pressurized conditions.

Air that has been entrapped in the form of bubbles can be expected to increase in volume according to the well-known gas laws as the temperature of the dough or batter rises. For example, 100 ml of air at 70°F will expand to about 128 ml at 212°F. In other words, the gas will expand about one-fourth as it goes from room temperature to near the boiling point of water. The full effect of this expansion will not be seen in the finished bakery product because there will be some slight restriction on expansion by the elasticity of the vesicle walls that inclose the gas, and a considerable amount of the gas will escape to the atmosphere.

Even if all the gas were retained within the product, however, its relatively small increase in volume as the temperature of the gases is raised from room temperature to about 212°F is not nearly enough to account for the expansion in the oven of air-leavened products such as angel food cake. It has been clearly shown that the additional volume comes from gases driven out of the liquid or dislodged from absorbants by heat, and from the increase in water vapor pressure. The last named factor is probably the most important leavening agent in many cases. It is not necessary for ingredient water to actually reach the boiling point for its vapor to become effective as an expansive force, since the partial pressure of water increases rapidly as the boiling point is approached (see the discussion on this point in the preceding chapter).

Although water vapor pressure certainly has an important leavening effect in many of the products that will be called "air-leavened" in this book, it would not have the desired effectiveness if small gas bubbles were not already present to serve as foci for the evolution of dissolved and adsorbed gases. It can easily be shown that a de-aerated dough, when heated, loses water vapor in ways not conducive to product expansion, for example, as evaporation from the product surface and in the form of large nonuniform bubbles that gradually coalesce and then reach the surface and burst. The advantage of structured foams such as the meringues used for angel food cakes is they have many small, uniform bubbles that retain their individuality throughout the baking process as gases are discharged into them from the liquid phase of the batter.

ANGEL FOOD CAKES

General Considerations

Meringues, which are baked shapes of foamed egg white and sugar, could be considered the simplest representatives of this class, but they are more closely allied to confectionery than to bakery products because they do not contain flour. The basic type of cake in this category is the angel food cake, which is based on egg white foams and contains no shortening. Cakes such as pound, chiffon, and sponge depend for their structure primarily on whole egg foams (in combination with flour, of course), and they do contain shortening, some times quite a bit of it. They may also contain some chemical leaveners. Egg foam cakes probably represent about 10% of the commercially manufactured cakes sold in the U.S.

In these days of increased awareness of the health impact of diet, it pays to give a little thought to the advantages of angel food cake. Here we have a product with no fat (well, anyway, less than 1%), no cholesterol, a substantial amount of high quality protein, a large proportion of a grain product ingredient, and a considerable part of its calories as complex carbohydrates (starch). It could also be made "all natural" with very little effort. If the portions are of modest size, it could serve as a relatively low calorie dessert. Of course, it is low in fiber and is not particularly high in vitamins and minerals, but if served with fresh fruit (and/or yogurt?) it should be good for at least two meals per day. It is surprising the product hasn't received more advertising support emphasizing these positive features.

Angel food cakes can be made by at least three kinds of processes: (1) The foam process, in which the egg whites are beaten to a fairly stiff foam before the other ingredients are added—this is the traditional method; (2) The meringue process, in which all (or most) of the ingredients are whipped together; and (3) The continuous process, in which automatic equipment is used to blend all of the ingredients and whip them into a foam in one continous flow, usually in pressurized chambers.

Ingredients and Formulas

The three essential ingredients for angel food cakes are egg whites, sugar, and flour. The usual proportions are about 30 to 40 parts flour, 100 parts liquid egg whites, and 80 to 100 parts sugar. Dried egg albumen and water can be used to replace the liquid egg whites, but otherwise water is not added. Cream of tartar (or other whipping aids and acidifiers), salt, and flavor are also found in nearly all formulas. The egg whites and flours act as "tougheners," that is, they contribute to the strength or resiliency of the foam structure, while sugar is the only "tenderizer"—there being no shortening in these cakes. Increases in the percentage of egg whites or flour in the formula will decrease the tenderness of the cake, while increasing the amount of sugar will make the product more tender. It is considered desirable to use a percentage of sugar just short of that which would cause the cake to fall, if optimum eating quality is to be obtained.

The sweetening agent is nearly always sucrose. Although the regular granulated form is satisfactory, it is preferable to use a finer particle size of sugar to speed up the dissolving of this ingredient in the egg white.

Characteristics of the flour have a strong influence on the quality of the finished product. A weak soft wheat flour is desirable. Gaines and Donelson (1985A) showed that height and tenderness of angel food cake decreased as flour protein increased through the range 7.1% to 12.5%, although relatively large increases (approximately 2%) in protein content were required to produce a noticeable change. This set of experiments was conducted with a 50% patent soft red winter wheat flour supplemented by protein concentrate removed from the same wheat by air classification methods. In another paper, Gaines and Donelson (1985B) reported than milling method (comparison of three different roller mills, pin milling, and turbo-milling) starch addition, and flour chlorination were flour variables that affected the height of angel food cakes. Increased height resulted from reduction of flour particle size, not from increased starch damage. They also concluded that angel food cake flour must be chlorinated to exhibit significant improvement in cake size from post-milling particle size reduction. Excellent cakes have been made from batters in which part of the flour was replaced by wheat starch.

The most critical ingredient is the egg whites. Cakes can, of course, be made with egg whites separated from fresh eggs, but this practice is rare or nonexistent in large-scale manufacturing. It may be possible for the baker to procure refrigerated fresh whites in bulk if a supplier is nearby, but it is much more common for wholesale bakers to use frozen or dried forms of this ingredient.

Both frozen whites and dried albumen can be used without compromising product quality, and they are about equally satisfactory, provided they have been properly processed from raw materials of good quality. Whiteness of the crumb, crust appearance, texture (closely associated with specific volume), and flavor are all strongly influenced by the functional properties of the egg white ingredient. Thinner egg whites whip to optimum volume quicker than more viscous whites do, and the final density of the foam is generally less, but thicker whites give a more stable foam. Frozen and dried egg products sold in the U.S. have been pasteurized to eliminate Salmonella, and this causes them to have a slightly different response than fresh eggs to the beating process. The only time this should be a problem to a technologist is when a cookbook recipe is being translated into industrial conditions. In the laboratory, formulas should be developed with plant-type ingredients, of course, so there should be no difference in egg performance.

Water is not usually mentioned as an ingredient in angel cake formulas if fresh egg whites or thawed frozen whites are used. In some cases, bakers will add up to 10% of water to liquid whites during whipping in order to get greater moistness and closer grain in the finished cake. If the crusts are becoming too brown during baking, addition of a slight amount of water to the eggs may lighten the color. A reduction in cake volume usually results when water is added, and the likelihood of collapse increases. If dried egg whites are used, the amount of water specified in the recipe is generally about the quantity needed to reconstitute the powder to the original moisture content of the liquid eggs. Dried egg whites must be completely reconstituted before the other ingredients are added to the mixer.

Whipping aids are important both in home preparation and in commercial manufacturing. They improve the foaming properties of albumen, so that a firmer foam with finer grain can be prepared quicker, i.e., with less whipping. One of these foam improvers is cream of tartar (potassium hydrogen tartrate), an acidic salt that adjusts the pH of egg white to a level conducive to maximum solubility of the proteins and reduces their denaturation during whipping. Without it, the foam does not reach its maximum potential specific volume, and the cake is coarser in texture. Cream of tartar also decolorizes the flavone pigments of flour, leading to a brighter crumb color, although much of the color change is due to the effect of this additive on bubble size. Smaller, more uniform bubbles lead to a whiter appearance of the cake crumb even when the intrinsic color of the batter is not changed.

Acids such as acetic, malic, tartaric, and citric also improve cake structure and color, but none seems to be as effective as cream of tartar for improving cake volume, so the latter substance is the additive of choice, though the cost factor has to be considered. Cream of tartar has the additional advantage of affecting flavor very little. About 1% to 2% (commonly 1.5% to 1.75%) based on weight of the liquid egg whites is the accepted range of addition for cream of tartar. Eggs that have been in cold storage a long time have whites that are more alkaline than those of fresh eggs, and albumen separated from them may require increased amounts of acidifier if they are to give cakes of good volume and color. Vinegar is said to have been used satisfactorily as a source of acetic acid for improving the whipping properties of egg whites in the preparation of angel food meringues. Surfactants that have been suggested and used for improving the whipping properties of dried eggs are sodium desoxycholate, triethyl citrate, triacetin, sodium oleate, and oleic acid. Some of these uses may be covered by patents or restricted by regulations.

Flavor variations of angel food cakes are rather limited because of the need for avoiding fatty materials. The customary or traditional flavors are vanilla and almond extract, while imitation rum flavor is sometimes used. Cocoa can be used, although it tends to decrease cake volume. Food colors are acceptable, provided they are not suspended in a lipid vehicle. Natural colors such as beet extract can also be used, but consideration must be given to the changes in hue that may occur at the pH of angel food batter.

Procedures

The traditional procedure for making angel food cakes is a two-stage operation. In the first stage, the egg whites are whipped with or without part of the sugar, then the rest of the sugar is mixed in with continued beating. The second stage consists of folding in the flour with the absolute minimum of disturbance needed to distribute this ingredient throughout the meringue. The reason for this sequence of additions is to keep to a minimum the bubble-collapsing effect that results from contact of the flour lipids with the protein solutions forming the cell walls of the meringue component.

A procedure in wide commercial use specifies whipping the egg whites (containing cream of tartar and salt) at medium speed until the foam begins to exhibit a soft structure. Then, about 50% of the total sugar is added slowly while whipping is continued. When the meringue forms a wet peak, the flavor ingredients, the remainder of the sugar and the flour are distributed over the surface while mixing is continued intermittently at the lowest possible speed. As soon as uniform distribution of ingredients is achieved, mixing is discontinued.

Angel food cake is very sensitive to changes in preparation method. There are not many other bakery products that have so many critical points in their processing. The beating of egg whites is the first critical step. If aeration is insufficient, the cell walls do not extend to their full capacity during baking and suboptimal volume and texture result. On the other hand, excessive whipping of the egg whites causes coagulation of some of the proteins so that the bubble walls lose extensibility and may break during baking. This leads to a reduction in cake volume and a coarser crumb. The whipping end point can be judged by appearance of the foam or by measuring the specific volume of a sample of the batter.

Different samples of egg white will vary in optimum specific gravity of their foam, but it is commonly recommended that they be beaten until a specific gravity between 0.150 and 0.170 gm per ml is reached. Overbeaten egg whites generally expand excessively during the initial period of baking, then shrink noticeably just before baking is completed. The specific gravity of the finished batter (with flour and all other ingredients) will typically be in the range of 0.26 to 0.32 gm per ml, although satisfactory cakes can be prepared with batters outside this range.

Angel food cakes are customarily baked in tube pans, not only because better heat distribution is permitted by this design, but also because the central tube supports the cake, preventing collapse at the center. Acceptable cakes can be baked in other types of pans. Obviously, the pans must not be greased and, in fact, must be entirely free of fatty materials.

Satisfactory angel food cakes can be baked over a rather wide range of baking temperatures. Consensus of experts seems to be that the best cakes result from baking at the highest temperature and for the shortest length of time consistent with the shape and weight of the cake. Examples are about 350° to 360°F for 1.5 lb cakes and 375° to 400°F for 12 oz cakes.

Batter weight, batter specific volume, pan type, pan size, baking time, and baking temperature are interrelated. Although it is essential to bake the cake long enough to firm up the internal structure and color the top crust, baking should not be continued longer than necessary because this drives out moisture and leads to an undesirable harsh texture.

The effect of altitude on cake baking times, which is primarily due to the difference in boiling point of water at different atmospheric pressures, is particularly noticeable when making angel food cakes. Higher altitudes lead to greater expansion during baking, and the cake becomes more tender. It may collapse, however, if expansion is excessive. Crust color becomes lighter at higher altitudes because the batter surface does not reach a high enough temperature. Some compensation of the effect of altitude can be accomplished by changing the ratio of sugar and flour in the formula.

Procedures for making a meringue layer base for tortes and two angel food cakes follow. Many details on formulating and processing angel food cakes can be found in "Formulas and Processes for Bakers" (Matz 1989).

Meringue Layer for Tortes

(1) Whip about 50 to 55 parts of liquid egg white, 25 to 30 parts of sugar, and 1 part cream of tartar until a stiff but not dry foam is obtained.

(2) Fold into the meringue 16 to 20 parts fine granulated sugar that has been mixed with 4 to 5 parts pastry flour.

(3) Scale 15 to 16 oz of the batter into greased pans 9 inches in diameter by about one-fourth inch high. Smooth the top.

(4) Bake at 290°F for one hour, more or less. The goal is to get dryness without much browning. Immediately turn out the layer on to paper. Cool for at least 30 minutes before using as part of assembled torte.

(5) These layers are often made with finely chopped (use conditions leading to minimum oil release) almonds or cashews, about 15 to 20 parts being coated with the flour then with the sugar described in part 2 above.

Foam Type Angel Food Cake

(1) Beat 4 lb liquid egg white to prescribed density.

(2) Add gradually, while mixing, 2 lb granulated sugar, 0.5 oz salt, 1 oz vanilla extract, and cream of tartar or other acidic material as required.

(3) Fold in 2 lb granulated sugar, 2 oz corn starch, 1.4 lb cake flour.

Continuous Mix Angel Food Cake

(1) Make into a slurry 30 lb liquid egg white, 30 lb granulated sugar, acidic ingredient, 4 oz salt, 6 oz vanilla extract (or equivalent), 9 lb cake flour, and 2.5 lb corn starch.

(2) Mix and beat in pressurized continuous equipment.

Patents have been issued for single-stage angel food cake mixes that contain chemical leavening components plus a hydrocolloid to increase the gas-retaining properties of the batter. For an example, see Shea (1969).

Trouble Shooting

One of the common causes of failure of angel food batters to perform properly is the presence of fats and oils. It is well known that lipids cause collapse of protein-based foams. Unsaturated fats seem to be somewhat more injurious than saturated triglycerides. Mineral oil and cholesterol do not have any appreciable effect. Even barely detectable traces of liquid triglycerides (food oils) will lead to significant decreases in volumes of the foam and of the finished product.

A common source of fat is egg yolk, which can contaminate egg whites when fresh eggs are being broken and separated for use as ingredients, but commercially frozen whites or dried albumen from reputable suppliers are remarkably free from yolk contamination. Inadequately washed bowls and agitators are often found to be covered with an invisible film of fat, and for this reason, many plants that make angel food have concluded that it is advisable to reserve a special set of utensils for these cakes. An extensive list of causes of failure of angel food cakes can be found in the previously cited publication of Matz (1989).

CAKES MADE WITH FOAMS OF WHOLE EGGS OR EGG YOLKS

Effects of Whole Eggs

The previous section described how egg whites can be whipped into light and stiff foams that have fairly good stability and can be made into cake batters that set up during baking to give foods having very pleasant eating qualities. Cakes can also be made from whole egg (or egg yolk plus egg white) foams. Sometimes these are categorized as "sponge" cakes.

Because of the egg yolk lipids they contain, foams made with whole eggs are softer (more fluid) than egg white foams, they are considerably denser, and they tend to collapse or drain quicker. Cake batters made from these foams are always denser than typical angel food batters. The crumb (internal structure) of the baked product may appear to consist of very fine bubbles and the cake may have a silky, tender texture but it does not closely approach the softness and resiliency of an angel food cake. Many formulas for foam cakes based on egg yolks also contain added shortening, which further changes the structural qualities of the batter and the cake. Some of these cakes require the separate addition of egg white foam and egg yolks (or whole eggs). If this maneuver is required, it must be conducted with great care, as excessive contact of the yolk lipids with the egg white foam can result in a failure to obtain adequate quality in the finished cake.

It is a fairly common practice to include chemical leavening substances in formulas for these cakes, although acceptable products can be made without them. As the amount of flour is increased and the egg content decreased, chemical leaveners become more essential, and we start to enter the class of layer cakes. The latter products will be discussed in detail in a subsequent chapter.

Pound Cakes

Pound cakes, sponge cakes, and chiffon cakes are examples of products based on whole egg foams and containing shortening. They are always denser than good quality angel food cakes.

Pound cakes were traditionally based on the very old formula of one pound each of flour, butter, whole eggs, and sugar. Modern formulas have departed considerably from this archetype. Most present-day commercial versions include at least some baking powder, although the amount is usually kept considerably less than in layer cakes so as to retain the relatively dense and firm but tender and somewhat crumbly texture expected in pound cake. Other changes often encountered in modern formulas are decreases in eggs and butter accompanied by an increase in sugar to give the sweeter, more tender cake preferred by many consumers. Very frequently, some or all of the butter is replaced by vegetable shortening to decrease the ingredient cost and improve shelf life. This change also improves the grain and increases the specific volume if the vegetable shortening is of the emulsifier type.

An example of a simple modern formula for pound cake that does not include baking powder is: 25 lb cake flour, 8 lb emulsifier type shortening, 28 lb sugar, 1 lb Salt, 12 lb liquid whole milk, 17 lb whole eggs, and 9 lb butter. Whipping improvers (except emulsifiers) and acidifying agents are not used. The quality of the eggs has a marked effect on the volume, texture, and flavor of the finished product. Cake flour meeting the usual standards is suitable for pound cake. Ingredient specifications are usually not as critical for pound cake as they are for many other types of cake.

The usual procedure for making the batter requires the following steps: (1) Cream the flour, shortening, and butter; (2) Add the sugar, salt, and milk and mix well; and (3) Gradually add the eggs while mixing, and beat for about five minutes. There are many modifications of the mixing procedure that have particular advantages under special circumstances. Excellent pound cakes can be made by continuous mixing processes.

Some minor variations that can be made in the formula without appreciably affecting the quality include replacement of part of the sugar with high fructose corn syrup or invert sugar syrup, addition of a small amount of glycerine to increase moistness of the crumb, increasing yolks or egg whites to secure desired textural improvements, use of reconstituted dry milk instead of fresh whole milk, and addition of baking powder. Many flavor variations are possible. The most common flavors are vanilla with a trace of citrus, although in some cases the citrus (usually lemon) flavor predominates. Butter flavor should be added if the shortening is predominantly vegetable. Excellent chocolate-flavored cakes can be made by replacing some of the shortening with chocolate liquor (melted) or by adding a good grade of cocoa. Marzipan cakes contain 5% to 8% of almond paste, or combinations of almond paste and kernel paste. Nutmeats can be added alone or in combination with almond and kernel pastes to give interesting flavor and texture variations. Spices, particularly cinnamon and/or nutmeg, are additions that are quite compatible with the base flavor. Raisin or currant pound cakes are well-liked in some regions. Table 13.1 gives starting formulas for some of these varieties.

Most customers expect pound cakes to be distinctly yellow in color. A sufficiently intense color may be hard to achieve with eggs of relatively light pigmentation. In these cases, use of one of the fat soluble yellow or orange colors might be considered.

Table 13.1. FORMULAS FOR POUND CAKE VARIETIES[1]

	Variety				
Ingredient	Regular	Navy	Raisin	Chocolate	White
Cake flour	25.5	25.0	20.7	24.4	25.1
Sugar	30.2	29.5	24.8	31.1	21.3
Emulsifier shortening	0	14.8	14.5	0	16.3
Butter	17.2	0	0	9.3	0
Liquid whole eggs	16.0	14.8	14.5	14.3	0
Liquid egg whites	0	0	0	0	16.3
Liquid whole milk	10.7	15.0	10.3	13.0	20.0
Salt	0.4	0.9	0.8	0.7	1.0
Raisins	0	0	14.4	0	0
Bitter chocolate	0	0	0	7.2	0

[1] Percent, as is basis. Formulas do not include flavors such as vanilla extract, which should be added "to taste."

Major variations of the pound cake formula include: (1) The Genoise, a specialty of French cuisine, calls for melted and clarified butter as the shortening ingredient and requires a complicated mixing technique involving beating of the whites before they are mixed with the yolks and—in separate steps—with the flour and butter. This overrated cake can easily be replaced by pound or sponge layers whenever it is called for as a component of pastries; (2) White pound cakes require only egg whites instead of whole eggs, and might be regarded as angel food batters to which butter or other shortenings have been added; (3) Certain types of fruit cakes are based on batters having a considerable resemblance to pound cake mixtures. These cakes, which contain a relatively small proportion of batter and a large amount of nuts and glacè fruit, generally are compatible with the dense, rather solid pound cake texture, although other types of cake batters can also be used successfully. Fruitcakes will be discussed in more detail in a later section.

Sponge Cakes

Sponge cakes can be regarded as a part of a recipe continuum that starts with the original formula for pound cake and continues through sponge cake and chiffon cakes to layer cakes. Some bakers call any kind of cake made with whole egg foams a sponge cake, and there is a certain logical justification and tradition behind this nomenclature, but the classification followed in this chapter is thought to be more informative. It is very common to find baking powder or soda plus some acidic ingredient in sponge formulas, and the shortening content is less than in a pound cake (sometimes none).

A formula for sponge cake that does not contain shortening or baking powder is 32.1% granulated sugar, 20.0% liquid whole eggs, 26.5% cake flour, 21% liquid whole or skim milk, and 0.4% salt. For maximum volume, the eggs can be beaten separately, the sugar, milk, and salt mixed in, and then the flour folded in with minimum agitation. If baking powder is to be used, it should be added in the final stage. Satisfactory results can generally be obtained with a one-stage mixing procedure, employing the wire whip at high speed to aerate the batter. An emulsifier must be added obtain proper volume development.

Flavor varieties are the same as those suggested for pound cake. Sponge cakes perform very well as the basis for jelly rolls, lady fingers, tortes, berry shells, and the like. Five formulas for sponge cake varieties will be found in Table 13.2. The wheat-free version does not have typical sponge cake texture and is very sensitive to processing variables.

Chiffon Cakes

Chiffon cakes are similar to angel food cakes in that leavening occurs mainly as the result of whipping the egg whites to a low density foam. In addition to egg whites, flour, and sugar—as found in angel food batters—chiffon cakes contain egg yolks and added fat, the latter characteristically in the form of vegetable oil rather than plastic shortening. Ingredients comprising the batter (shortening, flour, etc.) are mixed separately from the foam ingredients, then these two parts are combined by folding the batter into the foam. Sometimes the foam is folded into the batter, depending on the type of results the formulator wishes to obtain. "Chiffon" was the name given by the originators to the completed mixture before baking, but it is now applied to the cakes as well.

Table 13.2. FORMULAS FOR SPONGE CAKE VARIETIES[1]

Ingredient	Variety				
	Regular	Chocolate	Butter	Wheat free	Jelly roll
Cake flour	21.3	15.4	19.0	0	30.9
Sugar	25.6	26.1	30.3	30.7	25.8
Salt	0.7	0.7	0.8	0.4	0.6
Baking powder	0.2	0.2	0.6	0	1.9
Liquid whole eggs	35.3	35.8	15.2	42.3	12.0
Liquid egg yolks	12.5	12.7	15.2	0	6.1
Butter	2.2	1.8	7.5	0	0
Salad oil	2.2	1.8	0	0	0
Unsifted rice flour	0	0	0	18.0	0
Nonfat dry milk	0	0	0	8.6	0
Dutched cocoa, 10% fat	0	5.5	0	0	0
Invert syrup	0	0	0	0	5.1
Water	0	0	11.4	0	17.6

[1] Percent, as is basis. Formulas do not include flavors such as vanilla, lemon, or almond extract, which should be added "to taste."

Baking powder is often used to improve the oven spring in chiffon cakes, but the structure and volume are primarily due to the foamed egg ingredient. A typical formula, expressed in percent of batch weight, is: 10.7% egg yolks, 10.7% salad oil, 32.0% egg whites, 0.4% salt, 16.0% granulated sugar, 14.0% cake flour, 16.0% powdered sugar, and 0.2% cream of tartar.

The egg whites, cream of tartar, and salt are whipped until a soft foam is developed, then the sugar is added and beating is continued until a soft peak is obtained. The egg yolks are whipped in separate equipment until they are thoroughly blended and aerated. The egg yolk and oil mixture is carefully folded into the meringue using minimal agitation. The sugar and flour are sifted together and then folded into the eggs. If baking powder is to be added, it goes in with the flour.

Although chiffon cakes may be used in many of the same combinations suggested for pound and sponge cakes, the greater difficulty of making them and their somewhat coarser and less resilient structure reduces their utility in these items. Flavoring preferences are similar to those for sponge cakes, although orange and lemon chiffon cakes seem to be the most common varieties in retail bakery sections of supermarkets. Chocolate-flavored chiffon cakes are also well accepted.

The recommended temperatures for baking sponge cakes average about 350°F. Scaling weight, pan conformation, and batter characteristics will determine the baking time, but as a first approximation, allow 40 minutes for tube cakes, 20 minutes for sheet cakes, and 30 minutes for loaves.

CHEESECAKES

There are many varieties of cheesecakes. Some are light, some are heavy. Most are baked, but the refrigerator type is not baked. A few in a side and bottom crust of cookie dough, others are deposited in pans with greased and crumbed sides and bottoms, while others are baked without any crust. Some contain fruit or are topped with fruit after baking, others are topped with sour cream, a few neither contain fruit nor include toppings. Some contain no flour, but many formulas require flour as a means of establishing a lighter, more porous structure in the cake. Most cheesecake recipes demand the preparation of an egg white foam as the basic structural component but some of the heavier types do not require this step.

Cheesecakes of the type being discussed here, seldom if ever include chemical leaveners or yeast. The cheese used in most bakery-produced cheesecakes is bakers' cheese, which has a rather smooth, white, small curd of mild flavor and dry appearance; its moisture content will be close to 75%. It is by no means the same product as creamed cottage cheese that cannot, in fact, be made into a typical cheesecake. There is a dehydrated version of bakers' cheese that is often found to be satisfactory as an ingredient for cheesecake—it must be rehydrated before use, of course. Some formulas require cream cheese, an entirely different material that gives a rich, almost greasy, cake of solid texture and good flavor. Neufchatel cheese has been suggested as an ingredient; it contains an intermediate amount of fat, about 23%, which enables it to replace cream cheese in some recipes. Occasionally, one will encounter a specialty product that includes significant amounts of cheddar cheese or the like, primarily to give a flavor variation.

Cheesecake is usually baked in pans that are at least two inches deep. With normal scaling weights, this should leave enough free space above the deposit for the cake to expand without rising over the rim. Cheesecakes should be baked at low temperatures, never above 350°F. Many recipes call for oven temperatures in the range of 315° to 325°F. The reason for baking in a slow oven is that use of higher temperatures can lead to unbaked centers (crust forms before the center solidifies) and may cause excessive expansion during baking with resulant shrinkage and cracking during and after cooling. Steam batch baking is often recommended, and it certainly greatly reduces the chance of encountering the defects that have been mentioned, but is seldom necessary if the cake can be baked in an oven that can depended upon to hold below 350°F. Another tactic that can be tried if shrinkage and cracking are problems, is to use double pans to decrease the rate of heat flow into the cake. The formula below, attributable to Voorhees (1955), is instructive because it has several features common to many of the recipes for lighter-type cheesecakes containing flour.

Snow White California Cheesecake

(1) Place in cooking vessel and start at low heat:

    19 lb 8 oz Granulated sugar
    12 lb 12 oz Water
    9 oz Meringue stabilizer

(2) Place 12 lb liquid egg whites in mixer, install whip, but don't start mixer yet.

(3) Cream the following at medium speed until smooth. Keep bowl well scraped.

    30 lb bakers' cheese
    6 oz salt
    4 lb 8 oz bread flour
    1 lb 8 oz corn starch
    6 oz dried lemon juice
    3 lb nonfat dry milk

(4) To the step 3 mix, add the following ingredients gradually, scraping bowl frequently. Mix until smooth.

    9 lb liquid egg whites
    3 lb vegetable oil
    9 oz vanilla

(5) To the step 4 mixture, incorporate well 3 lb hot (180°F) water.

(6) When adding the hot water, start egg whites (stage 2), whipping on medium or high speed. Check syrup (stage 1) to ensure that it will be boiling across the surface by the time egg whites have been whipped to a wet peak. Pour the hot syrup slowly into the meringue while whipping at a reduced speed to avoid splashing. Continue whipping until a wet peak is again achieved. Now, fold batter (stage 4) into the meringue by hand until no streaks remain. Be sure to pick up the material at the bottom of the bowl when folding. The meringue should suspend the entire mass of batter.

(7) Scale at 29 oz into high-walled 8-inch pans that have been greased and lined with devils food crumbs. Bake at 300° to 325°F with the pans resting in water bath. Cheesecakes are finished when they feel firm to the touch and the top surface is even. Turn cakes out of the pan as soon as possible after baking. They will be snow white in color and fairly light in texture.

Chocolate cheesecake and marble cheesecake (chocolate batter and vanilla batter swirled together) are popular varieties. The following formula and procedure give a dense, very rich type of chocolate cheesecake. Beat 423 parts (grams, for example) cream cheese until it is smooth. Add 121 parts of sugar and 2 parts of vanilla extract, and beat until very smooth. Add 211 parts of semisweet chocolate which has been melted over a water bath and then cooled to between 90° and 100°F. Add 93 parts of fresh whole eggs in 3 or 4 portions (or gradually, in a thin stream) while mixing. Beat well after each addition. Add 150 parts sour cream and again beat until smooth. Deposit this batter in a crumb crust (chocolate wafer or devils food crumbs mixed with sugar and shortening are good choices), bake for one hour at 375°F with minimum radiant heat. The hot baked cake will be soft, not resilient. Cool the cake in the pan on a rack until it has reached room temperature. Serve cold with whipped cream.

Unbaked cheesecakes are preferred by some consumers and are made by many foodservice operators because of the ease of preparation. The recipe that follows requires no cooking and yields a kind of dense, rich cheesecake. Like most such combinations, it does not include any flour. Mix 6 lb cream cheese, 4 lb bakers cheese, 3 lb powdered sugar, lemon flavoring to taste, 1 oz salt, and 2 oz single-strength vanilla. When a smooth consistency has been reached, add 8 oz liquid egg yolks and blend well. Then add 24 oz liquid whole milk and mix to uniformity. Press the batter firmly into pans, with or without crumb lining. Smooth the tops and refrigerate until served.

Other types of refrigerated cheesecakes depend upon gelatin to help form the structure. These kinds often specify the preparation of a custard-like mixture as a preliminary step. They often rely on whipped egg whites, and perhaps whipped cream, for establishing a light, airy structure.

It is obvious from the formulas and the type of ingredients used that cheesecakes are quite perishable. Refrigeration will preserve them in acceptable condition for a few days, but freezing is required if a longer shelf life is required. Many varieties of cheesecakes do not freeze well without some formula modification because fluid tends to separate upon thawing and cracking may occur.

Distribution of most types of cheesecakes through normal bakery route channels is generally not feasible, but there is a large volume sold under national brand names through freezer sections of supermarkets. Cheesecakes prepared in supermarket bakery departments enjoy a reasonably good sale although surveys have indicated these products are of highly variable quality.

Baked cheesecakes are often topped with sour cream mixtures. A topping of this type can be prepared by mixing together 2 quarts of thick sour cream, 4 oz of sugar, and 1 oz of vanilla. A more complex formula with greater stability consists of 3 lb cream cheese mixed with 12 lb of sour cream stabilized with a mixture of 3 oz 150-bloom gelatin, 3 lb sugar, and 3 lb hot (180°F) water that is poured on to the cheese and sour cream and blended well (but not whipped). The lukewarm topping is poured on to the cake.

There are many quality problems that can occur during the manufacture of cheesecake. The following list includes a few of the most common defects, with suggestions for remedial measures.

(1) Batter is lumpy. May be due to using cheese that is too cold or to adding eggs and other liquids too rapidly. Corrective measures are obvious. Allow the cheese to warm to room temperature before incorporating it, and add eggs and other liquid ingredients slowly.

(2) Cake collapses during baking. May be due to baking the cake too long; correct by reducing the baking time. May be due to using an oven temperature that is too high; try reducing the oven temperature or baking the cake on a steam bath. The formula may contain too much egg white; try reducing the amount of meringue folded into the batter.

(3) Cake cracks or dries out and shrinks during cooling or distribution. These defects may be due to overbaking and, if so, can be alleviated by reducing baking time or by increasing the moisture content of the mix.

FRUITCAKES

The wide range of fruitcake types makes it difficult to generalize on the characteristics of these products. Some are made almost entirely of fruits and nuts, with just enough batter added to make the pieces cling together in the shape of a cake, while others have more batter than fruit. Expensive or gourmet fruitcakes often contain only traces of batter, the manufacturer seeming to regard this component as, at best, a necessary evil. On the other hand, fruitcakes made to be sold in slices as a snack item often contain as much batter as the consumer can be expected to tolerate.

Table 13.3. FORMULAS FOR FRUIT CAKES

	Variety				
Ingredient	Dark	Light	Army	Eco-nomy	Jubi-Jubilee
--Batter--					
Cake flour	11.9	15.0	13.0	13.3	12.6
Sugar	8.0	16.3	9.1	12.4	13.2
Butter (shortening*)	6.6	13.5	11.4	7.0*	7.7
Molasses	5.5	0	3.7	0	3.3
Liquid whole eggs	0	12.4	11.4	7.7	0
Liquid egg yolks	2.7	0	0	0	4.5
Liquid egg whites	0	0	0	0	5.9
Water	0	0	0	8.6	0
Salt	0.3	0.2	0	0.4	0
Spice mixture	0.3	0	0.7	0	0.3
Heavy cream	0	9.0	0	0.6	0
--Fruit and nut mix--					
Candied cherries	14.2	2.7	8.5	0	4.0
Candied pineapple	7.1	0	8.5	12.5	0
Candied citron	10.7	4.8	8.5	11.0	0
Raisins	4.5	21.2	17.0	11.0	14.0
Pecan pieces	0	4.8	0	0	31.5
Chopped figs	7.1	0	0	0	0
Almond pieces	14.0	0	0	7.5	0
Other ingredients	(1)	(2)	(3)	(4)	(5)

Notes: (1) 7.1 cider; (2) 0.1 grated lemon peel; (3) 8.2 mix of 16 parts cider, 4 grated orange rind, and 3 lemon juice; (4) 8.0 candied citrus peel; (5) 3.0 peach liqueur.

Many fruitcake batters are made with no leavener, relying on the gas brought in with the creamed shortening and eggs to give the minimal rise deemed necessary. In fact, some of the high fruit content products are not expected to show any expansion, and the manufacturer has not designed his containers to accommodate the effects of a leavening system. In this section, products both with and without leavening will be discussed, because the effect of gassing in the crumb is generally very minor in any case.

As implied above, recipes for fruit cake run the gamut from about 90% fruit and nuts to about 90% batter, and some of them specify very complex mixtures of fruits, nuts, and spices. The batter can be a very dark version with a high content of flavorful ingredients or a rather light colored batter which allows the flavor of the fruits and nuts predominate. The formula below is a fairly simple version of fruitcake.

(1) Soak the following fruits overnight in 2 qt sweet apple cider after cutting the cherries and pineapple into small cubes: 16 lb sultana raisins, 8 lb candied cherries, and 8 lb candied pineapple.

(2) Cream the following for about 10 minutes: 5 lb brown sugar, 4 lb shortening, and 2 oz salt.

(3) Add 5 lb liquid whole eggs to the above, then mix about 15 minutes.

(4) Mix in 6 lb bread flour until just well blended.

(5) Add the fruit and 5 lb pecan pieces to the above in a minimum mix step.

(6) Bake at about 300°F for about 90 minutes per pound of scaling weight, or as required to get the needed color and consistency.

Table 13.3 contains five formulas for fruit cakes; amounts are percent or parts (as is basis), and flavors such as vanilla, lemon, or almond extract are not included.

COOKIES

Cookies can be made by methods that involve air incorporation. Most cookies of this type are processed by deposit or spritz techniques. Certain types of macaroons are good examples of cookies requiring the preparation of an egg white foam—the recipes for macaroons cover a wide range of methods and formulas and some of them use egg white only as a binder. The following is one example of the type, which though it may not be typical, will illustrate some of the salient points. The formula and process are: (1) Mix 100 parts liquid egg whites and 175 parts granulated sugar at high speed until a thick foam is formed; (2) Add 100 parts finely ground almonds and 12 parts rice flour and mix at high speed until stiff; (3) Deposit through a 3 mm diameter tube on to parchment or a floured oven band. If the cookie spreads too much, increase the rice flour.

A somewhat similar formula, which does not specify a two stage mix but has a long enough total mixing to incorporate some air, is as follows: (1) Place 180 parts granulated sugar, 120 parts finely ground almonds, 20 parts vanilla sugar, and 100 parts liquid egg whites in the bowl of a vertical mixer and mix at moderate speed for about ten minutes; (2) Deposit through a tube of about 3 mm diameter on to a greased oven band.

There are hundreds of different recipes for brownies, and most of them specify some chemical leavener, but they can be made with an egg foam base, as in the formula and procedure given below.

(1) Beat 5 lb liquid whole eggs, 1 oz vanilla extract, and 10 lb fine granulated sugar until a light foam is developed.

(2) Blend 3 lb 8 oz cake flour into the meringue.

(3) Melt 6 lb margarine and add to it 3 lb bitter chocolate (shaved).

(4) When the margarine and chocolate are completely blended and liquefied, add them carefully and slowly to the egg, flour, and sugar mixture. Avoid overmixing.

(5) Add 6 lb coarsely chopped pecans by folding in until uniform distribution has been accomplished.

(6) Fill batter into a well-buttered cookie sheet or bun pan and bake at 300°F. Cool and frost with chocolate icing, then cut in two-inch squares.

Crumb cookies are a rather uncommon variety that, in the version below, combine the leavening effect of egg white foam with that of "prefabricated air" from cake crumbs.

(1) Beat 12 lb liquid egg whites, 8 lb granulated sugar, and 0.25 lb salt to a light peak.

(2) Fold 32 lb light cake crumbs, 4 lb medium fine coconut, and 10 lb granulated sugar into the above. Also add vanilla or other flavoring at this point.

(3) Mix the combined ingredients thoroughly and blend in: 4 lb white raisins or dark currants.

(4) Deposit at about one ounce on slightly greased pans and bake at 350°F until set.

Butter spritz cookies (a deposit type) rely on the air-entrapping qualities of egg for much of their texture. As a rule of thumb, deposit cookies will be made with about 35% to 40% sugar, 65% to 75% shortening, and 15% to 25% liquid whole eggs, based on the flour being 100%. The flour should be from soft wheat, unbleached, with 8% to 8.5% protein content, and 0.35% to 0.40% ash. It should have a minimum viscosity of 40°McM, and a spread factor of 79 or 80. Some of the formulas include chemical leaveners, but the following (Smith 1972) does not.

(1) Mix 310 lb granulated sugar, 360 lb shortening, 120 lb butter, 30 lb invert syrup, 3 lb salt, and 2 lb vanilla in a horizontal mixer at fast speed for two minutes.

(2) Add 120 lb liquid whole eggs to the above and mix 4 min at fast speed.

(3) Then add 600 lb medium strength flour to the mixer and blend for five minutes at slow speed.

A recipe for deposit cookies with a more definite whipping step is:

(1) Make a fairly light creamed mass of 10 lb 4 oz cake flour, 1 lb 6 oz nonfat dry milk, 1 lb invert syrup, 2 oz salt, and 7 lb margarine. Also add orange, lemon, or vanilla flavor at this point.

(2) Whip 2 lb 8 oz liquid egg whites and 2 lb 14 oz granulated sugar as in making meringue, then fold into the creamed mass of step 1.

(3) Place into pans or on band using deposit machine. Bake at about 375°F.

OTHER PRODUCTS

There are several confectionery products that do not rightly fall within the purview of this book but that should be mentioned here for the sake of completeness. The density of taffy, molasses crisps, marshmallow, and some other candy varieties is reduced and their texture and appearance modified by the incorporation of air bubbles. This is accomplished either by whipping a liquid mixture capable of holding bubbles (as in marshmallow preparation) or by repeatedly folding and stretching a hot low-moisture syrup (sometimes containing added structure-forming ingredients) as in making taffy and molasses crisps. Generally, no kind of chemical leavening agent is added to these products. This can be contrasted with peanut brittle, which is aerated by the addition of sodium bicarbonate just before the molten mass is spread out to cool. Marshmallow will be discussed in greater detail in the chapters on formulations and procedures for adjuncts.

BIBLIOGRAPHY

ANON. 1988. Putting on the glitz. Bakery 23, No. 8, 30-32, 38-40, 43

ANON. 1991. Whipping agent replaces egg white. Prepared Foods 160, No. 3, 62

ATKIN, L. 1966. Egg products and how to use them. Proc. Am. Soc. Bakery Engineers 1966, 248-254

BARMORE, M. A. 1935. Baking angel cake at any altitude. Colo. Agr. Expt. Sta. Tech. Bull. 13

BARMORE, M. A. 1936. The influence of various factors, including altitude, in the production of angel food cake. Colo. Agr. Expt. Sta. Tech. Bull. 15

BENNION, E. B., and BAMFORD, A. S. T. 1975. The Technology of Cake Making. Leonard Hill Books, London

BORDERS, J. H. 1968. A look at foam cakes. Bakers Digest 42, No. 4, 53-55, 66

DUNN, J. A., and WHITE, J. R. 1939. The leavening action of air in cake batter. Cereal Chem. 16, No. 1, 63-66

GAINES, C. S., and DONELSON, J. R. 1985A. Effect of flour protein content on angel food and high-ratio white layer cake size and tenderness. Cereal Chem. 62, No. 1, 63-66

GAINES, C. S., and DONELSON, J. R. 1985B. Influence of certain flour quality parameters and postmilling treatments on size of angel food and high-ratio angel cakes. Cereal Chem. 62, No. 1, 60-62

HARREL, C. G. 1960. Air-leavened bakery products. In Bakery Technology and Engineering. Edited by S. A. Matz. AVI Publishing Co., Westport, CT

HOOD, M. P., and LOWE, B. 1948. Air, water vapor and carbon dioxide as leavening gases in cakes made with different types of fat. Cereal Chem. 25, 244-254

MATZ, S. 1989. Formulas and Processes for Bakers. Pan-Tech International, McAllen, TX

SHEA, R. A. 1969. Single-stage angel food cakes. U.S. Pat. 3,459, 560

SMITH, W. H. 1972. Biscuits, Crackers, and Cookies, Vol. 2. Magazines for Industry, NYC

VOORHEES, E. M. 1955. Cheese cake production. Proc. Am. Soc. Bakery Engineers 1955, 304-314

chapter fourteen

CHEMICALLY LEAVENED BREAD AND ROLLS

INTRODUCTION

If we exclude yeast raised bread and rolls from consideration, most baked products depend upon sodium bicarbonate to provide a substantial part of the gas that expands the dough or batter during baking. Such products form the largest percentage of cakes and cookies prepared in the home and in bakeries. They also account for a considerable proportion of the quickbreads such as muffins, pancakes, and soda biscuits made at home and in commercial bakeries, and for a sizable share of the fried goods (doughnuts, etc.) market. This chapter will deal with quickbreads and similar products while the following chapter contains discussions on cakes, cookies, and other chemically leavened sweet goods.

The previous chapters included discussions of some products that were made with small amounts of leavening chemicals, but these ingredients were added mainly for the purpose of establishing an accumulation of bubbles for later enlargement by expanding water vapor or atmospheric gases. The products described in the following pages are much more dependent upon chemical leaveners for their structure and final volume.

CHEMICAL LEAVENING SYSTEMS

Effects of Air, Water Vapor, and Carbon Dioxide on Volume

In previous chapters, mention has been made of the relative contribution of gases from the air, water vapor from ingredient moisture, and carbon dioxide from chemical leaveners or yeast to the expansion of bakery foods in the oven and during other steps in their processing. It is certainly very clear that neither chemical leaveners nor yeast fermentation is necessary for generating a substantial increase in volume. There are two early papers (Dunn and White 1939; Hood and Lowe 1948) that discuss in a straightforward manner the relative effects of the various leavening agents in the expansion of bakery products.

It was shown by these investigators that a pound cake batter containing no chemical leavening ingredients, but well aerated as a result of the air bubbles formed when the egg-containing batter was beaten, gave cakes with specific volumes related in a linear fashion to the specific volumes of the batter. When batter was prepared by a method involving minimal air incorporation (by mixing at low speed with a dough hook, etc.), the final cake exhibited a volume increase of a little more than 40% compared to the batter. This contrasted with a volume increase of over

100% for the control cake. When the control cake mixture was placed in a vacuum chamber and stripped of the entrained air by repeatedly reducing the pressure, the batter did not expand during baking. In fact, it contracted slightly. The vacuumized batter could be brought back almost to its original performance by beating it in the mixer until it regained approximately the original specific volume; although this finished cake had good volume, there were indications of excessive gluten development, as might be expected.

By performing calculations based on the gas laws, the experimenters determined that about 52% of the total expansion observed in this pound cake batter, prepared under optimal conditions, was due to the expansion of entrained air as the temperature rose from 78° to 208°F. The remainder of the expansion (48% of the total) must have been due to the expansion of water vapor in the tiny air cells formed during mixing. In the vacuumized batters, the water vapor did not exert an expanding effect because it did not have preformed air cells to inflate. It is not intended to imply here that the relative proportions of these two forces (air and water vapor) will be exactly the same under other conditions.

Another investigator showed that of the 1,120 ml to 1,620 ml increase in volume during baking of angel cakes made according to the conditions of his experiments, only 350 ml could be attributed to the expansion of entrained air, the remainder being due to water vapor. It has also been observed that very few, perhaps no, gas cells are formed when chemical leaveners react. Instead, the carbon dioxide seems to enlarge air cells already present but does not form new bubbles.

When the increase of volume in batters made with three kinds of shortening and with chemical leaveners was studied, it was found that the major increase in cake volume was produced by carbon dioxide, followed by water vapor and air, in that order. The effectiveness of water vapor in the presence of air in leavening cakes varied with the type of fat used—it was most effective with oil, intermediate with butter, and least effective with hydrogenated lard. The effectiveness of carbon dioxide in expanding batter was greatest with hydrogenated lard formulas and least with oil formulas.

To sum up the results of these studies, both carbon dioxide from soda and water vapor from ingredients are quite effective in expanding cake batters, but there must first be a system of air bubbles formed during mixing or at some other stage during preparation before these two agents can exert an appreciable inflating force. Although the results are not conclusive on the point, it appears that neither size nor distribution of the bubbles is particularly important so far as the degree of expansion is concerned, though these factors undoubtedly have considerable effect on the appearance and texture of the cake crumb.

Characteristics of Chemical Leavening Systems

Chemical leavening systems depend upon the release of gas from a carbonate or bicarbonate that has been added to the dough or batter as an ingredient. This subject is discussed in great detail in the chapter on leavening systems. Only a very brief resume of the preceding material will be given here.

Nearly all modern formulas use sodium bicarbonate as the source of carbon dioxide, though some cookie recipes call for ammonium bicarbonate. Sodium bicarbonate, baking soda, is readily soluble in water, and when dissolved it dissociates into sodium ions and bicarbonate ions. Some of the bicarbonate ions then dissociate into hydrogen ions, carbonate ions, and carbon dioxide. The relative proportions of these ions in any given dough or batter will depend upon their concentration in the aqueous phase and on their partial pressure in the gas phase contacting the aqueous phase. Adsorption of the ions on the dough constituents and their reaction with these substances will also affect their absolute concentrations and their relative proportions in any system. Other, more obscure, factors may operate to modify the expected amounts of the ions.

This apparently complex situation is simplified for the baker by the observation that the quantity of gas released from a dough or batter containing a given percentage of baking soda is largely controlled by the pH of the aqueous phase and by the temperature. The pH is, in turn, dependent upon the acidic ingredients in the formula and the amount of sodium bicarbonate that has been added. The pH of the wet mixture can be decreased by adding chemical leavening acids or acidic food ingredients such as molasses or buttermilk. Leavening "acids" should be understood to mean chemicals that reduce the pH of the dough, even though they may not meet completely all of the points in the usual definition of an acid. Some examples are cream of tartar, sodium acid pyrophosphate, sodium aluminum phosphate, and monocalcium phosphate. The leavener chapter should be consulted for details on speed of reaction of these various leavening acids and the baking powders made with them.

It is risky to specify combinations of leavening acids for any given product without doing confirmatory tests. To remove some of this uncertainty, formulators often use "acid creams" obtained from bakery suppliers. These contain mixtures of leavening acids with diluents and other additives. They are often entirely satisfactory as the source of leavening acids for a new or improved product, at least in the initial stages of development.

The acidic effect of other dough ingredients must be taken into effect when designing a leavening system. Most acidic ingredients, such as molasses, some corn syrups, fruit juices, and cultured milk products, will exert their effect early in the preparation procedure. The effect of pieces of acidic fruit (e.g., raisins) is not as clear-cut and is likely to be very nonuniform throughout the dough. If possible, such fruits should be added to chemically leavened doughs late in the mixing process; this is the normal procedure anyway.

In preparing material balances for yield calculations and costing purposes, the loss of weight due to the evolution of carbon dioxide and its escape from the product during baking must be taken into account.

Adjusting Formulas for Differences in Altitude

The formulas given in this book, and nearly all recipes published for the benefit of commercial and home bakers, are calculated to give optimum results when the dough or batter is baked near sea level. When prepared at higher altitudes, the formulas may have to be adjusted to compensate for the lower atmospheric pressure. The question of below sea level usage is of very little importance since the percentage of the U.S. population living in areas below sea level is extremely small.

Often, satisfactory results can be obtained merely by adjusting the leavener. For more sensitive formulas, flour and eggs may have to be adjusted. Water quantity is also a possible variable. Correction factors suggested in the following paragraphs should be taken as only general guidelines.

Most recipes perform adequately at least up to an altitude of 2,000 ft, although this is not to say that identical results will be obtained at sea level and at, say, 1,500 ft elevation. At an altitude of 2,000 ft, a reduction of 15% in baking powder is advisable, and a further reduction of about 7.5% of the original amount should be made for each additional 1,000 ft of altitude until 8,000 ft is reached, when the reduction will reach a total of 60%.

Whole eggs and egg whites should be increased as the altitude increases. At 2,500 ft, the content of these ingredients should be raised by 2.5%, with increases of 2.5% for each 1,000 ft of altitude until 7,500 ft is reached, above which the adjustment will be 15%. Flour content should also be adjusted upward as the altitude of the bakery increases. At 3,500 ft, increase the flour by 2.5% and add to this about 1.7% for each additional 1,000 ft of elevation. Water must be increased to compensate for flour increase.

The crusts of products tend to be paler when they are baked at higher altitudes. An increased amount of radiant energy in the later stages of baking can help overcome this defect, but is not always feasible, of course.

FUNCTION OF INGREDIENTS

Although it is possible to prepare chemically leavened breads that have many superficial resemblances to their yeast-leavened counterparts (Irish soda bread is an example), it is obvious even to the untrained observer that most bicarbonate-leavened goods differ in internal structure and texture from fermented products. A baking powder biscuit would never be confused with a dinner roll. These differences are not entirely due to the leavening system, however, because flour characteristics and processing conditions also play important roles. The type of flour traditionally specified for chemically leavened products differs from the ingredient bakers are accustomed to use in white bread and rolls.

In most chemically leavened foods, the protein of the flour is inadequate in quantity and quality to support dough expansion to the extent it occurs in bread. This is one of the reasons soda-based products are of higher density than regular bread. Nonetheless, flour is not an inert ingredient in chemically leavened products, even in those cookies where a "dead," solid-appearing, non-extensible dough with very limited moisture content would seem to rule out any participation of gluten in the fine structure of the mass. Flour quality and amount must be understood as important factors affecting product characteristics in any formula in which this ingredient is used. Different types of chemically leavened products may require very different types of flour for optimum finished product quality. Therefore, careful attention should be given to the specifications of flour recommended for each particular use.

Sugars are present in most formulas for chemically leavened bakery foods. In addition to their obvious function as sweeteners, sugars have a tenderizing effect on the crumb and promote coloring of the crust. Sucrose is less effective in coloring the crust than are reducing substances such as invert sugar, glucose, and maltose. The situation is different than in yeast-containing doughs, where the invertase of yeast rapidly converts sucrose to glucose and fructose. No such action is observed in cakes, cookies, and pies, where the sucrose remains nonreducing throughout the oven stage and does not participate in the non-enzymic Maillard browning reactions.

Sugars retain moisture in the crumb of soda goods and therefore retard texture staling which, in these products, is related more to dehydration than to starch retrogradation. In this respect, glucose and fructose are more effective on a weight for weight basis than sucrose because of the lower molecular weight of the monosaccharides that tends to give them a higher water activity. Some sugar alcohols such as sorbitol and glycerol are particularly effective in retaining moisture and maintaining desirable texture in the crumb. Bennion and Bamford (1973), reporting English practice, say that "glycerine is normally used in flour confectionery" at the following levels: 12.5% of the fat in cakes, 10% of the egg in sponge goods, 10% of the egg whites in royal icing, 6.5% of the flour in powdered goods, and 2.5% of the liquid in fermented goods. This is considerably more of the ingredient than is normally used in U.S. practice, where it is rather rare to find glycerol specified in a formula.

Sugars compete with other ingredients for the water present in a dough. As the sugar content is increased, hydrocolloids will not be able to take up water to as great an extent and will not develop their maximum viscosity. This means that batters with more sweeteners will often be more fluid—this may not apply when high viscosity corn syrups are added. Generally, less air is entrained under these conditions, but the batter can be conveyed and whipped with lower energy expenditures.

An important function of the shortening component of batters is to entrap air during mixing—the "creaming" effect. Not only do these air bubbles contribute directly to the leavening effect, they help to control grain size by serving as foci for gas evolution. Microphotographs of batters have shown that the air bubbles in creamed mixtures appear to be inclosed in films of fat. Shortening also tenderizes the crumb and may contribute to the flavor of the product. Emulsified shortenings increase the amount of sugar and water that can be incorporated in the batter and thus contribute to the tenderness and resistance to staling of the finished product.

Fats and oils contribute to the "shortness" of baked products, hence their generic name. Shortness is widely understood as meaning tenderness, crumbliness, or crispness as contrasted with elasticity, springiness, or toughness. There is a level of addition beyond which fat will not be fully incorporated in the dough, and the product will look and feel greasy, a condition which generally, but not always, is considered undesirable. Crust glossiness, which often accompanies high levels of shortening (especially if the shortening has a low melting point) is a desirable feature in many cases.

The flour gluten in chemically leavened products seldom contributes to the formation of large air cells or thin cell walls. These deficiencies are remedied to some extent by using eggs in the formula. Egg whites are more effective than yolks or whole eggs in this regard. Proteins of the albumen in combination with gluten form the vesicle wall and facilitate the entrapment of air during mixing. In angel food cake, the entire vesicle structure originates from the air enclosed by the egg white during vigorous whipping. Of course, the vesicle walls in angel food cake are supported during baking by proteins from the flour that is added after the eggs have been whipped. Egg white proteins do not have sufficient mechanical strength, when in thin films, to withstand oven expansion or handling abuse after baking and cannot contribute the texture expected in many bakery products. These attributes must be obtained from flour.

Eggs also contribute flavors which are sometimes undesirable. Yolks are an important source of color and they contribute important emulsifying and tenderizing actions. Eggs are frequently the only ingredient that can compensate for an excessively weak flour or low amount of flour in cakes.

Milk accentuates crust color as a result of its content of lactose and protein. Skim milk, when it has been properly heat-treated before drying, appears to exert a toughening effect on the crumb, no doubt as a result of its high content of casein. With whole milk, this effect is offset by the lubricating or tenderizing action of milkfat. Milk (fresh or dried) which has not been heat treated to denature the serum proteins, will weaken gluten. The flavor contributed to a baked product by milk is generally considered desirable, and the lactose is slightly effective in retarding staling.

Water is, of course, a very important ingredient in chemically leavened bakery products, its quantity being critical in many formulas and its quality often having an effect on finished product characteristics. Formulas for chemically leavened goods generally contain less water than those for bread even when the moisture content of enriching materials is considered as part of the ingredient water. A small deviation in the amount of water added to a dough will often have dramatic effects on characteristics of the finished product, chemically leavened goods having less tolerance to these changes than more extensible doughs. Quite a few formulas for sweet goods will not call for any separate water addition, relying for the necessary moisture on liquid egg, fluid milk, and syrup components. A formulator should not hesitate to add additional water when adapting recipes which have previously relied entirely on ingredient moisture content. Often, significant and unexpected improvements can be obtained by this approach.

SODA BREADS

Most soda breads are similar to hearth loaves of yeast-leavened bread in shape, size, and usage, but are made from chemically leavened doughs. Their texture and flavor are considerably different from their yeast-leavened counterparts. Irish soda bread is a typical example of this group. There does not seem to be much demand for such products, but their novelty appeals to some consumers. There is also the ethnic attraction, which is not restricted to the Irish, because other nationalities have similar products.

For best results, a moderately strong flour is required, and the dough is developed much like the dough for yeast-leavened bread and rolls. Soda breads are often baked as hearth breads, usually in round (hemispherical) shape with a cross slashed in the top to promote oven spring. Some loaves described as "soda breads" are made from batter-like mixtures deposited in loaf pans. Home preparation is the rule; small retail bakeries may occasionally make this product as a novelty, but broadscale commercial distribution does not exist in the U.S.

A version of chemically leavened loaf bread was developed by the author for use in feeding the military, but there were no successful commercial adaptations of this development (Matz *et al.* 1961). Irish soda bread and allied products will be discussed here primarily as an introduction to the subject of quickbreads.

Table 14.1 gives five formulas for varieties of soda breads, and more detailed directions are included in the following subheads.

Table 14.1. FORMULAS FOR SODA BREAD VARIETIES[1]

Ingredient	Irish soda bread	Treacle	Raisin	Wheaten	Premium
Flour, all purpose	63.5	52.1	52.1	10.4	30.6
Sugar	0	2.9	0	0	10.6
Salt	0.8	1.2	0.9	1.0	0.3
Sodium bicarbonate	0.6	0.9	0.8	0.7	0.3
Buttermilk, cultured	33.0	27.2	36.9	32.5	30.9
Molasses	0	15.7	0	0	0
Butter	2.1	0	0	0	2.2
Cream of tartar	0	0	0.6	0.3	0
Currants	0	0	8.7	0	16.9
Whole eggs, liquid	0	0	0	0	7.4
Baking powder	0	0	0	0	0.8
Whole wheat flour	0	0	0	55.1	0

[1] Percent, as is basis.

Buttermilk Bread

Formulas for soda bread seldom call for baking powder. Sodium bicarbonate is, of course, required, and buttermilk is very often used as the acid-reacting component of the leavening system. Chemically leavened breads tend to be insipid, and the flavor contribution of buttermilk is helpful. When buttermilk is not included in the formula, cream of tartar is added to react with the soda.

Following is a very simple formula that makes an acceptable small loaf of bread, or the dough can be made into rolls. Blend together 6 lb to 7 lb all-purpose flour, about 1 oz soda, and 1 oz to 1.5 oz salt. To the dry mixture, add 3 lb 7 oz liquid buttermilk. After the milk has been blended in at low speed, increase to medium speed and mix until a light elastic dough is formed. Divide into 12 oz pieces and round them into smooth loaves with a diameter of about 6 inches. Cut a cross on top. Place on a greased baking surface. Bake at 350° to 375°F until a firm dark brown crust has formed.

Irish Soda Bread

Although "Irish" soda bread is the name commonly applied to the product to be described, no doubt other nationalities could claim similar recipes, if they wanted to. Following is a representative formula, of which there are many variations extant. This version does not include buttermilk.

Irish Soda Bread

(1) Blend together: 37.5 lb bread flour 4 lb dry skim milk, 4 lb granulated sugar, 4 lb shortening, 8 oz salt, and 3 lb baking powder.

(2) Add 32.3 lb water to the dry ingredients and mix at slow speed until the liquid has been incorporated. Then develop well at second speed.

(3) Add 18 lb raisins (preferably pre-soaked in part of the water held back from step 2) and mix at low speed just long enough to distribute the raisins.

(4) If desired, about 1 lb of caraway seed can be added with the raisins.

(5) Scale 19 oz pieces, round them up and place them in greased 7 inch layer cake pans. Make a cross-shaped knife cut in the top. Allow to rest about one-half hour before baking the loaves at 375° to 400°F.

Boston Brown Bread

This is a variety of chemically leavened loaf that is often steamed rather than baked. It is typically cooked in a tubular container, vertically oriented. Tin cans are sometimes used. At least one manufacturer had national distribution of Boston brown bread in a hermetically-sealed tin can. It is said this product was customarily eaten at a meal with baked beans. The formula given below is for a baked variety of the item, but it would probably perform satisfactorily if steamed. It will be seen that the preparation does not include a dough development step, and the finished product has a texture resembling muffins more than it does yeast loaves.

Boston Brown Bread

(1) Blend together at low speed: 10.5% corn meal, 13.2% all-purpose flour, 14.6% medium rye flour, 0.4% salt, 0.3% soda, and about 0.7% baking powder.

(2) Mix the following ingredients together before combining them with the step 1 blend: 5.4% seedless raisins, 6.0% chopped walnuts, 37.1% buttermilk, and 11.8% dark molasses.

(3) Combine step 1 and step 2 blends and mix well.

(4) Scale at about 5 lb 4 oz in well-greased bread pans measuring 4.5 inches by 14 inches. Bake in a 325°F oven for about 90 minutes or until done by the usual indications of piece firmness and dryness. This formula can also be baked as muffins or as small loaves.

Chemically Leavened White Bread

The introduction to this section mentions a chemically leavened bread developed for use in military rations as a direct replacement for yeast-leavened white bread. When this product is prepared as described in the cited patent, it bears a fairly close resemblance to loaves of regular white bread, but it is distinguishable from it in some respects. It is considerably closer in flavor, texture, and appearance to traditional white bread than is the average loaf of Irish soda bread or any other commercial or home-made chemically leavened bread. The patent also describes preparation of a dried flavoring material to be added to the dough. The flavor could be further improved by including a percent or so of ethanol in the dough.

A representative formula for the dry mix of this patent is: 70 parts flour, 5 parts shortening, 5 parts sugar, 7 parts glucono-delta-lactone, 3 parts baking soda, 5 parts nonfat dry milk, and 5 parts of a special flavor preparation. To this mix is added about 50% of its weight of water, and mixing is continued until the gluten is well developed. Dough pieces are scaled, formed, and baked without fermentation or rest periods. The original formula was intended to be baked as loaves, but hearth varieties are possible.

Other Bread Varieties

There are several refrigerated dough products that bake into simulations of yeast-leavened breads, bread rolls, cinnamon rolls, bread sticks, pizzas, etc. These are the types of doughs packaged under internally generated pressure in composite cans. They are sold at retail from dairy cases in supermarkets. All of these items are chemically leavened. Resemblance of the baked products to their yeast-leavened counterparts is superficial, at best, but apparently they satisfy many consumers.

QUICKBREADS

The category of quickbreads encompasses that vast array of muffins, soda biscuits, scones, and the like products, all made from chemically-leavened doughs or batters and not sweetened to the extent necessary to qualify them as dessert items. The author realizes there is an ambiguity in this classification that allows some overlap between these products and the ones discussed in the following chapter.

Soda Biscuits

Baking powder biscuits seem to have been developed in the U.S. many years ago and to have achieved their greatest popularity in the southern states where some families serve them at every meal. When properly made they have a great deal of appeal, with their light brown crusts, and tender crumb, and the rather bland flavor which makes them useful carriers for gravy, jams, and sandwich components. In the last 10 or 20 years, biscuits have been promoted nationwide by franchised fast food restaurants and have been enthusiastically accepted by millions of new customers

Biscuit doughs and processing methods for them differ greatly from the formulas and procedures used for yeast-leavened dinner rolls. Biscuit doughs are not developed to any great extent and, in many cases, the directions specify mixing only until the ingredients are incorporated. For some rolled and cut biscuit doughs, however, it appears that a slight amount of development does occur and is desirable.

The following recipe is representative of those used for traditional baking powder biscuits. Sift together or blend 50 lb flour, 3.2 lb baking powder, 4.4 lb sugar, and 0.6 lb salt. Cut in or rub in 7.8 lb shortening, as in making pie crust. Add 34 lb of cold whole fluid milk, blending at low speed for the minimum time needed to get a homogeneous mixture. Avoid developing the dough. Roll out the dough to make a sheet three-fourths of an inch thick, and cut circles with a cutter 2.5 inches in diameter. Minimize dusting flour. Set the dough pieces close together in pans having edges at least an inch high. Pass a rolling pin over the surface to make the tops flat and even. Allow the dough pieces to rest for five minutes, then bake at 400°F. It is not customary to wash the tops.

Large scale commercial preparation requires modifications in the formula and procedure. Some factors affecting quality and production will be listed here (Poehlmann 1985 and others). Strong flour is definitely contraindicated. Cake flour mixed with pastry flour or with bread flour is often used. As strength of the flour increases, biscuit height will increase and width will decrease. The softer the flour, the more uniform the biscuit contours and the deeper the furrow around the middle of the break. Strong flours give a silkier but tougher crumb, while the interior of biscuits made with weak flours are generally crumbly, soft, and coarse. With some formulas, cake flours will give a very light crust color, which is not usually considered desirable. This can be offset by including milk solids or some other coloring agent in the formula.

All ingredients should be thoroughly wetted. Presence of chunks of shortening or dry lumps in the dough will obviously lead to nonuniform products. The dough should appear as a weak, soft, wet mixture that barely holds together. Such doughs pose many problems when handled on a production line, so some compromises with the quality ideal may have to be made. A certain amount of development will occur as the dough is sheeted out for cutting. This is generally not fatal to good quality biscuits, but if it is desired to avoid it, biscuits can be made by dumping scoopfuls of the batter on to a pan, these "drop biscuits" have irregular contours and rough tops. If it is necessary to reprocess a large amount of dough from the cutting operation, some decline in quality may occur from overdevelopment.

A moderate amount of shortening is required to cause the necessary tenderness of the crumb and crust. Lard has long been the favorite shortening for home use, but hydrogenated vegetable oils also work well. Butter or margarine is seldom used. Excess shortening dramatically reduces oven expansion. Between 10% and 20% (FWB) is often recommended, although somewhat more can be tolerated in most formulas. Lowering the absorption allows more shortening to be used, but there is no increase in tenderness if this trade-off is made, so there is no point to it.

A small amount of sweetener is required to relieve the blandness of this unfermented dough. Sucrose (cane or beet sugar) of fine granulation is preferred. Dextrose can be used, but syrups are thought to be detrimental to the texture. Dextrose is more effective than sucrose in darkening the crust. If the biscuit is to be consumed as a fruit shortcake, up to 15% of sugar is added. For regular biscuits, the sugar addition is more often in the range of 2% to 5%.

Although biscuits can be made without any milk products, there is a beneficial effect on flavor and crust color of adding a few percent of nonfat dry milk. Buttermilk solids can also be used. Egg products are never used in standard baking powder biscuits.

The leavening system is a critical feature in biscuits. Sodium bicarbonate is the source of gas, of course, and the finest particle size is preferred since there is only a limited opportunity for the substance to dissolve, in the short mixing and processing time used for biscuits. If undissolved soda particles remain in the dough at the time it is baked, yellow spots will result. The acid components are usually selected to give a two-phase gas release, i.e., they should be double-acting. Monocalcium phosphate monohydrate may be used because its acidifying action leads to a quick release of gas, giving aeration to the dough during mixing. Sodium aluminum phosphate or one of the slower acting forms of sodium acid pyrophosphate can be used to force the release of more carbon dioxide during bench work and baking. Although some other chemically leavened products rely on acidic ingredients such as molasses to cause initial gas production, the only ingredient commonly added to biscuit doughs that has this effect is buttermilk.

Yeast is never used in regular baking powder biscuits. Its flavor would be regarded as foreign to the expected taste by most consumers. Certain specialty varieties of dinner rolls somewhat resembling biscuits in outward appearance are made with yeast in addition to a chemical leavening system.

Ranges for the most common ingredient used in biscuits are (FWB): shortening 10% to 40%, sugar 2% to 15%, baking powder 4% to 6.25%, salt 1% to 3%, nonfat dry milk zero to 13%, and water 60% to 70%. Many variations are possible outside these ranges and with ingredients not listed. Raisins, chopped peppers, whole wheat flour, cheese, and the like have been suggested as characterizing ingredients, but biscuits made with these additives have never attained significant popularity.

Table 14.2 includes representative formulas for five varieties of baking powder biscuits.

Table 14.2. FORMULAS FOR BAKING POWDER BISCUITS[1]

Ingredient	Standard	Navy	Army	Buttermilk	Cheese
Flour	51.8	48.6	45.7	49.0	47.1
Baking powder	2.1	3.0	2.9	1.0	2.1
Salt	0.3	0.6	0.7	0.6	0.7
Shortening	8.6	12.1	13.3	12.0	10.5
Fluid whole milk	37.2	35.7	0	0	28.0
Fluid buttermilk	0	0	0	37.0	0
Water	0	0	30.5	0	0
Evaporated milk	0	0	6.9	0	0
Baking soda	0	0	0	0.4	0
Grated cheddar	0	0	0	0	11.6

[1] Percent, as is basis.

Processing is relatively simple. Although most types of mixers can be used, it is preferable to use a type that can form a uniform blend without developing the dough excessively. Control of temperature is important both to avoid "conditioning" the dough too much and to prevent premature reaction of the leavening system components. If possible, the dough should be kept quite cool, in the range of 55° to 60°F.

Once the dough has been mixed, delays in processing should be avoided. Make-up should be started promptly and continued until all the dough has been cut and placed in the oven. It is often desirable to sheet and fold the dough one time, even though such a procedure seems contrary to the principle that development should not be encouraged. It is possible to extrude the dough, then thin and smooth the sheet by passing it through two or more sets of sheeting rollers, cut it with rotating hexagonal dies, and convey it automatically to ovens. Although hexagonal biscuits have some disadvantages, the minimal scrap generated by this form of cutter is definitely a positive feature in mass production.

Biscuits can be baked very satisfactorily in many kinds of ovens, including band ovens. A chamber with uniform temperatures throughout is highly desirable since any variation from side to side will lead to misshapen biscuits.

Scones

The word "scones" is almost unknown in the U.S., while great quantities of the very similar baking powder biscuits are made commercially and in home kitchens. Scones are a common type of quickbread prepared in the kitchens and retail bakeries of the U.K. They are usually made from a considerably richer dough that that used for baking powder biscuits, they sometimes include currants, and they are occasionally made in a pie-wedge shape.

Following is one of many recipes that have been published for this food. Mix 5 lb sugar, 6 lb butter, 0.5 lb salt, 3 lb liquid egg yolks, and 1.5 lb nonfat dry milk until well blended. Then mix in 14 lb water. Finally, add 20 lb bread flour, 12 lb cake flour, and 1.2 lb baking powder and mix to a smooth dough. Scale the dough into 12 oz pieces and round them up. Roll out to a thickness of about 0.5 inch. Place these large circles in layer cake pans and cut into six wedges. Bake at 400°F. This makes a very rich scone.

Another type of rich bread roll from the U.K. is the Sally Lunn. This scone was probably made originally from a yeast-leavened dough, since it dates back at least to the late eighteenth century, but present-day versions are often made with baking powder. Formula and procedure are: (1) Cream 105 parts granulated sugar and 105 parts hydrogenated vegetable shortening, then add 150 parts liquid whole eggs and beat well; (2) Add 270 parts fluid whole milk; (3) Sift together 350 parts bread flour, 18 parts baking powder, and 4 parts salt; (4) Add the dry ingredients to the creamed mixture and stir just enough to moisten the dry ingredients; (5) Dump mixture into a shallow pan and spread out to give a layer about one inch thick; and (6) Bake at 400°F.

Some Sally Lunn's are baked on a griddle from dropped dough. Softer, less viscous batters work better for this cooking method. As an initial approach, trials can be made using one of the above formulas but with about 5% to 10% added water.

Muffins

In the U.S., consumers generally expect a muffin to resemble a cupcake in size and shape, but to be somewhat less sweet. Recently, specialty shops have been established to sell muffins that are considerably larger than those commonly offered before—some probably approach four ounces in weight. There are many muffin formulas that overlap cupcake formulas in terms of sweetness, but most muffins are slightly more breadlike in texture than cupcakes, i.e., muffins are more irregular in grain, more elastic and less crumbly, and less tender. "English" muffins are an entirely different type of product, of course, and, since they are made with yeast, they will be discussed in another chapter. Cupcakes are made from essentially the same formulas as layer cakes and so will be covered in the next chapter.

The doughs and batters used for muffins can often be baked in the form of small loaves, etc. Generally, the larger the piece size, the denser the crumb. Moistness of the interior also tends to increase with increasing size.

A few examples of formulas for quickbreads will be described in subsequent paragraphs. All sorts of fruit and vegetable pieces can be added to basic formulas to give more variety of choice to the consumer, to enhance the image of "healthfulness." or to provide other advantages. Dairy products (butter, cheese, yogurt, sour cream, buttermilk, etc.) can be used to improve the flavor and imply added quality. Spices and other flavoring materials give opportunities for differentiating new products from competitive items. Even meat ingredients such as bacon bits, sausage crumbs, cracklings, etc., can be use to upgrade these items. No doubt many other variations will occur to the reader.

Corn bread and corn muffins are very popular quickbreads. When recipes and examples of corn bread are examined, a wide variation can be seem in density, crumbliness, and sweetness. The archetype was the journey cake, johnny cake, or hoe cake, which consisted of nothing more than corn meal, water, and perhaps a little salt made into a thin patty and baked before an open fire, sometimes on a shovel or hoe blade. The result was hardly in accord with modern enlightened thought and sugar, leaveners, shortening, etc., were gradually brought into the formula to upgrade the product. Purists have been heard to complain that modern corn bread is just a layer cake with some corn meal added for flavor. Characterizing ingredients that are popular in various regions include whole kernel corn, chopped roasted pimientos, and chopped jalapeno peppers.

The recipe that follows is a middle-of-the-road type of plain corn bread that will be found acceptable by most consumers. Blend together thoroughly 16.1 parts flour, 20 parts corn meal, 7 parts shortening, 7 parts sugar, 2.3 parts baking powder, 14 parts liquid whole eggs, 0.6 parts salt, and 33 parts whole milk. Blend the flour, sugar, baking powder, salt, and cornmeal. Beat eggs slightly, then add milk and shortening. Dump the liquid into the bowl of dry ingredients. Mix until the liquid ingredients are distributed; don't try to form a cohesive dough. Fill a two-inch deep pan about half full or a little more. Bake at 425°F for 20 to 25 minutes.

Five more recipes for corn bread will be found in Table 14.3.

Bran muffins are very popular. They are regarded by many as a health-oriented food even though they are often quite sweet and contain only minor amounts of bran. The deep brown color, which is preferred, is obtained either by using a considerable quantity of dark molasses or by adding caramel color. Raisins are nearly always incorporated in the batter. This type of quickbread is seldom baked as loaves or cakes. The formula to be found in the next paragraph is an example that will yield muffins having intermediate levels of sweetness and bran flavor. It can be varied in obvious ways to obtain greater lightness or heaviness, more or less sweetness, etc.

Mix until completely blended 7% high fructose corn syrup (or honey), 3% dark brown sugar, 4% butter (or margarine), 3.5% nonfat dry milk, 0.3% salt, 5.8% liquid whole eggs, and 2.2% baking powder. Blend in, with minimum mixing, 35.2% water. Add 19.5% bread flour and 19.5% wheat bran and mix to give a smooth batter. Scale the dough into muffin or loaf tins, filling the cavities slightly more than half full. Bake at 375° to 400°F. If raisins or currants are to be included, add 10% to 20% (depending on the degree of richness desired) at the last stage of mixing.

Table 14.3. FIVE VARIETIES OF CORN BREAD[1]

Ingredients	Old time	Yankee	Hush puppy	Fritters	Texmex
Flour	14.2	16.0	0	24.6	13.5
Corn meal, yellow	0	20.3	52.8	4.0	23.7
Corn meal, white	24.8	0	0	0	0
Shortening	5.3	6.9	0	5.7	5.1
Sugar	0	7.2	0	3.0	0
Baking powder	0	2.2	0	0.7	0
Salt	0.7	0.6	0.8	1.1	0.7
Sodium bicarbonate	0.4	0	0.3	0	0.5
Liquid whole eggs	11.8	13.8	0	18.9	11.3
Buttermilk	42.8	33.0	15.1	12.0*	40.9
Water	0	0	20.2	0	0
Other (see Notes)	0	0	(1)	(2)	(3)

[1] Percent, as is basis. * Whole milk, not buttermilk.
Notes: (1) 10.8 finely chopped onion; (2) 30.0 drained canned corn kernels; (3) 4.3 of a mixture of 1 part dried minced onion, 3 parts chopped canned pimiento, and 1 part chopped jalapeno peppers.

Instead of bran, rye meal (one of the darker grades) can be used to make an interesting muffin. A small amount of caraway seeds should be included to give the "clue" that signifies rye bread to most consumers.

There are several muffin varieties made with slightly sweet batter and including large pieces of fruit or whole berries. The most common example is blueberry muffins. These can be made with fresh or frozen or canned blueberries. If the fruit is canned, it must be thoroughly rinsed to minimize "bleeding" of the dark juice into the crumb. This will occur to some extent no matter what precautions are taken. A representative formula is: Cream until light and fluffy 17 parts granulated sugar, 2 parts high fructose corn syrup, 13 parts butter, and 0.7 parts salt. Add 5.4 parts liquid whole eggs in several small portions, mixing well after each addition. Add 25.8 parts liquid whole milk, 34.1 parts cake flour, and 2 parts baking powder while mixer is turning, and blend to a smooth batter. Add 25 parts individually frozen blueberries and mix only enough to distribute uniformly. Scale into greased muffin tins or fluted paper cups, filling about half full. Bake at 375° to 400°F.

Lemon flavoring is often added to increase the piquancy of these products. Cranberries can be used as the fruit ingredient, add at slightly less than the proportion given for blueberries. These must be fresh or individually quick frozen cranberries. Pieces of apples, dates, figs, prunes, or mixed candied fruit (in small dices) are also possible ingredients.

Especially in recent years, the addition of one or more kinds of chopped vegetable to a muffin recipe has led to good consumer acceptance of the product. The flavor is less important than the health image and the novelty of appearance. The formula and procedure which follow can be used as a starting point. Many consumers will prefer a less sweet "health" muffin.

Veggie Muffins

(1) Cream until light 27.4 parts sugar, 13.0 parts emulsifier shortening, 0.3 parts salt, and 2.0 parts baking powder.

(2) Add gradually, while mixing, 11.5 parts liquid whole eggs.

(3) When a smooth mixture has been formed, add gradually while mixing, 27.5 parts of a mixture of half bread and half cake flour, and 18.4 parts liquid whole milk.

(4) When the above has been blended to a smooth batter, add chopped or diced vegetables such as carrots, spinach, turnips, pimentos, beets, or whole corn. The vegetables should be cooked (but not soft), thoroughly drained, and rinsed. The amount to be added depends on the effect desired, but would seldom exceed 10% to 15% in any case. Some coloring of the crumb by highly pigmented vegetables such as beets is inevitable. This is not necessarily a negative feature.

PANCAKES

In what is perhaps an oversimplification, pancakes can be regarded as quickbreads baked on griddles from flowable batters. The batters are not highly sweetened, although pancakes, crepes, and the like are almost always served with sweet syrups, toppings, or fillings. Large quantities of pancakes are made for frozen distribution and by foodservice bakeries. There is also a retail—and perhaps a foodservice—market for frozen pancake batter, but the total volume is thought to be small. Nearly all commercially baked pancakes are chemically leavened, although yeast-leavened or sourdough pancakes have some popularity for home preparation.

Crepes

Crepes are available in frozen form filled with fruit- or cheese-based mixtures and are often topped with sour cream or the like. Automatic devices are available for making crepes in quantity with low labor input.

Restaurant chains have been established to specialize in items based on crepes; they generally use semi-automated equipment. The following recipe is given as a starting point for the product development scientist.

Sift together 250 gm flour, 50 gm sugar, and 2 gm salt. Beat 150 gm liquid whole eggs to a light foam. Add 360 gm whole milk and 30 gm melted butter. Combine liquid and dry ingredients. Mix at medium speed until batter is smooth. Lightly coat the inside of a hot skillet with melted butter or margarine. Pour in about two tablespoonfuls batter (for a 6- or 7-inch skillet) into the hot pan, tilting it to spread the batter evenly over the bottom. Brown the crepe on one side, then turn it over to brown the other side.

Plain Pancakes

The following recipe is typical of those used in quantity preparation of pancakes. Prepare the following dry mixture: 38 to 39 parts patent wheat flour, 15 to 16 parts fine corn flour, 22 to 23 parts rice flour, 7 to 8 parts sugar, 4 to 5 parts nonfat dry milk, 1.5 parts salt, 3 parts baking powder, 0.9 parts sodium bicarbonate, and 6 parts vegetable oil. To the preceding dry mix add 25 parts liquid whole eggs and enough water to give a batter of pourable consistency. Bake on a hot, lightly greased griddle, until the upper surface starts to appear slightly dull, then turn and cook the other side.

This high quality formula has been greatly modified to suit various purposes, primarily to get longer batter life for restaurants that cook pancakes over a period of several hours from a single batch of batter. Addition of gums and other hydrocolloids to adjust and maintain batter viscosity is common.

Rolled pancakes filled with savory mixtures including some meat ingredients have been offered on the retail market in frozen form in the U.K. (Anon. 1987). These appear to be derived from Chinese cuisine and are more closely related to egg rolls than to conventional pancakes as they are understood in the U.S. The ingredients for these pancakes are said to be flour and soybean oil (presumably, also water). They can be fried in deep fat, skillet fried, or baked by the consumer immediately before serving.

CRUMPETS

Crumpets are customarily made from a yeast batter to which some soda is added just before they are cooked. Although similar in some respects to English muffins, crumpets will be discussed in this chapter because they seem to be allied to pancakes in method of preparation. The formula also has some similarities to that of pancake batter. Sales of crumpets in the U.S. must be practically non-existent, but it is an interesting variant for the breakfast market that ought to be given some consideration as a new product, especially in view of the great success of English muffins.

Crumpets have contours somewhat similar to English muffins, being round and thick, with straight sides. The batter is deposited in a ring or "hoop" placed on a greased baking surface. It is characteristic of crumpets that the toop shows large, irregular holes and this coarse uneven structure extends throughout the piece. They tend to be moist and flexible instead of crumbly. It is said they are served in England at tea time, often together with muffins.

Using a batter of the correct viscosity is essential to obtaining the typical texture and appearance. The batter should be "runny"—of low viscosity—but not so liquid that it escapes from the ring. Part of the trick is selecting the proper flour, and the right kind, according to some English references, is half bread flour and half all-purpose flour.

Here is a recipe for home use which can be easily adapted to laboratory or pilot plant scale. Add 2 lb flour to 1 oz yeast, 1 pint milk, 1 pint water, 1 tbsp salt, 1 tbsp sugar, and 4 tbsp salad oil. Liquid ingredients should be warm—about 90°F. Disperse the yeast in the water. Mix in the other ingredients. Beat batter vigorously, then allow to ferment in a warm place for about two hours, or until the surface is a mass of bubbles. Stir until the mass collapses. Dissolve 1 tsp of baking soda in about 8 oz to 10 oz of warm water—the amount to be adjusted to give the proper batter consistency. Stir this liquid into the fermented batter. Grease griddle very lightly with oil or butter, place the rings (typically 4 inches in diameter and 0.5 inch high) on the griddle, and fill the rings about two-thirds full of batter. In about 8 to 9 minutes, the top surface should be almost covered with holes. Then, turn the crumpets and cook for 2 to 3 minutes on the other side. Rings should be removed before turning the crumpets. The finished product will have very little color, being at best a light tan or medium yellow. The texture will be soft and elastic, almost gelatinous.

SNACK CRACKERS

Many kinds of snack crackers are being produced from yeast leavened doughs, but satisfactory results can also be obtained from chemically leavened formulas. Stewart (1984) states that the main advantage of bicarbonate leavening for these items is the added versatility that it provides. Snack crackers can be produced in much less time (typically 4 to 6 hr) as compared to about 24 hr for saltines made from fermented doughs.

Soda crackers rely on the many reactions taking place during fermentation for a large part of the dough conditioning that is necessary for proper machining and good product quality. Chemically leavened snack crackers rely on enzymes, emulsifiers, oxidants, and reducing agents to achieve these effects.

Proteases are the main enzymes used in snack cracker production. By weakening the gluten network, proteases convert dough from a stiff, "bucky" mass to a pliable, extensible material which can be processed readily.

Because fermentation by-products, which contribute much of the flavor to saltines, are absent in a chemically leavened snack cracker, the latter must rely on added flavoring materials such as cheese, onion, spices, garlic, and bacon. The flavor ingredients are either mixed in the dough or applied to the outside of the dough piece by sprinkling or spraying devices, either before or after baking. In most cases, some sort of oil (flavored or unflavored) is applied to the baked product to enhance appearance and texture.

Following is a snack cracker formula slightly modified from one in Stewart's article, percentages are on a batch weight basis: Sugar 3.85%, salt 0.60%, corn syrup 1.90%, malt syrup 1.28%, cracker meal 0.96%, shortening 3.85%, sodium bicarbonate 0.71%, monocalcium phosphate 0.30%, flour 66.37%, hot water 18.10%, protease enzyme 0.03%, and ammonium bicarbonate 2.05%. To the basic formula would be added characterizing flavors.

BIBLIOGRAPHY

ANON. 1987. Pancake rolls: the inside story. Food Manufacture *62*, No. 5, 56

BENNION, E. B., and BAMFORD, G. S. T. 1973. The Technology of Cake Making, Fifth Edition. Leonard Hill Books, Aylesbury, England

DUNN, J. A., and WHITE, J. R. 1939. The leavening action of air included in cake batter. Cereal Chem. *16*, 93-100

HOOD, M. P., and LOWE, B. 1948. Air, water vapor, and carbon dioxide as leavening gases in cakes made with different kinds of fats. Cereal Chem. *25*, 244-254

MATZ, S. A., MILLER, J. A., and MC WILLIAMS, C. S. 1961. Yeast-leavened prepared flour mix. U.S. Pat. 2,969,289

POEHLMAN, R. W. 1985. Biscuits. Proc. Am. Soc. Bakery Engineers *1985*, 126-134

STEWART, J. 1984. Snack cracker production. How to choose ingredients and methods. Bakers Digest *58*, No. 4, 20, 22, 24

chapter fifteen

CHEMICALLY LEAVENED SWEET GOODS

INTRODUCTION

In the preceding chapter, formulas and procedures for chemically leavened quickbreads and allied non-dessert products were discussed. Much of the introductory material in that chapter is applicable to the dessert products that will be covered in the following paragraphs, but there are some general considerations to be reviewed before the details of formulas and processes are covered.

COMPOSITION

The gluten proteins of flour serve as the basic structural elements in chemically leavened sweet goods as they do in nearly all other bakery foods, but chemically leavened products normally have a softer, crumblier, weaker texture and higher densities than yeast-leavened bread and rolls. These differences result mainly from the use in chemically leavened goods of relatively small amounts of flour, the prevalence of less extensible protein in the soft wheat flours that are customarily used in such products, and the lower amount of protein in these flours. Also, the briefer and generally less intense mixing procedure applied to the typical chemically leavened sweet dough is a factor in that it does not lead to optimal dough development.

The great advantage of chemically leavened sweet doughs is that they are easier to process. Also, products can be made that would be difficult or impossible to manufacture using yeast leavening. For example, levels of sugar can be used in layer cakes that would be extremely inhibitory to yeast activity. Delicate flavors that would clash with, or be overwhelmed by, the aroma and taste of alcohol and other products elaborated by yeast can often be better appreciated in chemically leavened products.

The kinds of carbohydrates specified as ingredients for dessert goods do not differ much from those used in quickbreads, but they are present in larger quantity. A greater proportion of the total carbohydrate content is present as simple carbohydrates (sucrose, glucose, and fructose) rather than as starch or fiber. Consideration must also be given to the chemical state of the carbohydrate—is it present in solid form or is it in solution? Generally, it is desirable to have the simple carbohydrates in a dissolved state before the batter begins to bake, but in many types of cookie doughs the presence of sugar crystals is needed to give the desired amount of expansion and flow during baking. It is seldom desirable to have sugar crystals present in finished products, however, since they will be perceived as a gritty contaminant by the consumer. In a few cookie varieties, this kind of texture contrast is actually expected, but in nearly all other products it would be regarded as a quality defect.

Sweet bakery products tend to contain more shortening than is present in quickbreads and rolls. The high fat content affects processing response of the doughs and batters, as well as the texture, flavor, and appearance of the finished products. The caloric density of the food is also increased, sometimes dramatically. Texture staling of sweet goods is different in rate and in mechanism from that of bread and rolls, partly due to the high fat content of the former and partly due to the lower content of starch. Other factors may also be operative.

Many kinds of chemically leavened products contain substantial amounts of eggs. Layer cakes depend upon egg foams to establish the basic structure of the product, although, of course, the gluten and starch coming in with the flour also play their role. There is an emulsifying effect of the yolk phosphatides that is very helpful in dispersing the shortening and maximizing its tenderizing effect.

GENERAL RULES FOR DEVELOPING FORMULAS

It is very common for teachers and speakers at workshops and seminars to hear the question, "What are the rules for balancing cake [or other product] formulas?" The truth is, there are no hard and fast principles that can be applied to formula design. Many authors have published guidelines for "formula balance" which may have some slight merit in specific situations, but these rules can be very misleading if uncritically applied. A selection of guidelines that have often been used in formulation studies of standard types of layer cakes will be given below, but the reader should understand that slavish adherence to these implied limitations is not good practice. The "rules" may have worked fairly well as very general guidelines in the past, but as new ingredients and new processing methods are developed, they tend to become outmoded. In any case, they are not laws of nature and should not be allowed to hamper creativity in new product development.

Keeping these caveats in mind, it can be said that, on a flour weight basis, sugar should fall in the range 110% to 160% (FWB) in yellow and white layer cakes and 110% to 180% in devil's food and chocolate layers. Eggs as liquid eggs should equal or exceed the shortening. Total water, including the moisture in eggs and milk, should exceed the amount of sugar by approximately 25% to 35%. Shortening should fall in the range of 30% to 70%. Soda should be 1.2% to 2% and salt 3% to 4% of the flour.

If the amount of sugar in a formula is increased, the egg content should be increased an equal amount. More shortening should be added when the percentage of eggs is increased. Additional water is usually not added when the formula contains dried milk, but if the formula water is not sufficient to equal the reconstitution water for the milk, add about 1% of water for each additional percentage of milk solids.

The following differences are usually found. Rich formulas need less chemical leavening because they incorporate more air during mixing. For the same reason, such batters will have lower specific gravity and they perform better at lower baking temperatures. Batters baked in large piece sizes require less water and less leavener than those baked at smaller scaling weights. Other types of bakery products are generally too diverse to allow meaningful rules to be established, but in some cases a few guidelines will be given in the following sections as typical formulas for the different products are discussed.

LAYER CAKES

The category of layer cakes comprises many kinds of chemically leavened sweet goods that are both economically and theoretically important. Similar formulas may be baked in tube, sheet, loaf, and cupcake pans as well as in the traditional circular layer cake pans. They will be discussed in detail in this section.

Examples of Cake Formulas

Most authors consider yellow layer cakes the basic type of this class, but it is probably more logical to allocate this position to the white layer cake since good, typical layer cakes can be made without egg yolks—the additional ingredient in yellow cakes. A formula for a very lean white cake is shown in Table 15.1. Although this recipe is important for establishing an approximate lower limit of "richness," cakes that include considerably larger amounts of enriching ingredients are desirable from taste and texture standpoints.

Table 15.1. FORMULAS FOR WHITE LAYER CAKES[1]

Ingredients	Basic lean	Rich	Dry mix
Cake flour	25.6	21.0	40.3
Sugar	25.6	29.5	40.0
Shortening, hydrogenated	11.2	--	--
Shortening, emulsified	--	11.5	12.2
Egg whites, liquid (or *dried)	16.0	16.0	2.9*
Evaporated milk (or *MSNF)	10.2	--	2.4*
Milk, liquid whole	--	20.0	--
Baking powder (or *soda)	1.6	1.3	0.52
Salt	0.6	0.7	0.87
Sodium acid pyrophosphate	--	--	0.14
Monocalcium phosph. monohydrate	--	--	0.53
Vanilla	qs	qs	0.14
Water	9.2	--	--

[1]Quantities based on batch weight as 100%

An example of a formula for a rich white layer cake, which may be considered typical, is also given. Of course, flavoring ingredients must be added to these formulas. For white layer cakes, the flavor is nearly always vanilla. About 0.5% of single strength vanilla extract is a common level of addition. It is essential to use high emulsifying shortening in cakes having a high proportion of sugar to flour, the so-called "high ratio" cakes.

The principal difference between yellow layer cakes and white layer cakes is that the former are made with whole eggs instead of egg whites. In other words, the "additive" to the basic white mix is egg yolk. Of course, the flavoring is sometimes different, as well, with yellow cakes more likely to contain a lemon or orange flavor, and perhaps some spice. A possible formula would be the rich white layer cake recipe given above modified by replacing the egg whites with 12% to 13% whole eggs and increasing the milk by about 2% to 3% to supply an optimum amount of moisture. The ingredients for a typical yellow layer cake that has been formulated to take full advantage of the special properties of whole eggs would be: 21.5% flour, 30.0% sugar, 11.5% emulsifier shortening, 12.5% liquid whole eggs, 22.4% liquid whole milk, 1.3% baking powder, and 0.8% salt.

In addition to the flavoring alternatives already mentioned, yellow cakes are particularly suitable for the addition of materials such as pumpkin, applesauce, and mashed bananas to give variants having unusual properties and good natural flavors. The preceding formula will support moderate additions of these characterizers without failing, but large levels of addition may necessitate increases in the amount of flour and/or eggs.

Cakes containing cocoa or chocolate liquor can be divided into the classes of devil's food cakes and chocolate cakes. The difference between the color and flavor of these two types is largely due to the higher pH of devil's food. This has a pervasive influence on the organoleptic characteristics of the finished product. Chocolate cakes may be considered as a basic cake recipe to which has been added cocoa (usually dutched) or chocolate liquor, while devil's food cakes also contain extra soda to give a crumb pH that is definitely on the alkaline side. This pH difference has a pronounced effect on the color of the cocoa pigments, leading to the "mahogany" color of devil's food cakes. It also affects the flavor and texture, but to a lesser degree. Table 15.2 gives a comparison of the ingredients in these two cake types.

Cocoa takes up a considerable amount of water when it it added to a batter. The formulator can compensate for this by adding moisture to the base recipe. As a rule of thumb, add water equivalent to 75% to 100% of the weight of the cocoa, deducting an amount equal to the lost absorption of any flour displaced by the cocoa. Most authorities recommend reducing shortening by an amount equal to the cocoa butter contained in the cocoa or chocolate liquor. It is doubtful if this change is needed for any but the most delicately balanced formulas. If it is desired to account for cocoa butter in this manner, consider chocolate liquor to contain 50% fat that has a shortening value one-half that of hydrogenated vegetable oils. Thus, addition of 10 parts chocolate liquor would call for a reduction of 2.5 parts shortening.

Table 15.2. FORMULAS FOR DEVIL'S FOOD AND CHOCOLATE CAKES[1]

Ingredients	Chocolate cake	Devil's Food Cake
Cake flour	18.8	17.3
Sugar	27.5	26.8
Emulsifier shortening	10.6	9.6
Dried skim milk	2.5	3.8
Chocolate liquor (bakers' choc.)	3.5	--
Baking powder	1.0	0.7
Salt	0.8	0.8
Whole eggs, liquid	15.0	9.7
Egg whites, liquid	--	2.9
Cocoa, dutched, 10-12%	--	3.8
Sodium bicarbonate	--	0.5
Water	21.1	24.1

[1]Quantities in percent, batch weight basis.

Gingerbread formulas can be based on the typical yellow cake formulation, although there is a wide range of opinion as to what constitutes an acceptable gingerbread. Some people like it very moist, coarse, dark, and heavily flavored, while others prefer a much milder version, almost like a spice cake with some molasses added.

Lebkuchen and European-style gingerbreads are unusual products that deserve at least a passing mention. Although yeast is not usually added, one stage of the production of lebkuchen traditionally involves a lengthy period of storage in the dough form that must inevitably result in some bacterial or yeast action, so in a sense they are a type of sourdough product. Gingerbread doughs would undergo less of this lay time than lebkuchen. A brief review of this interesting process follows.

The first dough, also called a "boiled dough" is made by mixing rye flour and old gingerbread with a hot mixture of corn syrup and invert sugar syrup. Mixers with sigma-shaped blades are used because this dough is very heavy and tough. After about 20 minutes of kneading, the boiled dough is filled into special boxes and stored in a conditioned area for between one day and three weeks. During this storage period, the dough temperature decreases from about 140°F to about 70°F. After this "maturation" the final dough is made in another mixer by adding the boiled dough to invert sugar syrup, soda, leavening acid, and spices. The final dough is extruded on to baking plates and baked at 365°F for about one hour, then removed by a turning device and cooled. The large pieces are sliced and packaged. The basic product can be modified by adding candied fruits or pieces of sugar to the final dough, or by filling the cake with jam or marzipan. Further details can be found in an article by De Muynck (1968).

Processing Chemically Leavened Sweet Goods

There are perhaps five major categories of mixing methods for chemically leavened sweet goods batters and doughs, although what constitutes a minor modification is a matter of opinion. The five categories are: (1) single-stage mixing, (2) two-stage mixing, (3) creaming methods, (4) the flour batter method, also called "blending," and (5) sugar-and-water method.

The single-stage mixing process is the simplest and consists of dumping all the ingredients into a mixer bowl and beating them with the wire whip or batter beater until they are thoroughly blended. Variations include adding the leaveners near the end of the mixing period, or adding the eggs near the end and reducing the mixing time considerably. The main advantage of single-stage mixing is the saving of time, the main disadvantages are the poorer grain and texture or reduced volume that may result.

Two-stage batters are mixed by placing all of the dry ingredients and part of the liquids into the bowl and mixing them until a homogeneous mass is obtained. The remainder of the liquid is then added, usually in increments, and mixing completed. Variations include changes in the stage at which the eggs are added.

The creaming process requires that the sugar and shortening be beaten until a light and fluffy mass is obtained. The eggs are added while mixing, then the milk and flour added alternately in small portions. Usually, a substantial amount of air is entrapped by this method with a consequent good effect on the grain of the finished product. It also tends to reduce gluten development.

The blending method requires mixing the flour and shortening until the flour particles are thoroughly coated. The remainder of the dry ingredients is then added and mixing continued until the blend is homogeneous. Finally, the liquid ingredients are added in portions and the combination completely mixed. By thoroughly dispersing the fat, a very fine and uniform grain is promoted. Coating of the flour with shortening tends to reduce gluten development. Contrary to expectation, cakes made by this method are often tougher and have lower volume than products made by one- and two-stage procedures.

In the sugar-water method, which is seldom used, all the sugar and half its weight in water are placed in a bowl and beaten for 30 seconds at low speed. Then the shortening, flour, dry milk, salt, and baking powder are added and mixing continued at medium speed for five minutes. Advantages claimed are better crust color, tenderer crusts, and improved volume.

Generally, layer cakes are baked at oven temperatures of 360° to 400°F. Cooler ovens tend to give cakes that are flat on top and exhibit excess shrinkage around their circumference. The cakes may also be too tender for icing application and easy serving. Higher temperatures often result in peaked cakes with cracked centers; in addition, more holes and tunnels develop in the crumb and the products may be tough and low in volume.

Trouble Shooting Cake Faults

Volume too low.—Can be caused by insufficient leavening action, in which case the remedy is obvious—add more soda, or if the crumb is too alkaline, add more leavening acid. If batters are allowed to stand too long or at elevated temperatures a theoretically adequate leavening amount may be defeated by premature reaction of the leavening ingredients. This can be true even when double-acting leavening acids are used. Undermixing can cause low volume because of reduced air incorporation. An excessively high oven temperature can set the structure before the full effect of the leavening gases has been exerted. Improper balance of ingredients or improper type of ingredients (especially the flour or shortening) can reduce the volume markedly.

Defects of texture.—Gumminess, doughiness, or chewiness are often the result of underbaking or improper cooling before packaging. Such faults are readily corrected by increasing the baking time slightly or by thorough cooling before wrapping. If these faults are due to improper formulation, the exact cause may be harder to spot although the percentage of water and the type and quantity of shortening should be checked first. Toughness may be due to use of too strong a flour, overbaking, inadequate amount of water, overmixing with consequent overdevelopment of the gluten, not enough sugar, inadequate amounts or wrong type of shortening, or insufficient batter for the pan size being used.

Defects of crust appearance.—Spotted crusts can be due either to nonhomogeneous batter or to bubbles in the crust. The former problem can be corrected by using a different sequence of mixing or more vigorous mixing conditions. The latter difficulty may be the result of unsuitable types of leaveners, batters that are too viscous, or excessive oven heat. Condensation of water droplets on the crust at any time will cause spotting. Small spots, yellow to dark brown in color, in the crust or crumb, are probably due to undissolved soda.

Bursting of the crust may be due to high baking temperatures, overmixing, too much flour, or flour that is too strong.

Pale crust color can result from a baking temperature that is too low. The oven as a whole may be set at too low a temperature or the heat distribution may be faulty, with inadequate radiant heat reaching the crust. Conversely, crust colors that are too dark may result from undesirably high oven temperatures or an excessive contribution of radiant heat, as compared to conducted or convected energy. In addition, pale crust colors can result from underscaling with resultant shielding of the top crust from radiant heat by the pan sides.

Too much sugar, and particularly too much reducing sugars such as are found in corn syrup, can cause darkening of the crust even though baking conditions are correct as judged by the condition of the cake's interior.

Coarse or irregular grain.—Tunnels and large holes at the bottom of the cake may result from excessive bottom heat during baking. An oven that is too cool can cause the grain to be too open. Wet streaks are often due to underbaking. Undissolved spots of material in the crumb are not always the result of undermixing, although this is the usual cause. Some ingredients, particularly dry milk that has been improperly stored, will form agglomerates that are nearly indestructible by the usual mixing procedures.

Both undermixing and overmixing can lead to a coarse open grain in the finished product. An excessively close or fine grain is more often the result of overmixing.

CUPCAKES

As might be expected, cupcake formulas bear a great deal of resemblance to layer cake recipes. A good quality devil's food cupcake can be made by using the following ingredient proportions and process: Blend for four minutes at low to medium speed 3 lb emulsifier shortening, 5 lb cake flour, 7 lb granulated sugar, 1 lb dutched cocoa, 3.5 oz baking powder, 1.2 oz sodium bicarbonate, 2.5 oz salt, 9.5 oz nonfat dry milk, and 3 lb water; then slowly add 1 lb liquid egg white and 3 lb liquid whole eggs and blend for about three minutes; add 2.8 lb water and 1.5 oz vanilla and mix four minutes on low speed; then scale the batter at 1.5 oz in standard cupcake tins and bake at 350° to 400°F.

It is good practice to let the batter stand for 15 to 30 minutes after it has been deposited into the pans. This lets any large air bubbles rise to the surface and burst, leading to more uniform expansion in the oven and fewer cripples.

The amount of batter placed in the cups has an important effect on the appearance of the cakes. Ideally, the baked cupcake should show a dome above the top of the tin but should not overflow the edges. A few grams difference in the weight of the deposit makes a great deal of difference in the appearance of the cupcake. It is not possible to specify a scaling weight or weight range that will be applicable to all formulas and all baking conditions. If the specific volume of the batter varies, scaling weights may have to be adjusted to compensate for the variation. In setting a standard for the scaling weight of cupcakes, the technologist should run a simple experiment in which the deposit is varied in steps of one or two grams from an obviously inadequate amount to an obviously excessive amount, then make a judgement as to the desirability of the products' appearance.

If possible, a depositer should be used that can control the scaling weight within a range of two grams, i.e., within plus or minus one gram. This will help to maintain good and uniform appearance of the cupcakes. It is surely not necessary to remind the reader that different kinds of batter may require different scaling weights for optimum results. When it is necessary to sell a constant weight of cakes per package, formula or processing modifications may be required in order to keep the deposit constant for all flavor varieties. The other alternative is to give overweights for all varieties except the ones of lowest density.

Different amounts of expansion may be observed depending on location of the deposit within the tin, since different rates of heat flow will occur in different areas of the pan. Different expansions may also result from batters deposited at different times, especially if very large batches of batter are being made.

CAKE DOUGHNUTS

Formulation and Processing

Cake doughnuts may be somewhat reminiscent of layer cakes in flavor and in crumb texture, but the fact that they are fried rather than baked makes a number of changes in formulation and in pre-cooking processing necessary. Although cake doughnuts can be made by preparing a dough sheet and cutting pieces from it (as in preparing yeast-leavened doughnuts), this is very seldom done in commercial practice. The usual method for forming them is to make a flowable dough or batter that can be extruded directly into the frying vat. This not only saves much labor but eliminates the need for reprocessing scrap generated in a cutting step. The common types of doughnut depositers are the gravity-fed and the pressure-fed. Further descriptions will be found in the equipment chapters of this book.

Water temperature is a critical factor in controlling the dough response. Most standard processing systems now in operation call for a batter temperature in the range of 76° to 78°F for cake doughnuts. The most practical way of obtaining this condition is to adjust the temperature of ingredient water, or of other liquid ingredients, if water is not an ingredient. It is unlikely that small shops will be able to control batter temperatures within this narrow range.

Although frying times and temperatures vary according to the type of product being made, throughput, size of the piece, and other factors, the average fat temperature being used today is probably near 375°F. A considerable amount of fat will be absorbed by the doughnut, so the tank must be frequently replenished with fresh fat. This constant turnover helps to prevent the accumulation of highly deteriorated fat, but there must be means provide to remove scrap and other debris, which could otherwise attach to the product and spoil its appearance. Charred particles also hasten the development of off odors and bad flavors in the fat.

Traditional flavors for cake doughnuts include mace (or nutmeg), mild lemon, and cinnamon. Fillings, glazes, icings, toppings, sprinkles, and combinations thereof are limited only by the imagination. It is not uncommon for the busier doughnut shops to carry 50 different varieties (cake and raised), most of them being obtained by using many different adjuncts in combination with five or so different shapes made from two to five different dough formulas.

A very large proportion of commercial doughnuts made today start out as a premix bought from a bakery supply house or franchise distributor. Most of these premixes work very well.

Doughnut Trouble Shooting

1. Burst or cracked crusts. Frying fat may be too hot causing the crust to form before the internal expansion has finished. The crust may be too fragile as a result of excess sugar, insufficient flour, too much moisture, or some other formula defect. If the doughnuts are not turned at the proper time, bursting of the crust may result.

2. Brittle and/or dark crusts often result from frying temperatures that are too high.

3. Irregular sizes and shapes are often due to overdevelopment that does not allow proper flow of the dough, and can be corrected by reducing mixing time, using weaker flour or more cake flour in the blend, or changing the sequence of ingredient addition. The reverse condition may also cause misshapen pieces; very weak doughs will expand irregularly and be distorted unduly as they leave the depositer. Inadequate distribution of the leaveners and low frying temperature can also cause this condition.

4. Volume too low. May be due to insufficient leavener, dough that is too stiff, or frying fat that is too hot. Low batter temperatures resulting from the use of excessively cold water can also cause this defect.

5. Spots on the doughnut may be due to inadequate mixing or to frying fat that has deteriorated badly.

6. Toughness generally results from overdevelopment of the gluten or insufficient tenderizers in the formula. The batch containing flour and water should be mixed the minimum time needed to obtain a uniform blend. Increases in liquid, sugar, or shortening may correct the problem. Rarely, too much egg in the formula is the cause.

7. Solid cores inside doughnuts or overall sogginess is likely due to excess water or other liquid.

8. Greasiness can be due either to excess formula fat or excess absorption from the frying medium. The latter cause is more frequent. Some other possible causes are warm batters, undermixing, frying temperature incorrect (either too high or too low), frying time too long, or a suboptimal formula fat level.

COOKIES

Relationship of Formula to Processing Method

The formulas for some types of cookies are similar to those suggested for layer cakes. In fact, certain layer cake batters can be used to make quite acceptable cookies. For commercial cookie production, however, limitations of the standardized equipment that is usually available restrict the range through which the rheological properties of the dough can be allowed to vary. These, in turn, limit the range of variations of ingredients in the formula. Layer cake batters of the usual type are too fluid to be processed on most cookie manufacturing equipment and the resultant cookies are too fragile to be handled by conventional packaging equipment. Of course, many popular cookies are based on formulas far removed from the layer cake pattern.

Cookie formulas are generally classified according to the kind of equipment used to form the individual pieces. Stamping machines, rotary cutters, rotary molders, wire-cut machines (and similar extruding devices), and depositers are used for over 90% of large-scale cookie production in the U.S. Equipment has a strong influence on the texture of the cookie and it limits the formula variations that can be used.

Deposit cookies are the machine-made counterparts of hand-bagged cookies and many of the formulas for the latter can be successfully adapted to automatic production. Deposit cookies will contain (FWB) about 35% to 40% sugar, 65% to 75% shortening, and 15% to 25% liquid whole eggs. The flour should be milled from soft wheat, and it should be unbleached, with 8% to 8.5% protein and 0.35% to 0.40% ash. It should have a McMichael viscosity of 40° or more and a spread factor of 79 to 80.

Although wire-cut cookie equipment permits a wider variation in dough composition than any other type of cookie production machinery, there are still some rheological limitations that cannot be violated in these formulas. It is necessary for wire-cut doughs to be sufficiently cohesive to hold together as they are extruded through orifices, and yet they must be relatively nonsticky and short enough so that they separate cleanly as they are cut by the wire.

Wire-cut formulas may contain up to several times as much sugar as flour, and shortening up to 100% of the flour. Doughs may be almost as soft as some cake batters or too stiff to be easily molded by hand. The softest wire-cut doughs overlap deposit doughs in consistency, while the other extreme is close to the texture expected in many rotary molded doughs.

Some of the advantages of the wire-cut cookie over rotary molded varieties are a more open grain and a softer texture, and, as compared to deposit goods, a more uniformly shaped cookie. Disadvantages over rotary molded pieces are the lack of potential for making a surface design and somewhat less uniformity of size and shape. Doughs containing particles, such as chocolate chips and raisins, can usually be satisfactorily handled by wire-cut machines, within limits.

The principle of extruding dough through an orifice, which is the method used to form deposit cookies and wire-cut cookies, is also the basis of the manufacturing procedures used for rout press items, fig bars, and several other types of cookies. These products differ from wire-cut and deposit cookies in that a continuous strip of dough is extruded on to a belt or band. The strip can be severed into pieces either before or after baking. In the case of fig bars, and some other specialty items, two concentric extrusions are made so as to give a two component cookie. Each of these methods requires a somewhat different set of rheological properties and, consequently, different formulas and procedures.

The principal distinguishing feature of the stamping machine and rotary cutting operations is that the pieces are cut from a continuous sheet of dough by either a rotating cylinder or a reciprocating stamper. A rather large range of dough types can be handled by such equipment. It is necessary, however, that the dough be cohesive enough to form the continuous sheet from which the cookie shapes will be cut. It is also essential to hold the scrap, if any, together in strips so that it can be lifted away from the edges and from between the dough blanks. Reciprocating cutting machines, or stamping machines, are often regarded as though there were many points of similarity between them and rotary cutters. In fact, there are so many differences between the two types of equipment that it is not particularly helpful to consider them together.

For rotary molded cookies, the dough consistency must be such that it will feed uniformly and readily fill all of the crevices of the die cavity under the pressure existing at the bottom of the feeding hopper. The dough blank must be susceptible to being extracted from the cavity without undergoing distortion or forming tails of appreciable size, but it must adhere to the die roll long enough to prevent the piece from falling out of its cavity before it reaches the extraction roller. The blank must have sufficient cohesion to hold together and not break up at any of the transfer points before or after baking. The dough must flow very slightly or smooth out during forming and baking so that woodiness or undesirable irregularities in the surface pattern are not apparent in the finished cookie. Usually, the spread and rise should be minimized so as not to blur or distort the design. Doughs formulated to meet these requirements are, in most cases, fairly high in sugar and shortening and low in moisture. They can sometimes be almost claylike in appearance and rheology. Development of gluten, what there is of it, is definitely to be avoided.

Most cookie bakers use flour of about 8.1% to 8.2% protein content for rotary base cakes, but a range of 7.1% to 9.2% has been reported. Ash should be around 0.415%, with a known range of 0.33% to 0.47% being used satisfactorily. Oleo added in the liquid state is suitable for most of these doughs, but vegetable shortening can also be used. Powdered sugar and sugar syrups are the preferred sweetening ingredients. NFDM is often added, but it is thought by some that condensed milk is preferable since using the liquid ingredient removes any possibility of lumps appearing in finished cookies. Lecithin at about 0.4% will improve machinability.

One-stage mixing is often perfectly satisfactory for rotary sandwich bases but a creaming operation with most of the minor ingredients mixed before the flour goes in gives added assurance that lumps of undistributed ingredients will not appear in the cookie. The air entrapment function that can result from creaming is not a plus, however. Dough temperatures from 72° to 90°F are being used.

Ingredients

Basic concepts.—The materials used in cookies are often classified as either binding (toughening) or tenderizing ingredients depending on their expected effect on the finished product. Binding ingredients are thought of as those that either form the supporting structure of the cookie or harden this structure, while tenderizers either interfere with the formation of the basic framework or soften it.

The continuous structure of the cookie arises primarily from the flour. Although there is some disagreement about the role of starch in forming the structure, it appears that gluten is the principal contributor to the vesicular structure or other framework that holds the cookie together and provides at least some gas-retaining function. The basic structure is reduced in mechanical strength, or tenderized, by sugar, invert sugar, egg yolk, ammonia, soda, and shortening. It is firmed or toughened by water, cocoa, egg white, whole egg, nonfat milk solids, and leavening acids. Flavors and colors are usually not present in sufficient quantity to affect texture. Salt is usually considered to be a toughener.

There is some indication that, in cookies baked almost to dryness, sugar can form a continuous network within the cookie, leading to a hard or crisp texture. To function in this way, the sugar would first have to dissolve, then form a continuously contacting solution throughout the dough, then dehydrate to a glassy state. The theory is given some support by observations that confections formed by dehydrating and aerating sugars and syrups elicit sensory responses of this type. In such cases, sugar would have to be regarded as a toughener.

A summary of these guidelines follows. Binding materials or tougheners are flour, water (because it hydrates the gluten), milk solids (not very effective as binders in the amounts normally found in cookie doughs), egg whites, egg yolks (which act as tougheners because of their protein content and tenderizers because they contain fat and emulsifiers), cocoa or chocolate products, leavening acids, salt, oat flour, and soy flour. Tenderizing materials include sugar (probably the most important tenderizer in cookies), shortenings, emulsifiers, leavening (because a more porous, lighter structure seems softer), egg yolks, corn starch or wheat starch, corn flour, and ground raisins and dates. Generally, nonreactive (inert) substances act as tenderizers.

Specifications and functions.—Brief accounts of the basic requirements for the major cookie ingredients and their functions will be given.

A wide variety of flours are used in cookies, They range from a soft, very weak cookie flour to a rather strong sponge flour. The stronger the flour, the more shortening and sugar must be used to obtain an acceptable texture. High protein contents lead to hardness of texture, coarseness of internal grain, and rough surfaces. Chlorine bleached flours are not recommended for soft type cookies where relatively large amounts of tenderizing an moisture-retaining ingredients are used. Excessive amounts of enriching ingredients and inadequate flour lead to cookies lacking body and becoming fragile.

The particle size of sugar has a definite effect on the response of dough to oven heat and on the size and texture of the cookie. Sugars of different particle sizes can be used in combination to adjust spread and machining properties. For uniformity of spread, a specific granulation profile should be maintained. Finer sugars require less mixing, and they may reduce sticking to the band. According to Wittenberg (1965), invert syrup makes wire-cut cookies soft, light, and spongy, with an open texture. Large amounts of sugars, and especially of syrups, tend to make the dough sticky and hinder its release from dies and wires. A large excess of sugar can lead to undesirable hardness.

Whole eggs lead to a better structure and more delicate texture than do dried eggs. Frozen eggs seem to give greater volume and a more open grain (Velzen 1963). Use of egg yolk instead of whole eggs may give a more tender cookie, but the internal structure may not be as good (Flick 1964).

Shortening is one of the principal agents for increasing tenderness, at least so far as rich, sweet biscuits are concerned. Liquid shortening is in frequent use and oleo oil (liquid beef fat) is quite satisfctory in many formulas. For creaming, a hydrogenated vegetable shortening is needed. Substitution of liquid shortenings for plastic types usually necessitates a reduction in total shortening, and may require the adding of cold water or ice to adjust dough temperature to the proper level.

Lecithin seems to increase the shortening effect of fats. It promotes a tendency for the fat to cover damp particles or spread among slightly moist particles of sugar, flour, etc. It makes rich sweet doughs seem drier and improves their machinability. On rotary pieces, especially, better release from the die leads to a clearer impression of the engraving and cuts down on the number of cripples.

A salt of small crystal size should be used, except for topping purposes. Otherwise, standard non-iodized salt is satisfactory.

Milk mellows or ameliorates harsh flavors without contributing much flavor of its own. Crust color and gloss are generally improved. Seldom is more than 5% (FWB) of this ingredient needed to get maximum benefits. Whey has effects somewhat similar to NFDM, except that the stiffening, water-binding, and toughening effects are negligible. It is primarily useful where a non-binding filler of low sweetness is needed to reduce cost.

Representative Formulas

In this section, one or two simple formulas for each of the most important processing methods will be presented as a basis for product development personnel who may need a starting point for their formulation work. Original plant formulas were the source for this material, and the original proportions are quoted.

Cutting machine cookies.—Animal "crackers" or menagerie cookies are almost always made from a fairly lean formula. The formula shown in Table 15.3 is much richer than many current formulas, because the product has been cheapened over the years and is now salable only because of the packaging, the shape of the cookie, and the less-than-discriminating nature of the ultimate consumers. Animal crackers are often produced on a stamping machine, but in other plants on a rotary cutter. Both types of equipment do a satisfactory job, though the optimum formulas may be slightly different. In the same table is a formula for chocolate base cake which is known to process well on cutting machines.

Table 15.3. FORMULAS FOR TWO CUTTING MACHINE COOKIES[1]

Ingredient	Animal crackers	Chocolate base cake
Granulated (or *powdered) sugar	150	50*
Cookie flour	760	820
Arrowroot flour (or *dextrose)	25	95*
Sucrose syrup	100	150
Dark molasses (or *HFCS)	12	200
Honey (or *42 DE corn syrup)	32	50*
Vegetable shortening	155	175
Lecithin	3	4
Leavening acid compound ("cream")	5	--
Sodium bicarbonate	5	5
Salt	12	10
Liquid whole eggs	--	30
Ammonium bicarbonate	--	2
Vanillin	--	1
Dutched cocoa, 12% fat	--	60
Water (variable)	105	45
Batch weight	1,364	1,697

[1] Quantities are in pounds per batch.

Wire-cut cookies.—The two cookie formulas in Table 15.4 represent doughs that can be processed on wire-cut machines. One is for a rich vanilla wafer and the other is for a molasses cookie of the "old time" style. Spice cookies and the cheaper kind of chocolate cookie provide an opportunity to use "light meal" and "dark meal" as ingredients. These materials are ground cookies that have been rejected by quality assurance personnel because they have distorted shapes, are broken, or have weights outside the accepted range. In some shops, these scrap meals are made from stale returns, over-baked cookies, and formula errors, but this is in reality poor practice if the manufacturer intends to build up a loyal clientele. The proper outlet for off-flavor scrap is animal feed.

Table 15.4. TWO FORMULAS FOR WIRE-CUT COOKIES[1]

Ingredient	Vanilla wafer	Molasses cookie
Flour	400	900
Powdered (or *granulated) sugar	280	340*
High fructose corn syrup	40	80
Vegetable shortening	130	260
Liquid whole eggs	60	30
Sodium bicarbonate	3	12
Leavening acid mix ("cream")	1	--
Ammonium bicarbonate	1	--
Salt	5	--
Vanillin	1	1
Molasses, medium dark	--	200
Lecithin	--	2
Dark meal	--	50
Water (variable)	92	86
Batch weight	1,013	1,961

[1] Quantities are in pounds per batch.

Rotary molded cookies.—Most sandwich base cakes and many other types of cookies are made on rotary molding equipment, sometimes called dutch process machines. The big advantage of this method is that the dimensions of the cookie can be closely controlled, making packaging much easier. In addition, attractive designs can be impressed on the top of the cookies. The two formulas given in Table 15.5 include a spice-nut cookie that is often molded in a windmill shape, and a chocolate base cake of high quality. These formulas indicate a trend to proliferation of ingredients that often occurs when the recipe has been modified many times.

The chocolate cookie formula should result in a fairly alkaline crumb, which will help to intensify the color, but it is still necessary to use a highly dutched and heavily roasted cocoa if the color is to be sufficiently dark to satisfy the average consumer. Some manufacturers have been known to include carbon black to assist in darkening the cookie. It is not generally advisable to use artificial colors to simulate cocoa content. On a pound for pound basis, most other coloring agents are, in fact, less effective than cocoa as brown colorants, and they cost more. An artificial red color can, however, be useful in adjusting the hue to a warmer range.

Brownies baked in sheet form.—Brownies and some other cookies are being baked in continuous sheets on oven bands. The dough is extruded through a slit on to the band and no cutting of any kind is performed until baking is complete.

Because brownies can be made with high proportions of invert syrup and other hygroscopic ingredients, they can retain soft texture during several weeks of shelf life. This makes the product suitable for distribution.

as a vending machine item and through other routes that demand excellent stability. Many of these commercial items are packed in heat-sealed cellophane (often mylar-coated) and yet remain acceptable to consumers for up to nine weeks at room temperatures. The dark color, strong flavor, and rather dense crumb tend to disguise any minor problems that may develop during storage.

It is common practice to extrude a fudge-type icing on to the tops of the brownies before they are cut, and often to sprinkle them with nuts.

Table 15.5. TWO FORMULAS FOR ROTARY-MOLDED COOKIES[1]

Ingredients	Windmill cookie	Chocolate base cake
Flour	850	825
Medium dark molasses	50	--
Granulated sugar	200	100
High fructose corn syrup	75	--
Malt syrup	15	--
Powdered sugar	40	200
Vegetable shortening	220	165
Lecithin	3	3
Liquid whole eggs	30	--
Cinnamon (or *dutched cocoa)	10	65*
Allspice (or *chocolate liquor)	1	82*
Nutmeg, ground	4	--
Salt (or *vanillin)	10	2*
Sodium bicarbonate	4	7
Leavening cream	2	--
Ammonium bicarbonate	4	3
Almonds, finely chopped	30	--
Cashews, finely chopped	20	--
Dark meal	100	50
Water (variable)	60	100
Batch weight	1,728	1,602

[1]Quantities are in pounds per batch.

BIBLIOGRAPHY

ARCISZEWSKI, H ., PORZIO, L. A., CHIANG, B. Y., and SPOTTS, C. E., JR. 1990. Low sodium cake mix and process of preparing low sodium cake. U.S. Pat. 4,938,980

BANKS, L., BUSK, G. C., JR., CHIANG, B., and THULIN, R. 1989. Method for controlling the spread of soft cookies. U.S. Pat 4,873,098

BANKS, L., THULIN, R. R., ROSS, R. E., and SCHAEDER, W. E. 1989. Leavener-containing dough compositions bakeable to a moist matrix. U.S. Pat. 4,828,853

BENNION, E. B., and BAMFORD, G. S. T. 1973. The Technology of Cake Making. Leonard Hill Books, London, England

BOEHM, D. G., and FAZZOLARE, R. D. 1990. Filled cookie. U.S. Pat. 4,948,602

CONSTANCE, P., and POLIZZANO, R. A. 1988. Producing multi-textured cookies containing gum. U.S. Pat. 4,717,577

DARTEY, C. K., FINLEY, J. W., and THULIN, R. R. 1988. Process for preparing chocolate chip cookies containing low melting fat and product. U.S. Pat. 4,722,849

DARTEY, C. K., FINLEY, J. W., and THULIN, R. R. 1990. Processes and dough compositions for producing cookies containing low-melting fat. U.S. 4,894,246

DE MUYNCK, E. P. L. 1968. Bakery products of the European Economic Community. Proc. Am. Soc. Bakery Engineers *1968*, 144-156

DIXON, J. 1983. Cake doughnut production. Bakers Digest *57*, No.5, 26, 31, 34, 36

DOESCHER, L. C., HOSENEY, R. C., and MILLIKEN, G. A. 1987. A mechanism for cookie dough setting. Cereal Chem. *64*, 158-163

DOESCHER, L. C., HOSENEY, R. C., MILLIKEN, G. A., and RUBENTHALER, G. L. 1987. Effect of sugar and flours on cookie spread evaluated by time-lapse photography. Cereal Chem. *64*, 163-167

DONELSON, J. R., and CLEMENTS, R. L. 1986. Components of cake batter expansion in white layer cakes. Cereal Chem. *63*, 109-110

FINNEY, K. F., MORRIS, V. H., and YAMAZAKI, W. T. 1950. Effects of varying quantities of sugar, shortening, and ammonium carbonate on the spreading and top grain of sugar snap cookies. Cereal Chem. *27*, 30-41

FLICK, H. 1964. Fundamentals of cookie production, including soft type cookies. Proc. Am. Soc. Bakery Engineers *1964*, 286-293

GAGE, D. R., and MISHKIN, M. A. 1990. Texture equilibration in cookies. U.S. Pat. 4,892,745

GORTON, R. 1984. What happens while cookies baker? Bakers Digest *58*, No. 4, 12, 16

HAUMANN, B. F. 1987. Trends in frying fat usage. J. Am. Oil Chemists Soc. *64*, 789-795

JOHNSON, D. H. 1965. Correlating laboratory tests to production. 40th Annual Training Conference Biscuit Bakers Inst., Apr. 7

KISSELL, L. T., and MARSHALL, B. D. 1962. Multi-factor responses of cake quality to basic ingredient ratios. Cereal Chem. *39*, 16-30

LABAW, G. 1982. Chemical leavening agents and their use in bakery products. Bakers Digest *56*, No. 1, 16-18, 20-21

LOU, W. C., and FAZZOLARE, R. D. 1990. Shelf-stable microwavable cookie dough. U.S. Pat. 4,911,939

MARTIN, A. J., and FURIA, T. E. 1990. Shelf stable cookie. U.S. Pat. 4,965,077

MARTIN, A. J., and MOOI, R. 1990. Shelf stable cookie. U.S. Pat. 4,965,076

MARX, J. T., MARX, B. D., and JOHNSON, J. M. 1990. High-fructose corn syrup cakes made with all-purpose flour or cake flour. Cereal Chem. *67*, 502-504

MATZ, S. A. 1984. Snack Food Technology, Second Edition. AVI Publishing Co., Westport, CT

MATZ, S. A. 1989A. Formulas and Processes for Bakers. Pan-Tech International, McAllen, TX

MATZ, S. A. 1989B. Technology of the Materials of Baking. Elsevier Science Publishers, Barking, Essex, England

MATZ, S. A. 1991. The Chemistry and Technology of Cereals as Food and Feed, Second Edition. Pan-Tech International, McAllen, TX

MATZ, S. A., and MATZ, T. D. 1978. Cookie and Cracker Technology, Second Edition. AVI Publishing Co., Westport, CT

MIZUKOSHI, M. 1985. Model studies of cake baking. VI. Effects of cake ingredients and cake formula on shear modulus of cake. Cereal Chem. *62*, 247-251

MORROW, L., LORENZ, K., and BRENNEIS, L. 1974. Effect of atmospheric pressure and ingredient variations on cookie spread. Cereal Sci. Today *19*, No. 5, 200-206

NEVILLE, N. E., and SETSER, C. S. 1986. Textural optimization of reduced-calorie cakes using response surface methodology. Cereal Foods World *31*, No. 10, 744, 746, 748-749

NGO, W. H., and TARANTO, M. V. 1986. Effect of sucrose level on the rheological properties of cake batters. Cereal Foods World *31*, 317-322

PFLAUMER, P. P., and SMITH, J. P. 1988. Dual-textured cookie products containing a unique saccharide mixture. U.S. Pat. 4,752,484

SCHAAL, A. 1935. Cocoa & chocolate cakes. Proc. Am. Soc. Bakery Engineers *1935*, 1-26

VELZEN, B. H. 1963. Production of wire-cut cookies. Proc. Am. Soc. Bakery Engineers *1963*, 243-250

VETTER, J. L., BRIGHT, H., UTT, M., and MC MASTER, G. 1984. Cookie formulating. Bakers Digest *58*, No. 4, 6-7, 9

WHITE, D. C., and LAUER, G. N. 1990. Predicting gelatinizatin temperatures of starch/sweetener systems for cake formulation by differential scanning calorimetry. I. Development of a model. Cereal Foods World *35*, 728-731

WITTENBERG, H. L. 1965. Wire-cut cookies. 40th Annual Training Conference Biscuit Bakers Inst., Apr. 7

YASOSKY, J. J., HAHN, P. W., and ATWELL, W. A. 1990. Controlling the texture of microwave brownies. U.S. Pat. 4,933,196

chapter sixteen

YEAST-LEAVENED PLAIN BREAD AND ROLLS

INTRODUCTION

The emphasis in this chapter will be on plain loaf bread—those varieties called French, Italian, Vienna, white, wheat, etc. Plain rolls are essentially the same products, but baked in smaller pieces, which may be fancy shapes (such as Kaiser rolls) or decorated in some manner. Formulas and processes for other yeast-leavened products will be described in subsequent chapters, insofar as they differ from those used for plain bread and rolls.

The greater part of the present chapter will concern general principles, but specific examples will be introduced to illustrate important points. Procedures used in mechanized production will be stressed. Machines used for large-scale implementation of these procedures will be described in much more detail in the section containing chapters on equipment.

This chapter should be regarded as an introduction to the other chapters describing formulations and procedures for yeast-leavened products. Many of the principles set forth here are general in nature and therefore can be applied to products other than plain bread and rolls.

PRINCIPLES OF PLAIN BREAD AND ROLL PRODUCTION

Bread which is recognizable by the consumer as being within the conventional limits of appearance and flavor of white bread can be made from flour, water, salt, and yeast. Most consumers would not find such bread very palatable, however, and the baker might find it difficult to prepare, especially if uniformity is one of his criteria of quality. Very few loaves of bread made from such simplistic formulas are being sold in the U.S. today. Minor additions to the formula help immensely to simplify processing and improve uniformity of appearance and taste. Furthermore, most white bread made today includes added nutrients such as vitamins and minerals.

In order to make bread and rolls that meet the processing requirements of a specific plant or production line and have the flavor, texture, and appearance requirements of the targeted market, the formulator adds to the essential ingredients described in the preceding paragraph shortening for texture and flavor, sugars as fermentation substrates and flavor improvers, emulsifiers and other surfactants to improve dough handling properties and shelf life of the finished product, oxidizers or reducing agents to compensate for deficiencies in the flour or mixing procedure, and colors, flavors, and other characterizing substances to make the product more acceptable to the consumer. A small amount of malt (or other amylase source) is very desirable to give a continuous supply of substrate for fermentation, if sugars are not added. Sometimes this enzyme source is added to the flour at the mill, but the baker can also add it to the dough as malted barley flour or diastatic malt syrup. Wheat flour of various extraction rates up to 100% can be used to make "wheat" or whole wheat bread, and rye flour or triticale flour can be used as all or part of the cereal ingredient.

White Bread

French, Italian, and Vienna breads are generally made from lean formulas and can be regarded as basic breads from which other varieties can be developed. There is really no essential difference between these three breads, so far as formulation for the U.S. market is concerned. The chief characteristic differentiating them from other types of breads is their crisp or crunchy crust, and it is present only when they are fresh and properly made. Most, but not all, are baked as hearth breads. Another characteristic is their short shelf life, when measured against the requirements of our normal distribution systems. A typical formula is given below.

French Bread

(1) A sponge of approximately the following composition is fermented for 4 to 5 hours at 65°F:

    65 parts bread flour
    40 parts water
    2 parts compressed yeast

(2) To the fermented sponge, the following ingredients are added in a mixing and developing step:

    35 parts bread flour
    20 parts water
    2 parts sugar
    2 parts shortening
    2 parts salt
    5 parts nonfat dry milk (optional)

(3) The dough is brought out of the mixer at 80°F and made up into loaves or rolls by methods which will be described later.

The amount of water added to these lean doughs is a critical determinant of many of the finished product's characteristics and can only be determined by testing doughs made under the exact conditions of preparation and with the exact ingredients (particularly flour) that are to be used in mass production.

A crisp crust is not assured by any formula; it can be obtained only by applying proper processing techniques (especially baking) to an appropriate formula, and following them with suitable packaging and distribution practices. In any case, the length of time during which crispness is retained will be short, especially if a soft, silky crumb is also expected.

Rolls for hamburgers and hot dogs, as well as most soft dinner rolls, are made by somewhat similar formulas, but include considerably more enriching agents. The one given below has been widely used.

<u>White Rolls</u>

(1) Form sponge by mixing the following ingredients to a smooth blend:

150 parts bread flour
90 parts water
5 parts compressed yeast
1 part yeast food
1 part diastatic malt syrup

(2) Ferment the sponge for 4.5 hours at 78°F. Then mix in the following ingredients, developing the dough to its optimum:

50 parts bread flour
24 parts water (variable)
20 parts sugar
16 parts shortening
4 parts salt
8 parts nonfat dry milk
qs dough conditioners as required

(3) Dough should come out of the mixer at 76° to 80°F, and be given 5 to 10 minutes floor time before it is made up into shapes for hamburger, hot dog, or plain rolls, then proofed and baked according to standard procedures.

Bread sticks require stiffer doughs, and generally are not very rich. They can be made by either a sponge or straight dough method. The latter yields satisfactory products and is, of course, simpler. It used to be the practice of some bread stick manufacturers to add up to 6% (FWB) liquid egg whites to these doughs to give an internal structure and crust appearance they thought was desirable. This ingredient, though expensive, does seem to improve the texture and may be justifiable if the product is aimed at an upscale market.

Wheat Bread

"Wheat bread" has come to be the generic term for breads containing enough bran and other non-endosperm fractions of the grain to give a distinctive color and texture to the baked product. These varieties are not to be confused with "whole wheat" bread, which should, in theory, contain all the fractions of wheat in the same proportions as they exist in the unmilled grain. Whole wheat bread is by its very nature a coarse, dark, chewy, and rather highly flavored product, but wheat bread can be very close to standard white bread in density, texture, crust appearance, crumb color, and flavor. It appeals to consumers who believe there are some health problems with white bread but who have not yet been converted to the view that the worse a product tastes the better it is for you.

There is no Standard of Identity for "Wheat Bread," but any product purporting to be "whole wheat bread," "graham bread," "entire wheat bread," "whole wheat rolls," "graham rolls," "entire wheat rolls," "whole wheat buns," "graham buns," or "entire wheat buns" must conform to Federal Standards (21 CFR Part 136) for these products. They must be made from whole wheat flour, bromated whole wheat flour, or a combination of these. No white flour can be used.

Wheat bread is formulated and processed similarly to regular white bread. Because it contains structurally inert ingredients in the form of bran, germ, etc., supplementation by strong flour or even by vital wheat gluten is sometimes necessary in order to get volume and grain that will be accepted by the consumer. Examples of a formula and a process for a moderately dark example of wheat bread are shown below, but it is also possible to make satisfactory products by a straight dough process.

Wheat Bread

(1) Prepare a sponge from the following formula:

    40 lb first clear spring wheat flour
    40 lb whole wheat flour
    3 lb compressed yeast
    8 oz yeast food
    44 lb water
    28 lb shortening
    8 oz emulsifier-softener

(2) Set the sponge at 76°F and ferment it for four hours.

(3) To the fermented sponge, add the following and develop the dough:

    20 lb first clear flour
    16 lb water (variable)
    8 lb sugar
    2 lb salt
    3 lb corn syrup
    4 oz caramel color
    amylase and protease, as required

(4) The dough could come out of the mixer at 80°F and be given a floor time of about 25 minutes before make-up.

The preceding directions give starting points for formulating plain bread and rolls. More complex products will be discussed in subsequent chapters. The sections immediately following describe the effects of various processing methods. Many principles described in these discussions will be found to be applicable to both simple and complex yeast-leavened products.

TWO TRADITIONAL BREAD PROCESSING SCHEMES

In this section, descriptions will be given for two typical processing sequences used in traditional bakeries for making the kind of white loaf bread that is sold in greater quantity than any other bakery item.

Straight Dough Method

The straight dough process is not used much in larger bakeries for plain bread and rolls. Although it is certainly simpler than the sponge-and-dough method, it is less tolerant of production errors and of variations in flour and other ingredients. It also does not normally yield a product that is as flavorful and as soft. It is frequently used for specialty items, often for sweet doughs, and occasionally for white rolls.

The chief distinguishing feature of the straight dough method is that all (or substantially all) of the ingredients are mixed together and fermented at the same time. Occasionally, one hears of variant procedures in which patterns intermediate to the straight dough and sponge-and-dough procedures are recommended, but these are not sufficiently important or technologically interesting to be discussed in detail.

Kamman (1979) categorized straight doughs as (1) regular or full straight dough, which is given from 2 to 4 hours of fermentation, (2) short time straight doughs, which are generally fermented from 30 minutes to one hour, and (3) no-time doughs, which are taken directly to the divider with no more than 15 minutes floor time. The last category is discussed in considerable detail in the next chapter.

Four straight dough formulas for loaf bread are included in Table 16.1.

Table 16.1. FORMULAS FOR STRAIGHT DOUGH BREADS[1]

Ingredients	Basic white bread	French	Rich Vienna	Hearth bread
Bread flour	55.4	60.1	56.3	60.4
Shortening	2.8	1.0	3.5	1.2
Sugar	2.8	1.0	0.5	1.2
Diastatic malt syrup	0	0	0.5	0
Yeast, compressed	1.1	2.1	1.3	1.3
Mineral yeast food	0.1	0.1	0.1	0.3
Salt	1.3	1.0	0.9	1.2
Water (variable)	33.2	34.4	33.4	33.2
Dried skim milk	3.3	0	0	0
SS-2-L*	0	0.3	0	0
Liquid egg whites	0	0	3.5	1.2

[1] Percent, as is basis. *Sodium stearoyl-2-lactylate.

Sponge-and-dough Method

The most obvious difference between the sponge-and-dough and the straight dough method is in the mixing phase. The former system requires two separate dough mixing steps, while the latter requires only one. Of course, in either case, any number of premix operations may be conducted without making a significant difference in conditions of the dough development step. Figure 16.1 illustrates the steps required to produce bread by the sponge-and-dough procedure (adapted from a diagram by AMF).

The sponge process appears to have originated from the ancient technique of "seeding" each new dough with part of the preceding day's production or with a "sour' containing active microorganisms that contribute both flavor and gassing ability to the fresh batch.

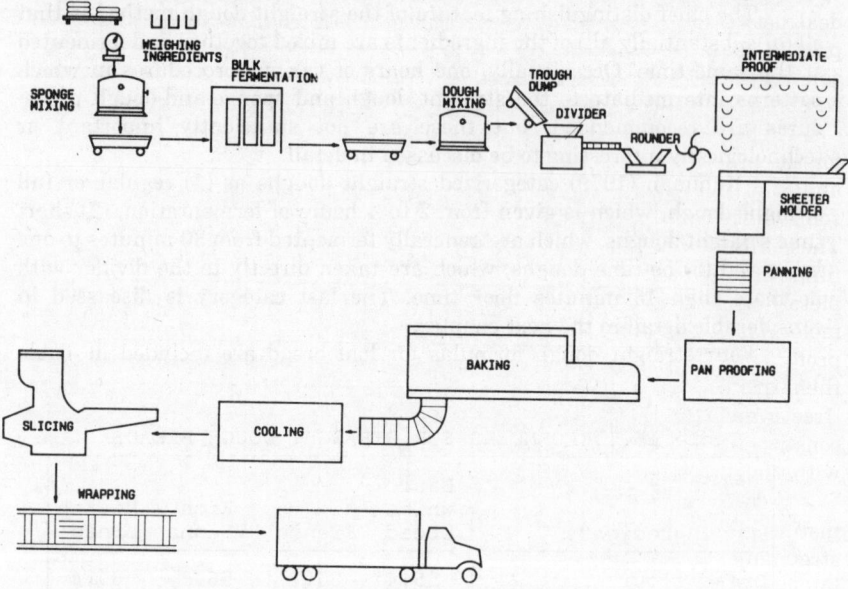

Figure 16.1. Producing bread by the sponge-and-dough method.

REACTIONS DURING MIXING

In the preparation of doughs for bread loaves and rolls, mixing has at least three important functions: blending the various ingredients into a homogeneous mass, establishing the basic vesicle structure that will entrap the gas emitted by fermenting yeast cells, and developing the dough. It is also widely accepted that "dough conditioning" occurs during mixing. Dough conditioning as that term is used in the literature is difficult to distinguish from some of the broader aspects of dough development, but it will be treated here as a separate subject.

Dough Development

Hydration of the flour, or more correctly of the gluten proteins, is an essential precursor of the development process. The rate of water uptake in the initial phase of dough mixing is related to the particle size of the flour, the amount and particle size of the soluble substances, and the rate at which the colloidal materials hydrate. It is generally agreed that hydration of the gluten proteins occurs rapidly, however, and does not vary a great deal between flours, while development of the gluten is a relatively slow process requiring the input of a considerable amount of ordered force and can vary widely for different flours. To a considerable extent, the mixing response of a flour is determined by the amount and quality of its gluten.

The peculiar property of wheat flours that makes them indispensable for the preparation of low density, well-aerated foods such as bread is the ability of the gluten proteins to form very thin continuous films that are somewhat resistant to the diffusion of water vapor and carbon dioxide. These films form the walls of gas vesicles, or bubbles, in the dough. In these films are embedded starch granules and other particulate masses completely or partially surrounded by the thin layer of hydrated protein. On the molecular level, the gluten films are probably composed of networks of protein molecules bound by forces of varying but relatively low strength. To them are bound water molecules undergoing constant exchange with the "free" water that is available to dissolve the sugars and other soluble dough constituents; a relatively constant quantity of water molecules is associated with the gluten molecules under any given set of conditions.

The kind of mixing action that appears to be the most effective in promoting gluten development is a repeated stretching and folding action. If stretching and folding are always performed in the same direction, the mixing process will be particularly efficient. Although no completely satisfactory explanation of the changes happening at the molecular level has been published, it is generally believed the chief result of the folding and stretching actions is an orienting of many of the gluten molecules so they become extended and parts of them lie side-by-side, rather than being coiled and interlaced in a brush heap structure. When positioned side-by-side, there would be greater opportunity for disulfide bonds and hydrogen bonds to form between adjacent protein molecules, leading to maximum strength and gas holding properties in the gluten network. No doubt the intermolecular bonds are constantly breaking and reforming in a dynamic interchange at a rate depending on the chemical and physical environment.

Notwithstanding the preceding comments, it is possible to prepare a loaf of bread from dough that has been mixed at very high speed in equipment that virtually whips it into a foam, such as the developers found in continuous bread making plants. These loaves tend to have very fine and uniform cell size, and are soft, highly hydrated structures with limited elasticity. It may be that the "developing" mechanism in such cases is the orienting of gluten in thin layers in the vesicle walls by the foam-producing operation and the subsequent expansion of these layers by gas evolution.

Modification of the chemical environment in the dough so that hydration and cross-linking of the gluten molecules proceeds to an extent suitable for the kind of process and product under consideration is part of conditioning, which will be more fully described later. It is often observed that, as the dough approaches peak development, it will begin to enfold considerable amounts of air. As a result of this gas entrapment, density of the dough will be markedly reduced just before the maximum power requirement is reached, the latter being readily measurable by wattmeters or the like. This phenomenon apparently marks a major change in status of the gluten (Fortmann 1967). There are also measurable changes in elasticity, adhesiveness, viscosity, cohesiveness, and extensibility throughout the mixing process.

The success of the mixing operation in forming a continuous gluten network that will have the maximum gas-holding capacity has a strong influence on the quality of the finished bread. Well-developed doughs can result in loaves having high specific volumes, a soft, silky, and uniform grain and texture, and good keeping qualities. If the dough has not been mixed to its optimum state, it is difficult if not impossible to compensate for this deficiency by changes in subsequent processing conditions. Factors tending to increase mixing requirements include (Fortmann 1967), but are not limited to: (1) fresh, not matured, flour, (2) short fermentation, (3) high salt level, (4) addition of iodate, and (5) low dough temperature. Factors tending to decrease mixing requirements include: (1) well aged flour, (2) longer fermentation, (3) low salt level, (4) no iodate, (5) higher dough temperature, (6) higher amount of alcohol present, (7) proteolytic enzymes, (8) modified yeasts, and (9) cysteine, a reducing agent.

Establishing Vesicle Size

The average size and the size distribution of the tiny bubbles or vesicle that establish the grain of the finished loaf are important quality determinants. These factors affect both the eating texture (mouthfeel) of the bread and the appearance of cut or torn crumb surfaces. They can also affect the specific volume of the loaf or roll. The total volume of all the vesicles in a loaf of bread is determined largely, but not entirely, by the gas generated in the pan proofing period, but the number and size distribution of these little bubbles is affected by all of the mechanical treatments given the dough, starting with the initial mixing step.

Some air is brought in with the flour and other dry ingredients, either as gas entrained by the mass or entrapped in microscopic cavities in the granules themselves. Part of these gases is displaced and escapes to the atmosphere or is dissolved by the liquids, but a considerable amount remains and is subdivided by the turbulence created in the dough while it is being mixed. Furthermore, the mixing process entraps additional air in the dough as it is folded, pressed together, torn and resealed, etc. This entrapment is partly offset by the squeezing action of certain types of mixers that press out some of the larger bubbles, and by tearing of the dough, which allows the escape of gas. The net effect of mixing is to subdivide the larger bubbles, decreasing the maximum size of the bubble population. In this way, mixing establishes numerous foci at which carbon dioxide can evolve from its dissolved form, and creates a base upon which further mechanical treatment can work to form good "grain and texture" in the finished loaf.

The bubbles initially formed in the dough are enlarged by gas evolving from dissolved carbon dioxide formed either by yeast fermentation or by the chemical reactions of sodium bicarbonate. Different bubbles tend to grow at different rates depending on thickness of their walls, activity of yeast cells in their vicinity, and initial size. Bubbles that are larger to begin with tend to grow faster. Furthermore, the films separating adjacent vesicles tend to break and allow the cells to coalesce. The net result is that vesicles in the dough tend to become larger and more varied in size. If this process is allowed to continue without interruption, the finished loaf will have a very coarse texture composed of extremely non-uniform vesicles, and many of the bubble walls will be thick and tough. Appearance and texture (mouthfeel) of the finished loaf crumb will then be unsatisfactory.

Many of the processing steps applied to dough as it proceeds through the bread have the effect of making the vesicle size more uniform. Dividing, rounding, sheeting, and molding all have this effect even though their apparent or major purpose is entirely different. The squeezing, compressing, tearing, and puncturing of dough pieces, which occur during these operations, burst the cells, collapse them, tear them open, flatten them, and in general reduce their size. Larger vesicles are more subject to this size reduction than are the smaller ones. Although the size differentiation of both the bubbles that remain intact and the newly formed vesicles begins anew after each of these steps involving compressive forces, the net results are the elimination of large cavities and an increase in the number of vesicles.

Conditioning the Dough

Correct mixing procedures, when applied to elastic yeast-leavened doughs of the type used for bread, improve gas retention and stability of the dough, contribute to a soft, silky, and close bread crumb having desirable mouthfeel, and extend shelf life. Part of this process can be called development and part conditioning—the dividing line is not entirely clear. Conditioning has sometimes been used to describe the action of oxidants, reductants, proteases, and other substances on the physical properties of dough, especially on the mixing tolerance, the extensibility, and the stability of the dough. This may be too narrow a definition, however, since the term "conditioning" has also been used, frequently, to describe the oxidation (or lack of it) that occurs during mixing of unsupplemented doughs (especially of the very vigorous type of mixing found in high speed equipment), responses to the strictly physical treatment aspect of intensive mixers (even at low oxygen tension), the phenomena accompanying hydration of flour components, and reactions largely attributable to yeast activity. Oxidants such as potassium bromate, reductants such as L-cysteine, and protein- or starch-complexing agents such as calcium stearoyl-2-lactylate are often referred to as "dough conditioners."

Many of the ingredients added to dough affect development and, by a logical broadening of the definition, might be called conditioners. Certain milk proteins (if not heat-denatured) will affect gluten and make the dough soft and easily mixed, although often weak and sticky as well. Shortenings have important effects, generally reducing the time and energy required to produce a fully developed dough. Salt has a pronounced effect on the energy requirement and mixing time, salt-free doughs being softer, probably because there is less sodium ion interference with hydrogen bonding of water molecules to the gluten strands.

Some chemical additives have effects that seem to be extreme relative to the small amounts normally added. These ingredients, which meet the usual definition of dough conditioners, are routinely added to bread doughs by many bakers, and they are absolutely essential to the success of high intensity mixing procedures such as the Chorleywood Bread Process.

Common oxidizing agents include potassium bromate, potassium iodate, calcium bromate, calcium iodate, calcium peroxide, azodicarbonamide, and ascorbic acid. These materials have been described in detail in a previous chapter and so need not be discussed further here.

The only pure substance added strictly for its reducing effect is L-cysteine. Glutathione, certain whey proteins, and other substances also have dough modifying effects that have been attributed to their reducing properties. In times past, sulfur dioxide and a substance called sodium metabisulfite were used as reductants to soften and increase the extensibility of doughs used for crackers and hard biscuits, but their use is somewhat questionable from a legal standpoint. They are, however, very effective in causing dough relaxation.

TEMPERATURE RISE DURING MIXING

As a result of the mechanical energy put into the dough during mixing, heat will be generated in the mass. In high speed mixers, especially, this temperature increase can easily reach undesirable levels. An excessive temperature rise can lead to wild fermentation, sticky doughs, and other unacceptable conditions. It can be offset to some extent by covering part of the mixer bowl with a water-cooled or refrigerated jacket. Chilled ingredients can also be used. Ice is commonly added for this purpose, but it interferes with dough hydration and development. Precooling the ingredient water to 35° to 40°F is a better approach, but this, too, slows down dough development and hydration. The usual procedure in large bakeries is to cool some part of the ingredient water to about 35°F and mix it with tap water to secure ingredient water having a temperature calculated to yield the desired dough temperature. Mixers with direct expansion jackets are also available.

Calculation of the ingredient water temperature (or what amounts to the same thing, the amount of chilled water) needed to give the desired dough temperature is a rather complex procedure if all factors are taken into consideration. The predominant item in this list is the mechanical energy taken up by the dough and converted into heat. Other factors are (1) the heat of hydration that results when a substance such as flour absorbs water, (2) the latent heat of solution that results when a substance such as sugar dissolves in water, and (3) the rate at which heat is gained or lost from conduction through the mixer parts. Factors that are seldom considered are the cooling effect of water as it evaporates from the dough during mixing and the heating effect of chemical reactions (mostly related to fermentation) in the dough during mixing.

Even in this day of readily available computers, few bakers are inclined to take into account all of these factors in calculating the amount of cold water needed to be added to a specific dough. Short cuts—simplified calculations—have been developed. They are satisfactory for all practical purposes and will be discussed in more detail in the chapter on mixers.

FERMENTATION

Yeast fermentation adds flavoring substances to the dough, affects the texture of both the dough and the baked product, and supplies carbon dioxide for increasing the volume of the bread. As yeast ferments the sugars in dough, it releases to the surrounding liquid dissolved carbon dioxide and ethanol, as well as metabolic by-products such as lactic acid and acetic acid. Small quantities of many other compounds are also formed and may have effects on processing responses of the dough, and the flavor, color, and texture of the finished product. Further details of yeast action can be found in the chapter on leaveners.

The points at which gas is released from solubilized carbon dioxide have never been clearly identified although they are probably small air bubbles incorporated into the dough during mixing. It is reasonably certain the foci are not the yeast cells themselves. Yeast cells fermenting in a fluid medium do not always show gas bubbles forming on the cell surface.

Two important conclusions that can be drawn from this point are that fineness of the grain, that is the number of gas vesicles in a given volume of bread, is not entirely controlled by the number of yeast cells present and that uniformity of grain is not governed solely by the uniformity of yeast cell distribution and activity. These characteristics must be controlled by other methods and are usually determined by the physical treatment accorded the dough, especially during mixing, dividing, laminating, etc. The mechanical punishment to which the dough is subjected divides the bubbles, increasing their number and decreasing their size.

Substances contributing the major portion of the characteristic aroma of bread and rolls undoubtedly arise either directly or indirectly from the activity of yeast. Some of these are flavor precursors that must undergo some additional reactions during baking before they contribute their desirable flavor notes to the finished products. A substance elaborated by yeast that is a direct flavor enhancer, not a precursor, is ethanol. This compound is a significant component of the odor of the crumb of fresh white bread and many other baked products.

It is well known that odorous substances are created in or near the crust as a result of nonenzymatic browning reactions. Aromas of these compounds will be quite different in character from those in the crumb, and generally are less desirable. The relative role of crumb and crust in bread aroma can be shown by comparing the odor of a yeast-leavened loaf and a chemically leavened loaf containing the same ingredient except for yeast. It is probably needless to say that the aromas are quite different.

Bulk Fermentations

During the sponge stage, the yeast becomes fully active, saturating the aqueous phase of the dough with carbon dioxide, forming ethanol, which mellows and softens the dough, and developing other substances that contribute to the final flavor and affect physical dough properties. Other microorganisms may flourish, ultimately making their own peculiar contributions to properties of the finished loaf. Characteristically, bread sponges become very gassy and full of large bubbles; they also become very aromatic.

Optimum time and temperature for bulk fermentations are variable depending on the formula, the conditions existing at a particular plant, and the effects desired. Temperature of the sponge as it comes out of the mixer has an important influence on the rate of reactions during bulk fermentation. Good bread can be made from sponges held from 3 to 6 hours, though some difficulties may be encountered at the extremes. It is probable the average time will fall in the range of 3.5 to 4.5 hours for sponge fermentation in white bread production. Temperature of the room will normally be held near 80°F and the relative humidity near 75%. The sponge temperature will increase about 10°F. Of course, in smaller plants and in retail bakeries, the sponge or dough may not be held in a special room but in a covered trough or other container placed in a warm area of the plant.

Excessive fermentation will cause the sponge to be too gassy, the gluten strands will be weak, the mass will be sticky, and there will often be a sour aroma indicating that bacteria are starting to take over from the yeast. On the other hand, if the sponge has not been fermented enough, it will be dense and heavy (indicating inadequate gas production), it will be tough and bucky (indicating acid and alcohol production are insufficient), and it will seem too dry.

If fungal enzymes are being added to reduce the remix time, or for other reasons, the sponge temperature should be somewhat less at the remix stage.

Proofing

Proofing, or intermediate proofing, refers to the rest stage following dividing and rounding, when the dough piece is in its final piece weight (except for weight loss due to evaporation and fermenation) but not usually in the final shape that will ultimately go into the oven. During proofing, moisture is redistributed throughout the dough piece, including the partially dehydrated and condensed skin formed as a result of the rounding operation. Gassing continues, and once more expands the bubbles that have previously been established in the dough. The gluten structure of the dough relaxes, presumably through repositioning of the protein fibers that have been stretched and distorted during the preceding steps. Enzymic reactions continue, forming maltose and dextrose from starches and peptides from proteins, among other important changes.

The moisture content of the dough piece may decrease during intermediate proofing, particularly if the outside layer has not been well sealed by the rounding process. It is very important to avoid the formation of a dry crust, since this dehydrated layer may not be fully absorbed during subsequent processing and may appear in the finished loaf as a distinct streak or layer. For this reason, controlled humidification of the intermediate proofing enclosure is highly desirable.

Important factors controlling the extent of dough modification that occurs in the proofing step include (1) the water content of the dough, (2) the soluble solids content of the dough, (3) the concentration of yeast cells, (4) the temperature of the dough, (5) the salt concentration, which must be considered separately from the other soluble solids, (6) the amount and type of conditioners present, (7) the damage done to the dough piece by the divider, (8) the effectiveness of the rounder in degassing the dough piece and sealing its surface, and (9) the humidity in the proofing enclosure, which affects the elasticity and moisture content of the surface layers of the dough piece but has very little direct effect on the overall moisture content.

Pan Proofing

Pan proofing is that stage in which a piece of dough, having previously undergone the hand or machine manipulation establishing the form of the final product, is allowed to expand and otherwise change into a condition suitable for baking. In ancient parlance, this was the "proof" of the dough, the stage during which performance of the dough showed whether or not the processing had been correct up to that point. Expansion and moisture redistribution takes place during pan proofing, the contiguous surfaces that have been pressed together while forming the loaf shape seal to each other so as to eliminate most visual evidence of the molding operation, and the dough begins to fit itself to the pan contours and establish a layer of coalesced vesicles that will be the basis of the crust.

MAKE-UP

For our purposes, make-up will be defined as those dough manipulations occurring between the dumping of the finished dough from the mixer and the placing of the formed piece on the pan or other baking surface, but not including the fermentation reactions described above. It will be obvious that dividing, rounding, molding, and the like are to be covered here.

Dividing and Rounding

At the divider, the remixed dough is cut into pieces of a size suitable for providing the finished product weight. Of course, the weight of the raw dough piece will be substantially greater than the finished product weight because of the provision which must be made for loss of fermentation products and water during the pre-baking processing and for the loss of volatiles during baking. Dough undergoes severe punishment in the divider. Much gas is pressed out of the dough and the bubbles are broken open. Cutting of gluten strands occurs and some redistribution of moisture can be expected. The dough piece resulting from the divider action has large areas of cut surface through which water vapor and carbon dioxide flow freely.

The function of the rounder is to heal some of this damage. As the dough is rolled around the divider surface, a ball is formed which has surface areas of oriented gluten that are partially dried by loss of moisture and addition of dusting flour. This layer acts as a fairly effective barrier to gas diffusion and allows carbon dioxide to accumulate in the interior. Thus, the gas vesicles that have been collapsed and subdivided during previous processing are inflated. One result is that the grain becomes finer and more uniform. Since the yeast can continue to ferment without excessively inflating the dough piece, more flavor compounds can be developed in the bread.

Bread-Molding Processes

In the bread-making plant, the molder receives pieces of dough from the intermediate proofer and shapes them into cylinders (loaves) ready to be placed in pans. Equipment for making rolls is markedly different from loaf-molding devices and will be discussed separately. There are several designs of bread loaf molders, but they all perform four functions: sheeting, curling, rolling, and sealing. The last two could be considered as one function since they are usually performed simultaneously. Details of the operation of bread molders will be given in the chapter on make-up equipment.

The dough exiting the intermediate proofer is a flattened globe. The molder shapes this spheroid into a thick sheet through the operation of sets of reduction rollers. Reduction is in stages so as to avoid excessive punishment, particularly tearing of the sheet. After the sheet is formed, it is curled into a cylinder; at this point the surface of the sheet is mostly intact and only slightly moist, and contact between the adjacent surfaces in the curled cylinder is not continuous. The next function of the molder is to thoroughly seal the contacting surfaces, and this is done by rolling the cylinder through a gradually narrowing channel. Ends of the dough piece are left rather loosely sealed so as to allow gas to escape.

As the dough passes through the molder, there is a tendency for the moisture content of the trailing edge to become increased at the expense of the leading sections. This redistribution of moisture results from the effect of compression on the dough structure. In a conventional molder, the trailing edge, which is of relatively high moisture content, ends up as the outside layer of the cylinder—that is, the outside of the loaf. Many bakery technologists have suggested it would be more desirable to have the wetter portion of the dough sheet folded into the center of the loaf. Observations made of hand-molded doughs formed according to this plan tended to confirm the superiority of "reverse molded loaves."

Some of the major modifications made in molder design are the result of attempts to avoid folding the dry end of the dough sheet into the center of the loaf. Successful developments include the cross-grain molder and the reverse sheeting molder. The former type curls the dough sheet at a right angle to its direction of travel through the sheeter rolls. The reverse sheeting molder curls the sheet of dough so that the wet end of the piece is folded into the center of the loaf. A third approach was to twist the dough piece so that a curled cylinder is formed; an advance on this method was to combine two thin cylinders and twist them together.

From the molder, the raw loaves fall into the pans in which they will be pan-proofed and, later, baked.

Roll-Forming Processes

Machines designed to form dough pieces into buns, rolls, etc., are often integral parts of a combination of machines that perform dividing, rounding, proofing, and molding. In bun dividers, dough from a large hopper is sucked into cavities in a large rotating cylinder by retracting pistons, which then cut off and expel the pieces onto a conveyor leading to the rounder. Since a dough trough will contain enough dough for at least 15 minutes running time, the change in dough properties from start to finish can lead to serious problems in maintaining uniform weights. Attempts have been made to overcome the density change by constant working of the dough to release gas during the time it is awaiting processing, or by placing the dough under pressure while subjecting it to a slight mixing action.

A common type of bun rounder consists of a conveyor belt running under a series of concave bars set at an angle to the belt's line of travel. Dough pieces drop onto the belt from the divider and are pulled along by the belt while the bar applies a sidewise force. These opposing forces cause the dough pieces to rotate and become rounded. Other types use cups reciprocated in a horizontal (circular) direction to round the dough pieces trapped beneath them.

From the rounder the dough balls travel to the intermediate proofer. On leaving this device, the dough is formed in desired shapes by molders, cutters, etc. Attachments can be obtained for making twin rolls, clover leaf rolls, hard rolls, Parker house rolls, Kaiser rolls, etc.

Table 16.2 includes five formulas for regular and specialty rolls, all based on the straight dough process.

Table 16.2. FORMULAS FOR STRAIGHT DOUGH ROLLS[1]

Ingredients	Soft rolls	Hard rolls	Brown and serve	Wheat rolls	Sour cream rolls
Bread flour	52.8	58.3	50.9	30.6	59.2
Whole wheat flour	0	0	0	26.3	0
Sugar	5.2	0.6	4.7	2.7	0.7
Nonfat dry milk	2.6	0	1.4	0	0
Yeast, compressed	2.1	1.6	0.9	1.6	3.9
Diastatic malt syrup	0	1.5	0	2.7	0.5
Salt	1.3	1.3	0.9	1.1	0.3
Shortening	4.1	1.8	6.6	1.5	0
Water (variable)	31.6	32.0	31.3	33.5	4.0
SS-2-L*	0.3	0	0	0	0
Liquid egg whites	0	2.9	0	0	0
Liquid whole eggs	0	0	3.3	0	0
Sour cream	0	0	0	0	31.4

[1] Percent, as is basis.   *Sodium stearoyl-2-lactylate.

BAKING

Under this heading will be found a review of the current knowledge of physical and chemical actions taking place in the dough piece while it is in the oven. Discussions of baking equipment, including more details on the processes of heat transfer, will be found in the chapter on ovens.

When the dough piece enters the oven, it begins a short period of intense chemical activity. Heat flows into the loaf as the result of radiation, convection, and conduction. Each of these modes of energy transmission affects different parts of the dough piece in different ways and, for a proper understanding of the reactions going on during baking, they must be considered separately.

Radiated heat.—Radiation's effect on dough pieces varies in two characteristics from the effects of the other means of heat transfer: (1) it is subject to shadowing, and (2) it is very responsive to changes in absorptive capacity of the dough surface, i.e., to changes in coloration in the case of infrared radiation or to changes in water content in the case of microwave radiation. Infrared radiation does not penetrate much beyond the surface layer of the dough, therefore its effect is mainly on the exposed crust area.

The darkening that accompanies baking indicates an increase in the absorption of visible wavelengths. An increase in the absorptive capacity of the dough surface for infrared rays, though not apparent visually, is an almost invariable concomitant of the visible change. That is, when the crust color darkens, indicating the absorption of radiation in the visible range, it is almost certain changes are occurring that result in increased absorption of infrared rays. As a result of this increase in heat absorption in the darkening areas, there is a tendency for color changes to accelerate after the first browning appears. This means that ovens relying heavily on radiant energy for heat transfer will tend to accentuate color differences. Such effects may be either good or bad, depending on the characteristics desired in finished products.

If heat transfer is unbalanced on the side of radiant energy, the products will tend to darken before the interior is completely baked. If, on the other hand, there is an insufficient amount of radiant energy, compared to convection and conduction, the loaves will come out of the oven with crusts that are too light in color, or, if baking is continued until a proper crust color is obtained, the interior will be too dry and the crust contacting the pan area (due to conducted heat) may be too dark.

The shadowing effect is most apparent with radiation having wavelengths near the visible range, such as infrared radiation, and is much less with microwaves. Infrared radiation impinges on the surface of the loaf at all angles, although its intensity will vary depending on the orientation of the dough piece. It originates from burner flames and from all the metal parts in the oven sides, top, band, etc. Radiation from below the band is completely intercepted by the band and partly re-radiated as infrared radiation and partly converted into conducted heat. sides of the pan shadow the top of the dough piece until the dough rises above the pan, at which time radiation becomes more effective in promoting crust color development.

If the dough piece is shaped approximately like a segment of a sphere, with a relatively smooth surface, and it sits on the oven band, the reception of radiation during its trip through the oven will be approximately equal over all parts of its exposed surface. Some cookies fit this description. Absorption of this radiation will also be approximately equal in all parts of the exposed surface as long as the color (an indirect indication of absorption in the infrared) remains the same over the entire surface. These comments also apply to flat-surfaced pieces covering most of the band.

Products with irregular surfaces, such as cookies with holes in the middle, twist bread, fancy pastry shapes, meringue topped pies, etc., will have some parts of their surfaces in a much better position than other parts to intercept radiant energy. If these surfaces are sufficiently absorptive, heating will occur at an accelerated rate in the prominences. The shadowed areas will receive less radiant energy and will tend to heat slower and brown slower. It should be understood that these effects of radiant energy can be offset to some extent by effects of conducted or convected heat.

Convected heat.—Convection is the transfer of heat from one place to another within a gas or liquid by the gross physical mixing of one part of the fluid (liquid, gas) with another. In the oven, molecules of air, water vapor, and combustion gases heated by whatever means circulate throughout the oven, constantly mixing with other gases and transferring heat by conduction when they contact solid surfaces. Within the dough piece, convection occurs as the result of the movement of water vapor and other gases within the dough structure. Furthermore, translocations of liquid water, melted shortening, and other liquids cause a transfer of heat from one location to another. There is also a flow of dough or batter, at least in some products, which causes a limited mixing of these semisolid materials and a transfer of heat energy by convection.

One of the principal effects of convection within the dough piece is a smoothing or blurring of temperature differentials. The hotter regions of the dough give off more water vapor than the cool regions, and the loss of this vapor in some areas and its increase in others tends to equalize temperatures. Generally, the more water that is present, the more convective transfer of heat occurs.

To generalize the overall results of convection within the oven, it can be said that it causes a smoothing or evening out of heat distribution that has become non-uniform as a result of conduction or radiation to the dough piece. The gases within the oven mix readily as long as there are no mechanical barriers and tend to make the temperature more uniform throughout the chamber. When different temperatures are required in different zones of the oven, it is necessary to isolate these zones in some manner to retard convective heat transfer between them. Ovens that create a high degree of turbulence within the chamber, as by burner flames or blowers, have a high amount of convective heat transfer and a relatively uniform baking rate at most points in the oven. Zones can be created within ovens by adding walls or baffles to isolate the convection forces.

Oven convection affects only the exposed areas of the product. The bottoms of the dough pieces, protected as they are by the band, do not participate directly in this type of heat exchange. It is doubtful that much convective transfer occurs at the bottoms even when mesh bands are used. All exposed parts of the dough pieces probably participate about equally in convective heat exchange, particularly if there is a good deal of turbulence in the chamber. Some protective effect of protuberances could no doubt be shown, but the high degree of turbulence known to exist in the gases above the band and the relatively low profile of most dough pieces suggest that variations in reception of convective heat by the different parts cannot be very great. Products at the edge of the band may receive substantially more heat, however, because of the more rapid flow of hot gases and higher temperatures in this area.

Conducted heat.—Conduction is the transmitting of heat from one part of an article to another part of the same body, or from one body to another body in physical contact with it, there being no appreciable displacement of the particles of the bodies. The rate at which heat is transferred by conduction depends upon the area of contact, the temperature differential (gradient), and the thermal conductivity of the materials. Equations are available to permit determination of the rate of conduction when all the terms are known. In situations where the parts are moving relative to one another, or where the temperature fluctuates markedly, an accurate determination of the rate becomes impractical.

When baking a dough piece in a band oven, conduction of heat occurs through the band and through the pan, if there is one. The band receives its store of energy from conduction through the supports on which it rides, radiation, and convection. Because of the localized nature of conductive transfer, steep gradients of temperature are set up within the dough piece, the hottest areas being the ones in contact with the pan and particularly where the pan is in contact with the band. Unwanted differences in the rates of heat-catalyzed reactions can easily occur unless these gradients are carefully controlled. Conduction from one part of the dough to another is a force tending to reduce temperature differentials, that is, to smooth out the differences.

Summary of heat transfer.—To summarize the effects of the three types of heat transfer during baking, it can be said that conduction and radiation tend to cause localized temperature differentials, conduction acting to raise the temperature of the bottoms and radiation acting to increase the temperature of exposed surfaces (especially darkened areas or protuberances), while convection tends to even out temperature gradients within the oven and, to a slight extent, within the dough piece.

These variables may make it difficult to determine when a dough piece is thoroughly baked; external clues may not give an accurate picture of what is happening inside the piece or at surfaces concealed by pans or bands. Some of the indications that a loaf is fully baked are: (1) The starch has gelatinized and the gluten has been denatured as a result of the center of the loaf entering the range of 206° to 210°F; (2) The crust color has reached a desired hue and intensity; (3) Moisture content of the interior has reached a desired level; (4) The internal characteristics are such that the loaf can be further processed (as in slicing) without seriously damaging or permanently distorting the loaf; and (5) The organoleptic qualities of the finished loaf meet customers' expectations.

Some heat-moderated changes in the product will continue after it leaves the oven and until it reaches room temperature. Among these changes are loss of water, continued browning (especially in those areas contacting hot pans), and changes in the protein and starch components of the crumb. These must be considered when establishing the oven dwell time.

Effect of Form and Size of the Dough Piece

Hearth Breads .–For millenniums, the only loaves that the baker made were hearth breads, lumps of dough placed on the oven surface and allowed to expand freely on all sides. This gave the product a thick crust covering all surfaces and helped to slow down dehydration during the fairly long periods during which some of these loaves were stored before they were consumed. In this book, hearth breads will be defined as those loaves (of whatever size) that are baked without side and end restraints, except for any restraints imposed by contiguous dough pieces. In other words, they are baked on a flat surface, not in pans. This difference, which at first may seem trivial, actually results in very substantial changes in the character of the finished products and often requires different processing techniques and formulations. In modern practice, many hearth breads are baked on sheets or pans of various sorts for the purposes of improved quality and processing convenience, and some are actually baked in pans with perforated side walls, so we must widen our definition to include those loaves that simulate the original hearth breads baked without any kind of pan or container. Now, the crucial difference between hearth breads and ordinary pan bread is simply that the "hearth" loaves have a greater amount of crust.

Rolls may be baked either hearth fashion or in individual cups. By far the greater number of rolls, comprising the categories of hamburger and hot dog rolls, are baked in pans that contain a large number of dough pieces and do not significantly restrain lateral expansion except by the presence of contiguous dough pieces. The pans usually do contain small depressions for each roll; these assist in the positioning of dough pieces when they are deposited in the pan and retain them in place during transfer of the pans, but they have little or no restraining effect on dough expansion during proofing and baking.

Pan Breads .–Pan breads are those loaves baked in containers that restrain the dough on four sides, and sometimes on the top as well (as in sandwich and Pullman loaves). These pans are generally rectangular in outline, possibly with outwardly sloping sides, but some breads are baked in totally inclosed cylindrical containers, tin cans, cake pans, and other shapes of non-conventional geometry. Input of heat, loss of moisture, and crust characteristics are all likely to be affected by these pans, particularly by the totally inclosed designs. In Pullman loaves, for example, the effect of radiant heat is greatly reduced, and must act by first heating the cover of the pan, then being transferred by conduction or convection to the dough. This makes it difficult to get a firm crust, which often leads to a greater number of cripples.

Rolls.–As suggested above, rolls are distinguished from loaves partly by piece size. The Federal Standard for Bakery Products (21 CFR 136) states that rolls and buns weigh less than one-half pound per unit while "bread" means the unit weighs one-half pound or more. Rolls usually do not approach the upper weight limit. Government regulations do not necessarily control definitions applied in retail bakeries or in this book.

Rolls often undergo special forming techniques that give easily recognizable varieties such as kaiser rolls, Parker House rolls, and butter flake rolls. Processing techniques up to the point of forming the pieces are usually very much the same as for loaves, but formulas for roll doughs are often richer and vary in other ways from those used for bread loaves.

Hamburger and hot dog rolls are baked in pans that allow the rolls to touch at their sides and ends, except for those dough pieces next to the side of the pan. Due to shadowing, the sides of the interior rolls receive only minor amounts of radiant energy and, for that matter, not much conducted heat, either. Consumers accept, or even expect, the white sides, but they seem to want the tops to be uniformly colored. This indicates a need for a rather flat upper surface and an oven that has a large contribution of diffuse radiant heat. It is practically impossible to balance the radiant and conducted heat so that the tops and bottoms achieve exactly the same color, but this is evidently not a merchandising problem.

Cooling and Depanning

When removed from the oven, the loaf or roll is very soft and fragile. To avoid distortion, it must be handled with extreme care and minimum force until it has developed greater mechanical strength through cooling and loss of additional moisture. Cooling is normally accelerated by blowing currents of air over the loaves. Sometimes vacuum cooling chambers or refrigerated air are brought into play.

TROUBLE-SHOOTING

In the next few pages, we will cover a few of the most troublesome problems observed in baking plain bread and rolls. It is not possible to cover all of the causes of each defect, but the suggestions should provide a basis for further investigations and may greatly reduce the time spent in finding a solution.

Defects of the Crust

Blistering of the crust.—This defect may be caused by (1) insufficient proofing, (2) insufficient development, (3) proofing at too high a humidity, (4) steam condensation in the oven, (5) insufficient salt, or (6) not molding tightly enough.

Cracking of the crust.—Cracks in the crust can be caused by (1) excessively fast cooling, or (2) formation of a dried crust on the dough pieces before they are put in the oven.

Crust too thick.—Can be caused by (1) insufficient sugar, (2) excessive fermentation, (3) exhaustion of fermentables in the dough, (4) overbaking, or (5) oven temperature too low.

Crust too tough.—Might be caused by (1) excessive amounts of sugar or malt in the dough, (2) excessive steam in the oven, (3) dough not fermented long enough, or (4) insufficient shortening

No shred.—Lack of the typical break at the join of the top crust and the side crust might be due to (1) insufficent steam in the oven, (2) insufficient time for pan proofing, (3) excessive humidity in the proof box, (4) fermentation too long, exhausting fermentable sugars, or (5) dough too young.

Shelling.—In cases where there is a very uneven break or even a separation of the top crust from the underlying crumb, look for (1) too short a pan proof, (2) crust formation during pan proof due to insufficient humidity, (3) young, inadequately fermented, dough, (4) dough too stiff, (5) too much salt, (6) too much top heat in the oven, (7) low protein flour, (8) dough too cold, or (9) pans too large or too shallow.

Crust color too pale.—Usually due to overfermented or old doughs. Other causes might be (1) insufficient top heat in the oven, (2) formula doesn't contain enough sugar or malt, or (3) dough pieces have formed a dry crust before they went into the oven.

Defects in the Crumb

Coarse texture.—If the interior of the loaf shows large or irregular cells, often with a grayish cast of color, the following possibilities can be considered, (1) proofing at too high a temperature, (2) baking at too low a temperature, (3) pan too large for the size of the dough piece, (4) dough brought out of the mixer at too high a temperature, (5) dough has been chilled at some stage, (6) too much pan proof, or (7) inadequate gassing in the rounding or molding steps.

Streaks or hard spots.—The appearance of streaks, either colored or a different shade of white, but usually noticeably denser than the rest of the crumb, can result from (1) excessive amounts of dusting flour, (2) crust formed on the dough piece before molding, usually the result of unduly low relative humidity during proofing, (3) improper mixing of the sponge with the dough ingredients, (4) unclean machinery or machinery that is dropping oil on the dough, or (5) flour that has formed lumps due to wetting at some stage before it gets to the mixer.

Holes in the bread.—Formation of tunnels in the bread is usually due to poor adherence of the dough layers as the formed loaf leaves the molder. Other causes that can be investigated include (1) dough is too soft, (2) too much dusting flour has been applied in the molder or elsewhere, (3) dough was not compressed enough during rounding, or (4) too much expansion occurred during pan proofing.

Dark or dull crumb color.—Grayish, dull crumb can be due to a number of causes. It often accompanies harsh and open texture. Some of the causes are (1) use of dark ingredients such as malt, (2) overfermented doughs, (3) dough is too wet, (4) young doughs, (5) dough too warm out of mixer, (6) contamination from equipment, or (7) crusting of doughs during any fermentation period.

Defects of Volume

Inadequate volume.—If the loaves are too small, as compared to previous batches, some of the possible causes are (1) not enough time allowed for pan proof, (2) too low a temperature during pan proof, (3) cold baking pans, (4) too much salt, (5) oven too hot in early stages of baking, (6) pans are too large, (7) dough pieces were too harshly treated in rounding or molding, or (8) all the sugar has been fermented before the pan proof stage. Of course, low piece weights due to divider errors should be one of the first things examined. Weigh the finished loaf, and compare results with your specification—*verify that your weighing equipment is accurate.*

Excessive volume.—If the loaf is too large, perhaps expanding out of the pan or showing an unduly large crown, the baker will first want to weigh the dough pieces coming off the divider to determine if there is an error at that point. If the dough weight is found to be correct, consider (1) flour may be excessively strong, (2) oven is too cool, especially in early stages, or (3) dough is overfermented.

Defects of Taste or Odor

The most obvious cause of off-flavor is the use of an unsuitable ingredient. Examine shortening for rancidity or near rancidity; perhaps it has absorbed flavors from tobacco, insecticides, cleaning materials, or the like. Dried eggs or dried milk can develop stale flavors, particularly if improperly stored. If you are using a whey product, this is one of the first places to look. It would be unexpected to find that sugar or salt is the culprit, but corn syrup, molasses, malt syrup, or invert sugar (and particularly the latter) can be undergoing fermentation or other types of biological spoilage. If ingredients are stored in bulk and transferred through heat-traced pipes, partial blockage of these pipes can lead to heat damage and off odors.

Artificial flavors can change drastically if stored too long or if stored at too high a temperature. It is advisable to store these ingredients in the refrigerator, but read the manufacturer's directions to make sure this will not cause separation, precipitation, or other undesirable changes. Inadequate quality control can lead to the acceptance of flavor shipments that are not similar to previous lots and that do not meet specifications. Yeast is not often a cause of off-flavors, unless it is badly deteriorated and this can be determined by inspection. Of course, use of too much yeast can lead to nontypical flavors in the finished product.

Other possible causes which may need to be considered are (1) errors in weighing ingredients, (2) use of unsuitable scrap material, (3) fermenting excessively, or not enough, (4) contamination by old dough from troughs, etc., which may have undergone considerable mold growth, (5) contamination by equipment grease, and (6) sabotage by deliberate contamination with all sorts of foreign substances.

Defects in Shelf-Life

If it has been stated by a customer, salesman, quality control representative, or other interested party that the keeping quality of bread or rolls manufactured by your company has changed significantly, the first thing to determine is whether or not this statement is true. It is an easy claim to make, but very hard to support by objective tests. Get a more complete description of the problem. Is the loaf staling as a result of hardening due to moisture loss, toughening due to starch retrogradation or other physicochemical changes, development of mold, loss of flavor, or some other standard? Once the situation has been adequately documented and the parameters of the problem established, remedial steps can be taken.

Baked products in the distribution system encounter widely varying types of storage conditions and it can be expected that their keeping quality will vary according to changes in the weather. In fact, items that never even get out of the store can be subjected to a fairly wide range of temperatures and humidities. Opportunities for contamination by mold, and subsequent spoilage, vary in unpredictable ways that are not necessarily related to characteristics of the bread as it leaves the bakery.

Other things to look at are: (1) Has the packaging material or packaging equipment been changed? (2) Have baking conditions been changed so that the bread is drier, or moister, when packed? (3) Has the blend of softener chemicals been changed, or has the formula been changed in any other way? or, (4) Is the bread being wrapped while it is too warm?

BIBLIOGRAPHY

BAKER, A. E., DIBBEN, R. A., and PONTE, J. G., JR. 1987. Comparison of bread firmness measurements by four instruments. Cereal Foods World *32* 486-189

BAKERY, J. C. 1939. The permeability of brad by air. Cereal Chem. *16*, 730-734

BECKER, J. A. 1975. Variety pan breads. Proc. Am. Soc. Bakery Engineers *1975*, 108-116

BOND, E. E. 1977. Australian non-time doughs. Am. Soc. Bakery Engineers Bull. *210*

BRADY, P. L., and MAYER, S. M. 1985. Correlation of sensory and instrumental measures of bread texture. Cereal Chem. *62*, 70-72

BRUINSMA, B. L., and FINNEY, K. F. 1984. Various oils, surfactants, and their blends as replacements for shortening in breadmaking. Cereal Chem. *61*, 279-281

CAMPBELL, S. P. 1979. Mechanical dough conditioning—new systems. Proc. Am. Soc. Bakery Engineers *1979*, 175-184

CARPENTER, D. H. 1977. Combining continuous mixing and batch-type systems for bread. Proc. Am. Soc. Bakery Engineers *1977*, 43-47

CHUNG, O. K. 1986. Lipid-protein interactions in wheat flour, dough, gluten, and protein fractions. Cereal Foods World *31*, 242-256

DAHLE, L. K., and SAMBUCCI, N. 1987. Application of devised universal testing machine procedures for measuring texture of bread and jam-filled cookies. Cereal Foods World *32*, 466, 468, 470

DERSCH, J. A. 1989. The use of steam in bread ovens. Am. Soc. Bakery Engrs. Bull. *218*

DIBBLE, W. E. 1977. Combining continuous mixing and batch-type systems for buns. Proc. Am. Soc. Bakery Engineers *1977*, 48-51

DUBOIS, D. K. 1981. Fermented doughs. Cereal Foods World *26*, 617-619, 621-622

DUBOIS, D. K. 1984. What is fermentation? Bakers Digest *58*, No. 6, 11-12, 14

ENDO, S., NEGISHI, Y., and SHIBA, K. 1989. New modified gluten product and bread improver composition. U.S. Pat. 4,871,577

ENDO, S., OKADA, K., and NAGAO, S. 1987. Studies on dough development. III. Mixing characteristics of flour streams and their changes during dough mixing in the presence of chemicals. Cereal Chem. *64*, 110-115

ENTRINGER, D. D., SR. 1975. Variety production from single pre-ferments. Proc. Am. Soc. Bakery Engineers *1975*, 52-57

FEINBERG, D. D., SR. 1975. Hearth and modified hearth-type products. Proc. Am. Soc. Bakery Engineers *1975*, 98-106

FISH, A. R. 1982. High speed dough development. Proc. Am. Soc. Bakery Engineers *1982*, 130-136

FORD, K. W. 1977. Specialty breads—update and new trends. Proc. Am. Soc. Bakery Engineers *1977*, 61-63

FORTMANN, K. 1967. Theory of mixing. Proc. Am. Soc. Bakery Engineers *1967*, 64-69

FREEMAN, T. P., and SHELTON, D. R. 1991. Microstructure of wheat starch: From kernel to bread. Food Technol. *43*, No. 5, 162, 164, 165-166, 168,

GLOVER, H. 1975. No-time dough methods. Proc. Am. Soc. Bakery Engineers *1975*, 59-64

GUY, E. J. 1984. Effect of sodium chloride levels on sponge doughs and breads. Cereal Foods World *30*, No. 9, 644-648

HAARASILTA, S., PULLINEN, T., VAISANEN, S. and TAMMERSALO-KARSTEN, I. 1991. Enzyme product and method of improving the properties of dough and the quality of bread. U.S. Pat. 4,990,343

HARINDER, K., and BAINS, G. S. 1990. High alpha-amylae flours: Effect of pH, acid, and salt, on the rheological properties of dough. Cereal Chem. *67*, 588-594

JACKEL, S. S. 1977. When is a loaf of bread baked? Proc. Am. Soc. Bakery Engineers EIS No. *57*

JOENSSON, T., and TOERNAES, H. 1987. The effect of selected surfactants on bread crumb softness and its measurement. Cereal Foods World *32*, 482-485

JOHNSTON, J. R., JR. 1975. Bread and bun softness. Proc. Am. Soc. Bakery Engineers *1975*, 93-97

KAMEL, B. S. 1987. Bread firmness measurement with emphasis on Baker compressimeter. Cereal Foods World *32*, 472-473, 475-476

KAMMAN, P. W. 1979. Recent developments in no-time dough systems. Bakers Digest *53*, No. 1, 26-29

KAMMAN, P. W. 1984. Oxidation. The do's and dont's. Bakers Digest *58*, No. 6, 18-20

KASPER, D. J. 1981. Troubleshooting at the bakery level. Cereal Foods World *26*, 390-393

KULP, K. 1983. Technology of brew systems in bread production. Bakers Digest *57*, No. 6, 20, 22-23

LAHVIC, R. 1989. New success with an old recipe. Bakery *24*, No. 8, 70, 72, 74, 76

LYNN, C. 1984. New fermentation technology. Proc. Am. Soc. Bakery Engineers *1984*, 47

MATZ, S. A. 1961. Yeast-free prepared flour mix. U.S. Pat. 2,969,289

MATZ, S. A. 1972. Continuous processing of bakery products. *In* Bakery Technology and Engineering, Second Edition. AVI Publishing Co., Westport, CT

MATZ, S. A. 1984. Modern baking technology. Scientific American *251*, No. 5, 122-126, 131-134

MATZ, S. A. 1989. Formulas and Processes for Bakers. Elsevier Science Publishers, NYC

MC NICHOLL, C. 1967. Fine breads of the past and present. Proc. Am. Soc. Bakery Engineers *1967*, 46-53

POMERANZ, Y. 1980. What? How much? Where? What function? in bread making. Cereal Foods World *25*, 656-661

POMERANZ, Y., MEYER, D., and SEIBEL, W. 1984. Wheat, wheat-rye, and rye dough and bread studied by scanning electron microscopy. Cereal Chem. *61*, 53-59

POULOS, G. A. 1978. Hearth bread production. Proc. Am. Soc. Bakery Engineers *1978*, 58-62

PYLER, E. J. 1982. Systems of accelerated dough development. Bakers Digest *56*, No. 4, 22, 24-26

SHIRLEY, E. H. 1977. The Canadian concept of no-time dough systems. Proc. Am. Soc. Bakery Engineers *1977*, 36-41

SIEVERS, R. 1978. New baking methods. Proc. Am. Soc. Bakery Engineers *1978*, 98-105

SKEGGS, P. K. 1985. Mechanical dough development—dough water level and flour protein quality. Cereal Chem. *62*, 458-462

THOMPSON, D. R. 1980. State of the art—bakery fermentation. Bakers Digest *54*, No. 3, 28-37

THOMPSON, D. R. 1983. Liquid sponge technology applied to high speed dough mixing. Bakers Digest *57*, No. 6, 11-17

TIPPLES, K. H., and KILBORN, R. H. 1975. "Unmixing"—the disorientation of developed bread doughs by slow speed mixing. Cereal Chem. *52*, 248-262

TURNER, J. E. SR. 1980. Liquid pre-ferments. Proc. Am. Soc. Bakery Engineers *1980*, 176-181

VARVELLO, A. 1989. Breadmaking method for the production of crisp long term preservation small loaves. U.S. Pat. 4,849,230

VETTER, J. L. 1979. Frozen unbaked bread dough: Past, present, future. Cereal Foods World *24*, 42-43

chapter seventeen

CONTINUOUS, SEMI-CONTINUOUS, AND EXPEDITED DOUGHS

INTRODUCTION

It is quite apparent that traditional dough preparation methods as described in the preceding chapter can be very labor intensive and subject to human errors at several points. They also require bulky equipment and much plant space. Many attempts have been made to reduce these inefficiencies by automating and expediting the whole bread making process from start to finish. These attempts were initially frustrated by the need for long holding times during sponge fermentation and by the damage to dough properties caused by ordinary methods of pumping, among other problems.

Bakery technologists generally accepted the concept that doughs needed to undergo "rest periods," stages during which fermentation could occur in the absence of mechanical punishment. After this conventional wisdom began to be questioned, some progress was made in automating the bread manufacturing process.

In this chapter, a discussion of continuous breadmaking plants will be presented first, since these plants attempted to integrate solutions to several important problems that had obstructed earlier efforts to make bread production a fully automated and continuous process. Next, we will examine various segments of the continuous plants separately and in greater detail. Later sections will describe other approaches that have been made and are being made to expedite parts of the breadmaking process; most of these can be, or must be, used in plants that do not support a continuous flow of product from ingredient proportioning to panning.

The main problems facing a bakery technologist or engineer who wishes to make the bread baking process more efficient are: (1) The need to reduce some or all of the time-consuming and space-requiring fermentation periods, (2) Providing a means of "conditioning" the dough that does not require lengthy rest periods, and (3) Automating the transfer and manipulation of dough.

There are several problems of some practical importance that are of less theoretical interest than those listed above; they will be given only brief attention. Some of these minor treatments deal with automatic weighing and metering of ingredients, measurement of dough qualities at various points in the process so that corrective measures can be applied to maintain uniformity, scheduling by data processing methods, simplifying molding procedures, transferring the pans in and out of the final proofer and oven, and refining oven controls. Many of these topics will be covered in considerable detail in the chapters dealing exclusively with equipment.

Continuous processing is not restricted to bread and rolls. Cake batters and many adjuncts such as marshmallow and icings can be prepared by continuous mixing and forming techniques, and some of these lines predate continuous breadmaking plants by several years.

CONTINUOUS PROCESSING OF WHITE BREAD AND ROLLS

History and Background

In the 1950s, successful plants for the continuous processing of bread were developed (reviewed by Matz 1972). The designs that made the most impact in the U.S. were the Baker Do-Maker and the AmFlow process. These two systems, which are no longer being installed, had many features in common. In its original form, the AmFlow process put the dough through a conventional rounder and molder before panning, but this was soon changed to direct panning of extruded dough as had always been done with the Do-Maker equipment. There were other minor differences that will be discussed later.

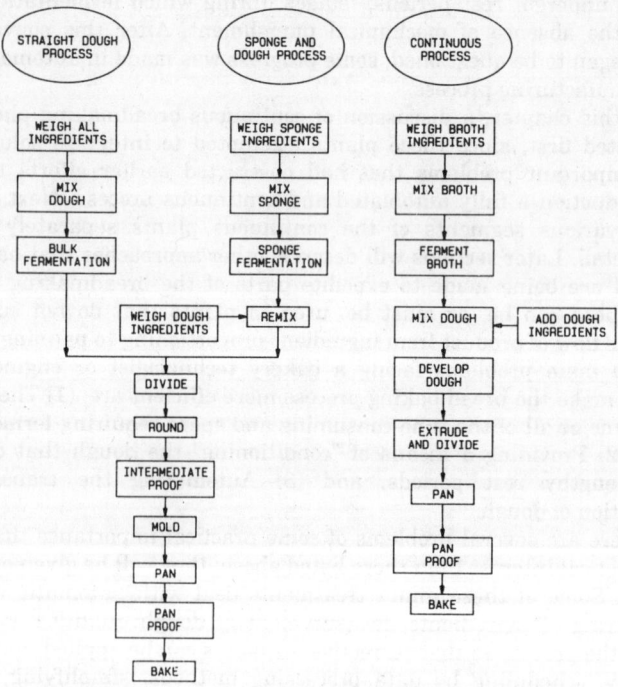

Figure 17.1. Comparison of three methods of making bread doughs

Principles of Operation

Both the AmFlow and Baker plants required liquid sponges or pre-ferments for flavor development, dough conditioning, and other functions. The pre-ferment systems can be considered as replacing the sponge mixer, the dough troughs, the fermentation room, and the trough hoists of the batch plant. Although different continuous plants use different formulas for the broth or liquid sponge, it is customary to find yeast, yeast food, liquid sugar, flour, and some of the previous sponge in the mixture. When fermentation is completed, the broth goes to a preliminary mixing apparatus that blends in the other ingredients. Principles underlying the replacement of a conventional sponge with fermented liquids are treated in more detail in a later section.

The complete mix is fed by a rate-controllable dough pump to the developer, which changes it from a poorly consolidated mass with little or no cohesion or structure to a smooth, moderately elastic, though soft, dough. The kneading work performed in the developer is done on a dough that contains very little gas in bubble form. The 20 lb to 60 lb pressure exerted on the dough and the high speed mixing action drive carbon dioxide into solution and into the gluten matrix.

A smooth cohesive dough emerges through an opening at the end of the high speed developer and passes into the extruder. The latter device forms an elongated cylindrical dough piece that is cut off by reciprocating knives and falls into a pan. The panned dough is conveyed to a proof box where it is allowed to ferment to height or for a given time. It is then delivered to the oven.

Processing the fermentation mixture.—The fermentation mixture is prepared at a definite interval in advance of the time it is to be added to the flour, shortening, and oxidizing agents. Fermentation begins when the yeast is added to a solution of sugar, milk, yeast food, vitamins, and mold inhibitor. After 2 to 2.5 hours (in the original systems), the fermenting liquid is pumped to the premixer. At this time, the yeast is fermenting at a rapid rate and its action brings the pH to about 4.7. The acid elaborated by the yeast has the important function of mellowing or conditioning the dough.

A properly fermented broth makes a positive contribution to the flavor of the finished bread. Long fermentations tend to produce a sour aroma and taste in the bread. Although this may be desirable for some variety breads, it is generally considered a defect in regular white bread.

Preferments influence dough properties after they are mixed with the other ingredients. In general, an overlong fermentation will weaken the doughs, while a fermentation period that is too short will not mellow the dough enough for an optimal response to mixing and machining. The preferment acts upon all fresh flour, and in this respect the dough made in continuous plants resembles that made by the straight dough process.

There is a temperature rise of 10° to 12°F during broth preparation, which may have to be corrected by a cooling step. Cooling exchangers are installed in the transfer line. The finished broth is pumped from the fermentation tank to a surge tank where it can be held for a few minutes. When it is needed, it flows through a constant level tank that provides a steady pressure to the feed pump, thence to the mixer.

Assembling and mixing the dough ingredients.—The flow rate of the broth, as well as that of other liquid and dry constituents, must be under precise control. Flow cannot be interrupted once the plant is started. Constant-rate pumps meter all ingredients into the premixer, which functions as an assembly point for the ingredients. Here occurs the first wetting of the flour with liquids and subsequent mixing to form a homogeneous dough. The ingredients are dispensed into the head end of a two-shafted mixing conveyor, each shaft of which has a series of blades. After mixing, the dough is discharged to a dough pump at the exit end.

The assembled dough is very weak and does not have much gas-retaining capability. It has undergone no development. The dough pump forces the dough under pressure to the developer, and is indirectly involved in shaping the developed dough piece.

Developing the dough.—The developer is one of the most important devices in a continuous plant, for it is this machine that changes the dough from a mass with virtually no structure, very little strength, and extremely limited properties of gas retention to a smooth film-forming substance having good strength and elasticity and the capability of retaining the leavening gas that will be generated.

The kneading work is done on a substantially de-gassed dough. Because of the external pressure and the high speed mixing action, however, carbon dioxide is driven into the dough in the form of very fine bubbles. Much carbon dioxide also dissolves in the aqueous phase. Such actions can in part explain the fine grain and texture of continuously produced bread. The temperature of the dough rises about 18° to 24°F as a result of the work performed on it.

In one design of continuous developer, kneading is done by two vertical impellers that turn at a speed designed to completely develop the dough in a minimum amount of time. Speed of the impellers may have to be adjusted if the type of flour or certain other factors are changed. In general, stronger flours require higher speeds than do medium strength flours. Other factors that may influence the mixing requirements are the amounts of some of the minor ingredients and the absorption. Oxidizing agents can affect mixing requirements. It was found that continuous operations require about ten-fold as much oxidation as conventional doughs.

The amount of electric power being consumed is shown by a recording wattmeter. If a change in mixing requirement occurs, it will be seen in the power curve. When deviations are observed, the operator can make adjustments such as changing the flow rate of cooling water through the heat exchanger. There are also some visual clues to guide the operator. The extruded dough piece, if undermixed, will show striations or laminations. Overmixing is indicated by a glossy surface and stickiness. The feel of the dough and its capacity to be drawn into films also helps the operator judge development and arrive at proper mixing speeds.

Forming and panning the dough piece.— The dough is continuously developed as it progresses toward the exit of the developer, and it should be fully developed as it passes through the slit leading to the extruder. After passing this point, the dough is shaped so that an elongated cylindrical piece can be cut off by opposed knives. The knives operate in synchrony with the pan conveyor, causing a dough piece to fall at the exact time a pan is correctly in place. The rate of extrusion and timing of the knife stroke are adjusted so that dough pieces of the required weight are cut off.

Once panned, the dough is conducted to the proof box where it is allowed to ferment to height or for a given time. From the proofer, pans are delivered to the oven. The proof time is generally in about the same range as required for conventional doughs.

Present status of continuous processing.—Although integrated continuous bread lines of the type described have advantages over traditional batch plants, and seem to yield bread of good quality, they were not as successful as originally expected. Manufacturers reported consumer objections to the bread, which does have some noticeable differences in grain and texture as well as in flavor, when compared with sponge and dough bread. Also, the systems were rather inflexible, not being readily adjustable to make different varieties of bread, and they are very sensitive to changes in some of the ingredients, particularly the flour.

In spite of their problems, several of these plants are still in operation, though in modified form. Other installations have been closed down. The principle seems sound and continuous plants may gain renewed favor in the future, but there will undoubtedly be considerable reluctance to invest in new designs after the less-than-satisfactory results some bakeries obtained with the preceding versions.

Formulating White Bread for Continuous Plants

Continuously mixed doughs have some different ingredient requirements than batch processed doughs. For example, they usually require higher oxidant levels. This may be due to the smaller amounts of oxygen incorporated into continuous doughs and the shorter times available for oxidation to occur. Potassium iodate, potassium bromate, calcium iodate, and calcium peroxide have been widely used. Oxidants are critical to satisfactory functioning of continuous plants, high intensity mixing will not work satisfactorily without them. On the other hand, it appears to be possible to make satisfactory bread at relatively slow mixing speeds if sufficiently high levels of oxidant are added.

Continuous mix formulations are more sensitive to lipid components than are conventionally made breads. Formulas often contain 2% to 5% shortening, usually a mixture of fat and emulsifiers. Adding hard fat (hydrogenated fat flakes) to the shortening results in improvements in grain and specific volume, while all fats that are liquid at the highest temperature reached by the dough produce poor quality bread. Adding hard fat at about the 10% level can correct this problem. It appears that neither the degree of saturation nor the fatty acid composition of the fats is extremely critical to dough properties if solid fats are present during mixing and proofing.

Milk has caused trouble in continuous bread processes. Addition of more than 1% NFDM can result in lower volume and poorer grain, crumb, and texture. These defects can be partially corrected by the use of stronger flours. Of course, the milk solids must be of the high heat type.

Yeast, sugars, and mold inhibitors can be the same as used in batch bread production. Some special additives are said to improve the tolerance and quality of the doughs. Sodium stearoyl fumarate (0.25% to 0.5%) extends the range of developer speeds at which good bread can be made.

MAKING FERMENTATION PROCESSES MORE EFFICIENT

In considering the problems that must be tackled if conventional batch processing of bread is to be made more efficient, it is quite clear that bulk fermentation stands at, or near, the top of the list.

Fermentation is the basis of many practical problems for the baker because large volumes of dough must be maintained at a constant temperature if uniform results are to be obtained. A uniform relative humidity is also desirable. These demands lead to the need for a large amount of space and considerable specialized equipment. In addition, fermentation is sensitive to the moisture content of the dough, salt content, and amount of fermentable sugars. Any fluctuation in one or more of these factors can lead to nonuniform bread and/or scheduling problems. Simplification and control improvement of the fermentation process would reduce capital costs, labor costs, and space requirements.

Any replacement process would have to (1) saturate the dough with carbon dioxide and form gas vesicles having a wide range of sizes, (2) develop fermentation products that are needed for the finished flavor of bread, and (3) modify the visco-elastic (rheological) properties of the dough so that it retains gas adequately and responds satisfactorily to subsequent processing steps, including baking.

If the sponge is replaced by a mixture that can be stored and transferred as a liquid, many of the difficulties of conventional bulk fermentation will be eliminated. Also, fermentation can be expected to proceed at a faster rate when the soluble solids content of the mixture is lower. These considerations led to the conclusion that bakery operations could be greatly improved if the conventional semi-solid sponge could be replaced by a flowable mixture of high moisture content, and, preferably, one with a lower percentage of flour. Working on these assumptions, technolgists developed fermentation broths, brews, liquid sponges, preferments, etc. The initial approaches tended to favor mixtures without flour, or "water brews."

Water brews were easier to handle than sponges, and in general caused fewer production problems, but doubts about consumer acceptance of the flavor of the bread caused a re-thinking of the problem. It is now generally agreed that the addition of flour to the brew tends to open the grain of the bread and improve slicing, stacking, and spreading characteristics of the loaf. It also seems to give more chewiness to the bread and reduces gumminess. One approach adds only a small amount of flour, so that the fermenting mix remains very fluid. A step nearer conventional sponge processing is the use of a considerable amount of flour, giving a liquid sponge having a fairly high viscosity, but still pumpable.

There is a wide variance in industry practice so far as brew formulation and processing are concerned, but all methods require the replacement of a high flour content, elastic sponge with a fluid, pumpable, stirrable fermentation mixture. Liquid sponges (or broths or brews or preferments—these names will be used interchangeably here) contain at least yeast, a fermentation substrate, and water. Some include flour, others do not include any flour. They all permit the use of tanks rather than dough troughs for fermentation and sanitary pumps for transfer. The liquid sponges can be mixed by equipment that is much cheaper and smaller and requires less power than conventional batch dough mixers. Of course, the final dough (containing all the bread ingredients) will have to be developed by some kind of mixer with high energy input, but the use of high speed horizontal mixers for sponges can be avoided.

Thompson (1983) stated that most continuous systems operating in 1980 were based on brews containing 50% to 60% of the total flour in the formula. Several plants that switched from continuous to more conventional breadmaking processes retained the liquid sponge portion of the continuous system. The space taken up by high flour liquid sponge systems is usually less than half that required when trough fermentation is used.

In Table 17.1 is shown a comparison (based on Turner 1980) of a typical early (about 1958 through 1972) pre ferment formula and a formula representative of more recent practice.

Three Kinds of Sponge Replacement Systems

Brews with no flour.—Flour-free brews usually contain water, yeast, yeast food, and a fermentation substrate such as sugar or corn sweetener. Kulp *et al.* (1985) showed that satisfactory bread could be made with flour-free broths. Their mixtures contained water, compressed yeast, sucrose, ammonium chloride, calcium carbonate, calcium sulfate, and salt. Fermentation was conducted at a constant 86°F.

Table 17.1. LIQUID SPONGE FORMULAS AND PROCEDURES[1]

Ingredient	Formula Early type	Recent type
Water	30.	20.
Yeast	3.	3.5
Sugar solids	2.	1.25
Salt	0.7	0.25
Buffering agent	0.25	0
Total sponge, lb	36.	25.
pH range of sponge	4.8-5.4	3.7-4.2
Conditions		
Starting temp., °F	85-86	84-85
pH at start	5.8	5.1
Fermentation time, hrs	2.	1.
Temperature rise, °F	5.	3-4
Temperature peak, °F	91.	89.
Foaming action	Mild	Vigorous
pH attained	4.8-5.2	3.7-4.2
Holding temp., °F	60.	48.

[1] Ingredients as percent of flour (FWB)

The pH tends to drop rapidly in water broths during the first 15 to 30 minutes of fermentation. Afterwards, pH continues to decline, but much more slowly. In an unbuffered (no calcium carbonate) broth, a pH of 3.4 was reached after 120 minutes of fermentation, while brew with 0.2% buffer reached pH 4.4 after 135 minutes, a level considered optimal for bread production. Fermentable sugars continue to be used and carbon dioxide, ethanol, and acid continue to be generated even though the pH does not change much.

One of the functions of the sponge stage is to bring the yeast to a fully active status. For compressed yeast, this takes very little time. Although yeast cells are essentially dormant at refrigerator temperatures, they adapt quickly to conditions in the broth provided the ingredient concentration is not itself a retarding factor and assuming a favorable substrate is available. Putting yeast in contact with a fermentable substrate before it is added to the dough appears to shorten the pan proof period.

Equipment for a water broth system will include holding tanks with special agitators, a refrigeration system, and pumps, pipes, valves, and meters suitable for the system. Cooling is needed because the yeast must be brought to a quiescent state after the predetermined pH has been reached.

One disadvantage of water broth systems is that doughs made from chilled brews require abnormally long mixing times to reach full development. This is caused by lack of conditioning of any of the dough flour and by the unsuitably low temperature of the pre-ferment. As a result, additional dough mixing capacity may be required in order to maintain production schedules. Other disadvantages were cited by Thompson (1983).

Advantages of water broth systems as compared to flour-containing systems were enumerated by Stakley (1985) who had much experience in designing these plants. For example: (1) Time—greater number of doughs from each sponge; (2) Labor—no additional manpower required; (3) Tolerance—tolerance is directly related to flour protein quality; (4) Sanitation—clean-in-place systems can be used and there are fewer sanitation man-hours as compared to other systems; (5) Equipment—great flexibility in tank and refrigeration requirements; and (6) Space requirements—a minimum amount of floor space is required and it need not be temperature-controlled.

Some bakers have found that systems combining two types of brews meet their purposes better than either the water brew or liquid sponge procedure used separately. A primary, or short-term, water pre-ferment is prepared and used as an ingredient for the second stage, short-time flour pre-ferment (Watkins 1985).

Broths containing flour.—When flour is added to the broth, the character of the fermentation changes somewhat. There is a conditioning effect on the gluten that is desirable so far as the texture properties of the bread are concerned. The flavor and aroma components and precursors are different from, and apparently better than, those in water brews. The broths, or liquid sponges, become more difficult to handle as the amount of flour is increased, however, so some compromise is necessary.

Another point to consider is the usefulness of the liquid sponge in varieties other than white bread. Some bakers wish to use one broth formula for several different products. The greater the amount of flour in the sponge, the less adaptable it is to variety breads. It is possible, however, to use high flour liquid sponges in varieties such as rye bread, soft rolls, and raisin bread (Fields 1985).

In plants using mostly conventional equipment, a weighing hopper is positioned above the tank used for sponge make-up. A squirrel-cage agitator incorporates flour into pre-metered water. Because of the high proportion of water to flour, mixing may cause the formation and separation of gluten strands, a highly undesirable condition. Part of the salt is usually added to the sponge to moderate yeast activity and prevent the generation of excessive gas. Too much gas in the sponge can cause transfer pumps to become locked, and it contributes to pressure build-up in the heat exchanger lines.

After the flour is added, the sponge is transferred by positive displacement pumps into one of the fermentation tanks, which are stirred by wide-sweep agitators operating at slow speed. There is a difference of opinion as to need for stirring during fermentation. On balance, it appears to do no harm and may be helpful in obtaining uniform conditions.

After completion of fermentation, as determined by the reaching of specified levels of pH and titratable acidity, the sponge is sent through heat exchangers that rapidly decrease its temperature to between 50° and 65°F. This halts yeast activity. Both swept surface heat exchangers and plate heat exchangers have been successfully used.

According to Thompson (previously cited), ferments using 50% to 60% of the total flour in the sponge give end products equal to those produced with more concentrated sponges or even with conventional sponges fermented in troughs. The ideal ratio of flour to water in a high flour sponge is said to be 1 to 1. This establishes a 65% sponge is about the maximum feasible for good handling properties.

Late model liquid sponge plants embody a positive flow concept that permits a considerable reduction to be made in the number of tanks and pumps. These systems combine the ingredients from the separate yeast and nutrient pre-mixes into a single chilled slurry and replace the multiple fermentation tanks with a patented "first in/first out" fermentation vessel having a series of internal compartments through which the sponge is transferred sequentially. In this way, intermixing is greatly reduced and a continuous discharge of sponge obtained. Because the sponge can be discharged at the same rate it is being pumped in from the incorporator, the system operates in a continuous mode.

All, or nearly all, equipment used for liquid sponges is suitable for clean-in-place sanitation. The product loss due to clean-in-place procedures is estimated to be less than 0.25% (Fields 1985).

Dehydrated ferments.—One recent variation on the pre-ferment concept has been the use of dried concentrated ferments (Lynn 1984). The powdered additives described by this inventor are intended to supplement the broth or pre-ferment thereby greatly reducing the amount of liquid sponge that has to be processed in the bread plant. In brief, the dry ferment system includes the following steps: (1) Yeast, water, and dry ferment are mixed in an "ingrediator;" (2) This pre-mix is pumped into the blending and fermenting tank where flour and water are mixed in; (3) After about 30 minutes, the remainder of the flour is added and mixed; (4) Fermentation proceeds for another 30 minutes; (5) Temperature of the slurry is brought to 45° to 55°F by passing it through a heat exchanger; (6) The chilled liquid sponge is held in an unjacketed holding tank until needed; and (7) Dough is processed subsequently by more or less conventional techniques.

In the late 1950s, the author of this book developed and later patented a chemically leavened bread mix flavored with dry ferments to be used in a field baking system for the armed forces (Matz 1961). Bread prepared by this method received good organoleptic ratings from consumer panels—panelists compared it with bread made in a pilot plant from the regular formula for field bakeries. It would appear then, that acceptable (not necessarily top quality) bread can be made if sponge fermentation is replaced by concentrated dry ferments. The economic advantage of such an alternative for commercial bread is not immediately obvious.

CONDITIONING BY MECHANICAL OR CHEMICAL MEANS

In the conventional breadmaking process, gas production is only one of the reasons for holding dough for extended periods in bulk or piece form. During these holding periods, the dough also undergoes other changes that are important to its proper functioning in subsequent operations. It develops, matures, conditions, relaxes, and is subject other complex and poorly defined modifications thought to be required for satisfactory molding and for baking into a good loaf of bread. These changes are needed to ensure the production of elastic, extensible doughs, and have no equivalents in the usual processing methods applied to chemically leavened doughs and batters. Because the changes generally occur more slowly than gas production, bread processing could be speeded up considerably if the conditioning and maturing periods could be eliminated or reduced by applying some other chemical or physical treatment.

High speed dough mixing, mechanical conditioning, short-time and no-time methods, and other variations have been suggested as ways of shortening or simplifying the breadmaking process. All, or nearly all, of these expedited methods rely heavily on chemical modification to speed up or completely alter the chemical and biological reactions that occur during conventional bread dough processing. Among the additives that have been used are oxidants, reductants, enzymes, and surfactants.

Systems Relying Principally on Chemical Modification

These expedited systems are based on, and can be considered as variants of, the traditional straight dough method. Seldom, if ever, do they include a sponge fermentation step, though, of course, liquid sponges or water brews can be included as ingredients. In emergency situations, bakers have for many years speeded up straight dough processing by increasing the amount of yeast added to the mix and by bringing the dough out of the mixer at a higher temperature than normal. These strategies may give products that are acceptable to the average consumer, but they are seldom of the best quality. Such doughs require increased mixing time, have poor machining quality, and exhibit irregular proofing. The finished products often have poor grain and texture and a short shelf life. In efforts to overcome these defects, bakery technologists have added reducing agents to shorten mixing time, oxidizers to strengthen the gluten, and yeast foods to accelerate fermentation. Enzymes (proteases) may be added to condition the dough and emulsifiers added to improve machining qualities.

The general principle underlying all these expedited processes is the use of chemicals and high energy inputs to substitute for reactions occurring over a much longer period of time in conventional doughs. Higher dough temperatures are often included as part of the system. The claims made for the various methods should be carefully evaluated, since unusual nomenclature is sometimes invoked to maximize the targeted customer's perception of advantages. For example, it is often insinuated that no-time doughs do not receive or require any fermentation or rest period between the initial mixing step and the pan molding step. This is, in fact, never the case, since a short period of bulk fermentation or intermediate proofing, described as "floor time," "processing delay," or with some other euphemism, always occurs. In addition, pan proofing is always required.

Of course, the reason for wanting to substitute expedited dough preparation methods for the traditional straight dough or sponge and dough schemes is the perfectly legitimate motive of economic advantage. Since less dough is in process at any moment, fewer pieces of equipment are needed, the equipment can often be of smaller size, floor space can be reduced, and less labor is required. Additionally, the shorter fermentation time reduces the amount of sugar that is converted to carbon dioxide and ethanol, resulting in a finished product with a higher level of residual sugar, or, conversely, less fermentables have to be added to get the same amount of residual sugar. There is less invisible processing loss.

The scientific rationale justifying the elimination of lengthy fermentation periods is said to include the following points: (1) Gas generation during bulk fermentation can hardly contribute importantly to final product quality because the dough is quite effectively degassed during the molding operation; (2) Most of the important flavoring constituents in a loaf of bread are formed in Maillard reactions occurring in the crust of the baking loaf and not as a result of fermentation, and (3) Modification of physical properties of dough by the slow processes of traditional breadmaking can be duplicated by proper combinations of high levels of energy input and intensified chemical reactions (Pyler 1982). Not all authorities agree that these statements are valid or conclusive.

It is generally agreed that loaves prepared by the modified methods are not exact duplicates of traditional loaves, although it is sometimes said they are better. Without a doubt, millions of pounds of bread made by these methods are being sold every day to consumers who find the products acceptable. It is said that 90% of the bread produced in Australia is made by expedited processes, as is most of the white bread manufactured in England, and a considerable part of the bread and rolls made in Canada. Whether bread made by any process, old or new, is acceptable in a given market is a fact determinable from the consumer reaction to that bread and not by a majority vote of a committee of experts. One thing that is lacking and that is needed is a study of the long term trend of per capita bread consumption in those areas where expedited processes are used to make most of the bread.

There are some formula changes common to nearly all so-called no-time doughs. These are in addition to some special requirements for individual systems that will be described in more detail later. Among the essentials are reducing agents, such as L-cysteine, which are added to reduce the mechanical energy required for adequate mixing and conditioning. Proteases (sometimes lumped in with reducing agents, although their action is very different), and sodium metabisulfite, a very effective reductant, have been used. Yeast nutrients are usually recommended for controlling proof time and oven spring.

Having used reducing agents to shorten mixing time and to reduce the energy requirement by weakening the network of gluten molecules, oxidants must be added to strengthen the dough at later stages when gas evolution begins to place increased strain on the gluten structure. Potassium bromate, potassium iodate, azodicarbonamide, and ascorbic acid are being added for this purpose. Emulsifiers and dough conditioners of other types are widely used to soften the finished bread and slow down staling reactions. These ingredients include mono- and di-glycerides, ethoxylated mono- and di-glycerides, calcium stearoyl-2-lactylate, and the diacetyl tartaric acid esters of mono- and di-glycerides. The absorption level can often be increased by up to 2% since no-time processes tend to give doughs with drier textures than fully fermented doughs. Fermentables (sugar, etc.) can often be reduced by about 1% because of reduced loss of these ingredients during fermentation.

Systems Relying Principally on High Intensity Mixing

A few years after continuous bread plants became available, expedited systems were developed using high intensity mixers to condition doughs so that sponge preparation and long intermediate fermentation were not essential. None of these systems involved continuous procedures ending with dough extrusion. They used modifications of traditional processes to divide, round, and mold the dough. Probably the best known of these mechanical development methods is the Chorleywood Bread Process (CBP). Advantages claimed for this procedure include: less elapsed time for bread production, decreased space requirements, increased product yield, savings on ingredient costs, and better performance of low protein flours.

The CBP mixing equipment uses five to eight times as much energy as required for mixing a conventional dough, yet it completes the mix in five minutes or less. Such doughs must be heavily supplemented with chemicals, usually the oxidants potassium bromate and potassium iodate. Ascorbic acid is sometimes used in combination with bromate and iodate. Figures that have been suggested are 40 to 120 ppm ascorbic acid, 10 to 20 ppm azodicarbonamide, and 10 to 60 ppm potassium bromate. Chemical reducing agents such as L-cysteine are often recommended to shorten the mixing time.

Also required in the CBP is the addition of at least 0.7% (FWB) hard fat (slip point of 140°F or higher) or solid monoglycerides or sodium stearoyl-2-lactylate to preserve the gas retention capability of the dough during the early part of baking. Higher levels of yeast, sweetener, and water are also needed. The absorption is increased on the order of 3% to 6%. Yeast requirements may increase as much as 50%.

The history of the development of the CBP has been closely connected with the Tweedy mixer. This mixer can be used in other expedited dough processes requiring high energy inputs in the mixing stage. It has a cylindrical bowl with a high speed impact plate at the bottom and a series of baffles around the side to rebound the dough onto the revolving plate. When the mixer is loaded and sealed, but before mixing begins, a partial vacuum is drawn on the bowl. After the mixer motor starts, the vacuum is held to 15 to 20 inches Hg, the exact pressure being set according to requirements for crumb grain and cell size. It is quite obvious that, under these conditions, very little gas will be enfolded by the dough during mixing, and most of the carbon dioxide which develops will be lost. More details on the Tweedy mixer are included in the chapter on mixers.

The CBP was not a success in the U.S. Apparently its failure was due in large part to the stronger flours used in the U.S. This led to the need for longer mixing times and thus to extremely high dough temperatures. From time to time, various modifications of the process have been introduced with a view to adapting the principles to market requirements in the U.S.

Research conducted in Australia during the period 1955 to 1965 led to the development of a no-time dough process involving the chemical acceleration of dough development under conditions of high and low speed mixing. The plant consisted essentially of conventional equipment. This system started to be used commercially about 1964 and eventually took over a large part of the production of bread and sweet goods in Australia. Factors said to have led to general acceptance of no-time doughs by both large plant bakeries and small bread shops in Australia include the high quality of the bread and the elimination or reduction of bulk fermentation and floor time.

The main technological advantages claimed, in addition to time saving are: (1) Saving of space, mostly in dough preparation and fermentation areas; (2) Maintaining better control over the dough room—temperature control is simplified by the fact that doughs can finish in the range of 80° to 85°F without adverse results and ambient temperature has little effect when doughs are taken immediately after mixing; (3) Possible loss of dough through production hold ups is greatly reduced because much less dough is in process at any time; (4) Dough handling is improved because of better uniformity of the batches and less sticking in make-up machinery; and (5) Finished product yield is greater because fermentation losses are greatly reduced.

The Australian no-time dough requires a high level of oxidant addition. Normally, ascorbic acid would be added at 100 ppm of flour and potassium bromate at 30 ppm. These oxidants are usually added by the baker in the form of compounded bread improvers that also contain cereal malt flour and yeast nutrients. Addition rates in this system can be compared to the general level of oxidizer supplementation in traditional straight doughs made in Australian bakeries of 10 to 15 ppm potassium bromate. Gluten softening ingredients, either L-cysteine hydrochloride or sodium metabisulfite are necessary to give optimum dough conditioning. They are used at levels of 15 to 75 ppm.

Most Australian bread is made from a slightly enriched dough formula containing nonfat milk solids, shortening, a small amount of sugar, and surfactants in addition to flour, water, salt, yeast, yeast nutrients, and oxidants. The low speed batch mixers used in Australia are two-arm machines having open, rotating bowls with capacities of up to 750 lb of flour. Dough mixing times with these machines normally falls in the range of 20 to 30 minutes. High speed mixers may be of the horizontal type, although vertical high speed mixers using the round bowl typical of the low speed machines are coming into use. With these units, mixing times range from five to eight minutes (Bond 1977)

Further information on expedited production systems can be found in the articles of Thompson (1983), Pyler (1982), and Campbell (1979).

BIBLIOGRAPHY

BECKER, J. A. 1975. Variety pan breads. Proc. Am. Soc. Bakery Engineers *1975*, 108-116

BINGAMAN, C. D. 1972. No-time dough systems. Proc. Am. Soc. Bakery Engineers *1972*, 88-92

BOND, E. E. 1977. Australian no-time doughs. Am. Soc. Bakery Engineers Bull. No *210*

CAMPBELL, S. P. 1979. Mechanical dough conditioning—new systems. Proc. Am. Soc. Bakery Engineers *1979*, 175-184

CARPENTER, D. H. 1977. Combining continuous mixing and batch-type systems for bread. Proc. Am. Soc. Bakery Engineers *1977*, 43-47

CHAMBERLAIN, N., and COLLINGS, T. H. 1979. The Chorleywood bread process: The roles of oxygen and nitrogen. Bakers Digest *53*, No. 1, 20-24

COTTLE, F. E. 1972. Production of bread by combination of continuous mixing and batch processes. Proc. Am. Soc. Bakery Engineers *1972*, 101-106

DIBBLE, W. E. 1977. Combining continuous mixing and batch-type systems for buns. Proc. Am. Soc. Bakery Engineers *1977*, Proc. Am. Soc. Bakery Engineers *1977*, 48-51

ENTRINGER, D. D., SR. 1975. Variety production from single pre-ferments. Proc. Am. Soc. Bakery Engineers *1975*, 48-51

FARIDI, H. 1980. Short-time saltine cracker. Bakers Digest *54*, No. 3, 16-21

FEINBERG, A. J. 1975. Hearth and modified hearth-type products. Proc. Am. Soc. Bakery Engineers *1975*, 98-106

FERNANDES, C. F., DUBASH, P. J. 1985. Accelerated breadmaking process at two fermentation temperatures. Cereal Chem. *62*, 413-415

FIELDS, E. T. 1985. Flour pre-ferments. Proc. Am. Soc. Bakery Engineers *1985*, 70-72

FISH, A. R. 1982. High speed dough development. Proc. Am. Soc. Bakery Engineers *1982*, 130-136

FORD, K. W. 1977. Specialty breads—update and new trends. Proc. Am. Soc. Bakery Engineers *1977*, 61-63

FORTMANN, K. 1967. Theory of mixing. Proc. Am. Soc. Bakery Engineers *1967*, 64-69

FRENCH, F. D., and KEMP, D. R. 1985. Automated mixing using Tweedy high-speed mixer. Cereal Foods World *30*, No. 5, 344-346

GEIGENBERGER, A. A. 1985. Straight/no-time dough process. Proc. Am. Soc. Bakery Engineers *1985*, 65-66

GLOVER, H. 1975. No-time dough methods. Proc. Am. Soc. Bakery Engineers *1975*, 59-64

GORTON, L. 1991. Catering to variety. Baking & Snack *13*, No. 4, 11-12, 14-15

HALLBERG, L. F. 1974. Pre-ferments. Proc. Am. Soc. Bakery Engineers *1974*, 61-66

JACKEL, S. 1977. When is a loaf of bread baked? Am. Soc. Bakery Engineers EIS No. *57*

JOHNSTON, J. R., JR. 1975. Bread and bun softness. Proc. Am. Soc. Bakery Engineers *1975*, 93-97

KAMMAN, P. W. 1979. Recent developments in no-time dough systems. Bakers Digest *53*,

No. 1, 26-29

KOVACH, N. C. 1988. Sponge dough process. U.S. Pat. 4,732,768

KULP, K. 1983. Technology of brew systems in bread production. Bakers Digest *57*, No. 6, 20, 22-23

KULP, K., CHUNG, H., MARTINEZ-ANAYA, M. A., and DOERRY, W. 1985. Fermentation of water ferments and bread quality. Cereal Chem. *62*, 55-59

LOUDENSLAGER, H. E., SR. 1974. Combination bread process. Proc. Am. Soc. Bakery Engineers *1974*, 69-74

LYNN, C. 1984. New fermentation technology. Proc. Am. Soc. Bakery Engineers *1984*, 47

MATZ, S. A. 1961. Yeast-free prepared mix. U.S. Pat. 2,969,289

MATZ, S. A. 1972. Continuous processing of bakery products. *In* Bakery Technology and Engineering, Second Edition. AVI Publishing Co., Westport, CT

MATZ, S. A. 1984. Modern baking technology. Scientific American *251*, No. 5, 122-126, 131-134

MC NICHOLL, C. 1967. Fine breads of the past and present. Proc. Am. Soc. Bakery Engineers *1967*, 46-53

MOSS, R., STENVERT, N. L., POINTING, G., WORTHINGTON, G., and BOND, E. E. 1979. The time-dependent interaction of oxidizing and reducing agents in breadmaking. Bakers Digest *53*, No. 2, 10-17

OJIMA, S. 1988. Method of and apparatus for making bread. U.S. Pat. 4,776,265

OLSEN, C. M. 1974 No-time doughs. Proc. Am. Soc. Bakery Engineers *1974*, 210-215

PARKER, H. K. 1959. Continuous bread processing. *In* Bakery Technology and Engineering, First Edition. S. A. Matz, Editor. AVI Publishing Co., Westport, CT

POULOS, G. A. 1978. Hearth bread production. Proc. Am. Soc. Bakery Engineers *1978*, 58-62

PYLER, E. J. 1982. Systems of accelerated dough development. Bakers Digest *56*, No. 4, 22, 24-26

RICHARD-MOLARD, D., NAGO, M. C., and DRAPON, R. 1979. Influence of the breadmaking method on French bread flavor. Bakers Digest *53*, No. 3, 34-38

SHIRLEY, E. H. 1977. The Canadian concept of no-time dough systems. Proc. Am. Soc. Bakery Engineers *1977*, 36-41

SIEVERS, R. 1978. New baking methods. Proc. Am. Soc. Bakery Engineers *1978*, 98-105

SPOONER, T. 1991. Are you ready for no-time doughs? Baking & Snack *13*, No.5, 28-30

STAKLEY, D. M. 1985. Water pre-ferments. Proc. Am. Soc. Bakery Engineers *1985*, 72-74

THOMPSON, D. R. 1983. Liquid sponge technology applied to high-speed dough mixing. Bakers Digest *57*, No. 6, 11-17

TOLLEY, J. H., JR. 1971. No-time dough systems—what's new. Proc. Am. Soc. Bakery Engineers *1971*, 40-42

TURNER, J. E., SR. 1980. Liquid pre-ferments. Proc. Am. Soc. Bakery Engineers *1980*, 176-181

UHRICH, M. G. 1975. Formulation of liquid pre-ferment. Proc. Am. Soc. Bakery Engineers *1975*, 42-46

WATKINS, F. H., JR. 1974. Fermentation systems. Proc. Am. Soc. Bakery Engineers *1974*, 157-162

WATKINS, F. H., JR. 1985. Continuous mixing process. Proc. Am. Soc. Bakery Engineers *1985*, 68-70

WINALSKI, R. 1972. Liquid ferments. Proc. Am. Soc. Bakery Engineers *1972*, 95-101

WOLFE, J. E. 1971. Continuous sponges—developments for continuous mixing or batch processes. Proc. Am. Soc. Bakery Engineers *1971*, 48-53

chapter eighteen

VARIETY BREADS

INTRODUCTION

This chapter will include descriptions of formulas and processing methods for many kinds of variety breads, that category being defined for the present purpose as any kind of yeast leavened bread product that is not intended to be served as a dessert but excluding the white and wheat bread and rolls discussed in the previous two chapters. As might be expected, the category now being considered includes a very diverse collection of products.

Discussions of yeast leavened products that differ considerably in processing method or formula from regular breads and rolls and are not sweet doughs will be found in a subsequent chapter. These items include English muffins, croissants, pizzas, bagels, pretzels, soda crackers and saltines, and some other products having an unusual feature in their processing.

Many additional formulas and methods can be found in the book "Formulas and Processes for Bakers" (Matz 1989).

SOURDOUGH BREADS

Before commercial yeast preparations became available, bread doughs were leavened with "sours," portions of old doughs that had been kept over from preceding batches for use in inoculating fresh dough with a mixture of wild yeasts and bacteria that had accumulated and stabilized during many such transfers. Although the leavening action, dough conditioning, and flavor development formerly performed by the microflora in sours or starters is now accomplished more uniformly and reliably by commercial preparations of bakers' yeast, there is still some demand for specialty breads having "that old time flavor."

The term "starter" is a term encountered in discussions of sourdoughs. A starter may be a blend of flour, water, and a portion of a previous dough that is fermented for a fairly long time or it may be a more complex mixture containing yeast or some scientifically compared culture of yeasts and lactobacilli in addition to flour, etc. Some starters rely entirely on new inoculations of microorganisms from the environment each time a fresh batch is made up, that is, no previous dough, sour, starter, or culture is added to the mixture of flour, water, salt, etc. Generally, a starter will contain less flour but more water than a sourdough and will be fermented longer.

Sourdoughs do give breads having different flavors (and, usually, different textures) than yeast leavened breads. Sours tend to cause an acidic taste (hence the name) and a more pungent aroma due mostly to the action of lactobacilli. It is true that yeast can produce a considerable amount of acidic compounds during lengthy ferementations but yeast leavened doughs seldom become as acidic as sourdoughs.

A serious problem with the use of sours is their fugitive nature—they tend to change character gradually over a period of time (or abruptly) for no discernible reason. It has been said that some bakeries have maintained their sourdoughs unchanged for more than a hundred years, but this claim must be viewed with some suspicion since it would seem to be impossible to compare the products made today with those made a hundred years ago.

In spite of the greater complexity of the processing method, certain specialty breads are still made with sours in order to achieve the more intense flavor and unusual texture characteristic of such fermentations. Sales of these breads constitute only a small fraction of total bread sales, but, from time to time, a type of sourdough bread will acquire a regional popularity that leads bakers in other parts of the country to attempt to duplicate it. New Orleans sourdough bread and Pacific Slope (San Francisco) sourdough bread are two fairly recent fads of this type. Such breads may actually represent the action of new mixtures of microorganisms as well as substantial modifications of formula and method, but, more likely, the novel features are not this extreme.

Bakers often find it impossible to closely simulate the successful product even when they use what is thought to be an authentic sample of the sour and the same formula and procedure used by the original producer. It is important to recognize that the typical flavors of such products are quite dependent on the organisms present in the culture or sour and on the conditions of fermentation. The other ingredients used in the dough also have an influence on flavor, of course, but it is futile to attempt to reproduce a specific sourdough flavor by manipulation of other components in the absence of the sour used in the original dough.

The "authentic" sample of starter used by a baker in an attempt to duplicate a successful sourdough bread may have undergone changes between the time it left one plant and was put into use at another. The culture that achieves such good results in the original plant may be composed of several different yeast and bacteria acting in conjunction or in sequence in very complicated patterns. Even when the predominant species in the sour is identified bacteriologically and pure cultures of this organism used to make bread, the final results may not be the same as those obtained in the original bakeries. Furthermore, transfer of samples of the sourdough from one plant to another may be accompanied by inadvertent and unrecognized changes, such as death of some of the desirable organisms or the introduction of foreign organisms, so that the transferred sour fails to perform satisfactorily. Additionally, adventitious inoculation of the doughs with organisms that are found on the equipment (such as dough troughs) in the plant of the succesful producer may be difficult to achieve in other plants.

Microflora of Sourdoughs

Leavening and flavor production resulting from the use of sourdoughs occur because of the activity of microorganisms that proliferate during the various phases of starter, sour, sponge, and dough processing. An inoculation of many different kinds of organisms occurs when water and a cereal product are mixed. Apparently, the organisms found in sourdoughs are nearly ubiquitous, being found in the air, on grain and grain products, and on bakery equipment. The type of organism that will survive and flourish depends, however, upon the conditions it encounters. A set of conditions very favorable to one species may be inhibitory or fatal to another.

In recent years, the microflora of sourdoughs has been given considerable attention by bacteriologists and food scientists. The principal acid producing genus of bacteria found in sourdoughs is apparently the lactic acid organism *Lactobacillus*. Some *Enterobacter* and *Citrobacter* have been found in certain preparations but probably do not occur at a level sufficiently high to have much of an effect on the flavor of bread. The yeasts found in sourdoughs are generally *Saccharomyces* species, with perhaps some Torula yeasts and even others.

The lactic acid species of major significance in sour rye fermentations are *L. plantarum*, *L. brevis*, and *L. fermenti*. Other species found in rye bread doughs are *L. delbrueckii*, *L. leichmanii*, *L. casei*, *L. pastorianus*, and *L. buchneri*. In San Francisco sourdough bread preparation, the predominant organisms seems to be *L. sanfrancisco*, a species first isolated from that product. In panettone sourdoughs, *L. brevis* is found. There may be other organisms present and responsible for different flavor notes in sourdoughs that have not been thoroughly studied.

Lactic acid bacteria all produce lactic acid and this substance has an effect on the flavor (and the physical properties) of baked products in which it appears. Some of these bacteria are heterofermentative and produce acetic acid as well. Factors affecting the vigor of individual species include water activity, oxygen tension, substrate availability, and pH.

Bacteria like those found in sourdoughs grow best in high absorption systems. The higher the level of soluble solids, the more the organisms are inhibited. At very high absorptions, however, the concentration of nutrients may become limiting. The pH at which cell multiplication stops is around 4.0. When this pH is reached, there is a sudden drop in the rate of acid production. The most favorable conditions for acidification of a typical rye sour include a temperature of 95°F and an absorption of 90%. Of course, factors other than temperature also affect the microorganism's metabolism.

Leavening effects are dependent upon the action of yeast, bacteria having essentially no effect on gasification of the dough. *S. cerevisiae* is probably present in most sourdoughs. *S. exiguus* is, however, the predominant species in San Francisco sourdough and in the Italian specialty panettone. Other species that have been found in various sours are *S. panis fermentati*, *S. curvatus*, and *S. chevalieri* (Lorenz 1981).

San Francisco (Pacific Slope) Sourdough Bread

This is an excellent example of a highly specific sourdough preparation that gives a product of unique organoleptic characteristics. A process for making it will be described in considerable detail in the following paragraphs, but it should be understood that other procedures may also achieve similar results.

It is necessary to have a starter sponge containing the specific organisms required for this bread. Without the correct microflora, it is useless to try any formula or procedure. The starter sponge is made up of 100 parts of the previous sponge, 100 parts of high gluten flour, and 46 to 52 parts of water. This mixture begins with a pH of 4.4 and, after about eight hours of fermentation at 75° to 80°F, levels off at a pH of about 3.9 or 4.0. The starter sponge is rebuilt in the same manner about three times a day, seven days a week.

The bread dough is formulated with about 20 parts of starter sponge, 100 parts of patent flour, 60 parts of water, and 2 parts of salt. After about one hour of floor time, the bread is made up, and the dough pieces proofed for five to seven hours. During pan proof, the pH drops from about 5.3 to 3.9. The dough surface is cut immediately before baking, and these cuts are said to be necessary to the development of the typical eating quality of this loaf. Baking is at 375° to 390°F for 45 to 50 minutes, the exact time depending on the oven conditions, piece size, etc. Low pressure steam is injected into the oven during the first half of the baking cycle or until the crust begins to color. The dough pieces are generally placed directly on the hearth. The pH of the crumb doesn't change much as a result of baking, so the final bread has a pH of 3.9 to 4.0.

Pure cultures of *L. sanfrancisco*, said to be the bacteria primarily responsible for the unique flavor of this bread, are available in freeze-dried or frozen form. The sourdough yeast, *S. exiguus*, has proven to be very difficult to stabilize for commercial distribution, but it has been shown that bakers' yeast can be substituted for *S. exiguus* if minor modifications are made in the process (Sugihara 1977).

Sourdough French Bread

Most bread sold in France is made by a straight dough process using commercial bakers' yeast (Richard-Molard *et al.* 1979). Minor amounts are made by a sponge dough method ("sur poolish") and by a sourdough procedure ("sur levain"). Compared with the bread made by the straight dough process, sur poolish bread has a stronger and more pleasant flavor. Levain bread is characterized by a marked acidic taste that differs considerably from that of the two other types.

Gas chromatographic methods showed that all three types of bread contained acetic acid with minor amounts of propionic, isobutyric, isovaleric, valeric, and caproic acids. When these constituents were quantitatively analyzed, it was found that sur poolish crumb contained twice as much acetic acid as the straight dough crumb, and the sur levain had 20 times as much. The level of isobutyric acid is six times higher in the straight dough bread as compared to the sur levain bread. The authors previously cited speculated that acetic acid acts as an enhancer of the flavor of sur poolish bread, making the consumer more aware of other aromatic components.

Panettone

This Italian specialty, a kind of sourdough fruit cake traditionally consumed during the Christmas season, exhibits a number of unusual features that justifies its discussion here. Most of the following material has been taken from the excellent review of Sugihara (1977).

The preparation process for panettone involves a fermentation process based on the yeast *S. exiguus* (the same organism found in San Francisco sourdough) and a heterofermentative lactic bacteria *L. brevis*. Other lactobacilli as well as *Enterobacter* and *Citrobacter* may also contribute to flavor development.

Panettone production begins with a 24-hour fermentation of a starter mixture composed of flour, water, and the necessary microorganisms. The ripened starter is used to inoculate a sour sponge composed of flour and water. The sour sponge is rebuilt two or three times to obtain a sufficient amount to make the "white dough." The latter composition is prepared by adding flour, butter oil, sugar, and water to the sour dough. White dough is allowed to ferment 8 to 10 hours at 85°F, and then mixed with flour, water, egg yolk, butter oil, raisins, and candied fruit peels to make the "yellow dough." Yellow dough is divided, rounded, and molded before proofing for 8 to 10 hours at 95°F and, finally, is baked for about an hour.

Salt-rising Bread

Salt-rising bread is a specialty product having some superficial resemblances to white bread. It has an unusual texture and a pungent aroma, which it gets from a combined yeast and bacterial fermentation. It was formerly prepared by using a natural sour or starter made by encouraging the proliferation of salt-tolerant organisms present in the environment and/or the ingredients. No doubt some home bakers still use this method for developing starters, but practically all commercial salt-rising bread being made in this country (and there isn't much) is based on a proprietary dry "yeast" preparation (Kohman 1959).

As is the case with many strong-flavored products, salt-rising bread exhibits a dichotomous distribution of acceptance. Some people find it very appetizing while many others dislike it intensely. There is a wide variation in texture and flavor of samples made by different producers, but a frequent description of the odor is that it is "like cheese." The specific volume is about 75% that of white bread.

Following is a method based on the use of a commercial type of salt-rising "yeast." Mix 2 lb of the special yeast with 24 oz of nonfat dry milk and stir into 12 lb of water near the boiling point. Cover to prevent drying and keep at 90° to 100°F for about nine hours. When gas begins to form, stir the mixture and allow to stand until the culture is light. Do not let the culture ferment until it becomes sour and thin because it will not make satisfactory bread in this condition. Make the sponge by adding the culture to 33 lb of water (110° to 130°F) which has been mixed with 40 lb of bread flour. Mix only enough to blend the ingredients uniformly. The sponge should be at about 95° to 100°F, and it should be kept warm for about two hours or until it begins to drop. Be careful not to age this sponge excessively. Add 20 oz nonfat dry milk, 40 oz shortening, 40 oz sugar, and 20 oz salt to 33 lb water at 120° to 160°F. Then add 80 lb of bread flour and, finally, the sponge. Mix at low speed just enough to make a smooth dough. At this time, the dough should be near 100°F and just stiff enough to handle well in make-up. Scale or divide within 15 minutes and mold the dough pieces immediately. Avoid chilling the dough. Pans should be of a size such that the dough fills them about half full. Brush the tops of the loaves with melted shortening. The loaves have a tendency to crack on the sides, so place two pieces of dough in each pan to allow the split to occur in the middle. a pan measuring 8.5x4x2.5 inches is suitable for a 1.5 lb loaf molded this way. Pan proof about one hour at 100° to 115°F or until the dough doubles its bulk. If the dough is over proofed, the bread's texture will be coarse and the loaves will not have much oven spring. Bake at normal temperatures for bread.

RYE AND MULTIGRAIN BREADS

Multigrain Breads

All multigrain breads are coarser in texture, darker in color, denser, and stronger in flavor than white bread. They are generally more difficult to process than white bread because the multigrain doughs tend to stick and tear in the make-up equipment and do not ferment in as uniform a manner. Baking response is often erratic, as well. On the other hand, consumers are less critical of differences in appearance, flavor, and texture from loaf to loaf do not demand the softness they equate with freshness in white bread. Texture staling is not quite as much of a problem in multigrain bread—it does occur but the change in firmness is not as obvious—but mold growth can be a greater problem.

Multigrain breads must include either strong wheat flour or vital wheat gluten to reinforce the gas-retaining structure that is necessary for the production of an acceptable finished product. Clear or straight flour from spring wheat is often recommended. Bran, germ, or other by-products of wheat milling may be present. These breads will also include one or more of the following in the form of meal, flour, flakes, or granules: triticale, durum, oats, barley, rye, corn, rice, millet, or sorghum. One of the soybean preparations, usually defatted meal, is a fairly common ingredient. Less common additives are buckwheat, linseed meal, cottonseed meal, potato flour, and bean flour. Absorption of these doughs can be expected to be significantly lower than that of white bread formulas. Table 18.1 gives the basic formulas for several multigrain breads.

Table 18.1. FORMULAS FOR MULTIGRAIN BREADS[1]

Ingredient	Honey whole wheat	Oat and wheat	Mixed grain	Corn and wheat	Wheat ama-ranth
Flour, strong	0	23.3	50.8	38.0	51.5
Water, variable	32.8	37.1	33.0	34.5	32.5
Salt	1.4	1.5	1.0	1.2	1.0
Yeast, compressed	1.1	1.5	1.5	1.4	1.9
Honey	3.3	2.3	0	0	0
Shortening	3.3	1.7	2.0	3.2	4.3
Yeast food	0.1	0	0	0.1	0
Dried skim milk	3.3	0	0	2.2	3.0
Whole wheat flour	54.7	0	0	0	1.9
Sugar	0	0	4.1	0	0
Corn meal	0	0	0	16.2	0
See NOTES	0	(1)	(2)	(3)	(4)

[1] Percent, as is basis.
NOTES: (1) 32.6% oatmeal; (2) 7.6% of a mix composed of 70% crushed wheat and 10% each of soy grits, rolled oats, and corn meal; (3) 3.2% molasses; (4) 3.9% amaranth flour.

The principal reason for adding non-wheat grains is their appeal to the consumer's desire for novelty or for a more "healthy" bread. In a multigrain bread containing several of these ingredients, it is likely some of them will be present at a level so low that their effect on the bread's organoleptic characteristics or nutritional quality is negligible. The nutritional or "health" image of the bread is frequently reinforced by using molasses or honey as the sweetener, polyunsaturated fat as the shortening, and buttermilk as the dairy component.

Preparation methods for these products are extremely variable, but some uniformity has been achieved by the commercialization of franchised varieties (e.g., Roman Meal) that require the use of standardized formulas and often of premixes. Incorporation of relatively large chunks of grain, as is often the practice with these ingredients, makes pre-soaking almost essential. Otherwise, dry or partially hydrated pieces carry through to the finished product as hard chunks that make for unpleasant eating. Mixing is generally at low speed or medium speed.

Multigrain doughs should be kept slightly on the underfermented side and the doughs should be cool—about 78°F. One hour floor time is generally sufficient. The panned dough piece should be proofed at 95°F for about 70 minutes, or until the dough is about one-half inch above the pan rim. These doughs do not have much oven spring.

A variety called sprouted wheat bread can be made by soaking entire wheat kernels (e.g., 100 lb wheat grain plus 111 lb water) for about 20 hr at 70°F, draining off the excess water, coarsely grinding the grain, and adding this material as the wheat component to a formula consisting of 6 lb water, 2.5 lb salt, 2.5 lb margarine, 0.5 lb lecithin, 3 lb nonfat dry milk, 6.5 lb molasses, and 2.5 lb yeast. The recommended procedure consists of mixing for 10 minutes at medium speed, bringing the dough out at 78°F, giving it a floor time of one hour, scaling 18.5 oz in a 1-lb size compact pan (8x4x2.8 inches), proofing for about 70 minutes at 95°F, baking 60 minutes at 400°F, and cooling two hours before slicing and wrapping.

Rye Bread

Since there are no Federal Standards of Identity for rye bread, there is an extremely wide range of characteristics and of quality in the products going by this name. They range from very light colored, fully expanded loaves with an extremely mild flavor to the dark sourdough breads such as pumpernickel, which are almost black in color, strong in flavor with distinct sour notes, dense (heavy), and have a texture that is moist, coarse, and rough. The nomenclature applied to different varieties is very confused and inexact. Many ethnic, regional, and other descriptions are applied without any clear rationale: American, Bohemian, German, Jewish, Polish, Russian, and Swedish—as well as New York, Milwaukee, Vienna, etc. Rye breads called by these names tend to have wide areas of overlap in characteristics.

The characterizing ingredient in all rye breads is, of course, some type of processed rye grain. Most of the possibilities are enumerated and described in the chapter on ingredients from "other" cereal grains. Commercially available rye products are white rye flour, medium rye flour, dark rye flour, rye meal, cracked rye, and rye flakes.

Other commonly used ingredients, the characteristics of which have a significant effect on rye bread quality are wheat flour, salt, sours or cultures, sweeteners, malt, shortening, and flavors (spices, etc.). Caraway is a spice that is found in the majority of rye breads, and most consumers regard it as an essential part of rye bread flavor.

A strong wheat flour must be included in rye doughs. Because rye flour is nearly inert so far as providing an effective gluten structure is concerned, this function must be taken over by the wheat flour if good machining properties are to be had in the dough and good volume and texture obtained in the bread. Most rye breads contain a fairly high percentage of salt, 2% (FWB) is not unusual and 3% can be found in some samples. Sweeteners may or may not be included. Many bakers prefer to add about 1% diastatic malt syrup instead of regular sweeteners; this material not only has its own sweetening effect but produces sugars from the rye starch through its saccharifying action. For the lighter types of rye bread, from 5% to as much as 10% of sweeteners can be added. Caramel color is an indispensable ingredient in darker forms of rye bread. Even with 100% rye flour processed by any practical baking method, it is impossible to obtain the very dark loaves desired by some consumers. Some formulas call for as much as 10% (FWB) of caramel color.

Shortening is used at zero to 2% in the darker and sour types of rye bread, and at somewhat higher levels in light hearth and pan rye breads. More shortening leads to a softer crust, and this can be a detriment in some types of rye breads.

Rye sours are commercially available. The true dehydrated cultured sours and the bacterial cultures that enable the baker to make his own uniform sours constitute one group, while the other group of sours consists of blends of organic acids and various flavoring materials. The compounded flavors almost always contain caraway. A small amount of anise may be added. Onion is occasionaly used to give a distinct variety with considerable appeal. Traces of dill, fennel, or fenugreek have been suggested.

Table 18.2. FORMULAS FOR VARIETY RYE BREADS[1]

Ingredient	Light	Honey	Onion	Pumper- nickel	Raisin
Flour, strong wheat	32.0	42.4	36.9	43.8	34.4
Flour, light rye	21.3	4.6	12.3	5.5	17.2
Flour, dark rye	0	4.5	6.1	5.5	0
Water, variable	41.6	34.8	36.9	35.6	34.4
Yeast, compressed	1.1	1.2	1.2	1.1	1.1
Salt	1.2	1.0	1.2	1.4	1.1
Dark molasses	0	2.4	0	1.2	0
Caramel color	0	0	0	4.4	0
Shortening	1.2	1.1	2.3	1.1	1.1
Dried skim milk	0	3.9	0	0	0
Caraway, whole	1.1	0.2	0	0.5	0
Caraway, ground	0	0	0	0	0
See NOTES	(1)	(2)	(3)	0	(4)

[1] Percent, as is basis.
NOTES: (1) 0.5% diastatic malt syrup; (2) 3.9% honey; (3) 3.1% chopped fresh onions; (4) 8.6% raisins, 1.6% diastatic malt syrup, and 0.5% sugar.

Mold inhibitors, emulsifiers, dough conditioners, and yeast foods are also found in the formulas for most modern rye breads. It is difficult to understand the justification for adding reducing agents or proteases to these inherently weak doughs, and yet some published formulas call for these additives.

Table 18.2 summarizes a few suggested trial formulas for variety rye breads.

Processing.—Most rye doughs are made by the sponge method, sometimes preceded by a sour fermentation. Straight dough methods can be used successfully, however. Rye doughs will typically be mixed in horizontal mixers at slow speed for 25 to 30 minutes, they are probably less sensitive to the agitator design and require less development than wheat flour doughs. As the percentage of rye flour in the formula increases, mixing times and speeds should be decreased.

Rye doughs should be set at a fairly low temperature, say 75° to 78°F, and allowed to ferment for a relatively long time, as compared to white bread doughs. For sourdough types, the percentage of sponge is kept at about 33% and it is composed of rye flour, water, malt, yeast, and about 2.5% to 3% of conventionally made sour dough. The mixture is allowed to ferment about four hours at 78°F. Generally, short intermediate proofing times are required.

Machine make-up procedures can be applied to most rye doughs, though these mixtures are definitely more troublesome than the average white bread dough. They tend to tear and stick and they recover from punishment more slowly.

Correct pan proof times for doughs with low levels of rye flour can be based on that used for white bread doughs. For hearth bread of this type, it is best to give the dough a full proof, i.e., the end point is when the dough will hold a finger impression without filling it up. At one time it was considered necessary to dock (puncture) the heavier types of rye bread with a wooden dowel or a metal spike just before the loaves are placed in the oven. With proper control of processing, this operation is either not needed or can be replaced by slashing across the top.

Most bakers believe that baking rye bread directly on the oven surface gives the best flavor, but this is impractical for most large commercial operations where sheet pans, screens, baskets, frames, sandwich bread pans, perforated pans, etc. are used to speed up transferring loaves into and out of the oven. Most doughs require a relatively high temperature and a stable heat. The optimum temperature will vary according to the size and type of dough piece. For the dense dark type, an oven at 450°F may be suitable, while pan breads of low rye content may perform better at 500°F.

It is very desirable to use a lot of low temperature steam (wet steam) in the oven, especially during the first part of the bake. The goal is to get moisture condensation on the crust so that it remains flexible and can expand without bursting. If this is not possible, somewhat the same effect can be obtained by washing the exposed surfaces of the loaves with a starch wash. To reduce loaf deformation and jamming in the slicer, rye breads should be cooled to an insided loaf temperature of 90° to 92°F before slicing.

Trouble Shooting.—Tough crusts can be caused by (1) doughs that are too soft, (2) using high pressure rather than low pressure steam in the oven, or (3) allowing the dough surface to dry out before baking.

Blisters can be caused by (1) using a weak flour, (2) excess proofing, (3) dough temperature that is too high, or (4) condensation of droplets of water on the unbaked crust.

Poor rye flavor can be caused by (1) mixing the dough at too high a temperature, (2) adding insufficient salt, (3) fermenting the dough too long, or (4) using stale rye flour.

Flaring or cracking near the bottom of the baked loaf may be due to (1) oven temperatures too low, (2) dough too young, (3) a dough that has been overmixed.

There are some rye bread faults attributable directly to flaws in the sour (Lorenz 1981). Some of these are listed below.

A volume that is too low can result from (1) a sour not fermented long enough, (2) a sour fermented so long that some of the microorganisms were inactivated, or (3) a sour that was too cold.

Gummy streaks in the crust can result from (1) a sour that was allowed to ferment too long or at too high a temperature, or (2) use of too much sour in the dough.

Cracks in the crust can result from (1) sour that was not fermented enough or (2) sour that was too warm.

Flat loaves result from using too much sour or sour that is too old.

Uneven crumb color can result from use of sour that is too young.

An excessively acidic taste can result from sours that are too old, too warm, or used in too large a quantity. Bland tastes usually result from use of insufficient sour or a sour that has not been fermented enough.

Crumbly interior structure can result from use of sours that are (1) insufficiently fermented or (2) held at too low a temperature.

Examples of formulas and procedures.— Rye breads of acceptable commercial quality can be made from relatively simple formulas.

Rye Bread Formula and Process

(1) A sponge of the following composition is fermented for 3.5 hr at 76°F:
   20 parts medium rye flour
   30 parts water
   2 parts yeast
(2) To the fermented sponge are added the following ingredients:
   80 parts strong first clear wheat flour
   35 parts water
   2 parts salt
   1 part diastatic malt syrup
   2 parts shortening
(3) The dough temperature, as it comes out of the mixer, should be about 80°F. Process as described earlier in this section.

Bread made by this formula will be light in color. It is common practice to add caramel color to make the crumb and crust more appealing and to correspond more closely to the customers' ideas of what real rye bread should look like. Dark molasses is sometimes used in place of caramel color, but many consumers do not appreciate the sweet and bitter flavors contributed by molasses. Caraway seeds or rye sour flavors may be added.

Pumpernickel.—A brief description will be given of pumpernickel, since it is a distinct type different from the rye breads previously discussed. The definitive publication on traditional pumpernickel is probably the article by Lorenz (1980), which reviews the history of this bread and describes several variations in formula and processing method.

Ingredients used in the old style pumpernickel include whole rye meal, water, salt, sour, and scrap bread. Optional ingredients are sweetener, a pre-ferment, and bakers' yeast. The whole rye meal should be medium coarse ground. The oldest formulas did not call for any sweetening ingredient, but relied on the formation of sugars as the result of enzymatic hydrolysis of starch and on the baking process. The dark color is at least partially due to the long baking time, caramel color is not used. The sour provides leavening action, but 0.3% to 0.4% yeast may be added.

The sourdough is prepared by a sponge and dough method, beginning with a starter containing acid-forming bacteria and sourdough yeasts. A rather lengthy process involving repeated transfers, additions of rye flour, and fermentation periods is used. The scrap bread is prepared by grinding and roasting stale loaves, then soaking the crumbs overnight in warm water.

The formula is as follows: to 220 parts full sour and 450 parts scrap mash is added 900 parts whole rye meal, 200 parts water, 15 parts salt, and 5 parts yeast. The ingredients are mixed for 20 to 25 minutes at low speed, after which the dough is rested for 15 minutes. Then, another 10 to 15 minutes of low speed mixing is applied. After the dough is dumped, it is immediately divided, rounded, shaped, and placed into baking pans that can be closed on all sides, like sandwich loaf pans. These pans have rounded corners and small holes in the bottom to increase access to steam. Pan proof time is about 50 to 60 minutes.

The filled pans are stacked side by side and on top of each other in the oven and baked for 16 to 24 hours at a temperature of 212° to 338°F. It is essential that the oven chamber be filled with steam. After baking, the covers of the pans are removed to allow moisture vapor to escape.

OTHER VARIETY BREADS

Breads with Vegetable Ingredients

General considerations.—The only vegetable used in commercial bread to any appreciable extent is potato, usually in the form of flour, and potato bread will be described in more detail below. Many other vegetable ingredients have been suggested for inclusion in bread doughs, however.

They are added primarily for their novelty appeal and supposed health benefits rather than for any significant improvement imparted to the bread's flavor or texture. Tomato products, particularly ketchup, keep turning up as bread ingredients in newspaper recipe columns, in cookbooks issued by churches and social organizations, etc. Carrots, beets, and other vegetables occasionally appear as bread ingredients in the same publications. It will be noted that these ingredients tend to be highly colored and so add some visual attraction to the bread. Although such variety breads can hardly be expected to ever command a large market, they might be of value to a commercial baker as a means of bringing attention to his other products. Most local papers would give a paragraph or two to Smith's Rutabaga French Bread.

Fruits are also rather uncommon as bread ingredients although raisin bread is available in most markets. This variety is mostly used for making toast, but sometimes for sandwiches. The dough portion of raisin bread may be slightly sweetened, but a very light sprinkling of cinnamon is often included between the dough curls—the powdered spice is sprinkled on the dough at the molding station after it has been sheeted out and before it is curled, if it is possible to arrange the machinery to do this. Loaf breads with fruit constituents other than raisins, such as bananas, dates, apple sauce, etc., are fairly common as dessert items but these delicacies are almost always "quickbreads," that is they are made from chemically leavened batters. They do not fit into the scope of the present chapter.

Semi-sweet mufins with vegetable components such as corn kernels or peppers, or sweet muffins with fruit components such as blueberries or apples are very popular, but nearly all of them are made from chemically leavened doughs or batters. Suggested trial formulas for breads containing vegetable and fruit ingredients will be found in Table 18.3.

Potato bread .—Potato bread can be made using a primary ferment that includes mashed cooked potatoes. This is the original method and it gives a sour dough type of flavor together with a moistening and softening effect arising from the potato starch. Some of the original potato flavor will carry through to the finished loaf if enough of the mashed vegetable is present. For many years, however, the potato bread found on the supermarket shelves has been made from a white bread formula with some potato flour added. Although this approach will not give the sourdough flavor that is obtained when a starter is used in the sponge, it does often cause an improvement in texture and a slight difference in flavor.

Shown here is a procedure that uses bakers' yeast but is fairly close to the original sourdough method since it includes a lengthy fermentation of a starter made with potato flour and wheat flour. Prepare a sour by mixing 3 lb bread flour, 2 lb potato flour, 4 lb water, and 2 oz yeast. Set at about 75° to 80°F and allow to ferment for 24 hr. Make a sponge mixture by adding 40 lb water to 70 lb strong bread flour, 3 lb yeast, and 6 oz yeast food. Ferment for 4 to 4.5 hr. Then make the dough by adding the sponge to 3 lb potato flour (yes, an additional portion), 30 lb bread flour, 21 lb water (variable), 1 lb shortening, 2 lb salt, and half (4 lb 9 oz) of the sour. Give the dough 15 to 20 min floor time, then make up. Bake at 425° to 450°F with steam in oven.

A formula and procedure that calls for the addition of potato flour in the dough stage, primarily for its texturizing and marketing advantages is given next. Make a sponge of 65 lb bread flour, 35 lb (variable) water, 2 lb 4 oz yeast, and 6 oz yeast food. The sponge should come out of the mixer at 77°F. Ferment 4.5 hr, then mix it for two minutes at low speed with 35 lb bread flour, 5 lb potato flour, 35 lb water, 2 lb 4 oz salt, 8 lb sugar, and 3 lb shortening. This dough should come out of the mixer at or near 78°F. Allow a floor time of 25 minutes. Make up and bake as for regular white bread.

Table 18.3. FORMULAS FOR FRUIT AND VEGETABLE BREADS[1]

Ingredient	Raisin	Tomato	Carrot	Pump-kin	Apri-cot & pecan
Flour, bread	39.1	53.4	54.1	47.3	53.6
Water, variable	23.8	23.5	27.1	20.3	10.0
Yeast, compressed	1.4	1.2	2.5	1.4	1.8
Salt	0.8	1.1	0.8	0.7	0
Yeast food	0.1	0	0.1	0	0
Shortening	1.4	3.2	3.3	3.2	9.8
Dried skim milk	2.2	3.2	1.6	1.5	1.0
Sugar	2.9	3.2	3.2	3.3	0.7
Liquid whole eggs	0.9	0	0	6.5	12.6
Diastatic malt syrup	0	0.5	0	0	0
See NOTES	(1)	(2)	(3)	(4)	(5)

[1] Percent, as is basis.
NOTES: (1) 27.4% of soaked and drained raisins; (2) 10.5% canned tomato juice; (3) 7.3% mashed cooked carrots; (4) 15.6% canned pumpkin and 0.2% of pumpkin pie spice mix; (5) 3.5% chopped pecans and 7.0% diced and floured dried apricots.

Breads with Dairy Ingredients

Most bread formulas contain a small amount of dried milk or milk replacer. Liquid milk is seldom used because of stability and handling problems and cost. Dried nonfat (skim) milk is by far the most common form of dairy ingredient, but dried whole milk and dried buttermilk are also used in considerable quantity. Dried whey, and combinations of dried whey with soy products, are rather widely accepted as cheap replacements for nonfat dry milk. Butter is regarded as a desirable shortening and flavoring ingredient but its use is restricted by its cost to premium and specialty breads. Although condensed milk and evaporated milk are used in some adjuncts, they are rarely employed as dough ingredients because they provide no special advantages and are more costly than dried milk. They are also rather difficult to store. Cheese, especially cheddar and American types, is used in some variety breads either in the natural form or as dry powders.

So far as their action on bread doughs is concerned, these ingredients fall into two categories—the nonfat portion and the butterfat. Nonfat dry milk, dry buttermilk, whey, and the milk replacers seem to add to the absorption and mixing tolerance of the dough, improve crust color, and mellow the flavor. It is important to use high heat milk solids, however, because the serum or whey proteins of milk can have a weakening effect on gluten. For this reason, all dairy products containing nonfat solids should have been processed by high heat methods if they are to be used in doughs. All reliable suppliers of milk powders will understand and comply with this requirement. If they have not been heat denatured the milk proteins will weaken the gluten proteins and make the dough sticky and hard to handle.

Use of a few percent of butter, buttermilk, or cheese, or fairly high levels of dried milk can give special character to the bread, in addition to permitting advertising claims that have some marketing advantage. There is little doubt that most consumers regard the presence of characterizing amounts of dairy ingredients as signaling quality improvements, especially in flavor. It should be noted that dried buttermilk contains about 5% milkfat. Butter can be procured in flavor intensified forms that are many times more effective than fresh butter in modifying the aroma and taste of bread.

The lactose of liquid and dried whole milk, skim milk, buttermilk, and whey is a reducing sugar that helps promote browning of the crust during baking. It has very little sweetening power and does not serve as a substrate for yeast fermentation. Since it does affect the osmotic properties (water activity) of the aqueous phases of dough, it may reduce the activity of yeast however. Lactose is not a substrate for yeast fermentation, but it can be used by certain bacteria.

DIETETIC BAKERY PRODUCTS

General Considerations

Many bakers have sought to tap the market for special dietary foods by producing breads meeting the requirements of persons whose choices of foods and beverages have been restricted by medical advice or personal health goals. There is a wide range of products falling into this category. Probably the biggest market segment is calorie-reduced and calorie-metered foods for weight reduction diets. Examples of products that can be expected to meet a more limited demand are reduced salt products for hypertensive persons, reduced cholesterol for those who are concerned about present or future arteriosclerosis, gluten-free for children who are afflicted with celiac disease, and sugar-free for diabetics. Bakery products have variable adaptability for these goals—it is much more difficult to make a low-calorie bread than it is to formulate a low calorie carbonated beverage, for example. On the other hand, it is easy to develop a cholesterol-free bread.

There are labeling restrictions affecting all of these categories and the manufacturer must be prepared to meet federal, state, and local regulations if the intention is to offer such products for sale.

In the paragraphs below will be given some basic concepts in formulating specific types of dietetic breads. Table 18.4 gives some preliminary concept formulas which can serve as a basis for experimentation.

Table 18.4. FORMULAS FOR DIETETIC BREADS AND ROLLS[1]

Ingredient	No salt added	No fat added	Gluten free	Chole- sterol free	High fiber
Flour, bread	56.7	57.9	0	53.6	50.3
Water, variable	35.0	34.7	35.8	34.9	35.2
Yeast, compressed	1.1	1.2	2.5	2.7	1.2
Salt	0	1.0	0.8	1.3	1.0
Shortening	2.5	0	2.5	0	3.0
Dried skim milk	1.7	1.7	0	2.6	2.0
Sugar	3.0	2.9	0	2.0	2.0
Liquid whole eggs	0	0	3.3	0	0
Diastatic malt syrup	0	0.6	1.2	1.3	0.5
See NOTES	0	0	(1)	(2)	(3)

[1] Percent, as is basis.
NOTES: (1) 53.9% rice flour, fine granulation; (2) 1.6% vegetable shortening; (3) 5.0% corn bran, food grade.

Reduced Salt

Salt is an important part of the flavor complex of bread. It also acts as a regulator of fermentation and has an effect on gluten strength. These functions make it a difficult task to prepare salt-free bread—it is not a matter of simply deleting salt from the formula while keeping all other factors constant. Replacement of salt with potassium chloride to make a reduced sodium bread is one possibility. Yeast does not respond to potassium chloride in the same way it responds to sodium chloride, so the baker will have to establish new times for fermentation and proof periods if this approach is being taken. Potassium chloride has a bitter note that is definitely discernible in bread containing this seasoner. If a chemically leavened product is being made, substantial amounts of sodium will be brought into the product by the sodium bicarbonate and probably by the leavening acids. Increasing sweetness of the product may mask the absence of sodium, to some extent.

Reduced Fat

Breads with low fat content can be readily formulated. This saves a few calories per serving, but the reduction in fat is probably of more interest to persons who are specifically reducing their intake of triglycerides than to weight-reducers. Both the processing response and the eating quality of the bread are affected by fat reduction, but not to the extent that either is unacceptable. Use of emulsifiers or surfactants in less than 1% quantities can improve dough and bread quality in low-fat products, and these ingredients do not necessarily increase the triglyceride content of the bread. However, diluents, carriers, and impurities in commercial versions of emulsifiers may be triglycerides.

Gluten-free

It is useless to try to make a normal-appearing loaf of bread that contains no gluten. The typical form, structure, and texture of breads are based on gluten networks expressed on the macro scale as elastic bubbles inflated by gas. No other edible substance functions in the same way as gluten. Celiac (coeliac) disease, the disorder that is related to gluten ingestion, can be triggered by wheat, rye, durum, or oat flour. Some writers have said that barley or even malt can also cause these symptoms, but there appears to be little or no evidence for this claim. Corn and rice are probably low-risk cereals for sufferers from celiac disease.

Of course, vital wheat gluten can't be used either. The best that can be done is to use eggs as the structure forming ingredient and rice or corn flour as the cereal or bulking component. Sometimes corn starch is used to eliminate any cereal protein. Most of the egg-based formulas will not give a batter that can be relied upon to support itself when in the form of a one pound loaf. Generally, the smaller the piece size, the more likelihood of success. Normal fermentation and proofing steps are out of the question for such products, although the addition of a fermented liquid at the final mixing might be helpful. De-gassed beer, added as a small percentage of the total liquid, might be helpful in simulating some parts of bread flavor.

This recipe for a gluten-free muffin can serve as a starting point, but the author has not verified it. Mix 9 parts water and 18 parts finely granulated rice flour with 2.5 parts of yeast. Bring out at 78°F and allow to ferment for 2 hr. Add 27 parts water and 36 parts rice flour to the "sponge" and mix until smooth. Ferment for 45 to 60 minutes. Scale into muffin tins (dusted with corn starch) about half full. Proof about 10 minutes. Bake at 385° to 410°F. This batter cannot be processed on bread equipment.

"Diabetic" or Sugar-free

In formulas for regular white bread, sugar is present in amounts too small to have much of an influence on the health of diabetics, assuming the usual consumption of a couple of ounces of bread per meal. Most of the carbohydrate in bread is in the form of starch. Some glucose and maltose is formed in the dough after water is added, provided amylases are present, but only a small quantity of sugar remains at the end of a normal fermentation. It is assumed that diabetics will have received dietary guidance from their physician and this will include advice on whether or not to moderate or cease their consumption of bread and rolls. Of course, sweet baked goods (cakes, pies, pastries, etc.) will probably be unsuitable for the diabetic diet.

In spite of the above statements, there does appear to be a demand for "sugar-free" bread. The term "sugar-free" can mean different things to different groups of consumers. Some health food buyers wish to avoid refined white sugar (sucrose, beet sugar, cane sugar), and would probably accept a product that contained honey, molasses, corn syrup, malt syrup, or even the so-called "raw" sugar. Few problems are encountered when one of these ingredients is substituted for the small amount of sugar usually added to bread dough. Even if sugar-free is interpreted to mean "does not contain added sucrose, glucose, or fructose," the demand can be met provided the baker is willing to make minor modifications in the standard bread formula.

Sugar is usually added at the level of only a few percent in white bread and it is rapidly converted by yeast into glucose and fructose and then mostly metabolized, so the amount present is continually reduced as the dough ferments. Sugar does not play an important role in establishing the structure of dough, but it has an indirect influence on the physical properties of bread as a result of its effects on fermentation. As a source of preferred metabolites, its effect on fermentation is substantial but it can be replaced to some extent by the glucose and maltose generated by diastatic malt syrup or fungal amylases. Malt syrup does include quantities of glucose, maltose, and higher saccharides—these constituents should be taken into account when making labeling claims. Incidentally, corn syrup, honey, molasses, etc., must also be omitted from bread described as being "free of added sugar(s)." Milk products (except caseinates) include considerable lactose, a disaccharide sugar. It is obvious that bread from which all sugars have been omitted or consumed by yeast will be less sweet than regular white bread and, therefore, less palatable to most consumers.

As an alternative approach, a chemically leavened loaf can be made and necesary sweetness supplied by saccharin or aspartame. Formulation and processing of sugar-free sweet doughs and cakes, where sugar has a definite effect on the texture of the normal product, is much more difficult.

Reduced Calorie

Significant reduction of calories per unit weight of white bread is very difficult, because there is no non-caloric replacement ingredient for gluten and starch that does not have severe effects on the organoleptic characteristics of the product when it is included at the level required. The starch that forms such a large proportion of flour and bread cannot be replaced by any substance of low caloric content (less than, say, 1 calorie per gram) without destroying most of the desirable characteristics of bread.

Most non-bakery products that are advertised as having reduced calorie content depend upon the replacement of most of the fat (about 9 calories per gram) by either water (no calories) or by carbohydrate and protein (about 4 calories per gram). If the normal product contains very little fat, significant calorie reduction per unit weight can only be achieved by replacing carbohydrates and proteins with water. For example, in low calorie beverages, the sugar or other caloric sweetener of the normal product has been replaced by water plus a very small amount of saccharin or aspartame.

Because of the complex nature of bread and its sensitivity to formula modification, the usual approaches to calorie reduction are seldom practical. Use of non-digestible substances such as purified cellulose (which theoretically has zero calories) to replace flour has received some attention. Other obvious candidates as replacements are ingredients having high dietary fiber contents such as corn bran or rice bran. Unfortunately, these materials also have severe effects on physical and sensory properties of the dough and bread, so much so that even the most dedicated weight watcher might find the food unacceptable. Also, white bread is a product covered by Federal Standards of Identity and virtually nothing of a calorie-saving nature can be done without violating these regulations. Designing the label to clearly indicate the product is not "white bread" is a way to avoid the restrictions of the Federal Standards.

An approach that has been tried is to reduce not the calories per unit weight but the calories per serving, a serving being defined as a certain number of slices, usually two. Comparison is then made between the calories per serving of the dietetic bread and the calories per serving of regular white bread. Calorie reduction is accomplished by reducing the weight of a slice, generally by making it thinner but occasionally by modifying the height or width. There is some logic to this approach. A large percentage of sliced bread is consumed as a sandwich component and, presumably, only two slices per sandwich would be consumed whether the slice weighed one ounce or three-quarters of an ounce. Some manufacturers have gone a step further and attempted to puff up the bread so that a slice has about the same dimensions but weighs significantly less than a slice of regular bread. There are regulatory uncertainties involved in all these approaches.

No Cholesterol

It is easy enough to make standard types of bread and rolls without cholesterol. This requires simply eliminating any animal fats or ingredients made from animal fats. Most authorities seem to agree that cholesterol is not found in any plant product, including vegetable oil, or is present in negligible amounts. Some published analyses do, in fact, show traces of cholesterol or cholesterol-like substances in vegetable lipids. Actually, a pure animal fat (pure in the sense that it contains triglycerides only) wouldn't contain cholesterol either, but lard, butter, and other common shortenings made from animal fats include some of this substance. The formulation changes required are, in most cases, minimal and any baker can easily make them with little or no effect on the finished product provided the changes involve substituting vegetable shortenings of equivalent physical characteristics to the animal shortening that is being replaced.

The producer must exercise caution in screening minor ingredients and processing aids if a "no cholesterol" claim is being made. Some emulsifiers are made from animal fats and thus may contain traces of cholesterol. Pan greases may contain animal fats. Washes to impart glossiness to the crust may contain materials with cholesterol content.

Kosher

Modifying non-kosher products so that they conform to Jewish dietary laws can lead to substantial ingredient changes, processing problems, and scheduling difficulties, particularly if the baker also intends to make non-kosher products in the same plant. It is nearly always desired to place on the product label the guaranty mark of some kosher-certifying person, agency, or group (these are religious organizations, not government entities) and in this case the baker will have to accept inspections of the plant, ingredients, ingredient specifications, products, packaging, cleaning materials, etc., by representatives of that agency and pay them a fee. The requirements of the different certifying agencies seem to vary somewhat and can be quite complex. It is advisable to get full details of the requirements from an agency whose guaranty mark the baker intends to use before any contractual commitment is made.

BIBLIOGRAPHY

AL-ZUBAYDI, A. H., AL-KAISSI, A. A., SHAKER, K. A., and HAMEL, S. M. 1983. Use of date syrups in breadmaking. Cereal Chem. *60*, 6-58

ANON. 1947. Variety Rye Breads. Service Men's Bulletin *138*. Standard Brands, NYC

ANON. 1952. Specialty Breads and Basic Sweet Doughs. Borden Food Products, NYC

BROEG, W. E. 1964. Down Maine sourdough bread. Baking Industry No. *1540*, 28-30

COLLAR, C., MASCAROS, A. F., PRIETO, J. A., and BENEDITO DE BARBER, C. 1991. Changes in free amino acids during fermentation of wheat doughs started with pure culture of lactic acid bacteria. Cereal Chem. *68*, 66-72

CRAMER, H. B. 1971. Flavor in bread by the Guthrie process. Am. Soc. Bakery Engineers Bull. *193*

GORDON, J. 1970. Production aspects of rye bread. Bakers Digest *44*, No. 5, 38-39, 67

GORTON, L. 1990. Put baked foods on a diet. Baking & Snack Systems *12*, No. 8, 15-18

KOHMAN, H. A. 1959. Formula for salt rising bread. H. A. Kohman, Pittsburg, PA

LORENZ, K. 1980. Pumpernickel—production and quality characteristics. Bakers Digest *54*, No. 6, 14-16

LORENZ, K. 1981. Sourdough processes—methodology and biochemistry. Bakers Digest *55*, No. 6, 33-38

MATZ, S. 1989. Formulas and Processes for Bakers. Pan-Tech International, McAllen, TX

MEIGS, H. T. 1987. Pacific Slope sour dough breads. Am. Soc. Bakery Engrs. Bull. *183*

MRDEZA. G. 1978. Trends for specialty breads. Cereal Foods World *23* , 635, 638-639

RICHARD-MOLARD, D., NAGO, M. C., and DRAPRON, R. 1979. Influence of the breadmaking method on French bread flavor. Bakers Digest *53*, No. 3, 33-35, 37, 39

SPIEL, A. 1985. Rye flavoring. U.S. Pat. 4,560,573

SUGIHARA, T. F. 1977. Non-traditional fermentations in the production of baked goods. Bakers Digest *51*, No. 5, 76, 78, 80, 142

chapter nineteen

YEAST-LEAVENED SWEET DOUGHS

INTRODUCTION

This chapter includes discussions of sweet or dessert-type baked goods made from doughs that derive most of their leavening action from yeast fermentation. Separation of the discussion into sections is done primarily on traditional bases, partly relying on differences in the methods of forming the dough and partly on cooking method (baking, frying).

PLAIN AND ROLL-IN SWEET DOUGHS

Regular sweet doughs are those mixed and fermented somewhat like bread and roll doughs, but which are considerably richer in composition (especially in sugars and syrups) and are often made up in fancy shapes. Doughs for individual sweet rolls and for coffee cakes are made in very much the same manner. These products are nearly always flavored with spices or extracts, and are usually filled and coated with icings or glazes, and often topped with mixtures containing fruits, nuts, cheese, etc.

Roll-in sweet doughs represent another type of bakery sweet goods. They differ from regular sweet doughs by being put through a laminating process in which shortening is layered in the product. This process resembles the laminating methods used in making puff pastry (described in an earlier chapter) but frequently calls for a lower proportion of fat and the layering conditions are not as critical since the finished product is not expected to show the same flaky characteristics as puff pastry. It does have some flakiness if well made, however, and it has more volume than Danish pastry.

Danish pastry can be considered as an extension or elaboration of the roll-in method. It uses more shortening for laminating than is used for lower quality roll-in doughs, and the conditions of laminating are more carefully controlled. Regular roll-in sweet doughs are sometimes made by the sponge method, but Danish doughs rarely are. Products made from roll-in doughs tend to be moderately high in specific volume and soft in texture, while Danish pastry tends to be flat (relatively high in density) and often rather crisp. Danish pastry production will be discussed in a separate section.

Sweet dough products are adaptable to many kinds of variations. Among the modifications that can be used to create new products are: (1) Modify the dough composition or processing conditions; (2) Vary the type of filling; (3) Vary the topping; (4) Modify the composition of the icing; (5) Change the shape or size of the finished piece; (6) Vary the size or shape of the baking utensil; (7) Alter the ratio of filling to dough; or (8) Change the packaging presentation. It is not possible to discuss all of these many variables in the present chapter; only the dough composition and processing conditions will be discussed here.

Additional formulas and process for yeast-leavened sweet doughs can be found in the book, "Formulas and Processes for Bakers" (Matz 1989).

Ingredients

Full details regarding ingredient specifications and their functional properties will be found in the first ten chapters of this book. Brief reviews of the important details will be given below.

Flour, water, yeast, shortening, sweetener, salt, flavors, and emulsifiers will be found in most sweet doughs. Eggs and milk products are also common ingredients.

Flour will vary from mixtures of bread flours and pastry flours as used in some of the smaller shops where manual make-up is the rule to very strong hard wheat flours used in extruder lines. Soft wheat flours tend to improve tenderness of the finished product, all other conditions being equal.

Quality of ingredient water is seldom a problem. Variations in municipal water supplies are generally not great enough to noticeably affect the characteristics of sweet doughs.

The range of sugar or other sweetener addition is probably 15% to 25% (FWB), perhaps higher. Roll-in products tend to have too much color, be slightly soggy, and have less volume when more than 20% (FWB) sugar is used. The concentration of sugar in sweet doughs is limited by the effect on fermentation rate of high sugar concentration. Above about 25% sugar, fermentation is severely restricted.

Salt need not be a special kind. The range of this ingredient will be from 1.5% to 2% (FWB).

Compressed yeast is used at the 5% to 10% level (FWB), with the higher levels being more common in cold processed Danish pastry and in high sugar doughs. Lower percentages perform adequately in sweet doughs of lower than average richness. Modern high sugar doughs should contain at least 8% yeast to give reasonable proofing times. Chemical leaveners are sometimes used to provide an extra boost of gas generation in the pan proof stage and in the oven.

The amount of yeast food and dough conditioner needed by sweet doughs is a matter of considerable debate. Oxidants, reducing agents, and enzymes may be helpful, depending on the processing conditions.

Egg ingredients may be added in the liquid form or as dried products. When developing formulas, many bakers like to start with an amount of liquid whole eggs about equal to the sugar percentage.

High heat NFDM is the dairy ingredient most often used in these products. The milk solids content of sweet doughs usually ranges from 5% to 12%, with many formulas calling for 6% to 8% of NFDM.

Shortenings are often the emulsifier shortenings based on hydrogenated vegetable oils supplemented with monoglycerides. Specifications for the roll-in fats vary considerably; special fats formulated and processed to give plasticity over a wide temperature range, but still giving minimum interference with eating quality, are available.

Formulas, General

Straight dough formulas are probably the first choice of small shop operators and specialty bakers. Sponge doughs are preferred when volume and softness are top requirements. Sponge fermentation may be of the two to four hour "short sponge" type, or longer as in white bread fermentation. Two typical formulas for regular sweet doughs are given below. These doughs can be made into many varieties of sweet rollss and coffee cakes by appropriate finishing techniques.

Straight Sweet Dough Formula and Procedure
(1) Cream until light: 4 lb granulated sugar, 4 oz salt, 1 lb nonfat dry milk, and 4 lb emulsifier shortening.

(2) Add 3 lb liquid whole eggs to the above and continue creaming.

(3) Disperse 1.5 lb compressed yeast in 9.5 lb water and add to the above.

(4) Then, add 12 lb hard wheat patent flour and 6 lb pastry flour and mix until smooth.

(5) Mix at high speed until the dough cleans the mixing bowl. It should come out of the mixer at 80°F for best results.

(6) Allow the dough to ferment about 1.5 hr. Don't punch. Scale pieces of desired weight. Form into strips and make into shapes as required.

Sponge Sweet Dough Formula and Procedure
(1) Cream until light 2 lb emulsifier shortening, 4 lb granulated sugar, 4 oz salt, 1.5 lb NFDM, 0.5 oz mace, and 1 oz rum flavor.

(2) Add 4 lb liquid whole eggs, then cream until light.

(3) Disperse 2 lb compressed yeast in 8 lb water and add to the above, mixing briefly. Then add 18 lb strong flour. mix until smooth.

(4) Bring out of mixer at 80°F and let ferment for 1.5 hr or until the sponge starts to fall.

(5) Disperse 1 lb compressed yeast in 1 lb of water and mix into sponge.

(6) Heat 2 lb of emulsifier shortening to 140°F and add to the above. Mix until smooth. Add 2 lb of bread flour and mix well.

(7) Give dough 20 minute rest, then scale pieces of desired size, Form into shapes, fill, etc.

(8) Let pieces proof to about 50% to 75% size increae. By adding nuts and mixed dried and glazed fruits, this dough can be made into stollen. It is also useful for other sweet goods.

(9) Bake at 300°F for large loaf sizes, 325°F or higher for smaller pieces.

The formulas used for roll-in doughs, where the doughs are sheeted out, a layer of fat applied, and sheeting repeated, are slightly different from those used for regular sweet doughs. An example is given below.

Roll-in Sweet Dough Formula and Procedure
(1) Cream until light 5 lb granulated sugar, 1 lb salt, 2 lb NFDM, 4 lb emulsifer shortening.

(2) Add 8 lb liquid whole eggs and cream until smooth.

(3) Mix 16 lb ice water with 3 lb compressed yeast, then blend with above.

(4) Add 12 lb pastry flour and 24 lb strong bread flour to the above, then mix to a smooth developed dough.

(5) Divide the dough into two equal parts. Sheet each piece into an oblong about three-fourths inch thick. Spread 8 lb roll-in shortening or margarine over two thirds of each sheet. Form three layers inclosing the shortening and sheet out to about the original thickness. Refrigerate for 15 to 30 minutes. Repeat the folding, rolling and refrigerating two more times (don't add more fat in these operations).

(6) Make into desired shapes using various types of fillings, toppings, etc. Proof to between 50% and 75% increase in size. Bake at 325° to 350°F depending on size.

Procedures

Traditional methods.—It is believed that most sweet doughs that are not otherwise described are being made by straight dough processes, especially in the smaller shops, but they can be made and are being made by other conventional processes and by any of the pre-ferment, accelerated, no-time, short-time, and continuous methods used for bread doughs. In general, sweet doughs are less sensitive to changes in preparation method than are bread doughs, because the latter must take full advantage of the optimum expansive qualities of the gluten, while sweet doughs can vary in specific volume and flavor over a fairly wide range without significant consumer complaints.

Mixing can be performed either in horizontal bread mixers, vertical mixers, or in the revolving bowl mixer often used for pie crust doughs. Straight doughs are mixed until the dough just starts to clean the mixer bowl—for roll-in doughs a little less, for regular sweet doughs a little more. Danish pastry doughs are generally mixed only until they are smooth. The richer the dough, the longer the mixing time is a pretty reliable rule.

Doughs for regular sweet goods, whether sponge or straight dough process, should come out of the mixer in the range of 74° to 80°F. Temperatures are critical in mechanical make-up plants. Doughs colder than 72°F are likely to be sticky, but have been recommended for some extrusion operations. Doughs above 82°F are also usually sticky and are troublesome to sheet.

With a sponge at 76° to 78°F, a three hour fermentation is recommended. Straight sweet doughs are given a full rise and then a short proof period before dividing or hand scaling.

Refrigeration is an important tool in making regular and roll-in sweet doughs and is almost indispensable in the preparation of Danish pastry. The temperature of the refrigerator should be just above freezing. Although little yeast activity occurs below 40°F, the colder temperature is needed to chill the large masses of dough as quickly as possible. About 10 lb of dough is the maximum that should be placed on a bakery sheet pan, and the piece should be flattened out to minimize thickness and expedite cooling. It is not advisable to use sub-freezing temperatures because they are not needed for the short holding times normally employed and they delay warming of the doughs to temperatures at which they can be readily processed. Very low temperatures also compound the problem of moisture condensation on the surface of doughs removed from the retarder and may cause some translocation of the soluble materials if some of the dough water freezes. Dough held in the refrigerator should be covered with plastic sheets, or protected by some other means, to prevent dehydration of the surface. When the pieces are removed from the cooler, the covering should be retained unless they are put in process immediately, since moisture will likely condense on the surface making them sticky and hard to handle.

Regular sweet doughs are customarily proofed at 95° to 100°F and 90% to 95% relative humidity, while roll-in sweet doughs are proofed at 85° to 90°F (but below the melting point of the roll-in fat) and 90% to 95% RH. Lower proofing temperatures will result in longer proof times. It is highly advisable to have the dough equilibrated to room temperature before proofing begins, otherwise different layers of the piece can be fermenting at different rates leading to a non-uniform product. Loaves or buns with a high content of fruit pieces are particularly sensitive to proofing time; they should be allowed to double in size. A proof that is too short gives a finished product that is too dense and has harsh texture while excessive proof leads to a product that appears wrinkled and shrunken, and has coarse grain and texture.

For final proofing and baking, the dough pieces should be placed on pans and sheets that have been dusted and lightly greased. Paper liners may be needed for some items. Of course, some sweet dough products have for several years been distributed in the pans (foil or ovenable plastic laminates and paperboards) in which they were baked. Sticky buns, upside down cakes, and the like require pan dressings that some bakers prefer to apply to warm pans, just after the previous load of rolls has been dumped.

Correct baking times and temperatures depend a great deal on the oven characteristics, but are also affected by piece size and pan characteristics. Sweet goods have more critical baking requirements than regular breads and rolls because they color rapidly and can acquire a burned appearance with very little overbaking, while slight underbaking gives products of poor eating quality. Individual pieces of regular and roll-in types are often baked at around 400°F. Cluster roll configurations can be baked at

400°F in a well-controlled oven. Coffee cakes should be baked at lower temperatures, typically 350° to 375°F. Heavy fruited items such as stollen call for even lower temperatures, 325°F being suitable in many cases. Varieties baked in tube pans should also be baked at this lower temperature.

Because of the weak mechanical strength of the freshly baked product and the irregular conformation of most of them, sweet dough items are often cooled on the baking sheets or in the pans. When they have reached 90° or 95°F, they can be dumped or otherwise removed and conveyed to the icing depositor. It is best to apply warm icings because they spread better and assume more rounded contours. Roller type applicators are often used. Formulas for icings, toppings, glazes, and other adjuncts can be found in subsequent chapters.

Other methods.—A kind of imitation roll-in sweet dough can be made by mixing flakes of hard fat into the dough. As in the blitz method for puff pastry, a certain amount of flakiness does appear in the finished product, but the eating texture is often somewhat waxy and the layering is not as pronounced as with the traditional roll-in method.

To obtain greater efficiency and promote uniformity, some manufacturers prefer to pump the dough from the trough that receives it from the mixer, and in which it may have undergone some fermentation, and force it through a slit to form a continuous strip. This method eliminates the need to handle chunks of dough manually, and it forms a sheet that is not only uniform along its entire length but has no breaks to cause scrap formation. Extrusion can also be applied to make individual dough pieces.

Generally, the dough formula requires only minor adjustments in order to adapt it to extrusion processing. Ingredient water should be reduced in these doughs. It is generally considered best to keep the dough on the underdeveloped side, although some operators recommend using well-developed doughs. It would appear that the dough would be more adaptable to pumping and extruding if it had less elasticity. A certain amount of "development" and "conditioning" occurs as a result of the sheeting done on the belt. A very undeveloped dough is, of course, not desirable.

Various opinions exists as to the proper dough temperature out of the mixer, and the best advice seems to be that the dough temperature has to be adjusted to fit the particular circumstances. Relatively high temperatures cause fast gas generation with consequent problems in maintaining dough dimensions through the sheeters and they usually increase the amount of tearing and surface disruption as the dough goes between the rollers. Some bakers prefer to bring doughs out of the mixer at 65° to 70°F, others say 80° to 82°F yields softer, fluffier sweet rolls and coffee cakes.

As mentioned elsewhere, continuous extrusion of dough for roll-in sweet doughs and Danish pastry provides the basis for automatic application of roll-in shortening, with substantial labor savings and improvements in uniformity.

FRUITED ROLLS AND STOLLEN

Most fruited rolls and stollen are based on regular sweet dough formulas but the method of preparation and their content of raisins and candied fruits make them appear to be quite different products. In some cases, the doughs are slightly to considerably leaner than those used for small sweet goods and coffee cakes, but never as lean as those recommended for regular bread. A rather complex recipe and procedure for a Christmas Fruit Stollen is given below.

<u>Stollen Formula and Procedure</u>

(1) Place in the mixer and cream until light: 2 lb emulsifier shortening, 4 lb granulated sugar, 4 oz salt, 1 lb 8 oz nonfat dry milk, 0.5 oz mace, and 1 oz rum flavor extract.

(2) Add 4 lb liquid whole eggs to the above and cream until light.

(3) Disperse 2 lb compressed yeast in 8 lb water; add to the previous mixture and blend for one minute.

(4) Add 18 lb bread flour to the above and mix until smooth. Bring out of the mixer at 80°F and let stand for 1.5 hr or until the dough starts to fall.

(5) Disperse 1 lb of compressed yeast in 1 lb of water, add to the above dough, and mix until smooth.

(6) Heat 2 lb of emulsifier to 135° to 140°F. Add to the dough. Mix until smooth.

(7) Add 2 lb of bread flour to the above and mix well.

(8) Wash in warm water 8 lb of white raisins, 7 lb mixed candied fruit cubes, 3 lb glazed cherries, and 2 lb glazed small pineapple chunks. Drain well. Mix 3 lb pecans (or large pieces of almonds) with the fruit. Add fruit and nuts to the dough. Mix just enough to distribute the fruit uniformly.

(9) Give the dough 20 minutes fermentation. Scale into pieces of desired weight. Shape into long oval loaves. Roll out the dough to medium thickness, wash with melted margarine, and sprinkle with cinnamon and sugar.

(10) Fold like a large Parker House roll and proof. Bake at 325°F for 1 lb size and 300°F for 2 and 3 lb sizes. Cool.

(11) Ice with white icing and sprinkle with nuts and cherry pieces.

DOUGHNUTS AND OTHER FRIED GOODS

Fried goods, both yeast-leavened and chemically leavened, probably exceed in dollar amount and tonnage any other type of sweet dough product. Although the basic doughs do not exhibit the wide variety of composition found, for example, in cookies, the many shapes and finishes applied to these basic doughs lead to a vast number of choices for the consumer. The familiar doughnut shape seems to predominate, but twists, sticks, honey buns, cinnamon rolls, and Bismarcks are also well known. These can be coated with powders, glazes, icings, and toppings, and filled with custards, jellies, fruits, and other semi-solid compositions. Space limitations obviously restrict the description in this section to a few typical or significant examples.

General Formulas

The range of variation of ingredients in regular yeast-raised doughnut formulas is given in Table 19.1.

Table 19.1. RANGE OF INGREDIENTS
IN YEAST-RAISED DOUGHNUTS[1]

Ingredient	Low %	High %
Sugars	5	12
Shortening	8	14
Nonfat dry milk	3	5
Soy flour	0	2
Salt	1.2	1.6
Eggs	0	2.5
Baking powder	0	1.5
Yeast	3	5
Water	40	50

[1] Flour weight equals 100%.

Often, pre-blended mixes are used as the basis for doughnut doughs. These most commonly contain all of the ingredients, except water and yeast, although some will allow the baker to add characterizing materials. There are many suppliers for these mixes, each of them having their own proprietary formulas. A typical mix, suitable for the doughnut manufacturer who is using the sheeting and cutting method of make-up, might have the following composition (Roth 1975): 55 parts bleached and bromated hard wheat flour of 13% protein content, 25 parts unbleached pastry flour of 9.5% protein content, 5 parts sugar, 10 parts emulsifier shortening, 2 parts nonfat dry milk, 1.5 parts salt, 1.5 parts chemical leavening, 0.5 parts dough conditioners, 0.3 parts yeast foods, 4.5 parts compressed yeast, and 41 parts water (variable).

Ingredient Specifications and Functions

The specifications for doughnut flour will depend on the process to be applied to the dough. If a pressure extrusion system will be used, an extremely high protein flour will be called for because this equipment punishes the dough severely. If the dough is to be sheeted and cut, a lower protein flour would be adequate. Bleaching and bromating are optional.

Full fat and defatted soy flours have been used in doughnut formulas as structure builders and tolerance improvers. Excessive amounts can have a weakening effect on gluten, causing an open grain. Soy flours increase water absorption and usually increase water retention

Sugar and dextrose can be used more or less interchangeably. Often a combination is employed. They act as fermentation substrates, crust darkeners, and sweeteners.

The main function of shortenings is to improve eating quality by tenderizing the finished product. They also improve dough processability by decreasing stickiness and increasing smoothness. Plastic shortenings made of partially hydrogenated vegetable oils are satisfactory.

Lecithin is occasionally added to dougnut mixes because it reportedly conditions the crust for better glaze retention. Mono- and di-glycerides are used as softeners and shelf-life extenders. Sodium stearoyl-2-lactylate is effective in improving dough machinability and crumb texture.

High heat NFDM is used as a structure builder and an improver of grain. It increases absorption, affects flavor, and darkens the crust color.

Dried whole eggs can be used as a structure building ingredient and to darken the crust. Dried egg yolk is effective as an emulsifier and it contributes to the structure of the dough. Both these ingredients are said to reduce the tendency of the white ring to collapse at the fryer turner.

Salt controls fermentation, and it affects flavor, of course. The more salt that is used, the slower the fermentation. It affects dough development and contributes to gluten strength during the proofing period. Insufficient salt produces dough of low tolerance and poor flavor.

Soda and leavening acids are nearly always added to these mixes to give a burst of gas in the fryer, because it is often found that adequate product expansion is not obtained when the formulator relies solely on the dissolved and occluded carbon dioxide that has originated from yeast activity.

Procedures

Mixing.—Either the straight dough method or the sponge-and-dough method can be used. It is believed that most of the yeast-leavened doughnuts made in the U.S. are processed by the straight dough method, but it has been reported (Fick 1971) that the sponge method gives more manageable doughs for extrusion forming equipment. Doubtless, any of the accelerated processes, liquid sponge methods, or continuous equipment being used for bread doughs could be applied to doughnut preparation if the volume was large enough. The re-mix method has been advocated by some producers. In this process, all ingredients are made into a sponge, which, after fermentation, is mixed until the dough develops. According to Braden (1976), the best yeast-raised fried goods are made from firm, well developed doughs.

Fermentation.—Fermentation times are determined by the formula richness, percentage of scrap dough added, percentage of yeast, and temperature. Generally, proper fermentation will demand times in the range of 45 to 75 minutes, but a warm dough containing 70% scrap could require as little as 20 minutes. The temperature of the room or cabinet in which the dough is being held should be in the range of 80° to 85°F.

Make-up.—After fermentation, the dough is cut into pieces, usually of 15 to 20 lb weight and allowed to rest 15 to 30 minute. The rested dough may be pre-sheeted before being fed to the sizing rolls on the make-up table. When the dough sheet has been reduced to the proper thickness, it is cut by either circular or hexagonal dies. Piece sizes are extremely variable depending on the product being made, but for conventional doughnuts, 1.25 to 1.75 oz will serve for the great majority of items. An alternative to sheeting and cutting is the pressure extruding method, in which dough is forced through nozzles that form rings. The dough pieces are collected on screens or cloth trays or belts, and proofed and fried on a continuous basis.

Proofing.—Proofing conditions are usually 95° to 105°F dry bulb and 85° to 95°F wet bulb, i.e., a 10 to 15 degree spread. Proof times can be from 30 to 45 minutes. If the humidity is high, the dough pieces may spread too much during proofing, and the finished product may show blisters and absorb excessive amounts of shortening. Low humidity can lead to the surface cracking during frying. Blistering is a common fault of under-proofed doughnuts.

Frying.—The frying fat is usually held within a range of 375° to 395°F. When dough pieces of 1.5 oz weight are being fried, about one minute frying on each side is required. Shrinkage of the doughnut after frying, or collapse of the white side ring due to weakness of the internal structure is usually due to insufficient frying time or temperature. If the frying time is too long, excessive absorption of fat will result. A 1.5 oz dough piece can be expected to absorb about 0.2 to 0.3 oz of fat.

In discussing the factors affecting fat uptake by doughnuts, clarity is added if the phenomenon of fat absorption into the mass of the doughnut is separated from that of fat adherence to the surface. Different factors affect the two processes. Probably the most important factor affecting fat absorption is the moisture content of the finished doughnut. Under normal conditions, the amount of fat absorbed is inversely related to the moisture content of the finished piece. This relationship is probably a function of the blanket of steam that covers a frying doughnut. Effusion of steam and leavening gases from the doughnut helps to reduce contact of frying oil with the crust. As the evolution of gas slows down with dehydration of the surface layers of the doughnut, the fat—which is in very turbulent motion around the doughnut—can contact the crust at more places and thus will have more opportunity to soak into the crust.

Since fat absorption is such an important factor in fried product quality, with excess absorption being very detrimental, it is worthwhile to discuss the effect of dough moisture in further detail. Firstly, the product when dropped into the fat has an essentially lipophobic surface—it is not readily wetted by the fat. This changes as the surface dries out. Secondly, gas (water vapor and carbon dioxide) is rapidly evolved from the surface of the product. This gas tends to form a variable (but effective where it exists) barrier to contact of the dough surface with the hot fat. Thirdly, the product does not present a continuous smooth surface to the fat. The outer layers ar ruptured and distorted in many places, forming protuberances that allow closer contact with the fat. When the surface is sufficiently dehydrated and chemically changed so that it soaks up fat this situation may be expected to exist as soon as browning starts—and when gas evolution slows down so that fat is not kept away from the surface, fat uptake will be fairly rapid.

It may be predicted from the preceding considerations that factors reducing fat absorption are: (1) A smooth product surface, maintained throughout frying; (2) Continuous carbon dioxide evolution during the time the product is in the fat; (3) Very short retention time in the oil after browning commences; (4) Use of fat with low viscosity at the temperature of frying; and (5) Good draining—that is, shaking, blowing, and tumbling the product as soon as it emerges from the fryer and continuing these operations until the fat is on the verge of solidification.

Extreme undermixing will often lead to high fat absorption, particularly if the crust of the doughnut is very rough and irregular because of the undermixing.

Finishing.—Doughnuts should be cooled briefly before they are glazed or iced. This allows the product to set slightly and the excess fat to drain off or be absorbed.

Variations

Basic formulas were given previously. Many varieties can be developed by simply changing spice combinations in the basic formula, incorporating characterizing ingredients such as pumpkin or applesauce, using specialized ingredients such as the flavored and colored "fruit" bits sold by bakery supply houses, using "health" ingredients such as yogurt or wheat germ, etc. One of the more complex fried sweet doughs will be described in more detail below.

Honey buns are fried sweet rolls that have attained great popularity in the last 20 or 30 years. The formula and procedure have changed considerably from the earliest examples, which were probably based on baked cinnamon rolls. Most present-day products contain little, if any, honey. The concept is a fried cinnamon roll covered with a sugar glaze. The list of ranges for ingredients in Table 19.2 has been adapted from Hildebrand (1980) and can be considered representative of much present day production.

Table 19.2. RANGE OF HONEY BUN INGREDIENTS [1]

Ingredient	Low %	High %
Flour	100	100
Sugar	7	15
Shortening	10	18
Yeast	4	9
Honey	0.75	8
Milk	2.5	6.5
Salt	1.25	3.1
Soy flour	0	6
Egg yolks or whites	0	3
Dough conditioners	0.25	1.5
Flavor	qs	qs
Total liquid	38	45

[1] Ingredient percentages are on a flour weight basis.

Procedure is as follows. Mix dough to clean up, then two or three minutes more. Bring out at 76° to 82°F. Floor time, or bulk fermentation, is variable depending on qualities required for the make-up line. For semi-automated systems, the bulk fermented dough is cut into large pieces of equal weight which are placed on flour-dusted pans until fed to the make-up line. There, the dough is first sheeted, dusting flour is removed, a thin layer of oil is applied, and then the cinnamon sugar mixture is sprinkled on top. The curling roller forms the spiral from which cross-sections of given weight will be cut. The raw buns are laid out on a belt, screen, or pan and proofed at wet bulb settings of 95° to 115°F and dry bulb settings of 115° to 130°F, keeping the spread at 15° to 18°F. The buns can be fried either on the surface, partially submerged, or fully submerged. Each of these methods has its own special advantages and disadvantages. Fryer settings range from 370° to 385°F. After frying, the buns are fully glazed or iced, usually with a thin vanilla icing.

DANISH PASTRY

Almost any sweet roll is called "Danish" nowadays, but the original meaning of Danish pastry was a product made from a rich yeast dough that had been layered with butter by repeated folding and sheeting steps in a process somewhat similar to that used for making puff pastry. The dough contained eggs, milk, and sugar in significant amounts. The result of this expensive formulation and the elaborate processing was a baked product having a silky tender crumb of characteristic appearance and a glossy flaky crust. The flavor reflected the presence of high levels of enriching ingredients.

The quality of Danish pastries seen in the marketplace today is highly variable, but the best examples are at least as rich as those made 60 or 70 years ago, while the worst are seldom as bad as those made of inferior ingredients by incompetent bakers in "the good old days." Ingredients are generally more uniform and fresher today, and quality control and automation have reduced the chance that a really horrendous batch will reach the store shelves. The real problem today lies in wrongfully describing roll-in sweet doughs or even regular sweet doughs as Danish pastry. They are not the same, even though the other types may be just as acceptable as Danish to many consumers.

History

Danish pastry was first developed in Vienna a couple of hundred years ago, according to some stories. In the U.S., it was first popularized starting in about 1920 by two master bakers from Denmark who traveled extensively in this country teaching the art of making the pastry. The formulas of these two artisans differed somewhat; Table 19.3 compares their two formulas according to the best available records.

Table 19.3. ORIGINAL FORMULAS FOR DANISH PASTRY

Ingredient and unit	Mr. Klitteng's formula	Mr. Jensen's formula
Bread flour, oz	56	32
Pastry flour, oz	0	20
Whole milk, quart	1	1
Sugar, granulated, oz	8	7
Yeast, oz	8	5
Fresh whole egg, oz	7	10.5
Shortening, oz	0	3.5
Roll-in butter, oz	32	56

The methods of preparation taught by these two experts also differed, primarily in the way the dough was folded and rolled after the butter was applied. In Klitteng's technique, the dough was chilled on ice between folding steps, while Jensen gave briefer rests and did not chill. It is to be noted that Jensen required a great deal more butter to get satisfactory results, as could be expected from a procedure that did not maximize the layering effects of the fat. In any case, the reported Jensen formula appears to contain too much roll-in.

Since the introduction of Danish pastry preparation, many changes have been introduced in the formulas and processing methods. These take advantage of the improved ingredients and better equipment that we have today, and are better adapted to requirements of the modern consumer. Techniques and ingredients have developed to maximize the effect of the layered shortening so that lesser amounts can be used, reducing the tendency to greasiness that was often noticed in the earlier products. Generally, enhanced amounts of adjuncts such as flavorings, fillings, icings, and glazes are used today, as compared to earlier practices that relied more on the dough itself for consumer appeal. It is likely that the best examples of true Danish pastry made today would rate higher with the average person than would products made according to the original formula and method.

Experimental Studies

In a series of articles, Glabau (1959) described experiments intended to clarify the effects of variations in type and amount of ingredients and of processing conditions on the quality of Danish pastry. The conclusions he reached then are still valid, in most respects. He found that bulk fermentation was not necessary but that it did no harm unless unduly prolonged. He showed that sugar improved tenderness and eating quality, as well as flavor, when added up to 18% (FWB). At levels of 22% and 27%, sugar hindered expansion and reduced flakiness.

Glabau's basic formula called for all bread flour, but he found that the pastry showed improvement if 15% or 20% of this ingredient was replaced by soft wheat flour. Greater or lesser amounts were not as effective in improving quality. The quantity of egg also had significant effects on several characteristics of the dough and finished products. Optimal results were obtained when liquid whole eggs were added at 25% of the flour weight.

The oven temperature had a marked effect on nearly all the scored characteristics. Although optimum temperature and time of baking were related to piece size, the best oven temperature was found to be 375°F, with hotter conditions not recommended.

When Glabau varied the water 20% (FWB) above and below the amount considered best for his formula, the time required for proofing to the same height varied over a range of 102 to 80 minutes. Doughs and products became softer with larger amounts of water.

Ingredients and Formulas

The flour should have properties that give the dough great tolerance so that continued folding and sheeting do not tear the roll-in combination. This indicates the need for a strong bread flour that can furnish a very extensible dough. Spring wheat flour having a protein content of 12% to 13.5% is desirable. Such a flour will, however, lead to a relatively tough finished product and the dough may be difficult to handle in early stages of laminating because it can get bucky and tough. As a compromise, it has often been the practice to add up to 30% of a pastry flour.

Butter is the traditional dough shortening, but margarine is satisfactory as are hydrogenated vegetable oil shortenings, including the emulsifier types. Roll-in shortenings can be butter, margarine, or specially fabricated vegetable oil shortenings, but they must have good spreadability and a plastic range extending down to 50°F so that they do not become brittle and rupture the layering when chilled. Proportion of roll-in to dough is said to be about 25%, as an industry average.

The eggs, sugar, salt, nonfat dry milk, and yeast do not need to be any different from those used in other good quality sweet doughs.

The ranges of ingredients in Danish doughs made in recent years are shown in Table 19.4, which is based on a report of Poehlmann (1979).

Table 19.4. RANGE OF INGREDIENTS USED IN DANISH

	Percent (FWB)	
Ingredient	Low	High
Flour	100	100
Sugar	15	22
Shortening	15	22
Whole eggs	5	12
Salt	1.5	2.5
Nonfat dry milk	4	8
Yeast	7	10
Flavor	0.5	0.8
Total liquid	55	67
Roll-in shortening	20*	30*

*As percent of the dough.

Procedures

In all cases, Danish dough should be given a minimum amount of development in the mixer bowl, otherwise the stretching and folding applied in the laminating step will overdevelop the dough and cause it to tear. Directions often say, "mix just enough to get a coherent mass." Probably, a little more mixing than this would give a dough that is easier to handle in the early stages of folding and sheeting. For hand laminating, the dough should be cool, as low as 60°F being recommended

Bulk fermentation before the dough is laminated is not necessary. A moderate and variable amount of floor time is inevitable and apparently does no harm. The usual procedure is to cut the mixed dough into chunks of convenient size and keep them in the refrigerator until needed. As the dough cools down, fermentative changes will be greatly inhibited.

Keeping the dough cool is one of the keys to developing good layering in Danish. Low temperatures help to maintain the continuity of the butter layers as the dough is repeatedly sheeted out. Proportion of roll-in fat to dough should be around 25%, more may give a somewhat greasy pastry while less may give a tougher dough and less flaky crust. The roll-in shortening should be applied as a layer of uniform thickness, either placed on the dough as a preformed sheet or extruded from a hopper on to the dough sheet. Alternatively, square and thin chunks can be cut from a block of the shortening and arranged to form a continuous layer on the dough.

There are several types of equipment that automatically combine the dough and shortening, sheet the combination, and fold. Although some of these start with flat sheets of dough and shortening, more recent designs make concentric tubes of extruded fat and dough, then sheet them out to flat sandwiches before further laminating them.

Ideally, the dough should be allowed to rest in a chilled area for several minutes or more after it has been folded. This makes maximum use of the shortening by toughening it, thus decreasing its tendency to be absorbed into the dough or to squeeze out the unsealed edges of the assembly. By increasing the amount of roll-in, some flakiness can be obtained in spite of extreme abuse of the dough, but this is not consistent with good eating quality in the finished product. It leads to perceptible greasiness in the finished product.

The so-called "blitz" method of Danish preparation calls for the addition of about 15% hard fat flakes toward the end of the dough mixing procedure. No special lamination steps are performed, the theory being that the flakes carry through more-or-less intact until the dough piece enters the oven, when they melt to form layers. This method is not recommended. Among other negative features is the need to use fat of high melting point, leading to a waxy sensation in the mouth.

Methods used in forming individual pieces are similar to those used for other sweet doughs. Small pieces do not exhibit the good points of Danish as well as larger pieces. Proofing practices are highly variable, but excess expansion at this point can partially obliterate the layers. For most pieces, it is satisfactory to proof at 80° to 90°F and at 90% to 95% RH until an increase of 50% to 75% in volume is attained. It is not to be expected that the specific volume of Danish will be as high as items made from regular sweet doughs, unless there are large internal voids in the Danish.

Individual pieces should be baked at 375° to 400°F with the preferred temperature depending somewhat on the piece size and the dough temperature. It is important not to underbake, keeping in mind that the crust will be relatively dark because of the richness of the dough.

For maximum appeal, much of the crust should remain uncovered by toppings so that its flakiness and crispness can be experienced by the consumer. In actual practice, many Danish pieces, especially the small ones, are almost 100% covered by icings and fruit toppings. Almond paste fillings and cinnamon flavor seem to go particularly well with the basic flavor.

Examples of Products

To give the reader a basis for practice and experimentation, specific formulas will be given for two different Danish products.

Almond Crumb Coffee Cake

(1) Mix together: 48 oz sugar, 4 oz salt, 20 oz nonfat dry milk, 16 oz emulsifer shortening, 16 oz margarine, 0.5 oz mace, 1 oz lemon flavor, 48 oz liquid whole eggs, and 32 oz cake flour.

(2) Disperse 20 oz compressed yeast in 129 oz water and add to the above.

(3) Add 240 oz bread flour to the mixture; mix well but do not develop.

(4) Scale 10 lb pieces. Using method previously described, roll in 2 lb of margarine to each piece, giving three folds three times. Rest 30 min between folds.

(5) Scale finished dough at 9 oz. Rest pieces 15 min. Roll into oblongs. Spread about 3 to 3.5 oz of an almond crumb filling over two-thirds of the surface. Fold the dough in thirds, completely inclosing the filling.

(6) Sheet out each piece to about 15 inches in length. Make three cuts from each side toward the center. Don't cut all the way to center. Curl the tails toward the center, turning so as to partially expose the filling.

(7) Wash with an egg wash and sprinkle a few granulated almonds or pecans on top. Fill the center top with pineapple filling.

(8) Give a 75% proof and bake at 350°F. Wash with hot syrup after baking and stripe with warm fondant when cold.

Apple Filled Coffee Cakes

(1) Scale 40 oz granulated sugar and 32 oz butter into mixer bowl and cream.

(2) Slowly add 40 oz liquid whole eggs to the above, while mixing at low speed.

(3) Disperse 20 oz nonfat dry milk, 4 oz malt syrup, and 20 oz yeast in 128 oz ice cold water and add the liquid to the preceding mixture.

(4) Add 192 oz bread flour, 64 oz cake flour, and 0.25 oz cinnamon or other flavor to the preceding mix and continue mixing only until uniform.

(5) Sheet out on a well-dusted bench to get an oblong shape about three-fourths inch thick. Spread 128 oz margarine or puff paste shortening over two-thirds of the length of the dough piece. Fold in thirds, enclosing the fat completely. Roll and fold three times, resting the dough 10 minutes between foldings, and 20 to 30 minutes after the third sheeting.

(6) Cut the dough into pieces of, for example, 9 oz. Roll into oblongs, and smear cinnamon spread over the surfaces. Put chopped apples over the cinnamon. Fold into three layers.

(7) Place pieces in pan. Wash with egg wash. Put streusel on top.

(8) Proof slowly at 80° to 85°F until a 50% to 75% expansion is achieved.

(9) Bake at 375°F. Glaze and apply icing.

YEAST-LEAVENED COOKIES

Yeast-leavened cookies have been overshadowed by the chemically-leavened type since baking powder became readily available many decades ago. It appears that a cookie, defined here as being different from the usual yeast-leavened pastry in that it is cooked to a much lower moisture content (typically, around 5% to 10%) and is smaller (typically, less than an ounce). They do not have much of the appealing fermentation aroma of most yeast-leavened goods because the odorous substances developed during fermentation are largely dissipated during the cooking process, and the silky resilient texture made possible by developed doughs is offset by the hard structure set up by baking nearly to dryness.

Yeast-leavened cookies can be either baked or fried. There are very few commercial examples of fried cookies, perhaps none, but recipes for products of this type can be found in some ethnic cookbooks and most of these are made from yeast-leavened doughs. Doubtless, some retail bakeries have occasionally made fried cookies as a novelty or to appeal to a special market. A discussion of these products is included here primarily to stimulate the imagination of product development technologists.

Frying has some advantages. Among these are the distinctive fried flavor ("like doughnuts") and the short duration of the cooking step which makes preparation of product for immediate consumption less tedious. The disadvantages of frying are all too obvious—the necessity for maintaining a bath of hot oil, the fact that the dough pieces are not supported during cooking, leading to irregular shapes, and, if they are made on a small scale, the labor intensive nature of the cooking method. An example of a fried yeast-leavened cookie formula and preparation method is shown below.

<u>Fried Yeast-leavened Cookie</u>

(1) Blend together at low speed: 13 parts granulated sugar, 9 parts emulsifier shortening, 1 part salt, 3 parts nonfat dry milk, 4 parts yeast, 1 part vanilla extract, 6 parts liquid whole eggs, 13 parts bread flour, and 28 parts pastry flour.

(2) Add 22 parts warm water to the above and mix about 3 min.

(3) Turn out on a floured board and give about 10 minutes rest time. Roll out the dough about one-eighth inch thick.

(4) Cut circles of 2 inches diameter. Dock heavily. Place in a wire basket and immediately submerge in fat held at 350° to 360°F. Instead of being docked, these cookies can be held between two wire screens not more than one-fourth inch apart while being fried. Remove from fat when the pieces are brown and firm.

(5) Decorate tops with half a pecan (or walnut) and sprinkle with confectioners sugar while still hot.

For other fried cookie recipes, see the "Golden Nuggets" described ty Newman (1974), "God's Favors" a Czech recipe reported by Howe (1975), "churros"—a Spanish-type recipe (Perry 1940), and "Rye Drops" (Ross and Disney 1963).

COMBINATIONS OF DOUGHS AND BATTERS

Some bake shops have had moderate success in promoting products made from combinations of yeast-raised doughs and cake batters. Unusual texture combinations and flavors can be obtained. A simple example illustrating the approach (Gunter 1967) is: Mix together 60 lb of previously prepared fermented sweet dough and 40 lb of cake batter, both being vanilla and butter flavored, and 1 lb of compressed yeast. Deposit 9 oz of the batter in an 8.75x5.75x1.125 inch foil pan. Give one-half proof and deposit 2 oz of prune, apple, cherry, pineapple, or any other flavor of pie filling on the cake. Cover with 1 oz of streusel and bake.

BIBLIOGRAPHY

ANON. 1976. A Study of Energy Conservation Potential in the Baking Industry. Federal Energy Administration and Management, Washington, DC

BRADEN, B. W., JR. 1976. Yeast-raised doughnuts. Proc. Am. Soc. Bakery Engineers *1976*, 127-131

DAVEY, V. F. 1965. Make-up procedures for roll-in coffee cake production. Proc. Am. Soc. Bakery Engineers *1965*, 281-290

DIXON, J. R. 1976. Ingredients in doughnut mixes. Proc. Am. Soc. Bakery Engineers *1976*, 144-166

EXETER, G. 1971. Automation in sweet yeast-raised bakery products. Proc. Am. Soc. Bakery Engineers *1971*, 192-199

FICK, O. B. 1971. Production of yeast-raised doughnuts. Proc. Am. Soc. Bakery Engineers *1971*, 174-180

FRANTZ, H. F. 1972. Danish production by various methods. Proc. Am. Soc. Bakery Engineers *1972*, 172-180

GLABAU, C. A. 1959. Danish pastry [a series of seven papers in Bakers Weekly, June 22, June 29, July 6, July 13, July 20, July 27, and August 4]

HARGROVE, W. W. 1973. Various degrees of mechanization in the production of sweet yeast-raised bakery foods. Proc. Am. Soc. Bakery Engineers *1973*, 78-86

HILDEBRAND, W. G. 1980. Honey buns. Proc. Am. Soc. Bakery Engineers *1980*, 85-95

HOWE, R. 1975. Cooking from the Heart of Europe. David and Charles, London

LEHAULT, W. B. 1964. The fundamentals of quality coffee cake production. Proc. Am. Soc. Bakery Engineers *1964*, 194-199

MEIGS, H. T. 1968. Sweet doughs. Am. Soc. Bakery Engineers Bull. No. *186*

NEWMAN, M. 1974. The Sweet Life. Houghton Mifflin Co., Boston

O'REILLY, M. 1976. The practical production of sweet yeast-raised varieties. Proc. Am. Soc. Bakery Engineers *1976*, 72-77

PERRY, J. 1940. Around the World Making Cookies. H. Barrows & Co., New York

POEHLMAN, R. W. 1979. Premium Danish production. Proc. Am. Soc. Bakery Engineers *1979*, 91-105

ROSS, A. L., and DISNEY, J. A. 1963. The Art of Making Good Cookies Plain and Fancy. Doubleday & Co., Garden City, NY

ROTH, R. L. 1975. Fried yeast-raised production. Proc. Am. Soc. Bakery Engineers *1975*, 149-155

SHAFFER, T. 1977. Automated sweet yeast-raised production. Proc. Am. Soc. Bakery Engineers *1977*, 117-123

VARNEY, H. D., JR. 1970. Coffee cake and Danish: Extrusion methods. Proc. Am. Soc. Bakery Engineers *1970*, 167-173]

VERHOEF, N. J. F. D., and ZOCK, H. F. 1990. Food product. U.S. Pat. 4,935,251

chapter twenty

OTHER YEAST-LEAVENED PRODUCTS

INTRODUCTION

The category of yeast-leavened specialty products to be discussed in this chapter includes those items that are not regular forms of bread and rolls and not sweet dough products. This leaves a rather wide field from which a selection had to be made because of space restrictions. Most of the products discussed here are of current interest and have not been described in readily available technical books. English muffins, bagels, croissants, pizzas, pretzels, saltines, and some others are included.

ENGLISH MUFFINS

A typical English muffin, as sold in the U.S., is about four inches in diameter and one inch thick, with flat tops and bottoms that are browned, and with rather straight side walls that are pale or relatively unbaked in color. Formulas tend to be on the lean side. The crumb is open and irregular, with some large bubbles, and it normally looks slightly gray and moist. English muffins are fairly tough in texture and have a well-fermented odor and taste. There are many variations on the basic theme—whole wheat, sourdough, rye, raisin, etc. There are even commercial English muffins that are chemically leavened. Most English muffins eaten in the home are split or the tops and bottoms torn apart and then heated in a toaster. This product has shown a steady increase in popularity in the U.S. during the past two or three decades.

Originally, muffins and crumpets were baked or fried on griddles, using a metal ring or hoop to prevent the fluid dough from spreading. After being cooked nearly to doneness on one side, they were turned over and finished. The similarity with pancake preparation is obvious. Some commercial English muffins are now baked much like buns, but most are probably still baked on a metal band while they are held within a circular ring.

For reference and comparison, an 80-year old formula for English muffins is reproduced here. Measure 80 oz water into a bowl. Dissolve 4 oz yeast, 1 oz sugar, and 2 oz salt in the water. Add 108 oz flour. Mix these ingredients well for about 5 min. Cover and allow to rise in a warm place for 45 minutes to an hour. Turn the dough out on a table well dusted with flour. Scale 3 oz pieces, mold round, and put on trays well dusted with rice cones. Proof in a warm place until the dough pieces are about the size of the hoops in which they will be cooked. Heat the griddle. Place greased hoops on griddle. Using a pancake turner or the like, lift the muffins and drop them in the hoops. When half-baked, turn them over and cook the other side.

Ingredients

The quality and type of flour are important factors affecting the characteristics of English muffins. A strong patent hard wheat flour with a protein content of 12% to 13% is considered optimal by many producers. If it is necessary to use a weaker flour, supplementation with vital wheat gluten will probably be necessary. A rule of thumb that has been suggested is to use 1% of gluten for each 0.6% the flour protein is below 12.5%. For flours of optimal type, and with other ingredient percentages in the average ranges, absorptions between 79% and 85% are required to secure the rapid flowing or spreading during proofing and baking that is need to get the typical conformation.

High absorption levels are also important to give adequate porosity of the crumb. Generally speaking, the higher the absorption, the greater will be the porosity. Consumer preference appears to dictate a crumb structure with many randomly spaced medium to large holes. Many gas bubbles of 0.125 to 0.25 inch in diameter should be present. A uniform bread-like or cake-like crumb would be regarded as an indicator of poor quality in most markets, although some English muffins are currently being made by methods that yield such structures.

Some formulators include proteases or reducing agents in the dough to decrease viscosity and insure adequate flowability. Since the conditions of cool dough and short floor time are not favorable to protease action, high levels of this enzyme may have to be added.

Compressed yeast will normally be added at the rate of 2% to 8% (FWB). Active dry yeast can also be used. Pfefer (1976) claimed good muffins can be produced using only chemical leaveners, but bicarbonate (alone or with yeast) does not seem to give optimal porosity. In fact, chemical leaveners are usually detrimental. For markets preferring sour flavors, cultures, proprietary sours, or sour doughs can be used in addition to yeast.

Any granulation and purity of salt that is suitable as a bread ingredient can be used in English muffins. Many formulas call for about 1% salt (FWB). This low level (as compared to about 2% in many bread formulas) is partly responsible for the bland flavor of English muffins. It also seems to improve flow during baking by allowing a weaker gluten network to form.

Very little shortening is added to English muffin doughs. A common level is 2%. Larger amounts tend to give excessive tenderness and a more uniform crumb. Non-emulsifier shortenings (e.g., lard) are satisfactory. Sweeteners are also kept at low levels because their flavor is not necessarily appreciated in goods of this sort. Sucrose, dextrose, and corn syrups are all satisfactory. About 2% of fermentable carbohydrate is sufficient to sustain fermentation during proofing and provide residual sugar for crust color.

Some formulas don't include nonfat dry milk, others rely on about 1% NFDM to supply lactose for crust coloration and to mellow the flavor.

Mold growth can be a problem because of the high moisture content. Many producers expect English muffins to have a longer shelf life than bread because muffins sell in smaller volume. These factors make the use of mold inhibitors very desirable. Some manufacturers will add as much as 4% (FWB) vinegar in the formulas, and propionates may also be included in the formula at the highest possible levels. Solutions of propionates or sorbic acid may be sprayed on the exterior of the baked muffin for the same purpose. Some consumers can detect an undesirable odor due to these additions, particularly when the muffin is toasted. If sour dough fermentation is involved, an inhibitory effect on mold growth should result from the lower pH of the dough and muffin.

Processing

A wide range of mixing procedures and equipment has been successfully adapted to the processing of English muffins. Some bakers prefer to undermix the dough, thinking this will accentuate the coarse crumb structure that is so much prized. Others overmix on the principle that such doughs will have good flowability, while coarse crumb will result from the weakened gluten network. The latter practice is probably more common at this time. Both batch mixing and continuous mixing are being used. Either horizontal or vertical mixers can be used in the batch processes.

Because these doughs must be slack and very extensible to yield the typical form and grain, processing difficulties can occur when the doughs are put through conventional dividing and rounding equipment. Bringing doughs out of the mixer between 62° and 63°F results in considerably better handling qualities.

The muffin pieces are usually well dusted with a blend of corn meal and corn flour before they are transferred to the proofer. This meal must be of the correct particle size; if too coarse, coverage of the dough will be inadquate, if too fine, uneven baking, carbon buildup on oven parts, and excessive adherence of the dusting material on the muffins will be seen.

Floor time should be kept to about 15 minutes. Shorter floor times will usually not allow the dough to relax sufficiently for good make-up. The dough pieces should go through a rounder immediately after dividing.

Before the dough pieces go into the proofer, they must be dusted with a coarse cereal meal, such as corn or rice cones. It has been recommended (Juers 1982) to proof the muffin on a flat surface coated with a blend of corn meal and corn flour. This permits the dough to flow out without rising too high. The proofer temperature setting is about 110° to 115°F. Excessive humidity will keep the outer surface of the dough too wet to deposit easily or uniformly on to the griddle, but dry atmospheres will cause the dough to crust, decreasing the flow and leading to small, non-uniform muffins.

When the proofed dough pieces are deposited on the hot baking surface, the dough is warmed and becomes softer. It immediately starts to flow and quickly fills the bottom of the retainer ring. Before the dough is well expanded, top covers are applied to the rings. At this stage, the gas vesicles are fairly small and relatively uniform. Within about 2.5 minutes, the dough enters the oven zone where the temperature is about 475°F. As the interior temperature becomes much hotter, water vapor pressure increases substantially and causes expansion of the bubbles. Some of these rupture and coalesce, so that they become quite large and the size distribution becomes much more uneven. The end result is the typical crumb containing gas bubbles, holes, and tunnels of widely varying sizes.

After about 4 minutes grilling time, the muffins are dumped from the cups and turned on their tops, then baked for about 3.5 minutes without retaining rings. Cooling in forced air for 50 to 60 minutes follows.

Although some muffins are sold without being sliced or split, by far the largest percentage are split or "forked" to make it simpler for the consumer to separate the muffin horizontally into top and bottom halves. Equipment has been developed to perform this operation automatically.

Examples of Formulas and Procedures

According to Noel (1963), most quality English muffins are made from lean doughs containing flour, salt, yeast, a small percentage of sugar, up to 78% (FWB) water, mold inhibitor, and perhaps a small amount of shortening. Juers (1982) says 80% to 84% is the normal range for ingredient water. Thompson (1981) recommends 17% above bread absorption for the flour. In some cases, chemical leaveners have been used to increase flowability of the dough in the oven—2% to 3% yeast (FWB) with 2% to 2.5% double acting baking powder has been suggested. Malt, milk, enrichments, enzymes, vinegar, and other additives are optional, but both proteases and amylases are helpful in keeping the dough slack and flowable during the early part of baking. Examples of formulas and procedures will be found below.

Straight Dough English Muffins

(1) Combine and mix 42 lb flour (14% protein, low ash), 6 oz yeast, 32 lb water (variable), 1 lb sugar, 12 oz salt, and 8 oz fungal protease.

(2) Dough should be at 85°F out of mixer; ferment 4 hr.

(3) Punch at 2.5 and 3.5 hr.

Sponge Process English Muffins

(1) Mix the following about 5 minutes: 145 lb bread flour (13% protein), 80 lb ice water (variable), 4.5 lbs compressed yeast, 1.8 lb malt, and 6 oz calcium propionate. Bring sponge out at 78°F.

(2) After the sponge has fermented 4 hr, mix it with the following: 50 lb bread flour, 50 lb water (variable), 3 lb salt, 2 lb nonfat dry milk, and 2 lb sugar.

(3) Bring dough out of mixer at 80°F. Give 5 to 15 minutes floor time and then make up.

CROISSANTS

Examples of Formulas

The method for preparing croissant dough has many similarities to the Danish process for making sweet doughs. In both cases, the same sheeting step using butter or margarine as an interleaving ingredient between yeast-leavened dough layers is applied.

A typical croissant formula, according to Rijkaart (1984), is 220 lb flour, 11 lb sugar, 4.4 lb salt, 24 lb liquid whole eggs, 22 lb shortening, 13 lb yeast, and 12 gal water. The dough is mixed thoroughly but without much development of gluten. One minute in a high speed vertical mixer is recommended, but other mixers can also be used. This base dough is laminated with 30% butter.

Croissants are mass produced on specialized make-up lines that first extrude the dough into a thick layer, extrude the required amount of butter on top, curl the two layers into a "giant Swiss roll" and then flatten the rolle into a sheet of, e.g., seven dough layers and six butter layers. Cross-rollers thin the sheet and two-roll sheeters size it. This basic sandwich or laminated sheet is then further laminated by automatic devices that operate by cutting and piling segments, or by giving it book folds, or by lapping it diagonally. Similar devices are used in soda cracker manufacture. For croissant dough, a total of 36 layers is satisfactory. This dough is formed into a block that is, preferably, rested overnight. It is then sheeted to the desired thickness, triangles are cut and rolled from the sheet, and the raw croissants placed on baking sheets with the points on the bottom. Proofing for 60 minutes in an inclosure maintained at 98°F and 80% RH is desirable. Baking is at 430° to 450°F for 14 to 15 minutes.

The above formula and process should yield a very high quality process. Most croissants being sold today are made from leaner doughs. A simpler formula and method have been recommended for retail bakery applications. Mix 64 lb whole milk, 6.5 lb yeast, 2 lb salt, 6 lb sugar, 10 lb shortening, and 112 lb bread flour to make a smooth dough. Sheet the dough and layer it with 50 lb butter or roll-in shortening. Give three turns as for Danish, and allow dough to rest overnight in the refrigerator. Sheet out, cut triangles of 1 to 1.5 oz weight, and roll into croissant shape. Proof 15 to 60 minutes (depending on temperature) in cabinet. Bake at 375°F

Sourdough Croissants

Sourdoughs can be used in the preparation of croissants to yield an unusual and tasty product. The following procedure is typical. Prepare a sourdough for white bread as described in one of the preceding chapters. Cut 9 lb sections of the dough immediately after removing from the mixer. Chill. Sheet out each block into a rectangle about 18x26 inches (sheet pan size). Apply 3 lb of roll-in margarine to two-thirds of the surface of the rectangle. Fold the uncoated end over half of the margarine-coated section, then fold the remaining half of the margarine-coated section over the top (formerly the bottom) of the uncoated piece. This is essentially the same as the three-fold operation used for Danish pastry. Sheet out to a rectangle about 60x24 inches. Give the sheet a four-fold and return to the refrigerator, After chilling, remove, sheet out, and give the dough another four-fold. Again chill, bring from refrigerator, and divide evenly into pieces of the size and shape suitable for processing through a crescent roll machine.

Allow to proof until about double in size. Brush with water, starch solution, or egg white wash. Bake, using a high temperature for a crisp crust and soft interior.

PIZZAS

There are hundreds of pizza variations. Some are yeast-leavened, some are chemically leavened. Some are baked, some are fried. There are thick, thin, and medium pizzas, any of which can be found in rectangular or circular versions. The dough can be breadlike or crackerlike, spiced or plain. Fillings can be on top or inside. The kinds of toppings are limited only by the imagination: pizzas topped with tomato, meat, fish, shellfish, cheese, vegetables, the ever popular anchovy, even fruit—in every conceivable combination—are being sold. Space limitations prevent an extended review of all these variations, but a few basic types will be examined and compared.

Pizza Dough Formulas

Although chemically leavened pizza doughs are known, the total amount of these in commercial distribution is thought to be small. However, refrigerated pizza doughs distributed in cans for consumer use are chemically leavened and dry mixes for home preparation are usually at least partially leavened by soda. Manufacturers of chemically leavened pizza doughs often include a small amount of inactive dry yeast to add a little character to the flavor, and some of them increase the amount of sweeteners, shortenings, and milk for the same purpose.

It is probable that the main interest of the reader will be in yeast-leavened pizza crusts, and they will be examined in greater detail. Commercial fried crusts for frozen pizzas have been prepared using the following formula and procedure (Westover 1980).

Formula and Procedure for Pizza Crust

(1) Mix the following ingredients at low speed for two minutes and then at high speed for four minutes: 60.65 parts flour, 36.04 parts water (variable), 1.28 parts active dry yeast, 0.93 parts salt, 0.30 parts sodium stearoyl-2-lactylate, and 0.80 parts soybean oil.

(2) Dump the dough (85°F) into an oiled trough and let rest for 40 minutes.

(3) Sheet to a thickness of 3 mm, dock with one-eighth inch docking pins

set one inch apart, then cut into circular pieces 10 inches in diameter and weighing 170 grams.

(4) Proof for five minutes at 115°F.

(5) Fry submerged for 40 seconds in 400°F fat. After draining, cool, apply toppings, and freeze.

A formula for a slightly different kind of crust was disclosed by Federico (1974). Disperse the following ingredients in 78.4 lb of lukewarm water: 4.5 lb compressed yeast, 9.0 lb sugar, 7.0 oz salt, and 1.5 lb dried whey. Mix the liquid formed in the preceding step with the following ingredients at low speed: 100 lb high gluten flour, 4.5 lb vegetable shortening, and 2.0 lb liquid whole eggs. Divide into 1.5 lb portions and round up. Proof until doubled in size. Roll out the pieces in rectangles about 15x21 inches, or cut into circles. Place dough in pans lined with paper. Baker at 450° to 500°F for 4 minutes or more. Freeze. Consumer removes crust from freezer, tops it with selected ingredients, and bakes a pizza.

Pizza Toppings

Most pizza toppings are based on a spicy tomato sauce and pieces of cheese. Nearly all pizzerias purchase the sauce already made, and many frozen pizza manufacturers purchase at least the basic sauces in bulk quantities from tomato canneries, although they may add other materials (such as spices and chopped vegetables) to the tomato product before applying the sauce to the pizza. Both pizzerias and mass producers often buy the topping ingredients in sliced or chopped form from specialized suppliers to the trade, though others go to the extreme of buying whole sausages, raw hamburger, fresh vegetables, and whole cheeses for further processing in their plant.

Pizza Processing Methods

Pizza made for sale as a frozen product is typically prepared by baking or frying the crust separately and then applying a topping just before freezing. This allows the manufacturer to obtain a much wider range of crust properties and permits him to cook the crust to an exact degree of doneness. If the cooked crust is cooled or even frozen before the topping is added, it will undergo less soaking of the liquid into the crust, thereby improving the texture of the product the consumer removes from his oven. Some pizzerias purchase frozen or refrigerated crusts prepared by an outside manufacturer.

There are two basic procedures for forming pizza crust. Either the dough is divided, rounded, and pressed into disc form or it is rolled out in a continuous sheet from which circles are cut. The latter method gives the manufacturer many more options for formulation and processing, requires less equipment, and produces a more uniform crust. The former method was thought by many producers to give a crust of superior texture, but it appears the average consumer is hardly able to detect, much less appreciate this difference

Pressed crusts are typically made from straight doughs with as much as 5% of yeast and about 1% of shortening. Sugar and dried milk (or whey) are sometimes used in small amounts. After the dough is dumped from the mixer, it is given some floor time, divided, rounded, sent through an intermediate proofer, and then pressed flat on the pan that will carry it through the oven. Oil is commonly applied during the pressing stage. The pressed dough is proofed until experience indicates that the crust will color well when baked and the dough has relaxed. The nature of the pressing operation is such that a perfect circle is not formed, and some shrinking and distortion of the dough must be anticipated. System modifications to alleviate these problems include using two pressing steps, pressing with heated platens, and docking heavily. One of the main arguments in favor of the pressed crust method is that it greatly reduces scrap generation, which is a predominant feature of the cutting process.

Sheeting and cutting is a straightforward way of producing circular pizza shells. This method uses standard continuous dough forming techniques and is applicable to many kinds of doughs, although of course not all kinds of doughs process equally well. Shrinkage and distortion should not be major problems in normal line operation, but scrap utilization is a problem, because a large amount of trimmings (30% to 50%) is generated in the cutting step. It is generally preferable to mix fresh scrap into the next batch, although some processors simply dump it into the extruder trough, allowing the dough pump and extruder to mix the fresh dough with the scraps. Fermentation and proofing practices vary widely. Generally, little floor time is given, and proof time in most high speed lines is limited to a few minutes travel through a warm tunnel. Elaborate fermentation cabinets were used in some of the early systems, but the difficulties that were encountered in transferring the fragile, sticky dough pieces gave ample justification for phasing out this equipment. Docking is essential in this method, as it is for all crusts that are cooked without the toppings (Thompson 1981).

BAGELS

Bagels have a characteristic shape (like that of a doughnut) and a characteristic texture (moderately tough and dense). The shiny surface and the preparation method are unusual. A simplified formula and processing method includes the following steps. Mix to a smooth dough, which should be rather tough and bucky: 62 lb strong bread flour, 31 lb ice water (variable), 1 lb salt, 1 lb yeast, 3 lb sugar, and 2 lb vegetable oil. Divide the dough into two to four equal parts and ferment them for six hours. Scale into 1.5 to 2 oz pieces. Roll out into strings (thin cylinders). Shape the strings into doughnut forms by overlapping the ends and pressing them until sealed. Proof for 25 minutes. Drop the bagels into boiling water. When the dough pieces come to the surface, remove them and drain off the excess water. Bake at 385°F for 18 to 20 minutes.

Some bakers add 4% to 8% whole eggs or up to 4% egg whites to the bagel formula to improve texture, flavor, and color. Recent developments include whole wheat bagels, rye bagels, etc. Forming the bagel from bulk dough is now done automatically by relatively inexpensive machines.

The layout of a wholesale bagel bakery shown in Figure 20.1 will illustrate the commercial process for manufacturing this item. Identification of the equipment numbers is as follows: (1) Ingredient storage silo; (2) Removable-bowl mixer; (3) Bowl dumper; (4) Heavy duty divider; (5) Bagel forming machines; (6) Maple top table; (7) Storage rack; (8) Proof boxes; (9) Walk-in cooler; (10) Rack ovens.

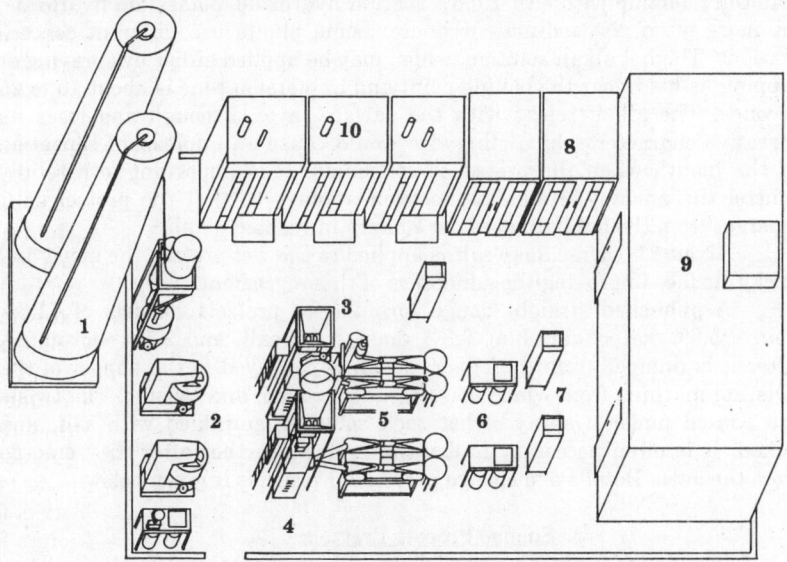

Figure 20.1. A batch process bagel bakery
Source: Bakery Machinery Distributors, Inc.

PRETZELS

There are two kinds of pretzels in commercial distribution: the large, soft pretzel that is perishable and must be sold fresh baked or in frozen form, and the small crisp pretzel that has about the same shelf life as a soda cracker. The following discussion relates to the crisp pretzel.

Pretzel doughs are made very stiff so they will withstand the punishment of machining without becoming sticky or misshapen and so they will give the desired texture in the finished product. Strong bread flours are often specified and sometimes vital gluten is added to make the dough tough and tolerant. On the other hand, Loving and Brenneis (1981) claim that high ash soft red winter wheat flour is being used in some plants.

Straight dough methods are used for some commercial pretzels, but probably the majority are made with sponges. In the latter case, sponges are fermented for a shorter time than cracker sponges, say 10 hr. Doughs may receive a short proof stage, but frequently are made up without additional fermentation. It is probable that most commercial pretzels contain sodium bicarbonate to supplement the yeast leavening. Continuous methods have been developed for mixing pretzel doughs (Blain and Zabrodsky 1988).

The machining steps, including formation of the pretzel shape, are handled automatically in all but a very few plants. The characteristic gloss of the pretzel results from treating the finished dough piece with an alkaline solution made up with either 0.5% sodium hydroxide, potassium hydroxide, or, more often, 2% sodium carbonate. Some plants use different concentrations. The hot alkali solution, which may be applied either by spraying or dipping, is held near the boiling point and immersion time is about 10 to 25 seconds. The alkali reacts with the surface layer of dough and loses its corrosive character, which otherwise would cause an unpleasant sensation in the mouth when the pretzel is consumed. It is important to carefully control the amount of alkaline solution applied, so that the pretzel as it emerges from the hot bath does not contain unreacted alkali.

About 2% coarse flake salt is applied to the wet pretzel, the moist and sticky surface improving the adherence of this ingredient.

A published straight dough formula for pretzels consists of 71.6% flour, 25.0% water (variable), 0.3% yeast, 1.0% salt, and 2.1% shortening. After it is dumped from the mixer, dough is conveyed to the hopper of the twisting machine from which it is extruded, rolled, and twisted. The twists are passed under a spray of hot soda solution, sprinkled with salt, and baked. It is often necessary to dry the pretzels further after they emerge from the oven. Details of a sponge process for pretzels is given below.

<u>Sponge Process Pretzels</u>

(1) Mix a dough containing the following ingredients: 200 lb strong flour, 100 lb water (variable), and 12 oz yeast.

(2) Ferment the sponge for 10 hours at 75°F.

(3) Remix after adding the following ingredients: 800 lb medium strength flour, 220 lb water (variable), 12 lb salt, and 28 lb shortening.

(4) Dump dough in hopper of pretzel machine. Dip the unbaked pretzels in sodium carbonate solution. Drain. Sprinkle with salt. Bake.

Figure 20.1 is a flow diagram of continuous pretzel making according to the patent of Blain and Zabrodsky (1988).

The temperature and time parameters for pretzel baking depend on the dimensions of the piece and its initial moisture content, among other factors. Conditions in a 50-ft oven that is in wide use are described as follows. The bake section, or top conveyor in the oven, is set at 475°F at the entry point and 425°F at the exit. Time spent in the bake section is controlled by a variable speed drive and is between 4 and 5 minutes. Moisture content of pretzels at the end of the bake period should be about 15%. The pretzels go down a slide from the bake section to the drying section, which is underneath the bake section and separated from it by heavy insulation. Pretzels that cling to the baking belt are removed by a doctor blade.

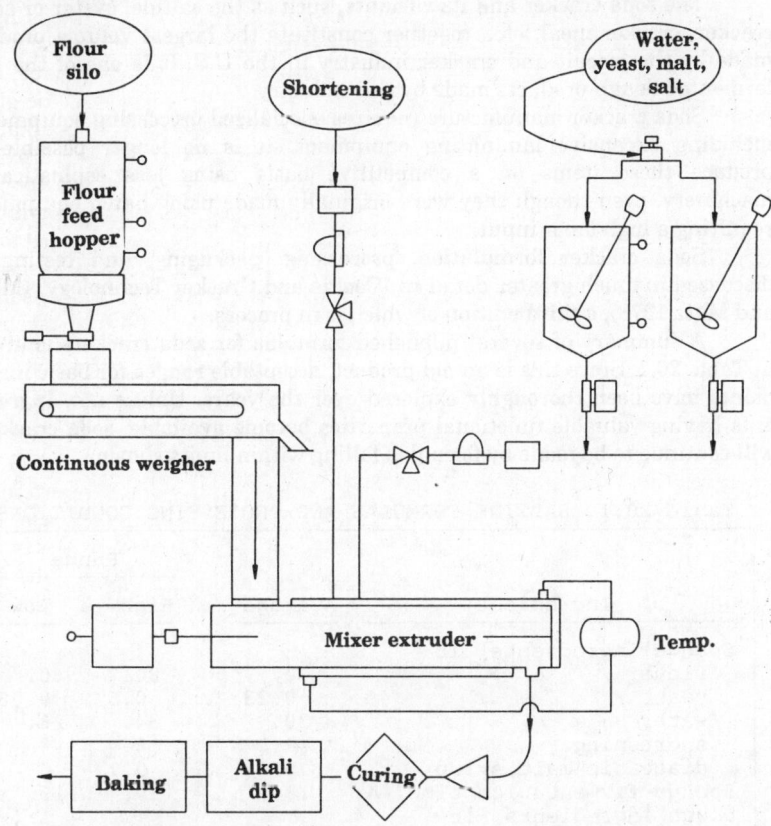

Figure 20.2. A continuous pretzel plant

Checking, or spontaneous cracking, of twist pretzels is a serious problem that can be minimized by closely controlling the baking, drying, and cooling conditions. The tension set up in the "knots" or overlapping joints in the pretzel during baking are often sufficient to break the crisp dough. The problem is not nearly as severe in stick pretzels, though it does exist, expecially in pieces of large diameter.

SODA CRACKERS AND SALTINES

The reader might question the classification of soda crackers as "yeast-leavened" products, since a final burst of carbon dioxide is supplied by sodium bicarbonate added at the remix stage. This product, however, derives many of its most important qualities from yeast fermentation, and so it is included in this chapter rather than in a preceding one.

The soda cracker and its variants, such as the saltine, oyster or soup cracker, cracker meal, etc., together constitute the largest volume product made by the biscuit and cracker industry in the U.S. It is one of the few fermented dough products made by this industry.

Soda cracker manufacture requires specialized processing equipment, including expensive laminating equipment. It is no longer possible to produce these items on a competitive basis using less sophisticated machinery, even though they were originally made using batch equipment requiring a high labor input.

Soda cracker formulation, processing, packaging, and testing is discussed in much greater detail in "Cookie and Cracker Technology" (Matz and Matz 1978), a third edition of which is in process.

A summary of several published formulas for soda crackers is given in Table 20.1. Since this is an old product, acceptable ranges for basic ingredients have been thoroughly explored over the years. Unless new ingredients having valuable functional properties become available, soda crackers will continue to be made by formulas falling within limits shown.

Table 20.1. SALTINE FORMULAS AND PROCESSING CONDITIONS

Ingredient	Average	Range High	Low
Sponge ingredients, lb			
flour	70.	80.	60.
yeast	0.23	0.5	0.06
water	30.	34.	28.
shortening	4.	8.	0
diastatic malt syrup	0.02	0.1	0
Sponge fermentation time, hr	18.	20.	16.
Dough ingredients, lb			
flour	30.	40.	20.
shortening	5.8	10.	0
salt	1.4	1.6	1.25
sodium bicarbonate	0.63	0.7	0.52
malt syrup	0.92	1.5	0
water	0.8	2.	0
Fermentation			
time, hr	4.	5.	3.
temperature, °F	82.	84.	80.

Ingredients

Since flour may be present to the extent of 80% or more of the finished product, its qualities are the principal controlling factors in determining the machining reactions of cracker dough. It also has an important influence on texture of the finished product, although moisture content is often the dominant factor. Due to its bland flavor, however, flour cannot be expected to exert an overriding effect on cracker taste and odor. Appearance is also considerably affected by ingredients other than flour and particularly by the machining and baking of the product.

The standards for flour to be used in cracker production are more stringent than for flours intended for cookies. Some very general recommendations can be made for flour specifications, but it should be understood that the suggested limits can often be exceeded without adverse results and, also, that some flours meeting all of the requirements will be found wholly unsuitable for cracker production. The influence of flour type on cracker flavor is poorly understood. Some authorities have indicated that hard wheat flours have superior flavor potential as compared to soft wheat flours. Long extraction flour is said to give a preferred, wheatier flavor.

The sponge flour should be relatively strong, unbleached, with an ash content of 0.39% to 0.42%, a protein content of 8.5% to 10.0%, and an acid viscosity value somewhere in the range of 60° to 90°McM., the exact value needed depending on the product and conditions. The dough flour should be weaker, with an ash of about 0.40%, a protein content of 8.0% to 9.0%, and an acid viscosity value of 55° to 60°McM. Strong flours tend to increase oven spring, but the crackers are often unduly tough. Weak flours lead to lesser amounts of spring, but give a tender, more friable cracker. The effect of fermentation is to mellow the gluten; weak flours and vigorous fermentation combine to yield flat, tender crackers. Flour for thick saltines (120 per lb) should be stronger than that needed for thin crackers (160 to 170 per lb).

Lard and oleo oil are widely used as shortenings. The flavor of crackers containing lard is widely regarded as superior to that of crackers made with oleo or vegetable shortening. Plastic shortenings are not essential, so liquefied fats handled by bulk transferring and metering systems are commonly employed. Hydrogenated shortenings are said to improve spring, while lard contributes tenderness but frequently detracts from expansion in the oven. Emulsifiers may be added.

The effects of variation in ingredient water quality on cracker properties are largely obscured by the lengthy sponge fermentation, which overcomes any alkaline tendencies in this ingredient.

Yeast foods are often added, but in formulas containing very small amounts of yeast, as in soda cracker sponges, their value is debatable.

The amount of topping salt was not shown in Table 20.1. About 2.5% based on dough weight is a good average figure. Salt suppliers sell a size specifically recommended for this purpose. Dough salt should be of a finer granulation, although this is not as important in crackers as in cookies.

Processing

Mixing.—Cracker sponges are mixed just long enough to wet the flour. Overmixing tends to develop the gluten and causes problems during fermentation. In some plants, mixing is stopped before complete wetting of the flour occurs, but this may be undesirable from the standpoint of obtaining a uniform fermentation.

Shortening is shown as being added to the sponges. One of the advantages is that shortening is certain to be adequately distributed. If any crust forms on the sponge, it is made softer and easier to incorporate by the higher fat content of the mass. The fermentation rate of the sponge is not noticeably affected by the shortening content.

Cracker doughs made with strong flours should be mixed for a few minutes at high speed to incorporate ingredients, but full development of the gluten at this stage will cause difficulties in machining. If the doughs are made up with relatively weak flours, full advantage can be taken of their limited gluten extensibility by developing the flour completely in the doughing-up process. This technique will tend to improve gas retention and, therefore, oven spring.

Fermentation.—The reactions of yeast fermentation have been discussed in considerable detail in an earlier chapter. There are special considerations involved in cracker fermentations that will be examined more fully at this point.

Micka (1955) showed that the yeast added to cracker sponges and the bacteria from ingredient flour or from deposits of material retained in the trough from previous batches will grow for 10 to 15 hr. After this period, both the yeast and bacteria are repressed, but bacteria are inhibited more than yeast. The acidity increases that are observed are largely due to bacteria and are favored by low percentages of yeast. Sterilizing the troughs retards bacteria and yeast fermentation as well as the development of acidity. When yeast addition is greater than 0.50% or the trough is sterile, acidity development is retarded to such an extent that the finished crackers are high in pH and have a nontypical flavor.

The rapidity of gas and acid development is related to the temperature of the sponge, and for a given formula is a function of the temperature at which the sponge is set and the temperature of the fermentation room. It is also related to dough composition—water, salt, enzymes, and sugars have important effects, as previously described.

The soda percentages shown in the formulas are only estimates and cannot be regarded as constant even in a given plant using a standard formula. The correct amount of sodium bicarbonate to be added to the dough is the quantity necessary to assure the obtaining of a predetermined pH in the cracker, and is therefore related to the amount of acid produced during fermentation. The amount of acid production cannot be predicted with certainty. Most manufacturers aim for a finished cracker pH between 7.5

and 8.0. Crackers outside this range are not likely to have the flavor the consumer expects.

Laminating.—All crackers of the type discussed in this section are made from laminated doughs. Formerly this step was performed on reversible dough brakes with a large amount of operator participation. At present, automatic laminators are used throughout the industry. The number of layers formed is somewhat variable, but must be at least 6 to 7 to secure any benefit from this operation. Excessive layering eliminates most of the benefits expected from this operation by breaking down the dough.

Laminating of soda cracker doughs is nearly always done without the benefit of an interleaving ingredient such as is used in puff pastry. In cream crackers, however, a small amount of a mixture of flour and shortening is added between the dough sheets.

Baking.—The average bake time for a 150 to 169 count cracker is about 2.25 minutes with variations in zones (up to eight) of 400° to 570°F in combinations that differ according to the processor's equipment and product specifications (Somers 1984).

BREAD CRUMBS, CROUTONS, AND STUFFING

In this section will be discussed three kinds of products which, at least in their initial commercial manifestations, were made from loaves of bread that had been returned as stale from retail outlets. According to current practice, most of these products are made from bread specially formulated and processed for these particular usages. There are also imitation products made by extruding and puffing dough pieces or by grinding a continuous band of baked material. Our discussion will concentrate on the more conventional type of product, that made from baked doughs.

Croutons

Most manufacturers of croutons prefer to use Pullman pans (i.e., sandwich style loaves) to bake the bread used as raw material. The more uniform grain of the crumb in these loaves is beneficial and the square cross section eliminates some problems in feeding and cutting.

A process called "tempering" is applied to the loaves to make the bread firm enough to process through the mechanical feeder and the crumb tough enough so that it will not tear or ball up as it is being cubed. Tempering is a staling and drying process, and can be conducted by exposing loaves to the air for one to three days, depending on ambient conditions of temperature and relative humidity. Rooms, cabinets, or other spaces with controlled temperature and humidity can be established to make the process more uniform and sanitary. After tempering, and before the loaves are sent to the slicers, the crust should be firm but not brittle and the crumb must be firm.

Cubing the tempered loaf can be done with the usual type of bread slicers, of either the conventional band or the reciprocating design. Because of the much firmer nature of the material being cut, blade wear is considerably greater when the slicers are making croutons as compared to slicing soft bread recently baked. Of course, at least three conventional slicers would have to be arranged in tandem to make the three directions of cuts on unsliced bread that are required to produce cubes. If the bread has already been sliced in the normal manner, only two cutting machines would be necessary for continuous cubing. The transfer mechanism must be designed to hold the loaves and strips together as they are carried from one of the slicing stations to the other. Three-eighths inch to one-half inch cubes are very common sizes, but some smaller sizes are seen, and there is no apparent reason why any of these sizes have been selected. In fact, there is no reason some shape besides cubes wouldn't be preferred by many consumers (discs?).

The cubes are dried after they are cut. A device that will turn or tumble the cubes while they are exposed to large volumes of hot air is the preferred approach. On the other hand, excessive agitation is to be avoided as this will break off and rub off pieces of the cubes, leaving a powdery residue that is unsightly and can create problems in the dryer and at subsequent processing points. A final moisture content of about 5% to 6% is considered satisfactory, though products having moisture contents of 3% to 10% are apparently being merchandised.

Salt, spices, cheese, and other flavorings can be added either to the dough or the cubes. If the bread is made from stale loaves collected from route operations, then there is no choice, a powder or liquid flavoring must be applied to the cubes in some manner. Problems of getting and maintaining uniform distribution are serious under these conditions. Powders tend to become dislodged and fall to the bottom of the package. If loaves are being baked specifically for the crouton market, then a more uniform distribution can be obtained by including flavoring ingredients in the dough. Most spices and flavorings will not significantly affect dough properties or fermentation rates, so the processing of the dough and finished properties of the loaf will not be noticeably different when the flavors are added with the other ingredients.

If the flavors are oil soluble, a mist of the oil can be sprayed into a rotating tumbler while the croutons are being carried through it. This method will generally give a sufficiently uniform distribution to satisfy the consumer, even though the flavor will be concentrated mostly on the surface of the cube. All authorities emphasize the necessity for using an oil of high stability—100 hrs AOM, at least. The dried and flavored croutons are cooled to 85°F or less and then packaged.

Various expedients have been suggested for delaying moisture absorption by croutons so they will stay crisp longer in soup. The usual approach is to coat the crouton with a water-repelling material (see, for example Verhoef and Zock 1990).

Bread Crumbs

Bread crumbs, which are frequently used by cooks to bread pieces of meat and the like, or as toppings for casseroles, are often packed in composite cans (fiber and foil construction) with sprinkler lids. Large users, such as manufacturers of breaded fish or chicken pieces for subsequent freezing, receive the crumbs in bags or drums. There is a large volume of industrial and foodservice demand for crumbs.

Loaves destined for bread crumb production are tempered as has been described for croutons. The loaves are then cut into pieces of the right size and shape to dry quickly in the next processing step. Cubes as prepared for croutons are quite satisfactory. The sized material is then dried in any kind of oven suitable for this operation. Uniformity of drying is important and the desired end point is 3% to 6% moisture content. Cooling and equilibration of the dried cubes is desirable to promote uniformity in grinding.

Grinding can be performed in a high-speed knife-type grinder. The screens in the grinder are selected to give the finished bread crumbs the particle size distribution required by the consumer. A U.S. Standard No. 8 screen is often used. Spices or other flavorings can, in some cases, be metered into the grinder input, but for gummy and otherwise troublesome materials, application in a tumbling mixer is often the best choice.

Stuffing Mixes

Stuffing mixes are prepared very much like croutons, but the cubical shape is not as important so the manufacturing process is somewhat less critical. Bread loaves are tempered, cut, dried, seasoned, cooled, and packed. Since stuffing is mixed with liquid and (usually) other seasonings, and sometimes adjuncts such as chopped giblets, before use, then baked in a mass, addition of flavoring ingredients to the dough is particularly suitable for this product. Surface impact on the consumer's taste buds is not an important consideration.

A published formula for a chicken-flavored stuffing mix is: 83.8% bread crumbs (62% medium, 20% fine, 18% coarse), 8.3% vegetable oil, 5.3% spice blend, and 2.6% dried vegetables (Sabhlok *et al.* 1990).

Some stuffing mix is shredded rather than cubed. This form is apparently regarded by some consumers as being of better quality than cubed stuffing (Gobble 1974).

RUSKS AND OTHER TOASTED PRODUCTS

There is only a limited market in the U.S. for rusks, zwieback, and other toasted bread products. In some European countries, considerable amounts of these items are sold, however. De Muynck wrote (1968) "In Holland, it [rusks] is found on each breakfast table." The type of rusk of which he speaks resembles a slice cut from a cylindrical loaf 3 or 4 inches in diameter, lightly toasted on both sides, with a crisp and rather fragile crumb that is light yellow in color and very bland in taste. It has a low density and a very fine and uniform grain. A typical formula, in parts by weight, is reported to be 100 wheat flour, 50 water, 10 yeast, 12.5 eggs, 12 corn syrup, 14 rusk jelly, 0.5 salt, and 5 sugar.

The rusk jelly mentioned as an ingredient apparently consists of a mixture of fat, corn syrup, and emulsifiers. De Muynck attributes the characteristic grain and color of rusks to the corn syrup and rusk jelly, but it would seem that the eggs, which are present in a relatively large amount for a yeast-leavened bread, must play an even more important role.

In the factories that make large amounts of rusks, the production line is automatic throughout. Doughs are mixed in vertical high speed mixers. After about 20 minutes of fermentation, the dough is divided into pieces of 30 grams each and rounded. Each of these small pieces of dough will end up as two rusks. The dough balls are flattened and deposited in cups, then proofed 45 minutes at 85°F and 65% RH. The cups, which have metal lids placed on them, are sent through an oven held at 500°F. Baking time is about 11 minutes.

Immediately after the cups emerge from the oven, the lids are removed to assist evaporation. The small "muffins" are sliced to give two equal halves, top and bottom. These are dried or toasted in a second oven, then packed. Packing is often in a corrugated tube that gives some support and protection to this fragile product.

BIBLIOGRAPHY

ADDO, K., POMERANZ, Y., HUANG, M. L., RUBENTHALER, G. L., and JEFFERS, H. 1991. Steamed bread. II. Role of protein content and strength. Cereal Chem. *68*, 39-42

AICHELE, W. J. 1981. Cookie and cracker processing. Cereal Foods World *26*, 161-165

ANON. 1972. Quinlan's non-stop pretzel production. Candy and Snack Industry *137*, No. 8, 36-38, 40

ANON. 1985. Pita baker lines pockets with accounts. Bakery Production Marketing *20*, No. 9, 110-112

ARTZER, R. 1990. Method of making a food product. U.S. Pat 4,966,781

BLAIN, W. A., and ZABRODSKY, J., III. 1988. Continuous pretzel dough manufacture. U.S. Pat. 4,738,861

BOYD, J. 1910. Hot-plate Goods, Tea-bread and Scones. Maclaren & Sons Ltd., London

CANZONERI, S. 1989. Method for preparing pizza dough. U.S. Pat. 4,834,995

COCOZELLA, A. 1975. Method of making a frozen pizza shell. U.S. Pat. 3,879,564

DE MUYNCK, E. P. L. 1968. Bakery products of the European Economic Community. Proc. Am. Soc. Bakery Engineers *1968*, 144-156

FEDERICO, A. 1974. Method of making high quality frozen pizza crusts. U.S. Pat. 3,845,219

FISCHER, H. A. 1981. Pizza crust production. Proc. Am. Soc. Bakery Engineers *1981*, 170-175

GLAROS, T. L., SOISSONS, F., and MC EVOY, J. 1991. Partially baked croissant and pastry and method of manufacture. U.S. Pat. 4,986,992

GOBBLE, H. G. 1974. Bread crumbs, croutons and stuffing. Proc. Am. Soc. Bakery Engineers *1974*, 138-143

GOGLANIAN, A. 1986. Method of preparing perforated pita bread. U.S. Pat. 4,597.979

GORTON, L. 1989. Pizza crust ouput doubles with automation. Baking & Snack Systems *11*, No. 4, 6, 7, 9

GORTON, L. 1991. On a roll. Baking & Snack *13*, No. 4, 6-7

HARIDAS R., P., LEELAVATHI, K., and SHURPALEKAR, S. R. 1986. Test baking of chapati—development of a method. Cereal Chem. *63*, 297-303

HESS, J. 1973. Out of the horse and buggy era. Snack Food *62*, No. 11, 25-28

ITOU, N. 1989. Process for preparing a food product having a food content and a dough for enveloping the food content. U.S. Pat. 4,814,194

JUERS, A. A. 1982. English muffins. Proc. Am. Soc. Bakery Engineers *1982*, 46-51, 78-79

LEHMANN, T. A., and DUBOIS, D. K. 1980. Pizza crust, formulation and processing. Cereal Foods World *25*, 589-592

LINGLE, R. 1989. The twisted world of J&J snacks. Prepared Foods *158*, No. 5, 218-222

MATZ, S. A., and MATZ, T. D. 1978. Cookie and Cracker Technology, Second Edition. AVI Publishing Co., Westport, CT

MC FEATERS, R. R., KOPPA, D. A., and BABIAK, T. P. 1989. Method of preparing thin uniformly bakable edible assortments. U.S. Pat. 4,865,862

MICKA, J. 1955. Bacterial aspects of soda cracker fermentation. Cereal Chem. *32*, 125-131

NOEL, E. M. 1963. English muffins. Proc. Am. Soc. Bakery Engineers *1963*, 252-259

PACYNIAK, B. 1991. Painting the west bialy. Bakery *26*, No. 4, 102-103, 105-106, 110

PAULUCCI, J. F. 1986. Process of making a dough crust. U.S. Pat. 4,574,090

PENCE, J. W., and HANAMOTO, M. M. 1963. Quality tests for selection of flours for pretzels. Presented at 48th annual meeting of the American Assoc. of Cereal Chemists

PFEFER, D. N. 1976. English muffins. Proc. Am. Soc. Bakery Engineers *1976*, 51-56

POULGOURAS, K. 1990. Method of making pizza dough. U.S. Pat. 4,954,357

PROSISE, W. E. 1990. Process for preparing reduced fat donuts having a uniform texture. U.S. Pat. 4,937,086

RIJKAART, C. 1984. Croissant production. Proc. Am. Soc. Bakery Engineers *1984*, 137-143

SABBLOK, J. P., HORAN, W. J., and CARLTON, D. K. 1990. Microwavable stuffing mix. U.S. Pat. 4,940,591

SATHE, S. K., TAMHANE, D. V., and SALUNKHE, D. K. 1981. Studies in saltine crackers (khara biscuits): I. Composition and certain physicochemical changes during baking. Cereal Foods World *26*, 404-409

SENEAU, B. 1989. Preproofed, partially-baked and frozen, crusty bread and method of making same. U.S. Pat. 4,861,601

SOMERS, J. 1984. Trouble shooting crackers. Presented at the 59th Annual Technical Conference, Biscuit Bakers Institute, Atlanta, GA. Jan. 24.

SPOONER, T. F. 1984. Pizza systems: A menu full of choices. Baking & Snack Systems *11*, No. 4, 10, 12, 14-15

STEWART, J. 1984. Snack cracker production. Presented at the 59th Annual Technical Conference, Biscuit Bakers Institute, Atlanta, GA. Jan. 24

SULLIVAN, N. D., and BAKER, F. E. 1986. Pizza docker. U.S. Pat. 4,573,388

THOMPSON, J. B. 1981. English muffins. Proc. Am. Soc. Bakery Engineers *1981*, 141-145

TOTINA, R. W., BEHNKE, J. R., WESTOVER, J. D., and KELLER, R. L. 1979. Fried dough product and method. U.S. Pat. 4,170,659

UMBACH, S. L., DAVIS, E. A., and GORDON, J. 1990. Effects of heat and water transport on the bagel making process: Conventional and microwave baking. Cereal Chem. *67*, 355-360

VERHOEF, N., and ZOCK, H. F. 1990. Food product. U.S. Pat. 4,935,251

WEAVER, J. A. 1978. Automation in the pretzel industry. Bakers Digest *52*, No. 5, 11-15

WESTOVER, J. D. 1980. Process for cooking dough products. U.S. Pat. 4,208,441

WOLF, A. 1985. Method for producing croissants. U.S. Pat. 4,526,795

WU, J. Y., and HOSENEY, R. C. 1989. Rheological changes in cracker sponges during an 18-hour fermentation. Cereal Chem. *66*, 182-185

chapter twenty-one

ADJUNCTS: WASHES, GLAZES, ICINGS, AND MARSHMALLOW

INTRODUCTION

The term "adjunct" as used in this book means a food composition that is not a dough or batter and that is applied to a bakery product to enhance the finished food's appearance, flavor, or texture, or to improve its acceptability by some other means. Although the adjunct is not usually in baked form when it is applied, it may in some cases accompany the dough or batter through the oven.

The adjuncts discussed in this chapter are washes, glazes, icings, marshmallow, and sugar paste fillings for cookies. These are defined, for the purposes of the discussion, as follows: (1) Washes are mixtures of low viscosity that can be applied to bakery foods either before or after they are baked to alter the color and/or texture (rarely flavor), and they are often expected to interact chemically with the crust if applied before baking. They may be either fat-based or water-based. (2) Glazes are generally sugar and water mixtures with flavors and other additives. They are usually applied after the product is baked, do not interact chemically with the crust, and are preferably translucent so the crust shows through. (3) Icings are mixtures of rather high viscosity, generally based on sugar and water mixtures but sometimes on fat systems, are applied in fairly thick layers after the crust is baked, do not interact chemically with the crust, and are usually opaque so they hide the crust. (4) Marshmallows have many similarities in formulation to icings, but are whipped to a low density. They are used as toppings, as fillings, and as bases for more complex mixtures. (5) Sugar paste fillings are based on finely powdered sugar and fat (or oil), are quite viscous mixes that set up to solids or semi-solids when cooled, and are sensitive to temperature changes.

Other kinds of adjuncts to be discussed in the next chapter consist mostly of solid or semi-solid materials such as streusels, fat-based enrobings, nut-based pastes, and pie fillings. A much more extensive collection of formulas, procedures, and specifications can be found in the book "Formulas and Processes for Bakers" (Matz 1989).

WASHES

Washes (sometimes called "washovers," especially in the U.K.) are the simplest kind of adjunct, often as simple as an aqueous solution of sugar or skim milk, or a brushed-on film of melted butter. They are applied to the surface of bakery products, either before or after these items are cooked, to modify the appearance (color, gloss, etc.) of the finished food. Washes may have other functions as well—improving the adherence of sprinkled-on granules, allowing increased expansion of the product by delaying crust dehydration, and modifying crust texture. Post-baking washes have been suggested as a medium for applying heat sensitive nutrients to bakery products. Although sprays of antimicrobial agents such as sorbic acid are not usually called "washes," there is some justification for putting these solutions in the present category.

Pre-baking washes are seldom used on batters or very soft doughs because the added moisture can have destructive effects on the surface layer and result in collapse of the piece in the oven. They are of greatest value on bread and rolls where a fairly tough and slightly dry surface layer can support the wash and delay its absorption; also, they are traditionally used on the top crusts of certain types of pies. They have been advocated for use on cookies and crackers to improve the gloss. Perhaps the main objection to their application is that the treatment sometimes leads to irregular patches of color, which many consumers do not like.

Examples

The basic types of washes will be discussed briefly. There are many possible variations of each type—in quantity, in method of application, and in composition—so the formulator has an opportunity to exercise his creativity in exploring these dimensions.

Melted butter or other fat is applied to baked crusts to improve gloss. The aroma of the baked product may also be improved. There is little effect on flavor because so little of the adjunct is added.

Milk washes have as their main purpose the darkening of crusts. Use liquid skim mik or dissolve a pound of NFDM in a gallon of water and apply with a spray or brush before the product is baked.

Egg washes modify both the color and gloss of the finished product. Beat well 2 lb of liquid whole eggs, then add 8 lb of water. Apply by brushing or spraying before the product is baked.

Egg and oil washes are applied to get unusual looking crusts. Add 1 oz salt to 8 lb liquid whole eggs and beat the mixture to maximum volume. Blend in about 2 lb salad oil. The amount of oil can be varied in the range of 8 oz and 4 lb to get different effects. Apply with a brush before baking.

Egg and milk washes give glossier and darker crusts. Mix one part of egg yolk with one part of whole milk; apply to crust before baking.

Egg white washes give glossier and probably crisper crusts. Mix liquid egg white with an equal amount of water and brush or spray a small amount on the crust before baking. The rapid spoilage that occurs in these washes can be prevented by including preservatives (Voss 1989).

Cream of any fat content is often brushed on pie crusts, especially in home baking, to improve the appearance.

Starch washes are used to improve the hardness or crispness of crust, especially of hearth rolls and breads such as rye, by brushing on before baking. To make a typical starch wash, disperse 3 to 5 parts corn starch in a little cold water, then add with vigorous agitation to 95 to 97 parts of boiling water. Cook a few minutes until the starch is thoroughly gelatinized. Apply hot or at least warm; do not allow to gel. A patented wash ("glaze") consists of starch in an oil-in-water emulsion (Holscher *et al.* 1988).

Sugar and milk washes darken the crust color, increase gloss, and may improve crispness when brushed on the surface of dough pieces before baking. Mix 1 lb of sugar and 1 lb of NFDM with 8 lb of water; strain to remove lumps before applying. Sugar, milk, and egg washes are made by mixing 1 lb of sugar, 2 lb of liquid egg, and 7 lb of liquid whole milk. Apply sparingly to unbaked dough.

Variations

Granulated sugar may be sprinkled on a washed pie crust to give a sparkling effect. Use of starch or starchy material in the wash leads to an accentuated texturing effect, often with many light-colored cracks in a dull dark layer. Readers with experimental tendencies can no doubt create many other interesting variations with little effort.

If the washes are to be applied by had, the procedure is simply to brush on an amount estimated to achieve the desired purpose. Use a wide brush with soft bristles. There are at least three mechanical methods of applying washes: (1) Conveying the pieces on a wire mesh belt through a "waterfall" of the liquid, a method most suitable for cookies or other very small pieces; (2) Spraying a patterned deposit from nozzles, best for pies; and (3) Using rotating brushes or cylinders coated with foam rubber or cloth to transfer the liquid to the tops of pieces.

GLAZES

Glazes are of two main types, the concentrated sugar mixtures that dry to a thin, translucent to nearly opaque layer, and are typically applied to doughnuts, and the high moisture, nearly transparent, almost gel-like materials used on fruit cakes, flans, etc. There are also types called "finishes" that are poured over fruit cakes, babas, rum cakes, and other bakery products that require a flavoring and moistening sauce to attain their maximum palatability. All these types are used on products that have already been baked and they are usually applied by pouring or dipping. Particulate materials may be included in, or sprinkled on, the glaze. There is no clear dividing line between glazes and thin water icings.

The main purpose of using glazes to increase the visual appeal of products, but they may also add positive flavor notes and textural contrast. Flavors that would be at least partially dissipated in the oven, such as vanilla, can exert their full impact when included in glazes. The high sugar content glazes give an initial effect of sweetness that is widely appreciated. An additional function of the high moisture type of glaze is to retard the drying of fruits on flans and tarts and of fruit cakes, etc.

A finish to be applied to rum cakes by pouring or dipping can be made as follows: Mix 65% granulated sugar, 16% water, 12% corn syrup, 6.7% invert syrup, and 0.3% salt. Bring to a boil while stirring. Remove from the heat and add artificial rum flavor when the mixture has cooled slightly. Real rum or other alcoholic or non-alcoholic flavors can also be used, if desired. As an interesting variation, try some of the brand name liqueurs in finishes for premium priced cakes.

The finer the grind of sugar used as an ingredient, the smoother the texture of the glaze. Acceptable glazes can be made with powdered sugar, but they may be grainy in texture. Still better quality is obtained by using fondant as a base, but this requires additional time-consuming preparations. Detailed descriptions of fondant preparation starting with granulated sugar can be found in "Formulas and Processes for Bakers" (Matz 1989). Fondant can, however, be obtained from bakery supply houses, usually packed in plastic bags inside boxes or in cans. The soft, creamy fondant can be used directly as an ingredient for icings, fudges, frostings, fillings, etc. Other types of fondants can be used as bases to which modifying materials are added to form the finished adjunct. Dry powdered fondants are commercially available; they are reconstituted by mixing them with a carefully measured amount of water. They are very convenient and uniform, but probably slightly more costly than fondants prepared in the plant.

Doughnut Glazes and the Like

A simple doughnut glaze, easily made with a minimum of ingredients can be prepared from 77.9% powdered sugar, 15.6% water, 4.9% corn syrup, 0.1% salt, 1.5% gelatin, and enough flavor and color to give the desired characteristics. Hydrate the gelatin in part of the water. Mix the other ingredients to form a smooth paste. The water (which must be adjusted to give proper depositing characteristics and appearance) should be hot at this point. Then add the gelatin and mix at low speed to avoid incorporation of air. The usual flavor is vanilla, but many other options are possible.

A slightly more complex version of a doughnut glaze can be made from the following ingredients: 13.20% water, 3.30% corn syrup, 0.05% cream of tartar, 0.82% nonfat dry milk 0.10% algin, 82.53% powdered sugar, and flavor as required. Bring the water, corn syrup, and cream of tartar to a boil. Place the other ingredients in a mixer bowl and add the hot syrup. Mix at medium speed until smooth. This glaze will retain its moisture somewhat better than the preceding formula because of the presence of algin, which can be replaced by commercial stabilizer mixtures.

Since honey has a strong appeal to many consumers, a glaze containing this ingredient should improve marketability. Honey glazed raised doughnuts are popular. Following is a formula that includes a significant amount of honey: 79.42% powdered sugar, 15.88% water, 3.97% honey, 0.24% stabilizer, and 0.49% powdered salt. The stabilizer (a commercial mixture) is hydrated in the water. The honey is warmed to assist dispersion and mixed with the water; this blend is then heated to about 200°F. The hot liquid is mixed with the other ingredients using minimum agitation to avoid the incorporation of air. This formula yields a translucent glaze that becomes opaque as it loses moisture.

A chocolate pouring icing, for which a formula will be given below, is not transparent or translucent, but it is a thin viscosity glaze or icing readily adaptable to being applied by pouring on to doughnuts, petit fours, etc. Since chocolate liquor is the flavoring ingredient, the quality will be quite good but the cost quite high. This ingredient adds a significant amount of fat to the glaze, another respect in which the formula differs from those described previously.

Chocolate Pouring Icing

(1) Mix together 70 lb fondant (12% moisture), 10 lb boiling water, 6 lb corn syrup (42 DE, 43 Be), and 14 lb melted chocolate liquor.

(2) Heat the above ingredients to 100°F while stirring.

(3) Allow to cool slowly to 85°F before using. The water content must be adjusted to give a workable consistency.

The top crusts of baked pies are occasionally washed, but they are seldom glazed. The crusts of fried pies, are, however, frequently glazed. There are several reasons for this. Greasiness of the fried pie crust is concealed by the glaze. If not so treated, the crusts are often dull and irregularly colored, appearance defects that are obscured when glaze is applied. Texture is improved, especially in pies several days old, when the filling has soaked into the crust and softened it. The initial flavor perception is improved by the sweet glaze, giving a boost to acceptability that is often needed because of the relatively large proportion of crust to filling. An example of a formula for a glaze for fried fruit pies is, 68.87% sugar, 5.36% stabilizer, 1.25% hard fat, 0.05% salt, 0.57% flavor and fruit pieces, and 29.90% water (adapted from Taylor 1971).

Gel Coatings for Fruit Flans, etc

Colored and flavored glazes are used as decorations and to prolong shelf life of cakes and tarts in many European countries. In England, these products are called "flan jellies," in Germany "tortenguss," and in France "nappage." They are especially useful to cover the exposed fruit slices that top many of these bakery products. Their glistening, clear, colored gel helps to mask irregularities and defects in the fruit while giving the tart an attractive overall appearance. Their high moisture content delays dehydration of the fruit that would otherwise cause a dulling of color and shrinkage.

Cakes and torts of this type are not very common in the U.S., but transparent, gel-like glazes are sometimes used on fruit cakes and the like. Ideally, these glazes should be clear gels with enough elasticity to minimize cracking, but they should be short and not gummy in eating texture. They should show very little syneresis during the product's normal shelf life. They should show good stability to repeated heating and cooling so they don't break down during holding periods on the production line. They should bind water well, so that they can hinder moisture migration. The basic gel should be nearly colorless and flavorless, except perhaps for sweetness and tartness, so that it does not mask the characteristic color and flavor of the cake to which the glaze is applied. They should be virtually transparent and maintain a good shine for a few days in the case of fruit torten and several months in the case of a U.S. style fruit cake.

The basis of these coatings is water plus some sort of gum. In fact, a very simple formula recommended for a fruit cake glaze is 87% water and 13% powdered gum arabic. This mixture is processed by bringing it to a boil, simmering briefly, and then straining. It should be applied hot to the cakes shortly after they have been removed from the oven. After it has cooled an set up, the glaze makes the surface glossy and retards dehydration of the cake. For a savory gel coating see patent of Best *et al.* (1988).

The composition of these gels is such that they are quite susceptible to microbiological growth unless the acidity is kept high enough to hinder this deterioration. The pH should be kept below 4.0.

Piping Jellies

Piping jellies are mixtures of sugar, color, preservatives, and gum systems that are often quite complex. Since their function is strictly decoration, flavors are not often added. They are usually applied by extrusion from a collapsible tube or a special air-assisted syringe, but are sometimes spread on the base icing to color larger areas. Because of the small amounts used, the specialized ingredients required, and other considerations, it is usually better to buy these products ready-made rather than try to prepare them in the bakery. However, a sample formula will be given for those readers who like to gamble. Mix the following dry ingredients: 3.3% modified waxy maize starch, 53.2% sugar, and 0.6% pectin (150 grade slow set). Add the dry ingredients to 42.5% water which contains the food color desired and heat to 212°F while stirring gently. Remove from the heat and stir in 0.4% of a solution made of half citric acid and half water.

ICINGS

The words "icing," "glaze," and "frostings" do not have definitions that allow them to be easily differentiated. There is considerable overlap between glaze and icing; many bakers will call any kind of icing a glaze if it is applied in a relatively thin coating. Water icings are practically the same in formulation as glazes. Frostings are applied primarily to cakes and cover the whole surface (except the bottom, of course) and sometimes form layers between sheets of baked product, while icings can be applied over the whole product or in stripes or other patterns. Dubois (1980) gave a summary of the composition of doughnut and honeybun glazes and icings that is reproduced in Table 21.1.

Table 21.1. RANGES OF COMPOSITION OF DOUGHNUT AND HONEYBUN GLAZES AND ICINGS[1]

Ingredient*	Glaze; product stored at--		Icing; product stored at--	
	Room temp.	Freezer temp.	Room temp.	Freezer temp.
Water	20-22	20-22	16-18	16-18
Stabilizer	6-8	4-6	8-12	6-8
Corn or invert syrup	0-2	2-4	0	2
Hard fat flakes	2-4	0	2-4	0
Non-emulsifier shortening	0	3-6	0	3-5
Granulated sugar	0-35	0-25	20-30	15-25

[1] Glaze to be applied to hot product; icing to be applied to cool product.
* Water percentage based on total formula, all other ingredient percentages based on powdered sugar weight.

The Different Types of Icings

There are several different methods of classifying icings, some based on the ingredients they contain, some on the preparation method, others on the appearance, etc. A classification scheme that is based on traditional usage was published by Pergiel (1966). It includes the categories of (1) flat icings, (2) creme icings, (3) fudges or fondants, (4) marshmallows, and (5) combinations. Flat icings were described as mixtures of 80% to 85% powdered sugar with 15% to 20% water and optional ingredients such as glucose or a small amount of shortening.

Cremes (such as buttercream) icings are generally whipped to a fluffy consistency and contain larger amounts of shortening than flat icings. A typical creme icing would contain 60% to 80% powdered sugar, 20% to 35% shortening, and 5% to 10% liquid. Optional ingredients are starches, gums, driers, and, of course, flavors and colors.

Fudge icings and fondant icings are similar in appearance with a fine dense texture and candy-like eating qualities. They are general purpose cake icings and are often recommended for cakes that will be enrobed or for little cakes, such as petit fours, that will have decorations applied to them. The very small size of the sugar crystals and the presence of considerable free syrup result in the smooth, glossy appearance of these icings.

Marshmallow icings are often called foam-type icings because of the large amount of air incorporated in the mixture. Gelatin or egg whites are used in conjunction with a syrup to permit the production of a highly aerated icing. A base formula for marshmallow icing includes 40% to 45% powdered sugar, 25% to 30% moisture, 1% to 2% gelatin, about 15% corn syrup, and about 15% invert sugar syrup.

Combination icings are blends of two or more of the other types, e.g., marshmallow and creme icing, and are intended to have some of the advantages of both. There are other formulas that do not seem to fit neatly into any of these categories, an example being German chocolate icing.

A very simple icing that is much used for decorative purposes is royal icing, consisting in its simplest form of nothing more than about 20% liquid egg whites and 80% icing sugar which have been mixed, warmed to about 96°F in a double boiler, and then beaten until light and fluffy. Often, about 0.5% cream of tartar is added, and, sometimes, a small amount of blue color to improve the whiteness of the finished icing.

Royal icing dries rather quickly, forming a hard crust, usually without cracking. It can be used on dummy cakes that are on display for weeks or months to show designs that are available on special order, etc. Because of its quick setting properties, it is advisable to keep royal icing in a mixer bowl with the motor running at the lowest speed while working with it.

Stabilizers

The word stabilizer has two distinct meanings when applied to icing ingredients. Icings based on fat systems, such as buttercream icings, require some sort of surfactant, such as monoglycerides, to assist in developing and maintaining their structure—these emulsifers/surfactants act as stabilizers. To give greater, more long lasting structure to aqueous-based icings—such types as flat, boiling, and marshmallow—a hydrophilic substance of the nature of gelatin, agar, or egg white is required, Stabilizers, when properly utilized, simplify preparation, prevent separation, reduce the tendency of icings to stick to wrapping material, and make the icing retain its moisture longer. Stabilizers are generally gums in the broad sense of that word, that is, they are starches, pectins, cellulose gums, and gelatin, as well as alginates, agar, carrageenan, guar gum, gum arabic, tragacanth, and furcelleran.

Most bakery supply houses can furnish proprietary mixtures of stabilizers for specific purposes, as for icing formulation. These materials will be available in plastic and powdered forms and are identified as either boiling or non-boiling types. Most premade icings stocked by these firms also contain stabilizers. The formulator will often find that specifically designed stabilizer mixtures give better results than these generic products.

According to Levine (1980), the most widely used stabilizer for white, boiling-type, flat icings is an agar-based gum system. Agar is not dispersible in cold water but readily dissolves in boiling water. It maintains good gel strength in saturated sugar solutions. Stabilizers based on agar do not become inconveniently viscous in sugar systems and they tend to retard the formation of large grainy sugar crystals. Agar will gel above room temperature, which is a useful feature when icing is being applied to hot products, such as doughnuts, yeast sweet goods, etc.

Formulating and Preparing Icings

Levine gave a representative formula for an icing suitable for application to Danish goods, coffee cakes, and similar yeast-raised sweet doughs. This is: 100 lb powdered sugar, 26.5 lb granulated sugar, 23.5 lb water, 9 lb icing stabilizer, 3 lb shortening, and 3 lb humectants. The granulated sugar, humectant, stabilizer, and water are boiled for one minute. Shortening is added to the hot syrup and the blended batch poured onto the sugar while mixing. Mixing is continued until proper consistency is reached. In these formulas, sugar of 6X or 10X fineness should be used to impart body and sweetness to the icing. Commonly used humectants are corn syrup and invert syrup. Granulated sugar aids in distributing the stabilizer during cooking and controls the rate of surface drying as the icing cools. The stabilizer suspends the water in the system and controls the size of sugar crystals in the finished icing. The fats can be regular hydrogenated shortening, oils, or hard fat flakes; the optimum type of fat is very much dependent on the drying time requirements, seasonal considerations, and the texture desired. Fat also serves as a lubricant for better machinability and forms a thin oil barrier between the icing surface and the wrapping material.

Levine also gave formulas for icings to be used on products packaged in very permeable containers (such as window boxes), containers of medium permeability (such as cellophane wrappers), and containers of relatively low permeability (such as heat-sealed polyethylene wrappings). The basic principle is that the greater the permeability, the more need for the icing to be able to retain its moisture. This can be accomplished by using more stabilizer and granulated sugar and less water as the permeability decreases; also lower melting point fats should be used as permeability increases.

Icings are usually prepared by putting the water in a mixing kettle, premixing the stabilizer with some of the granulated sugar to improve dispersibility and adding it to the water with constant stirring. The remainder of the granulated sugar is then added, and the batch brought to a full rolling boil as quickly as possible. After the mixture is boiled for three minutes, it is poured onto the powdered sugar in, for example, three portions while stirring continuously (Morley 1981).

Trouble Shooting

If the icing is too dry or stiff or becomes too hard as it sets up, it probably does not contain enough moisture. Ingredient proportions should be checked to determine whether the ratios seem logical. Analyze the cooked fondant to make sure that too much water is not being evaporated.

If the icing has too short a shelf life, some of the things to check out are: (1) Is the icing too hot when applied?, (2) Does the iced product stand around for hours before it is wrapped?, (3) Is the container permeable to moisture, either because the wrong type of film is being used or because the seals are poor?, (4) Perhaps the baked product is too dry and is dehydrating the icing layer from the inside out.

If the icing is too soft, too much water may have been added. The sugar granulation may be too coarse or too much granulated sugar may have been added. Too much syrup may have been added.

If the icing becomes discolored after a short time, there may be raisins or other fruits in the baked product that are leaking juice because they are too moist. Has the crust been overbaked so that charred or caramelized particles infiltrate the icing? Is machine grease contaminating the icing?

A common complaint is that icing sticks to the wrapper and pulls off the base product when the wrapper is removed. This is difficult to correct if the goal is to retain a soft icing until the product is consumed. Adjusting the formula by adding emulsifiers or gums may be necessary. If a slightly dryer icing can be tolerated, the problem should be alleviated by cutting back the moisture content. If the piece is iced while hot and then wrapped immediately, condensation of moisture on the inside of the package is almost certain to result, and almost any kind of icing will stick to the wrapper under these conditions. Redesign of the container to keep the wrapper from contacting the icing is effective, but may be quite costly.

Flat Icings and Buttercream Icings

A formulation guide for flat icings was given early in this section. These adjuncts are basically powdered sugar, water, color, flavor, and stabilizer. They are similar to glazes, except they are generally more viscous. Unless they are supplemented with some hygroscopic material such as invert sugar, glycerine, or gums, they lose moisture rapidly and become dull in appearance as well as hard and flaky in texture.

Buttercream icings are rather high in fat and intermediate in aeration between the flat icings and the whipped (marshmallow) icings. They are rather sensitive to temperature variations and do not have good storage stability except on frozen goods. The best examples have excellent flavor and texture, and they are generally preferred by consumers over all othe types of icing.

An example of a very simple formula for white buttercream icing that illustrates the essential ingredients and preparation method was published by Guckenberger (1977). Place in a mixing bowl 100 lb powdered sugar and 8 oz salt. Dissolve 8 lb icing stabilizer in 16 lb boiling water. Add the stabilizer solution to the mixing bowl and mix until smooth. Add 25 lb emulsifier shortening and cream to the desired specific volume.

As an example of a modification of the basic formula, a recipe for a fast setting creme icing is given. Place in a mixing bowl 10 lb powdered sugar and 4 lb 4 oz stabilizer. Add 17 lb cold tap water and mix at medium speed until smooth (about 6 or 7 minutes). Add to the bowl 100 lb 6X sugar,

4 lb nonfat dry milk, flavor, and color, then mix until smooth. Add 30 lb emulsifier shortening and cream until smooth and aerated.

Fudge Icings

Fudge icings are prepared by fondant methods. The fondant may be pre-made and incorporated with the other ingredients by a simple mixing step, or it may be made from granulated sugar and some of the other ingredients by boiling to a temperature giving a supersaturated sugar solution that is then crystallized to create the typical fondant system.

A chocolate fudge icing of typical characteristics can be made by following these directions. Soak 1.1 lb gelatin in 3.5 lb warm water. Bring 7.1 lb butter and 10.6 lb water to boiling. Mix 0.2 lb salt and 28.3 lb granulated sugar, then add the mixture to the boiling butter-water blend. Reheat to boiling, then boil for 5 minutes while stirring constantly. Remove from heat, add gelatin and beat well. Add 8.8 lb dutched cocoa to 4 lb egg yolks, mix well, and beat into the cooling batch. Then add 0.9 single strength vanilla extract and 35.5 lb confectioners sugar and beat until smooth.

Foam Icings

There are a large number of icings that depend on the mixing of an egg white foam, or the like, with a heated blend of other ingredients to form a light fluffy spread or filling. Some of these icings approach a marshallow in density and other characteristics. The storage stability is not very good unless the icings are heavily supplemented with stabilizers and, even then, problems can be expected in commercial distribution. A formula for a soft marshmallow that can be used as an icing is 24 parts water, 2.5 parts gelatin (200 Bloom), 38 parts granulated sugar, 35 parts corn syrup (62 DE, 43° Bé), and 0.5 parts single strengh vanilla extract. For a more extensive discussion see the following section on "Marshmallow."

MARSHMALLOW

Marshmallow formulations have many similarities to those for icings. They are high in sugar, intermediate in moisture content, and rely on gums and other stabilizers for maintaining their preferred physical state. In the case of marshmallow, the stabilizer is usually gelatin. The main point of difference between icings and true marshmallow is that the latter is beaten to a stiff foam. Also, true marshmallow never contains a fatty ingredient.

Types and Uses of Marshmallow

Marshmallow is used both by itself as a confection and as a component of bakery foods, ice cream, other confections, etc. The texture can be short or stringy, hard or soft. Though marshmallow is usually white, it can be colored many different hues with the available food dyes. When a flavor is added, it is most often vanilla, but other flavors are common, such as the banana flavor added to the children's confection "circus peanuts." Oil-based flavors cause problems, however, and good chocolate-flavored marshmallows are not available.

Marshmallow is frequently used in, or on, cookies. It can be placed between base cakes to form a sandwich—the popular "moon pie" is an example. It can be a shaped deposit on a single base cake, in which case it is either enrobed with chocoloate (or some other fatty coating) or covered with particles such as flaked coconut or chocolate sprinkles. The purpose of enrobing or covering with coconut is two-fold, it allows packing equipment to handle the pieces without coming into contact with sticky marshmallow and it avoids presenting the customer with a crusty dehydrated layer of marshmallow. The chewy texture of coconut conceals the defects of the dried crust while enrobing delays evaporation and dehydration.

If the enrobed piece is completely covered with a fairly thick and fairly uniform coating of chocolate, moisture interchange with the atmosphere is markedly reduced (though not completely prevented), but even enrobed marshmallow tends to dehydrate somewhat by vapor phase translocation of moisture, by gravitational draining of liquid, and by capillary absorption. In each of these cases, the base cake is the recipient of the translocated water or syrup. The amount of dehydration that will occur and the extent to which the marshmallow will toughen is largely determined by the relative proportions of base cake and marshmallow deposit. The equilibrium relative humidities (water activities) of the two components must also be considered. All other conditions being equal, drier base cakes will cause the marshmallow to dehydrate to a greater extent, but the composition of the marshmallow and of the base cake are also factors affecting the final equilibrium moisture.

Formulation

The fundamental structure in marshmallow is a stabilizer foam strengthened by the dehydrating effect of a concentrated sugar solution. Gelatin is the stabilizer most frequently used, but other types of marshmallow are based on egg white or on specially processed proteins derived from soybeans or milk, etc. All marshmallows are aqueous systems with, at most, traces of fat, and should be distinguished from the fluffy white fillings used in certain snack cake goods ("Twinkies," etc.), in cream horns for vending distribution, etc. These fillings are made by whipping mixtures of powdered sugar and low melting point fats, usually with some syrup and stabilizer.

A typical formulation for marshmallow would include granulated sugar, corn syrup, invert syrup, gelatin, and water. The types and amounts of sugar and the moisture content have a distinct effect on the texture of the finished piece. In a given solids composition, decreasing the moisture content leads to a firmer, harsher texture. Relatively large amounts of sucrose or invert sugar tend to give a shorter, less elastic, less stringy structure, while increasing the amount of corn syrup, especially if it is the low conversion type, leads to a stringier, more elastic texture. Most marshmallow formulations call for both sucrose and corn syrup, and often some invert syrup, to obtain an intermediate texture thought to be the most acceptable to the majority of consumers. Response of these mixtures to whipping differs as the proportion of ingredients is changed.

Manufacturers of bakery marshmallow generally agree that the consumer wants a tender (soft) marshmallow, not too stringy, in appearance very white, with small and uniform cell size, and sweet but otherwise bland in flavor. It is usually necessary to compromise on some of these details due to practical considerations such as compatibility with processing equipment and storage stability.

A review of a selection of formulas that have been recommended for cookie marshmallow resulted in the data shown in Table 21.2. The ranges shown should not be considered hard and fast limitations. Occasionally, formulas will be found that depart from the usual range and still, apparently, get good ressults. A simple formula is 50 parts granulated sugar, 50 parts corn syrup (43°Bé and 62 DE), 0.5 parts gelatin (200 Bloom), 1.5 parts dried egg white, and 10 parts water. Honey can be used as an ingredient, though its flavor contribution is not great. A typical formula for marshmallow with honey is 9.6% water, 1.2% gelatin, 48.2% granulated sugar, 28.8% honey, 12.0% liquid egg whites, and 0.2% salt.

Table 21.2. COOKIE MARSHMALLOW FORMULATIONS, AVERAGES AND RANGES

Ingredient	Average, %	Range, % Low	Range, % High
Granulated sugar	30	0	60
Corn syrup, 43° Bé	25	20	83
Invert syrup, 76% solids	NA	0	85
Gelatin, 200 Bloom	NA	1.25	2.25
Water, added as such	NA	10	20

Molasses can be added without significant deterioration of the processing characteristics or shelf-life of the product. A dark, highly flavored molasses should be used if the effect of this ingredient is to be noticed by the consumer. Maple syrup or malt syrup can also be substituted for part of the sugar and water to give other flavor variations. Mint oil gives a pleasant flavor to marshmallow.

Prolonging Shelf Life

Much effort has been devoted to finding moisture-retaining substances that will decrease the rate of hardening of exposed marshmallow deposits. The most hygroscopic substance available for this purpose is glycerol. All other solutions, including those made with low conversion corn syrups or sorbitol, will lose moisture to atmospheres of 50% RH or less, at normal temperatures. Getting a soft marshmallow to the consumer, in an open deposit, requires relatively fast turnover, a moisture-resistant package, and an initial moisture content that is as high as possible consistent with acceptable resistance to microbiological spoilage.

The heat treatment given marshmallow is inadequate to produce sterility and the material is often deposited under conditions conducive to massive contamination. Most baking plants have large numbers of yeast and mold spores floating in the air. Use of sterilizing lamps at appropriate places in the processing line will inactivate most yeast or mold cells in their immediate vicinity. These lamps can be used in skinning tunnels, in the head space of tanks containing finished syrups, and over the packing lines.

Preservation of marshmallow from fungal, yeast, and bacterial attack is related to the water activity of the solution (more simply, but less exactly, of the solids content), the pH, and the concentration of any inhibitors, such as sorbic acid, that are added. The number and kinds of organisms present at the time of preparation can also be a factor; the highest possible standards of sanitation are necessary if maximum shelf-life is to be obtained. Spoilage can become apparent through visible mold growth or detectable flavor changes, but the most common evidence of microbial deterioration is bursting of an enrobed piece as the result of an accumulation of fermentation gases. The presence of an alcoholic aroma is another characteristic indication of spoilage in enrobed marshmallow.

As a rule of thumb, a minimum total soluble solids content of about 68% is required in order to assure protection against spoilage. Higher proportions of solids may be necessary if the base cake is relatively small or if other adverse conditions exist. Most marshmallows, as made, contain between 28% and 32% moisture. This may decrease in storage to perhaps 22%. The requirement also varies according to the climate and weather, that is, according to the relative humidity and temperature encountered by the cookies in warehouses and supermarkets.

Changing of marshmallow formulas with the seasons has sometimes been practiced, particularly by firms who sell enrobed goods in southern states. The idea is to make a marshmallow of higher solids content for hot weather distribution, thereby gaining some additional stability at the cost of a tougher, less acceptable marshmallow. For open or unenrobed goods, it has been customary to increase the moisture content by about 1% to 1.5% in the winter months since the lower relative humidity encountered by the cookies during storage and distribution can be expected to cause more rapid dehydration of the deposit.

Processing Methods for Marshmallow

Marshmallow preparation begins with the mixing of a syrup containing all of the ingredients in an unwhipped form. If the sucrose content is high and there is very little corn syrup or invert syrup in the formula, the batch may be made by the cooked process, in which all of the ingredients except the gelatin and flavor are brought to boiling so as to ensure complete solution of the sucrose. The semicooked process, suitable for syrups of intermediate sucrose content, requires bringing the ingredients to 180°F and holding until a clear solution is obtained. In either the cooked or semicooked process, the syrups must be cooled below 140°F before adding the soaked gelatin. In the cold process, the sugars and water are mixed at about 120°F for a sufficient period of time to give complete solution. The soaked gelatin must be heated before it is added to cold process syrups.

After the gelatin and flavors have been thoroughly blended into the syrup, the mixture is beaten or whipped. Batch equipment consists of vertical mixers with bowls of various sizes and a wire whip, or the horizontal beaters especially designed for marshmallow production. The latter, which are more common in the confectionery industry than in bakeries, yield about 200 lb of marshmallow after 20 minutes of beating. Continuous equipment is more efficient in increasing overrun, is easier to control, and requires less labor.

In order to create the foam structure that is characteristic of marshmallow, a very turbulent condition must be developed in the syrup. This turbulence causes the syrup to envelop volumes of air which are then subdivided to small bubbles by the same forces. Whipping equipment and method should be designed to produce small air cells that are uniform in size and have thin walls. Cell wall thickness is a function of average cell volume assuming that the syrup is uniformly distributed over all surfaces. A foam of the desired type will be more stable than one composed of larger cells or more irregular cells, and it is firmer and shorter in texture. There are two or three designs of continuous whippers that make satisfactory marshmallow. All of them require the injection of air under pressure and the use of a pump to force syrup through the whipping chamber.

The overrun, or increase of syrup volume caused by whipping, is related to texture or mouthfeel in that the perceived resistance to chewing of a given volume of product becomes less with increasing overrun. The overrun which is obtained varies inversely with the viscosity of the syrup and directly with the moisture content. Other factors influencing the overrun, such as the temperature of optimum whip, change with variations in moisture content. A very thorough analysis of physical factors contributing to texture in marshmallow and their relationship to processing variables has been published by Tiemstra (1964A, B, C. and D).

Small marshmallows can be dried to give confection pieces that might be usable in decorating baked products (Meyer 1988).

SUGAR PASTE FILLINGS

These materials are mostly used as sandwich cookie fillings or creams, but they are also used for topping single base cakes, which are then enrobed, in sugar wafers, and as centers in rolled cookies. The principal constituents are always finely ground sugar and a fat or oil, usually in the approximate proportions of two to one. When warm or hot, they can be extruded very easily, but they set up to a moderately firm mass when held at room temperature. They become more fluid as the percentage of fat increases, as the solids content of the fat decreases, and as the sugar becomes coarser.

Flavors are nearly always added to the base mix. Colors may be added, but the vanilla flavored fillings, which constitute the majority of sandwich creams, are allowed to retain the normal whiteness of the base mix. Various texture-modifying, stability-adjusting, and nutritionally-justifiable ingredients can be used to meet various goals of the manufacturer. Although the basic ingredients are fairly economical, it is sometimes thought to be necessary to add cheapening materials such as dried whey, dextrose, or corn syrup solids. If a filling is considered to be too sweet for a particular application, lactose, dried whey, or maltodextrin can be used to replace some of the sugar.

Effect of Particle Size

The particle size of the sucrose ingredient affects the smoothness of the filling and thus its acceptability, grittiness due to large particles being regarded by the consumer as a detriment to eating satisfaction. Rheology or viscosity of the mix, which is related to consumer perception of mouthfeel and to the ease of dispensing the material in production, is also affected by particle size. A few large crystals can significantly decrease acceptability even though the average particle size indicates a very finely ground sugar. It is generally agreed that, for maximum acceptability, the particles should not exceed 40 microns in their greatest dimension. When the fillings are to be used as a relatively minor component in sandwich cookies, however, coarser sugar can be used without adverse comment from the majority of consumers, since the grittiness of the filling is partially masked by the crunchiness of the base cake. If the filling constitutes a large part of the finished product, or the filling comes into separate contact with the mouth (as in open-faced cookies), uniformly fine particle size is very desirable, and optimum acceptability can be assured by refining (milling) the cream.

The sugar's particle size also affects the amount of a particular fat or oil required to give the desired viscosity or plasticity to a filling. The critical parameter in this case is not the maximum particle size but the total surface area of the particles, which is related fairly closely to the average particle size, that is, the smaller the average particle size, the larger the surface area per unit weight of sugar. As the fatty material and sugar are mixed, the oil must first coat the particles before it begins to exert its full effect on particle mobility, the latter being observed as variations in the force required to mix the cream and the flowability of the material. The amount of oil required to attain this condition is obviously related to the total surface area of all the particles in the sample.

Effect of Fat Type and Amount

Extremely cheap, low quality fillings have been made with as little as 20% or 22% fat, but for the standard sandwich filling 30% to 35% is the common range. Up to 60% fat has been used where special effects are desired. The lower levels of fat content give fillings that are hard, do not adhere together well so that cracks and voids are seen in the uneven deposits, are nearly impossible to meter properly, and allow the base cakes to separate. It is poor practice to try to cheapen the filling by reducing the fat content to a bare minimum. On the other hand, the filling flows too freely and squeezes out of the cookie if the amount of fat is excessive. It is also likely to give a greasy sensation in the mouth and to soak into the base cake. If a cream of high shortening content is desired for some reason, a fat should be chosen that has a melting point higher than would usually be specified. The beneficial effect on filling texture of choosing the proper SFI for the fat component is described in the patent of Porcello and Manns (1989).

Coconut oil of intermediate hydrogenation, typically of 84 or 92 degree specification, is often selected as the fat ingredient in sandwich creams, but almost all available forms of shortening have been used. Mixtures of hard and soft fats can be made to achieve the consistency desired in the finished filling. The solids fraction index is a useful indication of the probable performance of a shortening in a sandwich cream. Flavor is a very important parameter, with perfect blandness being the ideal. Even a hint of rancidity or tallowy flavor makes the ingredient unacceptable.

Effects of Moisture Content

All ingredients should be at their lowest feasible moisture content. Free water should be rigidly excluded during processing. Any significant amount of water, more than 1%, will lead to serious difficulties by causing agglomeration of the sugar particles. The viscosity of the filling increases greatly, and large hard lumps can form and clog pumps and other machinery. Smaller amounts of moisture will significantly affect filling viscosity and cause fluctuations in deposit weight.

Lecithin has been recommended as an additive for sandwich fillings. It helps maintain a lower viscosity when traces of moisture are present. This contributes to smoother and more uniform depositing. Some filling fats contain lecithin added by the oil processor. A level of 0.3% to 0.4% lecithin (based on weight of the fat) is often found to be satisfactory. Larger amounts may adversely affect the texturizing action of the fat.

Other Ingredients

Sweeteners.—Powdered sucrose is the sweetener most often found in sandwich creams. It may be ground from cane or beet sugar in the factory, or it can be bought in bags or bulk bins from suppliers. The 2% to 5% of starch added to powdered sugar to reduce clumping, seems to have very little effect on filling properties. Syrups are not suitable as sandwich cream ingredients, because their moisture content interferes with satisfactory functioning. Brown sugar has been used as a minor sweetener, but the small amount of moisture it contains can cause problems, especially at high temperatures. Furthermore, it is virtually impossible to get brown sugar fine enough to yield a smooth filling.

Dextrose can be used in fillings to reduce sweetness. It also produces a cooling sensation in the mouth due to its negative heat of solution. Sometimes the hydrated form of this sugar is selected because of its lower cost, but above about 130°F the hydrate will break down into water and anhydrous glucose with disastrous effects on the filling, so processing temperatures must be kept below this level at all times. Maltodextrin might be a better choice to include in the filling at a moderate level for reducing sweetness. Lactose has been suggested, but its multiple hydrate forms can cause some of the same problems described for dextrose monohydrate.

There seems to be no technical reason why artificial sweeteners could not be used in fillings, but the dietary rationale for such a development is difficult to envision. A non-caloric bulking agent would need to be found to replace the sucrose; perhaps a dietary fiber material could be used.

Flavors and Colors.—Cocoa is ordinarily used as the characterizing ingredient for chocolate-flavored fillings since chocolate liquor does not normally provide enough added appeal to justify its much higher cost. For gourmet products, however, use of a considerable amount of chocolate liquor can give a very rich and appealing flavor and texture. Dutched cocoas of 10% to 12% fat are generally chosen because they are the most economical from a coloring standpoint and can provide a very acceptable flavor if properly selected; 10% of cocoa in the filling is a common level.

Flavors should be either powders or oil soluble types. Extracts or solutions in water are unsuitable, and flavors dissolved in propylene glycol tend to make the filling cheesy in texture. Essential oils, as from citrus, spices, and mint are suitable. Colors should be oil soluble versions or finely milled lakes.

Some cookie manufacturers use a small amount of of powdered skim or whole milk in sandwich creams. Sweetness is reduced and flavor improvement is often noted. Dried whey has been recommended as a filler and to reduce sweetness. Interconversion of lactose crystal forms must always be considered as a possible source of difficulty when dairy products are used. Also, these ingredients generally have a significantly larger particle size than powdered sugar, and may give a detectable grittiness to the cream.

Production Methods

Sandwich creams can be mixed in either horizontal or vertical batch mixers. Continuous mixers can also be used but offer relatively few advantages for this product. The mixing time is selected to be sufficient to give a homogeneous mass but not long enough to build up excessive heat. Sequence of ingredient additions is generally shortening first, then the minor ingredients, and finally the sugar.

Developing a slight overrun (air content) is helpful in improving the deposit operation and for improved eating quality. Both the correct weight and the volume of a package of sandwich cookies is dependent on close control of the cream's specific gravity. This control can be assured by correct ingredient specifications and processing methods.

Fillings for sandwich cookies are usually applied by machines that extrude the cream on to one of the base cakes through orifices in a metal roller. After baking, tube (rolled) cookies receive their filling from a nozzle through which a measured amount of cream is injected. In the case of patties and open-faced sandwiches, a more fluid cream can be deposited through fixed extrusion heads. High solids spreads can clog orifices and cause other difficulties unless the crystal structure of the shortening material and the particle size of the sweetener are carefully controlled (Barry *et al.* 1990).

Sugar wafer creams are applied by spreaders that usually take the form of hoppers with drum extrusion feeders. The filling is removed from the feeding rolls by heating them or by scraping them with a doctor blade so that the cream is laid on the wafers in the form of a continuous sheet.

To obtain the adherence of filling to base cake, as is necessary to prevent separation of these components during packaging and distribution, a considerable amount of liquid fat must be present in the cream when it is deposited on the cookie (and when the upper wafer is pressed on to the deposit). There seems to be no guide to the exact amount of liquid fat needed, or to the solids fraction index of the fat at the temperature of deposit.

BIBLIOGRAPHY

BARRY, D. L., DREHER, M. L., JOHNSON, A. A., and SCHROEDER, O. E. 1990. High solids filling material and comestible product. U.S. Pat. 4,919,947

BEST, C., MICHEL, J-P., and LEJEUNE, D. 1988. Colored food composition, in particular for decorative use. U.S. Pat. 4,759,936

CAMPBELL, E. J. 1971. Icings and fillings, the changing requirements for small variety cakes. Proc. Am. Soc. Bakery Engineers *1971*, 144-155

DUBOIS, D. K. 1980. Icings and glazes: formulations and processing. Cereal Foods World *25*, 390-395

GUCKENBERGER, J. D. 1977. Icings and fillings for cakes. Proc. Am. Soc. Bakery Engineers *1977*, 81-87

HOLSCHER, E. J., VERBOEF, N. J. F. D., and LIGEON, C. M. 1988. Oil-in-water emulsion glazing agent for foodstuffs. U.S. Pat. 4,762,721

LEVINE, L. W. 1980. Icing stabilizers. Proc. Am. Soc. Bakery Engineers *1980*, 96-101

MATZ, S. A. 1989. Formulas and Processes for Bakers. Pan-Tech International, McAllen, TX

MEYER, W. J. 1988. Method for drying confection bits. U.S. Pat. 4,785,551

MORLEY, R. G. 1981. Icings and glazes—trouble shooting. Proc. Am. Soc. Bakery Engineers *1981*, 99-105

PERGIEL, L. J. 1966. The wonderful world of cake. Proc. Am. Soc. Bakery Engineers *1966*, 268-302

PORCELLO, S. J., and MANNS, J. M. 1989. Soft soybean oil filler cream compositions. U.S. Pat. 4,865,859

TAYLOR, J. C. 1971. Fried fruit pies—production methods. Proc. Am. Soc. Bakery Engineers *1971*, 182-190

TIEMSTRA, P. J. 1964A. Marshmallows. I. Overrun. Food Technol. *18*, 915-920

TIEMSTRA, P. J. 1964B. Marshmallows. II. Viscosity and elasticity. Food Technol. *18*, 921-927

TIEMSTRA, P. J. 1964C. Marshmallows. III. Moisture. Food Technol. *18*, 1084-1091

TIEMSTRA, P. J. 1964D. Marshmallows. IV. Set and syneresis. Food Technol. *18*, 1091-1096

VOSS, G. D. 1989. Ready to use liquid bakery wash. U.S. Pat. 4,863,751

WILSON, L. L., PLAYER, K. W., PORCELLO, S. J., and MANNS, J. M. 1989. Lipid system for filler composition. U.S. Pat. 4,826,696

chapter twenty-two

ADJUNCTS: STREUSELS, PASTES, FILLINGS, ETC.

INTRODUCTION

The preceding chapter discussed those liquid or semi-solid adjuncts based primarily on sugar. The present chapter will deal with the other adjuncts that the baker can expect to encounter. These include simple dry additives as well as more complex products. Most of the items covered are solid or at least semi-solid. They are, in many cases, also relatively high in fat and low in moisture content. This division into two large categories of adjuncts is somewhat artificial and at times even awkward, but it is useful in several respects—the processing requirements, methods of use, and stability characteristics have certain similarities within the groups.

STREUSELS

Streusel toppings are characteristically in the form of dry lumps and coarse powders of nonuniform size and shape, and they are applied to the tops of dough pieces by sprinkling. Upon baking, they partially coalesce and adhere to the base cake, while at the same time retaining their individuality and, generally, their soft crumbly texture. The simplest version is cinnamon topping which is typically composed of about 93% sugar, 6% shortening, and 1% cinnamon. This topping departs from the norm in not containing any flour or other starchy ingredient.

The more common type of streusel is made with slightly less than one-fourth shortening, slightly more than one-fourth sugar, and about half flour. The pattern of mostly flour, somewhat less sugar, a little shortening, and minor amounts of flavoring and coloring ingredients is characteristic of streusels as a class.

Preparation methods for most streusels are simple. The sugar and shortening are creamed, then the flour is mixed in to form a light paste that is chilled and rubbed through a very coarse (one-fourth inch) sieve. When eggs are used, they should be creamed with the sugar and shortening. For small quantities of streusel, the shortening can be cut in or rubbed into the pulverulent materials, as in making a dough for flaky pie crusts.

Ingredient Requirements

Specifications for streusel components need not be as detailed or as stringent as for most other bakery ingredients. Most bakeries will probably not procure special ingredients for streusels but will use materials stocked for other purposes.

If the shortening is all or part butter or margarine, a flavor improvement can be expected, as compare to the results when emulsifier shortening is used. Because butter and shortening contain about 15% water, they make the flour slightly sticky and lead to the formation of larger lumps. The type of flour is seldom critical—bread, pastry, and cake flours all make satisfactory streusels. Sugar is usually of the granulated type, although some brown sugar may be added for flavor and color. Liquid egg can be added in small amounts, but it is not really needed and may give rise to undesirable tastes and odors if some of the streusel is scorched during baking. It is advisable to add from 0.2% to 0.7% salt to improve the flavor.

Streusels are often flavored with cinnamon, from 0.5% to 1.5% is the range. Chocolate streusel can be obtained by replacing about 6% of the flour with a good cocoa. Vanilla, lemon, rum, and almond flavors are sometimes added. Nuts are often added to streusels; they can easily double the ingredient cost with little effect on texture and not much improvement in flavor. To replace some or all of the flour, cake crumbs of compatible flavor can be used, often leading to a texture advantage.

Examples of Formulas and Procedures

Table 22.1 contains several formulas for streusel toppings. Considerable latitude in modification is possible without seriously damaging the textural qualities of these materials.

Table 22.1. FORMULAS FOR STREUSEL TOPPINGS[1]

Ingredient	Basic	Spice nut	Orange coco- nut	Cherry nut	Almond crunch
Sugar, granulated	34.9	29.0	19.3	22.8	66.4
Shortening	22.3	18.5	12.3	14.6	0
Salt	0.3	0.3	0.2	0.2	0.2
Corn syrup	0	0	0	0	0
Vanilla, 1-fold	0.3	0.3	0.2	0.2	0
Cinnamon, powdered	0.6	3.2	0.4	2.5	0
Liquid whole eggs	5.2	4.3	2.9	3.4	0
Flour, bread	36.4	29.9	33.7	23.7	0
Chopped nuts	0	14.5	0	16.3	10.0
Sweetened coconut	0	0	13.8	0	0
Liquid albumen	0	0	0	0	4.4
See NOTES	0	0	(1)	(2)	(3)

[1] As is basis. Chopped nuts can be pecans or almonds. NOTES: (1) 17.2% ground oranges; (2) 16.3% drained and chopped maraschino cherries; (3) 19.0% kernel paste.

Details that will enable the reader to prepare one of the more complex mixtures will be described. Cream until light 28% butter or margarine, 16% brown sugar, 16% granulated sugar, 1% cinnamon, and 4% whole eggs.

Then add to the mixer 30% cake or pastry flour, 3% chopped almonds, and 2% macaroon coconut. Mix by hand or at slow speed with a paddle only until the fat has solidified, then rub the mixture through a coarse sieve.

Peanut butter streusel can be made by adding enough peanut butter to a basic streusel formula to make a mix of slightly softer consistency than pie dough. The mix can be passed through a potato ricer or the coarse plate of a food chopper to give lumps of an appropriate size. Because the soft, oily nature of peanut butter tends to make the mixture stick together, the rice streusel should be chilled in the refrigerator before it is applied to the dough or batter—otherwise uniform distribution may be hard to accomplish. Chilling to freezer temperatures may may the mixture even easier to use. When baked on the top of coffee cakes these streusels take on a pleasant flavor and the appearance of small brown nuggets of peanut butter.

Including several percent of very small chocolate bits in a standard streusel formula will provide an interesting variation. For best results, the chips should be coated with a small amount of pastry flour before they are mixed with the other streusel ingredients. This helps restrain their tendency to spread when melted.

CRUNCH TOPPINGS

Mixtures very similar in composition to streusels but somewhat moister are baked in sheet pans until they become dry. They are then broken up and crumbled to the right size. These adjuncts are generally spoken of as crunch toppings though many of them are fairly soft and crumb-like. The following formula and procedure for a macaroon crunch topping will give the reader a base on which to design adjuncts meeting the requirements of a specific market. Mix together 32% almond paste, 28% light brown sugar, 5% nonfat dry milk, 6.5% liquid egg whites, 26% macaroon coconut, 0.3% salt, and 2.2% melted bitter chocolate. Spread this mixture in a thin layer on baking pans and bake in a cool to moderate oven until the top takes on a slightly toasted appearance. Remove, cool, and crush into particles having a size suitable for the purpose intended.

PAN DRESSINGS

Somewhat similar in composition to streusels and crunch toppings, but very different in their method of application and finished texture, are the pastes which are used to form the coatings of sticky buns, upside down cakes, etc. These pastes generally contain more moisture than crunch toppings. They are applied to the bottom, and sometimes to the sides, of the baking pan, and dough is placed on top. Upon baking, the glaze forms a very thick syrup. Often, pieces of fruits (cherries, pineapple) are placed on the glaze before the dough is applied.

A simple pan dressing for sticky buns and the like can be prepared from the following formula: 60% brown sugar, 10% shortening, 10% butter,

10% corn syrup, and 10% water. About 0.2% to 0.3% baking soda can be added to improve the product. Some bakers like to add a percent or two of corn starch to make the liquefied sauce a little thicker. Processing involves simply mixing the ingredients to form a slightly creamed product and spreading it in the baking container. The paste melts during baking and assumes a mildly caramelized color and flavor.

A more elaborate and costly pan glaze for pecan caramel rolls or coffee cake can be prepared from the following formula: 43% brown sugar, 11% granulated sugar, 9% invert sugar syrup, 8% corn syrup, 16% margarine, and 13% apple jelly. To the preceding should be added enough baking soda to neutralize some of the acid (about 0.1% to 0.2%) and a quantity of water sufficient to obtain a spreadable paste. The paste is used to coat the inside of the baking cups before the dough or batter is deposited in them, and chopped or whole nuts (pecans, walnuts, or almonds) are often sprinkled on top of the paste. After the rolls are baked and while they are still hot, the pan is inverted to allow the hot syrup to flow on to the rolls. Allowing the pan with the rolls to cool in an upright position will make it impossible to remove the pieces intact.

A honey and malt pan dressing can be made by creaming a mixture of 50% light brown sugar, 25% margarine or butter, 14% nondiastatic malt syrup, 10% honey, and 1% cinnamon.

Certain types of baked-on toppings have similarities to pan glazes. A topping for a sweet dough piece called, among other things, Philadelphia butter cake, can be made by mixing 56% granulated sugar, 19% butter or margarine, 9% emulsifier shortening, 2% cake or pastry flour, 3% nonfat dry milk, 6% liquid whole eggs, and 5% water. A sweet dough piece of 5 to 6 oz weight is placed in a 4x8 inch pan and topped with 5 oz of the above mixture, then baked at 380°F.

ALMOND PASTE AND ALLIED GOODS

The composition and manufacture of almond paste, kernel paste, marzipan, and allied goods has been described in considerable detail in the ingredient chapter dealing with nut products. The following formula for a filling for sweet dough products contains almond paste as a characterizing ingredient.

Almond Paste Filling for Sweet Doughs

(1) Mix together 29 parts almond paste and 29 parts granulated sugar.

(2) Add, and blend until smooth 15 parts margarine or butter, 14 parts shortening, and 8 parts pastry flour.

(3) Then add, and mix until smooth 5 parts liquid whole eggs.

A formula which can be used as a filling for tortes and other applications where the adjunct is used in a thicker layer than the above, is as follows. Mix 43 parts almond paste and 22 parts butter with a paddle until a smooth paste is formed. Add 9 parts pastry flour and 26 parts whole eggs and mix until smooth. Add lemon or other flavor to taste and adjust the consistency with a small amount of liquid whole milk, if necessary. This filling can be used on top of a layer of apricot jam in a short paste crust to make a European style torte.

TOPPINGS FOR PASTRIES

True jams and jellies are seldom used in bakeries as toppings for sweet dough products. Several considerations, not the least of which is the cost, dictate the use of ingredients specifically designed for this purpose. A very simple formula for a topping which is to be applied to a pre-baked product, typically a cheesecake, is: 10.5% sugar, 2.5% instant starch, 27% fruit juices and water, and 60% drained fruit. The starch and sugar are mixed together and then added to the liquid and stirred vigorously before pouring onto the fruit and blending to a uniform topping. Since no cooking is involved, a fresh fruit taste can be obtained, but of course the topping is quite perishable.

Many toppings for sweet rolls and Danish pieces can be adapted from pie filling formulas. Some obvious changes are to use smaller fruit pieces, increase the flavorings (because a smaller amount of fruit is used, compared to pie fillings), and avoid formulations that tend to brown excessively. Formulas for toppings suitable for applying to sweet rolls are described in Table 22.2.

Table 22.2. FORMULAS FOR SWEET ROLL TOPPING[1]

Ingredient	Peanut butter	Cheese	Lemon	Date	Butter scotch
Water	18.4	0	47.3	33.3	0
Liquid whole milk	0	0	0	0	72.3
Granulated sugar	0	17.8	28.3	0	0
Brown sugar	24.5	0	0	8.3	12.7
Corn syrup	0	0	8.5	0	0
Lemon juice	0	0	3.5	0	0
Corn starch	0	0	6.4	0	4.2
Liquid whole eggs	6.1	6.6	2.8	0	8.6
Salt	0.4	0.5	0.2	0	0.1
Peanut butter	18.4	0	0	0	0
Margarine	13.8	4.4	2.1	0	2.2
See NOTES	(1)	(2)	(3)	(4)	0

[1] As is basis.
NOTES: (1) 18.4% toasted cake crumbs; (2) 70.7% bakers' cheese; (3) 0.9% grated lemon rind; (4) 16.7% chopped almonds and 41.7% ground pitted dates.

FILLINGS FOR SWEET ROLLS

The fillings that are applied between the folds of cinnamon rolls (not as toppings) and other products formed in the same way are similar to streusels and pan dressings in many ways. They are usually made in the form of rather dry or stiff pastes to prevent them from being absorbed in the dough portion as it pan proofs. Most formulations are rather simple, as they present few problems, generally being substantially inert so far as the dough portion is concerned. A typical formulation for a cinnamon roll filling is: 37% powdered sugar, 29% margarine, 8% cake flour, 7% cinnamon, 1% salt, 11% liquid egg whites, and 7% cake crumbs. To prepare, mix the powdered ingredients and margarine, then blend in the egg whites. The cake crumbs, which should be of neutral flavor and well dried, are finally mixed in sufficiently to break them up and distribute them completely throughout the batch. The paste should be of spreadable consistency; if it is not, a small amount of water can be added.

A similar formula will be shown next to demonstrate the different approaches that may be used to obtain acceptable results. Mix 21% cake crumbs with 7% water. Blend in 31% powdered sugar, 10% brown sugar, 9% shortening, 10% margarine, 3% cake flour, 3% cinnamon, 1% salt, and 5% liquid whole eggs. To prepare, mix the cake crumbs with the water, add the remaining ingredients and whip until smooth and fluffy.

A rich almond sweet roll filling can be prepared from the following ingredients. Almond paste 10%, kernel paste 7%, cold water 23%, granulated sugar 12%, brown sugar 12%, 6% shortening, 1% salt, 6% liquid whole eggs, and 23% cake crumbs. Mix the almond paste and kernel paste with some of the water for a short time until a smooth consistency is obtained, then add the rest of the water and mix for 2 to 4 minutes at low speed. Put the remainder of the ingredients into the bowl and mix until the batch is well blended. It may be necessary to adjust the liquid to obtain a viscosity that will allow the filling to be dispensed and spread efficiently.

WHIPPED CREAM AND ITS SUBSTITUTES

Whipped cream is a traditional adjunct for premium bakery foods. It is especially prevalent in pastries made in France, Switzerland, Austria, and the Scandinavian countries. The instability of whipped cream has always been a problem, although the development of stabilizers that make possible the preparation of frozen whipped cream desserts has assisted in expanding distribution of the items.

Whipped cream is preferably made from cream having a butterfat content of 40%. Aging in the refrigerator for a day or two will improve the cream's whipping properties. The whipped product quickly separates unless it has been supplemented by some hydrophilic colloid. Gelatin is probably the most common stabilizer, although pectin, vegetable gums, carrageenan, and even starch have been used and may give good results under certain conditions. When using gelatin of 200 bloom strength, an amount of 1 oz per gallon of cream is suggested. Before it is added to the liquid, the gelatin must be hydrated by soaking it in warm water.

Nearly all whipped cream for desert application contains sugar added at the rate of about 12 oz per gallon of cream, and it can be dispersed in the product at various times, but often near the end of the whipping period. This adjunct is a useful vehicle for flavoring materials since no heating step is applied and, therefore, volatile flavors are not dissipated during mixing. Vanilla is a very desirable addition for whipped cream that is to be used in bakery goods. A stabilized whipped cream mix is 0.6% gelatin, 77.5% heavy cream, 13.3% water, 8.5% sugar (powdered or granulated), and 0.1% salt. Soak the gelatin in the water, then add the mixture to the cream. Allow the blend to stand for 12 to 24 hr in the refrigerator, then beat at medium speed with a wire whip until a medium firm consistency is obtained. Avoid excessive whipping as the fat will tend to separate under such conditions. Then, add the sugar, salt, and any flavor that is needed, and mix just enough to uniformly distribute these ingredients.

Complete whipped cream pre-mixes are available in pressurized containers of various sizes for immediate use by consumers, institutions, restaurants, and small factories.

"Cream" or creme filler, was described by Brody and Cochran (1978) as "a shelf-stable, aerated cream made up of sugar, shortening, water, milk solids or a substitute, and flavoring agents." These adjuncts are used mainly inside small snack cakes, being placed there either by injection or by folding a baked layer over them. These cremes must have a low specific gravity meeting a predetermined standard, a fair degree of stiffness (very important in folded layers, where the cream is expected to provide good support), good mouth feel, and resistance to syneresis and collapse. They should have a relatively bland flavor, be smooth and not gritty, and break down and disperse rapidly in the mouth (have fast "getaway").

Characteristics of the shortening ingredient are critical to the performance of the creme filler. Monoglycerides and highly hydrophilic emulsifiers are routinely added to get the desired processing response and the finished product characteristics required. Polysorbate and polymerized glycerin are examples of emulsifiers that have been suggested for use in these products. An example of a formula is 34.2% sucrose, 15.6% dextrose (corn syrup is often used instead of dextrose), 28.5% shortening, 13.7% water, 7.4% nonfat dry milk, 0.3% salt, and 0.3% vanilla.

FILLINGS FOR PIES AND OTHER PASTRIES

Fillings for pies are limited in their variety only by the bounds of the formulator's imagination. There are many cookbooks devoted to this subject and there is no possibility of matching their scope and detail here, but an attempt will be made to establish basic formulation principles and give a few examples.

Fillings Containing Fruit

There are several different ways fruit is packed for the baker. The small to medium size operator will probably be using No. 10 cans of fruit. Large factories will often find frozen fruit more economical and of better quality. Fresh fruit and dried fruit are also alternatives that can be considered, but they are used less often since they are not as convenient and often more expensive than the canned or frozen material. In the case of fresh fruit, seasonality is also a problem. Dried fruit always has a significantly different flavor than the fresh or frozen alternative; this may be either good or bad, depending on the intended effect. For example, pie fillings made with dried apricots are preferred by some consumers over the fillings made from the fresh, canned, or frozen fruit. The main steps in the preparation process for pie fillings using canned fruits are as follows:

(1) Drain the fruit. The solids content of the juice is an important factor in determining the amount of other ingredients to be added, and it will be related to the type of fruit, type of pack, sugar content of the pack, and extent to which the liquid has been allowed to drain from the fruit. Solids content may be calculated from the known variables or determined by moisture test or by refractometry. For proper body and stability in the finished pie, soluble solids should be in the range of 35% to 40%. They must not be much in excess of 45% in any event because such low moisture mixtures may inhibit starch gelatinization. The total weight of the filling, not just the amount of water present, must be considered when calculating the quantity of starch needed to thicken the product.

(2) Add water to the juice if necessary.

(3) Add to the juice enough sugar and corn syrup to increase the total solids to between 35% and 45%. The ratio of sugar to corn syrup should be approximately 4 to 1.

(4) Take out a small amount of the liquid to mix with the starch and bring the remainder of the liquid to a rolling boil.

(5) Disperse the starch, salt, flavor, color, acid, and other minor ingredients in the reserved cool portion of the water or juice.

(6) Add the suspension from Step 5 to the boiling juice and cook until the mixture is thick and clear, at which time the contents of the kettle should be near 195° to 200°F.

(7) Add the thickened juice to the drained fruit and blend.

(8) Cool fruit and juice blend to about 80°F before pouring into the crusts.

There are different types of starch that can be used to make pie fillings. Obviously, plain unmodified corn starch has been employed for this purpose by millions of home cooks for many decades, to the complete satisfaction of their families. The requirements for commercially prepared pies are somewhat different than those for home preparation and serving, however. The storage life of commercial pies is longer, the handling abuse is greater, and the serving conditions are different. Often, the ultimate consumer is far more critical.

Table 22.3. FORMULAS FOR APPLE PIE FILLING

Ingredient and unit	Form of the Apple Ingredient		
	Canned	Frozen	Fresh
Canned apple slices, lb	6.75	--	--
Frozen apple slices, lb	--	30	--
Fresh apple slices, lb	--	--	20
Sugar, oz	14	24	40
Juice and water, oz	16	96	64
Corn syrup	--	--	8
Cinnamon, oz	0.2	0.5	1
Nutmeg	0.05	0.1	0.25
Lemon powder	1	1.5	2.5
Modified food starch	2	6	4
Butter	1	3	2.5

For general purpose use, most bakers have found that modified waxy maize starch is preferable to other kinds. This material is available with different degrees of modification. A waxy maize starch of intermediate modification is recommended for fruit fillings when a thick syrup type of intermediate modification is desired. When the proper amount of such starch is used, the filling will be very clear and moderately flowable, not gel-like. There are more extensively modified types of waxy maize starch that give a firmer, more gel-like body to filling, if this is required for convenience of serving or for other reasons. A wide range of viscosities can be obtained by proper adjustment of the amount and type of starch.

In Table 22.3, formulas will be given for apple pie filing, one formula each for canned apples, frozen apples, and fresh apples.

With canned apple slices, mix sugar and apples and allow to drain for 3 hr. Add enough water to the syrup to make 1 lb. Disperse starch in 2 oz juice. Add flavorings to the rest of the juice and bring to boil. Stir in the starch suspension and cook while stirring until the mixture is thick and clear. Add butter and fruit. Mix thoroughly but gently. Cool before depositing in the pie shells.

With frozen apples, thaw fruit and allow to drain. To the juice, add enough water to make 6 lb. Suspend the starch in a small part of this. Add sugar, corn syrup, and flavorings to the rest of juice and bring to a rolling boil. Add the starch slurry quickly and cook with constant stirring until the batch is thick and clear. Add butter and apples, mixing thoroughly but gently. Cool before using.

When using sliced fresh apples, mix the fruit with sugar and allow to drain for 3 hr. Deposit slices in pie shells and place on top a dough circle with a single hole in the center. Bake at 450°F until apples are tender, about 45 minutes. Add sufficient water to the juice to make two quarts. Disperse the starch in a small amount of the juice. Add spices, corn syrup, and flavorings to the balance of the juice and bring it to a rolling boil. Add the starch slurry and cook until clear, stirring constantly. Allow the baked pies to cool five minutes, then pour 6 to 8 oz of the thickened juice into each pie.

Custard-type Fillings

In this category, we will consider both the true custards and the pudding-type fillings. A basic custard consists of milk, sugar, and eggs. After a cold or warm mixing stage, the ingredients are cooked without stirring to form a gel having its principal structure controlled by the milk and egg proteins. Many types of filling are based more or less loosely on this type of structure—pumpkin pies, some lemon pies, pecan pies, coconut pies, some chocolate pies, etc. The type of texture provided by the custard mix can be approximated by starch pudding mixes. To the basic starch pudding formula is usually added some type of shortening and an emulsifier to soften the texture of the filling and make it opaque.

A true custard filling can be prepared from the following formula: 62.8% fresh whole milk, 13.4% sugar, 14.2% liquid whole eggs, 9.4% egg yolks, and 0.2% salt.

Preparation requires that all of the ingredients be beaten together well before they are poured into the crust for baking. The batch may be warmed slightly to facilitate solution of the sugar. The shrinking and cracking of the filling sometimes observed is said to be alleviated by preheating the mix to 140° to 160°F, then cooling, before filling the crusts. If this is done, extreme caution must be exercised to prevent overheating and premature gel formation. Once the egg protein sets up, the gel is irreversible. Vanilla and nutmeg are the flavors most often added to plain custard pies.

Dried or frozen eggs can be substituted for fresh eggs according to the usual conversion factors. Of course, it is very important to completely dissolve the dry eggs if a successful custard is to be obtained. Furthermore, any off flavor that is present will be all too obvious in the finished filling.

There are many variations possible. Simple but effective combinations, such as apple rings placed on the crust before filing with the custard mix, provide interesting alternative choices for the consumer. Other fruit combinations can easily be imagined, but the fruit must not be too highly colored, or the custard may assume a peculiar mottled appearance. Simulated custards can be prepared by taking advantage of the action of certain gel-forming substances, such as carrageenan.

The original lemon pie fillings were essentially flavored custards. The current preference appears to be for fillings based mostly on starch with only a minor proportion of egg (usually egg yolk). A typical commercial formula is 19.46% sugar, 10.81% corn syrup, 0.21% salt, 59.46% water, 4.32% corn starch, 1.89% modified waxy corn starch, 1.08% lemon powder, 1.08% lemon puree, 0.20% citric acid, 1.35% shortening, and 0.14% dried egg yolk. The sugar, corn syrup, salt, and most of the water is mixed together and brought to a rolling boil. The dried egg is dispersed in the reserved water and, when rehydration is complete, the starch is mixed in, then the lemon flavoring and citric acid. This mixture is added to the hot liquid and cooked while stirring until the mixture has become thick and clear. The shortening is added and mixed well.

Pumpkin pies are also based on the custard type of gel structure. There is a wide variety of spices and other flavors that have been suggested for increasing the appeal of the bland pumpkin puree. One formula is: 16.2% dark brown sugar, 0.8% salt, 0.5% corn starch, 0.2% cinnamon, 0.1% mace, 0.1% ginger, 11.0% liquid whole eggs, 1.3% corn syrup, 33.6% canned pumpkin, 33.6% fresh whole milk, and 2.6% melted butter. The brown sugar, salt, starch, and spices are blended. The eggs and corn syrup are added and the mixture whipped. The pumpkin is blended in, and the milk added while mixing slowly. Finally, the melted butter is stirred in. Flavorings should be adjusted to meet local preferences. Canned pumpkin will vary in moisture from brand to brand, and the quantity of milk may have to be changed to compensate for these differences. Sweet potato pies are made with very similar formulas and can be almost indistinguishable from pumpkin. Use the pureed sweet potatoes ("dry pack") not the pieces packed in syrup.

Pecan pie fillings are also gels based on a coagulated egg protein structure, but few if any of these formulas specify milk as an ingredient and so they are not strictly speaking custards. Most pecan pie fillings are relatively simple and are based on sugar, whole eggs, and a syrup. generally corn syrup but sometimes honey or invert sugar syrup. Vanilla is often added, but seldom any other flavor. The amount of pecans added to these piece varies greatly, from about 10% to as much as 35%, based on the rest of the filling as 100%.

Most cheese pies are based on a custard-type filling. The following formula will give a filling of characteristic flavor and texture: 9.2% granulated sugar, 21.1% bakers' cheese, 0.5% cornstarch, 5.3% cake shortening, 0.4% salt, 0.4% vanilla, 15.8% liquid whole eggs, 5.2% nonfat dry milk, and 42.1% water. The milk solids are dispersed in warm water. The sugar, cheese, starch, fat, salt, and vanilla are mixed together until smooth, then the eggs slowly added with low speed mixing. Then, the milk and water is blended with the rest of the ingredients until a smooth paste is obtained, Bakers' cheese must be used, not cottage cheese. The filling mixture is deposited in unbaked pie shells. When the pies are baked and cooled, it is customary to put a fruit pie filling over the top, or at least around the edges. Pineapple, cherry, and strawberry toppings are popular.

Bavarian Cream

Nowadays, Bavarian cream is a rather poorly defined term. Traditionally, it meant a dessert consisting of whipped cream folded into a whipped flavored jelly based on gelatin. Very few commercial Bavarian creams are made according to this traditional recipe. Most bakeries would prepare this adjunct by whipping a starch gel containing some shortening. In this metamorphosis, it overlaps the cream pie fillings in composition and character, but is generally regarded as smoother and less cloying than the latter adjuncts. Compositions of this general type are often used as fillings in jelly doughnuts.

An example of a formula and processing method for a Bavarian cream type of filling is: (1) Prepare a dry mix by placing 46.8 parts extra fine granulated sugar in a mixer bowl, adding color and flavor dispersed in a small amount of water, and mixing until the color is uniform; (2) add 17.6 parts type 10 maltodextrin and 25 parts instant tapioca starch, then blend in 0.3 parts titanium dioxide (white color) and powdered vanilla to taste; (3) Add 10.3 parts emulsifier shortening and blend; (4) Prepare the cooked cream by adding 278 parts boiling water while stirring continuously; (5) Whip at high speed for 5 to 10 minutes, or until smooth; and (6) Chill thoroughly before serving.

Chiffon Pie Fillings

Chiffon fillings consist of a cream type base folded into a meringue or some other type of foamed mixture. They are light and fluffy in texture and mellow in flavor, but are rather difficult to make and have distinctly limited shelf life. They must be stored in the refrigerator.

A typical formula and procedure is as follow. Bring to a boil 60 oz water, 20 oz sugar, 6 oz lime juice, and about 0.5 oz grated lime rind. Mix 4 oz corn starch with 4 oz water and 12 oz liquid egg yolks and add to the boiling mixture. Cook until the mixture thickens. Remove from the heat. Beat 16 oz liquid egg whites and about 0.25 oz salt, adding 10 oz sugar gradually. Then add 1 oz gelatin that has been softened in 4 oz of water. Carefully blend the meringue and the lime cream until a uniform mixture is obtained. Do not overmix. Fill into prebaked pie shells. There is a difference of opinion as to whether this filling should be colored light green or left in its natural creamy white color. Some bakers prefer to omit the peel gratings; the specks left in the filling by the gratings are unacceptable to some consumers. Variations that immediately suggest themselves are orange, lemon, grapefruit, grape, and pineapple.

To get a successful blending of the meringue and the cream base, the latter should be semi-liquid at the time the two compositions are put together. The meringue must be stiff but not dry. The meringue constitutes between about 18% and about 35% of the total filling. There seems to be no rigid limitation on the proportions from a technical point of view, but, of course, the filling is fluffier when more meringue is added. Some recipes suggest slightly browning the top of the chiffon pie by placing it briefly under a broiler, for the purposes of adding to the appearance and setting the egg white to a firmer consistency. This operation is critical, only a few seconds separating the optimum color from disaster, so it is probably not advisable for most bakeries. Chiffon pies are often covered with whipped cream.

Miscellaneous Pie Fillings

There are so many variation of pie fillings that have been developed, it seems almost hopeless to attempt to make a representative listing of nontypical pie fillings. Given below are a few of the more unusual types which may give a boost to the creative talents of product development persons.

The Shoofly pie is a Pennsylvania Dutch creation that may arouse some customer interest because of its ethnic affiliation and novel features. The filling, a formula for which is described below, is filled into unbaked pie shells and bakes into a cake-like or cookie-like structure that seldom inspires second helpings. The crust can be made from most any formula.

For Shoofly pie filling, cream together 9.3 oz sugar, 4.7 oz shortening, 0.9 oz baking soda, 0.3 oz salt, 0.2 oz cinnamon, and 0.1 oz ginger. While creaming, add 5.1 oz fresh whole eggs. Then add and blend in thoroughly, 23.3 oz molasses of mild flavor and light color. Add in alternate portions 37.4 oz cake flour and 18.7 oz water. When the mixture is smooth and uniform, pour it into a pie shell and bake until firm.

There are other cake-in-crust combinations, most of which have more appeal than the one described above. A chewy brownie dough baked in a pie shell has interesting characteristics, especially if it is topped with whipped cream or a marshmallow icing. In designing new products along these lines, it is important to have a texture contrast while avoiding flavor dissonances. The flavor of pie crust of the ordinary type may not be compatible with other flavors. The filling should have considerable moistness and should be soft or chewy but not crisp. Consider the possibility of adding a sauce or other semi-fluid topping to give additional moistness to the filling. Another possibility is a rich fruit cake batter in a regular pie shell with hot rum sauce aplied shortly before serving.

A chocolate pie with a top "crust" that forms from the filling ingredients can be prepared from the following formula and procedure. Percentages are based on the total filling as 100%. Beat 19.6% whole eggs until foamy. Gradually add 21.1% brown sugar. Continue beating until the mixture is thick. Stir in 21.5% corn syrup, 13.6% invert sugar syrup or maple syrup, or honey, 1.2% pastry flour, 7.5% melted butter, 0.8% vanilla extract, 7.2% uncooked oats, and 7.5% semisweet chocolate bits. Make sure all ingredients have been dispersed uniformly. Pour this filling into standard formula pie crusts. Bake until the center of the pie has set up. Cool completely and garnish with sweetened whipped cream. This pie filling separates into an upper layer that is light in color and chewy, not crisp. It is composed mostly of the oats and appears porous and medium brown when baked. The bottom layer is chocolatey and rather pudding-like.

In this section, only dessert pie fillings have been covered. Many savory pies based on meat and/or vegetables are known (see, for example, Carroll 1990). The quiche has attained much popularity as a main course dish in recent years. It is basically a nonsweet version of custard containing meat and vegetables and baked in a conventional pie crust.

Trouble Shooting Pie Fillings

Fillings generally boil out because the baker is determining completeness of bake by the color of the crust. This is usually a suitable end point but may not fit the needs of some fillings. If the crust is properly formulated, it will brown to the proper color before the filling starts to boil. Here are some points to check if fillings boil over in the oven: (1) Check oven temperature—it should be at least 450°F; (2) Check filling temperature—it should be 70°F or lower when it goes into the crust; (3) Moisture content of the crust may need to be lowered to get quicker browning; (4) Thickness of the crust may have to be increased; (5) The top and bottom crusts should be sealed together well all around the rim; (6) Determine if larger vents or more vents are needed in the top crust; and (7) Check the weigh sheets to make certain the filling has been compounded correctly and the correct amount of filling is being put into the pie.

Is the filling too thick or too thin in the baked and cooled pie? This is usually due to some error in the type or amount of stabilizer that is being used, and often results from using one type of starch at the same concentration in every filling. Variations in the liquid amount of the fruit pack, in the amount of solids in the juice, and in the amount of pectin in the juice are among the things that can affect the consistency of the filling. Fruit pies require a relatively high percentage of waxy maize starch (or of proprietary stabilizer mixes containing this type of starch). Cream, lemon, and specialty types of pie fillings require considerably less of this stabilizer and various defects in appearance and texture may occur if excessive amounts are used. Furthermore, the starch must in every case be completely dispersed and completely hydrated or gelatinized if uniform and expected results are to be obtained.

Are the fillings breaking down before before the expiration of the normal shelf life? This is frequently the result of mistakes in the production method that affect the gel structure. Starch will not gelatinize properly if the total dissolved solids are substantially in excess of 45% and may not gelatinize at all if these solids are in excess of 55%. Some bakers attempt to get around this difficulty by holding out part of the sugar until the starch has been cooked. The problem with this strategy is that the sugar, when finally added, tends to destabilize the starch gel and the filling leaks syrup after a relatively short time. Loss of moisture during baking may lead to an excessively high solids content even if the amount calculated from ingredient additions indicates an acceptable level.

Is there an off-flavor in the filling? Often the source can be identified by a judicious use of comparative taste testing. Some of the defects to be considered are: (1) Scorched flavors from burning during cooking; (2) Spoilage or incipient spoilage of some ingredient; (3) Poor quality ingredients; (4) Contamination of ingredients or utensils with foreign materials such as cleaners, insecticides, preservatives, or machine grease; (5) Use of flavor extracts that are either unsuitable to begin with or have changed character because of aging; and (6) Attempting to use unsuitable scrap materials. Wrong amounts of ingredients or poor quality of ingredients are defects more difficult to detect. Obviously, if the cherries don't taste like cherries when they come out of the can, the filling made out of them isn't going to taste like cherries. If an ingredient has an unpleasant metallic or bitter flavor, that will be carried through to the finished product and nothing, probably, can be done to mask the off note. Balancing the acid and sweet notes of a filling is a difficult task which is, nonetheless, essential if optimal acceptability is to be achieved. The only sure way to determine if a satisfactory balance has been achieved is to taste the finished product.

ENROBINGS

Coatings or enrobings are fat-based mixtures that are solid at ordinary room temperatures but melt in the mouth. They are typified by chocolate preparations such as milk chocolate, and are always applied after baking and usually after cooling the product to room temperature. They do not react chemically with the crust, frequently require elaborate tempering processes, and are always opaque. In many cases, they are used to completely cover the product, and then they considerably inhibit moisture exchange between the contents and the atmosphere.

Bakery products that have been enrobed include individual cakes, which may be round, rectangular, or finger-shaped (plain or with cream fillings), doughnuts, Swiss rolls, petit fours, pretzels, and many types of cookies. Some of the advantages resulting from enrobing are (1) improvement of appearance, (2) enhancement of flavor, (3) improvement of shelf life by preventing moisture loss transfer, (4) shielding sticky surfaces, and (5) increasing structural strength (Wing 1975).

The principal ingredients in a coating are sugar and fat. The proportion of fat to nonfat solids, the melting point of the fat, and the particle size of the nonfat solids are major determinants of texture. The fat must have a melting point above the highest temperature expected to be encountered by the product during storage, distribution, and display for sale. It must, however, quickly melt in the mouth when the food is consumed. Cocoa butter is an ideal fat from the eating texture standpoint, although it has its storage weaknesses, and is quite expensive.

Sucrose is, by far, the most common carbohydrate ingredient in enrobing preparations, but corn syrup solids and dextrose are sometimes used. Rarely, lactose may be made a part of the carbohydrate mixture if the goal is to greatly reduce sweetness. The sugar must be finely powdered, with all of the particles preferably below 40 microns in their largest dimension.

Chocolate or imitation chocolate coatings as well as pastel-colored coatings of similar characteristics are used to enrobe many kinds of bakery products. They are probably most common on cookies and snack foods of the Swiss roll type. The coating may be a true chocolate (semi-sweet, sweet, or milk chocolate) or it may be a compound coating resembling chocolate in appearance. True chocolate coatings have the best texture and (almost always) the best flavor, but they are relatively expensive and are often replaced by compound coatings. Chocolate coatings, when described as such on the label or otherwise implied to be pure chocolate, are covered by federal definitions and standards of identity. These regulations specify with considerable exactitude the types and amounts of ingredients that must be used in coatings identified by any of the standard names. Both the chocolate and the cocoa used in coatings will normally be of the so-called "natural" variety, that is, will not be alkalized or dutched.

Many chocolate-colored or -flavored coatings used to enrobe bakery foods do not meet the federal requirements for chocolate. Some manufacturers feel that the standards result in coatings that are too strong in flavor to be compatible with certain fillings. Also, the requirement for a large proportion of cocoa butter causes the coating to be too expensive for popularly priced lines. Cheaper, less highly flavored coatings are prepared by using cocoa as the flavoring ingredient and some other fat besides cocoa butter. If properly formulated and processed, these types of coatings can have very good organoleptic properties.

Compound coatings, sometimes called confectioners' coatings, are basically white, but they may be colored to resemble chocolate, or given any other color for which a suitable food dye is available. Even the best compound coatings tend to have a somewhat waxy texture. On the other hand, they seldom develop fat bloom or sugar bloom. These coatings were formerly made from the so-called hard butters based on imported lauric oils such as palm kernel and coconut, but development of methods for fractionating and modifying other fats have resulted in specialized ingredients that are more satisfactory than the natural oils.

Most of the natural fats used for compound coatings are not compatible with cocoa butter and when a mixture of, say, a coconut oil fraction was used in combination with chocolate, the coated piece almost always bloomed in a short time. The newer modified fats can be used, with certain limitations, in combination with real chocolate to make superior type coatings which have a rather wide range of melting points.

Although the lower cost of a compound coating is a powerful motive for using it, there are some other advantages that can be more important in specific situations. They can be made softer than chocolate coatings, making them easier to cut and less messy to bite in cold weather. They can also be made harder, so that they do not soften in summer temperatures. Compound coatings are not as sensitive to tempering and setting conditions as chocolate coatings.

In addition to fat and sugar, coatings will contain flavor, color, and emulsifiers. Vanillin is a very common flavor in both pastel coatings and chocolate. Colors are usually lakes or non-certified colorants. Lecithin is usually added to control viscosity. Its principal function is to offset the traces of moisture, which tend to greatly increase viscosity of the melted coating and thus make the enrobing operation very difficult. Moisture in the finished coating should be around 0.5% and never above 1.0%.

Most commercial coatings now being offered have good shelf life provided the initial flavor is satisfactory. Contact of the material with copper lines or vessels is very undesirable, since the slightest traces of this element greatly accelerate oxidative reactions and the development of rancidity.

The amount of coating applied to a cake or cookie should be adjusted to give optimum eating quality in the finished piece. Thin coatings do not provide adequate protection against moisture transfer and are easily broken. The exact percentage needed for best results will be related to the size and shape of the enrobed part, i.e., smaller or irregular pieces take a higher percentage of coating than do larger or smoother or more uniform base cakes.

The thickness of the coating that will adhere to a given piece is related to the viscosity of the coating. This is controlled in practice by varying the percentage of fat in the coating or, occasionally, by temperature manipulations. Temperature can be adjusted only within a narrow range in the case of pure chocolate coatings, but the enrober temperature of some hard butter coatings can be adjusted more freely.

Coatings made with chocolate liquor and with mixtures of this ingredient and other fats require careful handling during application if fat bloom and dull surfaces are to be avoided. The tempering procedure recommended for chocolate must be strictly followed. This requires that the composition be fully melted by bringing it to 110°F; it is then cooled with constant stirring until it develops a mushy consistency. This can be expected to occur in the range 80° to 85°F, and typically at 84°F. At this point, "seed" or crystallization nuclei of the preferred form of fat crystals have been formed. The coating is then brought back up to 88° to 90°F to melt unstable crystal forms. At this point, the coating should have a viscosity suitable for proper application in the enrober and subsequent cooling should result in the formation of only stable fat crystals. Continuous and automatically controlled equipment is available for tempering chocolate coatings (Groen 1989). Various additives have been proposed for delaying or preventing the appearance of fat bloom in tempered or untempered chocolate (e.g., Sagi and Mori 1990, and Given 1990).

It is very desirable to have the temperature of the baked products in the range of 68° to 72°F when they pass through the enrober. The excess chocolate is blown off or shaken off. Coverage, or the thickness of the coating layer, is related to such factors as the baked product's temperature and the geometry of its surface, the viscosity and temperature of the coating, and the vigor and duration of the shaking and blowing process.

The enrobed pieces pass into a tunnel through which chilled air is blowing. Radiation coolers are also being used in some plants. After the pieces emerge from the far end of the tunnel, they should be stored at 72°F for at least 48 hours. During this period, various fractions of the fat continue to solidify and the relatively low temperature prevents remelting due to release of heat of crystallization. Under unfavorable conditions, a thin layer of relatively low melting fat may migrate to the surface and cause a dull appearance or even a white "frost," the so-called fat bloom that has been mentioned previously.

Of course, all these fat-based coatings have a very high caloric content and there is no simple way of alleviating this problem. Drastic measures such as substituting a non-digestible polyol fatty acid polyester for the natural fat, and an artificial sweetener plus a partially or wholly non-digestible carbohydrate bulking agent for the sugar have been proposed (Kong-Chan 1989).

BIBLIOGRAPHY

ANON. 1986. Modern Pie Technology American Maize Products, New York

ANON. 1990A. Balancing chocolate's advantages. Bakery 25, No. 1, 37-40, 42, 44-45

ANON. 1990B. Chocolate and cocoa in baking process. Bakery 25, No. 1, 69

BEST, D. 1987. Managing water in formulations. Prepared Foods 156, No. 7, 116-119

BRODY, H., and COCHRAN, W. M. 1978. Shortening for bakery cream icings and cream fillers. Bakers Digest 52, No. 6, 22-24

CARROLL, L. E. 1990. Stabilizer systems reduce texture problems in multicomponent foods. Food Technol. 44, No. 4, 94, 96, 98

CARTER, J. H. 1963. New developments in coatings for cake enrobing. Proc. Am. Soc. Bakery Engineers 1963, 282-290

EK, K. K. 1988. Preparation of a food coating. U.S. Pat. 4,767,637

FINKEL, G. 1989. Chocolate enrobed wafer products and method for preparing the same. U.S. Pat. 4,812,318

GIDDEY, C., and DOVE, G. 1989. Aerated food product based on raw milk and method for its preparation. U.S. Pat 4,818,554

GIVEN, P. S., JR. 1990. Method and composition for inhibiting fat bloom in fat based compositions and hard butter. U.S. Pat. 4,923,708

GROEN, J. W. 1989. Method of tempering edible compositions. U.S. Pat. 4,865.856

KONG-CHAN, J. L. Y. 1989. Reduced calorie and reduced fat chocolate confectionery composition. U.S. Pat. 4,810,516

LEVINE, L. W. 1981. Sweet yeast goods icing stabilizers and how to use them. Bakers Digest 55, 13, 16-17

MINIFIE, B. W. 1982. Chocolate, Cocoa, and Confectionery: Science and Technology, Second Edition. AVI Publishing Co., Westport, CT

SAGI, N., and MORI, H. 1990. Tempering accelerator and use thereof in chocolate. U.S. Pat. 4,910,037

SIML, G. J. 1952. Fried pies—filling formulas. Am. Soc. Bakery Engineers Bull. EIS-22

SPOONER, T. F. 1990. Mastering chocolate and its coating technology. Baking & Snack Systems 12, No. 4, 25-26, 29

TSCHEUSCHNER, H. D., and MARKOV, E. 1987. Instrumental texture studies on chocolate. III. Processing condition factors influencing the texture. J. Texture Studies 17, 377-399

ULINSKI, T. J. 1989. Flavoring low water activity fruit fillings for bakery goods. Cereal Foods World 34, 323-324

WING, D. H. 1975. Enrobing of bakery products. Proc. Am. Soc. Bakery Engineers 1975, 136-141

chapter twenty-three

BULK HANDLING OF INGREDIENTS

INTRODUCTION

For the purposes of this chapter, bulk ingredients are defined as those materials that are not delivered packed in containers of a given size, such as 100 lb bags, 30 gal drums, or 50 lb. cartons.

Water was the first bakery ingredient to be received and handled in bulk. It is still the material received in greatest quantity by bakeries, though much of it is used for non-ingredient purposes, such as steam generation and sanitation. The bulk handling of other ingredients—flour, syrups, sugar, oil, etc.—had to await the development of technologies that made the practice economically justifiable.

Implementation of bulk receiving by bakeries required a collaboration of suppliers, carriers, and purchasers that was relatively slow to evolve. In many cases, the final step was made when suppliers financed the installation of tanks and other necessary equipment, with payment being included as part of the ingredient cost.

Modern technology makes it possible to receive, store, and dispense in bulk virtually all of the ingredients normally used in bakeries, but it is usually not considered advantageous, even in the largest plants, to construct such facilities for more than 7 or 8 of the raw materials. Because bulk transfer is essential for computerized batching, however, a few factories have automated the handling of essentially all the ingredients, including such components as flavors and colors. Some lack of flexibility, in terms of the number of ingredients that can be introduced into the system, is inevitable in these plants.

Receiving, storage, and in-plant conveying of bulk ingredients can often be justified on the basis of economic advantages such as eliminating the cost of disposable containers, reducing waste, and lowering labor costs for materials handling. Additional benefits are frequently obtained in the form of improved sanitation, better control over measuring, and reduction in size of storage areas.

The author is a firm believer in the advantages of bulk handling. It must be admitted, however, that hope tends to outrun reality in the designing of some of these installations. Careful planning, with close attention to all present and future changes in costs, is essential when a proposal is being considered to install a bulk handling line.

Table 23.1 lists storage conditions required to maintain proper handling properties and/or stability of major food ingredients.

Table 23.1. RECOMMENDED STORAGE CONDITIONS[1]

Ingredient	Temperature range, °F	Relative humidity range, %
Flour	68 to 72	60 to 70
Sugar	60 to 80	dry
Salt	60 to 80	dry
Baking powder	60 to 80	dry
Chocolate	50 to 60	45
Cocoa	60 to 65	45
Coconut	40 to 60	40 to 50
Molasses	60 to 80	75 to 85
Nuts	40 to 50	40 to 60
Flavors	40 to 50	sealed
Shortening--		
-hydrogenated	70 to 75	dry
-mixed type	50 to 60	dry
-butter	0 to 5	40 to 50
-lard	40 to 50	dry
Milk products--		
-dried skim milk	40 to 50	dry
-dried whole milk	40 to 50	dry
-evaporated	40 to 50	sealed
-sweetened condensed	55 to 60	sealed
Eggs--		
-in shell	29 to 31	90 to 92
-frozen whole	-10 to -5	dry
-frozen whites	-10 to -5	dry
-frozen yolks	-10 to -5	dry
Fruit--		
-canned	40 to 50	ambient
-dried	30 to 35	dry

[1] From Anon. 1990A and other sources.

CONSIDERATIONS IN CHOICE AND DESIGN

Bulk storage facilities logically fall into two categories based on the physical state of the product—whether it is in liquid or solid (granular, powdered) form. In some cases, the baker has a choice of obtaining the product in either form. Flour is, of course, always handled as a powder and it is more common to transfer sucrose, dextrose, and salt in this form rather than as solutions. Shortenings, corn syrup, and invert sugar are almost always handled as liquids in bulk systems. When milk is received in bulk, the liquid form is often preferred, in spite of such negative factors as increased cost and greater potential for spoilage. Dried milk can be handled successfully, however. Dried eggs are not often handled in bulk systems, but liquid egg products are often treated in this way.

There are general principles applicable to all bulk handling facilities. Sanitation should be a primary consideration in the design. Surfaces that contact ingredients should be non-porous and resistant to corrosion and abrasion; they should be nontoxic and should not transfer odors, tastes, colors, or particles to the ingredients; and they must not accelerate deteriorative changes in the food materials. Physical changes (as in particle size) during transfer or storage should be held to a minimum consistent with the necessary design limitations. Tubes carrying powders should be grounded to prevent the buildup of static electricity. Changes in moisture content are to be avoided.

Cost and Convenience Factors

Sources of supply are more restricted for bakers who must rely on bulk delivery. Before a bulk system is installed, assurance should be obtained that an adequate supply of delivery conveyances will always be available. Shortages of trucks and rail cars occur, and are more common in some parts of the country than others.

Scheduling of deliveries is more difficult with a bulk system because storage space is absolutely limited. It is nearly always possible to find a place to put a few bags of sugar, but, if there is not enough space in the syrup tank when a truckload of this material arrives, nothing can be done to remedy the situation. "Running out" is also more serious in bulk systems, since it is often quite difficult to introduce bagged or drummed material into weighing and metering devices designed for bulk systems. Although suppliers will almost always be able to dispatch a truckload of commodity-type ingredient within a day or so after the order is received and get it to the delivery point within a few hours after that, tank cars are subject to the uncertainties of rail traffic, and allowing a considerable lead time should be regarded as a normal precaution when tank car delivery is used.

As is so often the case when changes are advocated for cost saving reasons, the economic advantages of bulk handling, as compared to receiving ingredients in bags or drums, are not as clear-cut as some experts would have us believe. The initial investment required for receiving bulk deliveries and for massive storage facilities is substantial, and seldom conforms to initial estimates. Although such equipment is normally rather long-lived and requires relatively little maintenance, some allowance must still be made for these expenses. Offsetting these costs are savings due to the elimination of material lost through bag and drum damage, reduced raw material spoilage through improved inventory control, and elimination of forklift damage to bags and drums. There are also substantial real and continuing savings due to complete elimination of unit containers such as bags, drums, and cartons. Reimelt (1987) says these savings make it desirable to receive sugar in bulk even at usage rates as low as 2,000 lbs per day. Companies not using this much should probably stay with bags, small totes, or other containers. In-plant logistics in smaller companies can sometimes be improved by utilizing larger bags, with capacities up to 2,000 lbs, that might be incorporated into an automatic conveying and weighing line.

RECEIVING BULK INGREDIENTS

Sampling and testing of bulk loads present some difficulties. The receiving department is anxious to unload the shipment quickly in order to avoid demurrage and other costs and complications, while the quality control department will not want to risk contamination of equipment or existing stocks of ingredients by taking in material that may be defective, and so will insist on completing an evaluation before unloading is started. There is usually no provision for retrieving unsatisfactory material that has entered the bulk handling system—an additional reason for completing tests before unloading.

The often disparate interests of the quality control department and the receiving department should be recognized at the outset, and a clear-cut policy on this subject promulgated by top management. The policy should assign responsibility and authority for approving the unloading of bulk shipments, and should be structured so as to promote close coordination of effort between departments and encourage maximum speed in sampling and testing incoming shipments.

Sampling of liquid loads for physical and chemical tests can be done using a simple bottle-on-a-stick type of device inserted through the loading hatch, but it is probably better to collect fluid from an appropriate port in the delivery vehicle or discharge line. Sampling of dry materials such as sugar or flour can be accomplished by inserting a long trier or specialized sampler through the opened manhole at the top of the tanker, and withdrawing and combining portions taken from several directions. There are also automatic sampling devices that divert a certain portion of the ingredient as it flows into the plant receiving system. Sampling problems resulting from stratification of both liquid and powder loads must be kept in mind constantly in order to avoid unpleasant surprises on production lines.

The importance of verifying delivered amounts can hardly be exaggerated. Unless all ingredient deliveries are checked for weight, and this includes bulk shipments, no control can be exerted over shipper's mistakes or deliberate fraud. Certified public scales and railroad scales are usually accurate but do not allow positive and direct control of the weighing operations by the purchaser. Buyers must recognize that it is possible some of their suppliers do not even have shipping scales and do not weigh their shipments in the carrier vehicle but only estimate them.

Weighing equipment used at the receiving point can include railroad track scales, motor truck scales, bulk handling scales, bag check weighers, and dock platform scales. By installing an automatic bulk materials receiving scale in the unloading line leading from the truck or rail car to the storage bins, and by installing automatic tank scales under the liquid storage tanks, shipping weights can be verified and inventories of bulk ingredients kept under close surveillance. In one type of bulk receiving scale, the material is air-conveyed to an overhead surge hopper, and then fed through a weigh hopper on a scale until a pre-set weight is reached, at which time the fill feeder stops and the weight is recorded. The weigh hopper then discharges its load of material to a designated storage hopper. When the weigh hopper is empty, the residual weight is recorded, and the cycle begins again. The computer adds each batch weight and subtracts each residual weight so that the total amount delivered by the shipping vehicle is known exactly at the termination of the receiving process.

Amounts of material retained in tank trucks can be considerable if viscous materials are being delivered. In the case of liquid chocolate, several percent of the load can adhere to the inside surface of the tanker. Therefore, the weight of material loaded into the tanker by the supplier gives only an upper limit on the delivery and is by no means a satisfactory figure to use in determining payment. Weighing the vehicle on a public scale before and after delivery is a possible check on delivered amounts, but can be subject to all the usual errors and tricks that accompany such measurements.

LIQUID INGREDIENTS

Since water was the first ingredient received and conveyed in bulk, it is to be expected that other liquid handling systems would be based to a considerable extent on engineering principles first established for water distribution operations. It was found necessary, however, to introduce many new design principles in lines intended for some of the other common fluid ingredients, such as the viscous, relatively unstable, and mildly corrosive syrups used as sweeteners.

Liquids delivered and stored in bulk include not only aqueous fluids such as sugar syrup, but oily materials as well. These oils and fats have requirements quite a bit different from those of the aqueous systems.

Product-contacting surfaces in pumps, pipes, valves, and meters should be made of stainless steel, if possible. In practice, some piping may be made of galvanized iron because of the cost factor, and occasionally copper is used. Plastic piping is a possible alternative for some applications. Piping must be installed so as to allow complete drainage of the system for cleaning. The entire transfer system is normally kept full if liquid sugar is being handled. Pipes in corn syrup installations are sometimes traced with heat tapes or steam pipes in order to permit the use of less powerful (and less expensive) pumps. This may lead to overheating and the delivery of discolored and off-flavored syrup. Overheating can occur during a shutdown, when a static load of syrup in the heated pipe encounters high temperatures for many hours or days. The obvious corrective measure is to shut off, or reduce, the heat when these conditions occur.

To design the most economical system for transferring a liquid food, the engineer must know the pipe diameter that will give a minimum resistance to flow, and thus requires the smallest pumps, while still conforming to restrictions on pipe cost and space. Rheology of the food or ingredient and required rate of flow must also be considered. Various schemes have been suggested for making these determinations (see Garcia and Steffe 1986).

Automated bulk handling systems obviously require electrically activated valves which are electronically coordinated with pumps, scales, etc. The valves must be of sanitary design and of materials compatible with the ingredient being handled. The newest type of "smart valves" will include, for example, a valve control unit mounted on a water-proof housing on top of the air actuator and consisting of a four-way air piloted solenoid valve, a microprocessor printed circuit board, and a photosensor printed circuit board. These will be connected to a switch/indicator control circuit that indicates the status of the valves and combines output transmitters and input receivers, each with its own light to indicate valve position. All of these will be connected to a master control unit that maintains two-way communication between the plant computer, the switch/indicator control units, and the valves (Anon. 1986).

Sweeteners

Bakeries of medium to large size will often find it to be economical and profitable to obtain fluid sweeteners, including corn syrups, sucrose syrups, invert syrup, and various combinations of these, in rail cars or trucks. Molasses, refiners' syrups, and other specialty items as well as made-to-order mixtures can be obtained by bulk delivery in many sections of the country. The economic advantages of buying cane or beet sugar as syrups rather than in granulated form vary in different geographical areas, and the financial aspects of this method of handling sucrose supplies should be carefully analyzed before a commitment is made to change from granular deliveries. Sugar syrup is not substitutable for granulated sugar in some formulas, especially cookie formulas. Anyone purchasing large volumes of corn hydrolysates would, however, almost certainly save money by installing a bulk system for this material rather than continuing to buy it in drums. Invert sugar, being available only in syrup form, is also cheaper to receive in bulk if the use rate can justify installation of the necessary equipment.

Stainless steel is the preferred construction material for storage tanks for liquid sweeteners. Many of these tanks are constructed of mild steel coated on the inside with a plastic lining meeting FDA specifications. Unlined aluminum tanks are sometimes used for liquid sugar tanks, but not for corn syrup or invert sugar tanks because the low pH of the latter materials makes them too corrosive. The top of the tank should be convex for strength and for good drainage inside and out. Outlets should be placed in the center of cone-shaped bottoms.

Sucrose syrups.—Since cane or beet sugar syrup at the maximum concentration of about 67% solids will allow the growth of certain microorganisms (particularly osmophilic yeast), these bulk products are subject to spoilage. Careful attention to good sanitary procedures and occasional cleaning of the tank with sterilizing solutions are essential. It is recommended that ultraviolet light appliances be placed in the headspace of the tank. Ultraviolet radiation inhibits microbiological activity above the liquid level, but it is effective only in a thin top layer of the liquid because the penetrating power of this radiation is very poor in aqueous solutions. Consequently, osmophilic yeasts may become established in lower levels of the liquid and begin a slow fermentation. Sucrose syrups of higher concentration are not feasible at normal temperatures, but combinations of sucrose and invert with solids up to about 76% are available and are definitely more stable. No matter how stable the syrup is expected to be, however, it is good practice to have plate counts run on the material at least every month and, preferably, weekly.

Air in the head space of the tank is saturated with water vapor in equilibrium with the water activity of the syrup, the latter factor being related to the temperature and solids content of the syrup. Some of this moisture can condense on the tank walls when the walls cool significantly. If this condensate runs down the walls and forms a film on the surface of the syrup, an environment is created that is very conducive to rapid growth of yeasts, molds, and bacteria. To prevent condensation from occurring, an air circulation system is regarded as an essential feature of tank design unless the whole tank is inclosed in a controlled temperature space. These systems include a fan to draw in the outside air and a filter to extract microorganisms from the air.

For sucrose-based syrups, a two-tank system is preferred, each tank being completely emptied before a new load is placed in it.

Regular conversion corn syrup.—Corn syrups are supplied at 76% solids or higher. These syrups will not be subject to microbiological attack unless they become diluted by condensate or water from other sources. Corn syrup can be heated, either for simplifying processing steps (as in manufacturing confectionery or icings) or for reducing the viscosity to facilitate pumping. Since corn syrups of low DE and the high solids syrups now being produced are extremely viscous at low temperatures, it will be necessary to heat them before they can be pumped, metered, and dispensed satisfactorily in a bulk system.

There are several alternative methods for warming the syrup. For example: (1) Inclose the tank in a room where the temperature is maintained at, say, 100°F, (2) build inside the tank a chamber containing heating coils so as to raise the temperature only in the lower section, and (3) place thermostatically controlled heating elements around the outside of the tank.

High fructose corn syrup.—HFCS is transported in either insulated tank cars or stainless steel trailers. The conditions for unloading and handling of HFCS are somewhat different from those for regular corn syrup and more like those for invert sugar syrups. This similarity results from the solubility characteristics of dextrose and fructose. Fructose crystallization does not occur in these syrups, so the newer generations of

HFCS, with high fructose:glucose ratios present fewer problems of crystallization, but the concentration of dextrose in the older and less expensive types of HFCS is high enough to cause precipitation if the temperature falls below about 80°F. HFCS 42 is loaded at a temperature of 90° to 95°F in the summer and 100° to 110°F in cold weather.

Glucose crystallization is reversible simply by heating the syrup. If the syrup is to be mixed with other aqueous solutions, there is probably no need to dissolve the crystals insofar as finished product quality is concerned. The real problem is the effect the crystals have on the physical properties of the syrup in the bulk handling system, where clogging of valves, pipes, and meters can occur. Generally, the crystals can be dissolved by taking the syrup to about 100°F, but heating must be done with care to prevent discoloration from taking place. It may take several hours for the syrup to become clear when heated at this temperature.

Dextrose syrup.—The limited solubility of dextrose necessitates the continuous application of heat to tanks containing solutions having concentrations greater than 50%. Therefore, if solutions of 65% to 67% are shipped considerable distances, the truck or railcar must be provided with heating facilities adequate to prevent crystallization. For short hauls in insulated vehicles, solutions that are filled hot may remain high enough in temperature to preclude crystallization without having to use of heating units.

Solutions containing 65% to 67% dextrose are usually stored at about 130°F, often in tanks covered with insulation. The localized heating systems used in most corn syrup tanks are not adequate for dextrose storage units. It is desirable to avoid the use of dextrose syrups, if possible.

Shortenings

Equipment requirements.—Bulk systems for edible fats and oils consist essentially of tanks, pumps, pipes, valves, and meters. Bulk oil shipments are usually made in standard tank cars containing 60,000 lb, jumbo cars containing 150,000 lb, or in tank trucks containing 20-, 30-, or 45-thousand lb. When oil or fat is delivered by truck, the driver connects a hose to the intake of the plant system and discharges the ingredient using a pump powered by the tractor engine. Plant personnel must take charge of emptying tank cars, using plant pumps and equipment. A basket strainer should be installed on the intake of the pump to prevent damage from scrap metal, and a finer filter on the pump discharge is desirable to remove extraneous material. Cartridge or bag-type filters with a porosity of 25 microns will remove visible particles. A bypass should be provided in case partially solidified fat must be pumped (Woerfel 1981).

Either positive displacement pumps or centrifugal pumps are suitable for moving oil. They may be made of either stainless steel or cast iron. Mechanical seals are preferred to packing seals. Rotary positive displacement pumps are quite good because lubrication by the oil gives them long life. They also give constant delivery rates regardless of the head. High pressure relief valves should be provided.

Both round and rectangular tanks are used. A convenient arrangement consists of two tanks for each type of shortening being procured, each tank having a capacity of 65- to 70-thousand pounds. Since each tank will hold the contents of a full tank car of oil, it will not be necessary to mix fresh oil with the residue left in the tank from previous shipments.

Stainless steel, type 302 or 304, is the preferred metal for constructing these tanks. Stainless steel has no adverse effect on shortenings and is not affected by common cleaning solutions, but it is expensive and difficult to fabricate. Consequently, most tanks are made of mild steel plate or even of black iron and they are satisfactory as long as precautions are taken to prevent rust formation. Oil will readily pick up the thin film of iron oxide that forms on a thoroughly cleaned steel surface. Therefore, oil-contacting surfaces should be wiped with oil immediately after cleaning, before rust forms. Tanks of fiberglass reinforced plastics have been suggested for storing oil, but it there may not be many such installations (Woerfel 1981).

Liquefied fats should be held about 10°F above the AOCS capillary closed-tube melting point—not the Wiley melting point. Lard will be completely liquid at 120°F, but oleo and some vegetable shortenings will require slightly higher temperatures. Transfer pipes are almost always heated and insulated.

Compounded fluid shortenings.—Development of "fluid" shortenings has simplified bulk handling of this ingredient, since th can replace melted shortenings that have to be Votated before being inc porated into doughs and batters. A fluid shortening may be composed of fat or oil with stearine, emulsifiers, and other additives. Some of these additives may be in the form of small solid (or semi-solid) particles floating in the liquid. These fluids should be kept under continuous agitation with a slow moving blade that circulates all the way around the inner surface of the tank. Pumps, pipes, valves, and meters used for other types of fats and oils are also suitable for these ingredients.

Stability problems.—Solid shortenings are more stable than liquid shortenings. Unless a solid shortening has been aerated with a gas containing oxygen (and this is rarely done) it will exhibit signs of oxidative rancidity only on the surfaces, and then only after several weeks. The situation is somewhat different with bulk shortenings because there is much greater opportunity for them to absorb oxygen.

Tanks should be thoroughly cleaned at least every six months or at the first sign of sediment or of off-odors suggestive of rancidity. If off-odors do appear, it is too late to save the contents of the tank and the oil must be sold for feed or soap use or for some other non-food applications. A new shipment of shortening should never be dumped on top of the residue from a preceding shipment. Antioxidants should be used up to the legal limit and bulk oils are often supplied with these additives.

Nitrogen blanketing has been recommended as a means of increasing the storage life of bulk shortening. Melted shortening will absorb oxygen while it is being manufactured and during transfer to the user's plant. Blanketing the shortening under a layer of nitrogen while it is in the user's tank will retard further uptake of oxygen, but the amount already present can cause deterioration sufficient to make the shortening unusable after a short time. Bubbling nitrogen through the fat in short bursts is a good method for establishing an oxygen free environment as well as for preventing stratification or settling of higher melting point fractions. Figure 23.1 is a diagram of a bulk transfer system including a nitrogen blanketing arrangement.

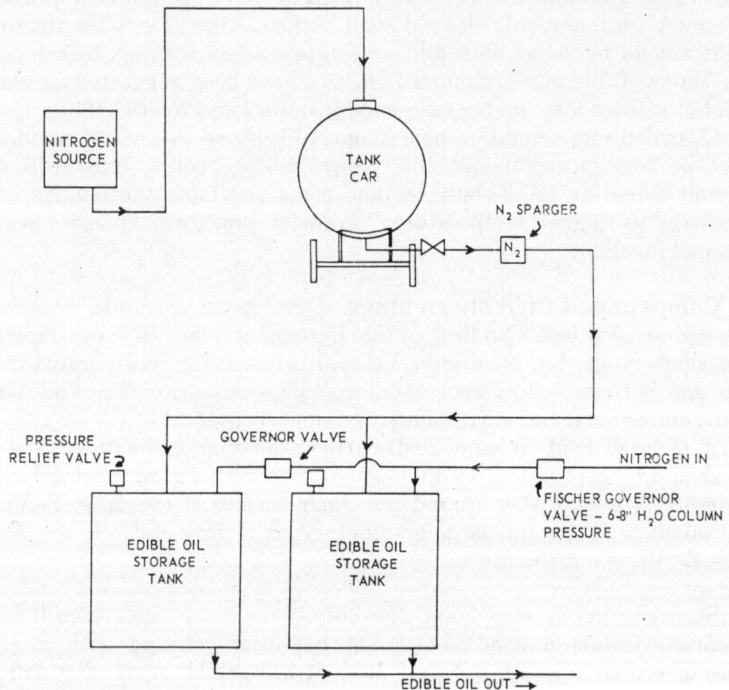

Figure 23.1. Receiving, storing and nitrogen-treating of bulk edible oil

Chocolate products.—In many parts of the country, chocolate, milk chocolate, sweet chocolate, and imitation chocolate coatings as well as other kinds of fat-based enrobing products can be procured in bulk. The liquid material replaces the usual paper-wrapped 10 lb blocks and eliminates the need to have a special unit to melt the chocolate at point of use. It is necessary to transport and store the bulk coatings at elevated temperatures in order to keep them in liquid form. If they are allowed to solidify at any point in the transport system, many problems result. Then, slow melting at moderate temperatures is absolutely essential if heat damage to flavor and other properties is to be avoided.

The usual tendency of production people is to apply excessive heat to speed up melting of the congealed mass, with the result that the entire content of the tank is spoiled. What is even worse, damage to flavor is sometimes not recognized, or is ignored, and the defective ingredient is used to produce many tons of inferior products.

Chocolate and similar enrobing materials are transported in insulated tanks, which may have a heating-duct system in the walls to permit delivery of the ingredient at nearly the same temperature at which it was loaded, i.e., in the range of 100° to 130°F. It is important that the tanks and fittings be clean and dry when the coating is loaded, since even traces of moisture can increase the viscosity of the product considerably and may be impossible to remove by any method available to the user. The tankers may have their own delivery pumps or it may be necessary for the customer to supply his own unloading system. Pipes 3 or 4 inches in diameter and jacketed with hot water or electrically traced are used. Heavy duty positive displacement pumps are recommended for rapid unloading.

GRANULAR AND POWDERED INGREDIENTS

Most granular or powdered dry ingredients can be received, transported, stored, and dispensed in bulk by either mechanical or pneumatic systems. Of course, combinations of these two methods can also be used. Which type of system is better suited for a particular purpose depends on the characteristics of the ingredient being handled, the rate of use of the material, the availability of suppliers who can meet the needs of the particular plant, acceptability of the cost parameters, and other factors peculiar to the specific situation.

The suitability of a specific dry granular ingredient for bulk handling will depend to a large extent on its flow properties. These affect its movement out of bins and through chutes and are also related to its adaptability to pneumatic transfer methods. Procedures for measuring the pertinent physical properties of a material will be discussed below. Readers who are interested in more details about this aspect of bulk handling can begin their search with Bureau of Mines Information Circular IC-8552 (Pariseau and Fowkes 1972) and an article by Peleg *et al.* (1973).

Factors Affecting Design of Bins for Powders

Certain physical characteristics of ingredients control the type of equipment required for transferring and storing these materials. Chief among these physical qualities are the rheological properties (viscosity or apparent viscosity) of liquid or semi-liquid ingredients and the flow properties of powdered and granular materials.

Factors affecting flow of powders.—Difficulties in handling bulk solids are generally caused by a lack of flowability or a strong tendency to floodability. These two properties are sometimes described as being at two ends of a spectrum with good flowability somewhere in between. A flowable material tends to move smoothly and evenly under the influence of gravity without requiring the input of vibration, stirring, pressure, etc. Poorly flowable materials tend to form bridges at outlets and clinging layers along walls, and to flow through tunnels they form inside the bulk of the material. Floodable materials move in a series of separate, irregular avalanches. These properties are manifestations on the macroscopic scale of microscopic features such as the dimensions of the particle, uniformity of particle size, conformation of the particle (whether spheroidal, cubic with protuberances, etc.), smoothness or roughness of the particles' surfaces, elasticity of the particles, tendency to entrap air, adhesiveness of the surfaces (whether due to "sticky" layers or to accumulation of static electricity), and true density.

Established procedures can be used to determine the relative position of an ingredient within the "spectrum" mentioned above, thereby furnishing a basis for predicting handling properties relative to other materials. The following descriptions of tests that can be performed omit many of the procedural details, but give an overall idea of the factors that are important in evaluating ingredient flowability. First, the bulk density of the material is estimated by filling a container of known volume, without applying pressure or vibration, and weighing the contents. Second, the "compressibility" of the ingredient is determined by compared the packed or tapped density of the material in the same container. Compressibility is expressed as the percentage increase in density; if it is high, say above 20%, the material will probably not flow smoothly and will tend to bridge in hoppers. If the compressibility exceeds 40%, there will very likely be problems in discharging the material from the hopper after storage.

Third, the particle size and shape are determined, partially by visual inspection. Powders and pellets are characterized by particle size, and fibrous or matting or interlocking strands by shape. Powders such as sugar and flour can be roughly characterized by finding the finest mesh sieve that most of the powder will pass through with shaking. Shredded or flaked material such as bran, wheat germ, or coarse rye meal present somewhat more difficult evaluation problems. The fourth test is measurement of the angle of slide and consists of pouring a small amount of the ingredient on a polished metal plate and tilting the plate slowly until the powder begins to run downhill under its own weight. The angle formed by the underside of the plate and the table surface is recorded. A high angle of slide indicates that the material is probably somewhat sticky and could bridge in bins and hoppers.

The final parameter to be determined in the usual series of preliminary tests is the moisture content, which is measured by any of several well known methods. Hygroscopicity is also a factor that may have to be considered. Other tests that can be conducted to give additional information on handling properties are the angle of repose, the angle of fall, the angle of difference, the angle of spatula, cohesion, uniformity, and dispersibility. Brief descriptions of these tests is given below.

Angle of repose is the acute angle formed between the side of a cone-shaped pile of the material and the surface on which it lies. The smaller the angle of repose, the more flowable a material will be and the more floodable a floodable powder will be.

After the angle of repose has been determined, a weight is dropped several times on the surface (plate) holding the material, then the angle formed by the side of the pile is measured again. The more free-flowing the powder is, the lower its angle of fall will be. A floodable material tends to collapse rather than to assume a uniform angle, that is, the side of the pile is somewhat rounded or irregular. The more floodable the material is, the smaller will be its angle of fall.

The angle of difference is obtained by subtracting the degrees of the angle of fall from the degrees of the angle of repose. The greater the angle of difference of a floodable material, the greater is its potential for flooding or fluidizing. It is possible for a floodable material to have a high angle of difference even though it has a low angle of fall.

The angle of spatula is obtained by drawing a spatula of given dimensions up through a mound of material and measuring the resultant angle on each side. This yields a so-called angle of rupture or relative angle of internal friction. A free-flowing material forms a uniform angle based on the internal friction of the particle sizes involved. A material that is not free-flowing forms a number of irregular angles on the blade. The greater the angle of spatula, the less flowable the material will be. Except for very free-flowing materials, angle of spatula is always greater than angle of repose.

Cohesion is a useful determination when dealing with very fine powders or with materials for which the force binding the particles to each other can be measured. The cohesion coefficient is a direct measurement of the amount of energy required to pull apart aggregates of cohesive particles in a specified time. A powder is less flowable when it has a high cohesion coefficient.

The uniformity coefficient is a value obtained by dividing the width of the sieve orifice that will pass 60% of the sample by the width of the sieve opening that will pass no more than 10%. This factor is more meaningful for granular and powdered material on which cohesion cannot be measured. The more uniform the size and shape of a mass of particles, the more flowable it probably will be.

Dispersibility can also be measured. As the dispersibility in air increases, dustiness and floodability also increase. Materials with dispersibility ratings of 50% or more, measured by a standard method, are considered to be very floodable and therefore likely to cause handling problems.

Materials which cause problems in bin discharge, either because of their floodability or because they fail to flow satisfactorily, require special bin geometry and/or special appliances such as bin vibrators.

Expedients for increasing flow.—Improving the gravity flow of powdered materials out of bins and through hoppers has been a problem ever since these ingredients have been handled in bulk form. Some ancient impromptu methods such as pounding on the side of the bin with a mallet or poking and prodding the material with a stick are still in use. More sophisticated equipment is available, however. Magnetic-powered and pneumatic-powered vibrators attached to the walls provide constant or intermittent movement to dislodge packed or clinging powders and to neutralize the avalanching of floodable powders. A wide variety of internal agitating methods have been developed. These include double-walled bins with the inner wall flexed by compressed air, injection of air directly into the powder at critical points, pulsating air pads, etc.

Attempts to overcome the limitations of manual prodding methods have led to the development of powered internal agitators such as screws, sweep arms, revolving scrapers, and the like. These devices function by pulling material through the bin opening. They work well with some powders, but do not function satisfactorily if the material tends to arch over the bottom or to tunnel. One successful design combines a bin activator (vibrating hopper) with a curved vibrating baffle affixed several inches above the outlet. See Figure 23.2 (Source: VibraScrew).

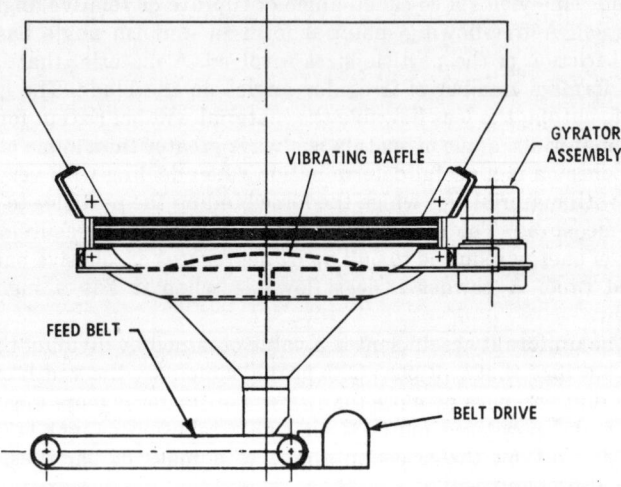

Figure 23.2. A bin activator assembly for improving the discharge of powdered ingredients

Pneumatic Transfer Principles

The essential feature of pneumatic handling, insofar as it refers to bakery ingredients, is the movement of particles through tubes by streams of air. The two general principles are dense-phase and dilute-phase transfer. Dense-phase pneumatic conveying methods involve relatively low air-to-solids ratios in which plugs of granular materials are pushed through the tubes. Dilute-phase pneumatic conveying methods involve high air-to-solids ratios in which the individual particles are surrounded by air currents.

Although low pressure (3 to 5 psig) systems transfer material at relatively low rates, the equipment is considerably less costly than high pressure equipment. Fans used in low pressure lines are less expensive than positive displacement pumps and generally require less maintenance and last longer. Venturi injectors can be used to introduce the ingredient into the air stream, and simple cyclone-type separators are suitable for removing the air from the powder at the discharge points. Such systems are used for moving low tonnages of material over short distances at low product-to-air ratios. They may also be used where a trickle feed is required or when it is necessary to cool the ingredient.

Dilute phase systems can be classified as (1) negative pressure or vacuum systems, (2) positive pressure systems, and (3) combination systems. See Figure 23.3. In many respects, vacuum systems are simpler and can be built from less expensive components, especially when ingredients must be conveyed from several locations to one discharge point. Pressure systems usually require a rotary valve and manifold at each pickup point, whereas only a manifold and cutoff valve may be needed for vacuum systems. Product is not blown out at leaks in negative systems, and, if bags or drums are to be dumped into the system, the conveying unit controls the dusts, thus eliminating the need for a separate air collector.

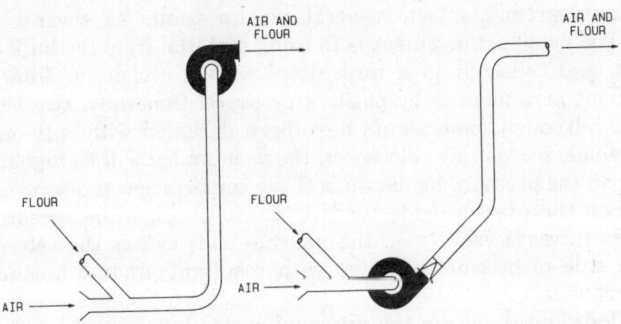

Figure 23.3. The basic pattern of negative (left) and positive (right) pressure pneumatic transfer of powdered ingredients

Vacuum systems permit conveying directly from a rail car or truck by simple suction nozzles, making it possible to use simpler unloading equipment. Less expensive diverter valves can be used because special seals are not needed. Diverter valves with sliding-type seals (available with multiple outlets) work well because product build-up in dead areas is minimized. When conveying from two pick-up points into a single line, a Y-shaped branch with cutoff valves in each leg can be used.

Positive pressure systems are best for conveying material from one pickup location to several discharge points. Cost is often the decisive factor in choosing these systems, because savings may result from not needing a rotary valve at each discharge point, though such valves are needed at the intakes. The discharge can often be a cyclone collector with a vent to the atmosphere on top and a simple spout connection at the bottom. If it is necessary to convey to several hoppers, a simple bag-type filter may suffice. Positive pressure plants require smaller pipelines because they operate with about 1.5 times the differential pressure of vacuum lines, and as a result the product-to-air ratio is much higher. Maximum operating pressures are usually 10 to 12 psig when rotary airlock seals are placed at the inlet. Most rotary valves can't tolerate pressure differentials much higher than this.

Negative systems usually operate on pressure differentials (vacuum) of about 7.5 psig. In dilute phase systems, such as we are discussing here, about 20 lb of material can be conveyed per pound of air, equal to about one cubic foot of product per 20 cu ft of standard air. If a separate venting system is needed to take care of blowback air or the dust generated at a dump hopper, the pressure system becomes more expensive.

Since the same amount of product is moved the same distance, the theoretical horsepower needed to operate the two types of systems is about the same, except for small differences in the efficiencies of the blowers.

Combination systems can combine some of the advantages of the vacuum and the pressure designs. They are particularly well adapted for conveying ingredients from several pickup points to several discharge points. The usual arrangement is to bring material from the bulk carrier by vacuum, and collect it in a tank fitted with a cyclone or filter receiver. Subsequent movement is by positive pressure. Generally, two blowers are required, although some plants have been designed with only one blower. With a single blower, air velocity on the vacuum leg will be higher than the velocity on the pressure leg because of the compression ratios involved. Low velocity on the pressure side tends to cause plugs, while speeding up the blower to increase velocity on the pressure side causes the velocity on the vacuum side to become excessive with resultant product breakdown and other problems.

Flour and sugar are the principal particulate ingredients handled by bakeries in pneumatic systems. The following operations are most often parts of these systems: (1) unloading of bulk railroad cars and trailer trucks; (2) transfer from unloading points to bulk bins; (3) transfer from sack blender to bins; (4) transfer from bulk bins to use bins and recirculation between bins; (5) transfer with in-line sifting; and (6) delivery to scales with return line.

Flour

Bakeries receive bulk flour deliveries from vehicles that may be either specially equipped freight cars or trucks. Mechanical equipment, primarily screw conveyors, can be used to unload the delivery vehicle, but pneumatic equipment is employed more often. If trucks are used, unloading equipent is often carried as part of the vehicle. Pneumatic unloading equipment for freight cars may be either the pressure or the suction type, with the pressure type probably the most common.

There is a self-contained wheeler unloader for GATX Airslide cars (Hallman 1987) that provides air for activating the slides of the car and also transfers flour at rates of 600 to 1,000 lb per hr. In the pressure system, flour is fluidized by injecting air which transports it to the top of the flour bin. Capacity of railroad cars is 90,000 lb while most trucks will carry 40,000 lb. Unloading rates will vary, but may reach 40,000 lb in 15 min. Unloading points may be located as much as 600 ft from the storage silos. Power and equipment costs usually become prohibitive for longer distances.

There are at least seven groups of equipment in pneumatic flour handling installations. These are:

(1) A mill-to bakery transporting vehicle with unloading means compatible with the bakery receiving system.

(2) Equipment for receiving flour from vehicles and transpor ing it to bins.

(3) Storage bins sufficient in number and capacity to hold the different types and required amounts of flour.

(4) Sifters and conveying means leading from the storage bins to sifters and from sifters to subsequent use points.

(5) Surge or service bins feeding the scale hoppers.

(6) Scale hoppers and means of conveying flour to and from them.

(7) Filter receivers discharging to mixers.

Figure 23.4 is a diagram of a dense phase conveying system for flour, while Figure 23.5 is a dilute phase conveying system (Adapted from literature of Whirl-Air-Flow, Inc.)

The different pieces of equipment are connected by conveying tubes made of metal (frequently aluminum) or plastic and having diameters calculated to efficiently carry the required volumes. The interior walls of these tubes should be very smooth to reduce friction, facilitate air flow, and minimize abrasion of the particles. Bends, turns, and elbows should be made on a wide radius for the same reasons. Grounding is essential to prevent the buildup of static electricity. The system should include quick-disconnect joints at critical points so that blockages may be quickly and easily corrected. Provisions should be made for withdrawing small amounts of flour for dusting doughs. It may be more efficient and economical, however, to simply procure a cheaper flour in bags for use in dusting.

In positive pressure systems, there will be blower-feeder groups at the car or trailer discharge point, a storage bin discharge, a central scaling unit, and use or service bins. Blowers may be of the positive-displacement type, having two close-fitting impellers rotating against each other like gears. Air is discharged through filters and it is important that plenty of filter area be provided to prevent pressure build-up in the bins.

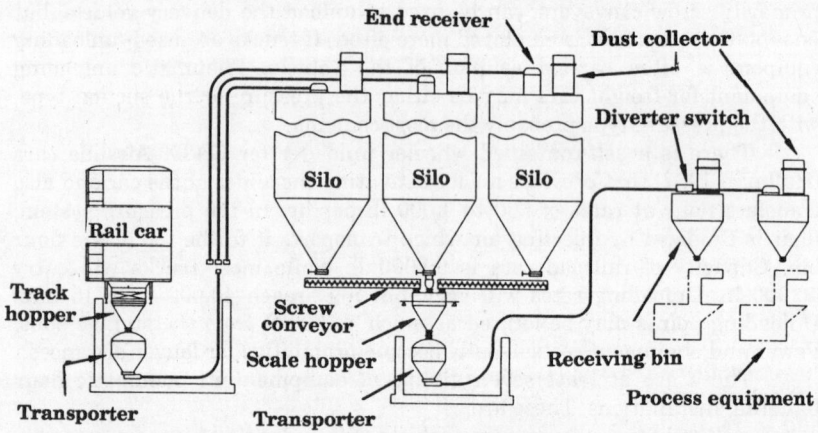

Figure 23.4. Dense phase pneumatic conveying of flour

Bins and silos can be either horizontally or vertically aligned, and are preferably of circular cross-section. It is often necessary to install flour storage bins outside the main building in order to avoid occupying valuable processing space. There are some negative features to this option. When outside, bins are exposed to rapid changes in temperature, so there is a possibility of condensate forming on the inner wall and contaminating the ingredient. In extreme climates, it is advisable to moderate temperature fluctuations by enclosing the bins in an inexpensive shelter. Condensation can be prevented by installing an air circulation system to exchange the air above the flour so that its relative humidity is always in equilibrium with the outside atmosphere. When the silos are placed outside the building, the cost of longer supply lines must be considered.

Coatings are seldom recommended for the flour-contacting surfaces of bins, clean polished metal surfaces being preferred. Flour has an abrasive effect that tends to keep the surfaces polished, but it removes coatings.

Flour should be sifted before use. The sifter should be placed as close to the mixers as possible. The two types of sifters in common use are the older design of rectangular shape containing a stack of wire or cloth screens moved in a horizontally reciprocating pattern by a motor and transmission, and the newer in-line design that can withstand pressure so powders can be conveyed directly through it.

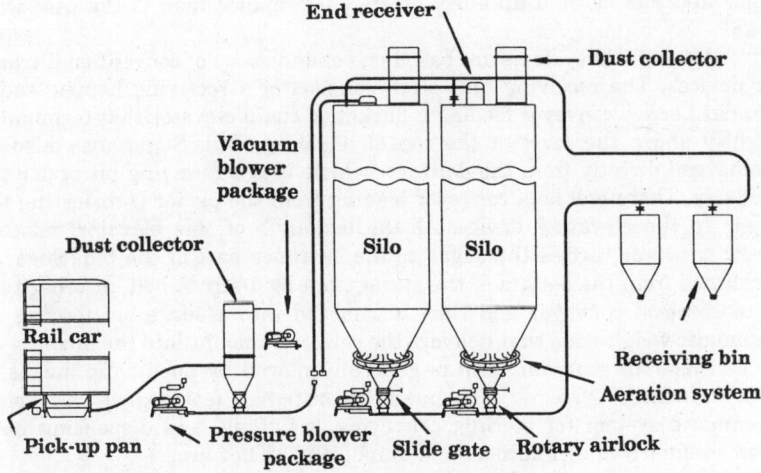

End receiver

Dust collector

Vacuum blower package

Dust collector

Silo **Silo**

Rail car

Receiving bin

Aeration system

Pick-up pan

Pressure blower package

Slide gate **Rotary airlock**

Figure 23.5. Dilute phase pneumatic conveying of flour

In any space where small combustible particles are suspended in air, the possibility of an explosion must be considered. Pneumatic flour, sugar, and starch handling plants have many points where explosions can occur, and they must be designed with full recognition of this hazard. See, for example, National Fire Protection Standard No. 66, "Pneumatic Conveying of Agricultural Dusts."

Sugar

Granulated sugar.—When it is filled with granulated sugar, the usual railcar of 5,000 to 6,000 cu ft capacity will hold 200,000 to 220,000 lb. Pressure differential and gravity discharge systems are practical. Air slide discharge is said to be of limited value because sugar cannot be fluidized with a significant degree of success. The pressure differential railcar is suitable for sugar and is designed on the principle of pressurizing the storage compartment at 14 psig. This allows relatively fast movement to remote receiving hoppers. Gravity discharge railcars are sometimes designed to include discharge-assisting means. Trucks are also used to convey granulated sugar in bulk. The discharge method is basically the same as for railcars.

Bulk sugar can also be delivered to the bakery in portable bins. They usually have capacities of 3,000 to 4,000 lb. These containers are received and moved by forklift trucks. A disadvantage of bins is that their transportation costs have to be paid both ways.

Sugar in granular form is generally moved by pneumatic conveyors in bulk handling systems, but mechanical conveying has the advantage that it causes less attrition, or particle breakdown. Attrition occurs more readily in sugar and has more of an effect on its performance than is the case with flour.

Mechanical systems are based on combinations of conventional transfer devices. The receiving unit often consists of a receiving hopper and a standard screw conveyor feeding a bucket or chain elevator that terminates slightly above the level of the top of a storage bin. Sugar may also be discharged directly from the delivery vehicle into a receiving pit under the roadway. There will be a conveyor leading from the pit for transferring the sugar to the elevating device. At the terminus of this elevator, another screw conveyor carries the sugar to the entrance part of the bin. Sugar is reclaimed from the bottom of the storage bin by a screw, belt, or other type of mechanical conveyor and then discharged into a surge bin feeding an automatic weigh scale that delivers the selected amount into the mixer.

Sugar in granular form is generally moved by pneumatic means in bulk handling systems. The main operational features in a typical pneumatic system for storing, conveying, weighing, and dispensing have been summarized by Pancoast and Junk (1980). They are:

(1) Air flow is developed by a blower located near the storage bin or under the bin skirt.

(2) Sugar is fed from the storage bin through a rotary valve airlock. It is picked up and conveyed by pipes to a receiver having a dust collector. The pipes are designed with long sweeping curves to reduce attrition of sugar.

(3) Sugar is fed by a rotary valve from the receiver into a weigh-hopper. When a pre-set weight is reached, a rotary valve above the hopper shuts off. Simultaneously, a rotary valve below the storage bin stops. The blower continues to run briefly to clean out the line, then it shuts off.

The devices making up a blower assembly are usually combined on one chassis and consist of a blower, filter, silencer, check valve, pressure gauges, motor, controls, drives, and guard.

The problem of most concern is caking due to moisture absorption. This can lead to bridging in the silo. Suppliers should load sugar at a maximum moisture content of 0.2% and a maximum temperature of 95°F (Hagedorn 1965). In the bins, an equilibrium is established between the water content of the sugar and the relative humidity of the ambient air. Flowability remains unchanged between 20% to 60% RH; in this range the sugar's moisture content changes little. At more than 60% RH, caking may occur.

The tubes through which the sugar is transferred to the silos are ordinarily six inches in diameter. Straight sections can be made of thinwalled aluminum tubing, but the elbows should be made of stainless steel.

Bins should be of steel, cylindrical in shape, and vertically oriented. They should be of sanitary construction, with a minimum number of cracks and crevices, and should be placed at an elevation such that gravity feed can be used to deliver sugar to the process area.

Of all the major ingredients, sugar is the one for which gravity feed assumes the most importance. Of course, all ingredients move by gravity at some point, even if only during the movement from the top to the bottom of a bin or silo, but we are concerned here with a transfer from one major unit to another. Granulated white sugar flows relatively freely and can, in certain circumstances, be moved efficiently by gravity transfer provided it has been held under appropriate storage conditions.

In all gravity transfer operations, it is important to remember that sugar, like all granular and powdered products, has a tendency to separate according to size when it is moved about or subjected to vibration.

Powdered sugar.—Powdered sugar is seldom if ever procured in bulk because of its poor flow properties and its pronounced tendency to consolidate into large lumps. Instead, it is either procured in bags or totes, or (usually) made in the plant by grinding granulated sugar.

Pneumatic conveying of granulated sugar to the pulverizer and of powdered sugar from the pulverizer to a use hopper or short term storage bin is practical. Granulated sugar is delivered from a silo to a receiving hopper above the mill by a system that is automatically controlled by sensors in the hopper. When it is necessary to replenish the stock of powdered sugar, an airlock at the bottom of the hopper meters granulated sugar into the mill. About 3% cornstarch is added at this point to improve the flow properties of the powdered sugar. Pulverized sugar is discharged from the underside of the mill into a pipeline through which it is carried by cooled conveying air until it reaches a dust collector, where the air is separated from the product. Pre-cooled air is used in the conveying system because it is needed to remove the heat generated by the grinding action. See Figure 23.6.

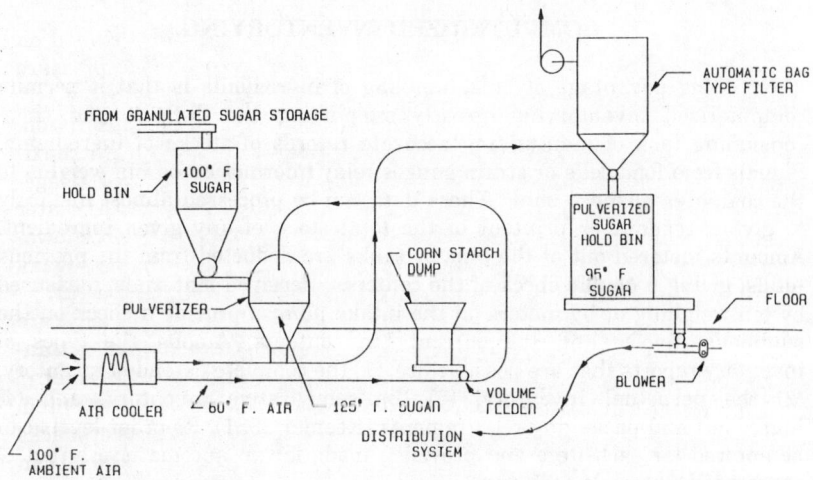

Figure 23.6. Air conveying of sugar to and from a pulverizing mill

Other Ingredients

Brown sugar is not a good candidate for bulk handling because of its strong propensity for caking. Possibly, some of the dried forms of this ingredient could by handled by mechanical conveying systems. A better strategy is to procure liquid brown sugar, or replace the ingredient entirely with a combination of molasses and either granulated or dissolved sugar.

Bulk granular dextrose can be shipped in trucks or Airslide cars. The handling systems and storage bins are much like those used for bulk sucrose. Pancoast and Junk (1980) say that mechanical handling of dextrose is preferred over pneumatic transfer because of the greater amount of crystal attrition occurring in the latter type of system. Crystalline dextrose tends to cake in storage silos and then clog handling systems. This problem can be alleviated by using a bin with a cone-shaped bottom and equipped with a vibrator. Other discharge-assisting means, such as live bottoms consisting of multiple screw conveyors placed under a large bottom opening, may be efficient.

Corn starch is stored in silos with Airslide bottoms and handled similarly to flour. Railcars can transport typically 40 tons of starch. This ingredient sometimes contains very fine particles, in the 10 to 20 micron range, that can escape through the pores of regular bin filter relief bags. Starch has a high shear friction when tightly packed, and this affects the internal design of feeders and diverters. Because of the explosion hazard of starch aerosols, explosion-proof gearmotors are used.

COMPUTERIZED INVENTORYING

A big advantage of bulk handling of ingredients is that it permits computerized inventorying, greatly simplifying the difficult and time-consuming task of maintaining accurate records of stocks of ingredients. Signals from load cells or strain gauges relay information on bin weights to the computer memory bank. These data can be processed almost instantly to give a readout or printout of the total stock of any given ingredient. Amounts metered out of the bins or tanks are deducted from the previous totals, giving a double-check of the contents. Received materials, measured by bin weighing or by meters on the intake pumps, provide a check on the supplier's invoice and the current bin contents. Among the types of inventory reports that are possible are: (1) the complete extended inventory, (2) the perpetual inventory, (3) the comparative inventory, and (4) ingredient and packaging requirements (Koehler 1981). Re-order levels can be entered for each item and provision made for an automatic printout of the needed materials each day.

A computer with the appropriate software permits the ready calculation and display or printout of: (1) recap of all products ordered, (2) bake shop production orders containing breakdowns for racks, pans, and pieces, (3) formula sheets for the mixing room, (4) raw material usage, (5) package material usage, and (6) cost of the day's bake with labor included (Cooper 1984).

A weak point in some bulk handling systems for flour is the difficulty of adequate inventory control. None of the methods currently used for measuring bin contents is completely satisfactory. Both volumetric and gravimetric devices are being used. Among the gravimetric types are strain gauges operating as part of an electronic indicating circuit and liquid load cells based on a combination of hydraulic and mechanical principles.

BIBLIOGRAPHY

ANON. 1985. Bulk storage system ensures 99% cleanout and uninterrupted flow. Food Engineering *57*, No. 11, 110

ANON. 1986. Smart valves save money at Palm Dairies. Prepared Foods *155*, No. 4, 82

ANON. 1990A. Flowability, floodability, and viscosity. Baking & Snack Systems *12*, No. 5, 20-21, 23

ANON. 1990B. Pressure sensors gauge tank level and fluid density. Prepared Foods *159*, No. 1, 134-135

ANON. 1991. Integrating ingredient systems. Baking & Snack *13*, No. 5, 20-21, 23

BORDEN, B. 1958. Bulk liquid sweeteners—engineering and economics. Proc. Am. Soc. Bakery Engineers *1958*, 79-84

COONS, J. 1979. Dust explosion hazards in bakeries. Proc. Am. Soc. Bakery Engineers *1979*, 206-211

COOPER, M. R. 1984. Computers for the baking industry. Proc. Am. Soc. Bakery Engineers *1984*, 99-104

DAVIS, L. B. 1953. Pneumatic conveying systems. Proc. Am. Soc. Bakery Engineers *1953*, 123-128

DIVER, J. J. 1982. Conveyors. Proc. Am. Soc. Bakery Engineers *1982*, 142-150

FARRAND, W. J. 1962. Flour packing, warehousing, and bulk transport. Biscuit Maker and Plant Baker, May 1962, 407-418

FISCHER, J. 1959. Conveying flour by air. Food Processing *20*, No. 9, 37-39, 43

GARCIA, E. J., and STEFFE, J. E. 1986. Optimum economic pipe diamter for pumping Herschel-Bulkley fluids in laminar flow. J. Food Process Engineering *8*, 117-136

GERCHOW, F. J. 1975. How to select a pneumatic conveying system. Chem. Eng. *82*, Feb.17

HAGEDORN, H. G. 1965. New practices in bulk handling of materials with special emphasis on instrumentation. Proc. Am. Soc. Bakery Engineers *1965*, 148-152

HAILE, F. 1973. Bulk material handling equipment. Proc. Am. Soc. Bakery Engineers *1973*, 178-184

HALLMAN, R. B. 1987. Personal communication. General American Transportation Co., Chicago, IL

HOWARD, R. M. 1956. Bulk flour. Proc. Am. Soc. Bakery Engineers *1956*, 78-84

IRWIN, J. 1976. Basic principles of pneumatic conveying. Bakers Digest *50*, No. 5, 31-34

KICE, J. 1985. Skilled Air Manual. Kice Metal Products, Wichita, KS

KOEHLER, W. H., JR. 1981. Computers in the bakery. Proc. Am. Soc. Bakery Engineers *1981*, 179-184

KOLLMAN, W. C. 1961. Some engineering and economic aspects of bulk systems. Proc. Am. Soc. Bakery Engineers *1961*, 199-206

LARSON,K. 1991. Tank gauges achieve new levels of accuracy. Control *4*, No. 6, 20-24, 26

LINGLE, R. 1990. Best way to get from here to there. Prepared Foods *159*, No. 5, 198-199

LONG, J. 1984. Minor ingredient systems. Proc. Am. Soc. Bakery Engineers *1984*, 92-98

MOORE, R. F. 1988. Flour: Handling your most important ingredient. Proc. Am. Soc. Bakery Engineers *1988*, 85-91

MORRIS, G. C. 1971. Pneumatic bulk handling systems in the bakery. Proc. Am. Soc. Bakery Engineers *1971*, 49-53, 66

PANCOAST, H. M., and JUNK, W. R. 1980. Handbook of Sugars, Second Edition. AVI Publishing Co., Westport, CT

PARISEAU, W. G., and FOWKES, R. S. 1972. Bin hopper engineering and bulk materials flow: A state-of-the-art report of empirical and theoretical analyses. U.S. Bureau Mines Inf. Circ. *8552*

PELEG, M., MANNHEIM, C. H., and PASSY, N. 1973. Flow properties of some food powders. J. Food Sci. *38*, 959-964

PETRICCA, T. 1976. Fluid bakery shortenings. Bakers Digest *50*, No. 5, 39-41

RADER, J. R. 1984. Automated packaged product system. Proc. Am. Soc. Bakery Engineers *1984*, 75-85

REIMELT, S. 1987. Personal communication. Sept. 21

ROTHFUS, P. R. 1968. Working concepts of fluid flow. V. Flow measurement. Instrum. Control Syst. *41*, No. 7, 105-108

SCHROEDER, W. 1956. Bulk fat handling. Proc. Am. Soc. Bakery Engineers *1956*, 85-90

SLATER, G. B. 1989. Ingredient feed systems. Proc. Am. Soc. Bakery Engineers *1989*, 158-167

SPOONER, T. F. 1990. Control through automated ingredient handling. Baking & Snack Systems *12*, No. 5, 12-16, 18-19

WAHL, R. C. 1978. Handling bulk materials—simple tests predict handling problems. Plastics World, No. 1978.

WOERFEL, J. B. 1981. Bulk handling of fats and oils. Cereal Foods World *26*, 446-448

chapter twenty-four

WEIGHING AND METERING EQUIPMENT

INTRODUCTION

The measuring of ingredients is obviously one of the most critical operations in the bakery. Not only is the accuracy of measurement directly related to the quality of the finished products, but it also affects costs and, therefore, the profitability and continued existence of the company. Since composition is regulated to some extent by federal, state, and local regulations in the case of standardized items such as bread and must, in any case, conform to the label declaration of ingredients, bakery management must be certain that the amount of each component found in the finished product will fall within acceptable tolerances if they expect to avoid legal entanglements.

The hand scaling of individual ingredients has been replaced at an ever increasing rate in recent years by automatic weighing and metering. Some of the advantages that result from these changes are faster batch preparation, reduction of human errors, lower manpower requirements, and improved sanitation. In practice, accuracy is usually improved. Automatic measuring is almost essential when bulk handling systems are used.

Designers of automatic measuring equipment for ingredients, doughs, and finished products have borrowed techniques freely from other industries. Water meters of various kinds have proved to be adaptable, with changes of varying degrees of complexity, to the measuring of other liquid ingredients. Weighing devices originally used in other food industries or in nonfood applications have been modified for bakery use. A great deal of ingenuity and expertise has gone into some of these adaptations and modifications.

Products and granular materials are generally measured by gravimetric techniques, while liquids are more often measured volumetrically. Volumetric equipment is less expensive, as a rule, but it is also inherently less accurate and dependable because its feed rate depends on the density and (usually) the flow characteristics of the material being measured, and these factors cannot be expected to be perfectly uniform, especially for powdered materials. As a practical matter, however, volumetric feeders function quite satisfactorily in many bakery applications for sugar and other relatively free-flowing ingredients.

Gravimetric measurement is usually somewhat more difficult to automate, but is theoretically of greater accuracy, at least for powdered and granular materials that can vary considerably in density. The subsequent sections of this chapter describe equipment that has been developed for the automatic weighing and the automatic metering (i.e., volumetric measuring) of ingredients. This chapter will not include discussions of measuring devices for dough or finished products, which are found in later chapters.

DEVICES FOR MEASURING MASS

The two major categories of mechanical weighing devices are force-deflection systems and balances. The simplest weight, or force, measuring system is the ordinary equal-arm balance. It is based on the principle of comparing moments, i.e., the tendency to produce motion about a point. The moment produced by an unknown weight is compared with that produced by a known weight. If the two arms of the balance are equal in length, a null balance will be obtained when the two weights are equal. For all practical purposes, a null balance is indicated when the beam forms a perfectly horizontal line. Usually, a pointer is attached to the bean at the pivot point so that the pointer is exactly perpendicular when null balance is achieved. When the two arms are unequal, the product of the moment and the length of the arm will be equal to the product of the weight and length on the other side. The device known as the beam scale results when the unknown weight is attached to a very short arm, the long arm is a beam with graduations along its length, and a known weight is slid along the graduated arm until a null balance is obtained. The ancient and still used steelyard is an example of a beam scale.

Some industrial equipment is based on the principle of the beam scale. An unknown weight on a short arm is balanced by moving a poise of known weight along a calibrated long arm. The farther it is necessary to move the known weight away from the fulcrum or pivot before the indicator becomes vertical, the heavier is the unknown weight. That is, the ratio of the arm lengths is varied to obtain a null reading. Muliple beam industrial scales introduce additional levers between the unknown weight and the beam to increase the ratio of unknown weight to poise weight, so that hundreds of pounds can be balanced by a much lighter poise. This scheme permits reduction in size of the equipment and often improves accuracy. Small capacity bench balances are examples of the uneven arm scale, while many platform scales and suspended hopper scales make use of the multiple beam design. Improvements that have been made in the design of these scales include electronic or electric readouts, automatic balancing systems, damping mechanisms, and recording devices.

Pendulum-balanced scales use one or more "pendulums," or short weights mounted on one end of a rigid rod that rotates about a pivot at its other end. The pendulum can balance increasing loads as it moves from vertical to horizontal. Because the weight which the pendulum will balance varies as the sine of the displacement angle, equal increments of weight will not cause equal rotation of the pivot and so cams are inserted into the system to give linear movement to the scale pointer. Metal tapes transmit the motion from platform to pendulum. These scales are commonly used ᵔere a dial indication of weight is required. They are available in recording and printing models, and with electric cutoff for batching.

Because the deflection of a spring or any other elastic element is directly proportional to the force applied to it, within its elastic limit, a calibrated spring, tube, rod, or plate can serve as a weight-measuring device. This principle is applied in the spring scale and the torsion balance, as well as in other kinds of weighing equipment. The spring, rod, or other elastic element is used to support a platform on which the unknown weight is placed. The larger the weight, the larger the deformation of the elastic element. The latter is measured mechanically, electrically, or electronically. These devices are subject to hysteresis, metal fatigue, and temperature errors, but can still be effective weighing devices when properly designed and used.

Other force-sensing elements adaptable to weight measurement include strain-gauge load cells and pneumatic pressure cells. In a sense, strain gauges are deflection plates, but the deformation is measured as a change in an electrical signal rather than directly as a change in dimensions.

The electrical resistance of an electronic load cell varies with the tension or strain on the cell. These cells are the basic measuring units in many types of automatic weighing devices. The design of such systems is that one or more of the supports for a tank, for example, is fitted with these elements. The load cell is distorted by an amount that is proportional to the weight resting on the support. An electronic circuit incorporating the load cell actuates a device that can transform the electrical charges into indications of weight. Equipment of this type is usually guaranteed to have an overall accuracy of 0.05% of the indicator's total capacity; at this accuracy, a load cell of 10,000 lb total capacity sensing the pressure of a 5,000 lb mixer and a 2,000 lb dough would report a load within 5 lbs of the actual weight.

In combination with the hydraulic load cell system, electronic load cells can be used in batching or other weighing operations, both to indicate the weight on the load cell and to automatically activate a valve or other control when a preset weight is reached.

The hydraulic or pneumatic load cell can also be used as part of the supporting member for an ingredient container. These cells generate pneumatic or hydraulic forces that vary with the weight they sustain and transfer them through the medium of a liquid contained in rigid tubes to an indicator or recorder. Accuracy of these units is said to be within 1% of load range.

Industrial Scales

The manual scaling of minor ingredients (sometimes major ingredients, too) is common practice in small bakeries. The scales may be stationary or mobile, mechanical or electronic, or vary in other characteristics. Inexpensive dial type mechanical scales with manual taring are frequently encountered pieces of equipment. They often have dial pointers and circular graduations where multiple revolution readings are necessary, and they may have either an adjustable or a fixed scale. Additive weighing is done with a fixed scale and absolute weighing with an adjustable scale. Mechanical scales are relatively inaccurate, difficult to read, and have no capacity for recording weights (Long 1984). Their resolution, or the smallest difference that can be read, is limited by the type of scale; customarily a dial with 1,000 lb total can be read to the nearest pound. In addition to their relatively low cost, their advantages are ease of maintenance and calibration, and the ability to cancel out the tare weight so the ingredient weight can cover the entire dial (or beam).

Mechanical scales are being replaced by electronic scales based on load cells and having digital readout and automatic taring. They can be obtained with metric or avoirdupois readouts, often interchangeable by pressing a button, and are available for all weight ranges, from micrograms to tons. For some models, readouts can be located at any reasonable distance from the scale and analytical programs of almost any degree of complexity can be put into use. Although these scales were initially too expensive for use in the smaller bakeries, many are now cheaper than equivalent mechanical scales. Sensors are usually electromechanical load cells of the compression-tension or deflector rod type. Advantages of electronic scales are their potentially better accuracy and resolution and their ability to be tared over their entire weighing range. Additionally, their output is suitable for transmission to a printer or for computer processing. In theory, they are not necessarily more accurate than mechanical scales, but in practice they are less subject to reading errors and to other operator's mistakes. They occupy less space than mechanical scales, but also may be less sturdy and more sensitive to environmental problems.

Continuous and Automatic Scales

Continuous and automatic operating scales for batch weighing can be based on the same weight-comparison principles found in manually operated unequal arm balances. Sensing means are used to energize the mechanisms that start and stop the flow of material into the weighing hopper. For example, weighing of flour in most modern bakeries is accomplished by an automatic flour scale located immediately above the dough mixer. Figure 24.1 is a schematic diagram of a flour hopper scale. In some cases, the hopper of this scale is carried on a trolley, and can be moved over several mixers, as required. The usual model consists of a conical steel hopper mounted on four point-suspension bearings of knife-edged pivots made from case-hardened steel. Once the scale beam is set for the required amount of flour and the switch is activated, operation is completely automatic. A mercury switch activated by the scale beam shuts off the flour input when a preset weight has been reached. At the proper time, the operator discharges the contents of the hopper directly into the mixer. Capacities range from

200 to 1,000 lb of flour. Transfer operations are dustless, the outlet of the hopper being connected to the mixer by a sliding sleeve. Air displaced as the flour goes into the mixer is conducted to the upper set of the hopper by a venting tube. The scale must be adjusted by the operator or automatically compensated for conveyor overrun to obtain satisfactory accuracy.

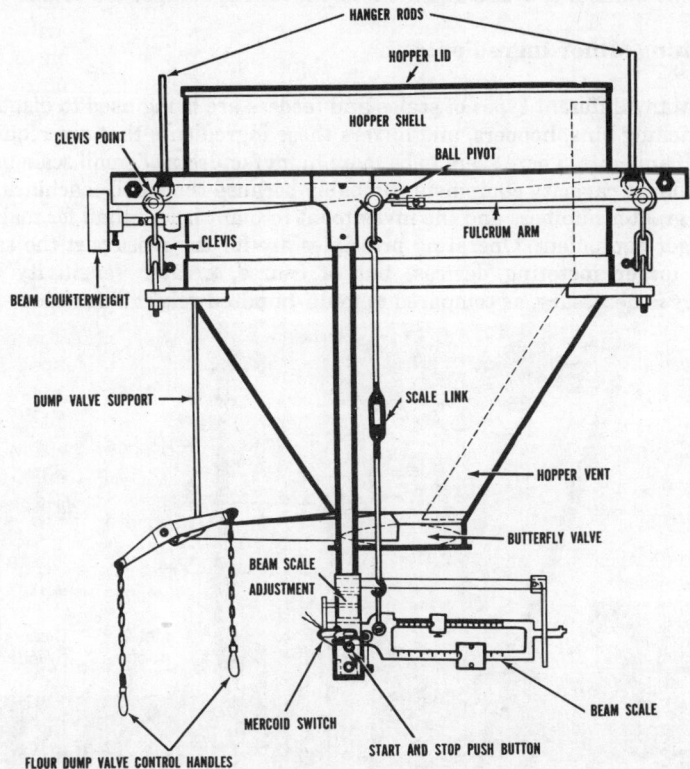

Figure 24.1. Flour hopper and scale, usually found above the mixer

In another type of automatic scale, a balancing weight is positioned by a reversible automatic motor. Deflection of the beam makes an electrical contact that causes the motor to move the weight in the direction necessary to restore balance, and the final balance position is translated into a signal by means of a potentiometer or digital encoding disc. The signal can be used for recording or control purposes, or both.

Automatic batch scales are adaptable to continuous flows of liquids, granular materials, or powders. If dry materials are being measured, the ingredient flows from a feed hopper through an adjustable gate into the scale hopper until the preselected weight is reached. Then, a trip mechanism closes the gate and opens the outlet. When the scale hopper is empty, the weight of the tare forces the door closed, resets the trip, and opens the gate so another cycle can begin. A dribble feed, resulting from a partial closing of the gate as the weight target is approached, reduces the rate of inflow so that the extent of overfill is reduced. A counter can be used to record the number of cycles and the total amount of dumped material.

Weighing Minor Ingredients

Many different types of scales and feeders are being used to dispense into batching bins, hoppers, and mixers those ingredients that are required in small amounts. There seem to be more manufacturers of small scale units than of large capacity equipment, probably because the small machines are sold in greater numbers and the investment in plant is less than for making the larger equipment. Operating principles are for the most part the same as for larger metering devices, but of course, greater sensitivity and accuracy is necessary, as compared to multi-hundredweight dispensers.

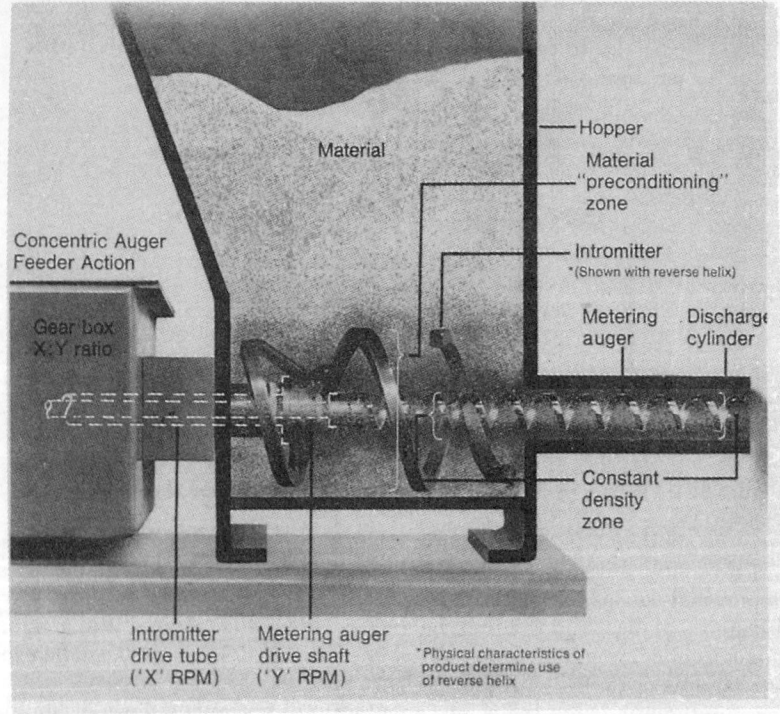

Figure 24.2. Cutaway view of ingredient feeder using counter-rotating helices

Counter-rotating augers, sometimes combined with live bins or vibrated hoppers, are frequently used to assist flow and make the density of powders more uniform as they reach the measuring region of the device. See Figure 24.2 (Source: Acrison).

In one unit suitable for measuring amounts as low as 0.15 lb per hr, a rotating and vibrating screw feeder is combined with a vibrating hopper or "live bin." These devices are said to be capable of handling many kinds of powders, pellets, flakes, and agglomerates that cause difficulties in other kinds of equipment. The hopper is subjected to continuous gyratory vibrations that are transmitted throughout the contents. This permits feeding from the hopper without bridging or flooding, producing a steady, positive flow of material into the screw chamber beneath the hopper. The vibrating action also tends to condition the material so that the bulk density is uniform when it enters the screw chamber (Anon. 1987).

Even in very large bakeries, there are usually facilities that require a certain degree of manual attention for weighing minor ingredients. In one arrrangement, a carousel carries small tubs past a stationary scale. As each container stops on the scaling platform, a worker deposits in it ingredients taken from bags or drums.

In one unit suitable for measuring amounts as low as 0.15 lb per hr, a rotating and vibrating screw feeder is combined with a vibrating hopper or "live bin." These devices are said to be capable of handling many kinds of powders, pellets, flakes, and agglomerates that cause difficulties in other kinds of equipment. The hopper is subjected to continuous gyratory vibrations that are transmitted throughout the contents. This permits feeding from the hopper without bridging or flooding, producing a steady, positive flow of material into the screw chamber beneath the hopper. The vibrating action also tends to condition the material so that the bulk density is uniform when it enters the screw chamber (Anon. 1987).

Even in very large bakeries, there are usually facilities that require a certain degree of manual attention for weighing minor ingredients. In one arrrangement, a carousel carries small tubs past a stationary scale. As each container stops on the scaling platform, a worker deposits in it ingredients taken from bags or drums.

Small ingredient storage bins can be mounted in a row along a wall. They are filled either by pneumatically conveying material from a dumping station or by dumping the ingredient manually into the top of the bin from a platform above it. An auger-fed dispenser at the bottom of the hopper leads into a mechanical scale or an electronically controlled weighing mechanism. Although the small silos are generally of the usual rigidly-attached metal construction, lift-type bins are also available, these are lowered so the top is near floor level for filling, then raised to a level convenient for dispensing ingredient form their bottoms. Such bins are available in sizes from 1 to 2 ft in diameter and 6 to 15 ft high, with capacities of 600 to 1,500 lb of material. To assist in dispensing materials that are not free flowing, bins can be fitted with mechanical cone wipers, discharge screws, or air fluidizing means.

In an automated version of minor ingredient scaling, a mobile weighing device holding a batch receptacle moves on a track or roller conveyor beneath a series of storage bins. A weighed portion of ingredient is discharged from each bin when the mobile scale is positioned directly below its outlet. The scale signal controls the shut-off point for ingredient delivery. A trailing cable running along the entire length of the track connects the computer's formula memory storage and carries commands to the mobile scale.

Weighing Materials on Moving Belts

Some scales are designed to determine the amount of material on a belt that is passing over the weighing mechanism. Although it might seem that movement of ingredient and interference from the supporting belt would seriously hamper accurate weighing, properly designed equipment can, in fact, deliver measurements sufficiently accurate for many purposes.

The simplest forms of this type of device weigh the ingredient but do not adjust the delivery rate so as to maintain a constant flow, that is, they do not have feedback control. They are useful in automatic batching, but are not readily adaptable to continuous processing where the rate of delivery and not the total weight is important. In one semi-continuous model, the scale belt runs continuously but is fed intermittently with loads that do not extend its full length so that an isolated load is being weighed at any given time. Since the increments are deposited at shorter intervals, they approximate continuous flow. The weigh belt is mounted on a scale mechanism that records and sums the amounts transported.

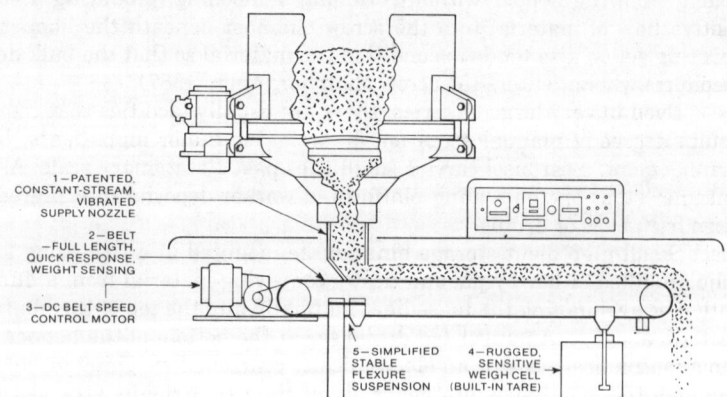

1—PATENTED,
CONSTANT-STREAM,
VIBRATED
SUPPLY NOZZLE

2—BELT
—FULL LENGTH,
QUICK RESPONSE,
WEIGHT SENSING

3—DC BELT SPEED
CONTROL MOTOR

5—SIMPLIFIED
STABLE
FLEXURE
SUSPENSION

4—RUGGED,
SENSITIVE
WEIGH CELL
(BUILT-IN TARE)

Figure 24.3. Principles of a weighbelt system receiving material from a vibrating bin and nozzle

Source: VibraScrew, Inc.

Another version of the belt weigher, the continuous conveyor scale, uses a scale-supported section of a belt conveyor to totalize the load that is being constantly deposited on it. The difference between this and the former type is that the entire conveyor (not just the belt) is supported by the weighing mechanism. The forms of weighing devices used in such equipment include spring-balanced beams, strain gauges, and pneumatic load cells.

Fully automated belt weighers with feedback to control the rate of delivery are useful in continuous or intermittent weighing. The most common type utilizes a conveyor belt balanced on a weigh beam. When the belt is driven at a constant speed and the total weight of the belt, material, and associated mechanisms is held constant, the rate at which the material comes off the end of the scale will also be constant and the total weight for any known time interval can be computed. Imbalance of the beam actuates a change of the rate of material deposition on the belt in the direction of restoring balance, by a mechanical adjustment of the feed gate or by varying the speed of a belt or screw feeding the weighing conveyor. Accuracies are claimed to be as high as 0.0001% (!) for certain products and equipment, but a more likely figure is about plus or minus 0.5% for continuous measuring scales used in the bakery.

Loss-in-Weight Feeders

Instead of measuring the amount of ingredient deposited in a batching receptacle by weighing that container and its contents, the loss in weight of the storage bin or hopper from which the ingredient has been withdrawn can be determined. In a typical loss-in-weight feeder, the entire feed hopper is mounted on a scale that controls the rate of removal of material from the hopper. Material may be released from the hopper by a rotating valve powered by a variable speed motor or by some other mechanism. If the counterpoise on the scale beam is retracted continuously by a constant speed drive, the rate of delivery will be constant and the equipment will be suitable for continuous processes.

Several modifications of loss-in-weight feeders are available for bakers. Vibratory, screw, pneumatic, and belt methods may be used to remove material from the hopper that is mounted on a multiple-beam scale mechanism. The hopper is filled and the scale beam balanced by manually adjusting the poise. The control dial on the rate adjuster is set to the desired rate of feed in pounds per hour. The rate setter, operated by a synchronous motor, retracts the poise by a lead screw at the exact feed rate desired. As long as the feeder delivers material from the hopper in a manner such that the hopper loses weight at the same rate the poise is being retracted, the scale beam will stay in balance. If the feeder delivers too much or too little ingredient per unit of time, causing the hopper to lose weight faster or slower than the poise is being retracted, the beam will tip and operate controls that cause the feeder to correct its rate. The beam is essentially in balance at all times.

When the loss-in-weight feeder is electronically controlled, it can be coupled to the flow from another loss-in-weight feeder or from liquid flowing through a Venturi tube, orifice plate, or other flow measuring device so that two or more ingredients are delivered in correct proportions. The metering can be continuous or intermittent, and in the latter case, the sensing of a predetermined amount of one ingredient leads to the operation of the feeder for a fixed number of seconds.

Control Methods for Gravimetric Feeders

Belt gravimetric feeders can be mechanically, pneumatically, or electronically controlled. Operation of belt gravimetric feeders is based on the principle of maintaining a constant weight of material on the moving belt through activation of a positive-acting gate on the feed hopper. The rate of feed may be changed by varying the belt load and/or changing belt speed. Net weight of belt load may be sensed directly by a force balance pneumatic transmitter and load cell or by a differential transformer that will transmit any variation from set load to the solid-state electronic controller.

The feedback actuates the control gate to maintain belt load at the set point and maintain weigh platforms in a null position. Electonically controlled belt gravimetric feeders are available with capacities from about 0.1 lb per minute to over 60,000 lb per hr and have accuracies of plus or minus 1%. The belt type with preset cutoff uses a scale and tachometer signal to provide an instantaneous indication of the rate of material flow by weight per unit of time. The resulting analog signal is converted into digital form by an integrator. A pulse counter records the digital information to provide visual indications of the total flow of material. The pulse counter can also be provided with a stop-point setting that will cause a contact to close and halt the conveyor when the prescribed amount of material has been transferred.

The proportional belt feeder also relies on a scale and tachometer output to provide instantaneous rate-of-flow measurement. In this case, however, the resultant signal is electronically compared with that from a percent-setter to regulate conveyor speeds. The system can be designed to have a stop-point similar to the arrangement described above. Two ingredients can be measured at proportional rates and blended on a conveyor. In belt systems, one of the chief factors affecting overall accuracy is the location of the sensing device in relation to the discharge point—the closer they are, the greater the accuracy.

Hopper weighing systems can be provided with either analog or digital controls. The analog system employs a scale and a conventional sensing apparatus. Other types of weighing devices such as load cells can be used as sensors, provided their output is electrical. The amplified signal is compared with the preset input through the balance detector. When the signals balance, indicating that the hopper weight is at the desired amount, a solenoid cutoff closes the feeder. The analog indicator (e.g., a large scale head with a thousand graduations) continually supplies progressive weight information.

The digital system employs a mechanical weighbeam and lever

arrangement and a conventional scale head. The basic sensor can assume a variety of configurations and use several kinds of components, but a pulse signal giving a number of pulses proportional to the material weight must be obtained. The remaining portion of the system includes a preset counter with digital weight indication.

VOLUMETRIC MEASURING DEVICES

A volumetric measuring device in its simplest form is a container of known volume, such as a tank, barrel, pipette, or volumetric flask. The container may be calibrated at various points—as in burettes, graduated cylinders, and some storage tanks. Volumetric measurements can be applied to solid and pulverulent materials as well as liquids; for example in home cooking procedures where nearly all proportioning is done volumetrically in spoons and cups. Large-scale manufacturing processes do not customarily include volumetric measuring systems for powders and the like because of the difficulty in maintaining uniform density in these materials.

Metering Liquids

Location of the liquid surface can be determined by several methods and used as a basis for inferring the quantity of liquid in the tank. A tape or chain connected at one end to an indicator and at the other end to a float on the liquid surface represents about the simplest possible method to use with an opaque tank. As the float moves up, the weighted indicator moves down along a calibrated scale, and vice versa. A calibrated or plain glass tube attached to outlets near the top and bottom of the tank can also be used for directly indicating liquid level since the top of the liquid column in the tube corresponds closely to the height of the surface of the liquid in the tank. The dielectric, conducting, or absorption properties of the liquid can also be used as the basis of this measurement. If the liquid rises between two vertically oriented plates of a condensor, a capacitance change will be produced that is proportional to the length of the conductor that is wetted and thus will be related to the surface level of the liquid. Absorption of radiation by the liquid lying between a radioactive source and a sensor will be proportional to the depth of the liquid. The electrical signals can, of course, be converted into analog or digital indications of volume and can, if desired, activate an alarm, pump, valve, etc. These volume measuring—or rather, depth measuring—devices are much more suitable for rough determinations of inventory than for controlling deliveries of ingredients to processing areas. Their precision is seldom satisfactory for the latter task.

In modern bakeries, the amounts of liquid ingredients delivered to processing equipment will be measured by totalizing flow meters wherever possible. Such equipment is almost indispensable in bulk-handling systems.

Much engineering expertise has gone into the design of water meters, and virtually all fluid control and measuring systems are based on instruments originally designed for water. Although it is rarely thought of in this way, water is a classical example of an ingredient received, transported, and dispensed by bulk transfer methods. Water is a rather difficult liquid to meter because of its lack of lubricity, its promoting of electrolytic erosion, and its corrosiveness (Hesley 1988). Other liquid ingredients add different or additional parameters to the measuring problem, and meters designed to meet the challenges of water dispensing may have to be substantially modified so they can handle hot, abrasive, and otherwise difficult materials.

Headmeters measure the loss in pressure between two points in a pipe containing a flowing liquid. The three most widely used headmeters are pitot tubes, orifice plates, and Venturi meters. Only brief discussions on the principles of these instruments can be included here; for more details consult Cheremisinoff (1979, 1985) and Anon. (1959). Four different kinds of head meters are shown in diagrammatic form in Figure 24.4.

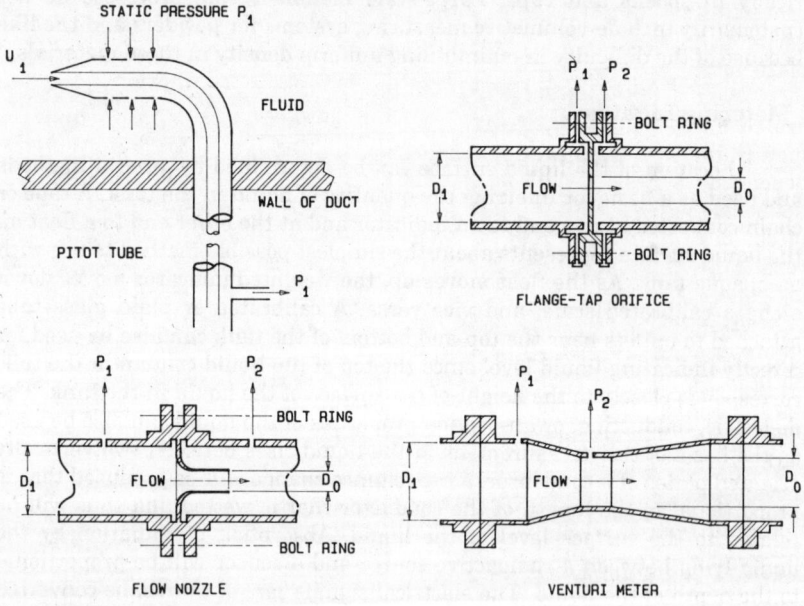

Figure 24.4. Variable head meters

The pitot tube is used for measuring local fluid velocities and consists of a tube inserted into the main pipe with its inlet turned upstream to receive the full impact of the flowing liquid. The impact is completely converted into pressure head and superimposed on the existing static pressure of the fluid. In practice, pitot tube instruments consist of both an impact tube and a piezometer tube to measure static pressure combined in an S-shaped tube, the combination allowing the static pressure to be subtracted from the total pressure—the difference being the velocity head.

An orifice meter consists of a thin plate with a hole of accurate size bored in it and placed across a pipe through which a liquid is flowing. In accordance with Bernoulli's equation, reduction of the cross section of the flowing stream as it passes through the orifice increases the velocity head at the expense of the pressure head. Gauges or manometers are used to measure the pressure upstream and downstream of the constriction to provide the data on which calculation of the flow rate can be made

A Venturi meter consists of a pipe of narrower diameter inserted in the main pipe. The measurement principle is based on determination of the reduction of flow pressure and increase in velocity. The pressure drop in the upstream connecting section is used to determine the rate of flow through the Venturi. On the discharge side, the fluid velocity is decreased and the original pressure is recovered. Practical applications of these devices require some method of automatically sensing the pressures, comparing them, and converting the differences to amounts of liquid passing through the pipe in each unit of time. When the rate is known, the duration of flow is a measure of the total amount delivered.

Several versions of flow meters sufficiently accurate for bakery use are commercially available. These have been classified as (1) inferential meters, in which the liquid actuates a screw, a vane, or some other inertia-dependent mechanism, and (2) positive displacement devices in which a defined volume of water is allowed to pass during each complete cycle of the mechanism. Both types are accurate to a few percentage points of the total reading at high rates of flow. At low rates of flow, the displacement meters are generally more reliable.

It is also possible to relate the flow rate to the area change needed to obtain a constant pressure drop. This principle is the basis of the rotameter, an inferential meter that is the most common type of variable area meter used in the food industry. Rotameters consist of a vertical tube, usually of glass, having its bore gradually tapered (becoming larger toward the top), with the fluid moving upward through it, and a float capable of unrestricted movement up and down the tube. The float will assume an equilibrium position such that fluid drag and buoyancy just equal the downward force of gravity. Fluid drag is related to the area of flow between the float and the sides of the tube. If the flow rate increases, the bob moves upward in the tapered tube so that the separation between the inner surface of the tube and the surface of the bob is increased. This increases the flow area and keeps the drag constant. The pressure drop through the instrument remains almost independent of the flow rate. The earliest versions of rotameters were designed so that the bob rotated, hence the name. A spinning float has more stability, is easier to read, and keeps itself cleaner. Most modern rotameters perform satisfactorily with non-rotating bobs.

The calibration of rotameters will vary with float dimensions, tube taper, and fluid properties such as viscosity and density. Special float designs are available that are relatively insensitive to viscosity effects, but in the bakery each meter will normally be used for one ingredient only, so viscosity changes should not be a complication that needs to be considered. Means for compensating for fluid density changes can be obtained, if needed. The mathematical treatment of fluid flow measurement is detailed in many texts on chemical engineering and hydraulics, but a good summary of this aspect of metering has been given by Rothfus (1968). By affixing a magnet or armature to the float and placing a sensing device outside the tube, rotameter readings can be transmitted to other instruments for recording and control purposes.

Turbine meters, another type of inferential meter, have come into use for measuring the flow of such liquids as water, invert syrup, and ammonium bicarbonate solution. Their small size and weight permit installation at almost any convenient point. These meters consist essentially of a sensing device that measures the turning of a rotor located in a tubular housing inserted as part of the pipe line. The flowing liquid impinges upon the turbine blades which freely rotate about an axis following the center line of the surrounding tube. The angular velocity of the turbine rotor is directly proportional to the fluid velocity through the turbine. The angle of the rotor blades to the stream affects the rotor velocity. Blade angles are usually made between 20° and 40° because greater angles result in excessive end thrust and bearing friction while smaller angles cause undesirably low angular velocity and loss of repeatability. Designs are available in which the rotor spins freely in a low pressure chamber, no thrust bearings being needed because there is established a hydraulically balanced rotor position that keeps it away from the chamber walls. Both the K factor and linearity of turbine meters are seriously affected by changes in viscosity when the viscosity of the fluid they are measuring exceeds 100 cp. For such liquids, positive displacement meters are recommended for determining volume.

In turbine meters, sensing of the rotation rate of the revolving element is done by magnetic interaction between the blade tip and a pickup coil located outside the tubing. The rotor blades are made of paramagnetic material and the pickup coil contains a permanent alnico magnet. The surrounding pipe is made of stainless steel so that it does not interfere with the magnetic interaction. Frequency of the magnetic pulses will be proportional to the flow rate. Pulses per unit volume may be reduced in meters of small capacity by making some of the blades nonmagnetic. In large diameter meters, resolution is increased by installing a large number of small magnetic buttons on a ring rotated by the turbine. An alternating current output proportional to the flow rate is created and sensed by calibrated instruments that amplify it and use it for recording flow rate, totalizing the delivered amount, or controlling other instruments. Turbine meters have, in addition to the flow sensing element, a frequency converter and an electric potentiometer. The frequency converter delivers a DC output directly proportional to the frequency of the AC input from the sensing element. A digital counter registers a proportion of the pulses.

Continuously flowing streams of liquid material can be measured volumetrically by displacement meters. There are several types based on nutating discs, reciprocating pistons, rotating vanes, etc. The piston meter is like a piston pump operating backwards and it is capable of accuracy to about 0.1%. For precise volume measurements, corrections for temperature must be made because of its effect on the density of the fluid being measured and on the dimensions of the volumetric device. Pressure is generally not a factor since common liquids are noncompressible under the conditions of measurement, and pressures normally encountered in bakery equipment do not have a significant effect on meter dimensions.

For many years, the common method for measuring water delivered to customers has been the nutating meter. In meters of this type, a disc piston fits approximately horizontally in a chamber defined top and bottom by truncated cones. A vertical diaphragm also separates the chamber. Liquid flows into the chamber on one side of the vertical diaphragm and pushes the disc up and down with a nodding (or nutating) motion. The disc does not rotate. At each complete cycle, the piston discharges a volume of liquid equal to the capacity of the measuring chamber. A spindle affixed to the large spherical bearing that supports the piston is made to describe a circle as a result of the disc's nutation and this motion is transmitted through a gear train to the register. The only moving part in the measuring chamber is the piston (Anon. 1963).

See Figure 24.5 for illustrations of the working principles of some commercial positive displacement meters.

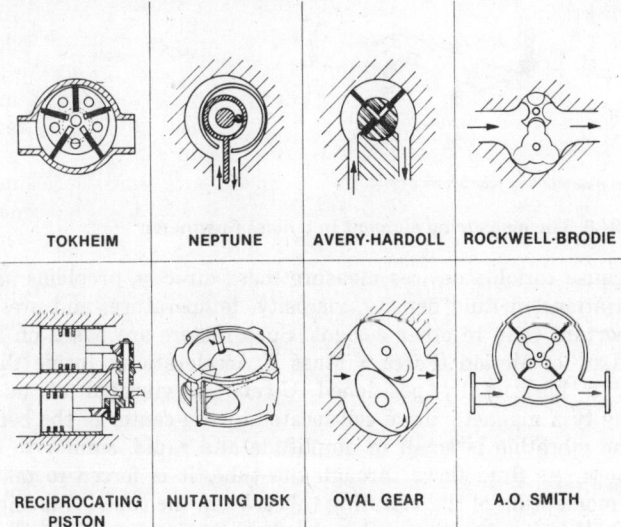

Figure 24.5. Measuring elements of positive displacement meters

Another common device for delivering precisely measured quantities of fluid, the positive displacement metering pump, is electrically actuated by a controller that has a synchronous motor drive. The motor moves the hands of an indicator that can be preset to shut off the flow when a desired quantity of liquid has been delivered. The metering cycle continues until another synchronous motor in the controller has counted the predetermined number of revolutions of the metering pump, after which the controller stops the two motors at the same time. Since both metering pump and controller are driven by synchronous motors energized by current of the same frequency, their motions will always be proportional. Each cycle of the pump will empty and fill a cavity of known volume.

Viscous fluids can also be measured satisfactorily by coriolis mass-flow meters (Hesley 1988). Figure 24.6 shows the method of function of the measuring element of a coriolis meter (Source: Micro Motion, Inc.).

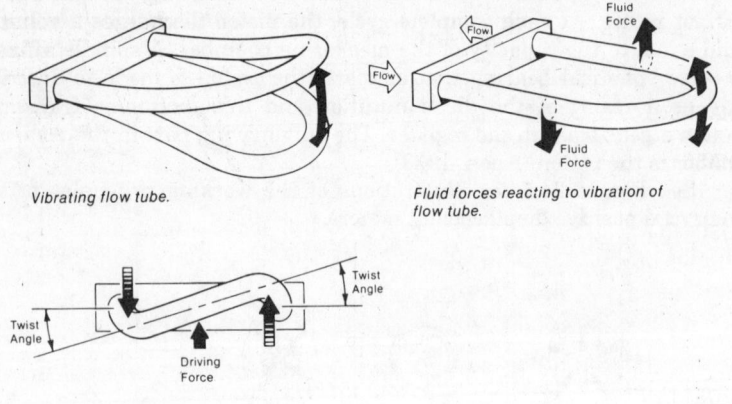

Vibrating flow tube.

Fluid forces reacting to vibration of flow tube.

End view of flow tube showing twist.

Figure 24.6. The measuring element in a mass flowmeter

Because coriolus devices measure mass directly, problems associated with variations in fluid density, viscosity, temperature, and pressure are less important than in other designs. Such meters are based on Newton's Second Law of Motion (Force = Mass X Acceleration). Inside the sensor housing, a horizontally positioned U-tube is vibrated at its natural frequency ty a magnetic drive coil located at the center of the bend in the tube. The vibration is small in amplitude and rapid, similar to that of a tuning fork. As fluid flows through the tube, it is forced to take on the vertical momentum of the vibrating tube. When the tube is moving upward (during half of its vibration cycle), the fluid flowing into the meter resists, thereby exerting a downward force on the tube. The fluid moving toward the outlet of the tube, having by that time been forced upward by the tube walls, resists the downward movement of the tube. These differently oriented forces cause the tube to twist—in one direction during the upward motion and in the opposite direction during the downward motion. Due to the tube's elasticity, the amount of twist imparted to it is directly proportional to the mass flow rate of the liquid passing through the tube. Magnetic sensors located on each side of the tube measure its up-and-down velocity and send this information to an electronics unit where the data is processed and converted into an output signal proportional to the mass flow rate.

Table 24.1. FLOW MEASURING DEVICES

Principle	Subclass	Suitable for measuring*	Linear or square root scale
DIFFERENTIAL PRESSURE:			
	Orifice	L, G, V	Square root
	Venturi	L, G, V	Square root
	Pitot	L, G	Square root
	Elbow	L, G	Square root
MAGNETIC:		EC L & S	Linear
MASS:	Coriolis	L, S	Linear
	Thermal	G	Linear
OSCILLATORY:			
	Vortex shedding	L, G, V	Linear
	Fluidic	L	
	Vortex precession	L, G	Linear
POSITIVE DISPLACEMENT:		Clean L & G	Linear
TARGET:		L, G, V	Square root
TURBINE:		Clean L & G	Linear
ULTRASONIC:			
	Transit time	Relatively clean L	Linear
	Doppler	L with entrained G or solids	Linear
VARIABLE AREA:	Rotameter	L, G, V	Linear
WEIRS & FLUMES:		L in open channels	Linear

* L=liquids; G=gases; V=steam; S=slurries; EC=electrically conductive.

Control of metering can also be accomplished by micro-switches activated by digital counters operated by cams on the pump shaft. When the shut-off point is reached the meter automatically resets itself to the original amount, ready to dispense the ingredient quantity for another batch. Accuracy of 0.1% has been claimed for positive displacement flow meters utilizing a system of oval gear wheels.

Any positive displacement pump in good condition can be calibrated for delivery at constant infeed and discharge pressures and used as a metering device. Revolutions may be counted by inserting a magnet in the pump coupling and using a sensor that detects the movement of the magnet. By counting the revolutions, the delivered quantity can be determined. If the pump is run at a constant rate, the delivery per unit of time can be used to make the pump serve as a meter. Accuracy is not of the best in such installations, but is sufficient for some purposes. For somewhat better accuracy, gear or lobe-type pumps can be used with constant speed drives for positive displacement metering of liquids of uniform density by operating them under constant suction and discharge pressure. An automatic time or automatic revolution counter can make the pump turn a selected number of revolutions equivalent to a desired quantity of material (Anderson 1976).

Table 24.1 lists virtually all the kinds of flow measuring devices currently available and identifies the principle of operation.

Metering Solids

Difficulties in accounting for variations in the density of the ingredient create problems whenever volumetric measurements are to be made on powdered or granular materials such as flour and sugar. Volumetric feeders for pulverulent materials can be classified on the basis of their action as: (1) a belt, disc, roller, or screw pushes or pulls the ingredient through a gate that usually can be moved so as to change the size of the opening; (2) a helix moves the material through a tube at a rate governed by the speed of the screw or the duration of a rotation; or (3) cavities in a disc or cylinder are first filled with powder as they pass under a hopper and then are rotated to dump their contents, the speed of movement of the pockets past the release point governing the rate of delivery.

Volumetric measurers relying on helical feed devices have been used in the baking industry for many years, as discussed briefly in an earlier section of this chapter. In one version of this type of feeder, two concentrically mounted and independently driven augers rotate in the same direction but at different speeds. The large outer helix tends by its slower rotation to create constant motion in a zone of material surrounding the faster speed inner auger (or metering auger). An optimum ratio of the two speeds is selected to give a constant uniform density in the material surrounding the metering screw. If product characteristics require it, a reverse helix can be added to further stabilize the flow pattern. Since the metering screw operates in an environment of stabilized density, it can deliver a constant rate of ingredient at any given speed. Metering accuracy of plus or minus 1% of the set rate is claimed to be achievable for most materials.

Still another type of volumetric feeder is frequently used in the food industry to dispense "micro" ingredients such as vitamins and oxidizers at low rates. Its feeding range can be varied from 4 oz to 60 lb per hr. The principle is that a vertically-movable slide or gate controls the depth of powder on a horizontally rotating feed disc that is drawing the material from a hopper. The powder, after it is removed from the disc by a screw, falls down a chute to the mixing vessel. Addition rates are controlled by varying the speed of the disc or the height of the opening in the hopper. Disc speed can be varied by changing the gears or the speed of the motor. The gate is adjusted by a micrometer screw to give a 1:20 variation in the height of the opening. As in all equipment of this type, feed rate is not necessarily directly related to the dimensions of the opening or the speed of the disc, and it is important to calibrate the settings by weighing the material discharged during a given time interval.

Another approach to auger feeding of small ingredients from loss-in-weight bins utilizes a flexible vinyl hopper against which two paddles press in alternating cycles. The undulating action of the paddles creates fault lines in the material and usually overcomes the common problems of bridging and rat-holing. It also conditions the ingredient into a uniform bulk density so that each flight of the feeding screw receives the same amount of material. The amplitude and frequency of paddle movement can be adjusted to meet the requirements of individual powders. Feeders of this type can be fitted with a microprocessor-based controller and a counterbalanced scale engineered for the unit. Loss-in-weight accuracies of 0.25% to 0.5% and volumetric accuracies of 0.5 to 2% are claimed by the manufacturer. Units sized to give flow rates of 0.0001 to 1,000 cu ft per hr are stocked.

AUTOMATIC BATCHING SYSTEMS

Weighing operations for flour, sugar, and some other ingredientes are integral parts of bulk handling systems. Ingredients which, for one reason or another, are not being handled in bulk transfer systems, can be dumped into receiving hoppers. Bag unloaders, sifters, and conveying systems (mechanical or pneumatic) will precede the receiving or surge hopper. Automatic conveying and metering or weighing devices are often used to eliminate manual transfer thereafter.

Automated minor ingredient scaling, as found in medium and large bakeries, involves programmed and pre-set (1) conveying to the scale, (2) weighing, and (3) subsequent discharging of weighed ingredients. One or more scales can be used. The sequence of weighing, as well as the weights for the individual ingredients in a formula, is pre-set, and dispensing proceeds automatically without need for manual interference (Long 1984).

Central batch weighing systems have one or more centrally located scales that deliver to several use points in a defined order. Hoppers can be located over each mixer, not as weighing hoppers, but as receiving or holding bins for ingredients weighed elsewhere. As a result, a weighed and fully assembled formula of dry ingredients is always ready to be dropped into each mixer as soon as the mixer is empty and ready to receive the next batch. This system is said to be particularly economical where a large number of use points is involved as well as where a large number of different ingredients is used. Such systems require computer control of the weighing process because several different formulas for several different use points must be stored in the computer's memory to be available on demand. There can be fully automatic checkout of the system, covering such things as verification of the condition of the scale, the conveyors, and tolerance, relieving the operator at the use point of responsibility for these checks. Central batch weighing can also include pneumatic mixing, providing the benefit of a homogeneous mixture of minor ingredients to be combined later with the major ingredients (Schraps 1982).

Automated bakeries generally use a central control panel registering and controlling the operation of many remote scales. In one form of the automated weighing system, formula weights are set in advance of each day's schedule by a supervisor who adjusts the weight selector dials behind the console. When the mixer operator signals readiness to begin a new batch, the central control operator starts the material flow by pressing a button. A further advance is the computerized system, in which recipes for several kinds of products are recorded in the computer's memory. After the mixer operator signals for his ingredients, the computer takes over all other functions. Changes, as for example to compensate for different flour moisture contents, can be made at will by typing them on an input keyboard.

The advantages claimed for automatic batching include: (1) elimination of human errors, (2) more consistent weights, (3) better sanitation, (4) less labor, and (5) reduction in loss of costly ingredients.

The automatic scale or meter is a system, or part of a system, made up of material handling devices, the weighing or metering equipment, data readouts, and the controls which program the entire series of operations for automatic cycling. All automatic scales transfer material from some type of storage to a scale and from the scale to some destination, usually a mixing vessel. From the scale comes information in the form of electrical signals that controls the weights of ingredients and which can also be used to print out weight data for quality control, inventory control, and other management requirements.

The simultaneous coordination of all feeders can be achieved by powering each of the critical drives with an induction motor receiving its electrical power from a central adjustable frequency source, such as a Varidyne power unit on the blender. The higher the frequency, the faster an induction motor revolves. A typical digital blending unit will include:

(1) A master unit with integral controls for setting system demand rate, batch size, valve ramp rates (up and down), and preshutdown point.

Automatic shutdown will be initiated by either measured or demand total. (2) Ratio unit (one or more) for setting individual component ratios by manual thumb switches. Multicomponent ratios are available, and 3 or 4 digit settings are optional.

(3) Individual component controllers, either pacing or memory, to provide control of the addition rates of the separate ingredients. Standard features include integrated total flow indication, manual valve control, and a low flow rate alarm to warn the operator when the measuring device is functioning below the range of linear flow.

Computers can be made part of the system to control any or all of the functions and to coordinate their operations. Automatic temperature compensation units can be used to continuously adjust quantity measurements for variations in density due to temperature fluctuations of liquid ingredients.

BIBLIOGRAPHY

ANDERSON, R. C. 1976. Weighing and metering systems for liquids. Proc. Am. Soc. Bakery Engineers *1976*, 63-70

ANON. 1956. Bread Baking. U.S. Dept. Army Tech. Manual. *TM 10-410*

ANON. 1959. Fluid Meters—Their Theory and Application. The American Society of Mechanical Engineers, New York

ANON. 1965. Conveyorized weighers. Food Engineering *37*, No. 12, 67-71

ANON. 1968. Omega gravimetric dry materials feeders and weighers. BIF, Providence, RI

ANON. 1985. Continuous Weighing and Feeding. Schenck Weighing Systems, Totowa, NJ

ANON. 1986. Dry Materials Feeding Handbook. AccuRate, Inc., Whitewater, WI

ANON. 1987. Vibra Screw Volumetric Live Bin Belt Feeder. Bulletin *BF-2A*. Vibra Screw, Totowa, NJ

ANON. 1988. Neptune meters. Neptune Meter Co., Long Island City, NY

BEATTIE, D. 1988. Personal communication. Liquid Controls Corp., North Chicago, IL

BENIER, J. 1983. Automated checkweighing. Proc. Am. Soc. Bakery Engineers *1983*, 113-119

CHEREMISINOFF, N. P. 1979. Applied Fluid Flow Measurement. Marcel Dekker, New York

CHEREMISINOFF, N. P. 1984. Fluid Flow Pocket Handbook. Gulf Publishing Co., Houston, TX

FULLER, W. S. 1970. Automatic weighing and dispensing of wet and dry sundry ingredients. Proc. Am. Soc. Bakery Engineers *1970*, 145-151

HAGEDORN, H. G. 1965. New practices in bulk handling of materials with special emphasis on instrumentation. Proc. Am. Soc. Bakery Engineers *1965*, 148-152

HESLEY, F. B., JR. 1988. Personal communication. S. J. Controls, Inc. Long Beach, CA

KOCHER, J. M. 1987. Personal communication. AccuRate, Whitewater, WI

LISK, I. 1989. Flow measuring equipment. Water & Wastes Digest *29*, No. 4, 8

LISK, I. 1990. Water meters and meter reading systems. Water & Wastes Digest *30*, No. 1, 8

LISK, I. 1991. Water meters and automatic reading systems. Water & Wastes Digest *31*, No. 1, 8

LONG, J. W. 1984. Minor ingredient systems. Proc. Am. Soc. Bakery Engineers *1984*, 92-98

OKLADEK, J. 1988. An overview of flow metering devices. Am. Laboratory *20*, No. 5, 92, 94, 96, 97-99

ROTHFUS, R. R. 1968. Working concepts of fluid flow. V. Flow measurement. Instr.

Control Systems *41*, No. 7, 105-108

RUBIN, M. 1991. How to keep turbine meters accurate. Control *4*, No. 6, 44-48

SCHRAPS, S. 1982. Automatic batching of major and minor ingredients in the baking industry. Bakers Digest *56*, No. 3, 12-18

SMITH, S. J. 1988. Personal communication. Micro Motion, Inc., Boulder, CO

SPANGLER, E. G. 1958. Storage and automatic dispensing of bulk lard and shortening. Proc. Am. Soc. Bakery Engineers *1958*, 71-78

SPOONER, T. F. 1989. Flowmeter measurement. Baking & Snack Systems *11*, No. 2, 20, 22

WILLIAMS, J. C., JR. 1955. Instrumental weighing and control in the baking industry. Baking Ind. *104*, No. 3, 62-65

ZIEMBA, J. V. 1965. Conveyorized weighers. Food Engineering *37*, No. 12, 67-71

chapter twenty-five

MIXERS AND MIXING

INTRODUCTION

Most bakery procedures are specific to the manufacturing of baked products. Mixing is an exception, and it has been said to be the only bakery processing step classifiable as a chemical engineering unit operation. As such, it has been thoroughly studied by many investigators.

Mixing has been defined as a process intended to put a plurality of materials, originally existing separately or in a nonuniform combination, into such an arrangement that each particle of one material lies as nearly adjacent as possible to a particle of each of the other materials. The reader will understand that mixing, as applied to doughs and batters has a broader purpose, encompassing aeration and development as well as other functions, some of them poorly understood.

It is probably safe to say that studies of the theoretical aspects of the unit operation of mixing have been of little help to bakery equipment designers, except possibly in the scale-up of equipment to larger models of the same pattern. Equipment designers had evolved an impressive array of efficient dough mixers long before there were college courses on dough rheology. Still, it is to be hoped that basic theoretical concepts can be applied to this art to establish relationships helpful in designing even more efficient machines to mix complex materials such as dough.

A fairly consistent body of data has been accumulated relating power input to mixer design and operating variables, but this has mostly involved simple equipment mixing nearly ideal fluids. On the other hand, there is little to rely upon in the design of mixers for highly viscous, pseudoplastic materials, except for intelligent trial and error in an experimental plan guided by practical experience. The main reasons for this situation are the numerous poorly understood factors affecting the response of doughs to mixing. Also, in any mixer operating on a dough of given formulation, viscosity and mixing velocity (two of the most important variables affecting power input) are interdependent. The apparent viscosity decreases with increasing rates of shear. It is almost impossible to define this relationship mathematically for purposes of equipment design, since most mixers must process several different formulas, each representing a different relationship between viscosity, mixing velocity, and power input. Consult Perry (1950) for a good discussion of the fundamentals of mixing, including clear definitions of the different kinds of fluids: ideal, plastic, pseudoplastic, thixotropic, dilatant, and rheopectic. Doughs and batters are principally pseudoplastic.

Blending or mixing can be accomplished by many different types of equipment, but they all rely on one or more of the following actions: (1)

Devices using blades, paddles, helical metal ribbons, etc., to push portions of the mix through other portions, (2) Devices relying on the elevating and dropping of all or a portion of a mixture so that the random rebounding of individual particles results in a redistribution of the particles, and (3) Devices creating turbulent movement by injecting currents of gas or liquids into a nonuniform body of material. There are changes occurring during the mixing of doughs and batters that are not included in the preceding definitions. For example, dough development is a separate phenomenon that happens to occur simultaneously with mixing when certain conditions exist. On the other hand, creaming and whipping do fit the definition, because they involve the entrapment and reduction in size of bubbles of gas within a mass of other material.

There are significant advantages, in many cases, to separating the mixing process into two or more stages. In a preliminary step, all or part of the ingredients can be roughly blended into a dry mix or slurry that is subsequently divided into batch size portions, possibly mixed with other components, and then subjected to intensive action to ensure uniformity and facilitate the physical and chemical changes needed to yield a finished dough or batter. Some of the implications of these premixing procedures are discussed in the following section.

PREMIXING

In bakery processes, there are some situations in which it is desirable or necessary to have a premix of part or all of the ingredients. A bakery "premix" is a combination of ingredients that must undergo additional mixing—usually with other ingredients or premixes—before processing is completed. Although a bakery premix often contains only a few of the total ingredients required to complete a product, it may contain all of them, or all except the gaseous ingredient, air. Premixing is used to accomplish several different objectives, some of which will be reviewed below.

Advantages of Premixes in Batch Operations

When it is desired to uniformly distribute a very small quantity of one ingredient (salt, vitamins, yeast, etc.) throughout a much larger viscous mass of other materials (such as bread dough), it is advantageous to premix the minor ingredients with the flour and other major dry components prior to adding water and starting the final mixing operation. This saves time and energy, reduces the heating that normally accompanies the mixing of doughs, and helps prevent localized concentrations of minor ingredients.

When a formula includes small quantities of several ingredients, and many batches of the formula are to be made, it is often helpful to prepare a large batch of premix containing the minor ingredients in their proper ratios. A calculated quantity of the premix is then added to each final batch. This saves a large number of weighing operations and reduces the expected frequency of errors in ingredient scaling. For this process to be efficient, the premix must be easy to prepare, store, convey, and meter. A pumpable aqueous premix containing dissolved or dispersed minor ingredients is a useful type of a premix.

The greater the number of minor ingredients that are included in the premix and the larger the premix batch, the greater will be the saving of weighing time. For example, a premix containing 10 minor ingredients that is made in batches large enough for 100 additions to the final dough mix would save 890 weighing operations (10 weighings for the premix preparation plus 100 weighings of the premix into the final mix versus 100 times 10 different weighings when the minor ingredients are added separately to each final batch). If only two ingredients are present in the premix, and it is made in batches sufficient for only 10 additions, then only 80 weighing operations would be saved for each 100 complete doughs.

When some of the ingredients require a strong shearing action to be dispersed but the final mix is of low viscosity, it may be difficult to obtain uniform distribution of all components when a single-stage mixing operation is specified. For example, it is difficult to disperse lumps of nonfat dry milk in water. But, if a high shear mixer is used to make a concentrated premix of the NFDM and part of the water, possibly with some of the other ingredients, the problem is solved. Although all the solid materials may not actually dissolve in the thick premix, lumps will be broken up and the particles uniformly dispersed by the high internal friction. As more fluid is added in the final mix, the dispersed particles dissolve (or are wetted) more readily. Gluten and gelatin are two other ingredients that may benefit from premixing with water.

For some industrial, military, foodservice, and domestic applications, prepared bakery mixes are customarily made up in large batches to save time and labor at the point of use. These can be packaged in batch size containers or in sacks or drums from which the baker weighs out enough mix for one batch. Although complete doughs and batters (including all liquid ingredients) are available for some products, it is often not possible to supply complete mixes, since they tend to be unstable, are difficult to handle, and lack versatility and flexibility. Consequently, dry premixes to which the baker adds water or some other liquid are more common than finished doughs and batters. Ready-to-bake doughs and batters in frozen or refrigerated form are widely distributed to retail and wholesale bakers, however.

Many of the advantages of premixes for batch operations are also applicable to continuous operations. There are, however, special problems in continuous mixing of doughs and batter that are greatly ameliorated by premix methods. Some of these will be discussed below.

It is theoretically possible to feed a continuous mixer by metering each individual ingredient stream separately through its own calibrated pump or gravimetric feeder. Very accurate metering is necessary since the continuous mixer must always operate on a dough or batter of uniform composition. Fluctuations of ingredient proportions could lead to malfunction of the equipment as well as to substandard products. Greater economy and (usually) better accuracy, result if several ingredients can be combined into a premix that is fed as one stream into the dough mixer. For instance, it is usually feasible to disperse in the water fraction all of the water-dispersible ingredients in a bread dough formula and meter this blend through a pump or other device. This premix can be prepared in batches (automatically or manually) or continuously.

It is rather difficult to feed dry materials directly into a continuous mixer operating at pressures exceeding atmospheric pressure. Special valving or a separate auger feeding section is required. A simple and convenient alternative is to assemble the ingredients in an open, atmospheric premixer, where batches in the form of a pumpable slurry are formed. Often, a storage tank or surge tank with agitators is provided between the blending unit and the continuous mixer. The liquid premix can easily be forced into the pressurized mixer by any of several types of metering pumps.

Premixing Equipment

If no fatty materials are to be added, satisfactory blending of bakery mixes can often be accomplished in blenders of the tumbling barrel type. Standard equipment in the industry is, however, the ribbon blender. Such a mixer will have a horizontal trough-shaped (U-shaped) bowl with a horizontal agitator shaft passing through the flat ends. Agitator elements are steel ribbons in an approximately helical design affixed to the shaft by radial supports. As the shaft rotates, these agitators lift and move the trough contents axially and radially. Other types of dispersing elements may be added to break up the mass as it is conveyed throughout the bowl. Figure 25.1 shows an agitator and bowl arrangement commonly found in ribbon mixers.

One advantage of the ribbon blender is that it is available in a wide range of sizes, from a one-cubic foot, fractional horsepower unit to a 500 cu ft, 50 hp unit. Maximum loading of the mixer should be the amount of mix that just covers the top of the agitator blades when the mixer is operating.

When shortening, especially plastic shortening, is to be blended into the dry mix, requirements are somewhat more exacting, but mixing can be done in conventional horizontal double-arm mixers, in ribbon blenders, or in vertical type planetary mixers. To add shortening to a ribbon blender, the fat is pumped to a manifold feeding a row of atomizing spray heads mounted in the cover but above the contents, so that the spray impinges on the dry solids as they are turned over by the agitator.

With some cake mixes, plastic shortening must be used. It is often pumped through a T-manifold and extruded in spaghetti-like strings onto the dry ingredients. The agitating action breaks up the shortening into discrete particles and eventually disperses it uniformly.

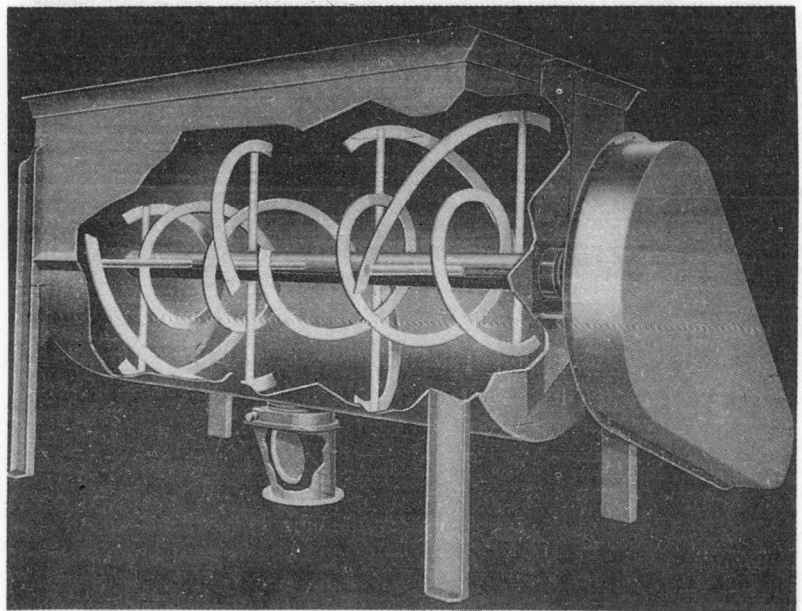

Figure 25.1. Ribbon mixer for dry blending

Minor ingredients are often pre-blended into a portion of the water. Among the many types of equipment used for this purpose is the Readco Ingrediator, which consists of a small vertical stainless steel tank with a direct-driven high speed agitator. When the tank is charged with water, the agitator creates a vortex that draws in the powdered material, then wets and dissolves (or disperses) it. Shortening may be incorporated in a liquid phase pre-blend if the mixture is subjected to a sufficiently intense emulsifying action. Anderson and Mullen (1951) reduced the fat-globule size with a dairy-type homogenizer to make an emulsion sufficiently stable to be held throughout an operating day.

Premixing is essential to the continuous cake-mixing process and may be done in one or two stages, depending on the nature of the final mixing process and the type of cake being prepared. The premixer is often a large planetary vertical mixer. Many operators find a 500-lb premix can be formed in as little as three minutes. If a vertical mixer is not available, a double-acting agitated kettle may be used for most cake premixes. For the highly aerated cakes such as sponge and angel food, all that is required for premixing is a propeller-agitated tank of suitable size.

For heavy, shortening type cakes, a two-stage premix works well. If easily emulsifiable shortening is used, all ingredients except flour and air can be batch premixed in a vertical tank having a high speed propeller agitator. This premix is then metered with a Waukesha-type pump to a Disc

Blender, along with a stream of flour from a gravimetric feeder. The Disc Blender is a low hold-up, highly efficient premixer containing a twin-cone agitator that maintains an open vortex and incorporates dry ingredients much more effectively than does a propeller type agitator. From the blender, the premix is pumped into the final mixer.

Oakes slurrry mixers consist of an electric motor and power train, a sealed mixing chamber, a sanitary pump, and a control console mounted on a frame. The stationary and rotating blades are capable of blending a premix into a uniform slurry in about one minute, without incorporating air. They were designed to supply a total ingredient preblend to the Oakes Continuous Automatic Mixer.

Figure 25.2. Stationary bowl mixer of 1,600 lb capacity

BATCH MIXERS FOR DOUGH

The mixers to be discussed in this section are bread dough mixers, which are also, of course, generally useful for sweet doughs and many other kinds of doughs, although the type of agitator and the horsepower may have to be adjusted to meet the needs of various types of doughs. There are also many types of mixers that can process bread doughs even though they were designed for other types of bakery products.

There are several possible ways to categorize dough mixers. It is convenient for the purpose of this section to classify them as horizontal dough mixers, planetary vertical mixers, continuous mixers, and others. Each of these types has sub-types. Figure 25.2 shows an example of a horizontal high speed dough mixer (Source: Baker Perkins).

Horizontal Dough Mixers

Many types of mixers can be, and are, used for batch mixing bread dough, but nearly all large wholesale bakeries use high speed horizontal dough mixers for this purpose. These mixers are popular because they have been specifically designed for mixing extensible doughs, and they do this job very well. They are sturdy, some units having been in almost constant use for decades, and they have the additional merit of being fairly versatile. The usual configuration of agitators, consisting of round bars running parallel to the bowl surface, is ideal for stretching, pressing, and folding the dough without tearing it. It is not, however, very efficient in mixing powders, batters, and other materials needing an intense, randomly directed, dispersing action, or doughs that should not be developed, like pie doughs.

Several manufacturers are producing mixers of this type. Whether used to mix sponges, doughs, straight doughs, or liquid ferment doughs, the mixer construction is basically the same. A horizontal mixing bowl, roughly U-shaped in cross section, is mounted on a rigid frame over a compartment enclosing the drive motor and its transmission. A single horizontal agitator shaft passes through the bowl from side to side and is turned by a sprocket and chain drive leading from the transmission. Mixer arms are affixed to two spiders mounted inside the bowl on the agitator shaft. The various mixer models may have 2, 3, or 4 rods attached to these spiders; some of the rods may be free to rotate, but usually they are fixed. One or more of the mixer bars may be angled so as to push dough from one end of the bowl to the other. Some mixers have stationary braker bars or baffles mounted inside the bowl parallel to the agitator shaft to prevent the dough from hanging on to the mixer bars through several rotations and to assist the mixing action in other ways. The axle can be mounted off center so that the free space on one side of the mixer is greater than on the other side; as a result, there is an increased squeezing and pressing action on one side.

The mixer is nearly always fitted with a two-speed motor to permit high and low speed mixing. Timers, or more sophisticated controls, are always included in the circuits, and there is also a provision for jogging, or giving the agitators a partial turn, to assist in throwing the dough out of the chamber during the discharge operation. Bowls and bowl covers can be fabricated of mild steel or stainless steel, the latter being preferred.

The standard agitator configuration described above is specifically intended for high speed mixers used mostly for developing dough. Slow speed horizontal mixers can be equipped with different types of agitator systems. They may even have two sets of axles. Double-arm mixers were formerly called creamers because they were used specifically for batters. They are now sometimes used for stiffer doughs, though heavier drives and motors must be supplied in these cases. Air can be incorporated by agitator arms of this configuration, as distinct from the action of figure-eight type arms. The latter type reduces gluten development and heat buildup. The range of speed in commercial mixers of this type will be from about 14 to 60 rpm, with an average of about 25 rpm. Sigma arm mixers, single- or double-arm, are recommended for cookie doughs, sweet doughs, etc. Figure 25.3 shows four types of horizontal mixers varying in bowl or agitator design.

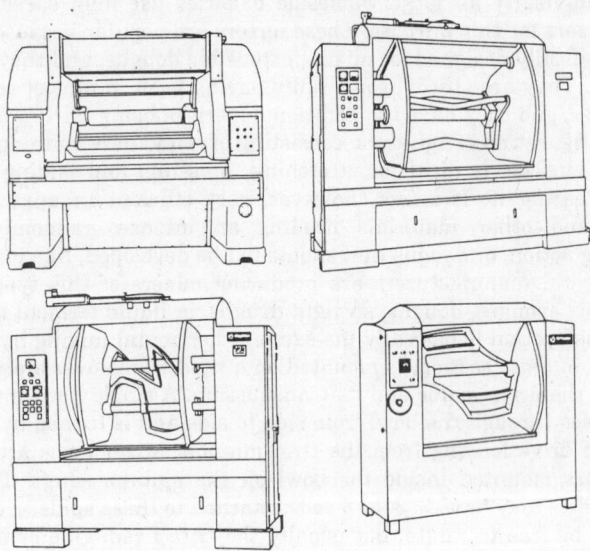

Figure 25.3. Four types of horizontal bowl mixers

The bowl is totally inclosed during the mixing process. Loading of ingredients can be performed by dropping them through ports in the top cover or by manually placing them in the opened bowl. The stationary bowl mixer has a tight fitting front panel that can be moved to expose the interior of the mixing chamber while horizontal tilt-bowl mixers of traditional design discharge their contents by turning the bowl about 90° so that the opening faces the side instead of the top. "Jogging" the agitators throws the dough into a trough or into a chute leading to make-up equipment on the floor below. Sometimes, dough must be cut out or pulled out of the bowl by the operator. The second type has a tight fitting front panel that can be moved to expose the interior of the mixing chamber so ingredients can be put in or dough removed.

A more recent development is the 140° tilt feature which almost turns the bowl upside down so the dough falls out with less operator participation.

The lower front center part of these mixers had to be redesigned so that troughs could be moved directly beneath the bowl or chutes installed there for gravity feed to a lower floor. Mixers are also being made with discharge action to either side, that is, the bowl tilts either backward or forward. Ingredients are put into these mixers through ports in the top cover. Sponges are fed in by tilting the bowl backward (relative to the discharging position) about 45° to open a space between the mixer bowl and the top cover through which a trough elevator can dump the sponge (Booth 1987). Another method is to have a special sponge door at the mixer's top front.

Size is usually specified in terms of the weight of dough the mixer can process. The most common sizes are probably Numbers 8, 10, 13, and 16, the numbers referring to hundredweights of dough. Motor size varies with the capacity of the bowl, and can be modified to the requirements for special doughs such as the generally stiffer pizza, pretzel, and bagel doughs.

It is necessary to have means for reducing the temperature rise that would otherwise accompany dough development, so mixer bowls are usually provided with jackets for either chilled water circulation or direct expansion of refrigerant gas. The direct expansion units seem to be more popular, and are available in sizes up to 25 hp for the largest mixers. In more recent designs, the flat ends of the bowl are also jacketed to achieve even greater heat exchange surface. Older jacket designs moved the refrigerant back and forth through channels of sustantially uniform cross-section. The newer style of expansion jacket has cooling channels that begin with a small cross-sectional area that increases as the coolant flows downstream and continues to evaporate. The abrupt right angle turns are replaced with gently curved radii, allowing the coolant to flow at a maximum rate with minimum pressure drop (Broaddus 1978).

Figure 25.4 shows the integration of a horizontal dough mixer with auxiliary equipment such as a weigh hopper and conveyors leading from a sack dump.

The latest models of batch dough mixers include a microprocessor to control and monitor ingredient feeding, mixing, temperature control, and discharge to an integral dough pump.

Other Types of Batch Mixers

It is possible and practical to mix small batches of yeast-raised dough on planetary-action vertical mixers. These machines are described in more detail later in this chapter. Retail bakers who must rely on one mixer for all products may mix sweet goods, pie doughs, and even bread doughs in such equipment. In a relatively few cases, wholesale bakers mix sweet yeast-raised doughs in batches of up to 200 lbs total weight on the largest size planetary mixers using an agitator called a dough hook. The dough hook is a single curved arm of bronze, aluminum, or stainless steel.

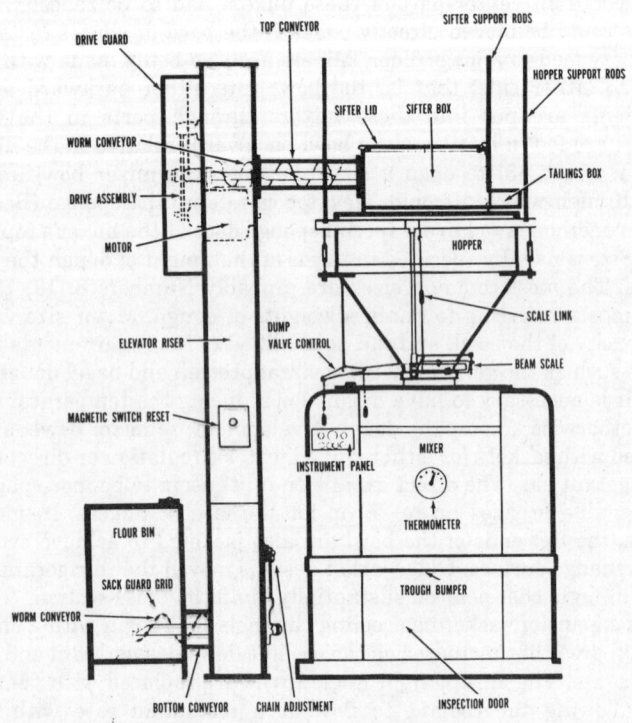

Figure 25.4. Horizontal dough mixer with allied equipment

The power of the agitator drive, which can be as much as 10 hp on the largest vertical mixers, would not be sufficient to drive an agitator with two or more arms at sufficient speed to mix bread dough. The transmission used in the largest cake mixers does not deliver the full horsepower of the motor at low speed. The action of these units is efficient, however, and the removable bowls add convenience.

Spiral kneaders have a rather long history of use in Europe, and a somewhat shorter one in the U.S. The kneading element is a strong stainless steel "spiral" (the geometry is more complex than this term indicates) that rotates rapidly in a fairly shallow and wide bowl. A slow speed is available for initial blending of liquid and dry ingredients. The bowl itself rotates and it has a large protuberance, about a third the height of the bowl, rising from the bottom center. Another version has a heavy rod that is fixed in the mixer head and goes to the center bottom of the bowl as the head is lowered. Advantages of these mixers are said to be short kneading times (3 to 8 minutes), minimal heating, and excellent developing action. Vertical dough mixers with planetary action can be used for high speed dough conditioning.

Much European dough mixer research has been concentrated on the Tweedy mixer and its variants. This machine is used in the Chorleywood bread process, one version of the "no-time" or mechanical dough conditioning procedures. Such systems depend on high speed, short time development of a straight dough that is "conditioned" with oxidizers, reductants, enzymes, and emulsifiers so as to eliminate the need for some of the fermentation and rest periods. Chemical aspects of these methods have been discussed in considerable detail in the chapter on formulas and processes for continuous, semi-continuous, and expedited doughs.

According to a review by Fish (1982), one form of the high-speed mixing complex consists of the mixing chamber, a top frame unit, a microprocessor to control the system, and an auxiliary fermentation and ingredient feed system. The mixer itself consists of a cylindrical bowl having a high speed rotating impact plate at the bottom and a series of baffles on the bowl's interior surface to force the dough onto the agitators. The system mixes to a predetermined energy input as measured by a watt hour meter. Desired input depends upon the formula, weight of dough, etc., but 6 to 7.5 watt hours per pound was required in a typical plant. Mixing times of less than five minutes are obtained. During mixing, a vacuum of ten inches or more is drawn on the chamber by a liquid ring vacuum pump.

Post-mixer Development

The desirability of making the dough's physical characteristics more uniform as it starts into the make-up equipment has led to the introduction of post-mixer devices that knead the dough just before it passes into the divider (Campbell 1979). These devices can themselves be regarded as mixers. Although one of their functions is the completion of the development begun in the horizontal dough mixer, they also reduce the variability resulting from changes in the bulk dough as it waits for processing. By kneading and compressing the dough until it enters the divider, the post-mixer developer substantially eliminates the density changes resulting from dough aging. Current designs are either self-contained devices that mount over divider hoppers and include both pumping and developing units or agitators that work within the divider hopper.

Since dough can be removed from the horizontal mixer before it is fully developed if further development is undergone in the kneading equipment described above, mixing time can usually be decreased and the number of mixer cycles increased.

OTHER SPECIALIZED BATCH MIXERS

Mixing of pie doughs introduces a special problem in that a very slight degree of overmixing results in a tough pie crust. Furthermore, the incorporation of air and the generation of heat are distinctly inadvisable. For these doughs, special mixers have been developed to simulate the folding, pushing, and pressing action of human hands. Generally, two agitator arms are used and they perform a fairly complex movement in a shallow bowl that is constantly rotated. The object is to just make the dough into a cohesive and fairly uniform mass that can be handled effectively in subsequent forming steps. Kneading and rolling to develop gluten are carefully avoided. This special mixer has been found to give the desired results in commercial pie production, and has also been used for many other kinds of doughs. The Artofex mixer was one of the earliest examples of this type, but many other companies are offering very similar designs, with various modifications to the mixing arms, bowl configuration, etc.

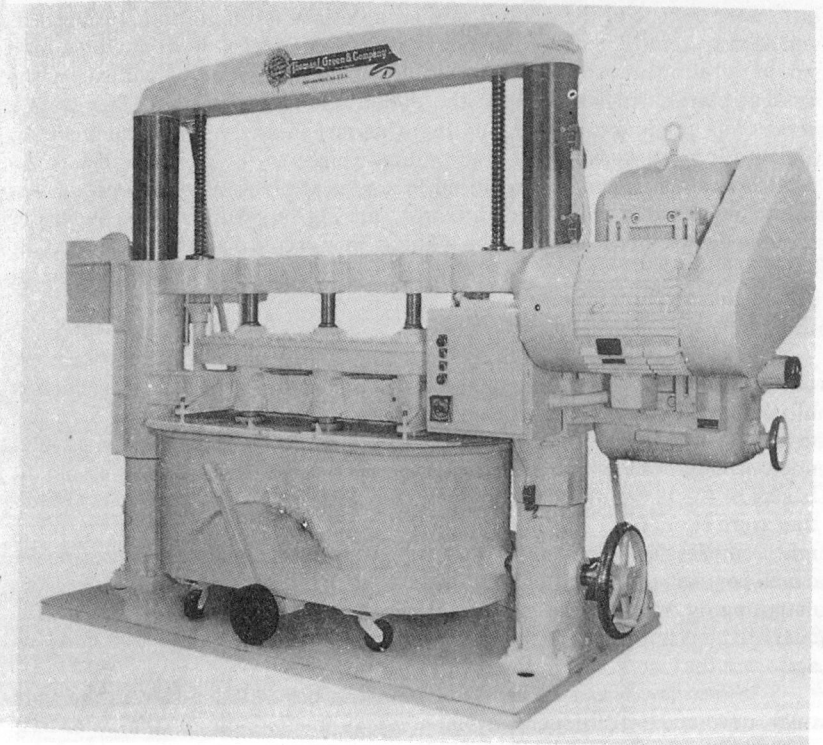

Figure 25.5. A three spindle mixer suitable for cookie doughs.

Cookie and cracker doughs represent a very wide range of properties. Some of these doughs can be mixed more or less well in vertical planetary mixers, horizontal dough mixers, or continuous mixers of various sorts. There are also special mixers that have been designed to mix certain types of cookie or cracker dough more efficiently. The spindle mixer is particularly suitable for cracker sponges, but can be used for heavy cookie doughs. This mixer accepts a transportable dough trough having rounded ends and a flat bottom. The sides of the trough are designed to match the turning of two or three agitator units having vertical shafts and several horizontal mixer blades of somewhat propeller-like configuration. The agitator speed is low and the motor and transmission are designed for high power input. Figure 25.5 illustrates a typical three-spindle mixer (Source: Thomas L. Green Co.)

CONTINUOUS DOUGH MIXERS

Discussions of continuous bread dough mixers in the U.S. generally refer to the complete systems developed by American equipment manufacturers beginning in the 1950s. These systems include machines for scaling, premixing, fermenting, mixing, depositing, and panning. Although the mixer was only one of the novel features of the continuous bread making systems, it is the aspect which will be dealt with in greatest detail in the present discussion.

The mixing system in these continuous lines has two components, the premixer (or incorporator) and the final mixer, or developer. The premixer is essentially a stainless steel screw or auger in a long stainless steel cylindrical housing. Ingredients are delivered to the feed end of this housing in three or more streams, then roughly incorporated into a dough form and discharged under pressure by the screw.

The three streams fed to the screw are (1) liquid ferment (broth, brew, or liquid sponge), (2) liquid shortening, probably containing some emulsifiers, and (3) flour and certain other dry ingredients which have not been added to the liquid ferment. After these ingredient streams have been blended together, they are forced through large stainless steel tubing to the inlet side of a positive displacement gear pump. Because there is some slip in the screw, this force-fed pump is the basic rate-measuring device for the dough production system and it must be kept hydrostatically full. It is not practical to perfectly synchronize all feed rates with the metering pump, so the streams feeding into the screw go through alternating high-low cycles with the high rate time kept constant and the duration of the low speed period varied according to the build-up of material in the feeder.

The metering pump forces the combined ingredients to the developer through a stainless steel tube. This final mixer has an internal cavity that is oval shaped in cross-section, with two counter-rotating double-arc paddle arms extending axially through it. The dough mass enters the cavity near one end and exits near the other. A hinged door at the front of the mixing head can be opened to permit access for cleaning and emergencies.

The dough exits from the developer through an intermittently opened slot that extrudes a dough piece broadside and drops it into a pan below. Extrusion is synchronized with the pan feed conveyor. The developer head will hold only a few gallons of dough, so the average residence time in the mixing chamber will be less than one minute. Mixing action during this short period is so intense, however, that the dough emerges in a homogeneous, full developed condition.

An important advantage claimed for systems using continuous mixers is that more accurate scaling of dough pieces is obtained, as compared to batch systems. This results from all the dough being of precisely the same age as it passes through the extruder cut-off slot. There is no change from old, gassy dough to fresh dough, as in dividers operating on a succession of batches. Another advantage is a labor saving of at least two operators.

Characteristics of continuously processed bread that were at first regarded as important advantages but later came to be regarded as possible disadvantages were the more uniform grain, finer texture, and whiter crumb. These features can be understood as among the results of the mixing action in the continuous developer. The extremely intense, very efficient agitation produces a more uniform mix of all components, including air and carbon dioxide. Since the air is distributed in finer bubbles and there are more bubbles, the total area of the cell walls will be greater and the cell walls themselves will be thinner, that is, the same amount of dough will be spread over a larger area. Therefore, the bread crumb will appear smoother, silkier, and softer. The finer grain is responsible for the whiter-appearing crumb. Finer-grained products always appear whiter, other conditions being equal, because the cells on the cut surface are relatively small and shallow, thus reflecting and refracting liqht more efficiently.

Aside from efficient mixing, an additional cause of grain uniformity in continuously mixed dough is that these mixers process only one physical phase whereas the batch mixer operates throughout its mixing cycle on two phases—the plastic dough phase and the gaseous phase. Continuous mixers function at 50- or 60-lb pressure and are kept hydrostatically full. Since the chamber contains no gas-filled space, new gas is not incorporated into the dough. Therefore, all existing bubbles receive the same dividing and dispersing action in the mixing cycle and are more uniformy distributed at the finish. Much more carbon dioxide is dissolved in the dough's liquid phase at 60 psi than at the atmospheric pressure existing in the batch mixer. In the latter, the agitator constantly draws new, and often large, gas air bubbles into the dough during mixing, and the bubbles enfolded near the end of the process will not be completely dispersed. One result is that bread from batch-mixed dough is generally coarser in grain and the crumb is less uniform that it is in bread made from continuously mixed dough.

The continuous mixing systems discussed above were designed to produce commercial white American bread, which is relatively high in specific volume due to efficient incorporation of gas in the dough and efficient retention of gas in the baking process. In the European market, there is less demand for light, fluffy white bread and, consequently, less need for highly refined gluten development equipment. Continuous bread dough mixers of relatively simple design were developed in Europe to meet their particular needs. Among these were the Strahmann and the Ivarsson mixers.

The Strahmann machine combines premixer and mixer-developer in one unit. The shaft has a plurality of screw-type, paddle-bladed units that are rotated to drive ingredients from the inlet port to the discharge port at the other end. Near the discharge end, the paddle blades are separated along the shaft by perforated baffle plates, mounted concentrically with the shaft but rotating in a direction opposite to the shaft's rotation. The baffles may be provided with a variety of perforations to give the desired developing effect. This mixer gives an intense shearing, cutting, mixing action. The Ivarsson device uses an ingeniously modified horizontal screw agitator to mix, knead, and propel the dough through the cylindrical housing. After it is discharged from the mixer, the dough is proofed and sent through conventional make-up equipment.

Ration development technologists of the U.S. armed forces have, from time to time, tried to develop a portable continuous baking plant that can be used to supply fresh bread to troops in the field. When the author was Chief of the Cereal and General Products Branch of the Quartermaster Food and Container Institute, a continuous mixer was designed for use with a chemically-leavened white bread mix. The mixer was light, compact, and simple so as to better fit it for field use. The dry mix metering feeder was volumetric, and had sufficient accuracy to keep the finished dough within acceptable limits. The premixer was a auger-fed machine that led to a Waukesha type metering pump, and it delivered the roughly mixed dough to the developer-mixer, a device that had many similarities to the developer used in commercial continuous bread plants and operated under 40 to 60 psig pressure. Dough was extruded from the discharge end through a rubber hose directly into pans. Because there was no conventional dough make-up equipment in the military process, variations in the absorption rate were not as critical as they would otherwise have been, so the volumetric dry feeder gave satisfactory accuracy. There were no provisions for cooling the developer chamber, and the dough was delivered much warmer than in a commercial plant. This shortened the baking time, however, and was not a source of major difficulties in the absence of the usual make-up procedures.

MIXERS FOR BATTERS

The mixers that have been discussed up to this point are particularly suitable for mixing yeast-raised doughs made from relatively strong, high gluten content flours. Efficient mixing of cake batters and the like requires an altogether different kind of agitator action. Less energy is needed to mix batters, their viscosity is less than that of the usual dough, and they do not require development, in the sense that a bread dough must be developed. They do require enfolding of air and the subdividing of it into small bubbles. Horizontal dough mixers do not function at all well in mixing fluids of this type. Many unleavened doughs present a still different set of problems, needing to be kept cool and to be mixed without any development.

From the standpoint of their response to mixing, cake batters can be divided into two types: (1) "Shortening" cakes such as layer cakes, pound cakes, etc., and (2) Sponge cakes, inluding conventional sponges, chiffons, and angel food cakes. Generally, the same mixers can can be used for both types; if somewhat different agitation is needed, it can be obtained by using specialized agitators and different speeds. Both batch and continuous mixers can be used for nearly all types of cake batters.

Batch Mixers for Batters

Vertical dough mixers, a class identified by the perpendicular orientation of the mixer shaft, are widely used in the food industry. They are relatively inexpensive, fairly versatile, and can be constructed in a wide range of sizes. A feature common to most vertical mixers is the use of removable bowls. Their other characteristics may be quite diverse—there may be one or more beater shafts, the beater shafts may move in a planetary action or remain stationary, and the designs of the agitators can be varied over a wide range. The types of vertical mixers of chief interest are the planetary mixers capable of preparing most batters and some doughs and often used for adjuncts such as icings, and the spindle mixers commonly found in cookie and cracker factories.

Vertical planetary mixers with removable bowls are used universally for the batch mixing of all types of cake batters. The agitator action is described at "planetary" because the beater has two types of movement: it revolves on its vertical axis at a relatively high speed while this axis is being moved around the inside of the bowl at a relatively slow speed. The latter, or planetary, action is in the opposite direction of the agitator rotation. The combination of motions is very effective in stirring all parts of the bowl's contents and reducing dead spots. When a rubber-edged beater is used, the entire inside surface of the bowl is wiped progressively as the planetary cycle is made. A small area at the bottom of the bowl may remain out of contact with the beater blades, but material in this area is generally picked up as the batter increases in viscosity.

This general type of mixer is produced by several U.S. companies and by manufacturers in several foreign countries. It may be obtained in bowl sizes of 20, 40, 80, 120, 140, 160, and 340 quarts. Even smaller sizes are available for home kitchens, bakery laboratories, etc. Using the usual two-stage addition method for layer cake batters, a 340-qt mixer can complete four 400 to 550 lb batches in an hour. The amount per batch depends largely on the specific volume reached. Whipped type cakes prepared with wire whips (sponge, chiffon, angel food), which may require specific gravities as low as 0.30, require smaller batches.

The larger units can raise the bowls and mixing heads automatically with an auxiliary motor. Bowl hoisting and dumping equipment is available for the largest mixers. Some of these mixers have four geared speeds from low to high, while others have infinitely variable speeds. On a 340-qt mixer of the latter type, the beater speed is continuously variable from 45 rpm to 325 rpm. The planetary action is only 25% as fast as the beater rotation (called a 4:1 precession ratio) in the standard single ration machine. In the dual ratio machine, a selection can be made between 4:1 and 2:1, or the planetary action can be stopped completely to create a vortex facilitating the addition of dry ingredients. Figure 25.6 shows an example of a 340-qt capacity vertical planetary mixer with removal bowl on dolly (Source AMF).

Figure 25.6. Vertical planetary dough mixer

A convenient feature of most planetary mixers is the easy removal and replacement of the agitator element. A large selection of agitators is available, making this machine the most versatile of all mixers in terms of mixing action. The most commonly used mixer elements are probably the dough hook, the wirewhip, and the batter beater. The wirewhip is an assembly of wires, wide at the top and coming to a rounded point at the bottom, designed to give maximum air incorporation and bubble dividing action. The wires are 0.125 to 0.1875 inches in diameter and are set in a pattern designed to give the maximum turbulence. Batter beaters are generally of cast aluminum, though large ones may be formed of stainless steel bars attached to a frame, and they have a shield-shaped outline. Batter beaters used for shortening-type cakes are of either the two-wing or the less common four-wing design. The outer edges of the wings are shaped to match the curvature of the bowl side wall and may have a white rubber insert along their edges for wiping the inside of the bowl. Their construction is strong enough to withstand high starting torque.

Bowls made be fitted with baffles to restrict the swirling motion of batters. This problem is greatest in the large mixers where very thin batters tend to swirl freely unless ridges are placed in the bowl to restrict or redirect the rotation of the liquid. Tinned baffles are available from stock for the largest mixers, along with the smaller diameter whips that are required when baffles are installed. Using a lower planetary ratio, say 2:1, is another way to prevent, or at least minimize, swirling. Bowl covers are available to cut down on ejection of liquids and powders from the bowl.

Old-style horizontal cake mixers, with kneader blades for shortening type cakes and a squirrel cage whip for foam batters have been all but completely replaced by the more efficient and versatile vertical planetary mixers. A batch mixer that gained some popularity for whipping cake batters, especially angel cake batters, is the air pressure whisk. They are comprised essentially of a vertical tank with a pressure-tight lid, and three rows of rod-shaped beaters, two of them powered and one stationary. Their mixing action is intense; the drive unit for a 200-qt bowl is 10 hp. In making angel food cake batter in this device, flour is charged to the mixer from an auxiliary tank, other ingredients are added, the tank is closed, and pressure raised to 5 to 22 psig. A batch of angel food cake batter can reportedly be mixed in 2.5 minutes, or pound cake batter in 1.5 minutes. Superior aeration and better uniformity are claimed. The batter is delivered to the depositer under slight pressure, through a plastic hose.

Wilkinson (1987) points out there are still some types of cakes best made by batch mixing, in spite of the advances in continuous mixing technology. He enumerated the previously known problems of planetary mixers: (1) Scaling of ingredients is not consistently accurate; (2) Mix speeds cannot be controlled accurately; (3) A stagnant film is always left on the side of the bowl, requiring the operator to scrape down the bowl regularly; (4) Design of the mixing bowl leaves an unmixed or poorly mixed residue in the bottom, often resulting in variable top-to-bottom quality; (5) Batch sizes are too small for large-scale production; (6) Sanitation and clean-up are constant problems; (7) Operator safety is a concern; and (8) The entire mixing process is operator dependent.

Wilkinson described a new type of mixer based on traditional planetary mixer principles but with features that give greater control over: (1) Variations in quality of the ingredients; (2) Accuracy in scaling the formula; (3) Time in the mix cycle; (4) Completeness of mixing the batch; (5) Temperature of the final mix; and (6) Attention and skill of the operator. The system includes "complex planetary mixing" together with electronic control systems. Complex planetary mixing refers to (among other changes) the addition of a second tool in the planetary head to give versatility that can't be achieved in simple planetary mixers. For example, a wire whip for foaming can be combined with a cross-beater for development. A tool for constantly scraping the sides is added.

Traditional open-bowl mixing depends on the incorporation of air at atmospheric pressure, making the time and speed of mixing and the type of agitator controlling factors determining the specific gravity of the finished batter. Much greater control over specific gravity can be obtained if the bowl can be pressurized. Achieving this requires some fairly elaborate modifications, but is being done routinely in many plants. The usual practice is to raise the pressure in the bowl to about two atmospheres, or say, 15 psig, during as much of the mix cycle as is necessary to get the predetermined specific volume.

Consideration must be given to the expansion that occurs when pressure is released. In these mixers, the batter would normally be conducted through tubes from the bottom of the pressurized bowl to a depositer. As the batter emerges into an atmospheric pressure environment, whether at the depositer or elsewhere, the higher pressure gas in the bubbles will cause the bubbles to expand very significantly. Some of the bubbles will coalesce or burst, and it is conceivable that the final specific volume could decrease because of these phenomena. The systems having complex planetary agitators, sealed pressurized bowl, and automatically fed ingredients are said to be applicable to sponge cakes, variety cakes of any kind, cremes and fillings, wire-cut cookie doughs, rotary molded cookie doughs, and light pastry doughs. Typical mix time is about one-third to one-half that requi. ed in a regular planetary mixer. From 5 to 8 batches per hour can be produced with most formulas. These systems can be automated for: (1) Delivery of ingredients according to a programmed formula and sequence; (2) Mixing for a predetermined time at a predetermined speed; (3) Adding pressurized air at a given time; and (4) Discharge to the depositer when the mixing cycle is complete.

Continuous Mixers for Batters

Semi-continuous mixing of cake batters was introduced in the U.S. in the mid-1940s. One of the first commercial continuous cake mixing systems was designed around a Votator scraped-surface mixer based on an ice cream freezer machine. Another early system used a modified Oakes marshmallow mixer. In both plants, the mixer operated continuously but was fed with a premix prepared batchwise in a standard batter mixer. About 1950, a truly continuous cake mixing plant based on the Oakes mixer was designed and installed. Since then, other manufacturers have introduced similar mixers.

The Votator mixer consists of one or more horizontal stainless steel cylinders containing axially mounted beater bars that can be set to scrape the inner wall of the cylinder. An outer cylinder is placed concentrically with the mixer tube so that a heat transfer fluid can be circulated through the annular space to heat or cool the batter as it is being mixed. Mixing action is intense, and the machine has the advantage of being operable under relatively high pressures.

The Oakes mixer has a stainless steel mixing chamber consisting of front and back stator halves, round in shape, and a circular rotor mounted between them. Concentric teeth on both inwardly facing stator surfaces mesh with teeth on the rotor. Premix batter is pumped in at the center of the back stator, and is sheared repeatedly as it is forced out around the rotor and from back to the center of the front stator, where it exits. Diameter of the rotor in the largest machine is 14 inches. Rotor speed is continuously variable over a fairly wide range. Only about 3 qt of batter is present in the chamber of the largest mixer at any one time, so that dwell time is very short and power requirements are low.

Air, or other gas, may be injected into the mixer with the other ingredients and distributed uniformly throughout the mass as very small bubbles. The stators are jacketed, allowing coolants to be circulated. Machines with capacities up to 6,000 lb per hr have been offered. There is a lab model with a nominal production rate of 30 to 200 lb per hr.

Figure 25.7. Complete system for continuous mixing of cake batter

The AMF mixer is similar in external appearance to the Oakes, but the mixing head is considerably different. Instead of splitting axially for dismantling, the stator separates radially. The rotor has several rows of teeth on its periphery; these mesh with rows of teeth on the inside of the stator wall. Rotor speed is continuously variable. These mixers are equipped with batter metering pump, air meter, and speed controls. A photo of a system including this mixer is reproduced as Figure 25.7. On the right is a vertical mixer for premixing; from it, premix is fed through a sanitary pump and a surge tank (middle of figure) to the AMF continuous mixer on the left.

The Goodway mixer/foamer has a slightly conical mixing chamber, pyramidal teeth, thermal jackets, and a working pressure of 150 psi. The Fedco mixer has a cylindrical chamber several inches long with hundreds of square-tipped teeth; it incloses a cylindrical rotor having many teeth on its periphery. Flow of product is straight through the annular space.

The intense shear applied to batter in mixing heads of this design is sufficient to emulsify air and shortening in a complete formula blend. Conventional batch mixers often require that the water be kept back until the shortening has been creamed with some of the dry ingredients. Their principal advantage, however, lies in the continuous mixer's unique ability to produce highly aerated batters such as angel cake batter from a rough premix. Air or inert gas is metered into the mixer head at a calculated rate. If the goal is to produce a foamed batter with a final specific gravity of about 0.25, the proportion would be three standard volumes of air to one of batter.

Continuous batter mixers can be incorporated into completely continuous systems if production schedules warrant, as in plants making a only a few varieties, and these in long unbroken runs. In such plants, liquid ingredients and plasticized shortening are premixed in vertical tanks equipped with high speed propeller agitators. The resultant emulsion is metered into an open vortex-type premixer to which the flour is fed by a gravimetric feeder. The premixer forms a slurry which is metered into the continuous mixer along with a stream of air.

Cake batter is much easier than bread dough to transfer through pumps, pipes, valves, and meters so that engineering for continuous production is easier for a cake plant than for a bread bakery. The economics of cake manufacture is such that expenditure of a large amount of money for continuous mixing equipment may not be warranted, however, particularly for small- to medium-size plants handling a large number of different formulas.

An example of a continuous mixing plant for cake batter was described by Shannon (1971). A slurry is prepared in a planetary mixer equipped with a valved mixing bowl of 340 qt capacity. When the batch is completely mixed, the valve is opened so the slurry can be pumped into a holding tank. From the holding tank, the slurry is fed to the continuous mixer at the desired rate. The continuous mixer (in this case, a rotor-stator unit) is provided with a valve that admits compressed air at the rate necessary to achieve a predetermined specific volume. A back pressure valve is adjusted to retain the batter in the continuous mixer chamber until it has been fully processed, as measured by specific volume or some other property. From the continuous mixer, finished batter is fed to the depositor.

Particulate ingredients such as nut pieces, chocolate chips, and raisins cause severe difficulties in continuous mix systems. The usual solution is to by-pass the continuous mixer and feed particles into the tube leading to the depositor at a rate consistent with formula requirements.

BIBLIOGRAPHY

AHLERT, D., BOERT, K., and MAISS, A. 1988. Method and apparatus for preparing dough. U.S. Pat. 4,766,766

ANON. 1987A. Mrs. Baird's bread and buns. DFI News *9*, No. 2, 2-6

ANON. 1987B. The Basics of Scraped Surface Heat Exchange. APV Crepaco, Chicago, IL

BARON, D. 1983. Dough temperature control systems. Proc. Am. Soc. Bakery Engineers *1983*, 100-105

BONAVIA, W. 1967. Techniques, operation, and engineering aspects of continuous production of cake batter. Proc. Am. Soc. Bakery Engineers *1967*, 301-307

BOOTH, M. D. 1987. Automated high volume dough mixing. Proc. Am. Soc. Bakery Engineers *1987*, 132-144

BROADDUS, M. R., JR. 1978. Soft roll equipment. Proc. Am. Soc. Bakery Engineers *1978*, 122-132

CAMPBELL, S. P. 1979. Mechanical dough conditioning—new systems. Proc. Am. Soc. Bakery Engineers *1979*, 175-185

CHEN, T-A. 1990. Cake manufacturing machine. U.S. Pat. 4,955,288

FISH, A. R. 1982. High speed dough development. Proc. Am. Soc. Bakery Engineers *1982*, 130-142

FISCHER, H. A., and GRUTTER, W. G. 1988. Mixer for baking doughs and the like. U.S. Pat. 4,767,214

JACKEL, S. S. 1975. Directions for future continuous mix. Cereal Foods World *20*, 314-316, 328

MATZ, S. A. 1989. Equipment for Bakers. Pan-Tech International, Inc., McAllen, TX

OLDSHUE, J. Y. 1983. Fluid Mixing Technology. McGraw-Hill Publications, New York

PIERCE, W. L. 1974. Pumping of bread and bun doughs. Proc. Am. Soc. Bakery Engineers *1974*, 92-99

SHANNON, T. A. 1971. A look at cake production by the continuous mixing process—equipment, procedures, and formulas. Proc. Am. Soc. Bakery Engineers *1971*, 138-144

SHIMAMURA, A. 1989. Process for preparing yeast raised doughnuts. U.S. Pat. 4,882,178

SPOONER, T. F. 1989. New approaches to continuous mixing. Baking & Snack Systems *11*, No. 8, 32, 34, 36, 39-40

SPOONER, T. F. 1991. Focus on mixing. Baking & Snack *13*, No. 1, 26-29

VALENTINO, F., BETTS, D. E., and ALESCH, E. A. 1989. Dough processing apparatus. U.S. Pat. 4,883,361

VALENTYNE, P. H. 1959. Practical aspects of heat balance in dough mixing. Bakers Digest *33*, No. 1, 40-44

WILKINSON, G. 1987. Cake mixing technology. Proc. Am. Soc. Bakery Engineers *1987*, 100-106

chapter twenty-six

DIVIDING, ROUNDING, SHEETING, AND LAMINATING

INTRODUCTION

This chapter will include discussions of the equipment involved in manipulating doughs after they leave the mixer and before they begin the forming process that defines the final product. The devices in question cut the dough mass into pieces that will become one unit of the final product, they round those pieces into balls that can retain gas and form an internal structure leading to good crumb and texture in the finished product, they form sheets that can be cut, rolled up, or otherwise subjected to shaping operations, and they can, if necessary, laminate the sheets with interleavings of fat or other material so as to further improve the internal structure of the baked item. Devices that form the final shape are, with a few exceptions, not included here but will be covered in a later chapter.

DIVIDERS

The function of dividers is to separate a dough mass of variable or indeterminate size into many smaller pieces of identical weight. In most, but not all, cases, the dough piece emerging from a divider will be carried through all subsequent processing steps as a single unit until it finally emerges from the oven as one finished product. Of course, the weight of the finished product will not be the same as the weight of the raw dough because volatile substances are lost through evolution of gases formed in fermentation reactions and evaporation of water and other liquids in the oven and elsewhere. This weight loss is offset to a slight extent by the accumulation of dusting flour picked up by the dough pieces as they travel through the make-up equipment.

Separating bread and roll dough into pieces of uniform weight is an operation that presents unusually difficult problems. Because of the elastic, sticky, cohesive nature of dough, it is unsuitable for metering by gravimetric procedures, and the constantly varying density resulting from fermentation interferes with accurate volumetric measurements. Of the two approaches, volumetric measuring has proven to be the more practical and economical. Campbell (1981) describes the four commonly used techniques of dough dividing as hand scaling, die or press methods, ram/shear/block dividers, and vacuum-assisted rotating drum and piston dividers. An additional method, extrusion dividing, has been developed and is being used commercially.

How Dividers Work

At the present time, all commercial dough dividers use some form of volumetric scaling. The principle is not much different from that used by the master baker working at the bench when he rolls a large chunk of dough into a long cylinder of uniform diameter and then cuts off pieces of uniform length so as to get multiple dough pieces of the desired weight. Experienced bakers can achieve a remarkable degree of accuracy with this type of scaling. The same volumetric principle is relied upon when the baker sheets out a dough, by means of a rolling pin or other device, to form a strip of uniform thickness, perhaps using rails to hold the rolling pin at a predetermined distance above the table, and then cuts the sheet with a device having one or more cavities of known (or at least, uniform) dimensions. Using a doughnut cutter on a sheet of dough is an example of the latter process.

The simplest type of automatic divider is the bench-top roll divider which separates a large dough piece into, typically, 18 or 36 portions of more or less equal weight, by pressing the dough into a disc of uniform thickness and then forcing through the dough a cutting head actuated by a spring and lever assembly. In brief, the process is to place a weighed amount of dough, more or less flattened out, onto the divider platen, lower a slotted pressure plate that forces the dough lump into a disc of uniform thickness, then release the knives which by spring action cut through the sheet. The knives have been so placed by the manufacturer that they cut out equal areas (and equal volumes) of the dough. More elaborate models are powered by a hydraulic system that receives its energy from a motorized pump. These bun dividers have the advantage that they quickly process all the dough in one small batch so that variations in density due to fermentation are not much of a problem. If the mixer delivers a quantity of dough requiring many divider operations to completely process it, this advantage no longer exists.

Some models of these bun dividers have a rounding mechanism built into the equipment. After the pieces are cut, the molding table or platen is driven by eccentrically-mounted wheels which give it a combined spiral and circular motion. Each dough piece remains in the chamber formed by the lowered cutter blades. As the table rotates, the upper or dividing disc is simultaneously lifted to the limit setting so that enough space is allowed for the height increase as the dough pieces become rounded. A recent invention (Beatty 1991) improves the ease of disassembly, making it simpler to clean these divider-rounders.

In traditional large-scale methods of bread manufacture, a mixer load of dough is placed in a trough that is transported to the divider area or to the floor above the divider. If a trough elevator is present, the trough is rolled into its brackets, then the elevator motor is started, first raising the trough above the divider then turning it through an angle of more than 90° to dump the dough into a hopper above the divider. If the troughs are on the floor above the divider room, a chute opening in the floor allows the dough to drop into the hopper. Doughs can also be pumped from the trough or from a post-mixer developer to the hopper.

Bread dough dividers currently available from equipment suppliers are based on one of the following systems: (1) Dough is forced into a pocket of known dimensions and the excess dough is sheared off, or (2) A cylinder of dough is extruded from an orifice at a steady rate and pieces of uniform length are cut off. The first method is the basis for most of the bread dough dividers in use today (see Figure 26.1), while the extrusion method is used in continuous bread plants and is also the basis of a few recently developed machines suitable for batch plants.

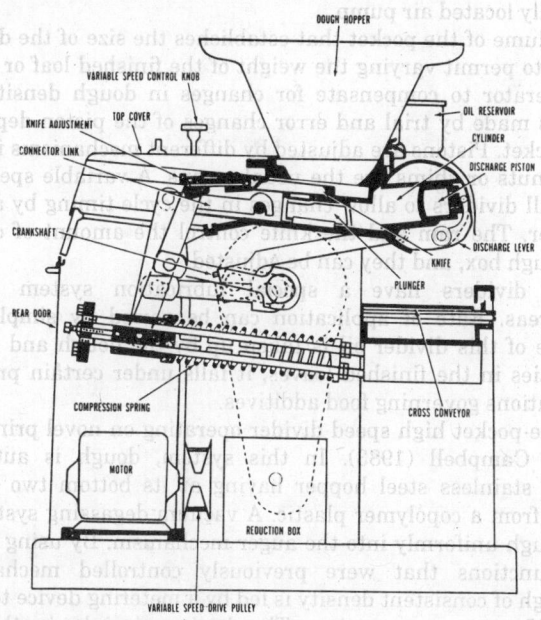

Figure 26.1. Schematic diagram of a common type of dough divider

In one of the most common dividers, the force of atmospheric pressure and the weight of the overlying dough mass force dough from a hopper into a compression chamber. At the start of the cycle, a knife moves horizontally to cut off a piece of dough near the hopper bottom. Next the ram, or piston, moves forward, pressing the severed dough piece into one or more chambers contained in a rotatable cylinder. At the end of the ram stroke, the cylinder turns, cutting off the excess dough. Each cavity will then be filled with a predetermined volume of dough that should weigh within the limits desired for the piece. Finally, the discharge lever ejects the measured dough piece on to a conveyor leading to the rounder. In the return cycle, the emptied cylinder is rotated back to its original position so that the now empty cavities face the compression chamber. The knife and compression piston withdraw, allow more dough to be drawn into the cavity by suction and gravity, and the cycle continues as before.

Commercial models have from two to eight pockets and operate at speeds up to 25 strokes per minute. The scaling range is from about 6 to 36 oz, and motors up to 7.5 hp are used.

In some dividers, a reciprocating division box replaces the rotating cylinder. In these machines, the box containing the pockets is forced downward after they are filled, shearing off the excess dough as a result of the movement of the pockets past the chamber edge. A recent invention (Schiek 1988) establishes a vacuum in the dough measuring area by means of an externally located air pump.

The volume of the pocket that establishes the size of the dough piece is adjustable to permit varying the weight of the finished loaf or roll and to allow the operator to compensate for changes in dough density. Volume adjustment is made by trial and error changes of the piston depth in each individual pocket. Pistons are adjusted by different mechanisms in different models; lock nuts or shims are the usual means. A variable speed drive is provided on all dividers to allow changes in the cycle timing by adjusting a wheel or lever. The ram and the knife control the amount of dough that enters the dough box, and they can be adjusted.

Dough dividers have a special lubrication system for dough contacting areas. Rate of application can be varied by simple controls. Because some of this divider oil is taken up by the dough and appears in small quantities in the finished loaves, it falls under certain provisions of federal regulations governing food additives.

A single-pocket high speed divider operating on novel principles was described by Campbell (1983). In this system, dough is automatically pumped to a stainless steel hopper having at its bottom two interfering augers made from a copolymer plastic. A vacuum degassing system assists in loading dough uniformly into the auger mechanism. By using electronics to control functions that were previously controlled mechanically, a degassed dough of consistent density is fed by a metering device to an orifice where a knife severs a portion. The basic principle is the familiar combination of extrusion at a fixed rate and cut-off at fixed (but variable) intervals which is so widely used in the plastics and snack food industries. Scaling accuracy is said to be in the range of plus or minus 3 grams. Dough piece sizes of 6 to 52 oz are said to be feasible. This divider uses neither dusting flour nor divider oil, and it incorporates a clean-in-place system.

Cummins (1990) describes an extrusion-type divider pumps dough through a manifold leading to several orifices. The output from each orifice can be controlled by a separate throttling valve so the rate can be kept very uniform at all ports. The cut-off mechanism uses a plastic knife mounted on a link mechanism driven by a continuous constant speed drive shaft.

Figure 26.2 is a process diagram for a rotary (extrusion) dough divider (Source: AMF).

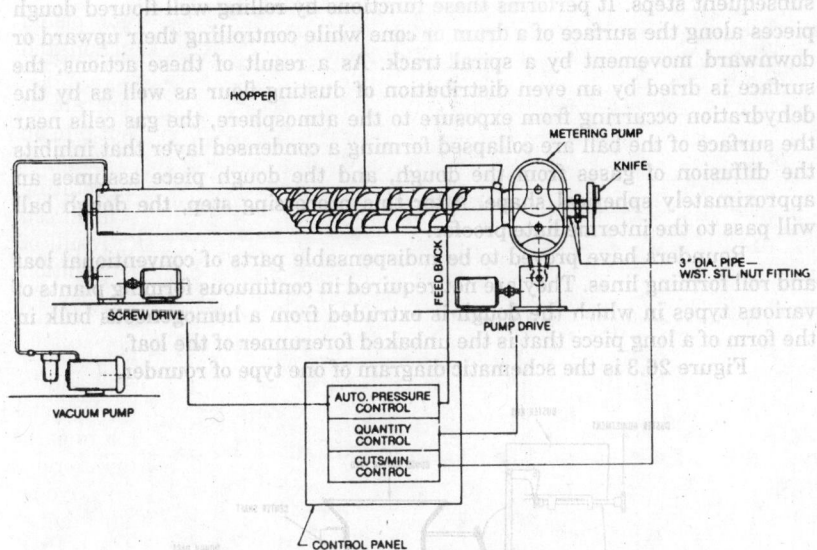

Figure 26.2. Process diagram of rotary dough divider

A new design of positive pressure dough divider has been patented by Jones *et al.* (1985). This machine consists of a dough hopper, a pair of sheeting rolls beneath the hopper, and a transfer chute through which the dough passes to a measuring chamber in a rotating metal wheel. The metal wheel, containing the cylindrical chamber, rotates slowly while the dough is entering the chamber, then rapidly moves to the discharge position. The measuring chamber is provided with a piston, that, in the usual fashion for dividers, moves downward to create suction when it is brought into contact with the dough, then moves in the opposite direction to discharge the dough piece as the wheel turns about 180°. The powered sheeting, or pressurizing, rollers are of relatively large diameter to provide adequate flow of dough through the passage to the measuring chamber while at the same time maintaining good dough quality.

ROUNDERS

When dough pieces leave the divider, they are irregular in shape with cut surfaces that are sticky and from which gas can readily diffuse. Their gluten structure is somewhat disoriented and so is not in suitable condition for molding. It is the function of the rounder to close these cut surfaces, giving the dough piece a smooth and dry exterior and forming a relatively thick and continuous skin around the piece. The rounder also re-orients the gluten structure and forms the dough into a ball for easier handling in subsequent steps. It performs these functions by rolling well-floured dough pieces along the surface of a drum or cone while controlling their upward or downward movement by a spiral track. As a result of these actions, the surface is dried by an even distribution of dusting flour as well as by the dehydration occurring from exposure to the atmosphere, the gas cells near the surface of the ball are collapsed forming a condensed layer that inhibits the diffusion of gases from the dough, and the dough piece assumes an approximately spherical shape. After this processing step, the dough ball will pass to the intermediate proofer.

Rounders have proved to be indispensable parts of conventional loaf and roll forming lines. They are not required in continuous forming plants of various types in which the dough is extruded from a homogeneous bulk in the form of a long piece that is the unbaked forerunner of the loaf.

Figure 26.3 is the schematic diagram of one type of rounder.

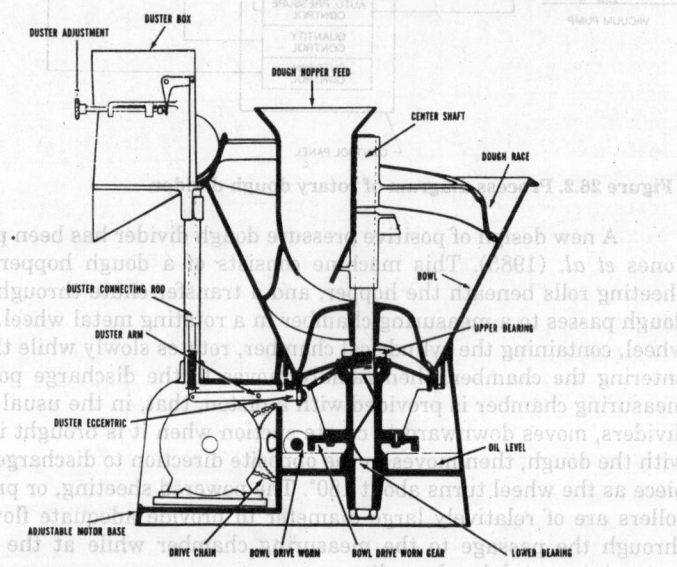

Figure 26.3. Schematic diagram of a bowl-type rounder

Types of Rounders

There are several models of rounders being offered for retail bakeries. Some of these are combined with simple, small dividers. One example is described in the divider section. Another is the Eberhardt rounding system, said to have outputs up to 1,000 lb per hr of pieces from 4 oz to 5 lb in weight. The rounder consists of a rotating center portion, circular in shape but having sides slanted inward, and an outer portion slanted slightly outward. These two parts create a circular channel that is about twice as wide at the top as at the bottom. The inner drum rotates off-center so that a dough piece placed in the channel is rolled and kneaded until it forms a ball.

Belt-type rounders are used in some of the most successful designs of roll and bun forming equipment. These rounders consist essentially of a fabric conveyor belt that moves small dough pieces under long metal guides having a rounded under surface. The guides are slanted with respect to the direction of belt travel. The combination of the forward motion imparted by the belt and the sidewise force exerted by the stationary guide causes the dough piece to roll. Because the dough adheres slightly to the belt, the surface of the dough is pulled into a relatively smooth outer layer. As a result of these combined actions, a piece of approximately ball shape is formed, very suitable for later molding into some sort of fancy bread roll or for proofing and baking without further forming to yield plain hamburger rolls or the like. These systems are rather sensitive to dough consistency, but when the formula is properly adjusted, they are very efficient. Registering the dough pieces as they come onto the belt is necessary to avoid doubles, which are very disruptive to efficient processing. This type of equipment has generally been regarded as being more suitable for dough pieces smaller than about 9 oz in weight and 4 inches in diameter than for loaf sizes, but there are now being offered belt-type rounders that can process pieces from 13 to 29 oz. They use tunnels constructed of Teflon, instead of the simple guides used on roll machines, and these channels are capable of being changed in curvature in two dimensions.

A type of rounder said to uniformly round large dough pieces and greatly improve registration of the emerging balls was invented by Voegtlin (1988). The rounding action is performed by a belt mechanism with a shaping channel not unlike the bun rounders described above.

Other types of rounders more suitable for buns than for loaves are based on cups that are moved in a circular motion above a fabric conveyor belt. The hand action used by bakers for rounding dough pieces on a bench top is duplicated quite closely by these machines. The cups are roughly hemispherical and may be made of Teflon or lined with Teflon to prevent sticking. They often have ridges radiating from the top center of the inside to the edge to give the cup a better grasp of the dough piece. Several cups are attached to a support extending across the belt, and several of these supports are attached to a power source that moves the whole assemblage in a circular pattern. Such rounders must be closely coordinated with the divider or with some other registering system so that the dough pieces are deposited on the conveyor belt in the exact positions which will later be covered by the cups. This need for precise positioning is the main drawback to the method, since the rounding itself is a gentle, non-destructive action applicable to doughs having a wide range of rheological properties.

Rounders used in medium to large commercial bakeries with conventional loaf bread equipment may conveniently be classified as bowl-, umbrella-, or drum-type. The bowl variety consists of a rotatable cone-shaped bowl around the interior of which is placed a stationary spiral track or "race." Dough pieces on the conveyor leading from the divider fall into the feed hopper of the rounder and then drop to the bottom of the rotating bowl. The chunks of dough are tumbled and rolled along the race as they attempt to follow the rotation of the bowl. Finally, the rounded pieces emerge from the top of the bowl and are discharged onto the belt leading to the intermediate proofer.

A second widely used type of rounder is the umbrella or inverted cone style (see Figure 26.4). These machines differ from the preceding kind in that the dough piece is carried around the outside surface of a cone that has its apex facing upwards. Because the dough first contacts the rounder cone at its largest diameter, its initial movement is more rapid than it would be in a bowl-type rounder. Opinions vary as to the relative merits of the two designs, but it can be said with certainty that many examples of both types have been performing satisfactorily for many years.

Figure 26.4. Race and molding surface of an umbrella-type rounder

A third type of rounder differs from the bowl and umbrella designs in that the cone segment has very little slope to its sides, i.e., the sides are almost vertical. Dough pieces enter a curved raceway near the bottom of the drum. It is obvious that the ball travels at a more uniform rate in these machines than in the other two types. This may or may not be a good thing. Among the advantages claimed for the drum rounders are that they require less floor space, allowing greater latitude in positioning the machine with respect to other make-up equipment. Not as many of these units as of the other two varieties are to be seen in bakeries.

A fourth style of rounder has concave sides. The round dough race is constructed in two or more sections on different planes. The dough pieces are fed in at the top, move through the sections of the dough race, and finally are discharged into the feed chute of the intermediate proofer.

In addition to their shape, rounding machines may vary in the texture or composition of the rotating surface, in the means provided for adjusting the relationship of the dough race to the drum or cone, in the method of applying dusting flour, etc. The rotating surface is usually corrugated vertically or horizontally to give it a better grip on the dough piece, but the design and size of the ribs varies considerably among manufacturers. The surface may be waxed or it may be coated with a plastic such as Teflon to reduce sticking. A device to shunt aside oversize dough pieces (doubles) is frequently positioned at the exit chute.

Still another type of rounder, usually combined with divider means for making bun-size dough shapes, is the drum rounder (sometimes the "third type" described above is also called a drum rounder, but its action is quite different). This consists of two drums arranged concentrically, one within the other and turnable about a common horizontal axis. The outer drum contains cavities for the dough pieces and the inner drum acts as the working surface by performing revolving movements. Generally, the circular recesses are formed as step-like concentric rings with a saw-tooth profile for securing adherence of the dough. The entire surface of the inner drum is fluted or corrugated. Even so, firm dough pieces with relatively dry surfaces may not be rounded properly on these devices, though they perform adequately with soft, moist dough pieces. Muller (1988) described an improved design for the circular cavity, consisting of a broken irregular formation in the working surface of the group of recesses, said to give improved rounding of firm, dry doughs.

SHEETERS

There are many operations in bakeries that require dough to be reduced in thickness and/or shaped into a sheet, web, or strip of relatively uniform thickness, either for the purpose of cutting from the sheet many pieces of constant linear dimensions and weight or for preparing the sheet for further manipulations, such as interleaving with fat, topping with some sort of adjunct, or curling into a cylinder. The machines performing these operations are called dough brakes, sheeting rollers, or gauge rolls and always consist of some combination of rollers designed for pressing dough pieces into thinner layers without tearing them. Sheeters and gauge rolls have more similarities than differences, and will be discussed together in this section. Pizza presses and the like, which compress dough pieces without using rollers, will be treated in the chapter on dough forming equipment.

Dough Brakes

Many doughs processed in bakeries and cracker plants go through multiple sheeting and folding steps before being made up into the final product shapes. In smaller factories, this can be done on manually-operated dough brakes. These machines are quite simple in principle, being a set of horizontal steel cylinders with provisions made for adjusting the clearance between them, and a return conveying means (belt or roller) for bringing the sheeted dough back to the operator. Dough brakes are generally stronger in construction than the usual sheeting rolls. They have been used for conditioning (developing) bread dough as well as for laminating puff pastry and cracker doughs. Their action can be characterized as "rough," and not suitable for preparing strips of uniform thickness and width. Figure 26.5 shows the working parts of one type of dough brake.

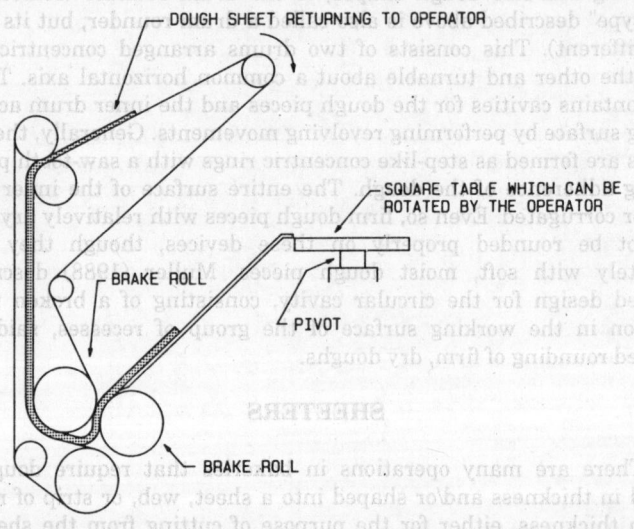

Figure 26.5. Working parts of one kind of dough brake

The cylinders of dough brakes rotate rapidly compared to regular types of reduction rolls and may be, for example, of 8 inches diameter and 20 or 26 inches wide. They are mounted on strong springs. A set of plates and chutes (and sometimes belts) is provided for guiding the dough into and out of the rolls. The brakes in most cases include automatic return devices that bring the dough back in front of the operator for the next pass. In one design, a revolving plate in front of the operator simplifies the tasks of folding the strip and turning it 90° for the next sheeting step. The job of operating a dough brake is both arduous and dangerous. Guard rails in front of the rolls as well as braking or reversing switches and other safety devices are essential parts of this equipment.

Sheeting Rollers

Sheeting rollers are used to change the dimensions of a dough sheet, making it thinner, wider, and longer. They can also be used to laminate dough, with or without the addition of interleaving material. Sheeting is also useful for combining strips of dough from end to end, so that a continuous web is presented to the next processing equipment. Their action is slower and more gentle than that of the dough brake. In the simplest form, sheeting rollers and gauge rollers consist of a pair of metal cylinders, either horizontally or vertically aligned, with provisions made for adjusting the separation ("gap") between them. Their axles are always parallel. A conveyor belt brings the dough piece into the nip of the rollers at a constant, usually adjustable, rate and a take-away conveyor removes the sheeted dough at a faster rate consistent with the amount of extension resulting from the rollers' stretching action. Dusting flour is often applied just before the dough enters the gap.

Cylinders may be made of stainless steel, chrome-plated metal, or other metals, and they may be Teflon-coated or covered with Teflon sleeves to improve their handling of sticky doughs. They may be chilled or warmed by fluids circulated internally, although this is not often done in conventional dough handling systems.

The web of dough is almost always delivered to the gap by a conveyor belt and the thinned down sheet is taken away by another belt. It is preferable to have the speeds of the rollers and delivery and receiving belts synchronized, though, of course, this does not mean their surfaces should move at the same velocity. Whether preset or manually adjusted, the absolute and relative speeds of these pieces of equipment are critical to proper performance. Usually, the sheeted dough web falls free a few inches before it contacts the offtake belt, and the dough is allowed to form wrinkles across its width at this point so it can relax somewhat from the punishment of reduction. If too much relaxation is permitted, however, there is some risk the dough will be carried under the roller with very messy consequences. In other cases, the offtake conveyor may be speeded up slightly to stretch the dough, preventing unwanted contraction and thickening.

Large diameter roll sets require smaller gaps than smaller rolls to achieve the same thickness reduction; they reduce the dough more gradually and so abuse the dough less (Levine 1985). Production-size rolls also impart much more energy to the dough than do the smaller diameter rolls commonly used in the pilot plant or laboratory. Dough rheological behavior is best regarded as that of a very viscous liquid instead of a solid. The primary mechanism associated with deformation of dough between rollers is shear development, and the main factor affecting performance is not the absolute compression ratio, but the length of dough contact and spacing and speed of the rolls. When sheeting lines are being designed, it is important to take into account the deflection of the mechanical components (rollers, shafts, bearings, and frames), which can be very significant to results when dealing with very thin products such as flatbreads and tortillas.

Efficiency of sheeter performance is related to roller speed relative to dough velocity, diameter of the rollers, surface texture of the rollers, width of the gap between them, rheology of the formula being processed, and the amount of dusting flour that is applied.

Sheeting rollers tend to develop the dough by causing a rearrangement of the gluten molecules (Levine 1985 and 1987; Feillet et al. 1975) that increases with the number of passes and with reduction in roll clearance. The desirability of this change depends on the state of the dough as it enters the sheeting system. Dough that is already well conditioned may be overdeveloped by repeated sheeting and folding, and will then start to break down, tearing at the edges and top surface and becoming sticky. Stenvert et al. (1979) describe the use of dough rollers for development and point out that sheeting equipment is very efficient in terms of energy consumption, requiring only 10% to 15% of the net energy consumed by a high speed mixer. Dough developed by sheeting can produce bread comparable to that produced by the Chorleywood bread process using a Tweedy intensive mixer.

When used as the principal means of dough development, roller processing can yield bread of exceptionally fine texture. In passing dough through rollers, one aim is to remove all large gas bubbles. This requires repeated sheeting and folding steps. Only doughs with good resistance to overdevelopment are able to tolerate the work input required to remove excess fermentation gases and still produce satisfactory bread.

The strip coming from the sheeting roller may be carried by a straight line conveyor leading to the next operation or it may be folded or rolled into a piece of size convenient for hand carrying to the next machine or to a retarding room. Simple devices are available for rolling strips on a cylinder of small diameter which may be picked up and carried to the next station (Siegenthaler 1990). Where multiple sheeting steps are required, with or without intervening folding steps, reversible sheeters may be used to avoid transferring the dough between each step.

Their versatility makes reversible sheeters practical for medium-sized shops that produce several different kinds of laminated products such as Danish, puff pastry, and snack crackers. Medium-duty equipment with automatic programming of the reduction steps can be obtained. A large conveyor surface permits folding and turning of the dough piece without removing it from the machine. Two operators can process 1,000 lb of dough per hour, giving each piece 3 or 4 three-folds. By proper adjustment of piece dimensions and the folding procedure, pieces can be finished off as long thick strips suitable for feeding through the reduction rollers on a forming line. For mass production of puff pastry and Danish doughs, and for the efficient running of all saltine lines, automatic laminaters are required. These will be discussed in a subsequent section.

Other Sheeting Devices

Cross-rollers.—Sheeting rolls are disposed transversely with respect to the movement of the strip of dough, consequently they stretch the dough mainly in a lengthwise direction. Of course, some sidewise extension also takes place, but this is relatively minor and is restricted by the width of the rollers. The repeated lengthwise stretching tends to introduce tension that may cause failure of the dough structure or distortion of the dough piece when it is baked. A device that may, in some cases, alleviate this problem is the cross-roller. It consists of a relatively small cylinder having its axle parallel to the movement of the dough, and associated machinery for carrying the roller back and forth fairly rapidly over the dough piece. As a result, the strip of dough is thinned and widened. The thinning is generally not as effective as sheeting rollers because the bottom thinning surface is the conveyor belt and the pressure that can be exerted is much less than achievable with sheeting rollers.

Dough "stretchers".—Dough stretchers or sheeters of the general type described by Hayashi (1986, also Anon. 1987) have come into use in recent years as a means of obtaining rapid thinning of dough without subjecting the sheet to excessive stress. These devices consist of groups of rollers of small diameter which rotate on their axes while simultaneously being carried on an oval or circular path above the dough while the dough is carried on a series of conveyors operating at increasing speeds. At the bottom of their circuit, they contact the dough and "massage" it to a thinner dimension by their repeated wiping and rolling action which is accentuated by the differential conveyor speeds. The manufacturers state that a device of this type only "500 mm long accomplishes the work done by a machine 10 meters or more in length and equipped with rollers 100 mm long and combined parallel in 70 stages." There is probably a natural excess of parental enthusiasm in this comparison, but it is generally agreed that such devices do accomplish rapid reduction in thickness of certain types of doughs. They have been combined with a laminator to form puff pastry doughs.

The beater sheeter.—A device patented by Vinas I Nigueroles (1989) combines dough lumps into a continuous strip and reduces the thickness of the strip, in part by a beating action applied to the strip by a short conveyor belt affixed to a reciprocating carriage above the strip. This device is said to be suitable for sheeting puff pastry doughs.

LAMINATERS

For many years, the standard equipment for laminating doughs was the hand-fed high-speed dough brake. A given quantity of dough, usually 40 lb or more, was formed into a thick strip on the brake and then folded into two, three, or four layers. If desired, an interleaving material such as shortening could be applied to the strip by hand and the dough folded to inclose it before additional folding and sheeting steps were applied. Additional materials were not applied to soda cracker doughs, the layer effect observed in the finished product being obtained solely from the orientation established in the dough by braking, plus some effect from the dusting flour. On the other hand, cream cracker procedures called for the application of a flour-shortening mixture between the layers.

The labor intensive and somewhat dangerous dough brake operation has been superseded almost everywhere in the world by automatic lamination, with resultant lowered costs, improved safety, and greater control. Cracker factories use highly specialized laminating equipment integrated into the production line, while Danish pastry, puff pastry, and croissant manufacturers can choose more versatile but somewhat less efficient machines for performing the shortening application and laminating steps.

Laminating Danish and Puff Pastry Doughs

If a layered dough or roll-in dough is to be prepared, as for puff pastry or Danish pastry, repeated sheeting and folding of the dough and fat combination is required. Dough brakes and reversible sheeters, which have been used for preparing dough and fat laminations for many years, have been described previously. Large scale operations will, however, generally use automatic laminators, which eliminate practically all the manual labor needed for operating dough brakes and reversible sheeters. To briefly recapitulate the laminating process used to make Danish and puff pastry, the following steps are required: (1) A dough, preferably undermixed but of good stability (resistant to breakdown when overmixed) is sheeted out to give a fairly thick layer; (2) fat, in either sheets or chunks, is applied to part of the dough layer; (3) the part of the dough sheet that is not covered with fat is folded over the fat; (4) the folded fat and dough combination is again sheeted out and folded (usually in three or four layers); and (5) the folded fat and dough combination is again sheeted out and folded, often after a rest period. Step 5 is repeated any number of times as necessary to yield the type and quality of product wanted by the baker. Usually, a rest period in the refrigerator is given to the dough piece after each sheeting and folding operation so that the dough can relax and the fat can congeal.

Three types of automatic laminators are used for quantity production of Danish pastry. In one version, dough is extruded in two continuous belts with a layer of shortening extruded between them. This three-layer sandwich is reduced in thickness by one or more roll stands, and the thinned sheet is cut into pieces about 18 inches long. Cut pieces are transferred in a shingled, or partially overlapping, fashion to a belt running at right angles to the original conveyor. After passing along a conveyor for a time sufficient to allow the dough to relax, the shingled sheets are pressed into a continuous strip by another reducing roller, or set of rollers. The strip is cut and shingled again before being reduced to about one-inch in thickness. This dough strip is cut to pan size and chilled for make-up 12 to 16 hr later.

In a more recently developed type of equipment, the dough strip is not cut but kept in continuous layers and overlapped upon itself in a diagonal pattern before it is reduced in thickness. The original dough-fat-dough sandwich described in the preceding paragraph is formed either by the same three layer extrusion method or by extruding a cylinder of dough inside of which is a cylinder of fat. In the latter case, the cylinder is flattened to make the three layer complex that starts the whole laminating process (Spooner 1988). Several different devices have been developed for making the overlapping layers.

Danish products can also be made by a continuous flow system that starts with extruding dough in a strip onto a conveyor belt. The dough strip is thinned out and widened by one or more pairs of reduction rollers. When the desired thickness is reached, several narrow bands of shortening, covering perhaps one-half of the dough's surface, are extruded onto the dough strip. This roll-in fat should equal at least 25% of the dough weight. A curling roller forms the dough and fat into a cylinder which is then flattened out by other sets of rollers. Results are similar to those from a three-fold operation done manually. A cutting wheel, or perhaps a guillotine, divides the strip of dough into lengths that will fit a bun pan. The dough is rested for a few hours in a 34° to 38°F room, then the sheets are folded to give four layers, sheeted out, folded again, and sheeted again. The dough can now be cut and shaped immediately, or retarded until make-up is scheduled.

Machines for coating sheets of dough with fat have been described, as in the invention of Siegenthaler and Zwahlen (1990), in which a conveyor roller with large saw-shaped teeth shaves cubes of fat from the contents of a packed hopper. The fat is conveyed along a cylindrical housing to a nozzle from the orifice of which a homogeneous strip of fat is discharged. It is claimed that uniform sheets of fat as thin as 2 mm can be formed, and that very little heat is generated during the operation.

Once the laminated structures have been formed, Danish dough can be made into sweet rolls and coffee cakes by the same kinds of equipment described elsewhere. The laminating process used for puff pastry and croissants differs little from that for Danish, although, of course, the doughs are very different in composition.

Laminating Machines for Cookie and Cracker Doughs

In cracker bakeries, combination machines for sheeting bulk dough and then lapping and cross-rolling it to form the structure that is characteristic of saltines are widely used. No interleaving of fat or other material is required for these products, and so the process is somewhat simpler than puff pastry preparation. Several ingenious methods have been developed for forming laminations. Two of these methods are diagrammed in Figure 26.6.

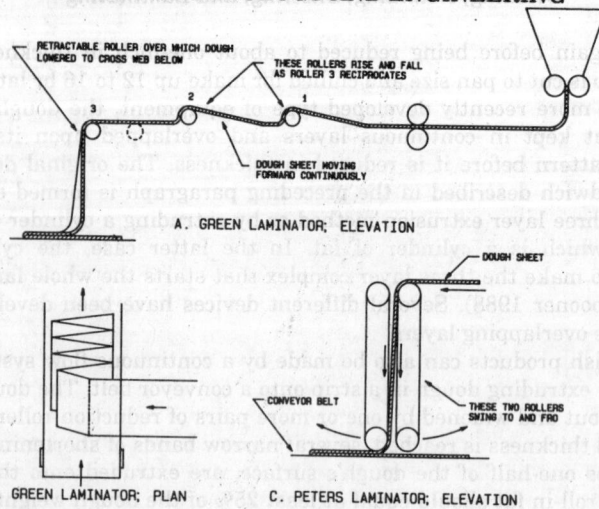

Figure 26.6. How the Peters laminater and the Green laminater work

A Werner-Lehara "laminator-three roll head" is described as follows. Bulk dough is fed to a sheeter head, which is a 3-roll sheeter with tubular steel rolls of 10-inch diameter. One of the rolls is corrugated, the other rolls are smooth, and they can be adjusted to give a roll gap of one-eighth to one-half inch. Sheeter hopper and rolls are 800 mm wide. The layering (laminating) carriage is composed of a main transport conveyor and a secondary compensating conveyor. These belts are arranged so as to lay the dough sheet across the supply conveyor for the subsequent stages. The action of the two layering conveyors is to continuously deliver the sheet of dough in a back and forth motion with the secondary compensating conveyor acting to control any slack that develops in the dough sheet during this back and forth motion. The layering carriage can be modified to supply 800, 1,000, or 1,200 mm wide dough sheets made up of 2 to 10 layers, with a maximum height of two inches. Options include gap gauges, turn counters, pick off rolls instead of fixed dough transfer knives, various conveyor materials, different number of layers, and modified drive systems. If the laminator is to be fed with pre-sheeted dough, a two-roll head machine can be supplied.

One design of combination sheeter-laminator includes a housing supporting two sets of primary feed-in rollers and two sets of secondary rollers. The initial dough sheet will be 2 to 3 mm in thickness. A reciprocating sheeting device is located between the secondary rollers and above the transport conveyor. This oscillating device grasps the dough sheet between two sets of endless belts mechanized so as to move the emerging sheet back and forth across the width of the transport conveyor, approximately at right angles to the conveyor belt motion. By adjusting the relative speeds of the sheeting device and the take-off conveyor, piles of any thickness up to 3.81 cm and consisting of any number of dough sheets can be made. The folded sheets are carried through gauge rollers and then to a rotary cutter or stamping machine.

Hydropneumatic laminators of Vicars design accept the sheeted dough, cut it into rectangles of appropriate dimensions, and deposit them in an overlapping stack on a belt moving transversely to the depositing conveyor. These devices use a hydropneumatic drive, enabling them to dispense with complicated cam-and-gear arrangements so they can achieve high operating speeds. Up to 15 laminations per minute can be made and a full range of adjustments is available to modify speed, length, and position of the dough sheet. Straight-out or cross laminating can be performed.

The semi-automatic compact laminator of Rykaart allows outputs of from 440 to 3,500 lb per hr, and is recommended mostly for medium-sized bakeries. The double lamination and double reduction of the dough in one section is claimed to be unique. By using the double-functioning twin multiroller (2x reduction 10:1) with 12 reducing rollers and a special relaxing device, optimal dough quality is said to be achieved.

Albrecht and Stanley (1974) described equipment consisting of a vertically-oriented horizontally-oscillating conveyor that delivers a strip of dough onto a horizontally travelling belt. Since the belt is concave, its upper surface forms a trough. Because the radius of the concavity is designed to equal the arc moved through by the bottom of the vertical conveyor, the dough strip travels an equal distance regardless of whether it is deposited on the center or the edge of the belt. This avoids the uneven stretching that would occur if the dough strip were deposited on a flat belt.

Morgenthaler and Seewer (1976) patented equipment consisting of a set of reversible conveyors adjustable in angle so that a piece of dough can be folded and lapped automatically in a predetermined sequence of steps. The three-layer dough piece formed in this operation is said to be less subject to breakage at the edges and to exhibit less squeezing out of the fat in subsequent sheeting steps.

Gugler (1975) described a method for forming folded dough sections. A relatively thin sheet of dough is severed into sections on a conveyor belt. Periodically, a part of the conveyor belt system is swung upward and to the rear, then forward and down to fold a forward portion of each dough section back over the following portion.

Swanson (1989) disclosed an in-line dough laminator, in which the strip supplied to the take-away conveyor is moved back and forth in a reciprocating fashion so as to form linear laps rather than cross-wise laps. This machine also has provisions for modifying the number of laps.

Currants or raisins can be rolled between two sheets of dough in a final step preceding the cutting of the cracker shape in order to form Garibaldi biscuits and the like (for example, see Chen 1987).

A totally different method of forming dough-fat layers and laminating them to form multiple layers is shown in Figure 26.7 (Source: Rheon).

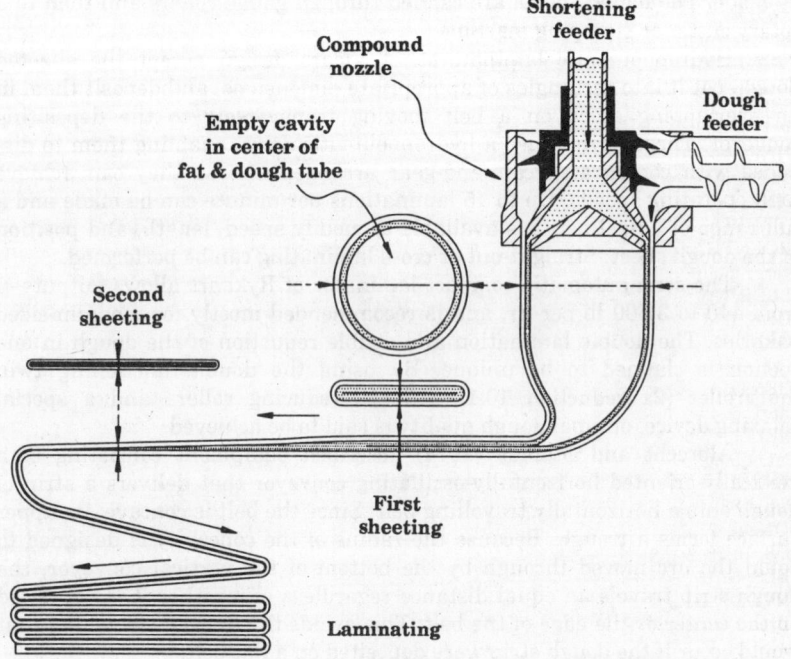

Figure 26.7. A method of preparing dough-fat layers and laminating them

BIBLIOGRAPHY

ALBRECHT, R. J., and STANLEY, A. J. 1974. Method for laminating sheet dough. U.S. Pat. 3,851,088

ALWES, M. 1985. A Quick Guide to Pumping Viscous Products. APV Crepaco, Chicago, Il

ANON. 1985. Hot air on rounder. Am. Soc. Bakery Engineers EIS Report 72

ANON. 1987. MM Line System and the Products. Rheon U.S.A., Irvine, CA

BEATTY, D. E. 1991. Divider head assembly. U.S. Pat. 4,984,978

CAMPBELL, G. P. 1983. Dough dividing. Proc. Am. Soc. Bakery Engineers 1983, 106-112

CAMPBELL, S. P. 1979. Mechanical dough conditioning—new systems. Proc. Am. Soc. Bakery Engineers 1979, 1175-186

CHEN, T. A. 1987. Automatic machine for making stone fruit biscuit. U.S. Pat. 4,711,166

CUMMINS, D. L. 1990. Method for dividing and cutting dough and the like. U.S. Pat. 4,949,611

FEILLET, P., FEVRE, E., and KOBREHEL, K. 1977. Modification in durum wheat properties during pasta dough sheeting. Cereal Chem. 54, 580-587

GUGLER, V. F. 1975. Method for folding dough. U.S. Pat. 3,865,963

HARRIS, R. W. 1985. Degassing and texturizing doughs. Proc. Am. Soc. Bakery Engineers 1985, 57-64

HAYASHI, T. 1986. Apparatus for producing strip of dough having constant dimensions and flow rate. U.S. Pat. 4,583,930

HAYASHI, T. 1988. Apparatus for continuously stretching a strip of dough. U.S. Pat. 4,731,008

JONES, D. A., WAWRA, G. F., and MOSS, W. R. 1986. Positive pressure dough divider. U.S. Pat. 4,573,898

JONSSON, O. T., and CARLSSON, S. R. 1989. Equipment for portioning out pieces of a doughy product. U.S. Pat. 4,813,860

KESSLER, H., and SPECTOR, G. 1990. Automatic apparatus for making strudel type pastry. U.S. 4,955,801

LEVINE, L. 1985. Thoughput and power consumption of dough sheeting rolls. J. Food Process Engineering 7, 223-238

LEVINE, L. 1987. Sheeting of doughs. Cereal Foods World 32, No. 5, 397

MISTRETTA, J. L. 1990. Sheeting head stripper wire adjuster. U.S. Pat. 4,966,641

MORGENTHALER, E., and SEEWER, R. 1976. Method of and apparatus for the transverse folding of dough band sections. U.S. Pat. 3,953,613

MULLER, G. 1988. Dough-rounding apparatus U.S. Pat. 4,793,789

SCHIEK, R. J. 1988. Dough feeding assembly. U.S. Pat. 4,731,007

SIEGENTHALER, P. 1990. Apparatus for winding sheets of dough on a dough reel and dough sheeter equipped with a dough sheeter winder. U.S. Pat. 4,954,064

SIEGENTHALER, P., and ZWAHLEN, A. 1990. Apparatus for coating sheets of dough with fat. U.S. Pat. 4,942,842

SPINELLI, L. A., and JENNIGES, J. M. 1989. Method of machining doughy material. U.S. Pat. 4,849,234

SPINNELLI, L. A., and JENNIGES, J. J. 1989. Apparatus of machining doughy material. U.S. Pat. 4,880,371

SPOONER, T. F. 1988. Producing quality croissants in quantity. Baking & Snack Systems 10, No. 8, 16-19

STEELS, G. 1972. Dough laminating. U.S. Pat. 3,698,309

STENVERT, N. L., MOSS, R., POINTING, G., WORTHINGTON, G., and BOND, E. E. 1979. Bread production by dough rollers. Bakers Digest 53, No. 2, 22-27

SWANSON, P. E. 1989. In-line dough laminator. U.S. Pat. 4,821,634

TASTET, C. 1988. Machine for automatically measuring portions of dough. U.S. Pat. 4,792,298

VINAS I NOGUEROLES, J. M. 1989. Process for the production by continuous rolling of a mass of dough for bakery products and buns and rolls. U.S. Pat. 4,877,632

VOEGTLIN, R. 1988. Apparatus for centering and shaping dough pieces for baked products or the like. U.S. Pat. 4,750,413

chapter twenty-seven

FERMENTATION ENCLOSURES AND BREW EQUIPMENT

INTRODUCTION

During the processing of yeast-leavened doughs, it is necessary to include stages, steps, and processes specifically intended to encourage the changes resulting from fermentation. Specialized equipment has been developed for these operations; it differs from much of the other equipment discussed in this book because it does not subject the dough or brew to mechanical change of form. Instead, the material is allowed to "rest" while the fermentation reactions are taking place. For the purposes of this chapter, the equipment will be divided into two types, that dealing with doughs and that dealing with liquids or fluids commonly called brews, broths, pre-ferments, liquid sponges, etc.

CONVENTIONAL FERMENTATION EQUIPMENT

Fermentation of a dough either as a sponge or straight dough has as its principal objects: (1) Saturating the liquid phase with carbon dioxide; (2) Forming the gas bubbles that will be, in the later processing, subdivided to form the basic cellular structure of the bread or roll; (3) Generating fermentation by-products, such as lactic acid, that mellow and soften the gluten; (4) Forming flavoring substances and flavor precursors that contribute much of the characteristic aroma and taste of bread; and (5) Adapting yeast so it can ferment maltose. In addition to yeast-mediated reactions, there are other changes occurring (such as those due to proteases and amylases) that are also of much importance to the processing and quality characteristics of the dough.

In the traditional sponge-and-dough system of breadmaking, there are three stages specifically intended to allow the combined ingredients opportunities for undergoing a more-or-less quiescent fermentation. These stages are: (1) sponge fermentation, (2) intermediate proofing, and (3) pan proofing. If there is no sponge, the straight dough may be allowed a fermentation period. Of course, doughs also continue to ferment and undergo other reactions in the intervals between the formal fermentation and proofing periods, and these changes can have significant effects on the dough's interactions with processing equipment and on finished product quality. Other yeast-leavened doughs, such as those for saltines, sweet doughs, and Danish pastry, also rely on fermentation and rest periods for some of their characteristic features.

Not all breadmaking processes involve sponge fermentation, intermediate proofing, and pan proofing. Sponge fermentation is omitted in all straight dough processes, being replaced by the bulk fermentation given the combined ingredients, and in the so-called mechanical development/conditioning procedures. A formal intermediate proofing step is dispensed with in no-time systems, although a certain amount of floor time always occurs and performs some of the same functions. It is difficult to imagine a system in which some pan proofing would not occur, but the time can be short and the proofing can take place on conveyors leading to the oven rather than in proofing rooms or cabinets. It is possible for all of the steps to take place in uncontrolled environments, in which case reliance must be placed on the starting dough temperature and on operator judgement of the completion of dough maturation to insure proper dough qualities at the time the dough is taken to the next step. For example, it is not uncommon for the sponge to be placed in a dough trough which is then covered with a piece of plywood or a plastic sheet before it is moved to a warm area of the bakery. This procedure leads to some fluctuation in sponge properties, but a skilled operator can usually compensate for these by adjustments at the doughing-up stage with, perhaps, additional adjustments at the intermediate proof stage.

In order to improve control over changes occurring during sponge fermentation, intermediate proofing, and pan proofing so that predictable results can be obtained, the dough is usually kept in enclosures where temperature and humidity can be regulated. Temperature should be controlled so yeast activity will proceed at a predetermined rate, and humidity should be controlled so the outer surface of the dough will not be too sticky or too dry. Equipment used to process, enclose, and convey the dough in these three maturing or conditioning phases will be discussed in this section.

There are many factors to be considered in designing systems for conducting fermentation, intermediate proofing, and pan proofing. Among these are temperature, humidity, and the mechanical shock imparted to dough by conveying mechanisms. When considering the influence of temperature and humidity on the dough, it is necessary to understand that the speed at which the product approaches equilibrium with its environment is as important as the actual conditions existing in the enclosure. In discussing theoretical situations, it is easy to lose sight of the fact that the temperature and humidity in any practical kind of enclosure are not only fluctuating constantly but vary from point to point within the enclosure. It should always be kept in mind that only by chance do the temperature and water activity of any dough piece, or of the atmosphere around it, match the average temperature and average relative humidity of the enclosure atmosphere at any given time.

Role and Control of Humidity

The effectiveness for their intended purposes of fermentation rooms, intermediate proofing cabinets, and proof boxes depends upon the accuracy with which they control humidity and temperature. To be sure, in practice the controls may be rather crude and poorly responsive to adjustment, but the value of maintaining humidity and temperature within fairly narrow ranges is well recognized.

In proofing enclosures, an atmosphere of high humidity is required to prevent drying out or crusting of the surfaces of dough pieces during the time they are in the enclosure. On the other hand, if the humidity is allowed to rise to near the dew point, there will exist the danger of water condensing on the surface of the dough, with the resultant development of a sticky or spotted surface and the possibility of splitting the softened skin as the dough piece expands. Best results can be obtained by carefully controlling the humidity within a narrow, high range. Control is made more difficult because, in many of these installations, artificial cooling is not provided and the operator is faced with a limited choice of dry bulb temperatures. The ideal situation would be to have both cooling and heating means available, but this is seldom found in practice.

There will always be substantial differences in the relative humidities at different locations in the room. One measure of the effectiveness of the temperature and humidity control and the air circulation systems is the range of these differences.

When a stream of air of controlled humidity is required, as in environmental cabinets to be used for testing storage stability, or in proof cabinets, accurate results can be obtained by mixing appropriate quantities of two streams of air, one of which has been thoroughly dried (thus at about zero RH) and the other saturated with water vapor, as by bubbling it through a reservoir of water. By varying the relative amounts of the two streams of air, it is possible to obtain any desired RH.

Humidity control according to this method requires fairly elaborate and costly installations. In proof cabinets and fermentation rooms, it is usually sufficient to maintain the RH at a fairly high level; reducing the humidity is not often needed in most bakeries.

In the simplest type of humidity modification, as found in the small cabinet proofing boxes used in retail shops, the air is conditioned by a manually adjusted heating coil and a valve or cock permitting steam to be injected for raising the humidity. In larger fermenting and proofing installations, both the temperature and relative humidity are automatically controlled. Water vapor can also be dispensed by intermittent injection of low pressure steam or by vibratory or centrifugal dispersion of liquid water. Forming water vapor by boiling water in the cabinet is seldom satisfactory as the amount of heat added to the enclosure is usually excessive and the amount of vapor created is usually inadequate.

The principal goals of the designers of proof boxes and fermentation rooms are (1) to provide for the efficient delivery and removal of dough containers, (2) to maintain the relative humidity at a uniform level, (3) to maintain a uniform temperature, (4) to provide sanitary conditions, and (5) to minimize physical shocks and other damage to dough pieces.

Fermentation Rooms

A major problem in designing fermentation rooms is selecting proper capacities for the air conditioning unit that will control temperature and humidity. Demands on this unit can be expected to be heavy and cyclic, because it will be called upon to compensate for the sudden influx of outside air as dough troughs are moved into and out of the enclosure.

The major unwanted causes of temperature changes in these rooms are: (1) Infiltration of air as doors are opened or through other openings in the walls; (2) Entry into the room of troughs and sponges that are of different, usually lower, temperature than the desired room temperature; and (3) Heat flow through the insulated walls, ceiling, and floor.

Cold air infiltrating into the conditioned room subtracts from the sensible or latent heat and can result in condensation, loss of heat, and reduction of humidity. Flow of heat through walls, roofs, floors, doors, etc., depends upon the area, the difference in temperatures, and the heat conducting properties of the wall.

The troughs and their contents, when moved into the room, will not be at the same temperature as the atmosphere. Steel has a specific heat of about 0.12, dry air of 0.24, and the average dough of about 0.88. Generally speaking, the weight of the trough will exceed the weight of the dough, but the higher specific heat of the latter makes it an important contributor to the heat exchange. All of these factors must be considered in calculating the capacity needed for the air conditioning unit.

The design temperature is the temperature that the system must be designed to maintain under the most difficult conditions expected to be encountered. It will be affected by the load placed on the system by the dough and pans, the climatic conditions (which influence the temperature of the infiltrating air and the differences between the cabinet and the environment), and the effectiveness of the insulation. Much of the following is based on some comments by Fred D. Pfening, and the general conclusions are applicable to cabinets for intermediate fermentation and pan proofing enclosures as well as fermentation rooms. Figure 27.1 shows some of the construction details to be discussed in the following paragraphs (Source: Fred D. Pfening, Sr.).

An air conditioning unit must be designed to provide sufficient air circulation and required amounts of heat, refrigeration, and moisture. In some systems, humidity can be controlled at three levels: high, low, and no addition. Lower relative humidity is preferred for use with silicone-coated pans or glazed pans, and for certain other purposes.

The conditioning unit should be able to provide cool air. The amount of cooling required is slight and the added cost is not great. Cooling is obtained by circulating chilled water or refrigerant through coils. All the cooling permissible with as little dehumidification as possible is the objective. Blower size is determined by calculation to obtain the desired velocity at the static pressure of the system. The blower runs continuously while heating or cooling devices function intermittently subject to signals from the thermostatic controls.

When the wet bulb thermostat causes moisture to be injected, a certain amount of evaporation occurs, dropping the dry bulb temperature of the atmosphere as much as 3°F. It the thermostatic control is sufficiently sensitive, this momentary cooling effect will cause the heating coil to react to restore the dry bulb temperature, if required. The best results are obtained when the water supplied for humidification is at the same temperature as the room atmosphere.

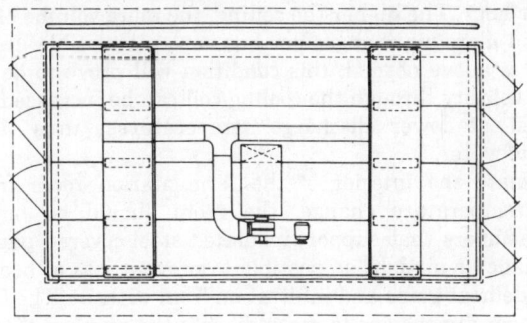

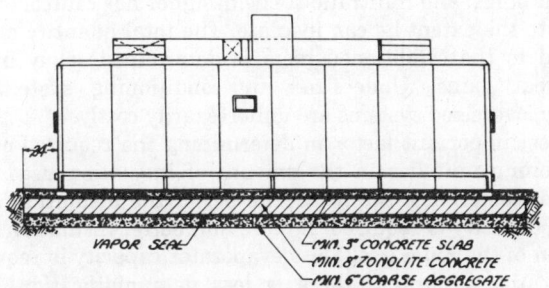

VAPOR SEAL   MIN. 5" CONCRETE SLAB
MIN. 8" ZONOLITE CONCRETE
MIN. 6" COARSE AGGREGATE

Figure 27.1. Construction details of fermentation room

To prevent condensation from forming on the side walls when the proof room is started up after a shutdown, it is very important to be sure the walls have heated up to operating temperature before humidity is injected into the chamber. The air heats faster than the steel and panels; the thermostat reflects the air temperature only until the steel equals it. A "humidity lockout" feature can be provided to prevent the humidification from being called for when a cold proof box is started up after a shutdown period. This disconnects the humidifier until the previously selected dry bulb temperature is reached so that an undesirable dew point and accompanying condensation are automatically avoided.

It is neither economically nor atmospherically desirable to dehumidify the air in a fermentation room, but the cooling coil does extract moisture from the air to an extent dependent on the temperature of the coil. The excessive elimination of moisture from the atmosphere passing through the coil face area causes the humidifying system to operate more nearly continuously to restore the cyclically eliminated water. Designers will usually plan to give the fermentation room six air changes per hour, therefore, the amount of air in the room will pass through the cooling coil six times per hour. The higher the ceiling, the more volume of air there is to circulate, and more air changes per hour are permissible. In the event the cooling load is above normal, this condition will prove to be advantageous because the velocity through the cooling coil can be increased and more Btu are obtained at lower discharge temperatures, thus decreasing the elimination of water.

To isolate the interior of the fermentation room from unwanted sources of temperature change, the room should be built with steel structural members that support insulated steel-covered panels. The room should be made as airtight as possible to prevent loss of heat from within, and to exclude heat gains and infiltration from without. The floor area must be of the proper dimensions to accommodate the number of troughs needed to satisfy the greatest anticipated production rate of the bakery. Heat accumulates from warm floors, walls, equipment, motors, people, troughs, dough, light bulbs, and infiltration. The designer has control over these heat gains only to the extent he can insulate. The total quantity of chilled air to be supplied to the conditioned room is determined solely by its internal sensible heat gains. Undersized air conditioning systems are never satisfactory, oversized systems are unnecessarily costly.

A most important factor in determining the required capacity of the air conditioning unit lies in the amount of insulation used in the walls, ceiling, and, sometimes, the floor. The better the insulation used, the less cooling coil capacity is required. If more and better insulation is used in the construction of the room itself, less evaporator capacity is required and less dehumidification occurs. If there is less dehumidification, there is less requirement for humidification. More money spent for insulation leads to savings on conditioning equipment and makes it easier to control the room.

Greater height is a distinct advantage because it permits dispersion of air and permits the additional air changes required to obtain the necessary cooling. The usual idea that volume of a conditioned room should be kept as low as possible to make it easier to maintain the desired temperature and humidification does not hold in this case. Also, high air velocity (encouraged by small rooms) has a marked drying effect on dough.

The reconditioned atmosphere should be distributed evenly in the fermentation room or proof box to prevent drafts or stratification. The number and design of air-diffusing outlets depends on the height of the room. An air stream should never be directed over a dough surface since it would have an evaporative effect and, therefore, would crust the dough. The fewer the air changes, the more beneficial the atmosphere remains. A conflict arises between setting up fewer air changes per hour and obtaining sufficient air velocity over the coil to transfer heat at a rate sufficient to maintain the room temperature.

Carbon dioxide is 1.5 times heavier than air. A blanket of carbon dioxide will form over the sponge surface until the sponge rises to the top of the trough. Then, the gas spills over the edge, flowing toward the floor. If sufficient gas accumulates, it may interfere with breathing of personnel who must enter the room. This situation is easily remedied by providing an opening in the room doors of about 10 inches in diameter. The opening should be a little higher than the highest trough. Gas reaching the level of the opening will flow to the outside and disperse into the atmosphere before it can rise to the breathing level.

Figure 27.2. A dough trough with conveyor pump in bottom

Dough troughs.—The dough trough is an important piece of equipment, but it is rarely given much consideration by the bakery technologist because it seems to have little direct effect on product quality. The production supervisor gives it some thought, but is mostly concerned about manpower requirements for trough handling and sanitary aspects. In sponge fermentations for saltine cracker manufacturing, the trough does have an effect on product quality because it serves as a source of inoculation for the sponge, furnishing bacteria of the types necessary to give the characteristic flavor and some of the gassing power to the dough. These factors may also function in bread sponge fermentations, but to a much lesser extent.

Troughs are customarily made from 10-gauge metal, either standard or stainless steel. They should be welded, with polished seams, and the rims should be rolled and sealed for sanitary reasons. Capacity of stock models range from about 14 to 56 cu ft to hold from 180 to 750 lb of sponge or 400 to 1,680 lb of straight dough. Considerable variation is possible in trough design. Most of the modifications are intended to offer better control over the removal of sponges from the trough. Among the familiar types are: (1) Slide-end, one end of the trough is like a gate that can be raised to give an opening through which the sponge can flow; (2) Sloping bottom, facilitates complete removal of the dough through one end; (3) Gate-end, the bottom part of one end is made as a gate hinged at its upper edge; (4) Chute-end, the lower third of one end can be opened, leading the sponge to an inclined pan or chute that guides it into the mixer; (5) Drop-side, the top third of one side is hinged and can be dropped down; (6) Controlled flow, designed primarily for overhead hoist operation, they have a gated end that can be raised in increments by a rack and pinion mechanism; and (7) Advanced models having a screw conveyor in a channel at the bottom of the trough to force dough directly to a processing line hopper (See Figure 27.2).

Several different systems have been devised for conveying dough troughs into, through, and out of the fermentation room. Manually pushing the trough on its casters from one point to another is, of course, the original way. Large fork lift trucks can also be used. Automatic handling is the rule nowadays, however. In one design, automatic handling in the proof room moves troughs in a line down the feed side of the enclosure, laterally across the end of the room, then back to the discharge door. A carriage, powered by a hydraulic ram, moves incoming troughs forward on their own casters and between two horizontal guides along the sides. Upon reaching the end of the room, the cross-carriage powered by a hydraulic ram moves the end trough transversely and positions it in the discharge line. At this point, another carriage identical with the feed unit moves the procession toward the discharge door. Troughs are moved onto and off the carriages by hand.

Figure 27.3 gives two views of an automatic system of the foregoing type (Source: Clock Associates).

Proof Boxes

There are many points of similarity between proof boxes and fermenation rooms. Duplication of the preceding points will be avoided unless repetition is necessary to insure clarity. Proof boxes can be classified as either intermediate proofing cabinets or pan proofing enclosures. The purose of a proof box is primarily heating and humidifying so as to maintain wet- and dry-bulb temperatures that will cause a dough piece to proof satisfactorily within a scheduled time, not necessarily the shortest possible time. The process relies heavily on an air-conditioning operation and is subject to all the vagaries of psychrometric measurement and control previously discussed. Another major problem is designing a mechanism that will efficiently and accurately move many small pieces of dough or pans.

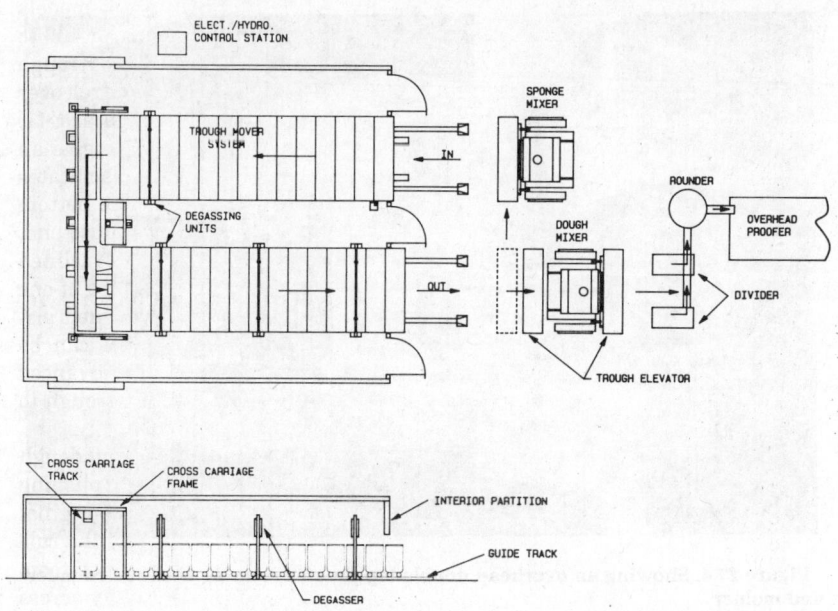

Figure 27.3. An automatic handling system for sponge troughs

Intermediate proofers.—When the dough piece leaves the rounder, it has lost much of its gas as a result of the punishment it received in that machine and in the divider. The dough lacks extensibility and tears easily. It is rubbery and would not mold satisfactorily. To restore a more flexible, pliable structure that will respond well to the manipulations of the molder, it is necessary to let the dough piece rest while fermentation proceeds and the gluten fibrils reorient themselves. This is usually accomplished in bread and roll lines by letting the dough ball travel through an inclosed cabinet for several minutes. The essential parts of these intermediate proofers (also called dry proofers, first proofers, or interproofers) are the enclosure or cabinet, the receiving mechanism, the internal conveyor, the power unit, and the controls.

In most cases bread and roll pieces will spend 10 to 15 minutes in the intermediate proofer. Optimum conditions are thought to be about 80° to 85°F and 70% to 73% relative humidity. Campbell (1990) said that intermediate proof time will range from 2 to 20 minutes, with an average falling between 6 and 9 minutes. Many of the intermediate proofers used at the present time in bread bakeries are the overhead type in which the principal part of the cabinet is raised high enough above the floor to allow space beneath it for other makeup machinery. See Figure 27.4 for an example of an arrangement of this sort (Source: Baker Perkins).

Figure 27.4. Showing an overhead double-lap proofer running between rounder and molder

When overhead space is not adequate, or when floor space is plentiful, a floor level proofing cabinet may be used. Smaller bakeries will use either overhead intermediate proofers or floor level cabinets into which racks of pans containing rounded dough pieces can rolled.

Intermediate proofers can be conveniently classified as belt type and tray type, the latter having many subtypes. Belt proofers consist of endless belts running in a closed cabinet. Dough pieces are carried forward to the end of the cabinet, then dropped down on the next lower belt, which will be traveling in the opposite direction. This process continues until the dough piece reaches the exit conveyor. A speed control allows adjustment of proofing time so requirements of different types and sizes of dough pieces can be accommodated. Flour applicators dust the trays before they are loaded.

Tray-type intermediate proofers have conveyors made up of segmented areas for carrying dough pieces. They include equipment that moves the dough in metal pans, troughs or buckets, wooden trays, or canvas loops. But for sanitary reasons, most of them use solid or perforated aluminum, stainless steel, or solid or perforated plated steel. Paraffined and plastic-coated wood trays have also been used. The trays are usually divided into segments or molded cups to prevent dough pieces from sliding together under the influence of the proofer's vibration. In some cases, liners of molded plastic are fitted to the trays to minimize or eliminate the need for dusting flour.

Each of the types has its special virtues and faults and, consequently, each has its proponents and detractors. Among the attributes of the dough carrying unit that are important in evaluating the suitability of an intermediate proofer are: (1) the ease of cleaning and of keeping it clean, (2) the ease of replacing parts and economy of repair, and (3) the effectiveness of the unit in preventing doubles and retaining the desired form of the dough.

In both tray and belt proofers, arrangements can be made to turn the dough pieces two or three times while they are in the cabinet. The invertings occur at the end of the belt when the dough ball drops to the next lower conveyor. When trays are used, they are tipped so the dough falls out and into a tray going in the opposite direction. By allowing all surfaces of the dough ball to be exposed to the humid atmosphere, there will be less crusting and the skin tends to be thinner. There is also, probably, a more uniform distribution of the gas bubbles when these inversions are made.

Proofer enclosure panels can be obtained in brushed aluminum, stainless steel, painted steel, or clear plastic. Some of the panels should be hinged or on slides for easy cleaning and examination of the interior.

Final proofers.— Final proofers (pan proofers) receive the shaped and panned dough piece and hold it for a short time before it is delivered to the oven. During this period, the dough pieces gain most of the volume they will have as finished loaves or buns, although oven spring will add some additional volume.

Final proofers are of several types. The most primitive example is the shallow box or drawer that controls humidity and temperature only by sealing off the dough piece from the bakery atmosphere. These are no longer in use, at least not in developed countries. Eventually, the advantages of better control became apparent and special rooms or cabinets were designed for final proofing. At first, the product was taken into the room manually, sometimes by pushing racks of pans into one end of the room and removing them in sequence from the other end. Injecting steam by a pipe leading from the boiler was the means of both heating and humidifying. Adjustment of conditions was manual and based on occasional reading of the wet- and dry bulb thermometers, if instruments of this degree of sophistication were available.

The high labor requirement for conducting the proofing operation by such methods led to the design of several different conveying systems. In the floor-type proof box, racks mounted on casters are used to hold many pan straps. There may be several lanes through the proof box, with a series of racks moved through each. Racks are manually or automatically pushed into one end of the box, thereby moving the preceding racks ahead one space, and pulled out of the other end at a rate calculated to give the necessary proof time. The enclosure is a steel frame covered with insulated panels and provided with an automatic air-conditioning system. Overhead rails or floor rails may be used to guide the racks. Continuous conveying of straps of pans through the final proofing enclosure is an advanced method requiring the minimum amount of personal participation.

Conditioning units will include blower, radiators, steam jet, spray units, and eliminators. In the larger units, stainless steel ductwork will be designed and positioned to distribute the conditioned air in a pattern that is best suited to the conformation of the room and the arrangement of the racks and pans. Air curtains can be installed in loading and unloading openings to reduce loss of conditioned air into the bakery.

Pan conveying systems somewhat similar to those found in traveling hearth ovens have been developed. Other automatic conveying means that have been suggested or designed include belt-and-chain driven mechanisms. Whatever the method used for conveying the pans, straps, or racks, it should not cause undue vibration, shock, or impact. Toward the end of pan proof, and perhaps before, the expanded condition of the gluten network and the relatively relaxed state of the proteins render the dough structure readily subject to distortion or collapse when subjected to minor shocks.

Modern proofers for large-scale operation automatically load pan straps onto racks that are integral parts of the proofer. In a multi-tray proofer, pans are grouped automatically and fed to the loading section. The loading conveyor is coordinated with the try unit, both operating intermittently. As each tray is loaded, the tray unit is indexed upward one tray pitch while the loading conveyor delivers another load. When filled, the tray unit is indexed upward once more and then pushed horizontally one space down the length of the proofer by the top ram. This action also causes the movement of one tray unit onto the elevator at the other end of the proofer. The elevator lowers the tray to the lower level where a bottom ram pushes it one space in the return direction. This movement automatically forces another tray unit onto the front-end elevator, which indexes it upward through the unloading position and then back to the loading position. If plenty of floor area is available, multitray proofers are the simplest, most economical type.

In multi-tier proofers, each tray after it is loaded is raised separately to the top tier of the proofer. Drive chains on each side of the loaded trays convey them back and forth through the length of the proofer, dropping them to a lower tier at each turning point until they reach the unloading station. The trays continue through the bottom leg to the loading station.

Another type of automatic proofer comprises eight principal functions: feeding, grouping, and discharge conveyors; automatic loaders; unloader; elevator; Lowerator; and double-deck tracks upon which racks are conveyed by roller chains. The racks are equipped with flanged wheels that roll along floor rails. A rack would typically have seven shelves, each holding eight straps of five 1.5 lb pans. Four endless conveyor chains are powered by sprockets at the ends of each of the four rails. Uniformly spaced projections engage slots at both sides of the racks and move them laterally on the upper rails, then transfer them to the Lowerator at the rear of the proofer. The Lowerator engages slots at the sides of each rack and moves it to the lower rail where the slots engage by brackets on the conveyor chains.

The Lowerator and the elevator consist in part of a set of two endless chains powered by sprockets. The chains operate in a vertical plane and are located on both sides and at the ends of the two sets of rails. Each set of chains is fitted with short lengths of rail, properly spaced to match the trucks. The elevator is more complex than the Lowerator, because it must index the shelves at proper intervals, keeping them level with both the feed and discharge conveyors. The loader and unloader consist of two steel pusher bars on rams mounted at opposite ends of heavy steel rods. As they move in a horizontal plane, the pusher bars simultaneously sweep straps off the feed conveyor and onto a shelf and off a shelf onto the discharge conveyor. A proof box about 18 ft wide, 12 ft high, and 68 ft long could accommodate about 8,120 loaves at a time.

In all types of automatic proofers, dwell time can be varied so as to fit most production needs (Valentyne and Hoag 1963; Petersen *et al. 1963*).

Bread, rolls, pizza, Danish, and other panned products can be final proofed in rooms provided with two connected spiral conveyors. The pans are placed on the conveyor by hand or by automated mechanisms.

Figure 27.5. A continuous rack proofer with automatic loading and unloading and a conveyor to oven

Automated and integrated pan proofing and baking.— In the late 1970s and the 1980s, systems were developed for continuous conveying of pans from the molder through the oven. For example, panned product is received from the molding machine and grouped. The grouper collects the pans and places a certain number of them in a specific array. The grouped pans are carried in this array to a rack-type proofer. where a loader transfers them on to the proofer shelf. A proofer chamber with associated conveyors for performing these functions is shown in Figure 27.5 (Source: Baker Perkins).

Grissinger (1973) lists four advances in the mechanical features of rack-type proofers: (1) Recent types of proofers have only one drive compared to the earlier versions that had four separate drives for moving the racks; (2) Rack movement is now accomplished with continuous drive motions compared to previously used intermittent motions; (3) Rack motions were electrically synchronized but are now mechanically synchronized, resulting in simpler electrical circuits and less than one-half the number of limit switches; and (4) Racks were free to swing during parts of their travel, leading to occasional hangups, but are now fully stabilized throughout their path.

The pans are unloaded from the proof room at the same end where they were loaded, and placed on another conveyor that carries them to the oven loader. They pass through the oven, then to the depanner where the pans are separated to return through the system while the loaves, buns, etc., are sent through the cooler, slicer, and packaging line. All these actions occur without manual intervention, except in the case of emergencies.

These lines were originally developed for loose pans that were carried on various types of conveyors, some of which grasped or positioned the pans. Problems in maintaining control of the pans tended to occur if they were distorted or damaged. Ultimately, these developments culminated in a conveyor to which straps of pans were attached and which carried these pans through a curving path inside an air-conditioned room until pan proofing was complete, then carried them to a room-like oven where they were baked. This automated system is a genuine innovation in processing. It reduced labor and promoted uniformity. More details will be found in the chapter on ovens.

Expedited proofing by microwaves.—Conventional bread baking systems include proofers that subject dough to a proofing environment of, for example 120° to 125°F and 80% to 85% RH for about 30 minutes in order to bring the temperature at the center of the unbaked loaf to about 110°F. Although the dough surface is relatively quickly raised to the desired temperature, considerable time is required before the center of the piece reaches 110°F. Microwave heating is a way of speeding up the heat rise and shortening the proofing period. Methods for implementing this process have been developed (Ingram *et al.* 1975). Generally, these methods combine conventional treatment in a conditioned air cabinet with a preliminary microwave-heating step. As with most microwave heating methods involving a continuous line, one of the major problems is shielding personnel from escaping radiation.

FLUID FERMENTATION EQUIPMENT

The sponge, which normally appears as a stiff dough when it is first mixed, is replaced by pumpable liquids in those processes that rely on liquid sponges or broths as the first fermentation step. Continuous or semi-continuous breadmaking systems require such intermediates, and modified batch systems can also make use of them. Temperature control is an essential part of these systems. Humidity control, of some sort, is also a factor, though it may not be maintained within a narrow range by equipment specially designed for that purpose. In fully continuous processing, only the final dough piece is proofed, the brew tanks taking the place of the sponge room and intermediate proofing being dispensed with.

The most obvious advantage of liquid sponge methods is that pumps, pipes, valves, meters, and tanks can be used to replace the cumbersome dough troughs and space-consuming fermentation rooms of the conventional bakery. The mixing equipment is simpler and less expensive for liquid sponge systems, and the time required to complete the initial fermentation is less. The effect of liquid sponges on bread quality is a question that has received many answers, but from a commercial point of view it appears obvious that satisfactory bread can be made with liquid sponges.

Although liquid sponges can be made by manually weighing and depositing the ingredients into mixers, it is considerably more efficient as well as more compatible with continuous processing to automatically meter materials into specialized liquid sponge makers. Typically, such equipment will continuously meter and blend controlled portions of flour, water, yeast, and additives to produce a uniform liquid sponge containing all the formula water and up to 70% of the formula flour. Most often, considerably less flour will be incorporated at this stage because the added viscosity of high flour content mixes increases the difficulty of handling the sponge as it ferments. Figure 27.6 shows an example of the equipment just discussed (Source: AMF).

Sponge temperature is regulated by adjusting the water temperature; tanks can be jacketed but seldom are for this type of operation. The finished brew can be put through heat exchangers if it becomes too warm for the final mix. Automatic valving, controls, and programmers are used to obtain a uniform and continuous flow at the rate required. Rates of up to 14,000 lb per hr are readily achievable with fairly small pieces of equipment.

The slurry is pumped from the blender to fermenting vessels where the liquid sponge undergoes those changes that ready it for incorporation into the dough. Fermentation vessels can be batch-type or continuous. The batch type will usually be adaptations of vertical tanks equipped with agitators designed to handle liquids of the viscosity expected to be encountered. Positive-flow continuous fermentors allow freshly mixed liquid sponge to enter a horizontally-aligned cylindrical tank at one end, and, after the desired fermentation time has elapsed, to flow out of the opposite end, giving a true first in-first out sequencing. A transfer reel turning slowly within the fermentor imparts positive flow to the liquid sponge through a spiraling in and out pattern. The standard units do not have heat control equipment, but this can be supplied as an option when ambient heat or other conditions require cooling of the fermentation mixture.

Figure 27.6. Automatic liquid sponge maker

From the fermenting vessels, the liquid will be transferred by an appropriate type of pump through a heat exchanger cooler to a refrigerated holding tank. If a continuous fermentor is being used, the speed of the pump must be automatically controlled to deliver fermented sponge at a rate that is synchronized with the fresh mix entering the system, so that all the liquid sponge receives a uniform amount of fermentation.

There are many variations in plant designs for liquid sponge lines. The following is given as an example of the equipment required for one such plant (Anon. 1987).

(A) Nutrient slurry make-up tank, 500-gal fiberglass, closed top.

(B) Centrifugal pump.

(C) Nutrient slurry supply tank; 150-gal fiberglass, closed top.

(D) Nutrient slurry feeder pump with variable speed drive.

(E) Yeast slurry make-up tank, 500-gal, "B" dome top, jacketed.

(F) Yeast slurry supply tank, 150-gal, "B" dome top, jacketed.

(G) Yeast slurry feeder pump with variable speed drive.

(H) Continuous liquid sponge mixer.

(I) Positive flow continuous fermentor.

(J) Sponge transfer pump with variable speed drive.

(K) Plate cooler for sponge

(L) Cold hold tank, 1,500-gal, "B" dome top, jacketed.

(M) Cold sponge pump with variable speed drive.

(N) Batch weigh tank.

(O) CIP tank and pumps, multi-compartmented.

(P) Control panel.

Pumps, pipes, valves and meters are preferably constructed of stainless steel and must be sized to meet the production needs of the bakery. It is seldom, if ever, necessary to jacket these elements for temperature control. Clean-in-place (CIP) sanitation procedures are readily adaptable to these installations.

Following is the description of a suggested dual temperature liquid sponge procedure developed for bakeries using conventional mix 50° to 65°F sponge at the remix stage and continuous mix 75° to 85°F sponge at the premixer or incorporator (Anon. 1988).

(1) Ingredients for the yeast slurry and nutrient slurry are scaled and blended with temperature controlled water in the slurry make-up tank. The liquid mixes are transferred to the appropriate supply tank, each of which is sized to store the requirements for several hours production.

(2) At the start of the production run, centrifugal pumps are used to maintain a flooded condition at the positive rotary transfer pumps that meter the slurries to the sponge blender.

(3) Flour is diverted from the overhead pneumatic flour conveying system into a hopper mounted above the sponge blender. Flour is continuously weighed onto a belt moving at a constant rate. At the end of the belt, the flour falls into a circular incorporation chamber housing a squirrel cage agitator. Metered amounts of yeast slurry, nutrient slurry, and temperature adjusted feed water are piped into the chamber for rapid incorporation with the flour to form a pumpable sponge containing up to 65% of the total flour.

(4) Liquid sponge mix is transferred at an uninterrupted flow rate to the inlet on the positive flow fermentor.

(5) The fermented liquid sponge is transferred by two variable-speed rotary pumps set to run at a combined flow rate equal to that of the transfer pump feeding the input end of the fermentor. Each pump transfers the required amount of fermented sponge through the dual temperature plate heat exchanger to the appropriate holding tank.

(6a) Sponge for the continuous mix operation is transferred directly to the pre-mixer or incorporator where the dough side ingredients are combined with the sponge before the final mixing. The surge tank helps to maintain a uniform metering rate and an uninterrupted operation.

(6b) Sponge for the conventional mix operation can be transferred by a reversible pump to the batch weigh tank and then back through the pump to a diverter valve, then on to the supply header serving the final mixers.

(7) With the exception of the automatic sponge blender, all system components may be cleaned in place with any desired level of automation.

A schematic diagram of this entire system is shown as Figure 27.7 (Source: APV Crepaco).

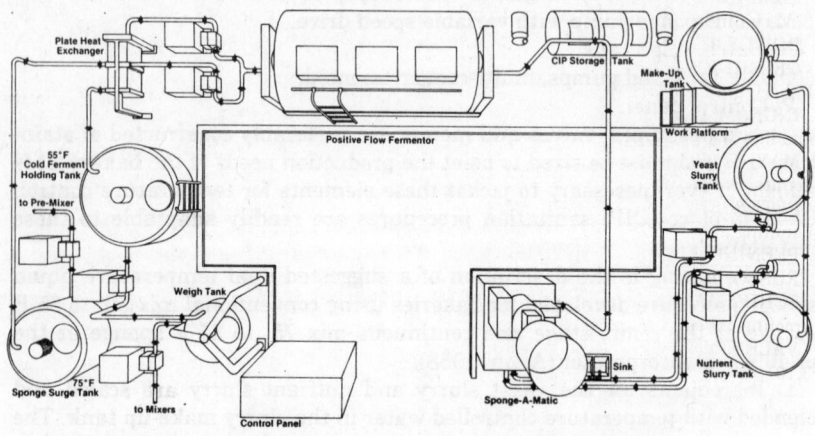

Figure 27.7. Dual temperature liquid sponge ferment system

An optional method using heat exchangers follows the above scenario through step 4, then transfers the liquid from the sponge fermentor through a single-function plate heat exchanger for cooling to 55°F, then into a jacketed cold sponge holding tank. On demand, a transfer pump removes the fermented sponge to the batch weigh tank, and a second pump transfers the batch to the supply header for the final mixers.

The dry ingredient incorporator recommended for the above systems is a tank-type blender suitable for batch make-up of yeast and nutrient slurries, and as a flour incorporator. A high-speed squirrel cage agitator causes a dual blending action combining an overall swirl with a deep draw vortex to quickly disperse the ingredients while minimizing the risk of gluten agglomeration. It is available in five capacities from 100 to 1,000 gal, and has a 15° cone bottom to facilitate unloading.

The automatic sponge blender is designed to continuously meter and blend controlled ratios of flour, water, yeast slurry, and nutrient slurry. It produces a uniform liquid sponge containing all or part of the formula water and up to 65% of the total formula flour. The sponge temperature is regulated during flour incorporation by adjusting the feed water temperature. Using metering pumps, automatic valves, and control programmers helps to assure a uniform and continuous rate of sponge flow to the fermentor. This piece of equipment is made in two models, to provide sponge for 7,000 or 14,000 lb of finished dough.

BIBLIOGRAPHY

ANON. 1987. CP Continuous Fermentor. Bulletin L-1-150. Crepaco, Inc., Chicago, IL

ANON. 1988. Liquid Sponge Ferment Systems. APV Crepaco, Chicago, Il

CAMPBELL, G. P. 1990. Bread production without intermediate proofing. Proc. Am. Soc. Bakery Engineers *1990*, 129-135

DOWDS, H. M. 1987. Baker's dough proofing and raising unit. U.S. Pat. 4,635,540

GRISSINGER, G. R. 1973. Automated proofing and baking advances. Proc. Am. Soc. Bakery Engineers *1973*, 128-137

INGRAM, C. E., BRUNK, R. H., and WITKOSKE, E. 1975. Apparatus for making bread and like food products. U.S. Pat. 3,881,403

MAY, L. 1962. Spaulding's three streamlined production lines for breads, rolls, and donuts. Bakers Weekly *195*, No. 9, 40-49

PETERSEN, C. W., WITTENBERGER, W. W., and ST. JOHN, J. M. 1963. Bread handling apparatus. U.S. Pat. 3,101,475

PFENING, F. D. 1972. Personal communication. The Fred D. Pfening Co., Columbus, OH

RUSSO, J. R. 1971. Microwave proofs doughnuts. Food Eng. *43*, No. 4, 55-58

SCHIFFMANN, R. F., STEIN, E. W., and KAUFMAN, H. B., JR. 1971. The microwave proofing of yeast-raised doughnuts. Bakers Digest *45*, No. 1, 55-57, 61

VALENTYNE, P. H., and HOAG, D. H. 1963. Dough processing apparatus. U.S. Pat. 3,101,143

chapter twenty-eight

FORMING AND MOLDING BREAD-LIKE PRODUCTS

INTRODUCTION

This chapter will first discuss the general requirements for bread and roll molding equipment, and then describe some specialized lines that make English muffins, pretzels, croissants, bagels, pita bread, bread sticks, and a few other products out of the same type of dough, that is, lean yeast-leavened extensible dough. Processing equipment for yeast-leavened sweet doughs and laminated doughs will be described in subsequent chapters. Most of the products described here, and others, are covered in considerably more detail in "Equipment for Bakers" (Matz 1988).

BREAD LOAVES AND PLAIN ROLLS

Principles of Loaf Molder Function

In bread-making plants, the molder receives pieces of dough from the intermediate proofer and shapes them into cylinders of loaf size ready to be placed in the pans. There are several types of bread loaf molders, and all of them except the extrusion type have four functions in common: sheeting, curling, rolling, and sealing. Some writers consider the last two as a single function, since they are performed simultaneously.

The dough as it comes from the intermediate proofer is a flattened spheroid. The first operation of the molder is to flatten this piece still more, forming a thick sheet that can be properly manipulated in the later steps. The sheeting is usually accomplished by two or more (usually three) consecutive pairs of rollers, each succeeding pair being set closer together than the ones before. The gradual reduction in thickness accomplished by this multiple roller system minimizes the punishment received by the dough so that tearing and similar problems are reduced. Sometimes, a single "flattening" roll is located above the infeed conveyor that leads to the molder. This flattening roller performs a slight initial reduction in thickness that facilitates engagement of the dough piece by first pair of rolls. It has become fairly common to encase some or all of the sheeting rollers with Teflon sleeves in order to prevent them from adhering to the dough pieces. When the molder sheeting rolls have not been treated in this manner, scraper blades are placed to assure separation of dough sheets from the rollers.

After the dough has been sheeted out, it is curled into a loose cylinder. This operation is normally performed by a special set of rolls. Alternatively, it is done by a pair of canvas belts—a lower conveyor belt moves the dough piece forward while the upper curling belt engages the front end of the piece and holds it while the rest of the piece continues forward, these opposing forces causing the sheet to curl up into a loose cylinder. A short length of woven metal mat or linked thin metal bars replaces the upper belt in some designs; in these machines the metal curling device is affixed just above the conveyor belt, with one end resting on the belt. As the dough piece passes under the curling device, the weight of the latter creates enough drag to pull the forward end of the dough piece up and delay it while the conveyor belt rolls the piece into a cylinder.

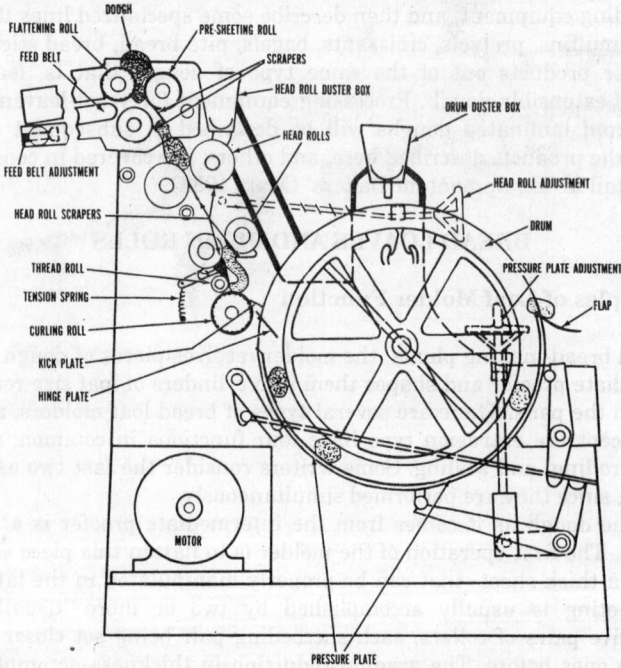

Figure 28.1. A simple drum molder for bread loaves

The layers in the cylinder of dough are not tightly adherent when it leaves the curling section. The next function of the molder is to thoroughly seal the layers together so that it will expand into the typical loaf shape when it is proofed. If sealing is not done properly, the curled shape can partially unroll when proofed, giving a misshapen loaf, or tunnels can develop between partially sealed layers. The cylinder of dough should be somewhat longer than the inside length of the pan. One way of sealing the curled dough is by rolling the dough cylinder between a large drum surfaced with canvas and a semi-circular compression board with a smooth surface. Clearance between the drum and the board is gradually reduced along the route of dough travel so that the piece is constantly in contact with both surfaces and gradually becomes compressed as it rolls through the narrowing channel. Molders of this type (see Figure 28.1) are appropriate for retail operations, but not for wholesale bakeries. The illustration is included because it clearly demonstrates the basic molding functions.

A more common arrangement for sealing is a flat pressure board combined with a powered belt that gradually squeezes the dough cylinder as the distance between the belt and board decreases. At high speeds, say 80 pieces per minute, dusting flour is usually applied just before the dough piece goes under the pressure board. Pressure boards range in length from about 24 to 48 inches, and their surface is often altered by some kind of "buildup" to give better control over the shape of the dough piece. A layer of sponge rubber covered by canvas is a common arrangement. Angles made of metal or wood strips or half-cylinders are sometimes attached to the pressure board, with points of the angles directed toward the intake, and the whole structure covered with canvas. Thick pieces of canvas belting are also used to build up the pressure board. These modifications are intended to permit use of a loose pressure board without getting pointed ends on the dough pieces. This leaves the ends of the dough pieces rather loosely sealed, allowing the gases to escape and giving a more even grain throughout the loaves.

An integral part of most modern molders is the automatic panning device. Empty pans are carried by a conveyor past the end of the molder, and the loaves are transferred from the molder and positioned in the pans by an apparatus operated by compressed air.

Types of Molders

As the dough passes through the sheeting rolls, the moisture content of the trailing edge increases at the expense of the leading sections. The redistribution of water results from the effects of compression on the dough structure. In the usual course of events in a conventional molder, the trailing edge, which is of relatively high moisture content, ends up as the outside layer of the loaf. It has been thought for many years that it would be preferable, from the standpoint of loaf performance during proofing and baking, to have the wetter portion of the dough sheet folded into the center of the loaf. Observations on hand-molded doughs formed in this manner seemed to confirm the superiority of "reverse molded loaves."

Commercially accepted developments that are intended to avoid folding the dry end of the dough sheet into the center of the dough cylinder include the cross-grain molder and the reverse sheeting molder. The former type curls the dough sheet at right angles to its direction of travel through the sheeter rolls. As a result, the wetter edge of the dough forms one end of the loaf rather than the outside layer. The crossover action is achieved by changing the direction of the dough 90° after it leaves the sheeting rollers. The first type of cross-grain molder used a turnover or flip-flop method of transfer, while a slide transfer or "shootover" method came into use later. A type of cross grain molder is shown in Figure 28.2 (Source: Stickelber).

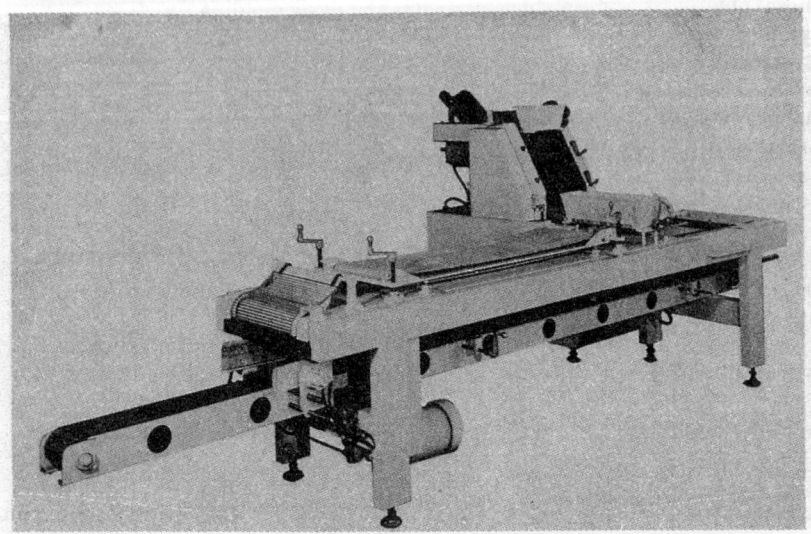

Figure 28.2. A cross-grain molder-panner for bread loaves

Pivonka (1988) describes a form of cross-panning, "W-folding," for loaves that differs substantially from the one previously described. The cylindrical dough piece is partly severed at three places, forming four approximately equal lengths held together by narrow strips, or "hinges." The dough piece is then held back at the center hinge so that it forms a V-shape, then held back at the two lateral hinges so that it forms a W-shape. Finally, the dough piece is squeezed laterally so the four sections line up side by side. This must be a primarily European development.

Reverse sheeting molders were designed to curl the dough sheet so the wet end of the piece would be folded into the center of the loaf. This is accomplished by turning over or reversing the piece between the second or third set of rolls, that is, between the center rolls and the sheeting rolls. This places the original trailing end (the wet end) in the leading position.

Another molder that was developed primarily to give loaves a more uniform cell structure twists the dough pieces after they have been rolled into cylinders. Two cylinders are twisted together to give a kind of rope shape. The unique appearance of these loaves is evidently attractive to some consumers, also. For whatever reason, twist bread has been popular in certain sections of the country for many years. The twisting operation was formerly performed entirely by hand, an obviously uneconomical practice in this highly competitive industry. Machines were developed that could perform the twisting at a rapid rate and with results at least as good as those obtained by hand twisting. In these molders, the curled dough cylinders fall into U-shaped cups, each end of a cylinder being supported by a separate cup, and the cups are then twisted in a rotary motion.

In a typical twist bread molder the sequence of events is as follows. As the dough pieces leave the molding conveyor, they first trip a flap that actuates the dough traps and the twisting mechanism of the molder; they then drop into the selecting trap. The latter device opens each time the flap is tripped and deposits pieces successively into each of two pockets of the collecting trap. When the collecting trap has accumulated two dough pieces, they are released into the first set of twisting cups, which then rotate 180°, but in opposite directions, to apply the first two twists. These dough pieces are now deposited in the second set of cups, where the twisting action is again applied. After this final operation, the loaf forms are deposited into pans for final proofing and baking by the usual means.

Extrusion Molders

Extrusion molders for bread loaves operate on a totally different principle from the molders described previously. They are used in continuous systems where the dough is pumped to the extrusion head as a homogeneous mass not divided into pieces. No dividing, rounding, or sheeting precedes or follows the extrusion.

In one widely used system, the extruder immediately follows the dough developer. The dough is continuously mixed as it progresses downward to the exit of the developer, where it passes through a narrow slit opening to the extruder. After passing this point, the dough is extruded as a cylinder that is cut off by opposed blades. The diameter of the cylinder is constant, but the knife action can be programmed to cut off lengths that give the desired weight. The blades are actuated synchronously with panner action, so that a pan will be properly placed when the severed dough pieces fall toward the pan conveyor.

The extrusion molder used with the AMF continuous breadmaking system is shown in Figure 28.3.

Bread Roll Molders

Buns and bread rolls are formed on equipment that differs in several important respects from loaf molding equipment. In some cases, dividers, rounders, proofers, and molders are part of an integrated unit that maintains dough piece registration throughout processing. There will be specialized shaping, cutting, and molding devices following the rounder or proofer to form kaiser rolls, split rolls, Parkerhouse rolls, etc. Applicators for poppy seeds, salt crystals, and the like may also be included in the line.

Figure 28.3. An extrusion molder for continuous production bread

Bun dividers and rounders have been discussed in an earlier chapter, but a brief recapitulation will be included here. A horizontal cylinder containing cavities rotates beneath a hopper filled with dough. Dough is sucked into the divider cavities by the retraction of pistons, then cut off and the pieces expelled onto the rounder conveyor. The most common rounder consists of a conveyor belt and a set of concave bars set at an angle to the line of belt travel. At the end of the rounder belt the dough balls fall into Teflon-line chutes that release four or six dough pieces simultaneously into proofer trays. Dough pieces leave the intermediate proofer and enter the molding device, where they are formed into desired shapes, such as hamburger buns, hot dog rolls, club rolls, salt sticks, etc. A typical molder will consist of (1) a molder chute having a gate operated by a cam mounted on a cam shaft synchronously driven by the proofer depositer, (2) a set of adjustable molder rollers, (3) a molding belt with an auxiliary curling mat,

(4) a standard auxiliary pressure board unit for forming hot dog rolls, (5) a set of hot dog dough gates, and (6) an indexing mechanism for synchronizing the release of the formed dough pieces with the cavities in the pan.

Many fancy bread roll shapes that were formerly done by tedious hand-forming techniques are now made by pressing designs into an unproofed or partially proofed round dough piece. Kaiser rolls, cloverleaf rolls, and split rolls are among these varieties. The imprinting machine is a simple assembly of several metal dies mechanized to press into the dough pieces in their pan. More elaborate shapes, such as triple-braid loaves are still formed by hand, even in the most automated bakeries (Gorton 1988).

A roll molder is shown in Figure 28.4. The molding bars are to the left of the divider and to the right of the intermediate proofer (Source: Clock Associates).

Figure 28.4. Divider-molder-proofer in a bread roll line

ENGLISH MUFFINS

The first fully automatic lines for producing English muffins were installed about 1960 (Noel 1962). They performed the functions of dividing, rounding, dusting dough pieces with corn meal, loading the proofer, proofing under controlled conditions, dusting trays with corn meal, transfer of dough pieces to a griddle, grilling, turnover of muffins, final grilling, elevating, conveying to cooler, cooling, discharge to packaging line, carton set-up, and automatic feeding to wrapper. Since 1962, a vast expansion of English muffin production has occurred, and pre-engineered lines are available from small semi-automatic operations to high speed fully automatic plants.

Details of English muffin production, especially as adapted to conventional roll equipment, were published by Pfefer (1976). Doughs can be mixed in horizontal dough mixers and vertical mixers, but not in the ultra-high speed mixers. A cool dough with high absorption is preferred, and the floor time should be kept to a maximum of 15 minutes between the end of mixing and the beginning of dividing. Any divider capable of cutting and dropping a soft dough can be used. The pieces can be rounded before proofing or dropped into the proofer trays without rounding. Muffins produced from rounded dough are more regular in outline. Before the dough chunks go into the proofer, they are dusted with corn flour by conventional dusting machines. Proof is approximately 30 min at 110°F wet bulb and 96% RH.

Dough pieces coming from the proofer are deposited into griddle cups by turning mechanisms that keep the top of the proofed dough piece uppermost as it falls into cup. At this point, the griddle cups are open at the top and are not at full baking temperature. After approximately 2.5 min of travel time, top covers are brought down to contact with the griddle cup. After four minutes grilling time, the muffins are dumped and inverted by a slide mechanism, then travel 3.5 min on a flat hearth without cups or rings. After they leave the griddle, muffins are cooled in, for example, a multi-tiered atmospheric cooler. Muffins may be split by machines employing stainless steel needles to perforate the roll on both sides.

The importance of high absorption doughs coupled with faster mixing, a cool dough, and a three-stage mixing process for efficiently producing high quality English muffins was emphasized by Juers (1982). Special mixer agitators also aid in the development of these doughs. Scaling of the dough is not particularly difficult, although a higher level of dividing oil may be required to insure a trouble-free run. To obtain good conformation, dough pieces should be proofed on a fairly flat surface that is coated with a blend of corn flour and corn meal. This permits the dough to flow without rising excessively. Good coverage of the dough with the right granulation (not too coarse) corn meal, corn flour, and/or rice flour is essential to proper handling in and out of the proofer. Poor coverage can result in cripples, while dusting powder that is too coarse can cause uneven baking, carbon buildup on the burners, excessive powder use, and possibly flash fires. Proofer design can affect dough response and product quality. If the cups in the proofer tray are too deep, proper flow will not be possible. To overcome this problem, various types of sleeves can be placed over the trays.

The proofer should be run at a dry bulb setting of 110° to 115°F. Relative humidity will depend on the system, the dry heat setting, and dough temperature. The lower the dough temperature and the higher the proofing temperature, the more humidity will be created by the dough itself. If excessive, this can be offset by using large temperature differentials between the dry and wet temperature settings or by installing a live steam injection system controlled by a wet bulb thermometer in the duct. Too much humidity in the proofer will make the dough pieces too wet to deposit easily and uniformly into the griddle, and a low RH will decrease dough flow and result in small, non-uniform muffins with a dull outer appearance. A commercially available English muffin proofer was described by Lupo (1987).

The depositer is another point where production problems can occur. The depositing mechanism is hourglass-shaped and turns the dough piece between its fall from the proofer tray and its landing on the grill. To improve performance of this mechanism, the depositor surface should be coated with a release compound and the depositor should be powered by a variable speed motor. Most of the time, the depositor is operated at a speed slow enough to just lay the dough pieces evenly into the griddle cups. Slight sticking to the depositor can often be corrected by slightly increasing its speed. The slide that, with the depositor, forms the transfer complex, can be improved by installing on its surface a piece of fiberglass cloth extending slightly slightly beyond the bottom end of the slide.

The griddle is probably the cause of most production problems. In one model, the top section consists of cups in rows of 12 across. Cups are usually three and seven-eighth inches in diameter and one inch high. Some griddles are merely a flat band with no cups. There are usually 18 burners located at the top section of the griddle, just below the traveling cups. Top flight plates are flat plates that travel above the cups for a part of the baking time. They are not present on all ovens. The positioning of these plates has a definite influence on the finished product.

To obtain a porous muffin, the plates should be situated far enough above the cups to permit the dough piece to expand without touching them. The last 18 inches of top flights should be placed so that they barely touch the top of the proofed dough piece and make a flat area about the diameter of a half dollar; if not low enough to flatten the muffins, the dough pieces will form peaks and be uncooked under the surface. If the plates are set too low, the dough piece will be restricted in its rise and the finished products will be very uniform but not porous. If the top plates are too high along their entire length, steam from the muffin will escape, sometimes causing the dough to set too quickly and resulting in non-uniform but porous muffins.

Clock (1987) gave a full description of a typical large-scale English muffin line. See Figure 28.5 for the complete layout of a similar plant. Key for the numbered equipment: (1) Mixer; (2) Dough pump; (3) Divider-rounder; (4) Proof cabinet; (5) Oven loader; (6) Double-plate oven; (7) Oven discharge conveyor; (8) Cooler; (9) Web slicing; (10) Scorer-splitter; (11) Muffin stacker; and (12) Packaging.

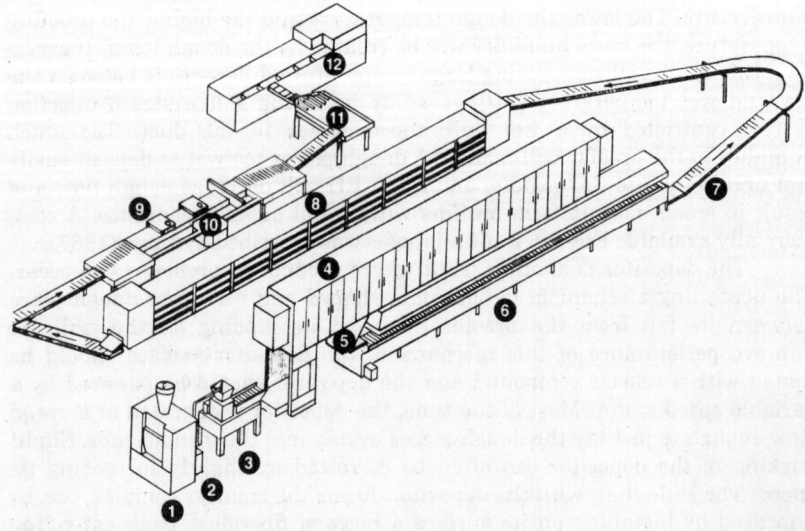

Figure 28.5. A plant for large-scale production of English muffins

A small, semi-automatic muffin griddle for use by small wholesale bakeries, in-store bakeries, and institutional bakeries was described by Lupo (1987). Also, see Matz (1988) for further details.

PRETZELS

There are three types of equipment used for forming the typical pretzel shape. One kind cuts a thin slice from a dough piece extruded through an orifice shaped like a pretzel, a second type forms a thin strand of dough and then twists it with mechanical fingers to form the pretzel shape, and the third design cuts pretzel shaped pieces from a flat sheet of dough. The latter type is used mainly in Europe, and probably mostly for cookie doughs, and it will not be discussed further in this section. The preceding descriptions apply to the traditional three-lobed pretzels. Evidently, all rod-shaped or stick pretzels are extruded. The following discussion applies to small dry pretzels of cracker-like texture, not to large soft pretzels.

Pretzel doughs tend to be very stiff, so either the mixer must be constructed to deal with strong resistances or smaller dough batches must be made. Horizontal dough mixers and vertical planetary mixers are being used. Blain and Zabrodsky (1987) describe the continuous manufacture of pretzel dough by a method in which the ingredients are continuously metered to an auger-type mixer conveyor.

In equipment made by the Reading Pretzel Machinery Co., dough is placed in a hopper from which an auger forces it through a slot in a die plate. Dough emerges from the extruder in small strips of circular cross section. An automatically-activated knife cuts the strips into pieces of predetermined length, allowing the segment to drop onto a canvas belt that carries it under a second belt. As the dough is gradually squeezed between the belts, it is rolled and formed to the desired thickness. At the end of the rolling process, the string of dough has its ends clipped so that all lengths are the same. The dough then enters a twisting machine that picks up the ends of the strip and performs the tying motions. After the shaped pretzel leaves the twister, it passes under a roller that exerts a slight pressure, thus fastening the "knots." AMF equipment has twisters that operate differently. Figure 28.6 shows three pretzel tying machines in operation (Source: AMF). Note that the dough strings are shown at three different stages in the tying operation.

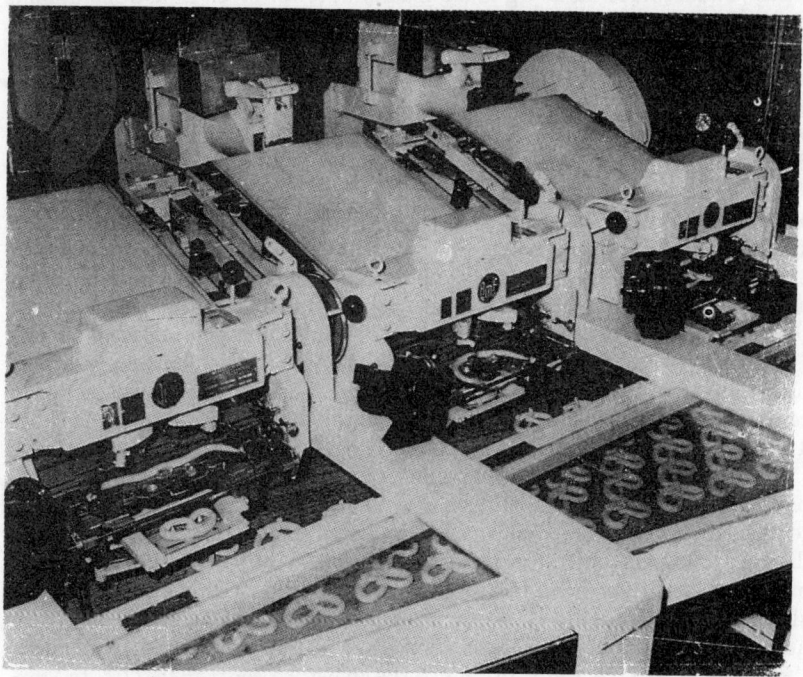

Figure 28.6. Three pretzel tying machines

The other type of pretzel former, now used for most of the pretzels made in the U.S., is similar in several respects to the wire-cut machines used for making cookies. A stiff pretzel dough is pushed by two rollers into the casing of a screw conveyor, the auger of which forces the dough under high pressure into a chamber having the lower surface penetrated by tubes leading to orifices shaped like pretzels. The dough continuously extrudes through these orifices and is sliced off in appropriate thicknesses by a blade held in a frame that is moved back and forth beneath the die plate. The blade moves forward for the cutting action while it is held close to the bottom surface of the die, and it is then dropped downward a slight distance for the return stroke so that it does not interfere with the extruding dough. As the dough pieces are severed, they drop on to a conveyor belt that carries them to the dipping and baking stations (Campbell 1988).

Regardless of the way the pretzel is made, the subsequent treatment is basically the same. By means of a reciprocating conveyor, the raw pretzels are placed across a proofing belt approximately 40 ft long. From the proofing belt the dough passes through a caustic bath, usually consisting of two tanks. There is a smaller tank through which the unbaked pretzels travel, and a larger make-up tank, usually at lower level. Caustic solution is pumped from the make-up tank to the upper container, in which its level is kept constant by adjusting an overflow pipe. The caustic solution of, perhaps, 1.0% to 1.5% sodium hydroxide is held at 186° to 195°F. If the concentration becomes too high, there will not be a complete conversion to sodium bicarbonate in the baking and drying cycles and the pretzel will be hot to the taste because of the residual caustic.

Immediately after the pretzels leave the caustic solution, they are salted. The salter consists of a supply hopper from which the salt is sprinkled by a grooved roller. Salted dough pieces enter an oven that is often about 50 ft long. One oven supplier offers modules 5 ft long that can be assembled to give a baking chamber any multiple of that size. As supplied, the ovens require manual lighting and manual adjustment of each burner. The baking section is the top part of the oven and it has burners over and under the conveyor that carries the pretzels. Time in the bake section is controlled by a variable speed drive on the conveyor, and is usually between 4 and 5 min. Moisture content at the end of the bake should be about 15%.

Baked pretzels go down a slide to a drying section underneath the baking section and separated from it by heavy insulation. Pretzels that cling to the baking belt are removed by a scraper blade. The conveyor in the drying section travels in the opposite direction to that of the belt in the bake oven. Speed of the drying belt can be varied, but it will always travel much slower than the baking conveyor. Pretzels form a bed several inches deep and remain in the drying section from 25 to 90 min. Temperature is held in the range of 225° to 250°F to reduce the moisture content to 2.0% to 2.5%. There has been much debate over the drying time and its total effect. It is said that a long drying time is needed to temper the pretzel so that it will not "check" and break during packaging and distribution.

There are continuous processes for making pretzels. Keller and Bowles (1988) described an assembly of machinery by which an essentially dry mixture containing flour, corn syrup solids, and salt is introduced into an extruder. Water is injected into the extruder barrel to bring the moisture level to between 19% and 25% (note the unusually low absorption). The dough is extruded at non-cooking temperature to form a self-supporting ribbon of extrudate that is sprayed with a caustic solution, then baked. This process is obviously only suited for forms that can be cut from a continuous ribbon, such as cylindrical, tubular, or (as the patent says) C-shaped.

Stick pretzels are extruded using, for example, a group of five extruding heads or die plates, each containing 10 to 12 holes. Dough is forced through the die orifices by means of a pressurizing helical conveyor (auger) and falls onto the proofing belt. As the dough strip nears the end of this conveyor, it is cut into the desired lengths by a group of circular knife blades that travel across the belt. When the knives reach the edge of the belt, they rise a few inches and return to their starting point. The raw stick pretzels pass through caustic and salting applicators similar to those previously described. Oven temperature is usually kept constant at 420°F and the bake time will be between 4 and 5 min. The drying section is held at 225° to 250°F, and the sticks remain in it for about 55 min. Log and nugget pretzels are made much the same way, except they are cut off at the extruder head.

BAGELS

It would seem at first thought that bagels could be formed in the same way as doughnuts. As a result of the requirement for very strong flour (or of flour supplemented with vital wheat gluten) bagel dough is, however, too tough to be cut or extruded as doughnuts are, and cut edges don't round off completely during proofing. Bench preparation of bagels involves hand rolling a cut piece into a cylinder, then pressing the ends together to form a circle. Automatic bagel machines generally perform the same actions.

Most modern bagel shapers take a cut, extruded, and/or rolled dough strip of proper weight and gradually reduce it in thickness and bend it into a circle between a sleeve type conveyor and a tapered mandrel. The gradually narrowing channel between conveyor and mandrel forces the ends of the strip together and seals them, forming a doughnut-like shape.

A machine patented by Patchell and Goldberg (1963) uses a different method. A piece of dough is forced onto the tip of a cone and then rolled up the cone by mechanical fingers until it assumes the proper shape and size. A later patent (Thompson 1974) discloses a machine in which a partially preshaped batch of dough of fairly uniform width is delivered by a conveyor to a dough dividing apparatus that forms the dough into two strips and then cuts them into rectangular pieces. These cut pieces are shaped between a stationary mandrel and moving forming cups into dough toroids, or bagel shapes. A further development of this theme (Thompson 1984) was a machine that divided bulk dough and formed it in somewhat the same manner as described in the earlier patent. According to the inventor (Thompson 1988), the latter patent can reasonably be regarded as representing the current state of the art and will be discussed below in greater detail.

The Thompson machine includes a dough divider of drum-like configuration having around its circumference rectangular dough receiving channels into which a pre-shaped dough batch is pushed by compression rollers. The intermittent movement of the drum can be adjusted to control piece size. Sensors are positioned above the drum to detect the buildup of dough at the divider drum before it passes beneath the compression rollers and to prevent flooding the drum with excess dough. A rotating cut-off knife and a dough wiping means are provided to complete the separation of a measured volume of dough from the divider cavity. The dough strips so formed are propelled by gravity and a rotating wheel through a chute and guide to the dough-forming station, which includes a series of articulated, toroid-forming, segmented, tubular cups mounted on a cup chain. These segmented cups open under the force of gravity as they move along the bottom pass of their conveying chain. They are closed by side guides as they approach the upper lay of the conveyor. A mandrel, which forms the internal circle of the bagel, is mounted on a single vertical support arm pivoted to facilitate moving the mandrel away from the forming cups. This permits the use of an alternative forming apparatus.

The patent describes a pair of top and bottom preshaping and dough-moving means positioned before the dough strips are engaged between the moving cups and the stationary mandrel so as to roll and squeeze the strips into a cylindrical form. The cylinder is gradually elongated and narrowed as the channel between the mandrel and cup is tightened. Finally, closure of the two ends of the strip occurs as they meet at the top of the mandrel, the hinged sides of the cups at that point having been brought together by guides positioned along the sides of the conveyor.

After forming, bagels are proofed. Provisions for proofing take many forms. The simplest proofing method involves placing the raw bagels by hand on wooden peels that are slid into racks. The proofing area may be simply a warm place in the bakery. More advanced procedures use intermediate proofing cabinets such as those described in a preceding chapter. Proofed bagels are often refrigerated to retard fermentation until the final steps of boiling and baking.

Immersion for a short time in water close to the boiling point forms the basis for the characteristic shiny brown skin of the bagel that is completed during baking. Hot water treatment can be performed in almost any kind of steam-heated kettler. Agitators are not required. For large scale production, dough pieces can be dropped into a rectangular vat, turned over after a short time, and then removed by some sort of skimming apparatus after they float to the top. The apparatus used for turning and removing doughnuts from a continuous fryer could doubtless be adapted for use in a boiling water bath. Some bagel bakers add low levels of molasses, malt, or caustic to the water to improve the surface gloss (Anon. 1991).

After a brief drying step, the bagels are baked in conventional types of ovens (Marracini 1986). A recent development is the baking of bagels without prior boiling; rack-type steam ovens are used to get a glossy crust. Opinions as to the quality of the non-boiled bagels differ among experts (Petrofsky 1986).

PIZZA CRUST EQUIPMENT

There are two main types of pizza crust production methods. The local pizzeria will normally use either a double sheeting process or some kind of pressed dough equipment, if it makes its own crusts and does not hand-shape them. Double-sheeting may be done with one small pair of rollers, the rounded dough being sent through the first time at a fairly wide setting of the rolls, then turned 180° and sent through the same rolls set closer together. Skill and some additional hand forming may be necessary to get the right shape. This type of crust forming is probably not used in factory production of pizza crusts.

There are several different kinds of pizza crust presses, including some suitable for individual pizzerias. The vast numbers of crusts that are made for frozen pizzas, and the fairly large number made for sale to pizzerias and other outlets for finishing, are made either by a sheeting and cutting process or by pressing lumps of dough into thin discs. Pizza gourmets claim crusts made by the two methods differ substantially in cooked texture.

Some details of the processing equipment used in the stamping methods of forming pizza crusts were described by Lehmann (1986). The dough is mixed 3 to 5 minutes in a conventional horizontal bread mixer, to give a soft, smooth, and relaxed dough that will flow out and exhibit minimum shrinkage at the stamping station. Dividing and rounding are done in conventional bread equipment. The dough balls are passed through an oil spray and enter an overhead proofer maintained at 95° to 100°F.

After 10 to 15 minutes of proofing, the dough pieces are deposited into pans designed to be compatible with the pizza press. These pans are then carried into the first stamping station, where the dough is pressed out to a specified diameter. In some cases, the initial stamping step extends the dough only part of the way to its finished size, and the crust must be further enlarged by a second pressing step after it undergoes a short relaxation period. For best results, the dough should rest at least two minutes between the stamping stations, but some bakers make do with only 45 seconds. The shorter time may lead to excessive shrinkage when the dough is baked.

Thin crusts will go directly to the oven after they are pressed. Thick crusts may either go directly to the oven, or receive an additional 5 or 10 minutes of final proofing at 90°F to promote greater crust thickness. Some bakers will press the freshly baked crusts under a compression belt or floating roller to reduce their thickness slightly and achieve greater uniformity of crust height. Texture, or eating quality, suffers as a result of these treatments, the crust taking on the cardboard-like characteristics that are frequently remarked upon by consumers.

Further information on preparing pizza crusts by large-scale equipment was given by Fischer (1981). For pressing operations, a straight dough with as much as 5% yeast and 1% or 2% of shortening is divided and rounded by conventional methods, such as those used for bread loaves. Dough pieces are given some floor time and then sent through an intermediate proofer, proofing being carried to the point that will enable the dough to color well when baked. Proofed dough is placed on an oiled pan and, usually, more oil is applied. Pressing can be done once or twice, or with heated platens. Pressed pizza crusts are baked in a pan and usually in a tunnel or tray oven. A major disadvantage of the pressing method is the large number of pans that are in use at any one time.

Preparation of pizza dough by sheeting and cutting methods is fairly straightforward. For large-scale commercial operations, horizontal dough mixers are perfectly satisfactory for blending the ingredients and developing the dough. Almost any other kind of mixer that can develop the rather stiff dough used for most pizza crusts can be used—vertical planetary mixers, for example. Dough temperatures of 78° to 82°F are considered desirable. The dough is allowed to rest for 5 to 10 minutes after mixing, then extruded on to the mixing line. The strip of extruded dough is passed through a series of reduction rollers to reduce its thickness to one-eighth to three-sixteenths of an inch for thin crusts or one-fourth to five-sixteenths of an inch for thick crusts. The dough then passes under a docker and, finally, is die cut to produce the desired shape and dimensions. Formed dough pieces are passed through a final proofer maintained at 90° to 95°F and 80% to 85% RH. Proof times are about 8 minutes for a thin crust and about 30 minutes for thick crusts. Immediately after proofing, the shells are baked at about 425°F.

For sheeting and cutting lines, the dough may or may not be fermented in the trough. Sheeting rollers may be arranged in a cascade so that the dough falls from one to the other before going underneath the cutter, or they may be arranged in the more common horizontal configuration. Rollers may be sheathed in Teflon, and pickoff rolls, rather than knives, may be used to transfer dough from the gauge rolls to the conveyor. Docking is considered to be necessary for crusts baked without topping. In some factories, the crusts are baked on the same band they have been proofed on, to eliminate a transfer of the soft, sticky disc of dough. In other installations, proofing is handled by transferring the cut pieces to a special carrier. This carrier allows the pickup nosing conveyor to get beneath the cut and proofed pieces and transfer them to the oven with no distortion. The sheeted and cut crust may be proofed before baking. Baking times for these crusts are on the order of 3 to 5 minutes. Band ovens are frequently used.

A large-scale method of preparing pizza shells by the sheeting and cutting procedure is described in a patent of Moline (1977). The production line described in the patent is composed largely, if not entirely, of conventional dough processing equipment. Dough is mixed in either a batch or continuous mixer and then transferred to a dough extruder that can form it into a relatively thin continuous strip. The dough web is then sheeted by conventional reduction rollers until it assumes the width and thickness deemed suitable for further make-up. The continuous strip is transported on an endless belt conveyor for the time required for proofing, after which the expanded dough is sheeted again to a predetermined width and thickness. Circles are cut from the web by conventional type roller cutters or by other means. Docking rollers, which punch holes in the dough to prevent excessive rise, may be applied at this point, although they are probably not necessary if filling is to be applied before baking. Trimmings generated in the cutting operation are collected on belt conveyors that carry them back to the beginning of the line where they are blended into newly mixed dough.

A patent obtained by Groth (1968) describes a type of apparatus that can be used to make pressed pizza crusts. A divider, presumably of any standard type, forms dough balls of the weight appropriate for one pizza crust. Each one of these balls is deposited on a separate aluminum plate having the approximate diameter of the pizza shell. The aluminum plates are conveyed on drive chains through a pressing mechanism. When a plate is centered in the press, the drive mechanism stops temporarily, and a hydraulic drive forces a circular mold the size of a pizza crust on top of the dough ball, causing it to assume the thin disc shape of a typical pizza shell. Subsequently, the aluminum plate with its raw crust is moved to a docking machine that perforates the outer surface of the shell to prevent excessive expansion in the pre-bake heating that follows.

Some inventors have concentrated their efforts on devising machines that duplicate the actions performed on the pizza sheet during hand preparation. The rather quick straight downward pressing motion of the usual pizza press machine has been thought by some pizza experts to be damaging to the textural properties of the crust, making it somewhat cracker-like. To improve these crusts, Pacilio (1987) invented a machine that simultaneously compresses and applies centrifugal force to a lump of pizza dough. A dough piece of proper weight is placed on a support surface or pan that can be rotated. While it is being rotated, the press slowly descends and at the same time pushes outward. Excessive spread of the dough is prevented by edges of the pressing surface. Other inventors have modified the design of the dough-contacting platen, as did De Christopher (1987), who provided the stamping platen with many downwardly projecting protuberances (bumps) that press the dough into a relatively flat disc having a dimpled surface. This leaves thick portions between indentations for the collection of gases. A later development (De Christopher 1990) consisted of a roller in the form of a cluster of balls on a polygonal support provided with ducts for olive oil. The cluster is rotated on a lump of dough to form a pizza crust.

Most pizza crusts are probably topped with sauce, cheese, and other adjuncts before they are baked. Many are prepared in pizzerias where topping application is essentially a hand operation, except, perhaps for some simple metering devices for sauce. This labor intensive step has been the object of considerable development work by equipment manufacturers. An integrated system for preparing crust, applying toppings, and baking was patented by Triporo and Eckels (1987), who disclosed a "tamping" press having a knobbed contacting surface that performs thrusting motions at successively different positions relative to the pan. This gradual and varying pressure is said to yield a crust similar in texture to those made by pressing with fingers, that is, similar to hand made crusts. A conveyor carries a pan with its portion of dough through this press and under outlets that automatically meter topping ingredients on to the crust, and then into the oven. The conveyor moves continuously in an oval path so as to bring the pan back to the dough extruding area after the finished pizza has been removed.

Some of the largest manufacturers of frozen pizza have changed to frying rather than baking the crusts before the topping is applied. The patent of Totino *et al.* (1979) is exemplary. There is no doubt that frying, done under proper conditions, can improve crust texture and flavor, and—most important—lead to better retention of quality during frozen storage. In a typical line of this type, the dough will be mixed in a conventional horizontal mixer, dumped into a trough and given some floor time, pumped through an extruder to form a fairly thick layer, passed through about three stands of reducing rollers (usually preceded by flour dusters), cut into circles by rotating die cylinders, proofed by passing for a few minutes through a tunnel into which steam is being injected, dropped into a vat of hot oil, carried through the oil by a wire mesh conveyor belt, scooped up at the other end by another wire mesh belt, shaken and blown to remove excess oil, cooled, topped, and frozen. After the circles are cut, the trimmings are removed and conveyed to the dough trough for recycling.

Docking is absolutely essential to prevent the dough pieces from expanding into a ball shape and the top and bottom surfaces from separating in the fryer. Proper choice of docking pattern prevents the formation of large bumps on the surface. These bumps are almost as objectionable as the ball shape, because they interfere with the application of topping and may make it difficult, if not impossible, to fit the pizza into its package. Different kinds of docking apparatus have been used, and it appears that thick pins rather than thin ones, and more rather than fewer pins, represent desirable choices. The pins should penetrate the crust, or nearly so. A mere dimple will not serve the purpuose. It has also been suggested to use heated bars or punches to tie the top and bottom surfaces together, but these appear to be needless elaborations.

Preparation areas or "kitchens" have been designed for use in delivery vehicles, so pizzas can be assembled and baked while the truck on its way to the consumer. One of these mobile kitchens is described in a patent granted to Abbott *et al.* (1986). The truck is divided into a driver's area and a pizza preparation station. The latter includes a pie case, a pizza preparation station, and a chair for supporting a cook while in transit. Pizzas are made from uncooked but proofed dough loaded in pans, and cooking is done in a conveyor oven that is part of the equipment.

OTHER BREAD-LIKE PRODUCTS

Croissants

The production of croissants includes, among other steps, the laminating of butter (or other shortening) into a yeast-leavened dough similar to bread dough, then reducing the finished laminate to a sheet of the proper thickness, cutting triangles from the sheet, and rolling the triangles into the typical croissant shape. It is said (Gorton 1989A) that the blitz or all-in method of roll-in shortening application is used by most large-scale producers of croissants in France, including a successful manufacturer of mini-croissants (20 gram).

Any and all of these steps can be partially or completely mechanized. Devices specialized for croissants are not required for mixing the dough, laminating it, and sheeting it. Cutting can be done by rotary dies that sever triangles from a sheet. In small retail bakeries, simple die rollers moved by hand can be used for cutting the triangles. For rolling, curling, and panning croissants, manufacturers offer equipment of almost any degree of automation and rate of production that could be desired. Laminating equipment and processes have been described in much detail in a previous chapter; that general information applies to croissants and will not be repeated here.

The manufacturer of a semi-automatic croissant line describes the process as follows (Anon. 1986). The dough is laminated into a sheet slightly thicker than required, thus saving considerable preparatory time. The strip is rolled on a wooden dowel that is placed on brackets situated above the infeed belt. An automatic device continuously feeds the dough to calibrating rollers that reduce it to a thickness that will give the desired finished product weight and also join the ends of sheets together to give a continuous feed. Operator participation is needed in the joining step. The triangles are cut in two stages by two rotary dies in order to prevent sticking in die cavities. Triangles are automatically conveyed to the roll-up machine with their bases parallel to the rollers. The rolling machine can be adjusted to give the dough as many curls as desired. The finished product has a raised spiral design and is delivered to the pan ready for proofing. About 4,000 croissants per hour can be made with this equipment.

There are a number of machines that satisfactorily roll croissants according to Rijkaart (1984). They are simple devices, consisting of two conveyor belts traveling at different speeds. Dough triangles are placed between these belts with the point trailing, the leading edge is pulled back by the slower traveling upper belt, starting the wrapping motions that continues until the entire triangle is curled up into the typical horn shape. The same type of machine can be used to form salt sticks, except the latter are generally rolled into tighter cylinders and are not curved into crescents after rolling. Other rolling machines have been described by Svengren and Wadell (1989, 1990), Hayashi (1990, 1991), Ueno (1988) The rolled dough is curved, usually manually, into the traditional crescent shape and deposited in trays for the final fermentation step. Proofing is usually at 98°F and 80% RH for 60 min. Baking conditions for a croissant of the usual size will be at 430° to 450°F for 14 to 15 min. Steam is added to the oven during the first minute of baking so the crust does not crack.

Rowe (1985) described a continuous automatic process for croissants that completely eliminates the retarding stage for finished dough blocks but does start with retarded unlaminated dough. The chilled dough is fed into a laminator that extrudes a hollow tube having an outer layer of dough and an inner layer of fat. The tube is flattened by a conventional roller, fed to a folding unit, and then sheeted by a "stretching unit" that has been described elsewhere. The stretched dough sheet is conveyed to the next folding and laminating table and then to another stretcher, from which it goes to another stretcher. The croissant molder fits on tracks over the make-up table and cuts the dough sheet of the proper triangular size, curls the triangle, and deposits the dough pieces on the make-up table. Capacity of the unit is said to be 15,000 croissants per hour and it requires one operator. Croissants are manually curved and panned for proofing, requiring another four persons. Proofing at 85° to 90°F and RH of 80% for 55 min is recommended, as is a baking time of 15 min at 400°F.

Pita Bread

Pita bread and the variations of it sometimes called Arab bread, pocket bread, etc., can be described as very thin pieces of baked dough, circular in outline, having the top crust separated from the bottom crust except at the circumference. Pita bread superficially resembles flour tortillas, but it is made from yeast-leavened doughs. The formulas generally define a lean dough, with a typical recipe calling for flour (usually strong flour, perhaps supplemented with gluten), water, yeast, salt, and (sometimes) sugar.

Most of the steps in processing of pita bread, before the shape is formed, are similar to those used for regular white bread. A flow diagram would show mixing, a relaxing stage, dividing, rounding, sheeting, final proofing, baking, and cooling (Cooper 1986). Straight dough procedures yield satisfactory products. Dough balls, rounded and given some intermediate proofing in the usual manner, are passed through a series of sheeting rollers that flatten each piece to a thickness of about one-sixteenth inch. Size, conformation, and skin characteristics are controlled so that the final "loaf" is as near a perfect circle as possible and the crust has no breaks or cracks. The amount of dusting flour should be kept to an absolute minimum. The flattened dough pieces proceed to a final proofer that, in large scale operations, may be a series of many conveyor belts stacked one above the other, so that the dough pieces can be carried back and forth several times before exiting the proofer. No pans or other supports are used. With a relative humidity of about 65% in the proofer, the crusts become tough and rather dry, characteristics that are important in obtaining the proper response during baking. The proofed loaves (discs) are baked on a mesh belt in a very hot oven having a high contribution of radiant heat. The temperature in the oven should be at least 700°F, and at some points perhaps as high as 1,000°F (Cooper 1986). Within 30 sec after they have entered the oven, the dough expands almost to a ball shape, the gas then bursts through at some point, and the dough piece contracts. Due to cooking and dehydration of the crust, complete collapse does not occur, and an interior space persists. Further contraction occurs during cooling, but it may be necessary to compress the loaf by hand or roller to get it into the package.

Some recent pita bread installations use a sheeting and cutting method to form the loaves, an obvious way to get perfect circles that are seldom achieved in the sheeted ball operation. The cut edges need not prevent the desired oven expansion.

Grissini and Breadsticks

There is a considerable production of breadsticks, the thin cylindrical pieces of bread sometimes baked almost to dryness but in other examples retaining some of the soft crumb texture. The small pieces found in individual serving packs and having a crisp texture throughout, are baked from dough that has been extruded through circular orifices by any suitable type of simple extrusion equipment. For more conventional doughs, bench top devices are available from Italian manufacturers for severing a strip of sheeted dough passed under a grooved roller. More elaborate automatic machines are available to perform essentially the same functions at a much higher speed and having the capability of varying the diameter and length of the bread stick. They include automatic and continuous dough kneaders and sheeters. A typical machine combines the sheeter with a loading hopper in the gauge roll section, to form the dough into a ribbon of the required thickness. Dough from the final pair of gauge rolls is allowed the necessary recovery time on the machine band, and, after this, is gang-slit and finally chopped into lengths by a reciprocating knife.

BIBLIOGRAPHY

ABBOTT, M. T., STREEPY, G. S., PAULUS, J. R., BARRERA, R., AND BREWER, D. E. 1986. Pizza preparation and delivery system. U.S. Pat. 4,632,836

ANON. 1985. Le Croissant Dore. Technomatik, Padova, Italy

ANON. 1986. New wrinkle to fully automated process. Prepared Foods *157*, No. 8, 201

ANON. 1989. Baking the best bun the automated way. Baking & Snack Systems *11*, No. 5, 7, 9, 16

ANON. 1991. Technology for today's hot products. Baking & Snack *13*, No. 4, 16-18, 21-22

BLAIN, W. A., and ZABRODSKY, J., III. 1987. Continuous pretzel dough manufacture. U.S. Pat. 4,691,625

BROADDUS, M R., JR. 1978. Soft roll equipment. Proc. Am. Soc. Bakery Engineers *1978*, 122-132

CAMPBELL, S. 1988. Personal communication. Atlanta, GA

CHIAO, T. T., and CHIAO, C. C. 1986. Apparatus for forming wrapped food products. U.S. Pat. 4,574,690

CLOCK, T. Q. 1987. Personal communication. Clock Associates, Portland, OR

COOPER, I. 1986. Pita/pocket bread. Proc. Am. Soc. Bakery Engineers *1986*, 151-156

CUMMINGS, R. P. 1987. Automation of specialty roll products. Proc. Am. Soc. Bakery Engineers *1987*, 145-153

DE CHRISTOPHER, E. L. 1987. Method of making a pizza-type product of dough. U.S. Pat. 4,696,823

DE CHRISTOPHER, E. L. 1990. Spherical roller for kneading a dough ball. U.S. Pat. 4,936,686

FISCHER, H. A. 1981. Pizza crust production. Proc. Am. Soc. Bakery Engineers *1981*, 170-174

GORTON, L. 1988. Automating hand-made bread and roll doughs. Baking & Snack Systems *10*, No. 9, 6-7, 9-10

GORTON, L. 1989A. Makes croissant process completely continuous. Baking & Snack Systems *11*, No. 8, 6-10

GORTON, L. 1989B. New plant relies on computerized processing. Baking & Snack Systems *1989*, 6-10

GROTH, F. A. 1968. Method and apparatus for forming pizza shells. U.S. Pat. 3,379,141

HAYASHI, T. 1990. Apparatus and method for rolling croissant dough pieces. U.S. Pat. 4,905,583

HAYASHI, T. 1991. Method for rolling croissant dough pieces. U.S. Pat. 4,994,293

JUDD, V. L. 1988. Apparatus and method for preparing patterned baked goods. U.S. Pat. 4,789.555

JUERS, A. A. 1982. English muffins. Proc. Am. Soc. Bakery Engineers *1982*, 46-51

KELLER, L. C., and BOWLES, C. A. 1988. Continuous production of pretzels. U.S. Pat. 4,759,939

LAHVIC, R. 1988. Canadian colossus. Bakery *23*, No. 1, 62, 64-66

LEHMANN, T. A. 1986. Pizza crust. Proc. Am. Soc. Bakery Engineers *1986*, 167-177

LORTZ, J. L. 1989. Apparatus for forming three dimensional food products. U.S. Pat. 4,886,441

LUPO, J. 1987. Personal communication. Production Line Equipment, Rockaway, NJ

MANI, D. 1989. Apparatus for the manufacture of perforated pita bread. U.S. Pat. 4,800,807

MARRACCINI, M. 1986. Bakery's growth attributed to bagel forming machine. Baking Industry *153*, No. 1868, 22

MATZ, S. A. 1988. Equipment for Bakers. Pan-Tech International, McAllen, TX

MOLINE, R. V. 1977. Method for forming dough shells. U.S. Pat. 4,046,920

MORIKAWA, M., and HAYASHI, T. 1990. Method for continuously producing at a substantially constant flow rate a strip of dough of substantially uniform dimensions. U.S. Pat. 4,902,524

NOEL, E. M. 1962. Fully automatic production of English muffins. Bakers Weekly *194*, No. 9, 32-34

PACILIO, V. C. 1987. Pizza dough spreading apparatus. U.S. Pat. 4,690,043

PATCHELL, H., and GOLDBERG, I. 1963. Apparatus for automatically forming dough rings for making bagels. U.S. Pat. 3,080,831

PETROFSKY, R. 1986. Bagels. Proc. Am. Soc. Bakery Engineers *1986*, 143-151

PFEFER, D. N. 1976. English muffins. Proc. Am. Soc. Bakery Engineers *1976*, 51-55

PIVONKA, J. K. 1988. Dough moulding and a dough moulding machine. U.S. Pat. 4,734,293

RIJKAART, C. 1984. Croissant production. Proc. Am. Soc. Bakery Engineers *1984*, 143-151

ROWE, C. S. 1985. Croissants. Proc. Am. Soc. Bakery Engineers *1985*, 137-145

SVENGREN, A. G., and WADELL, L. G. A. 1989. Preparation of a rolled pastry product. U.S. Pat. 4,828,862

SVENGREN, A. G., and WADELL, L. G. A. 1990. Apparatus for preparing rolled pastry products. U.S. Pat. 4,917,590

THOMPSON, D. T. 1974. Machine for forming bagels. U.S. Pat. 3,792,940

THOMPSON, D. T. 1984. Compact dough dividing and forming machine. U.S. Pat.. 4,478,565

THOMPSON, D. T. 1986. Personal communication. Thompson Machines, Los Angeles, CA

THOMPSON, J. B. 1981. English muffins. Proc. Am. Soc. Bakery Engineers *1981*, 141-145

TOTINO, R. W., BEHNKE, J. R., WESTOVER, J. D., and KELLER, R. L. 1979. Fried dough product and method. U.S. Pat. 4,170,659

TRIPORO, P. R., AND ECKELS, S. 1987. Apparatus for making pizza. U.S. Pat. 4,634,365

UNEO, S. 1988. Apparatus and method for producing croissants. U.S. Pat. 4,741,263

VANDERVOORT, D., and GRIFFITH, M. 1989. Method of subdividing dough. U.S. Pat. 4,812,321

chapter twenty-nine

FORMING COOKIES AND CRACKERS

INTRODUCTION

The manufacture of crackers and cookies in commercial plants requires certain kinds of equipment that are seldom found in other kinds of baked food factories. These devices fall mostly into the category of forming or shaping machines and will be discussed in this chapter. It is convenient to separate the machines into cookie equipment and cracker equipment, since the devices used for these two types of products are quite different.

Nearly all large-scale cookie and cracker production is based on the use of band ovens. Discussion of this equipment is included in the chapter on ovens and baking.

Much additional information can be found in Cookie and Cracker Technology (Matz and Matz 1978), a third edition of which is in process.

METHODS OF FORMING COOKIES

Types of Equipment

There are several types of cookie forming equipment, each type being limited as to the physical properties of the doughs it can process satisfactorily. The four broad types of forming or shaping devices that are used to manufacture the great majority of commercial cookies are (1) extruders which push dough or batter through a constricting orifice, exemplified by deposit machines, bar presses, and wire-cut equipment, (2) rotary molders which shape the dough in die cavities cut into the surface of a metal cylinder, (3) stamping machines or rotating cutters which force a relatively sharp die into a sheet of dough, and (4) Sugar wafer ovens, which bake thin batters in heated waffle-type molds. Each of these methods requires doughs of different rheological characteristics from those needed for the other methods, although it is true there is some overlapping. A more detailed classification is included below. It is probably unnecessary to say that there are types of equipment which do not fit neatly into this classification.

A. Machines which push bulk dough through a constricting orifice.

1. Extruders that do not cut the dough strand before baking.

a. Single-dough extruders. May have shaped orifices to give a pattern to the top surface. Bar cookie extruders and rout presses.

b. Combination dough/paste extruders. Two or more strands are combined in one, often as concentric extrusions. The fig bar machine is the most familiar example, but extruders for dual-textured cookies are probably in even wider use nowadays.

2. Deposit machines. Dough strands are separated into pieces by the moving apart of the orifice and the receiving surface (pan or oven band).

3. Wire-cut machines. Dough strands are separated into pieces by a knife or wire moved across the orifice.

4. Devices which form complex enrobing actions and then sever spheroidal shapes using rotating constrictors or iris mechanisms, etc. The familiar Rheon devices are exemplary.

B. Machines which force dough into cavities in a rotating metal or plastic cylinder and then remove the shaped dough by various methods.

1. Machines which remove pieces from the cavity by relying on their adhesion to a conveyor belt. The great majority of commercial machines rely on this method.

2. Machines which force the dough pieces out of the cavities by a plunger operated from within the rotating cylinder. Not very common but may be essential for processing problem doughs.

C. Machines which cut pieces from a continuous sheet of dough, sometimes applying an embossed design or docking pattern as part of the cutting action or in a separate operation.

1. Stamping machines. The flat cutting die moves up and down as the dough sheet moves beneath it. May including ejection motions to prevent dough pieces from remaining in the cavity during the upward (return) movement of the die. Nearly all soda crackers are so formed.

2. Rotary cutting machines. The cutting ridges are embossed (or formed of metal strips) on a metal cylinder which rotates above the moving dough sheet. Two, or possibly more, cylinders may be used in tandem, one to emboss or form a docking pattern, and another to cut the outline of the pieces. Ejection plungers are possible, but generally the adhesion of the dough to the underlying conveyor belt is relied upon to prevent cut pieces from clinging to the die cavity as it lifts off the dough sheet.

D. Sugar wafer ovens. A fluid batter is spread on one part of a baking mold and the other part of the mold is immediately clamped into position, forming an enclosed cavity that defines the shape of the finished product. In all cases, the mold is an integral part of the oven that heats the mold to cause the batter to expand and dehydrate.

1. Mold and oven combinations designed to form flat sheets that may, however, be rolled or otherwise formed into fancier shapes while they are still hot and plastic.

2. More complex molding devices, often quite different in operation from the traditional wafer ovens. Used mostly to form ice cream cones.

Interrelationship of Machine and Dough

Each type of processing machine can only process doughs with rheological properties falling within certain limits. Take, for example, the fluid batter fed to the sugar wafer molds. This batter would be totally unfitted for any other type of cookie molder, while, on the other hand, the sugar wafer machine would be unable to process any of the doughs or batters required by the other three major types of cookie machines. Nearly all the doughs that function well on stamping machines and rotary cutters would be impractical for commercial production on extruding or rotary molding equipment. There is overlapping, of course. The extruder is probably the most versatile, and can handle some of the doughs used in rotary molders, and perhaps even some of the doughs used in sheeters, though not very efficiently.

Stamping machines and rotary cutting machines must be fed continuous sheets of dough. An important requirement of these machines is that the scrap generated must be removed in one piece for efficient operation. Furthermore, thickness of the sheet must be held within a narrow range so the weight of the dough pieces will not vary significantly.

If dough is to be formed into a strip that will remain intact, be smooth on the surface, and maintain uniform thickness after sheeting, it must be cohesive enough to bear its own weight and have some elasticity. On the other hand, it must not shrink significantly after the piece has been cut, otherwise deformed pieces will result.

Doughs that run well on cutting machines are generally not suitable for forming into die cavities because when so treated they will not fill the die completely, they may not cut off cleanly, and they tend to shrink when baked, distorting the shape and design. These doughs seldom perform satisfactorily in extrusion equipment, since they tend to stretch and "string out" from the orifice, making it impossible to control weight and shape.

Rotary molded doughs, those formed by pressing into die cavities, should form a solid lump when pressed together, but they should possess little or no elasticity and should exhibit minimal stickiness. Some of these doughs have the general appearance and texture of crumbly lumps of shortening and sugar, others are clay-like in texture and appearance. Nearly all of them are quite low in moisture as compared to other types of cookie formulas. They must, however, possess sufficient cohesiveness so the individual dough pieces do not tear apart when they pass over transfer points, such as the transfer from the molder conveyor to the oven band. In spite of the seeming stringency of these restrictions on the physical characteristics of doughs for rotary molders, a wide range of cookies can be made by this method. Some of the cookies sold in the largest volume, both plain and fancy designs, including most sandwich cookie base cakes, are made by rotary molding. The process is generally not satisfactory for soft cookies.

Wire-cut, deposit, and rout press (bar press) cookies are formed by extruding doughs or batters through orifices. At some point before or after baking, the extruded strand is separated into individual pieces. For wire-cut goods, the dough is severed in a horizontal plane by a knife or wire operated at or near the orifice. The cut surfaces form the top and bottom of the cookie and lead to a more or less flat and featureless top surface. Bar goods go on to the conveyor in a continuous string that is cut into appropriate lengths by guillotines or gangs of disc knives, generally before baking but sometimes afterwards. By profiling the dies, the top surfaces of the strands can be given ridges or other longitudinal designs and their cross-section can be shaped. The familiar coconut bar is an example.

By extruding two different doughs and/or pastes simultaneously, filled cookies such as fig bars can be made. In this system, the filling is extruded through a tube inserted in the center of the dough orifice. Deposit cookies are made from very soft doughs (fairly stiff batters) that are extruded directly on to the oven band. Dividing into pieces occurs as a result of mechanisms that increase the distance between the band and orifice so that the batter band is stretched and breaks apart.

EXTRUDERS

Extruders vary in complexity from simple equipment consisting of a hopper with feed rolls that press dough through adjustable slits to very complicated devices that extrude deposit cookie batters through orifices moving in predetermined patterns. The most common type of machine consists of a hopper with one or more feed rolls to force dough through a number of tubes usually called die cups. These dies may have orifices of different shapes—square, round, oval, scalloped, etc. In wire-cut machines, discs are sliced from the continuously extruded cylinder of dough and allowed to drop onto the oven band or transfer belt.

Deposit Machines

In these devices, batter is extruded intermittently through shaped nozzles. Separation into cookie-sized portions is achieved by lowering the oven band during the time the extrusion is stopped. As a result, the batter on the band is pulled away from batter still in the extrusion orifice, resulting in a thinning and eventual separation of the two. Anyone who has observed an operator filling ice cream cones from a soft serve freezer knows how the principle works. The band is then moved up toward the nozzle and extrusion begins again. These machines are relatively simple, but are quite demanding so far as dough characteristics are concerned. In more advanced machines, the nozzles can be moved to form various patterns such as curves, wavy, fingers, swirls, and circles. A second depositor can be synchronized with the first one to put jelly or some other filling on top of the cookie.

Bar Presses

Bar presses are sometimes called rout presses, especially in the U.K. They employ a simpler method of forming than is used by deposit machines, since there is no need to separate the dough into cookie sized chunks at the extruder. A bar press extrudes continuous strings or strips of dough directly on to the oven band. Separation of these bands into individual bars can be made before or after baking by one of the usual cutting devices. If the die plate is inclined in the direction of the extrusion, the ribbon is supported for a longer period of time, an arrangement that reduces breaking or thinning of the dough strand due to gravitational pull.

Die orifices are usually slots with a straight lower edge to give a flat bottom to the cookie and a grooved top edge to give a ribbed upper surface. Usually, there are provisions for adjusting the thickness of the extrusion by moving the upper or lower edge. The scope of possible variations in surface appearance is rather limited, but some character can be given to the top by modifying dough characteristics to give smooth or rough texture, strong differentiation in browning between high spots and low areas, etc.

Fig Bars

Fig bars and other fruit-filled bars are made by extruding dough for the jacket and jam for the filling through concentric orifices in a bar press machine. Two hoppers and two sets of forcing rollers (or screw extruders) are required to feed the dies. Fig paste is led through the dough hopper portion to its designated orifice by tubes or chutes. Dies are of conventional design, as previously described. The extruder must be adjusted to deliver a ribbon of dough that is moving at the same speed as the oven band so as to avoid stretching, wrinkling, or breaking the dough strip,

Fig bars are baked in continuous strings that are cut into individual cookies when they come out of the oven. Some manufacturers (mostly British) have placed the cutters before the oven. The earliest examples of pre-oven cutters had a vertical knife that passed between two heavily oiled strips of felt before and after it contacted the dough strips. More recent versions separate the guillotine from the dough by a thin sheet of rubber. Users of this system claim the semi-sealed ends help to retain moisture during baking, but it seems doubtful this has much effect on finished product quality. Those manufacturers who bake in an uncut strip say it reduces distortion of the ends of the bars, prevents flowing out of the hot filling, and retards loss of moisture from the filling.

Guillotines or rotary cutters can be used to cut baked strips. The former type is similar to other reciprocating vertical-movement knives used in bakeries. Rotary fig bar cutters run two gangs of circular knives across the oven band. Cutter blades are heat treated and spaced along a shaft at the distance required to cut the desired cookie length. The shafts on which the knives are mounted are carried across the band by heavy roller chains running in guides. The chain speed must be regulated to coordinate with the oven band velocity. As the knives pass below the belt, they can be carried through a stainless steel cleaning tank. The tank is provided with an overflow for maintaining the level, and it can be heated. These provisions keep the knives reasonably free of jam and syrup. Rollers to support the oven band as it passes through the machine and under the cutting knives are integral parts of the equipment. The cutter is driven from the main oven band drive by means of line shafting and bevel gear box.

Dual-textured Cookies

There has been much interest in creating dual-textured cookies, often described as cookies with a crisp outer crust and a chewy interior. It is believed than many consumers prefer such cookies because the texture contrast is similar to that observed in freshly baked homemade cookies. It is evident that textural dichotomies of certain kinds are appealing to consumers, as shown by the popularity of chocolate chip cookies, marshmallow-containing cookies, cookies with nut pieces, etc. The crisp/chewy contrast in homemade cookies appears to be largely the result of uneven moisture distribution and, perhaps, crystal status of the sugar.

Many methods have been suggested for obtaining this texture differentiation in commercial cookies that spend several weeks or months in distribution before they are eaten by the consumer. One method is to extrude a continuous cylinder having around its circumference a dough high in crispness-inducing ingredients and in its center a dough containing ingredients contributing to chewiness.

Before it is baked, the continuous tube is cut into cookie-size pieces by a reciprocating die or roller that presses the outer dough through the inner dough and seals the outer dough all around. If the dough consistencies and dimensions are correctly chosen, this seal can be made by a guillotine blade with a flat bottom 0.25 inch or so in thickness, perhaps followed up by a sharp blade that cuts through the middle of the flattened area. Some rounding of the piece occurs as the doughs flow and expand during baking, so that the square edges are smoothed out. Under ideal circumstances, cookies that are almost circular will result. Reciprocating cutters that make a curved outline are also known to have been tried in attempts to get a more nearly circular piece. Other devices pinch the dough tube from the side.

Wire-cut Machines

These devices represent an advance in complexity over the bar press and deposit machines in that they include a device to cut off pieces of the extruded dough as it emerges from the die orifice. The cut-off device consists of a wire or blade that is drawn quickly through the dough by a "harp" moving back and forth below the orifice. Considerable information has been accumulated on the construction and operation of these machines. Figure 29.1 clearly illustrates the functional principles of wire-cut machines (Source: Weidenmiller).

Dough is fed to the hopper manually or by gravity. Mechanical devices for transferring doughs to the hoppers are also fairly common. Since the weight of the dough resting on the feed rollers affects their performance, greater accuracy and uniformity can be obtained by installing an auxiliary hopper that keeps a constant dough level in the machine hopper. Soft batters can be fed continuously by pumps and this would seem to be the method of choice when dough properties make it feasible.

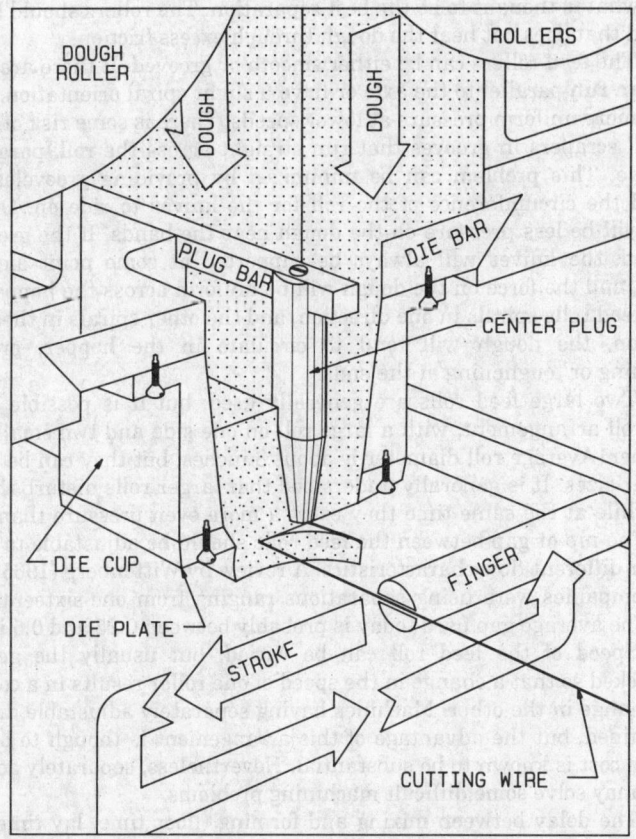

Figure 29.1. Operating features of the wire-cut machine

Vertical separator plates can be inserted in the hopper to allow feeding of two or more colors or flavors of dough at the same time. Some authorities have suggested using short partitions between each die cup to lessen the difference in feed rates between the outside and inside cups. Keeping the feed rate steady and maintaining hopper contents at about the same height at all times are the initial steps needed to assure a uniform pressure and constant rate of extrusion. Hoppers have been jacketed and warm air or warm water circulated to improve uniformity of extrusion rates. Ends of the hoppers have been curved so as to reduce the tendency of the dough to stagnate in this area.

Characteristics of the rollers that press dough through the die cups are important factors in maintaining uniform size and weight in the finished cookies. They may move either continuously or intermittently, depending on the result desired. In some extruders, separation of the rolls is adjustable to two inches or more, while in others the rolls are permanently set at what is thought to be the best separation. The rollers should be run at a speed that does not heat the dough through excess friction.

The feed rollers can be either smooth or grooved. If there are grooves, they can run parallel to the axle or have a slight spiral orientation. Grooves give a more uniform pressure at lower speeds. There is some risk of catching the roll scrapers in grooves that run straight across the roll, parallel with the axle. This problem can be minimized by providing grooveless bands around the circumference of the roll for the knives to ride on. Of course, there will be less pressure on the dough near the bands. If the grooves are spiraled, the knives will always be supported at some point along their length, and the force on the dough will be uniform across the hopper. If one of the feed rolls spirals in one direction, and the other spirals in the opposite direction, the dough will tend to circulate in the hopper, preventing hardening or toughening at the ends.

Two large feed rolls are generally used, but it is possible to use a three-roll arrangement, with a large roll on one side and two small rolls on the other. Average roll diameter is about 8 inches, but they can be obtained in other sizes. It is generally understood that larger rolls disturb the dough less, while at the same time they exert a more even pressure than smaller rolls. The nip or gap between the feed rolls should be adjustable to compensate for different flow characteristics. A review by Wittenberg (1965) showed that companies were using separations ranging from one-sixteenth to one inch. The average gap used today is probably between 0.25 and 0.5 inch.

Speed of the feed roll can be varied, but usually the gearing is interlocked so that a change in the speed of one roller results in a corresponding change in the other. Machines having separately adjustable drives can be obtained, but the advantage of this arrangement is though to be minor, and the cost is known to be substantial. Nevertheless, separately adjustable drives may solve some difficult machining problems.

The delay between mixing and forming (floor time, lay time) affects the response of cookie doughs to forming procedures. With longer floor time, flour in the dough tends to hydrate more, there is some drying at the surface leading to crusting, the chemical leaveners can react causing changes in dough density, and the temperature can change with effects on shortening crystallization and other physical attributes. All of the changes can affect the size and shape of the dough as it feeds through the wire-cut machine and give noticeable differences in weight, size, and appearance of the finished product. It is important to process batches quickly, and to establish a uniform schedule and adhere to it.

One method of improving the uniformity of extrusion across the width of the hopper is to insert a filler block. This device is a bar of machined metal placed up against the feed rolls and having a series of tubes running directly from the nip of the feed rolls to the die cups. This has the effect of giving each cup its dough supply directly from the feed rolls.

There are several designs of die cups. The common beveled channel cup tapers from the hopper nearly to the orifice and then has a straight section for a short distance. These cups are used for vanilla wafers and other cookies that require a thin edge. Other cups have a constriction inside of the exit opening, causing the dough to roll outward at the perimeter as they emerge from the cup. They are used when cookies with relatively thick edges are wanted. For cookies that are to have holes in the center and also for cookies that tend to rise too high in the center during baking, cups are made with a plug running down the center. Depending on the size of the plug and the consistency of the dough, the hole in the center of the extruded piece will fill up either partially or completely during baking.

Dough pieces coming out of the end cups frequently weigh less than those cut from center cup extrusions. To compensate for this effect and obtain equal weights across the band, different size cups can be used. This arrangement does not allow for equalling-out of flow rate differences if several doughs having different consistencies are used with the same set of cups. Flow can also be adjusted by inserting a screw through the wall of the cup and into the dough stream. By changing the distance the screw projects into the channel, the extrusion rate can be changed in small increments. Adjustments can be made to meet the requirements of whatever dough is being run. It is also possible to retard flow by using cups containing crossed wires in the channel, but they are not readily adjustable to meet the demands of varying conditions and different formulas.

It may be necessary to make the cup's orifice oval in cross-section so that a round cookie can be formed. This is intended to compensate for the distorting effect of the cutting wire that is forced through the dough at each stroke of the harp. Here again, there is no easy way to compensate for the different degrees of distortion that occur when different doughs are being processed. The die designer will generally base his calculation of the width to length ratio of elliptical dies (i.e., the minor and major axes) on a reversal of the ratio of length to width of a cookie baked from a round die of approximately the same size using the same dough and the same baking conditions. Most manufacturers of wire-cut dies are prepared to make these calculations if the necessary data can be supplied.

Most die cups made for wire-cut machines will be 1 to 1.5 inches in diameter, although the previously mentioned survey showed that companies were using from 0.25 to 2.75 inches in diameter. The cookies obtained ranged from 1 to 3.5 inches in diameter. It is generally observed that the larger deposits tend to spread less, percentagewise than do small deposits. Several of the die cups will be held on a bar that fits snugly into a channel at the bottom of the hopper. Usually, a handle is fastened to one end of the bar so it can be readily slid into and out of the channel; it also facilitates carrying the bar. As a result of this convenient design, changing from one variety to another is a matter of a few minutes, at least so far as the die is concerned. It also makes stripping the machine for cleaning very convenient. The outlet ends of the die cups should be parallel to the path of wire movement and they should be accurately machined and polished. Nicks and barbs resulting from mishandling can cause wire breaks.

The wire used for cutting pieces from the extruding cylinder of dough is held by a harp. A harp consists of metal frame holding the wire at each end and at intervals along its length. Wires from 0.013 to 0.031 inch in diameter have been used successfully. Wire 0.24 inch in diameter has been recommended for the most common types of dough while 0.029 inch wire is thought to be more suitable for certain dry or sticky doughs. Heavier wires are used when the dough contains particulate ingredients, such as chocolate chips, or when a rough-top cookie is desired. Thinner wires lead to smoother tops and they are also more suitable for soft doughs. Wires may be circular in cross-section or they may be saw-toothed or flat, like a narrow blade.

Teflon-coated wires have been suggested to reduce sticking of the dough pieces to the wire, a problem that can create much scrap. Wires may also be vibrated continuously in order to increase cutting effectiveness and to obtain better release of the dough pieces. Oscillating knives are driven in a side-to-side motion by a power unit placed at the side of the wire cut machine. A stationary back-up plate or board, which the wire can press against as it finishes its stroke, can be used to complete the cut in soft doughs. This design also reduces the tendency of thin pieces to flip over when they start to drop at the end of the stroke.

The mechanism controlling the travel of the harp is arranged so that the wire passes close to the orifice on the cutoff stroke while on the return stroke the wire is lowered slightly so that it does not interfere with the dough which is constantly extruding down into its path. Cuts may be made either in the same direction as the band is moving or in the opposite direction. If back-up plates are used, cutting can be done only against the flow. Burrs or rough spots on die edges cause rapid wire failure.

ROTARY MOLDING MACHINES

A simple rotary molding machine consists of a hopper, a feed roll, a cylindrical die, a knife or scraper, a cloth web or apron, and a rubber covered compression roller. There will also be a frame, motors, controls, etc. These machines may be permanently affixed to the oven band or they may be constructed as demountable attachments for cutting machine lines. They may also be mounted on casters so that the equipment can be moved out of the way when it is not in use. In any case, the frame must be very rigid so that the components maintain the same spatial relationships at all times.

Figure 29.2 shows the operating features of a rotary molder (Source: Vicars). Key to the numbered elements: (1) Feeding roller; (2) Scraper blade; (3) Forward and backward adjustment of scraper blades; (4) Quick release for scraper; (5) Adjuster for extraction roller; (6) Control for upward and downward movement of scraper; (7) Extraction roller; (8) Molding roller; (9) Extraction web; and (10) Dough hopper.

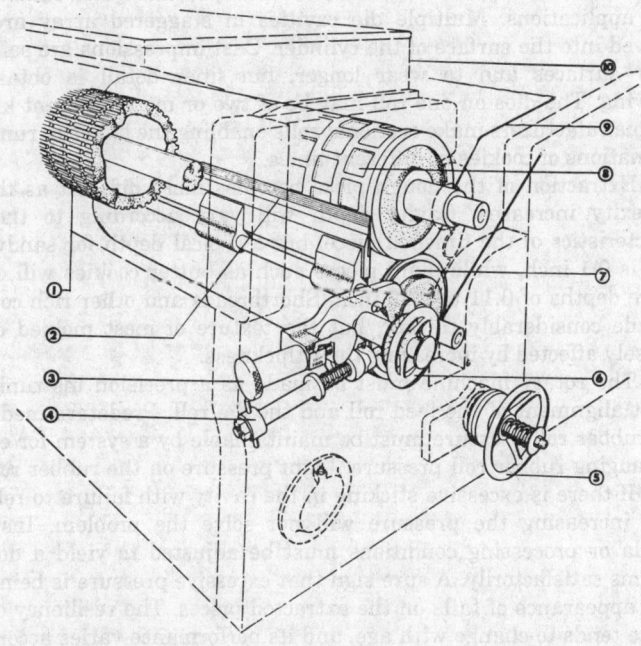

Figure 29.2. Operating features of a rotary molder

The basic principle of these machines is that dough is pressed into a shaped cavity and then removed from that cavity by adhesion to a belt. There have been different ideas of what actually causes the dough piece to be transferred from the molding roller to the conveyor belt. An early belief was that suction caused the transfer. Actually, the effective force is adhesion between the dough and the woven canvas belt. This adhesion is greater than that between the metal die and the dough, therefore the molded piece is transferred from the die to the belt, from which it finally is carried to the band of the oven.

The hopper should be internally guarded with properly placed bars as a safety feature, since the the operator may have to distribute dough across the hopper with his hand. Delivery of dough may be done manually by shoveling from a trough at floor level or by continuous transfer methods. At the bottom of the hopper is a feed roll and a die roll, having a gap between them of about 0.25 inch. Adjustment of this separation can slightly alter dough weights. The feed roll has serrations to force the dough more effectively. It must be made to be adjustable in pressure to accommodate doughs of different flow characteristics. This can be achieved by screw-type adjusters in combination with springs, or by air actuated cylinders.

Die rolls have been made of brass, bronze, or aluminum cylinders on steel shafts, sometimes with cast iron ends. Bronze is more resistant to wear and corrosion, while aluminum is cheaper and quite satisfactory for many applications. Multiple die cavities in staggered array are cast or engraved into the surface of the cylinder. Cast impressions are said to have harder surfaces and to wear longer, but finer detail is obtainable by engraving. The dies on one roll may be of two or more different kinds, and some manufacturers make sectional rolls enabling the baker to run different combinations of cookies at different times.

Extraction of the dough piece becomes more difficult as the design complexity increases. Cavity depth will vary according to the desired characteristics of the finished piece, but a typical depth for sandwich base cakes is 0.1 inch, while plain pieces such as butter cookies will ordinarily require depths of 0.11 to 0.12 inch. Shortbreads and other rich cookies can be made considerably thicker, but the texture of most molded cookies is adversely affected by increasing their thickness.

The rotary machine must be made as a precision instrument, with perfect alignment of the feed roll and the die roll. Predetermined and uniform rubber roll pressure must be maintainable by a system for equalizing and gauging rubber roll pressure. Light pressure on the rubber roll is desirable. If there is excessive sticking in the cavity with failure to release properly, increasing the pressure will not solve the problem. Instead, the formula or processing conditions must be adjusted to yield a dough that performs satisfactorily. A sure sign that excessive pressure is being applied is the appearance of tails on the extracted pieces. The resiliency of the roll surface tends to change with age, and its performance varies accordingly. A significant advance in machining capabilities was made when the coating of die cylinders with Teflon became possible.

The sharp edge of the knife or scraper bears on the molding roller and trims the bottoms of the dough blanks, separating the dough in the mold cavity from the mass of dough in the hopper. Knives are set about 0.125 inch below the center, slightly lower for extremely wide dies. Fractures on the knife indicate the position is too high. The knife should be kept sharp and its edge must be straight. Any nicks or burrs will cause uneveness on the bottom of the dough piece (perhaps a minor consideration) and can scar the molding cylinder, perhaps ruining it. The blade must be strong and rigid so that vibrations or other forces do not push a part of the edge into the mold cavities with resultant damage to the knife or to docker pins. If some of the dough is scraped out of the cavities, the pieces will be difficult to extract.

Locating the rubber roller in front of the die roll and equipping it with air cylinders to adjust the contact pressure evenly across the die roll eliminates or at least minimizes the tendency to produce wedge-shaped dough blanks (the pieces have thinner leading edges that show indistinct design impressions or they have an irregular leading edge) and tails (thin protrusions of dough from the bottom edge of the extracted piece). The arrangement allows misformed dough blanks to be completely released from the cavity before they come into contact with the extraction belt, or causes them to be so badly formed that they are immediately recognized.

The molding apron is an endless canvas belt of special weave. It can be made of linen. The tension is adjustable and the apron should be kept at the minimum tautness consistent with satisfactory running. Scrapers are used to remove any excess dough that may cling to the web. In some cases, steam is applied to the belt to improve adhesion.

Various depositing actions may follow the molding operation. Registration can be excellent if the depositing action is coordinated with the rotation of the molding cylinder and occurs on the apron, before the dough pieces are transferred to another conveyor.

A cookie former tradenamed "Jet-cut" is described as an advance on wire-cut devices, but appears to be more of a modification of a rotary molder. These devices are based on a rotary molding cylinder, with the die cavity ending in a piston head. The cavities pick up dough from the hopper with pistons in a retracted state, much like a conventional rotary molder. When the cylinder moves to the discharge position, the piston pushes the dough blank out of the cavity. Release of the dough from the piston head is assisted by an air jet. Advantages claimed are reduced weight variations, higher speeds, precise positioning, greater band coverage, and applicability to a wider range of dough types.

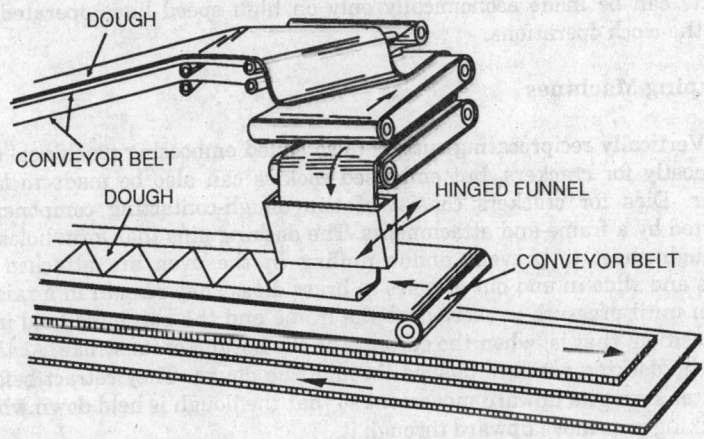

Figure 29.3. One method of laminating dough sheets

STAMPING MACHINES AND ROTARY CUTTERS

The traditional process for preparing soda crackers or saltines involves the cutting of square or rectangular shapes from a continuous web of dough. The dough will have been laminated by special machinery to ensure the flaky, layered structure that is typical of these products. Figure

29.3 shows the operating principle of a recently patented laminating method. Other laminating devices have been described in a previous chapter.

Most saltine cutters are reciprocating, or up-and-down, machines. Perfectly satisfactory crackers can be made with roller dies, though two consecutive roller cutters are generally necessary.

Doughs used in this method of forming must be capable of holding together in a continuous sheet during conveying and cutting. When scrap is generated, as is usually is, it is removed from between the biscuits and from the edges in a nearly continuous web and this imposes additional restrictions on dough properties. Tough doughs with a considerable amount of elasticity can be handled very well on cutting machines. High absorption, high flour content doughs that are completely unsuitable for wire-cut machines or rotary molders are particularly suitable for cutting. Such doughs are capable of considerable expansion in the oven and will bake into products of relatively low density compared to other types of crackers and cookies. On the other hand, hard sweets and semi-hard sweets, also traditionally made on cutting machines, undergo virtually no expansion during baking. The range of products adaptable to cutting machine processing is, then, rather broad.

The nature of the equipment needed for saltine cracker manufacture and consumers' perception of the product as a commodity make these items unsuitable for small shops and for most medium-sized bakeries. These products can be made economically only on high speed lines operated in round-the-clock operations.

Stamping Machines

Vertically reciprocating cutters (also called embossing machines) are used mostly for crackers, but embossed cookies can also be made in this manner. Dies for crackers consist of two dough-contacting components supported by a frame and attachments. The docking pins that form holes in the dough sheet to prevent undue puffing in the oven are attached to springs and slide in and out of holes in brass dies. They remain in a raised position until pressure is exerted on the frame and the bottom is held in a fixed position, that is, when the cutter is at the bottom of its stroke. At that point, the docking pins are pushed through the dough. They retract before the cutter starts its upward movement so that the dough is held down while the docking pins move upward through it.

Reciprocating cutters require a rather heavy framework and considerable head room to support the cutting mechanism, and these requirements can be negative features under certain conditions. They also generate more noise than most other machines in a bakery.

Figure 29.4 shows a stamping machine and a scrap collection system (Source: Vicars).

Figure 29.4. Stamping machine showing scrap collection method

The other part of the dough cutting apparatus consists of serrated strips or knives, often of brass. The serrations, or saw-toothed effect, can be either triangular or approximately rectangular. Their number and width must be adjusted so that the crackers break cleanly along the desired lines before they reach the packing station, but they must hold together in the required multiples during packing and distribution. The arrangement of serrations that accomplishes these goals may vary for different doughs. If there are two or more packaging options requiring that the sheet of crackers be broken in different combinations, separate cutters should be used for each.

To compensate for lengthwise shrinkage in the band of cracker dough, the knives are arranged to cut rectangles. The cracker before baking is about 6% longer than it is wide. For a two-inch cracker, the cutter is frequently made about 2.125 inches between centers of the knives from front to back. The side-to-side dimensions can be held satisfactorily if the proper kind of dough is being machined, and so the cut can be made equal to the desired baked product dimension. Similarly, cutters for round crackers must be made elliptical, with the long axis in the direction of band travel. Cracker length can also be adjusted by changing the speed of the apron leading to the oven band, this having the effect of stretching or contracting the piece depending on the relative speed of the two conveyors.

The number of docker pins in cracker cutters differs according to the ideas of different manufacturers, but a common pattern is 13 pins arranged in alternating rows of 2 and 3. Sixteen pins in 4 rows of 4 pins are also used. Number, size, and pattern of docking pins affects appearance and texture of the cracker. Increasing the number of docker pins will, in general, reduce the baking time.

Resiliency and firmness of the supporting surface under the cutting machine conveyor are important factors affecting cutter operation. For precision, high quality cutting, a sheet of hardwood having its cross-grain presented to the die is a very good choice for the cutting pad. The position of the pad must be changed frequently to prevent the development of deep grooves in the material. Linoleum is also a satisfactory material, but such pads will accentuate any differences due to unevenness in cutting edges and more resilient supports are far more common. One or more thicknesses of canvas will give a moderately firm pad that yields enough to compensate for minor variances in cutter height.

Aprons, the conveyor belts carrying the dough sheet under the cutting machine, are generally made of heavy canvas but, of course, various combinations of textiles and plastics can be employed. Some operators prefer to run them wet, others run them dry. Water or shortening can be used on them. Heavy applications of dusting flour should be avoided. A seamless belt would be best, but is rarely used.

Rotary Cutters

Rotary cutting machines will consist of a cutting cylinder geared to have a peripheral speed equivalent to the linear speed of the apron traveling under it, the canvas web or apron, and the supporting frame with motor and controls. Dies for these machines are either cast or fabricated cylinders, often of relatively small diameter. Cylinders fabricated from sheet metal are generally useful only for simple outline cutting, as for square or rectangular pieces, but fairly elaborate designs can be cut from cast cylinders. Dockers must be applied to cutters for hard sweets as well as to large base cake dies.

The main disadvantages of rotary cutting are the tendency to pick up and retain dough pieces in the cutter and the inflexibility of the method with respect to workable doughs and shapes. Advantages are less wear and less capital expense than with reciprocating cutters. Since there is less wear, the labor and down-time needed for maintenance are reduced and accuracy retention is improved so that more exact finished shapes are obtained. Rotary cutters are also much less noisy than stamping machines.

An improved unit for embossing and rotary cutting consists of two synchronized cutter cylinders. The first roller impresses the top design on the dough sheet and punctures the sheet with docking pins, while the second carries the ridges that cut the cookie outline. The embossing roller compresses the dough to the proper thickness, thus improving weight and dimensional control, and makes the dough piece adhere to the conveyor belt so that it is less likely to get stuck in the cutter. Scrap is lifted off the belt in the usual way, leaving the dough pieces to be transferred to the oven band.

Figure 29.5 clearly shows the method by which dual cutting and embossing rotors form the cookie (Source: Vicars).

Figure 29.5. Cutting machine with separate rolls for docking and cutting

Trouble Shooting Crackers

The following defects in cracker appearance can be related to certain processing errors (Somers 1984):

(1) Fishmouthing (gaping of laminations at edge of cracker) and poor separation at the cutoff knife can result from insufficient pressure on the cutting roll. If the cutting edges are not true, the edges of the crackers will spring open during baking.

(2) Setback or pyramid type separation of the cracker sheets can be due to the cutting machine running faster than the oven band or to intermittent motion as the dough sheet slips on the oven band.

(3) Streaks appearing on the baked cracker can result from improper mixing, particularly nonuniform incorporation of soda.

(4) Flat or dead areas on surfaces can result from inadequate mixing.

(5) Uneven or patchy blistering may be due to either improper setting of

burners or positioning of the cracker toward one side of the oven band.

(6) Cupping of the crackers can result from inadequate balance of top heat and bottom heat.

SANDWICHING MACHINES

When it is necessary to assemble two base cakes and a layer of creme filling to form a cookie of the Oreo type, sandwiching machines are used. Sandwich cookies, as originally made in pastry shops, resulted from hand spreading, with a knife or spatula, an icing or frosting on one cookie and topping it with another cookie. The next step was the stencil machine in which the base cakes were pressed against a plate with circular holes cut in it. Filling was forced into the holes with a spatula, and the bases cakes with filling sticking to them were knocked away from the plate. This process was gradually automated, step by step.

Modern sandwiching machines work automatically at a rapid rate, producing uniform products with very little scrap. Base cakes are received at the machines from cooling conveyors leading from an oven or from chutes that are hand fed from storage boxes. Vibrating conveyors jog the rows of cookies into a stacked-on-edge position. Half of these rows have the tops, with their embossed design, in front while the other rows contain cookies with the design trailing. Cakes are fed into magazines in the proper position for sandwiching and are removed from the magazines one at a time by means of double pins on double chains.

As the bottom cakes travel through the machine with their embossed side downward, they receive deposits of creme extruded through a rotating sleeve having shaped orifices. Extrusion pressure is supplied by a pump that moves creme from hopper to depositor. The creme deposit is cut off by adjustable stationary wires. Size of deposit can be adjusted by changing settings on the variable speed motors driving the auger paddles and the pump. An air valve halts the creme delivery in case the sandwich machine stops for any reason.

As the bottom base cake with its creme deposit reaches the second set of magazines, top cakes are dropped onto the filling. Then the sandwich is gently pressed together to assure adherence of the components and establish uniform thickness of the finished cookie.

A typical sandwiching machine will accept round base cakes from 1.5 to 2.62 inches in diameter, or rectangular, square, and finger-shaped base cakes up to 3.25 inches long and as narrow as 1.16 inch. Speeds are variable up to 1,600 sandwiches per minute on a two row machine. Operation can be made automatic except for filling the creme hopper. Peanut butter and cracker sandwiches are usually made on a different machine.

Sandwiches are conveyed to the packaging stations in stacked or flat positions, depending on the container to be used. Several machines can feed one packing conveyor. Sandwiching machines can be combined with tray loaders and overwrap equipment to give a completely automatic operation.

SUGAR WAFER EQUIPMENT

The forming of sugar wafer base cakes is inseparably connected with the operation of the wafer oven. Therefore, the wafer oven will be treated in this chapter, not in the chapter on ovens.

The type of sugar wafer commonly found in U.S. retail outlets is a cookie with top and bottom layers of characteristically crisp wafer sheets inclosing either one layer of creme or alternating layers of creme and wafer. The cookies are generally rectangular in form, but many other shapes are possible and there are many combinations of fillings and coatings which, in the most complex forms, resemble candy more than cookies. The equipment for ice cream cake cones and cups, hollow wafer sticks, fan wafers, shells, etc. appears considerably different, although the principles are the same. Rolled sugar cones are produced differently. The first part of this section will be devoted to explaining the equipment and method used for producing the common variety of sugar wafer cookie.

The sequence of steps in a factory equipped to make this product is:

(1) Ingredients are mixed in whisks and the batter pumped to a supply tank.

(2) Batter is dispensed by an accurate measuring piston pump onto wafer plates at the entrance to an oven. The dispensing device travels with the "book" (a pair of plates) while the latter is open and then withdraws and returns to its initial position as the plates close.

(3) After it closes on the batter, the book continues to travel through the oven absorbing heat and cooking the batter.

(4) The baked wafer sheets are removed from their plates by take-off units and conveyed on a steel band to collection containers from which they are transferred to the wafer-builder equipment.

(5) At the filling applicator, creme from the filling mixers is spread on the wafer sheet, which is now at room temperature. Alternate layers of wafer and creme are built up until the required thickness of cookie is obtained.

(6) Completed sandwiches are passed through a pressing unit which causes the components to stick together.

(7) From the pressing unit, the sheets pass through a cooler which sets up the filling.

(8) The sheets are collated into a stack of the required thickness and fed to the cutting machine to be sliced into individual cookies.

(9) After slicing, the cookies may be enrobed with chocolate or other fat-based coating.

(10) The finished cookies are packaged.

Figure 29.6 shows the layout for a fully automatic wafer production line (Source: Franz Haas). Key to the numbered devices: (1) Batter mixer and batter feeding installation; (2) Wafer oven; (3) Wafer sheet cooler; (4) Cream spreader; (5) Cream mixer; (6) Turning conveyor; (7) Marshalling conveyor; (8) Feeding conveyor; (9) Wafer cooling press; (10) Stacking and cutting machine; and (11) Packing conveyor.

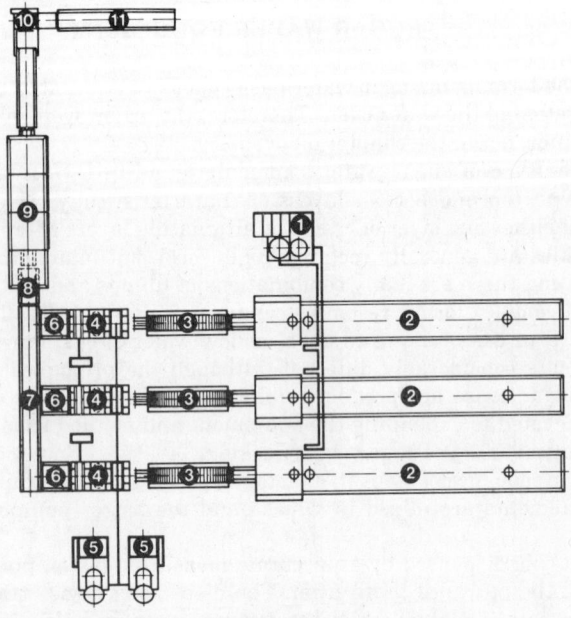

Figure 29.6. Automatic wafer production line

Ovens made by different manufacturers can vary substantially in structural details. The oven described below represents a hypothetical model of relatively simple design incorporating all of the important operating functions.

In the traveling book ovens, sets of two plates each (sometimes called "tongs") are mounted on wheels that support them on rails fixed on each side. A chain conveyor system pulls the books continuously through an upper course, then through a lower course in the baking chamber. The bottom plate is fixed solidly to the carrier chains and the top plate is hinged to the bottom plate. Books open automatically at the urging of cams to accept their charge of batter, then close and lock together. The closed books containing batter are carried through the heated chamber. When it reaches the front of the oven, the book opens, the baked sheet is ejected by mechanical means perhaps assisted by an air-blast. The book moves on to receive its next deposit of batter.

Wafer ovens are made in standard models containing 12, 18, 24, or 30 plates. Models with 36 plates, and perhaps even larger units, are available from some manufacturers on special order. The plates are typically 290 by 470 mm in length and width, but there appears to be a trend toward larger plates. Plates can either be mounted on frames or be self-supporting. The main advantage of the latter is that they contact the flames directly. Also, they can be adjusted easier. A special gray cast iron has been recommended for the construction material. Hard chrome plating can be applied to extend cleaning cycles and promote release of the wafer from the baking surface. Oven books are cured by the application of vegetable or animal fat to heated plates, similar to the treatment used for other baking surfaces.

Production rates vary depending on several factors, including thickness of the sheet, type of batter, exent of baking (how much moisture is removed), etc., but one manufacturer estimates a yield of about 320 lb from a 24-plate gas-fired oven in 5 hr (including 35 min preheating). This poundage refers to the wafer sheets only, not the finished cookies.

Figure 29.7. Wafer baker for making ice cream cones

Wafer ovens can be heated by gas or electricity. When gas is used, the entire chamber is heated, while electrical heating is done by means of elements built into each plate.

A modification of the traveling plate oven utilizes two sets of books conveyed side by side through a common baking chamber to increase output per unit of floor space and per dollar of capital expenditure. Another variation, the continuous band oven, is designed in such a fashion that the batter is deposited on the surface of a reeded drum similar in construction to the drive drums of band ovens. A reeded steel band forms the top plate, heat being applied to the inside of the drum and to the outside of the band. Batter is injected between the drum and the band, and a continuous wafer sheet is withdrawn from the outlet. Ovens for making ice cream cones are designed in a circular format and look quite different from wafer sheet ovens—see Figure 29.7 (Source: Franz Haas).

TROLLEY COOKIE EQUIPMENT

The process for trolley cookies has some unique points that might be interesting for the baker looking for new product ideas. The unusual aspects lie in the finishing operation; the base cake that forms the center of this confection is usually just a wire-cut cookie of more-or-less standard formula.

Trolley cookies are not a major factor in today's market. There has been a gradual decline in the number of firms offering them because the production method is slow, difficult to control, and costly in labor. The cookies do not have enough appeal over more economically manufactured goods to offset these negatives. As a result, older equipment is being abandoned and has not been replaced by equivalent capacity in new plants.

The distinguishing feature of trolley cookie plants is that base cakes are suspended on pins attached to a movable framework (the trolley) so that one or more coats of sticky or slow-drying coating can be applied to the entire surface of the base cake. In a typical plant, the trolley was four stories high and held tens of thousands of cookies at any one time (Anon. 1973).

It is possible to completely cover the piece with marshmallow, and then, after a drying period, enrobe it with a kind of water icing. This process may take more than a day to complete, especially in humid weather. Air-conditioned rooms and special drying facilities have speeded up the procedure to a total of about five to six hours.

The base cakes are usually wire-cut cookies although cutting machine base cakes are known to have been used. Many flavors of base cakes have been used, such as vanilla, chocolate, coconut, and devils food. Cookies with rather open texture, as exhibited by the usual wire-cut cookie, seem to contribute the best eating quality to the finished confection. Base cakes must, however, have sufficient structural strength and rigidity to hang on the trolley hooks during the dipping and transfer operations. Dipping the hooks or pins into corn syrup before they are pressed into the cookies helps to hold the base cakes and reduces scrap. Excessive tenderness at this stage leads to cookies falling from the pins, a very serious difficulty.

Base cakes are dipped two or three times. The first coat can be a jam, jelly, or marshmallow. The middle layer can be a chocolate flavored coating consisting mostly of sugar, corn syrup, cocoa, and shortening. The outside layer is generally a thin coating of glaze or water icing. Trolley marshmallow is usually a tougher, denser material than deposit marshmallow.

Other types of confectionery based on the trolley cookie concept are described in a patent (Yoon 1986) which sets forth a method for stabilizing the moisture content of the cookie and jelly and adding a "nutritive" coating.

BIBLIOGRAPHY

AICHELE, W. J. 1981. Cookie and cracker processing. Cereal Foods World *26*, 161-165

ANON. 1973. Distributors help Johnson Biscuit up sales 8% to 10% per year. Bakery Production Marketing *8*, No. 4, 106-107

BARTA, B. B. 1988. Personal communication. Franz Haas Machinery of America, Richmond, VA

GADAMS, F. 1984. Wire cut cookie production. Biscuit Bakers Institute 59th Conference. Biscuit and Cracker Manufacturers Association.

GORTON, L. 1989. Computer-integrated cookie line boosts productivity, improves product. Baking & Snack Systems *11*, No. 6, 6-7, 9, 12, 14

GREENE, H. L. 1982. Equipment manufacturer helped biscuit industry get its act together. Snack Food *17*, No. 2, 26-27, 40

HAAS, F., SR., HAAS, F., JR., AND HAAS, J. 1985. Apparatus for conditioning wafers. U.S. Pat. 4,524,682

HAAS, F., SR., HAAS, F., JR., AND HAAS, J. 1986. Process and apparatus for producing filled wafer blocks. U.S. Pat. 4,567,049

HEIDEL, D. J., and KENNEALLY, C. J. 1988. Method of and apparatus for producing individual dough pieces of substantially constant size and shape. U.S. Pat. 4,741,916

MATZ, S. A., AND MATZ, T. D. 1978. Cookie and Cracker Technology, Second Edition. AVI Publishing Co., Westport, CT

MC KEE, H. B. 1985. Method for feeding cookie preforms. U.S. Pat. 4,562,084

MORETH, N. W. 1967. Modern sugar wafer production—a technological breakthrough. Manufacturing Confectioner *47*, No. 11, 16-22

MORETH, N. W. 1982. Increased cookie production through laydown control. Bakers Digest *56*, No. 2, 8-10, 12, 14

PINTO, A. A. 1988. High volume dough piece production method. U.S. Pat. 4,786,517

POLIZZANO, R. A. 1988. Process and dough composition for producing multi-textured cookies. U.S. Pat. 4,717,570

REGET, G. 1966. Wire-cut cookie manufacture. Proc. Am. Soc. Bakery Engineers *1966*, 263-271

SMITH, A. 1970. Soft cookies. Proc. Am. Soc. Bakery Engineers *1970*, 114-123

SOMERS, J. F. 1984. Trouble shooting crackers. Biscuit Bakers Institute 59th Technical Conference. Biscuit and Cracker Manufacturers Association.

THORNTON, I., DE WITT, K. W., and ROBERTSON, S. A. 1985. Method of preparing a biscuit or cookie product. U.S. Pat. 4,517,209

VAN LENGERICH, B. H. 1991. Extruder apparatus for producing an at least partially baked product having a cookie-like crumb structure including a post extrusion microwave device. U.S. Pat. 4,984,514

WEIDENMILLER, E. A. 1966. Personal communication. Morton Grove, IL

WEIDENMILLER, T. 1988. Personal communication. Weidenmiller Co., Elk Grove Village, IL

WITTENBERG, H. L. 1964. Rotary cookie production. Biscuit Maker Plant Baker *16*, 26-30

WITTENBERG, H. L. 1965. Wire-cut cookies. Biscuit Bakers' Training Conf. *1965*

YOON, Y. 1986. Method for manufacturing a jelly confectionery coated with chocolate. U.S. Pat. 4,563,303

chapter thirty

FORMING OTHER PRODUCTS

INTRODUCTION

This chapter contains discussions of forming equipment for sweet doughs, pies, doughnuts, cakes, pancakes, tortillas, biscuits, and a few other items. Some of these products are made from yeast-leavened doughs, others from chemically-leavened or unleavened mixtures. When necessary, the auxiliary equipment that operates in conjunction with the forming devices will also be described. Much more information on equipment for making these products can be found in "Equipment for Bakers" (Matz 1988).

FORMING DEVICES FOR SWEET DOUGHS

The multiplicity of shapes and dough types found in yeast-leavened sweet goods leads to the need for many different combinations of the relatively few automatic devices available to the baker. Some of the most common pieces of equipment used for shaping these items are sheeters, applicators, curlers, plows, and cutters. These units are often combined with others to form pastry benches, automatic sweet goods machines, etc., that process the dough after it has been sheeted or extruded. Of course, any bakery that has been in operation for a considerable time will have developed gadgets, equipment modifications, and totally new devices unique to their plant. Large factories may have machines specifically designed for their particular needs and which are kept secret for competitive reasons. This article concerns the types of equipment offered as stock items by equipment manufacturers in the U.S. and abroad. A previous chapter has thoroughly covered sheeting, laminating, and size gauging equipment and that material will not be repeated here.

Dough extruders for sweet doughs use a screw or auger turning in a housing to move dough from a hopper through a large orifice that is is either rectangular or circular in outline. The dough strip falls onto a conveyor belt or into a sheeting roller for further processing. Since the dough is not forced through a small opening, little harm is done to its cell structure. In some cases, a cut-off mechanism is controlled by a variable electronic timer to give segments of desired weight. This equipment is particularly useful for extruding large (about 15 lb) dough pieces that are to be sheeted out as Danish pastry. In other cases, a continuous sheet is formed.

Many of the final forming devices—the curling rollers, guillotines, longitudinal cutters, etc.—can be used for any of the sweet goods doughs, such as Danish, roll-in sweet doughs, puff pastry, and regular. The following list describes equipment that would be found in a mechanical bench suitable for a medium-sized bakery making a wide variety of sweet dough products. Devices are listed in sequence according to the position occupied in the line.

(1) A conveyor to bring dough to the sheeting rollers.

(2) Three sets of sheeting rolls to reduce dough thickness in gentle stages.

(3) Optionally, a cross-roll sheeter could be installed next. For most doughs, it would not be needed.

(4) A make-up conveyor onto which the dough is transferred for subsequent operations.

(5) A tank with dispenser for applying oil or any other kind of liquid.

(6) A cinnamon and sugar dispensing unit, adjustable for rate and width.

(7) One or two curling rollers, for shaping strips into continuous cylinders.

(8) A sealing and guiding thimble for moving the coil back to the center.

(9) A rotating die or a guillotine cutter for severing the coil.

(10) A panning table with drop leaves on each side. Sweet rolls, coffee cakes, etc., are removed from the belt here and placed into pans by hand.

(11) Variable speed electric motors for driving the moving parts (including conveyor belts) of the equipment.

A sweet goods machine containing some, but not all, of these devices is shown in Figure 30.1.

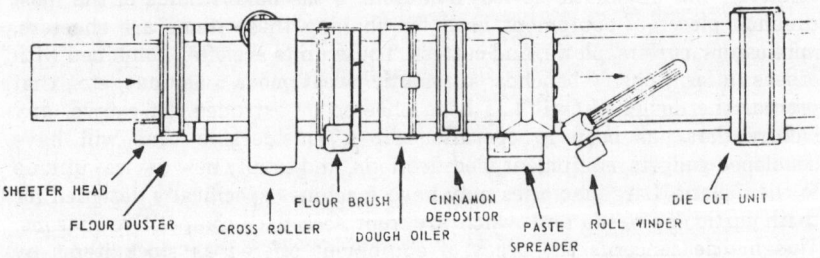

Figure 30.1. Arrangement of processing devices on a semi-automatic sweet goods machine

Curling Rollers

The master baker working at his bench will sheet out a piece of dough in an approximately rectangular shape and apply cinnamon "smear" to the sheet, avoiding both edges. He will then form the dough into a cylinder by grasping one of the longer edges near the end and rolling the sheet over on itself to make a cylinder of spiral cross section. The curling process will be continued until a long tube of fairly uniform diameter has been formed. During this manipulation, he will apply slight pressure on the upper surface to prevent entrapment of air and to assist the sealing process. When curling has been completed, the outward edge is usually sealed into the side of the roll to avoid "unraveling" and to provide an obstacle to leakage of the filling. He will then cut sections of, say, one-half to one inch from the dough cylinder and place these sections, with a cut side up, on the tray, pan, or peel that will hold them during the proofing and baking process. When baked and iced, this will be a cinnamon roll. There being an insufficiency of master bakers to supply the needs of the trade, there is a requirement for some mechanical method to automatically form cinnamon rolls and the like.

If a steel cylinder is placed slantwise on a conveyor belt carrying a strip of dough to which filling has been applied, with the proximal end of the roller near the edge of the belt and the distal edge somewhere near the center of the belt, and the cylinder is rotated (as by a motor) so that the motion of its lower edge is opposite to the motion of the belt, the cylinder will tend to pick up the edge of the dough and then continue to raise it up and roll it over the remainder of the strip. If conditions are correctly adjusted, a continuous roll of dough will be formed. Cross-cuts of this roll will show alternating spirals of dough and filling, the same pattern as found in the common sweet roll described in the preceding paragraph.

These curling rollers (also called roll winders) are found on nearly all mechanical benches for sweet dough products and are used for many varieties and styles of dessert items. By placing curling rollers on both sides of the belt, two dough strips can be curled at the same time. Some of these devices have segmented rollers so that one or more segments can be removed and the others moved to different locations on the axle, leaving a free space along the belt where curling will not take place. This allows two of the roll winders to be placed on the same side of the belt; the earlier-formed dough tube passes under the empty space on the second curler. If very thin strips are being formed (as for braided coffee rings) several small roll winders (rarely more than four) can be aligned parallel to each other to multiply the capacity of the line.

Most of these cylinders have shallow and narrow grooves alternating with broad ridges placed lengthwise to assist the roller in grasping the dough sheet. They are rotated by separate motors (not necessarily variable speed motors) and are, usually, mounted so that their angle to the belt can be adjusted. Their distance from the belt (gap) should also be adjustable, but it is not good to have the roller touch the belt since it rotates in a direction opposite to belt travel and the friction that could result from contact would not only cause much wear on both belt and cylinder but would heat the belt surface, cause tracking problems, and interfere with production in other ways. It is important to have the roller close to the belt, however, because there is a possibility the dough will not be picked up and will jam under the roller if the gap is too great. This is not likely to happen if the dough is rather dry and extensible and is fairly thick, but is a distinct possibility if the dough is wet, sticky, weak, and thin.

Cutting Devices

In the preparation of individual pieces from a continuous strip of dough, there comes a time when the strip must be cut. Cutting can also form part of the design of an individual piece. For lengthwise cutting, rolling disc knives (one or more on a shaft, powered or not) are suitable. For crosswise cutting, there are several options. The up-and-down motion of the guillotine is useful in many applications; disc knives rolled across the belt offer a more complicated solution; rotating cylinders with cutter blades are often used. For more complicated cutting, various types of rotating dies can be applied, as in the forming of doughnuts. Cutting with high pressure jets of air or water has been proposed and some commercial equipment does exist.

Guillotines are used to cut across the belt, severing the dough strand, strip, or sheet into segments. They have a reciprocating, up-and-down motion. Because the conveyor belt will usually move the dough continuously beneath the cutter while the blade is slicing through the dough, there will be some restraint on the dough's forward motion, possibly causing distortion of the piece. This effect is minimized by making the cut a rapid one and by advancing the guillotine blade a little as it completes the cut.

Another problem sometimes observed at the guillotine is sticking of dough to the blade, so that the strip is carried up and back when the blade retracts. If not corrected, this can cause serious repeated jamming. Suggested cures for the problem include stretching a thin rubber sheet beneath the cutter so the blade itself does not touch the dough, and passing the blade through oiled wipers before each cut. Blades can also be sheathed in Teflon.

Another type of cutting device is the rolling disc blade. The simplest are disc blades rotating freely on an axle. Usually, several blades are arranged along the axle at equal distances. They make lengthwise cuts in strips of dough passing down a conveyor belt. More effective, though more complicated, are the knives that are rotated at the same speed as the belt. Much more complicated are the disc cutters rolled across the belt by a mechanism that must take into account the forward motion of the dough sheet. The discs can complete their circle by moving above or below the belt. Such cutters are used on very sticky or tough products. Blades can be washed as they travel below the belt on their return path.

Many kinds of products can be formed from dough blanks cut from continuous sheets by rotary dies. Doughnuts, croissants, pizza crusts, tortillas, pita bread, and cookies are some of the many products that are partially or entirely shaped by rotating dies. Of course, there are alternate ways of preparing some of these items, extrusion for doughnuts and pressing for pizza crust, for example.

Rotary dies can be supported either on powered axles or rotated passively by their contact with the dough or belt. The former arrangement is more suitable for mass production, and it is necessary that the speed of the circumference of the die be closely coordinated with conveyor belt speed. Cutting surfaces of dies are usually constructed of thin metal strips soldered, welded, or otherwise affixed to the surface of a drum or cylinder connected by circular end pieces to an axle. It is also possible to construct such dies by machining ("engraving") cavities around the surface of a thick metal tube. When thick pieces are being formed, the reduction in dimensions as the walls of the cutters go toward the center of the cylinder should be taken into consideration. The difference in dimensions from top to bottom of the cavity is not necessarily a disadvantage, it can even assist in separating pieces from one another or pieces from scrap. If problems do arise, distortion can be minimized by using cutters of larger diameter.

Example of a Production System for Sweet Rolls

The following describes a commercial plant for producing sweet rolls and coffee cakes, and is based mostly on an article by Shaffer (1977). Dough is mixed for about 15 min in a horizontal mixer and brought out at 82° to 85°F. Bulk fermentation of 75 to 90 min is allowed. The fermented dough is pumped from the hopper to a continuous mixing developer operating at 65 to 80 rpm. Developed dough is extruded through a 4-inch stainless steel tube tapered to a 3-inch tube and provided with sanitary fittings to deliver a single dough strip on to a floured belt about 9-ft long. Dust is applied to the top, and the dough transferred to an incline belt about 18-ft long with a roller about 1-ft from the bottom of the incline. The roller flattens the dough and forms a thin skin on it. The dough is relaxed on another conveyor for 6 to 8 min, then transferred to make-up equipment.

The dough strip passes under three floating rollers that spread and shape the dough for uniform feeding into sheeting rollers. After sheeting, the strip is dusted again and passed under a cross-roller that gives it the desired width, say 24 inches. The sized strip passes under another floating roller that smooths the dough before it passes through the slitter and trimmer. These cutters divide the dough into two strips and remove any excess dough. The strips, now of uniform width and thickness, pass to a lateral switch conveyor and are carried to make-up belts. They are carried under a series of floating rollers that make the strips thinner and wider. A powered flour brush removes excess flour from the two thin strips of dough, about 15-inches wide at this point.

Fillings such as wet cinnamon, oil, preserves, jelly, etc., are pumped on to the dough strips. Rollers or spreaders smooth the filling to the desired width. Curling rollers are used to form the strips into cylinders that are transferred to an automated cutting and panning device that severs them into bun size pieces by a guillotine and drops the buns into foil containers.

A second make-up table is used for producing hand-panned coffee cake. A single large dough-and-filling cylinder is prepared for this product. There are panning aprons at the discharge belt so that personnel can hand pan the finished dough pieces.

PIE MACHINES

In discussing equipment for preparing pies, it is necessary to distinguish between baked pies, pressed crumb pies, and fried pies, because there is a considerable difference in the way these three types are formed.

Forming Equipment for Baked Pies

Two popular methods for forming pie crusts are (1) sheeting dough and cutting out circles (discs) and (2) pressing a lump of dough into circular shape between two dies. Satisfactory crusts can be made by both methods. The sheeting and cutting method is said to permit the achievement of better texture but it does generate a considerable amount of scrap that has to be remixed, re-sheeted, and re-cut. Stamping methods should lead to only a few percent of rework, at least as far as the forming operation is concerned.

Figure 30.2. A small pie crust press illustrating the method of pressure-forming dough in foil pans

Simple bench-scale machines can be obtained for press-forming pie crusts in aluminum foil tins or in regular pie pans. An upper die, shaped to form the interior surface of the bottom crust, is hydraulically actuated to press the dough, and it is electrically heated to increase plasticity of the dough mixture. A bottom die or form holds the pie tin that functions as a mold for the outer surface of the bottom crust. It is claimed these presses produce up to 700 pie shells per hr. Crust sizes from 1.5 to 10 inches diameter can be processed. The hydraulic drive is powered by an electric motor. Figure 30.2 shows an example of such a machine (Source: Ekco).

A pie-making machine using the pressing method of forming was described by Gageant (1964). Measured amounts of blended ingredients are fed through a series of stations that form it and place the crust in a pan. Filling is dispensed into the bottom crust, then a die-formed pastry cover is placed over the pan and its edges crimped to the bottom crust. Porous metal dies release dough from the forming surface by slight air pressure without the need for dusting flour. In some cases, the crust molding die may be heated, say to 250°F, to facilitate dough flow (Atwood 1964). Since the fat is substantially liquefied by this treatment, air-injection or other means must be used to release the dough from the molds.

The sequence of steps in a plant using the sheeting method is:

(1) An automatic divider converts bulk dough into multiple sets of two rectangular blocks that will become the top and bottom crusts.

(2) Dough blocks are conveyed from the divider to the crust rollers.

(3) One block is sheeted, cross-rolled, and deposited over a moving pie tin.

(4) A shaped plunger forces the sheet into contact with the pie pan, so it closely fits the sides and bottom of the tin. This hs been called "docking."

(5) A simple dispenser and applicator wets the upper rim of the bottom crust so that it will adhere to the top crust.

(6) Planetary spinning heads form and trim the edge of the lower crust.

(7) A quantity of fruit or other filling is deposited into the bottom crust.

(8) The second dough block is automatically cross-rolled and deposited over the moving pie pan containing the bottom crust and filling.

(9) Bottom and top crusts are sealed and crimped together around the rim.

(10) A wash or glaze can be automatically sprayed on the top.

(11) Dough removed in the trimming operation is returned to the divider.

It is said that 600 pies per hr can be produced with a labor force of three people operating a line of this type.

Forming Equipment for Fried Pies

The usual fried pie is a single serving pastry weighing about 4 to 6 oz. Consumers eat the pie out of hand, rather than with a fork. Shape may be semicircular, rectangular, or approximately triangular.

Doughs can be mixed successfully on vertical mixers equipped with a dough hook, on double armed kneading mixers, and on slow speed horizontal mixers (Burris 1979). In one operation, thought to be representative of general practice, batches of dough ranging from 250 to 1,000 lb are mixed in open bowl, double-arm mixers, then transferred either manually or automatically to a twin screw extruder that feeds a ribbon of dough through a series of sheeting rollers. To make crescent shaped pies, the dough is sheeted into a thin, narrow, and continuous ribbon that is draped over a series of opened pie-formers of clam shell shape. A Teflon-coated roller cuts excess dough from the molds.

Filling is metered and deposited on to the dough at intervals; then the clam shells close, enveloping the filling completely. Fluted edges on the dies crimp the dough and seal the filling within the pie, after which the pies are transferred by a conveyor to a submersing fryer. Conveyors within the hot fat hold the pies under the surface and carry them to the discharge end. While they are still warm, the pies are glazed with a sugar icing. They are then cooled and wrapped. Fat-based chocolate-flavored coating is sometimes applied to fully cooled pies (Anon. 1986).

Processing lines differ considerably between manufacturers. The following equipment sequence is another alternative. Bulk dough is conveyed under a corrugated roller that produces a strip from 0.5 to 0.75 inch thick. Three pairs of sheeting rollers reduce the dough sheet to its final thickness (0.125 inch) and carry it over aluminum molds mounted on conveyor chains. These molds are shaped like a square with rounded corners, and are hinged in the middle. A measured amount of filling is deposited on one side of the dough, then the opposite side is brought up and over by raising that side of the mold. As it continues, this action cuts off excess dough at the edge, and crimps and seals the pie. Trimmed dough is returned to the mixer.

Another approach to forming is to shape pies on the conveyor belt. One such system folds the dough over the filling, then aluminum molds mounted on the circumference of a wheel seal and trim the pies (Havighorst 1976). Still another method places a wide strip of dough across a conveyor belt before applying filling in continuous strips. The unfilled side of the dough strip is lifted up and over, then dropped down to cover the filling. Disc knives cut and crimp the pies into several continuous lines. A second cutter squeezes the filling apart, then cuts and seals the ends of individual pies. Mechanical transpositors can be used to line up the pies on the infeed belt of the fryer.

Fillings are mixed and cooked in steam kettles of standard type. Agitators of the slow-sweep type are needed in order to avoid excessive breakage of the fruit pieces. "Cream" or pudding fillings of chocolate, vanilla, lemon, butterscotch and banana flavor are also used and they are prepared either in steam kettlés or continuous jet cookers.

Frying is done in continuous deep fat fryers having submersing conveyors. The pies are often glazed in a waterfall-type coating device that applies about 0.5 oz to each unit. Air jets are used to blow off excess glaze. Coated pies are cooled for about 90 min on a spiral cooler or equivalent.

Forming Equipment for Pressed Crumb Crusts

Graham cracker crusts and other types of crumb crusts, such as those used for some cheese cakes and for some cream pies, are usually made by pressing to shape a mixture consisting of cracker or cookie crumbs with sugar, shortening, and flavoring ingredients. The pressing action is accompanied by a spinning motion of the upper mold that distributes the mix up the sides of the pan which forms the bottom mold. These crusts are not baked either before or after filling.

The basic steps in preparing a pressed crumb crust can be summarized as follows:

(1) The cookies are milled or crushed between rollers. Gentle action is required, since production of large amounts of fines must be avoided.

(2) The cookie crumbs are sieved to remove excessive fines or large pieces. A gently-acting sifting device is preferred to prevent further breakdown.

(3) The sieved material is gently mixed with melted or softened shortening, sugar, flavors, salt, and the rest of the ingredients.

(4) A weighed portion of the mix is deposited in a pie tin.

(5) The pie tin is placed in the plateholder of the pie press.

(6) The top mold descends with a spinning action, forcing the crumbs up the sides of the tin, and finally compresses the mixture into a compact layer.

(7) The top mold is raised.

(8) A measured amount of filling is deposited in each shell.

(9) Whipped topping is applied in a pattern to cover the filling

(10) The finished pie or cheesecake is automatically lifted from the plateholder and carried by a conveyor to the packaging area.

If the product is to be sold as an unfilled crust for home preparation, steps 8 ,9, and 10 are replaced by the application of a close-fitting, semi-rigid plastic cover bearing a paper label. The plastic cover is secured by crimping the extended rim of the aluminum foil pan over its edges.

Machines suitable for preparing and filling crumb crusts can be of either linear or circular configuration. Linear machines tend to be the higher speed equipment, and are often used for preparing the tart shells and cookie crusts that are sold in supermarkets. The circular machines are of variable capacities and are widely used by wholesale bakers as well as by some institutional bakeries. They are probably more versatile than the high speed linear units and certainly occupy less space. A typical unit would have nine stations, and produce 25 to 30 finished packaged pies per minute with two or more operators. These units include, among other devices, a pan depositer, a crumb dispensing station, an automatic spinning head, an orbital cream filler head, and an orbital topping head. The topping head can be fitted with different dies to give different topping patterns.

DOUGHNUT EQUIPMENT

Doughnuts are nearly all formed by either a sheet and-cut method or an extrusion method. Automatic doughnut production in a linear plant involves seven basic operations: (1) scaling ingredients, (2) mixing, (3) either extrusion forming or sheeting and cutting, (4) proofing, if the dough is yeast-leavened, (5) frying, (6) finishing, and (7) packaging. Some of the equipment alternatives available to commercial doughnut producers will be discussed below. Fryers will be covered in more detail in a subsequent chapter. Conventional horizontal or vertical mixers can be used for making doughs and batters for both yeast-raised and cake-type doughnuts, but efficient production requires specialized equipment subsequent to the mixing stage.

Yeast-raised doughnuts of the conventional hole-in-the-center type can be formed either by cutting hexagonal or circular pieces from a dough sheet or by extruding the dough through a circular orifice. Very soft doughs and batters are obviously not suitable for sheeting and cutting methods. Doughs varying in consistency from very soft to moderately tough, as well as batters, can be handled on extruding equipment.

Sheeting and Cutting Processes

The preparation and cutting of a sheet of doughnut dough varies little from the generalized system described for sweet doughs in previous sections of this chapter. Ingredients are scaled, the dough mixed (straight doughs with few exceptions), the dough passed through sets of sheeting rollers and gauge rollers or hand rolled, and pieces cut from the dough by die cylinders. The devices found on a complete sweet goods bench would be adequate for all these operations, although a special cutter is required.

The amount of trim or scrap dough generated during the forming operation should be a major consideration when choosing equipment. Cutting a sheet of dough with hexagonal cutting dies will reduce scrap. These cutters are often called "scrapless," though trimmings are generated along the edge of the strip of dough. The wider the dough sheet, the less scrap is generated in both the hexagonal and round cut, provided the rotary cutting die is sized to take full advantage of the width of the strip. Using a dough strip so narrow that the central part of a hexagon or circle falls on the outer edge of the strip is a sign of poor planning. Round cutters will generate perhaps 60% doughnuts and 40% scrap in the average well-run line, while hexagonal cutters can approach an 80% doughnut and 20% scrap ratio. Rectangular cutters (as for long johns) and square cutters (as for some Bismarcks) produce very little scrap.

It is important to keep the amount of scrap returned to the mixer at a minimum, not only because production capacity is reduced by reprocessing a material that has already gone through most of the line, but because scrap dough is more developed than freshly mixed dough and therefore changes the dough's consistency and its response to the whole series of processing steps. Since scrap cannot be avoided, it is important to keep the amount added to each mixer batch at the same level.

Center circles, or "holes," can be removed by a rotating picker attachment. These constitute a few percent of scrap to be reprocessed, or they can be fried separately to give a specialty item liked by many consumers. Figure 30.3 shows a hexagonal cutting bench equipped with "hole pickers" (Source: Moline).

Figure 30.3. Hexagonal doughnut cutter with hole pickers

After yeast-leavened doughs have been cut into finished shapes, they are usually allowed to proof. This is a critical step, and unusual conditions can be involved, sometimes with a view to developing a dehydrated layer on the dough piece so that a characteristic type of crust will appear during frying. Specialized types of proofers, often resembling intermediate proofing chambers or rack type cabinets are used. The three types of automatic proofing systems for yeast-raised doughnuts are:

(1) The proofing cloth system, in which the pieces are cut from a sheet of dough on the bench or make-up table and then transferred to a proofing cloth, screen, or proofing board. The dough pieces are then transferred on their supporting material to a conventional proof box. After a proof time of 25 to 35 min, the proofing cloths are taken to a feed table from which the dough pieces are transferred to a conveyor type fryer.

(2) A second type of production system involves the manual transfer of raw doughnuts from a conventional make-up table to the flights or baskets of an automatic proofer. Humidity and temperature are maintained by automatic controls. The uniform proof imparted to the product by the controlled conditions in the cabinet permits close control of product size and quality. Since a constant load is being sent to the proofer, and there are no doors to open and close, uniform temperature and humidity conditions can be maintained.

(3) The third type of proofing system uses microwave heating to speed leavening action. When irradiated by microwaves, there is a substantially uniform temperature rise throughout the dough, eliminating the slow transfer of heat by conduction or convection that must occur in conventional proofers. This is discussed in more detail in the chapter on proofing enclosures.

Extrusion Equipment

The extrusion method is the most efficient type of processing method since it is truly scrapless, at least so far as the forming operation is concerned. It is also less labor intensive. If it were not for the fact that the consumer, that fly in the ointment of all efficiency experts, often demands raised doughnuts, there would be no sheeting-cutting operations in existence.

Simple, inexpensive devices for extrusion forming are available for the retail baker. These doughnut cutters deposit the batter directly into a fryer. Extuders for yeast-leavened doughs, used mostly in large-scale operations, deposit scaled dough pieces directly into the infeed conveyor of a continuous proofer. Extrusion depositers do require that doughs have certain characteristics in order to operate satisfactorily, however.

Although it is possible to sheet a chemically-leavened dough and cut doughnut shapes from it (much like soda biscuits are made in large scale plants), cake doughnuts are generally extruded from a mass of soft dough (or thick batter) held in a hopper. Both vacuum-mechanical and pressure-extrusion systems are in use. In pressure extrusion, a rotary valve delivers batter from the hopper into a chamber where it is subjected to 4 to 10 lb of air pressure. Several tubes lead from this chamber and are closed at the exit end by cutting valves. When these valves are opened, pressure forces batter down the tubes and around the cutting dies. Closing of the valves severs the ring of dough, allowing the raw doughnut to drop from the end of the tube. Product weight is a function of the size of the opening, batter viscosity, air pressure, and length of time the cutter is open. The vacuum system creates a negative pressure by retracting cutters or plungers to draw batter from the hopper to the cutter cylinders. Each cutter has a separate cylinder for measuring the proper amount of batter. At a predetermined point, the cylinder is closed off, fixing the amount of batter that will be extruded in the form of a ring.

Extrusion methods drop the cut dough pieces directly into the hot fat. If a continuous fryer is involved, as there would be in all large-scale operations, the drop must be coordinated with the movement of the pusher bars or flights that move the doughnuts through the vat. Although this adjustment is critical, it is not difficult to maintain on modern equipment, assuming normal operator vigilance and a dough that does not hang up in the cutters. If the conveyor timing is improperly coordinated with the dough drop, distorted products can result from the pusher bars contacting the piece before it is firm enough to maintain its shape. Even worse is the dropping of the dough directly on top of the conveyor bar; this causes hangups in the fryer and a large amount of scrap product (Fisher 1976).

In the pressure methods, product weight is affected by batter viscosity, pressure on the batter, and length of time the die is open. Product size cannot be varied at the individual orifices because a single pressure chamber feeds all the cutters. The vacuum method is less sensitive to batter viscosity, which tends to increase as the batter ages, and the shape of the extruded ring is the same from all cutters because the opening does not change in size or shape.

Worn or damaged cutters cause scaling weight problems and appearance defects in finished products. Worn cutters leave strands ("whiskers") protruding from the cut surfaces and they drop small pieces of dough into the fryer. Badly worn cutters produce out of shape doughnuts.

By modifying the cutter plungers in a vacuum-mechanical system, different shapes of doughnuts can be produced. The star center doughnut cutter is equipped with a piston seal on the forming plunger and there is a row of degassing pins around the upper surface of the forming piston. The degassing pins change the rate of expansion in certain areas of the deposit, causing a "star" to form in the center, instead of a round hole. Star center doughnuts are surface fried.

Old fashioned doughnuts are characterized by a very rough surface with strong color contrasts. Cutter plungers for these doughnuts have piston seals and there is a degassing plate above the piston to assist in releasing gas. The latter action leads to a denser batter so the frying doughnut stays longer beneath the surface. The shape and position of the forming piston is changed to give a tubing effect to the cut. Lower frying temperatures and a special formula are generally necessary to get the best results.

Cutters for crescent, or semi-circular, doughnuts are made with attachments placed on the surface of the forming pistons for plain doughnuts. They are available in a variety of sizes for closing off a portion of the ring of cut batter. When the dough deposit fries, its expansion causes the cut to partly straighten out, so that a crescent is formed. A stick doughnut cutter plunger is equipped with a piston seal and sleeve in place of the usual forming piston. The sleeve has a slotted extrusion orifice through which the batter is forced during the cutting cycle. The rod of batter is flat, and should not round out during its expansion in the fryer, for this would lead to turning in the oil with generally poor cooking results.

Plunger cutters for French crullers are designed to include a counterrotating forming die and forming piston. The rotation of the die and piston impart a twisted shape for the batter deposit. This shape is held through the frying and finishing processes. It can be either surface-fried or submerge-fried. A special formula is required (Belshaw 1976).

A further development in vacuum-mechanical equipment is multispaced cutter heads. Since both the die shapes and the center-to-center spacings can be changed, several varieties and sizes of doughnuts can be formed simultaneously. When smaller pieces are being made, more pieces can be extruded on the same belt width, eliminating empty proofer spaces and increasing utilization of fryer capacity.

Extruder systems have been developed for depositing doughnuts containing a ring of jelly inside (Moyer 1986). Thus, instead of filling the doughnut after frying, it is filled before frying. In this equipment, a modified feed system draws jelly from a reservoir into a ring-shaped outlet placed in the same region where the dough is being extruded. The jelly must be a starch-based, lower moisture formula because standard fruit jellies based on pectin systems do not perform satisfactorily during extrusion or frying.

A completely automatic production system would include equipment for making both extruded and cut doughnuts from both yeast-leavened and chemically-leavened doughs. The line would require at least an extruder for yeast-raised dough, an automatic proofer, an automatic cake doughnut cutter, an automatic fryer, a fat melter and leveler, a sweep conveyor, an automatic glaze applicator, and a screen loader.

Frying, Cooling, and Decorating

Extruded doughnuts are almost always dropped directly into the frying vat, while sheeting methods require a transfer from the forming station to the frying vat. The transfer requires extra labor but allows considerably greater flexibility in scheduling the frying process.

Nearly all varieties of doughnuts must be turned over a little more than halfway through the frying process in order to get a symmetrical shape and a uniform crust color. In batch fryers, the doughnuts are turned manually, but continuous vat fryers are provided with conveyors that automatically turn the dough pieces at the proper time.

Doughnuts are usually cooled before they are packaged to prevent condensation from forming in the container. Cooling is usually conducted by conveying the fried products through a room temperature area, possibly with fans directed on the conveyor to assist heat transfer.

Most doughnuts are decorated and modified after frying by one or more of the following operations: (1) coating with powdered sugar, (2) covering wholly or partially with glaze, icing, or frosting, (3) sprinkling with nut pieces, coconut shreds, candy bits, or other particles, or (4) injecting fillings of the jelly, pudding, or jam type.

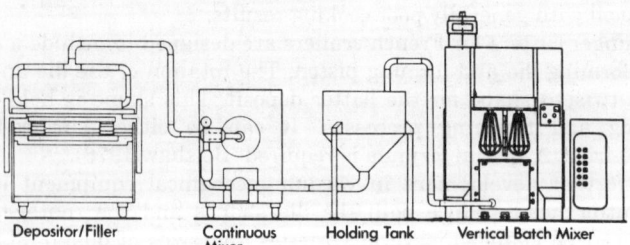

Depositor/Filler   Continuous   Holding Tank   Vertical Batch Mixer
Mixer

Figure 30.4. Continuous mixing and depositing line for cake

CAKES

Cakes and other products made out of fluid batters assume the contours of the containers in which they are baked, so the forming or shaping machinery can be regarded as the pans themselves and the pumps, pipes, and metering devices that deliver batter to the pans. Finishing equipment that enrobes, deposits, injects, spreads, or otherwise adds fillings, toppings, etc., has very important effects on the appearance, flavor, cost, and nutrition of the final products. Figure 30.4 shows an automatic depositing line for cake (Source: Western Bakery Imports).

Batter depositors may be either manifold-type or volumetric hopper types. Accuracy is a prime consideration. Ability to handle batters containing pieces such as raisins, nuts, and chocolate chips without reducing their size is important. The depositor should not markedly change the specific gravity established at the mixer. Whether deposited on the oven band or in open pans, the top surface of these cakes will be flat or slightly domed. Top contours of cup cakes and muffins are significant factors affecting consumer acceptance and, generally, the smaller the pan the more prominent the domed shape. Differentiation in the larger cakes must depend on post-baking operations such as cutting, rolling, layering, and decorating.

Of course, fancy pans to make cakes shaped like Easter eggs, or bunnies and lambs, are traditional. It is possible to bake cakes in pans shaped like Texas, and there are even people who want to do such things. The chief difficulties encountered when using these fancy pans are getting the batter to fill the cracks and crevices so the finer details of the pattern can be seen, and getting a relatively uniform bake in the thick and thin portions of the cake. The design problem is largely a matter of avoiding fine detail when doing the artwork, and adjusting the batter formula so the viscosity is low enough to allow the mixture to flow into all parts of the pan. Vibrating the pan strongly during and after depositing the batter is of considerable help, although it may tend to bring all the gas bubbles to the surface, with unfortunate effects on the appearance of the finished cake. Leavening should be on the low side, since substantial expansion during baking will tend to lift the batter out of small crevices. Large bubble size also tends to blur the finer details, making a small grain desirable. A slow bake will help to avoid a combination of unbaked areas in the thick part and burnt points and stripes.

Lining fancy pans with Teflon or some other nonstick coating improves detail and also reduces the possibility that some critical part of the design will remain in the pan when the cake is dumped.

Baking cakes as a continuous ribbon on an oven band has become common in large installations. Individual cakes are formed by cutting pieces from the baked strip and combining them in various ways. Of course, a somewhat similar procedure was followed when small shops used sheet pans for baking layer cakes and the like. Any non-rectangular shape results in the generation of a considerable amount of scrap that is difficult to utilize. Even with this limitation, however, many varieties can be obtained. In manufacturing band cakes, batter is prepared in a continuous mixer and pumped to a manifold, or batter distributor, positioned above the oven band. The manifold spreads the batter in a uniform depth, although more than one strip may be placed on the band if baked edges are preferred to cut edges, as they may be when preparing Swiss rolls (Freihofer 1985).

In addition to restricting the shape of finished products, baking cakes on a band also establishes limits on formulation. It is important that the batter does not spread significantly during baking. Sponge cake batters of high specific gravity are preferred. The finished cakes are often lower in moisture than is considered satisfactory for conventional cakes. Fillings, icings, frostings, and other adjuncts of reltively high moisture content are liberally applied to furnish the textural characteristics the consumer expects.

After the baked cake has been separated from the oven band by a knife, it is transferred in a continuous ribbon onto the cooling conveyor. When some cooling has occurred, the cake is cut into strips by disc knives and then, for the preparation of Swiss rolls, filling is deposited in a continuous stripe. Lateral cuts are made, often by rotating disc knives that move across the band. Individual pieces are then rolled mechanically or by hand to form the finished rolls. In preparing layer cakes, two iced or filled strips can be plowed up and over to form a double layer before the horizontal cuts are made.

Some very successful small cake manufacturers have found that many varieties can be produced from the same basic type of batter. Differentiation between varieties is established by changing the fillings, toppings, icings, and enrobings. Adding an automated machine for injecting fillings is one of the easiest and most effective ways to expand varieties in a line of small cakes. Newer automated finishing techniques include depositing creme fillings into dessert shells before enrobing. More personnel are required and some additional equipment is necessary for each variety, but the specialized equipment is generally considerably less costly than a new line. Consumers appear to appreciate the opportunity to choose something different, and greater sales volume results.

Totally oven-finished items are efficient to produce (Hokes 1977). These products involve depositing materials on top of cake batters or beneath the batter before baking. Among the materials that have been used in this way are jelly, streusel, raisins, blueberries, nut pieces, cheese pastes, coconut crunch, flavored crumbs, and cinnamon pastes. Equipment is available to do this automatically. Several oven-finished varieties can be produced in the same size pan and with the same batter, or with minor variations in the batter.

THE RHEON ENCRUSTER

This device, the basic design of which is now about 25 years old, is specified here by its trade name since it appears to be rather unique in the way it operates. Many kinds of devices have been suggested, and used, for enrobing a filling in a kind of dough, or for enrobing one kind of dough in another. Foods such as ravioli, apple dumplings, dual-textured cookies, and wafer shells with filling are examples. What appears to set the Rheon device apart from earlier equipment is its adaptability to many kinds of coatings and fillings, as well as its method of operation. It lacks versatility in shape, however, being limited to ball-shaped items for all practical purposes. No doubt a limited range of shaping procedures could be applied after the balls are formed. It can also be adapted to continuous extrusion of cylindrical products such as tamales. There are some limitations on consistencies of the filling and dough, and of piece sizes that can be extruded. Production rates are fairly low, as compared to certain other equipment designed for making filled dough products.

The unusual aspects are the actions by which the dough is transferred and gently shaped following its extrusion from the dough hopper. Dough is squeezed from the hopper by a set of two screw conveyors and a stability roller. The screw conveyors are designed to be without a center shaft for the final two-thirds of their length. When the dough reaches the compound nozzle assembly it is formed into a ring or doughnut shape. In the forming or ring assembly the dough is reformed in a continuous strip to completely enrobe the filling that has been directed by another extrusion method to the center of the dough forming ring. Sealing of ends to enclose a portion completely in a ball shaped mass follows. The machine is said to operate at a top speed of 3,000 pieces per hour.

PANCAKES, CREPES, BLINTZES, AND FRITTATEN

Automatic and semi-automatic devices are available for quantity production of pancakes, crepes, blintzes, and frittaten. There are simple low-capacity devices suitable for making crepes for restaurants and small retail bakeries. They consist of a motorized and heated conveyor serving as the griddle and a gravity dispenser for batter. A rectangular crepe results. The same manufacturer makes an industrial machine capable of producing 700 to 1,000 pieces 33 cm in diameter. This device includes a cylindrical rotating hearth bearing circular depressions for containing the batter. Cooked crepes are stripped off on a conveyor belt leading to an automatic receiving table (Anon. 1972). Other devices more suitable for restaurant use than for retail or wholesale bakery production include an electrically-heated machine for making circular crepes 6.5 to 12 inches in diameter and of adjustable thickness. It operates at the rate of 180 to 360 pieces per hr (Anon. 1973).

Blintzes could be formed on most kinds of crepe machines with simple modifications of formulas and processing conditions.

Another manufacturer describes the procedure for using his equipment, which is based on a circular horizontal rotating hearth. The hearth is divided into inner and outer sections. The crepe or pancake batter is prepared and filled into a dispenser. When baking temperature is reached, an oil spray and the batter spreader are started. The batter flows onto the baking plate in a continuous stream at a controlled rate. After one revolution of the inner baking plate, the batter is automatically turned on to the outer baking hearth, where final cooking takes place. The speed of rotation of both plates can be set to obtain the best baking time for the batter. Baked pancakes, either flat or rolled, are lifted from this discharge conveyor and transferred to the filling area where previously prepared compositions are applied. Accessories include a jam or cheese filling device for pancakes, a raisin spreader for Kaiserschmarren, filling and rolling devices for meat or vegetable rolls, and a shredding device for frittaten. Claimed production rates are 2,500 pancakes of 4.75 inch diameter and 175 lb of frittaten per hr. Baking times will be 0.5 to 2 min (Anon. 1982).

Ruhdorfer (1974) patented a method and equipment for making frittaten that involves feeding pancake batter to the upper roller of a pair of large heated rollers. The baked batter is removed to a conveyor belt and dried with a hot air blast. Cutting of the partially dried dough into strips is accomplished by cutting discs. The strips are severed lengthwise by a knife revolving with a roller and acting against a fixed blade. The partially dried frittaten are immediately guided to a vat of hot oil that further dehydrates them. The resultant product measures about 30 to 40 mm in length and 2 to 3 mm in width, and it has a moisture content of less than 7%. Advantages of the frying step are that the frittaten has improved flavor and much longer shelf life, as compared to the usual product.

TORTILLAS

Traditional tortillas are made of a paste (masa) formed by grinding corn kernels that have been soaked in hot lime water. Flour tortillas are made from a wheat flour dough. Details of processing can be found in a preceding chapter.

Havighorst (1971) and Clark (1981) described mechanized plants used to prepare corn tortillas. The cooking cycle begins with the dumping of 2,000 lb of white corn kenels and a measured amount of lime water into a kettle containing an upper perforated ring from which the water is sprayed over the corn. A steam injection ring in the bottom part of the kettle maintains the contents within a desired temperature range and agitates the corn kernels. After the corn is hydrated at about 120°F, the temperature is raised to 165°F to gelatinize the starch. During the cooking cycle, hot liquid is sprayed over the corn and continuously recirculated by a pump connected to the discharge valve.

After completion of a steeping period, the corn is flushed with fresh water into a draining conveyor. This conveyor discharges into a screw-type elevator in which the corn is again washed to remove free starch and other debris. The corn then milled by a buhr mill of generally conventional design, consisting of a stationary lower stone disc and and a rotating upper stone, both about 16 inches in diameter and 4 inches thick. The mill is powered by a 30 hp motor and grinds about 3,000 lb of corn per hr.

The ground alkalized corn dough, or masa, is conveyed to the hopper of a tortilla cutting head by a screw-type extruder. A thick sheet of masa is extruded between sizing rolls, and the resultant ribbon is cut into discs of appropriate size by the usual kind of rotating dies. Gas-fired ovens held at 600°F bake the raw tortillas in 30 to 32 sec. Tortillas reach 175°F at the discharge but are cooled to 85° to 90°F in a multi-tiered conveyor through which ambient air is circulated.

Machines have been developed to feed masa balls into a heated compression unit that forms them into tortillas of uniform weight and dimensions. Also, a compact tortilla press and oven has been patented. This device separates the masa into pieces suitable for one torilla, presses the unit into disc shape, and toasts each side. Presumably, this machine would be suitable only for small-scale use, as in restaurants.

Although the wheat flour tortilla is often formed in very much the same kind of equipment used for corn tortillas (Schmidt 1985, Roberts 1987), it is reasonable to assume it could be more efficiently processed in the type of plant used for pita bread and the like.

BISCUITS

The type of biscuit discussed in this section is the soda biscuit or baking powder biscuit, a kind of chemically-leavened bun or roll. Its formulation and processing has been described in a preceding chapter.

Doughs for this product should not be developed, so short mixing times at slow speeds will be used to blend the ingredients. A vertical mixer with dough hook will require about two minutes to cut in the shortening and one minute to mix in the water. Cool doughs are preferred, 55° to 60°F being the suggested range. If there is some question about the ingredients being completely hydrated, a 20 to 15 min rest after mixing is acceptable.

When the dough is sheeted by an extruder, it should be of a type that imposes minimum punishment on the dough. Roller feed devices would seem to be preferred to auger extruders. Dough is extruded at 1 to 1.25 inches thickness. The width of the strip should be just slightly more than that of the cutters, so that a minimum amount of scrap dough will be generated. Dusting flour should be kept to a minimum. The dough strip passes under a compression roller that has the functions of sealing the sheet and insuring that it will feed uniformly through the main head rolls.

The head rollers should normally have a clearance of 0.625 inch. They will have scrapers to maintain clean surfaces so that sticking or marking of the dough surface will not occur. The sheeting rollers smooth the top and bottom of the dough ribbon to form a skin that will retain leavening gases in the oven, produce a uniform expansion, and lead to an attractive crust.

The ribbon of dough, 0.625 inch thick, is transferred to the main conveyor. A small amount of shrinkage is induced by slowing the main conveyor speed to slightly less than the speed of the head rollers. This reduces any tension that would cause misshapen dough pieces.

Round or hexagonal biscuits can be cut with rotary dies. The round style, 3 inches in diameter and about 2.5 oz in weight, is traditional. Hexagonal biscuits are not as familiar, but have the advantage that scrap is greatly reduced. The finished dough pieces are conveyed on to sheet pans moving in a direction opposite to that of the dough conveyor. Biscuits are separated from each other by about 0.5 inches on the baking surface. It is customary to give the cut biscuits a few minutes rest to allow the leavening system to generate some gas before the pieces are put into the oven. The sheet pans are transferred to a 450°F oven and baked for about 15 min. Biscuits can also be baked directly on the oven band.

BIBLIOGRAPHY

ANON. 1972. Automatic machine for crepes flambees. Crepmatic, La Garenne, France

ANON. 1973. The Gyrocrepe. Gideco, Paramus, NJ

ANON. 1982. Automatic Pancake Baking Machine Type PKB. Franz Haas Waffelmaschinen, Vienna, Austria

AOKI, S., HAYASHI, T. and SUZUKI, Y. 1990. Apparatus for shaping and arraying spheroidal bodies of food materials. U.S. Pat. 4,936,203

ATWOOD, H. T. 1964. Mold for pie shells. U.S. Pat. 3,124,083

BELSHAW, T. E. 1976. Developments in automated doughnut production. Bakers Digest *44*, No. 4, 50-51, 54-56, 66

BRADEN, B. W., JR. 1976. Yeast-raised doughnuts. Proc. Am. Soc. Bakery Engineers *1976*, 127-132

BURRIS, J. B. 1979. Fried pies. Proc. Am. Soc. Bakery Engineers *1979*, 111-118

CANNON, A. S. 1987. Automated sweet goods production. Proc. Am. Soc. Bakery Engineers *1987*, 107-123

CHEUNG, Y. T. 1990. Method and apparatus for forming egg rolls. U.S. Pat. 4,913,043

CLARK, D. G. 1981. Corn tortilla and tortilla chip processing. Cereal Foods World *26*, 499

D'ALTERIO, J. C. 1990. Apparatus for encapsulating filler with dough. U.S. Pat. 4,941,402

DREISIN, I. 1988. Method for forming filled dough products. U.S. Pat. 4,794,009

DZIEZAK, J. D. 1989. Single- and twin-screw extruders in food processing. Food Technol. *43*, No. 4, 164-174

ESCAMILLA, R. M. 1988. Apparatus for forming and baking flat, thin discs of dough. U.S. Pat. 4,724,755

ESCAMILLA, R. M., ESCAMILLA, E., III, ESCAMILLA, E., JR., JOHNSON, G. E., ARNOLD, R. M., and TATNER, T. 1989. Method and apparatus for forming and baking flat thin discs of dough. U.S. Pat. 4,838,153

FINLAY, P. A. 1989. Apparatus for rolling circular dough product. U.S. Pat. 4,857,349

FISCHER, L. G. 1976. Cake doughnuts. Proc. Am. Soc. Bakery Engineers *1976*, 121-127

FREIHOFER, W. D. 1985. New trends in small cake production. Proc. Am. Soc. Bakery Engineers *1985*, 134-141

GAGEANT, L. M. 1964. Automatic pie machine. U.S. Pat. 3,093,062

GOODSELL, G. R. 1984. Cake doughnut production. Proc. Am. Soc. Bakery Engineers *1984*, 118-131

GORTON, L. 1989. Medallion gains control over production. Baking & Snack Systems *11*, No. 2, 6-7, 9-10

GORTON, L. 1990. Flexible processing yields made-to-order doughnuts. Baking and Snack Systems *12*, No. 4, 6-7, 9-11

GRIMMINGER, A., LAUSER, W., MULLER, F. J., PFAFF, G., and SCHLIPF, E. 1991. Screw-type extruder having a starting valve and throttle. U.S. Pat. 4,984,977

HAUCK, B. W. 1981. Control of process variables in extrusion cooking. Cereal Foods World *26*, 170-173

HAVIGHORST, C. H. 1971. Mechanizes age-old process. Food Eng. *41*, No. 6, 62-63

HAVIGHORST, C. H. 1976. Perky produces pies by millions. Food Eng. *48*, No. 6, 62-63

HAYASHI, T. 1989. Method for producing composite food having a controlled composition of materials. U.S. Pat. 4,877,623

HAYASHI, T., and TASHIRO, Y. 1989. Method for quantitatively extruding food material. U.S. Pat. 4,859,479

HOKES, J. J. 1977. Small cake production. Proc. Am. Soc. Bakery Engineers *1977*, 73-77

KOPPA, D. A. 1988. Method of triple co-extruding bakeable products. U.S. Pat. 4,748,031

MATZ, S. A. 1988. Equipment for Bakers. Pan-Tech International, McAllen, TX

MENDOZA, F. C. 1989. Tortilla dough forming machine. U.S. Pat. 4,854,847

MOYER, J. H. 1986. Doughnuts. Proc. Am. Soc. Bakery Engineers *1986*, 120-125

PACYNIAK, B. 1986. Pudding pies may firm up soft snack cake/pie market. Prepared Foods *155*, No. 9, 200-201

PLUTA, R. 1988. Personal communication. Colborne Manufacturing Co., Glenview, IL

POEHLMAN, R. W. 1979. Premium Danish production. Proc. Am. Soc. Bakery Engineers *1979*, 91-105

POEHLMAN, R. W. 1985. Biscuits. Proc. Am. Soc. Bakery Engineers *1985*, 126-134

ROBERTS, G. F. 1987. Apparatus for making filled food products. U.S. Pat. 4,691,627

RUBIO, M. J., DE LA VEGA, A., and LOBECK, E. M. 1990. Tortilla press apparatus. U.S. Pat. 4,938,126

RUCKH, A. B. 1986. Cakes. Proc. Am. Soc. Bakery Engineers *1986*, 125-131

RUHDORFER, A. 1974. Process for the production of frittaten. U.S. Pat. 3,830,946

SCHMIDT, C. O. 1985. Tortilla production. Proc. Am. Soc. Bakery Engineers *1985*, 114-126

SHAFFER, T. 1977. Automated yeast-raised production. Proc. Am. Soc. Bakery Engineers *1977*, 117-124

SIMELUNAS, W. J. 1988. High production method for forming filled edible products. U.S. Pat. 4,719,117

SIMELUNAS, W. J., POLIFRONI, N. R., SHOIKET, H. N., and MEYER, S. M. 1989. Method and apparatus for severing a coextrusion for making an enrobed food pieces. U.S. Pat. 4,882,185

SKARRA, L. L., EVANS, J. R., and MURTY, A. S. 1988. Food shell and method of manufacture. U.S. Pat. 4,781,932

SMIETANA, L. P. 1990. Method of making a conically shaped tortilla shell. U.S. Pat. 4,915,964

STEFANATI, P., STEFANATI, R, and STEFANATI, A. 1988. Machine for producing dumplings or troffiette. U.S. Pat. 4,755,121

STEVENSON, H. 1988. Personal communication. Colborne Manufacturing Co., Glenview, IL

UHROVIC, M. 1988. Apparatus and method for twisting pastry dough and the like. U.S. Pat. 4,767,638

VEY, J. E. 1986. Danish. Proc. Am. Soc. Bakery Engineers *1986*, 111-120

WIEDMANN, W. 1988. Method and apparatus for extruding a food product. U.S. Pat. 4,786,514

ZONES, J. J., and ROBE, K. 1976. 1,000,000 pies a week. Food Processing *37*, No. 6, 60-62

chapter thirty-one

OVENS AND BAKING

INTRODUCTION

In most bakeries, ovens are the most conspicuous and characteristic pieces of equipment. With their associated loaders, unloaders, coolers, panners, depanners, and conveyors, they dominate the layout and determine in large part the arrangement and location of other pieces of machinery. Baking is also the operation that limits output in most plants. For this reason, selecting the oven, maintaining it properly, and operating it at the maximum rate consistent with good product quality are key elements in the successful management of a bakery.

The oven has an important influence on product quality. It cannot compensate for all errors committed earlier in the processing sequence, but a well-controlled oven of the proper design can bring out the full potential of a well-processed dough piece. The factors of design and operation that govern an oven's effectiveness and optimize product quality are not completely accessible to scientific analysis. The mechanical details of oven construction are, of course, important in that they are related to labor requirements, efficiency of fuel utilization, frequency of product damage, and sanitation. But of more fundamental importance, and not as well understood, are the effects of heat transfer mechanisms on product quality. All ovens transfer heat by conduction, convection, and radiation, but the differences in the percentage of heat transferred by each method during each stage of baking determine the variation in baking results in different ovens.

There are many ways of classifying ovens, and each of the ways has some value for a specific purpose, but the two major categories used in this section are "Retailer Ovens" and "Wholesaler Ovens." This scheme was adopted mostly for the convenience of the reader, since there is necessarily considerable overlap between the two groups in technical details of heating devices, controls, enclosure construction, etc. It is expected that the individual reader, however, will have his or her attention concentrated on one of the two groups and so the classification method chosen will save time and make it easier to find pertinent information.

Heat Transfer Mechanisms

Heat may be generated within a mass (such as a piece of dough) by radiation, friction (work), or chemical reactions, but in baking we mainly have to deal with the transfer of heat from outside sources by convection, conduction, and radiation. The relative effectiveness of each of these mechanisms varies with oven design as well as with the conformation of the dough pieces, the size, shape, and construction materials of the container or pan, and the distribution of the dough pieces on the hearth.

The only types of radiation that are significant in baking are microwave radiation and infrared radiation. Transfer of heat by infrared radiation is a significant factor in most ovens. These radiations are not in themselves heat, but are converted into heat through absorption by, and interaction with, absorbing molecules. Radiation has two characteristics that make its action different from the other means of heat transfer: (1) It is subject to shadowing or blocking by intervening substances that are opaque to radiation and (2) it is very responsive to changes in absorptive capacity of the dough. Radiant energy comes from the burner flames and all hot metal parts in the oven. It is not necessary that the oven part be red hot, or otherwise visibly heated, for it to radiate infrared rays. This radiant energy travels in a straight line and much of it never reaches the dough piece because the rays are intercepted by some substance that is not transparent to the radiation. Shadowing, or blocking out of radiation by some intervening material, can occur from pan walls, parts of the oven, or parts of the dough piece.

Convection is the transfer of heat from one part to another within a volume of gas or liquid by the gross physical mixing of one part of the fluid with other parts. In the oven chamber, molecules of air gases, water vapor, or combustion gases, heated by whatever means, circulate throughout the oven, constantly mixing with other gases and transferring heat by conduction when they contact solid surfaces. Within the dough piece, convection occurs as the result of the movement of water vapor and other gases. Furthermore, translocation of liquid water, melted shortening, and other liquids can cause a transfer of heat from one region of the dough to another. If the overall results of convection can be generalized, it would be as a smoothing or evening effect on heat distribution.

Conduction is the transmittal of heat from one part to another part of the same body, or from one body to another that is in physical contact with it, there being no appreciable displacement of the particles contained in the bodies. When baking dough in a band oven, conduction of heat to the dough occurs only through the band. The band receives its store of energy from heat conducted through the supports on which it rides, and from radiation and convection. Because of the localized nature of conductive transfer, steep gradients of temperature can be set up within the dough piece, the hottest areas being the ones in contact with the pan and particularly where the pan is in contact with the band. The porous nature of most doughs greatly interferes with conductive transfer.

To summarize the effects of the three types of heat transfer occurring during baking, it can be said that conduction and radiation tend to cause localized temperature differentials, conduction acting to raise the temperature of the bottoms and radiation acting to raise the temperature of exposed surfaces (and especially darkened areas and protuberances), while convection tends to even out temperature gradients.

It is possible to heat dough products that conduct electricity if electrodes are placed on each side of the piece and a current passed through it. This is an old idea that is renewed occasionally. Yonezawa (1986) described an apparatus for electrical baking.

Electronic ovens generate heat within the product as the result of vibrations set up in some of the product's molecules when they absorb electromagnetic radiation of high frequency. The water molecule is particularly effective in facilitating this type of heating. The radiation in question is created by electronic circuits resembling radio transmitters in a very general way. There are two principal types of electronic ovens, the dielectric variety using frequencies in the range of 30 to 40 MHz and the microwave or radar types using frequencies of 915, 2,450, 5,800 or 22,125 MHz.

Microwave systems are the basis of radar ovens used in homes and restaurants for rapid heating of many foodstuffs. They can be very efficient because the oven cavity need not be held at a high temperature and therefore does not leak large amounts of energy to the environment as do conventional ovens. A very significant problem with microwave baking is that it does not contribute much to crust coloration and crust dehydration. Another problem is finding a cooking container that does not interact with the radiation. Many inventors have proposed combining microwave heating with conventional baking or irradiating with infrared rays to give products with a browned, firm crust and uniform textured interior. Rosenberg and Bogl (1987) reviewed recent publications on combination baking procedures.

Dielectric heat has been used to apply a final drying step to cookies, crackers, etc. (McCormick 1988). It is said to in commercial use in Europe for reducing moisture in baked products below 4%.

Energy Systems in Conventional Ovens

The energy systems in conventional ovens are generally considered to be comprised of the fuels, the devices that turn those fuels into heat, the control apparatus, and safety mechanisms.

The fuel crises that have occurred in recent years, sometimes taking the form of shortages of natural gas, low stocks of some kinds of fuel oil, high prices for electricity, etc., have made it difficult to predict which energy source will be the most economical over the long term. Some bakers have opted for ovens that can be quickly converted from gas to fuel oil and vice versa. It is probable, however, that most of the large ovens in the U.S. burn natural gas. Oil of different grades, manufactured gas, propane-butane, and electricity are other energy sources being used because of some special situation or requirement.

Electricity has many advantages as a heat source, some of them being cleanliness, low maintenance requirements, and ease of control. Its cost is prohibitive in all but a few locations, however. There may be some ovens burning coal or coke still being used, but the author knows of none in wholesale bakeries (a very few pizzerias may do so). These fuels have so many disadvantages as compared to natural gas that they can be regarded as of no current interest to the bakery technologist.

Average theoretical Btu availability per unit for electricity is 3,142 per KWH, natural gas 1,000 per cu ft, manufactured gas 550 per cu ft, light fuel oil 140,000 per gal, and coal 13,500 per lb. The average one pound loaf of bread will require from 150 to 200 Btu for baking to completion. Additional heat will be required for the pans, and some will be lost from the oven to its surroundings, so considerably more than the theoretical 200 Btu will be required. Heat taken up by pans will obviously vary depending on their weight and composition, as well as their initial temperature, but an average pan requirement of 40 Btu per lb of dough is often used in calculations.

Efficiency of the oven in utilizing fuel depends upon details of construction, such as type and thickness of insulation, manner of transferring the heat, etc. Skarin (1964) estimated that 400 Btu of gas were consumed per pound of bread in direct-fired ovens equipped with air agitating systems. With gas burning at 85% efficiency, 340 Btu are delivered into the oven (from the original 400), and of these about 50 Btu are lost through the walls or by other routes. Indirect-fired ovens require an additional 20% fuel because of the loss of efficiency in supplying heat to an enclosed system. For oil, about 80% of the theoretical heat content can be recovered in an efficient combustion system

On-and-off and modulating systems can be used for controlling the input of heat to the oven. On-and-off controls consist basically of a thermocouple that activates a thermostat switch; they can maintain the temperature within a range of about 10°F. The more expensive modulating-thermal-control systems can adjust the amount of gas flowing to the burner as required to maintain the temperature within about plus or minus 2°F.

There are three types of actuators used on ovens and driers: pneumatic, electric, and electronic. Pneumatic controllers receive a mechanical incoming signal and use a relatively complicated air-pressure balancing system to produce a pneumatic force for operating the heater valves. The sensing element can be a liquid-filled bulb connected by a capillary tube to the control instrument. A system of levers multiplies the slight motion of the liquid to an extent sufficient to activate the balancing section. Electrical actuators also receive mechanical incoming signals, and use a simple electric resistance slide wire balance to generate the electrical impulse that operates the gas valves. Electronic controllers receive incoming electric-voltage signals from thermocouples, and processes them through an electronic circuit to modulate the electric current that operates the valves. Most, if not all, modern equipment uses electronic controls.

Steam Injection

Steam is introduced into ovens primarily to modify crust characteristics. It tends to reduce the rate at which the dough surface dehydrates so that the crust remains elastic for a longer time, preferably during the entire period of dough expansion, and ragged breaks are avoided. The delay in crust stiffening may allow the development of greater loaf volume. The crust becomes smoother, leading to a glossier appearance. Browning reactions are also modified, giving better crust colors in most cases.

In order to achieve these improvements, it is necessary that moisture condense on the dough surface. Injection of high pressure steam is worthless for these purposes. Authorities agree that saturated steam of 2 to 5 psig should be injected into the chamber with orifice velocities of 200 to 500 ft per min. Violent turbulence is not desired, since it would tend to reduce the opportunities for moisture to condense.

As the crust temperature approaches 212°F, steam has decreasing effects, since condensation will not occur. The major effects seem to occur during the first 1 to 2 min in the oven, as the temperature of the crust is rising from about 90°F to near the boiling point of water.

According to Dersch (1960), the steam in a typical oven comes from the following sources: 2.7 cu ft per lb of dough from vaporization of water in the dough, 0.9 cu ft per lb of dough from products of combustion, and 9.25 cu ft per lb of dough from the steam injectors. It is obvious that far more water vapor comes from steam injection than from the other two sources.

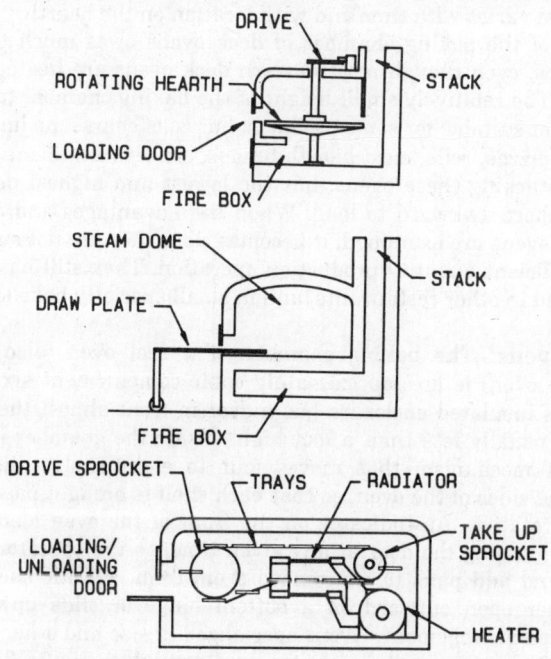

Figure 31.1. Top: rotating hearth oven. Center: draw plate oven. Bottom: single-lap tray oven.

RETAILER OVENS

Retailer ovens, so far as that description is used in the present chapter, are nearly all batch-type ovens such as deck ovens, reel ovens, rack ovens, and rotating hearth ovens. There are a few models of small continuous band ovens suitable for baking at individual outlets such as pizzerias. The operating principles of three types of ovens (rotating hearth, draw plate, single-lap tray) of historical interest are shown in Figure 31.1 (not to scale).

Deck ovens.—Deck ovens are often found in small retail bakery operations and at one time they were practically the only type of oven found in pizzerias. They are not particularly energy efficient and occupy a lot of floor space per unit of product baked. Bakers find them difficult to charge and empty, and the first row in, last row out, feature of the large models is not always convenient, although this is not a problem in the smallest models where only one row (or even just one pan) is baked at a time. Since there is no transport mechanism, these ovens tend to be cheaper and considerably easier to maintain than reel or rotary ovens. Heat distribution within the oven varies with time and with location on the hearth.

Design of the baking chamber of deck ovens owes much to the old coal-fired ovens, even though most modern deck ovens are heated by electricity or gas. The relatively small height of the baking chamber (about 7 to 16 inches) is not suitable for some products, but is, of course, no impediment when making pizzas, rolls, most hearth breads, etc. Space utilization can be improved by stacking these ovens, but the lowest and highest decks then become even more awkward to load. When the advantages and disadvantages of these ovens are examined, it becomes clear they are not suitable for any kind of efficient quantity production operation. They still have a place in pizzerias and in other restaurants, and in small specialty bake shops.

Reel ovens.—The baking chamber of a reel oven (also called a revolving tray oven) is an approximately cubic compartment six or seven feet high. This insulated enclosure has a door in front almost the width of the oven, but usually less than a foot high. Inside the chamber is a ferris wheel type of mechanism that moves four to eight shelves in a circle centered on the sides of the oven, so that each shelf is brought past the door during every rotation. An indicator on the front of the oven identifies the shelf which is passing the door at any given time, so the operator can stop the rotation and add pans to, or remove them from, specific shelves. The door will either open outward on a bottom hinge or slide upward in a counterbalanced arrangement. Ovens specialized in size and other construction features for cookies, rolls, pies, etc., are available. Figure 31.2 shows the mechanisms and construction of a reel oven (Source: Despatch Oven Co.).

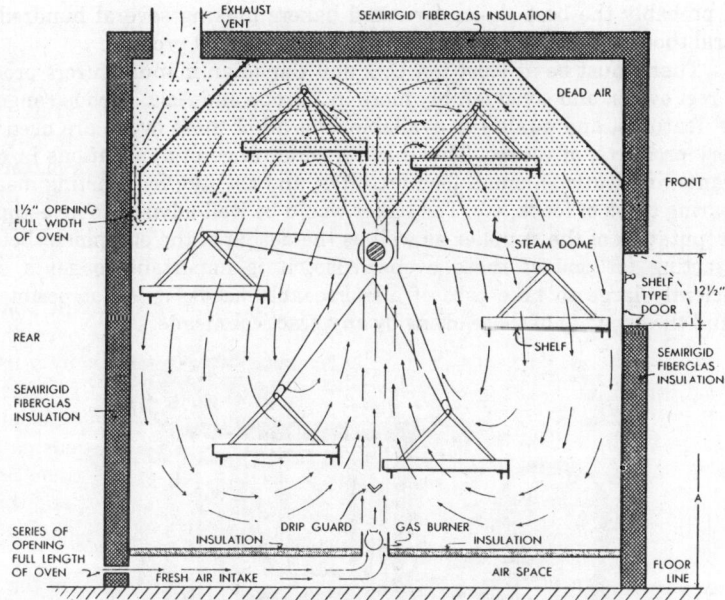

Figure 31.2. Schematic drawing of the important features of a reel oven

Reel ovens can be heated by gas, electricity, or oil. With gas or electricity, the heating means are placed on the floor of the oven. Gas ovens usually have a baffle placed above the burner to change part of the flame's energy to radiant heat. Indirect-fired ovens, generally oil heated, burn the fuel in a separate chamber located beneath the baking compartment; the hot vapors are conducted through radiators in the oven floor before exiting up the back and then out the flue. To apply steam, perforated steam sprayers effective in the entire chamber or in a partitioned zone can be installed.

There is a timer attached to the front of the oven. That is generally all it is attached to. It indicates the baking time and signals completion by a kind of alarm clock mechanism, but generally does not control heating time. Thermostats responsive to changes of about 3°F are the usual temperature control measures. This does not mean that products will encounter temperatures differing by only three degrees. There are side-to-side and top-to-bottom variations in temperature. The vertical differences are canceled out for all practical purposes by the reel's rotation, but the horizontal differences are not, and bakers often find there is a significant variation in the baking response of doughs placed on the left side and those placed on the right side of the shelf. Some fluctuations in temperature occur when the door is opened, allowing hot air to exit and cold air to enter in a draft that can affect sensitive products. In spite of these negative features, the reel oven has been found to be satisfactory for baking many kinds of products.

It is probably the best choice for retail bakers making several hundred to several thousand pounds per day of several varieties of product.

There must be at least ten U.S. and Canadian manufacturers producing reel ovens, and considerably more in Europe and Asia. A wide range of sizes, features, and quality is available. Not all of these ovens are used for bakery products, of course. They have a wide range of applications in restaurants, institutions, small food factories, and the like for roasting meats, preparing trays of foods, etc. The baker would be well-advised to investigate the reputation of the supplier as well as the design of the equipment before contracting for one of these ovens. Also, it is important to get a size sufficiently large to take care of all forseeable needs; it is not possible to expand the capacity of these ovens by any practical means.

Figure 31.3. Rotating rack oven. Loading door open.

Rack ovens.—A rack oven consists of a chamber into which are rolled, or otherwise transported, racks of shelves containing pans of dough products. The racks may remain stationary or be rotated while baking is taking place. Some kind of forced convection arrangement is almost always present in these ovens. Figure 31.3 is a photo of a small rotatable rack oven that would be suitable for a retail bake shop (Source: Babb Co.).

The following description of a commercially available rack oven has been taken from the manufacturer's literature (Anon. 1986) and gives a clear explanation of the operation of a typical rack oven. From initial loading, the fermented product can stay on the same rack through proofing, baking, and cooling without handling at each stage. A two-rack oven can be loaded easily in under 30 sec, or an eight-rack oven completely unloaded and reloaded in less than three minutes. The floor space is a fraction of that required for an equal capacity tunnel oven. A two-rack unit requires one-third the area of an equivalent reel oven or 45% of that required by a double deck oven having the same output.

The high efficiency heat exchanger and insulation coupled with cross flow forced air circulation reduce running cost. A two-rack oven producing mixed types of products averages one gallon of oil used per hour. The soft turbulent air heating system creates a faster heat transfer to the products, permitting a reduction in baking time or baking temperature. The capacity of the burner and heat exchanger is sufficient to permit continuous baking without having to wait for oven recovery between bakes. When the oven door is opened, the rotating turntable brings each rack to the loading position and stops automatically. When a rack has been loaded or unloaded, a simple operation of the indexing button brings the next rack into position. On completion of loading, the oven door is closed and the automatic control system starts the turntable rotation, air recirculation, and temperature control. Baking is then carried out by a horizontal forced air flow between the baking pans or trays, giving excellent bottom heat in addition to an evenly fired top coloring. The operator can separately switch off the burner, rotation, and air flow, if necessary. Air circulation is automatically turned off when the oven door is opened, and, as the fan drops in speed, air is drawn from the opening door into the heat exchanger, producing little or no loss of hot air into the bakery. During continuous production, the heat exchanger and residual heat in the oven have sufficient capacity to retain the oven temperature during the loading and unloading period.

The oven is fitted with a high humidity, self generating, steaming system suitable for the production of crusty bread. A damper controls the evacuation of steam from the baking chamber.

Maintenance is minimized by having only one bearing in a hot zone. All others are on top in ambient air and are lubricated from one point.

Other types of ovens.—Forced convection can be applied to almost any kind of oven. The units most often called "forced convection ovens" are shelf ovens that have been fitted with high capacity fans for moving strong currents of hot air through the chamber. Several manufacturers supply this equipment in a broad range of size and features (Lohrer 1987).

Some of the specifications for a 28-tray forced convection oven, non-rotating carriage, are given here (Pamart 1987). The trays are transported on a carriage. The oven is furnished with two of these carriages so that one can be loaded or unloaded while the other is baking. Surface area of the 28 trays is about 80 sq ft. A window in the door of the oven allows constant inspection of the interior.

Two reversible centrifugal turbines driven by 2 hp motors provide the convected air. An automatic programmer/timer can be used to reverse the operating direction of the turbines so that uniformity of heat distribution can be increased. When the door is opened, heat and air are turned off.

Oven temperature can be increased at the rate of about 20°F per min. Gas or electric heating can be specified. Optional accessories include humidifier, iodine vapor lamp, low voltage control, and stainless steel carriage.

WHOLESALER OVENS

According to Lugar (1962), manufacturers designing and building good baking ovens must take into consideration the following basic essentials: (1) Application of heat—in what manner is the heat to be applied; (2) Method of control of the required heat; (3) Best manner of insulating the heat for best efficiency; (4) Flexibility of the oven to bake a variety of products; (5) Cost of construction; (6) Overall ease of operation and maintenance of the baking unit; and (7) Ability to bake the most desired products in the most efficient manner. Being at that time vice president of the Thomas L. Green Co., Mr. Lugar was mostly concerned with biscuit ovens, but his words are still applicable to the design of ovens for all kinds of bakery products. Some of these general topics will be addressed in the following paragraphs before specific types of ovens are discussed.

Heat transfer systems.—The two main types of heating systems for modern large-scale ovens are ribbon burners in the baking chamber itself and combustion chambers located outside the oven proper. Ribbon burners are placed about 2 ft apart, while the recirculating ovens have a heating unit about every 50 ft. There has been a great deal of controversy about the relative advantages of these two systems, but it is well known that both types are being used satisfactorily. Open flame and surface combustion (ceramic) elements have been used, but the former type is more common.

Several burner designs have been developed to obtain maximum safety and accurate control of the heat sources within the oven. The open inspirator system uses gas at 1 to 5 psig and mixes it with room air drawn into the inspirator by the Venturi effect. Good combustion is obtained at or near the maximum output, but adequate air for complete combustion may not be entrained at the lower settings. The question arises as to the fate of solid particles drawn in with the room air. Smaller particles will undoubtedly pass through the jets and be burned without causing any problem. Large particles that might clog the burner can be entrapped by filters fitted over the intakes to the inspirator. Even so, some accumulation of deposits inside the burner occurs, and these systems are designed for easy and fool-proof cleaning of the inspirators and other critical parts.

The zone proportional mixer system uses air pressurized to

approximately 1 psig to draw gas at substantially atmospheric pressure into a proportional mixing unit. This gas is depressurized to zero gauge by a special valving arrangement. The combustible air-gas mixture is distributed to several burners, usually to all burners in a zone. Control is achieved by changing the volume of air going into the proportional mixer. Any change that is made affects all the burners in the zone, making this system somewhat inflexible. The air is filtered before being pressurized.

A modification of the zone proportional system mixes air and gas in a proper ratio at each burner. A zero pressure gas line and low pressure air line is led to each burner, and there is a separate proportional mixer and gas valve for each burner. This system provides good flexibility although it may be questioned how often its high level of control is actually necessary.

Gas and air for all the burners in an oven are premixed in a special device in the premixed gas system. The disadvantage of this method is the presence of relatively large quantities of an explosive mixture throughout the distribution system. Each burner must be fitted with a fire check to prevent backfires. The system is flexible because each burner can be adjusted separately, but because of the potential dangers it is not much used. Some ribbon burners can be adjusted so as to give different flame heights in three sections across the band.

In the exterior-combustion chamber type of oven, several arrangements are possible. Generally, there is one combustion chamber per zone, which restricts the number of adjustments that can be made. On the other hand, relatively close control of the temperature of the circulating gases can be achieved. The type of burner used in the exterior combustion chamber is more-or-less immaterial so far as effect on the dough piece is concerned.

Steam can be used to transfer heat from the combustion chamber to the baking tunnel. In one steam system, metal tubes sealed at both ends and partially filled with water or some other suitable liquid extend from the fire box into the oven. The flames vaporize the liquid, and turbulent vapor under high pressure carries heat throughout the length of the tube. Since heat is transferred to the product mainly by radiation in these systems, the tubes must reach very high temperatures before satisfactory baking conditions are attained. This heat transfer method was successfully applied in commercial operations but is no longer used to any great extent in bakeries. Experimental two-channel heat pipes have been described (Anon. 1989), although it is not known whether or not they can be adapted to ovens.

Zone control.—Although sequential application of different temperatures might be applied in convection ovens without moving the dough piece, and is even done sometimes in home baking, it is difficult to implement in ovens where the product remains stationary. If the dough is carried through a tunnel that is partitioned off into chambers, however, it is easy to apply different temperatures, as well as different top and bottom heating conditions, at different points in the baking process. For example, traveling hearth ovens have the advantage that baffles can be placed in the baking chamber to restrict heat circulation. If the heating elements can be adjusted separately in each of these zones, different temperatures can be applied to the product at different times in its baking cycle. this gives the baker more flexibility in adjusting conditions to the optimum for a given product. Generally, the burners can also be regulated separately for the top and bottom of each zone and the exhaust control dampers are separate for each zone. The use of zones is particularly helpful in baking crackers and cookies.

The number of zones in an oven will vary according to the specifications established by the engineer, who will take into consideration the needs of all the kinds of products the baker expects to make in the oven. In setting up baking conditions, it is often constructive to consider the oven as being divided into three sections, even though more zones are present.

Traveling Hearth Ovens

In tunnel or traveling hearth ovens, the baking hearth is made of steel segments that move through the baking chamber on conveying chains. Loading and discharging are at opposite ends of the tunnel, which is frequently a considerable advantage when positioning the auxiliary equipment. Straps, individual pans, or even unpanned dough pieces can be placed on the hearth. Because the baking surface is not divided into relatively small components, as in the traveling tray oven, it is more flexible in the size of pans it can accept and is often more efficient in capacity, especially where several sizes of straps are utilized. If pans are not at the loading area at the precise time a tray becomes available, the whole tray remains empty, but a traveling hearth oven can accept pans at any place on the hearth so that it is not necessary to leave empty spaces that are full multiples of the tray width. Thus, additional efficiency in hearth utilization may be obtained if timing happens to be somewhat irregular.

This type of oven seems to have lost some of its popularity in recent years. It is generally regarded as being more expensive and more difficult to maintain than a band oven of equal capacity, and traveling tray ovens are somewhat more flexible and no more expensive. Nonetheless, traveling hearth ovens can have a place in modern bakery practice.

Traveling Tray Ovens

Because provisions can be made for long horizontal runs, traveling tray ovens are more efficient than reel ovens in space utilization. Furthermore, they do not require high ceilings. Each tray is permanently fixed to a conveyor chain and holds several pans or straps. Trays are pulled by the chains from front to back of the oven, then moved to a lower track so baking can continue on the return trip to the front, where they are unloaded. In the early designs, problems were encountered in obtaining a smooth, vibrationless transfer as the trays were moved from the upper to the lower track. The jarring and vibration sometimes observed were not particularly harmful to bread, but could cause damage to delicate or fluid products such as pies and sheet cakes. Various methods of stabilization were invented, among them the shoe system and the transfer arm.

Small size traveling tray ovens may be operated as batch or as multicycle equipment. After the oven is loaded, the pans are permitted to make two or more round trips before they are unloaded. In longer ovens, however, the travel time required for one complete cycle is sufficient to complete the baking so the oven can be operated continuously, allowing automatic loaders and unloaders to be used.

Figure 31.4 shows a tray oven with its unloading arrangement and a conveyor leading to the hand depanning station (Source: Baker Perkins).

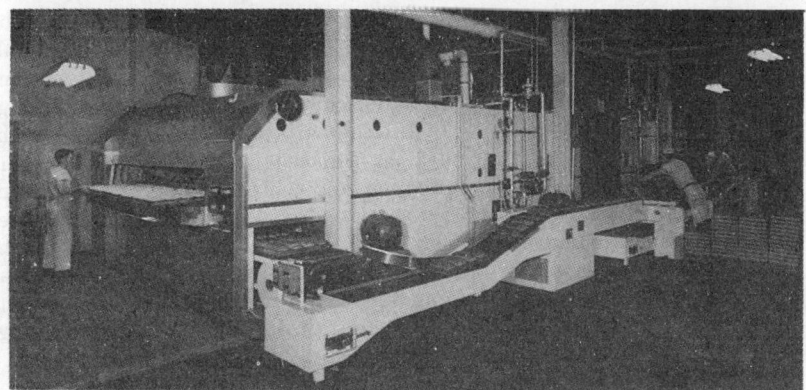

Figure 31.4. Traveling tray oven

By making the trays go through the oven two times in one baking cycle, approximately twice as much capacity can be obtained in the same floor space. Of course, the oven has to be much taller to contain the extra trays and machinery.

The shell of a traveling tray oven will consist of a steel frame resting on a level concrete foundation and supporting the steel lining sheets that form a rectangular baking chamber. Expansion joints allow the lining to expand and contract as the temperature changes without affecting the outer shell. A horizontal baffle divides the baking chamber into upper and lower compartments. The oven can also be divided into zones along its length to allow a sequence of different temperatures. The top, bottom, and sides of the oven are insulated with about two inches of rock wool, and then plastered with fireproof cement to meet sanitary standards. The insulation is covered and concealed by the exterior finish sheets, which are usually enameled.

Rows of direct gas-fired burners extend into the oven cavity below and above the tray conveyor. They are arranged in groups to form control zones for regulating temperatures in different parts of the oven. Every zone has separate air and gas supplies, a modulating temperature controller, and a group of burners. To permit adjustment of heat balance across the oven, some or all of the burners allow variation in flame intensity along their length. Each burner has an inspirator in which gas at about atmospheric pressure and air are combined. Ignition can be made continuous.

Indirect fired ovens will have one or more heating units located outside the chamber. Each heating unit will include a burner, combustion tunnel, heater body, radiator tubes, delivery and return ducts, circulating blower, exhaust stock with damper controls, and safety devices.

Band Ovens

The characteristic feature of band ovens is the continuous steel belt that forms the baking surface and which turns around two large metal drums, one at each end of the oven. There are many advantages in this form of construction. For example, the baking chamber can be made very long (300 ft is a fairly common length) leading to fast transit times and high production rates. There is no need for elaborate conveying and transfer mechanisms with all of the maintenance and control problems inherent in such designs. In fact, the band can be extended beyond the oven entrance sufficiently to accommodate certain forming operations so that no dough piece transfers are necessary, and extended past the exit end to allow a modest amount of cooling and some additional drying so that the product does not have to be removed from the belt until it is well set, thus providing support for the piece during the whole period of its maximum fragility.

Figure 31.5 shows the entrance of a band oven with the long lead in space over which forming devices can be placed. Also visible is the rotating drum with its tension-adjusting cylinder (Source: Baker Perkins).

Figure 31.5. Band oven

Because there is no need for elaborate transfer mechanisms, the baking chamber itself can be restricted in volume to almost the minimum theoretical space required to hold the product and the hearth, so that heat control is simplified and heat loss is reduced.

Although bands can be used as hearths for baking most kinds of bakery products, and as supporting surfaces for pans, their greatest utility has been for crackers and cookies. They seem to be nearly ideal for these products, and much of the information in the literature deals with the use of bands for biscuit baking. According to Fischer (1977), the wholesale baker expects from a band oven: (1) Uniformly baked product; (2) Constant baking rate; (3) Flexibility; (4) High baking rate; (5) Efficient removal of gases; (6) Automatic operation; (7) Minimum heat loss into the bakery; (8) Maximum efficiency of fuel use; (9) Stable baking surface; (10) Safety for people and machinery; (11) Mechanical and electrical dependability; and (12) Sanitation compatibility.

Modern band ovens are triumphs of engineering and technology. With little maintenance, an oven 300 ft long and 39 inches wide can bake 2,000 to 3,000 lb of cookie dough per hr continuously for long periods. On certain doughs, much higher output can be obtained. Assuming proper adjustment, the millions of units put out in 24 hr will be uniform enough to satisfy the most discriminating of consumers. Feeding and removal of dough pieces is routinely automated so as to require minimal operatior attention.

In a survey of the types of band ovens used in commercial cookie bakeries (Light 1965), the following information was elicited: (1) Ovens ranged from 100 to 400 ft ong, and the bands were from 26 to 60 inches wide; (2) Direct-fired, indirect-fired, and infrared means of heat generation were being used; (3) Energy sources were natural gas, manufactured gas, propane, oil, and electricity; (4) Ovens had been manufactured by Baker Perkins, Thomas L. Green, J. W. Greer, Spooner, Vicars, Werner, etc.; (5) There were single-ribbon, double-ribbon, high intensity, and double-flame burners, with premix, inspirator, and aspirator means for combining air and fuel. Sometimes blowers and heat tubes were used, as well as various types of baffling, dampering, and exhaust systems; (6) The baking surfaces were solid or perforated continuous steel bands and several types of wire mesh ranging from very open (for some kinds of pretzels) through continental types with smaller wire but still with open mesh, to heavy cord weave bands utilizing both straight- and crimped-wire designs; and (7) Basic adjustments that could be made included band speed, number of burners in top and bottom of each zone, pressure valves to regulate top and bottom burner flames separately in each zone, and dampers to remove or retain moisture in specific areas, vertical baffles between zones, and controllable exhausts. Many changes in design and improvements in materials have taken place since this survey was taken, but many of the same ovens exist and are working today.

The band oven chamber consists of a frame supporting the necessary rollers, guides, burners, and the like, together with insulation on top, sides, and bottom. Vents with dampers, clean-out doors, and observation ports are included as necessary. Oven chambers are usually manufactured in modular units, for example, in 10 ft lengths.

Baking surfaces can be solid steel bands, perforated steel bands, or wire mesh bands. Early mesh bands had a fairly open weave, but more recent versions have had a finely textured, closely woven structure. Perforated bands and wire mesh allow steam to escape from the bottoms of dough pieces and help to prevent gas pockets and distortions. They also tend to reduce spread. The unbaked dough or batter is either deposited directly on the oven band, or formed on auxiliary equipment and then transferred to the band by conveyors.

In long band ovens, even a slight amount of sideways movement will soon accumulate to the point where the band will be damaged and the oven jammed unless corrective measures are taken. This sideways drift is prevented by band guides that may be of several kinds. The simplest and least satisfactory consists of angle irons welded at strategic places along the band length. They will force a wandering band back into place, but they can also cause serious damage. Friction quickly wears out these simple guides. Spring-mounted vertical spools fixed at numerous places along the band are reasonably satisfactory. Canting the rollers supporting the band will guide it without edge wear, but requires close attention by the operator. A combined system utilizing spools a a sensing device to warn the operator when to adjust the support rollers is probably the best compromise solution. A patented system lets the spools themselves cant the rollers when the spools are driven off center by a wandering band.

CONVEYORIZED PROOFING AND BAKING SYSTEMS

The basic principle of the conveyorized proofing and baking method, is that pans containing the dough circulate continuously through the panning, proofing, baking, and depanning operations without the need of human intervention for handling or timing. In earlier versions of this concept, trays, straps, or racks may be subject to delays for some reason, as while waiting for an open space in the oven conveyor or while being transferred from one conveyor to another. In the continuous system, however, pans move from panner through proofer and oven without stopping and while attached to the same "endless" conveyor. In conventional processing, the pans would be handled individually (as straps, in some systems) and would be stationary at some points in their progress through the operations. The newer method greatly reduces the complexity of the equipment needed to handle pans. To fully achieve the benefits of this concept, it was necessary to design new types of proofers and ovens (Grogan 1980 and Wells 1983).

Traveling Tray and Rack Systems

There are four sets of equipment to be considered in the traveling tray and rack systems. These are the conveyor grouping machinery situated prior to the proofer, the proofer, the conveyor system prior to the oven, and the oven. A typical arrangement for a bread system of this type has a grouping conveyor for the proofer that is designed to separate a continuous flow of pans into groups of a predetermined size. There are two basic types, the full complement style and the random-load style.

The full-complement grouper separates pans into groups that have approximately the same length as the size of the tray being fed, and allows space between pans in the group. If a full group is not available for loading when a tray or shelf of the proofer is in the loading position, then that tray or shelf will circulate empty. The two-pan stop, full-complement grouper is said to be the most reliable design of this equipment for handling bread and roll pans in a high speed operation. This grouper is equally reliable for feeding both proofers and ovens. Conveyor grouping speeds greater than 100 ft per min are not recommended since such speeds could cause dough pieces to shift in the pans while grouping into a proofor or cause dough to collapse when grouping pans into the oven.

It is essential that sufficient conveyors be provided to allow for the accumulation of pans. Arrangements must be made to ensure that pans do not back up and cause unnecessary waiting of the production equipment. Back-up conveyors are usually located before the grouper. The required amount of back-up conveyor space is at least 2.5 times the length of the proofer tray or shelf. Any special feeding systems between the grouper and the proofer, such as a step or feeder preceder operation will decrease the amount of accumulating conveyor.

The second style of grouper, the random-load grouper, allows any size of pan group from one pan up to a full complement to be loaded into a proofer or cooler. This type of grouper should only be used as a proofer or cooler grouper. If used with the proofer, the pans must be regrouped into a full complement before the group is loaded into the oven. Random loading into the oven can upset the lateral heat distribution.

Load and discharge conveyors are mounted just outside the proofer's front end. Each of these conveyors has its own drive and the space between them is equal to the shelf spacing of the racks. Racks are made out of aluminum structural frames, with each rack having stabilization rollers affixed at its sides. The removable grids, or shelves for the racks, are made of stainless steel. The rack elevator section in front of the proofer consists of two vertical pawl assemblies, one set on each side of the machine. These movable pawls are moved by the main proofer drive and pick up the rack in a repeated stepwise action until the rack has moved to the top of the elevator.

The lowering mechanism for the racks at the rear of the proofer has a single chain circuit on both sides. Each chain is equipped with attachment lugs and swivel lengths to move the racks from the upper to the lower horizontal runs. These chains are driven continuously from the main proofer drive. Rack loaders and unloaders operate only while the rack is temporarily halted in its upward travel through the elevator. The loaders are driven by separate motors energized through an electrical cam switch so that they function only while the rack is at rest.

After pans leave the proofer, they are taken by a conveyor to the oven. All three arrangements that have been used transfer groups of pans in steps from one unit machine to another without the use of pan stops. The conveyors are designed to start and stop smoothly while holding the pans in separate groups spaced out between the unit machines. In each of these conveyor systems, the number of pans loaded on each proofer shelf will be the same as the number of pans loaded on each oven tray. The first type is the single-line conveyor, consisting of a single row of conveyors that take a group of pans laterally from a proofer and then in stages move them to the adjoining piece of equipment. The second type is the direct transfer system, which transfers a tray or shelf load of pans directly as separate groups or rows in a lengthwise direction from the proofer to the oven. The third type is a combination of the other two systems. In it, the pans are first transferred lengthwise out of the proofer for two or three pan groups, then advanced laterally in a single row to the oven. It allows slower conveyor speeds and is adapatable to seeding, slitting, and pan lidding operations.

Regardless of the system being used, there must be a sufficient number of storage spaces to prevent holding up proofer discharge because of delay in loading trays into the oven. The minimum amount of accumulating time required to prevent halting of the proofer under normal conditions is equal to the sum of the fastest cycle time of the oven and the cycle time required by the oven loader to clear the loading area. Bread usually requires five stages or conveyor sections and a high speed roll operation usually requires six stages for accumulation. Stages consist of the proofer discharge conveyor, three or four intermediate steps, and the oven load conveyor.

A conveyor carries the pans through the oven, which may be of the traveling tray design (taking in and discharging at the same end) or the tunnel type (entrance at one end, exit at the other).

Continuous and Integrated Proofer and Oven Systems

These lines represent advances in automation beyond the systems described previously. To achieve the full potential of these plants, it was necessary to redesign the proofer, the oven, and the conveyors. There are perhaps three major U.S. manufacturers making this equipment. They seem to have found their greatest acceptance in high volume bread and roll plants, although they are no doubt adaptable to any bakery producing long runs of any item.

The new conveyors have unique features making fully continuous and automatic operation possible. One circuit of the "endless" conveyor goes through the proofer and one through the oven. The two basic types of conveyorized proofer and oven systems in use today are (1) the style in which the pans or straps are center mounted on the conveyor chain and (2) the design in which the pans are side mounted on the chain drive. The side mounted style is constructed of universal joints that are linked together with steel bands. Each universal joint supports four ballbearing wheels, two on each axis. Other conveyors that have been reported are rod type belts for conveying pans or peel boards and another that uses triple strands of large-link chain. The latter type appears to have been used primarily in Europe.

Connected to the conveyor chain are grid support struts that run freely on an idler track constructed of angle iron. The carriage grids that fit into the support struts firmly hold the pans, which overhang the grids, and they are attached to the endless floor mounted conveyor chain. Grids are made of steel for the oven, and of stainless steel for the proofer. Advantages claimed for the side-mounted chain, as compared to the center-mounted, are a shorter turning radius, closer pan spacing, and a smaller module to house the conveyor. An important recent patent covering conveyor and other details of the continuous system is that of Bacigalupe and Doble (1989).

Details follow for a side-mounted version specifically designed for high volume roll production. The proofing module receives pans from a conveyor system interlocked with two make-up units. Pans enter the proofing module at a low level on the right side of the box, spiral upward to the top of the first loop, then over to the second loop where they spiral downward to a low exit point. The double spiral grid conveyor is supported by floor-mounted aluminum uprights and cross braces and runs on a steel track. Twin air-conditioning units are located on the floor between the double spirals; they control the proofing temperature and humidity. The outer walls are prepainted aluminum with a foamed polyurethane core.

Pans enter the oven module at a high level at one end of the box, and travel downward through a series of race tracks in a spiral to a low exit point. These units are fabricated of steel.

The oven is direct gas fired and uses ribbon burners that are located beneath the conveyor loops on each side. An air agitation system situated at each end of the oven module distributes hot air to the ends of the oven. Hot air from near the top of the oven is directed through ducts and past a damper that vents a portion out the stack and recirculates the balance into the turns. This process is said to result in good heat distribution throughout the oven. A section of the oven can be partly walled off as a steam zone. The enclosure has an aluminized steel interior and a sheet steel exterior painted white, with an 8-inch thickness of insulation between the walls.

A synchronizing feeder is used by both the proofer and oven modules during loading. Pans are positioned width-wise on a conveyor leading to the feeder. This continuously moving synchronizer positions the pans so they can be loaded onto the holding grid. Proper spacing is obtained through the use of springloaded synchronizing lugs. These traveling lugs hold the pans in position until the grid can move upward on the track and pick up a pan. Since the pans overhang the grid, a pair of stripper belts that overhang the grid can remove the pan at the end of the proofing or baking process.

In the proofer, the chain is hydraulically driven by multiple small load-sharing motors in a twin caterpillar chain drive mechanism. If excess pressure should be exerted on the chain, back pressure on the remotely located hydraulic power unit will automatically stop the drive motors and chain. Although either hydraulic or electric drive systems can be used, the former assures slow, easy starts and quick, smooth stops if the forward movement of the chain should be hampered. The chain in the oven is driven in the same manner, except the power unit is smaller and only one hydraulic motor, externally located, is present.

Factors to be considered in making a choice between tray-and-rack equipment and continuous conveyor equipment are the production rate (which appears to favor the continuous systems), floor space (greater amounts of product per unit space can be achieved in the tray-and-rack design), flexibility (variety of products and pan size can be accommodated better by tray-and-rack), and capital cost (probably lower for continuous conveyor). Maintenance and production people can more easily understand and service continuous conveyor equipment because it has fewer mechanisms and a smaller number of moving parts. The open construction of continuous conveyor systems makes sanitation easier and faster. Proofers for the rack or tray system use about half as much floor space as the continuous type, for equal production rates. Conveyor ovens probably take up less floor area than the others, but they occupy more cubic footage (Wells 1983).

BIBLIOGRAPHY

ANDERSON, R. C. 1970. Oven maintenance. Bakers Digest *44*, No. 8, 58-62, 76

ANON. 1986. Rotorack Ovens. Andrew Denholm, Lt., Midlothian, Scotland

ANON. 1989. Two-channel heat pipe moves heat fast and far. Designfax *11*, No. 3, 38

ANON. 1990. Pan-and-peel bread system built on flexibility. Baking & Snack Systems *12*, No. 4, 12-17

BACIGALUPE, C., and DOBLE, M. J. 1989. Continuous proof and bake apparatus having improved conveyor system. U.S. Pat. 4,882,981

BLUMEL, F., and BOOG, W. 1977. Five Thousand Years of Baking Ovens (In German). Deutsches Brotmuseum, Donau.

CHEN, T. A. 1989. Continuous processing machines for baking buns. U.S. Pat. 4,854,226

COPE, J. C., GRADY, M. E., and WARNOCK, D. G. 1988. Enchilada shell cooker. U.S. Pat. 4,754,699

DERSCH, J. A. 1958. Principles of heat distribution in baking ovens. Bakers Digest *32*, No. 5, 37-40

DERSCH, J. A. 1960. Bakery ovens. *In* Bakery Technology and Engineering. S. A. Matz, Editor. AVI Publishing Co., Westport, CT

DIXON, F. R., and CLEMENTS, R. G. 1963. Improvement in heat treatment of baking ovens. British Pat. 924,071

ESCAMILLA, R. M. 1988. Method and apparatus for baking thin dough discs. U.S. Pat. 4,751,876

FISCHER, H. A. 1977. Efficient oven design and imperatives for optimum fuel usage. Candy & Snack Industry *142*, No. 5, 17-18, 20-21

GRISSINGER, G. R. 1973. Automated proofing and baking advances. Proc. Am. Soc. Bakery Engineers *1973*, 128-137

GROGAN, P. E. 1980. Conveyorized proofing and baking systems. Proc. Am. Soc. Bakery Engineers *1980*, 113-118

HENKE, M. C. 1989. Hot air oven having infrared radiant surfaces. U.S. Pat. 4,881,519

HOLLAND, J. H. 1962. High frequency baking. Biscuit Maker and Plant Baker, Aug. 1962, 698 et seq.

HOLLAND, J. H. 1966. High frequency baking. Presentation at B&CMA Annual Meeting, Feb. 8, 1966

JOHNSON, L. A., and HOOVER, W. J. 1977. Energy use in baking bread. Bakers Digest

51, No. 5, 58-60, 62-64

KAISER, V. A. 1974. Modeling and simulation of a multi-zone band oven. Food Technol. *28*, No. 12, 50-53

KELLEY, H. N. 1969. A Brief Encyclopedia of Commercial Ovens. Middleby Marshall Oven Co., Morton Grove, IL

KOCH, A. 1983. Oven energy efficiency. Proc. Am. Soc. Bakery Engineers *1983*, 90-07

LIGHT, H. J., JR. 1987. Baking principles by zone. Biscuit Bakers Institute, 40th Annual Training Conference, Montreal

LUGAR, T. R. 1962. Economic Biscuit and Cracker Baking. Thomas L. Green & Co., Indianapolis, IN

MC CORMICK, R. 1988. Dielectric heat seeks low moisture applications. Prepared Foods *157*, No. 10, 139-140

MENDOZA, F. C. 1987. System for preparing tortillas. U.S. Pat. 4,715,272

MORETH, N. W. 1981. Optimal energy utilization in ovens. Bakers Digest *51*, No 5, 26-31

ORII, M. 1988. Baking apparatus and process. U.S. Pat. 4,767,639

PAMART, P. 1987. Personal communication. Arpen, Gennevilliers, France

PEI, D. C. T. 1982. Microwave baking—new developments. Bakers Digest *56*, No. 1, 8, 10, 12

PIRRIE, P. G. 1934. Use of steam in bakers' ovens. Am. Soc. Bakery Engineers Bull. *98*

ROSENBERG, U., and BOGL, W. 1987. Microwave thawing, drying, and baking in the food industry. Food Technol. *41*, No. 6, 85-91

RYCHNOVSKY, M. 1989. Accord reached in emissions control debate. Bakery & Snack Systems *11*, No. 9, 22-26

SEROTA, R. 1973. Heating with radio waves. Automation *20*, No. 9, 102-106

SHEI, S. M., HENKE, M. C., and SCHINDLER, J. W. 1988. Air flow system for a low profile impingement oven. U.S. Pat. 4,757,800

SIEVERS, R. 1978. New baking methods. Proc. Am. Soc. Bakery Engineers *1978*, 98-105

SKARIN, R. 1964. Selecting an oven for maximum performance. Proc. Am. Soc. Bakery Engineers *1964*, 88-93

SMITH, D. P. 1984. Thermal treatment of food products. U.S. Pat. 4,479,776

SMITH, W. H. 1966A. Steam, humidity, and damper control in bakery ovens. Biscuit Maker Plant Baker *17*, 730-732

SMITH, W. H. 1966B. What happens in the baking oven. Biscuit Maker Plant Baker *17*, 652-656

SPOONER, T. F. 1989. Production depends on efficient heating. Baking & Snack Systems *11*, No. 9, 28-29, 31,

STANDING, C. N. 1974. Individual heat transfer modes in band oven biscuit baking. J. Food Sci. *39*, 267-271

SUAREZ, P. E. 1963. Oven bands—their use and maintenance. Biscuit Cracker Baker *52*, No. 9, 74, 76

UNKLESBAY, K. B., and UNKLESBAY, N. F. 1985. Effect of dough temperature and infrared radiation on crust color of pizzas. J. Foodservice Systems *3*, 243-249

VARILEK, P., and WALKER, C. E. 1983. Baking and ovens—history of heat technology. Bakers Digest *57*, No. 5, 52-54, 56-57, 59. No. 6, 24, 26-27

VARILEK, P., and WALKER, C. E. 1984A. Baking and ovens—history of heat technology III. Bakers Digest *58*, No. 1, 24-26, 29

VARILEK, P., and WALKER, C. E. 1984B. Baking and ovens—history of heat technology V. Bakers Digest *58*, No. 3, 22-24, 26, 29

WADE, P. 1987. Biscuit baking by near-infrared radiation. J. Food Eng. *6*, 165-175

WELLS, H. D. 1988. Method of cooking. U.S. Pat. 4,758,442

WELLS, R. A. 1983. Proofing and baking systems. Proc. Am. Soc. Bakery Engineers *1983*, 119-124

WHITESIDE, R. L. 1982. Energy use in baking industry. Bakers Digest *56*, No. 4, 30-34

YONEZAWA, M. 1986. Apparatus for making bread. Apparatus for making bread. U.S. Pat. 4,592,273

chapter thirty-two

FRYERS AND FRYING

INTRODUCTION

Not all "bakery" products are cooked in ovens. All doughnuts, a large percentage of the crusts made into frozen pizzas, numerous snack products, and some other foods based on cereal ingredients are fried. The unifying principle in ovens and fryers is that they are designed to transfer heat from an energy source into the product. In ovens this is done by conduction from the pan, convection from hot oven gases, and radiation from flames and hot oven parts, while in fryers the heat is transferred to the dough piece by conduction from a liquid transfer medium, hot edible oil. In ovens, the product is supported in a pan or on a hearth during the whole time it is being baked, while frying products are generally unsupported (though they may be held under the surface) except by their buoyancy in the oil.

Radiation probably contributes very little to heat transfer during the frying process although convection currents in the oil contribute a great deal. Another important difference between baking and frying is that, in the latter process, some of the heat transfer medium (edible fat or oil) becomes part of the finished product.

Block (1964) states that frying differs from other heat-processing methods in the following respects:

(1) Cooking is accomplished in a relatively short period of time, generally within five minutes, due to (a) a great temperature difference between the heat source and the food, and (b) the small size of the individual food unit, which in some cases is less than one ounce in weight.

(2) The frying fat becomes a significant component in the end product, varying from as little as 10% by weight of the end product in breaded fish sticks to perhaps 40% by weight in potato chips.

(3) Fried products usually have crisper crusts than other cooked foods.

(4) The heat-transfer medium (i.e., the hot fat) is subject to changes in composition and often in performance characteristics during its process life.

(5) There are unique mechanical problems involved in commercial frying.

Several models of batch fryers and continuous fryers are available. Most batch fryers are used for purposes other than cooking dough products, but many are being used for doughnut frying and a few for specialty dough products. Probably more continuous fryers are being used for cooking potato chips, processing breaded meat products, and frying snack products than for dough products, but this equipment is important to the baked product market and will be discussed at length in this chapter.

CONTINUOUS FRYERS

An expert (Belshaw 1976) stated that four essentials for good automated frying systems are accurate temperature control, efficient heat transfer, minimum shortening contamination, and rapid shortening turnover.

Most continuous fryer systems consist of at least five independent sets of equipment: (1) The tank or trough containing the frying medium and providing a means of draining fat from the exiting product back into the kettle; (2) A conveying means for moving the food into, through, and out of the fat; (3) The fat system, which pumps and filters the frying medium and replenishes it from a bulk supply as needed; (4) A heating unit with a control system for generating thermal energy as required and transferring it to the fat; and (5) An exhaust system for removing the hot vapors emerging from the fat. The fat itself is an essential and interacting part of the whole system, and it strongly affects the functioning of the equipment and the results of the operation as reflected in the quality of the finished product.

Figure 32.1 shows a production fryer including conveyor, exhaust hood, oil sump, and other equipment (Source: Dawn Equipment).

Figure 32.1. Production fryer

Heating Methods

Direct heating.—Gas, oil, and electricity are being used as energy sources for food fryers. Dual-fuel systems convertible from oil to gas are available. A doughnut fryer equipped for using alternate energy sources has oil and gas supply lines leading into a pair of oil/gas "combustors" feeding flames into distribution manifolds from which the heat is diverted into a number of tubes crossing the vats.

The simplest heating system consists of gas flames directed against the bottom of a frying kettle, but this method has some deficiencies in controllability and efficiency. According to Belshaw (1976), heat is applied to automated doughnut fryers by (1) bottom-fired gas strip burners, (2) infrared gas heat on a V-bottom, (3) tube-fired atmospheric burners, (4) tube-fired premixed burners, and (5) electric tubular heaters with lift-out heaters

If the bottom of the vat is flat, solid matter such as dusting flour and pieces of batter accumulate on the bottom and form an insulating layer between the heat source and the fat. This results in a decreased rate of heat transfer, a loss of control, and accelerated fat breakdown due to localized overheating and contamination. By constructing the tank with a V-shaped bottom, this situation is alleviated to a certain extent, because the solid material collects in the lowest part of the vat, below the level at which the heat is being applied. An improvement on the V-shaped design uses a shortening circulating pump to flush solids to channels at the side of the tank.

Tubular heating systems transfer heat by passing burning gases through tubes that run through the vat from side to side. One advantage of this design, as compared to direct bottom heating, is that there is a cooler zone below the heating tubes; solids settle into this area away from the high heat and turbulence so they do not significantly interfere with heat transfer and do not deteriorate as fast. Tubular systems also provide a relatively large heating surface, giving a lower heat ratio per square inch that can be further improved by installing baffles inside the tubes to increase their heat transmitting efficiency. Disadvantages are the greater difficulty of cleaning tubes and the need for a larger quantity of shortening for the same output.

Two types of burners are used in tubular systems. In the atmospheric burner system, gas is fed in a thin stream to an orifice where it draws air into the burner. The gas and air mixture passes through burner ports and into fire tubes within the frying tank. Belshaw states these atmospheric burner systems are simple to install, easy to maintain, and provide good control as well as an acceptable level of efficiency. The second type of tube heater is based on a premix method in which gas and air are blended in the proper ratio and the mixture fed under slight pressure to burner orifices where it is ignited. This mixture burns with a high efficiency and requires no secondary air to complete the combustion. The premix system and power burners are rated superior in efficiency to all other gas-fired systems.

Electrical heating systems are convenient, though seldom economical as far as energy cost is concerned. They are used mostly in batch fryers, and sometimes in small continuous fryers. In modern systems, electricity is used to heat resistance elements inside small stainless steel tubes assembled in grids. These grids are fixed in the fryer just above the bottom of the vat. The grids can be positioned so that heat can be concentrated in some areas and minimized in others. Electrical heating elements can be installed in such a manner that the whole assembly can be raised up and out of the vat to make cleaning easier. In other designs, the entire heating complex can be removed quickly and completely for replacement or cleaning. Electrically heated fryers require relatively small amounts of fat.

Heat exchangers.—Oil can be heated in a heat exchanger located at an appreciable distance from the fryer. Hot oil is transferred to the vat by pumps and piping. Heat exchangers have been designed for direct and indirect heating of the fat. Capacities up to at least 14 million Btu are offered in horizontal direct-fired gas, oil, or propane models. Burner systems are completely automatic. Indirect systems have been designed to use chlorinated hydrocarbon heat transfer fluids for carrying the energy from an outside heat exchanger to tubes traversing the oil vat.

In one of the simpler designs of heat exchanger, fat is circulated through tubes traversing a chamber in which gas is burning. The constant circulation of fat tends to even out temperature differentials. The vat can be shallower, since it is not necessary to provide a space for heating elements or for collection of debris. This reduces the amount of fat that is required in the vat. On the other hand, additional fat is required to fill up the heat exchanger and the piping to and from it. Debris can be filtered out continuously as the oil is brought back to the heat exchanger.

A commercial low-pressure gas-fired cooking oil heat exchanger is available in sizes up to 1,500,000 Btu per hr. It features completely inspectable all stainless steel construction designed to meet USDA requirements. Heat is supplied by multi-port inspirator type low pressure gas burners of high thermal efficiency and has a proportioning temperature control. A patent (Bullock 1984) discloses details of one such system. Because oil is carried through the heat exchanger in very turbulent flow, heat transfer is very rapid and the temperature of the oil flowing through the pipe and the oil at the wall of the pipe will differ by only about 18° to 22°F from temperatures at the surface of the heating element. The lower temperature in the heat exchanger should cause less fat degradation.

Use of an external heat exchanger solves some of the temperature gradation problems resulting from placement of heating elements in the vat, but it creates others. For example, equipment cost is greater and maintenance is more complex. Generally the hot oil is pumped into one end of the fryer vat and removed from the other end, but there are some advantages to introducing the oil at one side of the tank so the current direction is from side to side (Miller 1990).

Frying temperatures and times.—Frying time, frying temperature and fat level in the vat are variables that can be controlled by the operator. The surface of the fat would ordinarily be kept within 2 to 3 inches above the top of the drop plate. Fat levels that are too low can produce misshapen or flat products, rough surfaces, and high fat absorption. If the fat levels are too high, the doughnut may crust over before it reaches the turner or it may float over the flight bars and fail to turn properly.

For yeast-leavened doughnuts, frying temperatures in the range of

375° to 395°F have been recommended (Braden 1976). Optimum frying times depend on the weight and configuration of the dough piece, among other factors. For regular round doughnuts weighing 18 to 19 oz per dozen, unfried weight, an average total frying time of 110 to 120 sec is considered normal. This allows about a minute cook on each side. Higher temperatures within the normal range may encourage greater expansion, but excessive temperatures firm up the skin too fast so that maximum expansion cannot occur. Frying at temperatures that are too low causes a slower coloring of the crust and allows too much fat to penetrate the crust before the interior is cooked. Settling, or collapsing of the white ring, is due to a frying time that is too short. Unduly long frying times lead to excessive fat absorption.

"Rise time" is the time it takes for the doughnut to come to the surface, measured from the time it drops from the cutter into the fat until it appears on top of the fat. Rise time is usually about 3 to 7 seconds depending on the size and type of the doughnut. Fluctuations in rise time can indicate problems with the leavening system, or other processing difficulties.

Figure 32.2. Fried pie cooker

In the cooking of fried pies, some special problems are observed. The crust must be thoroughly cooked to a medium brown color and the filling must be cooked to an optimal point before significant steam evolution occurs in the interior of the pie. The pie must often be rejected when this occurs. Also, boilout or bursting of the pie leads to contamination of the frying fat and its rapid breakdown. One authority (Taylor 1971) specified 3 min 22 sec at 385°F as suitable for a 4.5 oz fruit pie. Harding and Starwich (1965) recommended 3 min 45 secs for 3.5 oz pies frying at 355°F, and 4 min 15 sec for 4.75 oz pies fried at 380°F. These conditions are to be used with submerging conveyors.

Figure 32.2 shows an example of a large scale cooker for fried pies (Source: Dawn Equipment).

Temperature variation in zones.—There has been a gradually increasing recognition of the value of having different heating zones in fryers, especially in long conveyor fryers for doughnuts (Belshaw 1976). This is reminiscent of the development of zone heating in tunnel and band ovens. In large doughnut fryers, the demand for heat is greatest in regions where dough pieces enter the fat and, again, where the pieces are turned over. Also, the increased width and length of fryers being installed today make it impossible to get an even distribution of heat throughout the vat if the temperature is controlled and supplied by one set of heaters. When heaters and temperature sensors are located in areas of maximum demand, a rapid response can be obtained as the need for additional heat occurs.

An advanced version of a fryer with multiple temperature zones was described by Eves (1989). Oil is pumped from an external heat exchanger through separate pipes into separate zones. The amount of oil flowing into a given zone can be controlled individually. A continuous conveyor is part of the machine.

Radiation-assisted frying.—Stein (1972) discussed the cooking of cake doughnuts in a fryer that had an input of microwaves as well as heat from conventional sources. In this type of microwave frying, when dough-nuts are being cooked in the frying oil on their first side, microwave heating is also being applied. The microwaves heat the interior of the doughnut so that its temperature rises much more rapidly than it would in the absence of this radiation. The doughnut expands to its fullest while the first side is being fried, and there is no dense center ring. The total volume of the product is larger when it comes out of the fryer and fat absorption is reduced by 25%. However, Stein says these results are obtained only with blooming-type doughnuts, which are characterized by a relatively thin crust, low density, an open crumb, lower fat absorption, and a greater expansion.

Contact frying, or a simulation of contact frying, claimed to be suitable for pizzas, pancakes, and sandwiches, can be effected by infrared radiation, according to the patent of Dagerskog *et al.* (1986). The invention consists essentially of a single solid endless thin steel conveyor belt that is heated from below by short wave infrared radiation. Automatic control is provided by photocells and thermocouples connected to computerized heat modulating equipment.

Heat economizers.—Manufacturers of commercial fryers have offered equipment that conveys incoming product through the steam and vapor emerging from the vat. During its passage through this atmosphere, the raw products absorbs some of the oil and becomes heated, reducing the amount of heat and oil it requires when it reaches the fryer. In addition, the effluent gas continuing on to the exhaust is reduced in volume and its oil content is reduced, making it easier and cheaper to cleanse. These economizers have been applied mostly to potato chip fryers, but they may have some value in dough product frying.

Conveyors

Conveyors for transferring products from the entrance to the exit end of the oil trough include the following mechanisms: (1) Spacer bar conveying, in which the frying piece floats between transverse bars that push it over the surface at a rate adjusted to give it the desired cook by the time it emerges from the end of the vat; (2) Conveying by currents in the liquid fat, the currents being created by pumps; (3) Drop plate conveying, in which the product rests on shelves moving below the fat surface until the pieces develop enough buoyancy due to internal expansion to rise to the surface and contact the upper conveying means; (4) Submerger conveying, in which a mesh band moving just underneath the surface of the fat contacts the upper surface of the buoyant product and carries it along; (5) Conveyors for non-floating products, traveling well below the surface of the fat and utilizing baskets, belts, or other holding devices having no covers; (6) Restrained conveying, in which products are carried between two horizontal mesh belts; and (7) Compartmentalized conveying, in which dough pieces are held in small molds that may help shape the product as it cooks (see, for example, Cope *et al.* 1988).

The usual conveying means for yeast-raised doughnuts is of the spacer bar type, although some varieties of doughnuts require submerger conveyors. In cake doughnut fryers, conveyors are generally slatted drop plates onto which the dough pieces fall immediately after they are cut. The submerged plate moves in registration with the surface flight bars until the dough piece becomes light enough to float, after which the doughnut is moved by the flight bars. The conveyor is coordinated with the cutter so that doughnuts will be dropped in the proper position between the flight bars. In modern designs, this is accomplished by using a separate cutter drive, a mechanical adjustment to time the cutter signal from the conveyor, and a time-delay relay permitting an adjustment of the interval between the signal from the conveyor head to the cutter head drive. If the conveyor timing is not set in registration with the cutting mechanism, the dough piece as it is falling may strike the flight bars leading to misshapen products.

Speed of the conveyors should be adjustable to give the required frying time. The time at which a doughnut should be turned over is dependent on the rate of reaction of the leavening system, as well as on some other factors. If the doughnut is turned too soon, it will tend to be low in volume. When turned too late, it may become misshapen, too low in moisture, and too high in fat. The rate at which the leavening systems of cake doughnuts react depends upon the amounts and types of leavening chemicals used and on the temperature.

Some conveyor footage must be added to cool the product after it is fried and before it is coated or packaged. It is recommended that doughnuts be cooled to between 88°F and 92°F before packaging. One purpose of this cooling is to slow moisture migration from the crumb to the crust so that moisture droplets will not condense on the package surface. Another purpose is to allow the doughnut to become firmer so there is less chance it will be damaged in the packaging operation.

Some, perhaps most, fried pie cookers carry the pies between two mesh belts. The pie is completely submerged during the entire frying process. Pizza crust fryers generally use single-belt submerging conveyors because the buoyancy of the expanded dough creates enough friction with the belt to carry the crust through the fryer. For many other products, the conveyor is some sort of continuous mesh belt moving beneath the surface of the fat, usually with the discharge end emerging from the fat to dump the product on another wire belt for draining and cooling. Methods for transferring the cooked product out of the fat often involve mechanisms of considerable complexity. The raw product is often dumped directly into the hot oil, but certain items require more elaborate handling to register or position the individual pieces.

Various other types of conveying systems have been devised to transport kinds of foods requiring special treatment, but these have not generally been applied to dough and batter products. An example is the rotating drum conveyor described by Bullock (1984). In this device, the drum has internal shelves on which the product is placed. During part of the drum's rotation, the food is immersed in hot oil.

Exhaust Systems

A large amount of vapor is generated by fryers. This vapor is mostly steam but it also includes droplets of fat, gases given off by the food, and decomposition products of the fat. Even small batch fryers should be vented, but it is unacceptable to allow the vapor from a continuous fryer to escape into the processing area. Exhaust systems must be installed to collect and dispose of the hot gases in a safe and sanitary manner. The fryer may be completely enclosed in the exhaust system, or an overhead hood may be used. The totally enclosed design contributes very little net air movement within the room, but hoods exhaust large amounts of air from the processing area along with the steam, and it may be necessary to provide replacement air sources in order to compensate for the loss. All exhaust systems must be designed so as to prevent condensed materials such as fat from dropping back into the fryer.

It is inadvisable, and in some jurisdictions illegal, to vent the hood exhaust directly to the environment. Cooker vent scrubbers are available for oil emission control. Some of these are based on the cyclone separator method. Water spray is mixed with the cooker gases as they enter the centrifugal blower, where violent turbulence disperses the water and then throws the oil and water droplets to the blower walls by centrifugal force. Separation is completed in a tangential entry centrifugal separator that follows the blowers. There are no filters involved. Such units are quite effective in removing the oil, but other devices are needed for odor control.

For removing odorous compounds and other organic substances, thermal stabilizing units can be fitted to the exhaust system. They mix contaminated fumes with an intense flame in a combustion chamber. Sufficient time and turbulence allow the organic materials to be completely converted to carbon dioxide and water.

Controls

Pneumatic, electric, and electronic controllers are used for fryers. Pneumatic controllers receive a mechanical incoming signal and use a relatively complicated air-pressure balancing system to produce a pneumatic force that operates the heater valves. The sensing element can be a liquid-filled bulb connected by a capillary tube to the control device. A system of levers multiplies the slight motion of the liquid to an extent sufficient to activate the balancing section. An electric controller also receives a mechanical incoming signal, and uses a simple electric resistance slidewire balance to generate the electrical impulse that operates the gas valves. The electronic controller receives an incoming electric voltage signal from a thermocouple and processes this through an electronic circuit to modulate the electric current that operates the valves. Most, if not all, modern frying equipment is controlled by electronic equipment.

Either on-and-off or modulating control systems can be used for adjusting the input of heat to the fat. On-and-off controls consist of a thermocouple which activates a thermostat switch; they can maintain the temperature within a range of about 10°F. The more expensive modulating thermal control systems can adjust the amount of gas flowing to the burner as required to maintain the temperature within plus or minus 2°F.

Fryer Sanitation

The crucial points of a total sanitation program are (1) master cleaning schedules, (2) detailed cleaning procedures, (3) fundamentals of cleaning, (4) pest control programs, and (5) inspection program (McMurray 1976). The master cleaning schedule is an itemized list of equipment and utensils with predetermined intervals for cleaning. Detailed cleaning procedures are written out for virtually all utensils and machinery. Since the primary emphasis of this discussion is on fryers, a sanitation check list for a continuous fryer will be reproduced in modified form.

(1) Remove and clean exhaust hood filters.

(2) Pump shortening from reservoir into fryer.

(3) Unhook inlet and outlet pipes of reservoir.

(4) Hook up drain hose from fryer to drain.

(5) Wash reservoir and wipe dry. Close outlet valve.

(6) Turn off heat and filter hot shortening to reservoir.

(7) Attach hand hoist to conveyor, disconnect clutch, and lift conveyor out of fryer.

(8) Scrape out sides and bottom of fryer. Remove overflow pipe. Install

plug. Open drain valves.

(9) Lower conveyor back into frying position.

(10) Rinse fryer and conveyor. Flush with clean water.

(11) Close drain valve of fryer and start to fill with water. When water covers tubes by one inch, turn heater on. Pour in cleaner solution. Allow to soak 45 min at 200°F.

Various devices have been developed for expediting disassembly of the mechanisms that need to be cleaned separately. Woodworth *et al.* (1990) described an easily removable turner arm assembly.

EXAMPLES OF COMMERCIAL FRYING EQUIPMENT

In this section will be given details of a fryer which is being used for cooking both yeast-raised and cake doughnuts. It is available in lengths of 12, 16, and 20 ft, and in widths of 50 and 59 inches. The smallest model has a hot fat capacity of 151 gal if the heating tubes are below the conveyor and 130 gal if the tubes are between the conveyor belts, while the largest model has capacities of 358 and 275 gal, respectively. The kettle and all stationary parts within it are constructed of type 304 stainless steel, while the frame is sanitary heavy gauge tubular steel. There are independent heat controls for infeed and discharge sections, a shortening high temperature cut-out at 410°F with built-in fail safe operation, and a shortening low level shut down of the combustion system. There is independent electronic flame supervision of the infeed and discharge sections.

This fryer has a traveling baffle conveyor with a choice of 3.75 or 4.62 inch flights, and a choice of either a full submerging conveyor or partial front and rear submergers. The conveyor system is compensated for thermal expansion, and has self-aligning chemically inert bushings on all bearing surfaces. There is a conveyor synchronizing device. Ratchet assemblies enable the operator to make timing adjustments to both the conveyor and turner while the fryer is running. There is an automatic line-up device for use with automatic proofers.

The electrical system requires 230/460 volts, 60 Hz, three phase, and a 110 volt, 60 Hz, one-phase for the control circuit. Power required is 1.5 hp for the control circuit, 0.1 hp for the fat pump, 1 hp for the conveyor drive, 1 hp for the air pump, and 0.2 hp for the flue exhaust blower. Gas requirement for the smallest fryer is 500,000 Btu per hr of natural gas (6 inches WC minimum) and for the largest fryer is one million Btu per hr.

Another frying system made for outputs of 250 to 10,000 lb per hr is described as follows. A sealed tubular frame and insulated tank are combined in a hermetically sealed outer skin. Frying oil temperature is held at a pre-set operating level of approximately 400°F by a temperature sensor and controller and never exceeds 500°F. Since the heat is electric, the cooking oil is never exposed to open flame or intense heat. The food products on an endless belt or conveyor that travels just below the oil's surface. A screw conveyor in a V-shaped trough at the bottom of the fryer continuously keeps the oil free of submerged food particles. Material discharged by the screw conveyor, together with surface oil, is skimmed from the exit end of the fryer and pumped to a fine mesh vibrating screen from which it is circulated through a five micron filter.

Figure 32.3 shows product flow and oil flow in a doughnut frying operation (Source: Baking Industry).

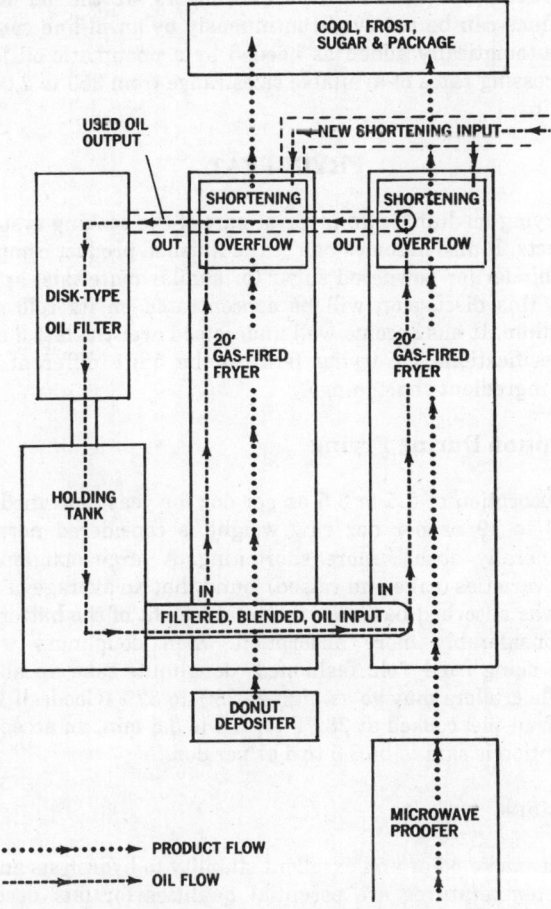

Figure 32.3. Fryers and related equipment in a doughnut plant

Fryers designed for corn or tortilla chip snacks generally consist of a product converyor belt, a tank containing cooking oil maintained within an optimum temperature range, a gas train that includes a pilot burner and a flame sensor, and a control panel. The extent to which the product is cooked is preferably determined by changing the time it stays in the fryer (through adjustments of the conveyor's variable speed drive) rather than by varying the temperature of the oil. In one such unit, angled stainless steel paddles meter chips to a submerger conveyor that holds them beneath the cooking oil until they are released at the discharge end. Heating of the oil is accomplished by the usual methods, i.e., direct heating of the tank, immersion tubes, or external heat exchangers. If the oil is circulated externally, fines can be removed continuously by an in-line catch box, and oil can be automatically added as needed by a pneumatic oil level control system. Processing rates of available sizes range from 350 to 2,000 lb per hr of tortilla chips.

FRYING FAT

The frying medium is an integral part of the cooking system for fried dough products. It also becomes one of the finished product components and it acts as a binder for powdered sugar (or similar materials) applied to the surface, but this discussion will be concentrated on its role as the heat transfer medium. It has become well understood over the last 3 or 4 decades that the specifications for frying fats can be quite different from those required for ingredient shortenings.

Fat Absorption During Frying

Fat absorption of 2.5 to 3.5 oz per doz for yeast-leavened doughnuts weighing 18 to 19 oz per doz raw weight is considered normal. Richer formulas generally absorb more shortening. A large doughnut operator frying many varieties (cake and raised) found that an average of 20% to 21% shortening was absorbed based on the total weight of the batters or dough. There is considerably more absorption when doughnuts with ragged surfaces are being fried; "old fashioned" doughnuts take up about 24% to 26% fat, while crullers may go as high as 28% to 32% (Goodsell 1984). For a 4.5 oz fried fruit pie, cooked at 385°F for 3.3 to 3.5 min, an acceptable range for fat absorption is said to be 3.5 to 5 oz per doz.

Specifications

A high smoke point and excellent stability to hydrolysis and oxidation at elevated temperatures are essential qualities for fats used in frying doughnuts, honey buns, etc. In most markets, the frying fat is supposed to contribute very little flavor of its own to the finished product, although consumers in some regions of the country are accustomed to the flavor of lard. Hydrogenated cottonseed oil, one of the most common frying fats, is bland.

The fresh shortening, as it is received by the doughnut manufacturer, may not be completely satisfactory for frying because its heat transfer characteristics (partly a function of viscosity) are not optimal. If the fryer is replenished from time to time with small additions of fresh fat, an equilibrium state can be maintained in which the finished product always has satisfactory properties. When the frying vat contains only fresh fat, it must be "broken in" by heating the fat at frying temperatures in contact with the product until a free fatty acid content of about 0.4% is reached, or until the product is being cooked as desired. The increase of viscosity is probably due mostly to the accumulation of polymeric substances that develop from oxidized fatty acids.

Some typical specifications for frying fats are:

(1) Free fatty acids (% as oleic): 0.05% max.
(2) Smoke point: 400°F min.
(3) Wiley melting point: 110° to 114°F
(4) Iodine number for vegetable fat: 69 to 71
(5) Iodine number for animal fat: 54 to 56
(6) Peroxide value (meq/kilo): 0.5 max.
(7) Stability (AOM hr): >90
(8) Odor: bland
(9) Color (Lovibond): 20 Y, 2 R
(10) Solids content index, percent:

50°F	37 to 43
70°F	25 to 29
80°F	20 to 24
92°F	15 to 17
104°F	10 to 12

(11) Crystallization rate (percentage solids when melted shortening is cooled for a given time at the given temperature):

92°F for 30 min:	1 to 7
92°F for 120 min:	13 to 16
80°F for 30 min:	14 to 17
80°F for 120 min:	16 to 19

The free fatty acids specification gives an indication of the effectiveness of the refining operation applied to the shortening and of the deterioration it has undergone since then. Melting point and solids fraction index are related to the eating quality of the doughnut and stability of the coating; an SFI that is too high may cause the doughnut to be waxy in texture and could result in poor adhesion of the coating sugar. An SFI that is too low may give a doughnut that is too greasy and that lets oil penetrate the coating. Smoke point is important becuse it may indicate poor performance if too low.

Fat will always break down to some extent during frying. Generally speaking, the higher the process temperature the faster the shortening deteriorates. This deterioration is accelerated if the fat is maintained at the frying temperature with no product going through the line. Any condition that brings a considerable amount of air into the fat—bubbling, spraying, spattering— will cause increased breakdown. Contact with brass or copper at any point will greatly increase oxidation

Excessive deterioration is evidenced by smoking, darkening, and foaming. Methyl silicone is often effective in reducing foaming. Filtration is effective in removing particles that can char and discolor the finished products, but it does not reverse oxidation that has already occurred and it does not affect the free fatty acid content or the viscosity of the fat (Moyer 1965). Some types of filtration, in which the fat is brought into contact with absorbent compounds, will reduce free fatty acids.

Cleaning Operations Applied to Fat

Various types of filters and other reconditioning equipment can be employed to prolong the useful life of frying oils by removing small particles and other debris that add dark specks to the fried object. When an operator determines that the oil in a fryer needs to be purified, the shortening is first pumped into a holding tank. There the oil is kept liquid until it can be pumped through a series of circular filter plates held in a press frame. A recent review of this topic was published by Stier and Blumenthal (1991).

A common type of filter pad is a disc of nonwoven cotton cloth, but other materials can be used. Filter aids, such as diatomaceous earth, are often mixed with the oil in the holding tank to absorb fatty acids, odorous substances, and other undesirable chemicals. These materials also improve particle retention. After the filtration step has been completed, the filter discs with their adhering coating of diatomite and entrapped residue, are discarded. The oil that has passed through the filter press may be withdrawn into drums, another holding tank, or a clean fryer. If the product that is being fried absorbs a large amount of oil, requiring the frequent replenishment of the frying medium with fresh oil, it may not be necessary to discard any of the "old" fat, if filtration is properly applied (Burns 1981).

Another type of filtering system uses a roll-stock filter cloth. In this equipment, oil flows by gravity through a concave filtering area formed by the conveyor belt that holds the filtering medium. An oil-level control, coupled to the conveyor drive, automatically advances the filter medium when the flow through it is reduced below the incoming flow rate. Oil that has passed through the filter cloth is collected on the sloping pan bottom and continuously discharged through a drain connection. A hood with a vent stack opening covers the entire filter area, and a clean-in-place spray ball is located under the hood for connection to the fryer's CIP system. USDA-approved filtering media for this equipment are available in 250-yd rolls in a range of porosities suitable for different requirements. The used filter pad can be collected in a portable disposal cart or other container.

One type and model of filter used in cleaning frying oil has the following characteristics. It is a 20-disc round plate and frame fabricated filter with 18-inch diameter plates and frames and 1.5-inch wide sludge frames built to USDA guidelines on an 87-inch long stand. It is equipped with a 3 hp motor and sanitary pump. The filter is dressed with #218 filter media between each plate and frame and changed every day after eight hour shifts during which 4,500 lb of product is cooked. The single stage medium is either 100% rag content pure cellulose or 100% pure nonwoven cotton. It removes particles as small as 2 or 3 microns.

One manufacturer describes their line of fat filters as follows. These square plate and frame filter presses are completely constructed of plates, bars, and forgings. Standard sizes run from 13 to 60 inches square. Standard construction material is #304 stainless steel, but carbon steel and #316 stainless can be used. Standard working pressure is 75 psi, and maximum working temperature is 425°F. The filter frames are of open construction with support bars between ports. Both sides of the plates are covered with heavy perforated sheet metal and have strong internal reinforcing and screen support bars to give the maximum clear filtration area. No cloth is required to support the filter media. Front and back heads are made of forged steel and are heavily clad with stainless steel. Standard unit construction is closed delivery, 2 or 4 ports, top or bottom inlet. All units are suitable for filtration using paper, canvas duck, synthetic fiber, or submicron filter media together with filter aid and diatomaceous earth.

These devices can be augmented with a drum type cooking oil pre-filter, especially if the foods being fried shed a lot of fairly large particles. The pre-filter passes all the oil in the circulating system through a revolving mesh screen drum. This removes large particles prior to final filtering. A continuous pneumatic system blows fines from the screen to a conveyor, which carries them to a steel drum or other receptacle.

Filters are also available for batch frying operations. One manufacturer supplies models with 100, 200, or 250 lb capacity. A typical arrangement is to have the filter, with its motor, pump, and tank on casters so it can be rolled into place near the fryer when required. This allows one filter to be used with several fryers. It is claimed that less than 10 min are required for draining the shortening and returning it to the kettle. Disposable filter pads are used. A movable filter assembly that can be rolled into place beneath fryer kettles, as needed, has been disclosed by Grob and Kinch (1990).

BIBLIOGRAPHY

BELSHAW, T. E. 1976. Cutting and frying equipment. Proc. Am. Soc. Bakery Engineers *1976*, 112-120

BLOCK, Z. 1964. Frying. *In* Food Processing Operations, Vol. 3. M. A. Joslyn and J. I. Heid, Editors. AVI Publishing Co., Westport, CT

BRADEN, B. W., JR. 1976. Yeast-raised doughnuts. Proc. Am. Soc. Bakery Engineers *1976*, 127-131

BULLOCK, R. F. 1984. Fryer with oil circulation and conveyor. U.S. Pat. 4,478,140

BURNS, N. R. 1981. Personal communication. Star Systems Filtration Div., Timmonsville, GA

COPE, J. C., GRADY, M. E., and WARNOCK, D. G. 1988. Food product cooker. U.S. Pat. 4,719,849

DAGERSKOG, M., GANROT, A. G., and JONSSON, K. O. G. 1986. Method and apparatus for frying. U. S. Pat. 4,565,704

EVES, E. E. 1989. Constant temperature fryer assembly. U.S. Pat. 4,882,984

FISCHER, L. G. 1976. Cake doughnuts. Proc. Am. Soc. Bakery Engineers *1976*, 121-126

GOODSELL, G. R. 1984. Cake doughnut production. Proc. Am. Soc. Bakery Engineers *1984*, 119-131

GROB, J. T., and KINCH, J. M. 1990. Deep fat frying apparatus having an improved cooking fluid filtration system. U.S. Pat. 4,890,548

HARDING, M., and STARWICH, B. G. 1965. Formulation and production of fried pies. Proc. Am. Soc. Bakery Engineers *1965*, 290-298

LEVINE, L. 1990A. Designing fryers for oil quality control. Cereal Foods World *35*, 962-963

LEVINE, L. 1990B. Understanding fryer operations. Cereal Foods World *35*, 272-273

LEVINE, L. 1990C. Understanding fryer operations II. Cereal Foods World *35*, 514

MC MURRY, T. K., II. 1976. Sanitation and safety. Proc. Am. Soc. Bakery Engineers *1976*, 132-144

MENDOZA, F. C. 1987. Oven for preparing fried food products. U.S. Pat. 4,711,164

MILLER, M. E. 1990. Deep fat fryer. U.S. Pat. 4,913,042

MOYER, J. 1965. Selection, maintenance, and protection of frying fats. Proc. Am. Soc. Bakery Engineers *1965*, 273-279

SIMS, R. J., and STAHL, H. D. 1970. Thermal and oxidative deterioration of frying fats. Bakers Digest *44*, No. 5, 50-52, 70

STEIN, E. W. 1972. Application of microwaves to bakery production. Proc. Am. Soc. Bakery Engineers *1972*, 46-51

STIER, R. F., and BLUMENTHAL, M. M. 1991. Filtering frying oils. Baking & Snack *13*, No. 5, 15-18

TAYLOR, J. C. 1971. Fried fruit pies, production methods. Proc. Am. Soc. Bakery Engineers *1971*, 182-191

TURMAN, W. C. 1989. Cooking oil filtering system. U.S. Pat. 4,826,590

WOODWORTH, F. G., AGATHOS, L. J., and MC CARTHY, J. P. 1990. Turner arm assembly for a doughnut fryer. U.S. Pat. 4,936,201

chapter thirty-three

PANS, PAN HANDLING EQUIPMENT, AND SLICERS

INTRODUCTION

The equipment discussed in this chapter includes pans and the handling devices they encounter outside the oven, as well as machines affecting the product, such as depanners, slicers, and coolers.

PANS

There are so many different sizes and shapes of pans, not to mention strapping features, materials, covers, etc., that a mere listing of the existing variables would exceed the space available for this chapter. The permutations must run into the thousands. The present discussion will deal with general principles, though a few specific examples will be given to clarify important points. Disposable foil, paper, or plastic baking pans will not be covered.

Baking pans can be considered as interacting with the oven and the dough during the baking process. It is generally recognized by both practical bakers and technologists that their conformation, construction, and surface characteristics (color, reflectivity, and adhesive qualities, for example) affect not only the finished product but also the efficiency of production.

The cost of pans for a bread bakery represents a considerable percentage of the total capital investment. About 6 to 8 times as many pans as are in the oven at any one time will be required for each variation. This allows two sets in the proof box, 3 to 5 sets in the cooling, greasing, and panning operation sequence, and one set in the oven. When the need for this many sets for each size and shape of bread is considered, it is obvious that substantial sums of money are involved. For this reason, careful evaluations of pan and pan set requirements must be made before a purchase order is signed. Thought should also be given to the possibility that a different production line, if that is being considered, may not be compatible with current or on-order pans.

Materials

The materials that have been used in baking pans include black iron (blued steel), tinplate, steel coated with aluminum alloy, aluminum, and type 3 stainless steel (Anon. 1973). Stainless steel has many advantages, but it is expensive as a material and to fabricate; it also has relatively poor heat transfer. Black iron is cheap, strong, and has good heat response, but has corrosion and resistance problems. Tinplate has good fabricating properties and strength, is relatively cheap, and has adequate heat absorption, but has problems with high temperatures, corrosion, and wear. Twenty or thirty years ago, practically the only sheet metal in wide use for pans was tinplate (either hot-dipped or electrolytic plated steel).

The usual form of tinplate for baking pans is low carbon steel coated with about 90 millionths of an inch of commercially pure tin. One difficulty with tin is that it has a melting point of about 450°F, well below some of the temperatures reached in bakeries today. Therefore, the tin coating may reach a temperature at which it melts and runs together to form drops and streaks on the pan surface. This leaves uncoated, or very thinly coated areas, that are susceptible to corrosion, so that the pans are permanently damaged.

The perforations often made in the bottom of bread pans to allow escape of air and moisture tend to corrode progressively in tinplate pans. Eventually, the round holes develop an elongated space from the center toward the ends, causing imperfect loaves and reduced pan life. The rusted and pitted areas that ultimately form in all tinplate pans will cause discolorations on loaves.

It was early recognized that aluminum could contribute many important advantages to commercial baking utensils, but there were many disadvantages to overcome before it became possible to design aluminum pans for mass production of bread and rolls. Of course, great quantities of baked foods are cooked in disposable foil pans for frozen distribution and other applications, but they require special handling techniques. Aluminum's structural weaknesses and its unsuitability for welding are serious defects. They have been largely overcome by using steel coated with aluminum alloys. This enables the baker to take advantage of aluminum's resistance to corrosion, excellent heat transfer properties, adaptability to deep drawing and forming into complex shapes, and relatively low density, while offsetting its relatively poor mechanical strength.

Aluminum will not melt at any temperature encountered during bakery processing, and aluminum-coated steel has the metallurgical, physical, and electrochemical properties necessary to make it useful as the structural material for baking pans (Inzerillo 1979). These properties are:

(1) Workability. It can be satisfactorily folded, drawn, and formed into the many sizes and shapes of pans used for bakery purposes.

(2) Strength. Aluminum-coated steel of the same thickness as tinplated steel can withstand the impacts encountered in automated pan handling over extended periods without greater changes (than tinplate) in the original configuration of the pan. One manufacturer claims their aluminized steel pans have a service life of 3,000 production cycles under normal usage.

(3) Corrosion resistance. The aluminum coating is more than ten times the thickness of the tinplate used for the same purpose. Coating of this thickness is essentially free of voids and micropores, making it highly resistant to the penetration of moisture.

(4) Temperature resistance. Aluminum coating is heat stable at 1,200°F, so

far above any temperature required for baking that melting is never a problem.

(5) Heat absorption. The material can be processed to impart a permanent heat absorptive coating.

Surface Treatment

There was formerly a requirement for "burning in" new pans. Bakers knew when they received a shipment of pans it would be necessary to modify their surfaces by a special heat treatment before the pans would perform satisfactorily. Burning-in was accomplished by heating for about 3 or 4 hours in an oven held at 400° to 420°F. This treatment produces a darker pan color that leads to better heat absorption and better coloration of the baked loaf, and it also produces an alloying or firmer bonding between the tin coating and the steel sheet. Manufacturers now will deliver pans having already oxidized tin surfaces or etched aluminum surfaces that do not have to be subjected to the burning-in treatment.

It is very common to apply silicone coatings to pans, especially to tinplate bread pans, to improve the release of loaves. This reduces cripples and often enables increased speeds at the depanning station without the use of pan oil. The pans usually remain cleaner, and there are some other advantages. Many bakers use pan oil (but smaller amounts) even though they have silicone-treated pans.

Silicone coatings are usually applied by firms that specialize in this service. Some professional applicators offer a program that includes monitoring pan condition and advising the user when re-coating is needed.

Sizes and Shapes

Bread.— The reader does not have to be told bread is baked in many different sizes and shapes of pans. Rectangular, square, round, and lidded are some common variations. And, of course, pans for hearth bread can be cleverly designed to give the impression the loaf was baked without a container. In this section, some of the more common loaf pans will be discussed.

For ordinary white loaf bread baked in open top pans, 5.8 to 6.0 cubic inches of pan volume for each ounce of dough is considered satisfactory. Pullman breads will require 6 cubic inches per oz of dough for a close-grained loaf, and 7 cubic inches per oz of dough for loaves having a more expanded texture.

It is necessary for the top of the pan to be larger than the bottom. This flare facilitates detachment of the bread from the sides when the loaf is depanned and makes it possible to stack the pans. Selecting the proper angle of flare is an important decision, especially when specifying deep containers such as bread loaf pans, because of the effect of flare on the ease of nesting straps. Straps of pans can occupy a large amount of space in a factory, especially if several different loaf sizes are being made, some of which are infrequently scheduled. Furthermore, nesting and de-nesting are essential operations in some conveying and transport systems. With large flare, release problems are reduced and pan life is increased because dented pan walls will not come in contact with one another. These pans do have less stability when stacked, however. With decreasing flare, there is less clearance between nested pan surfaces.

For bread pans 2.75 or 3 inches deep, the bottom length should be 0.5 inch smaller than the top inside length. The bottom width should be 0.625 inch smaller than the top inside width. These are general rules; obviously, there may be conditions making different specifications desirable.

There should also be a flare in pans for the ostensibly square pullman loaf, the loaf baked in a covered pan. If the top and bottom dimensions of this pan are the same, difficulties in dumping the bread will be encountered. Pans four inches or more deep should be flared 0.125 inch per side and end, or a total of of 0.25 inch. This provides ample clearance for release of the loaves and compensates for the usual shrinkage during cooling.

Construction and design of baking containers for hearth breads has proven to be a difficult task for pan designers. Of course, the term "hearth bread" implies that the loaf has been baked on the oven surface, as these breads originally were, but most present-day systems use some sort of pan, screen, tray, or sheet to hold the loaf during its movement through the oven.

For many years, pumpernickel and other rye breads were baked on perforated screens. Such containers were not very suitable for high speed production, so the perforated basket hearth pan was developed. These consist of an inner container with a rounded bottom having only a small flat area. To make these utensils run satisfactorily on conveyors, an outer pan or cover is put around them. The bottom of the outer pan must be mostly open so that the inner container is not shielded from heat. To offset the structural weakness caused by the open areas, the outer pan must be reinforced by adding a wire to the outer rim. This supports and strengthens the flanged edge. Panning bars are installed on the bottom to allow the indexing finger of the molder to slider under the pan without catching in a hole. Some of the outer pan constructions that have been used include full open bottom, flanged bottom platform, and corrugated sidewalls. In addition, other features include extended strapping, various sizes of holes in the inner as well as the outer pan, contoured wires to support the insert, strapping under the wire, welded pan rim corners, stitch welded pan rims, complete perforations in the insert, and many combinations of solid areas in the bottoms, sides, or ends (Inzerillo 1979).

Other types of hearth bread pans are combined in sets that are modifications of a regular pan bread set where the strapping provides some of the strength contributed by the outer container of the pans described above. The pan bottom is flat and there is a 0.625 inch radius along the bottom sidewall. The pans have wide flares to accommodate the contours of the hearth loaves. By eliminating the outer pan assembly, there are no perforations to catch in the conveyor or in the indexing finger of the molder-panner. Also, the pans are lighter in weight, nest better, and are cheaper and more sanitary than the double-walled hearth bread pan.

Rolls.—For many years, pan designers were extremely limited by the pan-forming methods they had available. Pan manufacturers relied mostly on two basic methods that have been used by tinsmiths for hundreds of years; these are cutting metal sheet and bending the pieces. No one seemed to have much interest in developing new pan manufacturing processes or new designs. Bakers were reconciled to using traditional type pans, because they worked reasonably well with their old-fashioned production techniques. Furthermore, they were making only traditional products for which they already had pans, and were not inclined to make the major investments that would have been required for replacing them with a new type.

As higher speeds and greater mechanization were forced on bun bakers by the pressure of competition, it became obvious that pans were, in many cases, the limiting factor in capacity and rate. Additionally, new bakery products were being developed that could not be made in the old pans. A few pan manufacturers met the challenge and made continual improvements, using new processing methods, new materials, and new designs. Some of their competitors could not adapt to the changing conditions and disappeared from the business world.

One of the first goals was to maximize the use of oven space by eliminating wasted area in the pan. Both in individual loaf pans and straps, as well as in bun pans, cupcake pans, etc., there were non-product-containing areas that contributed nothing to baking efficiency or product quality, but were included in the design because of tradition or because of the requirements of outmoded methods of pan manufacture. This wasted pan space meant fewer pieces of dough could be included on a given area of hearth and, consequently, the production rate was reduced by an equivalent amount. Wasted space is greater in roll pans than in loaf straps.

More rolls can be contained in a given area if the cups are square in outline. Some pans for brown-and-serve rolls are made this way, but consumers seem to have reservations about the appearance of the product. It was discovered that the circular cavities used for certain kinds of rolls could be placed closer together while maintaining the rounded configuration of the product. Sometimes the margin, or frame area, around the pan could be reduced. The cumulative effect can amount to an additional 20% to 25% of product in the same overall area. When cups or molds in cupcake frames and roll pans are over 0.75 inch deep, they are seamed into the panel. By eliminating the seaming of the molds, pan manufacturers were able to save as much as 0.5 inch between every row of cups in both directions. Normal seamed-in construction has a minimum spacing between cups of 0.625 inch.

According to Inzerillo (1979), a completely new concept was developed to obtain the minimum spacing that was made available to industry. Instead of bending the metal for the individual cups, then seaming the cups in a sheet which had holes punched in it, the cups were individually drawn with a rim of 0.0625 inch and welded together. The result is cups that have 0.125 inch spacing between them. Depending on the number of cups in a pan, the savings in space allow 20% to over 30% more cups in the same size frame, or an increase of the same amount in oven capacity.

The reader might ask, why not use close-packed geometry for the round cavities? This should allow some additional space saving, although the loss at the edges would take some of this back, the amount depending on the size of the tray and the size of the top of the cavities. The chief difficulty in this approach seems to be that such offset rows cannot be handled in current styles of panning machines or vacuum depanners.

Most pans for hot dog buns and the like do not have seamed-in cups. They are made of drawn sheet and require about 0.75 inch, or a little less, of separation between the depressions. The minimum separation needed depends on the configuration—whether the molds are round, square, oblong, or cluster shaped. Simply reducing the separation is not a feasible alternative in these cases. The solution was to bring the cavities closer together by squeezing the metal upward between the rows to form a ridge. The ridge can reduce spacing from the 0.75 originally thought to be the minimum to as little as 0.125 inch. If it is decided to reduce the width of the pan, the ridge would run lengthwise of the pan, and vice versa. It may not be practical at the present state of metal-shaping technology to run ridges both ways.

Pan manufacturers have learned how to make deeper depressions in drawn metal pans. For many years, the maximum depth was considered to be about 0.375 inch. Then, advances in the art made mold depths of about 0.55 commercially feasible. Further improvements in technique and equipment are leading to even deeper draws. The extra depth gives greater support of the dough piece during proofing and baking, so that buns are made more uniform in size and shape. Since the drawn pans are made as seamless panels, there are fewer crevices to impede release and trap dirt.

In designing pans where some knitting (flowing together at the edges) of the dough is expected and desired during proofing and/or baking, either because clusters are needed for the packing operation, or because the consumer expects joined rolls, this factor will have to be taken into consideration when calculating the separation allowable between dough pieces.

Interaction with Products and Equipment

Interaction of pans with products occurs as a result of the guiding effect of the container on the expanding dough, the support given the baked piece as it sets up, the rate of heat transmission to the product, and the shading effect on product surfaces, among other mechanisms. Some of these factors cannot be easily modified, but dimensions and slope of sides can frequently be specified within fairly wide limits. Once the pans have been purchased, however, the large investment tends to strongly restrict the options of the baker in future planning.

When baking bread, deeper pans result in better appearing break and shred. This part of the loaf becomes higher, there is less collapse of the break and shred, and the sidewalls are stronger. With greater flare, release problems are reduced. Greater flare does not have much effect on loaf size. According to Torrens (1964), corrugations give stronger loaf sidewalls and have no effect on oven spring or pan release. The chief purpose of corrugations is to increase strength of the pan.

In the early 1970s, a committee of the American Society of Bakery Engineers completed a two year test of open top bread pans having various structural features. The purpose was to determine how well pans withstood the wear and tear of actual bakery operations. Results of this study were reviewed in detail in "Equipment for Bakers" (Matz 1988); only a short summary is included here.

The committee concluded that a combination of the following features would lead to optimum life of bread pans: (1) No. 5 wire in the rim; (2) 4X tinplate for the body of the pan; (3) 90° corrugated bottom edges; (4) Balled bottom corners; (5) 90° overall corrugations; (6) Welded corners or anchored 4X tinplate under the pan strapping; and (7) Tempered strapping if pans are to be used with automatic depanners.

When highly automated roll plants started to come into use, new demands were placed on pans. At the time this changeover began, single-wire pans were common. These pans had a rounded top edge, usually formed by folding the rim of the metal around a thick wire. If these pans are handled in racks, or pass along a conveyor without touching each other, they function satisfactorily. But, when they push against each other on conveyors, as they frequently do in automated systems, they tend to shingle, i.e., the leading edge of one pan slides over the rear edge of the pan in front of it. For example, pans may stop while conveyors continue to run as they assemble groups for entry into a proofer or oven. When this takes place, the single-wire pans are subjected to forces that cause them to override one another, resulting in product damage or equipment damage.

An "anti-climb" feature was developed to eliminate this shingling. It consists of a second wire edge which was added below the first one, making a double tubular edge, the two wires being separated by a very short distance. The lower wire edge is commonly inset slightly from the upper one. Although this design did solve the shingling problem, it was expensive to make and had other problems. A more recent development is the replacement of the two wires with a solid bar of approximately rectangular cross section around which the top rim of the tray is wrapped.

Straps and Other Multiples

Usually, two or more pans are held together in a set by metal strips for efficiency in handling and conveying. These pan sets, sometimes called "straps," serve to separate the pans an optimum distance. Spacer lugs are attached to the side and end bands to keep the sets at a proper distance from each other as they go into the oven.

A method for strengthening sets is the welding of the pan material to the wire rim, or bringing strapping over the wire. In most cases, the strapping is made of 18-gauge tin or aluminized steel. Torrens (1964) says that one of the strongest sets available has a combination of 1.625 inch strapping over the wire and 1.375 inch strapping all around the bottoms and ends.

LIDDERS AND DELIDDERS

Lidders are used for pullman loaves (sandwich loaves) and a few other products. These machines fit into the production line between proofing and baking, automatically placing pan covers on pans containing proofed dough. Pan covers, with open side facing down, move into the machine on an accumulation conveyor at an upper level while the pans are moving along a conveyor at a lower level. The pan cover mechanism is synchronized to give the required rate of flow from the pan cover holding section. Covers move to a stop position, from which they are placed over the pans as demanded by the control system.

In older systems, the lids on bread pans could be removed manually or by magnetic appliances at the depanning station. The lids were then carried back to the lidding machine, or to storage. Pullman covers should be either a stacking or a nesting type for convenience in storing.

A later development makes the lid an integral part of each tray in a tray oven. The operator has the option of running the oven "lids down" for pullman and sandwich bread or "lids up" for open top breads. This arrangement neatly eliminates the need for lidding, delidding, and storing and transferring lids, at some cost in complexity of oven design.

PAN STACKERS, GROUPERS, AND CONVEYORS

In older systems, pan sets were taken off the depanning station by hand, placed on trucks that were pushed to the storage area by hand, and there removed and stacked by hand. When needed, they were removed from the stack by hand, placed on a hand truck, pushed or pulled to the panning machine area, and there transferred from the truck to the conveyor by hand. If forklifts were available, they could be used to transfer the trucks. This setup is obviously so slow and labor intensive that it had to be modified before any kind of automated system could be implemented.

Automatic stackers and unstackers were developed to make pan handling less labor intensive. A system based on magnetic grasping of the pans functions at rates up to 40 per min. The pan stacker receives pans from the conveyor system, stacks them to a predetermined height, and discharges the pan stack onto a storage conveyor or truck. The pan unstacker reverses this procedure, receiving pan stacks from a truck or storage stystem and feeding individual pans on demand into the conveyor system leading to the panning operation. When supply and demand are in balance, pans in the conveyor system flow through the stacker and unstacker without interruption.

Figure 33.1 shows three methods of handling sheet pans (Source: Pulver Systems, Inc.).

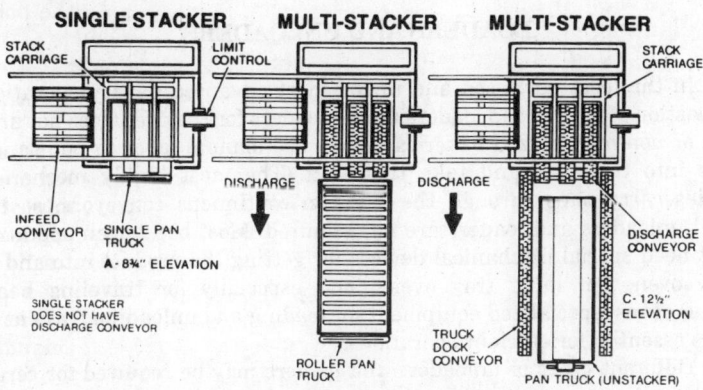

Figure 33.1. Optional systems for sheet pan stacking

The following description applies to a current model of pan handling system with automatic stackers. It can handle either bread or roll pans. The heart of the system is comprised of a pan stacker, an unstacker, a diverter, and the associated conveyors. It is designed to function with a minimum of operator involvement. The pan stacker can operate continuously—it does not stop for discharge of a completed stack. Instead, the stacking operation continues at the top of the machine as the full stack at the bottom is automatically moved out. The new stack is then lowered into place to complete an uninterrupted stacking cycle. This feature reduces the possibility of pan jams on conveyors, which can result from frequent starts and stops. The stacker operates at a maximum rate of 50 pans per min, while the pan unstacker operates at an average rate of 40 pans per min.

A "grouper" is essentially a conveyor that accumulates pans in a group of the size required for a certain operation, such as filling a proofer shelf or an oven tray. One commercial unit delivers a predetermined number of pans to the proofer loader conveyor in synchronization with the availability of proofer shelves. It has dual conveyors consisting of low friction table-top chains powered by separate DC motors. A gate at the discharge end stops the moving pans until a group has been accumulated, at which time the gate lowers and the set is delivered to the proofer. The unit's gate section conveyor chain runs at half speed during grouping to reduce pan impact and wear on the pan bottoms. A clamp holds the first pan of the next group until the previous set is loaded and the gate can return to its up, or stop, position. Proximity sensors control the operation of the gate and clamp. The grouper cycles in response to a signal from the proofer. For very high speed operations, there can be added on an optional traction system that employs variable electromagnets beneath the conveyor chain to increase the pan-to-conveyor friction. The magnetic pull can be varied to adjust for pans of different weights (Anon. 1975).

LOADERS AND UNLOADERS

In the least advanced and in the most advanced bakery operations, the question of specialized loaders and unloaders for the oven does not arise. Small or non-mechanized bakeries simply use manual labor to put pans or straps into the oven and take them out. The most highly mechanized bakeries carry pans through the oven on continuous conveyors, so that special unloaders and loaders are not required. Most band oven operations do not need special mechanical devices for getting the product into and out of the oven. For large tray ovens, and especially for traveling hearth (tunnel) ovens, specialized equipment for loading and unloading trays at the oven is essential for efficient operations.

Different types of unloaders and loaders may be required for certain products. For example, pies require very gentle treatment, with no change in level, and preferably no tilting as they move from the hearth to the removal conveyor. They are likely to be damaged by pusher bars or the like. Such products can be handled by "walking finger" unloaders consisting if two sets of long thin bars, oriented across the direction of travel. The set of fingers on which the pies rest rises slightly and moves forward a few inches, then moves downward to its base position, depositing the pies on the second set of fingers before retreating to its starting position. The second set of fingers picks up the pies and performs a similar set of operations. Then the first set repeats. The basic idea is that the fingers stay in about the same position from cycle to cycle, while the pans are moved along in short steps. Good support can be given to the bottoms of the pies by these conveyors and movement is very gentle even though it is not continuous.

The roller bed unloader may be used if small pans are not to be handled and high production rates for larger pans are required. Its action is essentially in accord with its name, the pans roll across a series of rotating cylinders. The pie and foil pan unloader uses a special fork lift mechanism to pick up a row of pans and gently transfer them to a take-away conveyor.

A fourth type, the multiple flat-top chain unloader has an elevating conveyor surface enabling it to unload both panned product and hearth breads. Panned bread is transferred from the oven hearth in a conventional manner. The flat-top conveyor can then be hydraulically raised, allowing hearth products to discharge directly down a slide plate to a belt conveyor underneath the flat top conveyor. Manual slide plate unloaders are useful for hearth products and some pan products. Loaves simply slide off the oven hearth down an inclined plate to a take-away conveyor.

A common type of loader utilizes a pusher bar, the movement of which is synchronized with the travel of trays into the loading area so that a complete line of pans goes into the hearth at the same time. The pans are transferred across the front of the oven and along the pusher bar by conveyor action. When a complete line is on hand, the inflow is temporarily halted and the pusher bar forces the entire line of pans into a tray as soon as a tray or hearth space becomes available. The loading platform may tilt upward to follow the travel of a tray as it passes the oven opening so that the oven conveyor does not have to stop. Unloading mechanisms either tilt the trays carrying the pans immediately before they reach the unloading area or they use horizontal pusher bars.

Traveling hearth ovens can be provided with a number of types of loaders and unloaders. The following description applies to a system that can load either peels or pans. If peels are used, the boards enter the loader via the infeed conveyor. When a full group is in position, stops on the infeed conveyor rise to prevent further peels from entering and, at the same time, the infeed conveyor stops. With the peel boards in position, the "wing" wire mesh conveyor starts turning while at the same time this entire conveyor is moved back toward the peel. The wing conveyor is a wire mesh band extending the width of the oven; it has an arc-shaped upper surface and a flat lower surface. Aided by a dough piece pick-up assist belt, the dough pieces are carried on to the wing conveyor and forward to its leading edge, at which time the mesh conveyor stops and the wing is moved towards the oven hearth. The speed of the carriage can be set by the operator to provide a wide range of spacings. Upon reaching its end position over the hearth, the carriage stops its forward motion and begins to retract, while the wire mesh conveyor re-starts, moving the dough pieces onto the oven baking surface at a speed about equal to the motion of the hearth. During this last operation, stop bars at the discharge end of the in-feed conveyor drop, allowing the empty peel boards to feed into the turn over chute and exit via the peel board return conveyor. At the same time, another line of fully loaded peels is entering the infeed conveyor for the next cycle.

When modified so that it can load pans, the wing conveyor is raised to a position that will allow it to pass over the pans being used. The pusher bar is, at the start, in the "up" position. Pans enter the loader in the same manner as the peel boards. When a group of pans is in position, the infeed conveyor stops and the carriage rides back over the pans. When the carriage frame and wing are over the pans, the air cylinder attached to the pusher bar moves the bar to the down position. The carriage frame with the wing and pusher bar now moves forward pushing the pans onto the oven hearth. With the pans loaded on the hearth, the carriage begins to withdraw, while the pusher bar retracts to the up position ready for the next group of pans which is now waiting on the infeed conveyor (Anon. 1980).

DEPANNERS

Manual depanning, as of bread loaves, is done by inverting the pan and dropping it on a frame that is open in the area where the loaves can fall through. Automatic depanners are of two major types, the gravity models by which the loaf is dislodged by machines that first invert the pans and then drop them a short distance to allow the loaves to fall onto a conveyor, and vacuum depanners that rely on a multiplicity of suction cups to lift the loaves or rolls out of the pan. Vacuum depanners will function properly only with certain types of pans. One of the earliest patents described a perforated drum, inside which a vacuum had been drawn, that did the lifting (Petersen and Heide 1963), but designs based on this principle were soon replaced by models using flexible vacuum cups.

Figure 33.2 shows a typical vacuum depanner transferring split top pan rolls to packages (Source AMF).

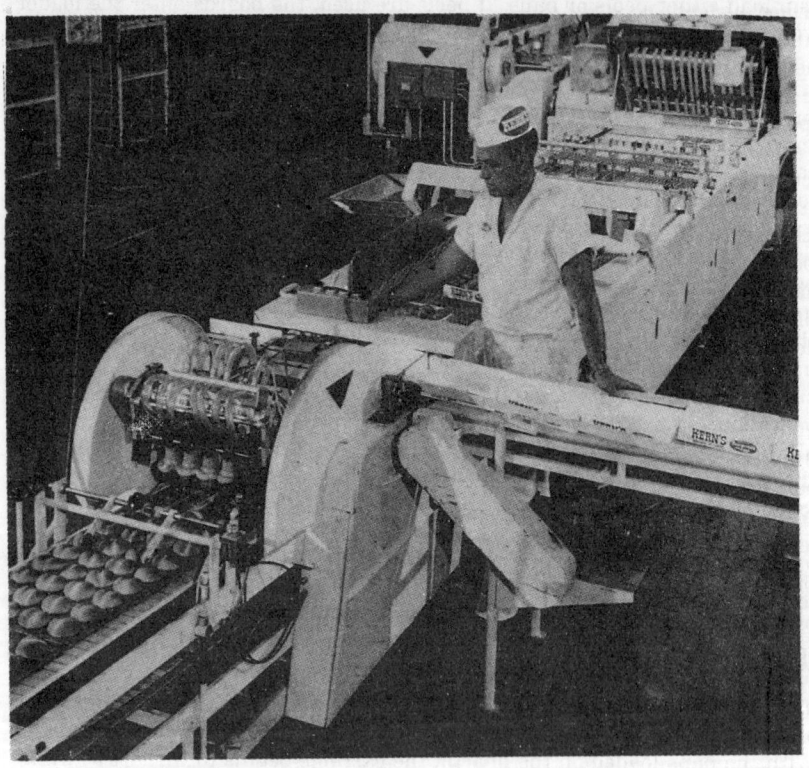

Figure 33.2. Vacuum depanner and packager for rolls

In a typical vacuum depanning installation, the roll-filled pans are placed on an infeed conveyor having a positive indexing finger to properly locate them in the pick up area. In older models, a vacuum pick-up head driven by a continuous crank mechanism swings in an arc above the pan.

The machine picks up, typically, twelve rolls simultaneously by placing a flexible vacuum cup on their tops and gently drawing them out of the pan. Pressure is reduced in each individual cup through a hose connected to the pump. The vacuum is slight and the cup is very flexible so as to avoid distortion of the roll. Emptied pans are then returned to a conveyer leading to the panning operation or to storage. Vacuum is supplied by a 3 hp turbine pump. Compressed air at 50 lb pressure is also required. These units work in combination with packaging machines.

Other versions of vacuum depanners use a silicone rubber belt on which are fitted numerous vacuum cups to pick up the rolls. The belt surface travels at about the same rate as the pan beneath it. Since the belt surface is slanted, it gradually comes into contact with the top of the rolls or loaf, and as it continues on an upward path, lifts the bread out of the pan. The pan conveyor has a magnetic rail to hold down the pans and can be fitted with a magnetic delidder. The vacuum cups then move up and around to deposit the loaf on a conveyor leading to the cooler while the pan continues on a lower level to a conveyor leading to the panner or storage. An average vacuum of 8 inches of water is used for some machines.

Conditions required to insure the best operation of the depanner-packer are (1) uniform make-up to give rolls of the same size and shape, (2) good pan greasing to give easy release of the rolls, (3) uniform proofing to maintain even size, (4) uniform production flow from oven to cooling, and (5) uniform cooling. Air jets directed into the corners of loaf pans are often used to loosen bread before it is depanned.

PAN GREASER

A properly designed and maintained pan greaser can assist in getting good release with a minimum application of oil. There are several types of pan greasing machines available for bread. They fall into two main categories, the multi-nozzle units and the single nozzle units. The former type is designed to produce a series of overlapping round spray patters to cover the entire interior surface of the pan. Single nozzle units feature a single spray head yielding a rectangular pattern of oil droplets conforming to the shape of the bread pan. Spray nozzles can be designed to meet specific needs. For example, equipment is available for applying pan oil to the ends and to a four inch square on the bottom of a perforated rye bread basket; the sides are not sprayed because the dough does not normally touch the sides. A properly designed spray pattern not only reduces the amount of pan oil required, but also improves sanitation.

Some of the most important factors affecting the performance of the bread pan greaser are: (1) Nozzle placement—height and centering; (2) Placement of the guide rails; (3) Pan flow control; (4) Spray pattern; (5) Air pressure; and (6) Heat control (Scott 1984). The flow of pans through the greaser should be adjusted so there is constant and even movement through the spray area. The spray pattern should be monitored daily by observing the oil pattern on a paper that has been folded to conform to the pan's inside contours then placed in a pan that is sent through the greaser.

The pan greaser generally works better with oil at 100°F than with oil that is substantially cooler. Scott recommends the following levels of pan oil per 1,000 pans: For open top pans, 15 to 20 oz for 1 lb loaf pans; 20 to 25 oz for 20 oz pans; and 25 to 30 oz for 24 oz pans. For sandwich or pullman pans, 20 to 25 oz for 1 lb loaf pans, 25 to 30 oz for 20 oz pans, and 30 to 35 oz for 24 oz pans.

Greasing of cake pans presents some of the same problems as bread pan greasing, as well as some different challenges. In addition to the usual nozzle type of sprayer, machines using spinning discs to apply the oil have been developed. Nozzle sprayers can be designed specifically for each pan cavity size and shape. Some greasing machines are mounted on the same chassis as the batter depositer, while others are separate units. Smaller bakeries may use hand spray guns that draw grease from a double-acting pump mounted on the oil drum. About 2% to 3% of grease based on batter weight has been recommended for cake pans. Factors to be considered are grease pattern, force of the dough being deposited, temperature of the pans, water left in pans, excess crumb, and product temperature when dumped.

COOLING EQUIPMENT

It is essential to cool many baked products before they are packaged. Loaf bread is removed from the pans shortly after it leaves the oven and cooled before it is sliced and wrapped. Rolls can be cooled before or after depanning. The situation varies with sweet rolls and the like, which often go through some sort of finishing operation.

Putting a hot product in a closed container, whether of plastic film or fiber will often lead to a greatly reduced shelf life because of moisture condensation and other factors. Cooling in ambient temperature systems, mainly by conveying product in dispersed array through air currents from fans, is very common practice and has been satisfactory in many cases. It does, however, involve rather lengthy delays in the processing line and long stretches of conveyors, and it exposes the product to contamination.

Most of the baked product cooling systems relying on ambient air movement use conveyors elevated above the processing area high enough to eliminate interference with operations taking place at floor level. These conveyors often have multiple spiral passes vertically disposed. Other systems have multilevel straight-ahead conveyor systems at floor level.

To overcome the disadvantages of heat removal by ambient air, accelerated cooling systems have been developed. Spiral, tunnel, and rack systems with refrigerated air are available. At least one manufacturer offers a compact, fully automatic, floor mounted rack model with washing and biological filtering of the cooling air.

Transfer of heat from low density porous products such as bread rolls and loaves is slow because of the porous nature of the product. Hot air tends to become entrapped in the product. It has been found that cooling can be greatly accelerated by use of vacuum. According to Fish (1980), modulated vacuum cooling systems are being used in many parts of the world to reduce the temperature of bread, buns, rolls, cake, melba toast, stuffing bread, and crouton bread. These systems use combinations of liquid ring pumps and water-cooled condenser with steam augmenters to create vacuum. Cooling chambers can be in-line high speed coolers with single or double tier conveyors connected to pivoting bridge conveyors at each end. The tunnel is clad with molded fiberglass panels supported by castellated beams.

SLICERS AND ASSOCIATED EQUIPMENT

Prepackaged sliced bread has been available at retail sale since the late 1920s. The first production slicers were based on the reciprocating (up-and-down) blade principle and could slice about 20 or 25 loaves of bread per minute. After the bread was sliced, it had to be put in a cardboard tray or bound with a paper circlet to keep the slices together through the wrapping cycle. It took about two years for the manufacturers of wrapping machines to make improvements in their devices so that they could wrap sliced loaves not held together by trays or bands.

The first bread slicers were rather crude machines. They made a lot of noise and were susceptible to mechanical troubles. Because they were slow, there was a tendency to crush the loaves as they were pushed through the blades. A large amount of crumbs was generated and it was necessary to cool the bread to about 90°F before it could be sliced.

Since wrapping machines in use at the time could handle the output of two of the early slicers, initial improvement efforts were directed toward increasing slicer speed. These efforts resulted in the development of slicers that could process 40 or 50 loaves per minute, or about the capacity of one wrapping machine. The principle of slicing the loaf with a set of parallel steel blades spaced about 0.5 inch apart and moving at high speed has remained the same since the earliest models. Some slicers with reciprocating blades are still being made, particularly for slicing specialty breads and for retail bake shops, but all high-capacity machines for white pan bread now use endless steel blades for cutting.

Automatic slicers for bakery products can be classified into three categories based on the type of blade they employ: (1) Slicers using straight blades; (2) Slicers using continuous bands; and (3) Slicers using disc shaped blades. The latter type is used almost entirely for splitting English muffins and buns. Some "forking" devices have been developed for splitting English muffins; these do not use saw-type blades.

It is known that experiments have been conducted in slicing bread by lasers and high pressure water jets. Bread can be cut by these two forces, but lack of a practical method of focusing allows the jet or laser to spread as it goes through the object. Until this method is solved, it does not appear that these two methods will find commercial application.

Bread Loaf Slicers

Reciprocating slicers.—The back-and-forth movement of blades in the reciprocating blade slicer is transmitted from the motor to the blade by a crankshaft and levers. The vibration and noise created by this mechanism was considered one of the most objectionable features of reciprocating slicers. Modern machines are constructed so as to minimize noise and vibration, however, and these factors should no longer be regarded as major objections to their use.

Blades are held in a rectangular metal frame, which may be made of cast magnesium. Each slice thickness requires a separate frame, and standard frames are available for several thicknesses. The time required to change frames is about 5 to 8 min. Each blade is held taut by a strong spring. When a blade is to be inserted in the frame, its spring is compressed by a special tool, allowing the blade pin to be slipped into a retaining notch.

Different slicer models vary in orientation of the blades and the direction loaves move during slicing. In the machines used in many retail shops, the loaf moves either straight through slanted saws or on a slanted path downward through vertical blades. Other versions have an elevator mechanism that moves the bread straight upward through horizontal blades. Each style has advantages for specific purposes, primarily for its adaptation to a particular packaging method. In one popular model, the knife frames are tilted 20° toward the top crust of the loaf so as to provide angle cutting and to accommodate the natural flow of bread through the saws.

Reciprocating slicers are often preferred for slicing raisin bread because build up of sticky substances from the fruit is not as severe a problem as in band slicers. They are also used for slicing hard crust breads such as French or Italian, heavy rye and multigrain breads, and iced loaves. As a generalization, machines of the reciprocating type can be said to be more verstatile but less efficient than band slicers.

Band slicers.—Band slicers are the preferred type for slicing uniform loaves of white bread at high rates of speed. They are also usable for many other types of bakery foods, but are less efficient for products that assume irregular shapes or have dense moist crumbs. Among the advantages of band-type slicers are: (1) Minimum vibration, (2) Greater cutting speed, (3) Less frequent need for blade sharpening, and (4) Continuously variable slice thickness, within limits. Three types of devices are found in all band slicers: (1) rotating drums that power the bands, (2) slicer blades, and (3) blade guides. Drum centers about 7 ft apart allow the band to twist sufficiently gradually that excessive heat generation in the knife guides does not occur. Considerable head room is required to accommodate these slicers because of the elevation of the top slicer drum. This situation can be alleviated somewhat by placing the drums in a slanted configuration. Such a machine is shown in Figure 33.3 (Source: AMF).

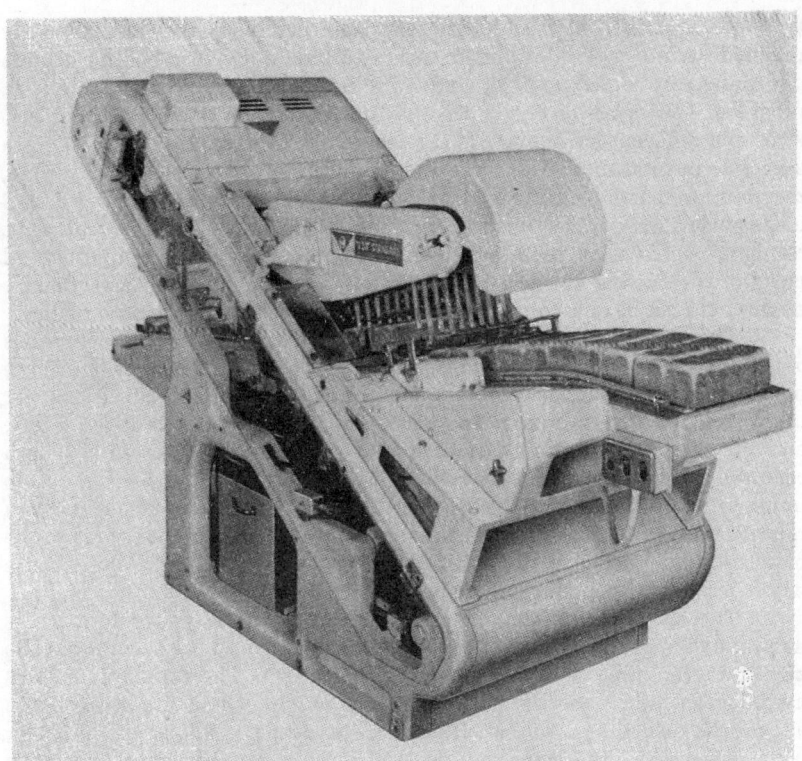

Figure 33.3. A band slicer for bread loaves

One type of endless band slicer has its bands placed around steel cylinders and crossed in the center so they form an elongated figure 8 as viewed from the side of the machine. The two passes of one band are separated by guides so they cut both sides of one piece of bread. The bread contact area is at the point where the blades cross. Another type uses four drums to give an approximately parallel orientation of blades in the slicing area. Since the blades must pass over the drums in a flat position and then turn to present their serrated edges to the bread, it is necessary to move them through a 90° angle between the time they leave the drum surface and the time they contact the bread. This turning function is performed by guides of hardened steel located above and below the line of travel of the loaves.

The knife speed in modern slicers is usually between 900 and 1,200 ft per min. There has been something of a trend to lower blade speeds since they reduce loaf distortion and temperature rise in the bands. Hot bands accelerate dough buildup on bands and drums. Blades can slice 500,000 to ' two million loaves of bread between resharpening if they are properly rehoned at intervals. Most band slicers include automatic honing devices and these can be activated by automatic timing devices while slicing is in progress. Two types of hones are the rotary and the fixed. Different grit sizes and different hardnesses of the binder are offered. Grits up to 600 are available in rotating hones, while the nonrotating variety is offered in fine, medium, or coarse grits. In many slicers, the hone is located about 5 or 6 inches below the point where the band meets the upper drum. At this point the band is vibrating with sufficient amplitude that the hone contacts all parts of the cutting surface. In the absence of this vibration, a stationary hone would not be able to process the complex beveling in a modern blade.

The useful life of a blade is determined mostly by the characteristics of the steel from which it was fabricated. Most, perhaps all, slicer bands are made of chrome-vanadium-steel conforming to close specifications for uniformity, hardness, dimensions, smoothness, accuracy of rounded edges, and the camber or straightness of the steel over the 20 ft or so of length required for a band. This relatively high priced alloy contains chromium to improve its hardness, so the edges will maintain their sharpness for a relatively long period of time, and vanadium to increase its toughness so the band can undergo repeated twisting and bending without breaking. Blades with specially hardened tips have been introduced.

The effectiveness of a blade in performing its intended function is determined largely by the design of its cutting edge and the accuracy of the manufacturing process in implementing that design. The standard shape is a scalloped tooth of specific dimensions and angles. The depth of the curve affects the smoothness of the sliced surface, deeper scallops giving better penetration and less crushing of the loaf but also causing more tearing so that the sliced surface is rougher. The type and direction of beveling also affect smoothness of the slice.

Blade guides were formerly made of chrome-plated steel with two opposing fingers contacting the blades. Tungsten carbide, or sometimes ceramic inserts, are now used in some slicers to improve wear resistance and decrease heat generation. The fingers have been offset to allow crumbs to flow through better (Wright 1988).

A description is of the AMF Slice-Master will be given here as an example of the construction and operation of a typical band slicer. In the AMF slicer, bread is received from racks or a cooling conveyor and deposited on a horizontal woven metal belt that transports it upward and against a rigid stop. An elevator mechanism releases loaves one at a time and delivers them into the flights of an infeed conveyor. The flights move down the infeed conveyor and then retract so that the gentle pressure of the accumulating bread moves the leading loaf toward the slicing area. A cushion of two loaves is set up between the blades and the positive feed.

Blades rotating around drums in a figure-eight pattern tend to pull the loaves forward, thus minimizing the need for force feeding. The sliced loaves are brought by a flighted discharge conveyor to the packaging machine. The blade drums are all steel but chrome-surfaced. They are precision ground and balanced. Support shafts are fitted with removable screw plugs on the operator's side to facilitate blade changes.

A heel control adjustment permits changes to be made to equalize heel thickness after the bread rails have been set to the proper loaf length. A slice thickness control handle allows changing slice thickness from 0.375 to 0.625, the current setting being indicated by and pointer and scale.

The slicing of bread into cubes for stuffing mixes and croutons can be done with special arrangements of bands. One model uses eight drums to cut up to 70 loaves per min into cubes 0.5 inch on each side, with automatic conveying of the loaves, strips, etc. from one station to the next.

Disc slicers.—Slicers with horizontal disc blades are used primarily for slicing hamburger buns and hot dog rolls so that the bun can be readily spread apart in more or less equal parts for inserting the meat. These slicers consist of two motor-driven discs with serrated edges. These saws are disposed in a plane horizontal to the bun conveyor and are separated a short distance (e.g., an eighth of an inch) so they leave hinges in adjacent edges of the pairs of rolls they are slicing. That is, each roll opens on its outside edge. The distance between the blades and the distance between the blades and the table or conveyor (height) are usually adjustable.

In the different designs of this general type, the characteristic operating element (toothed disc) remains the same while the method of orienting rolls and moving them through the slicing area differ. For example, a series of belts, moving in the same direction as the incoming conveyor but raised an inch or so above it, grasp a cluster of buns as they travel down the conveyor belt and carry them past the blades. Two vertical knives immediately in front of the saws split the clusters so they can pass by the spindles of the saws. Such equipment will process up to 35 clusters of 8 buns per minute.

Splitters for English muffins and the like.—It is possible to slice English muffins with the same kind of disc knives used to split hamburger buns, and some are processed this way. But nearly all large manufacturers use scoring machines that leave the two halves clinging together except at the edge. This simulates to some extent the fork separation that connoisseurs of English muffins are said to prefer. In a typical machine, a shallow razor cut is made around the mid-perimeter of the muffin by a continuously moving chain knife operating on a clockwise-rotating muffin (Clock 1988). After being scored, the product passes through a set of four wheels having many knife blades. The wheels turn at different ratios and serve to perforate the muffin through its entire diameter while leaving enough cell structure between the tines to hold the halves together.

Both scoring and splitting speed, as well as depth of cut, can be varied to meet the baker's requirements. A modification of this machine includes a web or hinge slicer with automatic or manual provision for moving the scorer and splitter elements away from the product flow so as to permit use as a single-file conveyor or hinge slicer. Other types of forkers use a straight line of tines that move back and forth on each side of the muffins as they move down a conveyor. Tines can be coated with Teflon or other nonstick coating.

It has been said the consumer wants the periphery of the muffin to be sliced inwardly about a quarter of an inch all around, so as to prevent unsightly raggedness along the edges of the muffin when it is pulled apart. A device to perform this operation, and at the same time score the muffin all the way around its periphery, is described in a patent of Hanson (1986).

There are available melba toast and bagel slicers that make many thin slices from loaves or bagels held in vertical magazines. They incorporate a high speed band blade and a plastic or wire flex belt take-away conveyor. Depending on the number of input product magazines, the unit can produce up to 320 pieces per min (Clock 1988).

BIBLIOGRAPHY

ANON. 1972. Report on project of research and study committee on bread pan structural feature study. Am. Soc. Bakery Engineers Bull. *194*

ANON. 1973. The whys and wherefores of tinplate's retirement. Ekco Bakery Engineering Review *3*, No. 1, 1-4

ANON. 1974. The case of the hot pans. Ekco Bakery Engineering Review *4*, No. 1, 1-4

ANON. 1975. The Teledyne Readco Grouper. Teledyne Readco, York, PA

ANON. 1976. Model M-44 Bun Pan Stacker. Alto Corp., York, PA

ANON. 1980. Operation of the Pan and Peel Oven Loader. Latendorf Conveying Corp., Kenilworth, NJ

CLOCK, T. Q. 1988. Personal communication. Clock Associates, Portland, OR

CRALL, R. D. 1980. Handling pans on air. Proc. Am. Soc. Bakery Engineers *1980*, 53-61

FISH, A. R. 1980. Vacuum cooling. Proc. Am. Soc. Bakery Engineers *1980*, 120-126

FITZMAURICE, D. T. 1970. Selection and care of slicer blades. Bakers Digest *44*, No. 3, 52-53

HANSON, D. R. 1986. Machine for prescoring English muffins or the like. U.S. Pat. 4,581,970

HARTMAN, W. W. 1948. The Story of Bread Slicing. Maine Machine Works, Los Angeles, CA

INZERILLO, A. N. 1979. Pan design. Proc. Am. Soc. Bakery Engineers *1979*, 64-71

JONES, G. W. 1991. Magnetic drive spiral conveyor. U.S. Pat. 4,981,208

JONGERIUS, S. C. E. 1987. Slicing device for bread or the like. U.S. Pat. 4,694,715

LECRONE, D. S. 1980. Automated roll-slicing and handling into packaging. Proc. Am. Soc. Bakery Engineers *1980*, 129-135

MARCKX, E. I. 1971. Bread and pastry processing apparatus. U.S. Pat. 3,614,933

MATZ, S. A. 1988. Equipment for Bakers. Pan-Tech International, Inc., McAllen, TX

PETERSEN, C. W., and HEIDE, H. A. 1963. Depanning apparatus. U.S. Pat. 3,099,360

SCOTT, E. A. 1984. Product release agents. Proc. Am. Soc. Bakery Engineers *1984*, 157-165

STUMPF, S. O. 1990. Bread pan fabricated of liquid-crystal polymer. U.S. Pat. 4,922,811

TORRENS, E. J. 1964. Pan care and maintenance. Proc. Am. Soc. Bakery Engineers *1964*, 147-153

WRIGHT, S. 1988. Personal communication. Hansaloy Corp., Davenport, IA

chapter thirty-four

APPLICATORS FOR ADJUNCTS

INTRODUCTION

This chapter contains descriptions of finishing and decorating equipment that is used to apply adjuncts to baked and fried goods of all kinds. Depositers of jellies, marshmallow, and other adjuncts, applicators of sugar, salt, colored particles, chocolate vermicelli, and the like, injectors for fillings such as whipped cream and Bavarian cream, pizza toppers, spreaders of icings, frostings, and cremes, sprayers for washes and oils, and enrobers for chocolate and other fat-based coatings are included. In this book the word "adjuncts" is used for the materials that are added because it seems to be the only common term broad enough to encompass all the many substances of very diverse qualities to be discussed here.

DEPOSITERS FOR GRANULES

Topping applicators are used with all sorts of bakery goods, even breads and rolls, but they are especially prominent in sweet goods production and biscuit manufacture. Salters are usually placed after the final forming operation and in front of the oven. In cookie lines, sprinklers for coconut, nonpareils, and the like are often placed after a marshmallow depositer and before the skinning conveyor to insure maximum stickiness of the marshmallow and therefore, good retention of the granules. Much of this type of equipment is portable so that it can be positioned on the line to suit the application being run at the moment.

Manufacturers offer machines that can be adapted to deposit particles of different materials. It may be necessary to use change parts, such as screens with different size apertures, to adapt the equipment to a particular ingredient. The machines are often among the simpler designs, since the more complex machines tend to derive their marketing advantage from a more efficient way of depositing a specific ingredient, and the design features leading to this efficiency often limit their applicability to other ingredients. As a result, general purpose depositers are often based on the principle of rolling, pressing, or brushing particles through a screen placed at the bottom of a hopper. Other use interchangeable types of rotating shafts to dispense the material.

Some specifications for an industrial dispensing machine that would be adaptable to depositing several different materials are as follows. The rotary dispensing shaft for dusting is a knurled rod in a choice of extra fine, fine, medium, coarse, or extra coarse to match the average particle size of the material to be dispensed. For depositing coarser materials, a grooved rod with shallow, medium, or deep corrugations is used. If seeds are to be sprinkled, a drilled shaft, with shallow, medium, or deep holes can be obtained. Two nylon brushes outside the hopper are counter opposed to the rotary dispensing shaft. Both brushes are secured in metal holders and are adjustable by thumb screws for regulating their contact with the dispensing shaft. Brushes are channel locked, a construction designed to prevent shedding of bristles. For larger particles, one of the brushes is replaced by a deflector plate or a pattern control plate. One agitator blade oscillates insider the hopper. It is linked to two movable walls inside the hopper. This combination improves flow of the material being dispensed and reduces or prevents bridging.

There are four adjustments that can be made on the above described machine to aid in obtaining the desired rate of deposit of the topping. The rate of rotation of the dispensing shaft can be varied by adjusting the motor controller unit. Four thumb nuts adjust the outside brush holder so contact of the brushes with the rotary dispensing shaft can be modified. Thickness of flow is controlled by the two density adjusting plates bolted to the outside of the hopper. These are positioned by elongated bolt slots and wing nuts. By loosening the wing nuts, these plates may be moved up to increase the flow, or downward to reduce the flow. Width and pattern of deposit are regulated by block-offs and slide adjusters operated manually from the end of the hopper away from the motor (Anon. 1972).

More flour dusters are made than any other type of dispenser. Almost any dough handling line requires at least one flour duster and most lines have several of these devices. Flour is a rather difficult powder to deposit uniformly because of its tendency to hang up in hoppers and to clog sieves. One important goal the designer must keep in mind is preventing the dumping of accumulations on the dough surface; these are very deleterious to dough properties.

The usual type of mechanism found in flour dusters is a rocker arm assembly moving above a screen. Often there will be a rotating spindle below the hopper outlet to further break up the flour and spread it more or less uniformly over the dough sheet. Rates of deposit can be adjusted by changing the distance moved by the rocker arm. The width of the slit beneath the hopper can often be adjusted by moving metal slats in or out. Starch dusters that surround dough pieces with a cloud of this powder in a slightly vacuumized chamber are also available.

Salt is sprinkled on many types of doughs: soda crackers, pretzels, and salt sticks being a few examples. Size of the granule determines to some extent the type of depositer that will be needed. If it makes little difference to the consumer whether the granule is large or small, or if there can be a wide distribution in particle sizes on the product, then the shaking depositers are adequate. If it is important to keep the particles as large as possible, an apparent advantage for salt sticks and pretzels, then a more defined pattern is desirable, suggesting that a more complex machine may be required. This is true for topping salt applied to soda cracker dough.

Simple mechanical sprinklers may use a vibrating or reciprocating screen or a rotating grooved bar to deposit salt, sugar, or spices from a hopper on to the product. Rotating brushes to push the powder into the dispensing element depressions and to pull it out again are common additions to the device. The brushes help to prevent the clogging that would certainly affect the amount of powder going through the screen. Pressure of the brush can often be regulated to modify the rate of deposit. Often, there is an adjustable damper regulating the infeed. The powder usually falls on to a distributor plate where it slides for a brief time before it falls off onto the product.

Coarse flake salt requires a dispenser that will feed it without involving mechanical action that can break down the particles. The electrostatic salt dispenser was developed to meet this requirement. Initially, it was used for adding salt to potato chips but it was later found to be suitable for baked products. The electrostatic dispenser encourages uniform spacing of particles during depositing by inducing a negative static charge on their surfaces, thereby causing the particles to mutually repel each other. Figure 34.1 shows one example of electrostatic salter (Source: Morton Thiokol).

Figure 34.1. Electrostatic salter

Pneumatic salters rely on air currents to transport salt to the dispensing area and to disperse it over the dough. Similar equipment is used for spices. In one type of equipment, an air-proportioning valve is combined with a clean sweep agitator to draw the salt or spice from a pressurized hopper. The granules are carried pneumatically to a spreader that dissipates the air and allows the material to shower down on the food product. Discharge may also be made through a variety of nozzles directly into tumblers or batch mixing vats. There are specialized valves to provide instant material flow at a predetermined rate. Some of the distribution control means that can be used are the wide pattern distributor, the fan pattern nozzle, and the cone pattern nozzle.

Other dispensers for salt, seasonings, and toppings rely on a belt distribution method. The mesh dispensing belt, moved by a variable speed drive, is as wide as the product belt and is placed a few inches above the product. A hopper, the width of the dispensing belt, holds the seasoning, and meters it onto the belt. Multiple belt shakers assure positive clearing of the mesh to prevent clogging.

Many of the units recommended for salt can be used for sugar. One of the simpler units consists of two stainless steel hoppers (one feeding the other to insure uniformity of flow), with a sloping vibratory distribution plate at the base of the lower hopper. The amount of vibration can be altered to control the amount of material fed.

A sugar dispenser used on cookie lines works in conjunction with the forming machine. A hinged mesh extension reaches between the die cups of the forming machine and the oven band. As products fall from the cutter, they drop onto the mesh conveyor that moves the pieces under a sugar-dispensing roll where they receive a deposit of the continuously falling granules. Excess sugar falls through the open meshes onto a cross conveyor for collection and re-use. The sugar-coated dough pieces are then discharged on to the oven band. The sugar discharge mechanism combines a hopper with an adjustable gate, a special fluted dispensing roller four inches in diameter, and a sugar agitator shaft controlled by a cam mounted on the dispensing roll shaft (Anon. 1986B).

Cinnamon and other spices of small particle size can often be deposited satisfactorily by machines very much like flour dusters and sugar sprinklers. When possible, the spices are mixed with sugar or some other carrier to make it easier to deposit the small amounts required.

Spices can be applied to doughnuts or snacks in rotating tumblers. A horizontally aligned cylindrical chamber, slanting slightly downward to the exit and rotated by a variable speed motor forms the basic device. The powder is either sifted into the cylinder or blown into it. Crumb and crunch pieces can also be deposited on doughnuts or small baked items in tumbling drums. These units are used in combination with a glaze applicator, the glaze forming the adhesive holding the crumb on the doughnut surface.

Seed applicators are available with patterned deposit capability. They place a round, square, oval or rectangular pattern of seeds on buns or bread. Pattern plates are easily changed. These depositers are said to function well with grain, bran, or flour as well as other toppings. Some nutmeat feeders have a belt running beneath the hopper. A gate at the hopper exit controls the rate of nutmeat removal as modified by belt speed. An agitator shaft with fingers spreads the pieces across the belt. One manufacturer advertises a unit for dispensing nutmeats directly into rotary molder cavities.

Coconut is particularly difficult to deposit uniformly, especially if it is in shredded form. The systems used to deposit the smaller size coconut particles conform in a general way to the concept of the other chunk dispensers described here. Rate of dispensing is controlled by the stroke length of an eccentric movement. The eccentric shaft drives a screen that controls the rate at which coconut drops from a hopper on to two rotating dispersing wheels. Screens of different mesh sizes are used for different granulations of the topping material. A gate is provided at the bottom of the feed hopper to control the amount of topping material fed to and by the Syntron feeder. A blower is furnished for removal of excess coconut from the product at the discharge end. With slight modifications, the same feeder can be used for chocolate sprinkles, nonpareils, etc.

Instead of dropping the nuts or other additive on the dough piece, a layer of nuts can be placed on a belt and dough dropped on the nuts, after which the dough is pressed down sufficiently by an idler roller to secure some adhesion of the nuts. Excess nuts are allowed to drop through a slot to a recovery bin at the transfer point. When caramel is dropped on the nuts, and the combination chocolate coated, the confection known as turtles is formed. Caramel nut cluster lines include a caramel depositer of the positive displacement piston type working out of a water jacketed stainless steel hopper. Also, a nut dispenser, conveyors, cooling tunnel, and recovery unit.

APPLICATORS FOR GLAZES AND WATER ICINGS

Glazes are among the main decorating and finishing adjuncts applied to doughnuts. Water icings are applied to doughnuts, cookies, and some cakes. These two materials overlap in composition and physical properties, the only real difference being that glazes are generally applied in thinner layers which are transparent or translucent, while water icings are likely to be present in thicker layers and are usually opaque. Water icings contain more sugar crystals, which accounts for their opaqueness and makes it necessary to apply them in thicker layers.

Icing of this type is applied to cookies by a thin (about 0.6 inch diameter) rotating cylinder that picks the icing (sometimes heated) off a larger roller (diameter about five inches) rotating at the bottom of a hopper. The two rollers are driven at about the same surface speed in the same direction, but by different motors. There is often a presser roll driven by its friction with one of the band return rollers. It helps to insure a uniform height in products passing under the icing roll. The latter is inflexibly mounted and cookies (or other pieces) that are too high can jam up the equipment. The bottom surface of the belt under the depositing roller is supported at a uniform but adjustable height by one of the band return rollers.

Band icers give more prolonged contact of the icing applicator with the product surface to achieve maximum adhesion of the coating. The icing is transferred to a belt the width of the product conveyor. The bottom surface of this belt is at the same height above the conveyor belt as the top surface of the product. Height is adjustable, and is generally fixed so that there is a slight tilt of the surface causing increased pressure on the product as it moves along. Icing not transferred to product is automatically scraped from the belt and returned to the hopper to be mixed with fresh icing. Band icing is often whipped slightly in the mixer to make it easier to apply and to give a somewhat less tough coating.

In retail shops, doughnuts are glazed while hot. They are transferred from the fryer screen to a glazing screen. A quick pass with the ladle of glaze over the top of the doughnuts gives a uniform covering to one side of the doughnut. The ladle is a two part scoop about the width of the glazer, it can be opened to give a slit at the bottom through which icing flows. Excess glaze drops into the sloping bottom of the glazer, where it is collected for future use. Continuous glazers of medium to high capacity are used in larger bakeries. They may have a temperature controlled tank holding a stock of icing, with provisions for receiving back the excess deposit. A pump, often of the sanitary type, forces icing from the tank through a hose to a simple waterfall depositer. This forms a curtain of glaze through which the products pass on a bar conveyor. The same type of unit can be used as a half icer by removing the depositer and pumping the icing into a shallow pan through which the doughnuts are floated.

CREAM ICING DEPOSITERS

Buttercream and other non-flowable icings cannot be satisfactorily applied by the machines described above. They require equipment that can extrude or sheet out a semisolid, plastic material without subjecting it to compressive forces that would squeeze out the entrapped air or the liquid fat on which the texture of the icing depends. It is important that the depositer meter the icing with a fair degree of accuracy to prevent unacceptable variations in the proportions of cake and adjunct.

Depositers that apply wide ribbons of icing to, for example, cakes in square or rectangular pans passing beneath the depositer on a conveyor belt, can be electronically controlled to precisely position the icing so that none is left on the edges of the pan or on the belt.

Devices for depositing whipped cream-type toppings on pies can be obtained from two or three manufacturers. Although small machines performing this function as a separate operation are available, the larger units are usually integrated into continuous or semi-continuous lines for forming complete pies. Large units are either linear or rotary in configuration. A typical rotary cream topping machine for semi-automatic operation would have six plates, with manual load and automatic unload. The topping is deposited through a cylindrical head having affixed to its bottom many vertically oriented tubes each of which deposits a small mound of whipped cream. The mounds can have simple designs such as rosette patterns on the upper surface. Retention of this pattern and of individuality of the mounds depends on viscosity of the whipped cream.

For cakes, cookies such as brownies, and snacks that are baked in a continuous sheet on a band hearth, icings, creams, other toppings, and fillings can be extruded in continuous ribbons on to the sheet before the cake is cut into units (Freihofer 1985). Filling depositers have been described that extrude a cylinder of cream slightly smaller in diameter than a layer cake. From the bottom of this cylinder, a slab is cut in the thickness needed for filling the cake, and the slab is dropped directly on the freshly baked and partially cooled layer (Kreisky 1965).

Figure 34.2. A cookie sandwiching machine

Highly specialized machines have been developed for depositing cream icing on base cakes in the preparation of sandwich cookies. These devices force the sugar-shortening paste through orifices on cylinders that rotate just above the base cake. The movements have to be closely registered. After the icing deposit has been severed from the main stream and adhered to the base cake, another cookie is placed on top of the deposit and the "sandwich" gently pressed together. The small amount of liquid fat present in the filling causes the assembly to assume a certain amount of structural strength so that it does not fall apart during packaging, distribution, and consumption. Figure 34.2 shows an example of a sandwich machine (Source: Peters Machinery). For clarity, a one-row device is shown; most cookie factories would use machines servicing many rows of base cakes.

FILLING INJECTORS

There are several kinds of fillings that are injected inside bakery products. Very familiar to most readers will be the "creme" that is injected into small cakes of the Twinkie type. Also widely used are the imitation jams and starch-based fillings injected into many kinds of doughnuts. Injectors take several forms over a wide range of sizes, from the simple one- or two-tube injectors found in most doughnut shops to the continuous and automatic manifold injectors with outputs up to 1,800 dozen pastries per hr.

Small injectors for doughnut shops consist generally of a base with motor, switches, etc., a removable hopper having at its bottom a simple pumping mechanism, and two large needles projecting from the pump. Controls allow adjustment of the amount of filling pumped through the needles at each cycle, for example, from a fraction of an ounce up to seven ounces. In operation, the baker will push a doughnut onto each needle and activate the machine with a push button, food pedal, or push bar.

Much larger units operate on the same general principle of inserting a spout or needle into the dough piece and forcing a measured amount of filling into the product. Registering and orienting the pieces is generally the most difficult part of engineering continuous filling operations.

APPLICATORS FOR FAT

Applicators are available for applying fats and oils to baked products, unbaked products, and pans. Fat can be transferred by mechanical means (brushes, rollers, etc.) or as a spray or curtain. Fat applicators are very common in the snack industry, since nearly all puffed snacks (popcorn, corn curls, etc.) are coated with oil. Most snack lines have continuous drum coaters into which stainless steel pumps force metered amounts of oil through multiple nozzles. The drum has guide tracks and drive traction channels on the outside to facilitate rotation by the external motor. Inside the drum, there will be ridges, variable in size and shape according to the product being coated, that cause the pieces to tumble and expose all their surfaces to the spray. The drum is tilted slightly downward to the exit end so that the product pieces falling into the drum from a slanted chute will gradually flow to the discharge point.

Certain types of dough products are oiled at some stage in their processing. Rounded dough pieces destined for pressing into pizza crusts are nearly always oiled. Dough oilers use three different application methods: (1) Oil flowing from a hopper through a slit or gate is deposited on a roller that transfers it to the surface of a continuous dough strip or pieces of dough; (2) Oil is sprayed in a fine mist onto a sheet or pieces of dough as they pass through an enclosure; and (3) Dough pieces pass through a curtain of oil, as in an enrober. Since oil is relatively expensive, enrober-style application is often contra-indicated, more oil being supplied by these devices than is necessary to achieve the desired result.

Some snack crackers are sprayed with oil to enhance their appearance and texture. Large scale automatic units are available for this operation (Anon. 1985A). Other oil applicators are more generalized in function. A self-contained oil spray machine for large scale production has the following characteristics. Product is carried through the spraying chamber on a balanced weave mesh belt driven by a pin roll drive pulley. A motor with variable speed drive is the motive force. The oil holding tank is a heated reservoir equipped with a recirculating pumping system and an immersion heater that can maintain temperatures up to 170°F. Oil is applied to a high speed rotating disc that disperses it into a mist. The amount of oil flowing onto the disc is adjusted by control valves. A dual piping system is supplied for metering the oil. The machine includes a set of flow controls for maximum oil consumption and another set of controls for minimum oil consumption. Excess oil falls into a drip collection tank and is passed through a screen before it is returned to the main holding tank. An electrostatic mist collection unit is mounted next to the spraying chamber to trap oil vapors. This unit condenses the mist into oil drops for re-use. Spray chambers can be 32, 39, or 48 inches in width. The two smaller chambers are equipped with three sprayers, one above the belt and two below it, while the large chamber contains four spray systems. The ratio of oil to product can be varied from 1% to 25% (weight basis).

Another type of dough oiler suitable for small or medium-size bakeries consists of a number of small oil reservoirs with drip type dispensers wetting rollers that ride on the dough surface. The reservoirs resemble in their construction details the small glass drip lubricators found on many kinds of small equipment. These oil tanks are made of transparent plastic. Fluid flow is controlled by a stepless adjustment measuring screw. Magnetic valves close off the oil flow when the production line shuts down.

A combination water splitter/butter applicator is offered by the Burford Corp. This unit uses a water jet to make the top cut in split loaves and applies butter to the slit immediately afterwards. The standard machine is provided with five nozzles to split the five loaves held in the usual strap. Water coming from a 0.017 inch orifice cuts the surface about one-eighth inch deep. Pressure is adjustable, firmer loaves generally requiring more pressure than soft white loaves. The small amount of residual water is said to have little or no effect on other crust characteristics. Jets are controlled by proximity switches for sensing the presence of pan bottoms. Immediately after the pans leave the splitting area, they pass under nozzles which deposit a strip of melted butter on the opening. Oil can be deposited as well as butter, and some bakers are adding a mixture of butter and honey (Ivey 1988).

WATER AND WASH APPLICATORS

Plain water is applied to improve adhesion of dry particles (seeds, salt, crumbs, etc.) to bakery products. Usually, this water is applied by spraying it on the unbaked dough. The spray may be in the form of a mist retained in a tunnel through which the dough piece is carried. Mist can be developed by forcing water through a nozzle or using one of the centrifugal type vaporizers.

Washes can be applied by belts or brushes. A unit that has been suggested for egg washes has a cloth belt carried around two small diameter rollers separated by about a foot on a frame pivoted in the middle. This belt assembly can be tilted so the bottom "nose" just touches the dough sheet passing beneath it and is driven at a speed that approximately matches the speed of the product conveyor belt. The bottom of the wash applicator also contacts a metal roller that turns in a pan containing the wash liquid. The metal roller thus transfers the wash from the pan to the belt. A thumb screw adjustment changes the pressure of the belt on the roller to control rate of wash transfer. The applicator belt is a lock-weave pre-shrunk single-ply cotton endless belt specifically woven for egg wash transfer. It can easily be removed for washing. This unit is said to be useful for water application, and presumably for other washes as well (Anon. 1971).

PIZZA TOPPING MACHINES

Spreading of cheese, sausage slices, ground beef bits, and the like on pizzas is a labor intensive operation and subject to considerable error in quantity judgements. It has proven to be rather difficult to mechanize this operation, but there are machines now available that do a respectable job in applying non-uniform chunks of mixed size and texture. Rotary pizza topping machines have been designed by one of the leading manufacturers of pie filling and topping machines (Pluta 1988). On a six-station rotary machine, sauce is deposited in a uniform pattern on the surface of a pizza crust, then fresh sausage or other topping is applied before pre-measured grated or shredded cheese is manually added. The semi-automatic unit consists of a positive piston filler, automatic sausage depositer, and cheese spreader mounted on a stainless steel rotary indexing table. Crusts of 9- to 16-inch diameter can be processed at rates up to 20 pizzas per minute, with change parts. The pizza sausage depositer is operated in the following manner: (1) Put ground sausage meat in hopper; (2) Set the control bar for the proper size; (3) Put pizza under end of depositer using the self-centering peel; (4) Push operating lever at side of depositer to move the large meat die plate under the hopper and force ground sausage into the die holes; (5) Pull the operating lever to return the plate to the depositing area, completing the filling cycle; (6) Press down on the spring-loaded handle to drop the sausage patties on to the pizza; and (7) Remove the finished pizza.

JELLY AND MARSHMALLOW TOPPERS

This section deals with equipment that deposits small amounts of jelled toppings and similar materials on cookies and cookie doughs. Most of these devices rely on some sort of piston arrangement for precise measuring and placement of the deposit. In one commercial unit, a positive placement piston and rotary valve system deposits jams and jellies onto the surface of preformed products. The operating mechanism is driven at a 1:1 ratio by the product forming equipment. Proper placement of the deposited mass is accomplished by linear movement of the entire dispensing unit relative to band conveyor direction. This topper can achieve up to 120 row deposits per minute. The minimum center-to-center distance of items across the width of the band is 54 mm. In operation, the material to be deposited is placed into the hopper of the unit and gravity fed to the piston-valve mechanism. Valves rotate to open and shut in synchronization with the piston stroke. A manual adjustment of the piston stroke determines the volume of the deposited mass. Horizontal head movement in relation to band speed and in coordination with deposits is controlled by an eccentric and linkage.

The Oven Pacer Depositer (Oakes 1983) is reputed to be particularly well adapted to the placing of marshmallow on base cakes (cookies) for later enrobing. The basic principle is that the depositing manifold travels with the base cake but does not interfere with the movement of the cookies. To accomplish this, the continuously fed pressure-depositing manifolds are mounted on a yoke assembly over the cookie conveyor. The yoke can move simultaneously in both the horizontal and vertical plane so the the the depositing nozzle can be positioned over the center of the base cake at the time the slider valve is opened. The deposit is formed while the manifold is tracking at the same speed as the conveyor. A synchronous vertical profiler is used to form not only the diameter but also the height and shape of the deposit. At a predetermined height above the base cake, the slider valve is closed and the horizontal motion is reversed, causing a rapid return to the start position.

PRINTING DESIGNS ON PRODUCT SURFACES

Colored designs can be formed on surfaces of baked products by using containers shaped to leave raised lines on the top. This technique is most successful with rotary molded cookies, with which good results can be obtained if the cookie normally bakes out to a light color and enough radiant heat can be applied to brown the raised lines. Some rather complex designs can be formed in this manner. Alternatively, the raised portions can be emphasized by the application of water icing after baking; this is seldom entirely satisfactory because of the smearing, dripping, and running characteristics of the icing. Of course, very elaborate designs can be applied to cakes and large cookies by hand application of colored icings.

There appears to be a demand for the printing of designs on cookies and the like that cannot be satisfied by these methods. This demand has been at least marginally met by systems that transfer edible inks either to the unbaked dough pieces or to the baked units. High speed forming operations can be serviced in this way, The patent of Krubert (1986), provides that the cookies first be iced and the design then transferred to the hard surface from a printing pad. Prior patents have discussed other methods, including inks applied before baking.

ENROBERS FOR FAT-BASED COATINGS

Applying fat-based coatings to a bakery product is often an excellent, though costly, way of increasing consumer acceptance of the item. These coatings are frequently applied to cupcakes, swiss rolls, doughnuts, and cookies, and can also be found on many other products. They have even been applied to pretzels, crackers, croissants, fried pies, and other unlikely candidates for this treatment. The highest quality fat-based coatings are the true chocolates, such as milk chocolate, but these are usually too expensive for use on baked goods for the general market. Analogous coatings with little or no chocolate content are available and are quite satisfactory in most cases. The chief problems encountered by users of these coatings are cost, difficult processing requirements, and susceptibility of the coatings to damage by ordinary ambient temperatures. In the following section, processing requirements and how they can be met by existing commercial equipment will be discussed.

Need for Special Treatment of Chocolate

Enrobing lines for applying fat-based, essentially moisture-free, coatings to small baked goods are common in the baking industry. Chocolate-flavored coatings are the most common, but other types such as white vanilla or pastel-colored coatings of different flavors (e.g., strawbery) are also available. Coatings containing vegetable fats other than cocoa butter are usually called compound coatings and they have substantially different properties than coatings containing real chocolate. Manufacturers of edible fats have spent much research time and money in trying to duplicate the organoleptic properties of chocolate with coatings that are cheaper and which do not have the temperature sensitivity of cocoa butter, but complete success has not been achieved.

In the enrobing process, the cooled baked items are carried from a textile or plastic conveyor belt on to a wire-mesh belt that is an integral part of the coating machine. The metal belt conveys the product through a curtain of liquid coating that covers the top and sides of the articles. A roller under the belt coats the bottoms of the pieces. A tank holding a supply of tempered coating is located nearby, often under the coating machine. A pump circulates the coating to a flow pan which forms the curtain by allowing the liquid to flow over one side of the pan. An air blower removes excess coating from the product, and helps to intensify the gloss, but it may leave slight ripples on the product. A vibrator shakes a section of the mesh conveyor belt and smooths out some of the ripples on the coating. The detailer rod (anti-tailing device) helps to control the amount of coating on the bottom and removes strings and tails.

Enrobing bakery goods with chocolate-containing coatings presents a number of problems not encountered in other finishing operations. Obtaining and retaining optimum texture (mouthfeel) and appearance of chocolate coatings depends upon carefully following a prescribed course of temperature treatments. This "tempering," as it is called, is very intolerant to temperature fluctuations outside acceptable ranges. Furthermore, products covered by even the best tempered coating will be irreparably damaged by exposure to temperatures above about 95°F—the exact temperature depending somewhat on the composition of the coating and the time of exposure.

All of these problems arise from characteristics of the fatty substances making up about 50% of pure chocolate. Melted chocolate liquor (also called bakers chocolate, bitter chocolate, and pure chocolate) is made up of a continuous phase of cocoa butter and a dispersed phase consisting of very fine particles of the nonfatty portions of the cocoa bean. When mixed with sugar, milk fat, or other components of coating chocolates (sweet chocolate, semi-sweet chocolate, milk chocolate, etc.) the basic system of continuous phase fat and discontinuous phase (everything not soluble in fat) persists. On cooling, the liquid chocolate behaves largely according to the crystalline status of the fat in this continuous phase. The fat can crystallize in many forms, only one of which (called the beta form) is stable. The unstable crystalline forms, if present, will revert in time to the stable form, but products manufactured from chocolate containing these unstable forms will be of poor appearance, suffer from fat bloom, and (in the case of molded products) be difficult to extract from molds due to reduced shrinkage. The purpose of tempering is to first remove the unstable forms by melting the chocolate and then to form a maximum percentage of stable crystals by cooling the liquid chocolate slowly according to an appropriate schedule. In an ideal situation, only the beta crystals will be present in the finished article.

If the tempered chocolate is placed on a hot product, all of the preceding effort will go for naught. Baked items should reach the enrober at a temperature of 75° to 85°F, and the room in which the enrober is located should be at the same temperature. The coating, after having been subjected to the tempering process, should be maintained at the appropriate holding temperature, which for pure chocolate is 90°F. Compound coatings which may include cocoa but normally do not include chocolate, may either require or not require tempering, depending on their composition.

Equipment for Tempering Chocolate Coatings

Five construction features are said (Anon. 1987) to be of great importance to the tempering of chocolate so that there is perfect microcrystallization of the mass. These are (1) many tempering sections, (2) large cooling surfaces, (3) perfect scraping and efficient mixing, (4) cooling time, and (5) accurate temperature control. If all these requirements are met, it is possible to get a finished product with high deep gloss, fine-grained and crispy break, good keeping qualities, short solidification time, and maximum contraction when cooled. For coatings, contraction is not much of a factor, because the product will not be removed from a mold, but there is some opinion that poor or inadequately controlled tempering can lead to spontaneous cracking of coatings, especially in products such as chocolate coated marshmallow deposits.

The initial handling of chocolate coatings will depend upon whether they are received from the supplier in melted condition or in slabs. There are melting devices specifically designed to reduce the solid chocolate to a fluid without causing any heat damage. In tempering, the melted chocolate must be brought through a number of temperature changes. These operations can be applied in separate heat exchangers, but most large users will employ unitary assemblages designed to continuously perform the desired sequence of operations.

A commercially-available tempering unit is described as follows. The unit is a free standing, self-contained machine consisting of the tempering tube with its drive, a control panel, and a water system, all mounted on a fabricated steel framework with stainless steel covers. The unit requires supplies of cold water and hot water. Four standard sizes cover a through-put range of 1,000 to 3,250 lb per hr. Capacity depends on the type of chocolate, milk chocolates requiring lower temperatures and longer hold times. The tempering tube is vertically mounted and divided into three sections: cooling, retention, and final temperature adjusting.

Using the tempering unit just described, untempered chocolate is continuously tempered during production. Liquid untempered chocolate is metered into the tempering tube where it is cooled in a swept film heat exchanger to a temperature at which stable beta crystals can grow. The chocolate then passes to the retention section, where these crystals grow and multiply. Without this retention time, it would be necessary to cool the chocolate to a much lower temperature in the first stage, and this could result in the growth of unstable crystals. As crystals multiply, there is an increase in mass temperature. In the last stage, another swept film heat exchanger is used to control the final temperature to within 1.8°F of that required for the enrober (Anon. 1984).

Figure 34.3 is a diagram of the heating system involved in tempering and applying chocolate coatings and the like.

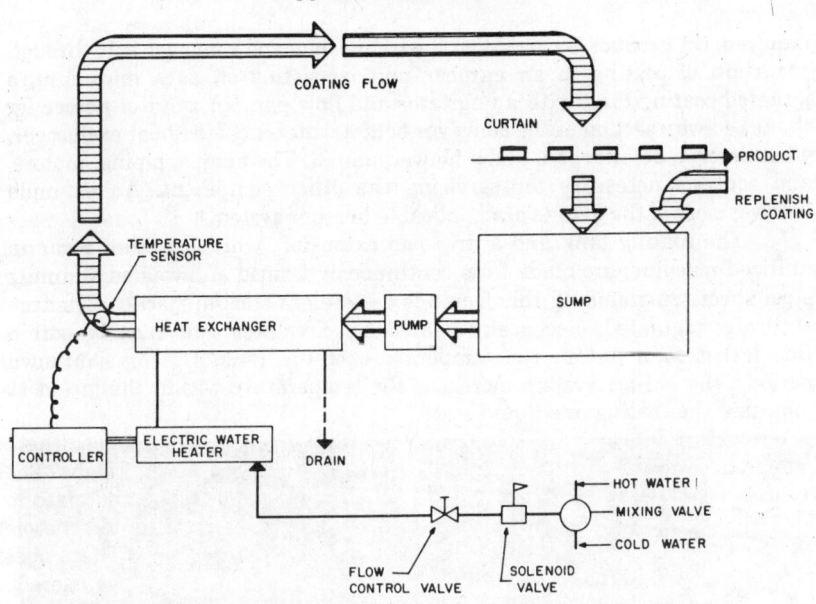

Figure 34.3. The heat control system for fat-based coatings

Chocolate holding tanks are of many different types and designs. A typical holding tank for use between the tempering equipment and the depositing machine might be comprised of a water-jacketed tank fitted with a stirrer and a vibratory sieve driven by independent motors. The tank itself might be a welded steel trough with hemispherical bottom swept by a reciprocating stirrer. There will be a water jacket on the trough and exit pipe. The piping in these systems may be of black iron and must be wound with industrial heating cable and insulated.

Pumps recommended for chocolate systems are slow moving rotary displacement pumps. A typical pump would have two moving parts, a rotor on the main shaft and a pawl. These parts and the pump body are made from high grade cast iron. Rotors have one or two lobes. The former should be used only when delivering against minimum head pressure. Removable plates give ready access to the pump cavity. Seals are in cartridge form for quick removal and replacement.

Enrobers

The majority of continuous enrobers used for bakery foods are of the curtain or waterfall type, in which the product is moved through a vertical sheetlike stream of liquid chocolate. Bottoms are covered by other methods. The usual sequence of operations in these machines is: (1) Properly conditioned coating from the tempering unit is delivered to the enrober as required; (2) Product is carried on a wire mesh or rod conveyor belt through a curtain of coating in an enrober unit consisting of, as a minimum, a jacketed coating tank with an agitator and flow pan, an agitator device for the take-away section of the conveyor belt, a water-jacketed heat exchanger, a bottomer, a detailer rod, and a blower; and (3) The pumps, piping, motors, and controls necessary for servicing the other equipment. An example follows; most of the details are applicable to other systems.

The coating tank and a drip pan extension, which together form an unitized machine, are made from continuously formed and welded stainless steel sheet. Surrounding this frame is a stainless steel air jacket. Thermostatically regulated, electrically heated air circulates continuously within this jacket to maintain the temperature of the tank. During shutdown periods, the hot air system increases the temperature within the jacket to maintain the coating in a liquid state.

Figure 34.4. Chocolate enrober

A stainless steel wire mesh belt with a 0.25 inch pitch conveys products through the coater. A shaker system adjustable in frequency and amplitude is provided to agitate the enrobed product. This vibratory action distributes coating more or less evenly over the product and also assists drainage of excess coating. The detailer rod is positioned at the end of the wire belt and rotates in a direction counter to belt movement. It can be adjusted up or down to eliminate trailing streaks of coating. Stainless steel flow pans allow a double curtain of coating to flow onto the belt. Melted coating flows either through a slit at the bottom of the pan or over one edge of the pan. The latter design is less likely to clog up. Pans can be designed to pour many evenly separated narrow streams of coating to stripe the product. Height of the pan can be adjusted in some models. Coating is pressure fed from the coating tank to a distributor that dispenses the melted material across the width of the pan.

Figure 34.4 shows a chocolate coating machine enrobing marshmallow puffs (Source: J. W. Greer).

Beneath the belt, a bottoming pan receives the excess coating. A supply of coating is pumped into this pan when bottomed goods are being made. The belt carrying the cookies or other products across the bottomer is generally composed of thin metal rods or wires transversely disposed, and it travels just below the surface of the chocolate so that the coating will be able to contact the bottoms of the pieces. The pan can be moved up or down to affect the amount of coating applied. A bottoming roller can be fitted to the pan to pick up coating and apply it to the bottom of the cookie.

Excess coating is removed by a high-pressure blower system. A damper on the blower intake controls flow of air through the nozzles. The nozzle, which is a tubular plenum chamber, gives uniform air distribution across the width of the belt. Nozzle height and angle, and width of air discharge, are adjustable. The detailer, a simple powered roller of small diameter located so as to contact the bottoms of the pieces, removes "tails" of coating which drop down from the product as it leaves the enrober belt.

The spray enrober uses a completely different method to apply confectionery coatings. It is based on using large orifice multidirectional spray nozzles through which the coatings are sprayed from the bottom and top onto the product to be coated. As contrasted with the standard enrobing curtain, this system has a large coating area that provides a very uniform coating at controlled rates on all surfaces. It is said that light, medium, or heavy coatings can be "dialed in". and uniform covering achieved. Enrobing speeds can be increased up to 50%, it is claimed, compared to more conventional enrober designs. Energy savings are also possible, since up to ten times more coating is applied to the product relative to the volume of coating being circulated (Anon. 1983) .

Cooling Tunnels, Slabs, and Conveyors

Enrobed products must be promptly cooled to solidify the coating so the pieces can be packed and to put the fat crystals in a more stable condition. Proper cooling of a well-tempered coating will give a product having good gloss and firm texture, and the gloss and texture will be maintained throughout a long storage period. If the coating is not firm, it will smear or retain fingerprint impressions from the packing operation.

Cooling equipment for enrobed goods generally takes the form of a tunnel with refrigeration units to chill the air or surfaces and a conveyor belt to carry the products through the tunnel. Suppliers offer these tunnels in module form so that plants may assemble any desired capacity. In counter-cooling tunnels, air temperature at the entrance should be about 65°F, and temperature should gradually drop until it reaches about 55°F at the discharge end. For more recently developed zone cooling tunnels, air temperature may be brought down from about 65°F at the entrance to 40°F near the middle, and then warmed up in the final zones to about 55°F so that the products are not cold enough to cause moisture to condense on them. Dwell time in the tunnel varies with products, but should be only a few minutes.

Contraflow cooling tunnels can consist of independently controlled cooling zones. They provide top cooling by radiation or linear convection and bottom cooling by conduction from a water-cooled slab. Zones are constructed from steel frames covered by insulated and reinforced plastic hoods that are removable for sanitation and complete accessibility to the conveyor and cooling module. Each section incorporates a water cooled table for bottom cooling. For top cooling, each section is split horizontally by a steel plate to form a supply return duct and product cooling area. The belt conveyor passes on top of the water-cooled slab through the product cooling area. Cooling air above the conveyor belt is horizontally distributed along the product zone against the product flow from the entrance of the tunnel to its middle and with the product flow from the middle to the tunnel end. Chilled water is circulated through the bottom bed and the cooling coils of each module. A radiation cooling system can be fitted, generally to the first third of the tunnel. Black-finished, water-cooled radiant panels are installed, replacing the steel sheeting above the product, and chilled water is circulated through them.

Cooling slab conveyors are used to cool and set bottoms of chocolate-coated bakery products. They are simpler and cheaper devices than cooling tunnels. They normally receive products from the prebottomer unit and transfer them into the main coating machine. The conveyor bed is an assembly of steel plates. Serpentine channels are formed between the plates so cold water or other refrigerant can be circulated. There will be adjustable nose pieces at each end of the conveyor to assist in smooth transfer. The delivery and feed ends are hinged to facilitate connecting transfers.

BIBLIOGRAPHY

ANON. 1965. Continuous delivery of uniform, stable, chocolate coatings. Greer Technical Information Sheet *BT-104*

ANON. 1971. Egg-wash Applicator. Anetsberger Bros., Inc., Northbrook, IL

ANON. 1972. Christy Industrial Dispensing Machines. Christy Machine Co., Fremont, OH

ANON. 1979. Salt/spice Dispenser. American Foods Machinery Corp., Memphis, TN

ANON. 1983. New Spray Enrober. Spray Dynamics, Newport Beach, CA

ANON. 1984. ACS Tempering Unit. APV (Werner-Lehara), Grand Rapids, MI

ANON. 1985A. Oil Spray. Vicars Group, Ltd., Merseyside, England

ANON. 1985B. Water Recirculating System. Aasted International, Farum, Denmark

ANON. 1986A. Chocolate Pump, Model 117 CP. APV (Werner Lehara), Grand Rapids, MI

ANON. 1986B. Portable Sugar Topper. APV (Werner Lehara), Grand Rapids, MI

ANON. 1987A. DMW Temperer. Assted International, Farum, Denmark

ANON. 1987B. Series-D Coater. APV (Werner-Lehara), Grand Rapids, MI

BOLLENBECK, G. N. 1965. Latest formulas and techniques for fondant and icing production. Proc. Am. Soc. Bakery Engineers *1965*, 266-270

CLIFFORD, F. J. 1972. Production of icings and creme fillings with continuous equipment. Proc. Am. Soc. Bakery Engineers *1972*, 159-162

DOOM, L. G. 1976. Cake filler. U.S. Pat. 3,999,691

DREIER, W. 1991. The nuts and bolts of coating and enrobing. Prepared Foods *160*, No. 7, 47-48

FREIHOFER, W. D. 1985. New trends in small cake production. Proc. Am. Soc. Bakery Engineers *1985*, 134-141

GUCKENBERGER, J. D. 1977. Icings and fillings for cakes. Proc. Am. Soc. Bakery Engineers *1977*, 81-87

HAYASHI, T. 1988. Method of injecting viscous fluid into bread or confectionery. U.S. Pat. 4,752,488

HAYASHI, T., and TASHIRO, Y. 1988. Method for quantitatively extruding food material. U.S. Pat. 4,788,071

ILLFELDER, B. 1964. Preparation and application of icings for sweet yeast raised products. Proc. Am. Soc. Bakery Engineers *1964*, 254-259

IVEY, D. 1988. Personal communication. Burford Corp., Maysville, OK

KREISKY, K. 1965. European baking equipment today. Proc. Am. Soc. Bakery Engineers *1965*, 118-129

KRUBERT, G. J. 1986. Printing of foods. U.S. Pat. 4,578,273

MINIFIE, B. W. 1980. Chocolate, Cocoa, and Confectionery. Second Edition. AVI Publishing Co., Westport, CT

MOSHIER, M., and POLITTE, R. 1990. Dual injection cake filler apparatus. U.S. Pat. 4,928,592

OAKES, W. P. 1983. Oakes Pacer Depositer. Frito-Lay Cookie Seminar, AIB, Manhattan, KS

PLUTA, R. 1988. Personal communication. Colborne Corp., Glenview, IL

PORCELLO, S. J., MANNS, J. M., PLAYER, K. W., and WILSON, L. L. 1987. Cookie filler composition. U.S. Pat. 4,711,788

STRIETELMEIER, D. M. 1969. On electrostatic salting. Snack Food *58*, No. 9, 60-61

WATKINS, H. E. 1970. Apparatus for flavoring of snack foods and the like. U.S. Pat. 3,536,035

WELCH, R. C. 1968. Chocolate and hard butter coatings. Proc. Am. Soc. Bakery Engineers *1968*, 242-263

WING, D. H. 1975. Enrobing of bakery products. Proc. Am. Soc. Bakery Engineers *1975*, 136-142

ZANETOS, T. and REEDER, P. E. 1990. Apparatus for molding chocolate. U.S. Pat. 4,950,145

chapter thirty-five

PACKAGING MATERIALS AND EQUIPMENT

INTRODUCTION

It is a matter of common observation that nearly all of the bakery products to be found in a present-day supermarket or convenience store are contained in some sort of manufactured package. The trend to in-store bakeries has reduced this practice to some extent, because part of the goods sold from these outlets is simply placed in a paper bag at the time of purchase. We are safe in assuming, however, that retailers have found the foodstuff to be only part of a marketable product. The other essential part is the container, and the bakery product manufacturer must give it just as much consideration as the formula and process used for making the food.

This chapter will contain details of packaging materials and machinery, and design considerations. Many more details about packaging equipment, materials, and testing, as well as information on technical and regulatory aspects of labeling can be found in "Bakery Technology" (Matz 1989).

FACTORS AFFECTING PACKAGE DESIGN

Studies reporting consumer attitudes toward existing food packaging indicate that consumers want containers that are reclosable, storable, reheatable, resealable, transportable, disposable, and biodegradable (Anon. 1988A). Copeland (1988) compiled a check list of what consumers want in packaging for foods in general (not just bakery items). This list included: (1) Packages that are lightweight, tamper evident, and microwave-heatable when appropriate; (2) Aluminum cans that are resealable; (3) Packaging that extends life and improves quality for fresh produce; (4) A single address to write to and a single telephone number to call for information or for registering a complaint; (5) Colors that help delineate lettering; (6) Packaging that looks good but isn't good enough to save; (7) Directions the entire family can use; (8) Freshness dates and expiry dates; (9) Accurate and simple directions and graphics; (10) Packages that are truly easy opening; and (11) Packagers who are responsible regarding littering, non-biodegradable material, and the environment. Some of these desires will be difficult to achieve and of limited marketing value. No doubt, many of the consumers who say they want these things will, when confronted with a choice, buy the unopenable, nondestructible, and poorly labeled package with a cartoon character on the front and contest coupon on the back.

Most people would agree that attractive packaging of foodstuffs in protective coverings is necessary for successful marketing. There are a few exceptions. For example, some success was had with cookies marketed in a printed kraft bag and French baguettes placed in a paper sleeve. Even these specialties, when packaged in such a manner, would be acceptable for retail bakeries having very short distribution channels and requiring only a few days shelf life—they would pose many difficulties for the wholesale baker.

Bakers expect the package to help sell the product, to assist in maintaining the maximum possible shelf life, to give at least some protection against mechanical damage during transport and handling, to provide surfaces on which to print legally required information as well as expiry dates, and to be convenient for the consumer to open and reclose. It is the task of the package designer to achieve all of these goals at the minimum cost in materials, equipment, and labor. A brief overview of design principles is included in this chapter. Readers who are interested in more detailed information can consult the references given in the bibliography.

Functions of Containers

There are many aspects of container quality and suitability for a given purpose that can't be considered here because of space limitations, or because they do not conform to the technical orientation of this book. It is important, however, to discuss the interactions of containers with products and with the equipment used to apply the packaging material, since these are facets of container design that the food technologist must often evaluate.

The package must protect against gross contaminants that are constantly or intermittently present in the environment. Dust, dirt, water droplets, loose or smeary material from other bakery products, insects, and the hands of customers or employees must be kept off the product to the greatest extent possible within the constraints of cost and labor faced by the manufacturer. To perform these functions, a hermetic seal and an impervious material are not absolutely necessary, but a tamper-proof seal and a moisture resistant film or board are highly desirable. Packages meeting only these minimum requirements may be satisfactory for in-store bakeries, pizzerias, and other operations making products to be sold in close proximity to the production area within a few hours of baking.

The package should also protect the product from damaging mechanical force, as from crushing, cracking (e.g., must offer a stable base for pies), and punctures (from fingers, corners of adjacent cartons, etc.). Inversion of the package can cause messy results with iced cakes, cheesecakes, pies, and most fragile items, but it is difficult if not impossible to design a container that gives good protection against this occurrence. Some protection should be provided against the effects of vibrations, which can have disastrous effects on pies, certain cakes, delicate pastries, etc. As a practical matter, this hazard can be defeated only by providing suitable transporation means and by training employees in preventive techniques.

Consumers do not expect all bakery products to be protected equally. A polyethylene bread bag gives only minimal protection against mechanical damage, but it is well accepted by consumers, partly because it gives them an opportunity to judge "freshness" by squeezing the loaf. Bread, buns, and the like are usually protected in transit from bakeries to retail stores by baskets, trays, and other multi-pack containers that prevent crushing.

Most bakery foods should be prevented from gaining or losing moisture after they have been placed in their package. If this is not done, crisp products (such as crackers) can quickly become soft or even soggy, and soft products (such as bread) can become tough and undesirably firm. Bakery products are very susceptible to flavor damage resulting from absorption of aromatic substances that are in their environment. Vapors such as those originating from gasoline, tobacco, insecticides, and toiletries are very harmful to the mild flavors and delicately balanced aromas of the typical baked product. The package should also prevent loss of volatile flavors from the product. Flavor may be absorbed into the container itself, a phenomenon sometimes called "scalping." In many cases, it is necessary to prevent movement of oxygen or some other gas across the package barrier. Some products require protection from light and ultraviolet rays, because radiation bleaches their pigments, causes vitamin deterioration, or accelerates rancidity development. An anaerobic or oxygen-reduced atmosphere may be desirable for controlling mold growth. A hermetically-sealed, opaque, rigid container such as a tin can would accomplish all of these functions, but is obviously impractical for nearly all bakery products. The package designer must do the best possible job using plastic and foil films, fiber boards, adhesives, and inks that are commercially available.

Since no single film will provide all of the desired protective features, it is common to laminate together several different films. For example, it may be considered necessary to use one layer for its heat seal properties, another for its printing compatibility, a third as an oxygen barrier, a fourth for its low water vapor transmission rate, and a fifth for grease resistance. It is not uncommon to find barrier structures with as many as eight layers, not all of them different, and some functioning only as adhesives. Of course, the material becomes more expensive as the number of layers increases.

Aluminum foil combines many of the protective features desired in food packages—virtually zero transmission rates for all common gases, water vapor, and odorous compounds, opacity, and good appearance—but it also has disadvantages. It is relatively expensive, it is difficult to economically recycle film containing foil, it prevents the product from being seen by the consumer, and it is incompatible with shrink or stretch wrapping

Occasionally, there is a need to provide protection against rapid temperature change. No thin film is good for this purpose. Foamed polystyrene has some insulating value, but it must be used in thicknesses that are awkward for many applications and impossible in others. It is also difficult to apply and has little mechanical strength. Paperboard has some value for insulating, but different grades vary greatly in their effectiveness. There is no good solution to the insulating problem in film packaging.

When a package is being designed, the Marketing Department will want to know if the package surface will accept the graphics they deem desirable for selling the product. The designer will have to inform them the kind of printing method that is feasible, the type of ink that can be used, the unprinted color and transparency of the film, compatibility with adhesive labels, and the opening and reclosure features that are available?

There must be sufficient space on the container for product identi- fication, selling messages, notices required by laws and regulations, bar codes, and other more or less essential words and images. If possible, the package must be constructed so it stands upright on the supermarket shelf, providing maximum visibility to the consumer. Some of these requirements may lead to the need for an overpack to contain one or more unit packages. The outer carton is seldom required to afford the protection demanded in the interior packages although it may, in fact, be cheaper to transfer the protective function to the outer container. In the latter situation, the interior packets can made of some cheap material such as thin polyethylene or coated paper. The kind of packaging is acceptable, however, only if it is reasonably certain that the interior packets will be used up before transfer of moisture, gas, or other substance renders their contents unacceptable.

Consumers must be able to open the package easily without using specialized utensils and without having to read complicated directions. The contents must not spill or soil the hands during opening. The product must not be damaged by the opening procedure. If the package is to be reclosed, the reclosure feature must be simple and reliable and it should be perma- nently attached to the main package so it does not become lost, fall down the garbage disposal, or otherwise infuriate the customer. In market research undertaken to determine what consumers disliked most about modern containers, difficulty in opening packages ranked high on the list.

It may be a marketing advantage to allow the consumer to use the package as a baking container, as for finishing off bread and roll doughs, pies, coffee cakes, Danish pastries, and the like. For many years, brown- and-serve rolls have been distributed in foil-paperboard pans for this purpose. Aluminum foil is a good choice for bake-off applications, although it is expensive in the gauges needed to give adequate handling properties. The big negative of foil is that it is unsuitable for use in microwave ovens.

In recent years there has been a great proliferation of foods packed in containers that enable the product to be heated in microwave ovens. Many of these products are bakery foods. Initial introductions were mostly fully cooked items requiring thawing and warming in the microwave oven, but these have been supplemented by an increasing number of products that require cooking as well as thawing, and therefore must be much more resis- tant to heat damage. Bakery foods particularly suitable for thawing and warming in microwaves include fully baked, single component structures such as pancakes, soda biscuits, bagels, and croissants. Full-sized loaves of bread do not respond very well because microwave penetration is too erratic, but small loaves and muffins are satisfactory. If the product is to undergo a baking process, it must be of a type which does not require crust browning since this is virtually impossible to achieve in most existing models of microwave ovens. Even microwave ovens with browning elements do not usually give typical crust colorations. Brownies and some layer cake batters respond reasonably well, but tend to give non-uniform contours and textures. Browning through use of susceptors such as metallic films or plates that concentrate heat is an improvement but needs to be perfected. There are many recent patents on the development of crust color, fried flavors, etc., through use of additives and package modifications.

Laws and regulations governing packaging of bakery products and other foodstuffs are becoming increasingly restrictive. All package designers must keep abreast of legal developments if they are to function effectively. It is no longer safe to rely entirely on supplier advice as to the legality of a particular food and package combinations, especially if the supplier ordinarily deals with non-food packagers. Salesmen's comments such as "This film is GRAS" or "This material is in the process of being approved by the FDA" are not adequate as bases for using a packaging material. After much time has been spent in design, it may be discovered the salesman has been overly optimistic in his interpretation of an off-hand comment made by some technical person in his own organization or by a competitive packer.

MATERIALS

Factors Guiding Selection of Materials

The requirements for an ideal packaging material for bakery products might include the following:

(1) The material should protect the product from harmful environmental influences. As a primary requirement, the product should be protected from drying out during its normal storage life. Not only must the material have a low rate of moisture vapor transmission, but it must also be capable of forming continuous seals that are as impervious as the intact film. If the film protects adequately against moisture transfer, it will very likely exclude mold spores, dirt, dust, and other foreign particles, and it will give some protection against the absorption of off-odors.

(2) The package should contribute to the dimensional stability of the product. Since most bakery foods are very susceptible to crushing, mechanical strength must be present in the container if the product is to survive storage, transportation, and merchandising without undergoing an unacceptable amount of distortion, breaking, etc. Packaging for fresh bread loaves is an exception to this requirement.

(3) The packaging material should be suitable for being formed into the finished package easily and quickly by mechanical means, and preferably by readily available equipment. A fundamental requirement for films is that the structure heat-seal readily. It should not crack, tear, or stretch during the rapid transfers and foldings it will encounter in the wrapping machine.

(4) The package should assist in selling the product. For bread loaves, this usually means the product can be squeezed so the customer can be confident

the bread is soft and, therefore, fresh. If visibility of the product is important, use of transparent films is imperative. A glossy surface definitely enhances consumer acceptance. Printability is necessary in most cases.

(5) The film should be relatively low in price. It must have a favorable cost per square inch (a much more important criterion than cost per pound), and the supplier's factory or warehouse must be located so as to make transportation costs acceptable. It must not deteriorate when stored under normal conditions, and must machine with a minor amount of waste.

Table 35.1. BARRIER PROPERTIES OF SIX BASE STOCKS

Base stock	Moisture vapor transmission rate	Oxygen transmission rate
PE, low density	1.4	500.
PE, high density	0.3	125.
PP, oriented	.4	150.
PET (polyester)	1.3	5.
Nylon	25.0	2.6
Aluminum foil	.007	.004

Abbreviations: PE=polyethylene, PP=polypropylene

Packaging films will exhibit different degrees of resistance to moisture vapor transfer, and will differ in their barrier properties to oxygen (and other gases), light, hydrocarbons, etc. They will also differ in cost depending on their specifications for base stock or resin (whether made of polyethylene, oriented polypropylene, nylon, etc.), gauge or thickness of film, coatings applied to the film, etc. Typical values for moisture and oxygen barrier properties of six kinds of base stock are shown in Table 35.1. The moisture vapor transmission rate is stated as the grams transmitted across 100 sq inches of film in 24 hours at 100°F and 90% RH, while the oxygen transmission rate is the cubic centimeters of oxygen transferred across 100 square inches in 24 hours at 23°C and zero RH.

A wide variation in properties of the different plastics is clearly shown in the table. Also shown is the lack of any obvious correlation between MVTR and oxygen transmission rate. The most nearly impervious film is aluminum foil. As might be expected, the thickness of a plastic film is related more or less directly (but not linearly) to the rate at which water vapor and oxygen gas can diffuse through the film. This gauge effect is shown in Table 35.2 (data adapted from Kale 1987).

Coatings are applied to the surfaces of films for three main purposes, improving the sealing properties, establishing a better substrate for printing inks, and/or improving the barrier characteristics. Saran is often used as a coating because of its superior barrier qualities. In Table 35.3 is shown the effect of applying three types of coating to an oriented polypropylene film having 0.4 MVTR and 150 oxygen TR in its uncoated state.

As implied by the preceding data, barrier properties may be changed in a desired directions by specifying base material, thickness, and coatings. Lamination of two or more films may also be used to modify barrier, sealing, and visual properties of the finished structure. Few, if any resins possess all of these qualities to an optimum degree. Shortcomings of one film may be compensated by using combinations of materials. Thus, the lack of strength and rigidity in one transparent film may be overcome, at least partially, by using bands or trays of tougher materials. Laminating of two or more films, particularly of aluminum foil with plastic, is a way of taking advantage of the best qualities of several materials. A brief survey of several basic packaging materials is given below.

Table 35.2. GAUGE EFFECT IN ORIENTED POLYPROPYLENE FILMS

Thickness, mils	MVTR	Oxygen TR
0.45	0.9	330
0.75	0.5	200
1.0	0.4	100

Cellulosic Materials

Among the flexible films that have been used for bakery products are cellulosic materials such as white bakery stock paper, waxed paper, cellophane, and glassine, and combinations of these materials with plastic or foil. Of course, other flexible cellulosic materials have been used in minor amounts or in experimental packages from time to time. A few decades ago, waxed paper was practically the only film used for bread packaging, and a minor amount is still used for that purpose. It was first supplanted by cellophane, then polyethylene became widely used, and finally polypropylene gained considerable popularity. Each of these films has some desirable features and some disadvantages. Cost ranks high on the list of factors the bakery manager considers in choosing a packaging material.

Bleached sulfite paper (usually 28 lb basis) is used for bakery bags in many retail and a few wholesale operations, primarily to package crisp-crusted breads such as French or Italian. In the wholesale trade, untreated paper may be glued into bag form on bag-making machines. This paper has no heat-sealing properties. For retail operations, bleached sulfite paper may be treated with hot melt wax to retain freshness of product. Coating is applied to one side only and penetrates the rather porous paper. This kind of paper can't be printed in bright and vivid colors due to its porosity. The chief advantages of the material is its high "breathing value" (rapid rate of gas transfer) and its wide and traditional acceptance for certain types of bread when unwaxed, and its low cost, whiteness, and good quality retention characteristics when it is waxed.

Table 35.3. EFFECT OF COATINGS ON BARRIER PROPERTIES

Coating	MVTR	Oxygen
Heat seal material	0.4	150
Saran	0.35	2
Metallizing	0.1	3

Greaseproof papers and glassine are not often employed by wholesale bakers for bread packaging although a few in-store bakeries use bags made of them for packing French bread and similar specialty items. Cookies, crackers, pastries, and brown-and-serve rolls are still packaged to some extent in greaseproof papers or glassine. Greaseproof paper is made from cellulose fibers that have been digested for a relatively long time during the pulping process and consequently retain a high moisture content after they pass through the paper-making machine. Glassine is prepared from greaseproof by a procedure that includes a supercalendering step in which application of heat and pressure makes the fibers mat densely and become rather transparent. Manila glassines range from a moderately dark brown to a very light amber in color while bleached glassine is virtually colorless.

Neither glassine nor greaseproof offers much resistance to the passage of water vapor, but coatings can be applied to improve this property. As indicated by the name of the basic material, these papers are quite resistant to the absorption and transfer of fatty materials ("grease"). This property is attributable to the high degree of hydration of the cellulose fibers. Protection against the transmission of off-odors and off-flavors is said to be good, but this presumes the existence of a good seal, which is a problem with both greaseproof and glassine.

. These two materials are not heat-sealable. Coatings of wax or lacquer can be applied to remedy this defect. They can be efficiently printed, except when coated, so they are printed before coating. The basis papers are obtainable in a weight range of 20 to 45 lb per ream (laminated) and as sheets or continuous rolls.

Vegetable parchment was developed to replace animal parchment, which is a thin, dried, treated animal membrane (often a layer taken from a cattle hide). It is made by immersing sheets of unsized paper in a bath of concentrated sulfuric acid, then washing and drying the sheets. Properties of the parchment are dependent to a considerable extent on the type of fibers laid down in the base sheet, but include greater grease resistance and higher mechanical strength than found in the base sheet. The reacted sheet can be plasticized, waxed, creped, or modified in other ways. It can be used as an extra bottom sheet in packages of bakery foods that are particularly greasy, but it is quite expensive per unit area.

When cellophane was first offered to bakers, there were only a few types available. Today suppliers offer many varieties with a wide range of properties. The film varieties are commonly identified by a combination of letter and number symbols that indicate some of their properties. For example, all heat-sealable coatings have an "S" in their number, while "P" indicates a plain film without coating or heat-sealing properties. "M" denotes moistureproof qualities, "T" signifies a clear or transparent film, and "C" is used for colored films. "A" indicates an anchored coating (which can be used for frozen foods), and "K" is a symbol applied to cellophanes that have vinylidene chloride coatings. The so-called PT cellophanes were never of any value to the baking industry because they would not heat seal and had high MVTR, contributing to rapid drying of the products. Coated cellophanes of certain types overcame these disadvantages and have been widely used for bakery food packaging.

Cellulose film has a grain direction resulting from the manufacturing process. It is weak across the grain and relatively strong in the other direction. In use, it is run through the wrapping machines in such a manner that minimum stress is placed in the cross-grain direction. If it is stored for long times at low humidities, the film can lose part of the 5.7% to 6.0% moisture content it needs to remain reasonably limp and pliable. Cellophane accepts printing inks readily, and has an unrivalled transparency that adds to the attractiveness of the package contents. For most baking applications, cellophane has been supplanted by polyethylene and polypropylene, which have much lower MVTR and can be almost as transparent as cellophane.

Paperboard is similar in protective characteristics to the flexible paper materials described previously. Both made from a suspension of wood pulp, which may be regarded as an impure preparation of chemically-treated cellulose fibers. This pulp is deposited on a moving screen or other apparatus that allows most of the water to drain off and provides a support for the web of paper or board until it dries. The amount of fiber deposited in a given area determines whether the product is called paper or paperboard.

Special properties can be given to paperboard by adding different ingredients to the pulp or applying them to the wet sheet. Among the grades of board are SBS (solid bleached sulfate), clay coated, calendered, and newsboard. To be suitable for use in making a folded box, paperboard must be able to withstand a 180° fold without cracking. Board meeting this requirement is called "boxboard." Bending paperboard is generally classified as (1) boards produced from waste papers and (2) boards produced from virgin chemical pulps. Some of the many types of the first class are called bending newsboard, bending chip, solid kraft lined chip, bogus kraft lined chip, white patent coated news, white clay coated news, bleached manila lined news, manila lined news or chip, and white vat lined news or chip. These usually have one side or neither side coated, but on demand both sides can be coated, White patent coated and clay coated boards are compatible with high fidelity printing processes. Types of chemical pulp boards include bleached or semi-bleached, cylinder coated or fourdrinier produced, coated or uncoated. Plastic films can be applied to paperboards to give moisture and grease resistance, better appearance, special printing properties, sealing capabilities, and other features.

Plastic Resins

Thermosetting and thermoplastic are the types of plastic commonly used in food-contact applications. The former is primarily found in re-usable plates, cups, and other dishes that do not have to withstand cooking temperatures, and for bottle caps and the like. Major varieties are phenolic, urea, and melamine resins. They will not be discussed further because of their very limited use in commercial packaging of bakery foods.

Thermoplastic resins can be softened or melted by heating and then become stiffer when cooled. It is this category that contains nearly all the resins used for food packaging. At room temperature, different resins assume different degrees of rigidity, some being quite stiff while others are soft and flexible. The cooling curve as well as the final temperature affect the mechanical properties of the finished structure, since stiffnes is related in part to the extent of "crystallinity" developed in the plastic. For some resins, the softening and stiffening cycle can be repeated many times without causing significant changes in their physical and chemical properties. Excessive heat treatment will, however, cause darkening and other changes in most thermoplastics.

Many of the the resins approved for food contact purpose are used largely in the form of films. Porner and White (1972) suggested that, to be successful, a film intended for packaging foods must have the following characteristics: (1) Good moisture barrier properties, (2) Aroma barrier properties, (3) Grease resistance, (4) Barrier properties against absorption of off odors, (5) Light resistance, (6) Acceptable coefficient of friction, (7) Good bond strength of coatings, thermal strips, and laminations, (8) Absence of blocking, (9) Good rigidity, (10) Good sealability, (11) Good appearance and feel, (12) Abrasion resistance, (13) Good machinability, (14) Good low-temperature durability, (15) Resistance to high temperature and humidity, (16) Toughness and tenacity, and (17) Protection of product freshness. Some of the most important members of the thermoplastic group of resins will be discussed in the following paragraphs.

Ethylene vinyl acetate is particularly suitable for the extrusion coating of paper, paperboard, and other substrates. It adds impact strength, softness, and flexibility.

Ethylene vinyl alcohol is a hydrolysed copolymer of vinyl acetate and ethylene. Its chief contribution to multiple film structures is to improve gas barrier properties. Rigid retort trays and aseptic packages without foil layers are being thermoformed from structures containing EVOH. This resin has limited use in packaging bakery products.

Mylar is a strong, tough, clear polyester resin. Uncoated mylar is used primarily as a substrate for laminating or coating with other materials. It promotes ink adhesion. Metallized coated and uncoated mylar films provide visually attractive packages and have excellent barrier properties.

Nylon is a family of compounds, some members of which have been used as one or more of the layers in composite films used to package foods.

Some have excellent gas barrier properties even after retorting, and are described as possessing high tensile strength and low water absorption.

Polycarbonate is a high clarity plastic, very tough, rigid, and dimensionally stable. It has been used for 5-gal drinking water carboys. Its cost is relatively high and it absorbs water vapor.

Polyesters are condensation polymers synthesized by reacting one or more dicarboxylic acids with one or more glycols. When biaxially oriented, PET resins provide a very good barrier against transfer of odors and oils. Thye can be used in trays that can be heated either in conventional ovens or microwave ovens, when properly conditioned and formed.

Polyethylene is a polymerized form of ethylene. The major classifications of importance to the packaging technologist are high density and low density. In general, high density (or linear) polyethylene is stiffer, tougher, denser, and more opaque. Low density is softer, more flexible, less crystalline, and more permeable to gases and moisture. There is also a medium density polyethylene, similar in many respects to the low density form. Polyethylene is used in great volume for packaging applications, being made into films, sheets, coatings, molded containers such as bottles and jars, lids and other closures, and liners. LDPE finds its greatest use in preformed bags for bread and the like because it is not stiff enough to run satisfactorily on most bread wrapping equipment. Medium density films combine good heat sealability with good stiffness, while high density films offer superior stiffness but comparatively poor heat sealability.

Cast polyethylene is a form that has been extruded, while molten, through a very narrow slit and immediately cooled by passing it over chilled metal drums. Oriented films are extruded by a different apparatus in which they are stretched in either one or two directions as they solidify. This orientation has very significant effects on many properties of the film.

Linear low density polyethylenes (LLDPE) are copolymers of ethylene and alpha olefins. Properties of these substances can vary substantially depending on the ratios of the materials and the conditions of manufacture. More on this subject can be found in the article of Parikh and Knight (1988).

Polyethylene can be drawn into very thin films and is satisfactory as a bread wrap at 1 mil, or even less, thickness, while many alternative materials have to be thicker to function satisfactorily. Some equipment can run 0.85 mil films while others require 0.95 or even thicker materials. As a rule of thumb, about 30,000 sq inches of 1 mil film can be obtained from one pound of plastic.

Polypropylene is a polyolefin somewhat similar in its properties to polyethylene, but is considerably stiffer and much tougher than either kind of PE. It also has superior machinability. PP films are available in cast oriented, cast coated printed, oriented coated, and laminated oriented forms. They are commonly used in 0.87 and 1 mil thicknesses, but can be obtained in other calipers. It has outstanding toughness and a stiffness that makes excellent end folds possible. Its higher sealing temperature and wider sealing range simplify equipment operation. Because of its toughness, the cutoff requires heated knives, preferably with acurate temperature controls. Cracking at low temperatures was a negative feature observed in some early films, but formulas were modified to overcome this disadvantage.

Polystyrene is made by polymerization of styrene using a peroxide initiator. Polystyrenes are light in weight per unit volume, have good processibility, can form rigid containers, exhibit glossy surfaces, and are relatively cheap. General purpose styrene is brittle, cracking readily when distorted, but it is glass-like in its transparency, has high dimensional stability, is odorless, and contributes no off-tastes. It has a relatively high WVTR. Modified, or so-called "impact" polystyrene, has improved strength and is not as brittle as the general purpose variety but it has reduced clarity. Extruded foamed polystyrene is used in thermoformed cups, etc.

Polyvinyl chloride or PVC is made with a wide range of toughnesses and flexibilities. MVTR is moderately high for flexible types and moderate for rigid varieties. These films are not widely used for baked goods.

Polyvinylidene chloride, PVDC or Saran, is used for films and coatings. Barrier properties are dependent on its copolymer content and the amount of additives. It is a heat sensitive material that gives off hydrochloric acid when it decomposes, but it has outstanding moisture and gas barrier properties, and is used to pack many kinds of foods including bakery foods.

Surlyn resins are derived from ethylene methacrylic acid copolymers. Some of the important properties of Surlyn films are low temperature sealability, outstanding hot tack, formability, toughness, clarity, oil and solvent resistance, and excellent adhesion to many other packaging resins. Other properties found in composite films containing Surlyn are low temperature impact resistance, puncture and abrasion resistance, easy deep draw, high melt strength, direct adhesion to foil and paper by extrusion coating and to nylon and other polymers by coextrusion, low sealing temperature, high sealing strength, transparency with low haze, and outstanding hot tack.

Table 35.4 (adapted from Butler 1984) summarizes the properties of materials commonly used for coating composite packaging structures.

Metal Films

For all practical purposes, aluminum foil is the only metal film used by the food industry in laminations for flexible packages. Some attempts have been made to laminate steel films with plastics such as polyethylene, but it is believed such materials are not commercially available at present. Aluminum foil is made by passing strips of the metal between a series of polished steel rollers until very thin webs are formed. Thicknesses from 0.00025 to 0.0015 inch have been used in bakery product packaging.

Pouch materials commonly include aluminum foil having a thickness of 0.00030 to 0.00035 inch. Foil adds great moisture transmission resistance. "Dead soft" foil is often used for flexible packages, but trays and the like require a harder foil to give increased stiffness. Unsupported foil wrinkles and tears easily, and for this reason, and to obtain seals, it must be laminated with other materials when used as a wrapping film. For bakery goods, it is often combined with paper, cellophane, polyester, and PE.

Table 35.4. COATINGS USED IN COMPOSITE STRUCTURES

Material	Primary purpose of the coating	Common method of application*
EVA copolymer	Heat sealability	Ext., Solv.
PVDC	Moisture & oxygen barrier, heat seal	Solv., aqueous soln.
Ionomer	Grease resistance, heat sealability	Ext., Solv.
Paraffin waxes	Low temp. heat seal, moisture & oxygen barrier	Melt., Solv.
Cellulose nitrate	Machinability, heat seal, grease resist.	Solv., aqueous
Alkyd amines	Gloss, TR*	Solv.
Silicones	Slip, release	Solv.
Polyester urethanes	Gloss, TR*	Solv.
LDPE	Heat sealability	Ext.
Polypropylene	High temp. heat seal	Ext.
Ethylene acrylic acid	Grease resistance, heat sealability	Ext., Solv.

* Abbreviations: TR = thermal resistance, Ext. = Extrusion, Solv. = organic solvent, Melt. = applied in molten form.

Laminations of aluminum foil with plastics are not much used for bread wrappings, except for some of the higher priced specialty loaves, but they have found a place in wrappers for other bakery products. A suitable foil lamination is virtually impervious to moisture vapor and grease and can be very attractive. Lack of transparency can be a disadvantage, however.

Technological advances have permitted the production of films coated with very thin layers of metal deposited from the vapor state. Buffed-on metallic dusts have also been used. The vacuum-coated materials, usually called "metallized" films, are being used extensively for candy packaging and for some specialty bakery items. Their principal advantage is added attractiveness; they do not add much to the film's resistance to transfer of moisture and oxygen.

PACKAGING EQUIPMENT

According to Manno (1966), the first commercial bread package (tied with a string) appeared in 1899, the first nonadjustable overwrap machine was reported in 1912, and the adjustable machine was marketed in 1925. Sliced bread appeared a little later, along with the first use of cellophane as a wrapping material. End labels were added in 1937. Ten years later, fortified waxes began to be used as improved coatings for the paper, and in 1958 plastic films were first used commercially for wrapping bread. In 1964, or thereabouts, some bakers started packaging bread in premade bags closed by tying or applying clips to the open end. Then came the simulated bag (a folded package sealed at one end) formed on a modified bread wrapping machine to which had been added an attachment for clipping or tying.

Variations in these bread bagging and bread wrapping machines are still being used for packaging millions of loaves of bread every day. The principles of operation of this equipment and some characteristics of currently available models will be discussed in this section Other types of equipment have been developed for packaging cakes, snack cakes, cookies, crackers, pizzas, doughnuts, and many other kinds of bakery products. The range is too great to cover in the available space, but examples of the most important types will be described.

Bread Wrapping Machines

In almost all modern bread baking plants, the bread wrapper is closely connected to the slicer. Not only does this arrangement avoid unnecessary conveyor lengths (always a good planning principle) but the transfer of sliced loaves is kept to a minimum, thus reducing opportunities for the slices to become disorganized. Units in which the slicer and wrapper are mounted on one framework provide the ultimate in integration of these functions. Flexibility of layout is not generally impaired by such designs, since a loaf is never sliced without being wrapped. It is true, of course, that some loaves are wrapped without being sliced.

Simplest of these units is a hand-wrapping machine, in which a loaf passes through a reciprocating slicer and then is delivered to the hands of the operator, who uses a folder jig and hot sealer plate to package the bread. Such units can be found in small retail bakeries. Equipment used in whole-sale factories is completely automatic and operates at a high rate of speed.

Basic mechanisms found in all automatic bread wrapping machines are the feed conveyor and guides, the elevator or lifting table, the folding mechanism, the heat-sealing stations, and the cooling plates. The infeed conveyor consists of flight plates supported and advanced by a pair of chain belts or link belts. It receives the loaf from the slicer and carries it into the wrapping machine. If slicer and wrapper are combined, the need for a sepa-rate conveying unit it eliminated. Sliced loaves are held together either by adjustable railings on each side of the conveyors or by flexible metal plates placed so as to compress the loaves slightly, insuring a tight wrap.

The lifter table or elevator receives the loaf either directly from the infeed chains or as the result of the action of a pusher plate and arm. As the loaf advances into the elevator, it moves into a pocket of packaging film that has been formed by retractable fingers. At this time, the film is cut to a predetermined length. The elevator now lifts the bread so that the paper or film is drawn across the top and passes down the trailing edge of the loaf.

Subsequently, the direction of travel of the loaf is reversed and the loose edge of the packaging material is drawn beneath it so that the film overlaps the outer cut edge.

Wrapping machines use tuckers to make end folds. The first fold is made by tucker blades or plates that are attached to, and sit astride of, the elevator that raises the loaf for the final heat-sealing operation. The bread is moved up 6 or 12 inches while being held by the initial tuckers and pressure plate, for action by the second set of tuckers. Three other folding operations follow to complete the wrapping operation. The third set of tuckers folds the side, while the fourth set folds up the bottom of the end folds. The sealing stations consist of electrically-heated plates, rollers, or belts. Resistance heating elements are usually employed; other options include infrared heated platens or Teflon-covered mesh belts contacting the film.

End labels, which give added strength to end seals, are attached before the package reaches the cooling plates. The labels can be affixed either by heat sealing or by adhesives. The latter materials are of two types, adhesives activated by heat and applied by conventional end labelers and permanently tacky substances that are protected by a release-backing until the moment of application and require the use of auxiliary equipment.

Top labels, coupons, and similar inserts are deposited on the loaf as it enters the conveyor leading from the slicer. Depositing devices range from relatively simple designs which "deal" labels from the bottom of a stack to more complex machines that use vacuum cups to transfer the leaflets, etc.

Bread Bagging Equipment

Bagged bread has taken over a large part of the market from wrapped loaves. The fundamental difference between these two kinds of packages is that the wrapped loaf has the film heat-sealed at both ends while the bag has one end closed by a clip or wire tie that bunches the material together 3 or 4 inches from the end. Buying pre-made bags may be more expensive for bakers (as compared to buying wrapping film), but consumers like bags because the reclosure feature is simple and effective. No effective and economical reclosure feature has been developed for wrapped bread.

A variant of the bagging process uses conventional wrapping equipment to form a container folded and sealed at one end and open at the other. The open end is gathered or twisted, then tied or clipped. The same type of films can be used as in standard wrappers, but a wider web is required to give the necessary 3 or 4 inches of loose film past the tie.

Much commercial bread is packed in bags made of polyolefins. Some authentic French bread is packed in paper bags in order to maintain a crisper crust. Bags may be purchased ready-made in wickets, or be made in the bakery from pre-printed roll stock. Wickets are simply bundles of bags held together by a metal fastener. Sometimes the term is applied to the metal rod that holds the bags on the machine. Bags are pulled off the metal clip as required by the packaging device. Among the differences in design between machines is the manner in which the bag is removed from the wicket. One design lets the loaf pusher thrust the bag from the wicket after the loaf has bottomed. Another style depends on the loaf itself pushing the bag off the wicket, while a third type removes the bag before the loaf is inserted in it.

There are manually operated baggers and automatic baggers. Equipment for automatic loading into preformed bags is relatively inexpensive. The two major types of automatic bagging machines are the paddle bagger and the reciprocating bagger. The former uses a pusher plate to insert the loaf into an opened bag while the latter uses a metal jaw to pull the bag over the loaf. Paddle baggers can reach higher speeds and size changes are easier to make, but reciprocating baggers are less subject to snagging.

In the loading process, bags are opened by air jets and held open by metal fingers or scoops while the loaves are pushed in. The cleanliness and dryness of the air affects the quality of the packaged bread, so the compressed air supply must be well filtered to remove oil droplets, water, and odor.

Pushing of the loaves into bags may be performed by overhead arms that move continuously or by reciprocating plates. While the bag is being filled, it is held in place by temporary adherence to metal scoops. When a loaf contacts the end of a bag, it pushes the bag loose from the scoop. Bags made from these machines must meet well-defined specifications for slip and side weld strength. Another system pulls a pouch over the product after the air-inflated bag has been removed from the wicket by a set of guides. A snug-fitting bag of minimum size can be used provided the loaf circumference can be maintained within a narrow range.

Wickets of bags are easily and quickly changed. Some advances in design include a double bag magazine that moves a new stack of bags into place without stopping the machine. In some systems, bags are brought up by a hand crank underneath the stack in use and threaded onto the existing wicket so the bagger can continue without stopping until a size change is required. Paddle baggers can be quickly changed over for a wide range of sizes. Bags are closed with plastic clips or plastic covered metal twist-ties, both being automatically applied.

Bag characteristics that tend to effect packager efficiency are: (1) Physical properties—slip, static charge retention, and tackiness; (2) Bag construction—uniformity of the lip and strength of the weld; and (3) Bag dimensions—symmetry and uniformity of width. If wicket packs are being used, the following factors are also important: (1) The size of the hole and its location relative to the lip and the tear slit, and (2) Alignment of the bags at the wicket. Bags can be fabricated at the bakery from rolls of folded film. This is nearly always more economical than buying ready-made bags and it eliminates the small torn area wher the bag has been torn from the wicket. Disadvantages are the added equipment cost and the problems in adjusting and maintaining the bag former.

Bun Packaging

There are three kinds of packages that have been widely used for bulk buns delivered to restaurants and institutions, particularly to franchised hamburger joints. These are: (1) Returnable cardboard boxes or bins—this was the only method available prior to the 1960s; (2) Disposable box and bag; and (3) Pillow or pouch pack, the application of which may be automated. Both the returnable and the one-way boxes are relatively inexpensive. The reusable type creates sanitary problems of the type always associated with repeated use of a food container. Plastic film packages containing 8 to 36 buns and measuring from 7 by 6 inches to 25 by 38 inches are now the predominant container for institutional buns.

Semi-automatic packagers for bulk buns require two operators for placing the buns in position and one person for taking off the packaged goods and stacking them. Capacities range from 300 to 340 buns per min. Fully automated machines pack buns between two layers of 1 mil polyethylene film. The film layers are then heat-sealed on all four sides to form a pillow pack. The pouch is transported to the customer multi-packed in returnable plastic trays.

In a typical automatic bulk packer, the buns are aligned, accumulated, channeled, metered, sliced, and indexed by the sealer control gate, then fed between two rolls of fill that are side sealed, end sealed, and cut off to form the pouch. Some machines feature hot air side sealers that help produce a tight pack. Alignment may be achieved by moving a series of pegs in a direction opposite to the bun flow or by a slide-type mechanism. One or more filled and sealed pouches (depending on their size), can be inserted into a tray supplied by a feed conveyor.

One of the most modern bulk bun packagers can bulk pack hamburger and hot dog buns at rates up to 800 buns per min. Operation of such machines is basically as follows. Buns flow from the cooling conveyor to the top of an accumulating conveyor. Adjustable guides direct hamburger buns, hot dog rolls, or submarine rolls into rows consistent with the final packaging configuration. A multi-way conveyor moves the aligned buns toward a metering gate. Photoelectric sensors detect the presence of product within the bun guides and electronically control the metering gate to select the proper number of buns for the package. Counted and aligned buns move into the slicing section. For accurate double and single through-slicing, two band slicers with adjustable blade guides and automatic tensioners are provided. Slip resistant conveyor belts hold the top of the buns so they can be sliced evenly and with minimum crumbing. For hinge-slicing of hot dog and sub rolls, a hinge slicer with 5, 6, or 7 blades is available. As the aligned buns emerge from the slicer section, they are pushed forward on the conveyor belt by an overhead brush and regrouped to eliminated any spacing errors. At the same time, side guides move the outside rows toward the center so that the buns are tightly grouped when they move into the film section. After they are wrapped, the buns move into the side-sealing section. The film is tightly gripped and the package is moved forward on the conveyor. During side-sealing, a vacuum system draws air from between the top and bottom film to further tighten the package and help maintain product freshness. As the bun group is conveyed through the film wrap operation, the exact amount of film is fed to the package, cross-sealed, and cut off.

Other Bakery Product Packaging Equipment

Vertical form-fill-seal machinery is widely used for snacks and sometimes for small bakery products such as oyster crackers and small cookies. Croutons, bread crumbs, and stuffing mixes are other bakery-related products that can be packaged efficiently on these machines.

A vertical form-fill-seal packager takes a strip of flexible film and wraps it around a metal tube open at both ends. The two vertical edges of the plastic strip are overlapped and heat-sealed, making the web into a continuous cylinder. A heat seal is made across this cylinder just below the forming tube and immediately thereafter a weighed amount of food pieces is dropped down the forming tube into the closed-off area. The clamp that has made the seal is meanwhile drawing the web downward, pulling more of the film along the forming tube. When it has drawn down a predetermined length, the sealing jaw returns to its original position for another sealing cycle. It makes the top seal of the bottom bag and cuts it off while it is making the bottom seal of the next bag. There are variations in the details of this process, but the basic design always involves forming the continuous strip of plastic into a tube sealed vertically, closing the bottom end, dropping the food particles on top of this seal, then heat sealing the top and cutting off the filled pouch.

Cartoning machines can be categorized according to (1) mode of operation (semi- or fully-automatic), (2) loading direction (vertical or horizontal), or (3) type of motion (continuous or intermittent). A semi-automatic cartoning machine requires the operator put the product in the carton manually. In the fully automatic mode, products are automatically loaded into cartons. Semi-automatic machines are said to be more appropriate when many different sizes are loaded and frequent changeovers are required. They normally complete 30 to 150 cartons per min.

Foil pans are generally sealed by crimping their edges around a precut paperboard cover. There are manually operated crimpers for doing this, as well as semi-automatic hydraulically powered units. Large-scale bakers will use fully automated equipment that can be integrated into the production line. In such machines, containers are automatically deposited into carriers on a chain-link conveyor that carries them through the filling stage. After the containers are filled, an automatic depositer places the paperboard cover on the container. Then, a serrated crimp closure is formed by rollers circling around the package.

BIBLIOGRAPHY

ANON. 1985. Mixing, make-up, slicing and packaging systems. AMF Inc., Richmond, VA

ANON. 1988   Behind package R&D lies consumer attitudes. Food Engineering *60*, No. 6, 64-65

ANON. 1989. Pillo-pak high speed bulk bun packers. Stewart Systems, Plano, TX

ANON. 1991. Nabisco and the three bears. Packaging Digest *27*, No. 1, 66, 68

ANTHONY, S. 1982. Package development. Cereal Foods World *27*, 264-266

ANTHONY, S. 1987. Package testing for distribution. Prepared Foods *156*, No. 12, 88-90

BRODY, A. L. 1989. Flavor interacts with packaging. Prepared Foods *158*, No. 10, 128-130, 132

BUTLER, J. P. 1984. Packaging with films. Packaging *29*, No. 4, 96-101

COPELAND, M. 1988. Consumers and packaging: A love/hate affair. Prepared Foods *157*, No. 10, 92-93

FERRERO, P. 1990. Package for food products, particularly confectionery products such as slices of cake and the like. U.S. Pat. 4,949,839

FOSTER, R. 1989. A guide to the packaging of taste and smell. Converting Magazine *7*, No. 4, 62, 64, 66, 68

JONES, J. P. 1989. Determining tension values. Converting Magazine *7*, No. 11, 64, 66, 68-71

KALE, E. L. 1987. Package power. Proc. Am. Soc. Bakery Engineers *1987*, 64-73

KIEFER, G. J. 1989. The bakery of the future—bagging. Proc. Am. Soc. Bakery Engineers *1989*, 197-203

MATZ, S. A. 1989. Bakery Technology. Pan-Tech International, Inc., McAllen, TX

PARIKH, D. R., and KNIGHT, G. W. 1988. Orientation and structure: Keys to PE film strength. Plastics Engineering *44*, No. 2, 47-49

PELEG, Y. 1990. Microwave composite sheet stock. U.S. Pat. 4,940,867

PORNER, F. E., and WHITE, O. L. 1972. Save time and money by running tests in proper sequence. Package Engineering *17*, No 9, 55-57

SIMELUNAS, W. J., SHOIKET, H. N., and ESPEJO, C. 1989. Automatic direct soft cookie loading apparatus. U.S. Pat. 4,799,583

chapter thirty-six

PRESERVATION METHODS

INTRODUCTION

In the present context, "preservation" means the retardation of any type of staling, including texture staling. Those preservation methods for bakery foods that have received substantial experimental effort and at least some commercial exploitation include low temperature storage (refrigeration and freezing), exposure to ionizing radiation, dehydration, heat treatment in hermetically sealed containers (metal cans, film pouches, and rigid plastic containers), use of special atmospheres, and inhibition of deteriorative reactions by chemical additives. Of course, various combinations of these methods have also been used or advocated.

Freezing has achieved great commercial sucess as a preservation method for baked and unbaked batters and doughs, so more space will be devoted to it than to the other methods. For more detail on any of these techniques, the reader may consult "Bakery Technology" (Matz 1989).

REFRIGERATED DOUGH PRODUCTS

The product originally marketed in this category was soda biscuit dough pieces packed in a composite container consisting of a foil wrapping and a cylindrical fiberboard can with metal ends. The product was well received by consumers, prompting several manufacturers to enter the field. The next step was a proliferation of varieties, and this led to a rather large number of clever modifications of the basic principle, few of which were purchased in large enough quantities to allow their survival.

The three preservation principles relied upon in refrigerated dough distribution are: (1) An anaerobic atmosphere resulting from the replacement of oxygen by carbon dioxide generated by the leavening system; (2) Relatively low water activities in the aqueous phase of the dough or batter; and (3) The low temperatures (32° to 40°F) at which the products are distributed. The initial population of spoilage organisms is kept low by choosing ingredients having minimal plate counts and by processing under sanitary conditions. There is not, however, any special sterilizing or pasteurizing process applied to these doughs.

The equipment for preparing the dough is conventional in design. Packaging involves the use of special cutting machines, devices for placing dough blanks in cans, and modified can sealers for closing the containers. A good example of a continuous automatic cutting and packaging machine was described by Watrous and Hood (1966). The usual container for biscuit and roll doughs is the so-called spiral-wound can having a cylindrical body composed mainly of laminated aluminum foil and kraft paper. The can may contain two or more compartments, one for the dough and another for icings, sauces, etc. The lid is of tin plate and has no sealing compound. It may be enameled on the inner surface, especially if the can is compartmentalized.

Sealing machines are modified to avoid the hermetic closure desired in foods that will be retort cooked; instead, a relatively loose seal is applied to the lid ("clinched") so that gas can escape through the lid-can interstices. Gas can pass through the seam but dough is prevented from escaping by its much greater viscosity. The cans are not completely filled at the time of sealing, but, as the leavening system continues to produce carbon dioxide, the dough expands so that it eventually fills the can completely and exerts a pressure of 5 to 20 lb per square inch against the internal surface. To get this pressure quickly, the gassing reaction may be accelerated by warming the sealed cans at, say, 90°F for a few hours.

Refrigerated leavened batters and doughs for cookies, nut breads, and the like have also been commercially packaged in chubs made of double-wound Saran sealed with metal clips at the ends. The clips are applied to a continuous tube full of the batter, so that diffusion of oxygen and carbon dioxide into and out of the finished container is hindered, not only by the tightly bunched film at the ends of the chub, but also by the dried batter filling the interstices. Steinke (1990) described an improvement on the packaging method by which the amount of batter remaining outside the clip is reduced.

FREEZING PRESERVATION

As a food processing operation, freezing is conducted for one of two reasons: the causing of desirable texture changes, as in the production of ice cream, or the improvement of storage stability. For bakery foods, the second reason is of primary importance. Nearly every variety of bakery goods has been offered in frozen form at one time or another, with the possible exception of low moisture products such as crackers. The technology is not quite as simple as it appears to the novice, however, and many commercial failures have occurred as the result of ignoring some very basic principles. The changes undergone by a product during freezing are rather complex, and it is important to understand them if top quality items with maximized storage life are to be produced.

In the freezing range of temperatures, the water molecules in a foodstuff undergo a change of state. Not all of them are formed into ice crystals, but many of them are. A relatively large amount of energy, called the latent heat of fusion, must be removed in order to change liquid water to ice at essentially constant temperature. For this reason, graphs of time versus temperature of a product held in a suitably chilled environment will show a leveling off of the temperature drop when the freezing range is reached. After all the latent heat of fusion has been removed, the temperature will again begin to drop.

If the liquid water present in a food dissolves some of the other substances, one or more eutectics, or mixtures that freeze at a temperature below 32°F, may be formed. A certain amount of the water molecules in a complex food will never form into ice because they are bonded to other molecules with forces too strong to allow them to migrate to ice foci. One result of these phenomena is that a graph of time versus temperature for a chilled complex food product will show that the line drawn during the freezing process is not straight but shows one or more breaks or steps. Moisture in bakery products will not lose all its liquid characteristics until temperatures considerably lower than 32°F are reached. Leaner doughs freeze solid at higher temperatures, richer doughs (having more solubles) freeze solid at lower temperatures. Many adjuncts with high contents of solubles and certain kinds of hydrocolloids, such as jams, jellies, and certain types of frostings, don't freeze solid until very low temperatures are reached.

It is reasonably certain that enzymatic and microbiological reactions in foodstuffs come to a complete halt when all of the water is converted to a bound form, ice for example. Deteriorative chemical changes such as the development of oxidative rancidity and physical changes such as the growth of ice crystals and the loss of water through sublimation can probably continue in the absence of any liquid water or water-containing eutectic. And, of course, strictly mechanical damage such as breakage is only slightly (or not at all) prevented by freezing.

There are disadvantages as well as advantages in the freezing of bakery products. Not all the reactions that occur are desirable. The principal objectionable changes affect mainly the textural characteristics and appearance of the product. Dehydration of hydrocolloids as ice crystals form cause collapse of gels when thawed. Mechanical damage to microscopic structure as a result of formation and growth of ice can destroy cell integrity in fruits, vegetables, meats, etc. Yeast cells can be damaged due to contact with the highly concentrated solutions formed as liquid water is gradually removed during the formation of ice crystals. Nutritive value, taste, and odor are seldom adversely affected by freezing, however.

Ice crystals are not stable in size. Water will pass in the vapor state between water crystals in frozen foods. As a result of this transfer, which occurs more rapidly at higher temperatures, large crystals will tend to gain water molecules at the expense of smaller crystals. Crystal growth is considered undesirable because large crystals break up the structure of the product and, when they melt, can cause localized sogginess. When most of the ice crystals formed during the freezing process are relatively large, the net translocation of moisture is slow. The surface energies of large crystals do not normally vary over a range that is large enough to cause pumping of water molecules at an appreciable rate. In such cases, the amount of water tied up in small crystals is insufficient to cause much growth even if all of it is transferred to the larger crystals. Growth will be most rapid when the bulk of the water is in the form of very small crystals with a generous sprinkling of substantially larger crystals. Rapid freezing generally causes the deposition of small crystals, since the eutectics formed as the pure water gradually separates out do not have time to coalesce into relatively large pools.

A second important motive for freezing bakery products as rapidly as possible is the existence of a rapid-staling range at cool temperatures, approximately between 20° and 70°F. Between 32° and 36°F, firmness increases about three times as fast as at room temperature. In this range, gelatinized starch retrogrades at a relatively rapid rate and the crumb acquires a harshness and firmness that it will retain in all subsequent steps unless it can be reheated under certain conditions. If the baked product is frozen relatively slowly, it will spend considerable time in the 20° to 70°F range and undergo texture changes that can adversely affect its acceptability even though all other processing steps have been optimal. Staling of this type is not much of a factor in rich cakes, but it can be quite important in bread and other lean products. It has no effect in raw doughs or batters that are baked after thawing.

Freezing Equipment and Methods

Commercial freezing of bakery products is accomplished by either subjecting them to blasts of mechanically refrigerated air or contacting them with liquid nitrogen or cold gas from this liquid or with carbon dioxide.

The older and more common type of freezing unit is the mechanical refrigeration system. These plants consist essentially of: (1) The refrigerant, a substance which is a gas at ambient temperatures and pressures but can be converted to a liquid by moderate pressure increases or temperature decreases; (2) A compressor that raises the pressure on this gas; (3) A condenser in which the hot compressed gas is converted to a liquid; (4) Fans to move ambient air over the hot condenser coils; (5) A reservoir or receiver for the liquefied refrigerant; (6) An evaporator equipped with an expansion valve allowing the liquid refrigerant to lose pressure as it enters the evaporator coils; (7) Fans to move air over the cold evaporator coils; and (8) Pipes, valves, meters, and controls. The basic principle is that the refrigerant is alternately expanded and condensed, taking up heat from the freezing chamber in one case and giving it up to the environment in the other.

Blast freezers consist of an inclosed insulated chamber containing some sort of arrangement for holding and/or conveying the bakery goods while exposing the maximum amount of their surface to the cold air currents, the evaporator coils of a refrigeration unit, and blowers to distribute cold air throughout the chamber. Mechanical freezing plants for bakery foods vary in complexity of design from simple holding rooms with refrigeration units and some method for circulating cold air around the stationary product, to fully automatic conveying arrangements with complicated ducting and fans. The simplest method of freezing baked goods is to place the products on large wheeled racks that are moved into a freezing room or tunnel provided with powerful fans that blow cold air over and around the items. A common air blast temperature is -20°F. The lowest practical temperature for a mechanical freezer system is about -40°F.

A modest improvement on the manual type of operation just described is the buggy tunnel through which racks are pulled at a fixed rate by a lugged motor-drawn chaing. A further advance is the continuous belt freezer consisting of a long metal belt passing through the freezing room. Othr belt-type freezers carry the product under a large number of cold air outlets. In these designs, product is fed onto the conveyor from the makeup line. They are said to be practical only for products having a very short freezing time. Still another type of freezer automatically positions products on moving trays that travel through the freezing compartment before discharging the product onto conveyors leading to the packing area.

Within the last 10 or 15 years, spiral freezers have taken much of the market away from straight line or multiple pass plants. Availability of efficient spiral conveyors have allowed the construction of relatively compact blast freezers having long product exposure paths. These freezers are not necessarily more economical from an equipment standpoint, but they do fit better into plant layouts than some other kinds. According to Gorton (1988), spiral conveyors can alse be used for ambient cooling, proofing, and setting (as of icings).

Although the single spiral configuration seems to be the most common one, the basic design can be formed into two helices to double the freezing path without product transfer from one conveyor to another. Presumably, additional multiples of helices could be constructed. There are two major types of conveyor driving mechanisms, the self-stacking and the cage-driven. In the former, the belt is constructed with flange-like vertical side links. When the belt is coiled into a spiral, each higher run rests on the vertical side links of the tier below it, so that no stationary rails or supports are necessary. Motive power is applied to the bottom tier and the remainder of the belt is carried along by it. In cage-driven systems, the helix is wrapped around a rotating cylindrical drum or "cage." The force driving the spiral belt is provided by friction between the inside edge of the belt and the outside surface of the rotating cage. The belt rests on slide rails made of ultra-high molecular weight polyethylene, which provides a tough long-wearing support with a low coefficient of friction. When it leaves the cage at the product outlet point, the belt is taken up from the cage by a separate drive, thus maintaining proper belt tension.

Bobbin-driven systems are a variation of the edge-driven design. By using rotating bobbins located along the inner circumference of the belt to provide the motive power, a spiral with oval cross-section can be constructed, economizing on floor space.

The time required to freeze a product can be reduced by: (1) Lowering air temperature in the freezer; (2) Improving cold air circulation by (a) exposing more product surface to the air current, (b) increasing air velocity, or (c) increasing air turbulence; (3) Reducing the distance-to-center in the product shape, i.e., making it thinner in one or more of its dimensions; (4)

Reducing the moisture content; and (5) Freezing the unwrapped product, or, if that is not possible, minimizing the free air space in the package or making the package of foil.

Freezing Doughs and Batters

Frozen doughs and batters have two major applications: (1) as a means by which a baker can prepare a quantity of raw material before the day when finished products are to be made, and (2) as retail products that will be finished by the consumer. Use of frozen dough as a reserve for baking purposes is rather uneconomical and time-consuming. Short term storage at refrigerator temperatures (retarding) is often practical for the average baker, but long term freezer storage ties up costly space. Both retarding and freezing require extra equipment and handling, and the energy cost is not negligible. Also, quality deterioration may occur, although this can often be recovered when proofing, making up, and baking the thawed dough.

The advantages of freezing are easier to document when frozen doughs are prepared in a central factory and transferred to bake-off installations in supermarkets and the like. Large quantities of dough can be prepared at one time in the central bakery and finished in units which may not have specialized mixing or make-up equipment. Better quality control can be enforced, since it is very difficult to adequately supervise the one or two person crews in the outlying bake-off shops and the fewer operations these usually untrained workers have to perform, the better the finished product.

Consumers benefit from the availability of frozen doughs. Bread doughs, pizza doughs, and bread roll doughs in frozen form give the consumer an opportunity to place "freshly baked" products on the table without going through the time-consuming, difficult, and messy steps of weighing out ingredients, mixing doughs, and bulk fermenting. Frozen roll doughs are, however, in direct competition with brown-and-serve products which often give comparable or better results without requiring as much work.

Yeast-leavened doughs.— Nearly all bakery technologists who have done extensive testing of frozen dough preparation have emphasized the need for minimizing fermentation prior to freezing. For example, Boyd (1980) said, "It has been found that when fermentation is allowed for any extended period of time, the dough becomes quite vulnerable to freezer damage. A straight no-time dough is used to obtain the stability we are looking for." One effect of over-fermentation is a weakening of the dough structure. A possible cause of this weakening is release of reducing substances by yeast cells that have been killed by the freezing process. The same weakening effect is observed when active dry yeast is used, a well-documented phenomenon. More recent versions of ADY with higher activity levels may not be so damaging.

Little or no floor time is normally given to bread doughs which will be frozen. They are taken to the divider immediately after having been dumped from the mixer. The dough pieces are then rounded and carried directly to the molder. The sheeter roller gap is widened so the dough will be flattened just enough to curl satisfactorily. After the loaf is molded, it can be Placed in a plastic tray with molded pockets that fit each loaf so that the dough pieces retain a uniform shape while going through the blast freezer.

Typically, trays are placed on a spiral conveyor that carries them through a blast of -30°F air moving at about 35 mph. Freezing time is 50 min under these conditions. During this treatment, the dough is "crust frozen." It will have a soft core about one inch in diameter in the middle of the loaf. After the product has been packaged, it is placed in a storage area held at -10°F and held there for at least 24 hours before it is shipped. Yeast viability is greatly reduced when dough is exposed to very low temperatures.

In a fairly recent discussion of the preparation of frozen bread dough either for later finishing in the bakery for for retail sale as dough, the following points were emphasized by Marston (1979). The dough should be fully matured, molded, and shaped before freezing. It should be completely developed in the mixer, but should undergo a minimum of yeast activity and gas generation. Storage life is improved by a minimum time interval between wetting the dough ingredients and freezing the fully prepared dough. For these reasons, a rapid or "no-time" process of dough development and maturing is the most suitable method for frozen or retarded dough. Preparation and maturing of dough by longer fermentation, either with a straight dough or a sponge-and-dough process, is less satisfactory.

When using a no-time dough method, the dough can be prepared about the same as for normal breadmaking, but the finished dough temperature should be relatively low. The effect of this temperature difference on dough consistency should be taken into consideration because the dough must be in suitable condition for molding within a few minutes after completion of mixing, yet be firm enough to retain its shape until it is frozen. A finished temperature in the range of 68° to 77°F is satisfactory. After the final molding, freezing of the dough pieces should commence without delay.

The most effective producton method, according to Marston, uses both a fast freezing chamber and a low temperature holding or equilibration room. Initial freezing is carried out on trays in a blast chamber equipped with either mechanical refrigeration or a cryogenic system. Plastic forms placed on the freezing trays are useful for maintaining the molded cylindrical shape of the dough pieces. The outer portion of each dough piece should be frozen rapidly, and the whole mass quickly chilled to the point at which a layer of hard, frozen material extends some 3 to 4 mm deep all around the piece and it is sufficiently rigid to be handled without distortion.

Once the interior of the dough piece has been reduced in temperature to approximately 32°F and the outer shell is sufficiently firm, reduction of the interior temperature can continue in a holding room at -4°F. This two-stage freezing operation reduces the time each piece of dough is held in the main freezing chamber, increasing both the plant throughput and product quality.

Unless the rigid surface-frozen dough pieces are placed directly into the baking pan, they should be filled into strong, moisture-proof bags prior to transfer to the cold storage room. Packaging materials must maintain flexibility at the low temperature of storage. Polyethylene film, plain or coated with polyvinyl chloride, is reasonably satisfactory.

The thawing and proofing steps required for making a frozen bread dough ready for the oven are undoubtedly regarded by most consumers as annoyances and inconveniences. Several inventors have secured patents on methods and formulations claimed to yield doughs that reduce the time required for thawing and proofing. In the patent of Felske and Silva (1988). the loaf can be proofed for 60 min in a warm oven before baking temperatures are applied. To make the dough, standard bread ingredients are supplemented with a hydrocolloid and a fermentation aid composition. The latter mixture seems to be a kind of fermented brew that has been dried to 4.5% to 9% moisture content. Hydrocolloids of choice are xanthan gum and various substrates that have been acted upon by specified microorganisms.

Although the quality of French bread baked from dough that has been frozen for some time is dependent to a large extent on oven conditions, as is that of all French bread, a reasonably good loaf can be prepared in home kitchens. One producer of frozen French bread dough (as reported by Jackel 1985) states that it is important to have a strong gluten structure. The following formulation guidelines are given: (1) Use a strong flour—12% to 13% protein content—and add 2% of vital wheat gluten; (2) Set absorption at 58%; (3) Add 90 to 100 ppm ascorbic acid; (4) Use 8 oz sodium stearoyl-2-lactylate per 100 lb flour; (5) Level of yeast—presumably compressed—should be 5%; (6) Add sugar and oil at 1% each and salt at 1.75%; and (7) Up to 20 ppm potassium bromate may be used if needed—larger additions will tend to inhibit yeast action after frozen storage.

Important processing considerations are: (1) Dough should be well-developed and brought out of the mixer at 72° to 74°F; (2) Dough should be divided and made up as quickly as possible, with no floor time, to overcome excess gassing; (3) Freeze fast, at -25° to -30°F, it is only necessary to fast freeze the crust; (4) Package the product immediately from the fast freezer; and (5) Place the packages in the holding freezer (0° to 10°F) and keep them there for 24 hr. When using a blast freezer, the conditions recommended are 45 to 80 min dwell time, depending on piece weight, at approximately -35°F, with a wind chill factor of approximately 100°F below zero. This type of freezing procedure is said to reduce dehydration and minimize the formation of large ice crystals. The producer claims this dough has shown good strength after extended shelf life in the freezer.

Doughs for other variety breads, such as rye, whole wheat, wheat, and raisin breads, should contain added vital wheat gluten (about 2%) to offset the loss in dough strength that occurs upon freezing.

To adapt a regular pizza dough for a frozen product, the following changes (compiled by Jackel 1985) have been recommended: (1) Increase yeast 30% to 50% to make up for cells killed during freezing; (2) Use 1.75%

to 2% salt; (3) Increase oil to 1.5% for better lubrication of gluten during proofing after thawing; (4) Use a good dough conditioner such as sodium stearoyl-2-lactylate to help lessen the shock of freezing and give strength and tolerance to the dough system; (5) Add 0.25% to 0.4% yeast food to help the yeast during thawing and proof periods. On processing the dough, these procedures will give good results: (1) Mix the dough cold—65° to 68°F; (2) Mix to full development, using a dough developer containing sulfite or cysteine, if necessary; (3) Allow only enough floor time to relax the dough enough for accurate scaling and good make-up, no more than 5 min; (4) Freeze immediately after processing; and (5) Thaw in a retarder 8 to 12 hr on a rack for the minimum time needed. If necessary, round thawed dough piece again and allow it to relax before hand make-up of the pizza crust.

Chemically-leavened products.—Many types of chemically-leavened batters and doughs are being sold in frozen form. A large part of this volume is cookie dough, most of which is used by the small "boutique" cookie shops. The leavening system is critical. One producer recommends a leavening system of sodium aluminum phosphate with sodium bicarbonate for soda biscuit doughs and corn bread. With such doughs, a pastry flour having 9% to 10% protein is often used.

A fairly good business seems to exist in frozen baking powder biscuits, baked, unbaked, and provided with fillings such as sausage and eggs. A recent patent describes a method for manufacturing a pre-baked chemically-leavened biscuit (Carroll 1988) that can be heated in an oven to give a product with crust and crumb characteristics closely resembling those of a freshly baked biscuit. Briefly, in this process a baked biscuit pre-form is tempered or moisture-treated to raise the moisture content of the top crust to above 16%, preferably above 20%. Moisturizing is accomplished by spraying water droplets on the crust or by exposing the biscuit to an atmosphere of high relative humidity. The treated product is frozen and distributed through commercial channels. Purchasers can place the biscuits in their ovens without the need for a defrosting step.

Frozen pancake batters that can be thawed and poured directly from the container onto a griddle have considerable convenience appeal, and have enjoyed a modest commercial success. They seem to have suffered to some extent from competition with pre-baked pancakes, French toast, and waffles which can be reheated in microwave ovens. The convenience of the latter items can hardly be matched by any other form except perhaps a product that can be heated in a toaster.

Typically, pancake batter will be mixed by conventional equipment, then passed through a heat exchanger to reduce the temperature, after which the batter will be filled, sealed, and coded by a standard milk packaging machine. The cartons are manually cased, then conveyed to a distribution center for frozen storage.

The market for frozen cake batters, muffin batters, and the like seems to be virtually non-existent.

Freezing Baked Products and Adjuncts

Because of the short storage life of freshly baked bread, any method of preservation that makes it possible to hold loaves for long periods is of great importance as a possible means of reducing stale returns. Mild cooling and distribution via the dairy case is not the answer—cold but unfrozen bread becomes stale (texture-wise) in much less time than bread held at room temperature. The maximum rate of staling for standard bread occurs at about 28°F. If bread is stored at 0°F or below, however, the rate of staling is very low. At -30°F, bread remains in good condition after a year of storage, provided the packaging is suitable. Since staling takes place most rapidly during the first few hours after baking, bread should be frozen as soon as possible after it comes from the oven.

Commodity-type white bread sold through supermarkets and most other retail outlets does not have a price/profit structure that will support the added cost of freezing and frozen distribution. Bakers find it preferable to accept a small number of stale returns rather than freeze their bread. There is very little doubt that consumers also prefer fresh distribution and probably would do so even if there was no cost differential. For specialty bread loaves—dietetic formulas, "natural" or "organic" recipes, richer formulas, and unusual shapes and flavors—freezing may be an acceptable alternative to other means of distribution. As the current market situation proves, frozen distribution of many kinds of pre-baked sweet and other dessert items is well accepted by manufacturers, retailers, and customers.

Prebaked products generally pose fewer problems in freezing and frozen storage than do unbaked doughs and batters. Those baked products with fillings, icings, and toppings are exceptions, because these adjuncts tend to be sensitive to freezing. In any case, it is important to take the baked product rapidly through the staling range by completely freezing it in the shortest possible time. The two-stage freezing process sometimes recommended for unbaked doughs is definitely not suitable for baked products. If possible, baked products should be frozen before they are placed in the carton or pouch, although there is little hindrance to cooling if they are frozen in aluminum containers. Both air blast and cryogenic freezers are satisfactory, although each has different advantages and disadvantages.

When frozen cakes were first introduced, some producers tried to use the same formulas for batter and icing that had been successful for cakes distributed in the traditional manner. Complaints about dryness of the cake and hardness of the icing were frequent, however. Improvement was obtained when the moisture contents of both icing and cake were raised. Moisture levels of 27% to 32% in layer cakes and 17% to 20% in buttercream icings are considered desirable. Pre-gelatinized starch and certain other colloids can be used to hold the moisture in bound form, restricting vapor phase translocation during storage.

Their high content of sugar and other solubles reduces the freezing point of most cakes to 15°F and under. The freezing points of some typical varieties made by traditional formulas was shown to be 15°F for chiffon cakes, 12.5°F for angel food cakes, 4°F for yellow layer cakes, and 2°F for pound cakes. As formulas vary, the freezing points will also change.

Mixing, make-up, and production processes for doughnuts that are to be frozen are not much different from those used in making doughnuts for fresh sale (Shannon 1981). It is important when producing doughnuts for freezing that moisture be bound in fillings and toppings by using appropriate emulsifiers, starches, or gums. Coating sugars of all types are tolerant to freezing and thawing processes. Sugar glazes and icings low in shortening have a tendency to become brittle and crack when frozen. Icings high in shortening are more suitable. Fruit fillings should be prepared with a freeze-thaw stable starch. Pectin fillings can generally be used with no changes. Doughnuts should be frozen before any kind of packing is applied. Shannon (1981) recommended a six month expiry date, with a possibility of going to eight months if conditions can be rigidly controlled.

Cryogenic freezing.—The two major categories of food freezing equipment are mechanical (contact or air blast) and cryogenic. Cryogenic freezing relies on liquid nitrogen or carbon dioxide as the source of cold. Nitrogen is purchased from firms that make a business of liquefying air and selling the oxygen from it to steel mills, welders, etc. For large, regular users of liquid nitrogen, installation of on-site equipment to liquefy atmospheric nitrogen is a feasible alternative. Carbon dioxide is obtained from various sources (underground deposits, by-product of fermentation, etc.) and purified, then compressed for storage in steel cylinders or as dry ice that can be transformed into liquid in converters operating in the 1,000 lb per sq inch range. Liquid nitrogen is shipped to customer plants in insulated containers or railroad cars, then stored at the plant in insulated tanks with distribution piping.

Liquid nitrogen will be at about -320°F and some of it remains in liquid form for a time before it finally boils away in the freezer. Carbon dioxide, as it it delivered on the product, will be at about -109°F. It is in liquid form in the pressure cylinder but flashes into solid form ("snow") as it emerges from the freezer nozzles. Carbon dioxide cannot exist as a liquid at atmospheric pressure, regardless of the temperature. Also the substance cannot exist as a liquid above 88°F, regardless of the pressure.

Pound for pound, nitrogen is a more effective refrigerant than carbon dioxide. One user reported that an 18 oz piece of dough will be frozen in about 12 to 18 min by nitrogen and about 22 to 30 min when carbon dioxide is the freezing medium. this compares to about 60 to 70 min required to freeze the same type of dough piece in a blast freezer having a -20°F airstream moving at 700 to 800 fpm.

In some of the original experiments on freezing with liquid nitrogen, the food was immersed in the liquid. Although extremely rapid freezing did occur, some disadvantages were noted. Violent boiling at the interface resulted in reduced contact between the article and the refrigerant, so that the full cooling potential of the liquid was not realized. Products cracked and surface layers peeled off because of thermal shock and violent contraction of the outer surface. These observations led to the development of systems in which the products were precooled with nitrogen gas and then either sprayed with liquid nitrogen or completely frozen by the gas.

The mechanical part of these installations consists of a conveying system (usually a wiremesh belt) operating inside an insulated tunnel. In order to take full advantage of the refrigerant capacity of the cold gas, a recirculating system is used to move it at high velocity over the products. The gas is exhausted near the entrance. It is not economical to recycle the gas, so the relatively warm nitrogen is vented to the atmosphere.

One type of installation that has been used successfully for several years is the Cryotransfer process of Liquid Carbonic Co. In this equipment, liquid nitrogen from the supply tank flows directly into an external, vacuum-insulated nitrogen reservoir or sump at the exit end of the freezer. Liquid nitrogen is usually under pressure of 10 to 20 psig at the storage tank, sufficient to transfer the liquid under the conditions existing in the usual installation. A centrifugal pump in the external reservoir pressurizes the liquid nitrogen (then at -320°F and atmospheric pressure) to between 5 and 7 psig and pumps the liquid into spray manifolds above and below the product. Nitrogen that remains liquid after spraying is accumulated in a collector pan and flows back into the external reservoir for recirculation.

There may or may not be economic advantages in using cryogenic freezers as compared to mechanical freezers. Their main advantage is the improved product quality that often results from extremely rapid freezing. Although the advantages of rapid freezing may be greater for particularly sensitive products such as shrimp and strawberries than for bread and cake, improved quality can often be demonstrated in the latter types of food. For example, cryogenic freezing confers the following benefits: (1) The product is rapidly brought through the zone of maximum texture staling so that minimal starch retrogradation occurs and much of the original softness is retained; (2) Proliferation of spoilage microorganisms, such as can occur in cream fillings, is greatly reduced; (3) Original flavor is sealed in by rapid surface hardening; (4) Dehydration is reduced; and (5) Crystal size of the ice is smaller and more uniform.

HEAT PROCESSING IN HERMETICALLY SEALED CONTAINERS

Bakery products can be preserved by enclosing them in containers that are then hermetically sealed and heat treated. Heat treatment for pasteurizing or sterilizing can be combined with the baking conditions necessary to convert a dough or batter into a finished food. The usual container is a round metal can, that is, a "tin can," but flexible pouches and flat metal pans shaped like steam table pans have also been used.

It is very difficult to bake doughs and batters inside hermetically-sealed cans because of the gas evolution that occurs. Some success has apparently been achieved by careful control of the amount of leavening and moisture, both of which are reduced from normal levels, and sealing the un-baked dough or batter under vacuum. Evidently, no commercial products of this type are being made. Instead, commercial and military canned baked products rely on baking the dough or batter in a can with a loosely clinched lid, sealing the can while hot, then cooling the can and contents.

A practical system for large-scale production of canned bread using a minimum of specially designed equipment involves the following steps: (1) The dough piece is proofed in a unsealed can until it reaches a volume known to yield a baked product that completely fills the container; (2) A lid is loosely clinched on the can, leaving a passage-way for egress of gases but effectively confining the dough completely within the can as it continues to expand under the influence of heat; (3) The can and its contents are baked in a conventional oven until the dough has filled the can and has "set up" so the crumb has a normal bread structure; (4) The can is hermetically sealed immediately upon its removal from the oven, so as to minimize the intake of contaminants from the atmosphere and to ensure the development of a high vacuum; and (5) The can is quickly cooled to develop a high vacuum within the container and to prevent heat damage, such as excess browning, in the bread. The method must be combined with formulation principles that give a finished product having water activity and pH within specified ranges.

The anaerobic atmosphere within the container tends to favor the growth of food poisoning organisms such as *Clostridium botulinum*. A combination of heat treatment, low water activity, and pH adjustment must be carefully developed for each product. Much additional information on this subject is contained in the book, "Bakery Technology" (Matz 1989).

MODIFIED ATMOSPHERE PACKAGING

Controlled atmosphere packaging (CAP) is the enclosure of food pro-ducts in variable gas-barrier materials which selectively control the gaseous environment so as to increase shelf life. Modified atmosphere packaging (MAP) is the enclosure of food products in packages made of gas barrier materials, in which the gaseous environment has been modified at the start so as to slow respiration rates, reduce microbiological growth, and retard enzymatic spoilage, with the final effect of lengthening shelf life. CAP seems to be of value mostly for raw meats and fresh fruits and vegetables where the product itself significantly influences the composition of the gases around it—this method seems to have little value for bakery products. Therefore, the following discussion will concentrate on MAP technology.

MAP has received an amazing amount of attention from technical and marketing people in the baking industry. The idea of modifying the gas phase in a container in order to extend shelf life is by no means new. It is in fact very old, having been used in prehistoric times to preserve olives and wine, among other things. The recent flurry of activity is probably due mainly to the availability of new types of plastic containers that can retain a mixture of gases free from interchange with the atmosphere for a long time.

Critical factors influencing the success of storage life extension include the pH and water activity of the product, the presence of antimicrobial additives or preservatives, and the respiration rate of the product itself. Often a single gas will be used, but the most common practice is to use a combination of carbon dioxide, nitrogen, and oxygen. If some oxygen is present, carbon dioxide evidently has a retarding effect on many spoilage that grow at refrigerator temperatures—the mechanism is not known. Nitrogen acts more or less as an inert diluent to reduce the concentration of oxygen and other gases in the package and to keep the container from collapsing as the carbon dioxide dissolves in the aqueous phase of the product. Oxygen inhibits the growth of anaerobic pathogenic organisms, but otherwise tends to decrease shelf life. A mixture that has been suggested as suitable for many nonrespiring products is 75% carbon dioxide, 15% nitrogen, and 10% oxygen. Modified atmospheres can be placed in the container by such methods as snorkel vacuum and back-flush, chamber vacuum and flush, use of engineered permeability films, and use of interactive inedible components (Hotchkiss 1988).

The package itself is a very important part of the system. Among its characteristics that affect the success of the process are headspace, form, resistance to damage, and selective permeability to gases and vapors. Headspace is related to the amount of gas that can be applied. Permeability affects the length of time the gas composition remains within a desirable range of compositions. Contours and dimensions of the container and the product determine contact of the gas with the food and gas flow within the package. Storage temperature is also very important. MAP is not a substitute for proper storage temperature. The effectiveness of MAP is decreased as the storage temperature increases because the solubility of the gas in the liquid phase decreases with increasing temperature.

In one study conducted in the UK (Smith *et al.* 1987), gas packaging was investigated as a means of extending the ambient temperature shelf life of intermediate moisture cream-filled and fruit-filled bakery products. Shelf life crumpets reached about 14 days before they became unacceptable either due to the development of mold spots or the production of carbon dioxide by lactic acid bacteria, the latter leading to puffing of the packages. Apple turnovers became unacceptable after about 18 days as the result of carbon dioxide production by yeasts. Mold growth limited the shelf life of gas packaged crusty rolls to 14 days. The authors used Response Surface Methodology to show that storage temperature, levels of water activity, and pH were the most important factors controlling the shelf life of crumpets. When this product was reformulated to give optimum levels of water activity and pH, then packaged under a suitable carbon dioxide concentration, its shelf life was extended beyond 21 days. Similar extension of shelf life for apple turnovers was obtained when ethanol modified atmospheres were used, while the shelf life of crusty rolls was extended beyond 60 days by incorporating oxygen absorbants into the gas-packaged product.

CHEMICAL PRESERVATION

Discussions of methods for the chemical preservation of foods generally concentrate on means for preventing microbiological deterioration, and particularly, the preventing of food poisoning resulting from the activities of yeasts, molds, and bacteria. Bakery foods lose their acceptability, or "spoil," for reasons other than proliferation of microorganisms, however, and it is worthwhile to consider how chemical additives can retard texture staling.

Bread is supposed to be soft, crackers are supposed to be crisp. Hardening of bread and softening of crackers are therefore deteriorative processes. Changes in water content can be the cause of these changes, and for low moisture products a gain of a few percent of moisture is about the only texture deterioration that occurs. Hardening, or toughening, of bread is more complex. Certainly, the loss of moisture will cause bread to become tough, or if it is carried far enough (as in the preparation of toast or croutons), to become crisp or hard. Even in the absence of moisture loss, however, bread crumb tends to become tougher with time. Temperature has an effect on the rate of this process, and, oddly enough, refrigerator temperatures accelerate it. When bread is solidly frozen, however, the reaction causing this change is brought to a very low rate or perhaps prevented entirely.

Texture staling of this type is thought to be due to a change in the status of starch molecules. As bread is baked, part of the starch is gelatinized and the long strings of glucose residues that compose the starch molecules become highly hydrated and disorganized with respect to one another. After the temperature of the bread drops to room temperature, or below, the conditions for hydration of the starch molecules is less favorable and they are less mobile. The net effect is that these molecules tend to become associated with one another in ordered arrays. It seems reasonable to call this aggregation a kind of crystallization (it is commonly called retrogradation). It gives a stronger and less mobile framework throughout the bread and this is perceived by the consumer as toughness and as an indication of staleness.

This texture change is one of the reasons for the very limited shelf life of bread. Many attempts have been made to develop ingredients or processes that will cause bread to remain soft longer, thus increasing consumer satisfaction. For example, monoglycerides of fatty acids apparently form a sort of clathrate or other association with gelatinized starch, and significantly retard the development of retrogradation. They have been used for many years as additives for the purpose of retaining softness. Other additives that improve initial softness and, at least under certain circumstances delay texture staling are sodium stearoyl lactylate, propylene glycol monostearate, and sorbitan monostearate.

Moisture loss or gain can be prevented by inclosing the product in a well-sealed film that is substantially impervious to moisture vapor transfer. For ordinary bread, the polyolefin bags and wrappers that are so predominant in bread packaging today are satisfactory. Of course, there will still be moisture transfer between various parts of the bread. The top layers of the crust are substantially completely dehydrated as the bread emerges from the oven, while parts of the crumb will contain around 40% water. As the bread cools, moisture redistributes, the crisp crust accumulating water and becoming soft and the crumb losing a little water. There seems to be no practical way of stopping this transfer of water molecules.

IRRADIATION

All irradiation currently being done uses either high energy electrons produced by machines or (usually) gamma rays produced by cobalt-60, a radioactive isotope of that element. Radiation dosages applied to the food or other substance can be measured by a number of methods and have been expressed in "rads." Recent publications use the SI unit of absorbed energy, the "Gray" (abbreviated Gy), which is equivalent to 100 rad. Very low doses of 5 to 10 krads inhibit sprouting of root crops such as potatoes with little effect on other characteristics of the product. The vegetable's ability to heal cuts is somewhat compromised by the treatment, however. The same low dose range also inhibits elongation and curvature of asparagus spears.

Higher levels of radiation are required to kill insects. A dose of 5 to 75 krads will stop insect development and reproduction, but may allow some of the pests to live and contaminate the product, and the food may itself be seriously damaged, especially if a fresh fruit or vegetable is involved.

Radiation doses of 175 to 200 krads will control postharvest fungi, but may also cause undesirable changes in texture, appearance, and flavor. Nutritive properties of the irradiated items may also suffer as a result of vitamin destruction. Radiation dosages in the range of 2,300 to 5,700 krads combined with heating will destroy microbiological life so that foods can be stored at room temperature for years without being spoiled by mold, yeasts, or bacteria. Of course, the food has to be in a hermetically sealed container when irradiated as there is no protection against subsequent contamination.

The preservation of bakery foods by treating them with ionizing radiation has been the subject of many studies conducted by U.S. government agencies and by industrial organizations. There is no clearance by the FDA for treatment of any bakery product by ionizing radiation and, so far as is known, no applications have been made by industry for clearance of a commercial bakery product. There have been discussions relative to approval of irradiated products of the bakery food type for Armed Force's rations.

Experimental treatment has involved exposing baked products to electron beams and cobalt-60. Because of convenience and lower initial cost of equipment, the latter method has usually been chosen. The effect of radiation on flavor, appearance, and texture depends, of course, on the dosage applied, but the results are seldom favorable. At high levels, browning reactions and development of stale flavors are often observed. It is believed that proper formulation and processing of the baked product combined with irradiation at low temperatures can minimize the undesirable changes.

OTHER METHODS

Reducing water activity to low levels is a common method of preserving bakery products, though the dehydration is frequently done primarily for reasons other than preservations. Crackers, cookies, pretzels, croutons, melba toast, flatbreads, and many kinds of snack products are given long shelf lives by bringing them to moisture contents below 5% during the baking process. The principal reason for baking these products almost to dryness is to give them the crispness and crunchiness the consumer expects.

Combination products such as the breakfast (toaster) tarts filled with jelly-like mixtures and sometimes partially covered with icing as well as small snack cakes and tarts, such as the familiar 2 to 3 oz pecan pies and the creme-filled or marshmallow-filled sponge cakes, rely on controlled water activity to give all of the components microbiological stability. Patents have been granted on pastie-like or burrito-like snacks filled with cheese or other savory mixtures and preserved by control of water activity and the use of chemical preservatives (see, for example, Kingham, *et al.* 1988). When designing these products, it is very important to consider the possibility that water may translocate from one of the components to another, causing a susceptibility to mold growth (or to bacterial or yeast attack) in the latter. It is certainly possible that a fruit filling, though stable itself as a result of its high content of soluble solids and its low pH, may contribute enough moisture to the crust to allow mold growth to start.

It may occur to the reader that water vapor translocation could not cause the water activity of the crust to rise above that of the filling since there would be no net flow of vapor from a region of lower to higher water activity. The situation is not quite that simple, however. The pH of the crust (which also affects microbiological proliferation) will almost certainly be higher than that of the filling, and the establishment of water activity equilibrium is not an instantaneous happening. Syrup emitted from the gel as a result of the syneresis that almost always occurs in these systems can soak into the crust causing localized susceptibility to spoilage.

There is really no substitute for actual storage-testing of products formulated, processed, and packaged in the exact manner expected to be specified for the commercial item. Theory will never give all the answers. Storage testing won't give all the answers, either, but it may identify some points that have been missed in theorizing or in studying model systems.

BIBLIOGRAPHY

ANON. 1989. Cryogenic gases improve bagel plant efficiency. Prepared Foods *158*, No. 9, 148-149

BOYD, B. E. 1980. Manufacture and processing of frozen dough. Proc. Am. Soc. Bakery Engineers *1980*, 38-43

FELSKE, L. V., and SILVA, R. F. 1988. Method for producing frozen yeast-leavened dough. U.S. Pat. 4,743,452

GORTON, L. 1988. Freezing takes a spiral turn. Baking & Snack Systems *10*, No. 7, 17-

18, 20, 22

HOTCHKISS, J. H. 1988. Experimental approaches to determining the safety of food packaged in modified atmospheres. Food Technology *42*, No. 9, 55, 60-62, 64

HUNG, Y. C. 1990. Prediction of cooling and freezing times. Food Technology *44*, No. 6, 137-138, 140-142, 144, 146-148, 153

JACKEL, S. 1985. Pizza formulation. Am. Soc. Bakery Engineers EIS Report *70*,

JACKEL, S. S. 1989. The control of bread staling. Cereal Foods World *34*, 430-431

KAMMAN, P. 1990. Frozen dough production. Bakery *25*, No.3, 90, 92

KINGHAM, C. G., CAINE, M., and DUFFIN, V. J. 1988. Shelf stable filled food and method of manufacture. U.S. Pat. 4,721,622

LANG, G. D., FINAN, D. S., and RHOADES, G. D. 1990. Helical conveyor freezer. U.S. Pat. 4,953,365

LANNUIER, G. L., and MATZ, S. A. 1967. Refrigerated dough products. Cereal Foods World *12*, 478-480

MARSTON, P. E. 1979. Frozen dough for breadmaking. Am. Soc. Bakery Engineers Bulletin *213*

MATZ, S. A. 1989. Bakery Technology. Pan-Tech International, McAllen, TX

PSZCZOLA, D. E. 1990. Food irradiation: Countering the tactics and claims of opponents. Food Technology *44*, No. 6, 92, 94-97

SHANNON, T. A. 1981. Frozen doughnuts. Proc. Am. Soc. Bakery Engineers *1981*, 90-97

SMITH, J. P., OORAIKUL, B., and KOERSEN, W. J. 1987. Novel approach to modified atmosphere packaging of bakery products. *In* Cereals in a European context. Edited by I. J. Morton. Ellis Horwood Lt., Chichester, England

STEINKE, G. L. 1990. Chub machine. U.S. Pat. 4,939,885

WATROUS, H.N., and HOOD, C. R. 1966. Continuous dough cutting and packaging. U.S. Pat. 3,273,300

chapter thirty-seven

COMPUTERIZATION IN PLANT AND LABORATORY

INTRODUCTION

It is certainly not possible to cover in the space available for this chapter all the important features of computer design and computer applications in bakery operations. The goals that have been adopted are to give an introduction to the subjects and to suggest sources of additional information for those readers who want to learn more. Brief summaries of the principles of computer operation will be followed by moderately detailed discussions of the type of equipment that has been found most useful for bakery operations. Some specific examples, with evaluations of their advantages and disadvantages, will be included. The articles listed in the bibliography include detailed reviews of topics that it was necessary to treat very superficially here.

COMPONENTS OF COMPUTER SYSTEMS

The elements in any computer system can be categorized as:

(1) Input devices. These devices are needed to transform some aspect of an event happening outside the computer into a set of electrical impulses that can be processed by the computer. The "event" may be the pressing of a button, fluctuations in the intensity of a beam of light, alterations in dimensions of a strain gauge, or any other phenomenon that can be translated into an electrical signal. A keyboard is an input device.

(2) Memories. Information storage facilities that can be in several forms, often semiconductor arrays on a chip or magnetic domains on a disc or tape. Recently, there has been a great increase in the use of optical discs that store data in the form of physical changes on a plastic or metal disc for sensing by optical devices. The memory will include a set of instructions, known as a program, that tells the computer how to perform its functions.

(3) Processor. A collection of microscopic electrical circuits on one or more silicon chips (plus the associated wiring) that processes the incoming signals to yield sorted and identified outgoing signals. The "brain" of the computer.

(4) Control unit. Governs the supply of data to the processor and to the output devices. Also controls the input of program instructions.

(5) Output devices. Translate computer code into a display on a monitor, a printed sheet, a control signal that affects some machinery function, or other useful action.

In addition, there are numerous pieces of auxiliary equipment, either necessary or optional, that aid in networking, restrict access to confidential information, allow use of phone lines for transmitting and receiving coded data, protect the system against environmental hazards (such as static electricity), and guard against excessive fluctuations in the line current.

Many personal computers are sold as a system and include the keyboard, internal memory as well as a flex disc drive (and perhaps a hard disc), a TV-type monitor and a printer (output devices), and cables that connect the units. There will be an internal permanent memory that includes the disc operating system (DOS); this establishes the basic functions needed to access programs. Personal computers of the most advanced designs can have a place in a bakery's analysis and process control, although their memory, speed, and networking capabilities may not be adequate to handle all the tasks encountered in a large or particularly complex plant.

When investigating larger computer installations, one will encounter the terms micro-computer, mini-computer, main-frame, and supercomputer. The dividing line between these classes is not clear, but the progression in the series as stated is from small to very large. Generally, the larger computers are not available as packaged systems; they are assembled from separate units, each obtained from a specialized supplier.

A consultant firm will often be retained to design the system, purchase the separate machines, assemble them into a functioning computer and controller, install the programs, and train plant personnel in use of the system. This process can be very expensive, disruptive to plant operations, and disappointing insofar as results are concerned. It is absolutely imperative to establish rigid cost, time, and results parameters when hiring a consultant firm on a turnkey contract, and to verify the consultant's past achievements and present abilities. Furthermore, reliable and computer-knowledgeable persons should be assigned to constantly police the consultant's activities and results and to report frequently to top management on progress and prospects.

LABORATORY INFORMATION SYSTEMS

Much has been written about the use of computers in laboratory information management systems (LIMS). It is generally conceded that a laboratory of any size needs, as a minimum, some sort of personal computer to acquire data, massage it, and deliver it in statistically-analyzed, reportable form. There are available a number of commercial off-the-shelf systems, which are said (often inaccurately) to be installable by the purchaser as turnkey operations. A good basic system of this type is a few orders of magnitude less expensive than a specially engineered setup, but may not fill all the needs of a bakery, especially if automated equipment is to form part of the network.

Add-on boards are offered by some companies to expand the capabilities of PC/XT/AT type computers destined for laboratory work. One supplier advertises that their boards will "turn your PC's into powerful multifunction analysis instruments, supporting a variety of industrial process control and data acquisition applications." One version is said to give 16 channels of 12-bit analog-to-digital conversion, 2 channels of 12-bit digital-to-analog conversion, 24 bits of TTL-compatible I/O, 5 timer/counters with 1 microsec resolution, menu-driven software, and support for all MS-DOS languages.

The successful utilization of a computer often depends as much on personnel attitudes as it does on the characteristics of the equipment. Misroch (1988) described a strategy or plan for implementing the installation of an LIMS. The salient points of this strategy include:

(1) A detailed functional specification.

(2) The identification of a system manager/administrator. This is mainly neccosary when multi-user systems or a PC network is involved.

(3) A detailed system implementation plan. The LIMS will alter some aspects of the laboratory's operation, provide new capabilities, and give new and different responsibilities to staff members. The implementation plan must smooth the transition from the original system of operation.

(4) A suitable growth projection plan.

(5) All networking and application interfacing requirements. This includes direct instrument interfacing with the LIMS. interfacing of robotics applications, and interfacing to manufacturing and accounting systems.

(6) A sample flow diagram to indicate how samples enter the laboratory, how work is scheduled, how results are entered and validated, and how reports are formatted and distributed.

(7) Information flow diagrams to indicate what information is required for sample identification, reporting, and retrieval purposes.

There is no doubt that many laboratories are successfully using personal computers in an LIMS. Larger units may sometimes be justifiable. Misroch (1988) mentions the advantages of starting out with a mini-computer such as the Hewlett Packard (HP-1000). The larger capacity of the minicomputer, as compared to the usual PC, is valuable, particularly where several users are involved and the sample load is consistently heavy. Selection of software available for LIMS application is large and changes constantly. It is good practice for the lab manager who is designing the system to survey as many software packages as time permits. The efficiency and success of the whole system depends on the selection of software applicable to the problems that will be encountered in the specific laboratory.

The full advantage of data processing by LIMS will not be achieved until it is interfaced with most or all the laboratory instruments. In order to interface an instrument to the computerized network, several problems must be solved. A list compiled by Davis *et al.* (1988) includes these factors:

(1) Compatibility. The instrument interface must be compatible with the LIMS computer. For example, an instrument having a parallel interface can't be connected directly to a serial port on the computer. Computer and instrument must be configured in exactly the same way.

(2) Synchronization. The computer must be synchronized with the instrument output so it is always ready to received data from the instrument. Synchronization may be achieved by defining commands to be sent to

the instrument and markers to define the start and end of messages or packets of data returned by the instrument.

(3) Recognition. It must be possible for the LIMS to recognize data it requires from the instrument. The ability of the computer to recognize the data is dependent on the type of report the instrument is able to supply. The system must be programmed with software enabling it to read a report, e.g., to recognize key words that define the location of a data item in the report.

(4) Identification. After recognizing the data acquired from an instrument, the LIMS must be able to identify the data with appropriate records in its database. The pieces of information required to identify a data item or result are (a) the name or identifier of the sample, (b) the name of the test or analysis, and (c) the name of each piece of data or result if more than one is produced during an analysis.

(5) Implementation. A method of operation must be chosen to define how the instrument fits into the LIMS environment.

Graphical and Statistical Analysis

Simple charts and graphs that give interesting, and perhaps even informative, representations of data collections can be made fairly easily using standard types of software. It is very likely most of these graphs could be made quicker and more elegantly by hand drawing, provided the technologist has a small amount of artistic ability. Complex graphs, such as response surface charts, fishnet graphs, and contour plots, involve somewhat different considerations. Plotting the tremendous amount of data involved and orienting the diagrams by hand can be very tedious. Understanding the software and adapting it to the particular problem can be tedious, too. When a large number of these graphs are going to be made in a continuing project, it is doubtless best to develop a method for drawing them by computer. Producing figures suitable for publication is less satisfactory, though many computer drawn figures can be found in today's journals.

There are many commercial software packages that promise to give versatile charting and graphing capabilities to the PC user, by converting raw data to high quality pictorial representations with little or no effort on the part of the operator. Most of these give disappointing results. Some appear to be essentially fraudulent, in that the examples shown in advertisements or as printed samples could never be obtained on the equipment for which the program is said to be designed. Part of the problem is that very detailed and fine-featured diagrams require an enormous amount of memory just for defining the pixel array or the printed dots. Furthermore, monitors and printers available to most PC owners do not have the capability of transforming the memory data into anything remotely resembling a halftone or a good line drawing. Advances of considerable magnitude appear to be in the offing, however, so it may be possible that, soon after this book is published, software will become available for making excellent quality charts, graphs, and pictorial representations using PCs.

The development of practical and relatively inexpensive optical discs having both read and write capabilities would be a giant step in this direction.

At this time, however, no recommendations will be made. If an immediate procurement is essential, check out the software on your equipment using examples of the data you intend to process. Do not depend on canned demonstrations, which may have taken thousands of man hours to produce and require equipment not available to you.

Collecting and Analyzing Sensory Test Data

Shortly after they became widely available, computers were used for statistical analyses of sensory test data, but the collection of sensory test data continued to be largely a manual operation. Recently, however, a computerized sensory analysis procedure based on an IBM-PC compatible local area network was developed by Findlay *et al.* (1986). Panelist input was simplified by use of a light pen and an interactive questionnaire program. The system was integrated to allow preparation of descriptive, hedonic, triangle, structured, and unstructured ballots; registration of panelists; collection of data; and statistical analysis and report generation. Among the benefits achieved by this system include the simplicity of response for panelists, flexibility for the sensory analyst to design questionnaires, and elimination of the time-consuming manual scoring and data manipulation involved in conventional sensory analysis.

In one use of the system, 26 panelists were divided into four separate groups to evaluate nine sugar cookie formulas. The purpose of the test was to determine optimal dextrose and sucrose levels. It required less than 10 min to evaluate each of the three attributes presented to the panelists. Four samples were presented each time. The accumulated data were analyzed and reported in less than 5 min. To illustrate integrative capabilities of the system, the data set was transferred to a mainframe computer for multiple regression analysis. The resultant data were used to generate three-dimensional response surface plots indicating the effects of the two independent variables on each attribute and permitting optimization of the formula.

Laboratory Robots

A more extensive discussion of robotics will be found in a subsequent section—Computer Assisted Manufacturing—but some space will be given here to robots in the laboratory. In a recent review, Fowler (1988) said there are between 1,000 and 1,500 robots in th 75,000 chemical and physical testing laboratories in the U.S. Probably less than 100 of these robots have a built-in capability to function in a coordinated way with an instrument controller or LIMS.

Fowler says there are three aspects of laboratory automation that can be integrated both conceptually and practically. These are (1) information (data and methods) flow, (2) instrument control, and (3) robotic sample handling. Four key strategic methods an organization can take to move forward in implementing integrated automation are: (1) Adopt a broadly accepted comunications standard; (2) Use instruments with intelligence and communications capability built in; (3) Use a broadly accepted computing platform; and (4) Use modular software split at the highest level by function/workcell supervision vs. peripheral control.

Bibliographic Searches

Almost any kind of computer can, with the addition of a modem, gain access to data banks that, for a fee, provide vast amounts of information on scientific, economic, engineering, bibliographic, and other areas of interest.

An example of the databases accessible by food scientists is Chemical Journals Online (CJO), a subsidiary of the American Chemical Society. This offers a full-text computer-powered on-line search system. It provides a CJO User Manual as well as an occasional CJO Bulletin. This system includes not only all the journals published by the American Chemical Society, but many other chemical and chemical-related journals, truly an enormous resourece for anyone working in these fields.

We are just beginning to see a proliferation of extensive data bases on optical discs. Already available on CD-ROM are the Oxford English Dictionary and some encyclopedias. Technical databases on discs are beginning to appear.

Appropriate software is needed to take advantage of the many data banks that can be accessed by modems. One version, called Scimate by its developer, eliminates the need to know the individual command language of each data base company. A search can be typed on an appropriate screen and then the search is sent electronically to the data base computer. As the search is completed, the program allows the user to save only selected references, store references in subject or project files, print bibliographies, and report and use the references in word processing programs.

COMPUTER ASSISTED MANUFACTURING

Processing

Engineers were building control systems using concepts of closed loop or open loop control before electronic computers and programmable controllers were invented. Computers and programmable controllers use many of these previously derived concepts. A programmable controller consists of logic circuits that function as a closed loop feedback system; it becomes a link in process control. According to Wolfe (1988), new graphics oriented PCs such as the Macintosh II and IBM PS/2 family are well suited as the bases of automated systems. The power of many PCs now surpasses that of conventional dedicated instrument controllers and systems based on mini-computers.

Cooper claims (1984) computerization can be justified because it reduces staff (or eliminates the need for increasing personnel) and yields more information from present staff. The main objectives when computerizing a bakery are:

(1) Choose programs that suit the specific bakery and staff. Look for programs first, then find the computer best suited for running the program.

(2) Be certain the system is easy to use. Pick a user-friendly, menu-driven setup.

(3) Find out if you will get good documentation. The printed material or directions should explain what is being shown in each menu. Documentation should be understandable by a first-time computer user.

(4) The supplier should have a good knowledge of the bakery business, and should also have the ability to support both hardware and software.

Among the production information that can be obtained from computerized production lines are: (1) Instant recap of all products that have been ordered; (2) Bake shop production orders broken down into numbers of racks, pans, and pieces; (3) Batch weigh lists for the mixing room, with formulas and total dough weights; (4) Raw material usage, including number of batches; (5) Packaging material usage; and (6) Cost of the day's bake with labor included. Some of this information will be sensitive and proprietary; confidentiality can be maintained by blocking user access at various levels in the program unless a proper password is entered.

Programmable Controllers

McCaffery (1986) described a high performance programmable controller applied to a bakery production line. As part of its functions of controlling and monitoring all of the key equipment in the plant, the controller can send information to, and receive it from, a personal computer. Components of the system include two high capacity advanced technology personal computers, one located in the production control center and the other in the chief engineer's office. There are ten remote input/output locations, each of which includes input cards, output cards, a rack to plug these cards into, and a serial interface module. The latter device takes the place of the microprocessor in a small independent programmable controller. Its main purpose is to provide a translating device to take signals from the input/output rack and route them through a specially designed coaxial cable that allows communication to remote locations up to 1,000 ft from the controller so that plant layout is not limited by system hardware.

Terminals for operator sending and receiving are located in both the QA lab and the floor control stations. The PC in the engineer's office is mainly concerned with maintenance functions, while the PC in production control primarily logs and records the operating characteristics of the plant (e.g., time, temperature, and humidity). The system can scan all points in 75 milliseconds. Human errors are minimized, according to McCaffery.

As pointed out by Booth (1987), automation of mixing and other bakery processes is best achieved by using a computer that can interface with microprocessors on the production equipment. Control of an automated mixing system can be achieved by interfacing a mainframe or mini- or micro-computer with ingredient dispensing operations and mixer, using a pprogrammable controller. The role of the computer is to: (1) Store recipes and ingredient tolerances that have predetermined as well as inventory data for usage records and re-order purposes; (2) Store and print out batch numbers, batch weights, individual ingredient weights, and batch temperatures; (3) Make changes in recipes, mix times, and temperatures; and (4) Control and monitor the production equipment.

The programmable controller performs the simple logic and sequencing of the system, receiving computer commands and passing them on after making the necessary decisions as to destination, timing, etc. The links between it and the process are sensors and activators. It interfaces with the hardware on the production equipment, opening and closing valves, and actuating the other mechanical devices. It can be programmed using standard relay ladder logic, familiar to most electricians and maintenance personnel.

Programmable controllers can be applied to existing equipment, i.e., retrofitted. If simple control circuits are needed to perform many rapid cycles, a programmable controller may be justified. Most mechanical control devices and switches will wear out after a few million cycles, which can be reached in a few weeks in modern automated plants. An example is a bulk bun packer having controls that may cycle 200,000 times per week. Solid state control devices are not limited by mechanical wear and tear. Cost of a programmable controller can be quickly paid back by eliminating down time needed for replacing mechanical switches.

Programmable controllers are flexible and can be adapted to a different application if their original use becomes obsolete. They are simply programmed to perform the new function. This flexibility is also helpful when add-ons are needed on the original machine. Generally, the controller can be programmed to encompass the additional operations.

Examples of equipment that can be benefitted by applying programmable controllers are pan handling conveyors and bulk flour handling systems. A pan handling conveyor can be improved by using a programmable controller that can count the pans in a certain area and make adjustments based on other factors in the system. This will reduce the number of persons needed to insure that the correct number of pans are on the proper section of the conveyor at a given time, and will give a steadier and more uniform pan flow. Bulk handling systems for flour will require accurate timing and precise control for satisfactory performance. With conventional controls, extra time must be allowed to ensure that the speed of the system is never exceeded. If this margin is not allowed, standard controls will begin to vary the set points as wear occurs, and stoppages may result. A reliable programmable controller will not need safety margins in timing and can make it possible to transport many more pounds of ingredient per hour (Bailey 1985).

Computer-controlled ingredient dispensing allows proportional batching. For example, the amounts of all other ingredients can be based on the amount of flour delivered to the mixer, thus retaining integrity of the ingredient proportions even though flour weight may have been adjusted because of moisture variations, etc. In a typical system, the supervisor selects the type of product to be made by pressing a button labeled with the appropriate name. The product category, a list of ingredients, or possible varieties then appear on the display screen of the instrument panel. Ingredient feeding is then actuated by the operator. As flour is loaded into the scale hopper, the actual weight will be displayed in one column and percentage variance in another column. If the actual amount fed is outside a preset variance limit, an alarm will signal the need for supervisory action. Assuming the flour weight is within acceptable limits, the remaining ingredients will be fed into the scale hopper in proportions adjusted to the actual flour weight. When the preceding batch has completed its mixing cycle and the bowl has been emptied, the total ingredient mix will be dumped into the bowl.

Automated dough temperature systems can be computer controlled. A dual output temperature controller/indicator works in conjunction with a time on the refrigeration system. One set point controls the final dough temperature while the second set point is adjusted to an upper temperature limit considered to represent an unacceptable dough. If the normal mix time is completed at a time when the dough temperature exceeds the upper limit, the mixer will continue running in slow speed with full refrigeration until the dough cools sufficiently to meet specifications. The refrigeration system is controlled by a temperature controller in addition to the programmable controller. The latter device controls the temperature until the mix is about half completed, after which the temperature controller becomes active. This insures that cooling is effective throughout the mixing period (Booth 1987).

From the monitor, visual indications can be obtained of the status of make-up equipment, status of the safey devices, and any failures of components. The advantages of a computerized automated mixing system, as enumerated by Booth, are: (1) Labor savings—no one is in attendance at the mixer; (2) Reasonable cost; (3) Inventory control—provides an accurate, constantly updated record of materials used and materials remaining in stock; (4) Product consistency—insures constant recipe balance regardless of batch size; (5) No formulation change—existing recipes can be kept when a switch to automated mixing is made; and (6) Instant recognition of problems such as tripped safeties and blown fuses simplifies trouble-shooting.

Sensors

Information about the characteristics of the object of interest, perhaps a loaf of bread, a peanut, a sugar solution, or a mixer load of dough, must be obtained from that item before the computer can do its job of analyzing and reporting the information that will be used by someone to evalluate the item or adjust the process which is acting upon it. This information is obtained and transmitted by sensors, of which there are many kinds. Only a few of the types can be discussed in this article.

Sensors are available for detecting temperature, pH, weight, distance, color, pressure, and many other attributes of samples and environments. They provide the computer with digitalized electrical signals that can be processed into a form useful for further handling or for reporting to a human observer. For example, a range or distance detector emits light or sound waves that are reflected from an object and then detected by the sensor. The time required for the light or sound to make the round trip is calculated and transformed by the computer to distance in common units of length. Sensors of this type (usually sonic) can determine dough doubles or detect loaves that are not properly oriented.

Proximity sensors can determine the presence of an object within their sensing area without the necessity for touching the item. The can be used to count pans, rolls, or almost any other object moving along a conveyor. Electromagnetic sensors are used to determine the presence or absence of metallic substances. Temperature sensors include contact types such as thermistors and thermocouples and non-contact types that measure radiation emitted by hot objects.

Chemical sensors convert chemical information into electronic signals. Typically, they are miniaturized devices that perform analytical chemical functions more frequently, closer to the point of interest, and at lower cost than conventional laboratory instruments (Goldman 1988). They are useful in process control and environmental monitoring, as well as in other applications, such as biosensory measurements, which we are not considering here. A chemical sensor is usually composed of a coating, a sensing substrate, a means of transmitting information to and from the remote sensor, electrical or electro-optic hardware to analyze the signals, and a computer for data reduction. Most of them can be classified as optical, acoustical, or electrochemical. A pH electrode and ion selective electrodes are chemical sensors that could be used in process control and lab tests.

Further information on this subject can be obtained from the article by Caro and Morgan (1991) and other papers listed in the biblography.

Inspection

Computers can provide important advantages to inspection systems by processing data obtained on the production line. To fully utilize the capabilities of computers in such applications, it is necessary to eliminate, as much as possible, the human element. Maximum efficiencies cannot be obtained if the computer is used only to collate and analyze measurements fed into the system by people who are looking at, weighing, and measuring product. The best results can be had when measurements are made by automated inspection systems. Such systems require specialized sensors and computers with software that can interpret them.

Egan (1988) quotes the following definition of an automated inspection system from a standard issued by the Automated Vision Association, "Devices used for optical non-contact sensing to receive and interpret automatically an image of a real scene in order to obtain information and/or to control machines or processes." He states that automated inspection offers speed and objectivity that are unattainable with manual inspection. As line speeds increase, it becomes impossible for human observers to make the necessary differentiation between objects on the conveyor. There is no fundamental limit to the speeds attainable with machine vision or automated inspection.

The color of most food products can be determined electronically by measuring light reflectance at one or more wavelengths. Measuring the entire spectrum of reflected visible light is neither necessary nor practical. Caramelization or non-enzymic browning reactions, such as occur in frying foods, are best measured at the longer wavelengths; there is generally a decrease in reflectance in the blue region, some change in the green, and a considerable drop in the red. The latter change frequently continues into the infrared portion of the spectrum (Coatney 1986).

In typical baking reactions, there is little change in the blue region of the spectrum, considerable change in green and red reflectance, and very little change in the infrared. Coatney described the use of the Agtron CA II color sensor in quantifying the appearance of potato chips. This device was developed as an intelligent color sensor capable of full communication with a process control computer system.

Shape and dimensions can be measured by optical sensors. Egan described the need for measuring the height of crackers as they exit the oven. The most important datum is the maximum height of the crackers. Crackers that have excessive thickness will not fit into the box when the predetermined number of units is assembled in the quarter-pound stack or "slug." If the height begins to increase, the computer can signal the sheeting rolls, causing them to make the dough web thinner. It is necessary to measure the height of the product relative to the conveyor, the conveyor itself varying in distance from the optical sensor depending on irregularities in the steel belt, bouncing, etc. Small changes in height (less than 0.003 inch) must be detected, and the sensor must be able to differentiate between bouncing of the conveyor, which is an unavoidable characteristic of the mechanism, and a true increase in cracker thickness.

Modified stock designs of nuclear magnetic resonance (NMR) spectrometers have been used as on-line process control analyzers, but they proved to be too difficult for plant operators to calibrate and they were difficult to maintain. To eliminate some of these problems and minimize the time required to train plant operators in the use of NMR, the spectrometers were designed to include several self-calibrating and self-adjusting features (Pearson *et al.* 1987). Before an NMR analyzer can be used for on-line process control, sampling and control system hardware must also be added. Moisture and oil contents of ground corn and moisture content of tempered wheat were satisfactorily determined by the modified equipment.

A paper by Lawson (1984), which dealt with computer applications in the cookie and craker industry, especially as that industry operates in the UK, describes the use of programmable logic devices to control ovens. This author states that information that can be acquired, stored, and distributed by an oven PLC include fault finding, maintenance procedures, fuel rate, output of product, efficiency of oven, heat exchanger temperatures, band temperature, flue analysis and volume, biscuit dimensions, state of oven, band tension, band wander, and data from other machines such as the forming machine or packer. Measurement of oven humidity can be done directly on line. The humidity of the gas in an extraction duct is representative of the humidity in the corresponding zone of the baking chamber and can be used for determining the adjustments needed to optimize oven conditions.

An instrument that can be used for this type of humidity measurement is based on determining the velocity of sound waves in the gas. Since velocity is dependent on the temperature as well as the humidity of the gas in the duct, automatic compensation is provided for temperature changes. On-line assessment of biscuit moisture may be made using the infrared energy absorption technique. If the sample being tested is irradiated alternately with beams of wavelengths strongly absorbed and weakly absorbed by water, then the ratio of reflected radiation at the two wavelengths is an indication of the moisture content. Since reflectance occurs essentially at the surface of the cookie or cracker, it is advisable to make the measurement just before packaging so the water within the piece has had more time to equilibrate. The technique is affected by formulation, so multiple calibrations may have to be entered into the memory—one set for each formula.

The importance of oven band temperature at the point of cracker depositing is well known. Adjustments to insure uniformity of temperature at this point can be based on measurements made with a spring-loaded temperature probe that presses against the underside of the band. Signals from this probe are used in a control system to modulate the heat input from the band pre-heaters. It is possible to provide a system that allows the oven to be started up and shut down from a remote location. When firing up indirect ovens, the operator would start the band and press a "start heaters" button. Each burner would then come under the control of its own hard-wired ignition sequencer, proving extraction and purging before lighting the burner. Once the burner was established, it would come under the control of the remote temperature controller, and extraction dampers would be driven from fully open to the required operating positions. With direct-fired ovens the start-up would be slightly different in that, once the purging is completed, burners are ignited in small groups. Remote shutdown of the oven would require the oven man to press a "stop" button. All gas valves then close, extinguishing the burners, and the extraction dampers move to fully open so as to purge the baking chamber. The band drive is stopped when the temperature in the baking chamber falls to a safe level.

Robot Operators

Robots have been defined as re-programmable, multi-functional manipulators designed to move materials, parts, tools, or specialized devices through variable programmed motions for the performance of a variety of tasks. The characteristic that qualifies a device as a robot is its ability to operate on its own using a built-in intelligence or a programmable memory or an arrangement of adjustable mechanisms that direct some kind of manipulation (Spooner 1985). From this definition it can be understood that a robot is not necessarily a computer and that it does not necessarily even have to be connected to a computer, but it is a fact that virtually all robots being designed today are controlled by computers.

Robots have been classified as the following types: limited sequence, playback with point-to-point control, and playback with continuous path control. The first type uses a combination of mechanical stops and limit switches to control the movements. These robots have no memory unit and cannot be programmed to perform their task but have to be set up in the same way an automated machine would be adjusted. The second type obtains positional control with a servo system that electrically detects and corrects errors. Memory units must be added to retain electronically all of the position commands before a true robot can be said to exist.

In programming the playback robot, the work cycle must be broken down into steps, and the arm and gripper are taken through the work sequence step by step. Each motion segment is fixed in the memory by pressing a control button. When the learning phase is completed, the robot is switched to an operational mode and will repeat the steps; there is no definition of the path to be traced by the limbs, only the points are fixed.

The first and second types, just described, are probably better described as manipulators than as robots. If it is necessary to control the path traveled by the robot hand as it moves between set points, the playback with continuous path control is used. This kind of robot is programmed in real time—the operator literally takes hold of the robot hand and leads it through the motions it is to perform. The desired speed of movement is also duplicated, so far as possible. During the teaching process, the robot continuously records in its memory the path traveled and positions taken by the arm and gripper. This requires a large amount of memory.

Although the jointed metal arms and plier-like fingers seen in so many TV specials on robots may not be visible in a modern bakery, the automated production lines that have been operating for years have most of the basic attributes of robots. According to Spooner, however, an industrial robot provides some additional benefits over automated machinery. These are:

(1) Availability—it may be possible to get an off-the-shelf (i.e., stock) industrial robot adaptable to an existing or planned production system, avoiding the extensive line design and construction of special equipment that might otherwise be required.

(2) Adjusting and debugging—when conventional automated bakery equip-

ment is installed, indexing devices, solenoids, actuators, and clamping mechanisms must be adjusted on the production floor after delivery, while the robot can be pre-programmed and put into use immediately after it is received.

(3) Resistance to obsolescence—robots provide a form of automation less subject to obsolescence. A robot need not be product- or operation-limited. It can be re-programmed to meet changing requirements.

A suggested bakery application for robots is forming products, such as rolls or loaves of bread, into patterns that can be easily fitted into boxes, bags, and baskets. Pallet loading of the assembled boxes or baskets is a similar task that can be handled by robots. In an operation of this type, stacked empty baskets would enter the plant, pass through an unstacker, trash dump, washer, and dryer, then enter the robotic pattern former and loader. Bread loaves enter the robot directly from the slicer and bagger. After the patterns are formed and baskets loaded, the baskets are discharged onto a conveyor system that directs them to the shipping area.

Some expected advances in robot design that will make these devices more useful in industrial applications are visual recognition and guidance capabilities, tactile sensing, computer interpretation of visual and tactile data, response to voice commands, and total diagnostic fault tracing.

Packaging

Virtually every type of packaging machine can be integrated into a control system that will ensure uniformity of weights, provide efficient channeling of products to the machines, and monitor package characteristics. Topken (1984) described the history of automating and computerizing packaging lines, and the following discussion is based, in part, on his paper.

Early control systems contained operator controls such as start and stop buttons, electrical timing devices with one or more limit switches, electromechanical devices such as solenoids, and the control logic to decide what the electromechanical devices were to do in response to input signals. Most logic operations were performed by relays.

Due to the demand for more automation, sensors were added to the machines and more output devices were added to the system. The output devices included additional electromechanical equipment, enunciators of various descriptions, and production monitors. With more components and electrical connections, reliability became a problem. Changes were more difficult to make because of the complexity of the system.

The programmable controller made the task of designing complex control systems much simpler and less expensive—many of the moving parts and much of the hard wiring were eliminated. As other forms of microprocessor controls became available, they were added to the system. Timing limit switches were replaced with programmable limit switches, which were more reliable. Servo-motors and stepping motors enabled the designers to eliminate bulk mechanical drives. For example, timing controls based on microprocessors maintained consistent patterns of glue on cartons even when the speed of the machine changed. This feature was needed because the speed of machines could change automatically for more efficient operation under conditions of varying product at the infeed.

Sophisticated enunciator systems were designed to help the operator maintain efficient machine functioning. Digital readouts became popular. One result of all these changes was that the operator control station became much more complicated. Elements that previously operated independently are now tied together with a central microprocessor or group of microprocessors. This system accepts inputs from both sensors and operator controls. Custom designed enunciator systems are replaced by cathode ray displays. Complexity of operator controls is dramatically reduced, leaving only four pushbuttons for routine operation. To ease the task of the operators and avoid errors from information overkill, an integrated system should also allow improvements to be achieved through software changes.

EXAMPLES OF AUTOMATED BAKERIES

The first attempt at designing and constructing a fully automated bakery along modern lines was the Kitchens of Sara Lee plant in Deerfield, IL. This operation went onstream about 1964. It is believed it never did achieve the original goals of complete "closed circle" controls, that is, all adjustments to processing conditions being made automatically according to feedback from sensors detecting quality factors in products and intermediates. Nonetheless, design features of this plant that were successful inspired many other innovations in wholesale bakeries.

A description of the Sara Lee plant in 1979 was published by Leonard (1980), and part of the following description is based on that account. The bakery produces 100,000 pound cakes, 77,000 fruit pies, and thousands of other items each day. There are 300 process variables that are controlled. Large-scale ingredients such as flour, sugar, and dairy products are weighed and conveyed to the mixer automatically. Minor ingredients are added manually and reported to the computer. Mixing conditions, including temperature and humidity, are controlled by the computer, as are the settings on sheeting and portion dispensing equipment. Some visual inspections and quality control tests provide data to supplement the information reported by electronic sensors. Packaging, freezing, palletizing, storing, and assembling of orders are largely under computer control. This plant has been closed because of obsolescence.

A modern Pepperidge Farm plant in Lakeland, FL was described by Bush and Lahvic (1989). Operations managers oversee entire processes from ingredient weighing through packaging from computerized stations in a central control room. A mainframe computer stores formulas and process parameters needed to produce 24 bread varieties and 50 cookies and crackers. Terminals monitor and control conveyor speeds, oven temperatures, bake and proof times, package counts, and inventories for bread and biscuit lines. Products are fresh loaf bread, bread rolls, hearth breads, cookies, and crackers. Dry ingredients for each batch are pneumatically conveyed to hoppers directly over the mixer. High speed mixers work the dough until a predetermined amount of energy is measured. The "no-time" doughs are conveyed to track-mounted troughs that move the intermediate to hoppers and dividers in processing lines where the dough is required.

Many of the high volume bakeries that have been built to supply buns to McDonald's and other hamburger-type fast food outlets are substantially completely automated. One of these was described by Gorton (1989). Processing is coordinated by a Westinghouse high performance programmable controller acting in concert with several IBM AT personal computers. The heart of the splant is a interlaced conveyorized proofer and oven. A bulk ingredient system supplies flour to two horizontal mixers, from which dough is moved by an AMF pump to a bun make-up line. Pan flow is automated by a Stewart pan stacker and unstacker. Wrapping, packing, and stacking in the freezer is done automatically, with minor operator attention.

BIBLIOGRAPHY

ALY, N. A. 1989. A survey on the use of computer-integrated manufacturing in food processing companies. Food Technology *43*, No. 3, 82, 84-85, 87

ANON. 1989. Baking the best bun the automated way. Baking & Snack Systems *11*, No. 5, 7, 9. 14

ARNOLD, G. R. 1989. Computer integrated manufacturing. Proc. Am. Soc. Bakery Engineers *1989*, 50-58

ARNOLD, G. R. 1990. More on CIM. Proc. Am. Soc. Bakery Engineers *1990*, 169-179

BAILEY, N. A. 1985. Programmable controllers and existing equipment. Proc. Am. Soc. Bakery Engineers *1985*, 190-195

BLASER, W. W., RUHL, H. D., and BREDEWEG, R. A. 1989. The challenge of on-line analytical instrumentation. American Laboratory *21*, No. 1, 69-70, 72

BOCKELMAN, J. 1990. Quality control brings sophistication to at-line testing. Baking & Snack Systems *12*, No. 6, 20-24

BOOTH, M. D. 1987. Automated high volume dough mixing. Proc. Am. Soc. Bakery Engineers *1987*, 132-144

BUSH, P., and LAHVIC, R. 1989. Pepperidge Farm's "Project Freshness." Prepared Foods *158*, No. 2, 122-124

CARO, R. H., and MORGAN, W. E. 1991. Trends in process control and instrumentation. Food Technology *45*, 62, 64-66

COOPER, M. C. 1984. Computers for the baking industry. Proc. Am. Soc. Bakery Engineers *1984*, 99-105

CURTIS, J. W. 1987. Robotics and artificial intelligence for the food industry. Food Technology *41*, No. 12, 63-64

DAVIS, A., BELTON, G., and MATTHEWS, D. 1988. Interfacing laboratory instruments to an LIMS computer system. Am. Lab. *20*, No. 9, 34, 36-41

DEMING, R., and YOUNG, L. A. 1989. Laboratory computer networking. Scientific Computing & Automation *5*, No. 4, 21-25

FOWLER, B. 1988. Integrated laboratory automation. Am. Lab. *20*, No. 9, 62, 64-68

GOLDMAN, D. S. 1988. Chemical sensor development for process and environmental monitoring. Am. Lab. *20*, No. 11, 102, 104-109

GORTON, L. 1988A. Computers integrate packaging, distribution. Baking & Snack Systems *10*, No. 4, 6-9

GORTON, L. 1988B. CIM put in control at new Danish plant. Baking & Snack Sytems *10*, No. 6, 6-8, 10-13

GORTON, L. 1989. From mechanization to true automation. Baking & Snack Systems *11*, No. 5, 24, 26, 28-29

HAAS, D. J., and MURPHY, L. 1989. Bar codes in the laboratory. Scientific Computing & Automation *5*, No. 10, 49-55

HETTICH, G. 1989. The basics of food automation. Prepared Foods *159*, No. 4, 132-133, 138

HUTCHISON, K. M. 1989. Rapid real-time monitoring and direct data storage techniques. Am. Laboratory *21*, No. 1, 102

JACKEL, S. 1984. Microcomputers, microprocessors, and robots in bakery operations. Cereal Foods World *29*, 258

JONES, G. Y 1985. Introduction to programmable controllers. Proc. Am. Soc. Bakery Engineers *1985*, 177-181

JOYCE, R. 1989. Advances in PC-based data acquisition. Am. Laboratory *21*, No.6, 48, 50, 52-54

LEONARD, L. 1980. The big computer bake-off at Sara Lee. Production Eng. *27*, No. 1, 39-43

MILLER, L. 1991. Computerized quality control system. Food Technology *45*, 102

MISROCH, M. 1988. Planning and evaluating a laboratory information system. Am. Lab. *20*, No. 9, 28, 30, 32

NEWMAN, F. P. 1991. Fourteen shortcomings of current control technology. Control *4*, No. 4, 53-55

PASDIRTZ, G. 1990. Laboratory automation, interface with the future. Hazelton Science Newsletter *34*, 1-5

RYAN, J. 1991. LIMS aid environmental labs. R&D Magazine *33*, No. 8, 59-60

SCHULTZ, T. M. 1987. Computer uses for plant maintenance. Proc. Am. Soc. Bakery Engineers *1987*, 162-168

SELLERS, C., and POPPITI, J. 1989. LIMS the QA equation. Environmental Lab *1*, No. 8, 18-24

SPOONER, T. F. 1985. Robotics. Proc. Am. Soc. Bakery Engineers *1985*, 168-177

SPOONER, T. F. 1989. Sensors emerge for artificial intelligence uses. Baking & Snack Systems *11*, No. 6, 21-24

VAIHIANATHAN, R. 1985. Using sensors in bakery productin. Bakery Production Marketing *20*, No. 2, 110, 112

WALULEK, S. C. 1985. Programmable controllers and energy. Proc. Am. Soc. Bakery Engineers *1985*, 181-189

WILSON, D. 1985. Retrofit equipment with electronics for competitive edge. Bakery Production Marketing *20*, No. 2, 106, 108, 110

WOLFE, R. 1988. New PCs are ideal platforms for automation. Scientific Computing Automation *4*, No. 6, 18, 20-22

YACU, W. 1990. Process instrumentation and control in food extruders. Cereal Foods World *35*, 919-926

YAZBAK, G. 1991. Fiberoptic sensors solve measurement problems. Food Technology *45*, 76-78

chapter thirty-eight

SANITATION AND SAFETY

INTRODUCTION

In the not too distant past, safety and health concerns were not thought of as being properly assignable to the technical departments of a bakery. They were considered as being more appropriately the responsibility of the production executive or, perhaps, the "human resources" group. As laws and regulations increasingly took on a highly technical content, it became necessary to involve scientists, engineers, and technical personnel in interpreting, enforcing, and auditing the sanitation and safety efforts of their company. In many ways, this has been a deplorable trend, since (for example) it has tended to divert the attention of the technically trained people from more creative efforts into routine and paper-shuffling duties. It is less than realistic to ignore these trends, however.

Discussions of sanitation and safety concerns have been combined in this chapter because they are inextricably connected in legislation and regulations intended to protect the health of workers and the jobs of bureaucrats. Due to the limited space available for the discussion, only the briefest of surveys of these two topics can be made.

GENERAL PHILOSOPHY OF HEALTH AND SAFETY COMPLIANCE

The comments under this head are essentially verbatim extracts (slightly edited) from NIOSH Health and Safety Guidelines (Anon. 1976).

Establishing and Managing a Health and Safety Program

Through the use of a health and safety program and actively supported employee training, existing unsafe acts or conditions should become apparent. For many of these there may not be specific standards. Nevertheless, it is important to find a solution to these recognized problems.

During the analysis of the workplace for health and safety problems, it may also become apparent that "the letter of the law" is not being met. This may be particularly noticeable where dimensions are given for ladders, stairs, railings, etc. If it is apparent to all concerned that the "intent" of the law is being met, instead of making changes, a variance may be requested. Considerable discretion must be exercised in this area and the decision not to make changes should be made with the concurrence of OSHA.

When new buildings are being constructed, renovations are being made, or new equipment is obtained, the standards must be followed.

Even where a citation is issued, it is desirable that the employer have demonstrated his willingness to comply with the intent of the law by operating effective, on-going safety and health programs, by correcting imminent dangers in the workplace, by maintaining records of purchases, installations, and other compliance-promoting activities. Therefore, after an OSHA compliance visit and a citation, the manager can substantiate his intent to provide a safe and health workplace for his employees by demonstrating records which document his purpose, and may be given the benefit of having shown "good faith," when penalties are determined.

Hazardous conditions or practices not covered in the OSHA standards are covered under the general duty clause of the Act which states, "Each employer shall furnish to each of his employees employment and a place of employment which are free from recognized hazards that are causing or likely to cause death or serious physical harm to his employees."

An effective method to assist in providing for a safe working environment is through a health and safety program. The purpose of such a program is to recognize, evaluate, and control hazards and potential hazards in the workplace.

Hazards may be identified by investigating accidents, reviewing injury and illness records, soliciting employee input (interviews, suggestions, and complaints), performing self-inspections, using material in the Guide (Anon. 1976), and other information sources. Typical examples are unsafe walking surfaces, unguarded machinery, electrical hazards, improper lifting, air contaminants, etc.

Those situations wich tend to occur most frequently or to cause the most severe problems should be given priority for corrective action. For more complex problems, such as those requiring engineering controls to reduce noise or airborne contamination, outside consultants may be needed.

Management may want to assign safety and health responsibilities in the area of both program development and implementation. Regular meetings or informal discussions can be held to discuss safety promotions, hazards, injury and illness records, etc. To ensure the success and progress of the program, management leadership is necessary. The person assigned responsibility, for instance the supervisor, must be delegated the authority and have management support to carry out the part of the program assigned. Likewise, everyone in the establishment should be aware of the activities of the program through a systematic interchange of information. Employees cannot take an interest in the program if they are unaware of what is occurring. Conversely, well informed employees will likely show interest and desire to participate.

Information of Specific Interest to Food Processors

Experience has shown that, in food processing plants, various factors such as the type of food processed, the seasonal nature of the industry, the long working day, the employment of inexperienced, untrained, and often fatigued workers can contribute to a potentially unsafe working environment.

The most hazardous departments, depending on the types of foods processed, are the receiving, husking, cutting, freezing, canned food processing, and maintenance departments. The following hazards have been observed in these areas.

(1) Broken ladders.

(2) Unguarded or inadequately guarded machinery. For example, belts, pulleys, gears, and other moving parts are exposed.

(3) Electrical hazards. Ground pins are cut from electrical plugs or power tools; extension cords and electrical equipment are not grounded; flexible cords are frayed, damaged, or are used in place of permanent wiring.

(4) Slippery floors. Floors are constantly being washed and so remain wet during the shift. Food spilled from conveyors gets squashed on floors, or grease, such as in deep-frying operations, makes floors slippery. Non-skid flooring is recommended in these areas.

(5) Hazardous maintenance procedures. For example, welding, cutting, or brazing are performed unsafely or the resulting toxic fumes are breathed. Hand tools as well as toxic or flammable chemicals, such as paints, solvents, cleaners, and the like, are handled or stored unsafely.

(6) Foods that contain acids may produce allergic reactions in some employees.

There are some general principles by which a safe environment can be maintained in food processing plants. Injuries can be reduced or eliminated altogether by constant awareness of possible hazards, by employee training directed toward avoiding them, and by the enforcement of established safety rules.

Frequently Violated Regulations

Persons working in food processing plants may be exposed to a variety of gases, dusts, vapors, mists, fumes, noise, etc. The most common exposures are the following, which are listed in alphabetical order.

(1) Ammonia—the most common refrigeration gas used in the food processing industry. Exposures occur most often in the compressor rooms as a result of leaks or when equipment is torn down for repair. Direct contact of liquid ammonia on skin causes severe burns. Ammonia in the vapor state is extremely irritating to the eyes, skin, and respiratory system. When there is a possibility of exposure, an individual should wear goggles or a face shield, rubber gloves, and (at times) a respirator.

(2) Caustics—such as sodium hydroxide are often used in peeling operations. Skin contact causes severe burns. Rubber gloves and a face shield or goggles should be worn when handling caustics. Any of these chemicals that contact the skin must be washed off immediately. A safety shower and eye wash fountain should be installed where caustics are handled.

(3) Chlorine—used in wash and rinse water. It is purchased in the liquid form, as a powder, or as a compressed gas. Respiratory protection should be available where chlorine is used or is stored in compressed gas cylinders.

(4) Carbon monoxide—propane or gasoline-powered forklifts produce carbon monoxide. The employee's exposure to carbon monoxide may be excessive where propane forklifts are used in low ceiling areas, cold storage areas, loading semi-trailers or railroad cars, etc. The use of electric forklifts in these areas eliminates this problem.

(5) Dermatitis—skin rashes can be caused by contact with or exposure to chemicals, microorganisms, foods, or other substances. Some persons may also be allergic to one or more substances. Good personal hygiene and protective clothing can aid in preventing an occurrence of these problems, but, if the allergies continue the employee should be relocated in the plant.

(6) Hot Environments—high temperatures are common in the food processing industry, especially in bakeries. Employees not accustomed to heat should be acclimatized over a period of several days by allowing them to work only a portion of the first day and increasing the work load and exposure time each succeeding day. Cool drinking water and salt tablets should be available to the employees. Engineering controls should be utilized, such as ventilation, to reduce environmental heat and humidity.

(7) Paints and Adhesives—epoxy paints and adhesives are being used in many plants. Where large areas are painted, such as floors, good ventilation is needed and respirators for use with paints should be worn. Skin contact with epoxy materials is to be avoided. Employess should be informed that rubber gloves should be worn and any materials on the skin should be washed off immediately.

(8) Sulfur Dioxide—used as a bleaching agent by some food processors. Sulfur dioxide is irritating to the respiratory tract and when used, respiratory equipment should be available.

(9) Welding Fumes—these gases contain the fumes of the metals being welded together, the filler material, and the coating on the welding rods. When extensive welding is done by an individual, there could be an excessive fume exposure to these materials. Local exhaust ventilation should be provided where extensive welding is done.

(10) Since protective techniques against all chemicals, such as gas, acids, etc., cannot be listed, management should be aware of the substances used in the plant so that proper protection can be provided. However, the above list represents the most common problems observed. Prominent signs should be posted to alert workers to the presence of hazardous chemicals.

Regulations of Special Concern to Food Manufacturers

Under "General Environmental Controls," NIOSH has listed (under the sub-head "Frequently Violated Regulations"), the following points to be taken into consideration by food manufacturers.

(1) Safe drinking water must be provided in all places of employment. The

use of a common drinking cup is forbidden.

(2) Receptacles for waste food are to be covered and kept in a clean and sanitary condition.

(3) Restrooms are to be kept in a clean and sanitary condition, including covered containers for sanitary napkins.

(4) Separate toilet facilities must be provided for each sex. The exception to this is if only one person at a time uses an toilet room and the door can be locked.

(5) One toilet and one lavatory must be provided for approximately every 15 employees.

(6) Each lavatory must have hot and cold or tepid running water, hand soap, individual hand towels, or warm air blowers.

(7) Beverages or food must not be stored or consumed in a toilet room or in an area exposed to toxic materials.

(8) Employees working with toxic substances should wash and remove contaminated clothing before eating, drinking, or smoking.

Recordkeeping Requirements

Recordkeeping requirements under OSHA are intended to establish permanent documentation about accidents that have happened. These records provide employers with a measure for evaluating the success of their health and safety activities and of identifying high risk areas of the business to which attention should be directed. Federal regulations require that employers with 11 or more employees at any time during the calendar year are required to complete OSHA Forms 100, 101 (or their equivalent), and 102. These records must be maintained for five years, excluding the current year. Forms 100 and 101 must be kept current to within six days.

The types of work-related injuries and illnesses which must be recorded are those involving fatalities, lost workdays, or those which are nonfatal and do not cause lost workdays for the employee, but do require medical treatment, job transfer or termination, or resulted in loss of consciousness. Employers are also required to report within 48 hours to OSHA any occurrence of a work-related fatal accident, or an accident requiring the hospitalization of five or more employees. An annual summary, Form 102, must be posted for the entire month of February.

Employers are required to maintain accurate records of certain potentially toxic or harmful physical agents which must be monitored or measured and to promptly advise any employee of excessive exposure and the corrective action undertaken.

For more detailed information, consult the booklet "Recordkeeping Requirements Under the Williams-Steiger Occupational Safety and Health Act of 1970", available from OSHA.

Safe Practices in the Workplace

All firms should make protecting employees from injury one of their top priorities. A safe workplace helps reduce injuries, with their accompanying financial liabilities and public relations problems, improves employee morale, increases efficiency, and minimizes intrusions by regulatory agencies. There is some question about where safety administration and responsibility fits in the table of organization—it is sometimes assigned to the Personnel Department/Human Resources Manager. Less often, the technical manager receives some or all of these responsibilities. It would seem to create conflicts to assign the ultimate responsibility for policing safety operations to the production department.

Industrial safety is an exceedingly complex subject, involving legal, psychological, engineering, medical, political, and financial aspects. Only a few of the engineering-related topics will be touched on here.

Safety Rules

Following are rules published by the Bakery Equipment Manufacturers Association (BEMA); they apply mostly to the operation of machinery. Most of the information on which the rules were based was collected from the American National Standards Institute, APV Crepaco, and FMC Corp.

General safety rules.—These are rules that should be communicated to all employees, and they employer should ensure that the workers understand and obey them. An operating zone should be established around all machines. A brightly painted guard rail or warning stripe should define the zone. Only the operator or other authorized personnel should be within the operating zone when machine control circuits are energized or the machine is running. No tools or other equipment should be kept within the operating zone.

(1) Equipment should not be operated with safety devices by-passed or guards removed.

(2) Only qualified personnel should operate a machine.

(3) Machines should not be started until all personnel are clear.

(4) Service or maintenance procedures should never be performed on a machine in motion.

(5) Most equipment requires a high voltage electrical system. To avoid shock or serious injury, only qualified personnel should perform maintenance on the electrical system.

(6) All air, hydraulic, and electric power must be OFF before servicing the machine.

General operating safety.—The following rules, similar to the above, but relating more particularly to line operations, should be communicated to all employees in an understandable manner.

(1) Do not operate the machine until you read and understand the operating instructions and become thoroughly familiar with the machine and its controls.

(2) Never operate a machine while a safety device or guard is removed or disconnected.

(3) Always wear safety glasses, safety hats, ear protection and other required safety equipment.

(4) Never remove "Warnings" that are displayed on the machine. Torn or worn labels should be replaced immediately.

(5) Do not start the machine until all other personnel in the area have been warned and have moved outside the operating zone.

(6) Remove any tools or other foreing objects from the operating zone before starting.

(7) Absolutely do not have loose clothing unrestrained long hair near operating machinery.

(8) Keep operating zone free of obstacles that could cause a person to trip or fall toward an operating machine.

(9) Never sit or stand on anything that might cause you to fall against the machine.

(10) "Horseplay" around a machine at any time is dangerous and prohibited.

(11) Know the emergency stop procedure for the machine.

(12) Air, hydraulic, and electrical power must be off when machine is not in use. Note: For maximum protection, the power source should be locked out using a lock for which only one person has the key. This prevents anyone from accidentally turning on the power to the machine while it is being serviced.

(13) Never operate machines above specified speeds, pressures, or temperatures.

(14) Never by-pass limit or other safety switches.

(15) Keep alert and observe indicator lights and warnings that are displayed on the machine.

(16) Never leave the machine unattended while the machine is operating.

(17) Do not operate faulty or damaged equipment. Make certain proper service and maintenance procedures have been performed.

(18) Avoid placing fingers, hands, or any part of your body into the machine or near moving parts when control circuits are energized.

Service and maintenance safety.—Persons responsible for maintaining and servicing machinery should be made aware of these rules.

(1) Do not service a machine until you are thoroughly qualified, trained, and familiar with the tasks to be performed. Only trained personnel should be operating machines.

(2) Never operate any controls while other persons are performing maintenance on th machine.

(3) Do not by-pass a safety device.

(4) Always use the proper tool for the job.

(5) Never open covers with power on.

(6) All air and hydraulic pressure must be relieved before performing maintenance or loosening connections on any pressurized system.

(7) Air, hydraulic, and electrical power are to be turned off unless absolutely required for the specific service being required. For maximum protection the power source should be locked out, using a lock for which only one person has the key. This prevents anyone from accidentally turning on the power to the machine while it is being serviced.

(8) Replace fuses only when electrical power is off (locked out).

Electrical safety.—These rules, similar in many respects to the preceding, are to be communicated to electricians and others who must work with electrical circuits.

(1) All electrical/electronic maintenance and service should be performed only by trained and authorized electricians.

(2) Assume at all times that power is "ON." Treat all conditions as live. This practice assures a cautious approach which may prevent an accident or injury.

(3) To remove load from circuit or equipment, open disconnect or breaker and lock in open position. Keeping a switch in open position using a lock for which only one person has a key prevents anyone from accidentally turning on the power.

(4) Make certain that the circuit is open by using the proper test equipment. Test equipment must be checked at regular intervals.

(5) Give capacitors time to discharge, or carefully discharge manually.

(6) There may be circumstances when "trouble shooting" on live equipment may be necessary. Under these circumstances, special precautions must be taken, as follows:

(a) Make certain your tools and body are clear of the ground.

(b) Take extra safety measures in damp areas.

(c) Be alert and avoid any outside distractions.

(7) Before applying power to any equipment, make certain that all personnel are clear of the machine.

(8) Open control panel doors only to check out electrical equipment or wiring. After the panel door is closed, make certain that (on the panels where applicable) the disconnect handle mechanism is operating properly.

(9) Close all covers on junction panels before leaving any job.

Hydraulic system safety.—A slightly different set of instructions was recommended by the BEMA for imparting to personnel who work with pressurized systems.

(1) Never operate a hydraulic system unless covers, safety devices, and indicators are operating and in place.

(2) Never operate a hydraulic system above the pressure specified.

(3) Never allow hydraulic fluid to collect on floors or equipment.

(4) Avoid skin contact with hydraulic fluid. Always wear protective clothing when handling hydraulic fluid.

(5) Never loosen any hydraulic connection when the system is under pressure.

(6) Never operate a machine that has leaks in the hydraulic system.

Cleaning safety.—Two sets of rules have been issued by the BEMA for cleaning safety, one for manual cleaning and one for CIP procedures.

(1) Manual cleaning procedures:

 (a) Do not use toxic and/or flammable solvents to clean a machine.

 (b) Turn off air, hydraulic, and electrical power (lock out) prior to cleaning machine.

 (c) Keep electrical panel covers closed and power off when washing a machine.

 (d) Always clean up spills around machine while it is operating.

 (e) Never attempt to clean a machine while it is operating.

(2) Cleaning-in-place procedures:

 (a) Make certain that all connections in cleaning circuit are tight to avoid contact with hot water or cleaning solutions.

 (b) When cleaning cycle is controlled from a remote or automated control center, establish fail-safe procedures to avoid automatic start-up while servicing equipment in circuit.

Example of a Checklist

The following checklist for guiding food sanitarians making inspections of manufacturing plants has been published by the Public Health Service (Anon. 1976). References found in this checklist refers to the appropriate sections of "General Industry Standards" (29 CFR 1910). All items allow for a "yes" or "no" answer. Due to continual changes in regulations, interpretations, and enforcement philosophies, it is advisable to contact the Department of HEW for the latest version of this checklist and the supporting citations before implementing the following.

WALKING AND WORKING SURFACES

(a) Aisles and floors (29 CFR 1910.22)

 Are all places of employment kept clean and orderly?

 Are floors, aisles, and passageways kept clean and dry and spills cleaned up immediately?

 Are floor holes, such as drains, covered?

 Are permanent aisles appropriately marked?

 Are wet surface areas covered with non-slip materials?

(b) Storage lofts, second floors, etc. (21 CFR 1910.22, .23)

 Are signs showing floor-load capacity present?

 Are platforms, storage lofts, balconies, etc. that are more than four feet above the floor protected with standard guardrails?

 Are all platforms, lofts, and balconies (where people or machinery could be exposed to falling objects) guarded with standard four-inch toeboards?

(c) Stairs (29 CFR 1910.24)

Are there standard stair rails or handrails on all stairways having four or more risers.

Are all stairways at least 22 inches wide?

Do stairs have at least a seven-foot overhead clearance?

Do stairs angle no more than 50° and no less than 30°?

(d) Ladders (29 CFR 1910.25, .26, .27)

Have defective ladders (e.g., broken rungs, side rails, etc.) been tagged as "DANGEROUS, DO NOT USE" and removed from service for repair or destruction?

Do portable rung ladders have non-slip bases?

Is it prohibited to use the top of an ordinary step ladder as a step?

Do fixed ladders have at least 3.5 ft of extension at the top of the landing?

Is the distance between the centerline of rungs on a fixed ladder and the nearest permanent object in back of the ladder at least seven inches or more?

Do all fixed ladders have a preferred pitch of 75° to 90°?

(e) Egress (29 CFR 1910.36-.38)

Are all exits marked with an exit sign and illuminated by a reliable light source?

Is the lettering at least six inches high with the principal letter strokes at least 3/4 of an inch wide?

Is the direction to exits, when not immediately apparent, marked with visible signs?

Are doors or other passageways, that are neither exits nor access to an exit, and located where they may be mistaken for exits, appropriately marked "NOT AN EXIT", "TO BASEMENT", "STOREROOM", etc.?

Are exit doors side-hinged?

Are all doors that must be passed through to reach an exit or way to an exit, always free to access with no possibility of a person being locked inside?

Are all exit routes always kept free of obstructions? •

OCCUPATIONAL HEALTH AND ENVIRONMENTAL CONTROL
(29 CFR 1910.93, .94, .95)

Is management aware of the hazards caused by various chemicals used in the plant (ammonia, chlorine, epoxies, caustics)?

Is employee exposure to such chemicals kept within acceptable levels?

Are eye wash fountains and safety showers provided in areas where chemicals, such as caustics, are used?

Are all containers, such as vats, storage tanks, etc., labeled as to their contents?

Are employees required to wear personal protective equipment when handling hazardous materials (gloves, eye protection, respirators, etc.)?

If internal combustion engines are used, is carbon monoxide kept within acceptable levels?

Is employee exposure to welding fumes controlled by ventilation, use of respirators, exposure time or other means?

Is vacuuming used wherever possible rather than blowing or sweeping dust?

OCCUPATIONAL NOISE EXPOSURE
(29 CFR 1910.95)

If a noise problem is suspected, have noise levels been accurately measured?

If a noise problem exists, have plans to reduce noise levels by engineering methods been formulated (e.g., enclosure, maintenance, different methods of processing)?

SANITATION

"Sanitation" encompasses the concept of cleanliness in preparing, distributing, and serving food, but for the food manufacturer it goes far beyond the usual understanding of cleanliness to include the preventing of (1) the food contamination by any filthy material or adulterant, whether or not that thing is readily detectable by the consumer (or, in fact, is detectable at all in the finished product), (2) early spoilage (however that state may be defined), and (3) the spreading of foodborne diseases by microorganisms in the product. It is important to recognize at the outset that a finding of actual physical harm to the consumer is not a prerequisite to a determination that a foodstuff is contaminated or could have been contaminated by conditions existing at the time and in the place of preparation. Therefore, the sanitarian must be concerned about the quality of food ingredients and food contacting materials (packages, detergents, air, etc.), the conditions existing in the plant and in the storage areas, the training and physiological status of employees, and (to some extent) the conditions existing in transport vehicles, warehouses, and retail facilities to which the finished products are exposed.

Federal regulatory activities in the sanitation field are largely based on the following clauses in the U.S. Food Drug and Cosmetic Act: "A food shall be deemed to be adulterated . . . if it bears or contains any poisonous or deleterious substance which may render it injurious to health . . . [or] if it consists in whole or in part of any filthy, putrid, or decomposed substance, or if it is otherwise unfit for food . . . or if it has been prepared, packed, or held under insanitary conditions whereby it may have been rendered injurious to health . . ." These basic considerations are expanded, elaborated, and confused by state, county, and municipal laws governing the preparation and sale of any commercial food article.

According to a publication of the Public Health Service, FDA (Anon. 1978) "Food sanitation programs should be based on uniform, nationally accepted public health principles and standards. Although the purposes and objectives of all food sanitation programs are the same, local customs and problems necessitate varying the methods needed to achieve such objectives. Accordingly, while there is a recommended uniform ordinance, there is no standardized, set method for effecting a food sanitation program. Such programs are concerned with motivating people to aply sound food sanitation principles, taking into consideration local desires, problems, and needs when implementing the program. However, basic principles must be understood and accepted if the program's objectives are to be achieved." In the view of McDonald (1982), the objective of a bakery sanitation program is to maintain a condition that is essentially free of insect and rodent infestations and produces wholesome foods free of extraneous material and microbial contamination. He also described two basic approaches to sanitation, the corrective method and the preventive method.

The corrective method seeks to discover unacceptable situations and remedy them. For example, insect or rodent populations in the plant are searched out and destroyed. Few, if any permanent and continuing preventive measures are taken.

The more effective preventive method is intended to forestall the occurrence of undesirable sanitation conditions. For example, possible entry ways for rodents and insects are identified and closed off. According to McDonald, four-fifths of preventive sanitation is made up of good housekeeping, which involves (1) maintenance housekeeping, (2) production housekeeping, and (3) janitorial housekeeping.

Regulatory Considerations

The regulatory responsibility and authority of the sanitarian is indeed a complex question and cannot be addressed here in any terms except the most sketchy type.

Section 402 (a) (4) of the federal Food, Drug and Cosmetic Act describes in the most general way the relationship of insanitary conditions and food adulteration. Section 701 (a) of the act authorizes the FDA to promulgate regulations for the efficient enforcement of the act. The FDA had trouble coming to grips with its assignments, but eventually developed a plant evaluation system consisting of standardized forms used by agency inspectors to evaluate various segments of the food manufacturing industry. Later, the FDA proposed generalized Good Manufacturing Practice guidelines. These were broad in scope and intended to cover the entire industry. Current versions of GMP can be found in 21 CFR 110. There were attempts to develop specialized GMPs for certain types of food manufacturing, but these encountered legal challenges and other difficulties. The present attitude seems to be to allow states and other sub-federal jurisidictions to develop the more stringent and specialized regulations.

Organizing a Sanitation Program

The following discussion is based largely on an article by Schultz and Smith (1963), brought up to date where necessary by other references and personal observations. Proper planning is essential in developing a sanitation program that is both effective and efficient. The sanitarian in charge can follow these steps in organizing and planning the program.

(1) A survey should be made of the plant so that all of the sanitation jobs can be listed and the frequency of performance determined. A floor plan of the building may be helpful in this listing of the pieces of equipment to be cleaned, the rooms to be cleaned, the utilities available, and other pertinent information.

(2) Personnel should be delegated to perform the various cleanup jobs that have been listed. A regular crew for building cleanup should be responsible for rest rooms, vacuuming, window washing, etc. Equipment cleaning may be assigned to the operator or to a regular equipment cleaning crew.

(3) After the various positions have been listed and classified, the equipment needed to do a satisfactory job should be determined. Among the equipment to be listed are ladders, pails, sponges, and cleaning supplies; also vacuum cleaners for dry cleaning. Enough equipment should be provided for everyone who needs it, and it should be of the proper size.

(4) Utilities (electric, air, and water outlets) should be listed on the building layout. A study of these utilities may indicate that additional outlets will save a good deal of time and labor. For equipment cleaning in areas where drains are available, a single temperature water system is recommended. Practically all hand cleanup jobs are bet accomplished with water at 110° to 120°F. By using a nozzle shutoff, a light weight hose, and a single temperature water system, savings can be made in water, steam, and labor. If hotter water is necessary, a conventional steam and water mixer system can be installed.

(5) The proper cleaning agent must be furnished for the particular job to be done. A single type of cleaner will not be adequate for all purposes. Cleaners are compounded specifically for certain jobs, such as washing walls, for use in a pressure washer, for CIP, etc. Measuring utensils or scales should be provided at each location where cleaning agents are dispensed or mixed.

(6) Help with this cleaning survey can be obtained from many cleaning product manufacturers. The have experienced personnel who can help establish the staffing requirements, suggest the best way to accomplish the tasks, and assist in writing specifications for equipment and supplies.

Duties of the Sanitarian

The duties assigned to persons responsible for sanitation procedures will vary widely from company to company. One view of the sanitarian's responsibility (Dimarco 1964) has been summarized in the following list of duties:

(1) Supervision of the fresh water supply.

(2) Maintenance of adequate clean-up procedures to prevent utilization of uncleaned equipment.

(3) Control of rodents, insects, and other vermin within the plant.

(4) Supervision of personal hygiene.

(5) Consultation in planning new, or altering old, equipment or buildings.

(6) Supervision of sewerage and waste disposal systems.

(7) Supervision of sanitation and health problems resulting from operation of company-owned eating establishment or housing units.

(8) Regulation of sanitary facilities such as toilets, rest rooms, and dressing rooms.

(9) Plant maintenance of general tidiness or housekeeping of the plant and premises.

(10) Supervision of sanitary warehousing of raw ingredients and finished products.

(11) Supervision of lighting, heating, and ventilation of the plant so far as these factors relate specifically to maintenance of sanitary concepts.

The following practices have been recommended for good bakery sanitation (King 1970).

(1) In the product zone:

(a) Daily washing of surfaces that become damp or wet, and daily emptying and cleaning of catch pans.

(b) Cleaning of conventional flour handling systems every three weeks, and bulk flour systems every four weeks.

(c) Weekly dismantling of brew and other liquid product lines that are cleaned daily by circulation.

(2) For non-product zone surfaces:

(a) Daily cleaning of floors and other surfaces that are exposed and become soiled.

(b) Weekly thorough cleaning and daily rough cleaning of all floors in warehouses and shipping areas.

(c) Twice weekly thorough cleaning of all surfaces that become coated with vegetable oil

(d) Regular dust removal from all non-product zone surfaces (overhead ledges, switch boxes, bases of equipment) to control insects.

(e) Application of residual insecticide weekly to one-quarter of the plant area and daily checking of traps when mouse activity is suspected.

(3) Use of detergents:

(a) Mild alkaline detergents (general purpose cleaners) remove soil without affecting painted surfaces. Complex phosphates do a better job of holding calcium and magnesium in solution and rinse more easily than does trisodium phosphate.

(b) Heavy duty detergents, including sodium hydroxide, are highly alkaline and will remove paint, burn hands, and attack certain metals.

(c) In instances where materials do not yield to alkaline detergents, acid cleaners such as phosphoric acid or mild organic acids must be used.

Equipment Sanitation

Equipment cleaning nearly always involves a sequence of initial rinse, wash, and final rinse. Pre-rinsing removes considerable soil, helps to keep the wash solution cleaner, and gives a more economical an better cleaning job. The wash operation removes organic films that have formed on the surfaces. The final rinse removes the small remnant of wash solution with its suspended soil. Sometimes equipment cleaning also involves the operations of filtering wash and rinse water and drying.

Three factors influencing the wash operation are: (1) time of contact of the wash solution with the object being cleaned, (2) concentration of detergent in the wash solution, and (3) temperature of the wash solution. The longer the contact time, the more effective the wash step. Up to a certain point, the hotter the solution and the higher the concentration of the detergent, the more effective the wash will be. There is an optimum for all three of the factors—these optimums should first be determined and then observed in each cleaning operation.

The five methods commonly used for cleaning equipment are: (1) hand brushing, (2) spray washers, (3) soak methods, (4) clean-in-place systems, and (5) pressure guns (Schultz and Smith 1963). Liquid sponge (brew) systems are particularly suitable for CIP, as are some other pieces of equipment in continuous bread making plants, but conventional bread making devices may be considerably less adaptable to this type of cleaning arrangement.

Washing of baskets and pans requires specialized equipment that automatically perform the required treatment under a rigidly prescribed set of conditions. Further information can be obtained from the article by Spooner (1988).

Designing and constructing bakery equipment that can be easily and completely sanitized and kept in a sanitary condition is a complex field of its own. The Baking Industry Sanitation Standards Committee, 521 Fifth avenue, New York, NY 10017, has issued 42 standards (up to this time) for specific categories of bakery equipment. These standards, which can be obtained from the issuer at a modest cost, are entitled:

(1) Flour handling equipment
(2) Dough troughs
(3) Mechanical intermediate proofers
(4) Pan, rack and utensil washers and industrial sinks
(5) Cake depositors, fillers, and icing machines
(6) Horizontal mixers and vertical mixers
(7) Conveyors
(8) Dividers, rounders, and bun machines
(9) Bread moulders
(10) Prefabricated enclosures and air conditioning equipment for fermentation, proofing, cooling, and retarding
(11) Ingredient water coolers and ice makers (atmospheric type)

(12) Coating equipment

(13) Bread, cake and roll slicing, wrapping and bagging machines

(14) Mechanical ovens

(15) Caster assemblies and wheels

(16) Doughnut equipment

(17) Pan greasers

(18) Emulsifiers and homogenizers

(19) Spindle mixers

(20) Liquid ferment and continuous mix processing equipment

(21) Dough chutes, dough hoppers, dough trough hoists and automatic dough trough hoists

(22) Depanners and delidders for bakery products

(23) Floor scales and ingredient scales

(24) Racks, pan trucks, dollies, pallets and skids

(25) Kettles and kettle agitators

(26) Liquid measuring systems

(27) Facilities for handling and storing refined liquid and dry sweetening products

(28) Facilities for handling and storing bulk edible fats

(29) Electric motors and accessory equipment

(30) Distribution cabinets and containers

(31) Pie make-up equipment

(32) Icing and glazing machines

(33) Coolers for bakery foods

(34) Portable ingredient containers

(35) Baking pans

(36) (Reserved)

(37) Package and package handling equipment

(38) Particle size reduction handling equipment

(39) Dough forming equipment

(40) Cookie and cracker sandwiching equipment

(41) Pretzel equipment

(42) Sugar wafer, wafer and sugar rolled cone batter systems

Sanitation Audits

The input of outside sanitation professionals can often be quite helpful in assessing the status of a company's sanitation program. There are several sanitation consultants that either specialize in, or are familiar with, the concerns of the baking industry. Representative of these is the American Sanitation Institute of St. Louis, MO. Their sanitation audit procedure results in two confidential reports: (1) Factual observations and recommendations compiled by the consultant during the audit and available to the client immediately afterward, and (2) A follow-up, typewritten report with practical recommendations and, if desired, a performance grade and rating. They also prepare recommendations covering:

(1) Advice on requirements and aspects of the Federal Food, Drug, and Cosmetic Act.

(2) Determine compliance with Environmental Protection Agency's FIFRA requirements for application of pesticides and certificatin of applicators.

(3) Check labeling of materials, such as insecticides and cleaners to determine compliance.

(4) Assist in developing a master sanitation schedule prescribing how hazards can be controlled on a periodic basis.

(5) Analyze cleaning, pest control, and general sanitation activities to determine where money can be saved through reduced labor or material usage.

(6) Recommend the redesign or location of equipment to improve cleanability.

(7) Consultation with any pest control operator on methods and safety of materials used.

(8) Check finished products for net weight discrepancies.

(9) Examine raw food ingredients for acceptance or rejection.

(10) Conduct a concluding conference with management covering the consultant's findings and recommendations.

Some of these consulting firms will conduct training seminars on the client's premises to assist in implementing the required changes and preventing future lapses. Other firms conduct industry-wide seminars at a central site, during which broader, more general topics will be presented.

The American Institute of Baking of Manhattan, KS has a department that specializes in sanitation topics.

BIBLIOGRAPHY

ANON. 1976. Health and Safety Guide for Food Processors. US Dept. HEW PHS NIOSH Pub. *75-166*

ANON. 1978. Food Service Sanitation Manual. US Dept. HEW PHS FDA *78-2081*

ANON. 1988. BEMA safety guideline booklet. Bakery Equipment Manufacturers Association, Chicago, IL

ANON. 1991. Managing the "new" microbes. Baking & Snack *13*, No. 6, 55-56

BRINK, R. C. 1965. Sanitation in the cake plant. Proc. Am. Soc. Bakery Engineers *1965*, 193-198

DIMARCO, G. R. 1964. Let detergents do your cleaning. Food Engineering *35*, No. 10, 54-56

DYKES, J. D. 1991. OSHA regulations. Proc. Am. Soc. Bakery Engineers *1991*, 114-119

FISHER, P. 1981. Coordination with sanitation. Proc. Am. Soc. Bakery Engineers *1981*, 130-131

FOLTZ, V. D. 1968. Salmonella control in the bakery. Proc. Am. Soc. Bakery Engineers *1968*, 283-289

GABIS, D., and FAUST, R. E. 1988. Controlling microbial growth in food processing environments. Food Technology *42*, No. 12, 81-82, 89

GENTRY, J. W. 1980. Inspection techniques. Cereal Foods World *25*, 310-311

GREEN, J. H., and KRAMER, A. 1979. Food Processing Waste Management. AVI Publishing Co., Westport, CT

GUTHRIE, R. K. (Editor) 1980. Food Sanitation, Second Edition. AVI Publishing Co., Westport, CT

HEGELE, F. A. 1989. Integrated pest management. Cereal Foods World *34*, 296

HESS, C. F., JR. 1977. Z50 safety standards. Proc. Am. Soc. Bakery Engineers *1977*, 164-170

HOBBS, B. C., and GILBERT, R. J. 1978. Food Poisoning and Food Hygiene, Fourth Edition. Food and Nutrition Press, Inc. Westport, CT

HOOVER, W. J. 1978. Basic sanitation principles. Proc. Am. Soc. Bakery Engineers *1976*, 147-154

KING, L. A., JR. 1970A. For better sanitation. Food Engineering *41*, No. 10, 34-35

KING, L. A., JR. 1970B. Sanitation: matrials and practices. Proc. Am. Soc. Bakery Engineers *1970*, 139-142

MC DONALD, G. E. 1971. The FDA looks at bakery sanitation practices. Proc. Am. Soc. Bakery Engineers *1971*, 229-232

MC DONALD, P. T. 1982. Bakery sanitation. *In* Baking Science and Technology, E. T. Pyler, Editor. Seibel Publishing Co., Chicago, IL

MC MURRY, T. K., II. 1976. Sanitation and safety. Proc. Am. Soc. Bakery Engineers *1976*, 132-161

MILLS, R., and PEDERSEN, J. 1990. A Flour Mill Sanitation Manual. Eagan Press, St. Paul, MN

NYBERG, K. V. 1977. Sanitation: Emphasis on self-inspection. Proc. Am. Soc. Bakery Engineers *1977*, 132-141

PURSLEY, W. E. 1986. Effective bakery sanitation. Proc. Am. Soc. Bakery Engineers *1986*, 104-110

PURSLEY, W. E. 1991. Sanitation update. Proc. Am. Soc. Bakery Engineers *1991*, 137-141

RASCO, L. C. 1971. Practical sanitation programs for bulk ingredient systems. Proc. Am. Soc. Bakery Engineers *1971*, 234-241

RICHTER, L. J. 1964. Today's report on bakery sanitation. Proc. Am. Soc. Bakery Engineers *1964*, 170-176

SADWITH, H. M. 1979. Machinery for cleaning and drying of plastic trays and baskets. Proc. Am. Soc. Bakery Engineers *1979*, 157-162

SCHULTZ, R. W., and SMITH, G. A. 1963. Bakery sanitation. Wyandotte Sani-Facts No. 2, 3-11

SMITH, C. A., JR. 1981. Flour mill sanitation. Cereal Foods World *26*, 451-453

SPOONER, T. F. 1988. In-plant washing of baskets and pans. Baking & Snack Systems *10*, No. 4, 18, 20-21, 23

SUHOVECKY, A. J., and HUGE, T. L. 1980. Plumbing cross-connections: Hazards to sanitation. Cereal Foods World *25*, 312-315

TSOURIDES, K. N. 1968. Quality control for the pie baker. II. Bacteriological aspects. The Bakers Digest *42*, No. 4, 34-37

WILSON, R. L. 1991. Hazard communication standard. Proc. Am. Soc. Bakery Engineers *1991*, 84-89

INDEX

INDEX

In this index, the entries have been placed in alphabetical order according to the word or words preceding the first comma in each entry. Spaces, hyphens, periods, apostrophes, italicization, and capitalization preceding the first comma were ignored when establishing the order of placement. Abbreviations were not treated as being spelled out.

curling rollers, 657, 659
currants, 194
cutters, 657
    for doughnut doughs, 666
    for fig bars, 637
cutting devices, 660
cutting dies, 660
cutting machines, dough rheology, 649

—D—
dairy blends, 158
dairy breads, 416
Danish dough processing, 583
Danish pastry, 423, 428, 434, 657
    factors affecting quality, 436
    history of, 435
    original formulas for, 435
    procedures for, 437
Danish toppings, 487
data banks, scientific, 800
date paste, 191
dates, 191
deck ovens, 684
dehumidification, 594
deionization systems, 131
deionized water, 131
dendritic salt, 137
dense-phase transfer, 515
dent corn, 35, 36
deodorization, of fats and oils, 85
depanners, automatic, 728
depanning, 724
    manual, 727
    vacuum, 728
deposit cookies, 318
    formulas for, 319
depositers, for cream icing, 742
    for English muffins, 617
    general purpose, 737
deposit machines, 633, 636
depth measuring devices, 535
desalinization, 129
design printers, 748
detailer rods, 749
developer, continuous, 560
    for bread dough, 559
development, of dough, 547, 548
devil's food cakes, 344
dextrinizing, 233
dextrinizing enzyme, 111
dextrins, 111, 235
dextrose, 107
    anhydrous, 108
    bulk handling of, 522

manufacture of, 108
dextrose equivalent (DE), 106
diastatic malt, 110
diastatic malt syrup, 410
dicalcium phosphate, 68
die cups, 64, 636
    design features, 641
die cylinders, for rotary molders, 644
dielectric baking, 681
dies for extruders, 636
dietary bakery products, 417
dietary fiber, definition of, 247
    determination of, 247
    effects on humans, 246
diglycerides, 90
dill, 222, 411
dilute-phase transfer, 515
disc slicers, 735
disinfection, of water, 127
dispenser, sugar, 740
dispersibility, 513
displacement meters, 539
distilled spirits, 11
disulfide groups, 239
dividers (see "dough dividers")
dividing, 374
docker design, 648
docking, purpose of, 646
docking processes, 625, 626
double-arm mixers, 554
dough brakes, 298, 578, 582
dough conditioners, 370, 399
dough conditioning, 366
dough-cutting wires, 642
dough development, 367
    by sheeters, 580
dough dividers, commercial models, 572
    extrusion-type, 572
    function of, 569
    how they work, 570
    lubrication systems of, 572
    reactions in, 374
    types of, 571, 573
dough dividing, problems in, 569
dough extruders, 657
dough hook, 555
dough mixers, 552
    horizontal type of, 553
dough mixing, 366
doughnut fats, specifications for, 712
doughnut flour, 430
doughnut fryers, heating methods, 702
doughnut glazers, 742
doughnut glazes, 466